2001

2001

WOMEN IN WORLD HISTORY

A Biographical Encyclopedia

WOMEN IN WORLD HISTORY

A Biographical Encyclopedia

VOLUME
6
Gab-Harp

Anne Commire, Editor
Deborah Klezmer, Associate Editor

YORKIN PUBLICATIONS

GALE GROUP

Detroit
New York
San Francisco
London
Boston
Woodbridge, CT

Yorkin Publications

Anne Commire, *Editor*
Deborah Klezmer, *Associate Editor*
Barbara Morgan, *Assistant Editor*

Eileen O'Pasek, Gail Schermer, Patricia Coombs, James Fox,
Catherine Cappelli, Karen Rikkers, *Editorial Assistants*
Karen Walker, *Assistant for Genealogical Charts*

Special acknowledgment is due to Peg Yorkin who made this project possible.

Thanks also to Karin and John Haag, Bob Schermer, and to
the Gale Group staff, in particular Dedria Bryfonski, Linda Hubbard, John Schmittroth, Cynthia Baldwin,
Tracey Rowens, Randy Bassett, Christine O'Bryan, Rebecca Parks, and especially Sharon Malinowski.

The Gale Group

Sharon Malinowski, *Senior Editor*
Rebecca Parks, *Editor*
Linda S. Hubbard, *Managing Editor, Multicultural Team*

Margaret A. Chamberlain, *Permissions Specialist*
Mary K. Grimes, *Image Cataloger*

Mary Beth Trimper, *Production Director*
Evi Seoud, *Assistant Production Manager*

Cynthia Baldwin, *Product Design Manager*
Tracey Rowens, *Cover and Page Designer*

Barbara Yarrow, *Graphic Services Manager*
Randy Bassett, *Image Database Supervisor*
Michael Logusz, *Graphic Artist*
Robert Duncan, *Imaging Specialist*
Christine O'Bryan, *Graphics Desktop Publisher*
Dan Bono, *Technical Support*

While every effort has been made to ensure the reliability of the information presented in this publication, Yorkin Publications and the Gale Group do not guarantee the accuracy of the data contained herein. No payment for listing was accepted, and inclusion in the publication of any organization, agency, institution, publication, service, or individual does not imply endorsement of the editors or publishers. Errors brought to the attention of the publishers and verified to the satisfaction of the publishers will be corrected in future editions.

Library of Congress Catalog Card Number Pending
A CIP record is available from the British Library

ISBN 0-7876-4065-4
Printed in the United States of America.

Library of Congress Cataloging-in-Publication Data

Women in world history : a biographical encyclopedia / Anne Commire, editor, Deborah Klezmer, associate editor.
  p. cm.
Includes bibliographical references and index.
ISBN 0-7876-3736-X (set). — ISBN 0-7876-4064-6 (v. 5). —
ISBN 0-7876-4065-4 (v. 6) — ISBN 0-7876-4066-2 (v. 7) — ISBN 0-7876-4067-0 (v. 8) — ISBN 0-7876-4068-9 (v. 9)
  1. Women—History Encyclopedias. 2. Women—Biography Encyclopedias.
I. Commire, Anne. II. Klezmer, Deborah.
  HQ1115.W6 1999
  920.72'03—DC21

99-24692

10 9 8 7 6 5 4 3 2 1

Gaboimilla

Queen of the South American Amazons of Chile.

Common from the time of Columbus' discovery of the New World, reports of Amazons in South America are also part of the legends of the numerous tribes of the region. Gaboimilla (meaning "Heaven of Gold"), queen of the Amazons of Chile, surfaced in the writing of Augustin Zarate, secretary of the Royal Council in Spain, as early as 1543. Gonzalo Pizarro encountered "some ten or twelve Amazons fighting in the front ranks of the Indians" who killed many of his soldiers. Francisco de Orellana, who explored South America in the 16th century, also reported encountering a women's army on the Maranon River (later called the River Amazon), near the Venezuelan coast, and the explorer Sir Walter Raleigh was also convinced of the existence of warrior women. However, 20th-century scholars, for the most part, ignored the evidence of Amazons until recently, when a group of modern field researchers made some startling discoveries. Anthropologists Robert and **Yolanda Murphy** found that even modern-day Brazilian tribal women live separate from men in a sisterhood that has authority over men in all practical matters. In 1970, German ethnologist Jesco von Puttkamer befriended a tribe of warring women who maintained an arsenal of firearms. He also discovered cave drawings and artifacts indicating that the legendary Amazons of the region were authentic. The artifacts included ancient helmets and guns that had belonged to early Spaniards possibly killed by these Amazons.

Gabors, The

Mother and three daughters whose flamboyant lifestyles, which included numerous marriages (18 between them), both astonished and entertained Americans for decades.

Gabor, Jolie (d. 1997). Mother of the infamous Gabors. Name variations: Mama Jolie. Born Jolie Kende around 1900; died in Rancho Mirage, California, on April 1, 1997; married Vilmos Gabor, a businessman (divorced); children: Magda Gabor (c. 1917–1997); Zsa Zsa Gabor (1919—); Eva Gabor (1921–1995).

Gabor, Eva (1921–1995). Hungarian-born actress. Born on February 11, 1921, in Budapest, Hungary; died from pneumonia on July 4, 1995, in Los Angeles, California; youngest daughter of Vilmos Gabor and Jolie Gabor (1900–1997); sister of Magda Gabor (c. 1917–1997) and Zsa Zsa Gabor (b. 1919); married Dr. Eric Drimmer (a physician), in 1939 (divorced 1942); married Charles Isaacs (a realtor), in 1943 (divorced 1950); married John E. Williams (a surgeon), on April 9, 1956 (divorced less than a year later); married Richard Brown (a stockbroker), on October 4 1959 (divorced); married Frank Jameson, an aerodynamics industrialist (divorced 1983).

Selected theater: made Broadway debut as Mignonette in The Happy Time *(1950); appeared as French countess in* Little Glass Clock *(1956); appeared in* Lulu *(1958) and* Present Laughter *(1958); portrayed Tatiana in* Tovarich *(1963); appeared in stock and/or touring productions of* Strike a Match, Her Cardboard Lover, Candlelight, The Play's the Thing, Affairs of Anatol, Blithe Spirit, Oh, Men! Oh, Women!, A Shot in the Dark, Private Lives, *and* The Happiest Man Alive.

Filmography: Forced Landing *(1941);* A Royal Scandal *(1945);* The Wife of Monte Cristo *(1946);* Song of Surrender *(1949);* Paris Model *(1953);* The Mad Magician *(1954);* The Last Time I Saw Paris *(1954);* Artists and Models *(1955);* My Man Godfrey *(1957);* Don't Go Near the Water *(1957);* Gigi *(1958);* The Truth About Women *(1958);* It Started With a Kiss *(1959);* Love Island *(1960);* A New Kind of Love *(1963);* Youngblood Hawke *(1964); (voice only)* The Aristocrats *(1970); (voice of Miss Bianca)* The Rescuers *(1977);* The Princess Academy *(1987); (voice of Miss Bianca)* The Rescuers Down Under *(1990).*

Made television debut in supporting role of French woman in L'Amour the Merrier *(1949); had her own interview program on television, "The Eva Gabor Show" (early 1950s); played Lisa Douglas on television series "Green Acres" for CBS (1965–71).*

***Gabor, Magda** (c. 1917–1997). Hungarian-born American actress and businesswoman. Born in Budapest, Hungary, around 1917; died of kidney failure in Rancho Mirage, California, on June 6, 1997; daughter of Vilmos Gabor and Jolie Gabor (1900–1997); sister of Eva Gabor (1921–1995) and Zsa Zsa Gabor (b. 1919); married and divorced six times; fifth husband was George Sanders; sixth and last husband was Tibor Heltrai (divorced 1975); no children.*

***Gabor, Zsa Zsa** (1919—). Hungarian-born actress. Born Sari Gabor in Budapest, Hungary, on February 6, 1919; daughter of Vilmos Gabor and Jolie Gabor (1900–1997); sister of Magda Gabor (c. 1917–1997) and Eva Gabor (1921–1995); married Burhan Belge (press director of the Turkish foreign ministry), in 1937 (divorced 1941); married Conrad Hilton (a hotelier), in April 1942 (divorced 1947); married George Sanders (an actor), in April 1949 (divorced 1954); married Herbert Hutner (a businessman), in 1964 (divorced 1966); married Joshua Cosden, Jr. (an oil magnate), in 1966 (divorced 1967); married Jack Ryan (an inventor), 1975 (divorced 1976); married Michael O'Hara (a lawyer), in 1977 (divorced 1982); married Felipe Alba (a Mexican businessman), in 1982 (declared invalid); married Prince Frederick von Anhalt, duke of Saxony, in 1986; children: (with Conrad Hilton) one daughter, **Francesca Hilton**.*

Filmography: Lovely to Look At (1952); Moulin Rouge (1952); The Story of Three Loves (1953); Lili (1953); Three Ring Circus (1954); Death of a Scoundrel (1956); The Girl in the Kremlin (1957); Touch of Evil (1958); Queen of Outer Space (1958); Pepe (1960); Boys' Night Out (1962); Picture Mommy Dead (1966); Arrivederci, Baby (1966); Jack of Diamonds (1967); Up the Front (UK, 1972); Johann Strauss—Der König ohne Krone (Aus./Ger./Fr., 1986); A Nightmare on Elm Street 3 (1987); Dream Warriors (1987); (voice only) Happily Ever After (1990).

The colorful saga of the Gabor sisters began in Hungary around 1916 when Jolie Kende's parents insisted that she marry after her return from a Swiss finishing school. Six months after the wedding, Jolie asked for a divorce from Vilmos Gabor, a businessman twice her age, so that she could pursue her dream of acting. But just when Vilmos agreed to the split, Jolie discovered that she was pregnant. The divorce was postponed, and the marriage unexpectedly endured for another 22 years before it was dissolved. After the birth of Magda, Sari (Zsa Zsa) and Eva, Jolie ran a jewelry boutique in Budapest. But the most important item on her agenda was the preparation of her girls for the glamorous world of high society that she felt had been denied her.

Jolie Gabor's first priority was that her daughters be attractive to men. Convinced that her own marriage had brought her down in the eyes of the world, she was determined that this would not happen to her children. Following in their mother's path and imbued with her buoyant self-confidence, the Gabor sisters were sent to exclusive schools in Switzerland, there to be polished, cultivated, and taught how to make the most of their beauty. "I wanted them to play the piano so magnificently that a Rubinstein would be green with envy," Jolie recalled years later. "They learnt to swim, to ride, to play tennis. They all went to the best finishing schools. Who wants a man who wants a dowry?"

By the late 1930s, having left a Central Europe tottering on the brink of war, Jolie and her daughters found themselves in the glitzy world of Hollywood. The quartet, as assertive as they were glamorous, soon became the talk of the town. Magda got on the matrimonial merry-go-round by marrying a glamorous Royal Air Force pilot. After divorcing him, she wed a successful New York lawyer. Spouse number three was also an attorney from New York. Her fourth husband was a Hungarian nobleman. Husband number five was the British actor George Sanders, who had previously been married to her sister Zsa Zsa. The marriage lasted only two months, the shortest of her unions; one reason given was that while Mrs. Sanders loved parties her aging husband did not. When not involved in nuptials, or courting celebrity, Magda acted on the radio with her mother Jolie and, in 1953, gave proof of her substantial business acumen by negotiating a lucrative contract for her entire family to appear on stage at the Last Frontier Hotel in Las Vegas. In a show they named "This Is Our Life," the Gabors faced competition that few performers wished to confront, namely *Marlene Dietrich, then the top nightclub act in Las Vegas.

Although Eva later proclaimed the show "horrible," the Gabors' singing, dancing and conversing in their unique brand of fractured English was immensely successful with audiences. The public fell in love not only with Jolie, more of an Auntie Mame than a conventional mother, but her glamorous daughters as well. A publicity still from the show depicted the Gabors in matching negligees, chatting with each other on telephones. After the Las Vegas success, Magda appeared occasionally on television, but she never displayed the dramatic ambitions of

Opposite page Eva Gabor, from the movie Princess Academy.

her sisters. Instead, she joined her mother in managing a string of jewelry boutiques catering to the upscale market in New York, Palm Beach, Florida, London, and Paris. By Gabor standards, Magda was somewhat retiring.

It was Eva, the youngest of the sisters, who enjoyed an acting career of considerable substance. Serious about her pursuit from an early age, she enrolled in acting classes at 15, but her parents, who at the time viewed the theater as a vulgar profession for a young lady, forced her to drop out. In the late 1930s, over her parents' opposition, she married a Swedish-born Hollywood physician and moved to Hollywood where she signed a contract with Paramount. Her early film career foundered, and she was eventually dropped by the studio, then fared no better on her own. In 1949, she made her television debut as a French girl in *L'Amour the Merrier*, after which her career took an upward swing. Thereafter, she appeared on a number of dramatic television programs, including a production of "Uncle Vanya" in which she played Helena. She also made guest appearances on variety shows, and even had her own television interview show for 18 months. Still hoping for an acting career, however, Eva accepted small roles in stock and touring companies, eventually earning the respect of the acting community. In 1958, Noel Coward, who called Eva "a damn good actress," cast her in his Broadway production of *Present Laughter*. Coward made Gabor change her orange chiffon costume to a more subdued champagne color on the grounds that the former would make the audience focus totally on her and not on him. She appeared again on Broadway in 1963, replacing *Vivien Leigh as Tatiana in *Tovarich*, then also toured. Her later film career included secondary roles in *My Man Godfrey* (1957) and *Gigi* (1958), but her image of the often-wed glamour queen kept her busy on the television talk-show circuit and eventually led to her role as the ditzy but dignified socialite Lisa Douglas in the television series "Green Acres," which ran on CBS from 1965 to 1971. Eva called it "really the best" show of her career. In the last decades of her life, Eva, who also had her share of husbands (five), headed a successful company that manufactured wigs. "We Gabors are supposed to do nothing but take bubble baths and drip with jewels," she told her friend and frequent companion Merv Griffin. "But I've worked like a demon. I didn't have time to sit in bubbles." Her autobiography, *Orchids and Salami*, was published in 1954.

Zsa Zsa, by far the most flamboyant of the three sisters, has also had the most husbands

(eight), among them Conrad Hilton, George Sanders, and Prince Frederick von Anhalt, her last. She has also been the most quotable member of the Gabor women: "I'm an excellent housekeeper. Every time I get a divorce, I keep the house," she said. Or, "A man is incomplete until he is married. After that, he is finished." Zsa Zsa's movie career was ongoing from 1952 to 1990, but her roles were mostly decorative. She also played in summer stock and in 1970 starred on Broadway in *Forty Carats*. Like her sister Eva, Zsa Zsa was a regular on television, notably as a guest on Jack Paar's late-night program, and as a panelist on the game show "Hollywood Squares." Prone to remarks that other celebrities (or their attorneys) deem libelous, Zsa Zsa has been in court on more than one occasion. In 1990, she made headlines when she spent three days behind bars for slapping a traffic officer. She has kept the world apprised of her career and her hard-learned lessons about the opposite sex with four books: *Zsa Zsa Gabor: My Story* (1960), *Zsa Zsa's Complete Guide to Men* (1969), *How to Get a Man, How to Keep a Man, and How to Get Rid of a Man* (1971), and *One Lifetime Is Not Enough* (1991). Always ready for new experiences and business ventures, in 1993 Zsa Zsa released a low-impact aerobic video entitled "It's Simple, Darling."

Starting in 1995, the colorful Gabor family began to be steadily and sadly diminished by the inevitable progression of time and human mortality. On July 4, 1995, Eva Gabor died in Los Angeles. Less than two years later, on April 1, 1997, matriarch Jolie Gabor died at the age of 97 in Rancho Mirage, California. The two remaining sisters were still reeling from their loss when Magda died of kidney failure in Rancho Mirage on June 6, 1997. Although the high-spirited sisters sometimes had their differences, according to Frederick von Anhalt, Zsa Zsa's eighth husband, "they loved each other very much." Underneath the style of zany flamboyance the Gabors exposed to the public, one could also discern that here were four highly intelligent and realistic women who had long ago made up their minds to be survivors. In a 1961 interview, Eva noted that "we're all doing well. . . . We worked very hard but we're also very lucky." Zsa Zsa, the last of the Gabors, spoke of the continuing pain of losing her mother and siblings: "It still hurts so much to talk about Mother. When she was alive, we were all alive."

SOURCES:
Brown, Peter H. *Such Devoted Sisters: Those Fabulous Gabors*. NY: St. Martin's Press, 1985.
Gabor, Eva. *Orchids and Salami*. Garden City, NY: Doubleday, 1954.
Gabor, Jolie, and Cindy Adams. *Jolie Gabor*. NY: Mason/Charter, 1975.
Gabor, Zsa Zsa, "assisted by, edited by, and put into proper English by Wendy Leigh." *One Lifetime Is Not Enough*. NY: Delacorte Press, 1991.
Geier, Thom. "Look Out, Jane Fonda," in *U.S. News & World Report*. Vol. 116, no. 1. January 10, 1994, p. 14.
Graham, Judith, ed. *Current Biography Yearbook 1995*. NY: H.W. Wilson, 1995.
Katz, Ephraim. *The Film Encyclopedia*. NY: HarperCollins, 1994.
"Magda Gabor," in *The Daily Telegraph* (London). June 9, 1997, p. 23.
"Magda Gabor," in *The Times* (London). June 10, 1997, p. 25.
Moritz, Charles, ed. *Current Biography Yearbook 1988*. NY: H.W. Wilson, 1988.
Oliver, Myrna. "Jolie Gabor: Matriarch of Flamboyant Family," in *Los Angeles Times*. April 3, 1997, p. B10.
———. "Magda Gabor: Eldest Sister in a Family of Actresses," in *Los Angeles Times*. June 7, 1997, p. A20.
Russell, William. "Magda Gabor," in *The Herald* [Glasgow]. June 12, 1997, p. 18.
Witchel, Alex. "The Lives They Lived: Jolie Gabor, Mother Dahling," in *The New York Times*. January 4, 1998, section VI, p. 24.

RELATED MEDIA:
Gabor, Zsa Zsa. "It's Simple, Darling" (videocassette), Best Film and Video, 1993.

John Haag,
Associate Professor of History,
University of Georgia, Athens, Georgia

Gabrielle, La belle.

See Estrées, Gabrielle de.

Gabrielli, Caterina (1730–1796)

Italian soprano. Name variations: Catterina; La Cochetta or La Cochettina. Born in Rome on November 12, 1730; died in Rome in April 1796; daughter of a cook; studied with Garcia, Porpora, and Metastasio; sister of Francesca Gabrielli.

Caterina Gabrielli, the daughter of Prince Gabrielli's cook, was known as La Cochetta or Cochettina. When she was 14, the prince overheard her singing a difficult song of Baldasare Galuppi's while walking in his garden. Under the prince's aegis, she became a pupil of Garcia and Porpora and made her triumphant debut at Lucca in 1747 in Galuppi's *Sonfonisba*. Beautiful, accomplished and capricious, she enjoyed further success in Naples in 1750, singing in Jomelli's *Didone*. In Vienna, she studied under Metastasio and charmed Francis I. Gabrielli was known for her bravura style and her many eccentricities.

In 1765, a very wealthy Gabrielli left Vienna for Sicily where she was imprisoned for 12 days by the king because she would not sing her role in an opera above a whisper. While incarcerated, she entertained, paid the debts of poor prisoners, and distributed gifts. The king had no choice but to set her free, and she became more popular than ever. From Sicily, she went to Parma; from Parma, she journeyed to Russia in 1768, where she asked for 5,000 ducats as salary at the court of *Catherine II the Great. When an astonished Catherine replied that the sum was more than she paid a field marshal, Gabrielli replied: "Then let your field-marshals sing for you."

Gabrielli appeared in London for the 1775–76 season, but Londoners were wary of her unconventional behavior. Charles Burney thought her "the most intelligent and best bred virtuosa with whom he had ever conversed, not only on the subject of music, but on every subject concerning which a well-educated female, who had seen the world, might be expected to have information." She sang with Pacchierotti at Venice in 1777 and with Marchesi in Milan in 1780. Soon after, she retired in Rome with her sister **Francesca Gabrielli**, who had remained with her throughout her travels as seconda donna. Gabrielli died of a neglected cold in April 1796.

Gacioch, Rose (1915—)

American pioneer in women's baseball who played for the Rockford Peaches. Born on August 31, 1915, in Wheeling, West Virginia; the youngest of four children; never married; no children.

Rose Gacioch, later known as "Rockford Rosie," was hooked on the game of baseball from the time her hand was big enough to hold a ball. She learned to pitch by throwing between two trees and trying to make the ball curve. Later, she pitched at a hole in a mattress. When she was 15, she was auditioned by *Maud Nelson, who let her play for the All Star Ranger Girls as pitcher and outfielder. After the end of "bloomer-girl baseball" in 1934, Gacioch played "barnstorming softball" in Ohio and Pennsylvania.

Gacioch was working in a Wheeling factory, during World War II, when she spotted a photo of a player for the All-American Girls Baseball League (AAGBL) in a New York newspaper. After a tryout, she was invited to attend the league's 1944 spring-training session in Peru, Illinois. Despite her advanced age, then 29, Rose made the cut. She started in right field and cred-

its coach Bert Niehoff for her skills as an outfielder. By 1945, she had been traded to the Rockford Peaches. Playing right field that year, she set an all-time AAGBL record of 31 assists from the outfield and also belted nine triples and batted in 44 runs (both league records). In 1946, she had 30 assists, and in 1947 she tied her own record of 31. Gacioch was proudest of her assists record, she said, "because that's most important to the team."

During the 1948 season, manager Bill Allington returned Gacioch to the pitcher's mound, where she remained until the league folded in 1955. In 1951, her best year, she posted a 20-7 record and a 1.68 ERA, making her the league's only 20-game winner that season. On August 26, 1953, she pitched a seven-inning no-hitter against South Bend. During the last years of league play, Gacioch combined pitching with play at third or first base. She was voted to the All-Star team as a pitcher in 1952, as a utility infielder in 1953, and as a pitcher again in 1954.

Gacioch also took up bowling and in 1954, with her partner **Fran Stennett**, won the national doubles bowling championship. Retiring to Michigan, she continued to bowl in senior tournaments. In 1988, she attended the opening of the Women in Baseball display at the Baseball Hall of Fame.

SOURCES:
Gregorich, Barbara. *Women at Play: The Story of Women in Baseball.* NY: Harcourt Brace, 1993.

RELATED MEDIA:
A League of Their Own (127 min.) film, starring **Geena Davis**, Tom Hanks, **Madonna, Rosie O'Donnell**, directed by **Penny Marshall**, Columbia Pictures, 1992.

Gadski, Johanna (1872–1932)

Prussian soprano. Born in Anklam, Prussia, on June 15, 1872; died in an automobile accident on February 22, 1932, in Berlin, Germany; studied with Schroeder-Chaloupka in Stettin.

Debuted at the Kroll Opera in Berlin (1894), Covent Garden (1898), Metropolitan Opera (1900), Munich (1905), Salzburg (1917); became leader of Wagnerian touring company (1920s).

Johanna Gadski was one of the first Victor Red Seal artists and made almost 100 recordings during her career. Singing in Germany between 1889 and 1895, she debuted at age 17 in Lortzing's *Undine* at the Kroll Opera in Berlin. When she joined New York's Metropolitan Opera in 1900, she became one of the company's leading Wagnerian sopranos although she performed

Johanna Gadski

Gág, Wanda (1893–1946)

American artist, writer, and translator who was much admired for the melodic style of her self-illustrated children's books. Name variations: Wanda Gag. Pronunciation: Gág (rhymes with cog). Born Wanda Hazel Gág on March 11, 1893, in New Ulm, Minnesota; died of lung cancer on June 27, 1946, in New York, New York; oldest of seven children (six girls and one boy) of Anton Gág and Lissi Biebl Gág (both artists); studied at the St. Paul Institute of Arts, 1913–1914, Minneapolis School of Art, 1914–1917, Art Students League, New York, 1917–1918; married Earle Marshall Humphreys, in 1930; children: none.

Was a teenage illustrator for children's section of the Minneapolis Journal; *worked as a schoolteacher (1912–13) and commercial artist (1918–23); exhibited extensively in New York, primarily at the Weyhe Gallery, across the country and abroad (beginning 1926); had major exhibits at Weyhe Gallery, NY (1926, 1930, and 1940 retrospective); exhibited in group shows at Museum of Modern Art, New York (1939) and Metropolitan Museum of Art, New York (1943).*

Selected works: collections in Metropolitan Museum of Art; Whitney Museum of American Art; Museum of Modern Art, New York; Art Institute of Chicago, Chicago, Illinois; British Museum, London; Bibliothèque Nationale, Paris; Kupferstich Kabinett, Berlin; and many other museums and private collections.

Awards: Millions of Cats (1928) was a John Newbery Award Honor Book (1929), given the Lewis Carroll Shelf Award (1958) and awarded first prize, Philadelphia Lithograph Show (1930); The ABC Bunny (1933) was a John Newbery Award Honor Book (1934); Snow White and the Seven Dwarfs (1938) was a Caldecott Award Honor Book (1939); Nothing-at-all (1941) was a Caldecott Award Honor Book (1942); received the Kerlan Award, University of Minnesota (1977), in recognition of singular attainments in the creation of children's literature; Purchase Prizes for lithographs, Metropolitan Museum of Art (1942), and Library of Congress (1944).

Selected publications (author-illustrator): Millions of Cats *(NY: Coward-McCann, 1928);* The Funny Thing *(NY: Coward-McCann, 1929);* Snippy and Snappy *(NY: Coward-McCann, 1931);* Wanda Gág's Story Book *(NY: Coward-McCann, 1932);* The ABC Bunny *(NY: Coward-McCann, 1933, with hand-lettering by her brother Howard Gág, and music by her sister Flavia Gág);* Gone is Gone: The Story of a Man Who Wanted to Do Housework *(retold, NY: Coward-McCann, 1935);* Growing Pains: Diaries and Drawings for the Years 1908–1917 *(NY: Coward-McCann, 1940);* Nothing-at-all *(NY: Coward-McCann, 1941).*

Mozart and Mahler ably as well. Also a recitalist, Gadski was one of the few to include songs by American composers on her program.

An extremely popular recitalist, Gadski was much loved by audiences but fared less well with critics who complained that her pitch varied, her interpretation was flawed, and that she had a limited emotional range. Numerous recordings, however, demonstrate that she had a large voice with a pure tone. Her recordings, in fact, are considered classics. Gadski was forced to discontinue her American career during World War I due to anti-German sentiment, but she returned as a popular performer after the Armistice. She formed her own Wagnerian touring company in the 1920s which performed in Europe and the United States. Johanna Gadski died in an auto accident on February 22, 1932. Records kept her voice alive, giving Gadski a much deserved reputation—far greater than the one she enjoyed in her lifetime.

John Haag,
Athens, Georgia

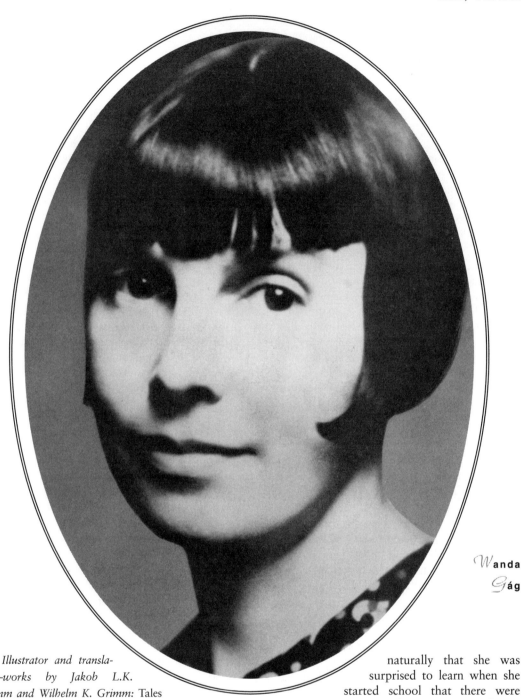

Wanda
Gág

*Illustrator and transla-
tor—works by Jakob L.K.
Grimm and Wilhelm K. Grimm:* Tales
from Grimm *(NY: Coward-McCann, 1936);*
Snow White and the Seven Dwarfs *(NY: Coward-Mc-
Cann, 1938);* Three Gay Tales from Grimm *(NY: Cow-
ard-McCann, 1943);* More Tales from Grimm *(NY:
Coward-McCann, 1947).*

Illustrator: Michael Wigglesworth, Day of Doom
(poems; Spiral Press, 1929); A Child's Book of Folklore; *contributor of illustrations and articles to various
magazines, including* The Horn Book Magazine.

Born on March 11, 1893, in New Ulm, Minnesota, Wanda Gág's love of drawing came so
naturally that she was
surprised to learn when she
started school that there were
some who never drew. Her passion for art
was fostered by her parents, both of whom were
artists from families with long traditions of artistic talent. Anton Gág, the son of a forest caretaker, was raised in Bohemia where he drew and
carved at an early age. Having immigrated to
New Ulm, Anton decorated homes, churches, and
public buildings and also worked as a photographer. A widower, he met his second wife, **Lissi
Biebl (Gág)**, when she applied for a position as
his photographer's assistant. Lissi came from a
creative family where the sons carved toys and
furniture, made musical instruments, cast statues

and painted primitive oils, and the daughters worked with watercolors and costuming. Wanda, her five sisters and one brother, were raised in an atmosphere of art, music, literature and love. Her childhood was a happy one, and her family, though poor, lived a comfortable life. Her parents instilled in her a curiosity about life that would lead to a wide range of artistic expression.

Since the family spoke German, Wanda did not learn English until she entered school. Much of her personality can be seen in her childhood diaries, published as *Growing Pains,* "a unique record of the evolution of an artist," wrote one reviewer. "The diary is not a conscious literary exercise," writes Thomas Craven; "it is the unaffected account of the struggles of a girl who was determined to make herself an artist, and who succeeded nobly." In the journal entries, we meet the child who was fascinated with drawing everything around her, while learning all she could. Her diaries reveal the high points of her childhood, such as having her drawings published in "*Journal* Junior" (the children's pages of the *Minneapolis Journal*), and of the difficulties, the overwhelming responsibility she experienced having to earn money to supplement the family income. The young girl longs for others to understand her artistic temperament, her "drawing moods." Her powers of concentration were such that she would spend years trying to explain that it was not in her control to stop drawing during a "drawing fit."

She enjoyed school, especially reading, but left high school in 1908 to care for the house and her baby sister due to her father's illness. After working in the damp, cold interiors of newly built churches and homes, Anton had succumbed to tuberculosis. "What Papa was unable to accomplish," he told her on his deathbed, "Wanda will have to finish." Gág understood this to mean both that she was responsible for the family and that she must pursue their shared dream of art as her life's work. Lissi Gág, who had cared for her husband in his illness and was shaken by his death, required care herself, so Wanda stayed home to manage the house and the children, and to carry the worrisome burden of how to bring money into the household. Her diary relates her concern over their financial state, and her lack of funds to buy drawing paper or another notebook to continue her diary. With almost no income, the family was forced to wear clothing from charity, so Wanda did alterations to conceal their identity from former owners. Because it was a small town, everyone knew of the Gágs' poverty. Many townspeople came to their aid, but there were those who criticized Gág for not working hard enough and spending too much time drawing and reading. These accusations cut deep, and she found solace in her family.

Wanda returned to school part time in 1909, supplementing the family income with earnings from drawing and painting for people in New Ulm. While still in high school, she entered her artwork in local and state competitions and was recognized with numerous awards. Her goal was to attend university after high school and to assure that her siblings at least finished high school. With the financial requirement for a college education out of reach, she applied to art school, not knowing how she would afford the tuition. Though awarded a scholarship, she put off attending to earn money for the family. Gág spent the year following her 1912 high school graduation teaching in a rural school. Known as an unorthodox teacher, she provided her students with what one biographer describes as "a never-to-be-forgotten year for the school children" and continued to teach until her next two sisters finished high school and found similar positions.

Gág's talent was well known in her town, and mentors came forward to support her art studies. In 1913, she left New Ulm for the St. Paul Institute of Art, sponsored by the editor of the *Minneapolis Journal*. There, she was known as a rebellious student, speaking out against the mechanization of art and straining against the school's traditions. She referred to this as her "wildness," but it was only humored by her teachers. Instead of studying painting, she turned to illustration, as she was faced with the immediate need of earning a living. Gág was somewhat conventional in her technical habits but by no means conventional in her attitude toward her chosen career; she earned her skills by hard work and developed her sense of color by working on her own with watercolor. In school, Gág was quickly set straight that the illustrators she adored, such as Charles Dana Gibson, were not serious artists. The instructors stressed the Postimpressionists and Cubists. Gág reluctantly took their advice, writing in her diary: "Dear God, suffer me to fight all my life . . . but do not let me stop at being a clever illustrator." She learned a great deal at St. Paul, including the full range of the tools of her profession. She benefited greatly from the association and encouragement of other students, including Adolph Dehn, Harry Gottlieb, and *Elizabeth Olds. Gág led an active social life and enjoyed extended discussions on philosophy and art.

After two years at St. Paul, in 1914 Gág's mentors made it possible for her to transfer to the Minneapolis School of Art. At this point, her future looked promising, but in February her mother died, setting Wanda's career and education on hold. As head of the family, she was responsible for her siblings, some of whom were still in elementary school. In 1917, she earned the coveted scholarship of the Art Students League in New York and sold her first paintings to Harry B. Wehle of the Art Institute of Boston. "But do you think he sat down and cried?" says Gág's character in her book *Nothing-at-all.* "Oh no, he had a plan." Gág resolved to continue her work in Minneapolis until such time as she could go to New York to use her scholarship. Despite the concern of family and friends, she and her siblings sold the family home and moved to Minneapolis. The next two oldest went to work, the third kept house, and the youngest children went to school. Two years of great hardship passed before Gág felt the arrangement had worked, and the family was secure. In 1919, she left for New York.

At first, she was unfavorably impressed with the city. Nonetheless, she studied hard. By the end of a year, New York had won her heart and in so doing changed her outlook. She told *Horn Book* (May 1947):

> The surroundings of the Middle West are not affected enough by the waves of progress and revolution in art. The people there seem a little too complacent in regard to their art. If anyone had accused me of that last year, I should have risen in indignation, but it was so, nevertheless.

Gág had been immediately drawn to Greenwich Village and became involved with the artists and writers who produced the leftist journals the *Liberator* and the *New Masses.* World War I was raging, and the young art community took an avid interest in the social implications of the war and the changes that were certain to follow. Fellow artist Lynd Ward claims that one of Gág's outstanding qualities, both as artist and person, was her social motivation. She was one of a group of artists who came together in the mid-1930s motivated by feelings of frustration and concern for the future brought by those years of economic and political crisis. She was one of the original signers of the *Call for an American Artists' Congress,* issued late in 1935, in which the dominant theme was that a "picture of what fascism has done to living standards, to civil liberties, to workers' organizations, to science and art; the threat against the peace and security of the world, as shown in Italy and Germany,

should arouse every sincere artist to action." In the resultant organization, something quite new in the art world, she took an active part in the work of the Graphic Committee.

After her first year in New York, Gág renewed her scholarship for another year, but financially strapped once more she was unable to take advantage of it. She left school and worked in commercial art, designing fashions and making lampshades. All but her expense money was sent home to the family. Gág pursued new sources of revenue. Interested in writing and illustrating books for children, she wrote stories for her friends' children, all of which were rejected by the major publishing companies. She was looking to set aside money for study in Europe and developed some children's games and story boxes she hoped to market, but the manufacturer's business failed and her savings were lost. Commercial art could provide her with a substantial living and likely success, but she was so disillusioned by this setback that she gave up commercial art for good.

Gág referred to her abandonment of the commercial art field as "going native." Her goal was to do what came naturally, preferably in a country environment. Aware of her artistic strengths and weaknesses, she set out to find her own distinctive manner, to capture simple things. With what was left of her meager savings, she rented a summer home in Connecticut in 1925, dedicating her life to her art and fulfilling her promise to her father.

Returning to New York City for the winter, Gág showed the result of her summer's labor to Carl Zigrosser, director of the Weyhe Gallery in New York. She was given her first one-woman show there in 1926; that same year, she was included in the *Fifty Prints of the Year* by the American Institute of Graphic Arts, an honor that was to be conferred annually on Wanda Gág for as long as the collection was presented. She was immediately recognized as one of America's most promising graphic artists. The following summer, she rented a New Jersey farmhouse that she called "Tumble Timbers" because of its worn condition. She worked diligently through a productive drawing mood that lasted for years, and many of her best known lithographs and woodcuts date from this period, including "Tumble Timbers," "Gumbo Lane," and "Lamplight." Gág developed a technique of using ink on sandpaper for the sparkling effects it gave the finished work. Zigrosser maintains that Gág was the only artist who made extensive use of this exacting technique. In 1928, the Weyhe Art Gallery gave her a second one-woman show which caught the attention of **Ernestine Evans,** director of the newly founded children's book department at Coward-McCann.

Evans wanted to revitalize the children's book industry. She was looking for talent to produce stories and illustrations that children liked, rather than stories that children ought to like. Unaware that Gág had already written for children, Evans arranged a meeting to discuss the possibility of illustrating children's books. Gág arrived with her manuscript and drawings for *Millions of Cats* from her "rejection box," explaining that she was not interested in just illustrating a story but needed to relate to the whole package of story and pictures. Gág left the meeting with a commission to complete and illustrate her book.

Hundreds of cats, thousands of cats, millions and billions and trillions of cats.

—Wanda Gág, *Millions of Cats*

Because she was not financially dependent on the publication of *Millions of Cats*, Gág decided to illustrate the book in her own fashion, bowing to no precedents. It is not known if the origin of the story is derived from a Bohemian folktale or from her own imagination. **Eleanor Cameron** notes in *The Green and Burning Tree* (1969) that the "charming narrative with its rhyme and repetition seems to be handed down from generation to generation of storytellers, smoothed and polished a bit more with each retelling." Gág chose the double-page spread because it strengthened the traveling aspect of the story, and the hand-lettering, done by her brother Howard Gág, suggested the childlike quality of the book's storyline. Her need to produce art for children which maintained the standards of art for adults made Gág a well-known and respected figure in the world of book publication. She insisted on working personally with the printer of the book, feeling that he needed to be educated about the matter of black ink. To Gág, black meant color, the rich sparkling blacks of her lithographs. Her desire to achieve deep, perfect blacks would cause some printers to object to her scrutiny of their work, but she would continue her role as overseer. "It was a happy day for her when the printer told her that other customers were asking for 'Wanda Gág black ink'," said **Rose Dobbs,** her editor at Coward-McCann, "and a happier day for the printer when she reached the point where she could say: 'You know how I want it; it isn't necessary for me to come down.'"

Because of her attention to every detail of the production of her first book, the final result was immediately judged a modern classic. Michael Hearn notes that with the publication of Wanda Gág's *Millions of Cats*, the modern American picture book came of age, setting the standard that every element of a volume's design should add to the pleasure of the whole. In her own day, Gág's work was celebrated primarily for bridging the fine and commercial arts. Gág was as distinguished a writer as an illustrator, and she was acclaimed for her integration of text and art. *Millions of Cats* was named an Honor Book by the John Newbery Award Committee in 1929. The Newbery Award goes to the best children's narrative each year, and the honor is not often granted to a picture book. Ironically, though she was often mentioned as a candidate during her distinguished career, Wanda Gág never received the Caldecott Medal, the award that *is* given yearly for the most distinguished American picture book.

Gág led an active social life in New York but did not feel that marriage was a possibility because of her art and her six dependent siblings. In the early years, "much as I liked men," she wrote in her diary, "I knew that art would always have to come first." She took the "unwomanly attitude" for the time that "I would marry no man unless he would promise to run the house during my drawing moods and would excuse me from scrubbing floors." Gág remained single until 1930, when, at age 37, she married Earle Marshall Humphreys, a businessman and labor organizer. They did not have children.

Her works *The Funny Thing* (1929), *Snippy and Snappy* (1931), *The ABC Bunny* (1933) and *Gone is Gone* (1935) were all published in quick succession. With the financial success of her early picture books, Gág was able to bring her family east. In 1931, she and Earle purchased a house in the mountains of New Jersey to share with her family. Gág named it "All Creation" since everyone who came to visit wanted "to draw, write poetry, paint, even sew." *The ABC Bunny* was a family affair at "All Creation." Howard Gág hand-lettered the text as he had for *Millions of Cats*, and **Flavia Gág,** her youngest sister, wrote the music and words for the song that appeared on the endpapers. Wanda's illustrations consisted of rich, velvety lithographs drawn on zinc plates with a wax crayon. Some critics lavished praise on this book, but Hearn feels the book does not measure up to the praise, the text being "only adequate." *The ABC Bunny,* however, was Gág's second Newbery

From Millions of Cats *by Wanda Gág. Illustrated by the author.*

Honor book. She went on to publish translations of Grimm from the original German, first a collection (1936) and then a single edition of *Snow White and the Seven Dwarfs* (1938) which was reportedly written in reaction to the Walt Disney movie of the same name. She also published another original story, *Nothing-at-all* (1941), followed by *Three Gay Tales from Grimm* (1943). *Nothing-at-all*, again done in the oblong format, was printed in color, a departure from her earlier works. Before the days of acetate overlays, Gág had to laboriously draw in black on ground glass to make each color separation. Although the story itself received lukewarm reviews, the book was named a Caldecott Honor Book for 1942.

While Gág was translating the German fairy tales for publication, the sentiment of progressive educators was that fairy tales and "fancies" had no place in the modern instruction of children who lived in an age of technology and wanted to read about practical things. Gág strongly disagreed, defending folklore as the precise antidote for a world too filled with steel, stone, machinery, and implements of war. Her translations of Grimm were, in her words, "true to the spirit rather than to the letter." She felt justified in the liberties she took, because the tales were not limited to German but had counterparts in many languages, with recurring motifs that resulted in an endless number of combinations. Her goal was to prepare a version of the story that would appeal to a child on the child's level, with special attention paid to the sound of the story when read aloud. Gág chose only those tales she felt were suitable for children, but she did not want to deprive the story of "salt and vinegar" as she believed a little "goriness" never hurt anyone, certainly not boys and girls. She rendered her versions of the old tales in the lilt of the storytelling of her Bohemian grandmother.

By 1940, though only working on books of her choosing, Gág was producing more than she wanted, and her heart was no longer in it. When her publisher pressed her to write a novel, she refused, but instead edited and published her teenage journals as *Growing Pains: Diaries and Drawings for the Years 1908–1917*. In the years that followed, she published some drawings and adapted her picture books as radio plays, while devoting the majority of her time to fine art.

In 1930, Gág had received the Mary S. Colliers Prize at the Philadelphia Print Club Show for the best lithograph, "Lamplight." During the years 1931 to 1940, her works were exhibited in Mexico, Russia, Sweden, and at the New York World's Fair. The Weyhe Gallery mounted a retrospective covering 35 years of Gág's work in 1940, at the same time that her diary *Growing Pains* was published. In 1943, she received a prize at the Artists for Victory Show from the Metropolitan Museum of Art for "Lamplight," and the following year she was honored with a Purchase Prize from the Congressional Library in Washington, D.C., for "Barns." Gág is permanently represented in leading American and European art galleries.

In the spring of 1945, Wanda Gág was diagnosed with lung cancer, but the nature of her illness was kept from her. Despite her long months as an invalid, she was able to continue the preliminary drawings for *More Tales from Grimm*. Her childhood friend **Alma Scott** was writing her biography at the time, and Gág took part in the effort, adding details and personal reactions. Gág and her husband spent the winter of 1945–46 in Florida; she wrote to her family of returning strength and of the work she was doing for her new book. She wanted to surprise her editor with the progress she had made, but, shortly after arriving back in New Jersey, Gág died on June 27, 1946. *More Tales from Grimm* was published by her family in 1947, with her unfinished drawings. Her indomitable artistic spirit had produced to the very end.

SOURCES:

Commire, Anne, ed. *Yesterday's Authors of Books for Children.* Vol. 1. Detroit, MI: Gale Research, 1977.

Craven, Thomas. "The Diary of a Working Artist," in *New York Herald Tribune Books.* September 29, 1940.

Dobbs, Rose. "Wanda Gág, Fellow-Worker," in *Horn Book Magazine.* Vol. XXIII, no. 3. May 1947.

Evans, Ernestine. "Wanda Gág as Writer," in *Horn Book Magazine.* Vol. XXIII, no. 3. May 1947.

Gág, Wanda. *Growing Pains: Diaries and Drawings for the Years 1908–1917.* NY: Coward-McCann, 1940.

Hearn, Michael Patrick. "Wanda Gág," in *Dictionary of Literary Biography: American Writers for Children 1900–1960.* Vol. 22. Detroit, MI: Gale Research, 1983.

The New York Times (obituaries). June 28, 1946.

Scott, Alma, *Wanda Gág: The Story of an Artist.* Minneapolis, MN: University of Minnesota Press, 1949.

Senick, Gerard, ed. "Wanda Gág, 1893–1946," in *Childrens' Literature Review.* Vol. 4. Detroit, MI: Gale Research, 1982.

Wanda Gág Tribute Issue. *Horn Book Magazine.* May 1947.

Ward, Lynd. "Wanda Gág, Fellow Artist," in *Horn Book Magazine.* Vol. XXIII, no. 3. May 1947.

Zigrosser, Carl. "Wanda Gág, Artist," in *Horn Book Magazine.* Vol. XXIII, no. 3. May 1947.

COLLECTIONS:

Correspondence, papers and memorabilia located in the New York Public Library; papers and memorabilia are on deposit in the Free Library of Philadelphia; papers, artwork and memorabilia are located in Walter Library at the University of Minnesota and the Minneapolis Institute of Art.

Laurie Twist Binder,
Library Media Specialist, Buffalo Public Schools, Buffalo, New York, and freelance graphic artist and illustrator

Gage, Frances D. (1808–1884)

American reformer and author. Name variations: (pseudonym) Aunt Fanny. Born Frances Dana Barker on October 12, 1808, in Marietta, Washington County, Ohio; died in Greenwich, Connecticut, on November 10, 1884; daughter of Joseph Barker (a farmer and cooper) and Elizabeth (Dana) Barker; married James L. Gage (a lawyer), on January 1, 1829; children: eight, including **Mary Gage.**

Frances D. Gage was born Frances Barker in 1808 in Marietta, a town on the Muskingum River in Ohio. She was the daughter of Joseph Barker, a farmer and native of New Hampshire, and **Elizabeth Dana Barker**, who was related to the Danas of Massachusetts. Frances attended a log-cabin school in the Ohio woods and assisted her father in barrel-making.

At age 20, she married James L. Gage, a lawyer from McConnellsville, Ohio. The couple had eight children, yet Gage still found time to write for leading journals and speak to gatherings about women's rights, temperance, and the evils of slavery. In return, she was subjected to ridicule and persecution. "Those who have never advocated an unpopular idea—who have not made principle, rather than policy, their guiding star—cannot appreciate the peculiar trials of those who are true in word and action," she wrote.

In 1851, while attending a Woman's Rights Convention in Akron, Ohio, Gage was chosen to be president of the meeting. In 1853, the family moved to St. Louis, Missouri, then a slave-holding state. Branded an abolitionist, she and her family endured threats and three disastrous fires on their property, probably started by arsonists, that effectively reduced the family's resources.

With her husband ill, Gage took the post of assistant editor of an agricultural paper in

Columbus, Ohio. Soon after, however, the Civil War began, destroying the newspaper's circulation. When four of her sons joined the army, Gage, along with her daughter Mary, began to minister to needs of soldiers and freedmen, while speaking to Soldiers' Aid Societies. In summers, Frances was an unsalaried agent of the Sanitary Commission, covering territory down the Mississippi to Memphis, Vicksburg, and Natchez. During this period, she was crippled in a carriage accident in Galesburg, Illinois, and laid up for one year. In August 1867, she suffered paralysis brought on by a stroke and was confined to her room, but she continued writing and became well known for her children's stories, written under the name "Aunt Fanny."

Gage, Matilda Joslyn (1826–1898)

Influential 19th-century radical suffragist whose work on behalf of the rights of women has been largely ignored. Born Matilda Joslyn in Cicero, New York, on March 25, 1826; died of an embolism in Chicago, Illinois, on March 18, 1898; daughter of Dr. Hezekiah Joslyn (a physician) and Helen (Leslie) Joslyn; married Henry H. Gage, in 1845; children: Helen Leslie Gage; Thomas Clarkson Gage; Julie L. Gage; Maud Gage.

Delivered her first public address advocating women's rights in Syracuse, New York (1852); formed the National Woman Suffrage Association with Elizabeth Cady Stanton and Susan B. Anthony and helped found the New York State Woman Suffrage Association (1869); named president of both state and national suffrage organizations (1875); co-wrote the "Declaration of the Rights of Women" (1876); was a founding member of the Equal Rights Party (1880); co-edited with Stanton and Anthony the first three volumes of the History of Woman Suffrage *(1881–86); formed the* Woman's National Liberal Union *(1890); published* Woman, Church and State *(1893).*

Along with *Susan B. Anthony and *Elizabeth Cady Stanton, Matilda Joslyn Gage was the third member of the great 19th-century triumvirate of women suffragists. Yet unlike Anthony and Stanton, whose names remain synonymous with the struggle for women's rights, Gage, a talented organizer, theoretician, and "one of the most logical, scientific and fearless writers of her day," is barely remembered. Recent scholarly work by feminist writers, including **Sally Roesch Wagner** and the radical theologian **Mary Daly**, have sought to correct this historical oversight. More radical than either Anthony or Stanton, Gage was also the most intellectually daring. While her contemporaries focused on political issues, particularly the vote, Gage concerned herself with the broader sociological and historical aspects of women's issues. While others worked within the system to improve the legal status of women, Gage's vision moved her outside the system and beyond the company of her fellow crusaders.

Matilda Joslyn Gage's interest in reform and her passionate dedication to women's rights was formed early. Born on March 25, 1826, in Cicero, New York, the only child of Dr. Hezekiah Joslyn and **Helen Leslie Joslyn**, Gage's upbringing from the first was decidedly unconventional. Unlike in most privileged bourgeois households of the 19th century, the dinner conversation in the Joslyn house was likely to turn to enlightened and lively discussions about abolition, temperance, women's rights and free thought—ideas her progressive-minded parents fervently advocated. Their home in Cicero was a meeting place for reformers and, reputedly, for members of the Underground Railroad.

Her father took it upon himself to supervise his daughter's education. Rather than attend school, Gage was tutored at home in Greek, mathematics and physiology. At age 15, she was sent to the Clinton (NY) Liberal Institute where she completed her formal education. Around 1843–44, Hezekiah Joslyn contacted an old instructor of his to find out if his daughter could receive a medical education. Nothing came of his inquiry.

Yet despite her unconventional upbringing, Gage, at least initially, set out on the very conventional course of marriage, children and housekeeping. In 1845, at age 18, she married Henry H. Gage, a merchant, and the young couple set up house in Fayetteville, New York. Over the next few years, her husband's business prospered, and she gave birth to five children (one died in infancy). Most of her energies during this time were directed towards raising the children and managing household affairs. Like her father, she was deeply interested and involved in her children's education, and by all accounts she was the dominant intellectual force in the household. One daughter later described her mother as "a character of independence of thought and action, decided convictions, courage of opinions, strong personality, great love of liberty and sympathy for the down-trodden."

Despite caring for her family and recuperating from her own recurrent bouts of illness, Gage became deeply interested in the burgeoning women's rights movement. In September

1852, at age 26, she made her first public address for the rights of women at the National Woman's Rights Convention in Syracuse, New York. Her appearance was a testament to her courage and determination. Gage was the youngest speaker at the convention and completely unknown. She suffered greatly from stage fright (a condition she never fully conquered), yet she ascended the platform and spoke passionately to the assembled suffragists, including Elizabeth Cady Stanton. In her speech, Gage urged that "self reliance [be] one of the first lessons taught to our daughters" and advocated legal and educational equality. Much of her speech was illustrated with notable examples of women's achievements throughout history. Extolling women's accomplishments, despite all the legal and societal obstacles placed in their way, was a theme that recurred in her speeches and writings for the rest of her life.

Two years later, while vacationing in the fashionable resort town of Saratoga Springs, New York, she encountered Susan B. Anthony. The distressed Anthony was attempting to organize a town meeting on women's rights but with little success; though she had hired a hall, she had no speakers; though she was distributing flyers, she would be hard put to pay for them; and, on top of that, her purse had been stolen. Gage agreed to help; she also agreed to overcome her fear of public speaking. The meeting was a triumph, due in no small part to Gage's speech and her involvement. Her stylish attire and youthful appearance helped to belie the conventional notion in the press and in the minds of the public that suffragists were not particularly feminine. One reporter described Gage as a "medium sized, and lady-like looking woman, dressed in tasty plaid silk with two flounces." She would pass muster.

Following her appearance in Saratoga Springs, Matilda Joslyn Gage became a key player in virtually every women's rights' effort over the next 40 years. In 1869, women's rights advocates split into two organizations. Conservative reformers and later members of the Women's Christian Temperance Union formed the American Woman Suffrage Association. The more radical-minded Matilda Joslyn Gage, Elizabeth Cady Stanton and Susan B. Anthony formed the National Woman Suffrage Association (NWSA). That same year, Gage helped found and became secretary and vice president of the New York State Woman Suffrage Association.

Though Gage continued to rally support by speaking publicly on behalf of women's rights, her real talents lay in organizing and writing. She was a voracious reader, a thorough researcher, and a creative thinker who used her pen deftly and brilliantly to record the past accomplishments of women, thus creating a historical framework for the women's suffrage movement. Susan B. Anthony credited her with "bringing more startling facts to light than any woman I know." Her series of pamphlets, including "Woman as Inventor" (1870) which contained evidence that a woman (*Catharine Littlefield Greene) invented the cotton gin; "Woman's Rights Catechism" (1871); and "Who Planned the Tennessee Campaign of 1862? Or *Anna Ella Carroll vs. Ulysses S. Grant" (1880) which argued that a woman planned the military strategy that changed the course of the Civil War, were widely read and enormously influential. Gage was also a regular contributor to the NWSA's newspaper, *Revolution*, and from 1878 to 1881 edited the monthly *National Citizen and Ballot Box* published by the NWSA. With Anthony and Stanton, she also edited the first three volumes of the monumental *History of Woman Suffrage* (1881–86).

Gage tried unsuccessfully to cast a ballot in the 1872 presidential election. When Susan B. Anthony successfully voted and was arrested, Gage was the only woman to join the speaking campaign that Anthony organized following her arrest. She and Anthony crisscrossed the country over the next year, making a series of public addresses. Her speech, "The United States on Trial—Not Susan B. Anthony," argued that the central issue was not whether the government should *grant* women rights; rather that the government had *denied* women rights to which they, as citizens and human beings, were naturally entitled.

In 1873, the NWSA called for a more organized national suffrage campaign under the revived motto of "no taxation without representation." The effort was launched on December 16, 1873, the centennial anniversary of the Boston Tea Party. At the New York Woman Suffrage Association, Matilda Joslyn Gage appealed to "the tax paying women of New York . . . to protest against the tyranny of taxation without representation." Gage once again laid the foundation for the protest by recalling that the original protestors in 1773 were women who had organized themselves and refused to buy tea from England. Though the campaign did not win them the vote, it legitimized their efforts, gained them new support, and moved the issue of women's suffrage more firmly to the center of public debate.

Matilda Joslyn Gage

In 1875, Gage testified before Congress on behalf of women's rights. That same year, she was elected president of both the state and national associations but turned over the post in the national association to the more visible Stanton in 1876, the centennial anniversary of the signing of the Declaration of Independence. In January of that year, the NWSA held a meeting in Washington, D.C. At Gage's urging, the members agreed to draft a "Declaration of the Rights of Women." Written by Gage and Stanton, the declaration asked for "no special favors, no special privileges, no special legislation" but rather called for "all the civil and political rights that belong to citizens of the United States, be guaranteed to us and to our daughters forever." At the close of the reading of the original Declaration of Independence at the July 4 centennial celebration in Philadelphia, Gage, Anthony and two other NWSA members marched to the stage and, before they could be stopped, presented the "Declaration of the Rights of Women" to the vice president of the United States. The bold move drew attention and newspaper coverage but accomplished little else.

Gage's efforts on behalf of women's rights remained undiminished. In 1877, she drafted a "Petition for Relief from Political Disabilities," and her congressional representative introduced a bill to declare Matilda Joslyn Gage "a citizen of the United States, clothed with all the political rights and powers of citizenship, namely the right to vote and hold office to the same extent and in the same degree that male citizens enjoy this right." Scores of women across the country followed her example, and Congress was flooded with similar petitions.

In 1880, Gage lobbied the national conventions of the Republican, Democrat, and Greenback-Labor parties in an unsuccessful bid to add women's suffrage to their platforms. Undaunted, Gage and other activists formed the Equal Rights Party with Gage acting as elector-at-large. The party nominated *Belva Lockwood for president and **Marietta Stow** for vice president under the slogan "Rally round the flag, girls/ Rally round the flag, Shouting the battle cry of freedom." The Equal Rights Party platform included equal justice for all, regardless of race, sex or nationality, as well as an international peace pact, self-determination for Native Americans, and civil-service reform. In the 1884 election, the Lockwood-Stow ticket received 4,149 popular votes.

[Gage] is a major radical feminist theoretician and historian whose written work is indispensable for an understanding of the women's movement today.

—Mary Daly

As time went on, Matilda Joslyn Gage was becoming far more radicalized than her NWSA sisters. Increasingly, she found herself at ideological odds with Anthony and Stanton. The decisive break came in 1890 when Anthony engineered a merger between the NWSA and the conservative American Woman Suffrage Association (which included members of the Women's Christian Temperance Union). Gage was completely opposed to this merger on ideological grounds. Her work in the women's suffrage movement was leading her to a belief that the established churches, namely Christianity, bore a preponderance of responsibility for the prevailing notion of male superiority. She left the NWSA and formed the Woman's National Liberal Union. The new organization was more extreme in its views and focused on a wider range of issues relating to women, including the oppression of women by the church. It also called for an end to prayer in public school and supported labor reform. That year, Gage also published a pamphlet, *The Dangers of the Hour,* which outlined the

development of her ideas through four decades of work in the women's movement. This manifesto constituted a clear warning to her friends in the movement that she was moving in a very different—and far more radical—direction than they were.

Gage expanded her views in her magnum opus *Woman, Church and State* (1893). The book's dedication said it all: "Dedicated to all Christian women and men, of whatever creed or name who, bound by church or state, have not dared to think for themselves." In *Woman, Church and State*, Gage set out to prove that the most egregious wrong ever inflicted upon woman was in the Christian teaching that God did not create her as man's equal. Gage traced this idea back to its origins in *Genesis* and claimed that this basic tenet of Christian faith had effectively stripped women of power and importance and sentenced them to lifetimes of subjugation.

Gage's assertion in *Woman, Church and State* was that in primitive, pre-Christian civilizations women exercised a great deal of authority and power. She referred to this period as the "Matriarchate" or Mother-rule. During the Matriarchate, women controlled social, political, and religious rituals and institutions. Gage then illustrated how Judaism and the rise of Christianity signaled the beginning of the "Patriarchate" or Father-rule in which men seized control of all aspects of society and systematically robbed women of authority and position. Gage went so far as to attribute the practices of infanticide, prostitution, and polygamy to the rise of the Patriarchate.

Woman, Church and State was widely read but offended many in the women's movement, particularly members of the Women's Christian Temperance Union. Gage was seen to have gone beyond the pale, with the result that she was written off by the mainstream leadership of the women's movement and written out of its history.

Matilda Joslyn Gage spent her later years in Chicago at the home of her youngest daughter. Declining health effectively ended her public appearances. Though she remained committed to women's suffrage, a budding interest in spiritual matters, including a flirtation with Theosophy, occupied much of her time. Gage, exceedingly ill, drafted but never delivered a speech for the 50th-anniversary convention of the women's rights movement in 1898. After two years of invalidism brought on by heart disease, she died of an embolism in the brain on March 18, 1898, at the age of 71. Upon her gravestone was carved her lifelong motto—"There is a word sweeter than Mother, Home, or Heaven: that word is liberty."

SOURCES AND SUGGESTED READING:

Buhle, Mari Jo, and Paul Buhle. *The Concise History of Women Suffrage.* Urbana, IL: University Of Illinois Press, 1978.

Daly, Mary. *Gyn/Ecology: The Metaethics of Radical Feminism.* Boston, MA: Beacon Press, 1978.

Gage, Matilda Joslyn. *Woman, Church and State.* NY: Arno Press, 1972 (reprint).

——, Elizabeth Cady Stanton, and Susan B. Anthony. *History of Woman Suffrage.* Vol. 1 (1881), Vol. 2 (1882), Vol. 3 (1886); *Ida Husted Harper and Susan B. Anthony, eds. Vol. 4 (1902); Ida Husted Harper, ed. Vols. 5 and 6 (1922). Salem: Ayer Company reprint, 1985.

James, Edward T., ed. *Notable American Women, 1607–1950: A Biographical Dictionary.* Vol. II. Cambridge, MA: Belknap Press of Harvard University Press, 1971.

McHenry, Robert, ed. *Famous American Women; A Biographical Dictionary from Colonial Times to the Present.* NY: Dover, 1983.

Spender, Dale. *Women of Ideas and What Men Have Done to Them.* London: Routledge & Kegan Paul, 1982.

Wagner, Sally Roesch. *A Time of Protest: Suffragists Challenge the Republic: 1870–1887.* Sacramento, CA: Spectrum Publications, 1987.

Zophy, Angela Howard, ed. *Handbook of American Women's History.* NY: Garland, 1990.

COLLECTIONS:

Gage Collection, Schlesinger Library, Radcliffe College, Cambridge, Massachusetts.

Matilda Joslyn Gage Woman Suffrage Scrapbooks, 4 vols., Library of Congress.

Suzanne Smith, freelance writer, Decatur, Georgia

Gahagan, Helen (1900–1980).

See Douglas, Helen Gahagan.

Gaidinliu, Rani (1915—)

Indian freedom fighter. Name variations: Rani Gaidinliu of Nagaland. Born in 1915.

The daughter of a poor farmer, Rani Gaidinliu joined the Indian freedom fighters in the 1920s, when she was just 13. At age 16, she led the Naga guerrillas against the British in a battle that led to her arrest and a 14-year imprisonment. In 1947, after India's hard-won independence, she was released by President Jawaharlal Nehru and later became a social worker in Nagaland. Her Zeliangrong Heraka Association worked to revive the cultural and religious heritage of the region. Professor Meijinlung Kamson created the Rani Gaidinliu Foundation in 1993.

Gaigerova, Varvara Andrianovna (1903–1944)

Russian composer, pianist and concertmaster who was interested in the musical heritage of the minority peoples of the Soviet Union, particularly in its southeastern regions. Born in Oryekhovo-Zuyevo, Russia, on October 4, 1903; died in Moscow on April 6, 1944; graduated from the Moscow Conservatory, 1927, where she studied piano and composition with the noted composer Nikolai Miaskovsky.

As a child prodigy, began her concert career in her early teens; served as concertmaster of the Bolshoi Theater Orchestra (1936–44).

The Bolshevik Revolution of November 1917 was a cataclysmic event in the lives of tens of millions not only in Russia but in the surrounding regions of the recently defunct Romanov Empire. In the musical world, the consequences were enormous. While many distinguished composers like Alexander Glazunov and Sergei Rachmaninoff fled the country for the West, others remained to preserve precious traditions and in some cases attempt to create a new, more socially conscious musical culture. For Soviet women musicians, considerable opportunities were opened by both the Communist ideology, which asserted the equality of the sexes, and the bitter realities of the day, which generated massive gaps in society because of loss of male lives in war, revolution, harsh industrialization and ruthless purges. Women of energy and talent were sometimes able to fill these gaps.

Varvara Gaigerova's abilities spanned the worlds of both performance and composition. An instrumentalist, she was concertmaster at the Bolshoi Theater, and she created over a period of two decades an impressive body of compositions reflecting the musical and political ideals of early Soviet society. Many of her works were inspired by the music of the less-developed nationalities of the Soviet Union. Among her compositions we find three symphonies, the second of which was based on Kalmuk themes. She also composed three orchestral suites for domra orchestra, utilizing the unique timbres of traditional instruments. One of her string quartets was inspired by Yakut themes, and a posthumously published piano sonatina derived its main themes from Buryat-Mongolian music. She also made many arrangements for Western instruments of traditional songs of the Bashkir, Buryat, Kazakh, Kirghiz, Tatar, Uzbek and other non-Russian peoples of the USSR. Gaigerova died in April 1944, during a trying period for Russia when the immense sacrifices of its people had not yet resulted in a final victory over Fascism.

John Haag,
Athens, Georgia

Gaisuenta (d. c. 568).

See Galswintha.

Gaite, Carmen Martín (b. 1925).

See Martín Gaite, Carmen.

Galard, Geneviève de (b. 1925).

See de Galard, Geneviève.

Galdikas, Biruté (1948—)

German-born primatologist and conservationist. Name variations: Birute Galdikas; Biruté M.G. Galdikas. Pronunciation: bi-ROO-tay GAHL-di-kuhs. Born Biruté Marija Filomena Galdikas on May 10, 1948, in Wiesbaden, West Germany; eldest of the four children of Anatanas Galdikas (a miner) and Filomena Galdikas; grew up in Toronto, Ontario, Canada; attended Elliot Lake High School, in northern Ontario; attended the University of British Columbia; B.A. (summa cum laude), 1966, M.A., and Ph.D. from the University of California at Los Angeles (UCLA); married Rod Brindamour, in 1970 (divorced 1979); married Pak Bohap (a Dayak tribesman and farmer), in 1981; children: (first marriage) son, Binti Paul Brindamour (b. 1976); (second marriage) Frederick Bohap; Filomena Jane Bohap.

Started the Orangutan Research and Conservation Project in Kalimantan, Indonesian Borneo (1971); became an Indonesian citizen; serves as a professor extraordinaire at the Universitas Nasional in Jakarta; under a special decree, served as a senior advisor to Indonesia's Ministry of Forestry on orangutan issues (March 1996–March 1998); won the prestigious Kalpataru award, the highest award given by the Republic of Indonesia for outstanding environmental leadership, the first person of non-Indonesian birth and one of the first women to be so recognized by the Indonesian government (June 1997).

It has been said that Canadian primatologist Biruté Galdikas simply knows more about orangutans than anyone else in the world. Indeed, since 1971, when she launched the Orangutan Research and Conservation Project in Kalimantan (Indonesian Borneo), Galdikas has lived and worked in the rain forest, studying and preserving "the people of the forest," which is how Malays refer to the orangutans. "To do what she does takes tremendous grit and a willingness to put up with not just the uncomfortable aspect of living out in the tropics but the politics and logistics of it all," said Dr. Gary Shapiro, a vice president of Orangutan Foundation International, which Galdikas established in 1987. "That's the whole reason there aren't more people doing these kinds of studies. It's extremely difficult to keep up that energy level, and she's done it." Along with ***Jane Goodall** and ***Dian Fossey**, who similarly researched chimpanzees and gorillas, respectively, Galdikas is one of "Leakey's Angels," a reference to the great anthropologist Louis Leakey who supported all three women in their work.

Of Lithuanian heritage, Galdikas was the eldest of the four children (two girls and two boys) of Anatanas and **Filomena Galdikas**. Born in Wiesbaden, in what was then West Germany, she grew up in Toronto, Ontario, Canada, where her parents settled when she was two. As a child, Galdikas was influenced by the natural world around her and by her mother's bedtime stories about ancient cultures. As a result, she developed into what she calls "that unlikely combination of bookworm and nature lover." She recalls that the first book she ever checked out of the library was H.A. and ***Margaret Rey**'s children's classic, *Curious George*, featuring a monkey as its title character, and that as she matured she remained fascinated by apes, jungles, and history. "Not just the written history, but all of it," she told Sy Montgomery. "Human history and beyond. . . . I remember thinking that if we understood our closest human relatives we'd understand our origins . . . maybe our own behavior."

Galdikas attended high school in northern Ontario, where the family moved after her parents lost just about everything in a bad real-estate transaction. While attending Elliot Lake High School, Galdikas became interested in orangutans, because, in her words, "I thought they must resemble our own ancestors who stood at the beginning of prehistory." She was particularly drawn to the orangutan's eyes, which unlike those of gorillas and chimps, resemble the eyes of humans, with irises surrounded by white. In time, Galdikas' fascination with the red apes solidified into a plan to study the animals in their natural habitat.

After high school, while her family was waiting for visas to join relatives in Los Angeles, California, Galdikas briefly attended the University of British Columbia. In 1965, she entered the University of Southern California at Los Angeles (UCLA), graduating with a B.A. in psychology in 1966. She immediately began graduate study in the department of anthropology, specializing in archaeology and taking every opportunity to join weekend excavations in order to gain field experience. She also spent a semester at the University of Arizona field school, working at the Grasshopper field site at the Fort Apache reservation. While still studying at UCLA, Galdikas met the two men who would greatly influence her future: Rod Brindamour, a 17-year-old Canadian whom she would marry in 1970, and Louis Leakey, who would help her realize her goal to initiate a long-term study of orangutans.

Galdikas first approached Leakey following a lecture he delivered at the UCLA campus in 1969. "As soon as I heard him talk about primates and great ape studies, and sending Jane and Dian into the field, I knew this was it," she later recalled. But first Galdikas had to qualify for Leakey's support, which necessitated submitting to a series of strange little "intelligence" tests. In one such brainteaser, Leakey spread out a deck of playing cards face down on the table and told her to identify which cards were red and which were black. The design on all the cards was identical, but Galdikas noticed that half the

Biruté
Galdikas

cards were slightly bent and half were not. When she told Leakey this, he fairly twinkled with delight, having confirmed to his satisfaction that Galdikas, like Goodall and Fossey before her, possessed the observation skills necessary to the study of animal behavior. (Leakey confided in her that men tended to fail his little test. He also shared his view that women were more perceptive and more patient then men, and less likely to excite aggressive tendencies in male primates the way men did.) Leakey was also impressed with Galdikas' enthusiasm and determination, which he prized even above formal education. He agreed to sponsor her and began looking into a research site and funding for her project. In the interim—"limbo," as she would later call it—Galdikas finished her Ph.D. course work, as Leakey had suggested. She spent time studying the six immature orangutans at the Los Angeles zoo and made two trips to what was then Yugoslavia to work on joint American-Yugoslav archaeological ventures. She also conducted a commuter relationship with Rod, who, following their marriage in 1970, had returned to Canada to finish high school and begin college.

By 1971, Leakey had raised $9,000, enough to get the orangutan project off the ground. (During the first decade of the project, Galdikas received additional funding from the National Geographic Society, the World Wildlife Fund, the L.S.B. Leakey Foundation, the New York Zoological Society, and the Chicago Zoological Society. From 1984, the bulk of funding for the project was provided by Earthwatch, a Massachusetts-based scientific organization which also supplied Galdikas with teams of volunteers who paid their own way to assist her in her research.) In November 1971, Galdikas and her husband finally arrived in the old hut that would be their home at Tanjung Puting, in the heart of the swampy forest of southern Borneo. "It was filthy and filled with all sorts of vermin," she told *People Weekly*. Beyond the primitive living quarters, which she christened "Camp Leakey," were perilous encounters with wild pigs, crocodiles, and poisonous snakes. But, as Galdikas later related in her book *Reflections of Eden*, the true hazards of the rain forest were really the "little nagging things like viruses, parasites, insects, and plant toxins. The leeches were so abundant that we lost track of how many we took off our bodies during the course of any one day. Bloated with our blood, leeches fell out of our socks, dropped off our necks, and squirmed out of our underwear." She also described a deep and painful skin burn she developed from sitting on a fallen log that was oozing toxic sap. There

were the additional hardships of constant humidity which permeated clothing and rotted books, and a limited diet consisting mainly of rice, canned sardines, pigs' feet, and bananas.

In addition to the struggle of day-to-day living was the enormous challenge of trying to locate the animals she had been commissioned to study. Although she sometimes spotted their night nests high in the trees, the orangutans themselves continually eluded her, disappearing into the foliage as soon as they detected her presence. If she did manage to close in on a group, they made it clear that she was not welcome, hurling fruit and dead trees in her direction. If Galdikas was successful in tracking one or more of the animals for several days, she found, more often than not, that "nothing happened." Unlike highly sociable chimps and gorillas, orangutans typically spend their days alone, often doing nothing more exciting than swinging from tree to tree looking for food. Moreover, when the animals do form groups, they seldom interact, tending to ignore each other. "Compiling data on the animals was considerably tougher for Biruté than for me," Jane Goodall once remarked. "Chimps are very sociable. It might take her a year to see what I can observe in one lucky day."

Galdikas, however, persevered, and in her years of research amassed an extraordinary amount of information about the species. She was the first scientist to discover that orangutans are not strict vegetarians, and the first to document the eight-year birthing cycle of the female. Although orangutans are notoriously solitary animals, Galdikas found that they are not totally antisocial. Adult females, who reach sexual maturity at about ten, nurture their offspring until they reach seven or eight, and adolescent females frequently forage for food in groups. The real loners of the species are the adult males, who only keep the company of a female for mating purposes and care little about offspring. Males will also occasionally rape a female, causing the female to bite her attacker and emit what Galdikas identified as a "rape grunt." Still, for the most part, orangutans do not require much contact with one another, a fact that profoundly affected Galdikas. "Orangutans forced me to come to terms with my own human nature, with the 'weakness' of simply being human," she wrote. "*Homo sapiens* is a sociable species. We need mates, children, loved ones, friends, acquaintances, even pets. Without intimate relationships, without communities, we are stranded."

In addition to tracking orangutans in their natural environment, Galdikas also became involved in the on going rehabilitation of ex-captive animals rescued from black-market traders. When feasible, the animals are nursed back to health and then released into the wild. Thus, Galdikas serves as a surrogate mother to large numbers of ex-captive orangutans, who in varying degrees interact with her and all of the other people involved in the project. Even Galdikas' first child, Binti Paul, born in 1976, played fearlessly among the animals when he was a baby. "Sometimes, I felt as though I were surrounded by wild, unruly children in orange suits who had not yet learned their manners," Galdikas wrote in a 1980 article in National Geographic. As of 2000, Galdikas had successfully returned more than 200 orangutans back into the wild, prompting the wildlife-conservation community to laud her efforts. Although some scientists have expressed concern about the impact of the ex-captives on the ecology, Galdikas argues that since orangutans have become an endangered species, the program is crucial. Others criticize her methods of introducing the ex-captives back into the wild population, saying it is frequently unsuccessful and risks transmitting fatal diseases to the wild orangutans. In contrast to Galdikas' approach, Dutch botanist Willie Smits, who oversees a orangutan reserve in eastern Borneo, limits human contact with the animals and releases them back into the jungle in places where there are no wild orangutans. Richard Wrangham, a primatology professor at Harvard University, upholds Smits' method, calling it "biologically appropriate."

As an adjunct to her work in returning captive orangutans to the wild, Galdikas is also involved in the preservation of the species whose numbers have been threatened partly by poachers, but more so by the clearing of vast areas of the forests by loggers. To raise money for this aspect of her work, Galdikas established the Orangutan Foundation International, a non-profit organization headquartered in Los Angeles. The commitment to conservation forced Galdikas to master the intricacies of the Indonesian bureaucracy, which she accomplished through diplomacy and by establishing good working relationships with government officials. She has earned the respect of many high officials and has enjoyed a number of significant victories, among them having Tanjung Puting declared a national park, thus bringing an end to trade in captive orangutans in the province.

Galdikas documented the early years of her research in her Ph.D. thesis, completed in 1978. Since that time, she has published very little of her research findings, a fact that draws sharp criticism from her academic colleagues, including Peter S. Rodman, a professor of anthropology at the University of California at Davis. "Here is someone who has this tremendous wealth of material. It could answer questions that the rest of us can only speculate about and we can't get at it," he told Mark Starowicz of The New York Times Magazine. "There are some implicit rules about what we do. If we seek support from some agency, then we receive it, and other people don't. So you expect something more than National Geographic articles, and descriptions of one's personal life with apes." In 1994, Earthwatch withdrew its support of Galdikas, citing, among other things, her failure to publish reports on her observations. Galdikas has responded to her critics by pointing out that her preservation work is simply more important. "When a species in threatened with extinction," she proclaims, "I don't understand how anyone can say it is more important to study than to save it."

Galdikas' dedication to her work has taken its toll on her personal life. In 1978, her husband Rod returned to Canada with Binti's Indonesian babysitter, with whom he had fallen in love. After so many years in Galdikas' shadow, he also wished to return to school and pursue a career of his own. In 1979, the couple divorced, and Binti ultimately went to live with his father. (Galdikas has visited him yearly from 1981, when she became at visiting professor at Simon Fraser University in Vancouver, British Columbia, where she is now a full professor.) In 1981, Galdikas married Pak Bohap, a Dayak tribesman who had been an employee at Camp Leakey. Since Bohap has never traveled outside of Indonesia, speaks no English (Galdikas is fluent in Indonesian), and has only a sixth-grade education, the marriage mystified some of Galdikas' Western colleagues. "He's as educated as I am, except he wasn't educated at a university. He was educated by experience," Galdikas told People. "He's a very smart and shrewd man—smarter than I am." The couple have two children—Frederick and Filomena Jane (named for Galdikas' mother and Jane Goodall)—and live in a large home Bohap built in his native village of Pasir Panjang. Though he respects her research and helps her with her fieldwork, Bohap has returned to farming, his occupation when the couple met, and he does not accompany Galdikas when she travels to lecture or teach. "Cross cultural marriages often become strained," Galdikas writes in her book. "Because Pak Bohap and I take equal delight in our children and our roles as parents, and because we have retained our individual identities, our marriage endures."

Most recently Galdikas has been targeted in a new controversy over her rehabilitation work. The primary charge is that she has kept nearly 100 orphaned orangutans at her home illegally and in poor conditions, and that many have died there of various communicable diseases, such as tuberculosis and hepatitis. Other allegations center on her alleged obsessiveness and mistreatment of her research assistants and staffers. Galdikas denies the charges, calling them a "smear campaign" conducted by jealous rivals, namely Willie Smits, whom she says "wants to become the undisputed king of the rain forest in Borneo."

Despite the dispute, Galdikas remains passionate about her life's work with the red apes, whom she calls gentle, noble creatures with great intelligence. "Looking into the calm, unblinking eyes of an orangutan we see, as through a series of mirrors, not only the image of our own creation but also a reflection of our own souls and an Eden that once was ours," she writes at the close of *Reflections of Eden*. "And on occasion, fleetingly, just for a nanosecond, but with an intensity that is shocking in its profoundness, we recognize that there is no separation between ourselves and nature. We are allowed to see the eyes of God."

SOURCES:

Galdikas, Biruté M.G. *Reflections of Eden: My Years with the Orangutans of Borneo*. Boston, MA: Little, Brown, 1995.

Graham, Judith, ed. *Current Biography Yearbook 1995*. NY: H.W. Wilson, 1995.

Hammer, Joshua. "A Typhoon in a Rain-Forest Eden," in *Newsweek*. Vol. 131, no. 22. June 1, 1998, pp. 58–60.

Montgomery, Sy. *Walking with the Great Apes: Jane Goodall, Dian Fossey, Biruté Galdikas*. NY: Houghton Mifflin, 1992.

People Weekly. January 16, 1989.

SUGGESTED READING:

Spalding, Linda. *A Dark Place in the Jungle*. NC: Algonquin Books, 1999.

Barbara Morgan,
Melrose, Massachusetts.

Gale, Zona (1874–1938)

Pulitzer Prize-winning author, regional writer, and political activist. Born Zona Gale on August 26, 1874, in Portage, Wisconsin; died of pneumonia on December 27, 1938, in Chicago, Illinois; daughter of Charles S. Gale (a railroad engineer) and Eliza (Beers) Gale (a teacher); graduated from the University of Wisconsin, 1895; married William L. Breese, in 1928; children: Leslyn Breese (adopted 1928).

Published Friendship Village *stories (1908, 1909); involved in Progressive Party activities, woman suffrage, and pacifism (1912–24); won Pulitzer Prize for the drama* Miss Lulu Bett *(1921); appointed to Board of Regents, University of Wisconsin (1923); named Wisconsin's representative to International Congress of Women (1933); elected to the University of Wisconsin Board of Visitors (1935). Honorary degrees from Ripon College (1922), University of Wisconsin (1929), Mount Mary College (1930), and Rollins College (1931).*

Portage, Wisconsin, was the center of Zona Gale's world, both literary and actual. The majority of her stories, novels, and plays are set in some version of the small town where she spent most of her life. More than just a regional writer chronicling a village, Gale brought an acerbic realism to her best work, similar to that of Sinclair Lewis' in *Main Street*. In her lesser writings, Gale sometimes tended to indulge in saccharine sentimentality, other times in a floating mysticism. Although she was among the first women to win a Pulitzer Prize in literature, her work is seldom included in current anthologies.

The Gale family formed a tight and private circle. As she was an only child and defined as "not strong," Zona's parents were exceptionally protective and discouraged her from active play with other children. She did little running, skating, or dancing. Instead, her early life seems to have involved quiet imaginative games, often played with her mother, and an unusual attentiveness to her parents. Until their deaths when Zona was in middle age, their beliefs and a quest for their approval defined their daughter's life.

Charles Gale was a mostly self-educated man who read widely in the great works of literature and philosophy. Considering himself a philosophical idealist, Charles imparted to his daughter a conviction that the supernatural co-exists as a higher form of human life, a view that would recur in her later, more mystical writings. **Eliza Beers Gale** and Zona were almost inseparable. In addition to infusing her daughter's religious and moral beliefs with her own Presbyterian faith, Eliza seemed to embody for Zona a "mother principle" that represented the essential harmony of all creation.

At an early age, Zona developed an interest in reading and writing. She read *Pilgrim's Progress* and *Paradise Lost* as well as the Bible and Shakespeare. As she completed each book, Zona recorded its plot in a notebook. Her summaries incorporate the canon of appropriate

Zona
Gale

novels for a young person of her era—works by Charles Dickens, Sir Walter Scott, ***Frances Hodgson Burnett**, ***Louisa May Alcott**, William Thackeray, and Nathaniel Hawthorne. Meanwhile, Gale produced her own literary creations, including poems and a book written on brown wrapping paper. Her mother's support stimulated Zona's early efforts at writing. Not only did Eliza Gale copy and keep all of her daughter's childhood literary creations, she also encouraged her at age 13 to submit a "novel" to *Youth's Companion*.

In 1891, Gale enrolled at the University of Wisconsin in Madison, a time when opportunities for women in higher education were still relatively uncommon. She seems to have had a mixed experience at the university. Her reticence, and possibly her naivete, kept her from being rushed by a sorority. For the remainder of her days, she argued against the Greek system that determined one's popularity and emphasized inequalities among students. Academically and artistically, Gale enjoyed greater success. She had above-average grades (especially in her English major), won several literary prizes, and published her first story in a Milwaukee newspaper for which she received a three-dollar check. On that fateful day, she boarded a train in Madison, traveled 40 miles to her home to show the check to her parents, and returned to school by another train that evening.

After graduation, Gale moved to Milwaukee, determined to find a job in journalism. She appeared at the office of the *Evening Wisconsonian* every day for two weeks asking for work, and her persistence ultimately paid off. She covered the subjects typically assigned to female reporters—weddings, social events, and theater. Occasionally, she had the opportunity to do interviews with visiting dignitaries, such as *Jane Addams. Gale rose in the newspaper profession, moving to the Milwaukee *Journal* and in 1901 to the New York *Evening World*.

In New York City, Gale had the opportunity to meet the up-and-coming stars of literature and the arts. In 1902, she left her regular position with the *Evening World* and became personal secretary to Edmund Clarence Stedman, who had gathered around him a group of young writers in a sort of salon called the "Sunday Club." Through Stedman and his contacts, she was able to place several of her short stories with fashionable magazines and to begin in earnest her career as a fiction writer.

At Stedman's gatherings, Gale also met poet Ridgely Torrence. Over a period of several years, Torrence and Gale carried on a romance marked by uncertainty—avowals of love followed by separations. Finally, in 1904, after announcing plans to marry, Torrence ended the relationship. A distressed Gale returned to Portage, Wisconsin, feeling that no one would ever replace Torrence in her affections. Twenty years later, she wrote to him, "I do hope that in our next incarnation we can be lovers again and [by] that time, [I'll] have enough more star-dust in me, to bring it off." Gale's parents were delighted with her return to Portage. During Zona's New York sojourn, Eliza Gale wrote to her daughter incessantly, warning her of the temptations and loneliness of the city as contrasted with the warmth of home. It seems clear that Zona's relationship with Torrence was not helped by her mother's disapproval.

Although Gale published her first novel, *Romance Island*, in 1906, and a collection of stories, *The Loves of Pelleas and Etarre*, in 1907, it was the "Friendship Village" stories written in Portage that brought Gale her first literary success. The first collection entitled *Friendship Village* was published in 1908. The same characters appeared in a total of 83 stories over the next 11 years, ending with *Peace in Friendship Village* in 1919. The popular tales reflected Gale's basic belief that people were the same regardless of education, class, urban or rural environment. Her characters represented the small-town population as good hearted, if unsophisticated. She sentimentalized domestic life, including household chores, though the women in her stories were also involved in civic improvement. The last collection in the series even introduced some fairly controversial topics, including racial prejudice, pacifism, and anti-Semitism.

In between writing the village stories, however, Gale pursued other interests. Each autumn, she spent several months in New York, where she placed her work in such magazines as *Harper's, Everybody's, Women's Home Companion,* and *The Outlook*. She also wrote a pamphlet in 1913 for the American Civic Association, "Civic Improvement in the Little Towns," which advocated the establishment of clubs and committees to enrich the quality of small-town life. Most important, she was developing her own political philosophy and a commitment to activism in support of liberal causes. Gale became a lifelong supporter of Wisconsin's "Fighting Bob" LaFollette and the type of Progressivism he embodied. Like other Progressives, Gale believed that economic competition must be replaced with cooperation, that the poverty and degradation that accompanied industrialization must be addressed by positive governmental programs. She supported animal rights, a vegetarian diet, and prohibition of alcohol and tobacco. As early as the 1920s, Gale came to believe in racial integration and the abolition of the death penalty. Her commitment to the latter issue is consistent with her involvement in the efforts to save the lives of Nicolo Sacco and Bartelomeo Vanzetti, Italian immigrants sentenced to death after a notorious trial that rested more heavily on prejudice against their ethnicity and radical views than on evidence of guilt. Gale, along with a vast number of other writers and intellectuals, publicized the injustice of the case and attempted unsuccessfully to prevent the executions.

Of all her interests in reform, Zona Gale devoted her greatest efforts to promoting pacifism and women's rights. Like many Progressives and feminists, Gale believed that war should be obsolete, that human beings should develop peaceful ways to resolve their differences. As the United States approached involvement in World War I, Gale published an antiwar novel, *Heart's Kindred* (1915). Although the book was not a success, she continued to pursue pacifist activities through the Women's Peace Party (later the Women's International League for Peace and Freedom), through support of efforts in the 1920s to outlaw war, by advocating an end to the production of violent toys such as soldiers and guns, and by opposing the teaching of military science in colleges and universities.

Likewise, Gale wrote and involved herself in efforts to enhance the position of American women. She greatly admired the work of Jane Addams and other female reformers dedicated to settlement work and industrial reform. She believed that women needed full political and economic rights in order to make a positive contribution to humanizing society. Gale's feminism was manifested in her fiction, which featured female characters attempting to escape from the narrow conventional definitions of womanhood in *A Daughter of the Morning* (1917), *Birth* (1918), *Miss Lulu Bett* (1920), and *Faint Perfume* (1923). In addition to her written depiction of women's issues, Gale worked for women's suffrage, and, after the vote was won in 1920, she helped draft the Wisconsin Equal Rights Law in 1923.

Critics consider the publication of *Birth* in 1918 the beginning of Gale's realistic period, the time in which she produced her best novels. These works continue to focus on small-town life but emphasize the vulnerability of average people who find themselves battered by forces beyond their control. In many ways, they are the opposite view from that portrayed in the Friendship Village stories.

Miss Lulu Bett, a short novel of only 45,000 words, was a bestseller and a critical success in 1920, competing with Sinclair Lewis' *Main Street*, another pessimistic tale of small-town existence. The book portrays a dull, narrow bourgeois society that entraps the unmarried woman of the title. The following year, Gale adapted the

story for the stage, and in 1921 the play won the Pulitzer Prize.

Her third realistic novel, *Faint Perfume*, appeared in 1923. The heroine of this work also finds herself confined in a bleak, small-minded town, prevented by conscience from marrying the man with whom she might find happiness. Here, too, Gale portrays the insensitivity and hypocrisy of the materialist culture. Although critics praised *Faint Perfume*, it was to be Gale's last truly realistic novel. Much of her remaining work would reflect her long-standing fascination with mysticism and the occult.

Just as Gale was beginning her next novel, *Preface to a Life* (1926), her personal world was drastically altered by the death of her mother in 1923. It may be that the daughter was seeking a way to continue her intimate devotion to her mother beyond the grave, but in any case Gale became more preoccupied with spiritualism. She claimed that she received hundreds of "spirit messages" from her mother, and she became even more convinced that the basic element of life was a universal "mother principle." These beliefs provide the underpinning for a number of Gale's works written during the late 1920s and the 1930s. In *Preface to a Life*, Gale attempted to portray a hero whose mundane life was relieved by glimpses of a higher consciousness, a spiritual awakening that allowed him to see that there was more than the everyday existence. Although rejecting all conventional religions as meaningless, Gale's work is permeated with the notion of a divine essence alive beyond mere human reality. Ironically, in works such as *Preface to a Life*, she is much more successful in her realistic descriptions of the ordinary world from which her hero longs to escape, than in explaining the supernatural plane which she believes is the alternative. In fact, in 1927 Gale produced a collection of short stories, *Yellow Gentians and Blue*, which is much more skillful in portraying commonplace life than in evoking the spiritual.

The following year, Zona Gale published *Portage, Wisconsin and Other Essays,* an anthology that includes several pieces describing the world in which she had lived, and a number of essays that define her theories about literature. Gale asserted that great literature was possible in the United States and could even concern itself with the everyday life of undistinguished people, as long as the literature attempted to "interpret the human spirit." She believed that fiction served a metaphysical purpose, but her own writing excelled when she left the metaphysical implicit and focused on describing the familiar and tangible.

While working out her literary theories and writing several other works—novels *Borgia* (1929), *Papa LaFleur* (1933), and *Light Woman* (1937) and collections of stories *Bridal Pond* (1930) and *Old Fashioned Tales* (1933)—Gale's real life included a number of significant events. Her father died in 1929. In 1928, at age 54, Gale had married widower, banker, and hosiery manufacturer William L. Breese, an old Portage acquaintance. They had met unexpectedly in California in 1927, and, upon their return to Wisconsin, Breese launched a quiet courtship. After the wedding, Gale moved into Breese's stately home, which he had enlarged by adding a study for his new wife. The household also included Breese's teenaged daughter, **Juliette Breese**, and a three-year-old girl, Leslyn, adopted by Gale and Breese. Gale was given to experimental methods of child rearing, which included a vegetarian diet and recording the youngster's every activity. Eventually the observation of Leslyn was delegated to governesses, while Gale carried on her political activities, her annual trips to New York, and her writing. She also became increasingly involved with the University of Wisconsin. In 1923, she had been named a member of the Board of Regents in recognition of her efforts to provide equal educational opportunities for women. In 1935, she was selected to serve on the university's Board of Visitors. In that capacity, she became embroiled in controversy surrounding the removal of the school's president, a dispute that led to an open quarrel with her longtime political ally, LaFollette. In 1937, seeking a change from her exhausting activities, Gale accepted an invitation to visit and lecture in Japan.

Eastern spirituality appealed to Gale, as did the beauty of the Japanese countryside. Although she planned to write of her trip when she returned to the United States and also to begin work on an autobiography, she delayed both projects to write a biographical work entitled *Frank Miller of Mission Inn* (1938) which paid tribute to Miller's creation of a hotel that combined a sense of peace with homage to California's history. That same year, she reworked a short novel, *Magda*, which would be published posthumously in 1939.

During the last years of her life, as World War II loomed, Gale continued her dedication to working for peace. She hosted an annual commemoration of the signing of the Kellogg-Briand Peace Pact for the Women's International League for Peace and Freedom. In October 1938, she ap-

peared with first lady *Eleanor Roosevelt at a National Peace Program in Green Bay, Wisconsin. In December, troubled by a prolonged cough, Gale went from Portage to Chicago for a medical consultation. There she entered the hospital, pneumonia developed, and on December 27, 1938, Zona Gale died. She was buried in Portage.

SOURCES:
Barlow, Judith E., ed. *Plays by American Women, 1900–1930*. NY: Applause Theater Book Publishers, 1990.
Derleth, August. *Still Small Voice: The Biography of Zona Gale*. NY: Appleton-Century, 1940.
Maxwell, William. "Zona Gale," in *Yale Review*. Vol. 76. Winter 1987, pp. 221–225.
Simonson, Harold P. *Zona Gale*. NY: Twayne, 1962.
Sochen, June. *Movers and Shakers: American Women Thinkers and Activists, 1900–1970*. NY: Quadrangle, 1974.

COLLECTIONS:
Zona Gale's papers are located at the State Historical Society of Wisconsin at Madison. Some of Gale's correspondence and papers are also found in the Ridgely Torrence Collection at the Princeton University Library.

Mary Welek Atwell,
Associate Professor of Criminal Justice,
Radford University, Radford, Virginia

Galeswintha (d. c. 568).

See Galswintha.

Galiana

Moorish princess. Flourished at the time of Moorish Spain; daughter of Gadalfe, king of Toledo.

From 1031 to 1492, Moorish Spain was divided into numerous kingdoms, known as "Taifas." The most important were Cordova, Seville, Granada, Jaen, Murcia, Valencia, Saragosa (Zaragoza), and Toledo. Galiana's father, Gadalfe, the king of Toledo, built a palace for his daughter on the banks of the Tagus River. It was so splendid that "palace of Galiana" became a proverb in Spain.

Galigaï, Leonora (c. 1570–1617).

See French "Witches" for sidebar.

Galindo, Beatriz (1475–1534)

Spanish scholar, essayist, and poet. Name variations: Beatrice or Beatrix Galindo; La Latina; M. Francisco Ramírez de Madrid. Born in Salamanca, Spain, in 1475; died in Madrid in 1534; buried with her husband at the Convent of Conception Jéronima, which she founded; married Francisco Ramírez de Madrid.

Selected works: poetry and essays, including the still extant Comentarios a Aristóteles y notas sabios sobre los antiguos.

Although her parents wanted her to enter the cloisters, and she is said to have dressed as a nun, Beatriz Galindo chose a secular scholarly life, studying Latin and the classics. She is known particularly for her influence on the Castilian court of Queen *Isabella I of Spain, where she educated people on these subjects and thus helped foster the growth of humanism in Spain. Christopher Columbus was educated at this court. The queen hired Galindo to teach her and her children, including *Isabella of Asturias, *Juana la Loca, *Maria of Castile, and ✥➤ Catherine of Aragon, then made the scholar a personal advisor and maid of honor. Galindo's greatest influence was made in her informal work in the court, although she also published treatises on classical authors and poetry.

She married Francisco Ramírez de Madrid, also known as "el Artillero" for his heroism at war in Granada. After he died, she left the court to devote her time to charity. Galindo financed the building of the Hospital of the Conception, which was later renamed La Latina after her. She also founded the Convent of Conception Jéronima, where she and her husband are buried.

Catherine Hundleby, M.A.
Philosophy, University of Guelph, Guelph, Ontario, Canada

Galindo de Topete, Hermila

(1896–1954)

Mexican revolutionary and feminist who was the leading woman supporter of the Constitutionalist forces led by Venustiano Carranza. Name variations: Hermila Galindo Acosta de Topete. Born Hermila Galindo Acosta in Ciudad Lerdo, Durango, Mexico, on May 29, 1896; died in Mexico City on August 19, 1954; daughter of Rosario Galindo and Hermila Acosta de Galindo; married Manuel de Topete; children: two daughters.

Although Mexico became free of Spanish rule in 1821, the nation's first century of independence brought considerably more turmoil than progress to the great majority of its citizens. After the possibility of a restoration of European rule ended in 1867 with the execution of the ill-fated Emperor Maximilian and the hospitalization of Empress *Carlota, Mexico enjoyed a brief period of relative stability under the administration of President Benito Juárez. Chaos ensued after the death of Juárez in 1872, but order was restored in 1876 when Porfirio Diaz (1830–1915) seized the reins of power. Ruling his country with an iron fist until he was forced to resign in 1911, Diaz profoundly transformed Mexico. Extensive railroad and telegraph networks were built, harbors modernized, a stable currency introduced, and public debts paid. But the masses rarely benefitted from these reforms, which created an environment in which the traditional landowning elite as well as foreign investors could amass immense wealth that was essentially free of taxation.

The condition of Mexico's peasants, most of whom were of Indian descent, was one of extreme poverty and exploitation when the Diaz regime began, and it never improved throughout his long rule. Illiteracy, estimated at 75% in the mid-1870s, had actually increased to about 80% by 1910. At the start of the 20th century, the majority of the Mexican rural population found itself trapped in dismal conditions. Reactionary legislation pushed farmers off communal lands, reducing them to a state of peonage or virtual serfdom. By 1910, an astonishing 96.9% of the rural heads of families owned no real property. Those who protested were imprisoned or, more often, murdered by local landlords and pliant officials. The banner of agrarian revolt was raised in 1910 by Francisco Madero, who succeeded Diaz in 1911 but proved to be an inept president and was assassinated in February 1913. Madero's successor, Victoriano Huerta, revealed himself to be no better in leadership skills, and the country sank into a state of civil war that raged until 1917 when Venustiano Carranza (1859–1920) emerged as the country's strong man.

Surface turmoil in Mexico often masked basic social conditions and attitudes that had changed very little over the centuries. Traditional patriarchal attitudes placed women in subordinate roles both within the family and in society at large. As noted by American observer **Edith O'Shaughnessy**: "How can a nation advance when the greater part of the women pass their lives grinding corn, making tortillas, and bearing children? There is no time or strength left to sketch in the merest outline of home-making, let alone a personal life or any of the rudiments of citizenship." Attempting to transform this bleak picture, a small but vocal group of Mexican feminists began to appear on the scene as early as the 1890s. Despite its essential social conservatism, the Diaz regime's economic modernization programs led to modest but real advances for a small but growing minority of Mexican women. The immense obstacles facing them,

◀✥
Catherine of Aragon. See Six Wives of Henry VIII.

both then and in later decades, included the traditional machismo attitudes, hostility from the Roman Catholic church hierarchy, ridicule by the press, indifference on the part of government, as well as tactical and ideological differences among the feminist activists themselves. Nevertheless, between 1888 and 1904 women began to be registered as students in the capital's schools of commerce, law, and medicine, and thousands of other women were already economically independent as schoolteachers, government employees, and sales employees in the private sector.

Hermila Galindo was born into a middle-class family in the city of Lerdo, Durango State, in 1896. After she lost her mother at an early age, Hermila was raised by her father and paternal aunt, Angela. While attending schools both locally as well as in Chihuahua and Torreón, she mastered not only typing and stenography but studied English as well. It was her father's plan to send Hermila to the United States to study chemistry, but his death crushed these hopes and she was compelled by economic necessity to terminate her studies and start work in order to support herself and her aunt. Galindo's political involvement began essentially by chance in 1909 in Torreón, while she was still a student. A lawyer, Francisco Martinez Ortiz, made an anti-Diaz speech, which Hermila transcribed. When the mayor learned of the speech, he demanded that all copies be turned in to prevent its publication, but Galindo retained her own copy of the text. Later that year, at a local celebration in honor of the universally beloved Benito Juárez, his son Benito Juárez Maza, a critic of the Porfirio Diaz regime, learned that a copy of the Martinez speech was still in existence. Juarez Maza requested it from Galindo and made copies that quickly received wide distribution in a political atmosphere that was increasingly hostile to Diaz.

In 1911, at age 15, Hermila Galindo moved to Mexico City. Already sensitive to political and social issues, she joined the "Abraham Gonzalez" Liberal Club, one of the many lively discussion groups that now took on a new life with the collapse of the Diaz system. By 1914, Mexico was a nation convulsed by civil war and chaos. Venustiano Carranza, one of the most powerful contenders for the presidency, had been politically active in Coahuila State during the Diaz epoch and quickly emerged as a major personality in the political coalition that opposed General Huerta. Described by **Anita Brenner** as "a cold-eyed, sensual, stubborn old patriot," Carranza had little of the idealist in him, but unalloyed idealism in the midst of revolution is probably a luxury successful leaders can ill afford. Carranza's attitudes on feminist issues were doubtless similar to his position regarding other political concerns, namely pragmatic, and determined by whatever tactical advantages he might derive from taking a particular stand.

In 1914, after President Huerta's resignation, Carranza entered Mexico City to celebrate the triumph of his Constitutionalist cause. Representing the "Abraham Gonzalez" Liberal Club, Hermila Galindo gave a speech in his honor, comparing him to the revered Benito Juárez. Evidently much impressed by her oratory, Carranza requested that she become his private secretary. She accepted his offer and as a result traveled throughout Mexico on behalf of his government during the next several years. Galindo organized revolutionary clubs in towns and villages in order to disseminate the message of Carranza's Constitutionalist ideology, which emphasized the dual imperatives of defending national sovereignty and bringing about social reform.

Although much of Galindo's energy went into propagandizing for the Constitutionalist forces in a bloody civil war, she did not neglect a specifically feminist agenda that she believed must constitute an important aspect of the Mexican revolution. The need for reforms in this area was staggering, as she pointed out when summing up the legal discriminations against women found in the Civil Code of 1884. At least on paper, this law granted to adult single women virtually the same rights as males. Married women, however, lost these rights and were defined as *imbecilitas sexus* ("an imbecile by reason of her sex"). Convinced that the gross inequities of laws then in force were self-evident, she pointed out how a wife "has no rights whatsoever in her home. [She is] excluded from participating in any public matter [and] she lacks legal personality to draw up any contract. She cannot dispose of her personal property, or even administer it, and she is legally disqualified to defend herself against her husband's mismanagement of her estate, even when he uses her fund for ends that are most ignoble and most offensive to her sensibilities. [A wife] lacks all authority over her children, and she has no right to intervene in their education. . . . She must, as a widow, consult persons designated by her husband before his death, otherwise she can lose her rights to her children."

In September 1915, along with **Artemisa Sáenz Royo** and several other feminists, Hermila

Galindo founded and became editor of the periodical *La Mujer Moderna* (*The Modern Woman*). It would be published until 1919, having had the same brief lifespan as Mexico's first important feminist journal, *La Mujer Mexicana,* which appeared between 1904 and 1908. Along with her feminist activities, during these years Galindo continued to defend the Carranza administration and its Constitutionalist program. In September 1916, she went to Havana to explain why the Carranza agenda of nationalism and social reform was important not only for Mexico, but for a Latin America challenged daily by the unequal power and wealth of both the U.S. government and foreign private corporations.

Back in Mexico, Galindo increasingly concentrated her efforts on advancing a feminist agenda. Although she had to function in a political environment that was almost totally male-dominated, she refused to admit defeat. As **Anna Macias** notes, in Mexico "to be female is to be reticent, subordinate, and self-sacrificing. To be male is to be decisive, dominant, and courageous." Thus, to achieve feminist goals "a Mexican woman must act like a man." Although her outspokenness outraged the overwhelming majority of Mexican males and most of the country's conservative females as well, Hermila Galindo's intelligence and courage impressed a minority of revolutionary leaders. Among the politically powerful individuals she could count on for support were two revolutionary leaders in Yucatán State, Salvador Alvarado and Felipe Carillo Puerto.

It was in Yucatán that the Mexican revolution would reveal some of its most radical tendencies, in large measure because of the local economic inequalities. While a tiny group of families (*la casta divina*) enjoyed a monopoly of power and wealth, the indigenous Maya and Yaqui Indian population found itself virtually enslaved, perpetually condemned to working in the fields for subsistence wages while harvesting the sole export crop, henequen. Both Alvarado and Carillo advocated a nondoctrinaire form of Socialism which would more equitably distribute wealth as well as guarantee for all citizens a free education, greatly improved working conditions, and equal rights for women.

Hermila Galindo was not in attendance at Mexico's first feminist congress, held in the city of Mérida, Yucatán, in mid-January 1916 (the first feminist congress in Latin America had taken place in Buenos Aires, Argentina, in May 1910). The paper she sent to be read to the assembly, entitled "Woman in the Future," proved to be a bombshell. Refusing to pull any punches, her address took a strongly anticlerical line, declaring that the Roman Catholic Church remained a major obstacle to the achievement of feminist goals in Mexico. By continuing to be institutionally impervious to healthy new ideas and reforms, the church functioned as a significant impediment to social progress. In other parts of her paper, she called for full women's suffrage, the legalization of divorce, and an end to the culture of machismo. Most shocking of all the assertions or proposals found in Galindo's paper were her ideas on female sexuality. Many of the more conservative members of the audience were stunned by her insistence that all Mexican schoolgirls should attend compulsory classes in anatomy, hygiene, and physiology so as to comprehend and control all aspects of their bodies. At least one fundamental reason why sexual enlightenment was necessary, Galindo argued, was because women possessed a sex drive as strong as that of males. Although many in the audience vigorously applauded the absent Galindo's address, a number voiced their opposition, and one member of the audience thundered from her seat that the essay deserved to be destroyed.

Despite the mixed reception her ideas had received at Mérida's feminist congress, Galindo refused to be discouraged. Despite mounting evidence that little was being achieved in the way of substantive reforms, she continued to work for the Carranza administration. She spoke out in favor of a drastic revision of a Civil Code which virtually destroyed all women's rights when they entered into a state of matrimony. Galindo and other Mexican feminists successfully pressured President Carranza into issuing a new Law of Family Relations in 1917. Her arguments for women's educational equality, which she presented both in print and in speeches, emphasized that women were themselves partially to blame for their own lack of social progress. Only when they had abandoned the pervasive notion that the only proper role for the earth's females was to bear and raise children would women finally be able to liberate themselves from an ancient yoke of ignorance that had reduced them to beings "without consciousness and without aspirations."

In December 1916, 20-year-old Hermila Galindo was the most visible female presence at the Constitutional Congress held at Querétaro to hammer out a fundamental political document for the new Mexican state. Although she was as eloquent as ever before, Galindo and the handful of other women present at the various meetings were laughed at or ignored. Only the head of the government's bureau of educational affairs, Felix Palavicini, made an effort to seriously argue the case for women's suffrage. Although many politically active Mexican men were adamantly opposed to granting women the vote, it was not only male chauvinism or rude indifference that explained the stand they had taken. Many of the most progressive and radical delegates at Querétaro saw the issue in terms of the delicate political balance between liberal and conservative. If women were given the vote, they reasoned, many women who remained strongly under the influence of the ultra-conservative and anti-revolutionary Roman Catholic Church would respond to the church's call to vote for traditionalist candidates, and that would in fact negatively seal the fate of the revolution.

Again refusing to be discouraged, Galindo ran in 1917 for the seat of a deputy from Mexico City's fifth electoral district. Although she stated during the campaign that she had no hope of being elected, and merely desired to bring the cause of women's suffrage before the nation, she was in fact elected in a stunning upset. In due course, she appeared before the electoral college of Mexico's Chamber of Deputies in order to claim her seat. However, that body decided to refuse to seat her because of her gender. Had they voted otherwise, Hermila Galindo would have been the first woman to serve in the Mexican Chamber of Deputies.

Throughout these tumultuous years of modern Mexican history, Hermila Galindo was not only an agitator, propagandist and advocate for women's rights, but a highly productive journalist and editor as well. Besides her work for the journal *La Mujer Moderna*, she wrote five books on various topics linked to the Mexican revolution, as well as a biography of Venustiano Carranza. With the approach of presidential elections scheduled for 1920, she wrote a laudatory biography of one of the major candidates, General Pablo González. By this time, many Mexicans had become frustrated with a Carranza regime that had promised major social reforms but had delivered virtually nothing to the millions of poor and dispossessed workers and landless peasants. In early 1920, Generals Obregón and González signaled the start of a revolt against Carranza when it appeared that the upcoming election might be rigged. Carranza fled the capital, was defeated in battle, and was murdered in Puebla State on May 21, 1920.

The bloody demise of the Carranza regime marked the end of the first phase of Mexican feminism as well as the abrupt termination of Hermila Galindo's public career. Although she continued to write and publish, Galindo retired into private life at the ripe age of 24. In 1923, she married Manuel de Topete and eventually gave birth to two daughters. For a number of years, she and her family lived in the United States, but they decided to return to Mexico. Hermila Galindo de Topete died in Mexico City on August 19, 1954. Despite Galindo's early retirement, and the consequent loss to the cause of Mexican feminism of one of its most talented and persuasive personalities, the cause of women's rights was slowed down but never completely halted in the years after 1920. Mexico's women had to wait until 1958 before they received full political equality, and in de facto terms much progress remained to be achieved at the start of a new millennium.

SOURCES:

Adams, Jerome R. *Latin American Heroes: Liberators and Patriots from 1500 to the Present.* NY: Ballantine, 1993.

———. *Liberators and Patriots of Latin America: Biographies of 23 Leaders from Doña Marina (1505–1530) to Bishop Romero (1917–1980).* Jefferson, NC: McFarland, 1991.

Brenner, Anita, and George R. Leighton. *The Wind That Swept Mexico: The History of the Mexican Revolution of 1910–1942.* Austin, TX: University of Texas Press, 1984.

Cano, Gabriela. "Feminism," in Michael S. Werner, ed., *Encyclopedia of Mexico.* Vol. I. 2 vols. Chicago, IL: Fitzroy Dearborn Publishers, 1997, pp. 480–486.

———. "Galindo Acosta de Topete, Hermila," in Michael S. Werner, ed., *Encyclopedia of Mexico.* Vol. I. 2 vols. Chicago, IL: Fitzroy Dearborn Publishers, 1997, pp. 549–550.

Carey, James C. *The Mexican Revolution in Yucatán, 1915–1924.* Boulder, CO: Westview Press, 1984.

Gilderhus, Mark T. "Many Mexicos: Tradition and Innovation in the Recent Historiography," in *Latin American Research Review.* Vol. 22, no. 1, 1987, pp. 204–213.

Macias, Anna. *Against all Odds: The Feminist Movement in Mexico to 1940.* Westport, CT: Greenwood Press, 1982.

———. "Felipe Carrillo Puerto and women's liberation in Mexico," in Asunción Lavrin, ed. *Latin American Women: Historical Perspectives.* Westport, CT: Greenwood Press, 1978, pp. 286–301.

———. "Women and the Mexican Revolution, 1910–1920," in *The Americas.* Vol. 37, no. 1, 1980, pp. 53–82.

Mendieta Alatorre, Angeles. *La mujer en la Revolucion Mexicana.* Mexico City: Instituto Nacional de Estudios Historicos de la Revolucion Mexicana, 1961.

Morton, Ward M. *Woman Suffrage in Mexico.* Gainesville, FL: University of Florida Press, 1962.

O'Shaughnessy, Edith. *Diplomatic Days.* NY: Harper and Brothers, 1917.

Reséndez Fuentes, Andrés. "Battleground Women: Soldaderas and Female Soldiers in the Mexican Revolution," in *The Americas.* Vol. 51, no. 4. April 1995, pp. 525–553.

Richmond, Douglas W. *Venustiano Carranza's Nationalist Struggle, 1893–1920*. Lincoln: University of Nebraska Press, 1983.

Soto, Shirlene Ann. *Emergence of the Modern Mexican Woman: Her Participation in Revolution and Struggle for Equality, 1910–1940*. Denver, CO: Arden Press, 1990.

———. *The Mexican Woman: A Study of Her Participation in the Revolution, 1910–1940*. Palo Alto, CA: R&E Research Associates, 1979.

John Haag,
Associate Professor of History,
University of Georgia, Athens, Georgia

Galitzin, Princess (1748–1806).

See Ney, Elisabet for sidebar.

Galizia, Fede (1578–1630)

Italian painter, one of the earliest still-life painters in Italy, who was also known for miniature portraits, landscapes, and religious subjects. Born in Milan, Italy, in 1578; died in 1630; daughter of Annunzio Galizia (a painter).

Little is known of the life of Fede Galizia, who was probably taught to paint by her father Annunzio Galizia, a miniaturist. Galizia was recognized for her talent at the age of 12, and by the time she was in her teens enjoyed an international reputation as a portraitist. Among her few authenticated works is a remarkable still life signed and dated 1604, when the artist was 24. By virtue of this painting (which was once held in the Anholt Collection in Amsterdam but is now missing), scholars have attributed to her a group of formerly unidentified still-life paintings.

Jesuit scholar and historian Paolo Morigia was one of Galizia's earliest patrons, and in a collection of short biographies published in 1595 he wrote that she showed signs of "becoming a truly noble painter." He praised one of her portraits of him, declaring this work "of such excellence, and such a good likeness, that one could not desire anything more." Although that particular portrait was lost, another of Morigia, painted a year later, survives. Describing it in *Women Artists, 1550–1958*, **Ann Harris** and **Linda Nochlin** remark that in the tradition of naturalistic portraiture in Northern Italy during the 16th century, the painting records Morigia in an almost photographic likeness, "unfiltered by either idealizing conventions or the artist's own personality." They further speculate that Galizia's father may have trained her to paint in the naturalistic style of *Sofonisba Anguissola, who came from Cremona, 50 miles southeast of Milan, and may have been known to him. Galizia may have also been influenced by Lorenzo Lotto, or even Raphael whose work she may have seen on visits to Florence.

The still life upon which the greater part of Galizia's reputation rests is described by **Germaine Greer** in *The Obstacle Race:*

> It is a small panel, showing a dish of fruit glowing in warm, focused light, against a mysterious background. The globes of fruit swell softly against the hard edges of the dish and its metallic sheen vibrates against the velvetness of their skin. Beneath and to one side stand a pear and a half. The hard enamelled skin of the pears indicates another extreme of the picture's frame of sensuous reference, while the sheerness of the face of the cut pear dramatizes the whole composition. As if to alert us still more to the frailty of these beautiful objects, the pears are balanced by a blowzy rose, lightly subsiding on the other side of the edgeless surface upon which they all exist.

According to Harris and Nochlin, Galizia may have been inspired to try the new genre of still life by Jan Brueghel, who was present in Milan in 1595. Two other still-life paintings, *Basket of Peaches* and *Still Life with Peaches* (Heusy, Belgium, E. Zurstrassen Collection), have also been attributed to Galizia. The restrained treatment of her still lifes did not endure, eventually giving way to an elaborate, lavish style reflecting the Flemish influence. Known to have prepared her will on June 21, 1630, the artist is thought to have died of the plague that overtook Italy at that time.

SOURCES:

Greer, Germaine. *The Obstacle Race*. NY: Farrar Straus Giroux, 1979.

Harris, Ann Sutherland, and Linda Nochlin. *Women Artists, 1550–1950*. L.A. County Museum of Art: Knopf, 1976.

Petteys, Chris. *Dictionary of Women Artists*. Boston, MA: G.K. Hall, 1985.

Barbara Morgan,
Melrose, Massachusetts

Galla (fl. 320)

*Byzantine and Roman empress. Flourished around 320; first wife of Julius Constantius also known as Constantius II, emperor of Byzantium and emperor of Rome (r. 337–361); children: one daughter and two sons, including Gallus Caesar (b. 325/326–354). Constantius II's second wife was **Basilina**.*

Galla (c. 365–394)

Empress of Rome. Born around 365; died in childbirth in 394; daughter of Valentinian I, Roman emper-

or (r. 364–375), and Justina (fl. 350–370); sister of Justa and Grata and emperor Valentinian II; half-sister of Gratian; became second wife of Theodosius I, Roman emperor (r. 379-395), around 387; children: three but only a daughter, Galla Placidia (c. 390–450), survived infancy.

A military officer of standing, Valentinian I was elevated to imperial status in 364 after the death of Jovian. Within a month of his elevation, Valentinian raised his brother Valens to co-imperial status in order to cover as many of the empire's hot-spots as possible. Their division of labor generally recognized Valentinian's authority in the West and Valens in the East, but in 367 Valentinian named his eight-year-old son Gratian (with his first wife *Marina Severa) an Augustus, so as to make manifest his choice of successors. Valentinian upheld his responsibilities admirably (if with choler or anger) until his death by stroke in 375. Gratian was then 16 and Valentinian II, another of Theodosius' sons (with second wife *Justina), was four. The latter's age did not prevent the troops around him from proclaiming him emperor upon the death of his father, but this status immediately came into question since neither Valens nor Gratian officially supported Valentinian II's imperial acknowledgment. Nevertheless, Gratian tolerated the elevation of his half-brother and granted him technical sovereignty over Italy, Africa, and Illyricum, although Gratian (with his handlers) maintained his real authority within these provinces. Then, in 383, a usurper named Magnus Maximus crossed to Gaul from Britain where his army had hailed him emperor.

Maximus was a Spaniard who, in an age of Christian theological controversies, followed the Nicene Creed. He had begun his career under the command of Theodosius, the father of the emperor Theodosius I. Maximus advanced his career in Britain, where he won victories over the Picts and Scots, and his army recognized his success by proclaiming him an emperor. His elevation put Maximus at odds with the established imperial hierarchy, which in turn prompted him to act decisively or perish. As a result, Maximus invaded Gaul, defeated Gratian, and put him to death. By defeating Gratian, Maximus became the de facto emperor of the West, although Valentinian II still lived in Italy with his mother Justina and sisters **Justa, Grata,** and Galla who was born around 365. For several years, Maximus controlled Gaul and Britain, his position apparently validated by the youth of Valentinian II and the inaction of Theodosius I, who himself had been elevated to the purple in 379 after the death of Valens in the East. Theodosius I did not take immediate steps to check Maximus because the two had ties which went back years: both came from Spain and were perhaps distantly related (although if so, Maximus appears to have been born to the humbler part of the family), and Maximus had served in the army of Theodosius I's father both in Britain and north Africa. Maximus probably also suspected that he had Theodosius' at least tacit support, because Maximus' usurpation of imperial authority had come at the expense of Gratian, whose house had been responsible for the political execution of Theodosius I's father. An open breach occurred between Theodosius and Maximus, however, when the latter attacked Italy in 387, probably because Valentinian II was nearing the age when he would begin to act more vigorously in his own interests. Before Maximus could capture them, Valentinian II and his entourage fled Italy to take refuge with the recently widowed Theodosius I, whom they convinced to intervene on their behalf against Maximus.

Theodosius' reason for supporting the remaining family of Valentinian I over a man who was once a member of his own political faction was alleged to have been Galla, whose beauty some suggested intoxicated Theodosius. Theodosius' primary reason for opposing Maximus, however, was probably more Machiavellian (although he may not have discounted Galla's reported comeliness), for the careers of both Maximus and his father should have forewarned Theodosius I against the unbridled ambitions of a political and military usurper—even one of past acquaintance. Who knew where such a man might stop? In addition, Theodosius I knew that by marrying Galla he could lay claim to the loyalties of a still significant political faction, a notable gain with all of the domestic and foreign troubles Theodosius still faced. Regardless of his reasons, Theodosius acted decisively after Maximus invaded Italy, defeating Maximus in battle several times during 387 and executing him in 388.

Before his campaign against Maximus, Theodosius had married Galla. Thereafter, Galla's public persona was fastidiously modeled after that of Theodosius' first wife, *Flaccilla (c. 355–386): that is, Galla was promoted as the emperor's devoted wife and as a Christian whose social activism helped those in society who otherwise could not help themselves. In terms of her political activities, Galla assiduously worked to promote her brother Valentinian II's imperial interests, and as such was an important liaison between the houses of Theodosius and Valentinian. Nevertheless, her work along these lines came to naught when Valentinian II died in 392, the victim of either suicide or murder. The latter is suspected because with Valentinian gone, another usurper, Eugenius, quickly seized power in the West, where he ruled until Theodosius exterminated him in 394. Thereafter, Theodosius elevated Honorius, the younger of his two sons with his first wife, Flaccilla, to the western post once held by Galla's brothers.

Galla was greatly distressed at the news of Valentinian II's death, both because she loved him and because his death marked the end of her father's dynasty. In fact, her loyalty to the house of Valentinian created difficulties between herself and Flaccilla's sons, Arcadius and Honorius. In 390, their relationship was so strained that when Theodosius was away from Constantinople on business, Arcadius even expelled her from the palace. Despite such animosities, Galla apparently got on well with Theodosius. Together they produced three children, although only a daughter, Galla Placidia, survived infancy. Galla did not live long enough to produce male rivals for Arcadius and Honorius, for she died during childbirth in 394, a year before Theodosius himself would expire. Galla Placidia matured to play a lengthy and influential role in the politics of the 5th century. She would long outlive her largely incompetent half-brothers, and among her accomplishments would be her rule as an Augusta from 421 until her death in 450.

William Greenwalt,
Associate Professor of Classical History,
Santa Clara University, Santa Clara, California

Gallagher, Kitty (fl. mid-19th c.)

Irish ex-convict and cattle drover who lived in Australia in the mid-19th century. Flourished in the mid-19th century; married Frank Gallagher; married a second time.

The little that is known about Kitty Gallagher comes down from William Telfer's account of the late 1830s and 1840s, but attempts to substantiate her background in Ireland and in Australia have failed. She is also remembered by two landmarks that carry her name: Gallagher's Mountain (near Scone) and Kitty Gallagher's Swamp (near Bundarra).

According to Telfer, Gallagher was the leader of the White Boys, an Irish insurgent group in Ireland during the late 18th century. She and her husband Frank participated in the 1798 Wexford Rebellion and were arrested and transported to New South Wales, where by 1839, they had their own small cattle run. After Frank died, Gallagher worked for William Telfer's father at an inn at Quirindi. She also spent six months working for a doctor at Tamworth and supposedly was the best nurse in the colony. Later, she and her second husband worked droving cattle for a man by the name of Henry Dangar. Dressed like a man and smoking a short clay pipe, Gallagher not only could drive a bullock team, but she could hoe and sickle a field of wheat, writes Telfer. A colorful figure, she is believed to have lived to age 96, spending the last years of her life near the swamp that bears her name.

Galla Placidia (c. 390–450).
See Placidia, Galla.

Gallegai, Leonora (c. 1570–1617).
See French "Witches" for sidebar.

Galli, Caterina (c. 1723–1804)
Italian mezzo-soprano. Born in Italy around 1723; died in London, England, in 1804.

Caterina Galli arrived in London in 1742, appearing at the King's Theatre in Brivio's *Mandane.* From 1747 to 1754, she sang for Handel at Covent Garden, creating mostly male roles in *Joshua, Solomon,* and *Jephtha.* From 1754 to 1763, she sang in Genoa, Venice, and Naples. Galli became the companion of the celebrated *Martha Ray, a singer and mistress of the earl of Sandwich, who strongly influenced naval appointments. Galli was in attendance when Ray was assassinated by James Hackman on April 7, 1779, while leaving the Covent Garden Theatre. Though she retired in 1771, a destitute Galli later returned to the stage at London's Covent Garden and continued singing until 1797.

Galli-Curci, Amelita (1882–1963)
Italian coloratura soprano. Pronunciation: GAHL-uh KOOR-chee. Born Amelita Galli on November 18, 1882, in Milan, Italy, of Italian-Spanish ancestry; died on November 26, 1963, in La Jolla, California; studied harmony, composition, and the piano under Vincenzo Appiani at the Royal Conservatory in Milan; was mainly a self-taught singer, though she studied briefly with Carignani and Sara Dufes; married Marquis Luigi Curci, in 1910 (divorced 1920); married Homer Samuels (her accompanist), in 1921.

poser, was intrigued by the unique timbre of her voice and encouraged her to sing. Though she took a few lessons and studied some opera scores, her vocal training was brief as she had to help support her family by teaching piano. Galli-Curci mainly relied on her ability to imitate the singing of birds and used phonograph records of her voice as a means of discovering defects of tone and delivery. She understood her unique abilities well enough to select operatic roles carefully. She sang Lakmé, Dinorah, and Manon, all roles which are typically performed by coloratura sopranos. She emphasized her electrifying high notes which were unlike any that listeners had experienced before.

Galli-Curci made her operatic debut in 1909 at the Teatro Constanzi, Rome, in the role of Gilda in Verdi's opera *Rigoletto*. During the following seven years, she sang in Spain (the country of her mother's birth), Italy, Russia, and South America. She made her first U.S. opera debut as a member of the Chicago Opera Association on November 18, 1916, once again as Gilda. Unprepared for her amazing voice, the audience went wild when she began to sing the "O caro nome" aria. Critics were as overwhelmed as average music listeners. Galli-Curci had come to the United States almost on a whim. Performing in South America, she had a letter from Victor Records in New York City and hoped to make recordings there. After her Chicago appearance, a tour of the United States and subsequent recordings solidified her popularity.

Two years later in New York, Galli-Curci proved she could be as popular on the East Coast as she had been in America's heartland. Singing Myerbeer's *Dinorah,* she was forced to make 24 curtain calls after the "Shadow Song" and 60 curtain calls at the end of the opera. "It wasn't a woman's voice but a bird's swelling throat," raved the critic for *The New York Times.* Each time she performed in New York, crowds well over capacity jammed the theater. Those who could not get seats waited outside. Throughout her career, her popularity never wavered. While remaining a member of the Chicago company until 1925, she also became a member of the Metropolitan Opera Company in New York City, making her debut at the Met as Violetta in Verdi's *La Traviata* (1920); she stayed with the Metropolitan until 1930. Her operatic repertoire also included the roles of Rosina in Rossini's *The Barber of Seville,* Mimi in Puccini's *La Bohème,* Lakmé in Delibes' *Lakmé,* Juliette in Gounod's *Roméo et Juliette,* and Elvira in Bellini's *I Puritani.*

Amelita Galli-Curci

Debuted as Gilda in Giuseppe Verdi's Rigoletto *(1909); was a sensation at the Chicago Opera (1916); sang with the Chicago Opera Company (1916–24); continued to sing with the Metropolitan Opera in New York City (1920–30).*

Amelita Galli-Curci's operatic career resembled that of a rock star, for she was enormously popular, especially in the United States. Tens of thousands of fans who had no tickets for her performances mobbed theaters outside to catch a glimpse of her. Once a crowd brought a piano, and she performed for them on the street. Many of her followers knew her voice through her recordings which sold as soon as they reached the stores. Her recording of "Caro nome" sold 10,000 copies of the first edition in Chicago alone. She continued to sell huge editions of recordings which only increased her popularity. Few opera singers have had such an adoring public.

Galli-Curci never trained for opera. When she attended the Milan Conservatory, it was to study piano. Pietro Mascagni, the opera com-

Shortly after Galli-Curci's marriage to her accompanist Homer Samuels, the couple built Sul Monte, a home in the Catskill Mountains in Highmount, New York. But a goiter caused by a thyroid condition increasingly interfered with her singing. Critics noticed that she began to sing under pitch which may have been caused by this condition. Her limpid voice, however, had such natural beauty that minor flaws were overlooked by her fans. Her best recordings were the acoustic ones made early in her career. Later recordings divulge a metallic quality which is an effect of the technology rather than of her actual voice. In 1935, Galli-Curci finally underwent an operation to remove her goiter. She attempted a comeback after the surgery, but the cheers were more for courage than performance, and she decided to retire from the stage.

One of the greatest recording artists of the early period, she was notable as a concert singer as well as an opera singer. At the Hollywood Bowl, she sang for 20,000; while touring Australia, she broke many box-office records. Amelita Galli-Curci was one of the best-known and most widely renowned coloratura sopranos of her time.

SOURCES:
Ewen, David. *Living Musicians.* H.W. Wilson, 1940.
La Massena. *C. Galli-Curci's Life of Song.* New York, 1945 (reprinted, 1978).

John Haag,
Associate Professor of History,
University of Georgia, Athens, Georgia

Gallienne, Eva Le (1899–1991).

See Le Gallienne, Eva.

Galliera, duchess of.

See Luisa Fernanda (1832–1897).
See Eulalia (b. 1864).
See Marie of Rumania for sidebar on Beatrice of Saxe-Coburg (1884–1966).

Galli-Marié, Célestine (1840–1905)

French mezzo-soprano. Name variations: Celestine Laurence Galli-Marie. Born Célestine Marié d'Isle in November 1840 in Paris, France; died on September 22, 1905, in Vence, France; studied with her father, Felix Mécène Marié d'Isle, in Strasbourg.

Debuted in Strasbourg (1859); appeared in Lisbon (1861) and Rouen (1862); debuted at the Opéra-Comique in Paris (1862); created Thomas' Mignon (1866) and Bizet's Carmen (1875).

Célestine Galli-Marié did not possess an exceptional voice. Described as having no range or volume, it did, however, have an exceptional timbre which was combined with clear diction and fine musical phrasing. She had a great ability to create characters on the opera stage, and her dramatic talent established her reputation. After Galli-Marié appeared in Rouen in 1862, the director of the Paris Opéra-Comique invited her to perform in his theater. From 1862 until 1902, her contribution to the Paris Opéra-Comique was considered to be of "incontestable dramatic worth." Galli-Marié created several operatic roles which include Mignon in Ambroise Thomas' opera of the same name; the roles of Taven and Andrelou in *Mireille;* and Dorothée in *Cendrillon.* She was most famous, however, for her creation of Carmen. She performed this opera over 100 times between 1875 and 1883.

John Haag,
Athens, Georgia

Galsonda (d. around 568).

See Galswintha.

Galswintha (d. around 568)

Frankish queen and saint. Name variations: Chilswintha; Gaisuenta; Galsonda; Galeswintha; Queen of the Merovingians. Died around 568 in Rouen, France; daughter of Athangild also known as Athanagild, king of the Visigoths, and Queen Goiswintha of Spain; sister of Brunhilda (c. 533–613); second wife of Chilperic I, king of Soissons (Neustria), king of the Franks (r. 561–584); no children.

A Visigothic princess, Galswintha was the daughter of Queen **Goiswintha** of Spain and King Athanagild of the Visigoths. She married the polygamous Frankish king Chilperic I, becoming his second wife. *Fredegund was jealous of his attraction to Galswintha. Fredegund had been the force behind Chilperic's separation from his first wife but had since been put aside herself in favor of the Visigothic princess; now she aimed to rid Chilperic of the pious Galswintha as well. Fredegund remained a servant at Chilperic's court (the position in which she had begun her career) and regained Chilperic's favor when his attraction to Galswintha diminished.

Galswintha, humiliated daily by Fredegund and Chilperic's relationship, asked to be returned to her own people. But the king was afraid of losing the large dowry Galswintha had brought him and refused to let her go. Some time later, Galswintha was strangled in her bed by a pageboy, and few people doubted Fredegund's guilt. The Frankish people despised the cruel Fredegund, now Chilperic's third wife, and mourned the loss of Galswintha deeply. They began to attribute miracles to the spirit of the murdered queen, and soon she was regarded as a holy woman for her patient suffering of Chilperic's ill treatment. She was eventually canonized.

The death of Galswintha prompted a war which lasted several decades between Fredegund (who reigned after Chilperic's death) and Galswintha's loving sister ✤ Brunhilda, who had become queen of Austrasia.

Laura York,
Riverside, California

✤▶
***Brunhilda.** See Fredegund for sidebar.*

Galt, Edith (1872–1961).

See Wilson, Edith Bolling.

Gamba Adisa (1934–1992).

See Lorde, Audre.

Gambara, Veronica (1485–1550)

Italian poet. Name variations: Veronica of Correggio. Born in 1485 in Pratalbiono, Italy; died in 1550 in Correggio, Italy; married Gilberto X of Correggio, in 1509 (died 1518); children: two sons.

Veronica Gambara was an Italian noblewoman and poet. She was born into the wealthy Gambara family of Pratalbiono, near Brescia. At age 24, she married Lord Gilberto X of Correggio, ruler of that small city-state. He died in 1518 and left Veronica with two young children and the burden of rule. She soon proved herself a competent leader, managing the administrative tasks required with skill. She even acted as military leader, fending off at least one invading army.

As a widow, Veronica also became a great patron of the artists and writers of the early Italian Renaissance, including the poets Pietro Bembo and Bernardo Tasso. Veronica herself composed poems, several of which are extant. She also was a busy correspondent, and many of her personal and business letters have survived. Her generosity and literary interests gained her many friends and admirers, including the powerful Holy Roman emperor Charles V. She died about age 65.

Laura York,
Riverside, California

Gan, Elena (1814–1842).

See Blavatsky, Helena for sidebar.

Gancheva, Lyuba (1912–1974).

See Yazova, Yana.

Gandersheim, abbess of.

See Hathumoda (d. 874).
See Gerberga (d. 896).
See Christine of Gandersheim (d. 919).
See Hrotsvitha of Gandersheim (c. 935–1001).
See Gerberga (r. 959–1001).
See Sophia of Gandersheim (975–1039).

Gandhi, Indira (1917–1984)

First woman prime minister of independent India who fought against political regionalism, casteism, and religious conservatism to advance her nation to a leading position in Asia. Name variations: Indira Nehru Gandhi; (nickname) Indu. Pronunciation: EEN-dee-raa GAAN-dee. Born Indira Priyadarshini Nehru, nicknamed Indu, on November 19, 1917, in Allahabad, in northern India; assassinated in New Delhi by two Sikhs on October 31, 1984; daughter of Jawaharlal Nehru (1889–1964, first prime minister of independent India) and Kamala Nehru (1899–1936); granddaughter of Motilal Nehru (Indian nationalist leader); attended International School, Geneva; St. Mary's Convent, Allahabad; Pupil's Own School, Poona; Somerville College, Oxford (did not complete degree); married Feroze Gandhi, on March 26, 1941 (died, September 1960); children: two sons, Rajiv (b. 1944, prime minister of India who was also assassinated on May 21, 1991); Sanjay (1946–1980).

Joined the Indian National Congress Party (1938); became a member of the Working Committee of the ruling Congress Party (1955); elected Congress Party president (1959); on father's death, became minister of information and broadcasting (1964); became prime minister of India as a compromise candidate between the right and left wings of the Congress Party (1966); saw a decisive military victory over Pakistan, helped create Bangladesh from East Pakistan, and received Bharat Ratna Award (1971); deprived of seat in Parliament by the High Court of Allahabad; declared emergency to establish authoritarian rule (1975); lost in general elections (1977); saw her supporters split from the Congress Party and form the Congress Party-I (I for Indira); imprisoned in December for one week (1978); won general elections to become prime minister again; son Sanjay Gandhi won a seat in Parliament (1980); elected chair of the Non-Aligned movement (1983); assassinated in New Delhi by two Sikh security guards (1984).

Invoke the words "20th-century heads of state" and, with the notable exception of seven or eight, rarely does the image of a woman flash into consciousness. The reason, of course, is that

Indira Gandhi

most heads of state have been, and still are, men. It does not discount the fact that in this century the world has seen a few exceptional women who defied the conventionalities of their societies, and that of the nation-state at large, to lead their nations. Despite their astounding capabilities, aptitude, education, and general competence when it comes to leadership of a democratic state, women have been denied equal status and opportunity. The issue is not an imponderable one: leadership of the nation-state remains the last bastion of most patriarchal structures.

Indira Gandhi, who keeps company with *Golda Meir, *Gro Harlem Bruntland, *Corazon Aquino, *Benazir Bhutto, and *Margaret Thatcher, led her nation for over two decades as prime minister of India. She demolished the twin forts of patriarchal control—the command over the nation-state and the male-dominated Indian society—to become Independent India's first woman leader.

Indira Gandhi's life began in British India and concluded in independent India. Since 1858, the Imperial Majesty of Great Britain was the ruler of India; the subcontinent was the acclaimed jewel in England's colonial crown. For 250 years, that Crown considered Indians incapable of independent rule, and English presence and policies had all but broken the spirit of India. By the early decades of the 20th century, however, Indians had organized and were galvanizing for what was to become a protracted and acrimonious battle for independence. The movement was led by the Indian National Congress, founded in 1885, which counted among its members, B.G. Tilak, *Annie Besant, and Indira's grandfather Motilal Nehru, and later, Mohammed Ali Jinnah, Sardar Patel, Mohandas Gandhi (no relation to Indira), and Indira's father Jawaharlal Nehru. The Indian National Congress, with Mohandas Gandhi at its helm, was transformed from a forum of intellectual discussion for urban gentry into a mass movement by the early years of the 20th century.

Indira Priyadarshini Nehru was born to Jawaharlal Nehru (who would be independent India's first prime minister) and ❧▸ Kamala Nehru on November 19, 1917, at Anand Bhavan (Abode of Joy) in the holy city of Allahabad; her grandfather Motilal Nehru, a freedom fighter, predicted that "this daughter of Jawahar . . . may prove better than a thousand sons." When Jawaharlal Nehru, a Harrow-Cambridge educated ardent nationalist, discarded his urban Westernized suits to don the hand-spun Indian cotton (a symbolic gesture with far-reaching consequences), it marked the end of four-year-old Indira's carefree childhood. The transformation from Westernized affluence to nationalist asceticism was carried out with the symbolic burning of all foreign clothes in her household: "I can still feel the excitement of the day and see the large terrace covered with piles of clothes," she wrote.

The life of the young girl was closely woven with the youthful struggle for India's independence; the chronic disturbances of the freedom movement deprived her of a normal childhood. Her parents were frequently in jail—arrested for seditious acts against the Crown. "At that t..... did resent the fact, perhaps, that my parents were not with me, as other children had their parents," she recalled. Indira was lonely during those years, not quite understanding the gravity of circumstances surrounding her, only aware that they deprived her of the security provided by the constant presence of her family. When her parents were not in jail, they were immersed in political activism outside the household and incessant political discussions within. She may not have understood the complexity of the arguments, but Indira did "imbibe something, even though not consciously. . . . It has an effect on one's thinking and development." Thus, the small child, dressed in the uniform of a young Congress volunteer, with close-cropped hair tucked under a Gandhian cap, was circulating among politically eminent visitors while absorbing the conversations of self-rule, independence, self-determination, and human rights. She rarely gave in to arguments with her scholarly father or lawyer-grandfather, and she re-enacted with her servants, sometimes even with dolls, scenes of police confrontations with freedom fighters; the freedom fighters always won. Having a flair for the dramatic, she would climb onto tables and give speeches to her servants, using language overheard from adults.

Though Indira's formal education began in 1924 at St. Cecilia's School, under Roman Catholic nuns, she received more valuable instruction through study at home. She roved freely through her father's well-stocked library, reading Shakespeare and Shaw. It was here that she first read about *Joan of Arc which fostered her sense of nationalism.

In March 1926, Indira accompanied her parents to Europe and attended the International School in Geneva where she learned French. Upon her return, she was enrolled at St. Mary's Convent School in Allahabad and learned Hindi at home. When her father was released from a British jail in 1933, Indira was sent to Rabindranath Tagore's Bisva-Bharati University at Santiniketan in Bengal. There she felt at peace with the world. She wrote of Tagore: "We had a glimpse of the universality of his spirit, the broadness of his vision and his strong sense of purpose." For further education, she was given a choice of studies in the United States or Britain. She opted for Britain.

Indira grew up in surroundings that could have easily subsumed her individuality. To some extent as a young adult, she had pressured herself into conforming to what was expected of her as a Nehru daughter. Her life would be consumed with being a Nehru and all that it entailed. Yet she developed a strong will of her own which first became apparent in the choice she made for a husband—journalist Feroze Gandhi, a young Parsi student she had met while in England. Feroze, who was studying at the London School of Economics, was a great admirer of Kamala Nehru, who inspired him to join the nationalist movement.

The Nehrus were an exclusive aristocratic family, and Feroze came from the lower-middle class (an origin for which he never apologized). For a caste-conscious society in which marriages were arranged between "equal" families, Indira's independent stance and determination were a surprise, at best. She held firm to her decision, despite the numerous reservations that her family expressed regarding Feroze's origins. "If I know what I want, it doesn't bother me if somebody opposes it," she said. "I go my way. And once I had made up my mind, there it was." According to a close relative, Indira actually reveled in the opposition confronting her. The fact that it was the issue of marriage on which she stood resolute is also remarkable, as she was extremely concerned about the emancipation of women in general, an idea that she extrapolated from the nation's subverted condition. Despite the lack of enthusiasm from both the Nehru family and the Parsi community to which Feroze belonged, the wedding took place on March 26, 1941. Indira Gandhi had won the first round in her personal life, but before the couple could settle down to ironing out the wrinkles of domestic politics, national politics intruded. In 1942, the world was at war, and India was asking for its freedom even more loudly and vociferously.

Like Indira, Feroze belonged to the radical wing of the Congress Party, and he was a modernizer. Because the newlyweds actively chose to put their nation's struggle foremost, contributing to Britain's escalating problems, the year 1942 proved to be a trying one. They were both arrested and put in jail. Indira accepted incarceration with characteristic stoicism. Experiencing firsthand the foul living conditions of the inmates, she set about demanding changes and improvements. She also commenced impromptu literacy classes for the women and learned childcare from those whose children had been jailed with them. Finally released in 1943, she was reunited with Feroze.

When India gained independence on August 15, 1947, Jawaharlal Nehru became its first prime minister. Since Kamala had passed away a few years earlier, the task of being the first lady

---

Nehru, Kamala (1899–1936)

Indian leader. Born Kamala Kaul in 1899; died on February 28, 1936; daughter of prosperous entrepreneurs in Delhi; married Jawaharlal Nehru (1889–1964, first prime minister of independent India), in February 1916; children: Indira Gandhi (1917–1984).

Kamala Nehru was called "gentle and unobtrusive" when, at age 17, she entered into an arranged marriage with 26-year-old Jawaharlal Nehru. Unsophisticated, provincial, she endured the ridicule of her more Westernized in-laws by withdrawing into herself, until the birth of her daughter and the Nationalist movement. "Kamala Nehru, indeed, was far more at home with the asceticism and austerity of Gandhism than with the Westernized affluence of the Nehrus," wrote Zareer Masani, "and she had vigorously led the nationalist transformation of the Nehru household."

"Many people know the part which was played by my grandfather and my father," *Indira Gandhi once said of her mother. "But in my opinion, a more important part was played by my mother. When my father wanted to join Gandhiji and to change the whole way of life, to change our luxurious living, to give up his practice, the whole family was against it. It was only my mother's courageous and persistent support and encouragement which enabled him to take this big step which made such a difference not only to our family but to the history of modern India."

In 1925, Kamala was diagnosed with tuberculosis. Despite this, she worked tirelessly as president of the Allahabad Congress Committee and later as a substitute member of the Congress Working Committee, the high command of the Nationalist movement. She was arrested on January 1, 1931, and spent six months in Lucknow Central Jail. When her husband Jawaharlal Nehru spent all but a few months of the period from the end of 1931 to September 1935 in jail, Kamala's health deteriorated throughout. His freedom in 1935 was brought about by her continued ill-health, and she finally succumbed to tuberculosis in February 1936. She was 37.

SOURCES:

Masani, Zareer. *Indira Gandhi: A Biography.* NY: Thomas Y. Crowell, 1975.

---

was handed to Indira Gandhi. It was a task that exacted payment; she had grown up a shy, diffident child, and now it was her responsibility to be the perfect host and suave socialite in her father's household at No. 3 Teen Murti Marg, New Delhi. The role held no appeal: "I hated the thought of housekeeping, and what I hated most was to be hostess at a party, as I always dislike parties and having to smile when one doesn't want to. But if one has to do a thing, one might as well do it well, so I grew into it."

The charming host who entertained foreign dignitaries and heads of state was also the mother of two growing boys (her first son Rajiv Gandhi had been born in 1944, her second son Sanjay in 1946). The prime minister's residence took on the appearance of a zoo, with the introduction of pandas, squirrels, parrots, pigeons, dogs, and tiger cubs. "Whatever other experiences we [various first ladies] might share," she observed, "I wonder how many of those ladies have had to chase a panda through their living rooms or to sit up nights with a sick tiger?"

Indira Gandhi's life was not restricted to the drawing room's gracious role playing. She traveled around the country, working hard to establish charity and welfare organizations in which she invested vast amounts of money and time. But for Gandhi, there was sacrifice; she subordinated her family life and personal aspirations to play an important, but backstage role, in not just her father's but also her country's interest. As a result, her relationship with Feroze suffered. The strains between husband and wife became fodder for unpleasant rumors until his death in 1960. Indira remained focused in her role as first lady, fascinated with the intricacies of factionalism and politics, involved in the complexities of political processes and lobbying. To say that Nehru was consciously molding her as his political successor is at best debatable. It is apparent, however, that the trajectory of her life was inevitably leading her towards increased participation in politics, if not a high-profile position in the political arena.

In 1955, she was asked by Congress Party president U.N. Dhebar to join the Congress Working Committee, the highest authority within the Congress Party. Once she accepted, her rise to the top was rapid. In 1959, she was elected party president, though many party leaders were unhappy at the notion that a dynasty was being formed. Concluding a disarmingly simple acceptance speech, she quoted from a Hindi song: "We are the women of India/ Don't think of us flower-maidens/ We are the sparks in the fire." Besides being committed to literacy and anti-poverty programs, Gandhi boldly made anticolonial statements, challenging various nations' strongholds in Africa and Asia, and assisting indigenous movements in colonized nations. From 1960 on, she was recognized as a political powerhouse in India and abroad. Among other honors, she received Yale University's Howland Memorial Prize for distinction in the field of government and was elected to the executive board of UNESCO.

While Gandhi was coming into her own, there were rumblings within the party that challenged her fast rise to prominence. It was widely rumored that her time was up, that, without her father who died in May 1964, she could not survive. Her opponents, the conservative wing of the party, believed that because she was a woman, Indians of every caste and creed would not readily accept her as the political leader. Besides, she had not inherited her father's magnetic personality. Or so it seemed.

Nehru's successor was Lal Bahadur Shastri, whose term was short-lived and largely unremarkable. In 1965, several crises arose. A minister was trying to impose the Hindi language on the south, about which the state of Madras was particularly unhappy. She flew to Madras and met with the Madrasi, who was charmed by her, believing her promise of "no imposition of Hindi." Then she flew to Kashmir, a city resentful of the central government's rigid control, and the Kashmiris were attentive to her advocacy for calm. In fact, she showed a quality of initiative and authority which no one dreamed she possessed. Gandhi then strengthened her position when Prime Minister Shastri sent her to London to attend the Commonwealth Prime Ministers' Conference.

Shastri's sudden death left the position of the prime minister vacant, and Indira Gandhi was a forceful and ambitious contender. Her political rival publicly claimed that he would politically slay "this mere slip of a girl." As the votes were counted on a sunny January day in 1966, it became abundantly clear that Indira Gandhi was to be India's new prime minister. "The lonely adolescent with her dreams of leadership had arrived."

Being the prime minister of the most populous democracy in the world was not an easy task. Gandhi was confronted with factional politics played out on a personal level. Not yet versed in *realpolitik* in the Machiavellian sense, she had to face constant challenges from within her own party. Though she was committed to their cause, the literacy and anti-poverty movements in the nation were only partially successful, not because of her ineptitude but because of the complex nature of a postcolonial democracy that was struggling to define its nationhood. But Indira soon remade the party in her own image and managed to silence opposition. In 1971, she called a general election a year ahead of schedule with the slogan *garibi hatao* (abolish poverty).

That same year, Bengali-speaking East Pakistan fought for its independence from Urdu-speaking Pakistan. The atrocities committed by the Pakistanis and the pitiful condition of the Bengali refugees forced Gandhi to the conclusion that East Pakistan had to be separated from Pakistan for the benefit of both the Bengalis and the Indian state. In October, she visited Russia and Western capitals and acted as an intercessor for the new country that would be known as Bangladesh. Gandhi was prepared for war against Pakistan if circumstances demanded. Remarking, "We got involved, first of all, for purely humanitarian reasons," she decided to help the Mukti Fauj (freedom fighters) of Bangladesh. Her performance in 1971 was brilliant, her decisions perfectly timed, as they had been when she came to power in 1966. Her triumph in Bangladesh and her election victory made 1971 a tremendous year for her. She defeated her principal opponent Raj Narain, a socialist, by a huge majority.

But in 1975 the High Court in Allahabad found that she had misused her official position during elections. Instead of stepping down, she declared a state of national emergency on June 25, giving her government supreme authority. On one hand, the declaration of emergency was deemed an unprincipled power grab motivated by her desire to prop up a weakened political position. On the other hand, the Jay Prakash movement and the activities of the opposition parties amounted to organized efforts to effect a coup d'état by paralyzing the government. Several critics and supporters alike disparaged her declaration of emergency when several excesses were committed in its name. Though these excesses have been associated with Gandhi, evidence indicates that she was not aware of each incident of political opportunism. But the emergency reflected her ambiguities. With tens of thousands of citizens jailed without charges or trials and her critics outlawed and silenced, she would calmly repeat to the astonishment of the opposition, "I am a democrat." Even so, the general public came to believe that she stood for them.

As a result of the Emergency, in 1977, she lost her seat in the next parliamentary elections only to gain it back in 1980. Though her son Sanjay's conduct during the Emergency had contributed to his mother's defeat, he was directly responsible for Indira's triumphant return to power. After Sanjay's tragic death in a plane crash in 1980, Indira planned to induct her son Rajiv into politics, but Rajiv Gandhi was reluctant to give up a career as an Indian Airlines pilot where he enjoyed high professional standing. Gradually, she induced him to participate in elec-

tion campaigns. When Rajiv was elected to the Indian Parliament from Uttar Pradesh, he filled the gap created by Sanjay's death. Indira hoped to offer him more responsible jobs in the party.

India had joined the community of nations as the tenth most industrialized power with nuclear capabilities; however, the battle for nationhood was not totally won. The early part of the 1980s were troublesome for the prime minister. To enhance her image, she involved herself with the international scene. In 1982, she visited both Moscow and Washington to demonstrate her nonalignment. The following year, she hosted a meeting of 101 nonaligned nations. But at home, she lost support in two states—Andhra Pradesh and Karanatak—and had to contend with escalating riots between the Muslim, Hindu, and Sikh religious sects. Sikh separatists assembled weapons within their sacred Golden Temple in Amritsar in the hope that the government would not enter the temple premises. But Gandhi was a secular-minded leader. After a long hesitation, she ordered the army to flush out the extremists from the Golden Temple. Since many Hindus and Sikhs were killed in the operation, this was to be her undoing.

With characteristic gusto, Indira Gandhi had returned to power intent on pursuing far-reaching programs that would take India into the next century. Her vision, however, was still in its conceptual stages when, in October 1984, four months after the incident in the Golden Temple, Indira Gandhi was assassinated on the grounds of the prime minister's residence and office by her Sikh security guards. Immediately following the shootings, her son Rajiv was sworn in as India's new prime minister, thereby keeping the Nehru dynasty in power. (Rajiv Gandhi would also be assassinated on May 21, 1991, but the dynasty would live on through his wife **Sonia Gandhi** who was elected president of India's Congress Party in 1998.)

Indira Gandhi is revered as a remarkable political leader and one of the most accessible in the history of India, who led her country with integrity and fortitude. To her political opponents, she was a ruthless autocrat bent on perpetuating a family dynasty. To the vast Indian masses, she was Mataji (revered mother). A compulsive reader with an incisive mind, she was always a pioneer in reform and became a role model for many Indian women. More than anyone else, she was acutely aware of her paradoxical position as a woman leading a male-dominated country. She admitted that the advantages of her family background and education gave her opportunities not available to most Indian women. While her example has been a stimulus that has encouraged numerous urban, educated women to discard the traditional yolks, it also produced a tendency to deify her. Indira Gandhi, always the pragmatist, pointed out to her sisters that aspirations could be achieved: "We have thought—our society has thought—that if you call a woman a goddess, you have done everything necessary, even if she is suppressed and has no rights. . . . I would like our women to be treated as human beings. They do not want to be goddesses, but they must have every opportunity to develop their talent, their capabilities, and to use those talents and capabilities in the service of the community." Though she totally dominated her country's political life, Indira Gandhi's service to the cause of India's modernization was immense, and she continues to be revered by Indians at home and abroad.

SOURCES:

Carras, Mary C. *Indira Gandhi: The Crucible of Leadership.* Boston, MA: Beacon Press, 1979.

Garnett, Emmeline. *Madame Prime Minister.* NY: Farrar, Straus, Giroux, 1967.

Masani, Zareer. *Indira Gandhi: A Biography.* NY: Thomas Y. Crowell, 1975.

Sahgal, Nayantara. *Indira Gandhi: Her Road to Power.* NY: Frederick Ungar, 1982.

SUGGESTED READING:

Jayakar, Pupul. *Indira Gandhi: An Intimate Biography.* NY: Pantheon, 1993.

Brahmjyot K. Grewal,
Assistant Professor of History,
Luther College, Decorah, Iowa

Ganeura (d. 470 or 542).

See Guinevere.

Gannett, Deborah Sampson (1760–1827).

See Sampson, Deborah.

Ganor, Ganora or Ganore (d. 470 or 542).

See Guinevere.

Ganz, Joan (b. 1929).

See Cooney, Joan Ganz.

Gaposchkin, Cecilia Payne (1900–1979).

See Payne-Gaposchkin, Cecilia.

Garbett, Cornelia Barns (1888–1941).

See Barns, Cornelia Baxter.

Garbo, Greta (1905–1990)

Film actress who, despite superstar status, left the film business after Two-Faced Woman *(1941) and carefully guarded her privacy and the "Garbo mystique." Born Greta Louisa Gustafsson on September 18, 1905, in Stockholm, Sweden; died in New York on April 15, 1990, of kidney disease; youngest of the three children of Anna and Karl Gustafsson; never married; no children.*

First appeared on film in advertisements for a Stockholm department store for which she worked as a teenager, followed by small parts in studio films while she attended a school of dramatic arts; came under the tutelage of Swedish director Mauritz Stiller, who trained her to act for the camera and gave her a major role in his drama, The Legend of Gosta Berling, *which was distributed internationally (1924); was subsequently offered a contract by MGM in Hollywood, where she played the mysterious foreign woman in a series of silent films and became America's favorite screen* femme fatale; *survived the transition to "talkies" with* Anna Christie *(1930) for which she received the first of four Academy Award nominations.*

Filmography in Sweden: En Lyckoriddare *(1921);* Luffarpetter *(1922);* Gösta Berling Saga *(1924);* Die Freudlose Gasse *(1925). In U.S.:* The Torrent *(1926);* The Temptress *(1926);* Flesh and the Devil *(1926);* Love *(1927);* The Divine Woman *(1928);* The Mysterious Lady *(1928);* A Woman of Affairs *(1928);* Wild Orchids *(1929);* A Man's Man *(1929);* The Single Standard *(1929);* The Kiss *(1929);* Anna Christie *(released in both a silent and a talking version, 1930);* Romance *(1930);* Susan Lenox—Her Fall and Rise *(1931);* Mata Hari *(1931);* Inspiration *(1931);* As You Desire Me *(1932);* Grand Hotel *(1932);* Queen Christina *(1933);* The Painted Veil *(1934);* Anna Karenina *(1935);* Camille *(1937);* Conquest *(1937);* Ninotchka *(1939);* Two-Faced Woman *(1941).*

She was Hollywood's most reticent star. "In my country," Greta Garbo once said of her native Sweden, "the papers talk about the King and Queen . . . and otherwise about bad people. I do not want to have things printed about me [since] I am not one of any of these people." True to her wish, Garbo's public knew little about the private life of the luminous celebrity with the perfect features and the provocative foreign accent. She was Hollywood's first superstar, but was so shy that she bolted from a Hollywood dinner party when she discovered that her table companion was gossip queen *Louella Parsons, and so insecure about her accented English that she asked a *Photoplay* reporter who landed one of the few interviews with her, "You laugh at me, maybe?" Journalists and photographers would pursue her relentlessly for the next six decades, even after Garbo voluntarily left the film business in the early 1940s, but she would not speak again to the press until very late in life,

Greta
Garbo

and even then only to a fellow Swede. "I am just an old movie star," she said then.

The thin little girl who had earned a few pennies by applying shaving cream to the customers of a Stockholm barbershop had hardly seemed destined for international fame. Indeed, Greta Louisa Gustafsson's major concern growing up in the poverty-stricken neighborhood of Stockholm's South Island during World War I was finding enough to eat. Born on September 18, 1905, Greta was the youngest of the three children of Karl and **Anna Gustafsson**. "My father had a sense of humor and always used to cheer people up," Garbo recalled. "His motto was: things will be better tomorrow." But Karl, a day laborer who barely earned enough to feed his family, died when Greta was just 14, putting an end to her six years of education at the Katerina Elementary School. It was the only schooling Garbo would receive, because all three Gustafsson children, along with their mother, were forced to find work to support themselves. While Anna cleaned houses, Greta and her sister and brother sold newspapers, among them the Salvation Army's journal *Stridsropet* ("Battle Cry"). It was at the Salvation Army's headquarters on South Island that Garbo first sang and danced to entertain those who were even less fortunate than she.

By the end of World War I, she was earning better money as a "lather girl" in a barber shop which counted among its customers the manager of Stockholm's Paul U. Bergstrom department store, the city's largest and most opulent. Garbo soon landed a job in the store that her mother considered a paradise, full of expensive merchandise and frequented by some of the best people in Stockholm society. When the store's publicity department decided in 1922 to produce a series of filmed advertisements to be shown in local movie theaters, Greta—tall and dark-haired, with her mother's long, luxurious eyelashes—was among the employees chosen to appear in them. In surviving publicity stills from these films, Garbo emerges as a generously proportioned, laughing young lady, not yet the thin, brooding *femme fatale* of later years. Greta would never confirm rumors that she took her first lover during this time, a wealthy Stockholm building contractor who was the father of one of her fellow employees; nor would she substantiate speculation that it was this doting gentleman who paid her tuition at the Academy of Stockholm's Royal Dramatic Theater, where she began her studies at 17 years of age. Small parts in two comedy silents came along to supplement her studies, since film directors regularly visited the school for extras to appear in their pictures.

Among the visitors to the Academy was Mauritz Stiller, one of the best-known directors in Sweden's lively postwar film industry. Stiller, born to Jewish parents in Russian-dominated Finland, had fled to Sweden to escape conscription into the tsar's army. Finding work as an actor, Stiller began directing films in 1912 and, ten years later, had become known for the lyrical, expressionistic style that made Sweden's film

industry as respected as Germany's. Stiller was casting a new film at the time of his visit to the Academy and his first sight of Greta Gustafsson. Not long after, Garbo was asked to audition for Stiller at Stockholm's Filmstaden ("Film City"), where she was asked to lie on a cot and pretend she was ill. "I was scared and laughed hysterically and kept moving my hands up and down over the sheet," Garbo recalled over 50 years later. "Stiller seemed displeased, and I was certain that I wouldn't have a chance after that." Nonetheless, he called her back, convinced her to abandon the stage training she was receiving at the Academy, and began schooling her in the basics of film acting. Stiller, Garbo later said, taught her the importance of subtlety before the camera, of using suggestion rather than the broad gestures and expressions demanded by the stage. It was important, Stiller said, that a film actor make the audience use its imagination.

As they worked together, student and teacher became an inseparable couple, growing close enough for Garbo to bestow the affectionate nickname "Moje" on Stiller. (His given Jewish name was Moshe.) Stiller, for his part, bestowed on Greta self-confidence and respect for the art of filmmaking. She was a good enough student that he cast her in what became one of the most famous films of the Swedish silent cinema, 1924's *Gösta Berling Saga*, a sweeping four-hour costume drama in which Garbo played an Italian noblewoman who redeems a fallen, alcoholic minister. "I wasn't a blonde, for one thing, which people abroad always expect Swedes to be," Greta offered as explanation for how she was given her first important film role. It was the first time a movie-house audience saw the name "Greta Garbo" on a screen, the name having been invented by Stiller for his new leading lady's debut. The picture was such a success in Sweden that it was subtitled in several languages, including English, and exported to Europe and the United States; and its popularity won Greta a supporting role in German director G.W. Pabst's *Die Freudlose Gasse* ("The Joyless Street"), playing a woman in desperate circumstances who considers turning to prostitution to support herself before being rescued by a handsome soldier. In an ironic twist of film history, Garbo's future Hollywood rival, ***Marlene Dietrich**, worked in the film as an extra. Like Garbo, Dietrich would rise to screen fame under the wing of a famous director—in her case, Josef von Sternberg.

Among the many admirers of *Gösta Berling Saga* was Louis B. Mayer, who called Stiller to Berlin during a European tour to scout new talent for the studio which bore his name, Metro-Goldwyn-Mayer. Mayer offered Stiller a directing contract which, according to Hollywood legend, Stiller refused to sign unless Mayer also signed Greta Garbo. "In America, men don't like fat women," Mayer allegedly complained, painting a picture of Garbo distinctly at odds with her later screen image. Nonetheless, Mayer accepted Stiller's terms. (An alternate version of Garbo's path to America came from a neighbor who lived in the same Stockholm apartment building as Greta, and who claimed years later to have heard her pleading with Stiller to take her with him to America.) Stiller and his young protégée arrived in Hollywood in September of 1925, joining a sizeable Scandinavian community already in place. Among their compatriots was Werner Ölund who, as Warner Oland, would become known to American audiences as the movies' first Charlie Chan, and Victor Seastrom, the only other Swede to equal Stiller's reputation as a director.

MGM was at first uncertain what to do with Garbo except to put her on a diet and give her lessons in English and American manners. But Stiller convinced the studio to cast Greta in the first film assigned to him, *The Torrent,* after the studio had passed over silent star ***Alma Rubens,** the wife of the picture's leading man who almost quit the picture rather than act with an unknown. Further troubles ensued when Stiller's artistic temperament got him fired from the picture and replaced by a director close to ***Norma Shearer,** reverently known at the time as the Queen of the Lot and the future wife of MGM's head of production, Irving Thalberg. But the Garbo mystique was already powerful enough to defy even Shearer's clout with the studio. With her first appearance in an American film, a Swede playing an exotic Spanish dancer who becomes the toast of the Paris Opera, the Garbo appeal became immediately apparent. More important, Greta met during production the photographer and lighting director William Daniels, who would be responsible for the exquisite softness of the Garbo screen image and with whom she would form a close working relationship.

Audiences were unaware that the foreign temptress who smoldered her way through such subsequent films as *Flesh and the Devil, The Temptress* and *A Woman of Affairs* was a shy young shopgirl from Stockholm who spoke only halting English; nor did they know the apprehension under which Greta worked: Stiller's European temperament, which regarded film as an art form, continued to conflict with MGM's American pragmatism and preoccupation with

the box office. As Garbo's fortunes rose, Stiller's fell precipitously. He was fired from *The Temptress,* was not offered another film in its place, and finally collapsed from nervous exhaustion in 1926. He returned to Sweden the following year, telling Garbo, "Don't argue, do as you're told," as he boarded the train for New York and a ship home. Guilt-ridden at the success that had come to her at Stiller's expense, Greta was even more distressed to learn of Stiller's death from pneumonia in 1928.

Garbo's own relations with the studio, meanwhile, were far from smooth. She wrote home that she had tried unsuccessfully to turn down the vamp roles MGM pressed on her; that the studio threatened to send her home if she refused to work; and that *The Temptress,* the second film from which Stiller had been fired, was hateful to her. "I have to apologize to everyone for it," she wrote to a friend back in Stockholm about her portrayal of a scheming seductress who drives her lovers to madness and suicide. "I've only got myself to blame. I was feeling low, tired, I couldn't sleep, everything was crazy. But the basic problem is that I am not really an actress." Audiences disagreed. *The Temptress,* the first film in which Greta was given star billing, was an enormous success at the box office and made Greta Garbo a household name.

By the time MGM cast her in 1927's *Love,* even Garbo had come to appreciate the power she now held. *Love* was the studio's lavish, if unfaithful, adaptation of *Anna Karenina,* performed in modern dress; but Greta refused to appear as Tolstoy's tragic heroine unless the studio agreed to her demands for a higher salary. It did, although Garbo in turn had to agree to shoot two endings to the film, since MGM was unsure how audiences would react to Anna's suicide in Tolstoy's novel and wanted a happy ending as insurance. The picture teamed Garbo for the second time with John Gilbert, with whom she had co-starred in *Flesh and the Devil.* Gilbert, who had been working in films as a handsome romantic lead for a dozen years when Greta came to Hollywood, was deeply in love with her and proposed marriage, the publicity value of which was not lost on MGM. While the studio's public-relations department worked overtime to promote the match, Garbo began to have her doubts and cut the affair short. Gilbert, studio insiders noted, was never the same afterward and his career began a sad, slow downward spiral.

By 1930, after five years in Hollywood, Greta had starred in 11 films for MGM, playing vamps, spies, amoral aristocrats, and even *Sarah Bernhardt (in *The Divine Woman*, directed by Victor Seastrom); and while the films themselves were not always well received, America's fascination with her continued unabated. William Daniels, who now photographed all her pictures, developed the ideal lighting for her almost mathematically perfect features. For close-ups, a small key light was placed next to the camera and focused softly on her face, while black curtains behind the camera were lit to reflect a shimmering glow into her dark eyes. She completed as many as four films in a year and was allowed to return to Sweden only once, in 1928, for Christmas with her family and a sad visit to Stiller's grave. Friends could hardly ignore the toll Hollywood and stardom had taken. "Garbo was a normal, ambitious and cheerful girl when she left Sweden," one of them said, noting that now she seemed nervous and depressed. Yet another challenge lay in store for Greta on her return to California. It was the microphone.

I have made enough faces.

—Greta Garbo, on her retirement from films in 1941

Like every other film star in the late 1920s, Garbo faced an uncertain future with the advent of "talking pictures." The soundtrack proved the undoing of many film actors, among them John Gilbert, whose thin, reedy voice destroyed his silent image of the torrid romancer and provoked outright laughter from audiences who heard him speak from the screen. Greta had the further handicap of her imperfect English and thick Scandinavian accent, although her rather deep, husky voice was thought to be an advantage. MGM was understandably nervous about its investment when the great Garbo spoke her first words on camera in 1930's *Anna Christie*, directed by Clarence Brown. It was the now famous line, "Give me a whisky with ginger ale on the side, and don't be stingy, baby," uttered as Anna sidles up to the bar at a dockside dive in search of her father, a Swedish sailor. ("Can you imagine a more stupid line?" Garbo marveled many years later from the depths of her retirement.) The studio had prepared a silent version of the picture just in case, but to MGM's great relief, no one laughed at Greta's portrayal of Eugene O'Neill's waterfront heroine with the shady past. Audiences turned out by the thousands in response to the studio's promotional slogan of "Garbo Talks!" A German version of the picture was shot simultaneously, requiring Greta to speak the same lines in German to an entirely different cast working under a different director.

Although Garbo disliked the film and her work in it, *Anna Christie* brought her the first of four Academy Award nominations, elevated her to superstardom, and gave her enough clout to make her the highest-paid woman in America by the mid-1930s.

The sound of her voice only increased America's fascination. Much was made of her open-mouthed kiss with Clark Gable in 1931's *Susan Lenox*, never before seen in the movies; of her rivalry with Marlene Dietrich as Hollywood's reigning Mysterious Foreigner; and the fact that Greta claimed to have started wearing trousers long before Dietrich made it fashionable. "For everyday wear and for the outdoors, trousers can be a healthy alternative," were the words that studio publicity put in Garbo's mouth. MGM, in fact, had found that Greta's reticence to speak in public or to the press made it much easier to control and mold her image. The public never knew of her quick temper on the set, of her disdain for the Hollywood glamour machine, or of her frequent *amours* with both men and women. (In another contest with Dietrich, it was said that screenwriter ❧ **Mercedes de Acosta** threw over Greta for Garbo's German rival.) In between pictures, Garbo followed a strict routine of rising early in the morning with yoga and breathing exercises, rushing to the beach for a swim before the usual droves of sun worshippers arrived, eating a lunch of salad and raw vegetables, and going to bed by seven in the evening. She rarely dined in public, especially after she was spotted at a Wilshire Boulevard restaurant one evening consuming quantities of spaghetti and meatballs with a soup spoon, followed by a large serving of strawberry ice cream. "Being a movie star . . . means being looked at from every possible direction," Garbo later said. "You are never left in peace. You're just fair game."

Only friends in Sweden knew of Garbo's growing disillusionment. "I am incredibly tired of being a 'star'," she wrote home, "tired of the films they offer me, just tired, in a word." Her interest rose, however, when MGM proposed that she play the most famous woman in Swedish history, Queen *Christina, admired by generations of Swedes for her courage in negotiating a peace treaty with the rest of Europe concluding the Thirty Years' War and then giving up her throne for the Catholic religion and moving to Italy. Christina was equally famous for her fondness for men's clothes, another attraction to the part for Greta. Laurence Olivier was originally cast as the love interest invented by the

de Acosta, Mercedes (1893–1968)

American screenwriter. Born on March 1, 1893, in New York; died on May 9, 1968, in New York City; youngest of eight children of Ricardo de Acosta; married Abram Poole (a painter), on May 11, 1920 (divorced 1935); no children.

Described in her obituary as a poet, playwright and scenarist, Mercedes de Acosta is best remembered for her liaisons with beautiful and famous women. The most significant incident of her years as a screenwriter at MGM was her firing by Irving Thalberg for refusing to write a scene for the movie *Rasputin and the Empress* (1932), about a meeting between Princess *Irina (1895–1970) and Rasputin that never occurred. Her sole publication, a memoir entitled *Here Lies the Heart* (1960), was dismissed at the time as untrue.

Mercedes de Acosta was born in New York City, the youngest of eight children. She always claimed Spanish (Castilian) heritage, though it was generally acknowledged that her family came from Cuba. A woman of many eccentricities, de Acosta adopted the habit of dressing in either black or white, or a combination of the two. Despite her dramatic persona and outward bravado, she was inwardly tormented. From early childhood, she suffered from deep depressions and as an adult was additionally plagued by insomnia and migraines. For a time, she owned a Colt revolver, taking comfort in the fact that if life became too unbearable she could "pop myself off this baffling planet." In later years, she sought relief from her suicidal depressions through Indian philosophy and spiritualism.

From 1920 to 1935, de Acosta was married to painter Abram Poole, for whom she professed genuine affection, though it did not prevent her from pursuing fascinating women. "To the outward form of sex which the body has assumed, I have remained indifferent," she wrote. "I do not understand the difference between a man and a woman, and believing only in the eternal value of love, I cannot understand these so-called 'normal' people who believe that a man should love only a woman, and a woman love only a man."

She gravitated to and had intimate relations with artistic women with complex personalities, among them *Eleonora Duse, *Isadora Duncan, Marie Doro, *Alla Nazimova, *Eva Le Gallienne, Ona Munson, *Marlene Dietrich, and, of course, *Greta Garbo, who was perhaps the great love of her life. Her numerous conquests fascinated a number of notables, including *Alice B. Toklas, who wrote: "A friend said to me one day—you can't dispose of Mercedes lightly–she has had two of the most important women in the U.S.—Greta Garbo and Marlene Dietrich."

De Acosta met Garbo in early 1931, shortly after arriving in Hollywood to work on a screenplay for *Pola Negri. Both had been invited to tea at the home of screenwriter *Salka Viertel. "As we shook hands and she smiled at me I felt I had known her all my life," wrote de Acosta, "in fact, in many previous incarnations." Mutually attracted, the two spent six idyllic weeks together in the summer of 1931, after which de Acosta moved next door to Garbo in Brentwood. De Acosta's passion for the enigmatic star endured for the rest of her life, although the relationship was by no means exclusive.

Following the publication of her tell-all autobiography in 1960, Mercedes never saw Garbo again. Indeed, she spent the later years of her life ill and alone. In 1961, de Acosta underwent brain surgery and, in 1963, a painful leg operation. Having earned little from her book, she was also in desperate financial straits and was forced to sell her jewelry to pay her hospital bills. Still, she declined an offer of $10,000 for her Garbo letters. They were ultimately sealed at the Rosenbach Museum in Philadelphia to be opened ten years after Garbo's death. De Acosta also donated Dietrich's letters to the museum with the same stipulation. During this difficult period, she was supported by her old friend, sculptor *Malvina Hoffman, and a new friend, Andy Warhol, with whom she regularly shared Thanksgiving. When Cecil Beaton became aware of de Acosta's deteriorating health, he entreated Garbo to at least send her a postcard, but Garbo refused. De Acosta died on May 9, 1968, an event recorded in Beaton's diary. "Now, without a kind word from the woman she loved more than any of the many women in her life, Mercedes has gone to a lonely grave. I am relieved that her long drawn out unhappiness has at last come to an end."

SOURCES:

Vickers, Hugo. *Loving Garbo*. NY: Random House, 1994.

SUGGESTED READING:

Acosta, Mercedes de. *Here Lies the Heart*. NY: Reynal, 1960.

Buckle, Richard, ed. *Self-Portrait with Friends: The Selected Diaries of Cecil Beaton 1922–1974*. NY: Times Books, 1979.

scriptwriters as Anna's reason for abdicating, but Garbo refused to do the picture unless the part was given to John Gilbert, desperately in need of a big-budget, heavily promoted film after his struggles with the transition to sound. (It proved to be his last film. MGM refused to renew his contract and Gilbert died of a heart attack three years later.) Although *Queen Christina* is Garbo's most famous film, and its final shot of Christina's departure on a ship for Italy with the wind streaming through her hair one of the cinema's most famous images, Greta hated the finished product. "I am so off balance that I can't tell you anything," she wrote to Sweden in distress halfway through production. "I am so ashamed of Christina, I often wake up and think with horror about the film coming to Sweden. It's really bad in every respect, but the worst thing is they'll think I don't know any better." Director Rouben Mamoulian had his doubts, too, when Garbo informed him on the first day of shooting that she never rehearsed a scene before the cameras rolled. His efforts to change her mind were fruitless and the first scene was shot cold. "Garbo was right," Mamoulian later said in admiration. "She was an intuitive actress. You didn't have to tell Garbo to look like this or that, for this reason or that. No, you just had to tell her which emotion you wanted to have produced for the scene in question. She really could act." Her opinion of *Queen Christina* was moderated somewhat when Winston Churchill once told her in the midst of World War II that he liked to screen the film in his private London shelter while the bombs were falling. "Well, perhaps I did help make Queen Christina known throughout the world," Garbo admitted 50 years after the film's release.

As early as 1934, after completing *Queen Christina*, Garbo was thinking of quitting the film business for good. "But," she wrote, "I am not satisfied with what I've got in the way of money, so I'll have to keep working for a while longer." Despite her high salary, bad financial advice and the onset of the Depression had much reduced her resources, and MGM was frank in its displeasure with her performance in *The Painted Veil*, a box-office flop adapted from the W. Somerset Maugham novel. Her fortunes improved with 1936's *Anna Karenina*, a more faithful telling of the Tolstoy tale than *Love* of the previous decade; and with two films released in 1937, *Camille* (based on the story of *Alphonsine Plessis) and *Conquest*. The former was directed by George Cukor, who shot three separate death scenes for Dumas' tubercular heroine with varying degrees of dialogue for Greta as she expired on screen. In the released version, Garbo says hardly anything on her deathbed. "It didn't really feel very natural talking that much when you've just about given up the ghost," she said. The choice was an effective one, for audiences were so moved by the film that one critic thought

"people were going home as though they had been to Mass. [Garbo's] very face is a work of drama. It can reflect feelings and sensations to such an intense degree that you are unable to analyze them. You are just carried away."

Greta's work in both *Anna Karenina* and in *Camille* brought her an award from the New York Film Critics as Best Actress as well as Oscar nominations, although neither produced the Academy Award that many felt was due her. (She was finally given a special Oscar in 1954 for her "unforgettable screen performances.") *Conquest*, in which she played opposite Charles Boyer as Napoleon's Polish mistress *Marie Walewska, was notable chiefly for the stunning wardrobe designed for her by Gilbert Adrian, who added high necks to his creations after Greta objected to revealing too much of her bosom to the camera. Completing work on *Conquest*, Greta ventured into the public eye by accompanying famed symphonic conductor Leopold Stokowski on a European tour which included a long overdue visit to Sweden. Stokowski gallantly refused to discuss his relationship with the world's most famous movie star, and although Greta allowed herself to be photographed in his company, she granted no interviews. The press now routinely referred to her as "the Swedish Sphinx."

Toward the end of that year, Garbo began work on what she later said was the favorite of all her films, 1939's *Ninotchka*. In her first romantic comedy, she played an unimaginative and pragmatic Communist bureaucrat who comes to Paris and falls in love with a wealthy and happy capitalist playboy. Scripted by Billy Wilder, Charles Brackett and Walter Reisch, and directed by Ernst Lubitsch, the picture was a sophisticated, wry examination of conflicting ideas in which love finally carries the day. Lubitsch was one of the few directors besides Mauritz Stiller of whom Garbo would speak respectfully. Lubitsch was especially understanding, she said, with her difficulty with a bit of dialogue in one scene in which she was required to say "Then I will kick you up the arse." Objecting to such "rude words," as Garbo thought them, she ran from the set in tears when the writers refused to cut the expression. Lubitsch, she said, comforted her "like a loving father" and saw to it that the dialogue was adjusted to suit her. In the film's best-known scene, the famously morose Garbo laughs boisterously after her playboy pursuer, having failed to move her with a series of jokes, loses his temper and falls off his chair. "Garbo Laughs!" trumpeted MGM's one-sheets for the

From the movie Queen Christina, *1933.*

film, correctly assuming such a rare sight would be box-office gold. In *Ninotchka*, Garbo gave a warm and accessible performance.

By the time *Ninotchka* opened in November of 1939, war had broken out in Europe, and Garbo was cut off from her beloved Sweden. "I do so long to go home," she wrote in a letter, "but the ocean is so unsafe now. If peace comes, what I most want is to go home and not make another film." Neither wish was to be granted as the war intensified and America finally entered the conflict two years later. Wartime tensions in Hollywood focused on a handful of European actors who, it was rumored, were either secret agents for Hitler or spying for the Allies. Garbo, it was said, had been assigned by American intelligence to spy on Swedish industrialist Axel Wenner-Gren, a suspected supplier to the Axis powers. Greta strenuously denied any such activity. "I would have died of shame if I had anything to do with spying," she said years after the war. In any event, there was another picture assignment, 1941's *Two-Faced Woman*, her second romantic comedy which again paired her with her co-star from *Ninotchka*, Melvyn Douglas. Garbo played a double role, as twin sisters, with Douglas bamboozled by both women in a running gag of mistaken identities. The film's frivolity and high-society antics did not sit well with a country just entering the war, and the Catholic Church complained that the picture's suggestion of a *ménage à trois*, however lighthearted, was immoral and urged the faithful to stay away. Artistically, Greta seemed ill-suited to the picture's madcap humor and seemed to be struggling to make each sister a separate, believable character. Reviews were the worst of her career. Some weeks after the film's release, Greta Garbo announced that *Two-Faced Woman* would be her last film. Typically, the news was communicated via a studio press release and Garbo herself never offered a public explanation for her decision, although the devastating reviews of her latest work must have played a role. Years later, she said she had agreed to do *Two-Faced Woman* only because her contract with MGM required it. Otherwise, she would have left the business much earlier. "I was tired of Hollywood," she said. "There were many days when I had to force myself to go to the studio. I really wanted to live another life."

There were the inevitable stories that the great Garbo would return to the screen once the sting of *Two-Faced Woman* had worn off; and Greta herself wrote in a letter from New York in 1945 that she was considering several offers. But a year later, she was telling friends back in Sweden that "I will never work again at my former job. I'm still living quietly and away from it all, so I've nothing exciting to tell you about. I have made no plans, neither for films nor for anything else. I am just flowing with the current." She would, in fact, spend the rest of her life "living quietly and away from it all." She resolutely refused to step in front of a camera again, dodged as best she could the prying lenses of tabloid photographers, and settled into the life of a celebrity jet-setter. She divided her time between her apartment on New York's East 52nd Street and the Hotel Pardenn in Klosters, Switzerland, which, she said, felt "like a piece of Sweden to me." There were frequent visits to Monaco for some genteel casino-hopping and a stop at the royal palace, and quiet days at sundrenched Greek villas. She hobnobbed with a coterie of fellow international celebrities as concerned with their privacy as she was with hers. Among them were the Kennedys, Aristotle Onassis, the Aga Khan, and the indefatigable Churchill, who ventured the opinion that a comeback late in life should not be discounted. "Look at me," he said. "I didn't become Prime Minister until I was over fifty years old, and I had to fight a World War." But Garbo was unwilling to even consider the possibility. "I have mostly wanted to be alone so that I can have peace and quiet," she said.

For over 30 years, Garbo's steadfast refusal of all requests for interviews perpetuated the mystery she gathered around her like a protective cloak. The world that had once adored her now saw her only in blurry photographs shot from a distance as she scurried across a busy New York street or boarded airplanes and ships for Europe or the Riviera. It wasn't until the late 1980s that she finally agreed to a series of interviews with Swedish journalist Sven Broman, held erratically over a period of two years in New York and Switzerland. Even though Garbo's health had by then become problematical, especially a kidney disorder that required occasional periods of dialysis, Broman was as awestruck as someone seeing her 50 years earlier. "The first thing that struck me was the beauty of her voice," he wrote. "It was so well preserved, so sonorous." And despite the advancing years, Broman said, the combination of shyness and self-confidence that had so marked her public career remained intact. "She was unpredictable," Broman delightedly noted. By the time Broman met her, Greta had stopped smoking, claimed that she limited herself to one cocktail a day, and confessed that her waning appetite restricted her to a diet consisting mostly of raw vegetables. Early in 1990, just as Broman's book was about to appear in bookstores in Europe, Greta returned to New York from Switzerland and was hospitalized with what would prove to be her final illness. On April 15, she died of kidney disease at New York Hospital. She was 84 at her passing and left an estate said to total some $200 million. Director Clarence Brown, who had guided her through her first talking picture, *Anna Christie*, noted that "Without having made a film since 1940, she is still the greatest."

The Greta Garbo that emerges from Broman's notes is hardly the mysterious vamp or the poignant lover of her screen years, nor the shallow, self-centered recluse of some biographers, but a practical-minded elderly woman with more than a few stories to tell about the old days. She is alternately wistful when speaking of her childhood in Sweden and her lifelong desire for privacy, disdainful about Hollywood's star system, and coy about the volumes of rumor and speculation that had grown around her over the years. "I always wanted to do my best," she told Broman. "I got nothing for free. I had to work hard. But I also got pursued and persecuted. That was no kind of life. It was not worth the price. I dreamed of being able to lead my own life." When she finally turned her back on Hollywood, Greta Garbo's fantasy came true.

SOURCES:

Broman, Sven. *Garbo on Garbo*. London: Bloomsbury Publishing, 1990.

Paris, Barry. *Garbo*. NY: Knopf, 1995.

Swenson, Karen. *Greta Garbo: A Life Apart*. NY: Scribners, 1997.

Norman Powers,
writer-producer, Chelsea Lane Productions,
New York, New York

Garbousova, Raya (1909–1997)

Georgian-born American cellist, renowned for the lyrical quality of her playing, who inspired major composers including Samuel Barber to write works for her. Born in Tiflis (now Tbilisi), Georgia, on September 25, 1909 (some sources cite October 10, 1905 or 1907); died in De Kalb, Illinois, on January 28, 1997; married Kurt Biss; children: Gregory, Paul.

One of the great cellists of the 20th century, Raya Garbousova was born in 1909 in Tiflis, Georgia, then a part of the Russian Empire. Her father, who was the principal trumpeter in the local symphony orchestra, was also a professor at the Tiflis Conservatory. By age four, Raya was a musical prodigy on the piano, until she heard a family friend, double bass player Serge Koussevitzky, perform. She then longed to study a stringed instrument like the cello. Initially her father resisted her pleas, noting that women simply did not play the cello. A determined Raya deliberately stalled further progress in her piano technique until her father changed his mind. In time, he relented, and on her sixth birthday she became the proud owner of a child-sized cello.

After a brief period of lessons at the Tiflis Conservatory, Garbousova made her local debut, with critics praising her for being much more than the typical "drilled prodigy." Although she spent countless hours practicing, she had many other intellectual interests both in her youth and throughout her life. As a child, her enthusiasm for great literature was encouraged by a tailor who lived in the same house, while a shoemaker who lived in the basement kindled a love of philosophy. Her view of life would remain all-encompassing, based on wide reading and eager traveling. At the time of her 80th-birthday celebrations, she would assert: "To this day I actually need the other arts. I object to any notion of the artist being isolated in his own discipline; we have to be citizens of the world of arts and thought."

The years in which Garbousova mastered the cello were difficult for her family and Russia (to be called the Soviet Union after December 1922). Civil war and chaos marked public life, and in her own home music was plentiful but food was often scarce. In 1924, Garbousova gave a triumphant Moscow debut. Critics compared her talent with another brilliant young virtuoso of the day, Emanuel Feuermann, suggesting that Garbousova had already left Feuermann behind in the emotional depths she could draw from her instrument. Despite war, revolution, and social upheaval, Muscovites had retained their enthusiasm for great music and the gifted young woman was acclaimed for her solo performances and invited to participate in chamber music recitals with other young stars like the violinist Nathan Milstein and the pianist Vladimir Horowitz. Deciding that she had exhausted her learning opportunities in Soviet Russia, Garbousova decided in 1925 to continue her studies in Western Europe, where she perfected her technique with teachers Diran Alexanian, Hugo Becker, Julius Klengel, and Felix Salmond.

After her Berlin debut in 1926, Garbousova rapidly became an international musical personality. In Berlin, she met Albert Einstein, an amateur violinist whose passion for performing chamber music sometimes exceeded his technical skills. Garbousova, who played chamber works with Einstein, later recalled not only the great physicist's profound love for music but also the fact that his fiddling was always a little bit out of tune and that he produced a "very odd" vibrato. Einstein became one of her most enthusiastic fans; when he faithfully attended her concerts in Berlin, he would always place a box of chocolates on the stage instead of the customary flowers.

In October 1926, Garbousova made a highly successful London debut. *The Times* critic praised her playing for its "pure and copious" tone, and for phrasing that revealed "a natural musical instinct." He predicted a great future for her, because it was clear that she would soon

Raya
Garbousova

mature into "a complete artist of unusual power." After an equally triumphant debut in Paris in 1927, Garbousova met Pablo Casals, who admired her abilities and allowed her to become one of his students. Casals, who in later years spoke of Garbousova as "the best cellist I have ever heard," invited her to perform as a soloist with his own orchestra in Barcelona.

Although she performed in Boston and Detroit in the late 1920s and made her New York debut recital in 1934, she made her home in

Paris during this period. In December 1934, Garbousova's New York debut turned her into a major artist overnight. Olin Downes, the influential music critic of *The New York Times*, wrote a long and enthusiastic review in which he stated that in "a very few minutes she proved her exceptional talent, sensibility and knowledge of her business." Commending her for her rare ability to end a musical phrase as effectively as she had begun it, Downes described the young cellist as "a figure to reckon with in the concert world."

Garbousova settled in the United States in 1939 as the clouds of war hung over Europe, becoming a citizen in 1946. A stunning woman with the charisma of a movie star, she was respected by colleagues and friends for her kind, gentle and considerate nature. She also had a delightful sense of humor. On one occasion, she bet five dollars that she would be able to kiss the renowned conductor Arturo Toscanini, who was sitting at the next table. Rather than being offended, Toscanini was delighted to be kissed by the beautiful young musician and offered her his other cheek as well. Encouraged by his enthusiasm, she kissed him on both cheeks, excusing herself by noting she could now collect not five but ten dollars on her bet.

Impressed by the passionate lyricism of her playing, several of the leading composers of her era composed major works for her. Perhaps the best-known was the *Cello Concerto* by Samuel Barber, a neo-Romantic work which was given its world premiere by Garbousova in Boston on April 5, 1946. Her recording of the Barber work remains the touchstone for all other performances of this modern classic. Other contemporary composers who composed for her included Karol Rathaus, Vittorio Rieti, and Gunther Schuller. Schuller composed a cello *Fantasy* for her in 1951, and then in 1990 composed a work in her honor entitled "Hommage a Rayechka." She gave many U.S. as well as world-premiere performances, among which were the cello sonata of Sergei Prokofiev (which she also recorded) and the third sonata for that instrument by Bohuslav Martinu. Soon after settling in the United States, Garbousova became interested in compositions by contemporary American composers including not only Samuel Barber, but Randall Thompson (she recorded Thompson's cello sonata in the early 1950s).

An inspirational teacher, Garbousova taught cello at the Hartt College at the University of Hartford from 1970 through 1979, and then at Northern Illinois University from 1979 until 1991. To her friends and students, she seemed to be virtually immortal. Appearing to be at least two decades younger than her actual age, and continuing to draw upon apparently unlimited reserves of energy, she enthusiastically taught master classes until the end of her life. Raya Garbousova died in De Kalb, Illinois, on January 28, 1997, leaving a void in the lives of family and friends. "The sadness can only be mitigated by gratitude for having had the chance to know this glorious woman," writes Steven Isserlis.

SOURCES:

Campbell, Margaret. *The Great Cellists*. North Pomfret, VT: Trafalgar Square Publishing, 1989.

———. "Raya Garbousova," in *The Independent* [London]. February 1, 1997, p. 18.

———. "Raya Garbousova," in *The Strad*. Vol. 100, no. 1193. September 1989, pp. 762–765 and 768.

"Concerts: Miss Raya Garbousova," in *The Times* [London]. October 23, 1926, p. 10.

Downes, Olin. "Raya Garbousova, 'Cellist, in Debut,'" in *The New York Times*. December 4, 1934, p. 22.

Inglis, Anne, and Steven Isserlis. "Raya Garbousova: Life Force at the Cello," in *The Guardian* [London]. February 8, 1997, p. 17.

Kozinn, Allan. "Raya Garbousova, 87, Cellist; Celebrated the New," in *The New York Times Biographical Service*. January 1997, p. 176.

"Loss Of Garbousova, cellist with joie de vivre," in *The Strad*. Vol. 108, no. 1284. April 1997, p. 361.

COLLECTIONS:

Georges Miquelle Papers, University of Virginia Library, Charlottesville, Virginia.

John Haag,
Associate Professor of History,
University of Georgia, Athens, Georgia

Garcia, Pauline (1821–1910).

See Viardot, Pauline.

Garcia, Sancha (fl. 1230)

Spanish abbess of Las Huelgas. Name variations: Sancia. Flourished in 1230 in Las Huelgas, Spain; never married; no children.

A Spanish noblewoman, Sancha Garcia was one of the last truly powerful abbesses of medieval Europe. She entered a convent as a girl, and eventually her piety, broad learning, and administrative abilities led her to be chosen head of the large abbey of Las Huelgas, putting not only a convent but also several monasteries under her direct control. Sancha did not believe, as the church's leaders did, that only men could perform the duties of a priest. Though she could not be ordained, she performed many of the same functions as a priest, including hearing confessions and blessing the nuns. She also acted, as did so many abbesses of large monasteries, as a business administrator, a spiritual counselor, and an educator.

Laura York,
Riverside, California

Garden, Mary (1874–1967)

Scottish-born American soprano. Born in Aberdeen, Scotland, on February 20, 1874; died in Aberdeen, on January 3, 1967; the second of four daughters of Robert Davidson (an engineer) and Mary (Joss) Garden; attended private school in Aberdeen; never married; no children.

Mary Garden was born in Aberdeen, Scotland, on February 20, 1874, the daughter of Robert Davidson and Mary Joss Garden. At the age of five, she made her first public appearance, singing for her grandmother's friends who had come to tea. Perched on top of a table, she sang, "Three Little Redcaps Growing in the Corn," all the while twirling her fingers around her head. From that time on, music was the center of her life, although as a child she never had the remotest thought of becoming an opera singer, nor could she have known she was destined to be a star. Brought to America while still quite young,

Mary Garden

she lived in Brooklyn, New York, and Chicopee, Massachusetts, before her family finally settled in Chicago. She studied the violin and piano, and at 16 began voice lessons with **Sarah Robinson Duff**, who encouraged her to study in Paris and even secured a wealthy Chicago patron to pay her way. In Paris, Garden rejected a number of teachers before deciding on Antonio Trabadello and Lucien Fugère, who kept her on as a student even after her sponsor stopped sending money. Quickly running out of funds for living expenses, Garden was dramatically rescued by *Sybil Sanderson, an American opera star living in Paris. Upon hearing of her plight, Sanderson decided to take Garden into her own home and to sponsor her.

Through Sanderson, Garden met the manager of the Opéra-Comique, Albert Carré, who was next in line to influence her budding career. Although Carré did not have an immediate opening in his company, he listened to Garden sing and then loaned her a copy of the new opera he was producing, Gustave Charpentier's *Louise,* urging her to study the score. On April 13, 1900, in another dramatic turn of events, Garden was called upon to step into the title role when the leading soprano took ill after the first two acts. She created a sensation and became a permanent member of the Opéra Comique, performing in *La Traviata, La Fille Du Tambour-Major*, and *L'Ouragon.* Carré later suggested Garden for the principal role in the world premiere of a new French opera, *Pelléas et Mélisande,* by Claude Debussy, which became her signature role. Later, one American critic called her portrayal of the elf-like character of Mélisande "vivid," but tempered his enthusiasm by also commenting that her vocal shortcomings were less evident in this role, which consisted largely of fragmentary, declamatory passages.

On November 25, 1907, Garden made her U.S. debut at Hammerstein's Manhattan Opera House in the American premiere of Massenet's *Thaïs,* an opera that the critics hated, though audiences flocked to see her. Her performance in *Louise* six weeks later confirmed her success, and she remained a star of the Manhattan Opera House until it closed in 1910, singing numerous roles with varying degrees of success. One of her most important Manhattan appearances took place on January 28, 1909, when she appeared in Strauss' *Salome,* stunning audiences as much with her erotic performance of the Dance of the Seven Veils as with her singing.

Critics generally agreed that Garden's voice, even in its prime, was never great, although her magnetism and dramatic flair often made up for her lack of technical skill. Oscar Thompson, in his book *The American Singer*, called her work "disturbingly irregular" and cited the wide divergence between the best and the average of her performances of the same role. "[H]er Carmen as an instance. Her Mélisande, in its early year particularly, stood alone. In *Thaïs* she could be glamorously convincing or she could attitudinize the evening long. Her Louise was hectic and tame by turns. . . . Out of these contradictions arose an imperious something to dwarf them all. Mary Garden was Mary Garden." Ian Fellowes-Gordon believes that Garden's reputation as a singer suffered because she was such a superb actress. "Her misfortune," he wrote, "is to be remembered in some quarters as a singing actress, rather than a singer."

With the close of the Manhattan Opera House, Garden joined the Chicago Opera Company, where she appeared in numerous roles, including Fiora in Italo Montemezzi's *The Love of Three Kings*, and the title role in *Monna Vanna*, by Henri Février, two of her favorites. When artistic director Cleofonte Campanini died in 1919, she was appointed to succeed him. The first woman to become the director of a major opera company, she held the post for one tumultuous year (1921–22), after which she happily resumed her status as a member of the company. One of Garden's last performances with the Chicago Opera was in the American opera *Camille*, by Hamilton Forest, in 1930. She retired from the stage in 1931 at the height of her career, deciding to leave quite suddenly one evening after a performance in *Le Jongleur de Notre-Dame*. Later, she went back to Aberdeen to live, although she returned to America for lecture and recital tours and to serve as a judge for the National Arts Foundation.

Garden never married, although it was not for lack of opportunity. There were numerous proposals, even one from Albert Carré, who was so incensed at her refusal that he tore up her contract. (He later apologized and presented her another.) Although she fell in love a number of times (once, quite seriously), she made an early decision never to marry. In her autobiography, *Mary Garden's Story*, she wrote that the real "romance" of her life was opera. "There never was anything in the world to take the place of my work—nothing and nobody." Mary Garden lived almost 30 years after her retirement, and to the end of her life was an encouragement to younger singers. She died in a nursing home in Aberdeen, Scotland, on January 3, 1967, at age 93.

SOURCES:

Fellowes-Gordon, Ian. *Famous Scottish Lives*. Watford, Herts., England: Odhams, 1967.

Garden, Mary, with Louis Biancolli. *Mary Garden's Story*. NY: Simon and Schuster, 1951.

McHenry, Robert, ed. *Famous American Women*. NY: Dover, 1983.

Sicherman, Barbara, and Carol Hurd Green. *Notable American Women: The Modern Period*. Cambridge, MA: The Belknap Press of Harvard University Press, 1980.

Barbara Morgan,
Melrose, Massachusetts

Gardener, Helen Hamilton

(1853–1925)

American author, feminist, suffragist, and federal civil service commissioner. Name variations: Alice Chenoweth; Alice Smart. Born Alice Chenoweth in Winchester, Virginia, on January 21, 1853; died in Washington, D.C., on July 26, 1925; third daughter and youngest of six children of Reverend Alfred G. and Katherine A. (Peel) Chenoweth; attended high school in Cincinnati; graduated from the Cincinnati Normal School, 1873; studied biology at Columbia University; married Charles S. Smart (school commissioner of Ohio), in 1875 (died 1901); married Colonel Selden Allen Day (a retired army officer), on April 9, 1902 (died 1919); no children.

The daughter of an abolitionist and itinerant Methodist preacher, Helen Gardener was born Alice Chenoweth in Winchester, Virginia, on January 21, 1853. She grew up in Washington, D.C., Greencastle, Indiana, and Cincinnati, Ohio, where she attended high school and graduated from the Cincinnati Normal School. A brief career as a schoolteacher was followed by her marriage in 1875 to Charles Smart, then school commissioner of Ohio. In 1878, the couple moved to New York, where Smart entered the insurance business and Gardener studied biology at Columbia University, lectured in sociology at the Brooklyn Institute of Arts and Science, and contributed articles on sundry subjects to newspapers (using various masculine pseudonyms). At this time, her friendship with the renowned agnostic Colonel Robert G. Ingersoll and his wife had a great impact on her life, and at Ingersoll's urging Gardener began giving a series of freethinking lectures which were heavily influenced by her new mentor. In 1885, the lectures were published as *Men, Women and Gods, and Other Lectures* (1885) under the name Helen Hamilton Gardener, a mysterious pseudonym that Gardener eventually adopted as her legal name.

Helen
Hamilton
Gardener

Gardener came to the attention of feminists in 1888 with her famous essay "Sex in Brain," a refutation of a widely publicized claim by Dr. William A. Hammond, a New York neurologist and former U.S. surgeon general, that female brains were inherently and measurably inferior to male brains. Gardener's well-researched rebuttal argued that Hammond's findings were invalid because all of the male brains he had studied were from intelligent, accomplished men, while the female brains in his study had come from indigents and criminals. To provide a suitable specimen for future research of this sort, Gardener magnanimously bequeathed her own brain to Cornell University.

Gardener achieved her greatest popularity with her novel *This Your Son, My Lord?* (1890), an outspoken attack on legalized prostitution, and the ridiculously low legal age at which girls were considered to be at the age of consent, told through the melodramatic story of a young girl's demise at the hands of seemingly respectable men. The book sold 25,000 copies in five months and was a source of shock and controversy among critics and readers alike. Gardener's next novel, *Pray You Sir, Whose Daughter?* (1892), with which she hoped to repeat her earlier success, dealt with the inferior status imposed upon married women. Gardener digressed somewhat in her next book, a fictional biography of her father, *An Unofficial Patriot* (1884), which is considered by some to be her best work. In 1899, it was successfully dramatized by playwright James A. Herne as *Griffith Davenport, Circuit Rider*. In two collections of short stories, *A Thoughtless Yes* (1890) and *Pushed by Unseen Hands* (1892), she returned to challenge the status quo, and her articles on social issues, which appeared in numerous journals, were collected in *Facts and Fictions of Life* (1893). A long-time contributor to the reform magazine *Arena*, Gardener was its co-editor in 1897. (Her husband Charles Smart served as *Arena*'s business manager for several years.)

After the death of Smart in 1901, and her second marriage to Selden Allen Day, a retired army officer, Gardener spent five years in world travel, during which time her interest in reform cooled somewhat. The couple settled in Washington in 1907, after which Gardener was called upon by suffragists to use her wide social contacts with government figures to advance their cause. In 1913, after members of the Congressional Committee of the National American Woman Suffrage Association resigned to back *Alice Paul's militant Congressional Union, Gardener was appointed to reorganize the association. She became its vice president in 1917, and through her personal contacts with President Woodrow Wilson and Speaker of the House Champ Clark, she was a central figure in steering the federal suffrage amendment to eventual ratification in 1920. That same year, at age 67, Gardener was appointed by Wilson to the U.S. Civil Service Commission, thus becoming the first woman to hold so high a federal position. Serving in the post until her death in 1925, Helen Gardener remained the consummate feminist, constantly finding ways to make federal service a more accessible and equitable career for women.

SOURCES:
James, Edward T., ed. *Notable American Women*. Cambridge, MA: The Belknap Press of Harvard University Press, 1971.
McHenry, Robert. *Famous American Women*. NY: Dover, 1983.
COLLECTIONS:
The Helen Hamilton Gardener Papers, Schlesinger Library, Radcliffe College.

Barbara Morgan,
Melrose, Massachusetts

Gardiner, Lady (1905–1991).

See Box, Muriel.

Gardiner, Marguerite (1789–1849).

See Blessington, Marguerite, Countess of.

Gardiner, Muriel (1901–1985)

American psychoanalyst who played an important role in the anti-Nazi Austrian Socialist movement in the 1930s and who, many feel, was the basis for Lillian Hellman's Julia in Pentimento. *Born Helen Muriel Morris in Chicago, Illinois, in November 1901; died in Princeton, New Jersey, on February 6, 1985; last of four children of Edward and Helen Swift Morris (both of whose fathers had made fortunes in the Chicago stockyards and meat packing industry); attended Wellesley College, Oxford University, and the University of Vienna; awarded M.D. in Vienna, 1938; married Julian Gardiner, on May 20, 1930 (divorced 1932); married Joseph Buttinger (an Austrian Socialist leader), on August 1, 1939; children: (first marriage) daughter* **Constance Gardiner.**

The possession of great wealth does not guarantee a productive life, but in the case of Muriel Gardiner it enabled an intelligent, sensitive woman to participate in some of the most dramatic events of modern European history. A person who matured slowly, both personally and politically, Gardiner was in her mid-30s before she involved herself in the dangerous underground work of Austrians who resisted Fascism. Though endangered herself, she played a key role in saving the lives of countless individuals.

Muriel Gardiner's life began not in the troubled Central Europe she loved so much but in Chicago, where she was born Helen Muriel Morris in November 1901. Her family was one of the wealthiest in that bustling city. Her paternal grandfather had founded the Union Stockyards of Chicago, while her maternal grandfather had started the meat packing firm of Swift & Company. Because her father was Jewish, Gardiner would later find it easy to identify with Jews and others who bore the brunt of discrimination or persecution. From her mother, who was of Anglo-Saxon New England stock, she learned the moral tradition of Puritanism and social duty. Her father imbued her with equally high ideals of honesty, hard work, politeness and fairness. Indeed, her sense of social justice was acute even in childhood, despite the dozen servants in her family's employ. Gardiner rarely saw her extremely busy father. A sensitive child, she was often lonely, having no friends her own age, even though in time she would be popular in school. The person she loved most was her nurse Mollie.

It is possible for even lone individuals to pit their strength successfully against the sinister forces of an unjust regime.

—*Anna Freud on Muriel Gardiner*

By the time she was eight, Gardiner was acutely aware that she lived in a different world from that of Mollie and the other servants. News of the sinking of the *Titanic* in 1912 only deepened feelings of the vast gap separating the privileged from the masses. When her parents' friends talked about the tragedy, they only mentioned the wealthy passengers who had perished, totally ignoring the hundreds in steerage who had also lost their lives. In 1910, when Muriel took her first trip to Europe, traveling with her family on a luxury liner, she would stare down from her enclosed first-class deck to the open steerage below. Poorly dressed passengers—men, women and children—sat shivering in rainy or rough weather while waves streamed onto their deck; some would gaze with pleading eyes at the warm and pampered passengers above.

Young Muriel's yearning for social justice expanded with each passing year. She read voraciously, asking countless questions of servants. Not yet ten, her social militancy first surfaced when she led her fellow female students in a suffragist parade. She delighted in devouring books brought home from college by her older brother Nelson, including such classics as the *Meditations* of Marcus Aurelius and Ralph Waldo Emerson's *Essays*.

In 1913, the early death of her 46-year-old father was a turning point, although the coming of war in Europe in the summer of 1914 left much deeper and more permanent wounds. Though not yet a teenager, Muriel followed the hostilities with interest. Her paternal grandfather had started life as an impoverished Jewish boy in Hechingen in southern Germany. Many of her family servants had been born in Europe and their colorful stories of poverty and oppression kindled her interest in social reform. The European conflict raised profound questions that a young girl could not easily answer. Why, for example, were the Germans now condemned as "Huns" when only a few months before most people, including the entire Morris family, had admired Germans for their industriousness and energy? The entry of the United States into the war in 1917 only accelerated Gardiner's evolution toward a radical rejection of the majority's political credo. Although deeply concerned about her older brother Nelson, who joined the army and was sent overseas, from the start of American military involvement she considered herself to be an uncompromising pacifist, convinced that if she had been born a male she would simply refuse to fight if called upon.

With each passing year, the youthful Gardiner became more confident in her beliefs. A number of strong-minded individuals helped her as she struggled to discover a system of values that best reflected her own mind. One of the most influential was her history teacher, **Helen Boyce**. Boyce was a rare woman for her time, who, after having earned a Ph.D. from the University of Chicago, decided on a career as a teacher in a girls' school. Miss Boyce brought out the best in her students, encouraging them to think independently. Gardiner's iconoclastic spirit was reinforced by a series of tragedies. Several of her brothers' friends, on whom the effervescent Muriel had developed one-sided crushes, died in their teens and twenties. As a result, Muriel decided before she was 20 that she could believe neither in God nor the notion of immortality as conventionally defined. Unlike her brothers, who exhibited a practical bent and went into the family business without completing college, Gardiner became more intellectually oriented. She entered Wellesley College as a freshman in the fall of 1918. Coming from a protective environment, Wellesley seemed almost paradisiacal.

The signing of the armistice ending World War I on November 11, 1918, was one of the most powerful experiences of her Wellesley years. Before dawn, the bells of the churches of Boston and surrounding towns began to ring. Excited, Gardiner went outside just as "the eastern sky showed streaks of red and orange heralding the sunrise of the first day of peace after more than four years of war." She walked along the wooded banks of the Charles River to ponder the meaning of the new world. But after 1918 there was precious little time for such reveries, given the fact that much of the world was in turmoil. Europe was tormented by starvation and bloody insurrections. At affluent Wellesley in the years after 1918, Gardiner formed a committee to send food and funds to those European students who, in the miserable postwar years, could scarcely afford fuel, new books, and journals.

Though she had made some attempts to simplify, her life style remained luxurious when compared to that of many of Europe's distressed students. Mortified, she gave away her fur coat and most of her jewelry, retaining only the string of pearls her dying father had given her and a necklace of semiprecious stones that had once belonged to her mother. At college, Gardiner had developed a passion for first editions with rare and beautiful leather bindings. After a long struggle, she decided that this obsession must be nipped if her campaign against excessive materialism was to succeed. Filling a large suitcase with most of her most cherished rarities, she lugged it to a Boston bookshop; the proceeds were immediately dispatched to the starving students of the University of Vienna—a place Gardiner had never seen but which would play a key role in her later life.

Muriel Gardiner's first encounter with postwar Europe took place in the summer of 1921, when she traveled through the Cotswolds, North Wales, and the Lake District between her junior and senior year. Intellectual stimulation that summer came from meeting and discussing the finer points of contemporary political ideas, including Socialism, with the eminent Marxist teacher and author Harold Laski. Returning home, she found more of the political and social intolerance that had gripped the United States since 1917, when pacifists, labor militants, and radicals were imprisoned, deprived of work, or in some cases deported as sowers of "un-American" ideas. Gardiner by now had developed a reputation as a campus radical and some conservatives felt she was another dangerous "Red" or "Bolshie." In a series of articles in *The Delineator,* then Vice-President Calvin Coolidge bitterly attacked college students who had in his opinion been seduced by radical ideas, suggesting that the origin of student militancy could be largely traced to cliques of ultra-liberal faculty members,

Muriel
Gardiner

including two of Wellesley's popular professors, *Vida D. Scudder and *Mary Whiton Calkins.

Graduating from Wellesley in 1922, Gardiner decided to travel to Europe in September of that year, arriving in Italy on the eve of the Fascist March on Rome. For all of her campus radicalism, she remained pitifully ignorant of the extent of European social turmoil, and her knowledge of Italian politics was virtually nil. Although she was an eyewitness to the March in October 1922, and was in fact detained by barbed wire spread in front of the gates of Rome by black-shirted militia members, Gardiner thought the situation ridiculous and dismissed Benito Mussolini's threat to democracy as minimal. Only her experiences in Austria in later years would make her realize how dire a threat to liberal civilization Fascism was, regardless of where it took root.

From the time of her graduation from Wellesley to the bloody suppression of the uprising of Austria's Socialists in February 1934, Gardiner's political interests stayed relatively dormant. While she remained at heart liberal, indeed often radical in her views, most of the ensuing 12 years were spent on rather desultory studies and travel. After returning from her year in Italy, she attended Oxford University from 1923 through 1925 but seemed unable to focus on a clear goal. Her Oxford thesis, on *Mary Shelley, required an oral defense, and Gardiner's uncompromising attitudes led to an explosive clash with one of her three examiners, a woman of a sternly moralistic bent. When asked if she condemned the act of suicide, Gardiner defiantly asserted that she did not, adding that the examiner's remarks were out of place in an examination setting. Not surprisingly, she failed the examination.

Although Gardiner was approaching her mid-20s, her wealth continued to act as a crutch, enabling her to delay choosing a career or even a serious avocation. In the spring of 1926, she first visited Vienna, hoping to be accepted as a psychoanalytic patient of Sigmund Freud. But Freud turned down her request without explanation, referring her instead to his pupil and colleague, American-born Ruth Mack (later ◄⚜ **Ruth Mack Brunswick**), a fellow Chicagoan and daughter of Judge Julian Mack, who had made his Chicago Juvenile Court a world-famous and respected experiment in social rehabilitation. In a situation not unusual at the time, Ruth Mack agreed to begin a course of analysis with Gardiner, providing Gardiner accompany her to New York

⚜► **Brunswick, Ruth Mack** (1897–1946)

American psychoanalyst. Name variations: Ruth Mack. Born Ruth Jane Mack in Chicago, Illinois, on February 17, 1897; died in New York City on January 24, 1946; daughter of Judge Julian Mack; graduated from Radcliffe College, 1918; graduated from Tufts Medical School, 1922; married (name unknown); married Mark Brunswick (an American composer), in 1928.

Refused entrance to Harvard Medical School because of her gender, Ruth Brunswick matriculated at Tufts before heading for Vienna to become an analysand of Sigmund Freud. Starting in 1925, she began her own practice in Vienna, became a member of the Vienna Psychoanalytic Society, an instructor at the Psychoanalytic Institute, and edited the American journal *Psychoanalytic Quarterly.* Following the annexation of Austria by the Nazis in 1938, 41-year-old Ruth and her husband, composer Mark Brunswick, moved to New York, where she went into private practice, preferring to tackle cases that were deemed hopeless. But Brunswick was suffering from poor health for a number of years, and she died in 1946, age 49.

City that summer. While there, Gardiner stayed with friends in Greenwich Village, meeting an intellectually varied group, including Princeton academics, legal scholars like Judge Learned Hand, and Jewish labor leaders including Sidney Hillman and Morris Hillquit. She returned to Vienna in September 1926 as a permanent resident, determined to understand all facets of the still-imposing former capital of a great empire. She was becoming increasingly enthusiastic about "Red Vienna's" pathbreaking social reforms in the areas of health insurance and education.

Muriel's years of aimlessness ended on May 20, 1930, when she married Julian Gardiner, a gifted young Brit. Soon a daughter Constance (Connie) was born, but by 1932 the marriage had broken down, and she and Julian divorced on amicable terms. After her divorce, a new maturity and determination began to surface. A decade older than most other students, she decided to earn a medical degree, enrolling at the University of Vienna. For the first time, she began to be an acute observer of a rapidly deteriorating social and political Viennese landscape. The world economic depression that began in 1929 impacted more severely on Austria than almost any other nation; public life became violently confrontational and radicalized. The long-festering tensions between "Red Vienna" and Catholics and other conservatives in the provinces, which had already led to a bloody riot that left almost one-hundred men and women dead in July 1927, now erupted on an almost daily basis. Armed units of unemployed young men prowled the streets looking for political foes to bludgeon into compliance. The government—which often sympathized with the forces of the extreme Right, including a growing Nazi party—customarily viewed these clashes with bemused impotence.

Gardiner was particularly shocked by the accelerating aggressiveness of Viennese anti-Semitism. As a student of the university's renowned Jewish anatomy professor Julius Tandler, she lived through episodes of pure terror on several occasions when Nazi students attempted to storm the Tandler wing of the anatomy building, where almost all of the students were either Jewish or Social Democratic, and in most cases both.

By 1933, democracy had been destroyed in both Germany and Austria. In Germany, Adolf Hitler's Third Reich created a reign of terror complete with concentration camps, whereas in Austria another year passed before the transition from parliamentary rule to a Fascist dictatorship under chancellor Engelbert Dollfuss transpired. During this time, Muriel Gardiner was in the process of completing her first two years of medical school. Given the unstable political climate in Central Europe, she seriously considered returning to the United States to complete her medical education. Then a series of events changed the direction of her life. One was a brief but passionate affair with the British poet Stephen Spender, whom she met on a vacation trip to the Dalmatian coast. More important was the radical transformation that took place in Austria in February 1934 when the Socialist movement was bloodily suppressed and a Fascist regime was set up with the enthusiastic support of the Italian dictator, Benito Mussolini. Given the fact that many of her closest Austrian friends were Social Democrats whose careers and lives were now in jeopardy, Gardiner felt she could not abandon them, believing that as an American with means she might in fact be of use to them.

Countless opportunities presented themselves immediately. Assuming the code name of "Mary" Gardiner, she became a member of the Socialist underground, lending her apartment to refugees from the police as well as hiding fugitives in her cottage in Sulz, deep in the Vienna Woods. From 1934 through March 1938, when Nazi Germany annexed Austria, she was involved in countless illegal actions designed to keep alive the spark of resistance against a repressive regime. Much of this work was sandwiched between the ordinary life of a wealthy American expatriate determined to earn a medical degree before returning home to begin a career as a teacher and psychoanalyst. But there were moments when the secret (and dangerous) side of her existence gave her the kind of emotional satisfaction that derives from the successful completion of a risky mission. For almost four years, she regarded it as perfectly natural to take overnight "sightseeing trips" by train to Prague in order to pick up false passports for her Viennese comrades. She was able to smuggle them back to Austria by taping them inside her corset.

During her underground work, Gardiner met and quickly fell in love with "Wieser," a courageous and intelligent leader of a militant Socialist cell who took refuge in her Vienna Woods cottage in order to grow a mustache and assume a new identity. Wieser's real name was Joseph Buttinger, and his life was one of almost total contrast to that of Gardiner. Born in 1906, his father was an impoverished worker of rural Austrian origins. On the eve of World War I, the struggling Buttinger family was in Germany's Ruhr region, where the father barely supported his wife and children working as a miner. When father Buttinger was killed at the front in March 1917, the family moved to an Austrian village in the region of Carinthia. The poverty they had always known became even worse, and the children often had to beg for food. Despite this, the boy grew into a youth who deeply desired an education. By his late teens, he was able to read difficult books of history and social theory and had become chair of the local Socialist youth group. He rose quickly in the Carinthian hierarchy of the Social Democratic Party and was secretary of the party district of St. Veit when the Fascist regime crushed Austrian democracy in February 1934.

Adolf Hitler's armed forces marched into Austria in March 1938, immediately placing Buttinger and countless Socialist friends of Gardiner's, many of whom were also Jewish, at great risk. As soon as Buttinger returned from party assignment in Czechoslovakia, he helped her destroy incriminating documents in her apartment, before rushing off to warn their comrades, urging them to leave Austria immediately. Fortunately, Gardiner had just received a large amount of American money which she began distributing among her endangered friends so they could buy railroad tickets and escape to freedom. While Buttinger departed for Paris, Gardiner's small daughter Connie was taken to Switzerland by trusted friends. Relieved, Gardiner could now concentrate on saving the lives of comrades. These included Manfred Ackermann and his family, for Ackermann was not only a leading underground Socialist functionary but also a prime target for the Nazi dragnet because he was Jewish. Gardiner was assisted by non-Jewish Austrian Socialists in her efforts to save Ackermann and other Jews. Although some of these "anti-Nazi Aryans" could still move freely in the first days of Nazi rule in Vienna, all of them risked their lives to assist Jewish comrades; in time, many of them would pay for their activities by being imprisoned in concentration camps.

Sometimes Gardiner's efforts, which constantly exposed her to arrest by the Nazis, failed to save endangered comrades. For example, she was able to procure passports for Hans and *Steffi Kunke, who could have departed Austria at that point, but they remained in Vienna with their friend Ferdinand Tschürtsch, who was weak and deformed. Procuring a passport fitting Tschürtsch's description was all but impossible. Because of the delay, the Kunkes and their friend were arrested, and all three perished in Nazi death camps. By the end of April 1938, Gardiner had been able to assist many Austrians in escaping from the Nazis, procuring passports for them, providing them with money and affidavits from the American consul in Vienna to prove they would have financial support as immigrants.

Gardiner successfully passed her medical examinations at the University of Vienna. Since Austria was now part of Nazi Germany, the graduating medical students were expected to raise their arms and offer "Heil Hitler!" at the graduation ceremony, held on June 18, 1938. Not surprisingly, Gardiner did not comply, but her insubordination was not noticed, and she received her degree. A few days earlier, she had filled out her final papers at the University of Vienna and had impulsively written down "Jewish" in the space on the form asking about her father's religion. According to the Nazi racial laws already in force, this classified her as a "person of mixed race, first degree," a very dangerous position at that time. Fortunately as an American she was still allowed to receive her degree, though she was compelled to sign a document stating she would never practice medicine in the German Reich (which now included Austria) even if she should acquire citizenship.

Gardiner departed Vienna immediately after her graduation, meeting Buttinger and her daughter in Paris. After a few months, she returned to Austria in November 1938 to establish contacts with some Socialist comrades. Although interrogated at her hotel by a Gestapo official, her mission was accomplished, and she returned safely to Paris. Notwithstanding Gardiner's aversion to matrimony, she married Joe Buttinger in 1939 in order to facilitate his immigration to the United States. Some of the bureaucratic red tape impeding their marriage was cut by Léon Blum, a Socialist comrade of Joe's and a former prime minister of France.

Almost immediately after arriving in the United States, the Buttingers began to work tirelessly to bring as many German and Austrian political and racial refugees to America as possible. They were able to make a persuasive case on behalf of their threatened comrades to the International Rescue Committee. *Eleanor Roosevelt heard these pleas and relayed the gist of their arguments to President Roosevelt; by the fall of 1940, the first boatload of several hundred refugees from Nazi-occupied France arrived in New York.

After World War II, Muriel Gardiner and Joseph Buttinger continued to be active in many causes. She had a busy psychoanalytical practice, taught at various universities, and published several well-received books in the field of psychology. At the end of her life, her memoirs were reviewed enthusiastically. One controversy which surfaced was whether Muriel was the anti-Nazi activist "Julia" *Lillian Hellman had depicted in her book *Pentimento*. (It was subsequently filmed as *Julia,* starring Jane Fonda and Vanessa Redgrave.) Gardiner dealt with the controversy with discretion and restraint, but many were convinced that Hellman had expropriated her life and achievements without proper acknowledgment.

While his wife led a productive professional life, Joseph Buttinger, whose formal education ended after the fourth grade, developed a reputation as an expert on Vietnam. Over a period of decades, he supervised the building up of a superb research library on Socialism and modern European mass movements which was housed for many years in the Buttingers' New York home near the Metropolitan Museum of Art. (The couple had a large country house in New Jersey as well.) In 1970, most of this library was given as a gift to the University of Klagenfurt in Austria, while the Vietnamese books went to Harvard University. Decades after their work of the 1930s, the Buttingers were honored by the Austrian government; she received the Cross of Honor First Class, and he the Great Golden Cross of Honor. Muriel Gardiner died on February 6, 1985, in Princeton, New Jersey.

SOURCES:

Berger, Joseph. "Muriel Gardiner, Who Helped Hundreds Escape Nazis, Dies," in *The New York Times Biographical Service.* February 1985, p. 156.

Buttinger, Joseph. *In the Twilight of Socialism: A History of the Revolutionary Socialists of Austria.* NY: Frederick A. Praeger, 1953.

Gardiner, Muriel. *Code Name "Mary": Memoirs of an American Woman in the Austrian Underground.* New Haven, CT: Yale University Press, 1983.

Godwin, Gail. "An Authentic Heroine," in *New Republic.* Vol. 188, no. 21. May 30, 1983, pp. 33–36.

Hellman, Lillian. *Pentimento.* Boston, MA: Little, Brown, 1973.

Lichtenberger-Fenz, Brigitte. "Eine Amerikanerin im österreichischen Untergrund," in *Wiener Tagebuch.* No. 12. December 1989, p. 38.

Locher, Frances Carol, ed. *Contemporary Authors.* Vols. 77–80. Detroit, MI: Gale Research, 1979.

Personal recollections of conversations with Muriel Gardiner, New York City, summer 1965.

Wright, William. *Lillian Hellman: The Image, the Woman.* NY: Simon and Schuster, 1986.

Young-Bruehl, Elisabeth. *Anna Freud: A Biography.* NY: Summit Books, 1990.

John Haag,
Associate Professor,
University of Georgia, Athens, Georgia

Gardner, Ava (1922–1990)

American screen actress, one of MGM's most popular stars, whose candor often had Hollywood wincing. Born Ava Lavinia Gardner on December 24, 1922, in Brogden, North Carolina; died of pneumonia at age 67 on January 25, 1990; youngest of seven children of Jonas and Mary Gardner; married Mickey Rooney (an actor), in 1942 (divorced 1943); married Artie Shaw (a musician), in 1945 (divorced 1947); married Frank Sinatra, in 1951 (divorced 1957); no children.

After a trip to New York City to visit a sister (1940), was called to the MGM casting office for a screen test and sent to Hollywood as one of the studio's group of young women with screen potential; appeared in her first film (1941), but was confined to bit parts and walk-ons until catching the public's attention in The Killers *(1946); for the next decade, held the position of Hollywood's reigning love goddess; nominated for an Academy Award for her work in* Mogambo *(1953); moved to Spain (mid-1950s) and lived there for some years while appearing in a number of well-received international film productions; returned to U.S. (1970s) and continued working in feature films and television until her death from pneumonia, age 67.*

Filmography: H.M. Pullham, Esq. *(1941);* We Were Dancing *(1942);* Joe Smith American *(1942);* Sunday Punch *(1942);* This Time for Keeps *(1942);* Calling Dr. Gillespie *(1942);* Kid Glove Killer *(1942);* Pilot No. 5 *(1943);* Hitler's Madman *(1943);* Ghosts on the Loose *(1943);* Reunion in France *(1943);* DuBarry Was a Lady *(1943);* Young Ideas *(1943);* Lost Angel *(1943);* Swing Fever *(1944);* Music for Millions *(1944);* Three Men in White *(1944);* Blonde Fever *(1944);* Maisie Goes to Reno *(1944);* Two Girls and a Sailor *(1944);* She Went to the Races *(1945);* Whistle Stop *(1946);* The Killers *(1946);* The Hucksters *(1947);* Singapore *(1947);* One Touch of Venus *(1948);* The Bribe *(1949);* The Great Sinner *(1949);* East Side/West Side *(1949);* My Forbidden Past *(1951);* Show Boat *(1951);* Pandora and the Flying Dutchman *(1951);* Lone Star *(1952);* The Snows of Kilimanjaro *(1952);* Ride Vaquero! *(1953);* The Band Wagon *(1953);* Mogambo *(1953);* Knights of the Round Table *(1954);* The Barefoot Contessa *(1954);* Bhowani Junction *(1956);* The Little Hut *(1957);* The Sun Also Rises *(1957);* The Naked Maja *(1959);* On the Beach *(1959);* The Angel Wore Red *(1960);* 55 Days at Peking *(1963);* Seven Days in May *(1964);* The Night of the Iguana *(1964);* Mayerling *(1968);* The Devil's Widow *(*Tam Lin, *1971);* The Life and Times of Judge Roy Bean *(1972);* Earthquake *(1974);* Permission to Kill *(1975);* The Blue Bird *(1976);* The Cassandra Crossing *(1951);* The Sentinel *(1977);* City on Fire *(1980);* The Kidnapping of the President *(1980);* Priest of Love *(1981);* Regina *(1982).*

It was the largest crowd of strangers anyone in tiny Smithfield, North Carolina, could remember, certainly for a funeral. Several hundred stood outside the barricades erected around the gravesite at the Sunset Memorial Park, hunched under umbrellas that rainy morning of January 29, 1990. A smaller group of more intimate friends and family of the deceased stood silently next to the grave as Smithfield's famous daughter, Ava Lavinia Gardner Rooney Shaw Sinatra, was laid to rest.

Four days earlier, Ava Gardner had died—far away from a muddy field bordered by a trailer park in rural North Carolina and in much more elegant surroundings—having succumbed peacefully at her flat in a fashionable London neighborhood near Hyde Park. In further contrast, Gardner's quiet passing was nothing like her often tempestuous life as one of Hollywood's most famous love goddesses and later as an internationally known actress and jet setter whose escapades and *amours* had been the delight of scandal sheets in the United States and Europe. As the minister who delivered the eulogy at her memorial service tactfully put it, "She was no saint."

Despite Gardner's very public and notorious life, friends often remarked that it was all merely the antics of a country roughneck made insecure by too much attention. Ava, born on Christmas Eve, 1922, was the youngest of five daughters and two sons raised by Jonas and **Molly Gardner** in tiny Brogden, North Carolina. (Gardner often referred jokingly to the place as "Grabtown," confusing some biographers who list her birthplace as "Grabton.") Brogden was little more than a collection of farmhouses sprinkled among the tobacco fields that Jonas worked, the nearest town of any size being Smithfield, and the nearest city a distant Raleigh-Durham. Despite later studio biographies that painted Gardner's childhood as poverty-stricken, the Gardners were relatively prosperous and hardly the leather-skinned sharecroppers MGM claimed. "Those stories really depress us all here [in Smithfield]," one of Gardner's nephews told a reporter for *Time* magazine, "and they depressed Ava sometimes." Jonas, described by another of the numerous local Gardners as "more than well-to-do," made a good profit on his tobacco crops, and owned a sawmill and a country store. Molly brought in extra money by working as a cook and housekeeper at a boarding house for teachers in Smithfield, and by all accounts the Gardner children were as respectable as any. "She was a tomboy back then," yet another Gardner relative once remembered. "She could hold her own." Even then, however, Gardner's good looks were much remarked on. She had inherited her mother's auburn hair and radiant, alabaster skin, while her high cheekbones and almond-shaped green eyes set her off from her older sisters.

The Gardners were strict Baptists, but Jonas and Molly had no objection to the normal pleasures of a country childhood. By great good fortune, Smithfield happened to boast a movie theater, to which Ava would thumb a ride when she had enough pocket money for a cheap balcony seat. Her attraction to the silvery images on the screen was that of any country girl dreaming of fame and fortune. "I always wanted . . . to be a movie star," she wrote to a friend when she was 13 years old. "I still do, but I know I can't so I have about given up hope." Near the end of her life, Gardner denied any such ambition. "If I . . . thought even for a minute that somebody like *me* could ever end up" on a movie screen, she wrote in her autobiography, "I surely don't recall it." One of Gardner's favorite films was 1932's *Red Dust*, starring Clark Gable and *Jean Harlow. She would have cause to remember the picture some years in the future.

In 1929, Gardner had just finished appearing in her first production—an operetta called *A Rose Dream*, presented by her first-grade class—when the stock-market crash reverberated across the country. The ensuing Depression years were as hard on the Gardners as on any rural family dependent for generations on the land. Jonas was eventually forced to sell his tobacco fields while Molly took her two youngest daughters, Ava and Myra, to Newport News, Virginia, where she had found a position as a cook in a boarding house catering to dockyard workers. Jonas failed to find work during the two years Molly was in Virginia and suffered from failing health. When his wife and daughters returned to Brogden, they found Jonas had developed a lung infection that eventually claimed his life in 1938.

By the time Ava graduated from Smithfield High School in 1939, her remarkable beauty had blossomed to such an extent that Molly felt compelled to keep a sharp eye on her, once following her daughter and an ardent suitor to a well-known necking spot at a nearby lake and dragging Ava from the car. Although Gardner spoke warmly of her mother in her autobiography, other family members blamed Molly for instilling in Gardner a deep suspicion of men and an insecurity about her appearance that plagued her throughout her life—two weaknesses they saw as the basis for Gardner's later troubled relationships. "She loved macho men," actress and friend **Arlene Dahl** once said. "She loved them because they knew who they were and were so positive and strong. She admired what she didn't have."

After her graduation, Gardner enrolled at Atlantic Christian College in Wilson, North Carolina, expecting to become a secretary. In 1941, Molly gave permission for Gardner to visit her eldest sister **Beatrice Tarr** in New York City over summer vacation. "Bappie," as everyone called Beatrice, had married photographer Larry Tarr, the owner of a chain of photography studios in the New York area. Bappie lived what seemed to Gardner to be a glamorous life in the world's most exciting city, and for months afterward she would remember meeting Henry Fonda and his date at an elegant nightclub frequented by Tarr. Like any man who caught sight of Gardner, Tarr was wonderstruck and persuaded her to pose for him, placing one of the resulting photographs in the window of his Fifth Avenue studio. The head shot showed Gardner shyly gazing at the camera from under a gingham bonnet and attracted a good deal of attention from passersby, including a clerk for MGM whose New York offices were just a block or two from Tarr's studio.

Gardner had only been back at school a few weeks when Bappie called excitedly with the news that MGM's Marvin Schenck, the studio's New York talent executive, wanted to meet her. Gardner would remember the meeting for the rest of her life. As she answered his questions about her background in her thick Southern drawl, she said, "[H]e listened attentively to the first few sentences I said, and a rather abstract expression gradually drifted over his face. I don't think he understood more than three words out of the twenty I'd spoken." (Howard Dietz, the studio's publicity director who was also at the meeting, recalled to reporters that Gardner dropped her g's "like magnolia blossoms.") But Schenck, like so many before him, could not ignore Gardner's radiant beauty and called for a screen test in which she was placed in a chair and merely asked to run through a series of emotions. With the exception of her appearance in her first-grade operetta, Gardner had never acted in her life, let alone faced the scrutiny of a motion-picture camera. This first experience would leave its mark. Even at the height of her career years later, she would admit that she still felt uncomfortable in front of cameras. Two weeks after the screen test, Gardner left for Hollywood with Bappie, to whom she declared that

she was going to marry "the biggest movie star in the world." Arriving on the MGM lot, she was forced to undergo another test for Louis B. Mayer himself. Mayer, unimpressed with her acting ability but predictably struck by her looks, signed her to a seven-year contract at $75 a week and added Gardner to his stable of potential young starlets. With her fellow hopefuls, Gardner embarked on a year's worth of studio-financed lessons in voice, diction, gymnastics, hair and makeup techniques, personal comportment and, last but by no means least, acting.

Gardner tried to learn as fast as she could, admitting many years later: "I didn't enjoy it. I didn't work hard enough at being an actress." Mayer also ordered up a studio biography for her, launching the legend of the starving sharecropper's daughter whom he decided had been born Lucy Johnson, to the great confusion of future biographers.

On a tour of the lot during her early days at MGM, Gardner was escorted onto the soundstage where *Babes on Broadway,* one of the lavish musicals for which the studio was famous, was in production. During a break in the shooting, a strange figure detached itself from the crowd and swept over to her. "Whatever it was," she remembered, "it looked like *Carmen Miranda*. It wore a bolero blouse, a long and colorful slit skirt, enormous platform shoes, and the biggest fruit-laden hat I'd ever seen." *It* turned out to be Mickey Rooney, *Judy Garland*'s co-star on the film and MGM's most valuable property after a successful series of "Andy Hardy" movies. Rooney later said that Gardner was the most beautiful woman he'd ever seen, so much so that his pursuit of her was relentless, starting with dinner at the old Chasen's with Bappie prudently along as chaperon. It was Rooney who gave Gardner her first useful lessons in film acting and who offered career advice. On January 10, 1942, less than six months after her arrival in Hollywood, Gardner and Mickey Rooney were married. He was 21, Gardner just 19.

I do it for the loot, honey—always for the loot.

—Ava Gardner

Partly because her Mayer-financed education was taking effect, and partly because of Rooney's clout with studio executives, Gardner appeared in her first film the year of her marriage. It was the beginning of many purely ornamental walk-ons until her initial small speaking role in 1942's *Kid Glove Killer,* and a minor role in a Dead End Kids comedy when MGM loaned her out to Monogram to give her more experience at someone else's expense. By the end of 1942, she had appeared in eight films and had attracted attention as Mrs. Mickey Rooney at the continual round of studio-arranged publicity events Rooney attended. At one of them, that heartthrob of the bobbysoxer generation, Frank Sinatra, made a point of introducing himself. "Why didn't I meet you before Mickey?" he told her, conveniently forgetting for the moment his own marriage to **Nancy Sinatra**. "Then I could have married you myself." Marriage was on Gardner's mind, too, for her union with Rooney

had been deteriorating for some time. "Mickey was so different from me," she remembered in later years. "He was enthusiastic, sure of himself, and good at everything he tried. I simply didn't fit into his world." The two were amicably divorced on May 2, 1943, after only 18 months of marriage.

Gardner's first substantial role in a film came soon after her divorce from Rooney. She played a seductive young woman hired by a prominent physician to test the moral character of a promising young intern; 1944's *Three Men in White* was one in a series of popular "Doctor Gillespie" pictures in which Lionel Barrymore played the sternly moral physician. During this same year, Gardner's extravagant romantic life began to accelerate. She plunged into a relationship with millionaire Howard Hughes which ended abruptly one night when Hughes, famously a teetotaler, arrived at the house he had bought for her to find a spirits-soaked party in full swing with Gardner as host. The ensuing argument culminated in Gardner throwing a heavy vase at Hughes, knocking him out cold, before fleeing the house with as many of her belongings as she could gather up before he came to. The year 1944 also marked her second, brief marriage to bandleader Artie Shaw, who had already married four times and was just divorced from Gardner's friend *Lana Turner*. "I suppose Artie was the first intelligent, intellectual male I'd ever met," Gardner later said, "and he bowled me over." But she began to balk at Shaw's constant hectoring about her lack of education, although she suffered through courses in English literature and economics in which Shaw had enrolled her at University of California in Los Angeles (UCLA). Matters only grew worse when Shaw insisted she see a psychoanalyst, the only concrete result of the visits being that Gardner's already considerable alcohol consumption increased. By August of 1946, after a mere ten months of marriage, the two were divorced. "I thought at the time that love could cure anything," she said after the divorce. "I found out the hard way it can't."

Although her personal affairs were in turmoil, Gardner's career took a decided turn for the better with her work in *The Killers,* based on a short story by Ernest Hemingway. She smoldered her way through the film as Kitty Collins, the gangster's moll who brings about the destruction of Burt Lancaster's Swede, his first starring role. The dark tale proved so popular that Gardner was named *Look* magazine's most promising newcomer in 1947. Encouraged by her reception, MGM increased Gardner's public exposure with product endorsements, guest spots on national radio programs, and larger roles in bigger-budget films while feverishly keeping the press away from her private life, including a rumored abortion after an affair with actor Howard Duff left her pregnant. *The Hucksters*, in 1947, marked her first work with Clark Gable, while the following year's *One Touch of Venus,* in which she played a statue of the goddess Venus who comes to life in 20th-century Brooklyn, showed her flair for comedy. By the time Gardner returned home to Brogden for a family visit, she was enough of a star for *Photoplay* to follow her there and induce her to pose on the porch of her childhood home.

Late in 1948, while Gardner was shooting *East Side/West Side* on the Metro lot, Frank Sinatra renewed their friendship. With his singing career suffering from the aging of his swooning teenage fans and a new acting career at MGM off to a shaky start, Sinatra found Gardner a willing commiserator. Before long, their tempestuous and very public courtship was in full swing. Fans of both were outraged at their dating and wrote torrents of sympathetic letters to Sinatra's wife and three children, while Gardner was portrayed as a homewrecker. One of the milder letters she received was addressed to "Bitch-Jezebel-Gardner." Ava confessed surprise at the controversy her affair with Sinatra touched off. "I didn't understand . . . why there should be this prurient mass hysteria about a male and female climbing into bed and doing what comes naturally," she complained. "It's blessed in weddings, celebrated in honeymoons, but out of wedlock it's condemned as the worst of sins." When the Roman Catholic Church's Legion of Decency called for a boycott of her films, MGM's answer was to ship Gardner out of the country to Spain to star opposite James Mason in *Pandora and the Flying Dutchman,* which Gardner noted late in her life was one of her favorite films and which is considered among her most charming performances. The picture was shot in Barcelona and was Gardner's first exposure to the culture that would captivate her for the next 15 years. Her passionate affair with a bullfighter during the shoot was much reported, as were the public arguments with a jealous Sinatra, who had followed her to Spain.

In 1951, MGM cast Gardner as the mulatto Julie in its remake of *Show Boat.* Although her musical numbers were dubbed by *Lena Horne in the final release of the film, Gardner insisted on doing her own singing for the soundtrack recording and astonished everyone with her performance. By the end of the year, and despite the fan magazine rumor mills about her love life (or perhaps because of them), Gardner was MGM's most popular female star. Also by the end of the year, Gardner had become the second Mrs. Frank Sinatra. The two were married on November 7, 1951, just days after Sinatra's divorce decree was finalized.

Her marriage to Sinatra marked the beginning of Gardner's most successful years on the screen. Henry King's 1952 adaptation of Hemingway's *The Snows of Kilimanjaro*, shot entirely on location in Africa, brought Gardner to international attention. The following year, she and an international crew braved searing heat, impending terrorist attacks, and wild animals to film *Mogambo* (the Swahili word for passion) in Kenya. The picture was a remake of none other than Gardner's favorite film as a teenager, *Red Dust*, and she played opposite Clark Gable, one of the original film's stars. Even Gardner, who never gave her acting much thought, admitted she did "a pretty good job" under John Ford's direction. So did Hollywood, which nominated her for Best Actress. She lost the award to *Audrey Hepburn (for *Roman Holiday*), although Sinatra's career was resuscitated by his winning the Best Supporting Actor award for his work as Maggio in *From Here to Eternity*—a role that Gardner was rumored to have pressured Columbia to give him. In 1954, Gardner gave to cinema what is still considered her signature role, as the Italian slum-girl-turned-aristocrat Maria Vargas in *The Barefoot Contessa*. The film's most famous scene, Maria's wild and sensual flamenco dance for her aristocratic lover, took several physically painful days to film and won Gardner the respect of her co-stars, Humphrey Bogart and Rossano Brazzi, and the entire crew.

The turmoil of Gardner's off-screen life attracted almost as much attention as her work on-screen. Her relationship with Sinatra was intensely emotional, marked by arguments in nightclubs and on the sets of various films along with what both frankly admitted was an exuberant sex life. "We were always great in bed," Gardner later remarked. "The trouble usually started on the way to the bidet." By 1954, Gardner and Sinatra had separated, Sinatra sinking into a deep depression and an attempted suicide while Gardner settled permanently in Madrid and began a new affair with a Spanish bullfighter. Their divorce was finalized three years later, in 1957. Years afterward, Sinatra still kept a picture of Gardner taped to his dressing room mirror wherever he went, and Gardner confessed to actress Arlene Dahl that Sinatra had been the only real love in her life.

Gardner's passion for bullfighting is reflected in her radiant performance in 1957's *The Sun Also Rises*, the third of her films to be based on a work by Hemingway. (Gardner was great friends with Hemingway and his wife **Mary Welsh Hemingway** and was devastated by the writer's suicide in 1960.) Gardner went so far as to take bullfighting lessons, which ended abruptly when her left cheek was gored by a bull. Rushed aboard a plane and flown to a London hospital for cosmetic surgery, Gardner later said the incident made her realize on how fragile a thing her career rested. The next decade included some of Gardner's best work in a series of high-profile international productions. She played the ◄❧ **Duchess of Alba** in *The Naked Maja*, based on the life of Goya (during which she was accused by *****Shelley Winters** of carrying on an affair with Winters' husband at the time, Anthony Franciosa, Gardner's co-star in the picture); traveled to Australia to appear to great acclaim in Stanley Kramer's *On the Beach*, playing one of a small group of survivors of a nuclear holocaust; played Tennessee Williams' gin-soaked hotelkeeper Maxine in 1964's *Night of the Iguana*; and captivated audiences as *****Sarah** in John Huston's epic *The Bible* in 1966, during which co-star George C. Scott was said to have suffered a nervous collapse when Gardner refused to marry him if he left his then-wife, *****Colleen Dewhurst**. Gardner considered Huston, who had also directed her in *Iguana* and would do so again in 1972's *The Life and Times of Judge Roy Bean*, the greatest director then working in the business. Huston was equally complimentary, publicly stating that Gardner was one of the most underestimated actresses in cinema.

The luster of Gardner's career, however, began to fade after these heady years. Indeed, after the poor reception for 1968's *Mayerling*, she stayed away from a studio for three years and swore to give up acting once and for all after her appearance in a disastrous Gothic thriller, *The Devil's Widow*, in 1971. Now entering her 60s, health problems began to plague her, including an illness at first misdiagnosed as cancer but which later proved to be a particularly stubborn infection. By now, Gardner had sold her home in Madrid and moved to London's fashionable Ennismore Gardens, near Hyde Park, telling friends she preferred the greater privacy London allowed her. She appeared in a number of highly commercial films during the 1970s, including Universal's wildly popular disaster film,

❧▶
Duchess of Alba (d. 1802). Maria del Pilar Teresa Cayetana, 13th duchess of Alba.

Earthquake, and the suspense film *The Cassandra Crossing*, in which she played opposite Burt Lancaster for the first time since *The Killers* in 1946. Her final theatrical film was 1982's *Regina*, although she continued to work by making her television debut in the mini-series "AD" in 1985 and in a recurring role as Ruth Galveston in the series "Knots Landing."

Her personal life in these later years was also more restrained. She now preferred quiet evenings at home in London and confined her relationships to a close circle of friends. She kept her apartment notably free of nostalgic mementos and accepted her aging with her usual, salty common sense. "Honey, there comes a time when you have to face the fact that you're an old broad," she remarked in 1989, at 66. "I've had a hell of a good time so my face looks, well, lived-in. You won't find me standing in front of a mirror, weeping." In 1986, Gardner had suffered a stroke which left her partially paralyzed and vulnerable to respiratory infections. With her illness, friends noted, Gardner's legendary fighting spirit seemed to disappear. She was confined to her bed after a bad fall in January of 1990, complicated by pneumonia. On the morning of January 25, she died quietly in her sleep.

There may have been no celebrities for that expectant crowd attending Gardner's funeral four days later, but everyone noticed the inscription on a huge wreath that stood by her coffin. "With my love," it simply said, followed by the name, "Francis."

SOURCES:
Fowler, Karin J. *Ava Gardner: A Bio-Bibliography*. Westport, Ct: Greenwood Press, 1990.
Gardner, Ava. *Ava: My Story*. NY: Bantam Books, 1990.
Green, Michelle. "Many Passions, No Regrets" (obituary), in *People Weekly*. Vol. 33, no. 6. February 12, 1990.

Norman Powers,
writer-producer, Chelsea Lane Productions, New York

Gardner, Edna (1902–1992).

See Whyte, Edna Gardner.

Gardner, Isabella Stewart
(1840–1924)

American art collector and socialite who designed and built the Isabella Stewart Gardner Museum in Boston. Born Isabella Stewart in New York City on April 14, 1840; died in Boston, Massachusetts, on July 17, 1924; eldest and one of four children (two girls and two boys) of David (a businessman) and Adelia (Smith) Stewart; educated by private tutors and at a small private girls' school in New York; attended a finishing school in Paris; married John Lowell Gardner (a businessman), on April 10, 1860 (died 1898); children: one son Jackie, who died at age two.

At Fenway Court in Boston, close to the Museum of Fine Arts, stands the Isabella Stewart Gardner Museum, an elaborate Italian palace designed and built by Gardner in 1902 as a residence and to house her remarkable collection of fine art. Upon her death in 1924, she left Fenway Court to the city of Boston "for the education and enjoyment of the public." Her will also contained the proviso that the building remain exactly as she left it, with nothing added, removed, or rearranged. Thus it stands, unchanged, a monument to the notorious "Mrs. Jack," a complex and fascinating woman who was one of America's most important art collectors.

Isabella Stewart was born and raised in New York City, the daughter of a successful businessman. She met John Lowell Gardner, one of Boston's most eligible bachelors, through his sister **Julia Gardner** with whom Isabella attended finishing school in Paris. The Gardners were married in April 1860 and established themselves in Boston, where young Isabella led an exceedingly quiet life for nearly a decade. Fragile in health, she had a meager social life during the early years of her marriage and was unnerved by a less than warm reception from Brahmin society. In 1863, Gardner was elated by the birth of a son and heir but sank into depression when young Jackie died two years later. A subsequent miscarriage, and news that she would be unable to bear another child, left her despondent. At the doctor's suggestion, she and her husband embarked on a restorative trip abroad. Upon departure, Isabella was purportedly so weak that she had to be carried aboard ship on a mattress. By the time she reached her destination, however, she was well enough for a grand tour, including Spain and a trek across Russia. She returned to Boston a few months later in renewed good health and exceedingly high spirits. "Quickly she became one of the most conspicuous members of Boston society," wrote Morris Carter, Gardner's biographer and the first curator of her collection. "Effervescent, exuberant, reckless, witty, she did whatever she pleased."

Indeed, over the next five decades, Gardner evidently took delight in shocking conservative Boston society with her behavior. She drank beer at Boston "Pops" concerts, while the other women sipped sherry, and sat in the front row at a Jim Corbett boxing match, when "proper" women generally did not attend sporting events. Some of her escapades may have grown more notorious as they were retold through the years, like the recounting of her supposed strolls around the Boston zoo with a lion on a leash or her Lenten penance at the Church of the Advent, where, dressed in sackcloth and ashes, she is said to have scrubbed down the steps on her hands and knees. One story has her arriving at an artists' ball dressed in a cerise and gold brocade gown, the train of which was held by a diminutive African in Malayan costume who carried a small dog in his arms.

C'est mon plaisir (It's my pleasure).

—**Motto over the Florentine door of the Isabella Stewart Gardner Museum**

Plain in appearance, Gardner made the best of her assets, playing up her hourglass figure and baring her extraordinary shoulders in dresses ordered from Paris. She surrounded herself with a who's who of artists and literary types, including Ignace Paderewski, Henry Irving, Henry James, James Russell Lowell, and Oliver Wendell Holmes. Among her few women friends were opera stars *Emma Eames and *Nellie Melba and authors *Edith Wharton and *Julia Ward Howe. Of her paramours, real and imagined, none was more notorious than John Singer Sargent, who traveled with the Gardners and was a frequent guest at Isabella's adjoining townhouses on Beacon Street and her summer retreat in Brookline. Sargent painted perhaps the most famous portrait of Gardner, a full-length likeness in which she is dressed in black with strands of pearls draped around her wasp waist. Her bare white arms caused such a stir when the portrait was first exhibited in Boston that her husband, who appeared to be unconcerned about her unconventional relationship with Sargent, never again allowed the picture to be shown. After John Gardner's death, Sargent would be Isabella's constant companion when he was in the country. (Their romance is the subject of Countess **Eleanor Palffy**'s 1951 novel *The Lady and the Painter*, although Palffy contends that the relationship was platonic.) Isabella Gardner was also captured on canvas by Swedish painter Anders Zorn and American James Whistler.

Beginning in 1874, the Gardners made frequent trips to Europe, where Isabella began to acquire rare books. Her acquisitions included a 1481 Dante, a Book of Hours that had belonged to *Mary, Queen of Scots, and a holograph manuscript of Longfellow's *Paul Revere's Ride*. It was not until 1888 that she purchased her first

important painting, a Madonna by Francisco Zurbaran. After that acquisition, she began to collect at an accelerated pace, especially after receiving a substantial inheritance from her father in 1891. From 1894, Gardner enlisted her friend and protégé Bernard Berenson to advise and assist her in her acquisitions. She had met and befriended Berenson in Charles Eliot Norton's art history class and later helped finance his studies in Europe. On his way to becoming the world's leading authority on Italian Renaissance art, he procured for Gardner some of her most exquisite paintings, including Titian's *Rape of Europa,* which Rubens called "the greatest painting in the world," and Rembrandt's self-portrait at the age of 23, which Berenson described as "one of the most precious pictures in existence."

Upon her husband's death in December 1898, Isabella Gardner inherited his considerable fortune and began to formulate plans for Fenway Court, a building worthy of housing her collection. In December 1899, on land purchased on the barren, swampy Fens, Gardner began construction of her Venetian palace, inspired by the Palazzo Bardini on the Grand Canal. She oversaw every detail of the project herself, exercising her will over everyone, including the Boston building inspector to whom, in the heat of battle, she once declared, "It will be built as I wish." Her architects and contractors were sworn to secrecy, and only a few of her intimates were allowed to view the building process.

On New Year's night, 1903, the building was officially opened. Following a concert played by 50 members of the Boston Symphony Orchestra, Gardner, resplendent in a black dress, with two enormous diamonds rising on wires from her head like antennae, rolled back the mirrored door of the music room and revealed to the 300 socialites the spectacular three-storied, glass-roofed inner courtyard of the building, with its masses of flowering plants, splashing fountains, and eight balconies hung with lanterns. If the splendor of the courtyard did not astound those in attendance, the artwork displayed on three floors of candle-lit galleries certainly did.

Fenway Court was first opened to the public on February 23, 1903, and thereafter was periodically available for an admission fee. Gardner lived in the house for 21 years, entertaining a host of distinguished guests and continuing to add superb works of art. In her declining years, she grew increasingly stingy, rationing food to the servants and barely eating enough herself. "When her husband died," recalled Bernard Berenson in *Rumor and Reflection*, "and the bills of the baker and butcher and electrician were brought to her, she got into a panic from which she never quite recovered." Around Christmas, 1919, she suffered a crippling stroke, after which she was carried around the palace in a gondola chair from Venice. She died on July 17, 1924, and was buried in Mount Auburn Cemetery, Cambridge, in the Gardner tomb.

At her death, Gardner's collection, minus manuscripts and rare books, or architectural elements set into the building, contained approximately 290 paintings, 280 pieces of sculpture, 60 drawings and prints, 460 pieces of furniture, 250 textiles, 240 objects of ceramic and glass, and 350 miscellaneous pieces. Among American collections, the Gardner Museum has been ranked fourth, after the Metropolitan and the Frick in New York, and the National Gallery in Washington. The building is as important as the collection. James J. Rorimer, director of the Metropolitan Museum, credits Gardner as a pioneer, the first person in the country to incorporate elements of Roman, Byzantine, Romanesque, and Gothic architecture in a building designed to exhibit paintings. Gardner's rival collector, Henry E. Huntington, called Fenway Court "the greatest work done by an American woman."

SOURCES:

James, Edward T., ed. *Notable American Women 1607–1950*. Cambridge, MA: The Belknap Press of Harvard University Press, 1971.

McHenry, Robert, ed. *Famous American Women*. NY: Dover, 1983.

"Mrs. Gardner: A Biographical Note," in *Selective Guide to the Collection: Isabella Stewart Gardner Museum*. Boston, MA: The Trustees of the Museum, 1989.

Saarinen, Aline B. *The Proud Possessors*. NY: Random House, 1958.

SUGGESTED READING:

Carter, Morris. *Isabella Stewart Gardner and Fenway Court*, 1925.

Shand-Tucci, Douglass. *The Art of Scandal: The Life and Times of Isabella Stewart Gardner*. NY: HarperCollins, 1997.

Tharp, Louise Hall. *Mrs. Jack*. Boston, MA: Little, Brown, 1965.

Watson, Peter. *From Manet to Manhattan: The Rise of the Modern Art Market*. NY: Random, 1992.

Barbara Morgan,
Melrose, Massachusetts

Gardner, Mrs. Jack (1840–1924).

See Gardner, Isabella Stewart.

Gardner, Julia Anna (1882–1960)

American geologist who identified the origin of a number of Japanese bombs used during World War

II. Born in 1882; died in Bethesda, Maryland, in 1960; the only child of Charles Henry (a physician) and Julia M. (Brackett) Gardner; earned a bachelor's degree from Bryn Mawr, 1905, master's degree, 1907; Johns Hopkins University, Ph.D., 1911; never married; no children.

An only child, Julia Anna Gardner lost her father when she was an infant and was raised by her mother. Money left to her by her grandmother paid her way through Bryn Mawr College, where she studied paleontology under *Florence Bascom. After receiving her master's degree in 1907, Gardner enrolled in the doctoral program in paleontology at Johns Hopkins University. There, and at Woods Hole Marine Biological Laboratory, she studied invertebrates, which became a lifelong interest. After earning her Ph.D. in 1911, Gardner stayed on at Johns Hopkins as a teacher and also did research on invertebrate paleontology at the Maryland geological survey. After a brief stint as a volunteer nurse during World War I, she joined the U.S. Geological Survey (USGS) and remained there for the rest of her career.

In 1920, Gardner moved to Texas to study Eocene invertebrates for the USGS Coastal Plain division, advancing steadily through the ranks there throughout the 1920s and 1930s. Her greatest achievement in this nonconventional field was her work during World War II, when she identified the origin of a number of Japanese bombs by analyzing the small shells in the sand used as ballast in the incendiary balloons.

After the war, Gardner studied the geology of Japan and the Pacific Island, mapping the area for the Office of the Chief of Engineers. For a year following her retirement in 1952, she served as president of the Paleontological Society, and the next year as the vice president of the Geological Society. From 1954, she suffered from ill health. Gardner died at her home in Bethesda, Maryland, in 1960.

Gardner, Mary Sewall (1871–1961)

American nurse and social reformer, who was a pioneer in the field of public health nursing and the force behind the founding of the National Organization for Public Health Nursing. Born in Newton, Massachusetts, on February 5, 1871; died on February 20, 1961, in Providence, Rhode Island; daughter of William Sewall Gardner and Mary (Thornton) Gardner; had half-brother, Charles Thornton Davis; never married; no children.

Opposite page

Isabella Stewart Gardner

Born in New England in 1871 into a distinguished family (her mother was a descendant of Declaration of Independence signer Matthew Thornton, and her father held a superior court judgeship), Mary Sewall Gardner grew up in an environment that emphasized civic responsibility and methodical thinking. When Mary was four, her mother died, and when her father remarried it was her stepmother **Sarah Gardner**, a pioneering woman physician, who gave her tangible evidence that whatever career she might choose could in fact be open to her in the future. Her affluent family sent the intelligent Mary to private schools, and for a while she also received instruction at home from a French governess. Having survived a bout with tuberculosis at age 16, she subsequently enrolled at Miss Porter's School, founded by ***Sarah Porter**, in Farmington, Connecticut.

By 1890, her father had died, and, with her stepmother now an invalid, Gardner chose to remain at home to run the household. In her spare time, she became active in community and volunteer work. In 1892, Mary and Sarah Gardner moved to Providence, Rhode Island, and it was during Mary's first years here that she began to consider a career in one branch or another of medicine. In 1901, at age 30, Gardner enrolled at the Newport Hospital Training School for Nurses. Upon her graduation in 1905, she became superintendent of nurses (later director) of the recently created Providence District Nursing Association (PDNA). To Mary Gardner's critical eye, the PDNA revealed more weaknesses than strengths, and she set about to the fortify the organization in as many ways as possible. Fully aware that much progress was taking place in the area of public health and nursing, she visited similar service organizations elsewhere. These included, among others, ***Lillian Wald**'s Henry Street Visiting Nurse Service in New York City. Both face to face and through correspondence, Gardner established lasting and valuable links to other public health nurses.

Many of the reforms initiated by Mary Gardner at her PDNA organization seem obvious to later generations and included such fundamental changes as introducing record systems, scheduling regular meetings, and requiring that nurses wear uniforms while on duty. Realizing that health issues were ultimately linked to broader societal problems, Gardner urged that not only nurses but all members of the health professions become involved in community organization and planning. Under its indefatigable director, the PDNA greatly expanded its services to become a model for other nursing associations not only in Rhode Island but throughout most of the United States. Starting in 1912, Gardner was able to more effectively share her experiences as an administrator because in that year she and her colleague Lillian Wald founded the National Organization of Public Health Nursing (NOPHN). In its first year, Wald served as president of NOPHN and Gardner held the post of secretary, but starting in 1913 Gardner became the organization's president, a position she held until 1916. In 1922, Gardner was named honorary NOPHN president, a distinction she shared with only the equally revered Lillian Wald. Although later generations of women often came to look upon such organizations as NOPHN as lacking in vision and concerned only with piecemeal reforms, in fact this group, in addition to the three others representing the nursing profession on a national basis, was progressive in spirit, advocating votes for women, calling for broader access to health and education, and generally believing in both the possibility and desirability of social improvement.

Of Mary Sewall Gardner's many contributions to American nursing, perhaps her greatest legacy was her classic textbook, *Public Health Nursing*. First published in 1916, the book was an immediate success, praised by reviewers and nurses alike for being "everywhere concrete, specific, and practical." *Public Health Nursing* became the Bible of nurses throughout the United States, appearing in revised editions in 1924 and 1936 and going through many printings (the last regular printing was in 1947, but in 1977 a reprint edition was included as part of the "Public Health in America" historical series published by Arno Press). A book that reflected its author's gentle manner as well as her "unusual understanding of, and respect for, human relationships," in time it became a global text, appearing in a number of foreign-language editions.

Global concerns took Gardner away from Rhode Island in 1918, when during World War I she served first as director of the American Red Cross' bureau of public health nursing, and then overseas in war-torn Italy. Here she was posted as chief nurse of the American Red Cross Tuberculosis Commission for Italy, a job she defined as one that stimulated local initiatives, including a rapid expansion of training programs for Italian women as nurses. In 1919, Mary Gardner returned from Italy to the United States, but she retained a strong interest in a continent devastated by four years of war and social upheaval. Believing she could still make a contribution in the

European public health environment, in 1921 she returned to study the state of child welfare and public health nursing in France as well as in war-ravaged Eastern Europe. Now enjoying an international reputation, Gardner was chosen in 1925 as chair of the standing committee on public health nursing of the International Council of Nurses, a post she held until 1933.

Mary Sewall Gardner officially retired in 1931, the same year she received the coveted Walter Burns Saunders medal for distinguished service to nursing. As busy as ever during much of her long retirement, she remained on call to give advice, continued her prolific production of journal articles, and supervised a third and final revision of her classic textbook, *Public Health Nursing* (1936). Gardner also published two works of fiction during her retirement years, *So Build We* (1942) and *Katharine Kent* (1946). Both books, obviously based on her many years of administrative experience, are thoughtful examinations of the day-to-day problems of managing a nursing organization.

By the time of Gardner's retirement, the nursing profession had been radically transformed by great social changes in American society. Circumstances that had created the need for public health nurses had largely disappeared with the virtual cessation of mass immigration, the growing role of hospitals, a dramatic decline in the occurrence of infectious diseases, and a significant diminution in public concern over society's poor and weak. By the early 1930s as the nation entered a decade of economic depression, American nurses had not become the highly respected profession they felt they should be regarded as, but instead found themselves suffering from marginalization within the health-care system. Mary Sewall Gardner was concerned by these new challenges in the final years of her life, but she could also look back with pride on a long and remarkable career of service and achievement. She died in Providence, Rhode Island, on February 20, 1961. In 1986, Mary Sewall Gardner was elected to the American Nursing Association's Nursing Hall of Fame.

SOURCES:

Buhler-Wilkinson, Karen Ann. "False Dawn: The Rise and Decline of Public Health Nursing, 1900–1930." Ph.D. Dissertation, University of Pennsylvania, 1984.

Bullough, Vern L., *et al.*, eds. *American Nursing: A Biographical Dictionary.* NY: Garland, 1988.

Dolan, Josephine A. *Nursing in Society: A Historical Perspective.* 4th ed. Philadelphia, PA: W.B. Saunders, 1978.

Fitzpatrick, M. Louise. "The History of the National Organization for Public Health Nursing, 1912–1952." Ph.D. Dissertation, Columbia University, 1972.

———. *The National Organization for Public Health Nursing, 1912–1952: Development of a Practice Field.* NY: National League for Nursing, 1973.

Gardner, Mary Sewall. *Katharine Kent.* NY: Macmillan, 1946.

———. *Public Health Nursing.* NY: Arno Press, 1977 (reprint of 1916 edition).

———. *So Build We.* NY: Macmillan, 1942.

Kantrov, Ilene, and Kate Wittenstein. "Gardner, Mary Sewall," in Barbara Sicherman et al., eds. *Notable American Women: The Modern Period. A Biographical Dictionary.* Cambridge, MA: Belknap Press of Harvard University Press, 1980, pp. 262–264.

Kaufman, Martin, ed. *Dictionary of American Nursing Biography.* NY: Greenwood Press, 1988.

Kersten, Evelyn Smith. "Industrial Nursing from 1895 to 1942: Development of a Specialty." Ed.D. Dissertation, Columbia University Teachers College, 1985.

Lewenson, Sandra Beth. "The Relationship Among the Four Professional Nursing Organizations and Woman Suffrage, 1893–1920." Ed.D. Dissertation, Columbia University Teachers College, 1989.

Monteiro, Lois A. "Insights from the Past," in *Nursing Outlook.* Vol. 35, no. 2. March–April, 1987, pp. 65–69.

Pennock, Meta Rutter, ed. *Makers of Nursing History.* NY: Lakeside, 1940.

COLLECTIONS:

Mary Sewall Gardner Papers, Schlesinger Library, Radcliffe College.

John Haag,
Associate Professor of History,
University of Georgia, Athens, Georgia

Gardner, Maureen (1928–1974).

See Blankers-Koen, Fanny for sidebar.

Garfield, Lucretia (1832–1918)

American first lady whose work to restore the White House with historical accuracy was cut short by her husband's assassination. Name variations: (nickname) Crete. Born Lucretia Rudolph on April 19, 1832, in Garretsville, Ohio; died on March 13, 1918, in South Pasadena, California; daughter of Arabella Green (Mason) Rudolph and Zebulon Rudolph (a founder of Hiram College); attended Geauga Seminary and Hiram College; married James Abram Garfield (1831–1881, later president of the United States), on November 11, 1858, in Hiram, Ohio; children: Eliza (1860–1863); Harry Augustus Garfield (1863–1942, president of Williams College and fuel administrator during World War I); James Rudolph Garfield (1865–1950, secretary of the Interior under Theodore Roosevelt); Mary Garfield (1867–1947); Irvin McDowell Garfield (1870–1951); Abram Garfield (1872–1958); Edward (1874–1876).

Lucretia Garfield's 200 days as first lady were beset by tragedy. Three months after her arrival in the White House, she was stricken with malaria and what was then called nervous exhaustion. On July 2, 1881, while recuperating at her summer home in Elberon, New Jersey, she received the news that her husband had been gunned down at the Washington train depot by a disappointed office seeker, Charles J. Guiteau. Still weak from her own ordeal, she rushed to Garfield's bedside, where she and her children kept vigil until he died of his wounds on September 19, 1881.

It was at Hiram College, founded by Lucretia's parents and other member of the Disciples of Christ Church, that Lucretia, known as Crete, began a long and troubled courtship with the handsome and dashing James Garfield. Early in the relationship, he transferred to Williams College in Massachusetts, where he was enormously popular, especially with women. He had doubts about continuing his dutiful relationship with Lucretia, whom he found intelligent and capable, but dull. He was also troubled by her progressive views on women's rights and some of her "notions concerning the relation between the sexes." The couple finally married in 1858, but doubts persisted right up to the ceremony. Lucretia, now 26 and earning her own money as a teacher, worried about losing her autonomy in "submission to that destiny which will make me the wife of one who marries me." James worried about his lack of passion for his new wife.

During the early years of the marriage, Lucretia kept her teaching job and lived largely on her own. Garfield was away most of the time, serving in the Union army and campaigning for election to the state legislature. After four years, the couple had spent only about five months together, and rumors circulated about another woman; Lucretia and James both agreed that their marriage was in trouble. It was at this time, however, that the relationship began to find direction, possibly due to the death of their first daughter in 1863. James resolved that he would not travel again without his wife, and gradually the two established a nurturing companionship, dividing their time between houses in Ohio and Washington. Another son died in 1876, but five children prospered. On her 42nd birthday, James thanked Lucretia for "being born and being his wife," and from then on they referred to their early relationship as the "years of darkness."

Lucretia was a private person and did not socialize easily. For a time, James Garfield became somewhat isolated as well. Forays into the Washington social scene were not always successful. One guest remarked after dining with the Garfields and some of their friends: "Very good people I am sure they are, but a plainer, stiffer set of village people I never met."

At the 1880 convention, in an effort to break the bitter deadlock between the Stalwarts backing Grant's third-term bid and the reform forces, the Republicans named Garfield as their candidate for president. Lucretia took pride in his eventual win and found the inauguration "the greatest spectacle she had ever seen." Her short tenure as first lady revolved around plans to restore the White House to historical accuracy. She undertook long hours of research in the Library of Congress, leaving little time for entertaining. Her work, which was greatly admired in Washington circles, was cut short by her illness in May 1881.

Lucretia survived her husband by 36 years. A widow's pension of $5,000 and a special subscription fund created by Cyrus W. Field, which raised $300,000, allowed her to live comfortably with her children in Mentor, Ohio. Devoted

Lucretia Garfield

to her husband's memory, she meticulously supervised the preservation of his papers and left the letters revealing the troubled years of her marriage intact. It was not until 40 years after her own death that her family finally allowed them to be placed in the presidential collection.

SOURCES:

Boller, Paul F., Jr. *Presidential Wives*. NY: Oxford University Press, 1988.

Caroli, Betty Boyd. *First Ladies*. NY: Oxford University Press, 1987.

Melick, Arden David. *Wives of the Presidents*. Maplewood, NJ: Hammond, Inc., 1977.

Paletta, LuAnn. *The World Almanac of First Ladies*. NY: World Almanac, 1990.

Barbara Morgan,
Melrose, Massachusetts

Garibaldi, Anita (c. 1821–1849)

*Hero of Brazil and Italy, possessed of exceptional physical and emotional courage, who actively participated in husband Giuseppe Garibaldi's struggles for liberty and national self-determination in South America and Italy. Name variations: Aninha; Annita Bentos. Pronunciation: Gah-ree-BAL-dee. Born Ana Maria de Jésus Riberio da Silva around 1821, in Morrinhos, Brazil; died at Guiccioli farm, Mandriole, near Ravenna, Italy, on August 4, 1849; daughter of Bento Ribeiro da Silva de Jesus (a peasant) and Maria Antonia; started to learn to read and write a few months before her death; learned to sign her name; married Manoel Duarte di Aguiar, on August 30, 1835; married Giuseppe Garibaldi, on March 26, 1842; children (second marriage): Menotti (b. September 16, 1840); Rosita (b. end of 1841 or, according to other sources, 1843 and died young); Teresita or **Teresa Garibaldi** (b. November 1844 or 1845); Ricciotti (b. February 24, 1847).*

Met Garibaldi at Laguna in southern Brazil (October 1839); fought in naval battle of Imbituba (November 3, 1839); fought in naval battle and involved in evacuation of Laguna (November 15, 1839); retreated through the mountains of Rio Grande do Sul (late fall-winter, 1840–41); with Giuseppe, departed for Montevideo, Uruguay (April 1841); arrived in Montevideo (June 17, 1841); stayed in Montevideo (1842–47); sailed for Italy (January 1848); arrived in Genoa and traveled to Nice (April 1848); left Genoa with Giuseppe Garibaldi and his volunteers for Livorno (October 24, 1848); stayed with her husband at Rieti, near Rome (February–April 1849); traveled from Nice to Rome, arriving during the siege (June 26, 1849); set out on retreat northward from Rome (July 2, 1848).

Giuseppe Garibaldi wrote in his autobiography:

> By chance I cast my eyes towards the houses on the Barra—a tolerably high hill on the south side of the entrance to the lagoon [of the town of Laguna, Brazil], where a few simple and picturesque dwellings were visible. Outside one of these, by means of the telescope I usually carried with me when on deck, I espied a young woman, and forthwith gave orders for the boat to be got out, as I wished to go ashore. I landed, and, making for the houses where I expected to find the object of my excursion, I had just given up all hope of seeing her again, when I met an inhabitant of the place, whose acquaintance I had made soon after our arrival.
>
> He invited me to take coffee in his house; we entered, and the first person who met my eyes was the damsel who had attracted me ashore. It was Anita, the mother of my children, who shared my life for better, for worse—the wife whose courage I have so often felt the loss of.

Much of the evidence about the life of Anita Garibaldi is incomplete or equivocal. She was born in the village of Morrinhos, Brazil, to poor peasants from the province of São Paulo. There were several other children, apart from Anita, but the exact number is unclear. Anita's father died when she was still a child, and soon afterwards her mother moved to the town of Laguna. Anita never received a formal education but learned at an early age, like other girls of the town, to be a good equestrian. She was vivacious and strong willed. About the time Anita was 14, a young man who had been courting her, without success, encountered her in a wood while she was walking home. Dismounting from his horse, he attacked and tried to rape her. Anita grabbed his whip, flogged him thoroughly, leaped on his horse, and rode to the nearest police station to file a charge.

Due to Anita's unruliness, her mother was eager to marry her off and pressured her to wed Manoel Duarte di Aguiar, a 25-year-old shoemaker. Anita, still 14, reluctantly agreed, though she expressed her misgivings to her close friend, **Maria Fortunata**. Although Anita and Duarte were together four years, their marriage produced no children, and, in 1839, the Brazilian army called Duarte into service, since he was a member of the national guard. Legend has it that an unlucky omen had occurred on their wedding day: as Anita walked into the church, she had tripped and lost a satin slipper. Some took this as a sign that she was destined to abandon her husband. Others speculate that the marriage had never been consummated, and that Duarte had been the one to abandon her. Whatever the truth, Duarte was out of the picture when Giuseppe Garibaldi spied her through his telescope.

The Anita who so captivated Giuseppe that he was ready to run off with a married woman was not a conventional beauty. Various sources describe her as having "large and stupendous eyes," freckles, and thick flowing black hair. Giuseppe was a short, handsome, 32-year-old Italian exile and sailor. He had been born in the city of Nice, which at that time was part of the Kingdom of Sardinia. In nearby Genoa, he joined the secret nationalist organization Young Italy, founded by Giuseppe Mazzini. The police of the Kingdom of Sardinia discovered Giuseppe Garibaldi's conspiratorial activities and forced him to flee Europe under sentence of death. He arrived in Rio de Janeiro in January 1836. There he made contact with the community of Italian political exiles, who put him in contact with the revolutionaries of the Brazilian state of Rio Grande do Sul. Rio Grande aspired to complete independence from the autocratic Brazilian empire. Giuseppe took up the cause of Riograndense independence and received the command of a ship.

Soon after his 1839 meeting with Anita, Giuseppe was ordered to raid the Brazilian coast, and Anita insisted on sailing with him. At Imbituba, 20 miles north of Laguna, his fleet of two ships came under attack from three better-armed Brazilian warships. Giuseppe tried to persuade Anita to go ashore while the fight lasted; she refused. When the battle reached its height, some of the crew lost their nerve and fled below deck, while Anita grabbed a musket and began to fire at the enemy. When the blast of a cannon ball exploded near her, two sailors were killed, but Anita remained unhurt. Giuseppe urged her to seek shelter below deck. For once, she listened. Within moments, she emerged back on deck with several sailors whom she had shamed into returning to the fray. Eventually, the enemy broke off the engagement and sailed away.

On another occasion, Giuseppe found himself on shore when a vastly superior Brazilian fleet attacked his ships. Most of his sailors, believing the struggle hopeless, either refused to return to their ships or hesitated to open fire. But Anita took matters into her own hands and shot the first cannon. This prompted the rest of the men to open up with cannon and small arms fire.

When it proved necessary to evacuate the town of Laguna, Anita took charge of removing supplies from the ships, while her husband directed covering fire against the enemy. The next 18 months were spent fighting inland. Anita was at Giuseppe's side the entire campaign. "She looked upon battles as a pleasure," wrote Giuseppe, "and the hardships of camp life as a pastime."

Despite the fact that she was several months pregnant, it is said that Anita led a munitions train to the front. Suddenly surrounded by Brazilian cavalry near the town of Curitibanos, she urged her fellow soldiers to fight on and not give in to the demands for surrender. Mounting her horse, she then galloped past the Brazilians and seemed on the verge of escaping. But the enemy shot her horse from under her, throwing her to the ground, and she was apprehended. Brought before a vindictive Brazilian commander, Anita denounced him and the Brazilian government. At night, she managed to escape and, after eight harrowing days, was able to rejoin her Giuseppe, or José, as she called him. Months later, in September 1840, Anita gave birth to her son Menotti, born with a scar on his head. Giuseppe believed that this had been caused by Anita's fall from her horse, but medical opinion deems this unlikely. Little Menotti soon had to face even greater dangers. Twelve days after his birth, enemy troops surrounded the farm where Anita was staying. Giuseppe was away at the time. Half naked, Anita seized her baby, leaped on a horse, and, together with some of Giuseppe's men, fled into the woods until the danger had passed.

New and powerful attacks by Caixas, the Brazilians' ablest general, drove Anita, Giuseppe, and the Riograndense forces into the western highlands of the province. The retreating army suffered great hardships. The temperature in the mountains of the western Rio Grande do Sul dropped below freezing at night. Heavy rains and flooded rivers and mountain streams made progress difficult. The band went hungry and were forced to live on small forest animals and berries. Sometimes Anita, sometimes Giuseppe carried Menotti in a large handkerchief tied around the neck to form a large sling, using their body heat and breath to keep him warm. Many died, and Anita was terrified that her son would not survive. Finally the Garibaldi family and the Rio Grande army reached safety in San Gabriel, 400 miles from their starting point.

Aware that he needed a rest and intent on contacting his parents in Italy, Giuseppe obtained leave, and he and Anita traveled to Montevideo, Uruguay, arriving on June 17, 1841. There, they took up residence in a small house shared with other families, and Giuseppe became a teacher of mathematics. Nine months later, the Garibaldis were married in a large Baroque church near their house. Why they married at this time is something of a mystery, although the historian Jasper Ridley suggests that it was because Anita had finally received news of the death of her husband. The truth cannot be established, since Duarte's death certificate has never been found and nothing is known of him after 1839.

Although Giuseppe Garibaldi had no immediate wish to return to the military life, he was soon drawn into the "Great War" of 1839–1851 between the Argentine dictator Juan Manuel de Rosas and Uruguay, a war complicated by the defection of a prominent Uruguayan politician to the side of Argentina. The Uruguayan Republic, which had been sympathetic to the Rio Grande revolutionaries, enrolled Giuseppe as a "colonel" in its navy. Later, he formed his famous Italian Legion to defend Montevideo against attack. During the five years that Giuseppe served Uruguay, Anita devoted herself to her growing family. After her arrival in Montevideo, she gave birth to three more children, Rosita in late 1841 (some sources give 1843), Teresa in February 1845, and Ricciotti in February 1847. Despite Giuseppe's rise to the posts of

Anita
Garibaldi

commander-in-chief of the Uruguayan navy and, for a brief time, head of the army in Montevideo, he survived on the salary of an ordinary soldier. For seven years, his family dwelt in one room, with shared kitchen privileges.

During the war, Anita did not serve, or lend her name, to the efforts of the Montevidean Philanthropical Society, which sought aid for the city's hospitals and money and comforts for the troops. Ridley suggests that this may have been because she was ignored by the upper-class women. Or it may be that, compared to the excitement of campaigning beside her husband, committee work appeared uninteresting. Contemporary accounts maintain that Anita felt a sense of inferiority and resentment toward the women of Uruguay's elite. Anita was known as a firebrand, jealous of their interest in her husband. On more than one occasion, she proffered her husband two pistols, one for him and the other for a suspected rival. She even compelled him to cut off his shoulder-length hair, which, she believed, made him too desirable.

Anita Garibaldi's life and death made her a national heroine in both Brazil and Italy, and a heroine of romance in many other countries of the world.

—Jasper Ridley

While Giuseppe was campaigning in western Uruguay in December 1845, their daughter Rosita died, probably of scarlet fever. Anita took the blow even harder than Giuseppe, who loved little Rosita dearly. Fearing his wife might go mad from grief, he suggested that she come to stay with him in Salto, despite the danger of the journey in wartime.

By the end of 1847, news of nationalist and liberal demonstrations in Italy persuaded Giuseppe to return to his homeland. A wave of revolutionary sentiment had swept across Europe, and many hoped that it might now be possible to throw out the Austrians, who were occupying Venice and Lombardy, and unite the different Italian states into one country. At the beginning of January 1848, Anita Garibaldi agreed to leave for Italy in the company of her children and a number of other wives and children of Italian Legionaries. Giuseppe was to follow. Unhappy at being separated from Rosita's body in the cemetery at Montevideo, Anita placed flowers on the grave the day before departing.

When she arrived at Genoa in April, she was greeted, to her surprise, by cheering crowds, crying out, "Long live Garibaldi! Long live the family of our Garibaldi!" She then made her way to Nice, where Giuseppe's mother lived, and where Giuseppe arrived to a great reception on June 21. Italian newspapers and nationalist propagandists, such as Mazzini, had already made the exploits of the Garibaldis well known in Italy.

Giuseppe's mother, who feared that his and Anita's marriage had been somewhat irregular, urged them to remarry in Nice. This they refused to do, and in September 1848, after Giuseppe's involvement in the vain struggle to drive the Austrians out of northern Italy, they moved to the cottage of an old sailor friend just outside the town. During the months she stayed in Nice, Anita began to learn to read and write.

In October, when Giuseppe elected to go with some volunteers to help the Sicilians against the despotic government of the Bourbon king of Naples, Anita demanded to accompany him. Menotti, eight years old, went to a boarding school in Genoa and the other two children stayed in Nice with friends. On October 24, the Garibaldis, and 72 volunteers, set sail from Genoa. When their ship landed in Leghorn, however, the people there begged Giuseppe to take command of the revolutionary Tuscan army. Subsequently, he decided to lead his volunteers in an expedition to Venice, which was holding out against an Austrian siege. Anita was persuaded to return to Nice. A difficult march through the Apennine mountains followed. Events in Rome, where revolutionaries had overthrown papal authority, caused Giuseppe to change his plans once again. Now he marched southward to assist the Romans. At Rieti, northeast of Rome, Anita met up with him, and stayed with him from the end of February until the beginning of April 1849. At Rieti, they decided to have their fifth child. When the new republican government in Rome, dominated by Mazzini, called Giuseppe's force to assist in the defense of the city, Anita again wished to join him. Giuseppe finally persuaded her, however, to return to Nice and care for their children.

On June 26, toward the end of the fierce campaign of the French army to wrest Rome away from the control of the Italian republicans and return it to the pope, Anita arrived at Giuseppe's headquarters unexpectedly. A few minutes after she had appeared, a cannon ball hit the building, blasting a hole in the roof and bringing down the ceiling plaster in the room where she and her husband were talking. The event did not disturb Anita who, as always, remained cool under fire. Giuseppe barely convinced her to stay away from the battle lines.

On July 2, the Roman Assembly decided to capitulate to the French, who had seized the western walls of Rome after a gallant fight by the outnumbered and outgunned troops of Giuseppe Garibaldi. That day, at 5 PM, Giuseppe addressed the remnants of the army in St. Peter's Square, with Anita on horseback by his side. "This is what I have to offer to you who wish to follow me," said Giuseppe: "hunger, cold, the heat of the sun; no wages, no barracks, no ammunition; but continual skirmishes, forced marches and bayonet-fights. Those of you who love your country and love glory, follow me!" Nearly 5,000 men, and Anita Garibaldi, would follow. Just before departing, she hurried from St. Peter's Square to change into men's clothing and have her hair cut short.

At Monte Rotondo, northeast of Rome, the Garibaldis stopped to rest, requisitioning supplies from the local inhabitants and paying for it with the paper money of the Roman Republic. Giuseppe sent Anita and a Swiss volunteer to obtain rations from a monastery outside the town. The Swiss volunteer recorded in his diary that the monks seemed to be terrified of Anita and produced the food and wine which were required. As the army swung north, the Garibaldis rode in front, the unarmed Anita wearing a green uniform with a broad-brimmed, plumed Calabrian hat. As French, Austrian, Spanish, and Neapolitan armies closed in on Garibaldi's band, the situation became more and more hopeless and desertions increased. Anita, however, remained cheerful. She inspired the men by her example, chatting with them on the march, and made a tent during the hours of rest. They responded toward her with many acts of kindness. If, on the other hand, any soldiers showed signs of weakness or grumbled, she subjected them to a good tongue lashing.

On July 17, the contingent crossed into Tuscany, where Giuseppe was welcomed at the town of Cetona. For the first time since the march began, he and his troops slept in houses. Anita bought and put on a woman's dress, now that her pregnancy was more advanced. On July 30, tired, hungry, and ever more closely followed by their enemies, Giuseppe's troops, now reduced to a force of 1,800, arrived at the border of the tiny Republic of San Marino, in northcentral Italy. While Giuseppe was negotiating to secure temporary sanctuary in the republic, an Austrian army came upon his forces and attacked. Most of the Garibaldean rear-guard panicked and fled, despite Anita's efforts to stop them.

In San Marino, the Garibaldis found a temporary haven, since the Austrians respected the international boundary. Giuseppe dissolved his army, leaving each man free to determine his own fate. On the evening of July 31, he decided to try to escape through the Austrian lines and make his way to Venice, which was still holding out against the Austrians. He, as well as the women of the town, urged Anita to stay in San Marino. After months of excellent health, she had developed a fever, perhaps malaria. But Anita insisted on staying with her husband. Her "noble heart was indignant at all my warnings," wrote Giuseppe, "and reduced me to silence with the words 'You want to leave me.'"

The Garibaldis, together with 200 followers, set out at midnight, after persuading a porter to secretly let them out through the town gates. They passed unnoticed through the Austrian lines and finally reached Cesenatico on the Adriatic coast, about 20 miles south of Ravenna. Here Giuseppe commandeered 13 small ships to transport his men to Venice. After they had hurriedly embarked, they discovered how short they were of drinking water. As Anita's fever became worse, she repeatedly asked for water.

The tiny expedition sailed north all day and night on August 2, passing Ravenna and arriving in the neighborhood of the swamps around Lake Comacchio, some 50 miles from Venice. Assisted by the light of a full moon, an Austrian naval patrol spotted the Garibaldi flotilla and succeeded in capturing 10 of the 13 boats, but the craft conveying the Garibaldis made it safely to the beach. Anita was too ill to climb out, however, and Giuseppe had to carry her ashore. He then ordered the 30 men who had reached safety to make their escape as best they could; he and one other companion, a Lieutenant Leggiero, would remain with his wife. With Anita in his arms, Giuseppe headed for a field, where they lay and rested, concealed by the corn. But Anita was delirious from fever and, though she spoke of her children, was becoming increasingly incoherent. Fortunately, Giacomo Bonnet, a local landowner and friend of Giuseppe, now found the little group and led them to a farm, with Giuseppe carrying Anita another two miles across the fields. There, they laid her on a bed and at last provided her with food and drink, but she could swallow only a little water and soup.

Initially, it was decided that Anita should be left in the care of a doctor, while Giuseppe tried to make his escape, since capture by the Austrians or the papal authorities meant certain death. But Anita clung to her husband, whispering, "You want to leave me," and Giuseppe could not bring himself to abandon her. On the afternoon of August 4, transported in a cart and resting on a mattress, Anita was brought to a large, isolated farmhouse owned by the Marquis Guiccioli, a farm managed by men sympathetic to Giuseppe. When a doctor arrived, Giuseppe pleaded with him to save her. Advised to quickly get her to bed, Giuseppe and the other men took hold of the mattress, carried her into the farmhouse, and up to a bedroom on the second floor. As they put her down on the bed, they realized that Anita Garibaldi had died while being conveyed up the stairs.

SOURCES:

Garibaldi, Giuseppe. *Autobiography.* Vols. I and II. Translated by A. Werner. London: Walter Smith and Innes, 1889.

Hibbert, Christopher. *Garibaldi and his Enemies.* London: Longmans, 1965.

Ridley, Jasper. *Garibaldi.* London: Constable, 1974.

Viotti, Andrea. *Garibaldi: The Revolutionary and his Men.* Poole, Dorset: Blandford, 1979.

SUGGESTED READING:

Bryant, Dorothy. *Anita, Anita: Garibaldi of the New World.* Ata Books, 1993.

Gerson, Brasil. *Garibaldi e Anita, Guerrilheiros do Liberalismo.* São Paulo: José Bushatsky, 1971.

Sergio, Lisa. *I Am My Beloved: The Life of Anita Garibaldi.* NY: Weybright and Talley, 1969 (a semifictionalized account).

Valente, Valentim. *Anita Garibaldi, Heroína por Amor.* São Paulo: Soma. 1984.

RELATED MEDIA:

1860, Italian historical film, directed by Alessandro Blasetti, 1934.

Anita Garibaldi, Italian film, starring *Anna Magnani and Raf Vallone, directed by Goffredo Alessandrini and Francesco Rosi, 1954.

Richard Bach Jensen, Assistant Professor of History at Louisiana Scholars' College, Northwestern State University, Natchitoches, Louisiana

Garland, Judy (1922–1969)

American singer, dancer, actress, and show-business icon in films and on stage for three decades, who had a devoted worldwide following. Born Frances Ethel Gumm on June 10, 1922, in Grand Rapids, Minnesota; died in London, England, on June 22, 1969, the official coroner's report listing an overdose of sleeping pills as the cause of death; the youngest of three daughters of Frank and Ethel (Milne) Gumm (both vaudeville performers); married David Rose (a musician), in 1941 (divorced 1945); married Vincente Minnelli (a director), in 1946 (divorced 1951); married Sid Luft (a producer), in 1952 (divorced 1957); married Mark Herron (an actor), in 1965 (divorced 1967); married Mickey Deans (a nightclub owner), in 1968; children: (second marriage) *Liza Minnelli (b. 1946); (third marriage) Lorna Luft (b. 1952); Joseph Luft (b. 1955).*

Made her stage debut with her sisters at the age of three (1925); signed a movie contract with MGM at age 13 (1935); secured position as a Hollywood star at age 17 with her portrayal of Dorothy in MGM's musical The Wizard of Oz (1939); appeared in a string of lavish MGM musicals to great acclaim; driven by professional and family pressures, began to suffer from depression and anxiety, struggling with addictions to various medications for the rest of her life.

Filmography: various shorts from 1929 to 1936; Pigskin Parade (1936); Broadway Melody of 1938 (1937); Thoroughbreds Don't Cry (1937); Everybody Sing (1938); Love Finds Andy Hardy (1938); Listen Darling (1938); The Wizard of Oz (1939); Babes in Arms (1939); Andy Hardy Meets a Debutante (1940); Strike Up the Band (1940); Little Nellie Kelley (1940); Meet the Stars #4 (short, 1941); Cavalcade of the Academy Awards (short, 1941); Ziegfeld Girl (1941); Life Begins for Andy Hardy (1941); Babes on Broadway (1942); We Must Have Music (short, 1942); For Me and My Gal (1942); Presenting Lily Mars (1943); As Thousands Cheer (1943); Girl Crazy (1943); Meet Me in St. Louis (1944); The Clock (1945); The Harvey Girls (1946); Ziegfeld Follies (1946); Till the Clouds Roll By (1946); The Pirate (1948); Easter Parade (1948); Words and Music (1948); In the Good Old Summertime (1949); Summer Stock (1950); A Star Is Born (1954); Pepe (cameo, 1960); Judgment at Nuremberg (1961); Gay Purr-ee (voice only, 1962); A Child Is Waiting (1963); I Could Go on Singing (1963).

Everyone on director Stanley Kramer's set waited in quiet anticipation one March morning in 1960 for the arrival of the actress whose few short scenes in Kramer's film *Judgment at Nuremberg* would be shot over the next few days. Heads turned when a thin, petite woman entered the studio; as she made her way toward Kramer, a spontaneous round of applause brought a deep blush to her cheeks. With a mock curtsey and a theatrical nod of her head to Kramer, Judy Garland reported for work on her first film in nearly seven years after a tortured career that had been nearly swamped by personal anguish and professional insecurity. But no one ever doubted her talent for exuberant song and dance and intensely focused acting when she was at her best. "There's nobody in the entertainment world today," Kramer said after completing his film, "who can run the complete range of emotions the way she can."

It was Judy's father, a vaudeville song-and-dance man named Frank Gumm, who had taught her to give an audience everything she had. Frank and **Ethel Gumm** had begun in the business by managing movie theaters which, in those early days, were really vaudeville houses that combined live entertainment with short, one or two-reel silent films. Frank had left a broken home and a college education in the Midwest to settle in Superior, Wisconsin, where he had turned a talent for singing into a job at the Savoy Theater. He was accompanied on the piano by Ethel Milne. The two were married in January of 1914 and soon moved to Grand Rapids, Minnesota, where friends told them a new movie palace had just opened.

Grand Rapids, on the banks of the Mississippi River in the southeast corner of Minnesota, had been settled by Irish and German immigrants who flocked to the New Grand Theater for their entertainment on weekends and holidays, where, along with "the flickers," they could enjoy Frank Gumm's rousing musical numbers, arranged by Ethel. Soon, the couple had bought the theater outright and had added amateur nights and fashion shows to the schedule. They also appeared together in a new act, billing themselves as "Jack and Virginia Lee, Sweet Southern Singers." The business ran smoothly enough that by 1918 the Gumms were able to buy a small house on a corner lot in which their two daughters were born— Mary Jane in 1915, Virginia in 1917. In later years, Judy would often claim that her mother never wanted a third child, that she was bent on having an abortion before a medical-student friend persuaded her otherwise. She even tried to induce a miscarriage. "She must have rolled down nineteen thousand flights of stairs and jumped off tables" Judy would say, adding that Ethel Gumm would delight in detailing her strategies to neighborhood ladies after Frances Ethel Gumm, soon to be Judy Garland, was born on June 10, 1922.

Judy's lifelong animosity toward her mother also included claims that she was forced into show business. Although it is true that Frances "Baby" Gumm made her public debut at the tender age of two-and-a-half in a fashion show Ethel had organized at a local dry goods store, she was already a willing participant, with her two sisters, in singing and dancing for neighborhood friends in garages and on street corners. **Virginia Gumm** once recalled her little sister's reaction to seeing a professional sister act, The Blue Sisters, perform at the New Grand. "Baby . . . was all but uncontrollable," she said. "She sat there

bouncing up and down and humming along," turning to her father at the show's end to ask, "Daddy, can *I* do that?" Soon, the three girls were appearing at the New Grand between movies, performing "When My Sugar Walks Down the Street" as their debut number. "The work of Frances, the two-year-old baby, was a genuine surprise," the Grand Rapids *Herald-Review* said of their first appearance. "The little girl spoke and sang so as to be heard by everyone in the house," a talent concisely summarized in another reviewer's description of her as "the little girl with the leather lungs."

"If I had any talent in those days," Garland once said, "it was inherited. Nobody ever taught me what to do on stage." She neglected to mention that it was Ethel who taught her basic dance steps and, later, saw to it that she and her sisters had professional training in dance; or that it was Frank who gave her an early repertoire of songs and coached her to sing them with as much enthusiasm as she could muster. That was the way, he explained, to put over even a mediocre song and win the audience's approval. By March of 1925, barely three years old, Frances was often appearing on the stage at the New Grand by herself, as well as with her sisters. The girls were famous enough by the following year to begin traveling to other towns to perform, and had polished their act to such an extent that they were added to their parents' act when the family departed on a two-month vacation to Los Angeles at the invitation of friends who had settled there. The rail tickets and hotel rooms were paid for by appearances in vaudeville houses and movie palaces in railroad towns from Grand Rapids to Seattle. Frank and Ethel were excited by the job opportunities in a movie industry just then turning a sleepy suburb of Los Angeles called Hollywood into an entertainment industry mecca. Although they returned to Grand Rapids in July of 1926, they relocated permanently the following October when Frank bought a movie house in tiny Lancaster, California, at the edge of the Mojave Desert some 70 miles northeast of Los Angeles. There were no picture palaces for sale in Hollywood and the real estate, in any case, was too expensive for the Gumms' limited resources.

Seventy bumpy miles over undeveloped roads were no obstacle for Ethel Gumm, who was intent on finding a spot in show business for her girls. Her determination may have been spurred by her increasingly troubled marriage to Frank, and it is likely that both she and her husband had begun by this time finding solace with other partners. The three-hour drive to Los Angeles finally paid off when the Gumm Sisters made their radio debut in Santa Monica on "The Kiddies Hour" and were invited to become a weekly feature. Even better, Ethel enrolled the girls at the Meglin Dance Studio, which she had learned was a favorite talent pool for Hollywood agents. *The Los Angeles Record* was already noting in its review of the 1928 Meglin Kiddie Revue at Loew's State Theater that "one small miss shook these well known rafters with her songs," and apologized to its readers for being unable to attach a name to the little girl who sang "I Can't Give You Anything But Love" dressed as Cupid. By 1929, Ethel had left Frank and moved permanently to Los Angeles with her daughters. The local Lancaster newspaper noted that the Gumm Sisters would be pursuing "special studies" in the city and added hopefully that the family would be reunited soon. Neighbors would not have agreed with Garland's later assessment of her mother as "the real Wicked Witch of the West"; the local gossip criticized Ethel less for being a stage mother than for neglecting her husband.

The Gumm Sisters soon became such a feature of "The Kiddies Hour" on radio that impresario Gus Edwards found them work in a series of short musical films made possible by the advent of sound, and put them in his "Hollywood Starlets Revue" in 1930. By 1933, they were touring the vaudeville circuit throughout the Midwest, where comedian George Jessel introduced them at Chicago's Oriental Theater for the first time as The Garland Sisters, perhaps taking the name from *On the Twentieth Century*, the film playing the theater along with the live entertainment, in which *Carole Lombard*'s character changes her name from Lily Plotka to Lily Garland. It was Jessel, too, who got them signed with his own agency, William Morris, and who suggested that it was the youngest Garland's voice that would sell the act. She sang, he said, "like a woman with a heart that had been hurt." After another year of touring, the Garland Sisters arrived back in Los Angeles for a spot on the bill at Graumann's Chinese Theater, their most prestigious venue yet. Garland was barely 12 years old but, *Variety* told its readers, "With the youngest, Frances, featured, the act hops into class entertainment. Possessing a voice that without a P.A. system is audible throughout a house as large as the Chinese, she handles ballads like a veteran and gets every one over with a personality that hits the audience." Virginia and Mary Jane, the review noted, "merely form a background."

The praise for little Frances Garland came at an opportune moment, for in 1934 Hollywood was fascinated with the success of six-year-old *Shirley Temple (Black)*, another alumnus of the Meglin Dance Studio, who had stolen Fox's musical *Stand Up and Cheer* from its adult stars. Equally riveted by the money the film raked in, rival studios were scurrying to find their own Shirley Temples, and it seemed inevitable that Garland would be in the running. Joe Mankiewicz, then a young writer at MGM and later to be a major figure in Garland's life, remembered the first time he saw the Garland Sisters' act. "[Judy's] voice was something incredible," he later wrote, "and you knew as you sat there that you were in the presence of something that wasn't going to come around again in a long time." Through Mankiewicz's influence, Garland was auditioned no less than three times at MGM, but Louis Mayer thought she wasn't pretty enough and especially heeded *Hedda Hopper*'s description of "a roly-poly girl with eyes like saucers" in telling his assistants that Garland was too chubby for the screen. In the meantime, she took a new stage name drawn from one of her favorite Hoagy Carmichael songs, with the line, "If you think she's a saint and you find that she ain't, that's Judy."

Finally, after her cause was embraced by Mayer's executive assistant **Ida Koverman** and a new studio composer and pianist named Roger Edens, Judy Garland was signed to a seven-year contract, at $150 a week, in September of 1935. Ethel counted her youngest daughter extremely lucky, for at the time MGM was Hollywood's most respected studio, with "more stars than there are in the heavens," as the studio's slogan went. Under Louis Mayer's paternal conservatism, MGM's talent was carefully nurtured and developed; actors' lives were strictly controlled to prevent scandal of any kind from tarnishing the studio's pristine reputation for quality family entertainment. Garland was assigned two hours of work a day with Roger Edens, who refined the skills her father had taught her and began to build her repertoire. Judy's ties to the studio were further tightened when Frank Gumm died unexpectedly of spinal meningitis. Garland suffered acute remorse at what she felt had been her abandonment of him and sobbed for hours in a locked bathroom—a habit she would repeat in years to come under more threatening pressures. With Frank gone, MGM's importance in her life increased. "It's hard to explain what it's like to have a film corporation for a parent," she said, "but when my father died Metro-Goldwyn-Mayer more or less adopted me."

Judy
Garland

Further anxieties developed when MGM insisted on delaying her debut before its cameras. The studio repeatedly withdrew offers of small parts in its musicals before finally, after a year, loaning her out to Fox for one of that studio's thinly plotted musical revues, *Pigskin Parade*, in 1936. Judy had by now learned from studio pros that a loan-out was a sure sign of impending dismissal, but she did her best in the Fox picture as one of a high-stepping chorus of collegiate beauties (a young ***Betty Grable** among them), each of whom were given chances at solo numbers, of which Judy was given three. Although *The New York Times* thought she was merely "cute, not too pretty," it noted her "fetching personality" and her ability to put a song over. But this slight encouragement could hardly compensate for Garland's shock when she saw herself on screen for the first time at the picture's preview. She had expected that the magic of lighting and makeup would compensate for MGM's litany of physical defects and was shocked at what she saw. "It was the most awful moment of my life," she recalled years later. "My freckles stood out. I was *fat*, and my acting was terrible." To make matters worse, *Deanna Durbin, who had entered the MGM stable at the same time as Garland but who had been aggressively promoted, had become an overnight sensation in her first film, *Three Smart Girls*. Ethel again found herself pounding on a locked bathroom door while Judy sobbed inside.

She just plain wore out.

—Ray Bolger

It was Clark Gable's birthday that saved Judy Garland's contract. The studio had arranged a gala birthday party for its biggest star's 36th birthday, at which Ida Koverman had convinced Mayer to let Judy sing. Koverman, Edens, and Garland worked up an act that came to be called "Dear Mr. Gable," in which Judy, doe-eyed and yearning, sang "You Made Me Love You" to a photograph of the star. Gable, along with everyone else, was enchanted and even strode on stage after Judy repeated her performance at a theater exhibitor's convention to give her a theatrically passionate embrace. By the time production began on MGM's *Broadway Melody of 1938* (shot during 1937), the number had been inserted into the film's score. "The sensational work of young Judy Garland causes wonder as to why she has been kept under wraps these many months," complained *The Hollywood Reporter* in its review of the picture. "Hers is a distinctive personality well worth careful promotion."

MGM took the hint, to the extent that Garland found herself working on two pictures at once—a racetrack comedy called *Thoroughbreds Don't Cry*, her first picture with Mickey Rooney in which she was required to do little more than sing; and *Everybody Sing*, another comedy about a wealthy family besotted with show business. MGM's publicists took Garland's image seriously in hand, promoting her on radio and arranging for a six-week concert tour starting in Miami and ending in Columbus, Ohio. Returning to the studio, Judy appeared in the first of three "Andy Hardy" pictures with Rooney. She was cast as the love interest that Rooney ignores for the more attractive *Lana Turner, to whom Garland's acting abilities were unfavorably compared. "Look at Lana!" Judy wailed. "I'm so ugly!"

To make sure they got a good return on their investment, studio executives put Garland on a strict diet and hired a physician to supervise a regimen of Benzedrine to control her appetite and Seconal to counteract its stimulant effects so that she might sleep at night. "My primary function was to work," Garland said later. "As long as I worked, the studio's investment in the property known as Judy Garland paid off. If I got fat, I couldn't work. So, I mustn't get fat." Even so, the studio's wardrobe department insisted that she wear a "figure flattener" when Garland was awarded the role which secured her reputation for generations of Americans, that of the plucky Dorothy in MGM's *The Wizard of Oz*. Running through two directors, 23 weeks of shooting (from October 1938 to March of 1939, the longest shoot in MGM's history at the time), and a budget three times that of most pictures in those days, *The Wizard of Oz* permanently implanted Judy's image as the virginal hometown American girl in the national consciousness. Her plaintive rendition of Harold Arlen and E.Y. "Yip" Harburg's "Over the Rainbow" especially won audiences' hearts. "She sang not only to your ears, but to your tear ducts," said Harburg. Hollywood was so moved by her emotional performance that Garland was awarded a special Oscar in 1940 for Best Juvenile Performance.

"Judy Garland's Dorothy is a pert and fresh-faced Miss with the wonder-lit eyes of a believer in fairy tales," gushed *The New York Times*, typical of the reviews that poured in with the film's release, just as Garland was beginning work on another MGM musical, *Babes in Arms*, directed by Busby Berkeley and teaming her once again with Rooney. The *Times'* depiction, unfortunately, belied the frictions and tumult that now surrounded the studio's most rapidly rising young star, already under pressure to compete and chafing at being an eternal adolescent. Her crushes on actor Jackie Cooper and bandleader Artie Shaw were in danger of advancing to something much more serious (Garland's bitter outburst at Shaw when his marriage to Lana Turner was announced being hastily concealed by the studio). Her relationship with her mother, assiduously portrayed by the studio as loving and benevolent, was in reality near collapse due to Ethel's remarriage to one of Frank's former rivals on the very anniversary of his death; and the 18-year-old Garland's demands for more adult roles were becoming increasingly strident. She was given a dual role—as a mother and, in a flash forward, as the daughter—in *Little Nellie Kelley*, despite Louis Mayer's serious reservations. ("You can't let that child have a baby!" he objected.) Critics hated her acting in the picture, but audiences turned out in force to see the film and earned MGM some $2 million on its $600,000 investment.

By now, Garland's drug addiction was causing serious problems on the sets of her pictures. She was often hours late for her calls and seemed to fly into fits of tearful anger at the slightest provocation. She disappeared completely from the set of *Babes on Broadway* in 1941, sending a telegram from Las Vegas to announce she had eloped with musician David Rose. "Please give me a little time and I will be back and finish the picture with one take each scene, love, Judy," she wired. An abortion in 1942 at Ethel's insistence and her subsequent divorce from Rose, finalized in 1945, sent Garland into a depression serious enough that medical help had to be sought. In 1943, after completing work on her second dramatic, adult role in *Presenting Lily Mars*, an affair with Tyrone Power ended badly when Power's wife *Annabella left him with much public accusation; Garland's succeeding lover, who happened to be Joe Mankiewicz, arranged a stay at the Menninger Clinic in Kansas for what was termed "nervous instability." Mankiewicz was familiar with psychological illness; his wife suffered from severe depression and paranoia and he, himself, had been in analysis for some time. "[Judy] was full of unconscious hostility toward the parent, represented by the studio, which she manifested by not showing up on time," he claimed. "She was treated by most people, including her mother, as a *thing*, not as a human being. The girl reacted to the slightest bit of kindness as if it were a drug." Mankiewicz was repaid for his concern by being hauled before Garland's mother and Louis Mayer, seething at what they saw as his interference. "All Judy needs is a mother's love," Mayer claimed. Mankiewicz promptly quit MGM, went over to Fox, and eventually became an Oscar-winning director with such pictures as *All About Eve* and *A Letter to Three Wives*.

Mayer immediately put Garland back to work in 1944's *Meet Me in St. Louis*, directed by a former art director, Vincente Minnelli, who handled Judy's aberrations on the set with great understanding and managed to produce an exu-berant turn-of-the-century musical that included such numbers as "The Trolley Song" and "Have Yourself a Merry Little Christmas." Their deepening relationship culminated in marriage in June of 1945, after Minnelli had directed her in their second film together, the melodrama *The Clock*. (Minnelli had taken the picture over from Fred Zinnemann when Garland's arguments with Zinnemann had shut down production.) By the time she began work with Minnelli on *Till the Clouds Roll By*, a sentimentalized biography of composer Jerome Kern, Garland was four months pregnant. By then, she had curtailed her reliance on drugs successfully enough to give birth to a healthy daughter, named **Liza Minnelli**, in March of 1946 before returning to work in another film directed by her husband, *The Pirate*, co-starring dancer Gene Kelly. But her fears that Kelly's dancing would overpower her own, and her jealousy over the time the two men spent together in rehearsals, brought back her drug habit to such an extent that by the time shooting began, the studio had budgeted for a session with a psychiatrist at the end of each day. Minnelli at last began to lose patience with her. Garland was absent or late to the set on 99 out of its scheduled 135 days, telling Hedda Hopper that everyone had turned against her. The crisis came to a head with Garland's first suicide attempt, barely prevented by Ethel, who broke down the bathroom door at Judy's home and grabbed away the shard of glass with which her daughter had already inflicted superficial wounds. Garland was confined to a sanitorium in northern California for several weeks while the studio delayed *The Pirate*'s release until she could return to reshoot several scenes. The picture fared badly in theaters and was quickly withdrawn.

Easter Parade was her next scheduled film, again with her husband, but by now the damage was irreparable. Garland refused to do the picture unless it was taken away from Minnelli. The studio was forced to concede, although it was not prepared for Judy's anger at co-star Fred Astaire when it was announced Astaire would be teamed with *Ginger Rogers on his next film, even though Garland claimed Astaire had chosen *her* as his permanent partner. After the usual outbursts, delays, and crises, *Easter Parade* finished production in July of 1947. Garland was promptly put under temporary suspension from her contract, the studio blaming her "temperament" for the decision while Garland blamed Minnelli. The truth was that Louis Mayer's power was being eroded by Dore Schary, whom Mayer himself had hired some years earlier as an assistant and who would eventually replace Mayer as general manager of the studio in 1951.

Judy was, in effect, losing the father who had grudgingly overlooked his rebellious daughter's behavior. In 1949, the studio's newly forming hierarchy took the drastic step of firing Garland from *Annie Get Your Gun*, noting it had only six minutes of usable footage after a month of shooting, and replacing her with ***Betty Hutton**.

Garland entered Peter Bent Brigham Hospital in Boston shortly after her termination, the press being told she was exhausted from overwork, although everyone knew the hospital's reputation for curing drug addiction. Judy revealed she had no money to pay for her treatment, blaming Ethel for investing her salary unwisely and borrowing money from the studio.

By the beginning of 1950, Garland felt well enough to make up with MGM and return to work in *Royal Wedding*; but after repeated arguments with director Stanley Donen and mounting tensions on the set, Judy was again replaced, this time by ***Jane Powell**, and at last permanently fired from MGM after 15 years of stormy employment. "Wish her well," Joe Pasternak, who had directed her in *Presenting Lily Mars*, said at a farewell ceremony on the studio lot. "Return her love, all you who cherish talent and genius and a great heart." Two days later, Garland again attempted suicide, again by locking herself in the bathroom, and again saved at the last minute; this time by Minnelli. She entered another hospital as she and Minnelli's divorce became final in 1951. Garland was granted custody of Liza.

As her career at MGM was waning, Garland had met a theatrical manager named Sid Luft. It was Luft who now proposed that Judy resuscitate her career by returning to the stage, and who found her an offer from London's Palladium. Garland's films, with their optimism and gay dance numbers, had always performed well in an economically depressed postwar England, and Luft was convinced her reception would be a warm one. He was proved right, even when Garland tripped on her gown and fell during opening night. "She melts even the flinthearts who came to gloat over a star who once fell to earth all screaming nerves and hysteria," *The Daily Express* enthused, while *The Evening Standard* told its readers "We saw a brave woman . . . but more than that, we saw a woman who has emerged from the shadows and finds that the public likes her as she is, even more than what she was." Luft followed this London success by booking Garland into New York's Winter Palace, where the reviews were no less positive.

In June of 1952, Judy and Sid Luft married. Judy was pregnant by then, giving birth to another daughter, Lorna, in November. Luft managed to keep a third suicide attempt, which Garland later blamed on postpartum depression, from public knowledge and arranged a six-picture contract for his wife at Warner Bros., with himself acting as producer on the first picture. Judy reported to work on *A Star Is Born*, her most famous film after *The Wizard of Oz*, in the fall of 1953. But by Thanksgiving, director George Cukor reported the picture was seriously behind schedule after six weeks of shooting. "This is the behavior of someone unhinged," he complained, although he admitted that Garland was "a very original and resourceful actress" and complimented her one day on the fact that she had given him six different screams on six different takes. "Oh, that's nothing," Garland replied. "Come over to my house anytime. I do it every afternoon."

Shooting stretched into the summer of 1954, but it was clear when *A Star Is Born* was released that Garland's career was reborn with her performance opposite James Mason as half of a show-business couple whose star is rising while that of her alcoholic, matinee-idol husband is in decline. Audiences were especially touched by her rendition of "The Man Who Got Away," and her delivery of "Born in a Trunk" was so convincing that such an odd manner of birth became part of the Garland legend. Judy won the Golden Globe award as Best Actress for 1955, and was nominated for the same Oscar category, but lost to *Grace Kelly*, for *The Country Girl*. By the time the award nominations were announced, Garland was again pregnant, giving birth prematurely to a healthy son, named Joseph, in March.

Despite the uplift to what had been a failing career and the six-picture contract Luft had negotiated, Garland never fulfilled her commitment to Warner Bros. and was absent from the screen for the next six years. There were reports that her health was deteriorating and that her marriage was again in trouble, the latter confirmed when she and Sid Luft divorced in 1957, and the former verified when Garland was diagnosed with severe liver malfunction. Doctors told her during a bout with acute hepatitis that her liver was swollen to four times its normal size and that she would have to terminate the excessive alcohol consumption that they felt was the culprit. Her recovery was so complete, however, that it seemed she was starting a new life in 1960 when she embarked on another concert

Opposite page
From the movie
Easter Parade,
1948.

tour and appeared that day on Stanley Kramer's set for the shooting of *Judgment at Nuremberg.* In 1961, she played a sold-out Carnegie Hall in what is still described as "the greatest night in show business history." She sang 24 numbers for two-and-a-half hours to a star-studded audience, with so many encores that Garland was finally obliged to tell her admirers that she had nothing else prepared. "Then just stand there!" a fan yelled. Everyone agreed that Judy had never looked or sounded better.

Now in the midst of a second renaissance, Garland was given her own television show, a weekly variety program on CBS. But the strain of turning out a new hour of entertainment once a week took its toll. By the time the show was canceled in 1963, Judy was again relying on pills to keep her going during the day and to put her to sleep at night. Friends advised her not to accept a concert tour in Australia, but in the company of a 30-year-old actor she had met at a party named Mark Herron, she left for Sydney. Herron got her through the tour as best he could, though Judy was often late for her calls and, at one point, inexplicably walked off the stage and disappeared into her dressing room for 25 minutes. One night near the end of the tour, Herron found her unconscious and perilously near death in her hotel room from an overdose of Seconal. She was revived at a hospital and later credited Herron with saving her life. The two married on board ship as they were returning to California in 1965, but she and Herron subsequently saw little of each other and went their separate ways after two years.

Her sixth marriage was announced in London, in March of 1969, to nightclub owner Mickey Deans, whom Judy had met some years earlier and whom, it was said, had once supplied her with drugs. Deans, an American who had permanently relocated to England, ran London's Talk of the Town club, and booked Garland there once they had settled into an apartment nearby. On the night of Saturday, June 21, 1969, Garland was seen by neighbors running into the street outside the apartment, some of them later claiming she had been screaming. A few minutes later, Deans left the apartment to search for her, telling friends that he and Judy had been quarreling. He remained away from home for several hours, not returning until early in the morning of the next day. Noting the closed and locked door of Garland's bedroom, he surmised she had gone to sleep until a phone call for her failed to elicit any response. Unable to break down the door, Deans was forced to run outside and crawl

From the movie The Wizard of Oz, *starring Jack Haley, Judy Garland, and Ray Bolger.*

through the window of Garland's bathroom, where she had obviously been lying dead for some time. The official coroner's report listed an overdose of barbiturates as the cause of death, but police refused to speculate if the overdose had been accidental. "The greatest shock about her death," wrote theater critic Vincent Canby, "was that there *was* no shock. One simply wondered how she survived so long."

While it is difficult for any account of Judy Garland's life to avoid the contrast between her screen image and the private torments she endured, the genuine affection and respect accorded to her by her industry peers is often ignored. Despite her travails, many remembered her indefatigable sense of humor and the loud, boisterous laugh Judy said she had inherited from Frank Gumm. "She was as lighthearted a person as ever I met in my life," Jack Haley, who played The Tin Man in *The Wizard of Oz,* said of her; and Joe Mankiewicz described her as "just the most remarkably bright, gay, happy, helpless, and engaging girl I've ever met."

Even daughter Lorna Luft, who had observed firsthand the vicissitudes of her mother's life, called Garland "one of the happiest people I knew," even when her mother's fortunes seemed at their lowest ebb. "She'd just look at me and say, 'Well, honey, things can't get any *worse*,'" Lorna remembers, "and then she'd have a darn good laugh."

SOURCES:

Geist, Kenneth. *Pictures Will Talk: The Life and Films of Joseph Mankiewicz.* NY: Scribner, 1978.

Katz, Ephraim. *The Film Encyclopedia.* 2nd ed. NY: Harper Perennial, 1994.

Shipman, Frank. *Judy Garland.* London: Fourth Estate, 1992.

SUGGESTED READING:

Shipman, David. *Judy Garland: The Secret Life of an American Legend.* Hyperion, 1993.

Norman Powers,
writer-producer, Chelsea Lane Productions, New York

Garner, Peggy Ann (1931–1984)

American actress and child star of the 1940s. Born in Canton, Ohio, on February 3, 1931; died in Wood-

land Hills, California, in 1984; married Richard Hayes (an actor), in 1951 (divorced 1953); married Albert Salmi (an actor), in 1956 (divorced 1963); married a third time, in 1963; children: (second marriage) one daughter, **Cass Salmi.**

Selected films: Little Miss Thoroughbred (1938); In Name Only (1939); Abe Lincoln in Illinois (1940); The Pied Piper (1942); Jane Eyre (1944); The Keys of the Kingdom (1944); A Tree Grows in Brooklyn (1945); Nob Hill (1945); Junior Miss (1945); Home Sweet Homicide (1946); Thunder in the Valley (1947); Daisy Kenyon (1947); The Sign of the Ram (1948); Bomba the Jungle Boy (1949); The Big Cat (1949); Teresa (1951); Black Widow (1954); The Cat (1966); A Wedding (1978).

Launched by her mother into a modeling career before she was six, Peggy Ann Garner arrived in Hollywood at age seven and appeared in small roles during the late 1930s and early 1940s. After displaying a mature acting talent in *The Pied Piper* (1942) and *Jane Eyre* (1944), in which she played the young Jane, she was cast in the key role of Francie Nolan in *Betty Smith's *A Tree Grows in Brooklyn* (1945), directed by newcomer Elia Kazan. The film became one of the biggest box-office hits of the year and won Garner a special Academy Award as the "outstanding child performer of 1945." However, none of her subsequent roles were as rewarding, and, despite consistently good performances and a huge teen-age following, her film career was all but over by the early 1950s.

Between 1950 and 1960, Garner lived and worked in New York, where she said she "learned her craft." In 1950, she made her New York stage debut in *The Man*, with *Dorothy Gish,* followed by other stage performances and numerous appearances in television dramas and series episodes. In 1955, she was said to have been the first choice of playwright William Inge for the lead in his hit play *Bus Stop*, but lost the role to *Kim Stanley.* Garner subsequently played the role on tour, but it did not reignite her career. By the 1960s, she was selling real estate. During the 1970s, though still maintaining an agent and considering herself in the running for suitable roles, she worked a full-time job as a sales manager for an automobile dealership.

Garner was married and divorced three times, and had a daughter with her second husband, actor Albert Salmi. The actress died of cancer in 1984, at the age of 53.

Garnett, Constance (1862–1946)

Prolific English translator of 19th-century Russian literature. Born Constance Clara Black in Brighton, England, on December 19, 1862; died on December 17, 1946, in Edenbridge, England; daughter of David Black (a coroner) and Clara (Patten) Black; educated by home tutoring; attended Brighton High School, Newnham College Association for Advanced Learning and Education among Women in Cambridge, 1879–83; married Edward Garnett (a writer), in 1889; children: David (b. 1892).

In 1879, Constance Garnett received the highest score of more than 3,000 candidates who sat the entrance examination for Cambridge University. The resulting scholarship to Newnham College allowed her, in the words of **Carolyn Heilbrun,** to "escape from the suffocating prison that was the life of the usual Victorian girl." Garnett had been born 17 years earlier, the sixth of eight children of David Black and **Clara Patten Black.** Her childhood had not been a happy one. She suffered from tuberculosis until the age of seven. Her father, who had been born of English parents in Russia and educated in law in England, worked as the coroner in Brighton. He was a severe and irritable man who terrified his many children. Her mother, from an artistic English family, died when Constance was only 13. Much of her early education came from her older siblings but was sufficient, given her natural abilities, for her to win the coveted scholarship and to gain the equivalent of a first-class university degree after four years at Newnham College.

Constance Garnett's disposition and her higher education, which was unusual for an English woman of this period, allowed her to live independently in London. She supported herself first as a tutor for girls of wealthy families and later as a librarian at the People's Palace. During the 1880s, she enjoyed the cultural life of the capital, became interested in social causes, and joined the Fabian Society. In 1889, she married Edward Garnett, a budding writer and literary critic. Three years later, during her only pregnancy, she started to study Russian at the suggestion of a Russian émigré living in England. She made sufficient progress that shortly after the birth of her son David she was able to translate Ivan Goncharov's *A Common Story* into English. Its appearance in print in 1894 began a career that over the span of the next 34 years witnessed the publication of 72 volumes of Russian novels, short stories, and plays in very readable English translations. This output made her, in the opinion of **Rachel May,** "the most famous translator of Russian literature of all time."

In the winter of 1894 Garnett traveled alone in Russia for three months, transmitting money raised in England for Russian famine relief, passing on letters to revolutionaries in that country, and visiting the novelist Leo Tolstoy. During this trip and another which she made with her son in 1904, as well as through her literary work and her association with Russians in England, she developed an affection for Russian life of the 19th century which she passed on to her readers through her translations. She introduced Dostoevsky and Chekhov to English audiences in addition to translating almost all of the writings of Turgenev and many of those of Tolstoy, Herzen, and Gogol. She deserves great credit for stimulating the interest of several generations of English-speaking readers in the classics of Russian literature. While some of her translations now seem dated, they exerted considerable influence on English literature during the first half of the 20th century. It is a tribute to their fluidity and accuracy that many remain in print a century after their original publication. Failing eyesight caused her to cease translating in 1928. She died two days before her 84th birthday in December 1946.

SOURCES:

Brailsford, H.N. "Garnett, Constance Clara, 1861[sic]–1946," *Dictionary of National Biography, 1941–1950*. Oxford: Oxford University Press, 1959, pp. 288–289.

Heilbrun, Carolyn G. *The Garnett Family: The History of a Literary Family*. London: George Allen and Unwin, 1961.

SUGGESTED READING:

Garnett, David. *The Golden Echo*. London: Chatto and Windus, 1954.

R.C. Elwood,
Professor of History, Carleton University, Ottawa, Canada

Garrett, Elizabeth (1836–1917).

See Anderson, Elizabeth Garrett.

Garrett, Emma and Mary Smith

American educators of the deaf.

Garrett, Emma (c. 1846–1893). Born in Philadelphia, Pennsylvania, around 1846; died in Chicago, Illinois, on July 18, 1893; one of at least six children of Henry (a businessman) and Caroline Rush (Cole) Garrett; younger sister of Mary Smith Garrett (1839–1925); graduated from Alexander Graham Bell's course for teachers of the deaf at the Boston University School of Oratory, 1878; never married; no children.

Garrett, Mary Smith (1839–1925). Born in Philadelphia, Pennsylvania, on June 20, 1839; died in North Conway, New Hampshire, on July 18, 1925; one of at least six children of Henry (a businessman) and Caroline Rush (Cole) Garrett; older sister of Emma Garrett (c. 1846–1893); never married; no children.

Little is known about the early lives of Emma and Mary Smith Garrett, whose pioneering work with deaf children in Pennsylvania parallels the ground-breaking efforts of *Sarah Fuller in Massachusetts, except that they were born and educated in Philadelphia, where their father was a businessman. Emma, the younger of the two, graduated from Alexander Graham Bell's first course for teachers of the deaf at Boston University School of Oratory in 1878, and that same year she took a teaching position at the Pennsylvania Institution for the Deaf and Dumb, at Mount Airy (Pennsylvania). As a champion of Bell's innovative approach of teaching deaf students to speak and read lips instead of signing, she was put in charge of the new Oral Branch of the institution in 1881, and she also began to teach summer courses that year in the techniques of speech instruction for other teachers. In 1882, Emma addressed the convention of American Instructors of the Deaf and Dumb, urging them to support the new vocal method. In 1884, after convincing civic leaders from Scranton that the new school for the deaf which they were planning to establish should teach the oral method, Emma was named principal of the new facility, which was called the Pennsylvania Oral School for Deaf-Mutes. Among her many duties, she headed a campaign for a new school building (completed in 1888). The following year, her sister Mary, who had been running a private school in Philadelphia to teach deaf children to speak, closed her school and joined her sister Emma in Scranton. Thereafter, the two became close collaborators.

The Garretts soon saw the need to begin training deaf children in oral speech at the earliest possible age, before the children were rooted in habits of manual communication. In 1892, with help from the Pennsylvania legislature as well as private benefactors, they established the Pennsylvania Home for the Training in Speech of Deaf Children Before They Are of School Age, which opened with 15 children in temporary quarters. When the state assumed financial responsibility for the institution in 1893, it became known as the Bala Home, because of its proximity to the suburb by that name. Children were accepted into the school at age two and spent an uninterrupted six-year period learning functional speech, with the hope that eventually they would be able to function in society. In the summer of 1893, the sisters were invited to present demonstration classes at the World's Colombian Exposition in Chicago. Although the exhibition was a huge success, the physical and mental stress of preparation, combined with a decidedly excitable personality, extracted a toll on Emma who began to display severe emotional problems. On July 19, 1893, the eve of her scheduled departure to a Wisconsin sanitarium, she ended her life by jumping from a Chicago hotel window. A memorial service for her at the University of Chicago was attended by Alexander Graham Bell, Edward Gallaudet, Sarah Fuller, and *Helen Keller.

Mary Garrett took over for her sister as principal at Bala Home and remained there for the next 30 years. She also continued an active campaign to promote speech education for the deaf, and through her lobbying efforts obtained passage of laws in 1899 and 1901 requiring the exclusive use of oral methods of instruction in all state institutions for the deaf. Gradually broadening her view to include a general concern for child welfare, Mary also joined *Hannah Dent Schoff in campaigning for a juvenile court and probation system in Pennsylvania. From 1902, Mary was a member of the National Congress of Mothers, and from 1916 to 1929 she chaired its department of legislation. During that time, she guided the department in work for juvenile-court legislation, child-labor laws, and marriage and divorce laws. She also served as vice-president of the Philadelphia Child Welfare Association and was a member of the Society for the Prevention of Social Disease. Mary Garrett died in 1925, at age 86, while vacationing in North Conway, New Hampshire. The Bala Home remained open under a new principal until 1935.

SOURCES:

James, Edward T., ed. *Notable American Women 1607–1950.* Cambridge, MA: The Belknap Press of Harvard University Press, 1971.

McHenry, Robert. *Famous American Women.* NY: Dover, 1983.

Garrett, Mary Elizabeth (1854–1915).

See Thomas, M. Carey for sidebar.

Garrett, Mary Smith (1839–1925).

See joint entry under Garrett, Emma and Mary Smith.

Garrett, Millicent (1847–1929).

See Fawcett, Millicent Garrett.

Garrett-Anderson, Elizabeth (1836–1917).

See Anderson, Elizabeth Garrett.

Garrick, Mrs. David (1724–1822).

See Veigel, Eva-Maria.

Garrison, Zina (1963—)

American tennis player who was the first African-American woman to reach the Wimbledon finals since Althea Gibson. Name variations: Zina Garrison-Jackson. Born in Houston, Texas, in 1963; the youngest of the seven children of Ulysses and Mary Garrison; graduated from Ross S. Sterling High School; married Willard Jackson.

The first African-American woman to reach the Wimbledon finals since *Althea Gibson in the 1950s, Zina Garrison is one of the few black women to have enjoyed a successful career in a game dominated by whites. When she retired from tennis in 1995, she was praised not only as a trailblazer and a role-model, but as a social-minded philanthropist who has given her time and money to improve life for the homeless and inner-city youth of Houston, Texas, where she was born and raised.

Garrison was the last of seven children. To prove it, her mother, who was 42 when Zina was born, saw to it that her name began with a "Z." When she was still a baby, tragedy struck the family. First, her father suffered an unexpected stroke and died; then her brother Willie developed a fatal brain tumor after being hit in the eye with a baseball. Garrison's mother cushioned the blows for Zina, as did her older brother Rodney, who let her tag along with him to MacGregor Park, a municipal playground in the neighborhood with tennis courts.

While Rodney went his way, Garrison hung around the courts, a persistent presence, watching local coach John Wilkerson give tennis lessons. He finally gave her a wooden racket and showed her how to play. Garrison had a natural talent for the game and before long Wilkerson was coaching her for major national tournaments. He also prepared her for the difficult road ahead, telling her that she would be up against better-trained players and that she would have to be two or three times better than her opponents.

Garrison was not daunted. In 1981, at 17, she won the junior titles at both Wimbledon and the U.S. Open. The following year, after graduating from high school, she turned pro, and by 1982, she was 16th in world tennis rankings. Employing Wilkerson as her full-time coach, she played tournaments in the United States, Europe, and the Far East, a hectic schedule that kept her away from her family in Houston. When her mother suffered complications from diabetes and died in 1983, Garrison was emotionally devastated and used tennis as an outlet for her grief. By 1985, she had risen to fifth in the rankings. That same year, she reached the semifinals at Wimbledon and the quarter-finals at the Australian and U.S. opens.

By 1986, however, Garrison's unresolved grief had erupted into a full-blown eating disorder that threatened her career, and she finally sought help. By the time of the 1988 Olympics in Seoul, Korea, she was back in top form. She won a gold medal in doubles with **Pam Shriver**, and a bronze in the singles competition. In 1989, she was ranked fourth in the world and that year became the last person to beat *Chris Evert** in a tournament. She hit her zenith in 1990, advancing to the finals at Wimbledon (where she lost to *Martina Navratilova**), and winning, by way of some lucrative endorsements deals, the recognition that had long been denied her as a black woman.

As she came into her own, Garrison used her celebrity and her money to help her hometown of Houston. Through the Zina Garrison Foundation, founded in 1988, she has supported various projects, including youth organizations and anti-drug programs, to help the homeless. In 1992, using a $20,000 award from *Family Circle* Magazine's "Player Who Makes a Difference," she established the Zina Garrison All-Court Tennis Academy, which provides tennis lessons for the economically disadvantaged children of the inner city. "The organizations were started because I noticed in Texas no one else was doing them," she said. "Tennis gave me the opportunity to learn more about myself and taught me I was capable of doing anything that I wanted to do. I want others to feel that way also."

Garrison, who is married to Houston executive Willard Jackson, retired from tennis in 1995 to start a family. As her career came to an end, there was talk of her sense of fair play and her grace under pressure. John Feinstein, in *Tennis* magazine, likened her to the great Arthur Ashe. "Like Ashe, Garrison-Jackson always has carried herself with a quiet dignity," he wrote, "even while suffering indignities that had nothing to do with who or what she was and everything to do with what color she is." Garrison credits the lessons back in MacGregor Park with giving her the strength to be successful. "You have to be meaner . . . to come from the parks," she told the *Chicago Tribune*. "Those scars . . . left me stubborn and tough and determined not to quit. I'm known for that. I never give up."

SOURCES:
Feinstein, John. "A Curtain Call for a Class Act," in *Tennis*. Vol. 31, no. 3. July 1995, pp. 24–26.
Johnson, Anne Janette. *Great Women in Sports*. Detroit, MI: Visible Ink, 1998.
"Star Profile: Zina Garrison-Jackson," in *Black Enterprise*. Vol. 26, no. 2. September 1995, p. 134.

Barbara Morgan,
Melrose, Massachusetts

Garrod, Dorothy A. (1892–1969)

English archaeologist and educator who was the first woman in any field to become a professor at either of the great British universities. Born Dorothy Annie Elizabeth Garrod in 1892; died in 1969; daughter of Sir Alfred Baring Garrod (1819–1907), English physician and professor of therapeutics; sister of Alfred Henry Garrod (1846–1879), a zoologist, and Archibald Edward Garrod (1857–1936), Regius Professor of history of medicine at Oxford; educated in France, where she studied Paleolithic archaeology under Breuil, Begouen, and Peyrony; never married; no children.

Dorothy A. Garrod was born in 1892, the daughter of Sir Alfred Baring Garrod, an English physician and professor of therapeutics; her brothers were Alfred Henry Garrod, a zoologist, and Archibald Edward Garrod, a Regius Professor of history of medicine at Oxford. Director of studies in archaeology and anthropology at Newnham College at Cambridge, Dorothy Garrod was the first woman in any field to be appointed a professor at Cambridge (1939). Working in the area of Paleolithic archaeology, she directed field investigations in England, Kurdistan, Bulgaria, Gibraltar, and Lebanon. Her most famous excavation was Mugharet et Tabun in Palestine where evidence was unearthed to provide testimony on the evolution of *Homo neanderthalensis* (Neanderthal man). Garrod served in the women's services in both world wars. After WWII, she used what she had learned of photographic evaluation to develop aerial photography as a finding tool for archaeology. She was the first woman to receive the Gold Medal of the Society of Antiquaries on London.

Garsenda (1170–c. 1257)

*Troubadour and countess of Provence and Forcalquier. Name variations: Garsende; Garsenda de Forcalquier; Gersende de Forcalquier; Garsinde of Sabran. Born in 1170 in southern France; died around 1257 in Provence; daughter of Garsenda and Bernard de Forcalquier (some sources cite father as Raimund of Sabran); grandmother of *Eleanor of Provence** (c.*

1222–1291); married Alphonse II, count of Provence (r. 1196–1209), in 1193; children: Raymond Berengar V (1198–1245), 4th count of Provence; Garsenda.

Garsenda was one of the female troubadours (poet-singers) who flourished in southern France in the 12th century. The daughter of Garsenda and Bernard de Forcalquier, she married Count Alphonse II of Provence, brother to the king of Aragon, in 1193. When Garsenda's grandfather took part of her dowry lands away from Alphonse and gave it to Garsenda's sister, Garsenda found herself in the middle of a bloody war between her family and her husband's family.

Despite the war, Garsenda created an important cultural center at her court, where she patronized several male troubadours. Two of them, Gui de Cavaillon and Elias de Barjols, were reputed to have been in love with her, according to their biographers. In 1209, Alphonse died and Garsenda became regent of Provence; she held this title until her son came of age as count of Provence. In 1225, she retired to an abbey, where she remained until her death, around 1257.

Garsenda's poetry was probably written during the years before her husband's death, although this cannot be confirmed. The one extant poem of hers is a tenson, written with a troubadour whose identity is obscure. The subject of the poem is Garsenda's elevated social position and the real danger inherent in their illicit love affair.

SOURCES:

Bogin, Meg. *The Women Troubadours.* NY: Two Continents, 1976.

Laura York,
Riverside, California

Garson, Greer (1904–1996)

Star of the English stage and the American screen who, despite her Irish origins, became the screen's image of the quintessential Englishwoman. Born Eileen Evelyn Garson in County Down, in the Presbyterian section of Northern Ireland, on September 29, 1904; died of heart failure on April 6, 1996, in Dallas, Texas; only child of George Garson and Nina (Gregor) Garson; educated at the University of London and at the University of Grenoble, France; married Edward Alec Abbot Snelson, in 1933 (divorced 1941), married Richard Ney (an actor), in 1943 (divorced 1947); married Elijah E. Fogelson, on July 15, 1949 (died 1987); no children.

Awards: Won Academy Award for Best Actress for Mrs. Miniver *(1943); nominated for Academy Awards for Best Actress for* Goodbye Mr. Chips *(1939),* Blossoms in the Dust *(1941),* Madame Curie *(1944),* Mrs. Parkington *(1945),* The Valley of Decision *(1945), and* Sunrise at Campobello *(1961); named honorary Commander of the Order of the British Empire (1984); received Golda Meir Award, Hebrew University of Jerusalem, for her contributions to making educational opportunities available to deserving young people (June 18, 1988).*

First appeared on stage with the Birmingham Repertory Company, Birmingham, England; appeared as Shirley Kaplan in Elmer Rice's Street Scene *(1932); toured in G.B. Shaw's* Too True to be Good; *made first London appearance in Shakespeare's* The Tempest *at the open-air theater in Regent's Park; also appeared in London in* Golden Arrow *(1934), and* Vintage Wine, Accent on Youth, Butterfly on the Wheel, Pages From a Diary, The Visitor, Mademoiselle, The School for Scandal, *and* Old Music *(1937); signed by MGM Studios and brought to America (1937).*

Filmography: Goodbye Mr. Chips *(1939);* Remember? *(1939);* Pride and Prejudice *(1940);* Blossoms in the Dust *(1941);* When Ladies Meet *(1941);* Mrs. Miniver *(1942);* Random Harvest *(1942);* The Youngest Profession *(1943);* Madame Curie *(1943);* Mrs. Parkington *(1944);* Valley of Decision *(1945);* Adventure *(1946);* Desire Me *(1947);* Julia Misbehaves *(1948);* That Forsyte Woman *(1949);* The Miniver Story *(1950);* The Law and the Lady *(1951); (as Calpurnia)* Julius Caesar *(1953);* Scandal at Scourie *(1953);* Her Twelve Men *(1954);* Strange Lady in Town *(1955); (as Eleanor Roosevelt)* Sunrise at Campobello *(1960); (cameo)* Pepe *(1960);* The Singing Nun *(1966);* The Happiest Millionaire *(1967).*

Television and radio: appeared in Shaw's "How He Lied to Her Husband" (BBC, 1937); "That Forsyte Woman" (Lux Radio Theater, November 11, 1951); "Career" (NBC, February 24, 1956); "The Little Foxes" (NBC's "Hallmark Hall of Fame," 1956); "The Glorious Gift of Molly Malloy" ("Comedy Spotlight," CBS, August 29, 1961).

Born in County Down, Northern Ireland (Ulster), Greer Garson was the only child of George Garson, a native of the Orkney Isles, and **Nina Gregor Garson,** a descendant of the famed Scottish warrior, Rob Roy MacGregor. (The name Greer is a contraction of Gregor.) By her own admission, she was a rather high-strung, "stuffy" child, who suffered from bronchitis and fainting spells and did not sit well with other children. Early on, she was reading books intended for grown-ups on which she would discourse; her first appearance on any stage was a recitation that she gave at the village town hall at the age of four. Soon, she was winning cups and prizes in amateur competitions but could not be taken to the theater because the experience proved too stimulating; coming home, she would relive each performance, reenacting the various parts.

After the death of her father when she was still a child, Garson accompanied her mother to London, where they lived outside the city in Essex County on rents from her father's properties. Young Greer continued to win awards for her recitations while attending the local county school. She came from a long line of teachers, doctors, and Presbyterian parsons, solidly middle class in her origins on both sides. Although her family intended she become a teacher, and she passed through the University of London in only three years with honors, she continued to develop her taste for acting. After graduation, though she went on to do advanced work at the University of Grenoble, Garson considered all this education to be a waste of time and later admitted that she attended only because of her family's wishes. It was in Grenoble that she decided to give up her graduate studies to pursue acting. Upon her return home, however, she met with firm opposition from her family, in particular her grandmother, a devout Presbyterian, who viewed the idea of a theatrical career with considerable alarm. Garson, therefore, took a job with the *Encyclopedia Britannica* and, after that, with an advertising agency. There she set up and operated a market-research library for the then handsome wage of £10 per week (around $50), amusing herself in her spare time by taking parts in amateur theatrical productions.

Greer Garson was turning 29 when she went on the stage. Emboldened by her limited success in amateur theatricals, she secured a letter of introduction to the manager of the well-known and respected Birmingham Repertory Company. Her interview went well, and in 1932 she made her professional debut in a black wig playing a Jewish-American "working girl" in the company's production of Elmer Rice's *Street Scene*, after which she appeared in a variety of roles over the next two years. Around this time, Garson met and, on September 28, 1933, married a young man named Edward Snelson, of the British civil service. This marriage ended abruptly five weeks later when Snelson announced that he was going to India, and his bride simply refused to accompany him. He left her for another woman. Garson was always reluctant to discuss her first marriage.

In 1934, Garson, who had been touring the provinces in a production of George Bernard Shaw's *Too True to be Good* and had already made her London debut in a production of Shakespeare's *The Tempest* in the open-air theater in Regent's Park, was required to have a throat operation after which she suddenly found it difficult to find acting jobs. While sitting in the University Women's club in London, she was approached by novelist-playwright *Sylvia Thompson, who was casting *Golden Arrow*. The play was to be directed by Laurence Olivier, who was also the star, and who, still less than 30 years old, was already one of the brightest figures in the British theater. Garson read the part (another American role) for Olivier, was given the job, and the two eventually became fast friends. In later years, many in Britain claimed to have "discovered" Greer Garson, but she always gave the credit to Sylvia Thompson and Laurence Olivier.

In less than three years (1934–37), Garson starred in eight popular plays: *Golden Arrow, Vintage Wine, Accent on Youth* (her first West End lead), *Butterfly on the Wheel, Pages from a Diary, The Visitor, Mademoiselle* (in which she was directed by Noel Coward), and *Old Music*. Though all of them were critical failures, she was always lauded and soon accounted one of the brightest young British actresses of the day. She also found time to appear in such classics as Shakespeare's *Twelfth Night* and Sheridan's *School for Scandal*. She was kept so busy that she virtually went from one play directly into another, so much so that during her days on the London stage she had only one two-week vacation. To the young working women who could afford only the cheapest seats in the highest galleries but were devoted theatergoers, she became known as "The Duchess of Garson" for her elegant manner, while to her peers in the theater she was known as "Ca-reer" Garson because of her ambition and drive. Swept up into the whirl of London theatrical society, she and her mother took a handsome flat in Mayfair, and, when not on the stage, she was soon hobnobbing, not only with Coward, Olivier, and Thompson, but with such luminaries as director *Margaret Webster and famed dramatist George Bernard Shaw. A significant incident, often overlooked in articles about her career, is that Garson made her television debut in Shaw's "How He Lied to Her Husband" for the BBC during the earliest years of British television.

One night in 1937, American film producer Louis B. Mayer was visiting London and saw

Greer
Garson

Garson on stage in the trivial costume melodrama *Old Music*. That evening, he invited her to dine with him after the show at the Savoy Grill. Though Garson brought her mother along as chaperon, Mayer was sufficiently impressed to give her a screen test the following day, after which she was handed a contract at $500 per week (said to have been at Garson's insistence and to have been the highest salary ever paid to a newcomer). She was told to appear at the MGM Studios in Culver City, California, as soon as she could extricate herself from the play. Mayer had eyes for other actresses as well, however, and on this trip to Europe he also acquired for his studio both the Hungarian blond *Ilona Massey, and the Austrian beauty *Hedy Lamarr.

For almost a year after arriving in Hollywood with her mother, Garson was paid to sit and wait while the studio decided how to use her. Altogether, she was allowed on the MGM lot only seven times and only for tests for films that were never made. Fed up with lounging around the five-room house that she had taken in Beverly Hills, she was about to return to London when she was handed the small but pivotal role of Kathy, the devoted wife who dies in childbirth, in the film *Goodbye Mr. Chips.* The film was made on location in England, the studio paying for her round-trip fare on an ocean liner. In effect, she had traveled 12,000 miles to make a film in what was virtually her native land. Produced in 1939, the year often celebrated as the most fruitful in Hollywood history, the film was a great success, even when measured against its competition: *Gone With the Wind, Destry Rides Again, Mr. Deeds Goes to Washington, The Wizard of Oz, The Women,* and *Stagecoach.* Garson was nominated for an Oscar for her performance and suddenly found herself an international star.

To be an actress, you need the sensitivity of a new-born mouse, plus the hide of a rhinoceros, coupled with a highly developed desire to please, and an ability to accept criticism without wailing. The paradoxes are endless.

—Greer Garson, 1945

Arriving in Hollywood about the time that *Norma Shearer retired and *Greta Garbo simply stopped making films, Greer Garson, with her cool, red-headed beauty and regal poise, was just the type needed to step into their elegant shoes. Emanating class and warmth, Garson appealed to both men and women and, in short order, became one of the leading members of what was called the MGM Stock company. She was cast opposite MGM's most glamorous leading men (Robert Taylor, Clark Gable), was directed by the best talent on the studio's lot (LeRoy, Cukor, Wyler, Negulesco), and was one of the ten most important box-office attractions of the 1940s.

Greer Garson's second film was a trivial comedy, *Remember?* (1939), co-starring the popular romantic leads Lew Ayres and Robert Tay-

lor, into which she was thrown by Louis Mayer to keep her in the public eye while he searched for a better vehicle to display her talents. He chose the role of Elizabeth Bennett in a gracious film version of *Jane Austen's *Pride and Prejudice* (1940). In this film, she was co-starred with her old chum Laurence Olivier, also newly brought to Hollywood. *Pride and Prejudice* was followed by *Blossoms in the Dust* (1941), the first of eight films in which Garson co-starred with Walter Pidgeon (1897-1984), and the film that earned her a second Oscar nomination as Best Actress. In *Blossoms,* the first to display the fullness of her beauty in technicolor, Garson played in a romanticized version of the life story of *Edna Gladney, a pioneer in the struggle for humane treatment of illegitimate children, and it was in this part that she began to elaborate on the role that she had first played in *Goodbye Mr. Chips,* and which she was to make her own: the noble, courageous, self-sacrificing heroine, or as she called them, "walking cathedrals."

In her next film, *When Ladies Meet* (1941), Garson appeared in a talky tract on women's rights that brought no luster either to her career or that of her co-star *Joan Crawford, but this was immediately followed by the title role in *Mrs. Miniver* (1942), certainly her best film and the one that would establish her reputation as one of the great Hollywood stars. Many stories still revolve around this particular film. Norma Shearer, for example, had turned down the part, unwilling to portray the mother of a grown son, while Garson was leery about the role for the same reason. Once in the film, however, Garson fell in love with Richard Ney, the very actor who played her son and who, at 26, was 14 years younger than herself. Though Mayer reluctantly accepted the relationship, he talked the couple into delaying their marriage until after the film was released lest the "incestuous" implications caused by their roles bring negative publicity for them and the movie. Only those who can remember how *Jennifer Jones damaged her career by portraying a trollop in *Duel in the Sun* after having just played the Catholic saint *Bernadette of Lourdes in *The Song of Bernadette* can appreciate the genuine risk run by an actor who violated the public's belief in his or her studio-built image during Hollywood's Golden Age.

Greer Garson received her third nomination and won an Oscar for Best Actress for *Mrs. Miniver,* for a performance that, incidentally, is said to have done an enormous amount to strengthen American support for the British cause in World War II. At the Academy Awards ceremony, however, she violated an unwritten rule of brevity by making a thank-you speech that lasted for five and a quarter minutes, later exaggerated to 45 minutes, an elaboration that has gained surprising currency.

Thereafter, Garson played in one variation of her standard Mrs. Miniver role after another, with little opportunity to display her natural vivacity or gift for serious drama. Whereas she might have been a British *Irene Dunne, she never really had the opportunity to become herself on the screen. In *Madame Curie* (1943), which *Time Magazine* called a "soberly, splendid, scientific romance," Garson played *Marie Curie opposite Walter Pidgeon and was nominated for her fourth Best Actress award; in *Mrs. Parkington* (1944), she was nominated for her fifth, playing the wife of Walter Pidgeon, a man who had earned his riches through sculduggery. Her sixth nomination was for her performance in *Marcia Davenport's *Valley of Decision* (1945), as an Irish servant girl, secretly in love with her employer, a Pittsburgh industrialist (Gregory Peck). At the height of her career after *Mrs. Park-*

ington, Garson was offered her second seven-year contract by MGM at very favorable terms.

In 1946, the enormously popular Clark Gable returned from wartime military duty to resume his movie career. Someone in the studio's publicity department dreamed up the crude but memorable slogan "Gable's back and Garson's got 'im," but the film, *Adventure*, in which Garson attempted to vary her role, was not a success, and she reverted to type for *Desire Me* (1947).

After this film, Garson's four-year marriage to Richard Ney came to an amicable end. No community property was claimed and no alimony was requested by either party. Garson then resumed her career with *Julia Misbehaves* (1948), a film which was stolen by a 16-year-old *Elizabeth Taylor, and then appeared with Pidgeon, Errol Flynn, and Robert Young in *That Forsyte Woman* (1949), a film version of John Galsworthy's novel *The Forsyte Saga*, the change of title said to have been due to studio executives who decided that the public would not know what 'saga' meant.

From the movie Mrs. Miniver, starring Greer Garson and Walter Pidgeon, 1942.

At this time, Garson married her third husband, Elijah E. "Buddy" Fogelson, a Texas oil millionaire, with whom she remained for the rest of his life. Married on July 15, 1949, she became an American citizen in Abilene, Texas, less than two years later. Thereafter, although she continued her career, her main interests lay elsewhere, and, while she maintained a lavish home in the Bel Air section of Los Angeles, she also luxuriated in a penthouse apartment in Dallas, her husband's ranch in New Mexico, an apartment in New York City, and another home in Palm Beach.

Garson's next film, *The Miniver Story* (1950), an ill-advised attempt to make a sequel to the original *Miniver,* was followed by an undistinguished remake of *The Last of Mrs. Cheney* retitled *The Law and the Lady* (1951). She followed that with a brief but significant appearance in a famed film version of Shakespeare's *Julius Caesar* (1953). Although Shakespeare did not create a significant female role for this play, *Julius Caesar* does contain a single scene between Julius Caesar and his wife *Calpurnia, the part that Garson requested. In this almost cameo appearance, she added the precise touch of dignity and "class" appropriate and necessary to the filming of a Shakespearean tragedy.

Garson's next few films were the easily forgettable *Scandal at Scourie* (1953), her eighth and final film with Walter Pidgeon; *Her Twelve Men* (1954), a comedy; and *Strange Lady in Town* (1955), an undistinguished western made at Warner Bros., but she bounced back with Warner's film version of the successful Broadway play *Sunrise at Campobello* (1960), dealing with the crisis in the life of Franklin D. Roosevelt, when he was suddenly struck down with polio at age 38. Garson played *Eleanor Roosevelt for which she received her seventh and final Academy Award nomination for Best Actress.

After a purposeless cameo in the quickly forgotten *Pepe* (Columbia, 1960), Garson waited five years before she undertook her next role, that of a mother superior in *The Singing Nun* (MGM, 1966). Her last screen appearance in *The Happiest Millionaire* (1967) was an undistinguished conclusion to what had been, at least in its earliest years, a most distinguished film career.

Garson continued to keep herself busy, leading a triple life as an actress, a winter resident of Dallas participating fully in its social and cultural life, and a summer vacationer at her husband's huge Pecos, New Mexico, cattle ranch. She had appeared on numerous radio programs in the 1940s and later on television in such plays as

"Reunion in Vienna" ("Producer's Showcase," 1955) and "The Little Foxes" (1956). She portrayed *Mary Ann Disraeli opposite Trevor Howard in *The Remarkable Mr. Disraeli* (1963) and made guest appearances as herself on the series "Father Knows Best" and "Laugh In." She also appeared in episodes of "Love Boat" and in 1971 undertook her last regular role, that of a woman lawyer in the series "Men From Shiloh," after which she appeared in "Crown Matrimonial" (1974). In 1978, Garson was seen in the series "Little Women," her last role as an actress. While none of these television appearances added any luster to her reputation, they did at least give Garson an opportunity to break out of her mold somewhat. In "Career," for example (NBC, February 24, 1956), she played a selfish movie star who adopts a child to polish her public image. Similarly, in "The Glorious Gift of Molly Malloy," she played an Irish schoolteacher whose educational methods upset the local authorities.

In 1958, Garson returned to the stage for the first and only time in over 20 years, taking over the lead in *Mame* from *Rosalind Russell and enjoying a huge success for eight months in New York. Ten years later, she appeared in Los Angeles as Lady Cicely Waynflete in The Center Theater Group's production of Shaw's *Captain Brassbound's Conversion,* a comedy that the Irish playwright had written for *Ellen Terry decades before. In July 1978, she added the role of producer to her many other activities, when she and Arthur Cantor brought Alec McCowen's solo performance in *The Gospel of Saint Mark* from London to New York.

In her private life, Greer Garson was lively, talkative, energetic, and optimistic. She took readily to life in the United States and was especially fond of New York. Extremely photogenic, she had green eyes, luxurious orange-red hair, and a flawless, bone-white complexion. Her voice, warm and rich, was only slightly accented and her diction was perfect. Devoted to the memory of Louis B. Mayer, to whom she was always grateful, she never blamed him for the narrow path that he had set her on and actively supported the Louis B. Mayer Foundation as one of her many charities. As late as the 1970s, she was still regularly offered opportunities to return to the screen but as these were usually for parts in horror films, she graciously but firmly refused them all. With no suitable roles available, she was content in her retirement. In later years, Garson and her husband took to raising horses on their land, and in 1972 they won the Eclipse Award as owners of Ack Ack, named Horse of the Year, a thoroughbred that they had purchased for $500,000. Rising oil prices had made the Fogelsons billionaires, and Garson had ample funds with which to support her numerous charities, among them Southern Methodist University in Dallas to which she gave $10 million to build The Greer Garson Theater and Film Archive.

Not everything in the life of Greer Garson went well. An early injury to her spine plagued her throughout her life, her first two marriages had been failures, her penthouse was robbed of $100,000 worth of jewelry in 1974, and one night, in the late 1980s, she was forced to look helplessly at a television newscast of her Bel Air home going up in flames. She not only lost all her personal belongings but her Oscar, which the Academy of Motion Picture Arts and Sciences graciously replaced. Her health, never especially good, also deteriorated in her later years. She suffered through an emergency appendectomy and in 1980 had to be fitted with a pacemaker.

In 1984, Greer Garson was named an honorary Commander of the Order of the British Empire, a full knighthood, which would have entitled her to be known as "Dame" Greer Garson had she not given up her status as a British subject. Usually, such awards were bestowed by Queen **Elizabeth II** at Buckingham Palace but, at 84, Garson's health was too precarious for her to attend in person. At the awards ceremony, however, she was cited for her work in the areas of environmental protection, wildlife conservation, the protection of antiquities and for her numerous endowments to several institutions of higher education both in the U.S. and Great Britain.

Buddy Fogelson died in 1987, and by 1990 Greer Garson had resettled in Los Angeles, but she was living in Texas when her last illness struck, and she died at Dallas Presbyterian Hospital of heart failure on April 6, 1996, at the age of 92.

SOURCES:

The Free Library of Philadelphia, Theater Collection.

Parish, James Robert, and Ronald L. Bowers. *The MGM Stock Company: The Golden Era.* New Rochelle, NY: Arlington House, 1973.

SUGGESTED READING:

Luft, H.G. "Greer Garson," in *Films in Review.* March 1961.

Troyan, Michael. *A Rose for Mrs. Miniver: The Life of Greer Garson.* University of Kentucky Press, 1998.

Wald, Malvin. "Greer Garson: Blue Ribbon Winner," in Daniel Peary, ed., *Close-Ups: The Movie Star Book.* NY: 1978.

Robert H. Hewsen,
Professor of History,
Rowan University, Glassboro, New Jersey

Garvey, Amy Jacques (1896–1973)

African-American nationalist. Born Amy Jacques in Jamaica, West Indies, in 1896; died in Jamaica in 1973; married Marcus Garvey (1887–1940, black nationalist and founder of the United Negro Improvement Association), in 1922; children: Marcus M. Garvey, Jr.; Julius Garvey.

Born in 1896 in Jamaica, West Indies, and influenced by her father who made her read the dictionary and foreign-language newspapers as a child, activist Amy Jacques came to the United States in 1917. In 1922, she became the second wife of Jamaican pan-Africanist Marcus Garvey, founder of the United Negro Improvement Association (UNIA) and advocate of the "Back to Africa" movement, whose first wife, from 1919 to 1922, was **Amy Ashwood.** Working alongside her husband, Amy Jacques Garvey became an activist in her own right. While Marcus was imprisoned for two years for treason (he was later pardoned), she worked to keep his message

Amy Jacques Garvey

alive, raising money for his defense and publishing the first two volumes of *Philosophy and Opinions of Marcus Garvey* (1923). From 1924 to 1927, she served as the associate editor of the UNIA newspaper *Negro World* and, as such, introduced a page called "Our Women and What They Think." In her own editorials, she expressed strong feminist views, encouraging black women to overcome male tyranny and demand their own positions of power in the Universal Negro Improvement Association.

When Marcus was deported in 1927, Amy toured England, France, and Germany with him, while continuing to write for *Negro World*. In 1934, when political pressure caused him to move to London, she stayed in Jamaica with their two young sons. After her husband's death in 1940, she continued to work for black nationalism, becoming a contributing editor to the journal *African* and founding the African Study Circle of the World in the late 1940s. She also wrote a biography, *Garvey and Garveyism* (1963), and published a book of articles (1966) before her death in Jamaica in 1973.

SUGGESTED READING:

Garvey, Amy Jacques. *Garvey and Garveyism*. Collier, 1970.

Garzoni, Giovanna (1600–1670)

Italian painter, best known for her studies of flowers, plants, and animals. Probably born in Ascoli Piceno, Italy, in 1600; died in Rome, Italy, in February 1670; never married; no children.

Selected works: Dish of Broad Beans *(tempera on parchment, Palazzo Pitti, Florence);* Dish of Grapes with Pears and a Snail *(tempera on parchment, Palazzo Pitti, Florence);* Still Life with Birds and Fruit *(watercolor on Parchment, c. 1640, The Cleveland Museum of Art).*

Much that is known about the life of 17th-century artist Giovanna Garzoni can be called into question, beginning with her place of birth which was probably Ascoli Piceno, although a Medici inventory cites it as Lucca. An oil painting, *Holy Family*, executed when she was 16, was still in Ascoli in 1830, suggesting that she began painting in her hometown. In 1625, she was in Venice, where she painted a miniature portrait of a young man. Her correspondence and other documents reveal that she subsequently worked in Florence, Naples, and Rome. Her patrons included the Medici, as well as other Italian and Spanish nobility. Garzoni reached the height of her popularity in Florence where she lived for some time and was evidently able to sell her work for top prices. She became quite wealthy and settled in Rome around 1654, where she contributed to one of the annual feasts of the Accademia di San Luca, of which Garzoni was probably made a member as early as 1633. She died in February 1670, leaving her possessions to the academy on the condition that they erect a monument to her in their church, which they eventually did in 1698.

Garzoni is best known for her studies of flowers, plants, and animals which are a blend of still-life and scientific drawing, and these include some of the finest botanical studies made in the 17th century. The largest grouping of her work is in the Palazzo Pitti in Florence. An album of 22 studies of insects, flowers, and fruits was bequeathed to the Accademia di San Luca, though **Germaine Greer** was unable to trace the album for her book *The Obstacle Race*. Four studies by Garzoni are in Madrid, and one of fruit and birds is in Cleveland.

Many of her paintings, such as *Dish of Broad Beans*, are simple in composition, usually consisting of one type of plant set on a dish or arranged in a vase, to which is added a contrasting species to complement or contrast textures and shapes. "Faint contour lines are filled in with color laid on in tiny parallel strokes or in stippled strokes that give many of her surfaces a characteristic speckled appearance like that of a bird's egg," note **Ann Sutherland Harris** and **Linda Nochlin**. "Her drawing is assured and her arrangement of the fruits and flowers sophisticated and far more complex than appear at first sight. She creates a feeling of concentrated mass that differentiates her work from that of predecessors like Ligozzi and Balthasar van der Ast."

A watercolor on parchment called *Still Life with Birds and Fruit* was one of four octagonal pictures attributed to Garzoni in 1964 by **Mina Gregori**, and this work displays the artist's skill at drawing birds as well as plants. Although Gregori was instrumental in helping to bring to light Garzoni's contributions to 17th-century art, the full extent of this artist's achievements has yet to be determined.

SOURCES:

Greer, Germaine. *The Obstacle Race*. NY: Farrar, Straus and Giroux, 1979.

Harris, Ann Sutherland, and Linda Nochlin. *Women Artists, 1550–1950*. LA County Museum of Art: Knopf, 1976.

Barbara Morgan,
Melrose, Massachusetts

Gaskell, Elizabeth (1810–1865)

Popular and critically acclaimed English writer of the Victorian period who wrote six novels, the authorized biography of Charlotte Brontë, several nouvelles, some 30 short stories, and numerous sketches. Name variations: Mrs. Gaskell; Lily; Cotton Mather Mills (early pseudonym). Pronunciation: GAS-kull. Born Elizabeth Cleghorn Stevenson on September 29, 1810, at Chelsea, London, England; died on November 16, 1865, at Alton in Hampshire; daughter of William Stevenson (a Unitarian minister, farmer, writer, teacher, keeper of the records of the Treasury) and Elizabeth (Holland) Stevenson; attended school at Barford and Stratford-upon-Avon; married William Gaskell (a Unitarian minister), in 1832; children: daughter (stillborn, 1833); Marianne Gaskell (b. 1834); Margaret Emily Gaskell (b. 1837); Florence Elizabeth Gaskell (b. 1842); William (1844–1845); Julia Bradford Gaskell (b. 1846).

Spent her childhood among deceased mother's family in Knutsford, Cheshire; spent five years at boarding school in her teens, then visited family and friends in London, Newcastle, Edinburgh, and Manchester until marrying at age 22 and settling permanently in Manchester; worked with her husband on philanthropic and educational projects among Manchester's working class in the early years of marriage, during which she gave birth to six children; began writing for publication (1845) after the death of her son; published Mary Barton, *her first novel (1848); met Charlotte Brontë, subject of her biography (1850); was a popular and successful writer (1850s–60s) while maintaining a strong family life, cultivating extensive social and professional relationships, enjoying foreign travel, and continuing her philanthropic activities among the poor; died at a new country retreat she had purchased for her and her husband's retirement (1865).*

Selected writings: (novel) Mary Barton: A Tale of Manchester Life *(1848);* (novel) Cranford *(1853);* (novel) Ruth *(1853);* (novel) North and South *(1855);* (biography) The Life of Charlotte Brontë *(1857);* (novel) Sylvia's Lovers *(1863);* (nouvelle) Cousin Phillis: A Tale *(1864);* (novel) Wives and Daughters: An Every-day Story *(serialized in the* Cornhill Magazine, *1864–66).*

Family relationships are at the center of Elizabeth Gaskell's writing; their permutations—for better or worse—shape the comedy, tragedy, pathos, and romance of her novels and stories, just as they inform the sympathetic reading she gives her subject in her distinguished biography of *Charlotte Brontë. Gaskell's preoccupation with the intricate and delicate nature of family ties—or the lack of them—can be traced to her own childhood.

Elizabeth Gaskell

Her father William Stevenson, from a naval family, became a Unitarian preacher. He left the ministry shortly before his marriage because he developed scruples about receiving payment for preaching the word of God. Her mother **Elizabeth Holland Stevenson**, whose family had its roots in rural Cheshire, was also Unitarian, a sect regarded at the time as the most unorthodox, and in some quarters, the most radical and dangerous of dissenting religious groups. The sense of community among Unitarians whenever and wherever they met, and the value they placed on education, tolerance, rationality, and humanitarianism, would have a lasting influence on Elizabeth's life.

After abandoning the ministry, William Stevenson was by turns a teacher, farmer, editor, and writer until he gained an appointment as keeper of the records of the Treasury, a post that finally guaranteed him the income to support a family. While he was finding his bearings, his wife gave birth to eight children, of whom only the first-born, John, and the last, Elizabeth, survived. Elizabeth Holland Stevenson died 13 months after her daughter's birth.

After the death of her mother, Elizabeth was sent, in what seemed at the time the best arrangement for the year-old child, to live with her maternal aunt, **Hannah Holland Lumb**, whom she later described as her "more than mother," in the small country town of Knutsford in Cheshire. Although her father married again when she was four, Elizabeth was not invited to return to his home in London, and she described her infrequent visits with her father, stepmother, and their two children as "very, very unhappy." Among her mother's relatives, however, she enjoyed a childhood in which the love of an extended family—Aunt Lumb and her daughter, her uncle Peter Holland, aunts, cousins, and maternal grandparents who lived not far from town—nourished a warm and impressionable nature. From the 12 years she spent in Knutsford, Gaskell gained a deep and lasting love of nature that finds expression even in those works of hers dealing almost entirely with urban themes and settings.

While it does not seem that her father, occupied by his second family, visited her in Knutsford, her brother John, 12 years her senior, did. Following the naval tradition of his father's family, John hoped for a career in the Royal Navy but, gaining no entree there, joined the Merchant Navy with the East India Company's fleet. Through letters and his visits, the brother and sister developed strong bonds of affection, and John was the first to encourage Elizabeth's gift for writing. He asked her to keep a journal so that she would have plenty to report to him in her letters. This warm and intimate relationship ended tragically when he was lost on a voyage to India around 1828. Elizabeth felt this loss deeply; she later transformed it imaginatively in several of her works that involve the return of a character who has been lost and presumed dead.

In 1822, Gaskell was sent to the Miss Byerleys' school, located at Barford and later at Stratford-upon-Avon, a boarding school where she received a good education for a woman of her day, in keeping with the liberal Unitarian tradition that offered women educational opportunities comparable in quality to those given men. At a time when most boarding schools prepared middle-class young women for marriage by emphasizing domestic and ornamental arts, Miss Byerleys' Avonbank School encouraged the development of Elizabeth's intellectual abilities and imagination with its emphasis on modern subjects: literature, history, and modern languages. She left school in 1827, shortly before her 17th birthday, and went with her Holland relatives for a six-week holiday in Wales, where the romantic wildness and grandeur of the Welsh mountains and sea provided a complementary dimension to the love of nature she had developed in the quiet and gently rolling rural landscapes of Knutsford and Stratford. Gaskell went to London at the end of 1828 or early 1829 to comfort her father when she learned of her brother's loss and was with him when he suffered a stroke and died in March 1829. Now motherless, fatherless, brotherless, she felt her lack of immediate family keenly, even though she knew she would always have a home at Knutsford. To her father's second family, she felt no strong connections; she did not see her stepmother and stepsister again for 25 years.

Elizabeth spent the winter of 1829–30 in Newcastle with **Anne Turner** and her father Reverend William Turner, a widowed Unitarian minister and schoolmaster related by his first marriage to Elizabeth's mother. In 1831, with Anne, Elizabeth visited Edinburgh and Manchester, where Anne's sister lived with her husband, the Unitarian minister of the Cross Street chapel, to whom William Gaskell was assistant minister. The dedicated and scholarly Mr. Gaskell, the city of Manchester, and the Unitarian tradition would shape the next 33 years of maturity for the motherless child of Knutsford and the bereaved young woman of London by giving her the three things that meant most to her: a family of her own, a sense of useful work in service to others, and a vocation as a writer.

When she married William Gaskell in 1832, Elizabeth Stevenson committed herself to the religious and philanthropic principles of the Unitarian community of family and friends she had known all her life. But these principles were to find their practice in Manchester of the 1830s, a prototypical north of England city created by the Industrial Revolution. In 1832, Manchester was a city with an economy based on cotton mills and calico-printers' works. Attracted by the work and wages offered by the rapidly growing cotton industry, the population had grown in 40 years from approximately 40,000 to over a quarter of a million. The cotton workers were housed in the center of the city in cheap, quickly constructed, back-to-back terrace houses and courts, which, because of lack of planning, overcrowding, and unsanitary conditions, rapidly degenerated into the worst urban slums in England. Although like most of the middle-class inhabitants of Manchester, the Gaskells lived on the edge of the city in a relatively rural setting, the social work they engaged in through the Cross Street Chapel brought both—unlike others of their class who never crossed the smoke barrier that separated the factories, warehouses, and working-class districts from their homes—into close contact with the conditions of physical, spiritual, and moral decay that were by-products of the "progress" of the Industrial Revolution. In her fourth novel, *North and South*, Elizabeth Gaskell describes from the perspective of her heroine Margaret Hale what may very well have been her own first impression of Manchester:

> They saw a deep lead-coloured cloud hanging over the horizon in the direction in which [the city] lay. It was all the darker from the contrast with the pale grey-blue of the wintry sky . . . . Nearer to the town, the air had a faint taste and smell of smoke. . . . Quickly

they were hurled over long, straight, hopeless streets of regularly-built houses, all small and of brick. Here and there a great oblong many-windowed factory stood up, like a hen among her chickens, puffing out black "unparliamentary" smoke, and sufficiently accounting for the cloud.

Into this paradoxical city of new wealth and poverty, the promise of progress and the evidence of deterioration, Elizabeth brought the sympathy that had been nourished by her Knutsford years and the conscience and egalitarianism instilled by the Unitarian values with which she grew up. In the early years of her marriage, she joined her husband in his work with Sunday schools and evening classes. In a letter written in 1836 she reports completing "compositions" on Wordsworth, Byron, Crabbe, Dryden, and Pope for a series of lectures William delivered at the evening school of the Mechanics' Institute for Working-Class Men. Throughout her life in Manchester, she engaged in social work, visiting prisons and factories; helping young women who had been seduced and abandoned to find new lives abroad; and teaching classes for the poor in her home. **Coral Lansbury** reports, "For her the slums were never a strange and alien world to be seen from afar, but familiar places of dismal wretchedness where she could see and smell poverty."

While her sympathy and energy were engaged in efforts to ameliorate the harsh conditions of working-class life in Manchester, she also suffered personally when her first child was stillborn in 1833. Her loss and subsequent depression caused anxiety about her next child, **Marianne Gaskell**, born in 1834, and she dealt with her feelings by keeping a journal, ostensibly to record her daughter's development, but apparently also to alleviate her fear and give expression to her own inner life. A second daughter, **Margaret Emily Gaskell**, called Meta, was born in 1837. Elizabeth had hardly recovered her strength after this birth when she went to Knutsford with her month-old infant to nurse her Aunt Lumb through her final illness. In the period of depression that followed her aunt's death, Gaskell found solace and distraction in writing to her growing circle of correspondents and in helping William research and write another series of lectures on "The Poets and Poetry of Humble Life."

One of her correspondents was ***Mary Howitt**, an established writer who wrote articles for literary journals with her husband William Howitt. In 1838, the Howitts announced plans to publish a work on *Visits to Remarkable Places,* and Elizabeth wrote suggesting they do a piece on Clopton Hall at Stratford-upon-Avon and describing her own visit there as a schoolgirl. William Howitt included her description in his volume and urged her to consider writing for publication. But at this point in her life, Gaskell wrote for the personal satisfaction she received from keeping up her lively correspondence and her daughter's journal, or from her conviction that the writing she and William were doing for his lectures would have a salutary effect on the lives of the working class. **Winifred Gérin** suggests, however, that:

> though as yet unconsciously, Elizabeth was finding the subject of her own future work—work that would be distinct from her husband's educational programme for introducing beauty and poetry into the lives of the working poor. What Elizabeth was discovering in her as yet early contacts with the sad lives of the operatives . . . was that beauty and poetry were already there in their lives; this revelation stirred her profoundly.

The Gaskells' third daughter, **Florence Elizabeth Gaskell**, was born in 1842, and in 1844, they were delighted by the birth of their first son, William. Elizabeth doted on her son and was shocked and grieved by his sudden death of scarlet fever ten months after his birth. Fearing a depression similar to the one she had suffered following the death of her Aunt Lumb, and knowing that writing had the capacity to absorb her fully, William suggested that Elizabeth write a full-length book to distract her from her grief. And so, in 1845, she began writing *Mary Barton,* the novel that would make her famous.

A good writer of fiction must have lived an active and sympathetic life if she wishes her books to have strength and vitality in them.

—Elizabeth Gaskell

Mary Barton: A Tale of Manchester Life, which Elizabeth described as a "tragic poem," grew out of both her personal sorrow and the sympathy she felt for the sorrows of Manchester's working poor. Set during the commercial crisis that ushered in the depression of the "hungry forties" and the Chartist and Trade Union movements, the novel develops a theme that would occupy the best minds of England for the next decades—the theme of the "two nations": the separate worlds of the rich and the poor, of "masters and men," explored in the writings of Benjamin Disraeli, Thomas Carlyle, Charles Kingsley, Charlotte Brontë, Charles Dickens, and Matthew Arnold. The novel aroused controversy because Gaskell's sympathies were clearly with her hero, John Barton, a worker driven by hunger, injustice, and despair to murder a factory owner's son. She does not condone what Barton has done any more than he can forgive himself for his crime; nonetheless, through her skillful plotting of the events leading to the murder, her insightful development of Barton's character, and her vivid descriptions of life among the working poor, Gaskell shows how a decent, intelligent man can be led to commit desperate acts when forced to live under intolerable conditions.

The novel, published anonymously in 1848, was a great success, not only because of the timeliness of its theme, but because of the power of its story, its characters, and its vivid evocation of urban life. In a short time, it became widely known that "Mrs. Gaskell" was the author of *Mary Barton*, and, when she visited London in the spring of 1849, she was greeted by the literary establishment as a celebrity and entertained at social events where she met such writers as Thomas Carlyle, Samuel Rogers, and Charles Dickens, with whom she would have a long if somewhat stressful professional relationship.

For the rest of her life, writing was a vocation to Elizabeth Gaskell; she loved her work, and she was more than pleased with the payment she received for her writing. Although by law she was obliged to turn over her earnings to her husband (the Married Women's Property Act, which gave married women a right to retain their earnings, was not passed until 1870), William Gaskell apparently was not strict about insisting upon his legal rights, and Elizabeth was able to save enough of her income to purchase a retirement home for them both. Unlike Charlotte Brontë or George Eliot (*Mary Anne Evans), Gaskell did not depend on writing for a livelihood, and so her sense of professionalism developed gradually. Ever mindful of the gap in her life she felt as a child for want of the love of a mother, she took up her writing only after she took care of family responsibilities. According to Angus Easson, after her last child, Julia Bradford Gaskell, was born in 1846, Elizabeth wrote in the evenings, when all household and family duties were done, or on holiday, or during family absences—whenever she found the chance.

Nor did she lose interest in the social work that had become part of her life in Manchester. In fact, she made use of her introduction to Dickens by writing to him in 1850 to ask his advice in arranging for the emigration of a young dressmaker's apprentice who had been seduced, sent to the penitentiary, lured into prostitution, and seemed destined for the short, hopeless life of an urban Victorian prostitute unless she had an opportunity to begin her life anew. Knowing that Dickens was interested in helping such young women gain a start abroad, she applied for and received his assistance. The story of the young woman inspired the plot of her next novel, *Ruth*, published in 1853, which again stirred controversy because of the sympathy and understanding the author creates for the plight of the all-too-common "fallen woman" of the Victorian age. Clearly, some of Gaskell's Manchester neighbors who burned the book did not share her perspective. However, literary and religious leaders who came to the defense of the novel turned the tide in its favor by praising Gaskell's courage in her choice and treatment of a largely unacknowledged social problem.

In 1850, Dickens had invited Gaskell to contribute to his new weekly, *Household Words*. She accepted his invitation and sent "Lizzie Leigh," a story based on Manchester life, for the first issue. Dickens was pleased with the piece, and thereafter pressed her to continue her contributions to his journal. Because of her other obligations, the pieces did not come as quickly and as often as Dickens would have liked; nonetheless, both he and his readers were delighted by the series of sketches she sent him from 1851 to 1853, the series that would become perhaps her most loved book, *Cranford*.

Cranford strikes an entirely different note than *Mary Barton* and *Ruth*. In place of the urban settings and pressing social problems of the earlier novels, *Cranford* reverts to the rural setting and slower pace of life in an early 19th-century village based on Gaskell's memories of Knutsford. The tragic tone of *Mary Barton* and the pathos of *Ruth* are replaced by quiet humor and gentle satire as Gaskell lovingly describes her "society of Amazons," the eccentric aging women who govern the village. They practice "elegant economy" and "friendly sociability" as they band together to protect one another and their way of life against all that threatens to invade their fragile world of declining fortunes and powers.

Because of *Cranford*'s great success in *Household Words*, Dickens was eager to secure a commitment from Gaskell for another work, and she agreed, with some hesitation, to the serialization of a novel still in the conceptual stage, a novel that was to contrast the landscapes, values, and social customs of the agricultural south of England with the industrial north. In *North and South*, Gaskell returns to the "masters and men" theme of *Mary Barton* in the central issue of the strike that pits workers against factory owners, but she sets this conflict in the larger social context developed through the two families who constitute her cast of major characters: the Hales, who move to Milton-Northern (Manchester) from the southern village of Helstone in search of a livelihood after Mr. Hale leaves his ministry because of "scruples"; and the Thorntons, a family made newly wealthy by the expanding industrial economy of the north. As Margaret Hale and John Thornton overcome their pride and prejudice in the love plot of the novel, Gaskell suggests that a similar honest attempt at understanding and communication between masters and men can lead to a reconciliation of class conflicts. In a letter to Dickens, Gaskell conceded after its completion that *North and South* was not the book she had hoped it would be; as she told him, "I meant it to have been so much better." Both her disappointment and Dickens' impatience with her during the serialization can be attributed to the fact that the pressures and conventions of weekly serial publication were not congenial to her temperament or talent.

The stress she experienced in writing the installments of *North and South* did not make her eager to take on another major writing project until 1855, when she was shocked to learn of the death of Charlotte Brontë as a result of complications of pregnancy less than a year after her marriage to Reverend Arthur Bell Nicholls. Elizabeth Gaskell and Charlotte Brontë had become fast friends and professional colleagues since their first meeting in 1850. Anticipating that Reverend Patrick Brontë, Charlotte's father, would object to a biography, Gaskell considered writing a memoir, not to be published for some time, in which she would record personal recollections of her friend still fresh in her memory. She was therefore surprised when Patrick Brontë proposed, with Nicholls' consent, that she write the authorized biography. Her motive in writing the *Life of Charlotte Brontë* was "to make the world . . . honour the woman as much as they have admired the writer," and she undertook her task in a spirit of friendship and professionalism that made it both an intimate portrait of an enigmatic woman and a compelling psychological study of the sources of Brontë's creative power. Gaskell's interpretation of Brontë in the context of the desolate Yorkshire landscape and her tragic family situation came naturally to a novelist whose works had always emphasized environment and family as the shaping forces of character. Although new information has come

to light since it was written, the *Life* remains a standard work on Brontë. According to Lansbury, it "has been acclaimed as the best biography of the nineteenth century and one of the finest in the English language."

Following the publication of the *Life* in 1857, Gaskell was occupied with the concerns of her maturing daughters and with relief work associated with the Manchester Cotton Famine of 1862–63. She published pieces from time to time in *Household Words* and in the new *Cornhill Magazine* while she worked on *Sylvia's Lovers,* a historical novel set in a Yorkshire fishing village during the Napoleonic wars, when men from English coastal villages had been kidnapped and pressed into service in the navy. In the tale of a harpooner who disappears and returns years later to find his love married to a rival, Gaskell develops a tragic plot set among the humble classes of the harsh Yorkshire coast. As in *Mary Barton* and *North and South,* she interweaves a public theme, in this case the tyranny of impressment and the evil it generates, with a love story. But whereas love served the theme of reconciliation in the earlier novels, *Sylvia's Lovers* explores the tragic aspects of passionate love, jealousy, and enthrallment. Through the vividly realized setting, the historical distancing, and the depiction of characters caught in conflict between love and morality, the novel becomes mythic in its evocation of powers beyond human control shaping human destiny.

Most critics agree that the works of Gaskell's final years, *Cousin Phillis* in 1864 and the unfinished *Wives and Daughters,* published in the *Cornhill Magazine* from 1864 to 1866, mark Gaskell's greatest achievement as an artist. Both works return to the village settings of her childhood, and each in its way is a perfect representation of a mood or tone over which she had gained mastery. *Cousin Phillis,* an idyllic nouvelle, captures a young woman and a family at a moment of transition between an agrarian way of life with its sense of rootedness in time and tradition and an industrial age in which people move optimistically toward a future with little time for backward glances. Through the story of Phillis, left behind in her old-world village by the young railroad engineer who seeks his fortunes in the new world, Gaskell creates a subtle mood that verges on both tragedy and nostalgia but avoids either as she brings her readers to full awareness of the irrevocable loss of the past and its innocence.

Wives and Daughters, Gaskell's novel of "everyday" life, reflects the full range of Gaskell's experiences and reflections on the nature of family relationships in the story of Molly Gibson's development through her motherless childhood, her beloved father's remarriage to a frivolous widow, her relationship with a stepsister whose vanity and thoughtlessness are faults of her upbringing, to her realization of the value of personal worth, love, and tolerance. Reminiscent of *Jane Austen in its treatment of three or four families in a country village, the open and leisurely plot of a young woman's coming of age allows for the full display of Gaskell's mature talents.

Elizabeth Gaskell died in 1865, while staying with three of her daughters at the country home she had recently purchased with earnings from her writing as a surprise for her husband for their retirement. Her sudden death came at a moment of fullness. She had lived to see her daughters grown and happy and her husband busy but content with his work; she had traveled throughout Europe and made enduring friendships with people she loved and admired; she was loved and respected by the working people of Manchester, whose lives she had touched personally and chronicled sympathetically; and she was esteemed as a writer who belonged in the distinguished company of Charles Dickens, George Eliot, and Charlotte Brontë in making the 19th century the great period of the English novel.

SOURCES:

Easson, Angus. *Elizabeth Gaskell.* London: Routledge & Kegan Paul, 1980.

Gérin, Winifred. *Elizabeth Gaskell.* Oxford: Clarendon Press, 1976.

Hopkins, A.B. *Elizabeth Gaskell: Her Life and Work.* London: John Lehman, 1952.

Lansbury, Coral. *Elizabeth Gaskell.* Boston, MA: Twayne, 1984.

The Letters of Mrs. Gaskell. Ed. by J.A.V. Chapple and A. Pollard. Manchester: Manchester University Press, 1966.

SUGGESTED READING:

The Complete Works of Elizabeth Cleghorn Gaskell. Knutsford Edition. Ed. by A.W. Ward. 8 vols. London: Smith, Elder, 1906.

Stoneman, Patsy. *Elizabeth Gaskell.* IN: Indiana University Press, 1987.

Uglow, Jenny. *Elizabeth Gaskell: A Habit of Stories.* NY: Farrar, Straus, 1993.

Patricia B. Heaman,
Professor of English, Wilkes University,
Wilkes-Barre, Pennsylvania

Gasteazoro, Ana (1950–1993)

Political activist in El Salvador during the late 1970s and early '80s, the most violent period of a 12-year "dirty war" waged by the Salvadoran military against the population. Pronunciation: Gas-tee-a-zoro. *Born Ana Margarita Gasteazoro Escolande on October 10, 1950, in San Salvador, El Salvador, Central America; died in San Salvador of breast cancer on January 30, 1993; daughter of Ana Marina Escolande (an antique dealer) and José Agustin Gasteazoro Mejia (a civil engineer); attended primary through high school at the American School in San Salvador; studied briefly at Bay State Junior College in Massachusetts and University of Central America in El Salvador; never married; no children.*

"Tell Mother I'm in paradise," Ana Gasteazoro said to the woman at the Ilopango women's prison receiving desk who asked her if she wanted to send a message to anyone. It was May 11, 1981, and she had just endured 11 days in a clandestine jail of the Salvadoran National Police. After spending three days blindfolded and tied to a bare metal cot, she had been brutally interrogated, repeatedly beaten, threatened with death, and groped by the guard who brought her food. Ana fully expected to die, as had so many of her friends at the hands of the paramilitary death squads in the past two years. Someone would "disappear" suddenly, just as Gasteazoro had disappeared, and a mutilated body would be found a few days later along a country roadside or in a city garbage dump.

Tied to the cot in her crude cell, Ana had listened to the screams of those being tortured in nearby cells. She had been told that no one knew where she was or had inquired after her. She had been told again and again that she was going to die. Finally, after a particularly terrifying beating, she had signed a false confession of terrorist activity.

Now, safely installed at the women's prison, having survived the horror of the "death squad" jail, Gasteazoro knew that she would live, that the most dangerous time was over. So the message she sent to her mother was optimistic. Though she was bruised, sore, and traumatized, the past 11 days had not broken her resolve. If the government saw fit to throw her in prison without a trial or due process, so be it. She would make Ilopango her trench from which to continue the war. As she would soon find out, the other female political prisoners had begun to plan a remarkable campaign of resistance in which Gasteazoro would become a key player for the next two years.

In 1981, El Salvador was still in the early years of a bloody civil war which, before it ended in 1992, would result in 75,000 deaths and over one million refugees. The smallest country in Central America, El Salvador is about the size of

Massachusetts. The causes of its civil war were not hard to understand. At the time Gasteazoro was imprisoned, 40% of the country's five million people were landless, while 2,000 large landowners held over 80% of the usable land. The majority of El Salvador's wealth was held by an oligarchy known as *los Catorce*, 14 families who had built cattle and coffee empires in the 19th century, while over half the population remained illiterate and with a daily caloric intake that was the lowest in Latin America.

By the 1970s, all avenues for peaceful change in El Salvador had long been blocked, beginning with an electoral process traditionally marked by fraud and coups. Demands for social and economic reform by trade unions, peasant organizations, human-rights commissions and land-reform agencies had been met with heavy-handed repression. As a result, a revolutionary process begun in the countryside in the late 1970s, with small groups of young guerrillas, spread to the urban areas. By 1980, a war had started in earnest. The United States chose to see the situation in El Salvador as a Cold War conflict. During the 12-year war, the U.S. contributed over four billion dollars to the Salvadoran government and its armed forces, despite well-documented evidence of the army's massive, unrelenting, human-rights abuses.

Ana Margarita Gasteazoro was an unlikely participant in such a war. She had been born on October 15, 1950, into an upper-class family who had long ago learned to live with and largely ignore the socioeconomic contradictions which would give rise to the civil war. As members of the Salvadoran elite, the family lived in a villa on the outskirts of the capital, surrounded by gardens, a swimming pool, and a coterie of servants. Ana described her father, a civil engineer who had been educated in the U.S., as a liberal-minded, gregarious man with interests ranging from photography to ham radio. Her mother, in contrast, was conservative, tradition-bound, and deeply religious. Both parents were strong-minded; even as a young child, Ana was aware of the irreconcilable differences and bitter conflicts between her parents. She always felt a great affinity for her father and was inspired by his subtle methods of undermining his wife's strict household and religious rules.

From childhood, Ana rebelled against the rigid social and moral conventions that circumscribed the upbringing and education of girls of her class. The only girl among three brothers (her sister was born much later), Ana shared their interests and pastimes, and fiercely resisted when, as school age approached, her mother directed her to wear dresses and engage in "proper" activities with girls from her own social class.

Ana's mother wanted Ana to attend a convent school where she would be under the watchful eyes of nuns, but her father insisted that all his children attend the American School, where they would learn English and benefit from a progressive curriculum and an international environment. In this conflict her father was immovable, and Ana and her brothers began their education at the elite American School in San Salvador.

By age 15, Ana had confirmed all her mother's fears about liberal education. She smoked and danced, dressed "improperly," went out with boys, and stayed out too late. It was 1965, and Ana argued that she was acting no differently than her classmates at the American School. She also argued that the same restrictions did not apply to her brothers. Her mother, concerned that she was ruining her chances for a good marriage, again insisted to her husband that Ana be sent to a convent school. Ana's father was determined that his daughter continue her education in English, however, so her parents finally compromised on a boarding school in Guatemala run by American Maryknoll nuns. Little did they realize that the year Ana would spend in Guatemala would initiate her into a world of political awareness and activism that would change her life forever.

Instead of the religious-based education her mother assumed she would receive at the Monte Maria school, Gasteazoro found herself in a school run by politically active nuns who considered it essential to instill in their students a sense of social responsibility. Under supervision, Ana was sent into the shanty towns of Guatemala City to distribute food, work in clinics, and give literacy classes in a community center. She saw poverty at close range for the first time, and her teachers were eager to answer her questions about the underlying causes.

One of Gasteazoro's major influences during her year in Guatemala was Sister Marian Peter, an American nun who lived at the school but had given up teaching the year before to devote herself to the poor. Sister Marian Peter had become involved in the liberation theology movement that began with the Catholic Church reforms of Vatican II in 1962. In Guatemala, she was secretly supporting the guerrilla movement, along with two radical American priests, the Melville brothers. After they were all expelled from the country for their political activities, Sister Marian Peter left her order and married one of the Melville brothers. As **Marjorie Melville**, she, her husband and brother-in-law became renowned in the United States as antiwar activists in the 1970s.

What you can do in the United States will have more effect on the future of El Salvador than anything we can possibly do here now.

—Ana Gasteazoro

But Ana's most significant friendship was with "Titina," a young Guatemalan psychologist and social worker named **Maria Cristina Arathon**, who had graduated from Monte Maria but still lived in the school dormitory. She took Ana to work as a volunteer dishwasher at The Crater, an inner-city drop-in center that sold cheap meals to poor university and high school students. Gasteazoro later discovered that The Crater was a meeting place for future leaders of the guerrilla movement, and that Titina was living a double life as a member of the Guatemalan revolutionary forces. Both Sister Marian Peter and Titina were careful at the time not to let Ana know about their double lives, but they provided the impressionable young woman with a glimpse into a new world of political activism.

Ana returned to El Salvador to finish high school at the American School, but she was changed by her year in Guatemala:

> [It] had awakened my social conscience. Since I had got used to walking in the poor barrios and sitting at the same table with working class people, I couldn't understand why we had to have such gulfs between rich and poor in El Salvador. It made me quite belligerent in school. I didn't have the historical or political background to know what I was talking about, but I was quite vocal.
>
> Still, I had no sense of what was really going on in El Salvador. That may seem strange, but you have to take into account that through the strict control of the media, Salvadorans had been kept ignorant of the political reality of their country for many years. It was only with the birth of the popular organizations and with their activities in the 1970s that the degree of social injustice became widely known, and that the political situation was volatile. We young Salvadorans were very ignorant of recent history in El Salvador, and most of us remained so as adults.

After graduation in 1967, Gasteazoro was sent to Boston for secretarial training. Although she had hoped to study landscape architecture or psychology, her family considered it more important to educate their three sons, who would eventually have to support their own families. Ana was expected to pick up a few skills and work as a secretary until she married well and was supported by her husband. But even her meager secretarial training came to an abrupt end in 1968 when a war between Honduras and El Salvador caused Ana's father to suffer considerable losses from business investments in Honduras. She was told to come home and continue her studies in El Salvador.

Infused with the new social and sexual freedoms of America in the 1960s, Gasteazoro returned to El Salvador and studied briefly at the University of Central America. But when she began to date a young acquaintance of her father's, an African-American Marine guard at the U.S. Embassy, Ana's mother decided it was time for her to embark on another education abroad. She arranged for Ana to study at the University of Nevarra, a conservative Catholic university in northern Spain, and live with an upper-class local family. Though unenthusiastic, Gasteazoro was still under age and had little say; she packed her bags and flew to Spain.

It was 1968, the height of the Franco regime under which Spain had become the most reactionary country in Western Europe. With her long hair, mini-skirts, dangling earrings and makeup, Gasteazoro felt like she had landed on another planet. She described this year as the unhappiest of her life. By spring, she had been expelled from the university for repeated infractions of their rules. She negotiated with the university to grant her a diploma to teach English as a second language (ESL) and pressured her mother to allow her to stay on alone in Spain another year.

At age 20, Gasteazoro was eager to be out from under parental control. She promptly landed a job as a secretary with a property management company in Madrid, then in May 1969 moved to the island of Ibiza, where she lived almost four years, working as a secretary to a wealthy Germany developer. Reveling in her independence, she supported herself with her work, lived with a lover, and went for long periods without contact with her family.

Ana spent the beginning of the 1970s in Ibiza. From 1974 to 1975, she became involved in politics while living in Jamaica with a government official, a member of the social democratic People's National Party (PNP), then Jamaica's government party. Gasteazoro's political apprenticeship opened her to the possibility of working for change in her own country. When her relationship ended, partly as a result of her political evolution, she returned to El Salvador. "Jamaica opened my eyes to the reality of my own country," Gasteazoro recalled, "and I returned with a very strong commitment."

It was 1975 and El Salvador was shaken by several ominous events. At a peaceful protest demonstration in July, the military shot and killed 25 or 30 high school students. Several months later, Roberto Poma, the director of tourism from one of the richest families in El Salvador, was kidnapped. A new armed group called the Army of Popular Revolution (ERP)

claimed responsibility. Their demands for ransom and the release of several ERP members from prison were met, but Poma was returned to his family dead. Ana felt touched personally by the escalating violence in El Salvador. Roberto Poma had been her father's godson.

She enrolled once again at the University of Central America where, at 25, she was older than most students. She rented a small house in a working-class neighborhood and supported herself giving English lessons and working with educational television.

Ana Gasteazoro

Feeling she was at last in a position to contribute to the political process in El Salvador, Gasteazoro began to look around for an organization to join. Since she did not believe in armed opposition at that time, she had to choose from among the legal opposition parties: the Christian democrats, the communists, or the social democrats. Guillermo Ungo, the secretary general of the social democratic party, the National Revolutionary Movement (MNR), was one of Ana's professors at the university. When she appeared at his office and announced she wanted to work for his party, Ungo was skeptical of this young bourgeois woman. Though he doubted the strength of her commitment and her grasp of the very real dangers, he allowed her to join.

Gasteazoro was soon heavily involved in MNR work, organizing a women's group, helping publish the party's newsletter, and arranging meetings. "Since we were such a small party it was not hard to advance quickly in the ranks. After not very long I was elected Secretary of Youth. Then I became a sort of glorified political secretary, doing much of the party's administrative work." Since she spoke English, she was often sent out of the country for international meetings and conferences, especially those of the Socialist International. Being young and attractive, and often the only woman at such events, Gasteazoro had to make her position clear early on: "I was fighting to be taken seriously by all these men around me, who related to me partly as a good friend and partly as a political colleague. I had to walk a careful line. I couldn't start sleeping with political acquaintances, because then I would lose my status as a colleague—that's part of the machismo."

In the summer of 1978, Gasteazoro was sent as one of two MNR representatives to the International Youth Festival in Havana, Cuba. Held every four years, this gathering of all the progressive youth movements of the world coincided with and helped celebrate the 20th anniversary of the Cuban revolution. "I picked up a huge feeling of solidarity in Cuba that was crucial to me as a Latin American," she remembered. "I arrived back in El Salvador feeling as though nothing was going to stop me in my political work or in my commitment to my country's struggle. I was ready to take up arms, and I knew that we could do it."

By 1979, the repression by state security forces and the brazenness of the paramilitary death squads escalated to the point of daily disappearances of student leaders, trade unionists, human-rights and political activists, journalists, and many whose only political act was to be a member of a community organization. Gasteazoro recalled the horror that had become daily life: "I'll never forget one morning when I left my house in Santa Tecla at 6:30. I went by an underpass and there was a body hanging from the bridge, a man in only his underpants. A placard signed by the death squads was stuck to him, saying 'death to the traitors of the country.' Further on, in the area of the American embassy, I saw another body. It had what was supposed to be the flag of one of the popular organizations on it. Then I saw a third body, this time on the sidewalk of the underpass by the Social Security buildings. This was a little bunch of bones that had been tortured and crushed. That was our daily routine."

It was also a year of demonstrations by popular organizations and strikes by the trade unions. In the countryside, peasants were occupying churches and government ministries, demanding land reform and better wages. All these actions were met with a murderous response by the authorities.

Gasteazoro increasingly felt that the state repression and death squads had effectively put her party, along with other legal opposition groups, on the political sidelines. Even though the MNR activities were legal and conducted openly, several of her colleagues had "disappeared" during her first two years working for the party. Many others were in exile. She realized the only useful work was now with the guerrilla organizations, and she determined to join one of the four or five armed groups while still carrying on her MNR responsibilities.

Through contacts at the university, Gasteazoro made it known she was interested in joining a particular group, the Popular Liberation Front (FPL); soon, she was receiving directions for tasks to carry out around San Salvador: locating safe houses for meetings, working on propaganda, and writing scripts for clandestine radio broadcasts. With her MNR connections, she was able to move around the city in her old car doing work considered legitimate. As she proved herself reliable and efficient, Ana's jobs for the FPL increased in responsibility but always concerned unarmed, support work based in the capital. Although the FPL, like all other guerrilla groups, had a military arm waging war in the countryside, it was of strategic importance to the organization that Ana remain in San Salvador and lead a double life. "Despite differences in ideology and strategy," Gasteazoro recalled, "the guerrilla groups realized the importance of an alliance with a legal party of the left. The MNR had a very solid reputation internationally, and excellent connections with the progressive governments of Europe through the Socialist International."

The 1979 triumph of the rebel Sandinista army in Nicaragua gave great hope to revolutionary movements throughout Latin America. The lessons of Nicaragua were not, however, lost on its neighboring right-wing governments, and the year 1980 marked new heights of repressive violence in El Salvador. The popular archbishop of El Salvador, Oscar Romero, who had spoken out against the government and defended the demands of the poor, was assassinated while saying Mass. Four American churchwomen working in El Salvador—**Maura Clark, Ita Ford, Dorothy Kazel,** and **Jean Donovan**—were raped and killed by National Guardsmen. Five leaders of the newly formed Democratic Revolutionary Front, an alliance of legal opposition parties on the left, were kidnapped by the military while meeting at the Jesuit university; they were tortured, assassinated, and their bodies dumped outside the capital. Gasteazoro was sent to identify and claim the barely recognizable body of a beloved colleague, the representative of the MNR party.

With the disappearance of so many of her party colleagues, and with most of the leadership in exile, Ana was forced to assume more and more responsibility in the MNR. In April 1981, she was sent to the Socialist International Congress in Madrid, where the focus that year was the struggle in El Salvador. To protect her identity so she could return to El Salvador, Gasteazoro gave her keynote speech to the Women's Conference under a pseudonym and in disguise.

Back in El Salvador, Ana continued her double life, working underground for her guerrilla group while carrying on her "legal" work with the MNR. She had maintained close contact with her family throughout her years of political work, and though they suspected and disapproved of her involvement with the guerrilla movement, she was still expected home at least once a week for the traditional mid-day family meal. Gasteazoro arrived home on April 23 to find that her father, who had been seriously ill with emphysema for years, had died of a heart attack earlier that day, at age 62.

Less than three weeks later, on May 11, 1981, Ana was arrested, along with two members of her clandestine group. They had recently moved into a house in San Salvador that was supposedly "safe" but in fact was already under surveillance by the security forces. In the early morning darkness, a large group from the National Guard surrounded their residential block. When Ana and the two men were awakened with a loud banging on the door, they knew immediately what was happening. A group of uniformed men rushed in, began ransacking the house, and tore the phone out of the wall as Ana attempted to make a call. Other security forces captured one of Gasteazoro's colleagues as he attempted to escape over the roof. He was brought back, beaten, and tortured with electrical shocks while the search of the house continued. Gasteazoro, restrained and forced to listen to her friend's groans, recalled thinking she might have one chance to save their lives. She identified herself to the captain in charge with her real name and stated her six-year association with the MNR social democratic party. She insisted that the two men in the house had nothing to do with her or her party. Thinking they had someone important, legal rights notwithstanding, the Guardsmen tied Ana and her two comrades up, blindfolded them, and transported them to the National Guard barracks in San Salvador.

Thus began 11 days of terror. Given Gasteazoro's experience of recent years and knowing she was being held in one of the notorious clandestine jails of the security forces, she had no expectation of surviving. She said later that she only hoped to die with integrity, without revealing any information that would bring harm to her comrades. After withstanding an initial interrogation, a beating and "mock execution" late the first night, Ana was handcuffed to a wire cot and not allowed to move or sleep for three days. Repeated abuse at the hands of the guards, violent interrogations and more mock executions followed. She was constantly threatened with death and told that no one knew where she was. On the tenth day of detention, Gasteazoro endured a particularly brutal beating, after which she finally broke and signed a false confession, admitting to several "terrorist" activities, from brainwashing foreign journalists to killing the chief of the national lottery. The next morning, she was presented to the media at a National Guard press conference as a "confessed terrorist."

Later that same day, she was taken to Ilopango Women's Prison. "The first night, after the lights were turned out," Ana remembered, "I lay in bed looking up through the iron bars of ventilation space in the wall. . . . After eleven days in the National Guard barracks that tiny bit of the sky above my heard was beautiful. There was life out there beyond the wall, and even if I was locked in this room at least I was there in the company of other women. And even if some of them were criminals, there was this chance of communication, maybe of building something together. We were here, we were alive."

Ana knew she was safe, but only later did she learn she owed that fact to a strange convergence of influences: her contacts within the Socialist International had brought international pressure to bear once her arrest was known (someone had apparently witnessed the early morning raid and contacted an MNR official), and her family had wielded their influence with government officials and officers high up in the military. Pressure from these two sources had forced the National Guard to admit they had Ana in her first few days of detention, and once they acknowledged she was being held in one of their clandestine jails, they had to produce her alive. Perhaps because of their connection to Ana, her two colleagues also survived and went to prison.

Ana Gasteazoro spent two years in prison, without charges or a trial. When she entered Ilopango, in May 1981, she was one of only seven women political prisoners. Until then the conflict in El Salvador had been largely a war without prisoners. The numbers of political prisoners soon began to swell, however, and Gasteazoro joined with the others to form a women's unit of the Committee of Salvadoran Political Prisoners (COPPES). The women's section of the prison had previously been run by nuns, who had left the country in protest after the assassination of Archbishop Romero. The organizational legacy of the nuns remained, however, and Ana recalled that the prison felt rather like a Catholic boarding school. The women prisoners were allowed to go about organizing every aspect of their daily lives. Among their many projects, COPPES established a prison store for personal supplies, a bee-keeping project, and a vegetable garden. With the help of the Red Cross, they negotiated to be allowed to cook their own meals, to increase visiting hours with families, and to set up a sewing workshop to earn money. To support their demands, the women managed a 33-day hunger strike. Despite internal power struggles and external repression, COPPES became an effective force in publicizing the Salvadoran struggle and the cause of women prisoners.

Gasteazoro was released under a mass amnesty for political prisoners in May 1983. She went immediately into exile, briefly in Mexico and Cuba before settling in Costa Rica, where she lived until 1992. In her years in Costa Rica,

she worked at various jobs, from teaching English to owning a successful restaurant on the Caribbean coast. As the 1980s came to a close, the Salvadoran government was increasingly under pressure from the United States to clean up its abysmal human-rights record and make a peace agreement with the rebel forces. In August 1991, as the war was winding down, Gasteazoro was invited to return to El Salvador as a delegate to the first open congress her MNR party had held in many years. To her surprise, she was honored with special recognition at the congress, along with others who had given distinctive support to their party and the revolution. Invited to run as an MNR candidate in the 1993 elections, Ana was considering a return to political life in El Salvador when her breast cancer, which she assumed had been successfully treated in 1991, recurred in mid-1992. She died in El Salvador at age 42 on January 30, 1993.

SOURCES:

Manuscript: "Tell Mother I'm in Paradise: Memoirs of a Political Prisoner in El Salvador," by Ana Margarita Gasteazoro with Judy Blankenship and Andrew Wilson.

SUGGESTED READING:

Baloyra, Enrique. *El Salvador in Transition*. NC: University of North Carolina Press, 1982.

Bonner, Raymond. *Weakness and Deceit: US Policy and El Salvador*. NY: Times Books, 1984.

Hochschild, Adam. "Inside the Slaughterhouse," in *Mother Jones*. June 1983, p. 18 (includes an interview with Ana Gasteazoro inside Ilopango prison).

Ross, Oakland. "Politics Splits Salvador Siblings," in *Toronto Globe and Mail*. May 31, 1983 (article about Ana and her brother, Javier Gasteazoro).

Shulz, Donald E., and Douglas H. Graham, eds. *Revolution and Counter Revolution in Central America*. Westview Press, 1984.

Tula, Maria Teresa. *Hear My Testimony: Maria Teresa Tula, Human Rights Activist of El Salvador*. Ed. and trans. by Lynn Stephen. Boston, MA: South End Press, 1994.

RELATED MEDIA:

Romero (film), fictionalized account of life and death of Archbishop Romero, directed by John Duigan, starring Raul Julia, Richard Jordon, **Ana Alicia**, and Eddie Vélez, screenplay by John Sacret Young, a Paulist Production.

Salvador (film), directed and produced by Oliver Stone, 1986.

Judy Blankenship,
photographer and writer who lived in
Latin America from 1985 to 1993

Gatehouse, Eleanor Wright

(1886–1973)

Australian golfer. Name variations: Nellie Gatehouse. Born Eleanor Wright near Geelong, Victoria, in 1886; died in 1973; married James Gatehouse, in 1909.

A golfer from her school days, Eleanor Wright Gatehouse, known as Nellie, was the winner of three Australian championships and five Victorian titles. In 1906, she was the first Royal Melbourne Women's Champion, a title she captured another ten times over a period of 30 years. She won her first national title in 1909, which was also the year of her marriage to James Gatehouse. Known for her administrative skills as well as her golf swing, she served as president of the Australian Women's Golf Union and of the Royal Melbourne Associates. In addition to golf, Gatehouse contributed a great deal of her time to the Royal Society for the Prevention of Cruelty to Children, serving seven terms as president. The Nellie Gatehouse azalea was named in her honor.

Gattilusi, Caterina (fl. 1440)

Greco-Italian noblewoman. Name variations: Catterina. Flourished around 1440; second wife of Constantine XI Paleologus, emperor of Nicaea (r. 1448–1453).

Caterina Gattilusi, a Greco-Italian, was the second wife and cousin of Constantine XI Paleologus. She died soon after her marriage. Constantine's first wife was *Magdalena-Theodora Tocco, who also died young.

Gattilusi, Eugenia (fl. late 1390s)

Greco-Italian noblewoman. Born into the Greco-Italian Gattilusi family, lords of the Isle of Lesbos; flourished in the 1390s; married her cousin John VII Paleologus, emperor of Nicaea (r. 1390).

From the Greco-Italian Gattilusi family, lords of the Isle of Lesbos, Eugenia married her cousin John VII Paleologus shortly after the end of his reign. It is not known whether she had any children who survived infancy.

Gatty, Juliana Horatia (1841–1885).

See Ewing, Juliana Horatia.

Gatty, Margaret (1809–1873)

British author and editor. Name variations: Margaret Scott; (pseudonym) Aunt Judy. Born Margaret Scott in Burnham, Essex, England, on June 3, 1809; died at Ecclesfield vicarage in Ecclesfield, Yorkshire, England, on October 4, 1873; daughter of the Reverend Alexander Scott (1768–1840) and Mary Frances (Ryder) Scott; married Reverend Alfred Gatty, D.D., *vicar of Ecclesfield, in 1839; children: ten, including daughters, Juliana Horatia Ewing (1841–1885) and Horatia Gatty Eden.*

Selected writings: The Fairy Godmother and Other Tales *(1851);* Parables from Nature *(5 vols., 1855–1871);* Aunt Judy's Tales *(1858);* Aunt Judy's Letters *(1862);* Aunt Judy's Songbook for Children; The Mother's Book of Poetry *(1862);* British Seaweeds *(1862);* History of British Seaweeds *(1863);* The Old Folks from Home *(1871);* Waifs and Strays of Natural History *(1871);* A Book of Emblems *(1872);* The Book of Sun Dials *(1872).*

Born in Burham, Essex, in 1809, Margaret Scott Gatty was the youngest daughter of **Mary Ryder Scott** and the Reverend Dr. Alexander John Scott, chaplain to Admiral Horatio Nelson. Her mother died when she was two, and her father and grandfather raised her and recognized her talent for drawing and calligraphy. She drew and etched on copper and vellum, and from the age of ten she was a regular visitor to the print-room of the British Museum.

In 1839, Margaret married the Reverend Alfred Gatty, vicar of Ecclesfield in Yorkshire, sub-dean of York cathedral, and the author of various works both secular and religious. In order to offset the costs of rearing a growing family, Margaret Gatty began writing. Her first publication, co-authored with her husband, was a biography of her father's life and his time with Nelson, published in 1842. Her first individual work, *The Fairy Godmother and Other Tales*, appeared in 1851. This book was a moralistic collection of fairy tales the inspiration for which came from the lively and active family life she enjoyed with her ten children, eight of whom lived to adulthood. Her second book surpassed the first in popularity. *Parables From Nature*, a series of five volumes, was published from 1855 to 1871. Gatty illustrated the parables, utilizing her own artistic skills.

In 1858, Gatty published *Aunt Judy's Tales* under the pseudonym Aunt Judy. She followed this with

Margaret Gatty

Aunt Judy's Letters (1862), *Aunt Judy's Songbook for Children*, and *The Mother's Book of Poetry*. As a result of the success of Aunt Judy, Gatty established *Aunt Judy's Magazine* in 1866. She edited and contributed to the magazine, which featured stories and articles of writers and poets of the 19th century, from 1866 to 1873. During this time, she developed a close relationship with her young subscribers. The magazine was popular due to many factors, not the least of which was Gatty's ability to see things from a child's point of view and communicate successfully with children on that basis.

Other writings included works of both fiction and nonfiction. An accomplished botanist, Gatty wrote *British Seaweeds* (1862) and *History of British Seaweeds* (1863) which she also illustrated. As a result of these authoritative works, she had both a seaweed and a sea serpent named after her. Gatty also published an account of a holiday in Ireland, *The Old Folks From Home*, and edited an autobiography in 1861, *The Travels and Adventures of Dr. Wolff the Missionary*.

Ill health forced Gatty to turn editorship of *Aunt Judy's Magazine* over to her daughters, *Juliana Horatia Ewing and Horatia Gatty Eden, in 1873. Increasing paralysis confined her to the vicarage at Ecclesfield, where she died later that year.

Judith C. Reveal,
freelance writer, Greensboro, Maryland

Gaulle, Yvonne de (1900–1979).

See de Gaulle, Yvonne.

Gautami, Mahapajapati or Mahaprajapati (fl. 570 BCE).

See Mahapajapati.

Gauthier, Eva (1885–1958)

Canadian mezzo-soprano and modern recitalist whose historic performances of modern masters—Ravel, Bartók, Hindemith, Schoenberg, and Stravinsky—were her legacy. Born Ida Joséphine Phoebe Gauthier on September 20, 1885, in Ottawa, Canada; died on December 26, 1958, in New York; studied with Frank Buris, Auguste-Jean Dubulle, Sarah Bernhardt, and Jacques Bouhy; married Frans Knoote, in 1911 (divorced 1917).

Eva Gauthier, who began her career as an opera singer, was destined to have an influential career in modern music. A soloist at St. Patrick Church in Ottawa, she left for Europe in 1902 thanks to the sponsorship of Sir Wilfrid and Lady **Zoe Laurier** (1841–1921). At the Paris Conservatory, Gauthier studied singing with Auguste-Jean Dubulle and declamation with *Sarah Bernhardt. A serious operation for nodules on the vocal cords interrupted her studies for several months. Her compatriot *Emma Albani engaged Gauthier for a tour of the British Isles in 1905. She was invited to sing at Covent Garden in 1910 but her tenure on the opera stage was not happy. Gauthier decided to devote her career to recital and concert. On an extensive tour of the Orient, she stayed in Java where she met her husband Frans Knoote, to whom she was married from 1911 to 1917. When she returned to a New York recital debut in 1917, Gauthier devoted the program to modern masters like Ravel, Bartók, Hindemith, Schoenberg, and Stravinsky. She gave the North American premieres of Stravinsky's *Trois Poésies de la lyrique japonaise* in 1917 and *Pribaoutki* in 1918. She also performed music of France's Les Six whom she met in 1920. On November 1, 1923, Gauthier performed a historic concert in Aeolian Hall singing the music of Jerome Kern, Irving Berlin, and George Gershwin with Gershwin at the piano. Paul Whiteman, the orchestra conductor, was in attendance and commissioned Gershwin to compose a work for piano and orchestra. *Rhapsody in Blue* was the result. Gauthier continued to perform premieres of modern works, and it is estimated that she gave some 700 during a career which also included recording. She was responsible for bringing much modern music to the concert stage.

John Haag,
Athens, Georgia

Gauthier, Marguerite (1824–1847).

See Plessis, Alphonsine.

Gautier, Felisa Rincón de (1897–1994)

Political leader who was mayor of San Juan, Puerto Rico, for over 20 years (1946–69). Born Felisa Rincón in Ceiba in Puerto Rico on January 9, 1897; died in San Juan on September 16, 1994; eldest daughter and one of eight children of Enrique Rincón Plumey and Rita Marrero Rivera de Rincón; married Jenaro A. Gautier (a lawyer), in 1940; no children.

The eldest of eight children, Felisa Rincón de Gautier was born in Puerto Rico in 1897 and left high school to care for her sisters and brothers after her mother died when Felisa was

11. As a young woman, she spent several months in New York working as a seamstress in a fashionable Fifth Avenue shop then returned to San Juan to open her own dress salon. She proved to be a savvy business-woman and within a short time had several stores including a flower shop. Her political career began in 1932, the year Puerto Rican women won enfranchisement, when she assumed leadership of San Juan's Liberal Party. In 1938, she became a member of the Popular Democratic Party founded by Muñoz Marin and as such worked to organize poor and disadvantaged voters. She served as president of the party's San Juan committee from 1940 and became mayor of the city in 1946, upon the resignation of Roberto Sanches Vilella, who left to take another government post. She was reelected to office unanimously each consecutive term until 1968, when she declined to run. "My opponents campaign just before elections and then they disappear," she once said. "I start campaigning the day after the election and never stop."

As mayor, Gautier was closely aligned with "Operation Bootstrap," a program introduced by Muñoz Marin in 1946 to industrialize Puerto Rico and raise the standard of living. Building on Marin's initiative, Gautier cleaned up the existing slums, built new schools and housing projects, and set up a network of neighborhood medical dispensaries linked to the city's hospitals. By far her most popular innovation was her Wednesday open house at city hall, when hundreds of the island's underprivileged visited her to solicit help and personal attention. As a good-will ambassador, Gautier toured Latin America and made frequent trips to the United States. Approaching her job at the level of human relations rather than politics, she delighted the local children by having planeloads of snow flown in for Christmas parties.

Felisa was married in 1940 to Jenaro A. Gautier, a lawyer who also served as assistant attorney general of Puerto Rico. Politics was something of a family affair to Gautier, who awarded a large number of city jobs to members of her family, a practice that rankled her detractors. "I wish I had 20 more nieces," she told critics. "They work better—for less."

Gautier also served as a member of the U.S. Democratic National Committee and, in 1992, was the oldest delegate to the Democratic National Convention, held that year in New York City. Felisa Rincón de Gautier died in San Juan on September 16, 1994, at the age of 97.

SOURCES:

Candee, Marjorie Dent, ed. *Current Biography 1956.* NY: H.W. Wilson, 1956.

The [New London] *Day* (obituary). September 19, 1994.

Graham, Judith, ed. *Current Biography 1994.* NY: H.W. Wilson, 1994.

COLLECTIONS:

Felisa Rincón de Gautier Museum, organized by the Felisa Rincón de Gautier Foundation, Box 6607, Loiza Station, Santurce, Puerto Rico 00914-6697.

Barbara Morgan,
Melrose, Massachusetts

Felisa Rincón de Gautier

Gautier, Judith (1845–1917)

French writer and Orientalist who was the first female member of the Académie Goncourt. Name variations: Judith Mendès; Judith Walter. Born Louise Judith Gautier in Paris, France, on August 24, 1845; died on December 26, 1917; elder daughter of Théophile Gautier (a poet, novelist, and journalist) and his mistress Ernesta Grisi (an opera singer); attended Notre-Dame de la Miséricorde for two years; tutored by Tin-Tun-Ling; niece of Carlotta Grisi

(1819–1899); married Catulle Mendès (a poet), on April 17, 1866 (judicial separation, July 13, 1878, and divorced, December 28, 1896); no children.

Selected works: (written as Judith Walter) Le Livre de Jade (1867); (written as Judith Mendès) Le Dragon impérial (1869); Iskender (1886); L'Usurpateur (1975); Le Collier des jours (2 vols., 1902 and 1903).

An Orientalist and France's first female academician, Judith Gautier was the elder daughter of the poet and critic Théophile Gautier and his mistress **Ernesta Grisi**, an Italian contralto. Théophile had earlier fallen passionately in love with Ernesta's sister, ballerina **Carlotta Grisi*, who at age 22 had danced in *Giselle* for which he had written the libretto. Although he called Carlotta "the true, the only love of my heart," she had only a platonic affection for him, leaving him to find a substitute in her elder sister.

Judith, favored over her sister **Estelle**, grew up in her father's house in Neuilly, where the likes of Delacroix, Flaubert, or Baudelaire often appeared at the dinner table. Her education began within the confines of her father's library and then, except for a few unhappy years at a French convent, was delegated to a variety of tutors. It was primarily Théophile, however, who indulged his daughter's intelligence and her love of the exotic East. As a teenager, he presented her with a Chinese tutor, Tin-Tun-Ling, and arranged for an entree to the Bibliothèque Impériale. Making the most of these unusual privileges, Judith emerged as a brilliant Sinologist.

Gautier grew into a classic beauty as well, possessing what was described as a languid quality in her movements and gestures that only added to her grace and appeal. Maurice Dreyfous, a man of letters, first met her when she was 17. "She was, and long remained, one of the most perfectly beautiful creatures that one could see," he later recalled. "The first time I saw her, she gave me the impression, which has never changed, of the Goddess of Nonchalance." Before the age of 21, and without her father's blessing, Gautier was married to the poet Catulle Mendès, a strikingly handsome man whom Parnassian poet Louis Ménard called "Apollo in person." A disastrous union from the start, the marriage ended in divorce and left Gautier contemptuous of men. Her subsequent paramours became the source of continuous speculation. She was probably the mistress of Victor Hugo and was undoubtedly the inspiration for Richard Wagner's opera *Parsifal*. John Singer Sargent did a series of portraits of her, and her salon in Paris and her seaside villa in Brittany were frequented by Pierre Loti (who carried on a correspondence with her in Egyptian hieroglyphs), Charles-Marie Widor, and Anatole France. Most disconcerting to Gautier's numerous male admirers was her late-in-life liaison with **Suzanne Meyer-Zundel**, a young girl of average intelligence who had the unusual occupation of modeling flowers out of breadcrumbs. The relationship, which began around 1904 and lasted until Gautier's death in 1917, was ill-defined; some speculated that it was a marriage, while others saw it more as a mother-daughter bond. Whatever the case, it brought Gautier a measure of peace and happiness that had previously eluded her.

Gautier's prolific output, which included novels, short stories, poetry, plays, translations, and criticism, was recognized in 1910 by her election as the first female member of the Académie Goncourt. Gaston Deschamps, writing for *Le Temps*, called the appointment "a proof of the good feminist feelings which move this literary company. . . . and the just reward for a life completely devoted to the pure cult of literature and the arts." The membership carried with it a yearly stipend that helped ease the fi-

Judith Gautier

nancial hardship that Gautier endured throughout her career. "You cannot imagine," she once confessed, "what it is . . . not to be able to pay your coal merchant or your cleaning woman." Earlier, in 1875, her novel about feudal Japan, *L'Usurpateur*, had been recognized by the Académie-Français. It, along with *Le Dragon impérial* (one of a handful of her books to be translated into English) and *Iskender*, a tale of ancient Persia, are considered some of Gautier's best works. However, it was when she was in her late 50s, ill, and feeling uncertain about the future, that she embarked on her autobiography *Le Collier des jours*, which her biographer **Joanna Richardson** calls "the work that was to remain one of her best titles to fame and to the affection of posterity." Published in two volumes, it was reviewed by Rémy de Gourmont, who was overwhelmed by both Gautier's genius and her youthful spirit. "Judith Gautier knows every language, living or dead; she knows every literature, philosophy and religion, and, when she writes, it is with the smiling innocence of a surprised and enchanted young girl."

During World War I, Judith Gautier's final days were spent at her villa, Le Pré aux Oiseaux; she was in ill health and devastated by the war. She died of coronary thrombosis on December 26, 1917, at the age of 72.

SOURCES:

Richardson, Joanna. *Judith Gautier: A Biography.* NY: Franklin Watts, 1987.

Barbara Morgan,
Melrose, Massachusetts

Gay, Delphine (1804–1855)

See Girardin, Delphine.

Gay, Sophie (1776–1852)

French novelist. Name variations: Madame Gay. Born Marie Françoise Sophie Nichault de la Valette or de Lavalette in Paris, France, on July 1, 1776; died in Paris on March 5, 1852; daughter of M. Nichault de la Valette and Francesca Peretti (an Italian); married M. Liottier (an exchange broker), in 1793 (divorced 1799); married M. Gay (a receiver-general of the department of the Roër or Ruhr); children: (second marriage) Delphine Gay Girardin (1804–1855).

Sophie Gay was the daughter of M. Nichault de la Valette and **Francesca Peretti**, an Italian woman. In 1793, Sophie married M. Liottier, an exchange broker, whom she divorced in 1799. Shortly thereafter, she married M. Gay, a receiver-general for the department of

the Roër (or Ruhr). When her husband was posted to Aix-la-Chapelle, a wealthy resort town, Gay began to hold a literary salon there and subsequently in Paris. She became friends with many celebrated personages, and her salon was frequented by all of the distinguished writers, musicians, actors, and painters of the time, whom she attracted with her intelligence, charm, and beauty. Her first literary effort was a letter written in 1802 to the *Journal de Paris* in defense of **Germaine de Staël's novel Delphine*. That same year, Gay published anonymously her first novel *Laure d'Estelle*, a controversial work which concerns a woman who, believing her husband killed in battle, has a series of amorous liaisons. *Léonie de Montbreuse*, which appeared in 1813, was considered by Sainte-Beuve as Gay's best work, but *Anatole* (1815), the romance of a deaf-mute, was even more highly regarded. Following the death of her husband, economic necessity prompted greater literary output, and from 1822 on she published regularly. Her other works include *Les malheurs d'un amant heureux* (1818), *Un Mariage sous l'Empire* (*A Marriage during the Empire*, 1832), *La Duchesse de Châteauroux* (1834), *La Comtesse d'Egmont* (1836), *Salons célèbres* (2 vols., 1837), and **Marie de Mancini* (1840). Gay wrote several comedies and opera libretti which met with considerable success, and her play *The Marquis of Pomenars* had a long run. An accomplished musician, she also composed both the lyrics and music for a number of songs. In 1834, she published her memoirs, *Souvenirs d' une Vieille femme*. Her daughter, Delphine Gay, wrote under her married name of Madame de Girardin (**Delphine Girardin*).

SUGGESTED READING:

Gautier, Théophile. *Portraits contemporains.*

Gayatri Devi (c. 1897–1995)

Indian-born spiritual leader of Ramakrishna Brahma-Vadin, a female religious order rooted in Hinduism. Name variations: known to her followers as "Ma," short for mataji, meaning reverend mother. Born in Bengal, India, possibly in 1897; died in La Crescenta, California, on September 8, 1995.

The Reverend Mother Gayatri Devi, the spiritual leader of a bicoastal religious order known as Ramakrishna Brahma-Vadin, was born in Bengal, India, around 1897, one of 19 children of a civil lawyer and a housewife. Forced into marriage at an early age, she was widowed at 19, after which she was allowed to

Châteauroux, Duchesse de.
See Pompadour, Jeanne-Antoinette for sidebar.

Gayatri Devi (1919—)

Maharani of Jaipur and member of the Parliament of India. Born on May 23, 1919, in London, England; one of five children of the Maharajah Jitendra Narayan Bhup Bahadur of Cooch Behar and Princess Indiraraje Gaekwar of Baroda; educated by private tutors; attended St. Cyprian's in Eastbourne, England; graduated from Shantiniketan University, Balpur, India, 1936; attended Brilliamount school, Lausanne, Switzerland, and the London College of Secretaries; married Sawai Man Singh Bahadur (the maharajah of Jaipur), on May 9, 1940 (died 1970); children: one son, Maharaj Kumar Singh.

Gayatri Devi, the daughter of the maharajah of Cooch Behar and Princess **Indiraraje Gaekwar** of Baroda, grew up in a sumptuous palace in what is now West Bengal, near the Himalayan foothills of eastern India. Her father died in 1922, when Gayatri was a small child, and she grew up in the care of her mother and attended by the 500 servants that inhabited the palace. Educated by tutors and in private schools, she graduated from Shantiniketan University in 1936, then attended finishing school in Switzerland. In 1940, she married Sawai Man Singh Bahadur (known as Jai), an internationally known polo player, and the maharajah of Jaipur, ruler of a 15,600-square-mile fief in the northwest Indian desert country of Rajputana.

Settling into a life of royal luxury in the 60-room castle on the outskirts of the "pink city" of Jaipur, the maharani encountered many unfamiliar customs, the most difficult of which was sharing married life with Jai's two other wives and his several children. Gayatri Devi, however, adapted well to her various social duties and combined them with a considerable interest in the welfare of her three million subjects, particularly in the areas of education and women's rights. She founded three schools, including the Maharani Gayatri Devi Public School in Jaipur, a progressive school for girls, a sewing school, and a school of arts and crafts, through which she hoped to perpetuate the handicrafts of Jaipur. She also served in the Red Cross and on the purchasing committee of India's National Museum.

After India won its independence from Great Britain in 1947 and the Republic was established, Jai lost his sovereignty and became the ceremonial head of the newly formed state of Rejasthan. Unable to maintain his standard of living on the $378,000 yearly salary the Indian government awarded him for life (a privy purse), he converted the Rambagh Palace into a luxury

Gayatri Devi (b. 1919), with husband Jai.

join her uncle, Swami Paramananda, in America. She was ordained at the Massachusetts center which her uncle founded in 1909, according to the teachings of Swami Vivekananda, who introduced Hinduism to America. The first Indian woman to teach Americans the Vedanta philosophy, which honors all religions, Gayatri Devi inherited leadership of the religious communities in La Crescenta, California, and in Cohasset, Massachusetts, after the death of her uncle in 1940. Although the mostly female order was disowned by its all-male parent order in India, it survived and flourished, eventually supporting two ashrams for underprivileged women in Calcutta.

In 1975, Gayatri Devi appeared with *Mother Teresa at the Conference of World Religions at the United Nations. She helped found the Snowmass Religious Leaders' Conference, and, at the invitation of the Dalai Lama, taught at the Harmonia Mundi Contemplative Congress in Newport Beach in 1989. Mother Gayatri Devi died in September 1995.

hotel and moved his family into the more modest Raj Mahal Palace. The added income from the business enterprise allowed the family to maintain, among other luxuries, several hundred servants, a fleet of 100 automobiles, a stable of polo ponies, and a herd of six elephants. In October 1949, Gayatri Devi gave birth to the couple's first son, informally known as Jagat.

As displaced nobility, the maharajah and maharani lost much of their political clout in the eyes of their former subjects. "The government tried to push us out of the public eye," Gayatri explained, "and we spent more and more of our time abroad." In 1961, the maharani joined the Swatantra (Freedom) Party, which was founded in 1959, as a rightist opponent of Prime Minister *Indira Gandhi's Congress Party. Shortly afterward, Gayatri announced her candidacy for the House of the People, the lower chamber of the Indian Parliament. "The Congress government was becoming rather like a dictatorship," she said, "and seemed to be trying to turn our country rather into a Communist country."

Gayatri campaigned by jeep, touring the 1,900 villages of Rejasthan and delivering up to 20 speeches a day in which she told her peasant audiences that the corrupt politicians were growing rich on the labor of the poor, and she intended to do something about it. The crowds that gathered to see her, however, seemed more impressed with the fact that their glamorous maharani had descended among them than with her political message, and showered her with marigold petals, and offered baskets of fresh fruit and vegetables at every stop. In addition to her field campaign, the maharani opened the palace grounds to the public and granted private audiences to those who volunteered to work on the campaign. On election day in February 1962, Gayatri Devi received 192,909 votes, the largest plurality of any candidate in the country.

During her first five-year term, Gayatri focused on the politics of her home state of Rejasthan. As the 1967 election approached, she was advised by Swatantra Party leaders, who hoped to oust the Congress Party from their control of the state government, to form an electoral coalition between the Rejasthan Freedom Party and the Hindu Jan Sangh (People's Party). The ploy was only partially effective. The Congress Party retained control of the state, although the Swatantra-Jan Sangh coalition succeeded in depriving it of a legislative majority. The maharani lost her bid for a state legislative seat but was re-elected to the national Parliament. When opponents of the Congress Party in Rejasthan protest-

ed the return of the party to power, violence broke out in Jaipur, resulting in 130 arrests. The maharani escaped arrest but made clear her support of the uprising. "I will not sit idle until the Congress goes, whether it is in a week, or two weeks or a month," she said. On March 9, 1967, she asked the federal government to take control of Rejasthan, dissolve the newly elected legislature, and set up a new state government. Ultimately, the Congress Party gained control, and the maharani became disillusioned with politics.

In June 1970, Jai, who had previously suffered a mild heart attack, collapsed while playing polo and died, after which the maharani secluded herself in mourning. In 1971, responding to Prime Minister Gandhi's dissolution of Parliament and her call for elections a year ahead of schedule, Gayatri reluctantly agreed to run for the opposition from Jaipur. Winning by 50,000 more votes than her Congress Party opponent, she came out of retreat to return to Parliament. However, Gayatri suffered a devastating political blow in December 1971, when both houses of Parliament passed a bill that "de-recognized" all former rulers, thus abolishing their privileges, titles, and privy purses, including those of her late husband.

Gayatri continued to serve out her term in Parliament, still concentrating her efforts on making life better for the villagers who comprised her constituency, but admitting that politics was a full-time job for which she did not have the time. She remained connected with the City Palace Museum, and in conjunction with her school of arts and crafts, she formed a company to export cotton rugs, or *durries,* made by the local weavers. Finally, her political life behind her, she moved from the palace to Lillypool, a house in the gardens of Rambagh Palace where she and Jai had planned to spend their later years.

SOURCES:

Gayatri Devi, and Santha Rama Rau. *A Princess Remembers.* Philadelphia, PA: J.B. Lippincott, 1976.

Moritz, Charles, ed. *Current Biography 1968.* NY: H.W. Wilson, 1968.

Barbara Morgan,
Melrose, Massachusetts

Gaynor, Janet (1906–1984)

American film and stage actress who won the first Academy Award for Best Actress. Name variations: (pseudonym) Augusta Louise. Born Laura Augusta Gainor on October 10, 1906, in Germantown, Pennsylvania; died on September 14, 1984, from complications of pneumonia, in Palm Springs, California;

daughter of Frank D. and Laura (Buhl) Gainor; educated in public schools in Pennsylvania, Chicago, and San Francisco; married Jesse Peck (a writer), on September 11, 1929 (divorced 1933); married Gilbert Adrian (a costume designer), in 1939 (died 1959); married Paul Gregory, in 1964; children: (second marriage) one son, Robin Gaynor Adrian (b. 1940).

Appeared in amateur theatricals as a child; was chosen at age 18 to appear in her first "bathing beauty" film; changed professional name to Janet Gaynor before embarking on a successful 15-year career as leading lady in films, winning the first Best Actress Award from the American Academy of Motion Picture Arts and Sciences (1927); retired from the business (1939); appeared sporadically on stage and television through 1981, but devoted most of her time to oil painting and her family.

Filmography: The Johnstown Flood *(1926);* The Shamrock Handicap *(1926);* The Midnight Kiss *(1926);* The Blue Eagle *(1926);* The Return of Peter Grimm *(1926);* Seventh Heaven *(1927);* Sunrise *(1927);* Two Girls Wanted *(1927);* Street Angel *(1928);* Four Devils *(1929);* Christina *(1929);* Lucky Star *(1929);* Sunny Side Up *(1929);* Happy Days *(1930);* High Society Blues *(1930);* The Man Who Came Back *(1931);* Daddy Long Legs *(1931);* Merely Mary Ann *(1931);* Delicious *(1931);* The First Year *(1932);* Tess of the Storm Country *(1932);* State Fair *(1933);* Adorable *(1933);* Paddy the Next Best Thing *(1933);* Carolina *(1934);* Change of Heart *(1934);* Servants' Entrance *(1934);* One More Spring *(1935);* The Farmer Takes a Wife *(1935);* Small Town Girl *(1936);* Ladies in Love *(1936);* A Star Is Born *(1937);* Three Loves Has Nancy *(1938);* The Young in Heart *(1938);* Bernadine *(1957).*

One evening in 1926, a select audience filed into a screening room on the Fox Studios lot in Hollywood for the first viewing of *The Return of Peter Grimm*. Among the spectators was a young German director, F.W. Murnau, who had made enough of a name for himself in his native country's motion-picture industry for Fox to offer him a contract to direct his first American film. Murnau was on the lookout for a leading lady, and he had heard that the young actress in *Peter Grimm* just might fit the bill. The actress was Janet Gaynor, who would be awarded the first Best Actress award from the American Academy of Motion Picture Arts and Sciences for her performance in Murnau's film *Sunrise*, still considered the last great silent film before the movies learned to talk.

Janet Gaynor, whose given name was Laura, was born in 1906 in a section of Philadelphia

then called Germantown for its high concentration of German immigrants; her mother **Laura Gainor**, for whom she was named, and her father Frank Gainor were second generation German-Americans. Frank, a painter and paperhanger by trade, made extra money on occasion by taking bit parts in the German language films made at the old Lubin Studios in Philadelphia, and he often took his children (the couple also had an older daughter **Helen Gainor**) to see the Hollywood films showing at the Mannheim Theater downtown. By the time she was in grammar school, "Lolly," as Gaynor was called, was entertaining her friends with imitations of *Mary Pickford and *Norma Talmadge. Noting her ability to memorize almost anything, Frank taught her songs and poetry and encouraged her mimicry. "I never dreamed she would become famous," he told *New Movie Magazine* in 1931, when his daughter had become very famous, indeed. "We just did it because it was fun."

With the Gainors' divorce in 1914, Laura Gainor and her daughters moved to Chicago to live with relatives, but Laura continued to encourage her younger daughter's talents. During World War I, when she was barely ten years old, Gaynor was entertaining at the Great Lakes Naval Training Station, singing for the recruits soon to be shipped off to duty in the North Atlantic; and during a winter spent in Florida with an aunt, she appeared in her first amateur theatrical, *Fascinating Fanny Brown*, playing an old woman. When Gaynor was 16, her mother remarried, and her stepfather—Harry C. Jones, a mining engineer—moved with his new family to San Francisco, where the two girls attended Polytechnic High School. Janet's performance reciting a dramatic verse at the Senior Rally in 1922 had the entire school buzzing about "that cute little Gainor girl."

Like Frank Gainor, Harry Jones ("Jonesy" to his stepdaughters) encouraged Janet's dramatic aspirations, especially when the family moved again, this time to Hollywood, where the girls went to secretarial school. On a lark in 1924, they auditioned at the old Hal Roach studios for one of Roach's trademark "bathing beauty" films, scantily plotted two-reelers in which young ladies posed and cavorted in full-body bathing suits that left everything to the imagination. The Gainor girls tested for a film called *All Wet*, to be shot over seven days in a park in downtown Los Angeles. To Janet's delight, she was offered a part; and to her further delight, her mother and stepfather gave their assent. The shoot made her eager for more.

Janet Gaynor, with Henry Fonda in The Farmer Takes a Wife.

Again, her parents acquiesced, as long as she didn't use her real name. It was Jonesy who came up with one she could use professionally. Instead of the name Laura, "he chose a name you couldn't diminutise," Gaynor once explained. "You can't put an 'ie' or a 'y' on the end of Janet." The change from "Gainor" to "Gaynor" was made only because her stepfather thought it looked better.

Two more Roach shorts followed. In 1925, Universal offered her $50 a week for the female lead in a two-reel western. Like the Roach films, such shorts were used to fill out programs featuring a studio's longer, more "serious" films, but at least Gaynor did not have to wear a bathing suit to play a western heroine. She did five more such roles, took small parts in Universal's bigger-budget productions, and was even loaned out by Universal to other studios for similar work. Her dedication and willingness to learn soon got her noticed, and it was the Fox Studios that first saw her box-office potential.

In 1926, Gaynor was offered the role of Anna Burgher, a young woman who braves a flood to warn her town of its impending inundation. *The Johnstown Flood* was Fox's silent epic based on the famous natural disaster in that Pennsylvania mining town in 1889, and it was Gaynor's chance at playing something other than a bathing beauty or a hand-wringing, peril-beset frontier girl. She gave up a sure $50 a week to take her first "emotional" role with feature billing, and played opposite George O'Brien, a former wrestler who would become one of the most popular early matinée idols. The film was well-received, and Fox offered her a five-year contract at $100 a week. Gaynor's gamble had doubled her money.

As you gain in years, you change mentally— or at least you should, if you have anything inside your head.

—Janet Gaynor

Moviemaking in those days was a much quicker business than it is now, and it was by no means unusual that Gaynor made four more pictures for Fox in 1926. *The Shamrock Handicap* was a family drama built around horse racing; *Midnight Kiss* was her first leading role in a romantic comedy, opposite another of her frequent leading men, Richard Walling; *Blue Eagle* was a naval adventure directed by a young John Ford in which she again co-starred with O'Brien. Her reviews ranged from raves to respectful restraint, but it was her fourth film for Fox—the one that Murnau came to see—that she later said made her a real actress.

The Return of Peter Grimm was a sort of supernatural melodrama, based on a 1911 play in which a father dies in such a troubled state over his daughter's pending decision on whom to marry that he returns from the grave to make sure she chooses the right suitor. *Photoplay* noted that Janet Gaynor "contributes some fine acting" to the film, notably in her father's death scene, in which her character had to gaily pretend ignorance of her father's passing while se-

cretly knowing his death was imminent. Faced with the challenge of laughing and crying at the same time, Gaynor turned to a veteran of the stage, Alec Francis, the actor playing her father, who taught her many tricks of the cinema trade over the course of the shoot. Before the camera rolled for the big scene, Francis looked her in the eye and said, "This is our big chance, little Janet. We mustn't fall down." Knowing how ludicrous the situation was, she laughed; but the thought of actually letting the great man down made the tears flow so copiously that audiences in theaters cried right along with her, and Fox upped her salary to $300 a week.

Murnau's *Sunrise,* in which she was teamed again with O'Brien, brought her to full maturity as an actress. The film tells the story of a man who tries to abandon, then murder, his wife at the urging of an alluring, vindictive mistress. Murnau cast Gaynor as the long-suffering wife; the role was not only a dramatic challenge for her but a physical one. The climactic scene in the film occurs when O'Brien takes her rowing on a lake with the intention of drowning her. Murnau, with his German Expressionist background (his *Nosferatu the Vampire,* made in Germany in 1922, remains a classic of the style) took great care in staging the sequence, with Gaynor spending several weeks neck-deep in water at Lake Arrowhead while O'Brien tried to drown her several times over. (In the end, O'Brien's character realizes the horror of what he's doing, relents, and remorsefully asks his wife's forgiveness.) Murnau would push her each day until, she said, "it seemed I had not a spark of life in me. Murnau would thank me simply, and when I arrived home there would be a great bunch of red roses, expressing his appreciation." Although Murnau's original ending for the film, in which the wife actually does drown, was changed at the studio's insistence, the film was a sensation. Sixty years later, Gaynor would still insist it was the finest performance she ever gave.

But it was only the beginning. While Murnau was still editing *Sunrise,* Gaynor embarked on another Fox film, *Seventh Heaven,* with another director with whom she would form a close working relationship, Frank Borzage, and with the leading man with whom she would do her most popular films, Charles Farrell. Farrell had been managing vaudeville acts and doing extra work before he was chosen for the male lead in *Seventh Heaven,* in which he plays a man who comes to the rescue of an abused woman intent on suicide. Gaynor's portrayal of a victim of emotional and physical abuse who pulls herself from the edge of self-extermination had a depth and poignancy new to her audience, leading the *New York Herald Tribune* to note that by "combining her idealistic prettiness with a skill at projecting believable emotions, she becomes immediately a novel screen personage."

When advance screenings of her next film with Borzage and Farrell, *Street Angel,* brought equally enthusiastic reviews, Gaynor was invited to attend a special awards ceremony organized by the new Academy for the Motion Picture Arts and Sciences. It was, in fact, the first Academy Awards ceremony, although the golden statuette given to each honoree would not be given the name "Oscar" until 1931 (because the librarian of the Academy mentioned one day that it resembled her Uncle Oscar). Gaynor remembered that first awards evening in 1928 as "more like a private party open only to members of the Academy than a big public ceremony." Even so, it was a memorable evening for her. Gaynor was given the first award for Best Actress, chosen over **Louise Dresser** and *****Gloria Swanson** for her work in *Sunrise, Seventh Heaven,* and *Street Angel* (the awards in those early days were often given for cumulative work rather than specific performances). In addition, two of her last three pictures won awards, with *Sunrise* honored for "Artistic Quality of Production" and Frank Borzage named Best Director for *Seventh Heaven,* which had also been nominated for Best Picture.

Now arguably the most honored actress in Hollywood, Gaynor was sought out again by F.W. Murnau for his next Fox epic, *Four Devils,* a circus melodrama in which Janet played one of four trapeze artists. Instead of days on end half-submerged in water, Murnau required her this time to learn basic trapeze work for the close-ups, which would be intercut with wider shots of stunt doubles doing the difficult work. Although the film received warm reviews, and Gaynor's performance was tagged as "sympathetic, sincere, and touching" by *Photoplay,* the real significance of the picture was its re-release in 1929 with several dialogue scenes added. The transition to talkies was a matter of some anxiety for her, as it was for most of her peers in the business, some of whose voices destroyed their silent film personas and their careers. But Gaynor needn't have worried, for her voice was judged "an immediate added attraction." Her future in the film business was assured.

Now in the third year of her Fox contract, she churned out three more pictures, two of them romantic comedies with Frank Borzage at the helm and with Charlie Farrell as her co-star.

She sang and danced on screen for the first time in *Sunny Side Up,* handling seven numbers and helping the film to win that year's vote as "most enjoyable production" in a magazine poll. Fox's publicity department was now billing Gaynor and Farrell as "America's favorite sweethearts," but Janet's real-life affections lay elsewhere. During 1928, she had met a young writer at Fox, Jesse Peck, who had ambitions to be a lawyer. The two were married on September 11, 1929. The marriage lasted only until 1933, but the divorce was a friendly one, and the fan magazines tiptoed around the breakup rather than besmirch their favorite star's reputation.

Gaynor had been such a hit in *Sunny Side Up* that Fox gave her two more musicals in 1930 (*High Society Blues* and *Happy Days*), but both flopped, and she knew why. "I know perfectly well I can't sing and that I didn't belong" in musical films, she told *Film Pictorial* in 1932. "I'd saved my money and I felt that I might just as well get out of films then and there with my screen reputation intact." She did precisely that after Fox refused to give in to her pleas for no more musicals. She took herself out of the business and moved to Hawaii for seven months, until Fox finally relented, having found *****Maureen O'Sullivan** as its new musical-comedy ingenue.

With her return in 1931, in Raoul Walsh's *The Man Who Came Back,* Gaynor embarked on what would be the last phase of her film career, starring in no less than 12 pictures over the next four years, in roles as varied as a drug addict, a scullery maid, a spunky Irish sweetheart, and a southern belle. Among the pictures were five more romantic comedies with Charlie Farrell and, despite her tiff with Fox, two more musicals, although she had to sing only one number in each. Her reviews seemed to grow more glowing with each picture, and her name was box-office magic for Fox. "I want people to forget their troubles and string along with the characters they see on the screen," she said, and her legions of fans turned out by the thousands to do just that.

Her last picture for Fox was 1935's *One More Spring.* The studio was then in the process of merging with Twentieth Century Films, and Gaynor chose not to renew her contract with the new Twentieth Century-Fox, risking her reputation as the country's favorite romantic leading lady. Just as she had known musical comedy wasn't for her, Gaynor, now 29, knew full well that she was reaching the end of her tenure as America's youthful sweetheart. "I had no desire to hold time in check," she said, "because each age has its own joys and compensations." She started looking for more mature roles and found one in William Wellman's *Small Town Girl* for MGM, playing opposite Robert Taylor. It was Wellman who, later in 1937, would give her what *Photoplay* called "her best work since the advent of talkies," the role of Esther Blodgett in *A Star Is Born,* written by the husband-wife team of *Dorothy Parker and Alan Campbell (and said to be based on the marriage of *Barbara Stanwyck and Frank Fay). "The story was perfect for me," she said with characteristic candor, "a little nobody without any great talent who suddenly finds herself a star." Her performance, as the South Dakota farm girl who reaches the heights of show business stardom at great personal cost, brought her a second nomination for Best Actress, although she lost to *Luise Rainer (for *The Good Earth*).

The next year, 1938, brought the two films which would be her last screen appearances for the next 20 years, *The Young at Heart* and *Three Loves Has Nancy.* The costume designer for the second picture was Gilbert Adrian, who would later build a successful fashion design house on his Hollywood reputation. He proposed to Gaynor while they were working on the film, and the two were married in August of 1939. At the same time, Janet announced her retirement from motion pictures. After working steadily for more than 15 years, she said, she wanted time to know other things. "I knew in order to have those things, one had to make time for them," she said. "Then, as if by miracle, everything I really wanted happened. Suddenly I was in a whole new world . . . a world Adrian exposed me to." An important part of that new world was a son, Robin Gaynor Adrian, born in July of 1940.

For the next 17 years, Gaynor devoted herself to those "other things." She took great joy in raising Robin, helping Gilbert establish himself as one of the leading *haute couture* designers of the 1950s, and indulging her passion for oil painting, a hobby she had developed throughout her film years, exhibiting many of her works under the name Augusta Louise. She and Gilbert purchased a ranch in Brazil in 1952 and became unofficial ambassadors for that country, with Gaynor receiving the medal of the Order of the Southern Cross for fostering relations between Brazil and the United States. She appeared on the new medium in 1953, taking a role in a television drama; and, in 1957, appeared in what would be her last film, *Bernadine,* a teenage romantic comedy in which she came full circle and played the mother of one of the young male leads.

In 1959, while Gaynor was in rehearsal for the Broadway drama *Midnight Sun,* her husband of 20 years died of a heart attack. Grief-stricken, she nonetheless went on with the show, earning respectful reviews in what was otherwise a short-lived production. She married for the third time in 1964, having met Broadway producer Paul Gregory several years earlier. Her interest in the Broadway stage brought her roles in 1980's *Harold and Maude* (in the role played by *Ruth Gordon on film) and in 1981's *On Golden Pond.*

Later that year she was with Gregory in San Francisco, where she was rehearsing with her friend, actress *Mary Martin, for the out-of-town opening of the comedy *Over Easy.* One night, as Gaynor, Gregory, and Martin were taking a cab to dinner, a drunk driver smashed into them. For the next two months, Gaynor lay in critical condition in a San Francisco hospital with severe damage to her internal organs. She never fully recovered, despite six operations over the next three years; on September 14, 1984, she died from complications of pneumonia at her home in Palm Springs, California.

During her 78 years, Janet Gaynor made some difficult decisions about the direction of both her career and her personal life. But she made them with a clear assessment of herself and her abilities. "For fifteen years I'd always ended in the fadeout where they were married and lived happily ever after," she told Hollywood columnist Earl Wilson in 1951, after she'd been away from films for 12 years. "And I wanted to go on into the fadeout and live happily ever after. And that," she said proudly, "is what I've done."

SOURCES:

Billips, Connie. *Janet Gaynor: A Bio-Bibliography.* NY: Greenwood Press, 1992.
Katz, Ephraim. *The Film Encyclopedia.* NY: Perennial Library, 1979.

Norman Powers,
writer-producer, Chelsea Lane Productions,
New York, New York

Gaynor, Mitzi (1930—)

American actress, dancer, and singer who starred in the film version of South Pacific. *Born Franceska Mitzie Gerber (sometimes seen Franceska Mitzi Marlene De Charney von Gerber), on September 4, 1930, in Chicago, Illinois; attended high school in Detroit, Michigan; married Jack Bean (a talent agent), on December 2, 1954.*

Filmography: My Blue Heaven *(1950);* Take Care of My Little Girl *(1951);* Golden Girl *(1951);* We're

Opposite page
$\mathcal{M}$itzi
$\mathcal{G}$aynor

Not Married *(1952);* Bloodhounds of Broadway *(1952);* Down among the Sheltering Palms *(1953);* The I Don't Care Girl *(1953);* Three Young Texans *(1954);* There's No Business Like Show Business *(1954);* Anything Goes *(1956);* The Birds and the Bees *(1956);* The Joker Is Wild *(1957);* Les Girls *(1957);* South Pacific *(1958);* Happy Anniversary *(1959);* Surprise Package *(1960);* For Love or Money *(1963).*

Reputedly a descendant of Hungarian aristocracy, actress Mitzi Gaynor followed her mother into dancing, making her stage debut at the age of three. By the late 1940s, she was in the corps de ballet of the Los Angeles Light Opera Company where she was spotted by producer-actor George Jessel, who arranged a screen test at Twentieth Century-Fox.

Signing a term contract, Gaynor made her film debut in *My Blue Heaven* (1950), receiving good notices, particularly for her rendition of the song "Live Hard, Work Hard, Love Hard." She subsequently made a string of musicals for Fox, including her personal favorite, *Golden Girl* (1951), in which she played *Lotta Crabtree, the renowned performer of the California gold-rush days. Despite her perky good looks and considerable dancing and singing ability, her films did poorly at the box office, and the studio dropped her option in 1954. That same year, she married talent agent Jack Bean, who helped get her career back on track. With a streamlined figure, blonder hair, and a more provocative image, Gaynor made a number of hit films at other studios, including *Anything Goes* (1956), with Bing Crosby, *The Joker Is Wild*, opposite Frank Sinatra, and *Les Girls*, co-starring Gene Kelly and *Kay Kendall (both 1957). Gaynor was chosen by director Joshua Logan for the coveted role of nurse Nellie Forbush in the much-heralded film version of *South Pacific* (*Mary Martin, who introduced Forbush to Broadway, was considered too old), but the movie was a failure and actually damaged her career. She tried to come back with a few romantic comedies, but by 1963 her days in film were over. "The movie musical thing was finished," she said, "the contract players were flooding the streets, and I was just part of the backwash."

Experimenting in other entertainment media, Gaynor appeared on television and initiated a nightclub act in which she sang, danced, and performed comedy skits. Opening in Las Vegas in July 1961, she continued to entertain at clubs. When she performed at the Westbury Music Fair in October 1979, *Newsday* praised her versatility. "She's not just a straight hoofer

and singer, but a first-rate musical comedienne, injecting wit and humor into her act that comes out charmingly." During the 1960s and 1970s, Gaynor made ten televisions specials, including her most elaborate "Mitzi and a Hundred Guys," which included guest appearances by Michael Landon, Bill Bixby, Andy Griffith, Monte Hall, and Bob Hope. As late as 1989, Gaynor was embarking on a 36-city national tour of the musical *Anything Goes*. "I got my Social Security card when I was twelve," she said at the time, "and I haven't been out of work a single day since then."

SOURCES:

Katz, Ephraim. *The Film Encyclopedia*. NY: Harper-Collins, 1994.

Parish, James Robert, and Michael R. Pitts. *Hollywood Songsters*. NY: Garland, 1991.

Gebbie, Grace (1877–1936).

See Drayton, Grace Gebbie.

Geddes, Barbara Bel (b. 1922).

See Bel Geddes, Barbara.

Geddes, Janet (fl. 1637)

Scottish religious dissenter. Name variations: Jenny. Flourished around 1637.

Janet Geddes is said to have been the originator of a riot in St. Giles' Church, Edinburgh, Scotland, on July 23, 1637. The church, in the High Street of the Old Town, is memorable for its associations with some of the most important events in the religious history of Scotland. Geddes reputedly emphasized her protest against the introduction of the English liturgy into Scotland by throwing her folding stool at the head of the officiating bishop.

Geddes, Wilhelmina (1887–1955)

Irish ecclesiastical artist. Born in Drumreilly, County Leitrim, Ireland, in 1887; died in 1955; attended Methodist College, Belfast; Belfast School of Art; Metropolitan School of Art, Dublin.

One of Dublin's first stained-glass artists, Wilhelmina Geddes was a member of *Sarah Purser's Studio of Ecclesiastical Art, An Túr Gloine. In addition to her glass work, Geddes illustrated books and designed book jackets, book plates, stamps and posters. Establishing an international reputation for her stained glass, she designed windows for churches in Ireland, New Zealand, and Canada. In 1929, she completed an eight-paneled window on the theme of the

Children of Lir for the Ulster Museum, and in 1938 she installed the Great Rose Window in the Cathedral of Ypres in memory of Albert I, king of the Belgians. Her work is represented at the Victoria and Albert Museum in London and at the National Gallery of Ireland in Dublin, which holds 30 of her designs for stained-glass windows.

Geiringer, Hilda (1893–1973)

German applied mathematician and statistician. Born on September 28, 1893, in Vienna; died on March 22, 1973, in Santa Barbara, California; only daughter and one of two children of Ludwig (a textile manufacturer) and Martha (Wertheimer) Geiringer; University of Vienna, Ph.D., 1917; married Felix Pollaczek (a mathematician), in 1921 (divorced 1925); married Richard von Mises (a mathematician), on November 5, 1943 (died 1954); children: (first marriage) one daughter, Magda.

The daughter of a Jewish textile manufacturer, Hilda Geiringer was born on September 28, 1893, in Vienna. She received her Ph.D. in pure mathematics from the University of Vienna in 1917. In 1921, after working for a year as editor of the *Fortschritte der Mathematik*, she accepted an academic position at the University of Berlin, working as the assistant to Richard von Mises in the Institute of Applied Mathematics. That same year, she married fellow mathematician Felix Pollaczek, with whom she had a daughter, Magda, the following year. In 1925, they divorced, and as a single parent Geiringer pursued her career. After six years at the university, she was recognized for her outstanding teaching as well as for her important research in probability theory and the mathematical development of plasticity theory, which led to the Geiringer equations for plane plastic deformations (1930). In 1933, when Hitler came into power and all Jewish educators in Berlin lost their jobs, Geiringer fled to Turkey, where, after learning the language, she obtained a job lecturing at Istanbul University. By 1939, however, even Turkey was not safe, and she and her daughter came to the United States. Shortly after her arrival, she secured a position as a lecturer at Bryn Mawr College.

In 1943, Geiringer married Richard von Mises, her former employer at the University of Berlin and now a full professor at Harvard University. She moved to Massachusetts in 1944, to chair the mathematics department at Wheaton College in Norton, a position she held until her retirement. In addition to her demanding teaching schedule, Geiringer continued to work on her own research into statistics, particularly the mathematical basis of Mendelian genetics. When von Mises died in 1953, Geiringer received a grant from the Office of Naval Research to complete his work at Harvard. In 1958, with Geoffrey Ludford, she finished one of her husband's incomplete manuscripts, published as *Mathematical Theory of Compressible Fluid Flow*. After her retirement in 1959, she continued to revise her husband's earlier works and to write her own articles, several of which supported her controversial view of probability theory (as a science based on observable phenomena rather than an extension of mathematical set theory). In 1964, she published a revised edition of von Mises' *Mathematical Theory of Probability and Statistics*, in which she removed an inconsistency present in the original work.

Late in her career, Geiringer was recognized by her alma mater, the University of Vienna, with a special ceremony honoring the 50th anniversary of her graduation. The University of Berlin, her former employer, made her a professor emeritus in 1956, and Wheaton awarded her an honorary degree in 1960.

Beyond her chosen field of mathematics, Geiringer was an avid mountain climber and also enjoyed literature and classical music. She died just six months short of her 80th birthday, while visiting her brother Karl, a noted musicologist, in Santa Barbara, California.

SOURCES:

Bailey, Brooke. *The Remarkable Lives of 100 Women Healers and Scientists*. Holbrook, MA: Bob Adams, 1994.

Sicherman, Barbara, and Carol Hurd Green, eds. *Notable American Women: The Modern Period*. Cambridge, MA: The Belknap Press of Harvard University Press, 1980.

COLLECTIONS:

Hilda Geiringer's papers are in the Harvard University Archives at Harvard University and the Schlesinger Library at Radcliffe College.

Barbara Morgan,
Melrose, Massachusetts

Geirthrud.

Variant of Gertrude.

Geistinger, Marie (1833–1903)

Austrian soprano celebrated in Vienna as the "Queen of the Operetta" whose superstar status helped popularize the stage works of Johann Strauss, Jr. Born Maria Charlotte Cäcilia Geistinger in Graz, *Styria, Austria, on July 26, 1833 (some sources cite July 20, 1828 or 1836); died in Klagenfurt, Carinthia, Austria, on September 29, 1903; daughter of Nikolaus Geistinger and Charlotte Geistinger; married August Kormann (1850–1930, an actor), in 1877 (divorced 1881).*

For almost half a century, Marie Geistinger was a power to be reckoned with in the cultural life of Imperial Vienna, not only as a celebrated soprano but also as a dramatic actress and as a theater manager. She was born in 1833 in the provincial capital of Graz, where her parents Nikolaus and **Charlotte Geistinger** were both engaged as actors. By age 11, Marie was appearing on stage in children's roles. In 1850, she made her official debut as an adult actress in Munich, followed two years later in Vienna where she performed at the Theater in der Josefstadt, delighting her audiences with her humorous parodies of the then-famous Spanish dancer **Pepita de Oliva**. She left Vienna for Berlin in 1854, remaining there for several years before moving on to successful engagements in Hamburg and Riga. Geistinger reigned over the Riga stage from 1859 through 1863, showing remarkable versatility as a star of opera, operetta and comic theater. The upward trajectory of Marie Geistinger's career continued in Berlin, where the singer and comedienne pleased countless theatergoers at that city's Viktoria Theater until she accepted an offer from Vienna in 1865.

From the start of her Vienna years, Marie Geistinger was the undisputed "Queen of Operetta." Her return to Vienna in 1865 marked an important milestone not only in Geistinger's career but in the history of Vienna as well. The year 1865 saw proud Vienna's inaugural of its grand new Ringstrasse, which in time could boast of such imposing edifices as the Parliament building, the new University of Vienna, and the Imperial Opera House. To entertain the prosperous and confident Viennese citizenry, Geistinger starred in Jacques Offenbach's *La belle Helene*, immediately creating a sensation. Although many regard Vienna as the cradle of operetta, it is in fact the city of Paris that deserves that distinction. The naughty sophistication and witty social satire of Offenbach's *operas bouffes* were imported to Vienna in the late 1850s, where they were avidly accepted by the increasingly sophisticated bourgeoisie of the burgeoning metropolis of Central Europe's key political state, the Habsburg Empire.

Marie Geistinger enjoyed the imprimatur of Offenbach because he had seen her on stage in

Berlin performing in a popular farce in which she was required to divest herself of various items of clothing. "I have never seen anyone undress with such beauty and discreetness," Offenbach told her backstage. "I will have a scene of that sort written for you in my next piece." After he saw her in *La belle Helene,* Offenbach felt she had given the best performance he had ever seen in the work's starring role and was the greatest operetta performer he had ever encountered. The only serious rival to Geistinger's fame in Vienna in the mid-1860s was **Josephine Gallmeyer** (1838–1884), whose comedic talents were considerable and who was renowned for her uniquely uninhibited cancan.

Geistinger was more than equal to challenges from Gallmeyer or any other Viennese star performer. By the end of the 1860s, she had appeared in countless performances of Offenbach (including his *La Grande-Duchesse de Gerolstein* and *Barbe-bleue*), as well as in other composers' works, invariably enjoying enthusiastic reviews and sold-out audiences. Energetic, confident and with years of stage experience behind her, in 1869 Geistinger became co-director of the Theater an der Wien, sharing management responsibilities with the versatile Maximil-

ian Steiner. By the early 1870s, Viennese audiences had grown tired of Offenbach and other foreign composers; the cancan was now regarded as somewhat absurdly frivolous and passé if not indeed downright decadent. The desire for a new and more homegrown operetta genre was growing and the Waltz King, Johann Strauss, Jr., was on hand to meet this need. In 1871, he set to music as his first operetta Maximilian Steiner's libretto *Indigo oder die vierzig Räuber* (*Indigo or the Forty Thieves*). Although the story line was muddled at best and it was far too long (four hours), Geistinger's performance turned this, the first indigenous Viennese operetta, into a smash hit from its premiere performance at the Theater an der Wien on February 10, 1871.

The next Strauss operetta, entitled "a comic operetta in three acts," was to prove to be his single most successful stage work, and indeed very likely the most famous operetta in history. This was *Die Fledermaus* (The Bat), with a libretto by Carl Haffner and Richard Genée, based on a French vaudeville piece by Henri Meilhac and Ludovic Halévy. The French work was first translated for use in Vienna as a straight play which took place at a *réveillon,* a midnight supper party. The problems this caused were only solved when the play was adapted as a libretto for Johann Strauss, who replaced the *réveillon* with a Viennese ball. Along with Strauss' sparkling music, a brilliant singer-actress is necessary in the soprano part of Rosalinde, wife of the wealthy and bored Gabriel von Eisenstein, for the witty plot of *Die Fledermaus* to shine. Even before the premiere performance, Geistinger gave a select group of Vienna's elite a sneak preview of Strauss' still-unperformed work when she sang Rosalinde's *csárdás* at a charity performance.

Marie Geistinger helped make *Die Fledermaus* an immediate success with the fickle Viennese public at its premiere performance at the Theater an der Wien on April 5, 1874. Her Rosalinde won her many curtain calls that evening. Despite the fact that Vienna had been profoundly shaken only months before by a catastrophic stock-market crash, the audience left its cares behind for a few hours, having been completely won over by both the new operetta's music and plot. The work was taken off the boards after only 16 performances, not—as some sources claim—due to lack of audience interest, but rather because of a theater schedule tied to a pre-booked visiting operatic company season; after this hiatus, in fact, the work returned to continue to delight the fun-loving Viennese—something

Marie
Geistinger

this frothy comedy of errors has continued to do not only in Vienna but throughout the world.

After the smashing success of *Die Fledermaus,* to which she contributed to a substantial degree, Marie Geistinger continued her multifaceted career as singer, actress and theater manager. In 1875, she resigned from the management of the Theater an der Wien, but remained as busy as ever on the stage. She created leading roles in the premieres of two more Johann Strauss operettas, *Carneval in Rom* (1873), and *Cagliostro in Wien* (1875), and remained a favorite as well with the Viennese public by starring in the always popular local dialect plays of Nestroy and Raimund. Geistinger was now at the height of her popularity in Vienna as the city's idol, adored for being uniquely vivacious, charming and enticing. Displaying stamina and versatility, in 1876 Geistinger began to emphasize her dramatic ability by appearing in classic stage roles at Vienna's Stadttheater. Here she starred as Queen *Elizabeth I in Heinrich von Laube's *Essex,* as well as taking the roles of Medea and *Sappho in the play by Grillparzer. She also successfully played the part of Beatrice in Shakespeare's *Much Ado about Nothing.* Encouraged by her Viennese successes, she then brought the same roles for the next several years to the major theaters of Berlin, Munich, Hamburg, Dresden and Leipzig.

In 1880, Marie Geistinger undertook a gruelling tour of North America which would take her to both coasts of the United States. In large cities as well as small towns and hamlets, she performed both as singer and actress to audiences that were considerably less sophisticated but perhaps even more enthusiastic than the ones she knew so well in Europe. In New York City, a large and enthusiastic audience saw her perform at the Thalia Theater in the Bowery. Several years after her return to Europe, she was forced to go into temporary retirement because of serious eye problems. By 1891, however, she had resumed her touring, again venturing to North America in April 1897. The following year, the aging Queen of the Viennese Operetta made her last major tour in Austria and Germany. In 1900, she gave her farewell performance in Vienna. In profound contrast to her stage portrayals, which Egon Gartenberg has described as being "realistic, charming, and persuasive," Geistinger's personal life was marked by instability and lack of direction. Her only marriage, to the actor August Kormann, was a failure, lasting only from 1877 to its dissolution in 1881. Despite her immense success over many decades, by the closing years of her life she had lost virtually her entire fortune through poor judgment and was forced to auction off her most precious possessions. Marie Geistinger died in Klagenfurt on September 29, 1903. She is buried in Vienna's venerable Zentralfriedhof (Central Cemetery), where her grave is designated as Ehrengrab (Grave of Honor) 32A/18.

SOURCES:

Brusatti, Otto, and Wilhelm Deutschmann. *Fle Zi Wi Csá & Co.: Die Wiener Operette.* Vienna: Eigenverlag der Museen der Stadt Wien, 1984.

Budig, Robert S. *Ehrengräber am Wiener Zentralfriedhof.* Vienna: Compress Verlag, 1995.

Gartenberg, Egon. *Johann Strauss: The End of an Era.* University Park, PA: Pennsylvania State University Press, 1975.

Grün, Bernard. *Kulturgeschichte der Operette.* Berlin: VEB Lied der Zeit, 1967.

Irmer, Hans-Jochen. "Jacques Offenbachs Werke in Wien und Berlin: Zum 150. Geburtstag des Komponisten am 20. Juni 1969," in *Wissenschaftliche Zeitschrift der Humboldt Universität Berlin.* Vol. 18, no. 1, 1969, pp. 125–145.

Jacob, Heinrich Eduard. *Johann Strauss, Father and Son: A Century of Light Music.* Translated by Marguerite Wolff. NY: Crown, 1939.

Kohut, Adolf. *Die grössten und berühmtesten deutschen Soubretten des neunzehnten Jahrhunderts.* Düsseldorf: F. Bagel Verlag, 1890.

Linhardt, Marion. *Inszenierung der Frau—Frau in der Inszeenierung: Operette in Wien zwischen 1865 und 1900.* Tutzing: Hans Schneider Verlag, 1997.

"Marie Geistinger Dead," in *The New York Times.* October 1, 1903, p. 5.

"Marie Geistinger Is Here," in *The New York Times.* April 12, 1897, p. 7.

Pirchan, Emil. *Marie Geistinger: Die Königin der Operette.* Vienna: W. Frick Verlag, 1947.

Traubner, Richard. *Operetta: A Theatrical History.* NY: Oxford University Press, 1989.

John Haag,
Associate Professor of History,
University of Georgia, Athens, Georgia

Gelfman, Gesia (d. 1882)

Russian revolutionary. Name variations: Guessia or Jessie Helfman or Helfmann. Grew up in Mozyr (Minsk province), Russia; died of peritonitis on February 1, 1882; children: one daughter (born on October 12, 1881).

To avoid an arranged marriage, at age 17, Gesia Gelfman fled her parents' home in Mozyr and moved to Kiev; there she enrolled in midwifery courses, the only courses available to women in Kiev, intent on making a living. She also joined a group known as the Fritsche, which advocated socialism and class warfare. *Vera Figner was a prominent member of the group. In 1875, Gelfman was imprisoned for serving as an intermediary for those engaged in propagandizing against the government. Four years later, she escaped. Her freedom was brief. Because the apartment she was sharing was used for preparatory meetings by those involved with the March 1, 1881, assassination Alexander II, tsar of Russia, Gesia Gelfman was again arrested. Weeks later, she was condemned to death. But Gelfman was pregnant, and, after demonstrations in Russia and abroad, authorities relented. Though her sentence was commuted, she was held in a large cell at the House of Preliminary Detention, with around the clock sentries, where she gave birth to a daughter on October 12, 1881. Under Russian law, her rights to keep the child were protected. Even so, authorities took the child away from her in the night and left it at a foundling home. Three months later, Gelfman died.

Gellhorn, Martha (1908–1998)

American journalist and fiction writer who was the leading female war correspondent of World War II.
Born Martha Ellis Gellhorn on November 8, 1908, in St. Louis, Missouri; died of cancer at her home in London, England, on February 16, 1998; daughter of Edna Fischel Gellhorn (a community activist) and George Gellhorn (a gynecologist); attended John Burroughs School, St. Louis, 1923–26; Bryn Mawr College, 1926–29; married Bertrand de Jouvenel (a journalist), in summer 1933; married Ernest Hemingway (a novelist), on November 21, 1940; married Thomas Stanley Matthews (a magazine editor), on February 4, 1954; children: (adopted) George Alexander.

Became war correspondent for Collier's Weekly, *Spain (1937–38), Finland (1939), China (1940–41), England, Italy, France, Germany (1941–45); was a freelance fiction and nonfiction writer.*

Selected publications: What Mad Pursuit *(Frederick A. Stokes, 1934);* The Trouble I've Seen *(William Morrow, 1936);* A Stricken Field *(Scribner, 1940);* The Heart of Another *(Scribner, 1941);* Liana *(Scribner, 1943); (play, with Virginia Cowles)* Love Goes to Press *(1946);* Wine of Astonishment *(Scribner, 1948, reprinted as* The Point of No Return, *New American Library, 1989);* The Honeyed Peace *(Doubleday, 1953);* Two by Two *(Simon and Schuster, 1958);* The Face of War *(1959);* His Own Man *(Simon and Schuster, 1961);* Pretty Tales for Tired People *(Simon and Schuster, 1965);* The Lowest Trees Have Tops *(Dodd, Mead, 1967);* The Weather in Africa *(Dodd, Mead, 1978);* Travels with Myself and Another *(Dodd, Mead, 1978); (editor)* The Face of War *(Atlantic Monthly Press, 1988); (editor)* The View from the Ground *(Atlantic Monthly Press, 1988);* The Novellas of Martha Gellhorn *(Alfred A. Knopf, 1993).*

Wearing gray flannel trousers, a sweater, and a warm windbreaker and carrying only a knapsack and some $50, Martha Gellhorn reached the Andorran-Spanish frontier in mid-March 1937 and crossed into Spain. Once over the border, the trim blonde took an antiquated wooden train to Barcelona and, after two days, reached the Spanish capital of Madrid, where she found herself in the midst of a particularly violent civil war. As she walked through the debris, bitterly cold and exhausted, Gellhorn saw how much the city itself had become a battlefield. She made her way to the basement restaurant of the Gran Via Hotel, the only designated eating place for correspondents. Ernest Hemingway greeted her with the words, "I knew you'd get here, daughter, because I fixed it so you could." Aware that the prominent novelist had really done nothing on her behalf, Gellhorn was furious over his braggadocio, not to mention his failure to give her credit for her own resourcefulness. As a novice in war reporting, however, she was utterly dependent upon such seasoned correspondents. Besides, she already felt strongly attracted to him.

Martha Gellhorn soon became a veteran correspondent. Together with Hemingway, she took blood to hospitals in Guadalajara, visited American trenches at Morata, and surveyed the Loyalist armies from the 4,800-foot Sierra de Guadarrama. She proofread Hemingway's dispatches, dashing down bombed streets to deliver them to the Spanish censors. She drove a station wagon for Norman Bethune, a Canadian medical doctor of pronouncedly radical views. She later remembered: "We were all in it together, the certainty that we were *right*. . . . We knew, we just *knew* . . . that Spain was the place to stop Fascism. This was it. It was one of those moments in history when there was no doubt." Little wonder Hemingway dedicated his novel of the war, *For Whom the Bell Tolls* (1940), with the simple words, "This book is for Martha Gellhorn."

She was born on November 8, 1908, in St. Louis, Missouri. Her German-born father George Gellhorn was a prominent gynecologist who taught at both Washington and St. Louis universities. Her mother **Edna Fischel Gellhorn** was a leading community activist, who was particularly involved in the suffrage movement. Both parents were strong nonconformists, raising their four children to be distinct individualists. Family discussions followed *Robert's Rules of Order*, with father George presiding. Disputes were resolved by consulting reference books.

Martha, or "Marty" as she was often called, spent grades one through nine at Washington University's Mary Institute. She then attended the experimental John Burroughs School, which had just been founded by such liberal St. Louis parents as her mother. In 1926, she entered Bryn Mawr College, Edna's alma mater. Though she excelled at writing poetry and involvement in contemporary politics, Gellhorn found the atmosphere too cloistered and left at the end of her junior year.

In the summer of 1929, she began her writing career with the prestigious New York weekly, the *New Republic,* but soon sought on-the-spot reporting. Hence, she simply walked into the office of Hearst's *Albany Times Union,* wearing dungarees and announcing, "My name is Martha Gellhorn. I want to work." Coverage of social events, deaths, and accidents quickly lost their charm, however, and within six months she left the paper.

In February 1930, Gellhorn bartered her way to Europe. In exchange for writing a laudatory article for the trade paper of the Holland-American line, she was given a free trip—third class in steerage. Settling on Paris' Left Bank, she went through a succession of jobs. At one point, she wrote advertising copy; at another, she did freelance work for the United Press. Her first real break came when she joined the Paris staff of the American fashion magazine *Vogue.*

By the fall of 1930, Gellhorn was engaged in special assignments for the *St. Louis Post-Dispatch.* Stories ranged from women delegates to the League of Nations at Geneva to striking textile workers in Roubaix-Tourcoing, France. By this time, she was traveling throughout Europe with Bertrand de Jouvenel, a radical French journalist of aristocratic background. A married man, Jouvenel had caused a scandal by walking out on his wife in order to accompany Gellhorn.

In the spring of 1931, Gellhorn returned to the United States, where she engaged in a brief affair with St. Louis poet Joseph Pennell. By the end of September, however, she was reunited with Jouvenel, with whom she traveled in the United States and Europe. In the summer of 1933, they married in Spain, though within a year the union was in trouble. Gellhorn was suspicious of Jouvenel's *idée fixe* that dedicated French and German youth could prevent another fratricidal world conflict, a position Gellhorn found particularly naive once Adolf Hitler had gained power. By 1935, the couple separated.

Excited by the prospects of working for Franklin D. Roosevelt's New Deal, Gellhorn arrived back in the U.S. in October 1934. She was hired by Harry Hopkins, director of the Federal Emergency Relief Administration (FERA) as investigator-at-large, though—as *Time* magazine noted—she was a most atypical bureaucrat: "Her face was too beautiful, her blonde hair too expensive looking, her long legs too distracting, her clothes too Paris-perfect."

> *I* was a writer before I met him, and I have been a writer for 45 years since. Why should I be a footnote to someone else's life?
>
> —Martha Gellhorn

Gellhorn toured the nation examining the condition of relief workers—their health, nutrition, morale, and likeliness of support. Her salary: $35 a month plus traveling expenses. Her reports covered union-busting in North Carolina, poverty in Boston, and graft in Rhode Island and New Hampshire. In the process, Gellhorn, never a conservative, became truly radicalized. To her, the American economic system was a brutal one.

An impolitic exposé of a contracting scam in Idaho led to her being fired from FERA, but the administration really had no hard feelings. An acquaintance of *Eleanor Roosevelt since her *Times Union* days, Gellhorn dined at the White House, where she reported on the conditions she had witnessed. In December 1935, when she was suffering from anemia, she wrote Eleanor Roosevelt, who persuaded her to stay at the executive mansion. In fact, Eleanor became a sort of second mother to Martha. Conversely, Gellhorn never warmed to Franklin, whom she later said treated her as "a sort of mascot or pet poodle."

All this time, Gellhorn was writing professionally. In 1934, she produced a semi-autobiographical novel *What Mad Pursuit,* dealing with the rude awakening of an immature female reporter. In 1936, her fictional account of the Depression, *The Trouble I've Seen,* was published. In his laudatory preface, British writer H.G. Wells wrote, "enlarge this book a million times and you have the complete American tragedy." Plugged by Eleanor Roosevelt in her daily column, the book catapulted Gellhorn into minor celebrity status. A striking picture of her adorned the cover of the September 26 issue of the *Saturday Review of Literature.* Soon her short stories were appearing in *The New Yorker* and *Scribner's Magazine.*

Eventually finding the promotional hoopla distasteful, Martha and her recently widowed mother Edna decided to spend Christmas 1936 in Florida. While visiting Sloppy Joe's, a bar in Key

West, they came upon Ernest Hemingway, who first impressed Martha as nothing more than "a huge, dirty man." Yet the magnetic novelist won the Gellhorns over, and when Martha left the town soon afterwards, Ernest pursued her.

In March 1937, Gellhorn went to Spain, covering the civil war there for *Collier's* and holding the title of special correspondent. The title was originally specious, *Collier's* editor Kyle Crichton bestowing it on her to remedy any problem with border guards. Hemingway was already there, reporting for the North American Newspaper Alliance.

Gellhorn proved her mettle. Not concentrating on combat, she wrote on the war's impact on individuals, combatant and noncombatant alike. Her "Only the Shells Whine," a story published in July 17 issue of *Collier's,* plunged her readers into the daily bombing of Madrid with an intensity that Hemingway himself could not capture. Moreover, *Collier's* now recognized her as a full-fledged staffer.

Gellhorn and Hemingway were soon lovers. They first tried to hide their affair by acting discreetly, but their liaison was public knowledge. Although still married to the former **Pauline Pfeiffer**, Hemingway was a jealous paramour, once admitting that he locked Gellhorn in her Madrid hotel room "so that no man could bother her." True, Ernest's possessiveness disturbed Martha. At the same time, she found him "instantly lovable" if "not a grown up."

In May 1937, the couple returned to the States, where Gellhorn publicized the Loyalist cause. Taking advantage of her ties to the Roosevelts, she arranged for a private White House showing of Hemingway's film, *The Spanish Earth*. That August, Gellhorn returned to Spain, where she again covered the war, more specifically, the battle-scarred cities of Belchite and Brunete and the fighting fronts of Teruel and Aranjuez. Broadcasting from Madrid, she conveyed the city's quiet stoicism to American radio listeners.

Hemingway admired Gellhorn's courage but was not always charitable in his assessment of her. During breaks in the fighting, he wrote a play, *The Fifth Column* (1938), in which he offered a veiled portrait of Martha that was not entirely cordial: "Granted she's lazy and spoiled, and rather stupid, and enormously on the make. Still she's very beautiful, very friendly, and very charming and rather innocent—and quite brave."

Soon after Christmas 1937, Gellhorn came back to the U.S., where she engaged in a lecture tour to raise money for the Spanish wounded. Within two months, she had spoken in 22 cities. Her audiences were huge: 3,000 at the University of Minnesota, 1,000 in St. Louis. "She spoke as an honest partisan," noted the *Post-Dispatch,* "and called Franco a butcher." Frustrated by American apathy, she returned to Spain that spring. She and Hemingway engaged in six more weeks of reporting.

In May 1938, Gellhorn covered peacetime England for *Collier's*. She found the island nation so complacent that she would personally harangue Britons about Hitler's might. "The English have always had the privilege of fighting their wars someplace else," she wrote, "but now England is preparing to fight in her own air, and the prospect is pleasing to no one." The title of her article, dated September 17: "The Lord Will Provide—for England."

Gellhorn was more encouraged by the attitudes of the French populace, though she found the nation's leadership inept. Visiting Czechoslovakia in the wake of the Munich conference, she conveyed her sadness in a *Collier's* piece appearing in the December 10 issue. This time the title was "Obituary of a Democracy." In early November, Gellhorn and Hemingway took their final trip to Spain. Despondent over the Republic's inevitable defeat, the couple left within the month.

By March 1939, Gellhorn and Hemingway were in Cuba. Martha called their status "living in contented sin." They resided in the impoverished village of San Francisco de Paula, 15 miles east of downtown Havana, where Gellhorn renovated a large house—Finca Vigia—for them. September found them in Sun Valley Lodge in central Idaho. There she followed the Hemingway regimen of writing in the morning, and riding, tennis, and shooting in the afternoon.

That November, with the onset of World War II, *Collier's* sent Gellhorn to Finland to cover its incipient war with Russia. She arrived at Helsinki on the 29th, just hours ahead of the first Soviet strike. The Finns, she claimed, would fight a defensive war and thereby repel the Russians. Returning to Cuba, then to Sun Valley, she and Hemingway were married on November 21, 1940, in the Union Pacific Railroad dining room in Cheyenne, Wyoming.

Early in 1941, *Collier's* gave Gellhorn an Asian assignment. Her task: to report on Japanese offensives and China's ability to resist them. She visited many spots, including Hong Kong, Chungking (Chongqing), Rangoon, and Singapore. Hemingway accompanied her as correspondent for the new liberal New York daily *PM*. Leaving Hemingway in Hong Kong, she flew to the Burma Road in bad weather in an unpressurized plane. Conditions equaled the most dangerous commercial flying in the world. In another leg of the journey, this one with Hemingway, Gellhorn traveled from Shao-kuan to Chungking by truck, horseback, motor boat, and sampan. As noted by Gellhorn biographer Carl Rollyson, her readers:

> learned about the nine war zones, the Japanese drive to divide and conquer China, the

Chinese army's lack of equipment and supplies (5 million superbly disciplined men who had no shoes), the gross underpayment of soldiers, and the hatred of the Japanese that made it virtually impossible to prevent Chinese soldiers from killing their prisoners.

In Chungking, they were twice the luncheon guests of Generalissimo Chiang Kai-shek and Madame Chiang Kai-shek (*Song Meiling) and also met Communist leader Chou En-lai (Zhou Enlai). Engaging in self-censorship, Gellhorn did not publicize her strong misgivings about the Chiang regime.

Martha Gellhorn

Amid all this reporting, Gellhorn kept producing fiction. In March 1940, her semi-autobiographical novel *A Stricken Field* was published. It dealt with a female war correspondent who arrived in Czechoslovakia just a week after the Munich conference. Later that fall, a collection of her short stories, *The Heart of Another,* came out. Again the settings were part of her own itinerary: Cuba, Finland, Germany, Spain, France. In 1943, another novel, *Liana,* made the bestseller list. The book centered on miscegenation in the Caribbean, an area Gellhorn had recently visited.

Marital tensions soon developed. Gellhorn (who always kept her maiden name) was increasingly exasperated by Hemingway's drinking and posturing. At one point, she would call him "The Pig." Hemingway in turn grew steadily intolerant of her globetrotting and lack of deference to "Papa," as he liked to be called.

In autumn 1943, *Collier's* sent Gellhorn to London as an official war correspondent. Here she covered Royal Air Force (RAF) pilots, cockney children, and Polish and Dutch refugees. In February 1944, she was on the Italian front interviewing American GIs. On the 27th, just before leaving Italy, she experienced enemy fire immediately outside Cassino.

When Gellhorn returned home to Cuba in March 1944, she and Hemingway renewed their incessant quarrels. She taunted him for avoiding the biggest story of the century—the war. She had written him in December: "You will feel deprived as a writer if this is all over and you have not had a share in it. . . . The place is crying out for you, not for immediate stuff but for the record." He railed at her for seeking to interrupt his idyllic life in Cuba. Ernest was certain that if he went overseas, he would be killed in the conflict and that Martha would be to blame.

Finally, in spring 1944, Hemingway offered his services as war correspondent to Gellhorn's employer *Collier's.* Because the press corps allowed only one front-line journalist per magazine, Ernest was able to preempt Martha's chance to cover the war in an official capacity. In May, he had the opportunity to fly to Europe while she was relegated to travel on a ship laden with dynamite and lacking lifeboats. Once the couple reunited in England, the mutual vilification continued. The marriage was already in ruins when Martha discovered Ernest's affair with **Mary Welsh (Hemingway)**, who would be his fourth wife.

On June 7, three days after D-Day, Gellhorn locked herself in the bathroom of an unarmed hospital ship that crossed the English Channel, then—under cover of darkness—went ashore. Unlike her husband, who saw the invasion from the bridge of a landing craft, Gellhorn was actually on Normandy beach, picking her way through the rice fields and barbed wire. Soon she was acting as a nurse, distributing water, food, and medication, and carrying urinals. Hemingway never forgave her for her accomplishment.

As her action was illegal, Gellhorn was sentenced to confinement at an American nurses' training camp outside London. She tolerated her situation for a day, then climbed a fence and hitchhiked to the nearest military airfield. Pretending she was a fiancée seeking her lover, she was able to secure an unauthorized flight to Naples. She sent an acid note to Ernest: "I came to see the war, not live at the Dorchester" (a prominent London hotel).

In Italy, Gellhorn was entirely on her own. She later recalled: "No papers, no travel orders, no PX rights, nothing. I was a gypsy in that war in order to report it." In July, Gellhorn attached herself to a Polish squadron stationed in the Adriatic, then traveled through France. Her *Collier's* article of November 4, "The Wounds of Paris," took readers on a tour of the city's torture cells. By October, she was accompanying General James Gavin's 82nd Airborne Division, reporting the Allied invasion of the Netherlands. Back in France by early December, Gellhorn experienced an auto accident en route to Toulouse. Despite a broken rib, she managed to visit a camp of Spanish refugees who had been interned for nearly six years. Soon, she was covering the Battle of the Bulge. At one point, she flew over Germany in a Black Widow night fighter, accompanying a pilot searching for a dog fight with Nazi war planes. Even the alienated Hemingway praised her work, saying in *Collier's,* "The things that happen to her people really do happen, and you feel it as though it were you and you are there."

In November 1945, Gellhorn sued for divorce, an event that made national headlines. Relations remained bitter. Hemingway offered a thinly disguised portrait of her in his novel *Across the River and into the Trees* (1950). Gellhorn never retaliated publicly. Privately, she expressed anger over portrayals in Carlos Baker's *Hemingway: A Life Story* (1969) and **Bernice Kert**'s *The Hemingway Women* (1983), though neither was particularly hostile.

Immediately after the war, Gellhorn covered Achmad Sukarno's rebellion in Java, the Nuremberg trials, and the Paris foreign ministers' meeting of December 1946. She lived briefly in Washington, D.C., but from 1948 to 1952 resided in the Mexican city of Cuernavaca. While reporting the postwar recovery of Italy, she adopted a 15-month Florentine boy Sandro ("Sandy"), whom she renamed George Alexander Gellhorn. In 1951 and again in 1953, she entered into a brief affair with Dr. David Gurewitsch, a pathologist at New York's Mt. Sinai Hospital and a protegé of Eleanor Roosevelt. In 1952, she bought a farm just outside of Rome, so that Sandy could attend school in his native Italy. However, she spent much of her time in London. All this time, she was a frequent contributor to the *New Republic*, the *Atlantic Monthly*, the *Saturday Evening Post*, and *Good Housekeeping*.

In 1954, Gellhorn married Thomas Stanley ("T.S.") Matthews, a widower who had just retired as editor of *Time*. The couple lived in London but traveled frequently. They divorced in 1963, T.S. finding Martha's continued rootlessness grating. In 1962, Gellhorn traveled to Africa and became so enamored with the continent that for 13 years she spent a part of every year there.

Much of Gellhorn's journalism centered on the state of Israel, a nation with which she always identified. In 1961, she covered the Jerusalem trial of Adolf Eichmann. Fascinated by the apparent blandness of the Nazi war criminal, she called him "the greatest organization man of all time." Her article in the *Atlantic Monthly* of October 1961 attacked Arab refugees for being interested only in "revenge and return." When she reported on the Six Day War of 1967, she found the Israeli army democratic and humane, its cause just.

From August to September 1966, Gellhorn reported on the Vietnam war. Infuriated by the blanket American bombing, she claimed that had she been a generation younger, she would have joined the Vietcong. Her milder accounts appeared in the *Ladies' Home Journal* and the *St. Louis Post-Dispatch*, her more hard-hitting ones in the British *Guardian*. Her indictment was severe enough to cause her to be the only correspondent ever blacklisted by the Republic of Vietnam. She later wrote of American military leaders:

> I told them they were inhuman. We were destroying a country and a whole innocent peasant population while we were saving them from Communism. Had they any idea how children looked and sounded when half flayed by napalm? Could they picture an old woman screaming with a piece of white phosphorous burning in her thigh? We had uprooted and turned into refugees millions of helpless people by unopposed bombing of their villages. We were hated in Vietnam and rightly.

Even when she was in her 70s, Gellhorn remained on the road. At age 75, she visited El Salvador, where she condemned the brutality of its government. Similarly, she found in Marxist Nicaragua a struggling but popular regime, not the Communist tyranny claimed by President Ronald Reagan. In 1986, after a 51-year absence, she return to Cuba. She was impressed by the lack of racial and sexual discrimination in Fidel Castro's regime, but appalled by his treatment of political prisoners.

During all the years after World War II, Gellhorn never neglected the writing of fiction. In 1946, her play, "Love Goes to Press," opened in London. Co-authored with American correspondent *Virginia Cowles*, it dealt with two manipulative women journalists on the Italian front. Gellhorn's novel *The Wine of Astonishment* (1947) centered on American troops fighting in northern Europe. In 1953, she published a series of short stories under the title *The Honeyed Peace*. The female protagonists had been in predicaments similar to Gellhorn's own.

Other fiction works included *Two by Two* (1958), a series of short stories focusing on troubled marriages; *His Own Man* (1961), a work dealing with romance in Paris; *Pretty Tales for Tired People* (1965), in which she again portrays the pitfalls of marriage; *The Lowest Trees Have Tops* (1967), a novel centering on Mexico; and *The Weather in Africa* (1978), which contained three novellas. None of these works met with the success of certain nonfiction works: *The Face of War* (1959, revised 1988), a collection of her *Collier's* dispatches; *Travels with Myself and Another* (1978), an account of her various voyages; and *The View from the Ground* (1988), a collection of various personal vignettes.

Gellhorn moved to an isolated cottage in Chepstow, Wales; she also had a flat in London. In June 1994, she wrote a short piece for the *New Republic*. Here she assailed the Washington press corps for not coming to the defense of President Bill Clinton. During her long life, Martha Gellhorn never stopped writing. She died, age 89, at her London home in February 1998.

SOURCES:

Gellhorn, Martha. *Travels with Myself and Another.* London: Allan Dale, 1983.

——, ed. *The Face of War.* NY: Atlantic Monthly Press, 1988.

———, ed. *The View from the Ground*. NY: Atlantic Monthly Press, 1988.

Kert, Bernice. *The Hemingway Women*. NY: W.W. Norton, 1983.

Orsagh, Jacqueline. "A Critical Biography of Martha Gellhorn." Ph.D. dissertation. Michigan State University, 1978.

Rollyson, Carl. *Nothing Ever Happens to the Brave: The Story of Martha Gellhorn*. NY: St. Martin's, 1990.

SUGGESTED READING:

Baker, Carlos. *Ernest Hemingway: A Life Story*. NY: Scribner, 1969.

Edwards, Julia. *Women of the World: The Great Foreign Correspondents*. Boston, MA: Houghton Mifflin, 1988.

Matthews, T.S. *Jacks or Better: A Narrative*. NY: Harper & Row, 1977.

Wagner, Lilya. *Women War Correspondents of World War II*. NY: Greenwood, 1989.

COLLECTIONS:

There is no archive of Martha Gellhorn papers. For Gellhorn correspondence, see the Edna Fischel Gellhorn Collection, Washington University, St. Louis; the Eleanor Roosevelt papers, Franklin Delano Roosevelt Presidential Library, Hyde Park, New York; the Joseph Stanley Pennell Papers, University of Oregon Library, Eugene, Oregon; the Crowell-Collier Collection, New York Public Library; the Patrick Hemingway collection, Princeton University, Princeton, New Jersey.

Justus D. Doenecke,
Professor of History, New College
of the University of South Florida, Sarasota, Florida

Gelman, Polina (1919—)

Soviet night-bomber navigator during World War II who received the Hero of the Soviet Union medal for bravery in combat. Name variations: Polya. Pronunciation: Puh-LEE-na Vlah-di-MEE-ruv-nuh GEL-mun. Born Polina Vladimirovna Gelman in October 1919 in Berdichev, Ukraine, USSR; daughter of Vladimir (a tailor) and Yelya (a worker) Gelman; undergraduate study in department of history, Moscow State University; trained as Spanish linguist, Military Institute of Foreign Languages; completed graduate dissertation in economics, earning Candidate of Sciences (Economics) degree; married Vladimir Kolosov (now a retired lieutenant colonel), in 1948; children: one daughter, Galina Kolosov, a historian (b. 1949).

Family moved to Gomel, Byelorussia (1920); entered Moscow State University (1938); joined Soviet Air Force (October 1941); served as navigator with 588th Night Bomber Aviation Regiment (later redesignated 46th Guards, 1942–45); served as military linguist; resigned from military service (1956) with rank of guards major; completed graduate education; served as senior lecturer (docent) and associate professor in department of Political Economy at Moscow Institute of Social Sciences; awarded Hero of the Soviet Union.

Polina Gelman, who received the Hero of the Soviet Union medal for bravery in combat, was a member of the famous "night witches" bomber regiment of Soviet female aviators during the Second World War. Of the 93 women who have received this, she is the only one who is Jewish. Gelman, who longed to fly since childhood, had been told that she would never qualify as a pilot because she was too short to reach the controls. But the exigencies of war allowed her to realize her dream; during her three years as a navigator, she flew 860 combat missions, nearly all at night, in the rickety old Po-2 biplane. The war gave her the chance to fly, but at a terrible price. Writes Gelman:

> I remember nights when I flew with tears on my face. We were pushed back from the Ukraine to the Caucasus. We were bombing the advancing columns of German tanks. They were advancing so fast that we had no time to change bases. We didn't even have maps. It was August and September of 1942. We could not harvest the grain, so they burned it. And so I was crying. Because it was my country and it was burning.

Gelman was a deeply patriotic woman. Her father Vladimir was a Bolshevik revolutionary during the civil war that followed the Russian Revolution. Throughout the course of the war, which lasted from 1918 to 1921, territory in the Ukraine changed hands repeatedly. In 1919, the hospital in which **Yelya Gelman** was giving birth to Polina was hit by enemy fire and half-destroyed. Five months later, Vladimir, the treasurer of a local Bolshevik organization, was returning from meetings in Moscow when his group was captured and then executed by a White Army unit. Yelya Gelman, now a widow, moved from the Ukraine to her parental home in Gomel, Byelorussia, where she later remarried. In 1925, Polina's half-brother was born.

While Polina's first love was always the social sciences—history, languages, and economics—she also became interested in flying at an early age; when she was a teenager, she joined a flying club with her best friend, **Galina Dokutovich**. The two girls completed the academics course and learned to parachute jump. But when Gelman was scheduled to begin flight training, she was disqualified from the program for being too short. "They were afraid that in difficult situations, for example in a spin, my feet wouldn't be able to reach the pedals," explained Gelman. She was extremely disappointed.

In 1938, after she had completed secondary school with an outstanding academic record, Gelman set out for Moscow. She had applied and been accepted at the Moscow Aviation Institute as well as to the department of history at Moscow State University. After long deliberation, however, she decided to study history at Moscow State while her friend Dokutovich entered the Moscow Aviation Institute. In 1940, Gelman joined the Communist Party.

The "Great Patriotic War," the Soviet term for the portion of World War II in which their country was involved, began on Sunday, June 22, 1941, when the Germans invaded the Soviet Union. Gelman was out of town, visiting a friend. Like any college student who had just finished exams, she was looking forward to a relaxing summer before returning to the university to complete her final year. Most students rushed back to the university as soon as they heard the news. When Gelman arrived on Sunday night, in time for an emergency party meeting, the students declared that they would all immediately volunteer to fight; but the women soon found there was no place for them in the military. "We had full equality before the war—in school, in sports, and so on. We were very offended when they wouldn't take us into the military."

During the summer of 1941, Gelman repeatedly went to the military registration offices, where volunteers were enlisted, and she was repeatedly told to go back to her studies, "war is not a woman's affair." Gelman's tiny stature did not make her a likely candidate for hard duty in the field. So she began studying at a school for military nurses, planning to join the medical corps after she completed training.

Hitler's armies swept across the western sections of Soviet territory; by the autumn of 1941, they were less than 50 miles from Moscow. Polina Gelman, along with thousands of other university students, was sent to help with the defense of the city, and she was put to work digging antitank ditches along the Belorussian road. On October 10, she heard a rumor that young women were being accepted into military aviation. Rushing back to Moscow, she sought out her friend Galina Dokutovich; as a student at the Moscow Aviation Institute, Dokutovich had already heard about the call-up, volunteered, and received her orders. Gelman quickly submitted the necessary paperwork, was accepted, and assigned the job of parachute packer. She wrote her mother that she had, at last, joined the army.

Gelman was assigned to ✥▶ **Marina Raskova**'s training group, Aviation Group No. 122. A famous Soviet pilot (the Russian counterpart of *Amelia Earhart), Raskova had been given the green light to form three aviation regiments to be staffed entirely by women. In mid-October, the entire company was loaded onto a train and sent to a training base at Engels, some 500 miles east of Moscow on the Volga River. As soon as they arrived, Gelman petitioned Raskova to be transferred to flight training. Because of her strong academic background, Polina was assigned to the navigator's group. Even though she was too short for normal flying duty, the 122nd desperately needed women who could swiftly learn the difficult task of navigation. Thousands of women had learned to fly in light aircraft before the war, but very few had received formal training as navigators. Two of the three regiments that would be formed from the 122nd would fly bomber aircraft and would require at least one dedicated navigator for every pilot. The student navigators worked 14 hours a day, cramming three years of normal military ground training into three months. Then flight training began—in January 1942—in the middle of one of the harshest Russian winters in memory.

Gelman was assigned to the 588th Night Bomber Aviation Regiment (later redesignated 46th Guards), which became active on May 27, 1942. The 46th was among the many Soviet night-bomber units that had to make do with one of the oldest aircraft in the inventory: the open-cockpit Po-2 biplane. More than 2,000 Soviet aircraft had been lost in the first year of the war, and the Soviet Air Force threw everything into the fight. Night-bomber regiments were used primarily to harass German troops, to disrupt the soldiers' rest, and to wreak what damage they could on military targets near the front lines. The Po-2 had very little instrumentation, could carry only a few small bombs, could fly only short distances, and had practically no defense against enemy fire. It was so vulnerable that it was impossible to use in the daytime, when it was easy pickings for German fighters. But at night, the small, quiet biplane made an effective short-range bomber. Po-2 units were based near the front and moved frequently to keep up with the army. They could land on rough fields and required only a minimum of support, compared to more modern aircraft. Still, no aviator would have flown the Po-2 by choice. During the war, writes Gelman, "men sometimes said, 'How do you manage to fly this piece of furniture? I would *never* fly this into combat!'"

The navigator in a Po-2 was responsible for keeping the aircraft on course and for finding the target; once there, the navigator dropped flares and bombs. Each combat flight required

✥▶
Raskova,
Marina. See joint
entry under
Grizodubova,
Valentina.

the crew to cross the front lines twice, braving the fire of antiaircraft weapons, light weapons, and the dangerously blinding glare of searchlights. Missions were relatively short, about half an hour in duration. Each crew flew anywhere from 5 to 15 missions a night, taking about 15 minutes to refuel and rearm the aircraft. Each flight was fraught with danger. It didn't take much to set a Po-2 afire; the old biplane was built of wood and canvas. And, until late in the war, Po-2 crews carried no parachutes.

When I announced that I had become a flier, my mama wrote to me that it was better to die standing on your feet than to live on your knees.

—Polina Gelman

"Of the three women's regiments formed from the 122nd Aviation Group," said Gelman, "only the 46th remained purely female until the end of the war. In the others, some men served alongside the women." While the 46th was one of many night-bomber regiments flying the rickety Po-2, it was the only one staffed by all-female personnel. According to Gelman, "the regiment was not only equal to the men's regiments in terms of combat effectiveness and other indices—it was among the very best." Combat effectiveness (the accuracy of each mission's bombing) was verified by both aerial and ground reconnaissance. Gelman believes that the women had a special quality of "thoroughness and responsibility" that accounted for their ability to conduct a high number of missions with such accuracy. The women of the 46th also accrued flight time because the regiment was never withdrawn from combat duty for leave or reequipping. "Without a break, over the course of three years, without rest or leave," says Gelman, "I flew an average of 5-10 combat flights a night in the fire of ground batteries and in the blinding beams of searchlights. That's the way it is in war."

Good leadership was the main reason why morale was especially high in the 46th. Throughout the entire war, a single commander, Lieutenant-Colonel **Yevdokia Bershanskaya**, guided the women of the night witches. "Our regiment was very harmonious and close-knit," wrote Gelman in 1992. "We were like sisters. . . . [Even now,] we rely on one another as if we were family. Our commander, Lt. Col. Bershanskaya, played a tremendous role in this. I'm very old, I served a long time in the army and worked in many places. I had many commanders. But I never met such a wonderful person as our commander."

Bershanskaya, who had been a civil-aviation pilot before the war, was not afraid to experiment or try new procedures. For example, the women of the 46th reduced the turnaround time between combat missions from 15 to 20 minutes, which was standard in the Soviet Air Force, to less than five. According to normal procedures, each aircraft was tended by its own designated ground crew. This led to duplication of effort. The 46th organized its maintenance into functional groups—one to meet aircraft as they landed, another to refuel each aircraft in turn, yet another to rearm. "It was not according to the regulations," recalls former chief of staff of the 46th, **Irina Rakobolskaya**. "But because of the better organization of our work, we managed to do more."

One of Gelman's duties in the regiment was that of "party organizer." As a Communist Party member with training in history, she was chosen to conduct political lectures for the squadron and classes on party history. Gelman tried to make these sessions interesting by instituting a "philosophy circle"; another navigator, **Yevgeniya Rudneva**, gave a lecture on Hegel's dialectic, while Gelman spoke on Feurbach's idealism. She also participated in other projects designed to keep up morale. "There was very little spare time, because we worked at night," she recalls. "Even so we published a literary magazine. We published it ourselves, writing and drawing everything by hand in a single copy."

The innovative procedures and sound morale of the 46th did not protect them from the risks of war. During the summer of 1942, when Galina Dokutovich suffered a back wound, the regiment called for a special ambulance plane to evacuate her. While waiting, they received orders to relocate immediately; with the Germans advancing, the landing strip of the 46th was in danger of being overrun. Dokutovich was vulnerable. If she was spotted by the enemy before her ambulance arrived, she had no way to protect herself. There was a shortage of handguns, so weapons were only issued to crews going on combat flights. Gelman could not bear the thought that her friend would be left behind, wounded and helpless. Before she left, she handed her own pistol to Dokutovich, just in case. Gelman later described this as her only heroic act of the war; she had a deadly fear of going down in enemy territory and being captured by the Germans. Without her pistol, she would be unable to defend, or kill, herself, which she swore she would have done to avoid becoming a prisoner. Fortunately, the ambulance plane ar-

Polina
Gelman

rived in time. On August 1, 1943, after months in the hospital, Dokutovich was permitted to return to flying duty. Tragically, her aircraft caught fire that very night, and she was killed—the same day that famous fighter pilot *Lidiya Litvyak died.

One of the most impressive feats performed by the crews of the 46th was the resupply of Eltigen. In late autumn 1943, a Soviet naval assault team landed near the small town of Eltigen, near Kerch in the Crimea. The team became cut off from the main body of forces without food, supplies, or ammunition. Terrible storms, combined with the precision required to drop packages on a tiny dark strip of beach, made resupply by plane difficult. But Gelman, along with her comrades in the 46th, resupplied the Soviet marines at Eltigen—for 26 consecutive nights.

The regiment developed barracks humor. Gelman claims that one of the funnier incidents was when she almost blew herself up because of a pair of gloves. Like other fliers who endured missions in open-cockpit biplanes, Gelman was issued a pair of fur-lined gauntlets to keep her hands warm. But the heavy gloves were too clumsy for manual work; she was forced to remove them, for example, in order to deploy flares, which had to be armed and then dropped over the side of the aircraft by the navigator. The gloves were connected by a leather thong, so they would hang from her neck when she took them off. One icy night, Gelman was preparing to drop flares to illuminate a target. She had already armed the timer when she realized that the cord to her gloves had gotten tangled in the tail fin of the flare. With seconds to spare, she had no time to unsnarl things; she was forced to pull her precious gauntlets from around her neck and pitch them out together with the flare. As she watched, they slowly descended to earth.

The 46th ended its combat duty in May 1945. On May 8, Gelman was sitting in the cockpit of her aircraft on alert, when word came that the Germans had capitulated. She cried on that day—from happiness, she says, but also because she knew that the way of life she had known for the past three years was ending. She would be leaving the company of her "sisters," and she would no longer be able to fly. The war had taken a heavy toll on the 46th; 31 women, or about 27% of the flying personnel, were killed in combat.

A total of 23 Hero of the Soviet Union medals was awarded to members of the 46th regiment: 18 pilots and 5 navigators—an astonishing number for a single regiment. "One of the fundamental criteria for the award was the quality and quantity of successful combat flights," notes Gelman; "our regiment firmly held first place among all the others for the number of flights." The fact that every member of the 46th was a volunteer was important. "Everyone was a patriot. Often they hadn't even completed a landing before they were already spoiling to carry out the next flight. The men even attempted to stop us. They said, 'the less you fly, the longer you'll live.'"

After the war, Senior Lieutenant Gelman found that she was reluctant to give up her career as a military officer. She enrolled in the Military Institute of Foreign Languages, where she studied Spanish. Despite missing several months of school due to a bout of encephalitis, she finished the difficult program. In 1948, she married Vladimir Kolosov, a fellow student at the Institute in the Polish department, who had been a border guard. When she gave birth to a daughter in 1949, she named her Galina in memory of her dear friend Galina Dokutovich.

Polina served on the faculty of the institute for several years. Later, she spent a year in Cuba studying its economy before she resigned from military duty in 1956. Soon afterwards, when she was in her 40s, Gelman decided to continue her education, and later completed an advanced degree as Candidate of Sciences in Economics. She then served as an associate professor and senior lecturer in Political Economy at the Institute of Social Sciences.

Back in Gomel, at the local flying club that refused to teach Polina Gelman how to fly, there is now a flagstone that carries the names of all its members who were awarded the Hero of the Soviet Union medal. Among those names, and the only name belonging to a woman, is that of Polina Gelman.

SOURCES:
Archival records, unpublished documents and personal interviews.
Bashkirov, B., and N. Semenkevich. "Geroini Sovetskogo neba [Heroines of the Soviet Sky]," in *Kryl'ia Rodiny.* March 1969.
Pennington, Reina. "Wings, Women and War: Soviet Women's Military Aviation Regiments in the Great Patriotic War." Master's thesis, University of South Carolina, 1993.
Staroselsky, L. "The Heart Cannot Forget," in *The Real Truth: Profiles of Soviet Jews.* Moscow: Raduga, 1986, pp. 135–147.
Viguchin, S., and E. Ignatovich. "Nezabyvaemoe kryl'ia," in *Komsomol'skoe znamia.* December 18, 1987, pp. 1–2.

SUGGESTED READING:
Cottam, K. Jean, ed. and trans. *In the Sky Above the Front: A Collection of Memoirs of Soviet Air Women Participants in the Great Patriotic War.* Manhattan, KS: Sunflower University Press, 1984.
Noggle, Anne. *Dance with Death.* College Station, TX: Texas A&M University Press, 1994.
Pennington, Reina. "Wings, Women and War," in *Smithsonian's Air & Space.* December–January, 1993–94, pp. 74–85.

Reina Pennington,
Ph.D. candidate in military and women's history,
University of South Carolina, Columbia, South Carolina

Geloria (d. 1022).

See Elvira Gonzalez of Galicia.

Gemmei (c. 661–721)

Japanese empress, 43rd tennō of Japan, who commissioned the Kojiki *(chronicle of ancient matters), the first written history of Japan. Name variations: Gemmei-tenno; Empress Gemmyo; Princess Abe or Princess Ahe (her name before she became empress). Pronunciation: Gem-may. Birth thought to have been in 661, most likely in Naniwa, then the capital; died in Nara (new capital) in 721 and buried in the tomb, "Nahoyama no Higashi"; daughter of Emperor Tenji and Nuhi; married Prince Kusakabe; children: Princess Hidaka (680–748), who ruled as Empress Genshō; Emperor Mommu (d. 707).*

One of Japan's most able rulers, this Nara Period empress (fifth of the ten empresses to date in Japanese history) reigned from 707 to 715. Born in 661, the daughter of **Nuhi** and Emperor Tenji, she was originally named Ahe. At Tenji's abdication in 672, several individuals ruled Japan including her uncle Temmu and her sister *Jitō. Ahe ascended the throne as Empress Gemmei, the result of a deathbed wish of her son, Emperor Mommu. In her mid-40s, reigning as the 43rd tennō, Gemmei was politically seasoned and wise, quickly proving that she was able to wield her power decisively yet in a spirit of moderation. She took steps to further strengthen the authority of the tennō (emperor-empress) and the central government by enforcing laws against peasants who fled their fields and by restricting property ownership of the nobility and Buddhist temples.

The empress' most significant contributions, however, were cultural. It had previously been the responsibility of the official reciters to memorize records of ancient events and narrate the epic tales. Through a series of decrees in 712 and 713, Empress Gemmei commissioned the transcription of the historical tales of Japan which were compiled in the three-volume *Kojiki*, a chronicle of the rise of the imperial clan and aristocratic families from the creation of the Japanese islands down to the reign of the 33rd tennō, Suiko. This history further strengthened the authority and legitimacy of Gemmei's family—the imperial clan. Gemmei ordered provincial governments throughout Japan to collect and compile their own histories, as well as information about soil, products, weather, and geological features. These historical gazettes contributed to a growing sense of national identity.

Aware of the importance of adhering to traditions, several years after ascending the throne she moved the imperial court from Asuka to Nara (Heijo) in Yamato province. Responding to the need to stimulate economic activity, she ordered the first striking of copper coins in the history of Japan.

As was the case with educated women and men of her time, Gemmei wrote poetry; several of her poems were included the *Manyōshu*, an imperial anthology of poetry commissioned in the mid-8th century. In it, she wrote: "Listen to the sounds of the warriors' elbow guards;/ Our captain must be ranging the shields/ To drill the troops." During a prolonged illness in 715, Gemmei abdicated in favor of her daughter Hidaka who reigned as Empress **Genshō**. Gemmei continued to supervise affairs of state, however, until her death in 721.

SOURCES:

Aoki, Michiko. "Jitō Tennō: The Female Sovereign," in *Heroic With Grace: Legendary Women of Japan.* Armonk, NY: M.E. Sharpe, 1991, pp. 40–76.

Miner, Earl Roy, Hiroko Odagiri, and Robert E. Morrell. *The Princeton Companion to Classical Japanese Literature.* Princeton, NJ: Princeton University Press, 1985.

Nelson, Andrew N. *The New Nelson Japanese-English Character Dictionary.* Rutland, VT: C.E. Tuttle, 1997.

Papinot, Edmond. *Historical and Geographical Dictionary of Japan.* Ann Arbor, MI: Overbeck Company, 1948.

SUGGESTED READING:

Tsurumi, E. Patricia. "The Male Present Versus the Female Past: Historians and Japan's Ancient Female Emperors," in *Bulletin of Concerned Asian Scholars.* Vol. XIV, no. 4. October–December 1982, pp. 71–75.

Linda L. Johnson,
Professor of History, Concordia College,
Moorhead, Minnesota

Gencer, Leyla (1924—)

Turkish soprano and coloratura who had a long and distinguished international career as a bel canto singer of the highest quality. Born in Istanbul, Turkey, on October 10, 1924 (though Gencer maintains she was born in 1928); married Ibrahim Gencer.

Considering the fact that she never made any commercial recordings or sang at New York's Metropolitan Opera, Turkish soprano Leyla Gencer enjoys a strong artistic reputation that continues to grow with the passage of time. Born in Istanbul (standard reference works note the year as 1924, but Gencer has told interviewers the correct year is 1928) to a Polish Roman Catholic mother and a wealthy Turkish Muslim father, she made her stage debut in 1950 in Ankara singing the role of Santuzza. She entered several singing competitions in Turkey, and although she never won any, the young singer remained confident about her future prospects, having received strong support from her coaches **Giannina Arangi-Lombardi** and Apollo Granforte. Only when she began to sing in Italy in 1953 did Gencer become a star. Her Italian debut, which took place in Naples, tested the young singer's ability to work under extreme pressure. After an audition, she was asked if she wanted to sing in *Cavalleria Rusticana*. Her answer was in the affirmative, but she noted in passing that while she had indeed sung the work on stage, it was in Turkish not Italian. With only five days to learn her role in Italian, Gencer mastered it so well that her appearance, before 10,000 demanding Italian opera fans, was a triumph.

Within months, Gencer was engaged by Naples' San Carlo Opera House to sing in both *Madama Butterfly* and *Eugene Onegin* (which she sang in Italian, as is customary in Italy, although it is a Russian opera). Over the next decades, she would perform at most of the world's great opera houses, working with noted conductors including the legendary Italian maestro Tullio Serafin. The venerable Serafin put Gencer on the path to her later career as a bel canto singer, and it was with him that she learned roles, including Aida and Norma, for a number of operas. By 1956, Gencer was appearing regularly at Milan's La Scala Opera House. In 1957, she had the signal honor of singing the "Libera me" from Verdi's *Requiem* at the La Scala memorial service for its greatest musician, Arturo Toscanini. She rapidly built up a loyal following of fans who cheered her at every performance. Gencer appeared in several world premiere performances at La Scala, including *Dialogues des Carmélites* by Francis Poulenc in January 1957 and *Assassinio nella cattedrale* by Ildebrando Pizzetti in March 1958.

By the end of the 1950s, Gencer had become a major figure in the opera world, presenting annual guest appearances at Florence's Maggio musicale and the San Francisco Opera. In 1959, she sang at the Spoleto Festival in one of the rare performances of Sergei Prokofiev's *The Fiery Angel*. In 1961, Gencer made her Austrian premiere, appearing on stage both at the Vienna State Opera as well as the Salzburg Festival, where her performance of Amelia in Verdi's *Simon Boccanegra* earned rave reviews from critics and standing ovations from audiences. Gencer thrilled her audiences with portrayals of well-known heroines, but also learned roles from a number of less well-known and virtually forgotten operas (by the end of her career, she had a repertory of 72 operas, overwhelmingly Italian but also including such modern works as Prokofiev's *The Fiery Angel* and Benjamin Britten's *Albert Herring*). In 1972, she appeared at Naples' Teatro San Carlo in the title role of Donizetti's long-neglected opera **Caterina Cornaro*.

Leyla Gencer brought not only great artistic talent to her singing and acting, but often provided new insights into old performing traditions that were in danger of becoming stale and hackneyed. Because she learned singing in a part of the world where European music was only one aspect of musical life, Gencer was not totally immersed in traditions: "Everything was new for me. When I studied, I remained very close to the score as written. I didn't imitate anyone. I sang according to my own musical conception, according to my own musical understanding. My colleagues had grown up in the verismo era and believed you always had to sing forte. Perhaps because I hadn't heard the others, I was untainted by any vestige of the infamous age of verismo [which placed an] emphasis on loud singing, on exaggeration. I sang with delicacy and nuance— a style that in a few years everyone imitated."

Leyla Gencer ended her opera career in 1983 but concertized until 1992. Since then, she has divided her time and energy between serving on competition juries and giving master classes. In 1995, a proud Turkish nation witnessed the first Yapi Kredi International Leyla Gencer Voice Competition. Held in Istanbul, it attracted young singers from around the world and was praised as a major cultural event that would only grow in importance in the future. By the end of the 1990s, a large number of Gencer live recordings from various phases of her long and remarkable career were available for opera lovers to enjoy and critique. Modern technology has thus been able to preserve the legacy of a great singing actress, an artist regarded by many critics as being "one of the last of the last prima donnas in the truly grand manner."

SOURCES:

Blyth, Alan, ed. *Opera on Record*. London: Hutchinson, 1979.

Cella, Franca. *Leyla Gencer: Romanzo vero di una prima donna*. Venice: CGS, 1986.

Celletti, Rodolfo. "Leyla Gencer," in *Opera*. Vol. 23, no. 8. August 1972, pp. 692–696.

Hathaway, J. "Turkish Delight," in *Opera News*. Vol. 61, no. 1. July 1996, p. 6.

Kellow, Brian. "The Road to Istanbul," in *Opera News*. Vol. 60, no. 13. March 16, 1996, pp. 36–37.

———. "Turkish Diva," in *Opera News*. Vol. 60, no. 13. March 16, 1996, pp. 38–39.

Luten, C.J. "Leyla Gencer," in *Opera News*. Vol. 62, no. 9. January 17, 1998, p. 39.

Mansel, Philip. "On the Bosphorus," in *Opera News*. Vol. 53, no. 16. May 1989, pp. 36–37.

Mark, Michael. "Leyla Gencer," in *American Record Guide*. Vol. 61, no. 4. July 1998, pp. 267–268.

Pines, Roger. "Another View," in *Opera News*. Vol. 58, no. 8. January 8, 1994, p. 33.

Sachs, Harvey. *Toscanini*. Philadelphia, PA: J.B. Lippincott, 1978.

Zucker, Stefan. "Leyla Gencer" (Bel Canto Society/Opera Fanatic/Internet).

John Haag,
Associate Professor of History,
University of Georgia, Athens, Georgia

Genée, Adeline (1878–1970)

Danish-born ballerina who founded the Royal Academy of Dancing and was the most famous ballerina of her day. Name variations: AG; Adeline Genee; Dame Adeline Genée; Dame Adeline Genée-Isitt. Pronunciation: Je-NAY or EYE-sit. Born Anina Margarete Kirstina Petra Jensen on January 6, 1878, in the Danish village of Hinnerup, in Aarhus, Jutland; died in Escher, Surrey, on April 23, 1970; daughter of Peter Jensen (a musician) and Kirsten Jensen (of Norwegian descent); at age eight, studied dance with her famous aunt and uncle, dancers Antonia (Zimmermann) Genée and Alexander Genée; married Frank S.N. Isitt, on June 11, 1910 (died 1939); no children.

Awards: honorary Doctorate of Music, University of London (1946); Dame Commander of the British Empire (1950); "Ingenio et Arti" from king of Denmark; Order of Dannebrog (1953); founder and president of London Association of Operatic Dancing (presently known as the Royal Academy of Dancing).

Ballet roles: Centifolie in Die Rose von Schiras (1896); a diamond in Monte Cristo (1897); Fairy Good Fortune in Alaska (1898); Lizette in Round the Town Again (1899); Variations in Sea-Side (1900); Queen of Butterfly Land in Les Papillons (1901); Swanilda in Coppelia (1902); Grand Adagio in The Roses of England (1902); Coquette in The Milliner Duchess (1903); the Hunting Dance and the Cakewalk in High Jinks (1904); the Bugle Boy in The Bugle Call (1905); title role in Cinderella (1906); Queen of the Dance in The Belle of the Ball (1907); lead role in The Soul Kiss (1908); title role in The Dryad (1908); Abbess Elena in Roberto il Diavolo (1909); divertissements in The Bachelor Belles (1910); title role in La Camargo (1912); principal dancer in La Dance (1912); Minuet in The School for Scandal (1915); a divertissement in Spring (1915); principal dancer in The Love Song (1932).

Adeline Genée was a major force in the world of dance who elevated the status of the dancer to a new level of respectability and brought the art of ballet to the masses as well as the cultured elite. The methods of teaching ballet in the British realm were meticulously standardized when she founded what was to become the Royal Academy of Dancing.

Genée was born Nina Jensen, the surviving twin in a Danish farm family. Her father was also a musician, and hers was a home filled with music. From age four, she displayed such a love of dance that her parents allowed her to be raised by her aunt and uncle, who were famous dancers of the day. It was understood that she would be trained to dance on the stage, an idea which pleased the young Nina. Alexander and **Antonia Genée**, who had formed their own ballet company and danced successfully throughout Central Europe and Russia, eagerly began their niece's training in 1886. Alexander had choreographed several dances in the opera *Carmen* for the famous opera singer *****Adelina Patti**, and he renamed his niece to honor Patti. Years earlier, he had taken the surname Genée from the composer Richard Genée, who had helped him greatly as a young artist. Thus Nina became Adeline Genée.

Dance lessons began immediately for Adeline. Antonia was Hungarian and spoke only Hungarian and German, while Adeline spoke only Danish, but Adeline was serious about her work and meticulous movement training broke down obstacles in communication. She was raised in the company of adults, a situation which fostered her mature demeanor. With a thorough knowledge of the backstage areas, she enjoyed watching her aunt dance on stage and longed to begin performing. Alexander ensured that her ballet training was pure and precise, passing on the fruits of his own ballet lineage. He taught Adeline what he had learned in Russia under Christian Johansson, who had been a student of August Bournonville, the most prominent man in Danish ballet. Bournonville was trained by none other than the greatest dancer of his day, the famous Auguste Vestris of the Paris Opera.

Owing to her uncle's theatrical work, Adeline had the opportunity to travel and live in various parts of Denmark and Sweden. She learned to adapt to new languages and surroundings, and she expanded her knowledge of various theatrical tasks and new balletic roles. Adeline's upbringing stressed the need to be fastidious in not only her dance movements, but also in her dress. Years later, it would be said that she was probably one of the most technically perfect dancers; if captured in a photo at any given moment, her movements would show perfect positioning. Such breeding was not the norm in the English dance world of that period. Genée learned the various roles in the ballet repertoire so well and quickly that she was easily able to fill in, with little or no rehearsal, if someone became ill. This was a greatly valued skill in the theater. Before long, she had many opportunities to play a wide variety of roles, winning critical acclaim. When she appeared in Munich, the *Allgemeine Zeitung News* commented on her lightness, grace, and the brilliance of her pointe work. The *Neuesten Nachrichten News* wrote that they had never seen such a dancer in the history of their theater.

In 1897, Genée received an offer to dance for six weeks in London at the Empire Theater to celebrate Queen *Victoria's Diamond Jubilee, and an important phase of her career began. What was supposed to be a six-week contract extended into a stay of ten years. Genée was to become the most popular ballerina of her day, both to com-

Adeline Genée

moners and royalty alike. Her achievement can be well appreciated in light of the status of ballet in her time. Early in the reign of Victoria, ballet was an important part of the opera, and foreign singers and dancers attracted the public, but there was no established British ballet school to provide the needed dancers, and so the fate of ballet in Victorian England was not very promising. Gone were the incredible ballerinas, such as *Maria Taglioni and *Fanny Elssler, of the 1830s and 1840s. Ballet by the mid-19th century was therefore less popular than opera. When British theater moved into what became known as the music-hall phase, characterized by huge spectacles in the variety show format, the programs attracted the masses rather than the cultural elite. The numbers in these spectacles were well choreographed, lavishly costumed and lit, and the motifs were kept light and happy rather than heavy and somber. The productions were expensive and often employed hundreds of artists, although the technical ability of the dancers left much to be desired. Some of the dancers were apprentices to the theater, and they received free lessons as part of their compensation but they were not required to attend. To counter the tendency of the shows to go flat, new ballerinas were brought in to keep the audiences coming back. Thus, because ballet was featured as part of the production, the general public—who may never have gone to see classical dance—was exposed to the art.

The London public loved Adeline Genée from the moment they saw her dance as a diamond in her debut in *Monte Cristo* in 1897. Her uncle insisted that she be given an additional dance to truly show off her expertise in her London debut. Genée was immediately compared to Elssler and Taglioni by some of the older audience members. It was said that she danced with her heart, not just with her body. Soon after, she went on to dance as the Fairy Good Fortune in a show called *Alaska*. Modern theatrical themes attracted large audiences, and this show's motif, the gold-rush, featured spectacular lighting, focusing on dancers who portrayed the Aurora Borealis. The newspaper reviews found the show positively enchanting. Genée was unique in her versatility: she could do classical work as well as character roles. Max Beerbohm commented in *The Saturday Review* that she was a born comedian, and such a fine actress in communicating her meaning without words that she made him forget his craving for words.

In *Round the Town Again*, Genée was the first leading ballerina at the Empire Theater to dance in high heels. She continued to win the hearts of the British and the establishment's management by filling the theater to capacity. An exceptionally hard worker, she practiced two hours every day, in addition to rehearsals and performances, under her uncle's watchful eyes. Intellectually curious, she began to study Shakespeare's plays. When Genée had to portray a character fighting a duel she studied fencing.

In the 1900 production *Sea-Side,* Genée attempted many varied dances and amazed viewers by the diversity of her dancing ability and character work. The following year, audiences were astonished by her portrayal of the Queen Butterfly in *Les Papillons.* This was the first time the public had witnessed a series of *entrechat six* (a series of beats of the feet) in pointe shoes. The dancers in this production wore costumes based on butterflies actually on display in the National History Museum.

The production *Our Crown* was mounted in honor of Edward VII's coronation in 1902, with Genée playing the Messenger of Peace who requests that the colonies bring their finest natural gifts in order to design the royal crown. The result was a breathtakingly beautiful work of art. Also in 1902, the Royal Theater in Copenhagen honored Genée by asking her to appear as Swanilda in *Coppelia.* Her partner Hans Beck asked the entire dance company to be present at a rehearsal in order to see Genée perform her *entrechat six* (a step the Danish did not perform). She surprised Beck by adding the step at the last minute during a performance, and he was so astounded that he forgot his entrance. The duo was graced by the presence of King Christian IX of Denmark and his daughters, *Alexandra of Denmark, queen of England, and *Marie Feodorovna (1847–1928), the dowager empress of Russia. A critic from the *Politiken* claimed that Genée's finely trained body made the Danish dancers look over-nourished, and he compared her toe to a steel spring because of her precise, controlled movement while quickly turning.

When Genée returned to London's Empire Theater in 1903, she danced one of her most famous roles as Coquette in *The Milliner Duchess.* By her exquisite technique, hard work, and example, she had raised the standard of dance in the *corps du ballet* at the theater. This ballet, especially, seemed infused with Genée's delightful personality. She played a country bumpkin employed in a millinery shop, who simply couldn't resist trying on every hat. The critics praised her as a born mime and comic.

The year 1904 hailed the production of *High Jinks,* which included one of Genée's most famous solo dances, "Return from the Hunt." Again, critics acclaimed her talent. Her determination to realistically portray her characters earned Genée the admiration of crowned heads of Europe. When King Edward VII invited her to give a performance, he enhanced the status and respectability of the dancer.

After the 1907 production of *The Belle of the Ball,* Genée sailed to America to star in a Ziegfeld production of *The Soul Kiss* at the Chestnut Street Opera House in Philadelphia. At age 29, she now had control of her own financial affairs. Before her departure, the Empire Theater celebrated the tenth anniversary of her debut there, and her devoted fans gave her countless curtain calls. Her years of work had changed the face of ballet in Britain, and now she hoped to do the same in the States.

Our grandchildren will never believe, will never be able to imagine, what Genée was.

—**Max Beerbohm**

Billed as *The World's Greatest Dancer,* she did not disappoint the public who jammed the Philadelphia opera house. Genée finished her American tour in a triumphant fashion and sailed back to her fans in London, where she renewed her "love affair" with her British public. When she returned to the United States for her second tour in 1908, she performed in 23 different theaters in 30 weeks. While there, rumors began circulating that the dancer was romantically involved with a prosperous businessman from London, Frank S.N. Isitt. Alexandra of Denmark, alarmed that the dancer might consider retirement, told her to weigh carefully her decision because "nobody can dance as you can." But after her third American tour, Genée nevertheless married Isitt, on June 11, 1910.

Following her wedding, Genée was busier than ever with performances and personalities. She continued to tour both in Britain and the United States, and in 1910 the American public had a chance to compare her with the visiting Russian ballerina *Anna Pavlova. Generally, Genée had more popular appeal than the Russian, because her light, quick, pleasant style induced a "happy" mood in the audience. Pavlova's style was more exotic, dangerous, deep, and full of melancholy. Despite their different appeal, the two ballerinas respected and admired each other. Genée and her husband also enjoyed the company of inventor Thomas Edison, who invited the couple to socialize over a meal.

Genée had a deep interest in the history of ballet, and she carefully researched the lives of professional dancers. Combining her academic and performance talents, she determined to educate the public about the history of dance and put together a revue, "La Danse," which related ballet's history from 1710 to 1845, by employing a series of tableaux. She was passionately devoted to this project and spent considerable sums of her own money to present the widely admired show on several continents.

In 1914, when Genée announced her intention to retire, several ballerinas—including Pavlova, *Tamara Karsavina, and **Phyllis Bedells**—published a letter of public appreciation for her magnificent contribution to ballet. Genée requested that her fans should not award her with monetary gifts, but should instead donate any gifts to **Topsy Sinden**, a dancer who had experienced a terrible accident. Genée's last audience gave her a 12-minute ovation.

Nevertheless, a great talent such as Genée could not really "retire." When World War I broke out, she helped raise money for the families of British war dead: she danced, she knitted socks for the soldiers, she auctioned off autographs—anything that would raise money. After the war, she focused on helping the ballet community standardize ballet instruction in Britain. Genée was well aware of the importance of technique and diligent training. When the concerned instructor Edouard Espinosa brought the standardization issue to Genée's attention in 1920, she gladly attended the meeting which he called. Five leading dancers represented the various schools of ballet at the gathering: one from the Danish-French Bournonville school, one from the French school, one from the present British system, and two from the Imperial Russian school. Genée presided over the group; in fact, she was the uncontested president of this fledgling Royal Academy of Dancing (RAD). Under her guidance, certain measures were adopted: British teachers must employ standardized ballet exams; dancers were to wear uniform attire in testing; and all who had an interest in the discipline should promote it for the masses, not just for the cultural elite.

Always quick to respond to requests for charity, Genée agreed to dance once more for a benefit to aid the Hertford Hospital in Paris in 1932. Even at the age of 54, she so awed her partner with her grace and style that the man had a difficult time concentrating on his steps. Genée was legendary for making the most difficult things seem easy. Even her husband was not permitted to watch her rehearse, for if he saw the sweat that such hard work produced, it might break the illusion of ease that she wished to portray in her dancing.

Genée spent much of her 50th decade caring for her ill husband, and she was deeply affected by his death in 1939. Her devotion to the cause of the Royal Academy of Dancing kept her strong during her difficult days. She was a powerhouse of energy in her toil and travels in the name of RAD. In 1954, after 34 years of unceasing service, she handed over the presidency of RAD to *Margot Fonteyn. By this time, Genée had received an honorary doctorate of music from the University of London; she had been named Dame Commander of the British Empire; and the king of Denmark had presented her with the Order of Dannebrog. In East Grinstead, Sussex, a theater was named in her honor. By many accounts, she was a wonderful host and put that skill to use while serving as chair of the Anglo-Danish Society in England. She also spent some of her later years meticulously recollecting a lifetime of memories for a biography that was written by Ivor Guest. By the time she died in 1970, at age 92, ballet had reached heights never previously imagined. Many changes in the ballet world were due to Genée's promotion of the finest ideals and standards of the art, beauty, and education of ballet.

SOURCES:

Chujoy, Anatole. *The Dance Encyclopedia.* NY: A.S. Barnes, 1949.

Clarke, Mary, and Clement Crisp. *The History of Dance.* NY: Crown, 1981.

de Mille, Agnes. *The Book of the Dance.* NY: Golden Press, 1963.

Guest, Ivor. *Adeline Genée—A Lifetime of Ballet Under Six Reigns.* London: Adam and Charles Black, 1958.

———. *The Empire Ballet.* London: The Society for Theatre Research, 1962.

SUGGESTED READING:

Pask, Edward H. *Enter the Colonies Dancing.* Melbourne: Oxford University Press, 1979.

Brigid Kelly,
ballet instructor at Desert Ballet Centre,
Yucca Valley, California

Genêt or Genet (1892–1978).

See Flanner, Janet.

Geneviève (c. 422–512)

Patron saint of Paris. Name variations: Genevieve; Genevieve of Paris; Genovefa, Genovefae. Born at

Nanterre (some sources claim Montriere), near Paris, between 420 and 423, most sources cite 422; died in Paris on January 3, 512; daughter of peasants, Severus and Gerontia.

According to popular tradition, Geneviève was the daughter of the peasants Severus and **Gerontia**, who lived in Nanterre, near Paris. She was remarkable for her piety and humility at a very young age and soon devoted herself to a life of holiness and purity. Having attracted the attention of St. Germanicus, Geneviève entered a convent at age seven and took the veil at age fifteen. Two years later, with her parents dead, she moved to Paris to be with her godmother in partial seclusion. Though she endured the scoffing of nonbelievers and, on one occasion, was only saved from drowning by the intervention of Germanicus, it is written that her active charity, and the extraordinary reputation for sanctity which she acquired, won for her a certain reverence, not just from the religiously minded, but even from the unconverted and the theologically indifferent.

Geneviève lived in a time of upheaval, during the waning days of the Roman Empire and the rise of the Frankish monarchy. In 451, when Attila and his Huns swept into Gaul, pillaging, raping and burning in a wide swath of destruction, Geneviève is credited with stopping a mass exodus of Parisians through her prayers and encouragement. She prompted the people of the city to trust in God and urged them to do works of penance, adding that if they did so the town would be spared. "The women let themselves be persuaded easily enough," wrote her chronicler in *Vita sanctae Genovefae.* "As for the husbands, she repeated to them that they had nothing to gain by flight; the places where they were counting on refuge were surely devastated, while Paris would certainly be preserved." Her exhortations prevailed, the citizens recovered their calm, and her words were prophetic. Leaving Paris untouched, Attila and his hordes moved toward Orléans where he met and was eventually defeated by the combined forces of Aetius, a Roman, and Theodoric, king of the Visigoths.

Years later, when Childeric, the pagan king of the Franks, besieged the city, Geneviève, with fellow religious women, set out on an expedition for the relief of the starving people and successfully brought back boats laden with corn from Arcis-sur-Aube and Troyes. By urging the Parisians to resist the power of Childeric, Geneviève earned his respect and successfully interceded with him for the lives of many of his prisoners.

When Childeric's son Clovis I became king, he embraced the Christian faith with the encouragement of his wife *Clotilda, around 496 or 497. Clovis also "granted liberty to several captives" at Geneviève's request, as his admiration for her was great. Saint Geneviève is also credited with the first designs for the magnificent church begun by Clovis. When Clovis died in 511, he was interred in Paris, setting a precedent and presaging the importance of that city in the future history of France. Geneviève died the following year, at age 90. When the church was completed by Clotilda, both Clovis and Geneviève were interred within the structure, a building for which they had done much. The numerous miracles wrought at Geneviève's tomb would eventually cause the name to be changed to the Church of St. Geneviève.

In 847, the church was plundered by the Normans but was partially restored in 1177. In 1764, Louis XV erected a new edifice in Geneviève's honor upon the supposed site of her tomb; it contains the famous murals of the saint, in several wall panels, by Puvis de Chavannes. In 1793, during the French Revolution, the government converted this church into the Panthéon, where busts of the famous of France are enshrined. St. Geneviève, the patron saint of Paris, is the subject of many popular and poetical legends. Her feast day is January 3.

Geneviève de Brabant (fl. 8th c.)

Saint. Name variations: Genevieve of Brabant; Genoveva or Genovefa. Possibly flourished in the 8th century; married Siegfried, count of Treves and Brabant; children: son Scherzenreich.

Geneviève de Brabant is the subject of a popular medieval legend which dates her life to about the middle of the 8th century. According to the legend, Geneviève, wife of Siegfried, count of Treves and Brabant, was falsely accused of adultery by one of her servants, the major-domo Golo. She was sentenced by Siegfried to be taken into the woods, along with her infant son Scherzenreich, and put to death. Abandoned in a forest by two executioners who were moved to spare their lives, Geneviève and Scherzenreich lived in a cave in the Ardennes nourished by red deer. Seven years later, Siegfried, who had discovered the treachery of Golo long after he was told that his wife and son were dead, was out hunting. A red deer he was pursuing took refuge in the cave, and Siegfried came upon Geneviève and Scherzenreich.

Genevieve of New France (1656–1680).

See Tekakwitha, Kateri.

Genhart, Cecile Staub (1898–1983)

European-born pianist. Born in 1898; died in 1983; studied in Europe with Feruccio Busoni and Emil Frey.

In 1924, Cecile Genhart joined the piano faculty of the Eastman School of Music in Rochester, New York, where she spent her entire career, becoming the most sought after piano teacher of that institution. Performing yeoman service in "the American provinces," she typified the European-born teachers who worked hard to create a rapidly growing level of musical culture in the United States in the first half of the 20th century. She introduced the Brahms Second Piano Concerto to Rochester.

John Haag,
Athens, Georgia

Genlis, Stéphanie-Félicité, Comtesse de (1746–1830)

Prodigious writer of novels and educational treatises who became the first woman to serve as the governor of royal princes when she was appointed to direct the education of the children of Philippe, duke d'Orléans. Name variations: Countess de Genlis. Born Stéphanie-Félicité Ducrest de Saint-Aubin on January 21, 1746, at Champçéry in Burgundy, France; died on December 31, 1830, in Paris, France; daughter of Pierre-Cèsar Ducrest or du Crest (a French noble who squandered most of his family fortune) and Marie-Françoise de Mézière; married Charles Alexis, Comte Brûlart de Genlis, later Marquis de Sillery, on November 8, 1763; children: Caroline de Genlis (1764–1783); Pulchérie de Genlis (b. 1766); Casimir (1768–1773); rumored to have given birth to two illegitimate daughters with Louis-Philippe Joseph (Philippe-Egalité), Duke d'Orléans: Pamela (1773–1831), the future Lady Edward Fitzgerald; and Hermine (1776–1822).

Married (1763); introduced into Parisian society (1765); became lady-in-waiting to the Duchesse d'Orléans (1769); made governess to her daughters (1777); made governor of the sons of the Duke and Duchesse d'Orléans; published Adèle de Theodore ou lettres sur l'éducation *(1782); published* Discours sur l'éducation publique du peuple *(1791); lived in exile in Europe during the French Revolution (1793–1800); published* Madame de la Vallière *(1804),* Souvenirs de Félicie *(1806), and* Mémoires *(1825).*

Stéphanie-Félicité Ducrest de Saint-Aubin was born in the last years of the reign of King Louis XV of France. The daughter of Pierre-Cèsar Ducrest, a member of one of the oldest noble families in France, and **Marie-Françoise Ducrest**, Félicité was born into a privileged élite who dominated the politics and economy of pre-revolutionary France. Her father was a known spendthrift, however, and her mother had come to the marriage without a dowry, so her father traveled the country in search of money while her mother dragged Félicité and her brother to a succession of country homes owned by friends and cousins in search of shelter and financial support. Félicité received little formal education in her youth; her father preferred to allow her to run around outside in boys' clothes to encourage her to be adventurous and hardy. Largely as a result of her mother's love of the stage, Félicité was introduced early to acting, dancing and playing music. She became a virtuoso on the harp.

Félicité was married at the age of 17 to Charles Alexis, Comte Brûlart de Genlis, a naval officer who had met her father while overseas. Genlis, according to rumor, had seen her portrait and had fallen in love with her on the spot. Delighted with the prospect of marriage into Genlis' prominent family (his uncle, the Marquis de Puysieux, was Minister of Foreign Affairs), Félicité agreed to the marriage. Charles' relations were infuriated by his marriage to a girl without a dowry, and so for two years they refused to recognize the union. It was only after the birth of **Caroline de Genlis**, in September 1765, that Charles' relations decided to recognize the marriage and introduce Félicité at court. Although her in-laws were initially cold towards her, Félicité soon won them over with her charm, vivacity, and tact.

Félicité's acceptance into her husband's family opened the doors to the most exclusive social circles in France. Her musical talents and gift for amusing conversation won her many allies during these years. Félicité gave birth to two more children in quick succession: her daughter **Pulchérie de Genlis** was born in 1766 and her son Casimir in 1768.

Soon afterwards, in 1769, she met Louis-Philippe Joseph "Egalité," known as Philippe, duke d'Chartres, who was the son of the duke d'Orléans. This meeting would change the destiny of her entire life. A romantic affair between the two began. At the time, Félicité was 22 and married; Philippe was 21 and negotiations were being feverishly conducted for his marriage to *Louise Marie of Bourbon, daughter and only heir of the wealthy duke de Penthiévre. Upon Philippe's marriage to Louise Marie in April 1769, the duke d'Orléans gave the couple the Palais-Royale in which to set up their household. Félicité was named lady-in-waiting to Louise Marie and the duke de Genlis received an appointment as the duke's Captain of the Guard.

Thus began a 19-year relationship between the Genlises and the heir to the Orléans house. Monsieur de Genlis developed a true friendship with Philippe and remained loyal to him until their deaths in 1793. Félicité attracted the loyalty and friendship of the younger Louise Marie, who seemed naively ignorant of Félicité's relationship with her husband. For several years, Félicité held the affections of both the husband and the wife.

As first princes of the blood, the Orléans family were nearly as prominent and wealthy as the royal family. The duke and duchesse of Chartres made the Palais-Royale the center of Parisian social life, where they entertained courtiers, literary figures and the intelligentsia of Europe. Félicité flourished in this environment. Older, more beautiful and more socially adept than Louise Marie, Félicité dominated the social scene at the Palais-Royale and soon became one of the most sought-after women in Paris.

The correspondence between Félicité and Philippe at this time reveals the intense passion shared between the lovers, as well as Philippe's submission to Félicité's stronger personality. In 1772, while Félicité was in Forge attending Louise Marie, who had recently given birth to a stillborn child, the lovers sent frequent letters to each other. At the beginning of their separation, she wrote:

> Yes, I am in despair. It seems to me that you have left me for always, that we shall never see each other again, or anyhow that the time of our happiness is over. . . .
>
> Why do I lose my head for a matter of one month? But you yourself, my love, what a state you were in yesterday; really I am alarmed by it. Well, I had more strength yesterday. . . . No, I do not *live* away from you. Oh! My child, my heart, to love each other to such an extent, to give oneself up to it so entirely that one should be sure of never having to leave each other for more than two days.

Philippe replied:

> How amiable, tender and charming you are, my child. Your letter enchants me, it is sad but consoling. Oh! Yes, it is true that we shall never be much to be pitied.
>
> It gives me a strange pleasure to see that we both write to each other the same thing

at about the same time. . . . I count the hours, the moments, and when I go to bed I am glad that another day has gone.

Philippe had little sympathy for his young wife, who had developed a toothache and had to have two teeth pulled. On hearing the news, he responded, "I would like the Chevalier to let me know tomorrow that they have pulled out the whole jaw and if the tongue went too I wouldn't mind." Félicité gently rebuked him, "Madame la Duchesse de Chartres has a beautiful soul. How pure, honest and tenderhearted she is!"

> *S*he would have invented the inkstand, if the inkstand had been uninvented.
>
> —Monsieur Sainte-Beuve

The affair between Madame de Genlis and the duke de Chartres became an object of speculation among the members of the aristocracy, especially when Félicité suddenly left the country with little explanation in 1773. Her son, Casimir, had died in a measles outbreak that year, but after his death she left France for Brussels, where she stayed for six weeks. When she returned, rumors circulated that she had borne a child of Philippe's. Another absence in 1776 provoked similar gossip.

In October 1773, Louise Marie gave birth to a long awaited heir, who was destined to become king of France as Louis-Philippe I in 1830. Other children quickly followed: Antoine, who became duke de Montpensier (1775), Louis-Charles, Comte de Beaujolais (1779), and twin daughters, though only *Adelaide (1777–1847) would survive infancy. Upon the birth of the twins, Philippe suggested that Félicité be made their governess. Félicité vacated her lavish apartments in the Palais-Royale and took the 11-month-old girls to live under her care in a pavilion designed by her in the grounds of the Convent at Belle-Chasse. In her memoirs, Félicité notes that she willingly moved out of her rooms at the Palais-Royale because at Belle-Chasse she could be away from malicious eyes: "I felt only joy in entering that peaceful sanctuary where I would be exercising such sweet rule." Monsieur de Genlis had already moved out of the Palais-Royale several years earlier to take apartments nearby with his mistress, **Madame de Buffon**.

Félicité continued to attend social events at the Palais-Royale, and even hosted visits from the best-known men of arts and letters at Belle-Chasse. At 31, she began not only her long career as a governess of royal children, but also a career as a writer, one which she would continue until her death. Many of her earliest writings contain her theories on education, but she also produced romances and a volume of comedies. Félicité's reputation grew more respectable as her writings became widely circulated.

Philippe shocked Parisian society when, in 1782, following the tragic death of one of the twin princesses, he dismissed the governors who had been in charge of the education of his sons and made Félicité the governess of all his children. Never before had a woman been named governor of royal princes. Public opinion, noted an observer, "murmured, then was silent." Louise Marie was opposed to the scheme, but she had never been a match for the strong wills of her husband or Félicité.

Madame de Genlis proved herself a rigorous instructor. She trained the princes not only in academic subjects like geometry and mathematics but also in how to "bear heat, cold, wind and rain, to sleep on bare boards, endure fatigue and fend for [themselves]." Louis-Philippe later recalled, "She brought us up with ferocity." Félicité later said of Louis-Philippe, "He was a Prince and I made him a man, slow and I made him

clever, a coward and I made him brave, but I could not make him generous." Félicité stressed the importance of charity and good works among the poor, which gave the Orléans princes enduring popularity among the people of France during and after the Revolution.

In 1785, two little girls were brought over from England to join Félicité's household. The eldest was named ❧▶ **Pamela** and the youngest **Hermine de Genlis**. The official explanation given by Madame de Genlis and the duke was that the girls had been taken from English families who could not provide for their upkeep. But public rumor maintained that the children were none other than the illegitimate daughters of Félicité and Philippe, who had been spirited off to England after their birth and were now being reunited with their mother. Although Félicité showed little interest in Hermine and gave her to her daughter Pulchérie to raise, Pamela became Félicité's favorite, rivaled only perhaps by Félicité's eldest daughter Caroline, who had married but died soon after in childbirth in 1783.

Philippe succeeded to the title of duke d'Orléans upon the death of his father in 1785. Showing considerable political foresight, Félicité took pains to teach the Orléans children the importance of popularity among the French people. She made the girl pupils dress as "Grey Sisters" and go out ministering to the poor. She convinced Philippe to sell the contents of his gallery at Palais-Royale and announced in the *Journal de Paris* in 1788 that the eight million francs brought by the pictures was to be spent in helping women in childbirth and distributing bread to the poor.

By 1789, widespread poverty and the impact of the new views of the *philosophes* were creating growing resentment of Louis XVI and his queen *Marie Antoinette. An Orléanist party arose which championed the idea of putting Philippe on the throne of France in a constitutional monarchy. When the Estates-General met that year and began the process of revolution, Philippe gave up his place at the head of the Princes of Blood Royal and instead walked in procession in the last row of the representatives of the Third Estate, to public acclamation.

As increasing numbers of ambitious politicians drew around Philippe, Félicité found her influence on him waning. Madame de Genlis' role in the French Revolution has remained unclear. In 1791, she published a call for reform in education, *Discours sur l'éducation publique du peuple,* which pushed for universal education of

Stéphanie-Félicité, Comtesse de Genlis

both boys and girls, although she maintained that nobles and the masses should be educated separately, using the same moral principles but different subject matter. She enthusiastically supported the reformers of the Orléans party, especially their plans for the creation of a Constitutional monarchy, but when the Revolution took a turn toward the more radical Jacobin party, Félicité seems to have abandoned the Revolutionary cause. As the Jacobins grew in power and influence in Paris, she took several of her young charges with her to the relative safety of England.

With growing unrest and anti-monarchical sentiment in Paris, Philippe found himself in a difficult position. In 1790 his son, Louis-Philippe, now a young man of 17, joined the anti-monarchy Jacobin club, to the distress of his mother, who blamed Félicité for her son's radical sympathies and begged her husband to dismiss her. Despite Louise Marie's vehement pleas, Philippe refused to remove Félicité from her post as governess. At Philippe's refusal, Louise Marie banned Félicité from the Palais-Royale. There is some evidence that she had finally been convinced of the affair between her husband and her children's governess. By this time, it is doubtful that Félicité and Philippe were still lovers in the full sense of the word, but Louise Marie's test of Philippe's loyalty placed him squarely on the side of Madame de Genlis. The conflict escalated as Louise warned her husband, "The person who, since she has had my children in her hands, has never ceased to cause disunion between us, is now going to separate us for ever." She insisted he choose between her and Genlis. After a terrible scene, Philippe shocked Parisian society by turning Louise out of the Palais-Royale with nothing but the clothes on her back. In 1791, Louise Marie returned to live with her father and asked for a separation from her husband.

Contrary to Philippe's wishes, Félicité bowed to public pressure and resigned her post. As the situation in France deteriorated, Félicité wrote from England to her husband, "I see that the good cause is very nearly lost. You can take one of two courses; either that of supporting the constitution and perishing in its defense; or that of accepting the changes that are proposed. . . . France will not be the freest country in the world, but it will not be under such a despotical government as before the Revolution." She advised him to sell their property and settle in England. Still loyal to Philippe, her husband Monsieur de Genlis refused.

Her advice to Philippe during this critical time was no better received. After her return to

Fitzgerald, Pamela (1773–1831)

*Daughter of Mme de Genlis. Name variations: Lady Edward Fitzgerald. Born in 1773 (some sources cite 1776); died in Paris, France, in 1831; daughter of Stéphanie-Félicité, Comtesse de Genlis (1746–1830) and Louis-Philippe Joseph, duke d'Orléans (Philippe-Egalité); married Lord Edward Fitzgerald (1763–1798, son of *Emily Lennox), on December 27, 1792.*

It states in her marriage contract to Lord Edward Fitzgerald that Pamela Fitgerald's parents were from Newfoundland. However, it is popularly supposed that she was the illegitimate daughter of *Madame de Genlis and Louis-Philippe Joseph (Philippe-Egalité), duke d'Orléans. Brought up as a ward in the Orléans household, Pamela journeyed to England in 1791 where she met Sheridan. The following year, she met the future Irish rebel Edward Fitzgerald in Tournay; that same year, Edward was ousted from the British Army for attending a revolutionary banquet in Paris where he toasted the abolition of all hereditary titles. Pamela married him in 1792 and accompanied him to Ireland where he became politically active, joining the United Irishmen who by then were openly calling for an independent republic. In 1796, Edward accompanied Arthur O'Connell to Basel to negotiate with General Hoche for France's help. He then led a military committee that made preparations for the French invaders. On May 19, 1798, Edward was shot in the arm while being arrested by Major Henry Sirr. Pamela attended to her husband in Newgate Prison but he died of his wounds on June 4. Pamela then left Ireland and eventually remarried, but she retained the name Fitzgerald.

France in October 1792, she warned Philippe that he was being used as a tool of the Jacobins and implored him to leave France with his family at once and flee to America until the Revolution was over. Philippe remained silent. The following day he sent Félicité, his daughter Adelaide, Hermine and Pamela away from Belle-Chasse to Tournay, where he hoped they would be safer. On the way, they were met by an Irish noble, Lord Edward Fitzgerald, who had met Pamela while she was attending the theatre with Monsieur and Madame de Genlis. Edward had fallen madly in love with Pamela and had intercepted the party to ask for Pamela's hand in marriage. Félicité gave her approval on the condition that Edward's mother, the widowed **Emily Lennox**, duchess of Leinster, was not opposed to the match. Edward rushed back to England to get his mother's approval. Edward's family assumed that Pamela was the daughter of Madame de Genlis and the duke d'Orléans, and despite their disappointment that Pamela had no

Lennox, Emily.
See Lennox Sisters.

dowry other than a small annuity settled upon her by Philippe, they welcomed the match. Edward hurried back to Tournay, where the marriage took place at the palace of the Bishop of Tournay on December 27, 1792. Both Félicité and Philippe signed the marriage contract, although little was said of the marriage publicly. Pamela left the party of exiles to join her husband in Ireland.

Events in Paris moved with increasing speed after Louis XVI and his family were caught trying to flee the country in 1792. The king was put on trial for treason, and the Jacobins called for his conviction and execution. Félicité heard the outcome of this tragic turn of events when Louis-Philippe left camp to bring her the news that his father, Philippe, desperate to save his own life, had voted for the death of the king. Félicité and Louis-Philippe were outraged at the duke's lack of courage and conviction. Rumor soon reached them that Philippe, in his panic, had told the Jacobins that he was not the son of the late duke d'Orléans at all, but of a coachman who had been his mother's lover. No one believed the story, and ultimately it did not save his life. After being interrogated by the Revolutionary Tribunal, Philippe was guillotined on November 6, 1793.

It must have been some consolation to Félicité to hear of her husband's actions. She received a letter from him shortly after the vote that condemned the king was taken. Monsieur de Genlis had refused to vote for the king's conviction and published his reasons in the newspapers: "I did not vote for death (1) because he does not deserve it, (2) because we have not the right to judge, (3) because I think their judgment the greatest political mistake that could be made. I know perfectly well that in pronouncing this opinion I have signed my own death warrant." Genlis gave himself up at the Abbaye Prison when he left the Assembly. He was executed with the other Orléanists in November 1793.

During this horrifying time, Félicité solicited help from friends to spirit her charges out of the country. Disguised as English ladies, the party journeyed through Germany and into Switzerland, where Félicité searched for protection. Many houses and convents were reluctant to take in a party of Orléanists, and Félicité found herself denounced by all sides. She was hated and slandered by the Revolutionaries, who considered her too aristocratic and too devoted to the Church, and by most of the French aristocrats who had fled the country, who accused her of influencing Philippe to vote for the death of Louis XVI.

Madame de Genlis would live in exile from her native country for seven years. Hounded by her political enemies and criticized publicly in the press, she kept her emotions in check and her finances secure by continual writing. Several lengthy novels and shorter works, many of which defended her educational methods, appeared during this time. Her writings were as popular as ever, even among those who claimed to disapprove of her. Félicité tutored the children of some of the wealthiest families in Berlin for a time as a way to support herself and her charges. Finally, in June 1800, her name was removed from the list of *emigres,* and she was allowed to return to France.

She brought with her a young boy she had adopted in Germany, whom she called Casimir after her own son who had died in childhood. As her own children and the Orléans children she had raised grew to adulthood, her relationship to them was often conflicted. Her adopted daughter Pamela had been widowed when Lord Edward died in an uprising of the United Irishmen in 1798. Upon Félicité's return to France, Pamela, anxious to remarry after two years of widowhood, confronted her about her true parentage. Félicité refused to acknowledge her as the child of herself and Philippe, holding to the story that Pamela was the daughter of a poor washerwoman who had sold her for a cash payment. Pamela was distraught, and she distanced herself from Félicité for many years afterwards. Two of Félicité's charges, Antoine, duke de Montpensier, and Louis-Charles, Comte de Beaujolais, died soon after, in 1807 and 1808. To make up for these losses, Félicité continued to adopt several other children until well into her old age, including a niece, **Georgette Ducrest**, and a grandson, Anatole de Lawoestine, son of her beloved oldest daughter Caroline.

Félicité's return to Paris was bittersweet. The inevitable changes caused by the Revolution distressed her. Her social position among the returning aristocrats was diminished by the role that Philippe had played in the Revolution. Her economic position was no longer secure; she found that her husband's property had been confiscated and sold by the Revolutionary Tribunal. Luckily for Madame de Genlis, the First Consul and soon-to-be-emperor Napoleon Bonaparte admired her literary reputation and took pity on her. He granted her an apartment in the Arsenal, adjoining the library, and offered her a modest annuity in return for a fortnightly letter from her, covering any topic she chose to write about.

The year 1804 saw Madame de Genlis' star begin to rise again. Her new book, *Madame de la Vallière,* was a fantastic success. Parisian newspapers described her newest work as "charming" and "ravishing." It was even said that the book brought tears to the Emperor Napoleon's eyes. Félicité found herself, at 58, once more becoming fashionable. Her salon was again crowded with the literary and intellectual élite of Paris. She continued to write prolifically, producing one of her most enduring works, *Souvenirs de Félicie*, in 1806. She also produced a number of historical works celebrating life under the early Bourbon rulers. In that year, she began a friendship with the 18-year-old Comte Anatole de Montesquiou, who exchanged letters with her daily and would remain her steadfast friend and ally for the rest of her life. Although 42 years apart in age, many of her contemporaries believed that Anatole became her last lover.

Félicité's frugal life could not compete with the luxury she had enjoyed in her early days at the Palais-Royale and Belle-Chasse, but she enjoyed the company of her children, her adopted children, and a growing brood of grandchildren. On several occasions, she took money from her own small funds to pay off the debts of one of her relations who had gotten into trouble. She wrote frequently to them, particularly to her adopted son Casimir, instructing them in how to get ahead in a society still driven by privilege and birth, even going so far as to draft letters of thanks for Casimir which she insisted he copy and send as his own. She was much relieved when Casimir married **Adèle Carret**, a young girl with a good dowry, in 1811, and settled down to the life of a country gentleman.

The fall of Napoleon in 1814 led to the end of Félicité's annuity, but the Orléans family was finally recalled from exile and she was reunited with Louis-Philippe and his younger sister Mademoiselle Adelaide, the only surviving children of the duke and duchesse d'Orléans. Napoleon's return for the Hundred Days in 1815 necessitated the flight of the Orléans family for another two years, and Félicité spent that time prudently out of harm's way at the country home of Casimir and his wife.

When Louis-Philippe again returned to France in 1817, he renewed his close ties with his former governess. His mother Louise Marie had taken up with a commoner after Philippe's death, much to the chagrin of her son. Her desperation for a rapprochement with Louis-Philippe was so great that, after years of enmity towards Félicité, she agreed to meet with her former rival. Louise Marie had aged considerably through her ordeals: "Her face was small and much wrinkled, her dress expensive but eccen-

tric." Félicité, now 69, was "thin and worn but her eyes were still bright and her teeth were perfect." Félicité and Louise Marie patched up their differences, and Félicité found herself again within the circle of the Orléans family.

By 1819, Félicité's last pupil had grown up and left her alone. She moved to a succession of small rooms accompanied only by her maid, but she remained something of a celebrity. Crowds followed her to visit wherever she lived, regardless of her humble surroundings. At the age of 76, she announced that she intended to rewrite the *Encyclopedia* from a religious point of view. The restored Bourbon King Louis XVIII was delighted with the prospect and offered her an annuity of 1,500 livres. In 1825, she published her own *Mémoires*. Although they shed no light on the scandals of her youth, they were praised in literary circles for their "purity of style and natural charm."

Félicité celebrated her 80th birthday in 1826. In reviewing her own life, she wrote to Anatole: "In rapidly going over in my heart the long succession of years, with what faith and what repentance do I implore the divine mercy! What heedlessness and what guilty steps! What agonizing sorrows, what misunderstandings by my own fault, what sadnesses of every kind did I bring upon myself! To what a point did I spoil my own destiny! How happy and beautiful it would have been had I had more sense and virtue!" In her last years, she was often sad and introspective, but she continued to write feverishly; during the final five years of her life, she published eleven new works. She remained an object of fascination among the literary circles of the day.

Political storms began to gather anew by 1830. The last Bourbon monarch, Charles X, had alienated the people with his reactionary policies. By July, Charles had been forced out of the country and Louis-Philippe, remembered as a hero of the Revolution and a friend of the people, was made lieutenant-general of the new republic. On December 31, messengers brought Félicité the news that her former pupil had been named king of France. She is said to have murmured, "I am very pleased." The following morning, when her doctor arrived, he found her sitting up in bed, her handkerchief pressed to her lips. He did not realize she was dead until he found her pulse had stopped.

Madame de Genlis was buried with great pomp and circumstance, at considerable expense to the new king, Louis-Philippe. Toward the end of her life, she had claimed, "I have tasted all the joys of the soul and all the griefs that can rend it and that Fate has heaped both blessings and sorrows upon me." She had published over 100 books and claimed to have brought up and educated 19 children. She inspired admiration and friendship among the greatest minds of her day. Although her works fell out of favor soon after her death, many modern scholars see her as an important bridge between the 17th and 18th centuries. Feminist scholars have praised her for supporting rigorous academic preparation for both men and women. She was one of the first educators to call for universal education for children of all classes up to the age of 16. Even her greatest detractors gave her credit for the education of Louis-Philippe, who not only survived the French Revolution but gave his country 18 years of peaceful rule during the tumultuous 19th century.

SOURCES:

Dobson, Austin. *Four Frenchwomen.* Freeport, NY: Books for Libraries Press, 1893, rpt. 1972.

Eifler, Margaret, ed. *Women in an Intellectual Context.* Rice University Studies. Vol. 64, no. 1. Winter 1978.

Harmand, Jean. *A Keeper of Royal Secrets: Being the Private and Political Life of Mme. de Genlis.* London: Eveleigh Nash, 1913.

Sartori, Eva Martin, and Dorothy Wynne Zimmerman, eds. *French Women Writers.* Lincoln, NE: University of Nebraska Press, 1991.

Stewart, Joan Hinde. *Gynographs: French Novels by Women of the Late Eighteenth Century.* Lincoln, NE: University of Nebraska Press, 1993.

Wyndham, Violet. *Madame de Genlis: A Biography.* London: Andre Deutsch, 1958.

Kimberly Estep Spangler,
Associate Professor of History and Chair of the Division of Religion and Humanities at Friends University, Wichita, Kansas

Genoa, Catherine of (1447–1510).

See Catherine of Genoa.

Genoa, duchess of.

See Maria Carolina for sidebar on Christine of Bourbon (1779–1849).

See Elizabeth of Saxony (1830–1912).

Genovefa, Genovefae, or Genoveva.

Variant of Genevieve.

Genshō (680–748)

Japanese empress, during whose reign the Yōro Code—which established the rule of her family, the imperial clan—throughout Japan, was promulgated. Name variations: *Princess Hidaka or Hitaka (before ascending the throne); Gensho-tenno.* Pronunciation: *Gen-SHOW. Born in 680 (some sources cite 679), most likely in the Japanese capital Naniwa; died in 748 in Nara, a later capital of Japan; daughter of Empress Gemmei (c. 661–721) and Prince Kusakabe; sister of Emperor Mommu; niece of Empress *Jitō (645–702); never married; no children.*

Born in 680, the daughter of Empress *Gemmei, Princess Hidaka would follow in her illustrious mother's footsteps by encouraging continued growth in the arts, sciences, literature, and economic life after her ascent to the imperial throne. In 708, age 28, she wrote a poem addressed to her mother on the eve of a battle: "Be not concerned, O my Sovereign; Am I not here,/ I, whom the ancestral gods endowed with life, Next of kin to yourself?"

As Empress Genshō, Hidaka reigned from 715 to 724 as the 44th sovereign during the Nara Period, the sixth of ten empresses who have reigned to date in Japanese history. She came to the throne upon the abdication of her mother, though Gemmei continued to oversee the affairs of state until 721. During Genshō's tenure, however, the high point of the centralization of the Japanese state was achieved. In 718, the Yōro Code was promulgated and extended the rule of the central government—particularly with respect to the administration of land and the establishment of the imperial bureaucracy—throughout Japan.

Following her mother's path, Empress Genshō also commissioned a second national history of Japan, the *Nihongi*, a meticulous chronicle of Japanese court and aristocratic life to the year 697 (it was completed in the middle of her reign, in the year 720). The *Nihongi* was more scholarly than the previous national history, the *Kojiki*. After nine years of rule, Empress Genshō abdicated in favor of her nephew Shomu when he reached the age of 25 in the year 724. She died in 748 at the age of 68.

SOURCES:

Aoki, Michiko Y. "Jitō Tennō: the Female Sovereign," in *Heroic With Grace: Legendary Women of Japan.* Armonk, NY: M.E. Sharpe, 1991, pp. 40–76.

Miner, Earl Roy, Hiroko Odagiri, and Robert E. Morrell. *The Princeton Companion to Classical Japanese Literature.* Princeton, NJ: Princeton University Press, 1985.

Nelson, Andrew N. *The New Nelson Japanese-English Character Dictionary.* Rutland, VT: C.E. Tuttle, 1997.

Papinot, Edmond. *Historical and Geographical Dictionary of Japan.* Ann Arbor, MI: Overbeck Company, 1948.

Linda L. Johnson,
Professor of History,
Concordia College, Moorhead, Minnesota

Genth, Lillian (1876–1953)

American figure painter who was noted for studies of nudes in Arcadian settings. Born Lillian Mathilde Genth in Philadelphia, Pennsylvania, in 1876; died in

1953; *daughter of Samuel Genth and Matilda Caroline (Rebsher) Genth; educated privately and in Philadelphia public schools; studied at the Philadelphia School of Design for Women with Elliott Daingerfield, and with James McNeill Whistler in Paris; never married.*

A popular artist at the dawn of the 20th century, Lillian Genth was known for her portraits and paintings of the female nude against a landscape background. Her work can be found in the National Gallery, Washington, D.C.; the Carnegie Institute, Pittsburgh; the National Arts Club, New York City; the Metropolitan Museum of Art, New York City; the Brooklyn Museum; and in private collections.

Gentileschi, Artemisia (1593–c. 1653)

One of the most celebrated women painters of the 17th century whose artistic influence, traceable from her native Italy to Spain and Holland, was obscured for centuries by the emphasis placed by many art historians upon her personal mores. Name variations: Aertimisiae Gentilescha. Pronunciation: Ar-tee-ME-zha Gente-LESkee. Born in Rome, Italy, on July 8, 1593; died in Naples, Italy, around 1653; daughter of Orazio Gentileschi (a painter) and Prudentia (Montone) Gentileschi; married Pietro Antonio di Vincenzo Stiattesi (a Florentine artist), in 1612; children: Palmira (or Prudentia), also a painter (b. 1618) and another girl (name unknown).

Painted earliest signed work, Susanna and the Elders *(1610); subject of rape trial of Agostino Tassi (1612); moved to Florence; worked in England for King Charles I (1638).*

Paintings: Susanna and the Elders *(inscribed ARTE GENTILESCHI, Schloss Weissenstein collection in Pommersfelden);* Judith and Her Maidservant *(Palazzo Pitti; another version resides in the Galleria Corsini in Rome; another in the Detroit Institute of Arts);* Judith Beheading Holofernes *(Galleria degli Uffizi, Florence);* Penitent Magdalen; Aurora; Rape of Proserpine; Lucrezia *(Durazzo-Adorno collection);* Cleopatra *(may be misattributed, Palazzo Rossi deposito);* The Portrait of a Condottiere *(or* Portrait of a Papal Knight; *inscribed on the back "Artemisia Getilsca faciebat Romae 1622");* Esther and Ahasuerus *(Metropolitan Museum of Art, New York);* Annunciation *(inscribed AERTIMISIAE GENTILESCHA F. 1630, Museo di Capodimonte, Naples);* Fame *(1632);* Self-Portrait as the Allegory of Painting; St. Catherine *(1635);* St. Januarius with Lions *(Pozzuoli Basilica, Naples);* Adoration of the Magi *(Pozzuoli Basilica, Naples);* Sts. Proculus and Nicaea *(Poz-*

zuoli Basilica, Naples); David and Bathsheba *(two versions, one of which is in the Columbus Museum of Art, Ohio, Schumacher Fund Purchase);* Birth of John the Baptist *(Museo del Prado, Madrid).*

Rome in the last quarter of the 16th century was a city in flux. Urban redevelopment was taking place under the leadership of Sixtus V, pope since 1685, and the new churches being built in the wake of the counter-Reformation brought with them an increased demand for the decorative skills of painters. Artemisia Gentileschi was born on July 8, 1593, the first child of **Prudentia Montone Gentileschi** and Orazio Gentileschi, an artist of Florentine descent, into the most auspicious environment in which to develop her skills: father, uncle, and godfather all being successful painters. By the time she was nine, one of her father's friends, Caravaggio, was causing a stir with his new style of painting—a style which Artemisia would adopt successfully and which would prove one of the greatest influences on art of the time.

Artemisia Gentileschi (self-portrait)

As a woman, Artemisia was ineligible to take part in the life-study, mathematics, or perspective classes which formed the usual course of training for an artist and was barred from entry to the Roman Accademia di S. Luca. Consequently, her artistic tuition was delivered by her father, probably at the expense of any other education; by the age of 19, she confessed that she could scarcely read and was unable to write. But the rewards of this specialization can be seen clearly in her first dated work of 1610, a painting on the theme of the Biblical tale of *Susanna and the Elders. Despite the obvious influence of Orazio, it is evident that by the age of 17 Artemisia demonstrated an unusual maturity of style.

The unavailability of traditional training coupled with her precocious skills conspired to cause the encounter, in 1611, between Artemisia and the man whose name would forever tarnish hers, Agostino Tassi. Recently arrived from Florence, Tassi was working with Artemisia's father at the Quirinal Palace in Rome when Artemisia visited that summer. Tassi's skills in architectural perspective made him the perfect tutor to further develop her talents. But in March 1612, Orazio Gentileschi sued his former colleague for damage and injury as the result of the rape of his daughter. According to the law of the time, Artemisia, as the property of her father, had no legal recourse to justice. Thus, her father, the owner of "damaged" (and therefore unweddable) goods, became the plaintiff in the case.

The trial lasted for seven months, during which a panoply of witnesses was brought forward by both sides to testify. According to Artemisia, Tassi had raped and then promised to marry her, following which she had consented to a continued involvement with him. Tassi, for his part, denied the whole affair, instead seeking to link Artemisia with a line of lovers and even an incestuous relationship with her father. (It was later revealed by historians that Tassi was no stranger to the law. "The list of Tassi's 'escapades' is impressive," note Rudolf and **Margo Wittkower**, "it includes rape, incest, sodomy, lechery, and possibly homicide. He served a term on a Tuscan galley, was sued for debts, and imprisoned for unruly behavior in Livorno and Rome.")

During the trial, Artemisia had to undergo physical examinations to determine the date of her loss of virginity. She was also subjected to the *sibille* (thumbscrew)—a type of torturous early lie-detector consisting of cords wrapped around the fingers and tightened. During the questioning, while Tassi looked on, she reiterated her innocence, shouting at her violator, "This is the ring you give me, and these are your promises!" In the end, Tassi spent only eight months in prison, the case being eventually dismissed. Amazingly, Orazio Gentileschi put all of this behind him and subsequently resumed a friendly working relationship with his former enemy.

Stylistically, Artemisia's work had changed in the previous few years to incorporate a heavy influence of Caravaggism with its dramatic use of light and shade. **Mary Garrard**, an art historian who has carried out the most extensive study of Gentileschi's work, dates the first of her five extant paintings on the theme of *Judith and Holofernes to shortly after her ordeals at the rape trial. Just as the story of Susanna and the Elders provided painters with the opportunity to portray a voyeuristic scene under the guise of Biblical reference, so the story of the beautiful widow who tricks the evil invader, beheads him and thus saves her nation, allowed for the depiction of violence and horror. It also gave Artemisia the opportunity to present the oft-used theme from the position of the woman. Painted with vigor and no lack of gory detail, *Judith Slaying Holofernes* presents the moment when a strong and determined Judith, assisted by her equally able maidservant, holds down Holofernes and commences decapitation. As Garrard describes it, "the bloody realism of the Naples 'Judith' places Artemisia in the vanguard of artists who pushed Caravaggesque naturalism to horrific extremes—in her case, for electrically intense expression." Many art historians analyze the working and reworking of this theme as Artemisia's attempt to exorcise her feelings of revenge against Tassi. Comparison of this Judith—muscular, powerful and determined—with, for example, Caravaggio's depiction of the heroine—petite and impassive—makes such an inference credible. And although Artemisia painted a wide range of subjects, from landscapes to portraits, it is her interpretation of the strong woman, manifested in Judith or Susanna or, later, *Cleopatra VII, which has interested most feminist art historians.

Despite expectations to the contrary, Artemisia was married in 1612 to a Florentine artist, Pietro Antonio di Vincenzo Stiattesi, with whom, in light of her prevailing reputation in Rome following the trial, she swiftly moved to Florence. Here artistic recognition came quickly, thanks to her friendship with the great-grandnephew of Michelangelo who commissioned her to work, at a highly paid rate, on the ceiling decorations of the house honoring his renowned relative. In addition, the support of Cosimo II, one of the Medici family, paved the way for her full acceptance into the artistic community. Artemisia soon became a member of the Florence Accademia del Disegno, the first woman to enter since its founding in 1563.

Unfortunately, many of the works completed during her time in Florence no longer exist—only their descriptions remain. From those that survive can be seen a slight change in style to accommodate Florentine tastes—her *Judith* of this period is dressed in lavish costumes and glistens with jewels—though essentially she continued to practice her art as a Caravaggist.

Some time around 1618, Artemisia gave birth to her first daughter whose name is recorded as both Prudentia and Palmira in later censuses. Evidently unhindered by this new responsibility, she extended her search for further commissions, accompanying her father on a trip to the north of Italy. The port of Genoa, made wealthy through banking and shipping, was a meeting point for artists of Northern and Southern Europe. Here, Artemisia met the Dutch artist, Anthony Van Dyck, and *Sofonisba Anguissola, probably the most renowned woman artist of the day who, though blind and in her

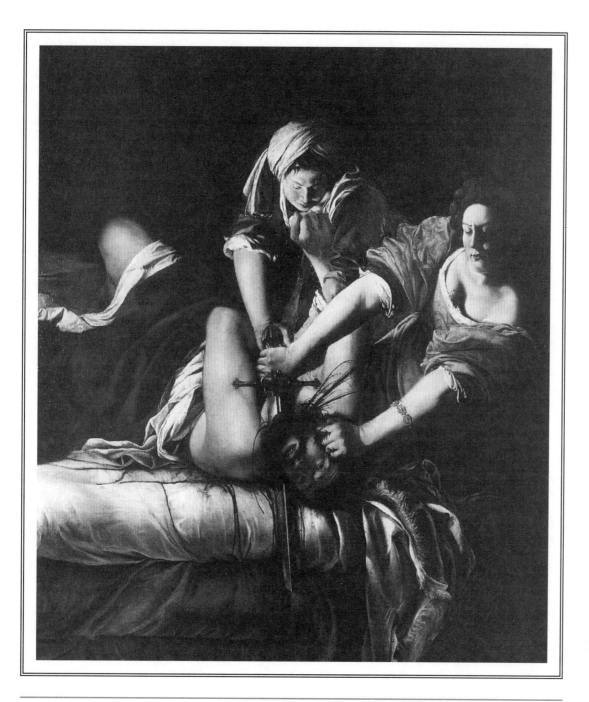

Judith Beheading Holofernes by Artemisia Gentileschi.

90s, was still offering advice and encouragement to her younger colleagues. Garrard suggests that it was at this time that Artemisia's influence made its way, through her paintings or copies made of them, from Genoa to Holland, where it can be identified in some of the works of the young Rembrandt.

By 1622, Artemisia had returned to her native city, Rome, to find that tastes had changed. While Caravaggism took hold in the rest of Europe, the Romans, tired of its naturalism, had begun to favor the more idealized style of Bernini. But Gentileschi continued to find commissions and her only extant portrait, of an unknown man in armor, dates from this period. For unknown reasons, she was now separated from her husband and lived in the city with her daughter and two servants.

She refused to deal in pathos and the softer emotions, and, as a result, alienated all those critics and historians of art who nurture the usual presuppositions about women.

—Germaine Greer

Judith and Maidservant with the Head of Holofernes, painted in 1625, is recognized by art historians as Gentileschi's greatest work and, notes Garrard, "is by universal acclaim one of the great masterpieces of the Caravaggesque Baroque." The subject is the aftermath of the decapitation of Holofernes, a moment of suspense as Judith and her maidservant, perhaps fearing discovery, freeze in their escape. The light of a single candle throws into effect the positions and gestures of the two women, and, contrasting with the darkness of the rest of the canvas, brings them to the focus of the viewer. Its sophistication "displays the artist's mature talent for dramatic narrative, dynamic chiaroscuro, and the creation of monumental heroes."

By the late 1620s, the search for work had led Gentileschi to move again. Naples, the second largest city in Europe after Paris, was ruled by Spanish viceroys who were renowned patrons of the arts. Home to many wealthy merchants, it was the center of artistic activity at the time. Artemisia soon established a market for her works with patrons including *Maria Anna of Spain, sister of the king of Spain. One commission, in 1630, was for a self-portrait, the result of which now hangs in St. James's Palace, London. In *Self-Portrait as the Allegory of Painting,* Gentileschi achieved what her male peers were unable to do: combining the traditional symbols associated with the allegorical (female) figure of "painting" with her own image, she becomes her art. Again she displayed an inventiveness of composition, writes Garrard, as "she has posed herself with one arm raised upward, the hand stretched toward its invisible target, suggesting the higher, ideal aspirations of painting, with the other arm resting firmly on a table, the hand holding the brushes and palette which are the physical materials of painting."

Despite her avowed dislike of the city, Naples held the few sources of work available to Caravaggist painters. Church commissions and religious paintings delivered the income she now needed to provide her daughters with a dowry. (A second child, about whom little is known, was born some years after Prudentia.) By now all links with Stiattesi, her husband, had been broken and, although no evidence exists to certify that he was the father of either child, it is likely that the dowry problem prompted Gentileschi to write from Naples, in 1637: "Please send me news of whether my husband is alive or dead." This, of course, provided legions of future anecdotists with the evidence required to prove her defiant neglect of wifely duty.

For a working woman in 17th-century Italy, life was not without its difficulties. As a working woman separated from her husband, these difficulties were multiplied. In many instances, her brother, Francesco, provided support by maintaining her affairs and representing her where a male presence was required. It was he who brought the offer, which Gentileschi accepted, to travel to England to work under the patronage of King Charles I.

Charles I's reputation as a connoisseur of fine art was supported by his collection which boasted works by Raphael, Titian, Caravaggio, and some of Artemisia's paintings. Orazio Gentileschi had been invited to work there eight years earlier, but, now in failing health, he desired the assistance of his daughter on the decoration of the Queen's House in Greenwich. Within a year of her arrival, he had died, leaving Artemisia to complete the commission. It is speculated by some art historians that she was helped in her task by her daughters who were also practicing artists.

Political unrest in England, which would lead to the Civil War and Charles I's execution, combined with a desire to return home, brought Gentileschi back to Naples in 1642 where she was to spend the last decade of her life. Although an established figure in the art world with a reliable and important patron, Don Antonio Ruffo of Sicily, she was finally forced to dramatically alter her style, in part a response to changing tastes, in part to elicit more money. According to the arrangement with her patron, the cost of a picture was dependent upon the number of figures depicted, naked figures being more expensive than clothed ones. And so we can see in her later works a tendency towards a softer approach to her subjects, with themes like the story of *Bathsheba, allowing as it did for the portrayal of lucrative bodies, taking over from the heroines of her earlier years. Gone too, is the hallmark of the Caravaggist—the exciting effects of light and darkness which had characterized so many of her previous paintings. The letters of this period present an Artemisia who confidently negotiates her prices and knows her worth, a woman of experience and acumen who is not afraid to assert her rights in the often disreputable dealings of the art market.

The dates of Gentileschi's final work and her death are not known; historians tend to favor the year 1653, when the following insulting epitaph was published in Venice:

> By painting one likeness after another
> I earned no end of merit in the world;
> While, to carve two horns upon my husband's head
> I put down the brush and took a chisel instead.

It was this short verse, reprinted and translated throughout Europe, which formed the basis for a lasting opinion of Artemisia Gentileschi. She had excelled at her work, influencing artists across Europe. She had worked for some of the most important patrons of the day. She had left paintings, recognized both then and now as masterpieces. But in a world where artists were almost expected to be eccentric, to take lovers, to drink and carouse, the double standard already prevailed.

For centuries, interest in Artemisia Gentileschi centered upon the details of her personal life: her promiscuity, as evidenced through the rape trial, and her dismissive treatment of her husband. This was to be the legacy of the denigration of her talents which began immediately after her death. Where she was mentioned in art historical texts, it was usually as a footnote in a study of the work of Orazio Gentileschi, to whom some of her work was attributed. Only with the publication of her letters in the 19th century, and a study of her work with her father earlier this century, did art historians begin to document the significance of the work of this singularly independent and magnificently skilled woman.

SOURCES AND SUGGESTED READING:

Banti, Anna. *Artemisia.* Translated by Shirley D'Ardia Caracciolo. University of Nebraska Press, 1995.

Bissell, R. Ward. "Artemisia Gentileschi: a new documented chronology," in *Art Bulletin.* Vol. 50, 1968, pp. 153–168.

Garrard, Mary D. *Artemisia Gentileschi: The Image of the Female Hero in Italian Baroque Art.* Princeton, NJ: Princeton University Press, 1989.

Greer, Germaine. *The Obstacle Race.* NY: Farrar, Straus, and Giroux, 1979.

Slatkin, Wendy. *Women Artists in History: From Antiquity to the 20th Century.* Englewood Cliffs, NJ: Prentice Hall, 1990.

Wittkower, Rudolf and Margo. *Born under Saturn.* NY: Random House, 1963 (pp. 162–165 for an interpretation of the rape trial).

RELATED MEDIA:

Artemisia (French film), starring **Valentina Cervi** and Michael Serrault, 1998. ("The film's got it all wrong," said Mary Garrard, who published an English translation of the Tassi trial transcripts. The film "portrays them as voluntary lovers. But the only emotion on record is hostility.")

Diane Moody,
freelance writer, London, England, with a B.A. in Art History, Princeton University, Princeton, New Jersey

Genville, Joan de (fl. 1300).

See Mortimer, Joan.

Geoffrin, Marie Thérèse

(1699–1777)

One of the most famous of the 18th-century salonnières, whose salon was the intellectual home of influential writers, philosophers, and artists of the period, including the Encyclopedists, many of whom received her financial support. Name variations: Geofrin. Pronunciation: Marie Tur-ESS Jeff-RAN. Born Marie Thérèse Rodet in 1699 in Paris, France; died on October 6, 1777, in Paris; daughter of Pierre Rodet (a valet de chambre of the French royal court) and the former Mlle Chemineau (daughter of a banker); married Pierre François Geoffrin, on July 19, 1713; children: Marie Thérèse Geoffrin, later the Marquise de la Ferté-Imbault (b. 1715) and a son (b. 1717) who did not survive childhood.

Attended salon of the Marquise de Tencin, which opened her intellectual world (1730); established her salon (1737); supported the work of the Encyclopedists, including Diderot, D'Alembert, and many others (1750s–60s); commissioned many works of art, including over 60 paintings (1750–70); was guest of King Stanislaus Augustus of Poland and Empress Maria Theresa of Austria-Hungary (1766).

It has been said of uneducated women that "Ignorance forces a woman who is not stupid to make great use of her brains," and there is probably no better example of this axiom in history than the 18th-century Frenchwoman known as Mme Geoffrin. Orphaned at age seven, poorly educated, and married off at the age of 15 to a man 33 years her senior, she became a patron of the arts, a supporter of the intellectual enterprise known as the *Encyclopédie,* and the most important social and literary arbiter of her age. Among her correspondents she counted the Empress *Catherine II the Great of Russia, King Stanislaus Augustus of Poland, and Empress *Maria Theresa of Austria. Her Paris salon at no. 372 Rue Saint Honoré remained a gathering place of artists and women and men of letters for more than a quarter century. Although she acquired great social power and influence, she was known chiefly as a generous patron and friend of the poor, epitomizing the spirit of the period of the Enlightenment in which she lived.

Mme de Tencin.

See Salonnières.

Marie Thérèse Rodet was born in Paris in 1699, daughter of Pierre Rodet, a *valet de chambre* at the court of King Louis XIV. Her mother, the former **Mlle Chemineau,** was the daughter of a banker, whose family passed on its solid bourgeois values to Marie Thérèse. Mlle Chemineau died giving birth to a son Louis when Marie Thérèse was a year old. When Marie Thérèse was seven, her father died, leaving both children to be brought up by their maternal grandmother, **Mme Chemineau,** a traditionalist who did not endorse education for women. Marie Thérèse was taught to read, but writing was little emphasized, and her spelling was notorious. Throughout her life, many would note her lack of education. Deprived of disciplined studies, she learned to enter into the feelings of others rather than express her own opinions, a skill she developed into a fine art. But the limitations of her upbringing were typical of the time. "She taught me in my childhood simply to read," wrote Geoffrin of her grandmother, "but she made me read much; she taught me to think by making me reason; she taught me to know men by making me say what I thought of them. . . . My education was continual."

On July 19, 1713, Marie Thérèse Rodet married François Geoffrin, whom she had met at daily mass at the Church of St. Roche. François had been left wealthy by a brief first marriage to an elderly widow and had invested his inheritance in the Compagnie de Saint-Gobain, the glass works of which he became administrator. Mme Chemineau viewed the union as ideal, since François was a well-to-do, respected man, who could also serve as a father figure to both his young wife and her brother. Marie Thérèse brought a substantial dowry to this marriage, and after two years the couple had a daughter, Marie Thérèse, born in 1715. Two years later, a son was born who died at the age of ten. Mme Chemineau did not live to see her grandson born.

At age 18, the young Geoffrin was thus in charge of her two young children and her brother Louis. A sensible soul given to an ordered life—who knew the value of money and never indulged in flashy dress or jewels—she adhered to a soberly bourgeois lifestyle. But in 1730, the life of the Geoffrin family was forever changed, after ◄ **Mme de Tencin** (1685–1749) came to live nearby on the Rue Saint Honoré. Famed for organizing notorious fêtes for Philippe II, duke of Orléans, regent to the young King Louis XV, at Saint-Cloud, Mme de Tencin was not one who would be expected to share many interests with the sober and industrious Mme Geoffrin. Nevertheless, the two became friends, and the younger woman became a frequent guest in the home of Mme de Tencin, where she entered a new world inhabited by such illustrious intellectuals as Montesquieu, Fontenelle, and La Motte-Houdard. The table at the home of Mme de Tencin was not sumptuous, however, and when Geoffrin began to invite the same prominent figures to dinner at one o'clock on Wednesday afternoons, the good food, wine, and conversation she offered was a real drawing card. Thus was the salon of Mme Geoffrin born.

In 18th-century France, it was possible for women to reach great ascendancy. A succession of royal mistresses formed a virtual dynasty based on authentic political power. Other women achieved equal influence in literature and the arts by acting as host in their salons. To create a salon required a good host and literary lions who would attend, and it was said of such *salonnières,* "Hostesses, like poets, are born, not made." In essence, these women were in charge of the clearing houses for the creative and intellectual thought of their time, because a philosopher, playwright, poet, or artist could find it difficult to gain recognition without their stamp of approval. Compared to Hollywood in the late 20th century, these women of Paris were the superagents of their age.

The salons were also important in raising the general status of artists. Prior to the 18th century, artists had generally been treated as servants rather than as independent creators capable of unique contributions, and the patronage provided by the nobility reinforced their lowly status, allowing them to be ordered about. In the salon of

Marie Thérèse Geoffrin

Mme de Tencin, the prestige of artistic accomplishment was on the rise, according some artists the same status as aristocrats, while the role of the hostesses in their salons expanded beyond the confines of social entertainment. Gifted artists, writers, and philosophers were launched through these social mentors, who advertised their work, provided them with desirable contacts, and gave financial assistance.

Geoffrin was in no sense an intellectual luminary, but in her time she was the most powerful of the *salonnières*. Never overawed by the prominent and powerful, she disliked controversy, so politics were rarely the topic under discussion in her salon. If other talk became too heated, she might halt the conversation with the phrase, *"Voilà qui est bien."* Religious, even somewhat devout, she was also open minded, welcoming members of the intellectual group known as the Encyclopedists at her table, although she did not share their anti-clerical ideology. Montesquieu, Voltaire, Diderot, d'Alembert, Lord Shelbourne, and Stanislaus Augustus, later king of Poland, were regular guests at her dinners, as well as Horace Walpole, Grimm, and Bernardin de Saint-Pierre. Following the dinner, there would be other guests to join in an invigorating exchange of ideas. Some described no. 372 Rue

Saint Honoré as the place where the aristocracy of genius met the aristocracy of birth.

Mme Geoffrin's salon was considered the center of the philosophical movement partly because of her sponsorship of the *Encyclopédie*. She was known as the "foster mother of the philosophers," and her contributions to this immense undertaking were greater than many realized at the time. The very first enterprise of its kind, it took many years to complete, and there is evidence that the publishers were on the verge of ruin in 1759. Geoffrin provided much of the funds for Diderot and D'Alembert as well as lesser contributors like Marmontel and Morellet, to carry out the basic research and writing of the encyclopedia's entries. Providing regular stipends as well as publicizing the work and introducing the writers to influential members of her extensive network, she made a critical difference, in ways great and small, leading to the work's publication. In sheer monetary terms, her daughter later estimated that she had contributed the vast sum of more than 100,000 livres and some estimates are as high as 200,000 livres. With typical largess, she also refurnished the study of Diderot, supplying leather chairs, deep-red damask for the walls, an intricate marquetry desk, and a gold-and-bronze clock. In response, Diderot was inspired to write a pamphlet, *Regrets sur ma vieille robe de chambre,* a comedic lament for his old furniture.

Lespinasse, Julie de. See *Salonnières.*

Deffand, Marie. See *Salonnières.*

*ℰ*quality of sex, of mind, and of person was never more conspicuous than in the salon of the 18th century.

—Helen Clergue

Mme Geoffrin did not confine her support to literature, however, as she also sponsored an artistic salon. Noticing that the artists always drew apart at her Wednesday receptions, she began sponsoring a Monday dinner just for them which was organized by M. de Caylus, the artist and archeologist. Although china, bronzes, tapestries, sculpture, and furniture were all pleasing to her, she personally preferred paintings and commissioned at least 60 between 1750 and 1770. Sponsoring the works of Van Loo, Vernet, Boucher, La Tour, and Greuze, she provided other artists with stipends and gifts. Her two most famous commissioned paintings, by C.A. Van Loo, *La Conversation espagnole* and *La Lecture,* were sold to Catherine the Great in 1772 and now hang in the Hermitage Museum in St. Petersburg. Hubert Robert, an artist she supported, painted his patron and himself. He is in a gray suit standing by his easel, while she is in a stiff, black-lace bonnet.

Women other than the hostess were usually excluded from salons, and for a while Geoffrin moved almost exclusively in male circles. A sociable person with many friends, she instituted *petits soupers* for her women friends to share light meals and conversation. Apart from Mme de Tencin, her friendships with women included **Julie de Lespinasse,** a companion and helper of the celebrated marquise **Marie Deffand,** who was much loved by D'Alembert. The salon of Marie Deffand declined as she became blind and increasingly cantankerous in old age, and when conditions became intolerable for Lespinasse, Geoffrin provided her young friend with funds for an apartment and servants so that she could begin her own salon.

Although Geoffrin was unobtrusive in her giving, stories of her generosity were legion. One friend who called on her unexpectedly on a Sunday found her making up bags of coins to distribute to the poor. When the artist Van Loo died, she bought two of his pictures for 4,000 livres and sold them shortly thereafter to a Russian prince for 50,000 livres; she then sent the difference to the artist's widow. When two workers delivered a vase from the famous sculptor Bouchardon, she pointed out a broken lid, and the men acknowledged the breakage, saying that the third worker who was responsible had been afraid to make the delivery. Geoffrin promised not to mention the breakage and later sent a servant with money for the hapless worker and his friends. Since many donations were made unobtrusively, no one knows the full extent of her generosity.

As the 18th century progressed, Geoffrin's reputation became international. She corresponded with the empresses Maria Theresa and Catherine the Great. She was also a great friend of King Stanislaus of Poland who had arrived in Paris at the age of 19 as Stanislaus Augustus Poniatowski. When he was put in debtors' prison after a short sojourn, Mme Geoffrin paid his debts, and a close friendship ensued. In fact, he called her "Maman," and she referred to him as her "son," perhaps hoping to replace her son who died. Stanislaus later became a favorite at the court of Catherine the Great, who rewarded him with the crown of Poland.

When Geoffrin was 67, she was invited by Stanislaus to his capital. She was ecstatic at the prospect, having rarely left Paris, and was unaware of the conditions awaiting her on the roads and in filthy inns along her journey, which took several weeks. As she had a poor opinion of Frederick the Great, she bypassed Berlin in favor of traveling through Vienna and was given a royal welcome at the court of the Empress Maria Theresa, the future emperor Joseph II, and the little archduchess *Marie Antoinette. From Poland, she wrote enthusiastic letters about the new king, and reports of her progress circulated throughout Europe. After the journey, however, her correspondence ceased with Catherine the Great, who was annoyed that Geoffrin had not chosen to extend her journey as far as St. Petersburg.

Little is recorded about the husband of Mme Geoffrin. A quiet presence, he attended the Monday and Wednesday dinners but rarely said a word, and lived to be 84. Shortly after his death, a guest inquired about the whereabouts of the elderly gentleman, wondering who he was. His widow replied: "That was my husband. He is dead."

The excellent relationships that Geoffrin enjoyed with people from all stations in life unfortunately did not extend at all times to her daughter. The young Marie Thérèse complained constantly about patching up quarrels between her parents,

which may explain something of their rift. Her daughter also did not share much of her enthusiasm for Enlightenment ideas. Like her mother, however, young Marie Thérèse was placed in a loveless marriage, to the Marquis de la Ferté-Imbault, when she was 18 and he was 21. She lived with his family for four years until his sudden death. Then, as a 22-year-old widow with a seven-month-old daughter, she returned to the home of her mother. The young marquise began writing and sponsored a counter-salon, called the Order of Lanturelus, which was a forum for the intellectual movement of anti-philosophers.

Despite her association with many who considered themselves agnostic, Geoffrin was religious throughout her life. She often went on retreat at the Convent of the Abbey of Saint Antoine, where she is immortalized in a painting by Robert, shown seated among the nuns. During religious exercises for the jubilee of 1776, she took a chill and was incapacitated shortly thereafter by a stroke. Her daughter kept watch by her bedside, deciding who could see her ailing moth-

Madame Geoffrin (third from right), presiding over her salon.

er. Since many of the philosophes were turned away, there was bitterness over the Marquise de la Ferté-Imbault's control over the patient. During the yearlong illness, Mme Geoffrin was visited by the future emperor of Austria, Joseph II, who stayed for two hours, but her contacts were limited. She died on October 6, 1777.

Had she reached the end of the century, Geoffrin would probably have been surprised by the bloodiness of the French Revolution, which claimed its ideological inheritance from those who met regularly in her salon. Such revolutionary upheaval surely would not have met with her approval. Yet the concepts of freedom, equality, and representative government frequently aired in her salon were the ideals fought for then and are the ideals that continue to be cherished.

SOURCES:

Batiffol, Louis, André Hallays, Raul Reboux Nozère, and André Bellessort. *The Great Literary Salons*. London: Thornton Butterworth, 1930.

Besterman, Theodore. *Voltaires Correspondence*. Geneva: Institut et Musée Voltaire, 1961.

———. *Voltaire*. Chicago, IL: University of Chicago Press, 1976.

Clergue, Helen. *The Salon*. NY: Burt Franklin, 1907 (reprint 1971).

Ducros, Louis. *French Society in the Eighteenth Century*. NY: Putnam, 1927.

Glotz, Marguerite and Madeleine Marie. *Salons du xviiie Siècle*. Paris: Hachette, 1945.

Gooch, G.P. *Catherine the Great and Other Studies*. London: Longmans, Green, 1954.

Goodman, Dena. "Filial Rebellion in the Salon: Madame Geoffrin and Her Daughter," in *French Historical Studies*. Vol. 16, no. 1. Spring 1989, pp. 28–47.

Grand, Serge. *Ces Bonnes Femmes du XVIIIe*. Paris: Pierre Horay, 1985.

Grimsley, Ronald. *Jean D'Alembert (1717–83)*. Oxford: Clarendon Press, 1963.

Kastner, L.E., and Henry Gibson Atkins. *A Short History of French Literature*. Port Washington, NY: Kennikat Press, 1970.

Lougee, Carolyn C. *Le Paradis des Femmes: Women, Salons, and Social Stratification in Seventeenth-Century France*. Princeton, NJ: Princeton University Press, 1976.

Lough, John. *The Encyclopédie in Eighteenth-Century England and Other Studies*. Newcastle-upon-Tyne: Oriel Press, 1970.

Mason, Amelia Gere. *The Women of the French Salons*. NY: Century, 1891.

Nitze, William A., and E. Preston Dargan. *A History of French Literature*. NY: Henry Holt, 1938.

Quennell, Peter. *Affairs of the Mind: The Salon in Europe and America from the Eighteenth to the Twentieth Century*. Washington: New Republic Books, 1980.

Roustan, M. *The Pioneers of the French Revolution*. NY: Howard Fertig, 1969.

Scott, Barbara. "Madame Geoffrin: A Patron and Friend of Artists," in *Apollo*. Vol. 85, no. 60. February 1967, pp. 98–103.

Tallentyre, S.G. *The Women of the Salons*. NY: Putnam, 1926.

Wade, Ira O. *The Structure and Form of the French Enlightenment*. Vol. I. Princeton, NJ: Princeton University Press, 1977.

Karin Loewen Haag,
freelance writer, Athens, Georgia

George, Fanny Lloyd (d. 1941).

See Lloyd George, Fanny.

George, Gladys (1900–1954)

American actress of stage and films. Born Gladys Anna Clare on September 13, 1900, in Patton, Maine; died, 1954; the daughter of an actor and actress.

Selected films: Red Hot Dollars *(1919)*; The Woman in the Suitcase *(1920)*; Home Spun Folks *(1920)*; The Easy Road *(1921)*; The House That Jazz Built *(1921)*; Straight Is the Way *(1934)*; Valiant Is the Word for Carrie *(1936)*; They Gave Him a Gun *(1937)*; Madam X *(1937)*; Love Is a Headache *(1938)*; *Marie Antoinette *(1938)*; I'm from Missouri *(1939)*; The Roaring Twenties *(1939)*; A Child Is Born *(1940)*; The House Across the Bay *(1940)*; The Way of All Flesh *(1940)*; Hit the Road *(1941)*; The Maltese Falcon *(1941)*; The Crystal Ball *(1943)*; The Hard Way *(1943)*; Christmas Holiday *(1944)*; Minstrel Man *(1944)*; Steppin' in Society *(1945)*; The Best Years of Our Lives *(1946)*; Millie's Daughter *(1947)*; Flamingo Road *(1949)*; Bright Leaf *(1950)*; Lullaby of Broadway *(1951)*; He Ran All the Way *(1951)*; Detective Story *(1951)*; It Happens Every Thursday *(1953)*.

Born into a theatrical family, actress Gladys George made her debut at age three and later played vaudeville, stock, and on Broadway. Although she made a few silents, George is mainly known for the films she made in the 1930s and 1940s. Cast as the leading lady or second lead in melodramas, her most notable roles were in *Valiant Is the Word for Carrie* (1936), for which she won an Oscar nomination, *The Roaring Twenties* (1939), and *The Way of All Flesh* (1940). George played character roles later in her career and worked until shortly before her death in 1954.

George, Grace (1879–1961)

American actress. Born in New York on December 25, 1879; died on May 19, 1961; educated at Notre Dame Convent in New Jersey; studied at the American Academy of Dramatic Arts, 1893; married William A. Brady.

Grace George made her debut at the Standard Theater in New York on June 23, 1894, as one of the schoolgirls in *The New Boy*. Her first appearance of note was in the part of Juliette in *The Turtle* at the Manhattan Theater (September 1898). In 1903, she appeared as *Peg Woffington in *Pretty Peggy* and subsequently toured in the same part with great success. Her London debut was in 1907 at the Duke of York Theater as Cyprienne in *Divorçons*. Among a long list of appearances, George took on many of George Bernard Shaw's plays, portraying Barbara Undershaft in *Major Barbara* (1915) and Lady Cicely Waynflete in *Captain Brassbound's Conversion* (1917). She was last seen at the National Theater in New York as Mrs. Culver in *The Constant Wife* in December 1951.

George, Megan Lloyd (1902–1966).

See Lloyd George, Megan.

George, Mlle. (c. 1787–1867).

See Georges, Marguerite J.

George, Zelma Watson
(1904–1994)

African-American sociologist, musicologist, and performer. Born in Hearne, Texas, in 1904; died in Cleveland, Ohio, in July 1994; graduated from the University of Chicago; master's and doctoral degrees in sociology at New York University; studied voice at the American Conservatory of Music, Chicago; studied pipe organ at Northwestern University, Evanston, Illinois.

A Texas native and a graduate of the University of Chicago, Zelma Watson George was a trained soprano and organist. She worked briefly as a social worker in Evanston, Illinois, before becoming a probation officer in Chicago. From 1932 to 1937, she was dean of women at Tennessee State University, then helped organize the Avalon Community Center in Los Angeles. During her early career, George also lectured on the cultural contributions of African-Americans, and in 1935 she began research on black music. With the aid of a Rockefeller grant in 1942, she traveled the country collecting data from libraries and private collections. The result of her research, "A Guide to Negro Music," an annotated bibliography, served as her thesis for a doctoral degree in sociology from New York University. She later donated the compendium of over 12,000 titles to Howard University.

In 1949, George sang the lead in a black production of *The Medium*, a folk opera by Gian Carlo Menotti, at the dedication of the Karamu Lyric Theatre in Cleveland. Upon hearing of her performance, Menotti brought her to New York to recreate the role for the 1950 production of the opera at the Arena Stage in the Hotel Edison. Becoming the first black woman to take a white role on Broadway, George was praised by the critics. "She has great personal force," wrote Brooks Atkinson of *The New York Times*. "She sings with power and imagination."

In 1960, George was appointed by President Dwight D. Eisenhower as the only African-American member of the U.S. delegation to the 15th General Assembly of the United Nations. In the late 1960s, she was executive director of the Job Corps center in Cleveland. She remained a resident of Cleveland until her death in 1994.

Georges, Marguerite J.
(c. 1787–1867)

French actress. Name variations: Mlle George. Born Marguerite Joséphine Weimer or Wemmer at Bayeux, France, in 1786 or 1787; died in Paris in January 1867.

Some juvenile performances of Marguerite Joséphine Georges' at Amiens attracted the notice of actress *Mlle Raucourt, by whose influence Georges was brought to Paris and educated. Her imposing beauty and powerful acting produced a sensation at her first appearance as Clytemnestra and led to successful engagements in other European cities (1808–13). In Russia, Tsar Alexander I became so infatuated with her that he would not consent to her returning to France, but later Napoleon, one of her warmest admirers, secured her reappearance at the Théâtre Français (1813–17), where the French actor François Joseph Talma added polish to her style. From 1821 to 1847, she was connected with the Odéon and the Porte Saint-Martin theaters, sustaining her reputation as an impassioned and majestic tragedian in such roles as Semiramis (*Sammuramat), *Agrippina the Younger, *Lucrezia Borgia, and *Catherine de Medici.

Only rivalled by **Mlle Duchesnois**, Georges received costly presents from emperors, princes, and a host of other admirers; yet on retiring from the stage in 1849, her poverty impelled her to become a teacher at the conservatory.

Georgia (d. 6th c.)

Saint. Name variations: Georgette. Died at the beginning of the 6th century.

According to Gregory of Tours, her near contemporary from Auvergne, Georgia was a young girl living at Clermont in the beginning of the 6th century who withdrew from public life in order to meditate, fast, and pray. When she died a flight of doves, said to be angels, accompanied her body as it was borne in funeral procession from the house where she perished to the church. During the service, the birds hid in the roof, then reappeared when the funeral procession left for the cemetery. After the interment, they flew toward the heavens. Saint Georgia's feast day is February 15.

Geraldine (1916—)

Hungarian-American who was queen-consort of Albania. Name variations: Geraldine de Nagy-Appony. Born Geraldine de Nagy-Appony in 1916; daughter of Cyula Apponyi, count de Nagy-Appony; married Ahmed Bey Zogu, also known as Scanderbeg III or Zog I or Zogu I (Ahmed), king of Albania (r. 1928–39), in 1938 (died 1961); children: son Leka I (b. April 17, 1939); possibly others.

Ahmed Bey Zogu was one of Albania's largest landowners. In January 1925, he was elected president of the Republic, superseding the Council of Regency that had been established in 1921. By March, he was tailoring the constitution to enhance his power. On December 1, 1928, he declared himself King Zog I of Albania, using his powers for reform. But poverty in Albania was widespread.

In 1938, when he married 22-year-old Geraldine, an Hungarian-American, his country was in close collaboration with Benito Mussolini's Italy. So powerful was Italy's control that Albania became its vassal state. On April 19, 1939, two days after Geraldine gave birth to the Albanian heir, planes droned over the capital city of Tirana, dropping leaflets proclaiming that friendly Italian troops were about to enter the country to "reestablish order, peace, and justice." As Mussolini invaded Albania, Zog put his still-bedridden wife and newborn child into an ambulance and sent them down 160 miles of rough road to neighboring Greece. On arrival, Geraldine released an appeal to the world: "I left my husband leading his troops—his poor insignificant little Army—into battle. What could Albania do against such armed might as that which ground down on us?" One day later, Zog, along with 115 court followers and 10 cases of valuables, joined her in Greece; then the family spent their years in exile in Egypt. At the end of World War II, the monarchy was not restored, and Queen Geraldine and King Zog were officially deposed in 1946. Zog's sister, Princess **Sania**, married a diplomat and lived in Paris. His two other sisters were **Majida** and **Muzayaj**.

Geraldine

Geraldine the Fair (c. 1528–1589).

See Fitzgerald, Elizabeth.

Gérard, Marguerite (1761–1837)

French artist who was the first woman in her country to succeed as a genre painter. Name variations: Marguerite Gerard. Born in Grasse, France, in 1761; died in Paris, France, in 1837; sister of Marie Anne Fragonard (1745–c. 1823); studied with Jean Honoré Fragonard, her brother-in-law; never married; no children.

The daughter of a perfume maker and purportedly one of 17 children, Marguerite Gérard was eight years old when she went to Paris to live with her sister *Marie Anne Fragonard, a miniaturist who was married to the artist Jean Honoré Fragonard. As a member of the Fragonard household, Marguerite was informally apprenticed to one of France's greatest masters, welcomed into his menage at the Louvre, and given access to the outstanding private art collections of the day. Able to devote herself completely to her work, she ultimately became a successful genre painter, even surpassing her mentor, Fragonard, to whom she remained passionately devoted, as he was to her. (Scholars presume their relationship to have been one of cohabitation as well as collaboration, although there is no definitive proof of either charge.) After Fragonard's death in 1806, and the death of her sister in 1823 (also given as 1824), Gérard presided as the matriarch of the Fragonard clan until her own death in 1837.

Unlike her female contemporaries *Anne Vallayer-Coster, *Elisabeth Vigée-Le Brun, and *Adelaide Labille-Guiard, who were recognized in the minor fields of still life and portraiture, Gérard excelled in genre painting, an area previously reserved for men. Genre painting, as explained by **Ann Sutherland Harris** and **Linda Nochlin**, was "the nearest approximation of history painting for an artist lacking the requisite academic education," and as such "supposedly required a degree of inventiveness and imagination that placed it a notch above portraiture and still-life painting in the hierarchy of eighteenth-century art." After 1790, when the Salons were opened to women, Gérard exhibited regularly and was honored with three medals. Her works were purchased by Napoleon and Louis XVIII, adding further to her credibility. Her professional career flourished for nearly 50 years and brought her considerable personal wealth. **Germaine Greer**, who apparently buys into the theory that Marguerite was a homewrecker, finds more than a little irony in Gérard's popularity. "That she could have become famous as a pictorial moralist while living openly as an adulteress with her sister's husband exceeds all possibilities of hypocrisy."

Gérard's genre scenes, small in size (rarely exceeding 19 by 22 inches), were inspired by Dutch masters like Gabriel Metsu (1629–1667) and Gerard Terborch (1617–1681) and were admired for their "old master" ambiance and meticulous technique. Gérard emulated the *trompe l'oeil* effect of the 17th-century Dutch masters and also employed a painstaking glazing technique used to eradicate all traces of brushstroke. One of her most famous genre paintings, *The Piano Lesson* (1780s), well represents the artist in both theme and technique. The scene depicts a devoted mother, the bourgeois heroine of many of Gerard's genre scenes of the mid-1780s, overseeing her young daughter at the piano (a less erotic treatment of Fragonard's music lesson in which a male instructor hovers over a female pupil). In the accurate rendering of the mother's satin gown, which Harris and Nochlin refer to as "a Gérardian cliché," is seen the glazing technique that Gérard borrowed from the Dutch *petits maitres*. (It is interesting to note that Gérard probably used a draped mannequin to achieve the realistic effect of

Marguerite Gérard

the fabrics in the ladies' gowns. An inventory of her estate in 1837 contains a description of four very worn mannequins of different sizes.)

Gérard's portraits and miniatures, also small in size, were more spontaneous and dynamic ("Fragonardesque"), with colors applied directly on the surface of the canvas allowing the brush marks to remain quite visible. Among these, *The Architect and His Family* (c. 1787–89) and *The Attractive Art Student* (c. 1780–1790), a self-portrait, are representative. In her less constrained portrait style, some suggest that Gérard may have been an 18th-century precursor of Impressionism. While that is debatable, it is most certainly true that as an independent woman who chose a career over marriage, Marguerite Gérard was well ahead of her time.

SOURCES:

Greer, Germaine. *The Obstacle Race*. NY: Farrar, Straus and Giroux, 1979.

Harris, Ann Sutherland, and Linda Nochlin. *Women Artists, 1550–1950*. LA County Museum of Art: Knopf, 1976.

Petteys, Chris. *Dictionary of Women Artists*. Boston, MA: G.K. Hall, 1985.

Barbara Morgan,
Melrose, Massachusetts

Gerbage or Gerbega.

Variant of Gerberga.

Gerberga (d. 896)

*Abbess of Gandersheim. Name variations: Gerbega. Died on July 24, 896; daughter of Ludolf or Liudolf (c. 806–866), count of Saxony, and *Oda (806–913).*

*Hathumoda was the first abbess of Gandersheim. Upon her death, she was replaced by her sister Gerberga. Another sister, *Christine of Gandersheim, replaced Gerberga.

Gerberga (r. 959–1001)

Abbess of Hildesheim and Gandersheim. Died in 1001; daughter of Judith of Bavaria (c. 925–987) and Henry I the Quarrelsome (918–955), duke of Bavaria (r. 947–955).

Gerberga, the daughter of *Judith of Bavaria** and Henry I the Quarrelsome, duke of Bavaria, became abbess of Gandersheim in 959.

Gerberga of Saxony (c. 910–969)

*Queen and regent of France. Name variations: Gerberge de Saxe. Born in Germany around 910 (some sources cite 913 or 919); died in France on May 5, 969 (some sources cite 984); daughter of Henry I the Fowler (c. 876–936), Holy Roman emperor (r. 919–936), and Matilda of Saxony (c. 892–968); sister of Otto I the Great (912–973), king of Germany (r. 936–973), Holy Roman emperor (r. 962–973), and *Hedwig (c. 915–965); married Duke Giselbert also known as Gilbert, duke of Lotharingia (Lorraine), in 929 (died 931); married Louis IV (918–954), king of France (r. 936–954), in 939; children: (first marriage) Gerberga of Lorraine (who married Adalbert, count of Vermandois); (second marriage) several surviving children, including Lothair (941–986), king of France (r. 954–986); Charles (b. 953), duke of Upper Lorraine; *Matilda Martel (943–c. 982).*

Gerberga was a Saxon princess, the daughter of Henry the Fowler of Germany and *Matilda of Saxony**. At age 19, she married Duke Giselbert of Lotharingia, but was widowed only two years later. She then married Louis IV of France as part of an alliance between the French monarch and her father. In the tradition of politically active French queens, Gerberga headed peace delegations and negotiated treaties. Widowed again in 954, Gerberga ruled France as regent until her son Lothair came of age. She was a valiant queen-regent who used her substantial army to keep herself in power, and thus ensure the throne for Lothair. In one example of her militancy, she captured a city from a besieging traitor and had the traitor beheaded in public to discourage further acts of disobedience by her subjects. After Lothair took over the reins of government, Gerberga retired to her own estates, where she died in 969.

Laura York,
Riverside, California

Gerberge.

Variant of Gerberga.

Gerberge of the Lombards (fl. mid-700s)

Queen of Austrasia. Name variations: Gerberga. Flourished in the mid-700s; married Carloman (c. 751–771), king of Austrasia (r. 768–771); children: several.

Gerdrud.

Variant of Gertrude.

Gerg, Hilde (1975—)

German skier. Pronunciation: Gairg. Born on October 19, 1975, in Bad Toelz, West Germany.

Finished 15th overall in World Cup standings (1995–96); finished 3rd overall in World Cup standings and in the top four in all seven World Cup Super G's (1996–97); won the bronze medal in the Super G and the combined in the World Championships in Sestriere (1997); finished 7th in World Cup downhill standings (1997); won the Olympic gold medal at Nagano in the women's slalom (1998).

Hilde Gerg was born in Bad Toelz, West Germany, in 1975. Her family home was in the mountains of the Bavarian Alps, where she had to ski down the slope daily to attend school. In 1998, after over five years on the tour, Gerg won the gold medal at Nagano in the women's slalom; *Deborah Compagnoni won the silver, and Zali Steggall of Australia came in third. Gerg also won a bronze in the combined for a German sweep, coming in behind *Katja Seizinger who took the gold and Martina Ertl who took the silver.

Gerhardt, Elena (1883–1961)

German-born British mezzo-soprano universally recognized and honored as one of the greatest lieder singers of the 20th century and a master interpreter of the great cultural tradition embodied in the German Romantic song. Born in Leipzig, Germany, on November 11, 1883; died in London on January 11, 1961; married Fritz Kohl.

Born in Leipzig in 1883 into a family that loved music but had produced no professional musicians, Elena Gerhardt exhibited remarkable talent from an early age. While still a student at the Leipzig Conservatory, she was discovered by the renowned conductor Arthur Nikisch, with whom she began to present song recitals. Her first recital, given on her 20th birthday in November 1903, was a huge success and her future was assured. At first, it was assumed that she would become an opera singer, and Gerhardt did in fact appear briefly on stage as an opera singer. She quickly decided, however, that her strength was not in the spectacular theatricality found in standard operas or in the vast music dramas of Richard Wagner. Instead, she chose to explore the infinite variety of human experience to be found in the miniature universe of lieder, the psychologically and emotionally complex German art song. For the remainder of her long and successful career, Elena Gerhardt sang only lieder, mastering to perfection the vast repertory of songs by Brahms, Mendelssohn, Schubert, and Schumann, as well as songs by Richard Strauss and Hugo Wolf, composers who were her contemporaries.

After achieving a spectacular success with her Leipzig debut, Elena Gerhardt toured throughout Germany and Central Europe. Her singing elicited the highest praise, including a compliment from the Italian-born British composer Francesco Paolo Tosti that he believed her to be almost unique among German singers in her ability to sing in the "bel canto" style (she began her singing career as a soprano, but her voice deepened to mezzo-soprano during her maturity). In 1906, she made a profound impression on British music lovers during her first tour of the United Kingdom. One of Gerhardt's British recitals, which included Queen *Alexandra of Denmark in the audience, was so wildly successful that she had to encore every one of the 15 songs on the program. During the next years, before the start of World War I in 1914, Gerhardt concertized not only in her native Germany, but in most European countries, including Spain, and in Russia. In January 1912, she made her American premiere in New York City, earning glowing critical reviews. *The New York Times* praised her for having given a performance that "penetrated deeply into the essence of the German song," going on to state that she was "in fact, a mistress of variety and characteristic interpretation of a wide gamut of moods and emotions." *The New York Tribune* joined in the chorus of critical praise, describing Gerhardt as "an artist of the finest grade calibre" and pointing out that her phrasing "was truly exquisite." At a subsequent New York recital two weeks later, the *Times* again commented on the young German singer's "versatility and variety of expression," as well as her ability to project charm and vivacity by means of a voice that combined with rare artistic excellence the attibutes of "beauty, power, and sympathetic quality."

Although she continued to concertize in Germany and Austria-Hungary during World War I, Elena Gerhardt was cut off from her admiring audiences for a number of years because of the war and the period of chaos that followed it. By the mid-1920s, however, she was again an international musical celebrity, performing not only in the major cities of Europe but in the United States as well (by the time she retired, Gerhardt had made 16 tours of the U.S.). In 1928, when she toured the States to commemorate the centennial of Franz Schubert's death, Gerhardt's loyal and enthusiastic audiences, many of whom had been introduced to her artistry through her numerous recordings, now showed up in sold-out recital halls for virtually every one of her appearances. Olin Downes, music critic of *The New York Times,* reported that the net effect of one of her recitals "was one of uncommon satisfaction and pleasure for an audience which packed the hall." Several weeks later, another enthusiastic New York audience heard Gerhardt give a memorable performance of Schubert's song cycle "Die Winterreise," a setting of 24 lyrics which include some of the Austrian composer's most hauntingly beautiful creations including "Der Lindenbaum," "Die Post," and "Der Leiermann." That evening and on countless other occasions, audiences and critics alike felt that they had experienced what Desmond Shawe-Taylor has described as a performance "of memorably exalted and tragic character." Although "Die Winterreise" is more often than not performed by a male singer, Gerhardt was able to project this tragic figure so effectively that her audiences completely ignored her gender.

The world economic crisis of the early 1930s and the rise of Nazism in Germany resulted in dramatic changes in Elena Gerhardt's life and career. In 1932, on the eve of the establishment of the Hitler dictatorship, she married Dr. Fritz Kohl, director of Radio Leipzig. In 1933, with the onset of Nazi rule, Kohl was arrested for having encouraged broadcasting policies that were "un-German." After Kohl's release from incarceration, Elena Gerhardt and her husband immigrated to Great Britain and found a country where personal security and artistic freedom were assured. Already highly acclaimed by British audiences, Gerhardt continued her concert career. At the same time, she began teaching advanced pupils, both through classes at London's Guildhall School of Music and by giving private instruction.

Soon after arriving in London, Gerhardt continued to make recordings. The most important of these, in the 1930s, were her renditions of the lieder of Hugo Wolf, the Austrian composer whose reputation was still on the rise in the English-speaking world and many of whose songs had not yet been transcribed. In 1931, even before she fled Germany, Gerhardt had been approached by the His Master's Voice recording firm to sign up for a recording project of Hugo Wolf lieder. When she asked for an advance royalty of 300 guineas, a substantial sum, the company replied it was impossible in the midst of a world depression and an uncertain market for the music of a relatively obscure composer. Nevertheless, she went ahead without payment, and recorded the discs as the first installment of the limited-edition subscription set known as *The Hugo Wolf Society.*

When the first Wolf set sold out immediately after release, many recording executives were astonished but also gratified, and *The Hugo Wolf Society* recording project continued until 1937 with the issuance of five additional volumes (an additional 20 lieder were recorded in 1937–38, but the projected seventh volume was never issued because of the start of World War II). The Wolf project enlisted other noted singers besides Gerhardt, including John McCormack, Alexander Kipnis, *Tiana Lemnitz, and *Elisabeth Rethberg, but Elena Gerhardt's recordings remain incomparable in their interpretation of the art of Hugo Wolf. Many critics continue to regard Elena Gerhardt's recordings of Hugo Wolf songs from this phase of her career as the best imaginable introduction to his lieder, and indeed to the art of the German lied in general.

Deeply grateful to her adoptive country for having granted her and her husband refuge from Nazism, Gerhardt performed on many occasions during World War II at the National Gallery concerts in the heart of London. Organized by the renowned pianist Dame *Myra Hess, these lunchtime recitals played a crucial role in maintaining the morale of London's population during the worst days of the Blitz. Although the British nation found itself in a life-and-death conflict with Nazi Germany, Elena Gerhardt's wartime audiences were as appreciative as ever of the artistry of a German-born singer who sang the greatest of German lieder in such a heartfelt fashion.

Despite her international celebrity, Elena Gerhardt never took on the airs of a prima donna. As pointed out by her accompanist, Gerald Moore, she was "charming and unpretentious as most great artists are." Before a concert, she would sit quietly, chatting with Moore or others about any subject other than music. In a career than spanned more than four decades, Gerhardt was able to entrance many thousands of music lovers who experienced her ability to dramatically change moods from song to song. In Brahms' "Immer leiser wird mein Schlummer," she was an ailing woman, while in the same composer's "Feldeinsamkeit" she could produce a tone so dematerialized that the world seemed to have stood still. Elena Gerhardt enjoyed a recording career of extraordinary length, making her first recordings in 1907 and her last in 1953, when she was 70. Even in her earliest discs, Gerhardt revealed an astonishing level of artistry, being able to express not only many different moods, but virtually transforming herself into a different personality within each lied.

Elena Gerhardt was, in the words of Gerald Moore, "an instinctive singer, born to sing." Her audiences sensed that all of her subtle effects of tone color, mastery of rhythm and structure of phrasing were not the result of probing analysis or coldblooded calculation, but flowed directly out of her deeply artistic personality. Although she was by any standard a great artist, Gerhardt was at the same time able to remain in many ways a remarkably normal human being. A physically attractive woman, she possessed a lively sense of humor and was extremely sociable, becoming an expert practitioner of the games of bridge and poker. A no-nonsense person who disliked sentimentality, in March 1947 she simply informed her longtime accompanist Gerald Moore, "Gerry, this next concert at Liverpool is going to be my last." Unbeknownst to her Liverpool audience, she simply gave her last recital without any prior announcements, ending her extraordinary performing career of 44 years by partying afterwards with close friends, exhibiting neither melancholy nor tears, displaying instead laughter and high spirits.

After the death of her husband in 1947, Gerhardt continued to live in the charming house they had purchased in the Hampstead district of London, and where she taught pupils from all over the world. She lived her last years "with the same simplicity and dignity" that had marked her long and acclaimed singing career. By the time of her death in London on January 11, 1961, few would dispute the fact that Elena Gerhardt had been successful in her life's mission of converting "the English-speaking world into worshippers of Schubert and his royal succession."

SOURCES:
Downes, Olin. "Elena Gerhardt Sings," in *The New York Times.* February 1, 1928, p. 30.
"Elena Gerhardt, Singer, 77, Dead," in *The New York Times.* January 12, 1961, p. 29.
"Elena Gerhardt's Recital," in *New York Tribune.* January 10, 1912, p. 7.
Gerhardt, Elena. *My Favorite German Songs.* Boston: Ditson, 1915.
———. *Recital.* St. Clair Shores, MI: Scholarly Press, 1972 (reprint ed.).
———, et al., eds. *The Hundred Best Short Songs.* 4 vols. London: Paterson, 1930.
"Miss Gerhardt's Recital," in *The New York Times.* January 25, 1912, p. 11.
Moore, Gerald. *Am I Too Loud? Memoirs of an Accompanist.* London: Hamish Hamilton, 1979.
———. *Furthermoore: Interludes in an Accompanist's Life.* London: Hamish Hamilton, 1983.
"Opera Has No Lures for Elena Gerhardt," in *The New York Times.* January 15, 1912, p. 13.

Radford, Winifred. "Elena Gerhardt," in *Recorded Sound.* No. 40. October 1970, pp. 671–677.
"Recital by Elena Gerhardt," in *The New York Times.* February 19, 1928, p. 27.
Steane, John. "The Art of Elena Gerhardt," in *International Classical Record Collector.* Winter 1996.

RELATED MEDIA:
The Christmas Album: Holiday Melodies from Around the World [Sony MHK 63309].
Gerhardt/Nikisch: Lieder Recordings [HMV HLM 1436031].
Hugo Wolf Society, 1931–1938: The Complete Edition [EMI CDHE 66640/2, five CDs].

John Haag,
Athens, Georgia

Gérin-Lajoie, Marie (1867–1945)

Canadian educator and first Francophone champion of women's rights in Quebec. Name variations: Gerin-Lajoie. Pronunciation: Jay-REEN Laj-OO. Born Marie Lacoste on October 19, 1867, at Montreal, Quebec, Canada; died on November 1, 1945, in Montreal, Canada; first child of Sir Alexander Lacoste (a lawyer and politician) and Marie Louise Globensky; attended the Hochelaga Convent, Montreal; married Henri Gérin-Lajoie, in 1887; children: Marie Gérin-Lajoie (b. 1890, who founded the Congrégation de Notre Dame du Bon Conseil); Henri (b. 1892); Alexandre (b. 1893); Léon (b. 1895).

Canadian women granted the right to vote in Federal elections (1918); all women, except in Quebec, granted right to vote in provincial elections (1921); women admitted to the Canadian Senate (1929); start of World War II (1939); Quebec women given vote in provincial elections (1940).

Selected writings: Traité de Droit Usuel *(1902);* La Femme et le Code civil *(1929).*

Born on October 19, 1867, in Montreal, in the province of Quebec, Canada, Marie Gérin-Lajoie came from one of the most distinguished French-Canadian families in the province which, in accordance with its prominent social position, occupied a large house on the Rue Saint-Hubert, then one of the elite districts of the city. Sir Alexander Lacoste, Marie's father, had been called to the bar in 1863 and quickly rose to become one of the most celebrated lawyers in the province. In 1882, he was appointed to the legislative council of Quebec and two years later was selected to sit as one of that province's representatives in the Senate (the senior chamber of the Canadian legislature). Although designated as speaker of the Senate in 1891, Sir Alexander did not hold that post for long. Later the same year, he resigned to take up a new post as chief justice of Quebec, a position which he held until his retirement in 1907.

Marie's mother (also called Marie) was the epitome of a strict Victorian matriarch. An austere and deeply religious woman, she sought to instill in her children a strong sense of self-control and restraint. This disciplinary regimen was to some extent mitigated by her husband's innate sense of good humor, and his constant encouragement to his children to read widely, discuss important issues of the day, and to engage in such activities as singing, dancing, and even amateur theatricals.

Like all female members of the Lacoste family, young Marie was sent as a boarding pupil to the highly prestigious Hochelaga Convent. There she proved to be a very unwilling student; the strict discipline imposed by the nuns was all too reminiscent of that of her mother. Marie constantly found herself in trouble with her teachers, and she responded by adopting an uncooperative and temperamental attitude. She refused all attempts by the nuns to make her handwriting neat and elegant; to the end of her life, her script was practically illegible.

Gérin-Lajoie hoped that her rebellious nature would encourage the authorities to dismiss her from the convent. This they refused to do, and, until approximately the age of 12, her unhappiness continued. For his part, Sir Alexander was well aware of his daughter's condition, but he urged her to persevere. Recognizing that his daughter possessed a genuine intellectual ability, he encouraged her to carry on her studies by herself. Sir Alexander permitted Marie free use of his extensive library, and soon she began to read widely in a variety of diverse fields such as philosophy, history, literature, and the natural sciences (specifically chemistry, physics, and astronomy). Marie was also interested in religious works, particularly those by Père Gratry, a French theologian who strongly opposed Pope Pius IX's proclamation on papal infallibility. Her main interest, however, lay in her father's judicial books, and, indeed, it was a study of the law that progressively became the main interest of her life. Through this study, she became aware of the many legal and social restrictions then placed on women in Quebec.

Gérin-Lajoie formally graduated from the Hochelaga Convent in 1882 when she was 15. After solemnly swearing never to send any of her own future daughters to boarding school, she made her first entry into Montreal society. For the next several years, Marie led an increasingly rich and varied social life. She attended all the most prominent parties and dances in town, and there she came into contact with representatives of all the most important families in Quebec.

Throughout this period, she did not neglect her program of private study. Increasingly drawn by the arguments of contemporary feminists, she came to believe that marriage was incompatible with her new ideals. Her father, though respectful of his daughter's beliefs, nevertheless persuaded her that a prominent marriage into the ranks of Quebec society would in fact help promote the principles which she now espoused. Accordingly, in 1887, she married Henri Gérin-Lajoie, an aspiring lawyer and son of one of Quebec's most famous authors and public servants. The couple were happy together and between 1890 and 1895 had four children. Their only daughter Marie later became an important social reformer in her own right, founding the Congrégation de Notre Dame du Bon Conseil, which operated social centers and schools for family and social education.

For the next few years, Gérin-Lajoie divided her time between raising her children and pursuing her own study of the law. In 1902, she published a brief manual on legal rights, the *Traité de Droit Usuel,* which eventually became widely distributed in schools and colleges throughout Quebec. It was also translated into English, an unusual distinction at this time given the intense cultural and linguistic jealousy that generally prevailed between the Francophone and Anglophone communities in the province. Marie was greatly helped and encouraged in the preparation of this manuscript by **Mother Saint-Anaclet,** a nun in the Order of the Sisters of Notre-Dame.

At the turn of the century, the two main feminist organizations in Quebec were the National Council of Women (NCW) and the Montreal Local Council of Women (MCCW). Originally, both were comprised of almost entirely of English-speaking Anglophones who, though mainly of middle-class origin, espoused a radical and militant form of feminism. Gradually, however, a number of Francophones, including Marie, joined the MCCW where they rapidly learned the methods and structures of action proposed by their English colleagues. Despite this, however, the principal concern of French feminists remained quite distinct. In other words, whereas Anglophones tended to concentrate their demands solely on women's suffrage and equal rights, Francophones focused their main concern on a broader range of issues, such as urban reform, infant mortality, health care, prostitution, and alcoholism. They believed that a program of legislative reform that would address these general issues would have the correlative effect of improving the specific conditions of all women in society.

Gérin-Lajoie recognized the strengths of both these positions. Her legal studies had convinced her that women deserved the same legal rights as males, including the right to vote. At the same time, however, she consistently rejected the militant tactics of Anglophone feminists and argued instead that change should come about through the existing order of institutions. She particularly emphasized the necessity of retaining the traditional family structure as this was the best guarantee of maintaining a woman's role in society.

It was this essentially conservative vision which led her, in 1907, to co-found (with **Caroline Béique**) the Fédération Nationale St-Jean-Baptiste (FNSJB). The impetus for this new organization arose because it was increasingly felt that neither the NCW nor the MCCW were suitable vehicles for Francophones to express either their patriotic or religious ideas. The latter was particularly important in the predominantly Catholic environment of Quebec. For many years, the Catholic Church had consistently denounced any Francophone who had sympathized or collaborated with the secular and chiefly Protestant NCW and MCCW. In contrast, the new society was viewed by the church as a vehicle that would maintain Catholic doctrine regarding the proper place of women in society while, at the same time, advocating certain mild proposals of social improvement and reform.

Under Marie's leadership, the FNSJB acted as an umbrella organization coordinating the activities of 22 affiliated associations. These associations grouped together several thousand members into three broad areas, charity, education, and working women. The federation held annual conventions, organized a wide variety of study sessions and, under Gérin-Lajoie's editorial guidance from 1913, published *La Bonne Parole*, a magazine which had a circulation of over 2,000 copies per month. Members of the FNSJB were instrumental in founding the Sainte-Justine Hospital for children in Montreal which had a woman as its first president. They also supported the Gouttes de Lait which, at that time, did much to address the problem of infant mortality. In addition, they organized lectures on hygiene, agitated against alcoholism and prostitution, demanded special courts for children, insisted on the need for policewomen to be stationed in

every police station, and worked for other charitable causes such as the Red Cross and the Fonds Patriotique (a nationalist organization committed to the protection of Francophone culture in Quebec).

Although the aim of the FNSJB was to fight for reforms in the status of women, its focus was centered on the home and family which its members considered a woman's natural and rightful place. Their struggles thus conformed to what Mgr. Bruchési, the Catholic archbishop of Montreal, called "the zealous pursuit by women of all the noble causes in the sphere that Providence has assigned to her." In short, the principal activities of the FNSJB were in harmony with the dominant clerical-nationalist ideology that prevailed within the Francophone community in Quebec during this era.

Gérin-Lajoie's public role in these activities eventually caused her to become known as the "mother" of the federation. Although this word was employed affectionately, it tended to mask a certain centralizing, authoritarian disposition inherent in her style of leadership. Moreover, a certain ambiguity slowly arose in her public pronouncements. Thus, while continuing to profess a belief in full equality between men and women, Marie gradually came to suggest that the latter enjoyed some special and unique role in formulating social improvements.

In 1913, Gérin-Lajoie extended her work by founding the Ligue des Droits de la Femme (League of Women's Rights). At that time, married women in Quebec had virtually no independent judicial standing. For instance, they could not own property independent of their husbands nor could they initiate any legal action by themselves. The aim of the League was to agitate for reforms to those parts of the Quebec Civil Code that affected the standing of women (although in this endeavor it had little direct success).

In 1918, the Federal Canadian government passed legislation granting the right to vote to all adult women. This measure was bitterly resisted by many leading French-Canadian members of parliament as well as journalists and clerics. In their view, this development represented a fundamental threat to the social order, because women did not have the necessary abilities to properly participate in the political process. Their protests, however, could not prevent women exercising their franchise in the 1921 federal election. A year later, women's suffrage was extended to the provincial level as well. The only exception was Quebec where the local legislative assembly refused to implement a similar measure.

In these circumstances, Gérin-Lajoie took it upon herself to convince the conference of Quebec bishops that there was nothing in Catholic doctrine that could be interpreted as forbidding women's suffrage. Along with a number of Anglophone colleagues, she helped found the Provincial Franchise Committee which sought to mobilize women to put pressure on members of the legislative assembly to change their decision. This committee was publicly opposed by Monsignor Eugène Roy of Quebec City who organized a petition, eventually signed by tens of thousands of women, in support of the assembly's stand.

In order to counter this opposition, Gérin-Lajoie appealed directly to the Vatican. She traveled to Rome where the World Union of Catholic Women's Organizations was holding its regular convention. Her appeal had the desired effect, and the convention prepared to pass a strongly worded resolution in support of women's suffrage. At the last moment, however, the pope's personal representative, Cardinal Merry del Val, insisted on an amendment to the resolution which stated that although the church was agreeable to the principle of women's suffrage, it would be left to the discretion of the bishops in each country whether or not to endorse this proposal.

Marie had no more success when she appealed to the leader of the Quebec government, Premier Elzéar Taschereau. The latter was adamantly opposed to any suggestion of bringing Quebec's policy into line with that of the other provinces. Moreover, he flatly declared that women would never receive the right to vote in a provincial election so long as he and his party were in office. These failures, combined with intense pressure from the Catholic hierarchy that she obey the position of the church, led to Marie's resignation from the franchise committee. With her departure, the impetus behind the struggle for the provincial vote was lost. It was not until 1927 that another French-Canadian feminist, **Idola Saint-Jean**, managed to persuade a sympathetic member of the provincial assembly to introduce a bill giving women the right to vote. This bill was defeated, as were similar measures every year until the franchise was eventually granted to Quebec women in 1940.

Gérin-Lajoie's last major intervention on behalf of Quebec women came in 1929. In that year, a commission of women's civil rights was set up, with Judge Dorion as chair. Its purpose was to study proposed changes to the Civil Code affecting marriage law. Although no women were permitted to sit on the commission, they were permitted to make submissions and give evidence. In this regard, Marie's testimony was influential in the commission's recommendation that a married woman should have the right to dispose of the income of her own labor without the permission or authorization of her husband.

During her last years, Marie Gérin-Lajoie was appointed as a part-time teacher at the University of Montreal where her lectures on law were enthusiastically received by a new generation of Francophone feminists. After her husband's death, however, her own health began to decline, and she suffered from frequent bouts of ill-health. Shortly before her own death, Marie Gérin-Lajoie was awarded a medal by Pope Pius XI in recognition of her work for the welfare of women as well as the prestigious Palmes Académiques by the government of France for her contribution to improving the legal status of women. Gérin-Lajoie died of a heart attack at her home in Montreal in November 1945.

SOURCES:

Hulet, Michelle. *Mère Marie Gérin-Lajoie.* Quebec City: Édition Canadiennes, 1979.

Linteau, Paul-André. *Quebec: A History, 1867–1929.* Toronto: James Lorimer, 1983.

SUGGESTED READING:

Cleverdon, C.L. *The Women Suffrage Movement in Canada.* Toronto: Toronto University Press, 1974.

Dave Baxter,
Department of Philosophy,
Wilfrid Laurier University, Waterloo, Ontario, Canada

Gerloc (d. 963)

Duchess of Aquitaine. Name variations: Gerletta. Born before 912; died in 963; daughter of Rolf or Hrolf also known as Rollo (d. 931, the Norse conqueror of Normandy) and *Poppa of Normandy; married William III, duke of Aquitaine; children: William IV, duke of Aquitaine.

Germain, Marie (1776–1831).

See Germain, Sophie.

Germain, Sophie (1776–1831)

French mathematician and winner of the French Academy of Sciences' gold medal. Name variations: Marie Germain. Born Marie-Sophie Germain on April 1, 1776, on rue St. Denis, Paris, France; died on June 27, 1831, rue de Savoie, Paris, France; buried in Père Lachaise cemetery, Paris; daughter of Marie-Madeleine (Gruguelin) Germain and Ambroise François Germain; self-taught; never married; no children.

Began study of mathematics (1793–94); École central des travaux opened in Paris (1794); began correspondence with J.L. Lagrange under the pen name M. le Blanc (1794); began correspondence with Carl Friedrich Gauss under pen name M. le Blanc (1804); concerned about Gauss' safety after the French Invasion of Prussia (1807); had her true identity revealed to Gauss (1807); submitted essay to the French Academy of Sciences on vibrating elastic surfaces (1811), essay rejected; submitted second essay and received honorable mention (1813); submitted third essay and awarded grand prize of the French Academy of Sciences (1816); permitted to attend public sessions of the French Academy of Sciences (1822); diagnosed with breast cancer (1829).

Selected publications: Recherches sur la théorie des surface élastique (Paris: Huzard-Courcier, 1821); Recherches sur la nature, les bornes et l'étendue de la question des surface élastique (Paris: Huzard-Courcier, 1826); Considération generales sur l'État des sciences et des lettres aux différentes époque de leur culture (Armand-Jacques Lherbette, ed. Paris: Huzard-Courcier, 1833); Oeuvres philosophiques de Sophie Germain (H. Stupuy, ed. Paris: Paul Ritti, 1879).

Sophie Germain was born in Paris on April 1, 1776, at a time when French science flourished, as did the growth of educational institutions which catered to it, though women were excluded from admission. Even so, Sophie Germain has been called one of the founders of mathematical physics.

We know little about Germain's mother save her name, **Marie-Madeleine Gruguelin**. Sophie's father was Ambroise Germain, a prosperous silk merchant, who was elected to the Estates General in 1789 and later became a director of the Bank of France. The Germain home was a frequent meeting place for those interested in liberal reform. Sophie grew up in the final turbulent years of the Ancient Regime and was 13 years old when the Bastille fell. Fortunately, the Germain family was wealthy enough to protect itself from the worst excesses of revolutionary violence.

Sophie spent many solitary hours in the family library, where she read Isaac Newton, Leonhard Euler, and Étienne Bérout's *Traité d'Arthmétique*. The most influential author of her early education, however, was J.E. Montucla, who describes the death of Archimedes in his book *History of Mathematics*. During an invasion of his city by the Roman army, Archimedes was so engrossed in the study of a geometrical figure which he had drawn in the sand that, when questioned by a passing Roman soldier, he failed to respond. As a result, he was speared to death. Thus for Germain, mathematics came to represent a repository of truth and knowledge, and Archimedes, the great scientist of antiquity, became her role model.

The choice of mathematics as an area of study was an unpopular one with her family. Although France had a tradition of female intellectuals, there was a common reaction against such pursuits, as typified by Molière's satire *La Femme Savante*. Fearing that rigorous study would imperil their daughter's health, the Germains fought a desperate rear-guard action to prevent her from undertaking strenuous research. They confiscated the candles in her bedroom, denied her heat, and took away her clothing at night. Not to be outwitted, Germain waited until her parents were asleep before wrapping herself in a quilt and treading her way carefully down to the library by the light of contraband candles. After discovering their daughter asleep one morning, with the ink frozen in the ink well and papers scattered about her covered with calculations, the Germains relented. Thus, during the Reign of Terror (1793–94), Sophie Germain spent the period teaching herself differential calculus.

In 1794, the École central des travaux, later known as the École Polytechnique, was established in Paris for the training of mathematicians and scientists. Women were not admitted. Nevertheless, Germain managed to obtain the lecture notes of various professors. One who sparked her interest was J.L. Lagrange, one of the outstanding mathematicians of the 18th century. Using the new practice of allowing students to hand in written observations at the end of the course, Germain set forth some of her theories under the pen name of M. le Blanc. Lagrange was suitably impressed. After learning the true identity of his correspondent, he sought Germain out, praised her ideas, became a lifelong supporter, and introduced her to many of France's leading scientists. Despite this, notes **Margaret**

Sophie Germain

Alic, "she was viewed by her contemporaries as a phenomenon, not as a serious student in need of teaching and guidance."

All abstract knowledge, all knowledge which is dry, it is cautioned, must be abandoned to the laborious and solid mind of man. For this reason, women will never learn geometry.

—Immanuel Kant

Then Carl Friedrich Gauss published his masterpiece *Disquisitiones Arithmeticae* in 1801. Germain was so taken with his theories of cyclotomy and arithmetical forms that in 1804 she sent him a copy of her own calculations, again employing the pen name M. le Blanc. The pair began a lively correspondence. Germain was particularly anxious to learn of Gauss' reaction to Adrien Marie Legendre's *Essai sur le Théorie des Nombres*. When Napoleon's forces invaded Prussia and besieged Breslau, near Gauss' home, Germain apparently feared that Gauss might suffer a fate similar to that of Archimedes. She interceded on his behalf with General Pernety, a family friend. But Gauss denied knowledge of anyone named Sophie Germain when the general sent a messenger to enquire after Gauss' safety. The misunderstanding was cleared up when Germain admitted that she was not M. le Blanc. Replied Gauss:

> The tastes for the abstract sciences in general and above all, for the mysteries of numbers, is very rare: this is not surprising, since the charms of this sublime science in all their beauty reveal themselves only to those who have the courage to fathom them. But when a woman, because of her sex, our customs and prejudices, encounters infinitely more obstacles than men in familiarizing herself with their knotty problems, yet overcomes these fetters and penetrates that which is most hidden, she doubtless has the most noble courage, extraordinary talent, and superior genius.

Gauss' admiration was not reserved for Sophie's ears alone. He also sang her praises to his colleagues, as a letter written to H.W.M. Oblers on July 21, 1807, demonstrates:

> Lagrange is warmly interested in astronomy and the higher arithmetic; the two test-theorems (for which the prime 2 is a cubic or a biquadratic residue), which I also communicated to him some time ago, he considers "among the most difficult to prove." But Sophie Germain has sent me the proofs of these; I have not yet been able to go through them, but I believe they are good; at least she has attacked the matter from the right side, only somewhat more diffusely than would be necessary.

Germain's early research focused exclusively on number theory. However, by the turn of the century, the interests of French mathematicians were turning increasingly to the work of Ernst Chladni, a German physicist living and working in Paris. Chladni's research involved the vibration of elastic surfaces. By sprinkling sand on a metal sheet and striking the edge with a violin bow, he conducted experiments on elastic surfaces. The pattern formed by the sand's nodal lines was then recorded on a piece of paper.

Interest in the vibrations of elastic materials dated back to the Pythagoreans, but no mathematical theory existed to explain the phenomenon. Napoleon was greatly impressed by Chladni's research and ordered the French Academy of Sciences to hold an essay competition on the subject. The question to be answered was: formulate a mathematical theory of elastic surfaces and indicate just how it agrees with empirical evidence. French mathematicians refused to enter the contest, following assurances from Lagrange that contemporary mathematical methods were unequal to the task.

Sophie Germain, however, was intrigued by the challenge. She completed her entry in eight months and submitted the results anonymously on September 21, 1811. She was the sole entrant. Lagrange, who was a member of the selection committee, thought that her method of passing from a line to the surface was neither accurate nor complete. Thus, her entry was rejected. The Academy informed her that her mathematical equation was incorrect, although her hypothesis was plausible.

The deadline for entries was extended until October 1813. For the next year and a half Germain worked on her second essay. Adrien Legendre, who also sat on the selection committee, wrote to her on December 4, 1813, having just read the results:

> Mademoiselle,
>
> I do not understand the analysis you send me at all; there is certainly an error in the writing or the reasoning, and I am led to believe that you do not have a very clear idea of the operations on double integrals in the calculus of variations. Your explanation of the four points does not satisfy me any more. . . . There is a great lack of clarity in all this. I will not try to point out to you all the difficulties in a matter that I have not especially studied and that does not attract me; therefore it is useless to offer to meet with you and discuss them. . . . In any case, there is the possibility of having your research published, reestablishing the correct analysis or down playing it.

In 1813, Germain's essay received an honorable mention from the French Academy of Sciences. Again the deadline for entries was extended. Germain, however, was concerned about the impartiality of some of the judges sitting on the selection committee. In a letter to an unknown correspondent she wrote:

> I enjoin your probation of memoir No. 1 carrying this epigram: But by far the greatest obstacle to the progress of science and to the undertaking of new tasks and provinces therein is found in this: that men despair and think things impossible.
>
> If I had found the occasion, I would have consulted you before adopting this quotation, since it has an air of pretentiousness, which hardly suits me, having so many reasons to mistrust my own skills and, indeed, not seeing any strong objection to my theory other than the improbability of having it meet with justice. I fear, however, the influence of opinion that M. Lagrange expressed. Without doubt, the problem has been abandoned only because this grand geometer judged it difficult. Possibly this same prejudgment will mean a condemnation of my work without a reflective examination.

Three years later, in 1816, Sophie Germain's third essay was awarded the grand prize. She exposed the laws of vibrating elastic surfaces by describing a fourth-order partial differential equation which explained what was happening in Chladni's research.

For her efforts, she was awarded a one kilogram gold medal, worth 3,000 francs. To the disappointment of the public, however, Germain refused to participate in the awards ceremony, which was held on January 8, 1816. One can only speculate as to the reason. It should be noted, however, that Germain was not allowed to attend public sessions of the French Academy of Sciences until 1822, when Joseph Fourier was elected permanent secretary.

Winning the grand prize was the highlight of Sophie Germain's career. As a result, she was welcomed into mathematical circles and met Augustin L. Cauchy, André Marie Ampère, M.H. Navier and Siméon D. Poisson. A published version of Germain's work appeared in 1821. It was celebrated by Navier, who was so impressed with Sophie Germain's powers of analysis that he wrote of her research, "It is a work which few men are able to read and which only a woman was able to write." The Baron de Prony, a member of the French Academy, referred to Germain as the *Hypatia of the 19th century.

Germain continued to pursue research on elasticity and published several other works on the topic. The most significant of these included an essay on the qualities and binding abilities of elastic surfaces and another work which explored the mysteries of the curvature of elastic surfaces. Her best work, however, was in the field of number theory. She proved Pierre de Fermat's Last Theorem. In 1909, the American algebraist Leonard E. Dickson generalized her theorem to primes less than 1,700, and, more recently, Barkley Roser extended the upper range to 41,000,000.

The interests of Sophie Germain were varied—from chemistry to physics, from geography to history. Like her predecessors, such as *Maria Gaetana Agnesi and *Émilie du Châtelet, Germain was interested in philosophy and hoped to apply scientific methods to the study of psychology. The thrust of her musings entailed the thesis that human behavior could be analyzed and predicted with the mathematical precision which contemporary scientists used to define the natural world. This philosophical stance, which emphasized the holistic nature of the physical and moral order of the world, anticipated many of the features of Auguste Comte's positivistic approach.

Despite an extensive correspondence, Gauss and Germain never met, but Gauss demonstrated his enduring respect by recommending that the University of Göttingen award her an honorary doctorate. Before she could travel to Göttingen, however, Sophie Germain died of breast cancer in Paris on June 27, 1831, at the age of 55. Ironically, Germain's death certificate listed her profession, not as a mathematician or a scientist, but merely as a landlord.

Guillaume Libri wrote in her obituary that she "carried throughout everything" a "forgetfulness of self; in the science which she cultivated with entire self denial, without dreaming of the advantages that success would procure, applauding even, on occasion, the sight of her ideas fertilized by others who had seized them; saying it was not important where an idea came from but only how far it could go, and [she was happy], as long as her ideas bore their fruit for science without furthering the reputation, which she disdained; and [she] proclaimed ludicrous the glory of the bourgeois, [calling fame] the small place which we occupy in the minds of others." Now, a commemorative plaque appears outside her house at 13 rue de Savoie in Paris.

Sophie Germain is principally remembered for her work on elasticity, although her confirmation of Fermat's Last Theorem was by far her best work. In either case, her research has stood the test of time. As Alic points out, however, "Germain's . . . work was all being done within a community that excluded her so completely that she did not even realise what was happening. It was her sex, not her mathematical ability, that was the determining factor."

Unlike other women who had husbands, friends, and even lovers, through whom access to the scientific community could be gained, Sophie Germain was bereft of such support. Thus, much of her work suffered from the professional isolation in which it was conducted. As Louis Bucciarelli and **Nancy Dworsky** noted:

> Every conversation was a formal social event requiring lettres of invitation, planning for transportation, requests for permission. Sophie Germain could not stop to chat with friends at meetings of the Institute nor get into a serious conversation over cigars and brandy after dinner.

Germain was a woman outside the male scientific community. Self-educated, she never benefited from the educational opportunities which France offered. Although her work furthered our understanding of elasticity, when the Eiffel Tower was built her name was not included at the base of the structure along with those scientists whose research had made the construction of this Paris landmark possible. As well, Sophie Germain was denied membership to the French Academy of Sciences. She shares this sad distinction with such eminent scientists as Maria Agnesi, *Sophia Kovalevskaya, and Nobel Prize-winner, *Marie Curie.

SOURCES:

Bell, Eric Temple. "The Prince of Mathematicians," in *The World of Mathematics.* Edited by James R. Newman. NY: Simon and Shuster, 1956.

Bucciarelli, Louis L., and Nancy Dworsky. *Sophie Germain: An Essay in the History of the Theory of Elasticity.* Dordrecht, Holland: D. Riedel, 1980.

Dunnington, G. Waldo. *Carl Friedrich Gauss: Titan of Science.* NY: Hafner, 1955.

Edwards, Harold M. *Fermat's Last Theorem.* NY: Springer-Verlag, 1977.

Fère, Guyot de. "Sophie Germain," in *Nouvelle Biographie Générale.* Edited by J.C.F. Hoefer. Paris: Firmin-Didot, 1842.

Mozans, H.J. *Women in Science.* Cambridge, MA: MIT Press, 1974.

Todhunter, Isaac, and Karl Pearson. *A History of the Theory of Elasticity and of the Strength of Materials.* NY: Dover, 1960.

SUGGESTED READING:

Alic, Margaret. *Hypatia's Heritage.* London: The Women's Press, 1986.

Hugh A. Stewart, M.A.,
University of Guelph, Guelph, Ontario, Canada

Germany, empress of.

Germany, queen of.

Gersenda (fl. 1000).

*Countess of Bigorre. Flourished around 1000; married Bernardo, count of Cousserans; married Bernard I, count of Foix; children: (first marriage) *Gilberga (d. 1054); (second marriage) *Estefania of Barcelona (fl. 1038).*

Gersende de Forcalquier (1170–1257?)

Gerster, Etelka (1855–1920)

Hungarian singer. Born in Kaschau (Kosice), Hungary, on June 15 or 16, 1855; died in Pontecchio on August 20, 1920; married Pietro Gardini (her director), in 1877.

Etelka Gerster was born in Kaschau, Hungary, in June 1855. She studied with *Mathilde Marchesi and made her debut at Venice with great success as Gilda in *Rigoletto* (January 1876). The following year, she married her director Pietro Gardini, and after a tour of Europe visited the United States, singing at the Academy of Music, New York, in 1878, 1883, and 1887. In 1890, when she reappeared in London, her vocal powers became suddenly impaired, and she retired from public life. She set up a singing school in Berlin which had *Lotte Lehmann as one of her pupils. Gerster was one of the favorite prima donnas at the old Academy of Music. It is said that she had a voice of exquisite beauty and was an artist of extraordinary vocal and dramatic genius.

Gertrud.

Variant of Gertrude.

Gertrude of Andrechs-Meran
(c. 1185–1213)

*Queen of Hungary. Name variations: Gertrude of Meran. Born around 1185; murdered in September 1213 by nobles; daughter of Bertold or Berchtold III of Andrechs, marquis of Meran, count of Tirol, and duke of Carinthia and Istria, and Agnes of Dedo; sister of *Agnes of Meran (d. 1201), *Hedwig of Silesia (1174–1243), and Eckembert, bishop of Bamberg; became first wife of Andrew II, king of Hungary (r. 1205–1235), before 1203; children: *Elizabeth of Hungary (1207–1231) and Bela IV (1206–1270), king of Hungary (r. 1235–1270). Andrew II's second wife was *Yolande de Courtenay (d. 1233); his third wife was *Beatrice d'Este (d. 1245).*

Gertrude of Eisleben (1256–1302).
See Gertrude the Great.

Gertrude of Flanders (d. 1117)

*Duchess of Lorraine. Name variations: Gertrude of Lorraine. Died in 1117; daughter of Robert I, count of Flanders (r. 1071–1093), and *Gertrude of Saxony (fl. 1070); married Henry III, count of Louvain, count of Brussels (died 1095); married Thierry of Alsace, duke of Lorraine; children: (first marriage) four daughters (names unknown); (second marriage) Thierry of Alsace.*

Gertrude of Flanders became a powerful and active widow. She eventually buried two husbands, each time increasing her own wealth and individual power. When her second husband died, Gertrude refused to marry again; instead, she seemed quite content with the feudal powers she gained through her extensive properties and by the very fact that, without a husband, she had no legal guardian to keep her from acting as she wished. Gertrude's independence led to her involvement in the politics of the Holy Roman

Empire, including plotting against the royal family and sending her troops into battle to defeat her enemies.

Laura York,
Riverside, California

Etelka Gerster

Gertrude of Hackeborne (1232–1292).
See Gertrude the Great for sidebar.

Gertrude of Helfta (1256–1302).
See Gertrude the Great.

Gertrude of Hohenberg (c. 1230–1281).
See Anna of Hohenberg.

Gertrude of Lorraine (d. 1117).
See Gertrude of Flanders.

Gertrude of Meissen (d. 1117)

Duchess of Saxony. Name variations: Gertrude von Meissen. Died on December 9, 1117; daughter of Ekberts I, margrave of Meissen; married Henry the Fat, *duke of Saxony, margrave in Friesland, around 1090; children: *Richensia of Nordheim (1095–1141).*

Gertrude of Meran (c. 1185–1213).

See Gertrude of Andrechs-Meran.

Gertrude of Nivelles (626–659)

Frankish princess and abbess. Name variations: Saint Gertrude of Nivelles. Born in 626 in present-day Belgium; died in 659; daughter of Pepin I of Landen, mayor of Austrasia (d. 640), and Ida of Nivelles (597–652); sister of ◄⚜ Begga (613–698); cousin of Saint *Modesta of Trier (d. about 680); never married; no children.

Gertrude was born in 626 in present-day Belgium, the daughter of Pepin I, mayor of Austrasia, and *Ida of Nivelles. Although her parents tried to arrange several different marriages for her, the pious Gertrude refused to wed, declaring that she would live her life with Christ and no mortal man. As a teenager, she entered the convent of Nivelles, where she remained the rest of her life and was eventually elected abbess.

Nivelles was a double monastery, meaning that Gertrude had responsibility for the care of both monks and nuns. She proved a competent manager and earned admiration for her selflessness and for her total devotion to the welfare of her charges. When Gertrude's father died in 640, her widowed mother Ida became a nun at the abbey. Gertrude of Nivelles died about age 33 and was canonized several years later; her moth-

er was also canonized. Many miracles were attributed to Gertrude's powers, and followers of the abbess took her personal belongings as relics to be revered. Her feast day is March 17.

SOURCES:

Anderson, Bonnie S., and Judith P. Zinsser. *A History of Their Own.* Vol. I. NY: Harper and Row, 1988.

Klapisch-Zuber, Christiane, ed. *A History of Women in the West, vol. II: Silences of the Middle Ages.* Cambridge: Belknap/Harvard, 1992.

Laura York,
Riverside, California

Gertrude of Ostend (d. 1358)

Dutch mystic and saint. Name variations: Gertrude van der Oosten; Saint Gertrude. Died in 1358 at the almshouse in Delft.

Blessed Gertrude of Ostend, of lowly parentage, was betrothed to a young man who jilted her for the sake of another woman with a larger dowry. Gertrude was known for having the stigmata or five wounds, for having worked many miracles, and for her ecstasies, in which she would sometimes remain for weeks. Her surname came from her practice of singing a song about her country, "Het dagbet in den Oosten" (Day breaketh in the East), applying the words to Christ. Gertrude of Ostend's feast day is January 6.

Gertrude of Poland (d. 1107)

Grand princess of Kiev. Died on January 4, 1107; daughter of Mieskzo II (990–1034), king of Poland (r. 1025–1034) and *Richesa of Lorraine (d. 1067); married Yziaslav I (Izyaslav), grand prince of Kiev (r. 1054–1078), around 1043; children: Sviatopolk II (b. 1050), prince of Kiev.

Gertrude of Saxony (fl. 1070)

Countess of Flanders. Flourished around 1070; married Robert I, count of Flanders (r. 1071–1093); children: *Gertrude of Flanders (d. 1117); Robert II, count of Flanders (r. 1093–1111).

Gertrude of Saxony (1115–1143)

Duchess of Bavaria and Saxony. Born on April 18, 1115; died on April 18, 1143; daughter of Lothair II (b. 1075), Holy Roman emperor (r. 1125–1137), and *Richensia of Nordheim (1095–1141); married Henry the Proud (c. 1100–1139), duke of Bavaria and Saxony, on May 29, 1127; children: Henry V the Lion (1129–1195), duke of Bavaria and Saxony.

⚜► **Begga (613–698)**

Belgian saint. Name variations: Beggha; Beggue of Austrasia. Born in 613; died in 698 (some sources cite 693 or 694) at Ardenne; daughter of *Ida of Nivelles (597–652) and Pepin I of Landen (d. 640), mayor of Austrasia; sister of *Gertrude of Nivelles (626–659); married Ansegisel also known as Auseghisel, Anchises, and Ansegisal, mayor of Austrasia (r. 632–638, son of St. Arnulf of Metz and *Dode); children: Pepin II of Heristal (c. 640–714), mayor of Austrasia and Neustria (r. 687–714).

Upon the death of her husband Ansegisal, the mayor of Austrasia who was killed around 638 while hunting, Begga made a pilgrimage to Rome. Returning home, she retired to the abbey that she had founded at Ardenne in present-day Belgium. She also founded six other churches at Ardenne of the Meuse. Begga's feast day is celebrated on December 17.

Gertrude of Saxony (c. 1155–1196)

*Queen of Denmark. Name variations: Gertrude of Saxony; Gurtrude. Born around 1155; died on July 1, 1196; daughter of Henry V the Lion (1129–1195), duke of Saxony and Bavaria, and either *Matilda of England (1156–1189) or *Clementina of Zahringen; married Knud or Knut also known as Canute VI (1162–1202), king of Denmark (r. 1182–1202), in 1171.*

Gertrude of Sulzbach (d. 1146)

*Holy Roman empress. Died on April 14, 1146; daughter of Berengar II of Sulzbach; sister of *Bertha-Irene of Sulzbach (d. 1161); married Conrad III (1093–1152), Holy Roman emperor (r. 1138–1152); children: Henry (1137–1150); Frederick IV (b. around 1145–1167), duke of Rottenburg (r. 1152–1167) and duke of Swabia (who married Gertrude of Brunswick).*

Gertrude of Swabia (c. 1104–1191)

*Countess Palatine. Born around 1104; died in 1191; daughter of *Agnes of Germany (1074–1143) and Frederick I, duke of Swabia (d. 1105); married Hermann, pfalzgraf (count Palatine) of Lotharingen, in 1125.*

Gertrude the Great (1256–1302)

German nun from the monastery of St. Mary at Helfta in Saxony whose mystical visions and devotion to God earned her the title "the Great," making her the only woman in Germany to be given such an honor. Name variations: Gertrude of Helfta; Gertrud von Helfta; Gertrude of Eisleben. Born on January 6, 1256, somewhere in Germany; died on November 16, 1302 (some sources cite November 17, 1301 or 1311), in the monastery of St. Mary at Helfta in Saxony, Germany; there is only speculation regarding her family and heritage; educated in the monastery at Helfta where she learned Latin, church history, and theology.

Entered the monastery at the age of four or five; at age 25, had her first mystical experience (1281); was a recipient of the stigmata (1283), prophetic visions (1292 and 1294), and minor miraculous events; began writing the Legatus *and the* Spiritual Exercises *(1289); recognized as a saint by the Catholic Church though never formally canonized (1677); given the title "the Great" (1738); November 16 is honored as her feast day.*

In 1281, wrote Gertrude the Great, the Lord first appeared to her in the form of a 16-year-old youth. Having sensed her lack of passion with her faith, He took her right hand in His own and said to her, "You have licked the dust with my enemies and have sucked honey among thorns. Now return to me and I shall make you drink from the torrent of my delights." At that moment, she notes, she was so in awe of God that she recognized her own inferiority and gave herself up with total and joyful abandonment.

Like other religious women of the 13th and 14th centuries, Gertrude saw divine images that allowed her to have a direct relationship with God. Mysticism was not just one event, writes **Evelyn Underhill**, but a succession of insights and revelations about God that gradually transformed the recipient. Mystics, who could either be men or women, experienced things as opposed to accepting them through faith. Mystical communication could be in the form of voices, symbols, or visions of a member of the Holy Trinity or other revered individuals, such as *Mary the Virgin. These experiences generally occurred spontaneously without regard to time or place and usually were out of the control of the recipient. For women, mysticism afforded them an extremely unique opportunity—a direct relationship with God. The Catholic Church forbade women to perform any of the sacraments. To receive the Eucharist or confess one's sins, a cleric was needed to act as an intermediary between the woman and God. However, if a woman was chosen by God to be the recipient of visions or symbols, she had an avenue with which she could bypass the male cleric and engage in a unique relationship of her own with the Lord. It is for this special relationship as well as her devotion to God that Gertrude is known.

Gertrude was born on the Feast of the Epiphany, January 6, 1256. Nothing is known of her childhood, including her birth name, prior to her entry into the Benedictine monastery of St. Mary at Helfta in Saxony, Germany, at age five. She was named after Helfta's abbess, ❧▶ **Gertrude of Hackeborne** (1232–1292), with whom hagiographers have often confused her. A fellow nun of Gertrude's indicated that her birthplace was a distance from Helfta, and that Gertrude was "exiled from all her relatives, so that there should be no one who should love her for the sake of ties of blood." Nothing is known for certain of Gertrude's parentage either. Sister Maximilian Marnau suggests that Gertrude was probably not a member of a noble or wealthy family since a surname was not transcribed for her in St. Mary's registry. As a rule, a monastery recorded its association with a powerful family and often required payment of a dowry for the young girl, to cover educational and boarding expenses, before they admitted her. The recording of this payment,

See sidebar on the following page

along with other welcome financial donations, would have been necessary for proper bookkeeping. However, monasteries were often charitable and received those less fortunate; it is therefore likely that the omission of a family name for Gertrude reflected her impoverished status.

Gertrude's early years as an oblate, or child in the care of a monastery, consisted mainly of an introduction and education into the ways of the Catholic Church. She learned Latin fluently, was well-versed in rhetoric, and studied the works of the church fathers, Augustine and Gregory the Great, and contemporary spiritual writers such as Hugh of St. Victor and Bernard of Clairvaux. When not studying, Gertrude's life consisted of prayer and work. This tripartite scheme of study, prayer, and labor is the bastion of Benedictine monasticism, founded by St. Benedict of Nursia (480–550). Due to consistently poor health, however, Gertrude's portion of any manual labor, such as tending the crops or working with the farm animals, was greatly reduced. Instead, her work consisted of spinning and copying manuscripts. She also wrote explanations and simplifications of the Scriptures. The portion of the day devoted to prayer would have combined individual worship with communal daily services.

Until her conversion, Gertrude had only systematically lived the life of a nun. She followed the monastic rule and looked to God as her spiritual leader, yet she lacked fervor in her devotions. Her conversion experience then, was not one

from a life of sin to one of virtue, but rather the beginning of a life completely and totally devoted to God with a new found fervor. Gertrude, however, treated this experience as a complete turning point in her life. She saw herself as someone who had taken too much pride in her accomplishments and had not paid enough deference to the Lord's power. Prior to her conversion, Gertrude's dedication to her studies led her biographer to note that by "attaching herself with such enjoyment to the pursuit of human wisdom, she was depriving herself of the sweet taste of true wisdom." After her conversion, Gertrude's studies did in fact move from grammatical matters to only those that dealt with theological issues. She wrote to God, "I offer you my laments for the very many infidelities and sins which I have committed in thought, words, and deed . . . but especially for being so unfaithful, careless, and irreverent in the use of your gifts."

Gertrude's displeasure with her own behavior stemmed from an intense feeling of unworthiness in contrast to the awesomeness of the Lord, for her sins were only those of impatience, vainglory, and negligence. It is ironic then that her cries of humility earned her the respect and admiration of her contemporaries who wished they could aspire to be like her. They often sought out Gertrude for spiritual guidance and as their own intercessor. Her mystical relationship with God caused many to ask Gertrude to pray for them, thinking that her prayers were more likely to be heard than their own. While she often complied in order to aid fellow nuns, she herself would turn to others for prayers and guidance, noting her own unworthiness as a cause for God not to respond to her. Such confidantes included fellow mystics at Helfta, *Mechtild of Magdeburg (c. 1207–1282) and ◄ Mechtild of Hackeborne (1241–1298), sister of Gertrude of Hackeborne. It was with Mechtild of Hackeborne that Gertrude collaborated on many writings, possibly contributing prayers and biographical vignettes to Mechtild's volume of revelations, *Book of Special Grace*.

Though Gertrude's own writings have proved to be important, it took the mystical intercession for her to write them down. Gertrude wrote that God told her, "Know for certain that you will never leave the prison of your flesh until you have paid the last farthing that you are keeping back." She understood this to mean that she would never be received into Heaven until she shared with others her unique mystical experiences and revelations. She then began composing a volume of works that later generations would find invaluable.

❧► Gertrude of Hackeborne (1232–1292) and Mechtild of Hackeborne (1241–1298)
German sisters and mystics.

The monastery at Helfta was only 20 years old in 1251 when Gertrude of Hackeborne became abbess. Its great days continued after her death in 1292, until the death of *Gertrude the Great. in 1302. Gertrude of Hackeborne's sister Mechtild, the choir mistress of Helfta, also had visions; an account of her revelations, compiled by two nuns, is titled *Liber specialis gratiae* (*Book of Special Grace*). Since Mechtild was always accessible to the community, her visions concerned messages of love from Jesus to sustain her in helping her fellow sisters. Her grief at the loss of her sister Gertrude as well as *Mechtild of Magdeburg in 1282 was also assuaged by these visions. Mechtild of Hackeborne once saw the newly departed Mechtild of Magdeburg dancing around Christ in heaven, celebrating the goodness of the nuns at Helfta.

In 1289, Gertrude started *Liber Legationis divinae pietatis* (or *Herald of God's Loving Kindness*). Written as a simple essay, the *Legatus* was addressed to God and offered an account of her inner thoughts, feelings, and devotions. What was significant about the work was the openness with which Gertrude discusses her intimate relationship with God. The *Legatus* reads like a diary, allowing others a private look at God's dealings with a soul. Often combined with the *Legatus* in later collections are writings by fellow nuns who tell of Gertrude's accomplishments and provide her biography. It is only through these anonymous voices that anything is known of Gertrude's life, since her humility prevented her from believing that her life was in any way noteworthy. Surpassing the popularity of the *Legatus* was Gertrude's *Spiritual Exercises*. No date is given for the writing of this work, except that it was begun after her conversion experience in 1281. A kind of handbook for Christians, *Spiritual Exercises* consists of reminders of the privilege of being part of God's family and the necessity of preparing for the next life through the words and deeds of this life. Topics in the work include conversions, preparations for death, the love of God, and the renewal of faith.

Reflective of her training in rhetoric, Gertrude's writing relied on comparisons, similes, and an overabundance of adjectives to describe her ideas. Later nuns at Helfta mimicked this style, most notably in the *Precis Gertrudianae* (*Gertrudian Prayer*), a work comprised of extracts from many of Gertrude's writings as well as new prayers composed in her unique style. Despite her fluency in both her native German and in Latin, only her Latin texts have survived.

Gertrude was also devoted to the symbol of the Sacred Heart of Jesus, the heart of the Lord in its human, physical form. In church tradition, the Holy Spirit formed the Sacred Heart while Jesus was still in Mary's womb. Thus, it represents both the divinity and the humanity of the Lord. But the Sacred Heart is not just a symbol of the Lord but rather of the Holy Trinity. The physicality of the Heart was merged with God (the creator of humanity) and the Holy Spirit (the creator of the Heart) into the person of Jesus.

Along with Mechtild of Hackeborne, Gertrude gave shape and prominence to the devotion of this symbol. She enjoyed special images of the Sacred Heart, along with visions of its earliest associated saint, John the Apostle. In what modern scholar, Jean Bainvel, called the beginning of "an epoch in the history of the devotion to the Sacred Heart," Gertrude had a dialogue with St. John and asked him why he had not spoken of his devotion to the Sacred Heart until their conversation. Responded St. John, "It was my task to present to the first age of the Church the doctrine of the Word made flesh. . . . The eloquence of that loving pulsation of His heart is reserved for the modern age so that the world grown old and torpid may be rekindled by the love of God." For Gertrude, love was at the core of all her devotions and writings, and what better symbol to exemplify this notion then the heart of the Lord.

The culmination of all of Gertrude's spirituality, writings, and passion for God took three forms; receipt of the stigmata, the gift of foreknowledge, and the power to perform small miracles. When Gertrude was 27, she was given the stigmata by God, physical proof that God recognized Gertrude's piety and devotion. The stigmata, which represent the five wounds received by Christ during His crucifixion, were emblazoned on her heart. In May of 1292, Gertrude had her first prophetic experience. At that time elections were being held to choose an emperor to replace Rudolf I Habsburg, Holy Roman emperor, who had died the previous year. Before the choice of a new emperor had been made, Gertrude informed the abbess that Adolph of Nassau had been chosen and that he would perish at the hands of his successor. Gertrude could not have received that information from a human messenger since the election took place after she envisioned it, and Adolph was not killed until 1298. In 1294, Gertrude foresaw that the monastery would be saved despite an assault from outside invaders. It was also recorded by Gertrude's biographers that God had given her miraculous power in addition to the favors he had already granted. It was said that, because of her prayers, an intense and unseasonable cold spell ended on one occasion, and on another, a rain which had threatened the harvest ceased.

Gertrude the Great's blessed life made her a dynamic figure in the history of medieval religious women. Her death on November 16, 1302, left a void for the nuns at Helfta who had looked to her for spiritual camaraderie and guidance. Gertrude's impact was not confined to just the 13th and 14th centuries alone. Translations of her writings were made from the 16th century onward as more and more of the faithful turned to her comforting words and insights. In 1677, Pope Innocent XI added her name to the Roman martyrology and Clement XII later directed that her feast day, November 15, be observed throughout the Western Church. Spain declared

Gertrude the patron saint of the West Indies, while the cities of Urbino, Italy, and Tarrangona, Spain, both later recognized her as a minor patron. And finally, tradition has placed Gertrude above all other notable women in Germany's history. In 1738, Cardinal Prosper Lamertini (later Benedict XIV) accorded her the title Gertrude the Great, the only German woman to ever be given the exalted title.

SOURCES:

Finnegan, Mary Jeremy. *The Women of Helfta: Scholars and Mystics.* Athens, GA: University of Georgia Press, 1991.

Gertrude of Helfta. *The Herald of Divine Love.* Edited and translated by Margaret Winkworth. NY: Paulist Press, 1993.

Gertrude the Great, Saint. *Love, Peace, and Joy: Devotion to the Sacred Heart of Jesus According to St. Gertrude.* Edited and translated from the French by Reverend Andre Prevot. Rockford, IL: TAN Books, 1984.

Petroff, Elizabeth Alvilda, ed. *Body and Soul: Essays on Medieval Women and Mysticism.* NY: Oxford University Press, 1994.

SUGGESTED READING:

Beer, Frances. *Women and Mystical Experiences in the Middle Ages.* Rochester, NY: Boydell Press, 1992.

Johnson, Penelope. *Equal in Monastic Profession: Religious Women in Medieval France.* Chicago, IL: Chicago University Press, 1991.

Ellen T. Bastio,
graduate student, University of Maryland at College Park

Gertrude von Helfta (1256–1302).

See Gertrude the Great.

Gessner, Adrienne (1896–1987).

See Christians, Mady for sidebar.

Gestring, Marjorie (1922–1992)

American diver. Name variations: Margaret Gestring. Born on November 18, 1922; died on April 20, 1992.

In 1936, at age 13 years, 9 months, Marjorie Gestring won the gold medal in the springboard competition at the Berlin Olympics, the youngest person ever to win an individual medal in any sport. Gestring's record withstood **Fu Mingxia**'s gold-medal win in platform-diving in Barcelona. Fu Mingxia was 11 weeks older.

Geva, Tamara (1906–1997)

Russian-born actress and dancer. Born Tamara Gevergeva or Gevergeyeva in St. Petersburg, Russia, in 1906, of Russian, Swedish, and Italian descent; died at her Manhattan home on December 9, 1997; studied at State Ballet School of Maryinksy Theatre (Theatre Street School); married George Balanchine, in 1923 (separated and divorced soon after); married Kapa Davidoff (divorced); married John Emery (divorced).

Tamara Geva trained as a dancer at the Theatre Street School (formerly the Russian Imperial Ballet School). In July 1924, at age 16, she left Russia with a small company that included George Balanchine and *Alexandra Danilova and danced in recitals in Frankfurt and Ems, Germany. In October of that year, she appeared at the Empire in London with Balanchine, whom she had married. She then toured the Continent with the Diaghilev Monte Carlo Ballet. Engaged by Nikita Balieff, Geva made her debut in America with his Chauve-Souris company at the Cosmopolitan Theater in New York on October 10, 1927, dancing "Grotesque Espagnole" for which she received glowing reviews. The following year, she turned her attention to musical comedy, appearing in Florenz Ziegfeld's *Whoopee* with Eddie Cantor. In 1933, Geva performed in her first straight play, as Lania in *Divine Drudge.* At the Adelphi in 1935, she danced Balanchine's ballet *Errante* at the first performance of The American Ballet, but her subsequent career was devoted to musicals, plays, and films. Other stage roles included Vera Baranova in *On Your Toes* (1936), Irene in *Idiot's Delight* (1938), and Helen of Troy in *The Trojan Women* (1941). Geva appeared in and directed Sartre's *No Exit* for the Coronet Theatre in Los Angeles; created choreography for the film *Spectre of the Rose;* and appeared in the movies *Night Plane from Chungking* and *Orchestra Wives.*

Geyra (fl. 980s)

Princess of Wendland. Name variations: Geira. Flourished in the 980s; daughter of King Burislaf of Wendland; married Olav I Tryggvason (968–1000), king of Norway (r. 995–1000).

One of Olaf I Tryggvason's marauding expeditions took him to Wendland, an area of northern Germany occupied by a fierce Slavic people in the late 10th century. There, King Burislaf, allowed his daughter Geyra to marry Olaf. The union was brief, however, as Geyra died three years later. Olaf's response to her death was to initiate another round of plundering, this time concentrating on areas from Frisia to Flanders.

Ghevardini, Lisa (b. 1474).

See del Giocondo, Lisa.

Ghica, Helene (1828–1888).

See Chica, Elena.

Ghika, Elena (1828–1888).

See Chica, Elena.

Ghika, Princess (1866–c. 1940).

See Barney, Natalie Clifford for sidebar on Pougy, Liane de.

Ghisi, Diana (c. 1530–1590)

Italian sculptor and engraver. Born around 1530 into a Mantuan family of engravers; died in 1590; daughter of Giorgio Battista Ghisi, called Mantuano (a painter, sculptor, architect, and engraver); sister and pupil of Giorgio Ghisi (b. 1524).

Diana Ghisi was born around 1530 into a Mantuan family of engravers; her father Giorgio Battista Ghisi, called Mantuano, was a painter, sculptor, architect, and engraver who flourished about the mid-16th century. Her brother and teacher was Giorgio Ghisi, also an eminent engraver born in 1524, whose works were esteemed by collectors. In contrast to another brother Adamo, Diana Ghisi was considered the best artist and executed some plates of great merit. They were all called Mantuano.

Giannini, Dusolina (1900–1986)

American soprano. Name variations: Gianini. Born on December 19, 1900, in Philadelphia, Pennsylvania; died on June 26, 1986, in Zurich, Switzerland; daughter of Ferruccio (a tenor) and Antonietta (Briglia) Giannini (a violinist); sister of Euphemia Giannini (1895–1979), a soprano who taught at the Curtis Institute, and Vittorio Giannini (1903–1966), a composer; studied with her father.

Debuted in Hamburg (1925), Teatro alla Scala debut (1928), Metropolitan (1936); retired (1962) and became a teacher.

Dusolina Giannini could no more remember her first singing lesson than her first breath as she was vocally trained her entire childhood. Her father was an operatic tenor and impresario while her mother was an accomplished instrumentalist. An older sister, **Euphemia Giannini**, became a well-known voice teacher at the Curtis Institute, and Dusolina's younger brother, Vittorio, was a composer of merit. Dusolina first appeared at her father's theater at age nine. During her childhood, she was known as "the Little Duse." As the family could not decide if Dusolina was a soprano or contralto, she was sent to study with *Marcella Sembrich at age 16. On March 14, 1923, a series of events prevented Genei Sandero and two backup performers from

appearing at Carnegie Hall. Giannini was plucked out of Sembrich's class and placed on the stage, an appearance which was a triumph. She received offers to perform with major orchestras and a recording contract with the Victor Talking Machine Company as a result.

Giannini appeared at La Scala in 1928 and was so popular that she was invited to make a complete recording of *Aïda* in 1929. Although she was asked to sign a contract with the famous Italian opera house, she refused, deciding that she would never become a formal member of any opera company. On February 12, 1936, she walked onto the stage of the Metropolitan, with no rehearsal, to perform *Aïda*. Once again her presentation was a triumph. She withdrew from a performance of *Norma* on February 26, 1936, because the Met would not grant her enough rehearsal time. Giannini returned to Salzburg that same year at the request of Arturo Toscanini to sing Mistress Ford in Verdi's *Falstaff*. Siegfried Wagner invited her to sing Kundry in *Parsifal* at Bayreuth, but as Giannini explained, "a man named Hitler interfered with my plans." After the war, she settled in Zurich where she taught master classes and was proud of the title, "The Musician's Singer," given by her peers. She was also proud to be considered Marcella Sembrich's successor as a teacher.

John Haag,
Athens, Georgia

Gibb, Roberta.

See Samuelson, Joan Benoit for sidebar.

Gibbons, Abby Hopper (1801–1893)

American philanthropist, abolitionist, and Civil War nurse. Born Abigail Hopper in Philadelphia, Pennsylvania, on December 7, 1801; died in New York City on January 16, 1893; daughter of Isaac Tatum Hopper; attended Friends' schools; married James Sloan Gibbons (an author and abolitionist), in 1833; children: six.

Born into a strong Quaker family, Abigail Gibbons assisted her father in the formation of the Isaac T. Hopper Home for discharged prisoners. During the Civil War, she and her daughter rendered valuable service as nurses in the Federal camps and hospitals in Washington, D.C. Her home in New York was sacked in the riots of July 1863 because of her prominence as an abolitionist and her activities in the Manhattan Anti-Slavery Society. When the conservative

Quakers disowned her husband and father for their work in the abolitionist movement, Gibbons stood up in the meeting and resigned her membership.

In 1871, she helped found the Protestant Asylum for Infants, and it was chiefly through her efforts that the New York State reformatory for women and girls was established by the legislature in 1872, an act which was considered Gibbons' crowning achievement. She had lobbied for the bill for a very long time, even appearing before the legislative committee at age 91. *The Life of Abby Hopper Gibbons Told Chiefly through Her Correspondence* was edited by her daughter and published in 1897.

Gibbons, Stella (1902–1989)

British novelist and poet, best known as the author of **Cold Comfort Farm.** *Name variations: Stella Webb. Born Stella Dorothea Gibbons on January 5, 1902, in London, England; died in December 1989 at age 87; eldest child of Telford Charles Gibbons (a north London doctor) and Maud Williams; educated at home by governesses until age 13, when she attended the North London Collegiate School; took journalism course at University College, London; married Allan Bourne Webb (an actor and opera singer), in 1933; children: a daughter.*

Worked as a decoder for the British United Press; spent ten years in Fleet Street working on various jobs—literary and drama criticism, fashion writing, special reporting, while doing some creative writing of her own; published first novel Cold Comfort Farm *(1932), which brought her instant fame; over the next 40 years, wrote 25 novels, together with four volumes of poetry, and three collections of short stories (none, however, were to achieve the same success).*

Selected works: The Mountain Beast and Other Poems *(1930);* Cold Comfort Farm *(1932);* Bassett *(1934);* Nightingale Wood *(1938);* Christmas at Cold Comfort Farm *(1940);* The Bachelor *(1944);* Gentle Powers *(1946);* Conference at Cold Comfort Farm *(1949);* Collected Poems *(1950);* Here Be Dragons *(1956);* The Charmers *(1965);* Starlight *(1967);* The Snow Woman *(1969);* The Woods in Winter *(1970).*

Stella Gibbons did not have a happy childhood. Her father's medical practice was in a poor part of London, and the grinding poverty she saw around her, combined with the sterility of her family life, depressed the young girl. Not being allowed to go to school until she was in her teens did not help. As a means of escape, she made up fairy tales which she told to her two younger brothers. She also buried herself in books with exotic settings, such as Disraeli's *Alroy* and Thomas Moore's *Lalla Rookh.* When she finally went to school, at age 13, she was no happier. In a very funny and clearly autobiographical passage at the beginning of *Cold Comfort Farm,* Flora Poste is asked by her friend how she managed to survive a school career of organized games without getting to like them:

> Well—first of all, I used to stand quite still and stare at the trees and not think about anything. . . . But I found that people would bump into me, so I had to give up standing still and run after the ball like the others . . . until I found they didn't like me doing that, because I never got near it or hit it or did whatever you're supposed to do with it. So then I ran away from it instead, but they didn't seem to like that either.
>
> And then a whole lot of them got at me one day after one of the games was over, and told me I was no good. And the Games Mistress seemed quite worried and asked me if I didn't really care about lacrosse . . . and what did I care about?
>
> So I said, well, I was not quite sure, but on the whole I thought I liked having everything very tidy and calm all round me, . . . and going for country walks, and not being asked to express opinions about things (like love, and isn't so-and-so peculiar?) . . . and after that she left me alone. But all the others still said I was no good.

After graduating from a course in journalism in 1922, Gibbons embarked on what she later described as her life in "the vulgar and meaningless bustle of newspaper offices." She did admit, however, that working for the British United Press taught her to write, and reviewing novels encouraged her gift for satire. Nevertheless, she was clearly not enamored with the life of a press scribbler. As she wrote her friend and mentor, Antony Pookworthy, just after the completion of her first book:

> The life of the journalist is poor, nasty, brutish and short. So is his style. You, who are so adept at the lovely polishing of every grave and lucent phrase, will realize the magnitude of the task which confronted me when I found, after spending ten years of my life as a journalist, learning to say exactly what I meant in short sentences, that I must learn, if I was to achieve literature and favorable reviews, to write as though I were not quite sure about what I meant but was jolly well going to say something all the same in sentences as long as possible.

For her first novel, Stella Gibbons decided to go for the burlesque, and the subject she chose to parody was the rural tradition in English literature.

The Romantic movement of the early 19th century—particularly the poetry of William Wordsworth—first postulated the idea of the harmony between man and nature. It was a reaction to the increasing mechanization and urbanization of English society and was inclined to romanticize country people and, at its worst, patronize and exploit them. This was not, however, a view held by perhaps the greatest of all 19th-century rural writers—Thomas Hardy (1840–1928). Although believing that the landscape in which people lived could either be used as an illustration of human moods and feelings, or have human moods and feelings imposed upon it, he increasingly abandoned the idea of "the land" as tilled and cultivated by man as being a predominant symbol of harmony. It is indicative of the mood of a mainly urban readership that his last novel, *Jude the Obscure,* was intensely unpopular with a hitherto admiring public.

In the first decades of the 20th century, however, there was a string of lesser writers such as *Sheila Kaye-Smith (1887–1956) and T.F. Powys (1875–1953), who nostalgically over-sentimentalized the rural world in purple passages or what Stella Gibbons described as "sheer flapdoodle." In her novel *The Golden Arrow,* *Mary Webb had her lapses:

> The sky blossomed in parterres of roses, frailer and brighter than the rose of the briar, and melted beneath them into lagoons greener and paler than the veins of a young beech-leaf. The fairy hedges were so high, so flushed with beauty, the green airy waters so far back into mystery, that it seemed as if at any moment God might walk there as in a garden, delicate as a moth.

The effect of such writing, as critic G. Cavaliero comments, leads "to a kind of clotted chaos . . . and self-indulgence, most clearly manifest in the sentimental transformation of God Himself into something suggestive of a pixie." (It should be stressed, however, that much of Mary Webb's prose is of a very high standard, and her books, particularly *Precious Bane,* 1924, convey a rich and intense impression of the Shropshire countryside, and a sense of impending doom not unlike the works of Hardy.)

Clearly such a style, together with the conventions of rural plot, characterization and atmospheric description, laid themselves open to satire. But Stella Gibbons in *Cold Comfort Farm* not only parodies the hackneyed purple passages (obligingly asterisked for the benefit of the "common reader"), but exercises a more serious criticism by causing her down-to-earth heroine, Flora Poste from smart metropolitan Lambeth, to reorganize the lives of that collective embodiment of rural literary mannerism, the Starkadder family. Such a character had long been anticipated by critics and reviewers. *Katherine Mansfield, for instance wrote that she had:

> grown very shy of dialect which is half prophecy, half potatoes, and more than a trifle impatient of over-wise old men, hot-blooded young ones, beauties in faded calico, and scenes of passion in the kitchen while the dinner is hotting up or getting cold.

Stella Gibbons also takes a swipe at D.H. Lawrence (1885–1928), and others who saw rural working men and women as the embodiment of vigor, libido, and cultural alternative set amidst a countryside throbbing with dark passions and sexual undertones.

An acute and witty parody of the rural novel . . . , [Cold Comfort Farm] both makes and exploits the hysterical intrigue, emotional turmoil and lugubriousness of the genre.

—Ian Ousley

Most rural novels of this period set the scene with atmospheric fantasy. Compare the opening lines of **Nora Kent**'s *Barren Lands* (1926):

> Stilehouse Farm lay back from the road on the rising ground between Durham and Tarring Neville. The house, mellowed by age and the sun, stood foursquare to the salt winds blowing inland from the Channel.

with Flora Poste's first sight of the Starkadders' farm:

> Dawn crept over the Downs like a sinister white animal, followed by the snarling cries of a wind eating its way between the black boughs of the thorns. The wind was the furious voice of this sluggish animal light that was baring the dormers and mullions of Cold Comfort Farm.

(This passage received two asterisks from the author.)

The Starkadder family that Flora encounters at the farm is a rural caricature. The matriarch, Aunt Ada Doom, rules the roost from the attic and only emerges twice a year for "the counting"—that is to make sure that none of her numerous progeny have left. Her only two phrases are "they'll always be Starkadders at Cold Comfort Farm," and "there's something nasty in the woodshed"—an unexplained encounter she experienced when she was two (a phrase that has subsequently entered the English language, meaning something sinister in arcadia). Her son, Amos, is the quintessential fundamentalist preacher who weekly spits fire and brimstone to an appreciative audience in the appropriately named village of Howling—"Ye miserable, crawling worms, are ye here again then? . . . to hear me tellin' o' the great crimson lickin' flames o' hell fire?" His wife Judith suffers from some obscure and inconsolable sorrow, while her extensive brood of young men fight and intrigue and push each other down the well that never quite manages to get finished. Reuben, the stolid farmer, and Seth, the earthy womanizer ("I eats women," he says), are the most prominent sons in the book. In a passage marked with three asterisks, displaying shades of D.H. Lawrence and *Emily Brontë's *Wuthering Heights,* Stella Gibbons describes Seth's reaction to finding an interfering woman in his house:

> The man's big body, etched menacingly against the bleak light that stabbed in from the low windows, did not move. His thoughts swirled like a beck in spate behind the sodden grey furrows of his face. A woman . . . Blast! Blast! Come to wrest away from him the land whose love fermented in his veins, like slow yeast. She-woman. Young soft-coloured, insolent. His gaze was suddenly edged by a fleshy taint. Break her. Break. Keep and hold fast the land. The land, the iron furrows of frosted earth under the rain-lust, the fecund spears of rain, the swelling, slow burst of seed sheaths, the slow smell of cows and cry of cows, the trampling bride-path of the bull in his hour. All his, his . . .

All this about a character who ends the book by becoming a film star.

Other characters include Elfine, the daughter, who spends her time floating around the countryside in long dresses pretending to be a nymph; Mr. Myburg, an intellectual writer who sees sex and phallic shoots in every aspect of nature; and Adam the cowman who sits in the barn "coddling the 'dumb beasts'" (the cows, Graceless, Pointless, Feckless, and Aimless, with bull, Big Business).

Meanwhile:

> The country for miles, under the blanket of the dark which brought no peace, was in its annual tortured ferment of spring growth; worm jarred with worm and seed with seed. Frond leapt on root and hare on hare. Beetle and finch-fly were not spared. The trout-sperm in the muddy hollow under Nettle Flitch Weir were agitated, and well they might be.

Flora Poste's self-imposed task is to create order and "tidiness" amongst the heaving undercurrents of countryside life—which of course she does in her down-to-earth fashion over the space of 200 pages. Aunt Ada Doom is persuaded to embark on a round-the-world airplane trip; Amos goes to America in a Bedford van to convert the heathen; Stolid Reuben takes over the farm; passionate Seth becomes a film star and goes to Hollywood; Flighty Elfine stops being clever and marries the son of the local squire and cultivates an interest in horseflesh; and Adam continues to coddle his "dumb beasts" in pastures new.

Cold Comfort Farm remains a very funny book. Although it only damaged the more hackneyed rural novels of the day, it served as a warning to avoid absurdity or pretentiousness for writers attempting to describe a more elemental way of life. It has certainly outlived most of the books that were its occasion. A musical version in 1965, deriving its title from the most quoted line in the book, *Something Nasty in the Woodshed,* was also adapted for television in 1968. A film, directed by John Schlesinger and starring **Kate Beckinsale**, was released in 1996.

Stella Gibbons' success with this book came with a price, however. Nothing she subsequently wrote was regarded as its equal, and her later books suffered from the comparison, "like a mother with unusually precocious offspring who continually overshadows the quiet, worthy members of her brood," as one reviewer put it. Other critics felt that her later fiction, though well written, tended to dwindle into magazine entertainment.

Although she often saw herself as primarily a poet (her *Collected Poems* came out in 1950), Gibbons had marginally more success with her novels and stories. *Christmas at Cold Comfort Farm* (1940) and *Conference at Cold Comfort Farm,* both collections of stories, attempted to capitalize on earlier successes. Many of her later novels were set in literary north London, which Gibbons knew well, and show a sharp eye for social contrasts. Two works, *Gentle Powers* and *Here be Dragons,* deal with a young woman's education and disillusionment.

For *Cold Comfort Farm,* Stella Gibbons received the Femina Vie Heureuse Prize, and she was elected a fellow of the Royal Society of Literature in 1950. She continued to write until the year she died in December of 1989, at age 87.

SOURCES:
Bradbury, Malcolm. *The Modern British Novel.* Penguin Books, 1994.

Cavaliero, Glen. *The Rural Tradition in The English Novel, 1900–1950.* Macmillan Press, 1977.

Gibbons, Stella. *Cold Comfort Farm.* Penguin Books, 1932.

———. *Gentle Powers.* Penguin Books, 1946.

———. *Here be Dragons.* Penguin Books, 1956.

———. *The Wood in Winter.* Penguin Books, 1970.

SUGGESTED READING:

Cunningham, Valentine. *British Writers of the Thirties.* Oxford University Press, 1989.

Drabble, Margaret. *Oxford Companion to English Literature.* Oxford University Press, 1990.

Shattock, Joanne. *The Oxford Guide to British Women Writers.* Oxford University Press, 1991.

RELATED MEDIA:

Something Nasty in the Woodshed, musical, 1965, British television version, 1968.

Cold Comfort Farm (8 cassettes, audio), read by **Anna Massey**, Sterling Audio, 1993.

Cold Comfort Farm, film starring Kate Beckinsale, **Joanna Lumley, Maria Miles,** Ian McKellen, and Stephen Fry, directed by John Schlesinger, released in 1996.

Christopher Gibb,
writer and historian, London, England

Gibbs, Georgia (1920—)

American "pop" singer. Born Fredda Gibson (also seen as Lipson or Gibbons) in Worcester, Massachusetts, on August 17, 1920; one of four children of a widowed mother; never married; no children.

Discography—singles: The More I See You/ In Acapulco *(Vi 20-1660);* You Keep Coming Back Like a Song/ Willow Road *(Maj 12000);* So Would I/ Wrap Your Troubles in Dreams *(Maj 12008);* How Are Things in Glocca Morra?/ Necessity *(Maj 12009);* Ballin' the Jack/ As Long as I'm Dreaming *(Maj 12010);* Ol' Man Mose/ Put Yourself in My Place, Baby *(Maj 12014);* While We're Young/ While You Danced, Danced, Danced *(Mer 5681);* Kiss of Fire/ A Lasting Thing *(Mer 5823);* He's Funny That Way/ Say It Isn't So *(Mer 70218);* The Bridge of Sighs/ A Home Lovin' Man *(Mer 70238);* Under Paris Skies/ I Love Paris *(Mer 70274);* Baubles, Bangles and Beads/ Somebody Bad Stole de Wedding Bell *(Mer 70298);* My Sin/ I'll Always Be Happy with You *(Mer 70339);* Tweedlee Dee/ You're Wrong, All Wrong *(Mer 70517);* Dance with Me, Henry/ Every Road Must Have a Turning *(Mer 70572);* Get Out Those Old Records/ I Still Feel the Same About You *(Cor 60353);* A Little Bit Independent/ Simple Melody *(with Bob Crosby, Cor 60227).*

LPs: Swingin' with Her Nibs *(Mer MG-20170);* The Man That Got Away *(Mer MG-25199);* Her Nibs, Georgia Gibbs *(Cor CRL-57183);* "Her Nibs" *(Rondo-lette 876).* CD: Her Nibs Miss Georgia Gibbs *(Good Music Records).*

Born in Worcester, Massachusetts, in 1920, Georgia Gibbs was placed in an orphanage at the age of two because her widowed mother could no longer support the children. She began her singing career as a young teenager, performing on local radio shows and at clubs throughout the state. After several years, she auditioned and won a spot on the Jimmy Durante-Garry Moore radio show. It was Moore who dubbed her "Her Nibs, Miss Georgia Gibbs," a title she has been known by ever since. Gibbs' early career also included a three-year tour with Danny Kaye, whom she credits with turning her into a versatile performer. Her first club date as a single, at the Waldorf Astoria in New York, led to television guest appearances, record deals, and her own bi-weekly show on NBC, "Georgia Gibbs' Million Record Show."

In 1953, her career went into high gear with one of her first Mercury recordings, "Kiss of Fire," which sold over 2.5 million copies and also became her first gold record. It was fol-

Georgia Gibbs

lowed by three additional gold records: "Dance With Me, Henry," "Arrivederci Roma," which she brought to the U.S. from Europe, and "Tweedlee Dee." ("Tweedlee Dee" had originally been recorded by *LaVern Baker, an African-American, and had risen to #14 on the charts, but in the practice of the day it was "covered" or rerecorded by a major label with a white singer, this time Gibbs.)

Over the course of her career, Gibbs sold over 30 million records and performed on some of the great stages of the world, including Lincoln Center, in New York, the Palladium and Albert Hall, in London, and the Empire Theater in Glasgow. She also played every major club in the U.S., including New York's Waldorf, Copacabana, and Persian Room, Chicago's Empire Room, and the top clubs in Las Vegas, San Francisco, and Los Angeles. Possessing a voice that lends itself to any kind of song, in later years Gibbs continued to perform in major cities in the United States and appeared on a PBS television special, "Sentimental Journey."

Gibbs is an avid reader, a collector of art, and a student of politics. A tiny woman, just over five feet tall, she also designed her own gowns.

Gibbs, May (1877–1969)

Illustrator and author, especially of fantasy for children, who was one of the first creators of a popular Australian imagery. Pronunciation: Gibbs with a hard "G." Born Cecilia May Gibbs on January 17, 1877, in Lower Sydenham, Kent, England; died in Sydney, Australia, on November 27, 1969; daughter of Herbert William Gibbs (an artist), and Cecilia May Rogers (an amateur artist); attended Miss Best's School for Ladies (Perth); Art Gallery of Western Australia; Cope and Nichol Art School (London); Chelsea Polytechnic (London); Henry Blackburn School for Black and White Artists (London); married Bertram James Ossoli Kelly, on April 17, 1919.

Arrived in Australia (1881); studied in London; published first book (1912); moved to Sydney (1913); published eight books (between 1918–53); published weekly comic strips (1924–67); published last book (1953).

Major works written and illustrated: Tales of Snugglepot and Cuddlepie *(Sydney: Angus and Robertson, 1918);* Little Ragged Blossom and More About Snugglepot and Cuddlepie *(Sydney: Angus and Robertson, 1920);* Little Obelia and Further Adventures of Ragged Blossom, Snugglepot and Cuddlepie *(Sydney: Angus and Robertson, 1921);* The Story of Nuttybub and Nittersing *(Melbourne: Osboldson, 1923);* Two Little Gumnuts—Chucklebud and Wunkydoo, Their Strange Adventures *(Melbourne: Osboldson, 1924);* Scotty in Gumnut Land *(Sydney: Angus and Robertson, 1941);* Mr. and Mrs. Bear and Friends *(Sydney: Angus and Robertson, 1943);* Prince Dande Lion . . . A Garden Whim Wham *(Sydney: Ure Smith, 1953).*

May Gibbs was an unconventional woman for the late-19th to mid-20th centuries. Unmarried until late in life, childless and unconcerned with the usual scope of women's affairs, she possessed a passion for drawing and was determined to forge a career in the competitive, largely male, field of illustration. She was successful. With a childlike quality, she reveled in imagining and creating, but when met with opposition she stuck solidly to her own opinions. She was also a shrewd negotiator.

Significantly, Gibbs' passion was not only for drawing; she was also concerned with the Australian environment. As she recognized the ecological threats, she directed her stories to teach her readers a sympathy and understanding for the natural world. After a life of drawing Australian plants and animals, Gibbs was able to encapsulate an essence of the Australian environment and produce, for the first time, a complete fantasy world based upon it. One the eve of World War I, Gibbs developed an amusing set of characters—sturdy, down-to-earth creatures of the gum trees—and applied them to bookmarks and magazine covers, and finally a series of stories. Somewhat bereft of national symbols, Australians grasped onto these "gumnut" characters and have delighted in them ever since.

May Gibbs was born on January 17, 1877, in Lower Sydenham, Kent, England, and spent her first four years in the comfortable, loving company of parents, older brother, and extended family in Surrey. Her parents, who had met at the Slade School of Art in London, were both skillful artists. Though the couple would later have two more sons, it was May, their first daughter, who followed most closely, and successfully, their fascination with art and illustration.

In 1881, the family decided to try their luck in the relatively new colony of Australia. Property was cheap and the climate was seen to be healthier and sunnier than in England. They sailed for three months to the tiny settlement of Port Adelaide, in South Australia. After a few distressing months clearing land, building a hut, and trying to farm in poor soil, the Gibbs family moved to an already established homestead in the outskirts of Port Adelaide.

Taught at home by her parents while her brother was sent to school, May was given a generous helping of artistic and literary instruction. She had a ready interest in drawing, an interest that was encouraged by her parents' enthusiasm. In a 1968 oral-history interview, Gibbs recalled: "I could draw almost as soon as I could talk and. . . . I used to lie down in the grass so that my eyes were on the same level amongst the grass stalks as the ants; and I naturally loved all those things."

When May was about eight, the family sailed north to Western Australia, first to a rural property and later to the Swan River, near the growing township of Perth. She continued her drawing, sketching the new range of flora and fauna, and was encouraged when a page of her sketches won a competition and was published in the *W.A. Bulletin* in 1889. She joined the Wilgie Sketching Club that her father had helped to establish, constructed caricatures as her father was doing for newspapers, and took over part of his studio at the top of their large, rambling house. "My interest in drawing at this time was everything—everything I saw," she recalled, "and I was particularly keen on making fun of things; and when I was old enough I used to do caricatures of everybody and they were really, although I shouldn't say it, tremendously good."

During the mid-1890s, Gibbs attended classes in art at the new Art Gallery of Western Australia. Her teachers were keen for her to extend her drawing skills by going to England for art classes. Though May was also eager, her parents felt differently, knowing how precarious an artist's career—let alone a woman artist's—could be. Instead, Gibbs was expected to settle down and start looking for a spouse. Despite the pressure, in 1900, at age 23, she made the first of her three trips to London. On each sojourn, she studied and drew obsessively. Seven hours of drawing a day, six days a week, was standard at the art schools she attended, then on to life drawing at night. Gibbs was restless on Sundays, painting and sketching and anxious to get back to school. She also spent time looking for illustration commissions, sometimes successfully.

Each time Gibbs returned to Australia it was to recover the health she had crushed by overwork, self-neglect, and the general damp and smog of London. While convalescing in Perth, restless under the controlling hand of her mother, she concentrated on developing stories

May Gibbs
(self-portrait)

and illustrations for children's books and tried to find publishers. But she was attempting to break into a closely knit field that was predominated by men, and commissions remained fitful.

On her second trip to London in 1904, age 27, Gibbs concentrated on black-and-white line drawing—a media that had only become available to illustrators since the 1870s thanks to the development of photographic reproduction, ending their reliance on wood cuts. The popularity and status of this new pen-and-ink medium as a form of art and illustration was rising rapidly. Gibbs attended drawing classes at the Chelsea Polytechnic and Henry Blackburn's School for Black and White Artists, obtaining first class passes. Her drawings from this period are confident and technically impressive, lucidly conveying human form and character.

While British publishers declined to publish Gibbs' Australian children's stories, claiming they needed English settings to ensure good sales, one publisher, George Harrap and Company, was impressed by the wide range of well-developed artistic skills demonstrated in her portfolio. Harrap gave her three historical novels to illustrate: Wilmot Buxton's *The Struggle with the Crown,* **Estelle Ross'** *Barons and Kings,* and **Susan Cunnington's** *Georgian England.* In between intensive research on early England, Gibbs recast her Australian "Mimie and Wog" story, setting the action around the London rooftops with personified fog and gruff chimney pots forming some of the new characters. Titled *About Us,* the story was published in England and America in 1912. She also secured commissions with the National Union of Women's Suffragette Societies, illustrating their public debates.

May Gibbs . . . mapped out a world of her own—and conquered it completely.

—*Advertiser,* **Adelaide, 1917**

One of the English suffragist society members was **Rene Heames,** a socialist and boarder in the same lodging house as Gibbs. They became firm friends and remained so for life. By the end of Gibbs' third stay in London, from 1909 to 1913, she was battling her health. Her relatives encouraged her to try again to establish a career back in Australia, this time in Sydney. Gibbs liked the idea, and both she and Heames set sail for Australia early in 1913. Sydney was a propitious move. As the burgeoning publishing and population center of the continent, the demand for illustrators ran high. Gibbs, at last, was able to find work immediately. Illustrating story books, a New South Wales school magazine, textbooks, and 25 covers for the *Sydney Mail* newspaper, she had finally fomented, at age 35, a demand for her skills.

Throughout 1913, Gibbs worked steadily on these commissions in her city studio, occasionally taking time off to walk in the Blue Mountains near Sydney. Commissioned to design a bookmark, she had one shaped and painted like a eucalyptus leaf, but something was missing. That something woke her up one night. She added a plump cherub with long-lashed, wide eyes, peeking over the top of the leaf, wearing a round, eucalyptus seedpod cap. From behind, tiny triangular wings stuck out from its shoulder blades, and its feet were tucked up beneath its bare bottom. Sydney-siders bought the bookmarks as quickly as Gibbs painted them. The print run was just as successful.

For the cover of *The Lone Hand,* she multiplied this little creature to make a cluster of them clinging to a bunch of gum leaves. The paper's editors and reviewers were impressed. Gibbs then published booklets that extended the idea of creatures related to native plants, dressing them in a particular plant's petals and leaves: *Gum-Nut Babies, Gum-Blossom Babies, Wattle Babies, Boronia Babies,* and so on. Soon after the booklets were published in 1917, a reviewer for the Sydney *Evening News* wrote: "These little creatures belong to the same category as the leprechauns of Irish fairy tales. The artist gives a quaint individuality to her little people and, if the world is not getting too materialistic, she may perhaps be laying the foundation of a new Australian folklore."

The uniquely Australian quality of Gibbs' creations was what reviewers commented on repeatedly. Although there were high-brow representations of Australia in art galleries and libraries, Australians lacked an accessible, comfortable imagery with which they could readily identify. May Gibbs gave Australians images of recognizable native flora and fauna co-existing in a realistic habitat with characters who, though imaginary, were plausible creatures of the harsh Australian environment. They were robust and matter-of-fact, a long way from the floating, thinly fragile fairies of European folklore.

The outbreak of war in Europe in 1914, in which Australia—as part of the British Empire—was intimately involved, unified the Australian public in the face of a common enemy. It was perfect timing for Gibbs' pictures. As historian **Marcie Muir** has pointed out, those at home were looking for patriotic images that could communicate sentiments and bring some humor to cheer the spirits. Scores of Gibbs' amusing postcard vignettes of domesticated kookaburras and gumnuts dressed as soldiers were sent to the Australians at the front lines in Europe and the Middle East.

Happy with her newfound characters, Gibbs now turned her efforts to creating adventure stories for them. "I thought to myself 'I'll make the pictures first, and write the stories round them, because the pictures will sell the book,'" she said. "The stories just rolled out of me, I had plenty of them, I'd no trouble at all." By the end of 1918, after much negotiating with Angus and Robertson, she secured a publishing agreement that suited her and completed *The Tales of Snugglepot and Cuddlepie.*

The story was set in the branches and cluttered floor of a eucalyptus forest. It was a world full of two-inch-high gumnut people, of all different professions, living in towns and cities amongst the forest, or "bush," with the animals—friendly and otherwise. Part of the appeal for children lay in the realistic, gripping depiction of a natural world with predators and prey; Mrs. Snake and her gang of Banksia men both terrified and fascinated their audience. *Snugglepot and Cuddlepie,* and the further adventures she published in the years following, were filled with pictures: vibrant color plates and countless line drawings set within the text pages. They were funny, often satirical, scenes of a well-thought-out world, full of detail.

Gibbs wrote well, using as much imagination in the construction of speech for her characters as she had in drawing them. The gumnuts, birds, possums, and snakes spoke with expressions picked straight from the bush—"give me the twigs of the whole thing," "he's deadibones," "smoke and burn him," "Gum it all!"—a mix of invention and complete disregard for grammar that delighted child readers. "Deadibones" is one of many of Gibbsian words that entered the Australian language.

The first page of *Snugglepot and Cuddlepie* features the two gumnuts scrawling on a leaf banner, "Humans: please be kind to all Bush

"The Picture Gallery," from Snugglepot and Cuddlepie *by May Gibbs.*

Creatures and don't pull flowers up by the roots." Clearly committed to educating against cruelty to animals and the needless destruction of flora and fauna, Gibbs' entire approach—giving readers the names and exact appearance of native flora and fauna, mirroring how animals tended to behave, showing how both animals and plants could be hurt by humans—appears to have been directed to this end. She gives the reader a view of the world from the animals' perspective, looking out at humans with their traps and cages. At a time when koalas had been hunted almost to extinction and so much of the continent's forests had been cleared, Gibbs' message was a much-needed one. There had long been groups who sought to educate against the wanton destruction of Australia's resources—The Australian Forest League, the Wattle Society, the government's Botanical Gardens—but few of their publications had the appeal of Gibbs' work.

The first three editions of *Snugglepot and Cuddlepie* sold out at lightning speed. Within a year, 14,414 copies had sold in Australia and 700 in England, and the book has remained continuously in print ever since. Gibbs was now firmly established—along with *Beatrix Potter, Norman Lindsay, and *Ida Rentoul Outhwaite—as one of a new group: the writer-illustrators.

In 1918, during a stay at Perth when she was 42, Gibbs met J.O. Kelly, a mining manager. A firm friendship blossomed not long after, and they decided to marry in Perth at Easter, 1919. "He and I were such tremendous pals," she said, J.O. "was always immaculately dressed, quite unconscious of himself, beautifully spoken and friends with everybody. . . . He encouraged me tremendously with my work." J.O. and Gibbs settled in Neutral Bay, Sydney. After a few months, they invited Rene Heames and another friend, **Rachel Matthews**, to come and share their home, so Gibbs continued to enjoy their company and support.

J.O. gave up his previous job and took on, to Gibbs' delight, the more mundane business matters involved with her career, though he was not prepared to go to battle with publishers. Though she found it distasteful, Gibbs found herself wrangling over royalties, paper choice, and printing quality. "I had a very decided feeling about doing things," she said; she refused to be taken advantage of or to have her work altered. A skillful negotiator, Gibbs managed for many years, writes **Maureen Walsh**, to have publishers agree to a 15% royalty, surpassing the standard 10% being granted to the great pillars

of Australian literature: Banjo Patterson, Henry Lawson, C.J. Dennis, and Norman Lindsay.

Because children had been writing to publishers Angus and Robertson asking for more adventures of Snugglepot and Cuddlepie, in 1920 Gibbs gave them *Little Ragged Blossom and More about Snugglepot and Cuddlepie*. The story was set largely under the sea with an entertaining cast of fish folk going about the dubious ways of human folk. These characters continued to delight their audience—child and adult alike—in *Little Obelia*. "May Gibbs brings the breath of the bush," wrote a reviewer for the Melbourne *Age*, "the stirring of gumleaves and the twittering of feathered inhabitants. One loses the reality of trains, desk and the countinghouse."

Gibbs had plenty of ideas for further stories and products to which the gumnut and blossom characters could be applied. She produced posters, handkerchiefs, calendars, badges, dolls, fabric, pottery, and her ideas did not end there. "I used to have a little sketch book in one pocket and a pencil in the other," she said in 1968, "and would go 'round gardening, and that's how I got my best ideas, out in the open. Then I'd go into the studio and measure my board and start drawing them, draw onto the board and then ink them in, and send them across to have them printed, and there they were."

It was her unique stories and her witty, confident line drawings that brought Gibbs most acclaim. She also sketched portraits on commission. In 1917, one writer for the *Sun* described them as "of a remarkable standard, the artist reproducing a fleeting mood or expression in an exquisite water color that seems more nearly to reveal the soul of the sitter than any more set styles of portraiture." Nevertheless, when in 1921 and 1922 she submitted some watercolor portraits to art society exhibitions, reviewers were critical, calling them "unfinished." Gibbs vowed she would never again submit to art societies.

Keeping to her formula of a book a year for the Christmas market, Gibbs produced *Nuttybub and Nittersing* in 1923 and *Chucklebud and Wunkydoo* in 1924, both with a new set of bushland characters. It was also in 1924 that she pursued and gained entry into the sphere of newspaper comic strips. She drew and wrote, in verse, episodes in the precarious life of two inquisitive gumnuts, Bib and Bub, and their bush friends and foes—each week's episode tending to revolve around who was eating whom. These were the first cartoons produced in Australia for young children. Before long they were being used in schools as reading lessons and, as Walsh points out, would have been an entertaining source of reading for children in families where virtually the only bodies of written material in the house were newspapers.

The 1930s bought hard times to the Gibbs enterprise as it did for all, and the sales of her work dropped. A friend went to America in 1932 to promote Gibbs' books but failed to find willing publishers. "Australia's depression," her friend wrote back, "is kindergarten compared with here." The depression had a similar effect in England. J.O. fumed over it in a letter to Gibbs' parents: "The beasts of publishers in England are too narrow minded to embrace Australia. . . . What a kid likes, he very seldom gets a chance to say. It appears to us that the stereotyped fairy with butterfly wings and the dear old fatuous stories appeal to the publishers. Why, they even seem to object to the fact that the 'Gumnuts' are unclothed!"

Ironically, Australian material was becoming harder to sell in Australia itself, due to foreign syndication, a certain vogue for things American, and local publishers preferring cheap imports. Although alarmed, Gibbs, with typical steadfastness, refused to change her style, and she defended her stand to one of the papers who sought to reduce her pay: "I am the only feature Artist exploiting purely Australasian matter and fauna. I have maintained this style of work as I feel the children of Australasia should have the opportunity of becoming familiar with their own animals." At least Gibbs knew, from the "wealth of correspondence" sent by children, that her audience appreciated her work.

Just before the outbreak of the Second World War, her husband died of heart trouble, marking the beginning of a sad decade for Gibbs. When her father, who had been one of her dearest friends, her teacher, and guide, died in 1940, Gibbs was increasingly alone with her garden and the Scottish terriers she doted on.

She kept herself busy, incorporating wartime rationing and long waiting lines in her comic strips, making jokes of frustrations. By 1941, with encouragement from Heames, Gibbs had written another book, using her dogs as models for *Scotty in Gumnut Land*. It was refreshingly successful. In 1943, now 66, she produced *Mr. and Mrs. Bear and Friends* and then her last book, *Prince Dande Lion . . . A Garden Whim Wham*, which was, she said: "For older children, and I hope, some quite old ones." The story was bursting with puns and gave life and

character to flowers—not wild, but garden variety. This was fitting, for Gibbs now rarely ventured out of her own house and garden.

In 1955, now nearly 80, Gibbs was still drawing the Bib and Bub cartoon each week. With her perpetual enthusiasm and drive, she continued to look for new projects, write in her notebook, and construct humorous verses. To her delight, she was awarded an MBE on June 9, 1955, in recognition of her contribution to children's literature. In 1967, at age 90, after fighting her way back to mobility and memory after a stroke the year before, she finally decided to submit her last Bib and Bub comic strip. It had run, with only one short break, for 43 years. Gibbs refused to accept the "charity" of a pension and managed without until March 1969, when the Commonwealth Literary Fund realized her straitened situation and gave her an annuity.

An unfinished letter, penned just before she died in Sydney on November 27, 1969, shows Gibbs busy with gardening, the housework, and pleased with her special recipe for irresistible apple pie. She had dealt with the distribution of her estate and the ownership of her works. "It must have been a toss-up whether her estate went to children or conservationists," said one of her childhood fans. It went to the United Nations' Children's Fund (UNICEF), the New South Wales (NSW) Society for Crippled Children, and the Spastic Centre of NSW. Another legacy of her works, the understanding and regard for the bush that she has inspired and continues to inspire in generations of children, has gone to the conservationists, and the plants and animals that surround them still.

An unconventional woman, May Gibbs was able to produce works that were unconventional enough to appeal to children. Those works helped give expression to the feeling of Australians for their country at a time when little else was available, and continue to do so.

SOURCES:

Cooper, Nora. "A Cottage for Fairy Fancies," in *The Australian Home Beautiful*. United Press, Melbourne, March 12, 1926, pp. 17–20.

Frizell, Helen. "May Gibbs—Lover of Children and Australia's Bush," in *Sydney Morning Herald*. Sydney, November 29, 1969, p. 6.

Lang, J. *Pathway to Magic: The Story of May Gibbs in Western Australia*. Perth: Challenge Bank, 1991.

Marshall, Marie. "The Art of May Gibbs," in *Australasian Book News and Literary Journal*. Sydney, September 1947, pp. 153–154.

Muir, Marcie. *A History of Children's Book Illustrators*. South Melbourne: Sun Books, 1977.

"Queen of the Gum-Nuts," in *The Sun* (Sunday edition), Sydney, March 11, 1917, p. 14.

Saw, Ron. "Boyhood not the same without the Banksia Men," in *Daily Telegraph*. Sydney, June 9, 1970, p. 10.

Saxby, H.M. *A History of Australian Children's Literature 1841–1941.* Sydney: Wentworth Books, 1971.

Sayers, Andrew. *Drawing in Australia: Drawings, Watercolours, Pastels and Collages from the 1770s to the 1980s.* Melbourne: Oxford University Press, 1989.

Walsh, Maureen. "Gibbs, Herbert William and Cecilia May," in *Australian Dictionary of Biography*. Vol. 8. Edited by B. Nairn and G. Searle. Clayton Victoria: Melbourne University Press, 1981, pp. 644–646.

———. *May Gibbs, Mother of the Gumnuts; Her Life and Work.* North Ryde: Cornstalk Publications, 1985.

SUGGESTED READING:

Holden, Robert. *A Golden Age*, Vol 1: *Visions of Fantasy, Australia's Fantasy Illustrators: Their Lives and Works.* Pymble NSW: Angus and Robertson, 1992.

McVitty, Walter. *Authors and Illustrators of Australian Children's Books.* Sydney: Hodder and Stoughton, 1989.

RELATED MEDIA:

"Conversation with May Gibbs," recording, 1968, DeB 356, National Library of Australia, Canberra.

COLLECTIONS:

Original works, illustrated books, and ephemera, located in the James Hardie Library of Australian Fine Arts; May Gibbs Papers, located in the State Library of NSW, Sydney.

Jenny Newell,
research and editing assistant at the Centre for Cross-Cultural Research, Australian National University, Canberra, Australia

Gibbs, Pearl (1901–1983)

Aboriginal activist. Name variations: known as Gambanyi (in Ngiyamba). Born in Australia in 1901; died in 1983; daughter of Maggie Brown and stepdaughter of Dick Murray; attended school at Yass and Cowra; married a man named Gibbs (an English sailor), in the 1920s (separated); children: one daughter and two sons.

Pearl Gibbs was born in Australia in 1901 and spent her childhood near Yass and later in the Brewarrina area. During the 1920s, while working as a maid and cook, she became a political activist, assisting Aboriginal "apprentices" (girls indentured by the Aborigines Protection Board as domestics). Her marriage to an English sailor ended in separation, leaving her to raise their daughter and two sons. During the 1930s, Gibbs organized strikes among the Aboriginal pea pickers and initiated protests against Board controls. From 1937, she gained status as a member of the Aborigines' Progressive Association, which campaigned for full citizen rights and an end to the Aborigines Protection Board. Known as an articulate and passionate speaker, she focused her attention on issues of concern to women: "apprenticeships," school segregation, health, hospital segregation, and Board rationing.

Serving as secretary of the all-Aboriginal Aborigines' Progressive Association from 1938 to 1940, she helped unite regionally based factions and spoke frequently for the Committee for Aboriginal Citizen Rights, a predominantly white organization formed in 1938 to mobilize public opinion. Participating in radio broadcasts and writing newspaper articles, she supported Northern Territory Aborigines in their conflicts with the frontier "justice" system and lobbied for Aboriginal representation on the New South Wales Welfare Board.

In 1946, with Bill Ferguson, Gibbs helped establish the first formal link between Aborigines in two states, by setting up the Dubbo branch of the Australian Aborigines' League (founded by William Cooper in 1933). In 1953, after serving as vice-president and then secretary of the branch, she became organizing secretary for a new Melbourne-based Council for Aboriginal Rights. From 1954 to 1957, she served as the elected Aboriginal member of the Welfare Board, although as the only woman member, she was often excluded from the real decision-making processes of the male bureaucrats and academics who comprised the rest of the Board.

In 1956, with *Faith Bandler, Gibbs established the Australian Aboriginal Fellowship, which included both Aboriginal and white members, and for which she served as vice president. Utilizing her organizational skills and her numerous contacts, Gibbs attracted a high turn out of Aborigines for the public rally in Sydney in 1957. The rally kicked off the campaign to remove discriminatory clauses in the federal constitution, a goal that was finally realized in 1967. Gibbs continued her political activities, establishing the first hostel for Aboriginal hospital patients and their families in Dubbo in 1960, and organizing a Fellowship conference in 1965. She attended most major Aboriginal conferences in New South Wales until ill health curtailed her traveling. Pearl Gibbs died in 1983 after years of commitment to Aboriginal rights, which she viewed as part of the larger struggle for human rights and international peace.

SOURCES:

Radi, Heather, ed. *200 Australian Women.* NSW, Australia: Women's Redress Press, 1988.

Gibson, Althea (1927—)

American tennis champion, known as the "Jackie Robinson of Tennis," who was the first African-American to win tennis titles, as well as the first black female to compete on the Ladies Professional Golf tour. Born Althea Gibson on August 25, 1927, in Silver, South Carolina; first daughter and one of five children of Daniel and Annie (Washington) Gibson; Florida Agricultural and Mechanical University, B.S., 1953; married William A. Darben, in 1965.

Won the National Negro Girl's Championships (1944, 1945, 1948–56); won the French Open (1956); won women's singles and doubles at Wimbledon (1957 and 1958); won Wightman Cup (1957), national singles championship at Forest Hills (1957 and 1958) and the Babe Didrikson Zaharias Trophy (1957).

Was a singer, musician, product representative, and actress (1958–63); was a member of Ladies Professional Golf Association tour (1963–67); served as tennis coach, member of athletic commissions, and associate of Essex County, N.J., park commission (1970–92).

Selected publications: (autobiographies) I Always Wanted to Be Somebody *(Harper, 1958) and* So Much to Live For *(Putnam, 1968).*

How does a wayward youth become world champion? A high-school dropout become a university instructor? A teenage welfare ward become a good-will ambassador for the U.S. State Department? A street fighter learn how to curtsey before the queen of England? A poor black ghetto kid gain highest honors in the rich, exclusive, all-white world of professional tennis in the 1950s? It takes desire. "I knew that I was an unusual, talented girl through the grace of God," Althea Gibson once said. "I didn't need to prove that to myself. . . . I only wanted to prove it to my competition." It takes passion. "The only thing I really liked to do was play ball." It takes courage. "Uncle Junie hauled off and slapped Mabel as hard as he could, right across the face. Well, that was all I had to see. . . . I sashayed right up to him and punched him in the jaw as hard as I could and knocked him down on his back." It takes hard work. Describing one of her matches, a *Daily Telegraph* reporter wrote, "Gibson, ever pressing netwards, ever on the attack, fighting every point, recoiling only to spring again, played as relentlessly as [any woman] ever did." It takes poise. After a New York City tickertape parade in her honor, Gibson told the crowd at the Waldorf Astoria, "I can't describe the joy in my heart. God grant that I wear this crown with dignity and humility." And in Althea Gibson's case, it also took many a helping hand.

An unemployed musician, volunteering as a Police Athletic League play-street supervisor, saw her tennis potential. A part-time cab driver and tennis coach believed in her game when she was beginning to doubt herself. The dynamic director of the Ladies Professional Golf Association (LPGA) supported her attempt to break the color barrier in golf. A Cosmopolitan club member bought Gibson her first tennis dress and helped her grow both on and off the court. Two doctors gambled that she might become what New York's mayor would eventually call, "A credit to our city, [and] a credit to our nation."

When Althea Gibson was first noticed, she was a rough, tough teenager. At age 13, she had a great basketball jumpshot and polished boxing moves, but few people skills. She was moody, temperamental, tactless, and arrogant. Early in her tennis career, her relationship with the press was so rocky that she was referred to as Jackie Robinson without the charm, and Ted Williams without the ability. It took a great deal of hard work for Gibson just to control her temper, play by the rules, and moderate her hostile attitude toward responsibility. The enormous stress of moving rapidly from the streets to the courts to the spotlight, and into the role of champion and role model, often made her withdraw. Even her friends described her at times as sullen—a turtle-like personality who often retreated into an impenetrable shell. Ultimately, by her 30th birthday, Gibson gained peace with herself and fully blossomed. Along the way, she managed to pack a good deal of excitement into her life.

Althea Gibson was a Depression child, born two years before the stock-market crash, on August 25, 1927, in the tiny farming town of Silver, South Carolina. Her parents, Daniel and **Annie Gibson**, lived in a cabin on a farm but owned no land. Instead, Daniel helped his brother farm five acres of cotton and corn. The Gibsons were sharecroppers who, for the first three years of parenthood, faced falling prices, bad weather, and brutally hard work. In 1930, Daniel spent a third of his $75 yearly income to purchase a train ticket and headed to New York to find a better life for his family.

Althea was sent to live with her Aunt Sally in Harlem, where her parents also lived for a while before they found an apartment of their own. Since Aunt Sally sold bootleg whiskey, Gibson's earliest memories include accidentally drinking from the wrong jug and sometimes sipping spirits with her aunt's customers. For two years, Althea lived in Philadelphia with her Aunt Daisey, where she began to be known as mischievous. It wasn't until she returned to her family in New York, at age nine, as they settled into a place of their own, that Althea began to get herself into serious trouble.

Unlike her four younger brothers and sisters, Gibson hated authority and rarely went to school. No degree of discipline from her teachers or her father helped. At the time, physical punishment was not only acceptable but encouraged. Sometimes her teachers would spank her "right in the classroom," wrote Gibson in her 1958 autobiography:

> Daddy would whip me, too, and I'm not talking about spankings. He would whip me good, with a strap on my bare skin, and there was nothing funny about it. Sometimes I would be scared to go home and I would go to the police station on 135th Street and tell them that I was afraid to go home because my father was going to beat me up.

But she didn't change her ways, although truancy, shoplifting and minor thefts were the worst of her crimes. She roamed the streets, traveled throughout the city on the subway, and often escaped into the movies. Away from school and home, Gibson overcame her problems by playing sports.

It has been a bewildering, challenging, exhausting experience, often more painful than pleasurable, more sad than happy. But I wouldn't have missed it for the world.

—**Althea Gibson**

The athletic teenager was taller and stronger than other girls her age, eventually growing to 5'10½", and weighing 145 pounds. Daniel Gibson actually wanted his daughter to be a professional boxer on a circuit rumored to be in development, but it was never formed. Wrote Althea:

> I know it sounds indelicate, coming from a girl, but I could fight, too. Daddy taught me the moves, and I had the right temperament for it. . . . He would say, 'Put up your dukes,' and I had to get ready to defend myself or I would take an even worse beating. He would box with me for an hour at a time, showing me how to punch, how to jab, how to block punches, and how to use footwork. He did a good job on me, maybe too good. I remember one day he got mad at me for not coming home for a couple of nights, and he didn't waste any time going for the strap. When I finally sashayed in, he just walked up to me and punched me right in the face and knocked me sprawling down the hall. I got right back up and punched him as hard as I could, right in the jaw, and we had a pretty good little fight going and we weren't fooling around, either.

She earned a reputation for not backing down in a fight with anyone. She also earned a reputation in sports. The block she lived on—143rd Street between Lenox and 7th—was designated a "play" street and closed to traffic by the Police Athletic League to keep children "on the courts and out of the courts." At age 14, Gibson earned medals playing paddle tennis, a sport played with wooden paddles in a fenced-in area about half the size of a tennis court. That's where Buddy Walker first noticed Gibson's natural athleticism and tenacity. Walker purchased two used racquets for five dollars and taught Gibson the basics of tennis. Impressed by her quick ability to absorb the game and by her powerful strokes, he arranged an exhibition for her at New York's premier black tennis club.

Although blacks were banned from playing at white clubs and from competing in national tournaments against whites, black tennis players had their own leagues and clubs. The American Tennis Association, founded in 1916, is the nation's oldest African-American sports organization. The Cosmopolitan Tennis club, where Gibson's first match caused a stir, was composed of wealthy and prestigious members. Althea demonstrated enough talent and promise to merit the Cosmopolitan's encouragement and support. President Juan Serrell and club pro Fred Johnson convinced fellow members to donate money to develop Althea's game. **Rhonda Smith**, who had lost a daughter of her own, helped clothe, feed, and sometimes shelter Gibson. Within six years, Althea Gibson became the best black female tennis player in the nation.

While developing her tennis game, Gibson graduated from junior high school at age 17 and worked several odd jobs for pocket money. She started to attend technical high school but dropped out. As her relationships at home soured, the welfare department paid her a stipend and gave her shelter. At age 18, Gibson competed in the primarily black American Tennis Association (ATA) national women's singles championship at Wilberforce College in Ohio in 1946. Though **Roumania Peters** defeated her in the finals, Gibson was noticed by two men who helped change her life. Robert W. Johnson of Lynchburg, Virginia, and Hubert A. Eaton of Wilmington, North Carolina, were wealthy African-American doctors. They were also tennis fanatics.

The doctors saw in Althea both a prodigy and a potential force for attacking segregation. At the time, blacks were prohibited from competing against whites in all sports. The doctors proposed that Althea split her time living among their families while she pursued a college athletic scholarship. Stunned by her announcement that she had never received a high-school diploma,

Althea
Gibson

they came up with a plan to send Gibson back to high school while developing her game at Eaton's house in North Carolina.

Althea returned home and faced a tough decision. She was tired of being poor and had little

to keep her in New York, but she was wary of the segregation and racism in the South. One night she noticed Harlem's premier celebrity Sugar Ray Robinson at a bowling alley. Althea, who as a young teenager bowled in the 200s, brazenly challenged the world-champion boxer to a match. Sugar Ray and his wife **Edna Robinson** befriended her, became lifelong supporters, and encouraged her to pursue tennis and especially the opportunity to get an education. "You'll never amount to anything just banging around from one job to another like you've been doing," declared Sugar Ray. "No matter what you want to do, tennis or music or whatever, you'll be better at it if you get some education."

That summer of 1947, Jackie Robinson broke the major-league baseball color barrier. That September, Gibson stepped off the train at the Wilmington station. North Carolina was a huge transition for Althea. The Eatons had a full-time maid, a private tennis court, and they provided a supportive family environment. In contrast, Wilmington was an insular town, which, like all Southern cities, had humiliating regulations concerning where blacks could eat, what fountains they could drink from, and where they had to sit on the bus.

After a five-year absence from school, Gibson pushed herself, graduating from high school, "tenth in my class if you please," and then accepted a scholarship to Florida A&M. But she had a hard time bonding with her younger classmates and fitting in as a female athlete. A saxophone that Sugar Ray had given her as a gift helped her find musicians on campus. They seemed better able to accept Althea for who she was.

Gibson's tennis continued to improve as she practiced religiously on Eaton's court. In 1947, she and Eaton won eight out of nine mixed-doubles tournaments on the ATA circuit. The following year, Althea captured her first of nine consecutive ATA singles championships. By 1949, her mentors felt she was ready to pursue the chance to play on the all-white tour. Gibson agreed.

Though Gibson was ready, the entrenched opposition at the U.S. Tennis Association built seemingly insurmountable roadblocks. The press rallied to Althea's cause. Writers highlighted the unfairness of a bogus argument; that players had to first prove themselves in the preliminary matches—none of the major pre-Forest Hills grass eliminations allowed blacks. The biggest assist came from a fellow player. In July of 1950, *Alice Marble, one of America's greatest players, wrote in *American Lawn Tennis*:

> I think it is time we faced a few facts. If tennis is a game for ladies and gentlemen, it's also a time we acted a little more like gentle people and less like sanctimonious hypocrites. If there is anything left in the name of sportsmanship, it's more than time to dis-

play what it means to us. If Althea Gibson represents a challenge to the present crop of women players, it's only fair that they should meet the challenge on the courts, where tennis is played. . . . I can't think of one who would refuse to meet Miss Gibson in competition. She might be soundly beaten for a while—but she has a much better chance on the courts than in the inner sanctum of the committee, where a different kind of game is played. . . . Eventually the tennis world will rise up en masse to protest the injustices perpetrated by our policy makers. Eventually—why not now?

A Forest Hills invitation soon found its way to Gibson. Despite a large media gathering and feeling "pretty emotional deep down inside," Gibson, the initial black to compete in a major tennis tournament, won her historic first-round match. In a dramatic second-round match, she fought back from a poor start and had three-time Wimbledon champ *Louise Brough on the verge of defeat before a thunderstorm forced a delay of the match. Brough won the following day, but Gibson had proved that she could compete against the world's best.

In 1951, Althea Gibson became the first black to compete at Wimbledon. Joe Louis, the boxing champion, lent her an apartment near her training area and helped raise money for her trip. Although Althea was defeated in Wimbledon's third round, she again proved that she belonged.

For the next five years, Gibson ranked among the top ten female players in the world, but she failed to win the biggest tournaments. Her rising fortunes seemed to reach a plateau and then begin to fade. She was often unhappy and did not handle the press well. She also had trouble carrying the torch for racial equality. Gibson was criticized for not being outspoken enough, and she disappointed friends and fans who thought she had the talent to prove that a black player could win the toughest matches. *Jet*, a prominent black magazine, called her "the biggest disappointment in tennis." She also suffered financially. Before the age of television, amateur athletes, especially women, were barely paid expenses. A job as a physical education instructor in Missouri helped financially but left her unfulfilled, and she felt hemmed in by the divisive racial climate in the midwest.

Losing interest, Gibson nearly joined the service on the advice of a U.S. army captain she was dating. Two things kept her from changing paths. Sydney Llewellyn, a part-time taxi driver and tennis coach, revamped and reenergized her tennis game. And the U.S. State Department invited her to participate in tennis exhibitions throughout Southeast Asia to promote American good will. Her answer came quickly, "Not only would I consider making the trip but I was dying for something interesting to do."

Gibson traveled with Ham Richardson and Bob Perry and roomed with **Karol Fageros**, all tennis players. Althea loved the excitement, the attention, and the camaraderie, and the foursome earned rave reviews in every city. "I've never done anything more completely satisfying," Gibson wrote, "or more rewarding, than that tour." The stimulation helped bring her out of her shell; it also reinvigorated her tennis game.

At the second to last stop on the tour, Gibson's game came together. She won the women's singles championship at the All-Asian Tennis Tournament in Rangoon, Burma, and then won 16 out of the next 18 tournaments she entered. On May 20, 1956, Althea Gibson became the first black to win a major singles title when she captured the crown at the French Open. Even though she lost again at both Wimbledon and Forest Hills, she had jumped to number two in the 1956 world rankings.

Finally, in 1957, Gibson defeated *****Darlene Hard** in straight sets in the finals at Wimbledon, and Queen *****Elizabeth II** presented Althea with the silver tray commemorating her championship victory at centre court. Upon her return to New York City, the girl from the Harlem ghetto was treated to a tickertape parade. She also received the following telegram which read in part:

> Millions of your fellow citizens would, if they could, join with me in felicitations on your outstanding victory at Wimbledon. Recognizing the odds you faced, we have applauded your courage, persistence and application. Certainly it is not easy for anyone to stand in the center court at Wimbledon and, in the glare of world publicity and under the critical gaze of thousands of spectators, do his or her very best. You met the challenge superbly.
>
> With best wishes,
>
> Dwight D. Eisenhower

Two months later, Gibson became the first black to win the U.S. national women's singles championship at Forest Hills. Amazingly, the following year, she successfully defended her titles, taking first place at both Wimbledon and Forest Hills, and then abruptly retired at the top her game. Gibson was, she wrote, "as poor as when I was picked off the back streets of Harlem and given the chance to work myself up to star-

dom. . . . I am much richer in knowledge and experience. But I have no money." At that time, before *****Billie Jean King** and others on the tennis circuit made waves, women could only earn money under the table from tournaments sponsors, and a black woman in the 1950s had little chance of signing with a mainline sponsor.

So Gibson attempted to switch careers, and her fame helped get her in the door of the music world. She had a rich, resonant singing voice. At age 15, she had won second prize in a talent competition at the Apollo Theater. She had played saxophone in the band and sang in the choir at Florida A&M. She had made test recordings in 1956 and hired a voice coach in 1957. After performing at a testimonial dinner in 1958, she signed an album contract with Dot Records. Gibson appeared twice on the "Ed Sullivan Show," the most popular television variety show of its time. She also released an album. But her records did not sell, and the requests for appearances never came.

Next, she turned to acting. John Ford cast her in an important role in his Western *The Horse Soldiers*, where she played alongside William Holden and John Wayne. In the 1950s, however, there were few roles available for black actors, and her acting career never blossomed. But a surprise offer took her into a different area of show business.

In 1959, when Abe Saperstein offered Gibson the chance to stage a tennis exhibition as an opening act for his Harlem Globetrotters basketball team, Gibson formed a corporation with Sidney Llewellyn and her lawyer. She also convinced Karol Fageros, her traveling roommate in Southeast Asia, to join the tour. The matches were a hit with fans. Gibson, inspired by her first significant income-generating venture, decided to branch off and go out on her own. It was a disastrous business move. Without the pull of the Globetrotters, the tour failed.

Althea Gibson Entertainment's bankruptcy was a damaging blow, perhaps the lowest point in her life. But another helping hand reached out, in the form of a corporate sponsor. The Ward Baking Company signed Gibson to a $25,000-a-year personal appearance contract and sent her around the country to give motivational speeches. She spoke on radio and television shows, at school assemblies, and at charity affairs. Gibson was very popular, but she found the work difficult. She was often lonely and had trouble talking about the past instead of focusing on a future goal. "Everything worth living for," she wrote, "it seemed to me then, existed in the past: money, glory, prestige, popularity and publicity, love and friendship all glowed with the yellow luster of unpolished trophies."

Earlier, friends had introduced Gibson to the game of golf, and, to kill time during speaking engagements, she played wherever she traveled. At age 33, after "hibernating" for two years, she decided to pursue professional golf and dedicated most of 1962 and 1963 to developing her game. Althea had to adjust her mental approach—in golf there was no chance to blow off steam by spending herself physically. She started with a terrific disadvantage, competing against younger players, most of whom had developed their games as children. And once again she had to fight racism.

Although the barrier was the same, the Ladies Professional Golf Association (LPGA) was set up differently than the Tennis Association. It was possible for Althea to be proactive during the fight. Players made up the LPGA, not a governing committee, and players were generally open to competition of any kind. Many country clubs banned blacks altogether. But it was difficult for a club to keep an LPGA member off the greens. Any player who finished in the top 80% of three-out-of-four consecutive tournaments qualified for an LPGA card.

Gibson set out to obtain a card. Despite a slow start, by the summer of 1964 her scoring average dropped to 77, at a time when the elite players averaged around 74. After finishing in the top 80% in two tournaments, she was allowed to compete on the next course but, because of her skin color, was barred from entering the clubhouse. Instead of exploding, Gibson dismissed the pettiness and took out her revenge on the course. She had one of her best days ever and qualified for the LPGA player's card. LPGA director Leonard Wirtz readily accepted Althea and championed her right to play.

Gibson made slow progress. By the end of 1964, she had collected $561.50 in prize money. Unfortunately, Ward reluctantly dropped her as a sponsor because the obligations of the tour took too much of her time. A personal bank loan kept Althea on the tour. The following season, she collected $1,595 in prize money, but her winnings were not nearly enough to make her loan payments.

In 1965, her Las Vegas wedding to longtime suitor Will Darben, brother of her good friend **Rosemary Darben**, provided emotional and financial support. The following year, she broke

the course record at the Pleasant Valley Country Club in Sutton, Massachusetts, lowered her average to 74 and doubled her earnings. Gibson improved her game again in 1967, but it would ultimately be her best year. Though she worked hard for three more years, she never managed to separate herself from the middle of the LPGA pack. Althea Gibson opened the door and paved the way for younger players, but she never reached the top or covered her tour expenses.

After retiring from golf, Gibson and her husband settled in New Jersey. She briefly considered a tennis comeback, enticed by the huge prize money available, but ultimately settled on teaching tennis and investing in a tennis center. She also accepted an offer from the city of East Orange, New Jersey, to manage the Department of Recreation. For 20 years, she was a source of inspiration to thousands of young players, lending a hand to kids just as needy as she had been.

Gibson retired in 1992. As to how she continued to fare, there have been conflicting reports. She was said to be "still active," and she told a reporter in 1994 that she was still hoping for a women's Seniors LPGA so she could compete again professionally. But in 1996, *Time* magazine reported that Gibson was living in East Orange as a virtual 69-year-old recluse, barely subsisting on Social Security. A major fundraiser was held in California.

In Harlem, they still speak of Althea Gibson with the reverence usually reserved for freedom fighters like Dr. Martin Luther King, Jr. Jackie Robinson is described as having fiery up-front courage, Joe Louis quiet dignity, Muhammad Ali outrageous panache. The champion Gibson, like the champion Arthur Ashe she helped inspire, had a straight-forward, low key, strength and confidence. In an interview about her role in the desegregation of sports, she said, "I set a good example. I didn't think about anything but the sport I was involved in and playing as well as I could, talent shows up better, quicker than anything else."

SOURCES:

Angelou, Maya, and Brian Lanker. "I Dream a World," in *National Geographic*. Vol. 8, 1989, p. 220.

Biracree, Tom. *Althea Gibson*. NY: Chelsea House, 1989.

Brunt, Stephen. "Althea Gibson, Remember Her?, Is Still Swinging," in *St. Louis Dispatch*. February 24, 1991, Section F, p. 2.

Contemporary Black Biography. Detroit, MI: Gale Research, 1994.

Current Biography. NY: H.W. Wilson, 1957.

Gibson, Althea. *I Always Wanted to be Somebody*. NY: Harper and Row, 1958.

———. *So Much to Live For*. NY: Putnam, 1968.

Higdon, Hal. *Champions of the Tennis Court*. Englewood Cliffs, NJ: Prentice-Hall, 1971.

Pizer, Vernon. *Glorious Triumphs: Athletes Who Conquered Adversity*. NY: Dodd, Mead, 1980.

Pratt, John Lowell. *Sport, Sport, Sport: True Stories of Great Athletes and Great Human Beings*. NY: Franklin Watts, 1960.

Jesse T. Raiford,
president of Raiford Communications, Inc., New York, New York

Gibson, Irene Langhorne (1873–1956).

See Astor, Nancy for sidebar.

Gibson, Perla Siedle (d. 1971)

South African pianist and concert singer, known as "The Lady in White" during World War II. Name variations: The Lady in White. Died in 1971; married; several children, including daughter Joy Liddiard.

Known as "The Lady in White," Perla Siedle Gibson was a classical pianist and concert singer as well as a volunteer at a dockside canteen at Durban harbor, a South African port for troopships carrying millions of soldiers during World War II. In April 1940, while she was minding the canteen in her regulation white overalls, a soldier aboard one of the giant ships shouted down to her, "Hey Ma, sing us a song! Give us 'Land of Hope and Glory!'" Gibson obliged the young man by cupping her hands around her mouth and sending the patriotic song soaring up toward the ship, while delighted soldiers joined in the chorus. She continued with an impromptu concert of songs from the Great War, including "Pack Up Your Troubles," and "It's a Long Way to Tipperary." From that day forward, she serenaded every convoy—a total of 20,000 ships and three million men—that entered port, never missing a day, even after she learned of her own son's death in action while serving in Italy. Following Gibson's death in 1971, newspapers throughout the world ran stories about this middle-aged woman who lifted the spirits of, and gave hope to, so many frightened and homesick young men. An adaptation of Gibson's original autobiography, *Durban's Lady in White*, which had gone out of print, was published in 1991, with a foreword and postscript by her daughter **Joy Liddiard**.

Gideon, Miriam (1906—)

American composer, the first woman commissioned to write a complete synagogue service, who was probably the most recorded woman composer of her era. Born in Greeley, Colorado, on October 23, 1906; daughter of

Perla Gibson

Henrietta Shoninger and Abram Gideon (a professor of philosophy and modern languages); had one sister, Judith; studied at the Yonkers Conservatory of Music with Hans Barth, the pianist, with her uncle, Henry Gideon, and with Felix Fox at Boston University; studied with **Marion Bauer**, Charles Haubiel, Jacques Pillois, a distinguished French composer, Lazare Saminsky, a well-known Russian composer, and with Roger Sessions at New York University; received her master's in musicology at Columbia University in 1946 and a Doctor of Sacred Music in Composition from the Jewish Theological Seminary in 1970; married Frederic Ewen (a professor of German literature).

Taught at Brooklyn College, City College of the City University of New York, the Manhattan School of Music, and the Jewish Theological Seminary; saw Lyric Piece for Strings premiered with the London Symphony Orchestra (1944); won the Ernest Bloch Prize for choral music (1948); won the National Federation of Music Clubs National Award to a woman composer (1969); was elected to the American Academy and Institute of Arts and Letters (1975).

Miriam Gideon credited the public schools of Colorado for the excellent training she received in reading music. Outside of school, opportunities for her to hear music were rare. "My sister and I were taught solfège from the first grade," she said. "We used 'movable doh,' and everybody learned this system until it became automatic, which is the only way it can be useful. This has remained a permanent help to me." When she was nine, the family moved to Chicago and then to New York where opportunities for training her considerable talent expanded. Although her first interest was piano, composing became more and more important to her. She was fortunate to be able to study with Roger Sessions in New York who taught a few students privately, including *Vivian Fine, the dance composer.

One of Gideon's early compositions, *Lyric Piece for Strings,* was performed by the London Symphony Orchestra in 1944. Later a string quartet and orchestral version of the work appeared. Gideon was probably the most recorded woman composer of this century. Works like *The Hound of Heaven, The Seasons of Time,* and *Symphonia Brevis* are only a few of her recorded compositions. Gideon's music was widely performed in the United States, Europe, and the Far East.

SOURCES:

Page, Tim. "Gideon and Talma at 80—Composers and Neighbors," in *The New York Times Biographical Service.* October 1986, pp. 1276–1277.

John Haag,
Athens, Georgia

Gies, Miep (1909—)

Austrian-born Dutch hero who aided Anne Frank and her family while they were in hiding. Name variations: Miep Van Santen in Anne Frank's original diary. Born Hermine Santrouschitz in Vienna, Austria, in February 1909; adopted by the Nieuwenhuises; married Jan Gies (known as Henk in the diaries), on July 16, 1941 (died 1993).

Known as Miep Van Santen in *Anne Frank's diary, Miep Gies introduces her book *Anne Frank Remembered* with a disclaimer: "I am not a hero. I stand at the end of the long, long line of good Dutch people who did what I did or more—much more—during those dark and terrible times. . . . Times the like of which I hope with all my heart will never, never come again. It is for all of us ordinary people all over the world to see to it that they do not."

Born Hermine Santrouschitz in Vienna, Austria, in 1909, Gies was five when she eagerly ran beside a parade of men and horses as World War I marched into her city along with the Germans. By war's end, she was severely undernourished, and her parents were warned that she might die. In December 1920, under the auspices of a workers' program, 11-year-old Gies was name-tagged, along with scores of other children, and shipped off to an unknown family in the Netherlands, where there were no food shortages, to be brought back to health.

When she arrived at the train station of Leiden, recalls Gies, a strong man spoke to her in a foreign language, then took her hand, walked her through town in the moonlight, and they arrived at a house where a woman with "soft eyes" greeted her, while four boys peeped from above stairs. The woman gave Gies a glass of milk and took her into a small room with two beds. There was another girl her age in the other bed. "The woman took off all my layers of clothes," wrote Gies, "removed the bow from my hair, and put me between the covers in the center of the other bed. Warmth enfolded me. My eyelids dropped shut. Immediately, I was asleep. I will never forget that journey."

Gies was sent to school to learn Dutch, and her schoolmates eagerly offered their guidance. By January's end, she spoke a few words in Dutch; by May, she was the best in the class. Originally her stay was to be three months, but she was still weak, and the doctors repeatedly recommended three-month extensions. Her adoptive family, the Nieuwenhuises, began to see her as their own and gave her the nickname Miep.

When Gies was 13, the Nieuwenhuises moved to South Amsterdam. Though at age 16 she revisited her actual family in Vienna, all agreed that she was now acclimatized and more Dutch than Austrian, so she remained with her adoptive parents. In 1933, after a two-week tryout making jam from fruit and pectin in the company kitchen of Opekta, 24-year-old Gies was hired by a man named Otto Frank to type, keep the books, answer telephone questions from his homemaker customers, and sell kits for making jam.

In 1938, when Gies applied to renew her Austrian passport, she was handed a German passport bearing the Nazi swastika. The Germans were now the occupiers of Austria, and Miep had become a German citizen. Soon, a Dutch Nazi sympathizer arrived at her door and invited her to join the Nazi Girls' Club. Miep brushed aside the invitation, complained of Germany's handling of Jews, and the woman retreated in anger. When the Germans conquered Holland in the spring of 1940, Gies was summoned before them. To her horror, they invalidated her passport and told her that she must return to Vienna within three months' time. They then asked if it was true that she had declined to join the Nazi Girls' Club; Miep admitted it was.

For Gies, there was only one solution. In order to stay in the Netherlands, she had to become a Dutch citizen: she had to somehow obtain her birth certificate from Vienna and marry her boyfriend Jan Gies within the three-month timeframe. After a hair-raising attempt to keep the German bureaucracy ignorant of her invalidated passport while obtaining a marriage license, the couple married on July 16, 1941. Anne Frank and her father Otto were in attendance.

One year later, at considerable danger to themselves, Miep and Jan were helping their friends the Franks to become *onderduikers* (Dutch for "dives under" or goes into hiding) in the Secret Annex. One evening, Anne begged Miep and Jan to stay the night. Wrote Gies: "All through the night I heard each ringing of the Westertoren clock. I never slept; I couldn't close my eyes. I heard the sound of a rainstorm begin, the wind come up. The quietness of the place was overwhelming. The fright of these people who were locked up here was so thick I could feel it pressing down on me. It was like a thread of terror pulled taut. It was so terrible it never let me close my eyes. For the first time I knew what it was like to be a Jew in hiding."

Following the publication of Anne Frank's diary, Gies became a frequent speaker, begging for tolerance—tolerance for everyone. When Connecticut College bestowed an honorary doctorate on her in 1996, she wrote the college thanking them for the honor but claiming she was not heroic. It was Anne that was heroic, she said. Besides, at the end of the war, said Gies, she hated the Germans. At one point, she lashed out at German tourists who were visiting the Annex. She learned later that these German tourists had been imprisoned in a concentration camp for opposing Hitler.

SOURCES:
Gies, Miep, with Alison Leslie Gold. *Anne Frank Remembered*. NY: Simon and Schuster, 1987.

Giesler-Anneke, Mathilde Franziska (1817–1884).

See Anneke, Mathilde Franziska.

Miep Gies, with husband Jan, on her wedding day.

Gifford, countess of.

See Blackwood, Helen Selena (1807–1867).

Gilberga (d. 1054)

Queen of Aragon. Name variations: Hermesenda. Died in 1054; daughter of Bernardo, count of Cousserans, and Gersenda, countess of Bigorre; married Ramiro I, king of Aragon (r. 1035–1069), on August 22, 1036; children: Sancho V (b. 1042), king of Aragon; Garcia of Aragon (d. 1186), bishop of Pamplona; *Teresa of Aragon (b. 1037, who married William VI, count of Provence); *Urraca of Aragon (a nun); *Sancha of Aragon (who married Pons, count of Toulouse, and Armengol III, count of Urgel).

Gilbert, Anne (1821–1904)

Anglo-American dancer and actress. Name variations: Ann; Mrs. Gilbert; Mrs. George H. Gilbert. Born Anne Jane Hartley in Rochdale, Lancashire, England, on October 21, 1821; died in a Chicago

Anne
Gilbert

Gilbert was best remembered as old Mrs. Gilbert, one of the famous members of Augustin Daly's Company, which she joined in 1869. A stage star for 47 years, she became identified with eccentric elderly women roles, such as Mrs. Candour in *The School for Scandal* and Mrs. Hardcastle in *She Stoops to Conquer.* The ensemble team of Gilbert, *Ada Rehan, John Drew, and James Lewis became known as "The Big Four." After Augustin Daly's death, Gilbert came under Charles Frohman's management. In 1904, at age 83, she began her farewell tour in Clyde Fitch's *Granny,* which had been commissioned specifically for her. After receiving standing ovations in New York and Chicago, she died one month into the tour on December 2, 1904. Gilbert is known to have held a unique position in the American theater due to the esteem, admiration, and affection she enjoyed both on and off the stage.

SUGGESTED READING:

Martin, Charlotte M., ed. *The Stage Reminiscences of Mrs. Gilbert.* 1901.

Gilbert, Eliza (1818–1861).
See Montez, Lola.

Gilbert, Mrs. George H. (1821–1904).
See Gilbert, Anne.

Gilbert, Mrs. John (1893–1985).
See Joy, Leatrice.

Gilbert, Katherine Everett
(1886–1952)

American philosopher. Born on July 29, 1886; died on April 28, 1952, in Durham, North Carolina; Brown University, B.A., 1908, M.A., 1910; Cornell University, Ph.D., 1912; married Allan H. Gilbert, in 1913; children: two sons.

Was editorial assistant at the Philosophical Review *(1915–19); was a research fellow, University of North Carolina (1922–29); served as acting professor of philosophy, University of North Carolina (1929–30); was a professor of philosophy, Duke University (1930–40); was chair of the Department of Aesthetics, Art and Music, Duke University (1942–51). Honorary D.Litt., Brown University (1942).*

Selected works: Maurice Blondel's Philosophy of Action *(1924);* Studies in Recent Aesthetics *(1927); (with Helmut Kuhn)* A History of Esthetics *(1939);* Aesthetic Studies *(1952); many articles in philosophical journals.*

In addition to her papers which appeared in many philosophical journals, including *Philo-*

hotel on December 2, 1904; studied dance in the ballet school of Her Majesty's Theatre, Haymarket; married George H. Gilbert (a dancer and manager), in 1846 (died 1866).

Anne Gilbert was born Anne Jane Hartley in Rochdale, Lancashire, England, on October 21, 1821. By age 15, she was a pupil at the ballet school connected with the Haymarket theater. Ten years later, in 1846, she married George H. Gilbert, a fellow performer, and together they filled many engagements in English theaters. In October 1849, they moved to America, intent on giving up the stage for a farm in Wisconsin. When that enterprise did not pan out, they joined a Chicago theater company.

In the role of Wichavenda in Brougham's *Pocahontas,* Anne Gilbert had her first success in a speaking part (1857). She and her husband then moved to New York in 1864. That September, Anne made her Manhattan debut in *Finesse,* presented by Mrs. John Wood (*Matilda Wood).

sophical *Review* and the *Journal of Philosophy*, Katherine Gilbert published several books of philosophy. Her interest in the philosophical treatment of art—aesthetics—was sparked by her undergraduate studies in philosophy at Brown University with Alexander Meikeljohn. After completing her Ph.D. at Cornell University in 1912, Gilbert went to work as an editorial assistant at the *Philosophical Review*. From 1922, she worked as a research fellow and eventually a lecturer at the University of North Carolina. Finally, in 1930, her career brought her to Duke University, where she became the school's first full female professor. When the departments of music and art were merged in 1940, Gilbert moved from the philosophy department to become chair of the new department of aesthetics, music, and art. She remained in that position until her retirement in 1951. Despite her move away from mainstream philosophy to a concentration in aesthetics—with a particular interest in art criticism, dance, literature and architecture—she claimed that her approach to art could never be anything but philosophical. Gilbert died in Durham, North Carolina, on April 28, 1952.

Catherine Hundleby, M.A.
Philosophy, University of Guelph

Gilbert, Lady (1841–1921)

See Mulholland, Rosa.

Gilbert, Linda (1847–1895)

American prison welfare worker. Born Zelinda Gilbert on May 13, 1847, probably in Rochester, New York; died on October 24, 1895, in Mount Vernon, New York; one of two daughters of Horace and Zelinda Gilbert; attended St. Mary's Convent, Chicago; never married; no children.

Little is known about Linda Gilbert's childhood except that when she was about five her family moved from Rochester, New York, to Chicago, where she attended St. Mary's Convent. Purportedly, each morning on her way to school, she passed Cook County Jail where she became acquainted with an inmate who expressed interest in her schoolbooks. She subsequently brought him a book from her father's library and resolved that when she was old enough she would see to it that the prison had a library. In 1864, aided by an inheritance, she donated some 4,000 volumes to the prison facility. Hoping to establish a library in every prison in Illinois and provide other services for prisoners, Gilbert sought to raise funds by setting up a lottery modeled after a successful one sponsored by

the owner of a Chicago opera house. However, when her sponsors realized that she was advertising unrealistic prizes and withdrew support, she was forced to abandon the scheme.

Around 1872, after suffering losses in the Chicago Fire, she moved to New York City and renewed her efforts. Although the city already had two prison associations, she chose to establish her own Gilbert Library and Prisoners' Aid Fund. In addition to raising money, she visited prisons, bringing gifts of food and flowers and writing letters for inmates. When prisoners were released, she often provided them with clothing, lodging, and assistance in finding employment. Another of Gilbert's grandiose money-making schemes went awry in 1875, when her "Grand Testimonial Concert" at the Barnum Hippodrome was poorly attended. Undaunted, she sought to attract a permanent endowment for her work through her publication *Sketch of the Life and Work of Linda Gilbert* (1876), which, although well-meaning, was filled with inflated claims. At the same time, she incorporated her Gilbert Library and Prisoners' Aid Society, which continued to provide limited prison services until 1883.

Linda Gilbert

To further support her prison work, Gilbert was thought to have patented several inventions, including a noiseless rail for railroads and a wire clothespin, although her name is not included in the index of women inventors given federal patents. Linda Gilbert died on October 24, 1895, at the age of 48.

SOURCES:

James, Edward T., ed. *Notable American Women 1607–1950*. Cambridge, MA: The Belknap Press of Harvard University Press, 1971.

McHenry, Robert, ed. *Famous American Women*. NY: Dover, 1980.

Barbara Morgan,
Melrose, Massachusetts

Gilbert, Marie Dolores Eliza Rosanna (1818–1861).

See Montez, Lola.

Gilbert, Mrs. R. (1895–1994).

See Cooper, Whina.

Gilbert, Ronnie (1926—)

American singer, actress and author who was a member of the famous folk-music group The Weavers and a successful survivor of McCarthyism. Born in Brooklyn, New York, on September 7, 1926; daughter of Charles Gilbert and Sarah Gilbert; married Martin Weg (divorced 1959); children: daughter, **Lisa Weg.**

Performed with The Weavers (1949–52); rejoined the group after its revival (1955–63); began a successful solo singing career (1960s), turning to acting as well; earned a professional degree in clinical psychology and practiced as a therapist; recorded with Holly Near (1980s); combined her acting, singing and writing to present her play Mother Jones: The Most Dangerous Woman in America *(1990s).*

Ronnie Gilbert was born into a Jewish-American working-class family in Brooklyn during the height of the Roaring '20s but grew up during the economically depressed 1930s when labor activism and the specter of fascism and war became basic facts of American life. From her parents, Gilbert absorbed political idealism and a faith in the possibilities of creating a world free of poverty, war, and racism. As a high school student, she took a stand against racial stereotyping when she refused to appear in a blackface minstrel show with white students. Citing Paul Robeson's denunciations of racism, Gilbert would not back down, even when her teacher threatened with denial of graduation. Ronnie graduated as scheduled.

Gilbert was deeply influenced by the internationalist aims of the Left. From her earliest years, she was exposed to revolutionary songs and sang them with enthusiasm while marching in the annual May Day parades in Manhattan. During the summers, she attended Camp Wo-Chi-Ca (Workers Children's Camp), where **Naomi Feld**, a counselor and choral conductor, made singing a part of the daily camp routine. Feld reminded the campers that music always existed in a broader social and political context, that "singing is a form of battle."

Ronnie's mother **Sarah Gilbert** was born into a poor ghetto family in Warsaw. Orphaned as a child, Sarah came to America at age 16 after having already absorbed the traditions of the Polish-Jewish Bund, a Socialist organization that emphasized economic victories for workers as well as cultural and moral enlightenment. In a 1990 interview, Gilbert gave credit to her mother's labor idealism as having played a major role in her own formative years, noting that the Bund was an "inspired and inspiring movement [that] was full of culture, full of songs and poetry and theater and writing of all kinds." A woman who loved to sing and an active member of the International Ladies Garment Workers Union, Sarah Gilbert would often return home from union meetings with her book of labor songs. This and other songbooks and recordings, including songs inspired by the Spanish Civil War as well as pop music of the period, were always available in her home. Ronnie Gilbert's political involvement began around this time as well, when she stood on New York street corners to collect money for Spanish refugee children. At the start of World War II, she went to Washington, D.C., to work for the Federal government. In her spare time, she continued her activism, joining a leftist singing ensemble called the Priority Ramblers—its priorities being to sing about the necessity both of winning the anti-fascist war overseas and working for an expansion of social and racial justice on the home front.

Growing up in New York became even more challenging for her family after Sarah Gilbert divorced her husband, but Ronnie matured into an attractive, confident and talented young woman. The world around her was rapidly changing, however. Now, with victory over fascism and the achievement of a hard-won peace, a new era was dawning. In December 1945, folksinger Pete Seeger was instrumental in founding People's Songs, a group closely linked to the Communist Party whose avowed goal was to raise the morale of the labor movement and disseminate the progressive agenda.

People's Songs reached its apogee during the presidential campaign of 1948, when Henry Wallace, the Progressive Party's candidate, challenged the rapidly emerging ideological orthodoxies of the Cold War. Folksingers were invariably on hand at Progressive Party rallies, and both Pete Seeger and Paul Robeson sang at the Philadelphia convention that nominated Wallace for the presidency. It was during this time that Ronnie Gilbert began to combine her political idealism with her love of music, singing on behalf of Wallace throughout a campaign that was marred by incidents of red-baiting and threats of violence. While employed as a secretary for CBS, she also worked for social and political change. Art, she was convinced, could play a vital role in modifying the world for the better. Decades later, she recalled: "I had a lot of faith in the effectiveness of songs because of my own experience of songs getting so deeply to me. . . . I expected them to have the same effect on others."

Although most of her friends during this period were either members or sympathizers of the Communist Party and accepted its rigid discipline, Gilbert chose to define her beliefs in a socialist society as one in which "nobody had to worry about clothing and housing and medical care [so that] people could turn their attention to how to make the products they made better." She envisioned the new society as one that was economically decentralized, and which emphasized lifelong educational opportunities that enabled individuals to change course if they discovered "that there was something that they did better or wanted to do. There would be a lot of singing and painting and plays." In view of the fact that her *Weltanschauung* was as much based on her artistic ideals as on political and economic ideology, Gilbert found herself irritated by Communist meetings and the know-it-all attitudes of the party leadership, noting

decades later: "I am not a good organizational person. . . . It's very hard for me to follow regulations or discipline. I tend to laugh a lot when I should probably be serious."

Despite the enthusiasm of millions who supported Henry Wallace, the progressive and leftist forces faced an increasingly repressive environment. Anti-Communism, which became the official ideology of American public life in the late 1940s, covered a broad spectrum, ranging from genuine concern about Stalinist tyranny and Soviet territorial expansion to a belief on the part of ultra-conservatives that any impulses toward domestic reform should be stigmatized and crushed as an expression of subversive "un-Americanism." By 1949, the American mood had become extremely ugly as "subversion" was being uncovered by self-proclaimed patriots in every state. In Washington, D.C., the House Committee on Un-American Activities (HUAC) sought headlines by issuing subpoenas to individuals whose ideas appeared to be a threat to an American Way of Life; this group had detect-

Ronnie Gilbert and The Weavers.

ed subversive tendencies in folk music as early as May 1941, when a HUAC special committee labeled Woody Guthrie and other folk-based entertainers as red balladeers whose cultural deviance was alleged to pose a clear and present threat to national security.

Ronnie Gilbert, a few days shy of her 23rd birthday, experienced the new mood in America, ominous in its near hysteria, at a Paul Robeson concert in Peekskill, New York, in late August 1949. Decades later, Gilbert could vividly recall a day when a peaceful crowd that had assembled to enjoy a folk-music concert found itself being violently attacked by a mob of rock-throwing "patriotic" vigilantes, while police, some smiling, were visible on the sidelines doing nothing. As Gilbert and thousands of others attempted to depart, they were mauled and insulted by a screaming mob. Rocks were thrown, while on a nearby hill a burning cross could be seen. Over 150 in the audience were seriously injured; cars and buses were smashed. Several years later, Gilbert and The Weavers would recall that frightening day in a song titled "Hold the Line" but avoided scrutiny by professional red-hunters by recording it for the little-known Hootenanny label and using the billing of "Pete Seeger and Chorus."

As early as 1948, during and after the ill-fated Wallace presidential campaign, Gilbert found herself singing at hootenannies organized by People's Songs. Along with Pete Seeger, the initially unnamed quartet also included Lee Hays and Fred Hellerman. The group was heterogeneous: Seeger was born into a WASP background in Manhattan in 1919, while Hays, the son of a Methodist minister, was born in Little Rock, Arkansas, in 1914. A social activist in the 1930s, Hays had written both a play and produced a documentary film about the plight of America's sharecroppers. Hellerman, born in Brooklyn in 1927, was gifted both as a guitarist and singer. As the foursome coalesced, they would often meet for songfests at Seeger's home on MacDougal Street in Manhattan's Greenwich Village, in which the rumbling bass of Lee Hays would contrast dramatically with Ronnie Gilbert's soaring contralto.

Appearing in their debut on Oscar Brand's "Folk Song Festival" on municipally-owned radio station WNYC, the group was still searching for a collective persona when it was announced to listeners as "The No-Name Quartet." This situation changed instantly when they decided to identify themselves as The Weavers. Taken from the title of a 19th-century play about impoverished weavers by the German

dramatist Gerhart Hauptmann, the name was both simple and memorable but also evoked a spirit of social militancy. As the group's only woman, Ronnie Gilbert brought an artistic maturity to the ensemble that was extraordinary in view of her youth (she was one year older than Hellerman, but twelve years younger than Hays and seven years younger than Seeger). In their performances and recordings over the next 14 years, Gilbert was able to provide The Weavers with what Robert Cantwell has described as a "protean and brilliant" voice, one that was capable of revealing innumerable facets, "by turn gentle as a nursing mother's, innocent as a child's, [and] lusty as the Wife of Bath."

In December 1949, The Weavers received their first booking at Max Gordon's Village Vanguard. Uncertain of their appeal, Gordon offered the group only $200 a week and all the hamburgers they could eat. Not having properly assessed how healthy the singers' appetites were, he quickly insisted on renegotiating their salaries to $250 weekly without kitchen privileges. The Weavers' new sound and fresh material, which included songs by then relatively little-known African-American folk singers such as Leadbelly (Hudson "Huddie" Ledbetter), who had died only a few weeks before their Village Vanguard debut, delighted audiences, and their reputations quickly soared. Soon, the Manhattan press was singing the group's praises, as when the critic of the *Herald-Tribune* enthused about their "unspoiled . . . spontaneity." Carl Sandburg, who happened to see their show, declared enthusiastically, "When I hear America singing, The Weavers are there." Pleased by The Weavers' popularity, Max Gordon extended the ensemble's contract, keeping interest alive through newspaper ads in which he declared them to be "the most exciting act" that had appeared at the Village Vanguard in a decade.

One of the most important members of the Vanguard audience for many nights was bandleader Gordon Jenkins, whose enthusiasm for The Weavers only seemed to increase with time. Jenkins was convinced that these musical neophytes could be commercially successful and was certain that he could convince his recording company's director, Decca Records' Dave Kapp, into offering a contract. Kapp was somewhat skeptical, however, and wavered until Columbia's producer Mitch Miller offered to sign them up. Only then did Decca make the decisive move. Advised by their new manager Harold Leventhal, The Weavers signed with Decca. Pete Seeger echoed the group's sentiments when he voiced their hope to "do for folk music what Benny Goodman did for jazz."

In May 1950, with the ink on their contract barely dry, The Weavers began recording their repertoire. At their first session on May 4, they recorded a catchy Israeli soldiers' tune, "Tzena, Tzena, Tzena." A few weeks later, they taped the flip side, a song composed by Leadbelly that was dear to their hearts. "Goodnight, Irene" shot up the national charts, became the #1 single, and earned a gold record. "Tzena, Tzena, Tzena" also caught the attention of America, peaking at #2. For much of 1950, Decca Records could not press the vinyl fast enough to meet the nation's demand for The Weavers' discs.

For the next two years, The Weavers enjoyed immense popular success, earning another gold record and a #2 chart rating with "On Top of Old Smokey," a folk ballad from America's Southern Highlands. They achieved another smashing success in 1951, reaching #4 on the charts with their spirited rendition of Woody Guthrie's "So Long (It's Been Good to Know Yuh)." The group also recorded Guthrie's "Hard, Ain't It Hard," as well as "Lonesome Traveler," with words and music by Lee Hays who was inspired by fragments of an old American hymn. The group's astonishing success gratified Decca Records—pulling the company out of debt—but was as much a surprise to Gilbert and her Weavers colleagues, who had hoped to earn enough to pay their basic, and rather modest, living expenses. Between 1950 and 1952, The Weavers would sell more than 4 million records. They also enjoyed choice engagements at plush night clubs in major cities throughout the United States.

The Weavers' success, however, did not create a situation of unalloyed happiness. As overnight stars, each member of the group indulged in varying degrees of soul-searching and artistic unease; all could easily remember their days of political activism. Each chose to deal in a different fashion with the ambiguities of success; for example, Pete Seeger wore red socks along with his tuxedo. The Weavers' hit records and well-paid night-club engagements were the result of the group's conscious decision to formalize their repertoire, limiting their freedom of improvisation so as to present shows that were smooth, polished and audience pleasing.

With the Cold War now at its chilliest, The Weavers decided to avoid being ideologically controversial. From the first days of the group's public appearances in 1949, they had chosen to bypass songs that made political statements.

Their tunes now contained innocuous lyrics, and they were careful to delete verses that might offend conservative sensibilities, like the line in Leadbelly's "Goodnight, Irene" that concluded: "If Irene turns her back on me/ I'd take morphine and die." They even avoided singing "If I Had a Hammer," a new composition by Pete Seeger and Lee Hays. Writing in the leftist folk-song journal *Sing Out!* in February 1951, Irwin Silber noted with considerable annoyance: "The Weavers would have sounded far better in the more vital and vibrant Hootenanny setting than they did in their formal evening attire on the Town Hall stage."

The Weavers' retreat from artistic activism delayed but did not prevent their becoming embroiled in the worst excesses of the Cold War. Since 1947, a group of disgruntled ex-FBI agents, convinced that the U.S. government remained soft on Communism and incapable of effectively fighting internal subversion, had been publishing an anti-Communist newsletter named *Counterattack*. On June 22, 1950, *Counterattack* issued a special report entitled *Red Channels: The Report of Communist Influence in Radio and Television*. Listing 149 "prominent actors and artists" it accused of having lent their names to organizations "espousing Communist causes," *Red Channels* was sent to media executives and quickly became universally accepted by the industry as the Holy Writ of radio and television blacklisting. There was little if any resistance to the intimidationist tactics from the entertainment world. The music industry's trade journal, *Billboard*, chose to add some additional fuel to the fire by reporting that "the Commies are hell-bent on taking over."

Red Channels did not list The Weavers as a group, but the blacklisting bible did devote fully two pages to document the "un-American" activities of Pete Seeger, who was accused, among other things, of having performed before such groups as the Progressive Citizens of America and the Committee for a Democratic Far Eastern Policy. The Weavers were, however, collectively accused of pro-Communism in the June 9, 1950, issue of *Counterattack* in an article that took pains to note that the group was "well-known in Communist Party circles" and had publicly performed the "fighting songs of the Lincoln Brigade . . . and other Communist song favorites," also pointing out what the blacklisting journal regarded as a glaring discrepancy, namely between the songs the ensemble had recorded for Decca and performed in night clubs, which were "not the folk songs they sing for the subversive groups they frequently entertain." The appearance of both the *Red Channels* listing of Seeger and the *Counterattack* piece on the entire group had an immediate and dramatic impact on the professional future of The Weavers. Without warning, plans for them to appear as regular guests on a television series were canceled by the program's sponsor, Stokely-Van Camp. Terrified of the prospects of a total blacklisting, The Weavers' manager promised the editors of *Counterattack* that the singers would henceforth turn down all future invitations to perform before left-wing groups.

At first, The Weavers appeared to have successfully weathered the storm unleashed by *Counterattack* and *Red Channels.* If imitation is the height of flattery, then The Weavers were flattered indeed when Dennis Day, Vic Damone, and Frank Sinatra all made recordings of "Goodnight, Irene," which *Billboard* hailed as being quite possibly "the biggest hit of the era." For the 122 weeks between the release of "Goodnight, Irene" and the termination of their relationship with Decca Records in November 1952, a Weavers song appeared on *Billboard*'s weekly bestseller chart an astonishing 74 times. Even more amazingly, for 25 of these weeks, not one but two Weavers songs appeared on that listing. "Goodnight, Irene" remained immensely popular even at the end of 1951, fully 18 months after its release. Even though they were banned on television, The Weavers continued to flourish as live performers, appearing at the best night clubs in New York, Las Vegas, and Hollywood. Audience response remained enthusiastic, and at their opening at New York's Blue Angel the group was greeted with what the *New York Post* described as "the greatest ovation ever accorded an act at this club."

Despite the blacklist, The Weavers' career continued to flourish throughout 1951. Nevertheless, an event that took place in Chicago in June of that year foreshadowed serious trouble. The group had been scheduled to perform on a national television program on the NBC network. When word of this was somehow relayed to Rabbi Benjamin Schultz, founder of the American Jewish League Against Communism, Schultz organized call-ins to pressure NBC to cancel their appearance. Despite the fact that only a handful of complaints had been received by the network, NBC capitulated to pressure. Even with the television blacklist, The Weavers generally continued to enjoy broad-based popularity throughout 1951. Several of their recordings, including "On Top of Old Smokey" and "Kisses Sweeter Than Wine," rose quickly into the upper reaches of the

charts, and *Newsweek* described them as "the hottest singing group around." But pressure groups continued to target the singers. The American Legion was able to frighten the director of the Ohio State Fair into canceling a Weavers appearance even though they had already signed a contract. The year ended optimistically with a packed house for a Christmas concert at New York City's Town Hall.

The year 1952 began hopefully, with Decca Records announcing that they were inaugurating an "all-out" campaign to promote several of their leading recording artists, including The Weavers. Another positive sign was the fact that The Weavers' latest release, the South-African tune "Wimoweh," was rapidly climbing the charts. The American Legion in Ohio, however, continued to hound the group. During The Weavers' visit to Cleveland, the Legion noted that all four members of the group had been kept under "constant surveillance" during their stay in that city. While The Weavers performed at Akron's Yankee Inn, local Legionnaires regularly showed up, presumably in order to monitor the content of their music. For a while, the owner of the Yankee Inn resisted the Legion's pressure tactics, but eventually he bowed to economic realities and announced that his contract with the musicians had been terminated "by mutual consent."

In February 1952, a former Communist named Harvey Matusow, who had become a professional anti-Communist working for the notorious Senator Joseph McCarthy, testified before a HUAC panel in Washington, D.C., accusing the Communist Party of misusing folk music, and particularly popular groups such as The Weavers, to entrap young people to join their movement. Matusow insisted that he had proof positive that Gilbert, Hellerman, and Seeger were all card-carrying Communists. In his 1955 autobiography, *False Witness,* Matusow admitted that most of his voluminous HUAC testimony was fabricated and that his work as a paid government witness had done great harm to the lives of innocent women and men. Ronnie Gilbert was one of Matusow's intended victims, but she exhibited remarkable powers of decency and resistance during an indecent period of American life. When subpoenaed by HUAC, she simply ignored it (fortunately, she never received another). In 1950, at the onset of The Weavers' overnight fame, she married Martin Weg, a dentist. Soon a daughter Lisa was born, and, as the intimidating pressures of the blacklist took hold and The Weavers received fewer and fewer invitations to perform in public, Ronnie settled into the role of wife and mother. Not all was normal, however, for a young woman who never hid her beliefs. On several occasions, FBI agents visited her husband's office, frightening off his patients and inflicting economic damage on the Weg family.

"Wimoweh" was the last Weavers song to appear on the charts, and the management of Decca began to distance itself from the quartet that had earned their company large sums of money. When other Decca artists, such as Louis Armstrong and Guy Lombardo, failed to appear on the charts, the company invested in a promotional campaign to rekindle their popularity. But when The Weavers found themselves in a similar situation in late 1952, Decca dropped them from their roster. Soon after, the group decided to disband. The Weavers were brought down not by an aroused public angry at their political ideals or by fans who had grown tired of their singing, but by a small band of Americans who created blacklists and intimidated employers even though millions of Americans were attending their concerts and buying their records.

Ronnie Gilbert survived the era of Senator McCarthy and the blacklist and continued performing. In December 1955, with McCarthy politically discredited and the worst excesses of the era that bears his name diminished, The Weavers were back together as a group. Performing in New York's Carnegie Hall, Gilbert and her colleagues gave a stunning performance which the group self-recorded because record companies were still fearful. (Vanguard Records eventually purchased rights to the tapes and released discs derived from them.) For the next several years, The Weavers once again enjoyed success throughout the United States despite continuing protests and occasional bomb threats before concerts. Pete Seeger departed from the group in 1958, replaced in quick succession by Erik Darling, then by Frank Hamilton and finally by Bernie Krause. Fred Hellerman and Lee Hays stayed on to continue singing with Gilbert. After a 15-year existence, the group finally disbanded in 1963 with an emotional farewell concert in Carnegie Hall. Shortly before, they had been offered an appearance on ABC's "Hootenanny" but declined to sign a loyalty oath demanded by the show's director.

The original Weavers quartet, Gilbert, Hays, Hellerman, and Seeger, performed for a final time in a pair of concerts in Carnegie Hall in late November 1980. By this time, it was obvious that Lee Hays, who had lost both legs because of severe diabetes, did not have long to live. He died in August 1981.

After touring as a solo performer in the 1960s, Gilbert's energies were channeled into earning a master's degree in clinical psychology. She then practiced throughout the 1970s as a therapist. Music was, however, never banished from her life, and, by the 1980s, she was again active on stage and in the recording studio. She made a number of solo recordings before making two recordings with **Holly Near**, "Lifeline" (1983) and "Singing with You" (1986). Gilbert toured with Near in 1983-84 and sang with the group HARP (consisting of Holly Near, Arlo Guthrie, Ronnie Gilbert, and Pete Seeger). Gilbert also appeared in a number of films, including *The Loves of Isadora, Windflowers, Loin de Vietnam, Going On, Hard Travelin'*, and *The Hopi: Songs from the Fourth World*. She enjoyed performing as an actress on stage and was seen in many plays in New York and London, as well as in Canada and France, even once appearing at the Venezuela Festival in Caracas. She also became a decades-long member of Joseph Chaikin's experimental drama troupe, The Open Theater. Gilbert also released the solo albums *The Spirit Is Free* (1985) and *Love Will Find a Way* (1989); the latter was self-produced with her new manager and life partner, **Donna Korones**.

In 1993, Gilbert's considerable talents came together in her play about *Mary Harris Jones titled, Mother Jones: The Most Dangerous Woman in America*. In her portrayal of the legendary union organizer, Gilbert set out to reveal a woman who was at once "spunky and sarcastic, fearless and opinionated." The show's songs, most of which were written by Gilbert, provide its audiences with indelible portraits of an age of resistance to injustice when the Knights of Labor, John D. Rockefeller, and Mrs. O'Leary's cow all made their marks on the history of an exuberant and raucous young nation.

In the 1990s, Ronnie Gilbert could look back on a remarkable career that spanned the turbulent eras of the Great Depression, the New Deal, World War II and the Cold War. She had found the strength to survive the McCarthyite hysteria and never abandoned her ideals, continuing to believe that, despite some errors of judgment made by her generation, she had been part of a movement whose aspirations had been on balance "good and true and clean and wonderful." Ronnie Gilbert has never grown tired of quoting Mother Jones, who said, "Women have such a power, but they don't know how to use it." Gilbert's career is a testament not only to this power in one gifted woman's life, but also to her remarkable ability to use it often and well.

SOURCES:

Cantwell, Robert. *When We Were Good: The Folk Revival.* Cambridge, MA: Harvard University Press, 1996.

Denisoff, R. Serge. *Great Day Coming: Folk Music and the American Left.* Urbana, IL: University of Illinois Press, 1971.

Duberman, Martin. *Paul Robeson.* NY: Alfred A. Knopf, 1988.

Dunaway, David King. *How Can I Keep from Singing: Pete Seeger.* NY: McGraw-Hill, 1981.

Fariello, Griffin. *Red Scare: Memories of the American Inquisition, An Oral History.* NY: W.W. Norton, 1995.

Gilbert, Ronnie. *Ronnie Gilbert on Mother Jones: Face to Face with the Most Dangerous Woman in America.* Berkeley, CA: Conari Press, 1993.

—— and Herbert Haufrecht. *Travelin' on with the Weavers.* NY: Harper and Row, 1966.

—— and Robert De Cormier. *The Weavers' Songbook.* NY: Harper and Row, 1960.

Hampton, Wayne. *Guerrilla Minstrels.* Knoxville, TN: University of Tennessee Press, 1986.

Jackson, Bruce. "The Folksong Revival," in *New York Folklore.* Vol. 11, no. 1–4, 1985, pp. 195–203.

Klein, Joe. *Woody Guthrie: A Life.* NY: Alfred A. Knopf, 1980.

Lieberman, Robbie. *"My Song Is My Weapon": People's Songs, American Communism, and the Politics of Culture, 1930–1950.* Urbana, IL: University of Illinois Press, 1995.

Mackey, Heather. "Ronnie Gilbert: Resurrecting Mother Jones," in *American Theatre.* Vol. 10, no. 7–8. July–August, 1993, pp. 47–48.

Matusow, Harvey Marshall. *False Witness.* NY: Cameron & Kahn, 1955.

Mitchell, Pam. "Ronnie Gilbert: 'We are either going to make it together or we're not going to make it,'" in *The Progressive.* Vol. 54, no. 6. June 1990, pp. 32–35.

Post, Laura. *Backstage Pass: Interviews with Women in Music.* Norwich, VT: New Victoria Publishers, 1997.

Reuss, Richard. "American Folklore and Left-Wing Politics, 1927–1957." Ph.D. Dissertation, Indiana University, 1971.

Rodnitzky, Jerome. *Minstrels of the Dawn: The Folk-Protest Singer as a Cultural Hero.* Chicago: Nelson-Hall, 1976.

Spector, Bert. "The Weavers: A Case History in Show Business Blacklisting," in *Journal of American Culture.* Vol. 5, no. 3. Fall 1982, pp. 113–120.

Spector, Bert Alan. "'Wasn't That a Time?': Pete Seeger and the Anti-Communist Crusade, 1940–1968." Ph.D. dissertation, University of Missouri—Columbia, 1977.

Willens, Doris. *Lonesome Traveler: The Life of Lee Hays.* NY: W.W. Norton, 1988.

RELATED MEDIA:

Brown, Jim. "The Weavers: Wasn't That a Time!," Warner Reprise Video, 1992.

John Haag,
Associate Professor of History,
University of Georgia, Athens, Georgia

Gilbreth, Lillian Moller (1878–1972)

*American engineer, industrial psychologist, household efficiency expert, pioneer in management theory, inventor of the field of scientific management, and mother of 12 children. Born Lillian Evelyn Moller on May 24, 1878, in Oakland, California; died of a stroke in Scottsdale, Arizona, on January 2, 1972; oldest daughter of nine children of William Moller (a partner in a successful retail hardware business) and Annie (Delger) Moller (daughter of a wealthy Oakland real-estate developer); University of California at Berkeley, B.A. in literature, 1900; University of California at Berkeley, M.A. in English, 1902; Brown University, Ph.D. in psychology, 1915; earned 13 additional master's and doctoral degrees in science, engineering, letters, and psychology at Rutgers, Brown, Michigan, Syracuse, and Temple, 1928–52; married Frank Bunker Gilbreth, on October 19, 1904 (died 1924); children (all have middle names of Bunker or Moller): **Anne Gilbreth Barney** (who married Robert E. Barney); Mary Elizabeth (died at a young age); Ernestine Gilbreth Carey (who married Charles E. Carey); **Martha Gilbreth Tallman** (who married Richard E. Tallman); Frank Gilbreth, Jr.; William Gilbreth; **Lillian Gilbreth Johnson** (who married Donald D. Johnson); Frederick Gilbreth; Daniel Gilbreth; John (known as Jack) Gilbreth; Robert Gilbreth; **Jane Gilbreth Heppes** (who married G. Paul Heppes, Jr.).*

Was the first to introduce the concept of the psychology of scientific management (1911); with her husband, established the consulting engineering firm, Gilbreth, Inc., in Providence, Rhode Island, and later in Montclair, New Jersey, where a laboratory and school of scientific management for managers, educators, and other professionals was located in their home (1910–20); named honorary member of Society of Industrial Engineers (women were not admitted at that time); following husband's death (1924), headed Gilbreth, Inc., and became lecturer at Purdue University, then full professor of management in School of Mechanical Engineering (1935–48), the first woman in that position; served as a member of the President's Emergency Committee for Unemployment Relief (1930); honored by American Women as one of ten outstanding women of the year (1936); replaced Amelia Earhart as consultant at Purdue on careers for women (1939); made an honorary life member of the Engineering Woman's Club (1940); was head of the Department of Personnel Relations at Newark School of Engineering (1941–43); served as educational advisor to the Office of War Information during World War II and member of the Civil Defense Advisory

Commission (1951); awarded Gantt Medal by the American Society of Mechanical Engineers (1944); given the American Women's Association Award for Eminent Achievement (1948); appointed visiting professor of management at the University of Wisconsin at Madison (1955); was the first woman to receive the Hoover Medal for distinguished public service by an engineer; honored by the American Society of Mechanical Engineers with the Gilbreth Medal, awarded during the Gilbreth Centennial marking the 100th anniversary of Frank Gilbreth's birth (1968). Honorary degrees awarded throughout her life from such institutions as the University of California, Smith College, Brown University, and Rutgers; she was also an honorary member of Phi Beta Kappa.

Selected writings: The Psychology of Management *(1914); books co-authored with her husband include* Motion Study, A Primer of Scientific Management *(1912),* Motion Models *(1915),* Fatigue Study *(1916),* Applied Motion Study *(1917), and* Motion Study for the Handicapped *(1920); other writings include* The Quest for the One Best Way: A Sketch of the Life of Frank Bunker Gilbreth *(1926),* The Home-Maker and Her Job *(1927),* Living with Our Children *(1928), (with Edna Yost)* Normal Lives for the Disabled *(1944),* Management in the Home *(1954); contributed chapter on "Women in Industry" to* American Women: The Changing Image *(1962), and many articles in popular magazines such as* Better Homes and Gardens *and* Good Housekeeping.

Lillian Moller Gilbreth's life was remarkable. Following her marriage, a shy Lillian was encouraged by her husband Frank to work with him as a partner in their innovative consulting business that sought to change attitudes towards workers and increase their productivity. By 1921, at her induction as an honorary member of the Society of Industrial Engineers, she was cited as "the first to recognize that management is a problem of psychology, and her book, *The Psychology of Management,* was the first to show this fact to both the managers and the psychologists." Seven years previous, the same ground-breaking book had been attributed to "L.M. Gilbreth," because the publisher feared using a woman's name on such subject matter. When Frank Gilbreth died in 1924, Lillian stepped out of her socially defined role as "Frank's helpmate" and, for the next 50 years, became a pioneer in industrial engineering and management in her own right. She also raised their 12 children.

The first-born of nine siblings, Lillian Evelyn Moller was the daughter of William and

Annie Delger Moller, a wealthy couple of German heritage who were leading citizens of Oakland, California. Because she was an extremely introverted child, Lillian was tutored at home until she was nine, then attended public schools. The Mollers encouraged her early interest in poetry and music; as a high school student, Lillian studied with composer John Metcalfe and wrote the lyrics for "Sunrise," one of his popular melodies of the 1890s. Annie Moller, who was prone to illness, entrusted the upbringing of her youngest daughter Josephine to Lillian, who soon learned to schedule her time carefully.

After overcoming her father's initial objections to women attending college, Lillian entered the University of California at Berkeley and excelled. "I had decided very young that since I couldn't be pretty, I *had* to be smart," wrote Gilbreth. By the time she graduated in 1900 with a major in English and a minor in psychology, she managed to set aside her diffidence long enough to become the first female commence-

Lillian Moller Gilbreth

ment speaker at the college. She then traveled to New York, having been advised to study at Columbia University for a master's in English with Professor Brander Matthews. Upon enrollment, however, she was told that he, and many other male professors, refused to accept female graduate students.

Before long, sick with pleurisy, she returned to California to pursue her master's degree, then a Ph.D. In 1903, Lillian interrupted her doctoral work to accompany friends on a trip to Europe. En route, the travelers stopped in Boston where their chaperon **Minnie Bunker** introduced Lillian to her cousin, an up-and-coming builder named Frank Bunker Gilbreth who had "a yacht, smoked cigars, and had a reputation as a snappy dresser," wrote Frank Gilbreth, Jr. and **Ernestine Gilbreth Carey** in their bestseller *Cheaper by the Dozen*. He also had a reputation for being fast. Frank was a speed builder who had earned international recognition for designing techniques to maximize productivity, and he had offices in New York, Boston, and London. Starting as an apprentice bricklayer, he had worked his way up in the construction business. As industries developed, businesses valued the speed and quality in building that Frank Gilbreth could deliver.

Age needn't determine what one is able to do. It's really a matter of marshaling your resources, using time sensibly and well.

—**Lillian Moller Gilbreth**

That November, when 25-year-old Lillian returned from Europe, 36-year-old Frank met the boat and followed her back to Oakland where he proposed, promising a partnership in career and family. When they married on October 19, 1904, the Oakland paper reported the event: "Although a graduate of the University of California, the bride is nonetheless an extremely attractive young woman." Biographer **Edna Yost** assessed the marriage as "primarily of the husband's inception and the wife's creative acquiescence." Frank had "almost no sense of personal limitations and living with him helped [Lillian] discover her own limitations were sometimes of self-imposed origins."

At the time, although there was no formalized science of management, Frank had already invented work systems and labor-saving devices, for what he termed time-and-motion study, that anticipated the pioneering work that he would pursue with Lillian Gilbreth. Immediately, Lillian began learning management techniques of business and technology. Frank took her along on construction jobs, where she climbed scaffolding and inspected brickwork. She even learned how to run a small steam engine. As a bricklayer, Frank had invented a rising scaffold that held the loose bricks and mortar level with the top of the emerging wall so workers did not waste time bending down for bricks. The Gilbreths would study a worker's motion, cut down on the amount of motion, and redesign machinery to cut down even further.

Lillian wanted a large family, but it was Frank who settled on the number 12. When Lillian cheerfully inquired as to how she could have so many children and a career, Frank replied that as a team they could do anything and do it successfully. "We teach management," he said, "so we shall have to practice it." Over the next 17 years, Lillian Gilbreth would give birth to six girls and six boys.

With their first four girls—Anne, Mary (who would die of diphtheria in 1912), Ernestine, and Martha—the Gilbreths moved to Plainfield, New Jersey, where Frank, Jr., was born. Although Frank Sr., continued to work in the construction business through 1911, Lillian saw her husband as an engineer, not a contractor. Frank encouraged Lillian to pursue psychology rather than English for her doctorate. When Brown University agreed to let her do original research for her thesis on the application of psychology to industry, the Gilbreths moved to Providence, Rhode Island, in 1912, to accommodate Lillian's studies.

In the summer of 1913, the Gilbreths launched the first of four summer schools of scientific management for professors of psychology, engineering, economics, and other allied fields. (The summer schools would continue at Pennsylvania State College.) By 1915, Lillian had earned her doctorate in Applied Management and given birth to her sixth child William. Young Lillian, Fred, Dan, and Jack would also be born in Providence.

As outlined in *Cheaper by the Dozen,* the Gilbreths managed their household with their own techniques. They instituted a Family Council which organized work and made decisions. For extra pocket money, children put in sealed bids for jobs that went to the lowest bidder. Purchasing committees were responsible for food, clothes, furniture, and athletic equipment, even making a deal with one store for wholesale rates; a gift buyer bought the presents for everyone's birthday. "When it came to apportioning work on an aptitude basis, the smaller girls were assigned to dust the legs and lower shelves of furniture; the older girls to dust table tops and upper shelves." The older boys would push the lawnmowers, the younger ones would do the weeding.

A projects committee monitored work schedules, and a utilities committee fined those who wasted water and electricity. When one brother discovered that a dripping faucet had filled the bathtub, he roused the sleeping culprit and insisted that he take a second bath so as not to waste the water. The children soon learned that council meetings could be used for their own advantage and once moved to spend five dollars they had saved to buy a puppy. Though Frank was horrified, convinced that any animal that did not lay eggs was a luxury, Lillian seconded the motion.

Frank and Lillian founded and worked as partners in the consulting engineering firm of Gilbreth, Inc. Their first contract was with the New England Butt Company. Their goal: to increase productivity and eliminate workers' fa-

tigue. Workers were more important than the tools they used, maintained the Gilbreths, and they should not be slaves to them. The benefits: more efficient workers, more profitable businesses, and industrial harmony. Using motion pictures, Frank illustrated how workers' motions could be simplified. Lillian pointed out that fatigue on the job was not only physical but psychological.

They demonstrated the "one best way" of doing work. "Multiplying the number of bricks laid in constructing one large building alone," writes Yost, "the waste motions of the workmen were tremendous. But multiplied by the number of bricks used everywhere year after year, the number of waste motions, costing human strength and human fatigue, became almost astronomical." Motion-study expert Frank could "always find the most efficient work plan that would use the fewest and easiest motions, but psychologist Lillian was quick to understand whether those so-called 'best' motions gave also the happiest results for the people who used them; for nothing could really be 'best' that did

From the movie Cheaper by the Dozen, *based on the life of Lillian Gilbreth.*

not take into account the way those who used them felt about them." Their consulting practice became international, and American clients included Eastman Kodak and U.S. Rubber. From 1910 to 1920, the Gilbreths promoted their concepts through lectures, professional association meetings, and publications.

Frank Gilbreth could charge high fees for consulting jobs because clients saw quick results in profitability. The fees supported not only the family but the Gilbreths' research which became a family affair. While Lillian held the stopwatch, Frank buttoned his vest from the bottom up, rather than top down: bottom-up took three seconds while top down took seven. When the Remington Company hired Gilbreth, Inc., to help develop the world's fastest typist through motion-study techniques, the Gilbreths enlisted the children to learn to touch type in two weeks, using incentives such as a white typewriter with blind keys to spur them on. Frank color coordinated the children's fingers to the correct typewriter keys and documented their movements on film. On all these experiments, Lillian would take her turn with the children to see if the effects were salutary for the workers.

Though they had a business staff, Lillian was Frank's only partner. The true dimension of her contribution to modern industrial engineering, according to **G. Kass-Simon** and **Patricia Farnes**, has "not been understood or widely discussed by historians or by engineers." Her expertise focused on the integration of psychology and mental processes with time-and-motion study, but historians only refer to her contributions to domestic engineering, the design of kitchens and appliances. On consulting jobs, she would visit each plant at least once, preferably when the initial survey was to be conducted. She would observe all aspects of the operation and talk to the workers, seeking their advice for better efficiency, eliciting their level of satisfaction.

At the Dartmouth College Conference on Scientific Management, Lillian Gilbreth was the first to publicly introduce the psychology of management. Though workers were the most essential part of industry, she told the group, they were receiving scant attention. But, writes Yost, while Frank was alive, Lillian "would never lay claim to being anything more than her husband's pupil and helper though partner she certainly became." Despite close collaboration, publications reporting on their work for the construction aspect of their business, including *Field Systems, Concrete System,* and *Bricklaying System,* only indicate Frank Gilbreth as author. Other collaborations with her husband included management classics: *Motion Study, A Primer of Scientific Management, Motion Models, Fatigue Study, Applied Motion Study,* and *Motion Study for the Handicapped.*

Based on her Ph.D. research, Lillian's *The Psychology of Management* (1914) is considered a major contribution to the field. Although others were studying industrial psychology, Lillian Gilbreth consolidated the basic components of management theory—knowledge of individual behavior, the theory of groups, the theory of communication, and a rational basis of decision-making. She succeeded in translating time-and-motion study into fundamental modern management practices. Frank and Frederick Taylor, who was also a major proponent of scientific management, were not professionally trained in psychology to analyze connections between psychology, management, and work. Her sensitivity to the human aspects of work differed from Taylor and was a harbinger of sensitivity training popular in management circles in the 1960s.

Enlisting in the army during World War I, Frank was commissioned a major in the Engineers Officers Reserve Corps and soon became involved in revamping jobs and redesigning machinery to meet the needs of disabled soldiers. At Fort Sill, in Oklahoma, his assignment was to make films for new recruits in an effort to shorten their training. When Frank became ill with rheumatism and severe uremic poisoning, he worked long-distance with Lillian, sending his film to her and consulting with her on how to hold the interest of the recruits. After taking her own children to the movies, watching their reaction and questioning them, she wrote back to Frank with some suggestions.

Even when family crises, like Frank's illness, occurred, and uncertainty over Frank's bad heart became a part of her life, Lillian Gilbreth resorted to Frank's work philosophy: she would survey the situation, lay out the job, and decide on the "one best" way to handle it. During his long convalescence at The Shoe, their new summer house in Nantucket, he worked jointly with Lillian, selecting clients carefully to reduce the strain. By the time they moved to a 14-room house in Montclair, New Jersey, in 1920, they were both overworked; there were papers to write, children's education to monitor, some financial problems, and new babies. Bob had just been born in Nantucket. (Jane, the last child, would be born in the Nantucket Cottage Hospital in June 1922, the only child not born at home.)

Motion study had its detractors in the Taylor camp which rankled Frank. His paper, "Time Study and Motion Study as Fundamental Factors in Planning and Control: An Indictment of Stop-Watch Time Study," created controversy; conflict made Lillian uncomfortable, and the lack of recognition hurt them both. Some vindication came with Lillian's honorary membership in the Society of Industrial Engineers.

Frank, enjoying renown abroad, traveled constantly around the world on consulting jobs and promoted motion study with missionary zeal. But, on June 14, 1924, days before he and Lillian were to sail to Europe for several important conferences, Frank Gilbreth dropped dead of a heart attack. "There was a change in mother," wrote the Gilbreth siblings:

> A change in looks and a change in manner. Before her marriage, all Mother's decisions had been made by her parents. After the marriage, the decisions were made by Dad. . . . While Dad lived, Mother was afraid of fast driving, of airplanes, of walking alone at night. When there was lightning, she went in a dark closet and held her ears. When things went wrong at dinner, she sometimes burst into tears and had to leave the table. She made public speeches, but she dreaded them. Now, suddenly, she wasn't afraid any more, because there was nothing to be afraid of. Now nothing could upset her because the thing that mattered most had been upset. None of us ever saw her weep again.

With her eldest child only 18 and all her children still living at home, Lillian Gilbreth called a Family Council. There was little money, she told them, because most had gone back into the business. Therefore, they could move back to Oakland to live with their grandmother or they could stay in Montclair with the children running the house while she would continue Frank's work. The children voted to stay in Montclair, and Lillian set out for Europe, despite her shyness, to give Frank's speeches to the World Power Conference in London and the First International Congress of Scientific Management (created at Frank's suggestion) at the Masaryk Academy in Prague.

Although the large corporations canceled consulting contracts with her when Frank died, convinced that a woman could not command the respect needed from shop foremen to handle the job, Lillian Gilbreth was determined to keep her husband's work alive. She would remain in business and promote research projects, spread his ideas and techniques to new generations, and seek new clients. She would also see to it that her 11 children went to college. "The speech in Chicago will go for Martha's new overcoat," she'd say. "The one in Detroit will be for Ernestine's college wardrobe."

Johnson & Johnson suggested that she start a school in the Montclair home to offer Gilbreth-style training, which she did for six years. She addressed fatigue problems for Macy's department store through micromotion techniques. She reconnected with her husband's international contacts and presided over the first summer school of an international association created to study human relations. According to Yost, Gilbreth had a talent for mediating, viewing work as "the constructive channel of cooperation between management and the worker."

Lillian had to work hard to counteract the critics. A textbook *Scientific Management since Taylor* was published with no mention of the Gilbreths' motion studies, and misstatements of Frederick Taylor about the Gilbreths' motion-study work, which had been made 14 years earlier, were reprinted. She lectured frequently, emphasizing motion study as an essential part of industrial engineering curricula, and spurred the establishment by 1930 of motion-study laboratories at several colleges. *The Engineering Index* finally included "motion study" as an independent classification. Lillian continued to write. *The Quest of the One Best Way: A Sketch of the Life of Frank Bunker Gilbreth* was published in America as well as Germany and Czechoslovakia in 1925 and 1926. As a management consultant, she measured and observed 4,000 homemakers to evaluate their movements doing chores in the home, resulting in her 1927 book, *The Home-Maker and Her Job.*

The stock-market crash in 1929 stimulated the acceptance of improved management; economic opportunity meant survival. In the 1930s, Dr. Gilbreth served on the President's Emergency Committee for Employment, organizing a "Share the Work" program that involved women's club members around the country. From 1929 to 1933, she served on the New Jersey State Board of Regents.

In 1935, at age 57, having originally replaced Frank as a lecturer at Purdue, Lillian returned there as the first woman professor of management on an engineering school faculty. For 13 years, until she retired from Purdue in 1948, she not only taught but also researched diverse disciplines; the motion-and-time-study lab she helped create served students in the School of Agriculture and students in the School of Home Economics. She also replaced *Amelia

Earhart as career advisor to women students after Earhart's disappearance. As a student, Gilbreth earned another 13 master's and doctoral degrees in various arts and sciences at universities around the country between 1928 and 1952. She was head of the Department of Personnel Relations at the Newark College of Engineering from 1941 to 1943, which developed students' aptitudes and taught them how to handle personnel problems. Gilbreth also lectured at Bryn Mawr and was a professor of management at Rutgers.

World War II was yet another spur toward modern management. Wartime industries sought easier ways to do work, and the Gilbreth technique applied to everything from training films to process charts. At 65, Lillian Gilbreth worked as a consultant for rehabilitation of disabled war veterans, and *Normal Lives for the Disabled*, written with Edna Yost, was published in 1944. As a consultant to New York University Medical Center's Institute for Rehabilitative Medicine in 1950 when she was almost 80, Lillian designed features that could ease the lives of disabled homemakers, enabling them to use one hand to break an egg, open a can, or peel a potato. "Mother really loved work," one of her daughters recalled; she was not just working to support her family.

Gilbreth received numerous honors. In 1940, she was made an honorary life member of the Engineering Women's Club. In 1944, the American Society of Mechanical Engineers and the American Management Association had jointly awarded the Gilbreths the Gantt Medal "in recognition of their pioneer work in management and their development of the principles and techniques of motion study." The Wallace Clark Award in 1951 recognized "thirty years of service in applications of scientific management principles in industry." *American Women* chose her in 1936 as one of the ten outstanding women of the year, and the American Women's Association chose her as Woman of the Year in 1948. During the Gilbreth Centennial, sponsored by the American Society of Mechanical Engineers in December 1968 to mark Frank Gilbreth's birth, Dr. Howard Rusk, director of the Institute of Rehabilitation Medicine, called the Gilbreths' contribution to rehabilitation of the disabled "a phenomenal one both in concept and substance."

Lillian Gilbreth, who died of a stroke in 1972 in Scottsdale, Arizona, at age 93, also left a personal legacy—her family of 12 children and their numerous offspring. Three of her children were engineers, several were homemakers, and there was a journalist, a schoolteacher, an exporter, and a department store buyer. *Cheaper by the Dozen* and *Belles on Their Toes* became bestsellers and then popular films, both starring *Myrna Loy. Lillian Gilbreth, wrote Yost, was a "management engineer who understands that industry's most important problem is the human being who works in it."

SOURCES:

Gilbreth, Frank B., Jr. *Time Out for Happiness*. NY: Thomas Y. Crowell, 1970.

———, and Ernestine Gilbreth Carey. *Cheaper by the Dozen*. NY: Thomas Y. Crowell, 1948.

Kass-Simon, G., and Patricia Farnes, eds. *Women of Science: Righting the Record*. Bloomington, IN: Indiana University Press, 1990.

Krebs, Albin. *The New York Times*, January 3, 1972, p. 30.

Rothe, Ann, ed. *Current Biography*. NY: H.W. Wilson, 1951.

Sicherman, Barbara, and Carol Hurd Green, eds. *Notable American Women: The Modern Period*. Cambridge, MA: Belknap Press-Harvard University, 1980.

Stoddard, Hope. *Famous American Women*. NY: H.W. Wilson, 1970.

Yost, Edna. *Frank and Lillian Gilbreth: Partners for Life*. New Brunswick, NJ: Rutgers University Press, 1949.

SUGGESTED READING:

Gilbreth, Lillian M. *Living with Our Children*. NY: W.W. Norton, 1928.

———. *The Psychology of Management*. NY: Sturgis and Walton, 1914.

May, Elizabeth Eckhardt. "Lillian Moller Gilbreth, 1878-1972," in *Journal of Home Economics*. April 1972, pp. 13–16 (information about Gilbreth's work for the disabled).

Spriegel, William R., and Clark E. Meyers, eds. *The Writings of the Gilbreths*. Homewood: Richard D. Irwin, 1953.

RELATED MEDIA:

Belles on Their Toes (89 mins.), starring Myrna Loy, Jeanne Crain, **Debra Paget**, Jeffrey Hunter, Edward Arnold, Hoagy Carmichael, **Barbara Bates**, Robert Arthur, **Verna Felton**, and Martin Milner, directed by Henry Levin, 1952 (sequel to *Cheaper by the Dozen*).

Cheaper by the Dozen (85 min.), starring Clifton Webb, Myrna Loy, *Jeanne Crain, *Mildred Natwick, Edgar Buchanan, directed by Walter Lang, 1950.

COLLECTIONS:

Lillian Gilbreth Collection, Department of Special Collections and Archives, Purdue University Library, contains professional and personal correspondence, films, photographs and other visual media, newspaper clippings, and conference records. (The Frank Gilbreth Collection also is located at Purdue.)

Laurie Norris,
intercultural relations consultant
and freelance writer, New York, New York

Gilder, Jeannette Leonard (1849–1916).

See Blanc, Marie-Therese for sidebar.

Gildersleeve, Virginia Crocheron

(1877–1965)

Outstanding educator and dean of Barnard College, during the years of its greatest development, who was also U.S. delegate to the UN conference held at San Francisco in 1945, thereby holding the highest political appointment then given to an American woman.
Born Virginia Crocheron Gildersleeve on October 3, 1877, in New York City; died in Centerville, Massachusetts, on July 7, 1965; daughter of Henry Alger Gildersleeve (a judge) and Virginia (Crocheron) Gildersleeve; attended Brearley School; graduated Barnard College, A.B., 1899; Columbia University, A.M., 1900; Columbia University, Ph.D., 1908; never married; lived with Elizabeth Reynard (a professor of English at Barnard); no children.

Was an instructor in English, Barnard College (1900–07, 1908–10), assistant professor (1910–11), and professor and dean (1911–47); served as U.S. delegate to United Nations conference on international organization in San Francisco (1945).

Selected publications: Government Regulation of the Elizabethan Drama *(Columbia University Press, 1908);* Many a Good Crusade *(Columbia University Press, 1954);* A Hoard for Winter *(Columbia University Press, 1962).*

One December day in 1910, while riding on the uptown elevated train in New York City, Nicholas Murray Butler, the president of Columbia University, chanced upon an old acquaintance. "Judge Gildersleeve," said Butler, "I have good news for you. I've decided to make your daughter dean of Barnard." Judge **Henry Gildersleeve** paused a moment, then commented, "I am not surprised." Though only after her tenure was the title changed from dean to president, one thing was certain: the appointment eventually launched Virginia Crocheron Gildersleeve into the position of being an internationally known leader of women's education in the United States.

Virginia Gildersleeve was born in New York City on October 3, 1877, the youngest of five children born to Virginia Crocheron Gildersleeve, for whom she was named, and to Henry Alger Gildersleeve. Her father was an eminent city jurist, serving successively as judge in the Court of General Sessions (a criminal court), the superior court, and the state supreme court. Raised in a brick house with brownstone trim just off Fifth Avenue, Virginia grew up amid upper-middle class comfort. "We were not 'in society' exactly," she would later write. "We were professional people." The household did,

however, maintain two fulltime maids. Nonetheless, Virginia experienced personal tragedy when a brother died of typhoid fever as she was just turning 14. "At that moment a black curtain cut my life in two," she said.

Gildersleeve attended the Brearley School, whose headmaster, James Croswell, sought to turn adolescent girls into budding scholars. In 1895, she entered Barnard College, which occupied a shabby brownstone on Madison Avenue. She later referred to herself as "a shy, snobbish, solemn freshman" but soon found she was quite popular. Though Barnard was still small and poor, Gildersleeve claimed that its tie to Columbia University gave her an education without parallel. She was taught by a succession of renowned Barnard and Columbia faculty, including George Odell in English, Nicholas Murray Butler in philosophy, and Franklin Giddings in sociology. *Emily James Putnam*, Barnard's dean and professor of Greek, made a particularly profound impression on her, contributing what Gildersleeve recalled as "exhilaration of adventure, illumination of the mind, and great joy in beauty." She later termed historian James Harvey Robinson "by far the greatest teacher I have ever studied with."

Gildersleeve, who received her A.B. in 1899, was elected to Phi Beta Kappa, graduated first in her class, and was class president. Winning the Fiske Graduate Scholarship in Political Science, in 1900 she received an A.M. in medieval history from Columbia. Robinson directed her thesis, a critical bibliography entitled "Some Materials for Judging the Actual Workings of Feudalism in France—Twelfth and Thirteenth Centuries." Shortly thereafter, she began teaching English composition and argumentation at Barnard. Her salary: $250 a year.

In 1908, Gildersleeve was awarded a Ph.D. in English and comparative literature from Columbia, having completed the doctoral program in three years. A leading Shakespearean scholar, Ashley Thorndike, directed her dissertation. That year, Columbia University Press published Gildersleeve's thesis under the title *Government Regulation of the Elizabethan Drama*. In 1908, she also joined the Barnard faculty as lecturer, directing the required sophomore program in English and teaching a course on Shakespeare at Columbia. In 1910, she was promoted to the rank of assistant professor of English and was elected secretary of the faculty. She held, she later said, a "magnificent teaching position, probably the best one held by any woman in the whole United States, or indeed the world."

Gildersleeve turned down the offer of an associate professorship from the University of Wisconsin because she did not want to leave her parents, with whom she would live until their deaths in 1923. In December 1910, when she was only 33, Nicholas Murray Butler—then Columbia's president—offered her the deanship of Barnard as well as the rank of full professor. Reluctant, she accepted only on the ground that she receive autonomy in hiring and fiscal matters. Indeed, Gildersleeve turned the Barnard deanship into the equivalent of a presidency. She possessed much freedom, dealing with a separate board of trustees and drawing up the budget. Having held office in Barnard's alumnae association, she had a working knowledge of the school's graduates.

During the 36 years she held the college's highest office, the name of Virginia Gildersleeve was synonymous with that of Barnard. "Miss Gildersleeve was Barnard," Barnard faculty member, Joseph Gerard Brennan, once noted to contemporaries, "just as de Gaulle was France." According to *The New York Times*, Gildersleeve was sparely built, of medium size:

> She had startling dark and brilliant eyes gleaming out under heavy curved eyebrows. Her nose was finely chiseled, her lips restrained and thin, and her voice was rich, her hair dark. . . . She moved briskly about in English tweeds and Queen Mary-like hats, like "a well-oiled steam engine," as one officer of Barnard once said of her.

Author *Alice Duer Miller, whose friendship with Gildersleeve went back to undergraduate days, wrote, "Everyone knows that the Dean is a good executive, a magnificent speaker, a wise woman, an intellectual, but not everyone knows she can lose her temper over examples of stupidity and spite, and that, therefore, her tact and calm are the more to be admired, since they are achieved and not wholly innate."

It was under Gildersleeve's direction that Barnard gained an international reputation. Always working closely with Butler, she modernized the curriculum. Compulsory Latin was dropped. In the 1920s, Barnard required students to take courses in each of the broad areas of human knowledge and pioneered in the practice of substituting the first year of professional school for the final undergraduate year. Moreover, she added physical education, home economics, and political science to the program and instituted a freshman course that included sex education, a move quite radical at the time. In 1938, acting on the conviction that students should understand the way of life they would soon be called upon to defend, she introduced the budding field of American Studies. During World War II, Gildersleeve saw to it that Barnard became one of the first colleges to establish practical war courses, particularly those centering on mathematics.

During the Gildersleeve administration, Barnard had a number of distinguished faculty members, including Edmund W. Sinnott in botany, Raymond J. Saulnier in economics, Frederic G. Hoffherr in French, Douglas Moore in music, and *Mirra Komarovsky, William F. Ogburn, and Robert MacIver in sociology. Raymond Moley, later one of Franklin D. Roosevelt's brain-trusters, headed Barnard's government department. History was particularly strong, possessing such names as René Albrecht-Carrié, Basil Rauch, David Saville Muzzey, and Edward Meade Earle. Prominent visiting scholars included British medievalist *Eileen Power and Tudor specialist A.F. Pollard. The services of distinguished Columbia professors were utilized, including Douglas Moore in music, Allan Nevins in history, and Hoxie Fairchild in English.

As a matter of policy, Gildersleeve promoted only those female junior faculty whom she saw as "unusually competent." At the same time, she would reserve most senior positions, which required Columbia approval, for males. Only by such means, she maintained, would there be a needed balance between the sexes. Fully aware that militant feminists were accusing her of betraying "our cause," she replied, "In one sense perhaps they were right, for I would always, I think, have placed the welfare of the whole institution above the present advancement of our sex." At the same time, she successfully fought to have Barnard graduates admitted to all of Columbia's professional schools. Architecture and journalism opened their doors quickly, though opening the schools of Medicine, Law, and Engineering took a carefully designed strategy that combined prodding with patience.

During the 1920s, Gildersleeve put Barnard on a healthy financial footing. Even during the Great Depression, the college experienced just a modest retrenchment. Only during her last years was its financial status shaky.

Under her tenure, Barnard pioneered in undergraduate services. Campus facilities were enlarged, a placement office established, and academic advising instituted. An elaborate student center, Barnard Hall, was constructed. Sororities were abolished. The unique Greek games, combining

Virginia
Crocheron
Gildersleeve

athletic contests with originally created performances in the fine arts, became a major event.

By no means did Barnard monopolize Gildersleeve's talents. In 1919, with Bryn Mawr president *Martha Carey Thomas, Gildersleeve helped organize the International Federation of University Women, a body that sought to elevate educational standards through personal contacts. Serving twice as its president, she presided at sessions in Krakow (1936) and Stockholm (1939). She also chaired the American Council on Education and was instrumental in the founding of the Seven College Conference of Women's Colleges. Her francophile sympathies inspired her to become board chair of Reid Hall, a center for visiting scholars in Paris.

Given her many involvements, Gildersleeve was one of America's leading advocates of higher education for women. She once said:

> There seems to survive in some quarters the antique idea that a woman who is a graduate from college is thereby necessarily and inevitably a portentously learned and scholastic person, quite removed from the ordinary run of human beings, an inspirer of awe in the rest of the world. Yet, I have never discovered that the young man graduated from Columbia or Yale or Harvard is looked upon as necessarily a paragon of learning, rather the opposite.

Gildersleeve opposed the "double curriculum," by which high school girls who were headed for college were separated from those who were not. Such practice, she believed, could discriminate unjustly against those "late bloomers" who discovered themselves fully capable of education beyond high school. Wives and mothers, she further maintained, needed college training just as much as working women.

Early in her career, Gildersleeve undertook major civic tasks. During World War I, she coordinated activities of several women's war-work organizations. Appointed by New York mayor John Purroy Mitchell to the city's Committee of Women on National Defense, she devised a program whereby urban young women would serve as farm volunteers. Under her leadership, nearly 80% of Barnard's student body devoted spare time to the war effort. She chaired the University Committee on Women's War Work and was a member of the Committee on War Service Training for American Women, in which capacities she traveled frequently to Washington. Always a strong advocate of international cooperation, she spoke on behalf of the League to Enforce Peace and later the League of Nations Associa-

tion. A Democrat, she campaigned for Al Smith and later Franklin D. Roosevelt for president.

During the 1940s, Gildersleeve's internationalism became even more visible. In the fall of November 1939, Columbia historian James T. Shotwell appointed her to the Commission to Study the Organization of the Peace, a 28-member research body that met weekly for five years to study world organization. In the late spring of 1940, she joined William Allen White's Committee to Defend America by Aiding the Allies. That June, in a radio broadcast, she warned that the U.S. faced great perils if Britain and France fell.

World War II found Gildersleeve more active than ever. Although many Barnard faculty engaged in some form of war employment work "for the duration," she was able to manage a greatly increased student body with a skeletal staff. Even before the Japanese attacked Pearl Harbor, she attended national meetings in Washington on women and defense. From 1942 to 1945, she chaired the advisory council of the women's reserve of the navy. Called the WAVES, or Women Accepted for Volunteer Emergency Service, the unit involved some 80,000 women.

Gildersleeve visited England in 1943, where she witnessed the British system of army education. Upon her return, she urged the United States to adopt some form of adult education for the armed forces. Noting their prominent role in wartime Britain, she accused the U.S. Congress of treating females as though they were "perishable dolls rather than sturdy, respectable citizens." Indeed, she favored conscription of women, believing it "hard for our young women to expect all the rights and privileges of citizenship without owing any required service in exchange."

During the war, Gildersleeve repeatedly urged the American people to avoid hatred. Towards its end, she called for exiling Hitler and claimed that all Germany should suffer a hard peace. "After all, " she said, "this is the third time that Germany has behaved like this. It isn't all Hitler. The German people must take some responsibility."

In February 1945, Gildersleeve was one of the six American delegates, and the only woman member, to the San Francisco conference convened to draft the charter of the United Nations. "For some weeks," she said, "I was the most conspicuous woman in the United States." Once the plenary sessions had ended, she did not play a leading role in such controversial matters as the veto and the seating of Poland and Argentina. Rather, she was assigned to two technical committees, one dealing with the actual charter draft and the other focusing on economic and social cooperation. It was Gildersleeve, with her aide **Elizabeth Reynard** (1897–1962), who drafted the opening of the preamble which read:

WE THE PEOPLES OF THE UNITED NATIONS

Determined to save succeeding generations from the scourge of war, which in our time has brought untold sorrow to mankind . . .

Gildersleeve also had a hand in the very name of the organization: the United Nations. When most of the Latin nations called for a collective noun—such as league, union, or association—she formally advanced the American position, declaring that it had been the term favored by the late President Roosevelt:

As I look back over the years, Mr. Chairman, to some of the darkest moments of this war, when it seemed as if victory for the cause of all of us was perhaps impossible, I begin to feel that perhaps some particular good fortune, some talisman of good luck, is attached to the name of the United Nations.

One of the creators of the United Nations Educational, Scientific and Cultural Organization (UNESCO), Gildersleeve pushed to have the word "educational" as part of the title. She drafted Article 55 of the UN Charter, dealing with economic and social cooperation. In 1947, she was appointed an alternate delegate to the General Assembly but was too ill to serve.

In March 1946, Gildersleeve was a member of the U.S. Educational Mission to Japan. In helping the Japanese design a restructuring of their educational system, she vigorously opposed those delegation members who sought to impose far more egalitarian American practices. She was particularly critical of any desire to eliminate a merit system, warning that "in a democracy it was absolutely essential that there should be able, trained, highly educated leaders."

For many years, Gildersleeve took an active interest in Middle Eastern affairs, being long influenced by such figures as diplomat Charles R. Crane, archeologist James Henry Breasted, and historian George Antonius. In 1924, she became a board member of the American College for Girls in Istanbul and in 1944 became its chair. She was also a board member of the Near East College Association, an organization that included American institutions in Turkey, Greece, Bulgaria, Baghdad, and Beirut.

Strongly critical of the Zionist movement, in 1945 she warned against massive Jewish immigration "to a section of the world where they will have as neighbors many millions of enemies." Though attacked by many Zionists for her stand, she found a kindred spirit on Palestinian-Jewish matters in Rabbi Judah Magnes, president of the Hebrew University in Jerusalem. In that same year, she made her own proposal for alleviating the plight of homeless Jews. Every member state of the UN, she said, should accept a proportionate share of such refugees. The U.S. quota, she claimed, would possibly come to 200,000.

In 1948, Gildersleeve became chair of the Committee for Justice and Peace in the Holy Land, an organization that opposed the creation of a Jewish state in Palestine. Leaders included Henry Sloane Coffin, president emeritus of Union Theological Seminary, and Rabbi Moses Lazeron, a leading member of the National Conference of Christians and Jews. In her memoirs, she wrote that she considered the proposed formation of the nation-state of Israel as "directly contrary to our national interests, military, strategic and commercial, as well as to common sense."

Gildersleeve always remained single, forming intense friendships with *Caroline Spurgeon (1869–1942), a prominent British expert on Chaucer, and later Elizabeth Reynard, a professor of English at Barnard and her longtime personal assistant. On the eve of her retirement, which took place in 1947, Gildersleeve sought to have Reynard succeed her as dean. The proposal met with strong opposition from Barnard's trustees and faculty as well as from Columbia president Butler. Upon retirement, Gildersleeve—accompanied by Reynard—moved to a refurbished mansion in Bedford Village, New York, 40 miles north of Manhattan. Here she wrote her memoirs, *Many a Good Crusade* (1954), and edited a collection of articles entitled *A Hoard for Winter* (1962).

During her lifetime, Virginia Gildersleeve received so many honorary degrees that in 1936 the *Literary Digest* claimed she possessed "enough caps and gowns to fill an ordinary New York apartment closet." In 1947, France bestowed its Legion of Honor upon her. In 1969, the Virginia Gildersleeve International Fund for University Women was established. On July 7, 1965, Virginia Crocheron Gildersleeve died of a heart attack in a nursing home in Centerville, Massachusetts.

SOURCES:

Gildersleeve, Virginia Crocheron. *Many a Good Crusade.* NY: Columbia University Press, 1954.

SUGGESTED READING:

Brennan, Joseph Gerard. "Barnard: Gildersleeve & Mrs. Mac," in *The Education of a Prejudiced Mind.* NY: Scribner, 1977.

Miller, Alice Duer, and Susan Myers. *Barnard College: The First Fifty Years.* NY: Columbia University Press, 1939.

White, Marian Churchill. *A History of Barnard College.* NY: Columbia University Press, 1954.

COLLECTIONS:

Gildersleeve's papers are in Special Collections, Columbia University.

Justus D. Doenecke,
professor of history, New College of the
University of South Florida, Sarasota, Florida

Gilette of Narbonne (fl. 1300)

French physician. Flourished around 1300 in Narbonne, France; daughter of Gerard of Narbonne, a physician.

Gilette of Narbonne was a French townswoman, the daughter of the physician Gerard of Narbonne. Gilette learned the science of medicine from her father; after his death, she continued treating his patients. She was a highly respected doctor, and Giovanni Boccaccio wrote of her in one of his books, calling her *Donna Medica* ("Lady Doctor"). It was reported that she was so renowned that the French king summoned her to treat him, and that she cured him of fistula.

Laura York,
Riverside, California

Giliani, Alessandra.

See Trotula for sidebar.

Gillars, Mildred E. (1900–1988)

American-born radio personality who was convicted of wartime treason for broadcasting Nazi propaganda from Germany during World War II. Name variations: Axis Sally; Mildred Gillars Sisk. Born Mildred E. Gillars in Portland Maine, in 1900; died in Columbus, Ohio, on June 25, 1988; attended Ohio Wesleyan College.

Born in 1900 and raised in Portland, Maine, Mildred Gillars tried her hand at acting after college in both New York and Europe, with little success. In Germany at the onset of World War II, she worked as an English teacher before taking the radio position that made her an overnight success and would lead to her imprisonment for treason. "Axis Sally," as she was known, was highly paid for her programs of Nazi propaganda which often began, "Hello, gang. Throw down those little old guns and toddle off home. There's no getting the Germans down." Heard by American and Allied troops in Europe and North Africa, she was also known

to sometimes describe, in graphic terms, how the men on the homefront were seducing the wives the soldiers had left behind. Her notoriety found its way back to the U.S. through the American press and by letters home written by soldiers who served within the sound of her broadcasts.

At the end of the war, Gillars was tracked down and returned to the United States, where, in 1948, she was tried in federal court. By some reports, she said she did it all for love, implicating a staff member of the foreign ministry. In other accounts, she maintained her innocence, pleading that she had been mistaken for another woman broadcasting from Rome and using the same name. Whatever the case, she was convicted on a single count of treason and sentenced to 10 to 30 years in the women's federal prison at Alderson, West Virginia. Another famous inmate then serving time in that penitentiary was said to be *Iva Toguri, better known to American GIs as "Tokyo Rose."

Paroled in 1961, Gillars spent some time with her half sister in Ashtabula, Ohio, and then went off to live and work with the Sisters of the Poor Child Jesus, who ran a girls' boarding school in Columbus. Having been converted to Catholicism in prison, Gillars lived in the convent and received a small salary as a music teacher. Apparently, the parents of the schoolchildren were nonchalant about having the notorious "Axis Sally" in their midst. The Mother Superior praised her as "a good influence on the students," and said she was now living a productive life. In 1973, it is believed that Gillars returned to college to complete a bachelor's degree.

Until her death in 1988, Gillars remained reluctant to discuss the past, avoiding interviews and shunning photographers. To the end, she maintained that she had received an unfair trial.

SOURCES:

Lamparski, Richard. *Whatever Became of . . . ?* 2nd Series. NY: Crown, 1968.

Parrish, Thomas, ed. *The Simon and Schuster Encyclopedia of World War II.* NY: Simon and Schuster, 1978.

Read, Phyllis J., and Bernard L. Witlieb. *The Book of Women's Firsts.* NY: Random House, 1992.

Barbara Morgan,
Melrose, Massachusetts

Gillespie, Mother Angela
(1824–1887)

American educator. Name variations: Eliza Gillespie. Born Eliza Maria Gillespie near Brownsville, Pennsylvania, on February 21, 1824; died at Saint Mary's Convent in South Bend, Indiana, on March 4, 1887; attended private school and a girls' school run by the Dominican Sisters in Somerset, Ohio; graduated from the Visitation Academy in Georgetown, Washington, D.C., 1842.

Mother Angela Gillespie was born Eliza Maria Gillespie near Brownsville, Pennsylvania, on February 21, 1824. In 1853, after years of charitable work and teaching positions in Lancaster, Ohio, and at Saint Mary's Seminary in Maryland, she felt called to the religious life and devoted the remainder of her days to the Sisters of the Holy Cross. Taking her final vows that year, she became director of studies at Saint Mary's Academy in Bertrand, Michigan, and was made superior of the convent in 1855. At the academy (which later became St. Mary's College and was moved to a new site near Notre Dame), Mother Angela, who strongly believed in full educational rights for women, instituted courses in advanced mathematics, science, foreign languages, philosophy, theology, art, and music. In addition to preparing the sisters to teach in Chicago's parochial schools, the order established Saint Angela's Academy in Morris, Illinois. In 1860, Mother Angela began publishing *Metropolitan Readers*, a graded textbook series used in elementary through college courses.

During the Civil War, she supervised some 80 nuns who provided nursing services in army hospitals across the country, as well as aboard hospital ships on the Mississippi. The nuns also converted a riverfront warehouse in Mound City, Illinois, into a 1,500-bed military hospital that became the finest facility of its kind in the country.

Under Mother Angela's direction, the order of the Holy Cross and its educational work was greatly expanded, with 45 institutions founded between 1855 and 1882. In 1866, Mother Angela also began editing *Ave Maria*, a Catholic periodical started by Father Edward Sorin, founder of the University of Notre Dame. When difficulties between American and French branches erupted in 1869, the order helped facilitate an independent American branch with Mother Angela as provincial superior (under authority of Father Sorin as superior), thus establishing her as founder of her order in America.

Barbara Morgan,
Melrose, Massachusetts

Gillespie, Eliza (1824–1887).

See Gillespie, Mother Angela.

Gillian.

Variant of Julia.

Gilman, Caroline Howard
(1794–1888)

American author. Name variations: Caroline Howard; (pseudonym) Clarissa Packard. Born Caroline Howard on October 8, 1794, in Boston, Massachusetts; died on September 15, 1888, in Washington, D.C.; daughter of Samuel Howard and Anna (Lillie) Howard; sister of **Harriet Howard Fay**; *her education was, she noted, "exceedingly irregular, a perpetual passing from school to school, from my earliest memory"; married Samuel Gilman (a Unitarian minister who wrote the poem "Fair Harvard"), in December 1819; children: Caroline Howard Jervey (1823–1877);* **Eliza Gilman**; *as well as five other children, three of whom died in infancy.*

Selected works: Recollections of a Housekeeper *(1834);* The Lady's Annual Register and Housewife's Memorandum Book *(1838);* The Poetry of Travelling in the United States *(1838);* Recollections of a Southern Matron *(1838); (editor)* Letters of Eliza Wilkinson *(1839);* Tales and Ballads *(1839);* Love's Progress *(1840);* The Rose-Bud Wreath *(1841);* Oracles from the Poets *(1844);* Stories and Poems for Children *(1844);* The Sibyl; or, New Oracles from the Poets *(1849);* Verses of a Life Time *(1849);* A Gift Book of Stories and Poems for Children *(1850);* Oracles for Youth *(1852);* Recollections of a New England Bride and a Southern Matron *(1852);* Record of Inscriptions in the Cemetery and Building of the Unitarian . . . Church . . . Charleston, S.C. *(1860); (with C.H. Jervey)* Stories and Poems by Mother and Daughter *(1872);* The Poetic Fate Book *(1874);* Recollections of the Private Celebration of the Overthrow of the Tea *(1874); (with C.H. Jervey)* The Young Fortune Teller *(1874).*

Author Caroline Howard Gilman, who lost her father when she was two and her mother when she was ten, spent her childhood moving from one Boston neighborhood to the next. She found her first genuine stability after her marriage to Samuel Gilman in 1819, when she settled in Charleston, South Carolina, where her husband became a Unitarian minister. Gilman had seven children, three of whom died in infancy.

Gilman wrote verse as early as age 11, but her writing career was slow to develop. In 1832, she began publishing *Rose-Bud*, or *Youth's Gazette*, one of the earliest children's magazines in America. In 1833, it was renamed *Southern Rose-Bud* and in 1835 became *Southern Rose*, gradually developing into a broader family magazine before ceasing publication in 1839. Within its pages, Gilman serialized her first novel *Recol-*

lections of a Housekeeper, which appeared in book form in 1834 under the pseudonym Clarissa Packard. The book, written as a first-person narrative, presents the domestic life of a housekeeper in New England and was followed by its counterpart, *Recollections of a Southern Matron* (1838), which was set on a Southern plantation. In these two books, as in much of her work, Gilman sought to compare the two sections of the country on a domestic level, thereby hoping to ease some of the tensions between North and South on the political front. Unification as a theme also dominates *The Poetry of Travelling in the United States* (1838), in which Gilman's stated goal is to "present something in the same volume which might prove attractive to both the Northern and Southern reader" and "to increase a good sympathy between different portions of the country."

Once under way, Gilman proved prolific and turned out a variety of work, including novels, short stories, travel books, children's books, poetry (some with her daughter ◀❦ **Caroline Howard Jervey**), and a biography of her husband. **Susan Sutton Smith**, in *American Women Writers*, calls Gilman "a humorous chronicler of middle-class domesticity, North and South—a sort of early *Erma Bombeck." She adds, however, that as time went on "this New England-born Unitarian gave her sympathies to her adopted South."

During the Civil War, Gilman was forced to flee inland to Greenville, South Carolina, where she was active as a Confederate volunteer. When she returned to her home in Charleston in November 1865, she found that most of her personal possessions, including her papers, had been destroyed. She would never write again. Gilman remained in Charleston until 1882, after which she lived with a daughter in Washington, D.C. Caroline Howard Gilman died there on September 15, 1888.

❧▶ **Jervey, Caroline Howard** (1823–1877)

*American novelist. Name variations: (pseudonym) Gilman Glover. Born Caroline Howard Gilman in South Carolina in 1823; died in 1877; daughter of *Caroline Howard Gilman (1794–1888) and Samuel Gilman (a Unitarian minister); married; children.*

Caroline Howard Jervey's novels include *Vernon Grove* and *Helen Courtenay's Promise.*

SOURCES:

Edgerly, Lois Stiles, ed. *Give Her This Day*. Gardner, ME: Tilbury House, 1990.

Mainiero, Lina, ed. *American Women Writers*. NY: Frederick Ungar, 1980.

McHenry, Robert, ed. *Famous American Women*. NY: Dover, 1983.

SUGGESTED READING:

Kelley, Mary. *Private Woman, Public Stage*. NY: Oxford University Press, 1984.

Barbara Morgan,
Melrose, Massachusetts

Gilman, Charlotte Perkins

(1860–1935)

American feminist and socialist writer and orator who was controversial in her day for criticizing the nuclear family and for advocating careers for women. Name variations: Charlotte Anna Perkins (1860–1884); Charlotte Perkins Stetson (1884–1900); Charlotte Perkins Gilman (1900–1935). Born Charlotte Anna Perkins in Hartford, Connecticut, on July 3, 1860; committed suicide in Pasadena, California, after cancer treatments had proved ineffectual on August 17, 1935; daughter of Frederick Beecher Perkins (a librarian) and Mary Fitch Westcott; educated at home and at the Rhode Island School of Design; married Charles Walter Stetson (an artist), in May 1884 (separated 1887, divorced 1894); married her cousin George Houghton Gilman (a New York lawyer), in June 1900; children: (first marriage) one child, Katherine Stetson (b. 1885).

*Moved to Pasadena, California (1888); published short story "The Yellow Wallpaper" (1892); published In This Our World (1893); edited, with **Helen Campbell**, The Impress, organ of the Pacific Coast Woman's Press Association (1894); was resident of Jane Addams' Hull House (1895); went on lecture tours (1895–1900); appointed delegate to the International Socialist and Labor Congress in London (1896); published Women and Economics (1898), Concerning Children (1900), The Home (1903), Human Work (1904); founded and edited The Forerunner (1909–16); published What Diantha Did (1910); published The Man-Made World, Moving the Mountain, and The Crux (1911); founded, with Jane Addams, the Woman's Peace Party (1915); published His Religion and Hers (1923); lived in Norwich, Connecticut (1922–34); diagnosed with cancer (1932); moved to Pasadena, California (1934); published Charlotte Perkins Gilman: An Autobiography (1935). Unpunished, a detective novel, was published by The Feminist Press in 1997.*

Charlotte Perkins Gilman scandalized most of her contemporaries when she condemned the middle-class family as outmoded and oppressive. She was one of the most active Progressive reformers of the late 19th and early 20th centuries, prolific as a writer, inexhaustible as a traveling lecturer, and fearless as an advocate of unpopular ideas. Like many of her contemporaries, she lived to see part of the feminist agenda completed but not in the way she could approve, so that her success was tinged with regret.

The daughter of **Mary Perkins** and Frederick Beecher Perkins, Charlotte was the third of four children born in rapid succession (two of whom died) to a well-connected New England family. When Charlotte's mother learned that further pregnancies would endanger her life, Charlotte's father, a distinguished librarian, abandoned the family. Mary and her children were obliged to depend on the charity of relatives, many of whom belonged to the influential Beechers, and on money Mary could raise by occasional grade-school teaching. The Perkins family moved 18 times in 19 years, and Charlotte had little sense of home stability. After the first decade of abandonment, Mary Perkins sued for divorce, lost some of her relatives' sympathies, and moved to a life of genteel poverty in Providence, Rhode Island, where Charlotte enjoyed one of her few periods of formal schooling, at the Rhode Island School of Design.

Afraid that Charlotte would develop the same kind of emotional attachment that had made her vulnerable, Mary became cold and remote. Charlotte grew up lonely, outwardly severe, while inwardly building an imaginary world of warmth and affection. The outward character dominated, especially once Mary ordered her 13-year-old daughter to stop writing fantasy fiction. As biographer Carol Berkin notes:

> Her childhood diaries reveal a self-consciously stoical Charlotte, a character ruthlessly creating itself, always disciplining and reprimanding, always self-critical, trusting in rigorous programs for self-improvement to overcome unacceptable character-traits.

Gilman also believed in strenuous physical exertion, then and later. As an adult, she walked five miles a day, and she joined Barnard College's basketball team when she was 42.

Having resolved in her late teens never to marry and to dedicate herself to social uplift, she met and fell in love with Walter Stetson, an aspiring and talented artist. They were married in 1884, when she was 24, but after a happy honeymoon she became morose and introspective and was diagnosed as suffering from neurasthenia. She gave birth to a daughter, Kate, in March 1885 but again fell into a severe depression, so that her mother had to take care of the baby. As Gilman wrote in her autobiography: "Here was a charming home, a loving and devoted husband; an exquisite baby, healthy, intelligent, and good; a highly competent mother to run things; a wholly satisfactory servant—and I lay all day on the lounge and cried." The episode was the basis for her superb short story "The Yellow Wallpaper" (published 1892) about an unhappy woman with postpartum depression steadily descending into madness. Based closely on her own experience, it has greater power than most of her later didactic, hastily written fiction. Walter Stetson was supportive and sympathetic to his sick wife and offered her a separation, if she thought marriage was the source of her illness. She declined at first, but a journey to Pasadena, California, in 1886, transformed her into a healthy and happy woman. On the Pacific coast, she met her father as well as a close friend, **Grace Channing**, and seemed cured.

Gilman relapsed as soon as she returned to New England, however, and now visited Doctor Weir Mitchell of Philadelphia, an authority of that era on women's health, who believed that serious intellectual pursuits by women damaged their ability to be good mothers. She tried to follow Mitchell's orders for a calm home life (he told her not to read, write, or draw), but domesticity irritated her beyond endurance. She and her husband separated in 1887, but he remained close by, visiting often and always solicitous, mystified by what had happened. Still weak, Gilman decided to go West again, this time taking her mother and daughter along, and there began her career as a public lecturer and reform writer. It was a precarious living at first, and she had to supplement her income by managing a boarding house, but she gained literary celebrity with a poem in support of Darwin's theory of evolution entitled "Similar Cases."

Early solace came from an intense friendship (possibly an affair) with another reformer, **Adeline Knapp**, whom Charlotte nicknamed Delle, or Dora. But Knapp often treated Gilman like a housewife, the role she had tried to escape, and, after a stormy relationship, they separated in 1893. Gilman again blamed herself and wrote that she was permanently emotionally damaged by her unsuccessful marriage. In fits of recurrent illness, she was able to read for only about an hour each day, and to write for no more than three hours, before suffering disabling headaches. In view of these limitations, her lifelong literary productivity is astonishing. Already in 1894, she was editor of a weekly San Francisco journal, *The Impress*, for which she wrote a string of stories in imitation of the great Victorian authors. Despite praise from the president of Stanford University, as well as William Dean Howells and other literary figures, her reputation as an unconventional divorcee caused adverse publicity and the magazine's sponsors withdrew, forcing it to close after six months. More broad-minded readers and reviewers acclaimed her book of poetry, *In This Our World*, published the following year.

At the same time as her literary reputation developed, and despite her low self-esteem, continuing money problems, and psychological stresses, Gilman was becoming a well-known speaker on the reform circuit. After reading Edward Bellamy's enormously popular utopian novel *Looking Backward* (1888), she converted to socialism and, from that time, argued for a rationally planned society in Bellamy-inspired "Nationalist" clubs. She believed socialism could be accomplished peacefully, however, and was never a Marxist or revolutionary. *Lucy Stone, *Elizabeth Cady Stanton, *Jane Addams, and other prominent women reformers met and admired her, all impressed by her oratorical skill and persuasive writing. Gilman spoke on behalf of votes for women, women's right to work, and a child-care system for working women.

These themes were the subject of her best-known book, *Women and Economics*, which she wrote at high speed (17 days for the first draft) and published in 1898. It explained the economic basis of women's exploitation and purported to trace gender inequalities back to the prehistoric era. Influenced, like most of her contemporaries, by the ideas of evolution and progress, she argued that women at home were stuck in an evolutionary blind alley, doing the same dreary, psychologically stultifying tasks again and again while men, in the wider world of work and technology, carried civilization forward. Both sexes had suffered in consequence, and the divergence between men and women was now much wider than nature had intended. Housework and family life, as currently organized, were inefficient, she said, and should be collectivized. Rather than each family living in its own home, with each wife cooking, cleaning, and looking after the babies, these tasks should become specialized careers for a small number of women, leaving the rest to take up serious careers and to enter fully into public and work-life. Her plans for changed social arrangements were backed up by elaborate architectural and town-

planning schemes, and, as **Polly Wynn Allen** writes: "Changing neighborhood architecture to support women's participation in a unified world was the most sustained, practical focus of Gilman's lifelong feminist, socialist campaigns." Her fellow progressives shared her faith in science, systematic study, temperance, and political reform, but few joined her in advocating an end to the nuclear family. Nevertheless, the biting satire of *Women and Economics*, its cogent development and assertive tone, made it a bestseller. It changed her image. Previously known mainly as a satirical poet, she now joined the ranks of social theorists.

In 1895, her ex-husband Walter Stetson married Charlotte's great friend Grace Channing. Far from taking offense at this match, Gilman, who was by then working at Jane Addams' Hull House Settlement in Chicago, was delighted and sent her daughter **Katherine Stetson** to live with them. Newspaper editors who knew of her as a public figure in the reform movement professed to be scandalized and said she had renounced her "natural" role as a mother, though Gilman believed the decision to send Katherine back to her father was in the child's best interest: she saw herself as acting dutifully, not selfishly.

In 1900, Charlotte married her cousin George Houghton Gilman, whom she had known and liked as a child. The ceremony took place in a Unitarian church because the first Protestant minister she asked refused to officiate at the marriage of a divorcee. George was seven years younger than she, worked as a New York attorney, and shared few of her reform interests, but they made a compatible couple, and he proved to be a valuable editor of her work. For four years before the wedding, they enjoyed a large, affectionate correspondence, with him staying in New York, managing her business affairs, and she traveling throughout America (and twice to England) to lecture on reform and women's suffrage. They wrote to each other every day when her tours kept them apart. At the time of her marriage, *Women and Economics* was a success, selling widely enough and enhancing her fame to such a degree that she was earning high lecture fees and becoming prosperous. Gilman had also won the admiring notice of many prominent reform intellectuals, notably the economic and social theorists Edward Ross, Thorstein Veblen, and Lester Ward. She thought Ward to be one of the greatest living thinkers and was flattered by his esteem.

The era between 1900 and 1914 was the most productive in her life, and she wrote nine

Charlotte
Perkins
Gilman

more books. None were so famous as *Women and Economics*, but some, particularly *The Home* (1903), were equally skillful and eloquent. *The Home* advocated the "kitchenless home" for most families, and praised utopian communities which had minimized domestic drudgery and made child-raising a scientific collective business. A characteristic passage of that book, showing her debts to evolutionary thought, reads:

> The home *in its essential nature* is pure good, and in its due development is progres-

sively good; but it must change with society's advance; and the kind of home that was wholly beneficial in one century may be largely evil in another. We must forcibly bear in mind, in any honest study of a long-accustomed environment, that our own comfort, or even happiness, in a given condition does not prove it to be good.

Between 1909 and 1916, she was editor (and sole contributor to) a feminist magazine, *The Forerunner*. Though it never made a profit, she kept it going with subsidies from her lecture fees and royalties. The 86 issues of the magazine each had 28 pages, blending stories with investigative journalism and reports on women's and socialist causes. She churned it out with prodigious speed. For the 1915 issues, Gilman wrote a serialized novel, "Herland," about a women's utopia, a land populated only by women, and run with collectivized kitchens and child care. The food was good, there was plenty of nurturance and a sensible way of life in Herland but, as Gilman admitted, there were no competitive sports, no dramatic literature, and no great science (all, in her opinion, the creations of men). "Herland," as historian **Rosalind Rosenberg** writes:

> illustrated women's special gifts but it also revealed women's unique weaknesses, their lesser variability (and therefore want of genius), and their lack of ambition. For civilization to realize its highest potential, Gilman concluded, it must be able to draw on the full range of human talent. High civilization required one whole humanity, not two halves.

⟨⟩ f all the great feminist writers, [Charlotte Perkins Gilman] made the finest analysis of the relation between domesticity and women's rights, perhaps the most troubling question for liberated women and sympathetic men today.

—**William O'Neill**

Some of her feminist contemporaries, including Sweden's *Ellen Key, saw feminism as a movement to bring women's nurturing qualities into public life through the vote, but warned that the idea of women's careers was "socially pernicious, racially wasteful, and soul-withering." For Key, the gender differences were too great ever to permit women to pursue careers. Gilman dissented strongly in a series of public disputes with Key, answering "that the main lines of human development have nothing to do with sex, and that what

women need most is the development of *human* characteristics."

For Charlotte Perkins Gilman, as for many Progressive Era reformers, the outbreak of the First World War in 1914 was a shattering disappointment, a supremely irrational event which seemed to destroy her hopes of a disciplined, reasonable solution to all national and international frictions. Although she was a socialist, she was equally horrified by the brutality of the Bolshevik Revolution in Russia three years later. Ironically, however, she had become convinced by 1917 that America *should* intervene in the First World War, in order, as President Woodrow Wilson said, to "make the world safe for democracy." Most of her New York feminist friends, members of the Heterodoxy club, disagreed with her hawkish views, and the dispute led to a temporary rift (which would heal by the early 1920s). Further disillusionment was in store in the '20s. Women's suffrage, assured by the 19th Amendment to the Constitution (1918), for which Gilman labored hard in the National Women's Party, did not lead to the social and political improvements she had anticipated. Neither did she approve of the social customs of the '20s and the rapidly developing idea (helped by popular Freudianism) that sexuality was a liberating form of self-expression.

For 20 years, she and her husband had lived in New York, though she was often crisscrossing the country by rail on her extensive lecture tours (she lectured in all but four of the states). In 1922, they moved to Norwich, Connecticut, partly to get away from the polyglot population of the city. Like most Anglo-Saxon Americans of the time, she was a racial supremacist, believing that she belonged to the most gifted and civilized race in world history. By modern-day standards, her remarks about black, Jewish, and Asian people are insufferably condescending, and she admitted that she found it a relief in her last years to be living in an ethnically homogeneous white community. Her idea for immigrants was not the "melting pot" but rather a form of forced Americanization, and her novel *Moving the Mountain*, serialized in *The Forerunner* then published intact in 1921, had an ugly eugenic side, which advocated sterilization or even killing of the genetically "unfit."

When she discovered she was suffering from breast cancer in 1932, Gilman bought a bottle of chloroform and vowed she would use it when the disease became acute. Meanwhile, she settled down to finishing her autobiography, with which she had been tinkering since 1925. When her husband died in 1934, she returned to Pasadena. The following year, true to her word and self-disciplined to the end, she killed herself with the chloroform, leaving her autobiography to be published posthumously.

SOURCES:

Allen, Polly Wynn. *Building Domestic Liberty: Charlotte Perkins Gilman's Architectural Feminism.* Amherst, MA: University of Massachusetts Press, 1988.

Berkin, Carol Ruth. "Charlotte Perkins Gilman," in *Portraits of American Women.* Edited by G.J. Barker-Benfield and Catherine Clinton. NY: St. Martin's Press, 1991, pp. 311–338.

Cott, Nancy. *The Grounding of Modern Feminism.* New Haven, CT: Yale University Press, 1987.

Lane, Ann J. *To Herland and Beyond: The Life and Work of Charlotte Perkins Gilman.* NY: Pantheon, 1990.

Meyering, Sheryl L., ed. *Charlotte Perkins Gilman: The Woman and Her Work.* Ann Arbor, MI: University of Michigan Research Press, 1989.

Rosenberg, Rosalind. *Beyond Separate Spheres: Intellectual Roots of Modern Feminism.* New Haven, CT: Yale University Press, 1982.

Scharnhorst, Gary. *Charlotte Perkins Gilman.* Boston, MA: Twayne, 1985.

SUGGESTED READING:

Gilman, Charlotte Perkins. *The Home: Its Work and Influence.* Urbana, IL: University of Illinois Press, 1972 (originally published in 1903).

———. *The Living of Charlotte Perkins Gilman.* NY: Arno Press, 1972 (originally published in 1935).

COLLECTIONS:

Mary Ingraham Bunting Institute and Schlesinger Library at Radcliffe College, Cambridge, Massachusetts.

Patrick Allitt,
Professor of History, Emory University, Atlanta, Georgia

Gilmer, Elizabeth Meriwether

(1861–1951)

American newspaper columnist who wrote under the name Dorothy Dix. Name variations: (pseudonym) Dorothy Dix. Born Elizabeth Meriwether in Woodstock, Tennessee, on November 18, 1861 (some sources cite 1870); died in New Orleans, Louisiana, on December 16, 1951; eldest of three children of William Douglas (a plantation owner) and Maria (Winston) Meriwether; attended the Female Academy, Clarkesville, Tennessee, and Hollins Institute in Virginia; married George O. Gilmer, in November 1888 (died 1929 or 1931).

When Elizabeth Meriwether Gilmer died in 1951, age 90, over 60 million readers throughout the world were familiar with her advice column and knew her as Dorothy Dix. From 1896, when she began writing a weekly "sermonette" for the *New Orleans Picayune*, until 1949, just one year before she was hospitalized with a stroke, Gilmer fielded questions on every subject from romance to superfluous hair removal. For 15 years, when she worked for William Randolph Hearst's *New York Journal,* she also covered sensational murder trials, vice investigations, and special-interest stories, acquiring the oft-used pejorative for women columnists: "sob sister." Admired for the sympathy and compassion she brought to her work, Gilmer attributed her sensitivity to the unhappiness in her own life.

Elizabeth Meriwether Gilmer grew up impoverished, amid Southern gentry, her father having lost most of his land during the Civil War. Her education was minimal, though she read widely from the family library and distinguished herself in grammar school with her essays. At 18, she married, following what she referred to as the "tribal custom" of the day. Almost immediately Gilmer became concerned with her young husband's wild and costly business schemes and abrupt mood swings (a symptom of the mental illness that would eventually cause his death). Although she tried to keep up appearances through the first two years of the union, the strain of an uncertain future ultimately caused her to suffer a nervous breakdown. During her recuperation at a resort on the Mississippi coast financed by her father, she began writing sketches about her early life. One story, about how their trusted family servant, Mr. Dicks, had saved the family silver during the Civil War by burying it in a graveyard, caught the attention of *Eliza Jane Nicholson, owner of the *New Orleans Picayune*. She bought it for three dollars and offered Gilmer her first job.

After a spell of writing obituaries and recipes, Gilmer was given a column, "Sunday Salad," which soon evolved into "Dorothy Dix Talks." She purportedly chose the name *Dorothy,* because she thought it dignified, and *Dix* in honor of Mr. Dicks. Struggling to learn her trade, Gilmer put her early columns through several drafts. "Writing is like firing in the dark," she once said. "You never know whether you hit anything or not. And so it is good to hear the bell ring every now and then." She was an instant success, mainly due to her fresh insights and straight-forward colloquial style. Some readers, however, preferred the prevailing romantic attitude, with one reader criticizing, "You're just about as sentimental as a mustard plaster."

In 1901, Gilmer went to work for Hearst's *New York Journal,* lured away from New Orleans by a $5,000-a-year salary. Leaving her husband and taking a room in a boarding house, Gilmer began producing three advice columns each week but was soon pulled into the more sensational reporting that fueled the circulation war between Hearst and rival Joseph Pulitzer. Hoping to exploit Gilmer's "mother confessor" image, Hearst sent her to New Jersey where a woman had murdered her husband's 18-month-old baby from another marriage. Although officials and relatives had offered no information to the press, Gilmer managed to find the former boyfriend of the accused woman. He not only offered to drive her around to find sources but, by her account, proposed marriage. The resulting story was all that the paper had hoped for. Written with Gilmer's characteristic empathy, it not only covered the crime in detail but provided insight into the community and those involved in the case. For the next 15 years, in addition to her advice column, Gilmer covered the crime beat and was present at all the sensational murder trials of the period, including the **Nan Patterson** trial in 1904 and the Harry Thaw trial in

Elizabeth
Meriwether
Gilmer

1906 for the murder of Stanford White. "I was on speaking terms with every criminal in America," she once boasted. Gilmer much preferred her column, however, which she felt provided a genuine service to her readers. "Time and time again I received letters telling me how someone had taken my advice, and that it had solved his or her problem."

Although her own marriage was strained by her husband's illness and frequent separations, Gilmer believed that divorce was out of the question. When she was well into her 70s, she confided in a reporter that she could not offer advice to others that she would not follow. "I could not say to others: 'Be strong!' if I did not myself have the strength to endure. If I turned my back on a hard job, it would ruin any influence for good my work might ever have—and I took my work pretty seriously."

In 1917, Gilmer accepted a contract from the Wheeler Syndicate which allowed her to devote herself exclusively to her column. Returning to New Orleans, she published six times

weekly: three columns of her sermonettes and three columns in a question-and-answer format. Of the thousands of letters she received (100,000 in 1939 alone), those bearing a signature and a return address were either answered within the column or sent a personal reply. After her husband's death in 1929, Gilmer continued her column for another 20 years, bringing her a new generation of readers. She now addressed a number of new problems, including the hasty marriages of the war years:

> Watch your step, boys, and go slow. You will worry a lot less about the sweetie you left behind you than you would over a wife.

And the new sexual freedom:

> Love is only the dessert of life. The minute you try to live on dessert, you get sick of it and you can get sicker of love than you can of anything else in the world.

Her common sense approach prompted one young male reader to write to her syndicate, "This old girl makes sense. Are you sure she isn't younger than that picture you're running?" Gilmer took pride in never missing a deadline and kept three months worth of columns locked in a bank in a safety deposit box to be used in case of illness or travel. Her writing career also included five books: *Mirandy* (1914), *Hearts à la Mode* (1915), *Mirandy Exhorts* (1922), *My Trip Around the World* (1924), *Dorothy Dix: Her Book,* based on her columns (1926), and *How to Win and Hold a Husband* (1939).

Gilmer held firm to the belief that being a woman was the hardest profession in the world, and, as a career woman, she particularly empathized with working women. In 1931, upon receiving an honorary doctorate from Oglethorpe University in Atlanta, Georgia, she urged women students to consider a career in journalism. "What is a newspaper, anyway," she said, "but the aggregate gossip of the world." Dorothy Dix died in New Orleans on December 16, 1951.

SUGGESTED READING:

Belford, Barbara. *Brilliant Bylines.* NY: Columbia University Press, 1986.

Barbara Morgan,
Melrose, Massachusetts

Gilmore, Mary (1865–1962)

Australian poet, journalist, and social activist. Name variations: Dame Mary Gilmore. Born Mary Jean Cameron at Cotta Walla, near Goulburn, North South Wales, Australia, on August 16, 1865; died in Sydney in 1962; first daughter and eldest child of Donal (Donald) (a building contractor) and Mary (Beattie) Cameron; educated at home except for two years at a school in Wagga Wagga, 1875–77; married William Alexander Gilmore (a shearer from Western Victoria), in May 1897; children: William Dysart Cameron Gilmore (1898–1945).

Selected works—poetry: Marri'd and Other Verses (1910); The Tale of Tiddley Winks (1917); The Passionate Heart (1918); The Tilted Cart (1925); The Wild Swan (1930); The Rue Tree (1931); Under the Wilgas (1932); Battlefields (1939); The Disinherited (1941); Pro Patria Australia and Other Poems (1945); Selected Verse (1948); Fourteen Men (1954). Prose: Old Days, Old Ways: A Book of Recollections (1934); More Recollections (1935); Letters of Mary Gilmore (selected and edited by W.H. Wilde and T. Inclis Moore, 1980).

In a literary life that encompassed nearly a century of Australian history, Mary Gilmore recorded in poetry and prose the social and political changes that transformed her country from a colony into an independent nation. She was also a political and social crusader.

She was born in 1865 at Cotta Walla, near Goulburn, the daughter of a building contractor of Scottish heritage who instilled in his young daughter a love of the land and a passion for Aboriginal history and lore. Gilmore was an extremely bright child who could read the newspaper by the age of seven. She attended school in Wagga Wagga for two years (1875–77) but credited her parents with providing her with most of her early education. By the time she was 12, she was a teacher's assistant in small schools around Cootamundra, Albury, and Wagga and, at 16, was contributing verse to local newspapers. From 1888 to 1889, she taught school in the militant mining town of Silverton, near Broken Hill, which aroused her life-long interest in the labor movement. While teaching in Sydney during the early 1890s, she supported the maritime and shearers' strikes and aligned herself with the newly formed Australian Workers Union.

Gilmore supported William Lane's venture to establish a Utopian socialist settlement in Paraguay and helped him launch his first voyage there in July 1893. In 1896, at his request, she sailed to South America to teach in the colony of Cosme, which was formed after Lane's initial colony, New Australia, failed. Life in the colony was difficult, and Gilmore was often ill and overworked. While there, she married William Gilmore, a shearer from Western Victoria, whom she had spent hours reading while he recovered from an accident. The couple, who had a son in 1898, returned to Australia in 1902, after the Cosme settlement disintegrated.

After a brief stay in Sydney, where Gilmore was able to renew her contact with the literary and journalistic world, they settled on an isolated farm at Strathdownie near Casterton in Western Victoria. It was a lonely period for Gilmore, who was left alone much of the time and endured what she referred to as a "want of educated conversation or discussion." Around 1903, Gilmore moved to Casterton to facilitate her son's secondary education. At that time, she resumed her contact with the literary world, publishing both verse and prose in the *Bulletin*, the *Worker*, and other newspapers. In 1908, she was hired by Hector Lamont, editor of the *Worker*, to edit the paper's Women's Page, a post she held for the next 23 years. Her first volume of poems, *Marri'd and Other Verses*, which included poems from her days at Cosme and Casterton, was published in 1910. By 1912, Gilmore's husband William had joined his brother in Queensland, and she had settled permanently in Sydney. After her son Billy completed his education, he joined his father, and the family was rarely together after that time.

From the Women's Page of the *Worker*, Gilmore aired her grievances and launched a wide range of campaigns for social and economic change. Aligning herself with the cause of Aboriginal rights and the plight of the working man, she became a voice for outcasts and the socially disadvantaged. A feminist, she also championed equal status for women and improved health care for children and expectant mothers.

Between 1920 and 1940, Gilmore published six volumes of poetry and three of prose. Her second collection of poems, *The Passionate Heart*, expressed her horror over the war of 1914–18 and the treatment of the returning soldiers, to whom she dedicated the work. Gilmore relinquished its royalties to blind soldiers, saying, "I would have felt like eating blood had I kept them." Her first book of prose, a collection of essays called *Hound of the Road*, was published in 1922, followed by a third volume of poems, *The Tilted Cart*, a collection of ballad-like verse accompanied by copious notes detailing early outback life.

Mary Gilmore retired from the *Worker* in 1930, at age 65, but continued her writing and her impassioned crusades. That year, she pub-

lished perhaps her best collection of verse, *The Wild Swan*. It was followed by *The Rue Tree* (1931), a volume of mostly religious poems, and *Under the Wilgas* (1932), which emphasized Aboriginal themes. Her reminiscences were encompassed in two volumes which appeared in successive years: *Old Days, Old Ways* (1934) and *More Recollections* (1935). In 1937, in recognition of both her literary achievement and her activism, Gilmore was made a Dame of the British Empire. A volume prophetically called *Battlefields* was published in 1939, just before the outbreak of World War II.

In 1945, Gilmore suffered the double loss of both her husband and son; William died of blood poisoning in February and Billy succumbed to pneumonia in July. As was her custom, she took refuge from her grief in her writing and her numerous social causes. She remained active well into her 90s, residing during her later years in a tiny flat in the heart of Sydney's bohemian Kings Cross. In 1952, she began writing for the Communist newspaper *Tribune*, an action prompted by her zeal as a pacifist but causing some controversy. At age 90, although somewhat slowed, she published her final volume of poetry, *Fourteen Men* (1954), in which she acknowledged her impending death as "the last thing left to defeat." Yet another birthday, her 92nd, was marked by the unveiling of a portrait commissioned by William Dobell, who pronounced her "a splendid person with a tremendous vitality and dignity."

Gilmore, a beloved national figure, was the recipient of numerous honors. Her birthdays were publicly celebrated and scholarships were awarded in her name. She died quietly in December 1962, just three years short of her 100th year. Her death was marked by a ceremonial state funeral through the streets of Sydney.

SOURCES:

Buck, Claire, ed. *The Bloomsbury Guide to Women's Literature*. NY: Prentice Hall, 1992.

Wilde, W.H., Joy Hooten, and Barry Andrews. *The Oxford Companion to Australian Literature*. Melbourne: Oxford, 1985.

———, and T. Inglis Moore. *Letters of Mary Gilmore*. Melbourne, Australia: Melbourne University Press, 1980.

RELATED MEDIA:

"When Butter Was Sixpence a Pound" (one-woman dramatic interpretation of Gilmore's life and work), starring **Joan Murray**, produced by ACT, 1983.

"To Botany Bay on a Bondi Tram" (one-woman show), starring **Beverly Dunn**, produced by Melbourne Theatre Company, 1984.

Barbara Morgan,
Melrose, Massachusetts

Gilot, Françoise (1922—)

French painter, author, and paramour of Pablo Picasso. Born in France in 1922; daughter of Emile Gilot (founder of Parfums Gilot); attended Catholic boarding school; received a licence in literature (equivalent of an A.B. in an American or English university) and studied law at the Sorbonne; lived with Pablo Picasso (1881–1973) for a decade beginning in 1943; married Luc Simon (a painter), in July 1953 (divorced); married Dr. Jonas Salk (1914–1995, a physician who developed the first vaccine against polio), in 1970 (died 1995); children: (first marriage) daughter, Aurélia Simon; (with Picasso) Claude Picasso (b. May 15, 1947); Paloma Picasso (b. April 19, 1949).

"The creative fire is hard to bear," said Françoise Gilot, one of Pablo Picasso's many paramours and the mother of two of his children. "It is not small stuff. It is a very serious thing." Gilot, who lived with the famous artist for a decade and had two of his children, walked away from the relationship seemingly unscathed, which cannot be said of all the women in Picasso's life. "He did not destroy me because I was of the stuff that cannot be destroyed," she said in a 1996 interview for *Mirabella*. "I do not need another consciousness to define my own. Picasso used to say that I have my own window on infinity. I did not need him or anything he did to have my own being complete." Indeed, Gilot went on to become a respected painter in her own right, as well as a poet and author.

Gilot was born in 1922 and grew up in a well-to-do Parisian home dominated by her father, a strong-willed man who was disappointed that his only child was a girl. In response, she was dressed in boyish fashion, with her hair cut unfashionably short, and was encouraged to excel in athletics. Her father took her hunting and fishing, and grew angry if she expressed any fear. Later, Gilot began to conquer her fears, not for her father, but for herself. "And when I met Pablo, I knew that he was something larger than life, something to match myself against," she writes in her memoir *Life with Picasso*. "The prospect sometimes seemed overpowering, but fear itself can be a delicious sensation."

Their meeting took place in May 1943, during the German occupation of France. Gilot was having dinner with friends at a small restaurant frequented by writers and artists on the Left Bank, where Picasso was also dining with his own coterie, including his companion since 1936, *Dora Marr (Picasso, 40 years Gilot's senior, had already been involved with numerous women and was then married to ballerina **Olga Khoklova**, from whom he separated in 1935 but because of Spanish law was unable to divorce. He had a son Paulo with Olga, and a daughter Maya with **Marie-Thérèse Walter**, his mistress before Dora Marr.) Gilot, then 21, had just lost her long-time painting teacher (a Hungarian by the name of Endre Rozsda) and was grappling over how to tell her father that she intended to give up university studies to pursue art full-time, a decision that she knew would cause a split between them. She had also been rejected by a boyfriend, one with whom she was quite serious. Noticing Gilot across the room, Picasso openly flirted with her, then came over to her table, bringing with him a bowl of cherries and offering them around. His small talk included an invitation to his studio, which Gilot responded to the following week. Over the course of the next few months, she continued to call on Picasso, frequently bringing her work for him to critique. "When I did go back to see him, it wasn't long before he began to make very clear another side of the nature of his interest in me," she wrote. During this time, Gilot also made up her mind to confront her father, who was so enraged over her desire to paint that he attempted to have her declared insane. She left his house and went to live with her grandmother, sacrificing not only the relationship, but the allowance her father had provided for her. She did not see her father again until 1951, at her grandmother's funeral.

Gilot's relationship with Picasso continued to intensify, but, although they became lovers, she refused his persistent invitations to move in with him until the spring of 1946. She was wary of Picasso's notorious mood swings and his ongoing involvement with Dora Marr, but eventually the challenge of the relationship overcame her doubts. She would later discover that Picasso's ties to the past did not end with Marr. He regularly visited Marie-Thérèse and her daughter Maya, while Olga's son Paulo spent summers with him. Olga, devastated by her separation from Picasso and in fragile mental health, followed the artist everywhere; she would ultimately begin to harass Gilot as well.

During their decade together, Picasso and Gilot divided their time between his Paris studio at Rue des Grands-Augustins and Vallauris in the south of France, where Picasso made his pottery and where he eventually purchased the villa La Galloise. Gilot gave her life over to Picasso and his work, expecting nothing for herself, she maintains, "beyond what he had given the world by means of his art." In 1947, having been persuaded by Picasso that a "child would complete her as a woman," Gilot gave birth to their son, Claude Picasso. A daughter, *Paloma Picasso, followed in 1949. Picasso was always in a happy mood when she was pregnant, writes Gilot, and her decision to have a second child was based partly on her desire to keep him on an even keel.

For the first three years with Picasso, Gilot had stopped painting, convinced that her work would "reflect his presence." Picasso, however, as he did with each new lover, produced a series of portraits of Gilot, including 11 lithographs executed during the first month she lived with him, and a number of paintings, including *La Femme-Fleur*, a likeness of Gilot that resembles a flower. Among his later portraits of Gilot is the lithograph *Françoise–grave or sad?* and a sculptured portrait *Tête de Femme*, as well as numerous portraits of the children, alone and with their mother. During her hiatus from painting, Gilot spent her free time drawing. In 1948, she picked up her brushes again, first working in gouache, then in oils. Claude, restless and energetic, was a constant source of interruption to his mother, but Paloma was an ideal baby who basically slept and ate. "She'll be a perfect woman," Picasso used to say. "Passive and submissive. That's the way all girls should be. They ought to stay asleep just like that until they're twenty-one."

Picasso was generous as Gilot's mentor, and her early work does reflect his influence. He was outwardly pleased at any success she attained during their time together. In 1949, when D.H. Kahnweiler, Picasso's off-and-on dealer, offered her an exclusive contract on her yearly production of paintings, Picasso encouraged her to accept. Gilot's work sold well, and within two years she had doubled her income. In the fall of 1951, she had a successful showing at la Hune Gallery in Paris, and the following spring she had a full-scale exhibition at Kahnweiler's.

Following the birth of Paloma, Gilot was ill for a time and grew quite thin. Picasso began to criticize her appearance. He also started to chafe under the confines of domesticity and withdrew, while Gilot began to want more from the relationship. Picasso had directed her metamorphosis, writes Gilot, then wanted no part of the woman she had become. Their affair, however, took several years to play itself out, despite numerous bitter encounters. In 1953, Gilot left permanently, moving to Paris with the children and taking up with Luc Simon, an artist she had known in her teens. But Gilot continued to see Picasso on occasion, sometimes accompanying the children on visits. He was alternately welcoming and dismissive.

A year after they had parted, Picasso invited Gilot to participate in the opening of the first bullfight in Vallauris, an event at which he was to be honored. "You deserve to leave with the honors of war," he told her. "For me the bull is the proudest symbol of all, and your symbol is the horse. I want our two symbols to face each other in that ritual way." Gilot agreed. Her performance at the event, which involved circling the stadium several times on horseback, was triumphant, indeed, and served as the ending of the 1996 Merchant-Ivory film, *Surviving Picasso*, based on Gilot's memoir and starring Anthony Hopkins and **Natascha McElhone**. In reality, the couple's last encounter, far less dramatic, was in 1955, when Gilot told him that she was marrying Simon. "I hope it's a fiasco, you ungrateful creature," he said. Gilot never saw Picasso again, but he continued to exercise his disdain, seeing to it that she was excluded from several salons and that her contract with Kahnweiler was terminated.

Gilot wed Simon and had a second daughter Aurélia, although the marriage did not endure. In 1970, she married Dr. Jonas Salk, the renowned American physician who developed the first vaccine against poliomyelitis. Meanwhile, she pursued her art in earnest, producing paintings, drawings, and prints that are included in the permanent collections of museums throughout the United States and Europe. A recurring theme in her work, which encompasses 1,300 oils and more than 300 works on paper, is mythology, stories of the ancient gods and goddesses. "During my adolescence, I started to envision these myths as a kind of metaphor for life," she writes in the artist's preface to **Ariana Huffington**'s *The Gods of Greece* (illustrated with some 60 of Gilot's paintings and drawings done over a 50-year period), "and I took particular solace in the inventiveness these tales elicit, reinforcing human skill . . . in defeating negative occurrences, sometimes even those of fate itself." Gilot exhibited her mythological paintings in the United States in 1966, and again in 1993–94, in a traveling exhibit titled *Past-Present: Mythology of the Gods (1940–1993)*. In 1990, she was awarded the Legion denier in her native France, and in January 1994 she received the Jean Cocteau International Style Award, presented annually by the Severin Wunderman Museum in Irvine, California, to a person whose "personal style and participation in the arts reflect the spirit of Jean Cocteau."

Gilot has also authored nine books, including *Interface: The Painter and the Mask, Françoise Gilot: An Artist's Journey* and *Matisse and Picasso: A Friendship in Art*. Her memoir, *Life With Picasso*, published in 1964, was said to have angered the artist, who by then had obtained his divorce from Olga Khoklova and was married to *Jacqueline Roque.

SOURCES:

Champa, Paula. "Past-Present: The Mythological Paintings of Françoise Gilot," in *American Artist*. Vol. 57, no. 617. December 1993, pp. 38–48.

Gilot, Françoise, with Carlton Lake. *Life with Picasso*. NY: McGraw-Hill, 1964.

Moritz, Charles, ed. *Current Biography*. NY: H.W. Wilson, 1986.

Nicksin, Carole. "Sassing Picasso," in *Mirabella*. Vol 7. September–October 1996, p. 40.

RELATED MEDIA:

Surviving Picasso (film), based on Gilot's memoir, starred Anthony Hopkins and Natascha McElhone, produced by Merchant-Ivory, 1996.

Barbara Morgan,
Melrose, Massachusetts

Gilpin, Laura (1891–1979)

American photographer who documented the lives of the southwest Navajo, among other subjects, and gained renown in the last decade of her life after 70 years in her field. Born on April 22, 1891, in Austin Bluffs, Colorado; died on November 30, 1979, in Santa Fe, New Mexico; daughter of Frank Gilpin (a furniture maker) and Emma (Miller) Gilpin; attended Baldwin School, 1905–07; attended Rosehall, 1907–09; attended New England Conservatory of Music, 1910; attended Clarence H. White School of Photography, 1916–17; never married; lived with Elizabeth "Betsy" Forster (d. 1972); no children.

Began experimenting with photography (1903); resolved to become a professional photographer and entered Clarence H. White School of Photography (1916); met Elizabeth Forster (1918); began documenting the Navajo of the southwest (1931); published first book (1941); awarded honorary doctorate from University of New Mexico (1970); awarded Guggenheim Fellowship (1974).

Frank and **Emma Gilpin** married in Chicago on April 23, 1890, and shortly thereafter moved to Colorado where their first child Laura was born in Austin Bluffs on April 22, 1891. Emma Gilpin was an ambitious woman who enjoyed intellectual pursuits, while her husband enjoyed the challenges of frontier life. Their daughter was influenced by both these perspectives. When Laura was still an infant, the Gilpins moved to Perry Park in the mountains near Colorado Springs. A son John was born on May 10, 1892, but died five months later. The family relocated to Manitou Park, where Emma tried to recover from the loss. For several years, Frank ran cattle and managed a summer hotel. When he did not find his fortune in ranching, the family moved again in 1896 to Colorado Springs, where he managed a mine. This pattern of relocation and failed business ventures dominated their lives. Three years later, on July 24, 1899, Emma had another son, Francis Gilpin, Jr. At the time, Laura was eight years old.

She was given a Brownie camera on her 12th birthday and, that Christmas, received a developing tank from her parents. These gifts began what was to be her lifelong passion for the art and science of photography. The year was 1903, and the family now lived in Mexico where Frank was managing a mine while Laura and her brother were left in the care of the directors of Laura's private school. Two years later, Laura was sent to Pennsylvania to attend the Baldwin School in Bryn Mawr. In 1907, she transferred to another private school in Greenwich, Connecticut, but she never excelled in her academic work. With the complication of a severe illness in 1908, Laura left Connecticut for good in 1909 and returned to Colorado Springs. She never earned a high school diploma.

In these years, Gilpin cultivated her photographic skills and taught herself how to make autochromes (plates that had been created by the Lumiere brothers, pioneers of photographic techniques, only a year earlier). With these plates, which were coated with colored dyes to create soft-colored images, Gilpin made noteworthy portraits and still-lifes. Having earlier studied the violin in high school and shown some talent for music, Gilpin returned to the East Coast in 1910 to attend the New England Conservatory of Music in Boston. Music and photography, she found, had much in common as forms of artistic expression. "Photography uses waves of light, composed and harmonized to express an idea," she wrote. "Music uses waves of sound for the same purpose."

After only a few months, Gilpin was forced to leave the conservatory when another failed business venture meant another family relocation and no money to keep her in school. Returning home to her parents' new cattle ranch in Austin, Colorado, Laura started a poultry business, raising turkeys to contribute to the family income. Her enterprise proved surprisingly successful, although she gave most of the profits to her father. In 1915, the Gilpins sold the ranch and returned to Colorado Springs.

The same year, Gilpin traveled to California to visit the Panama-Pacific Exhibition in San Francisco and the Panama-California Exhibition in San Diego, where she renewed her interest in photography. While in California, she met **Anne Simon**, a musician and poet, who became a close friend and inspired in Gilpin the desire for artistic excellence. They remained in contact after Gilpin returned to Colorado and Anne to Washington, D.C. Deeply attached to the older woman, Gilpin credited her with having "awakened my spirit." Indeed, Anne quickly became the most important person in Gilpin's life. When Anne died suddenly in August 1916, Gilpin became despondent and traveled alone to the Grand Canyon to mourn the death in solitude. In her grief, she resolved to follow the path that she believed Anne wished her to follow, that of a serious artist engaged in the study of photography.

Genius is nothing but an uncommon aptitude for patience.

—Laura Gilpin

Gilpin moved to New York to study at the Clarence H. White School of Photography in October 1916. In New York, she made the acquaintance of sculptor **Brenda Putnam**, one of Anne's friends, and moved in with her and two other women artists. Putnam would remain a confidant, advisor, and supporter for the rest of Gilpin's life. At school, Gilpin studied the pictorial style of photography emphasized by Clarence White, a contemporary of Alfred Stieglitz. Pictorialism, which would dominate most of Gilpin's work in the 1920s, was characterized by soft-focus, romantic images conveying strong emotional impact through careful composition. Although she thoroughly enjoyed her studies with White, Gilpin contracted a severe case of influenza in the fall of 1917 and was forced to leave New York and return to Colorado Springs, ending her formal studies.

Elizabeth Forster, a 32-year-old registered nurse from South Carolina, was hired to look after 27-year-old Gilpin in early 1918. As Elizabeth—"Betsy," as Laura called her—nursed her back to health, the two developed an intense, loving relationship which would affect both their lives for the next half-century, an alliance each would call the most important in her life. The two women shared similar interests in literature, music, exploring the outdoors, and in maintaining their independent careers. Laura remained in Betsy's care until the fall of 1918,

when Betsy left Colorado Springs to join the Red Cross. She returned the next year. During the next several years, Betsy and Laura were a familiar sight at town social events, and Frank and Emma Gilpin accepted Betsy as a member of their family.

Gilpin's professional career began after her recovery in 1918. She opened a studio in Colorado Springs and obtained a position teaching at the Broadmoor Art Academy in town. Most of her commissioned works were portraits, first of friends, then, as her reputation expanded, of families. She also produced many fine landscapes of the Colorado desert. With considerable success as a commercial artist, Gilpin submitted her prints for exhibition in galleries and museums throughout the country. In 1922, Gilpin traveled to Europe with her old friend Brenda Putnam. She studied classical art and architecture on her own in many European art museums, and returned to Colorado several months later with renewed energy and motivation. For the remainder of the decade, Gilpin continued working as a commercial photographer while her reputation spread across the United States and Europe. "Despite her geographical isolation and her increasing load of local commissions," writes **Martha Sandweiss**, "Laura remained active in the national and international photographic world."

In 1927, Emma Gilpin died, leaving Laura as her father's only means of emotional support. Within a few years, Frank's advancing age and deteriorating health led to his financial dependence on his daughter as well. This did not diminish Gilpin's professional activities. By 1930, her work had been shown in museums and galleries from Honolulu to Edinburgh. That same year, she applied unsuccessfully for a Guggenheim fellowship, which had never been awarded to a photographer, since photography was not then considered one of the fine arts.

In 1931, Betsy Forster moved to Red Rock, on the Navajo Reservation, to become a field nurse for the New Mexico Association on Indian Affairs. Visiting her often, Gilpin began to photograph the members of the Navajo community, developing a great understanding and empathy with the Navajo and earning their trust and admiration. Her images of the Navajo were direct and in sharp focus, a departure from the style of her previous pictorial work.

In the early 1930s, as the Depression strengthened its grip on the American economy, Gilpin slowed down the pace of her exhibitions in order to concentrate on earning a living. In the fall of 1931, she presented a series of slides at an archaeological conference held at the Laboratory of Anthropology in Santa Fe, New Mexico. Jesse Nusbaum, director of the laboratory, wrote her: "In selection of subjects, in photographic quality, and from the artistic standpoint, your lantern slides are in a class by themselves, seldom approached and never excelled. The particular set shown here . . . merits wide distribution among the scientific and educational institutions of this country."

In 1932, Gilpin again applied for a Guggenheim, intent on making a series of slides of the Yucatan for educational purposes. Again her application was denied. But Gilpin journeyed to the Yucatan anyway and photographed the ruins at Chichen Itza. She was able to exhibit her Yucatan images at several different museums, including the American Museum of Natural History in New York City.

As part of the Depression-induced cutbacks at the New Mexico Association on Indian Affairs,

Betsy Forster lost her job at Red Rock in April 1933. Gilpin urged her to assemble a small book about her nursing work with the Native Americans, consisting of Betsy's letters and Laura's photographs. Before Forster could begin the work, however, she obtained a new position with the Emergency Recovery Administration (ERA) in Park County, Colorado, and soon became the state supervisor of the ERA's nursing program. The next year, Gilpin presented her work both of the Yucatan and of the American southwest at the Library of Congress. This exhibition resulted in the sale of 42 of her prints, which became part of the Library's permanent collection.

In 1935, Gilpin and Forster began a poultry business which briefly proved successful. When the ERA disbanded in 1936, Forster concentrated all her efforts on the turkey farm, but in 1939 the poultry business failed (possibly due to sabotage by a competitor), and Forster started a guest house for vacationers in Colorado. In 1941, Gilpin's first book, *The Pueblos: A Camera Chronicle*, was published; its images, depict-

Laura Gilpin

ing the southwest and its impressive history before the Europeans arrived, represented 20 years of her photographic work.

The following year, Forster was forced to resume her nursing career when the boarding house she had been leasing was sold. In November, Gilpin, who wanted to contribute to the country's war effort, was offered a job as photographer for the public-relations department at the Boeing Company in Wichita, Kansas. But events spiraled downward. In July 1943, Frank Gilpin died. In August 1944, Forster was diagnosed with acute encephalitis and, after hospitalization, was further diagnosed with polio as well. When her health deteriorated further, Betsy was declared legally incompetent and soon moved to her sister's home in Nebraska. Though Laura wanted to care for Betsy herself, she was not allowed to do so, probably because she was not a blood relative. Another tragedy came in 1945, when Laura's brother Francis was killed in an automobile accident.

Gilpin had relocated to Santa Fe, New Mexico, that fall. The following year, Forster, who had mostly recovered from her illnesses (the declaration of mental incompetency was annulled), moved to Santa Fe. After 27 years of companionship, she and Laura were finally able to set up a household together. Both came to love the tolerant, open atmosphere of Santa Fe, remaining in that town for the rest of their lives.

To distract herself from her sorrows, Gilpin had traveled to New York, where she signed a contract for a second book, to document the course of the Rio Grande. The project took four years to complete, during which time she found a publisher for a third book on the Yucatan. She combined her traveling for both books and was rewarded in 1948 with the release of *Temples in Yucatan* by Hastings House, which was followed in 1949 by the publication of *The Rio Grande: River of Destiny* by the firm of Duell, Sloan, and Pearce. Both works were praised by archaeologists, anthropologists, and geographers for their depth, spirit and clarity.

In 1947, Gilpin made a third application for a Guggenheim and received her third rejection. Elected an active member of the Indian Arts Fund, by the following year she was a trustee and vice-chair. She continued her work with the organization for a number of years, illustrating her concern and commitment to supporting Native American artists. Although Gilpin had received considerable acclaim, in the late 1940s she and Forster, who remained too ill from polio to work,

still struggled financially. With the concern and support of close friends, however, Gilpin was able to continue her photographic work. In the prospering economy of the 1950s, she returned to commercial photography, although true financial success continued to elude her. She struggled to find new projects and sought a publisher for a book she wanted to produce on the Navajo people. Her fortunes continued in much the same vein throughout the 1960s.

However, in 1968 her last book, *The Enduring Navaho*, finally found a publisher in the University of Texas Press. Combining prints made from the 1930s to the 1960s, the work was dedicated to Betsy Forster, whom Gilpin credited with leading her to an understanding of the Navajo people. Thoroughly integrating the photographic illustrations with the text (adapted from Betsy's letters written 30 years earlier), Gilpin created a book which found scholarly and popular praise as a documentary history of the 20th-century Navajo. More important to her, however, was the admiration the book received from the Navajo.

In the winter of 1969, Gilpin was awarded an honorary doctorate from the University of New Mexico as "one of the pioneers in the recognition of photography as a fine art." The award encouraged her to apply for the fourth time to the Guggenheim Foundation for a fellowship, although, yet again, her application was turned down. Despite this disappointment, Gilpin was finally finding the recognition she had long sought. *The Enduring Navaho* had introduced her work to a new generation of photographers and galleries were anxious to exhibit her prints. But Betsy Forster's health continued to deteriorate. Gilpin, now in her late 70s and facing her own declining health, was taxed to her limits to tend to Betsy's needs but was reluctant to place her life companion in a nursing home. In autumn of 1971, Gilpin was forced to place her under professional care. Betsy Forster died only a few months later, on January 1, 1972. She and Gilpin had been together over 50 years.

After Forster's death, Gilpin sought to fill the void with a new photographic project. She was given a grant for a book on Canyon de Chelly, but, due to advancing age and ailing health, she did not complete the work. Still, her reputation continued to expand during the 1970s, and in 1974 at long last she was awarded a Guggenheim Fellowship. With the endowment, she was to produce platinum prints, much as she had created in her first years as a photographer. But Gilpin was unable to begin this final project, as the demands of visiting with her ever-increasing followers kept her from her work. In 1977, she received the Governor's Award in the Arts and Humanities from the governor of Colorado; two years later, a documentary film was produced on her career. On November 30, 1979, Laura Gilpin, a photographer for more than 70 years, died of heart failure at her home in Santa Fe. At the end of a life lived largely in obscurity, she was hailed by Ansel Adams as "one of the most important photographers of our time."

SOURCES:

Sandweiss, Martha A. *Laura Gilpin: An Enduring Grace.* Fort Worth, TX: Amon Carter Museum of Western Art, 1986.

SUGGESTED READING:

Gilpin, Laura. *The Enduring Navaho.* Austin: University of Texas Press, 1968.

———. *The Pueblos: A Camera Chronicle.* NY: Hastings House, 1941.

———. *The Rio Grande: River of Destiny.* NY: Duell, Sloan, and Pearce, 1949.

———. *Temples in Yucatan: A Camera Chronicle of Chichen Itza.* NY: Hastings House, 1948.

Heather Moore,
freelance writer in the history of photography and women's studies,
Northampton, Massachusetts

Gimbutas, Marija (1921–1994)

Lithuanian-born archaeologist and educator who shaped much of the field of pre-Indo-European archaeology (7000–3000 BCE). Born Marija Alseika in Vilnius, Lithuania, on January 23, 1921; died of cancer in Los Angeles, California, in 1994; daughter of Daniel and Veronica (Janulaitis) Alseika; Vilnius University, M.A., 1942; Tubingen University in Germany, Ph.D. in archaeology, 1946; married Jurgis Gimbutas, in 1942; children: three daughters.

Selected works: Goddesses and Gods of Old Europe (1974); The Language of the Goddess (1989); The Civilization of the Goddess (1991); The Living Goddess (1999).

Born in 1921 and educated in Vilnius, Lithuania, Marija Gimbutas received a doctorate in archaeology from Tubingen University in Germany. In 1949, she immigrated to the United States where she undertook post-graduate work at Harvard University. Gimbutas joined the University of California at Los Angeles (UCLA) in 1963 and served as professor of European archaeology until her retirement in 1990. During this time, she directed five major archaeological excavations in southeastern Europe and was the author of 20 books and more than 200 articles on European prehistory and folklore. She was also considered an authority on the Prehistoric

incursions of Indo-European-speaking people into Europe and the ways in which they changed society there.

Most notable among her books are *Goddesses and Gods of Old Europe* (1974), *The Language of the Goddess* (1989), and *The Civilization of the Goddess* (1991), the last being the most comprehensive of the three. Together, these works present an interpretation of the Neolithic period of Europe that challenges traditional views of prehistoric societies. Her most controversial thesis suggests that the world was at peace during the Stone Age, when goddesses were worshipped and societies were centered around women; this harmony was then shattered by patriarchal invaders and the subsequent worship of warlike gods. Through her studies and interdisciplinary approach, Gimbutas created a new field called archeomythology. Although skepticism about her thesis was widespread among scholars, it was embraced by many feminists and by the renowned mythologist Joseph Campbell.

Marija Gimbutas

Commenting on Gimbutas' book *The Language of the Goddess*, historian *Gerda Lerner of the University of Wisconsin said that although her theory could never be proven it could "challenge, inspire and fascinate" simply by presenting an alternative to male-centered explanations. Gimbutas died of cancer in Los Angeles in 1994, age 73. Before her death, she had been working on *The Living Goddess*, a distillation of her life's work. Edited by **Miriam Robbins**, the book was published in 1999. "As in her previous work," noted a reviewer for *Publishers Weekly*, "Gimbutas's aesthetic and spiritual sensitivity adds a depth unusual in archeological writing. This book is a major contribution to cultural history, especially the history of religion; clearly no one but Gimbutas could have produced this masterful contribution to the archeomythology of Europe."

SOURCES:
The Day [New London]. February 4, 1994.
Publishers Weekly. March 15, 1999, p. 39.

SUGGESTED READING:
Gimbutas, Marija. *The Living Goddess*. Edited by Miriam Robbins. University of California, 1999.

Ginevra (d. 470 or 542).

See Guinevere.

Gingold, Hermione (1897–1987)

British-born actress of stage and screen. Born Hermione Ferdinanda Gingold on December 9, 1897, in London, England; died on May 24, 1987, in New York, New York; daughter of James (a stockbroker) and Kate (Walter) Gingold; educated privately; attended Rosina Filippi School of the Theatre, London; married Michael Joseph, a publisher (divorced); married Eric Maschwitz, a program director with the BBC (divorced); children: (first marriage) two sons.

Selected films: Someone at the Door *(1936);* The Butler's Dilemma *(1943);* The Pickwick Papers *(1952);* Around the World in 80 Days *(1956);* Gigi *(1958);* Bell Book and Candle *(1958);* The Naked Edge *(1961);* The Music Man *(1962);* I'd Rather Be Rich *(1964);* Harvey Middleman-Fireman Rocket to the Moon *(*Those Fantastic Flying Fools, *1967);* A Little Night Music *(1977);* Garbo Talks *(1984).*

Selected theater: Herald *in* Pinkie and the Fairies *(professional debut, His Majesty's Theatre, 1908);* Jessica *in* The Merchant of Venice *(Old Vic Theatre, 1914);* Liza *in* If *(Ambassadors' Theatre, 1921);* Old Woman *in* The Dippers *(Criterion Theatre, 1922); second daughter in* From Morn to Midnight, *Lavinia in* One More River, *Lily Malone in* Hotel Universe, *and Vidette in* I Hate Men *(Gate Theatre, 1931–33);*

Camille in Mountebanks *("Q" Theatre, 1934); May in* Laura Garrett *(Arts Theatre, 1936); Leading Lady in* In Theatre Street *(Mercury Theatre, 1937);* The Gate Revue *(Ambassadors' Theatre, 1939);* Sweet and Low *(Revue, Ambassadors' Theatre, 1943);* Slings and Arrows *(Revue, Comedy Theatre, 1948); Mrs. Rocket in* Fumed Oak *(Ambassadors' Theatre, 1949); Jane Banbury in* Fallen Angels *(Ambassadors' Theatre, 1949);* It's About Time *(Revue, Brattle Theatre, Cambridge, Massachusetts, 1951);* John Murray Anderson's Almanac *(Revue, New York debut, Imperial Theatre, 1953); Mrs. Bennet in* First Impressions *(Alvin Theatre, New York, 1959);* From A to Z *(Revue, Plymouth Theatre, New York, 1960); Clara Weiss in* Milk and Honey *(Martin Beck Theatre, New York, 1962); Madame Rosepettle in* Oh Dad, Poor Dad, Mama's Hung You in the Closet and I'm Feelin' So Sad *(Phoenix Theatre, 1963); Celeste in* Dumas and Son *(Dorothy Chandler Pavilion, Los Angeles, California, 1967); Agnes Deringdo in* Highly Confidential *(Cambridge Theatre, London, 1969); Madame Armfeldt in* A Little Night Music *(Shubert Theatre, New York, 1973, and Adelphi Theatre, London, 1975).*

Hermione Gingold was born Hermione Gingold—"Would I have chosen such a name?" she once asked—on December 9, 1897, in London, the daughter of James, a stockbroker, and **Kate Gingold**. She made her stage debut at age 11 and spent her early career in serious roles, until finding her niche as a comedian in *The Gate Revue* (1939). It was followed in 1943 by *Sweet and Low*, which in continually updated versions (*Sweeter and Lower, Sweetest and Lowest*) occupied London's Ambassadors' Theater for almost six years. During the run of the revue, critic T.C. Worsley commented on Gingold's quirky portrayal of a theater gossip: "To watch Miss Gingold's tongue roll around a familiar name and then quietly drop it off with all the mud sticking on is to watch art raising a foible to the stature of a Humour." Captivated by her in *Slings and Arrows* (1948), Harold Hobson noted: "Miss Gingold blossoms into gargoyles as if she were Notre Dame itself."

In 1951, the wild-maned, bass-voiced, and notably eccentric Gingold made her American debut at the Brattle Theater in Cambridge, Massachusetts, in the revue *It's About Time*, which was followed in 1953 by her first New York appearance in *John Murray Anderson's Almanac*. In 1959, she delighted Broadway audiences in the role of Mrs. Bennet in Abe Burrows' *First Impressions*, a musical adaptation of *Jane Austen*'s *Pride and Prejudice*. "Mrs. Bennet is no longer the vague, fussy provincial matchmaker of Jane Austen's imagination," reported Kenneth Tynan, "but a burbling dragoness fully capable (as she never is in the novel) of withering her husband with a single fire-darting glare. . . . No actress commands a more purposeful leer; and in nobody's mouth do vowels more acidly curdle."

Gingold, who called herself "very chintzy" with her money, was selective about her roles, working only when she wanted. From the 1950s on, she traveled back and forth between the London and New York stage, and also made a few memorable appearances in films, notably *Gigi, Bell Book and Candle* (both in 1958), and *A Little Night Music* (1977), the Stephen Sondheim musical in which she recreated her stage portrayal of the indomitable matriarch, Madame Armfeldt. She made numerous television appearances, often in the role of raconteur on talk shows with Steve Allen, Jack Paar, Garry Moore, and Merv Griffin. She also published two books: her autobiography, *The World is Square* (1945), and *Sirens Should Be Seen and Not Heard* (1963).

The actress was married and divorced twice. Her first marriage to publisher Michael Joseph, produced two sons, one of whom is the founder and director of a theater in England. Her second husband, Eric Maschwitz, was a program director for the BBC. Hermione Gingold died in New York in 1987.

SOURCES:

McGill, Raymond D., ed. *Notable Names in the American Theatre.* Clifton, NJ: James T. White, 1976.

Moritz, Charles, ed. *Current Biography 1987.* NY: H.W. Wilson, 1987.

Morley, Sheridan. *The Great Stage Stars.* London: Angus and Robertson, 1986.

Barbara Morgan,
Melrose, Massachusetts

Ginsburg, Ruth Bader (1933—)

American advocate, specializing in sex-discrimination cases, and the second woman to sit on the U.S. Supreme Court. Born Joan Ruth Bader on March 15, 1933, in the Flatbush section of Brooklyn, New York; younger of two daughters of Nathan Bader (a clothier and furrier) and Celia (Amster) Bader; attended James Madison High School; graduated Cornell University, B.A., 1954; attended Harvard Law School; graduated Columbia Law School, 1959; granted honorary degree, University of Lund, Sweden, 1969; married Martin D. Ginsburg (a lawyer), 1954; children: Jane Ginsburg (b. 1955); James Ginsburg (b. 1965).

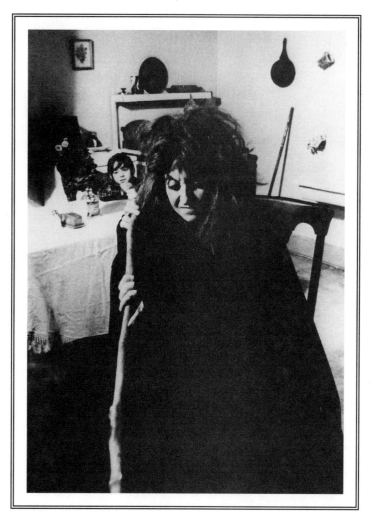

Hermione Gingold

Born in Brooklyn, New York, on March 15, 1933, Ruth Bader Ginsburg was raised as an only child from age one, when her older sister Marilyn died from meningitis. Ginsburg was strongly influenced by her mother, **Celia Bader**, a dynamic woman who shared with her daughter a love of reading and language. Celia also shared her frustration in the socially circumscribed life for a woman with ambition in the 1930s. In 1950, the day before Ginsburg graduated from James Madison High School in Brooklyn, her mother died of cervical cancer, an illness she had been fighting for four years. Determined that her daughter have a chance for the career she had longed for, Celia Bader had salted away several thousand dollars toward Ruth's education. When Ginsburg won a scholarship to Cornell University, she gave the money to her father.

Upon graduation from Cornell, Ruth married Martin D. Ginsburg, a fellow graduate and fellow lawyer. They both then entered Harvard Law School where Ginsburg was one of only nine women in a class of over 500. At a welcoming reception, Erwin N. Griswold, dean of the law school, asked each woman to justify the filling of a slot better served by a man. To prove her worth, "Ruthless Ruthie" studied intensely during her years at Harvard, and, though women were barred from the periodical room of the Lamont Library, she was elected editor of the *Harvard Law Review*. In their second year, Martin was diagnosed with testicular cancer. While he underwent radiation, Ruth added his classes to her agenda, taking notes and typing his papers.

When Martin, who graduated on schedule, took a job with a law firm in Manhattan, Ruth transferred to Columbia University Law School, worked on the *Columbia Law Review*, and, upon graduation in 1959, tied for first place in her class. With her law degree and a passing of the New York Bar exam, she signed up for every law job interview available. "Not a single law firm in the city of New York bid for my employment," she said, citing not only her gender but the fact that she was a Jew and a mother. Supreme Court Justice Felix Frankfurter refused to interview her because he was not interested in hiring a woman, while Judge Learned Hand refused to work with women because it would inhibit his freedom to curse. She was finally hired as a clerk with Edmund L. Palmieri, a federal district judge in New York. Completing her clerkship in 1961, she worked on Columbia Law School's International Procedure project for two years as well as studying at the University of Lund in Sweden. Three books came out of that experience, *Civil Procedure in Sweden* (with Anders Bruzelius, 1965), *Text, Cases, and Materials on Sex-Based Discrimination* (with Herma Hill Kay and Kenneth M. Davidson, 1974), and *The Swedish Code of Judicial Procedure* (translation with Bruzelius, 1968).

In 1963, Ginsburg joined the faculty of Rutgers University Law School, only the second woman to do so and one of the first 20 women to teach in an American law school. She had undergone a long series of setbacks and slights because of her gender but was not fully aware of the pattern until she read *Simone de Beauvoir's *The Second Sex*. Simultaneously, the New Jersey chapter of the American Civil Liberties Union (ACLU) began to refer sex discrimination cases to her. "I repaired to the library," noted Ginsburg, "and spent the better part of a month reading every article written and every published federal case in the area since the nation's start." This was not a daunting task, however, since "there was so little." "In the process, my own consciousness was awakened. I began to won-

der, How have people been putting up with such arbitrary distinctions? How have I been putting up with them?" Her first major case was *Reed* v. *Reed*, and the U.S. Supreme Court agreed with her brief, reversing an Idaho law that preferred men over women for executorship of an estate. It was the first time a law was overturned because of a woman's complaint of unfair sexual bias.

In 1972, Ginsburg was hired as founding counsel, then general counsel, to the ACLU's Women's Rights Project. "The project's goal was to get decision-makers to understand what sex stereotyping is and how the notion that men are this way (frogs, snails, puppy dogs' tails) and women are that way (sugar, spice, everything nice) ends up hurting both sexes." She also joined the staff of Columbia Law School as its first tenured female professor. Preferring to stick with cases that she felt had a good chance of winning, Ginsburg's box score before the U.S. Supreme Court was 5 wins, 1 loss.

In 1980, President Jimmy Carter appointed Ginsburg to the U.S. Court of Appeals for the District of Columbia. During her tenure, she wrote 300 opinions, mostly taking a moderate position. When she was nominated to the Supreme Court by President Bill Clinton in 1993, her position as a centrist alarmed many liberals, and she was not endorsed by the ACLU. In the area of abortion, a bone of contention with many of her critics, Ginsburg had maintained that the 1973 Supreme Court law should have been grounded in the equal protection clause which outlawed sex discrimination rather than cast as a privacy issue. Generally, Ginsburg refused to discuss controversial issues during nomination hearings, but she did testify on July 21, 1993, that abortion is "something central to a woman's life, to her dignity. It's a decision she must make for herself. And when government controls that decision for her, she's being treated as less than a fully adult human responsible for her own choices."

As regards the Equal Rights Amendment, Ginsburg had long been an advocate. In 1981, she had told **Lynn Gilbert** and **Gaylen Moore** for their book *Particular Passions*: "We know the Founding Fathers in the eighteenth century did not think men and women were or should be equal before the law. . . . It's hard to read into provisions written over a century ago our modern concept that men and women should have equal opportunities, so far as government action is concerned. Yet the Supreme Court Justices have been doing just that. They have done so be-

*R*uth
*B*ader
*G*insburg

cause our Constitution is meant to survive through the ages; there must be some adaptation to changing times and conditions. But it would be so much cleaner if the Constitution were amended to state the sex equality principle expressly. A case by case approach could achieve the same end, but not as solidly or securely. The same issues would have to be fought out again and again and again."

Ginsburg's nomination was confirmed by the Senate with a vote of 96-to-3. In her acceptance speech, she spoke of her mother, "the bravest and strongest person I have known. . . . I pray that I may be all that she would have been had she lived in an age when women could aspire and achieve and daughters are cherished as much as sons."

SOURCES:
Gilbert, Lynn, and Gaylen Moore. *Particular Passions.* NY: Clarkson Potter, 1981.
Graham, Judith, ed. *Current Biography.* NY: H.W. Wilson, 1994.

Ginzburg, Natalia (1916–1991)

Leading Italian novelist, known for her neorealistic style, and whose most memorable works were novels on the difficult relations between the sexes. Name variations: (pseudonym) Alessandra Tornimparte. Born Natalia Levi on July 14, 1916, in Palermo, Italy; died in Rome on October 9, 1991; daughter of Giuseppe Levi (a professor of anatomy at the University of Palermo) and Lidia (Tanzi) Levi; private study at home to 1927; attended secondary school in Turin, 1927–33; studied briefly at University of Turin, 1933; married Leone Ginzburg (an academic, writer, and anti-Fascist activist), in 1938 (died 1944); married Gabriele Baldini (a professor of English at the University of Trieste), in 1950 (died 1969); children (first marriage) two sons, Carlo and Andrea, and one daughter, Alessandra Ginzburg; (second marriage) one daughter, Susanna Baldini.

Moved with family to Turin (1919); her first short story published and her father arrested by Fascist government (1934); started work as editor at Einaudi publishing house (1938); followed husband Leone Ginzburg into exile in the village of Pizzoli (1940); published first novel under pseudonym (1942); fled to Rome during period of German occupation, her husband arrested and handed over to Nazis (1943); on death of husband, took refuge with her children in Florence (1944); resumed work with Einaudi (1944); returned to Turin (1945); joined Communist Party (1946); won Tempo Literary Prize (1947); left Communist Party (1951); moved to Rome, won Veillon International Prize (1954); won Viareggio Prize (1957); lived in England (1959–62); won Chiancino Prize (1961); won Strega Prize (1963); completed first play (1965); elected to Italian Parliament (1983); reelected (1987).

Selected works: La strada che va in città *(The Road to the City, 1942);* Tutti i nostri iera *(All Our Yesterdays, 1952);* Le voci della sera *(Voices in the Evening, 1961); (collection of essays)* Le piccole virtù *(The Little Virtues, 1962);* Lessico famigliare *(Family Sayings, 1962);* Serena Cruz, or True Justice *(1990).*

From the late 1940s until her death in 1991, Natalia Ginzburg was a leading Italian writer, whose life was intimately linked to the tragic experience of her country in the era of Fascism and World War II. Nonetheless, this prolific author, with a stream of novels and novellas as well as ten plays and numerous essays following 1945, put no emphasis in her work on the momentous political and military events of the Fascist, wartime, and postwar eras. The basic themes of her fiction were the courses of intimate relationships within the family, and these she explored with unrelenting—some critics say deepening—pessimism. Professor Sergio Pacifici of Yale University in his study of Italian literature described her themes as "the solitude and anguish of life as well as the impossibility of communicating our despair to other humans." For Alan Bullock, the "basic stimulus" for her writing was her rejection of "submission or exploitation . . . in a society where women are still more often than not relegated to positions of inferiority and where masculine values are correspondingly seen as naturally and necessarily predominant." Nonetheless, he notes, Ginzburg's male characters likewise show a lack of creativity, drive, and ambition. To add a paradox: Ginzburg, who used the political upheavals of her time only as an occasional background element for her fictional writing, ran successfully for the Italian Parliament in 1983 and again in 1987.

She was born Natalia Levi in Palermo on July 14, 1916, to an academic family of mixed religious heritage. Her father Giuseppe Levi was a member of a Jewish family that traced its origins to the city of Trieste. Her mother **Lidia Tanzi Levi** was a Roman Catholic. Natalia was the second daughter and the fifth and last child in the family. When Natalia was only three, her father's career as a professor of anatomy led to the family's relocation northward where Giuseppe Levi received an appointment to the faculty of the University of Turin. Most of the rest of her life, except for a harrowing period during World War II when she was in exile in a southern Italian village, she spent in the cities of northern Italy.

Home life revolved around her autocratic father who tried to dominate his wife and children much as he ruled over his university laboratory. To shield Natalia from infectious diseases, her father insisted on keeping her at home, and she was educated by private tutors. When she entered her first communal classroom at age 11, the young girl discovered that, as neither actively Jewish nor Catholic, she was a permanent outsider.

Although her father had no interest in literature, it became a central concern for the Levi children. By the time Ginzburg began attending school with other children, she had already decided to become a writer. While still a teenager, she began to publish fiction. Her regular studies drew little of her energies and attention, and she failed many of her courses in secondary school, although she still managed to enter the University of Turin.

A crucial thread running through Natalia Ginzburg's teenage years was her family's opposition to the Fascist regime. Her father and one of her brothers were imprisoned in 1934, a second brother was arrested the following year, and her third brother avoided the Fascist police only by a daring escape to Switzerland. Natalia joined an anti-Fascist organization in Turin. Critic Wallis Wilde-Menozzi finds the roots of her passion for exploring human relationships in her "somber childhood." There "as a girl and a Jew in a family in which science, political opinion, and physical danger took precedence over art and feeling, her impulse to express herself became a painful, solitary, lifetime task."

Ginzburg later described the struggle at the heart of her early writing. She had problems finishing her stories, and sometimes even writing the first lines of a piece was nearly impossible. Taking Anton Chekhov as a model, she saw herself constricted by her Italian identity. "It pained me to have been born in Italy, to live in Turin because that which I would have loved to have described in my books was Nevsky Prospect."

The tragic events of the era leading up to World War II soon overtook her life. In 1938, Natalia married Leone Ginzburg, the leader of the anti-Fascist group in Turin that she had joined a few years before. Born in Russia, Leone was a former professor of Russian literature who had lost his academic post due to his open opposition to dictator Benito Mussolini's Fascist regime. For the first years of their marriage, she joined him in working as an editor and translator for the Einaudi press, which he had recently helped to establish. The newlyweds immediately began a family, and they soon found themselves and their children in a deeply hostile environment. Both the Ginzburgs' Jewish background and their political sympathies placed them in peril in the Italy of the late 1930s. Mussolini's growing ties to Adolf Hitler led his dictatorial government to adopt increasingly severe restric-

tions on Italy's small Jewish community. The Racial Laws of 1938, for example, made marriage between Jews and non-Jews illegal and barred Jews from teaching in universities, publishing books, or even being listed in the telephone directory. Moreover, the Fascist government had from its origins dealt severely with open political opposition and especially with avowed critics from the socialist side. In these difficult years, Natalia's father was forced out of his position at the University of Turin and immigrated, along with Natalia's mother, to Belgium.

When Italy joined World War II in May 1940, the Ginzburgs were affected immediately. Leone, as a known left-wing leader, was exiled to a remote part of the country, the town of Pizzoli in the Abruzzi. Natalia, by now the mother of two young children and pregnant with her third, soon followed her husband to this remote locale in the extreme southern part of the Italian peninsula. Always prone to writer's block, Natalia found the dullness and isolation of her primitive new home a useful backdrop for a period of substantial creativity.

Italy's fortunes and that of the Ginzburgs changed dramatically in 1943. Mussolini was deposed in late July, and, in early September, Italy abandoned its alliance with Nazi Germany. Following the fall of the Fascist dictator, Leone immediately left the family's place of exile and settled in Rome. There, he continued his political activities. But the shift in the Italian government's composition and policies led to a brutal response from Adolf Hitler. The German army now rushed in to occupy the territory of their erstwhile ally, and anti-Fascists like Leone Ginzburg were in serious danger.

The German occupiers also took control of Pizzoli. To escape being arrested as a Jew, Natalia traveled to rejoin her husband. Posing as a refugee from Naples and a relative of a member of the village population, she managed to secure a place on a German army truck bound for Rome. In November, she had a rendezvous with her husband, but the couple spent less than three weeks together before Leone was arrested. Natalia soon learned the tragic news that her husband had died in early 1944 as the result of torture in a German prison.

In 1942, while the war was still going on, Ginzburg had published a short novel entitled *The Road to the City*. In those days of a Fascist government, the book could not be presented to the public under her real, obviously Jewish, name, so it appeared under the innocuous pseudonym of Alessandra Tornimparte. In 1944, in the aftermath of Leone's death, she now resumed her literary career. Natalia settled in Turin where she worked for the publishing giant Einaudi. Another brief novel, *The Dry Heart*, appeared in 1949. These novellas were marked by the absence of any extensive plot. Typically her heroine (and narrator) is a young woman who seeks but fails to achieve personal happiness in a secure emotional relationship.

A perceptive novelist capable of distilling so much of our own anguish in simple and unusually poetic stories, she deserves to be read.

—Sergio Pacifici

In an early venture into political affiliation, Natalia Ginzburg joined the Italian Communist Party in 1946. In 1951, she would abandon this tie, stating that a writer had to be free to pursue truth and reality, not to stand always on the side of the oppressed as the party tried to do.

In 1950, the young widow remarried. Her husband, the distinguished scholar Gabriele Baldini, was professor of English at the University of Trieste, and in 1952 he was appointed professor of English at the University of Rome. His career subsequently took him and Natalia to London from 1959 to 1961, where he served as head of the Italian Cultural Institute. The couple had a severely handicapped daughter, Susanna, whom Ginzburg cared for at home and refused to institutionalize.

Starting in 1952, Ginzburg published a number of full-length novels to accompany her continuing flow of novellas. Several were set in the World War II years, but her emphasis remained on her characters' evolving personal relationships rather than the impact of great political and military events upon their lives. The basic themes of her writing were now becoming evident: anguish, solitude, despair at life's problems, an inability to connect in a meaningful way even with one's spouse. Suicide and murder are frequently the only way the lives of many of her characters can find some resolution for their problems. As Pacifici noted, "The world they live in is surely a strange one; although the action acknowledges the existence of an external world, little or no attention is paid to it." He saw her heroes "living in a glass bowl, unhappy with their condition and yet doomed to it." A clear statement of Ginzburg's literary aims comes from Alan Bullock: "Dissatisfaction, frustration, and a sense of alienation are almost invariably crucial to Ginzburg's characters."

American reviewers compared her work with that of her childhood idol, the turn-of-the-century Russian writer Anton Chekhov. Like Chekhov, Ginzburg concentrated her talents on everyday life events and the subtle depiction of her characters' maturing personalities.

By the early 1950s, European critics were also impressed by her work, and she received growing recognition such as the prestigious Veillon International literary prize, which she won in 1954. In 1957, she was awarded the Viareggio Prize, in 1961, the Chiancino. Despite her success, she was frequently the target of Italian literary critics who objected to her simple style, a mode of writing notably removed from what Bullock has called "the ornate traditions of Italian literary composition."

The decade of the 1960s brought a number of new accomplishments. Still afflicted by writer's block, Ginzburg found that her residence in England, just like her enforced exile in the south of Italy from 1940 to 1943, eased her return to productive work. An important collection of essays that she had written between 1944 and 1962 appeared in Italian as *Le piccole virtù*. Its subsequent English translation, *The Little Virtues*, appeared in 1962. A notable essay in this collection, "Winter in the Abruzzi," recorded the Ginzburg family's experiences in their southern Italian place of exile from 1940 to 1943. Her novel-like memoir of 1962, *Lessico famigliare* (*Family Sayings*), was written in less than a month, and it soon won the prestigious Strega Prize. The success of *Family Sayings*, which recounted her life up to her second marriage, encouraged Ginzburg to strike off in a new literary direction. Thus, she wrote eight plays between 1965 and 1971. The plays, like her novels, downplayed dramatic events in the lives of her characters. Using dialogues and soliloquies, Ginzburg sought to show her audiences the characters' natures. Critics had a mixed response, with some suggesting that her work was crippled by her inexperience in writing for the theater, and others finding her willingness to transfer the techniques of her novels to her stagework effective in a delicate and subtle fashion.

In the view of Wilde-Menozzi, the publication of *Family Sayings* and the award of the Strega Prize created a basic dividing line in Ginzburg's career. In that critic's view, Ginzburg's role in Italian society as the widow of an anti-Fascist hero dropped away, and she was known first and foremost for her literary achievements. Moreover, the Italian writer's confidence grew in a way that opened the door to

larger achievements. For example, she now began to publish highly regarded articles of personal opinion in Italy's newspapers.

Tragedy struck Ginzburg in 1969 when her second marriage, like her first, ended with her husband's death. Nonetheless, her steady production of novels filled with carefully wrought and incisive studies of family life continued for several more decades. Ginzburg's basic interest in the family remained the dominant element in her work, and her bleak and pessimistic views on the impossibility of deep personal happiness remained ever present. Along with a final novel that appeared in 1987, she wrote a critical biography of the renowned Italian poet and novelist of the 19th century Alessandro Manzoni and translated the works of Marcel Proust into Italian. In the last years of her writing career, she took up the celebrated legal case of a Filipino girl who had become the center of an ugly controversy between officials of the Italian government and the couple that had adopted her. The resulting book, *Serena Cruz, or True Justice*, appeared in 1990.

Although her fiction was largely devoid of concern for the great political events of the time, Ginzburg became increasingly linked to the political world in the last decade of her life. As a candidate of the Sinistra Indipendenza Party, which was positioned on the non-Communist left of the political spectrum, she was elected to the Italian Parliament in 1983 and reelected four years later. Even before entering the political arena, she had taken up the cause of Palestinians whom she saw suffering as a result of actions by the state of Israel. In a revealing article written in 1972, Ginzburg had explored her complex feelings toward her Jewish background. This was only one of a number of essays that she devoted to subjects of current concern. All the while, her fictional work held closely to the world of private emotions. In an interview with American novelist **Mary Gordon** in 1990, Ginzburg spoke about her life's experiences and her views on writing. "Of course I wrote about the war," she remarked. "I think of a writer as a river; you reflect what passes before you." Nonetheless, she remained convinced that she had properly devoted her talents to family life. "I write about families because that is where everything starts, where the germs grow."

Following her death in Rome on October 9, 1991, Natalia Ginzburg's children decided that their mother should be buried as a Roman Catholic. While she had given great weight to her Jewish identity, nonetheless she had converted to Catholicism during her marriage to Gabriele Baldini.

In his introduction to *Family Sayings*, D.M. Low gave an apt summary of Ginzburg's literary achievement. In contrast to earlier Italian writers, she had left behind "the opulent and florid styles once so popular, in favour of a pregnant economy of phrase." With this "severely controlled writing," she conveyed "a deeply felt sense of the inseparable blend of comedy and tragedy in life."

SOURCES:
Bullock, Alan. *Natalia Ginzburg: Human Relationships in a Changing World*. NY: Berg, 1990.
Current Biography Yearbook, 1990. NY: H.W. Wilson, 1990.
Ginzburg, Natalia. *Family Sayings*. Translated by D.M. Low. NY: Dutton, 1967.
Gordon, Mary. "Surviving History," in *The New York Times Magazine*. March 25, 1990.
Pacifici, Sergio. *A Guide to Contemporary Italian Literature: From Futurism to Neorealism*. Cleveland, OH: Meridian Books, 1962.
Wilde-Menozzi, Wallis. "Anchoring Natalia Ginzburg," in *Kenyon Review*. Vol. 16. Winter 1994, pp. 115–130.

SUGGESTED READING:
Bowe, Clotilde Soave. "Narrative Strategy of Natalia Ginzburg," in *Modern Language Review*. Vol. 68. October 1973, pp. 788–795.
Merry, Bruce. *Women in Modern Italian Literature: Four Studies Based on the Work of Grazia Deledda, Alba De Céspedes, Natalia Ginzburg and Dacia Maraini*. Townsville, Australia: Department of Modern Languages, James Cook University of North Queensland, 1990.
Russell, Rinaldina, ed. *Italian Women Writers: A Bio-Bibliographical Sourcebook*. Westport, CT: Greenwood Press, 1994.

Neil M. Heyman,
Professor of History, San Diego State University,
San Diego, California

Gioconda, La (b. 1474).
See del Giocondo, Lisa.

Giovanna.
Variant of Joanna.

Giovanna I of Naples (1326–1382).
See Joanna I of Naples.

Giovanna II of Naples (1374–1435).
See Joanna II of Naples.

Giovanna of Austria (1546–1578).
See Joanna of Austria.

Giovanna of Italy (1907—)

Queen of Bulgaria. Name variations: *Giovanna of Savoy; Giovanna de Savoi; Joanna of Italy. Born on November 13, 1907; daughter of Victor Emmanuel III, king of Italy (r. 1900–1946), and *Elena of Montenegro (1873–1952); married Boris III (1894–1943), king of Bulgaria (r. 1918–1943), on October 25, 1930; children: Simon II (Simeon), king of Bulgaria (r. 1943–1946); *Marie Louise of Bulgaria (b. 1933).*

Giovanna of Savoy (b. 1907).
See Giovanna of Italy.

Giovanni.

Variant of Joan or Joanna.

Giovanni I of Naples (1326–1382).

See Joanna I of Naples.

Giovanni II of Naples (1374–1435).

See Joanna II of Naples.

Gippius, Zinaida (1869–1945)

Russian Symbolist poet, playwright, novelist, short-story writer, critic, and memoirist, whose emigration after the 1917 revolution prevented her from receiving the critical attention she deserved until the disintegration of the Soviet Union. Name variations: (spelling) Hippius; Z.N. Gippius, Zinaida or Sinaida Nikolaevna Gippius-Merezhkovskaia, and Zinaida Nikolaevna Merezhkovskaia or Nikolayevna Merezhkovski; (pseudonyms) Anton Krainii (Anthony "The Extreme"), Tovarisch German (Comrade Herman), Lev Pushchin, Roman Arenskii, V. Vitovt, and Anton Kirsha. Pronunciation: Zin-ay-EE-da Nik-a-LI-yev-na GIP-pee-us Me-rezh-KOF-ska-ya. Born Zinaida Nikolaevna Gippius in Belev (district of Tula), Russia, on November 8, 1869; died in Paris, France, on September 9, 1945; daughter of Nikolai Gippius (assistant procurator of the St. Petersburg Senate and later chief justice of Nezhin, a district of Chernigov); name of mother unknown; married Dmitrii Sergeevich Merezhkovskii (the Symbolist writer and philosopher) in Tiflis (Tbilisi), on January 8, 1889.

Initiated the Religious-Philosophical Meetings in St. Petersburg (1901); began publication of the literary journal, The New Path (1903); moved to Paris (1906); returned to Russia (1908); emigrated from Russia to Poland (December 24, 1919); left Warsaw for Paris (October 20, 1920); organized the literary society, The Green Lamp, in Paris (1926).

Poetical works: Collected Poems: 1899–1903 (Moscow, 1904); Collected Poems: Second Book (Moscow, 1910); Final Poems: 1914–1918 (St. Petersburg, 1918); Poetic Diary: 1911–1921 (Berlin, 1922); Radiances (Paris, 1938); The Last Circle (and the Modern Dante in Hell) (Paris, 1968).

Prose works: New People: Stories (St. Petersburg, 1896); The Victors: A Novel (St. Petersburg, 1898); The Mirror: Second Book of Stories (St. Petersburg, 1898); Third Book of Stories (St. Petersburg, 1902); The Scarlet Sword: Fourth Book of Stories (St. Petersburg, 1906); (co-authored with Dmitrii Merezhkovskii and Dmitrii Filosofov) Le Tsar et la Révolution (Paris, 1907); (signed Anton Krainii) Literary Diary: 1899-1907 (St. Petersburg,

1908); (co-authored with Merezhkovskii and Filosofov) The Color of Poppies: A Drama in Four Acts (St. Petersburg, 1908); In Black and White: Fifth Book of Stories (St. Petersburg, 1908); The Devil's Doll: A Biography in Thirty-three Chapters (Moscow, 1911); Lunar Ants: Sixth Book of Stories (Moscow, 1912); Roman-Tsarevitch: The History of One Beginning (Moscow, 1913); (signed Anton Kirsha) How We Wrote to the Soldiers and What They Responded to Us (Moscow, 1915); The Green Wheel: A Play in Four Acts with an afterward "Green-White-Scarlet" (Petrograd, 1916); Heavenly Words and Other Stories (Paris, 1921); (co-authored with Merezhkovskii and Filosofov) The Kingdom of the Antichrist (Munich, 1921); Living Faces (2 vols., Prague, 1925); The Blue Book: Petersburg Diary, 1914–1918 (Belgrade, 1929); (co-authored with V.P. Kocharovskii) What Is the Russian Emigration To Do (Paris, 1930); (co-edited with Merezhkovskii) Literary Review: A Free Anthology (Paris, 1939); Dmitrii Merezhkovskii (Paris, 1951).

Giovanna of Italy

Zinaida Gippius was an influential figure in Russian Symbolism, a literary movement which endured from around the turn of the century to the 1920s and had a distinctly religious and mystical orientation. She wrote poetry, plays, short stories, novels, memoirs, and literary criticism, though she is best known for her poetry, which is characterized by its religious and metaphysical themes and its innovative versification patterns. In addition to distinguishing herself as a first-rank poet, Gippius hosted one of the leading literary salons in St. Petersburg and later, in emigration, in Paris. She also organized the Religious-Philosophical Meetings in St. Petersburg, which played a major role in the Russian religious renaissance at the turn of the century. Playfully dubbed "Miss Tification" by her contemporaries, Gippius was as notorious in her day as she was influential. Among other things, she held idiosyncratic views of sex and marriage, assumed contradictory gender roles in her life and art, and fostered religious views that were considered heretical.

The eldest of four daughters, Gippius was born on November 8, 1869, in Belev, Russia, in the district of Tula. Her father Nikolai Gippius served as assistant procurator of the St. Petersburg Senate and later as chief justice of Nezhin in the district of Chernigov. During Gippius' childhood, her family moved frequently in search of an adequate climate for Zinaida and her father, who both suffered from tuberculosis. In 1881, Gippius' father died, making it necessary for Zinaida and her family to take up residency with various relatives in Moscow and later in the Crimea and Caucasus.

Because of her family's constant moves and her ill health, Gippius never completed her formal education. With the exception of a few months spent at the Kiev Institute for Girls from 1877 to 1878 and at a classical gymnasium in Moscow in 1882, she received her education at home from governesses and private tutors. Despite her unsystematic education, Gippius became well versed in literature, history, music, and foreign languages. She spoke French, English, and German fluently as well as her native Russian and was familiar with the literary traditions of these languages. She was particularly fond of Russian literature and developed a profound interest in the works of the novelist Fyodor Dostoevski (1821–1881), whose influence can be felt in her poetry as well as her prose.

Gippius reportedly developed an early interest in poetry. Her secretary, Vladimir Zlobin, maintains in his memoirs, *A Difficult Soul,* that she began writing poetry as young as the age of seven. According to Zlobin, the lyrics that Gippius wrote as a young girl display "the invariable masculine gender [of her lyrical "I"] and the same attitude toward the world—offended and contemptuous" that are characteristic of many of her mature poems. While scholars have been unable to confirm that Gippius began writing poetry at such a young age (let alone that she chose to identify with the masculine gender so early on), it is known that she spent much of her adolescence writing poetry. While living with relatives in the south of Russia, she wrote comic verses about friends and family members, which she frequently read aloud, as well as more serious poetry, which she reportedly hid or destroyed. Like many youths of the day, Gippius was taken by the civic poetry of Semion Nadson (1862–1887), whose popular verses were often set to music. Her first published poems were written in the style of Nadson and appeared in the avant-garde journal, *The Northern Herald,* in 1888, under the signature Z.G.

That same year, Gippius met the well-known Symbolist poet, writer, and philosopher, Dmitrii Sergeevich Merezhkovskii (1865–1941), in the town of Borzhom in the Caucasus. Gippius, who had been dubbed "our little poetess" by the inhabitants of the resort town, was initially jealous of the attention that the famous Merezhkovskii received. Gradually, however, her competitiveness with Merezhkovskii dissipated and, as she writes in her memoirs, *Dmitrii Merezhkovskii,* "we—and it was important that it was both of us—suddenly began to speak as if it had been decided long ago that we would marry and that it would be good if we did." On January 8, 1889, Gippius and Merezhkovskii were married in a simple religious ceremony in Tiflis (Tbilisi), beginning what was to become one of the most intriguing, yet creative, literary marriages.

Gippius' marriage to Merezhkovskii was hardly "typical" in the traditional sense. Although the couple lived together for 52 years, never parting for so much as a day, they never had any children and purportedly never engaged in conjugal relations. In her memoirs, Gippius recalls that after the marriage ceremony which occurred "by itself," as if in some kind of a dream, they each retired to their separate quarters:

> [Dmitrii Seregeevich] went to his hotel rather early, and I went home to bed and forgot that I was married. I forgot to such an extent that in the morning I barely remembered it, even when my mother called through the door: "You're still sleeping, and your husband has arrived. Get up!"

"Husband? What a surprise!" [thought Gippius.]

She clearly intimates in this passage that their marriage was not consummated on their wedding night. Whether or not this was the case, Gippius actively fostered the myth that their marriage remained chaste. As her contemporary Sergei Makovskii recalls in *On the Parnassus of the "Silver Age,"* Gippius would appear in society with "her thick, gently wavy, bronzish-red hair in a long braid as a sign of her virginity (in spite of her ten-year marriage)."

While the Merezhkovskiis' marriage may not have been productive in the traditional, reproductive sense, it was very productive in the intellectual sense. The couple collaborated on numerous projects and developed a creative relationship that seemed to replace the need for a procreative one. Vladimir Zlobin clearly suggests this:

> Strange as it may seem, at least at first glance, the guiding male role belonged not to him, but to her. She was very feminine and he masculine, but on the creative and metaphysical plane their roles were reversed. She fertilized, while he gestated and gave birth. She was the seed, and he the soil, the most fertile of all black earths.

Zlobin's usage of a reproductive metaphor to describe the Merezhkovskiis' intellectual and artistic relationship is hardly arbitrary. Like many of the Russian Symbolists, Gippius and her husband substituted intellectual affiliation for filiation. Not only did they prefer to produce works of art, rather than children, but they readily formed intellectual and social affiliations that served as a substitute for filiation or the family. This is a fact that Gippius and Merezhkovskii clearly alluded to in their later years, when they referred to the young writers and poets who attended their salon in Paris as their "embryos," thus envisioning themselves as spiritual parents of Russian literature in emigration.

The Merezhkovskiis began their distinctly Symbolist "family" in 1889 in the capital city of St. Petersburg. And it was here that Gippius distinguished herself as a major figure in the Russian Symbolist movement. Together with Merezhkovskii, Gippius began hosting their famous literary *soirées* or "Sundays," which were attended by the leading poets, writers, and philosophers of the day. Gippius seemed to relish playing the role of grande dame of their salon. According to the accounts of her contemporaries, she would appear in the salon in outrageous feminine costumes and hairstyles that not only overstepped the boundaries of so-called "good taste" but pushed cultural notions of fem-

ininity to a parodic extreme. As Sergei Makovskii recalls:

> [Gippius] dressed in a fashion that was not customary in writers' circles and not typical for "society," in a very unique manner, with the obvious intention of being noticed. She wore dresses of her "own" design that either clung to her like scales or had ruches and flounces. She loved beads, chains, and diaphanous scarves. Need I even mention her infamous lorgnette? Not without affectation would Gippius draw her lorgnette up to her nearsighted eyes and peer at her interlocutor. With this gesture she emphasized her absent-minded arrogance. And her "make-up!" When she grew tired of her braid, she concocted a hairdo that gave her a ridiculously unkempt look with curls flying about in every direction. In addition, there was a time when she dyed her hair red and put on an excessive amount of rouge. (In Russia, "proper" ladies refrained from such maquillage.)

Despite the fact that Gippius projected an ultra-feminine image in salon society, she managed to distinguish herself as more than simply a salon "poetess" or the wife of the famous Merezhkovskii. She received major critical acclaim with the publication of her poem, "The Song," in *The Northern Herald* in 1893. In "The Song," the speaker of the poem yearns, "I need that which is not of this world,/ Not of this world," expressing the concern with "other-worldliness" and metaphysical ideas that was the earmark of Russian Symbolism. Shortly thereafter in 1896, she published her first collection of short stories, *New People,* and in 1904 she came out with her first anthology of poetry. Gradually, Gippius expanded her creative endeavors to all major literary genres, including novels, plays, memoirs, and literary criticism, a genre which, at that time, was practiced almost exclusively by men.

*As soon as I would speak in verse,
Like now this very moment with you,
I quickly metamorphosed into a man.*

—Zinaida Gippius

In *On the Parnassus of the "Silver Age,"* Sergei Makovskii praises Gippius' poetry for its "masculinity." Masculinity or, more appropriately, androgyny is a characteristic that Gippius aspired to in her writing. She sought to write, in her own words, "like a *human being,* not just like a woman." Accordingly, she frequently employed the masculine voice in her poetry, rather than the feminine voice, typical for a female poet. (That is to say, she used unmarked masculine adjectives and past tense verbal forms for her lyrical "I.") In addition, she exclusively employed the gender-neutral signature, Z. Gippius or Z.N. Gippius, for her poetry, rather than the feminine signature, Zinaida Gippius or Zinaida Gippius-Merezhkovskaia, which would mark her not just as a woman, but also as the wife of Dmitrii Merezhkovskii. As she explicitly stated to one of her editors, "My signature should, of course, be Z. Gippius. I have never in my life signed as 'Zinaida.'" For her literary criticism, she frequently used the masculine pseudonyms, Anton Krainii (Anthony "The Extreme"), Tovarisch German (Comrade Herman), Lev Pushchin, Roman Arenskii, and V. Vitovt.

Besides distinguishing herself as a major figure in the Russian Symbolist movement, Gippius, together with her husband, played a leading role in the Russian religious renaissance at the turn of the century. The couple envisioned their primary religious mission to be the creation of a new church. They felt that the Russian Orthodox Church, based on the principles of what they termed "Historical Christianity," put too much emphasis on the spirit at the expense of the revitalizing potential of the flesh. Only through a synthesis of Historical Christianity's emphasis on the spirit with paganism's emphasis on the flesh could humanity be saved through the creation of a third type of religion based on "consecrated flesh." The attainment of this new religion, which they called "Apocalyptical Christianity," would herald the beginning of a new era based on the Second Coming of Christ and the establishment of "the kingdom of God on earth."

Gippius and Merezhkovskii worked toward the establishment of Apocalyptical Christianity through discussions with other philosophers and intellectuals of such issues as the "unsolved mystery of sex" and its relationship to God. Eventually, however, Gippius came to believe that their mission could best be served if they created a secret inner body that would be completely devoted to their religious mission, which they referred to as "The Cause." Gippius decided that this secret body should be comprised of three members, Gippius, Merezhkovskii, and their young friend and colleague, Dmitrii Filosofov, in imitation of the Holy Trinity. Therefore, on March 29, 1901, the three signified their initiation into this new religion by performing a secret religious rite based on Russian Orthodox Church practices. This marked the birth of the Merezhkovskiis' mystical *ménage à trois*. For the next two decades, Gippius, Merezhkovskii, and Filosofov lived together, working toward the promotion of "The Cause."

A temporary rift between the Merezhkovskiis and Filosofov in 1901 led them to seek a larger forum for the discussion and promotion of their religious ideas. In 1901, Gippius and Merezhkovskii organized the Religious-Philosophical Meetings, which were attended by members of the intelligentsia as well as members of the Russian Orthodox Church hierarchy. Through these meetings, the Merezhkovskiis attempted to increase the number of their converts as well as to mend the ever-widening gap that was occurring between the intelligentsia and the Russian Orthodox Church. These meetings were held regularly from November 29, 1901, until April 5, 1903, when Konstantin Pobedonotsev, the procurator of the Holy Synod of the Russian Orthodox Church, abolished them on the basis of their "outspoken character."

As well as organizing the Religious-Philosophical Meetings, Gippius and her husband founded the monthly journal, *The New Path,* in 1903. The journal not only served as a medium for the religious issues discussed at the Religious-Philosophical Meetings, but also for literature and literary criticism. With the abolishment of the Religious-Philosophical Meetings in 1903, the journal lost one of its primary functions, and, in December 1904, Gippius stepped down as editor of the journal. At this point, Sergei Bulgakov and Nikolai Berdiaev assumed editorship of *The New Path* which they renamed *Questions of Life* and began devoting the journal primarily to sociological and political questions.

With the 1905 revolution, Gippius and Merezhkovskii turned their attention from religion to politics. Like many Russian intellectuals, they supported the 1905 revolution and were disillusioned by its inability to yield concrete results. Disenchanted with the political and social climate in Russia after 1905, the Merezhkovskiis, together with Filosofov, moved to Paris in the spring of 1906. While in France, the three collaborated on *Le Tsar et la Révolution* (1907) which discusses the failed 1905 revolution and the problems inherent in autocracy. They also met with various political émigrés, including the Socialist-Revolutionary terrorist, Boris Savinkov. Sensing the Messianic element in the political ideas of many of these revolutionaries, Gippius tried unsuccessfully to convert them to her unique form of mystical revolution.

In 1908, she and her husband returned to Russia, where they resumed their literary and religious activities. For Gippius, the period after her stay in France was particularly productive. In 1908, together with Merezhkovskii and

Filosofov, she published the play, *The Color of Poppies.* In this same year, she issued a collection of short stories, entitled *In Black and White,* as well as an anthology of literary criticism, *Literary Diary: 1889–1907.* Two years later, she came out with her second volume of collected poems. Shortly thereafter, she published the first and third sections of her uncompleted trilogy, *The Devil's Doll* (1911), the collection of short stories *Lunar Ants* (1911), and *Roman the Tsarevich* (1913).

Gippius continued to work and live in Russia through World War I and the revolutions of 1917. Although she supported the February revolution and the abdication of Tsar Nicholas II, she did not support the October revolution and the Bolsheviks' seizure of power. Believing the Bolsheviks to be the embodiment of the Antichrist, Gippius, along with Merezhkovskii and Filosofov, fled Russia on December 24, 1919, for Poland, where they began organizing a military opposition against the Bolsheviks. Having lost faith in the White counter-revolutionary effort, they staked their hopes in Polish president Jozef Pilsudski's military offensive against Russia. They invited Boris Savinkov to join them in Warsaw to assist them in their anti-Bolshevik efforts. However, once Pilsudski signed a peace agreement with Russia, the Merezhkovskiis realized that their "Russian cause" was hopeless. On October 20, 1920, Gippius and her husband left Warsaw to settle permanently in Paris, leaving Dmitrii Filosofov behind to work on the Communist opposition with Savinkov.

For Gippius, the period in emigration was particularly trying. Not only had she suffered the loss of her homeland, but also of Filosofov, who, with the Merezhkovskiis, had formed a mystical trio for the last 19 years. Despite her sense of profound loss, Gippius resumed her former literary activities. Believing that it was her duty to keep Russian literature and culture alive in emigration, she set about reestablishing her elaborate web of literary and cultural affiliations. In the 1920s, Gippius and Merezhkovskii reintroduced their famous "Sundays" or "Resurrections" (the words are the same in Russian), which served as a meeting ground for Russian writers and philosophers in exile until 1940. And in 1926, they organized the literary society, *The Green Lamp.* Conceived of as "an incubator of ideas," this society drew a much larger audience than their "Sundays," including a host of emerging writers.

In addition to fostering the renaissance of Russian literature and culture in exile, Gippius

continued her own writing. In 1921, she published *Heavenly Words and Other Stories.* Five years later, she published her memoirs, *Living Faces,* which recount her meetings with some of the major writers, philosophers, and personalities of the day, and in 1938 she published her final book of poetry, *Radiances.* With the death of Merezhkovskii in 1941, Gippius turned her literary attention to the subject of her husband. She wrote her reminiscences of Merezhkovskii, detailing the complexities of their 52-year literary marriage. And, in the final years of her life, she paid homage to Merezhkovskii by making him the "dark-eyed" (male) muse of her own modern version of Dante's *Divine Comedy,* titled *The Last Circle (and the Modern Dante in Hell).*

Gippius continued working until almost the very end of her life. She died from paralysis in Paris on September 9, 1945, at age 75. Because of her status as an émigré writer and her inimical stance toward Communism, Gippius was denounced as a "decadent" in Russia, and her works were rarely published or read until the recent political changes. In the West, she has long been considered a major Symbolist poet and one of the most influential and intriguing figures of the time.

SOURCES:

Gippius, Zinaida. *Dmitrii Merezhkovskii.* Paris: YMCA Press, 1951.

Makovskii, Sergei. "Zinaida Gippius," in *On the Parnassus of the "Silver Age" (Na Parnase "Serebriannogo veka").* Munich: Izdatel'stvo Tsentral'ngo Ob'edineniia Politicheskikh Emigrantov iz SSSR, 1962.

Matich, Olga. *Paradox in the Religious Poetry of Zinaida Gippius.* Munich: Wilhelm Fink Verlag, 1972.

Pachmuss, Temira. *Zinaida Hippius: An Intellectual Profile.* Carbondale, IL: Southern Illinois University Press, 1971.

Zlobin, Vladimir. *A Difficult Soul: Zinaida Gippius.* Ed. and intro. by Simon Karlinsky. Berkeley: University of California Press, 1980.

SUGGESTED READING:

Gove, Antonina Filonov. "Gender as a Poetic Feature in the Verse of Zinaida Gippius," in *American Contributions to the Eighth International Congress of Slavists.* Vol 1. Linguistics and Poetics. Ed. by Henrik Birnbaum. Columbus, OH: Slavica, 1978, pp. 379–407.

Matich, Olga. "The Devil and the Poetry of Zinaida Gippius," in *Slavic and East European Journal.* Vol. 16, no. 2, 1972, pp. 184–192.

———. "Dialectics of Cultural Return: Zinaida Gippius' Personal Myth," in *Cultural Mythologies of Russian Modernism: From the Golden Age to the Silver Age.* Ed. by Boris Gasparov, Robert P. Hughes, and Irina Paperno. Berkeley, CA: University of California Press, 1992, pp. 52–72.

———. "Zinaida Gippius and the Unisex of Heavenly Existence," in *Die Welt der Slaven.* Vol. XIX–XX, 1974–75, pp. 98–104.

TRANSLATIONS:

Between Paris and St. Petersburg: Selected Diaries of Zinaida Hippius. Trans. and ed. by Temira Pachmuss. Urbana, IL: University of Illinois Press, 1975.

Modern Russian Poetry: An Anthology with Verse Translations. Ed. by Vladimir Markov and Merrill Sparks. Indianapolis, IA: Bobbs-Merrill, 1967.

A Russian Cultural Revival: A Critical Anthology of Émigré Literature Before 1939. Ed. and trans. by Temira Pachmuss. Knoxville, TN: University of Tennessee Press, 1981.

Translations: Selected Works of Zinaida Hippius. Trans. and ed. by Temira Pachmuss. Urbana, IL: University of Illinois Press, 1972.

Women Writers in Russian Modernism: An Anthology. Trans. and ed. by Temira Pachmuss. Urbana, IL: University of Illinois Press, 1978.

Jenifer Presto,
Assistant Professor of Slavic Languages and Literatures,
University of Southern California, Los Angeles, California

Gipps, Ruth (1921—)

English composer and conductor. Born on February 20, 1921, in East Sussex, England; one of two children of Bryan and Hélène (Johner) Gipps; attended Brickwall School for Girls, Northiam; attended "The Gables" (a preparatory school for boys where she was allowed to enroll because her brother had also attended); attended Bexhill County School; studied music at the Royal College of Music, London; married Robert Baker (a clarinetist), in March 1941; children: one son, Lance (b. 1947).

Selected works: The Fairy Shoemaker (first composition, 1929); Mazeppa's Ride (Op. 1 for female chorus and orchestra); Rhapsody (Op. 18 for soprano and small orchestra); Quintet (Op. 16, for oboe, clarinet and string trio); Brocade (Op. 17, piano quartet); Oboe Concerto (Op. 20); Variations on Byrd's Non Nobus (Op. 7); Knight in Armour (Op. 8); Symphony 1 in F Minor (Op. 22); Death on the Pale Horse (Op. 25); Violin Concerto (Op. 24); Jane Grey Fantasy (Op. 15 for viola and strings); Symphony No. 2 (Op. 30); The Cat (Op. 32 for contralto, baritone, chorus and orchestra); Piano Concerto (Op. 34); Goblin Market (a tone poem for two soprano soloists, three-part female choir and strings or piano); Sinfonietta (for ten winds and tam-tam); Concerto for Violin, Viola and Small Orchestra (Op. 49); Symphony No. 3 (Op. 57); Horn Concerto (Op. 58); Symphony No. 4 (Op. 61); Symphony No. 5 (Op. 64); Ambarvalia (Op. 70).

English composer and conductor Ruth Gipps characterized herself as a born rebel and used her defiant nature to open doors normally closed to women in the world of classical music. Born into a musical family (her mother was a pianist and her father and brother violinists), Gipps (known as "Wid" to friends), was a child prodigy, beginning piano lessons at four and performing her first composition at the age of eight. She entered the Royal College of Music at 15, where she took up the oboe and also began to compose seriously. She studied composition with R.O. Morris, Gordon Jacob, and Vaughan Williams, whose influence can be heard in her early compositions. In 1941, Gipps married Robert Baker, a clarinetist whom she had met in 1939.

During her early career, Gipps worked as an orchestral oboist and also appeared as a concert pianist. Through World War II, she was a member of the Council for the Encouragement of Music and the Arts (CEMA), which was founded by three women, **Seymour Winyates**, **Gladys Crook**, and **Mary Glasgow**, in order to stimulate interest in the arts and provide entertainment for those working in factories. CEMA's concerts took place at all hours, some even starting at midnight for workers on the night shift. In 1947, Gipps received her doctorate in music from Durham University and also gave birth to her son, Lance. She continued her study of conducting with George Weldon, who gave her lessons despite his strong bias against women conductors. She subsequently left Weldon to study with Stanford Robinson for whom she had played oboe in the BBC Theatre Orchestra.

From 1948 to 1950, Gipps was choirmaster of the City of Birmingham Choir. In 1954, at age 33, she began suffering severe pain in her right hand, back, and neck, the result of injuries sustained in a bicycle accident when she was 12. After a period of uncertainty, she decided to abandon the piano and concentrate more on conducting. Gipps led the London Repertory Orchestra from 1955 to 1961, when, after receiving a small legacy, she founded the Chanticleer Orchestra, a group of mostly young London musicians. The orchestra was acknowledged for its high standards and "perfect balance," but it suffered from sporadic support by patrons and a general lack of respect from the musical establishment.

Gipps also built a distinguished teaching record, including a professorship at Trinity College (1959–66), ten years as a professor of composition at the Royal College of Music (1967–77), and a year as a principal lecturer at Kingston Polytechnic (1979). She is a Fellow of the Royal Society of Arts and was made a Member of the British Empire (MBE) in 1981. Amid all her musical activities, she always found time

Ruth
Gipps

to compose. Her works include five symphonies, concertos for violin, piano, violin and viola, and horn, several choral works, and chamber music. In an article on Gipps for *The Maud Powell Signature*, **Margaret Campbell** points out that discrimination was a recurring occurrence in Gipps' career and that her work has never received the recognition it deserves. "[W]hat she would prize above all would be to have her symphonies and major works performed professionally. Apart from her music she considers her life to be of little value to the world."

SOURCES:

Campbell, Margaret. "Ruth Gipps: A Woman of Substance," in *The Maud Powell Signature.* Vol. 1, no. 3. Winter 1996.

Barbara Morgan,
Melrose, Massachusetts

Giralda de Laurac (d. 1211).

See Guirande de Lavaur.

Girardin, Delphine (1804–1855)

French author. Name variations: Madame Émile de Girardin; Madame de Girardin; Delphine Gay; Delphine de Girardin; Delphine Gay de Girardin; (pseudonyms) Vicomte de Launay or Le Vicomte Delaunay; Charles de Launay. Born Delphine Gay on January 26, 1804, in Aix-la-Chapelle, Prussia; died on June 29, 1855, in Paris, France; daughter of Sophie Gay (1776–1852, a novelist) and M. Gay (a receiver-general of the department of the Roër or Ruhr); married Émile de Girardin (1806–1881, a journalist and economist), in 1831.

Selected writings: Essais poétiques *(1824);* Nouveaux Essais poétiques *(1825);* Le Lorgnon *(1831);* Contes d'une vieille fille à ses neveux *(1832);* Le Marquis de Pontanges *(1835);* La Canne de M. Balzac *(1836);* L'École des journalistes *(1839);* Lettres parisiennes *(1843);* Judith *(1843);* Cléopâtre *(1847);* C'est la faute du mari *(1851);* Lady Tartufe *(1853);* Il ne faut pas jouer, avec la douleur *(1853);* La Joie fait peur *(1854);* and Le Chapeau d'un horloger *(1854).*

Delphine Girardin, daughter of M. Gay, a receiver-general of the department of the Roër, and novelist *Sophie Gay, grew up in a brilliant literary society thanks to the influence of her famous mother. A talented poet and writer, Delphine was also a beautiful woman who displayed spirit and was widely considered the queen of Romantic *cénacles* (literary circles).

Girardin's romantic writings, *Essais poétiques* (1824) and *Nouveaux Essais poétiques* (1825), best reflect the sensitivity and spirituality for which she was known. Her writing was so popular that, during a trip to Italy, she was crowned in the tradition of *Germaine de Staël's *Corrine.* Her trip produced various poems including the popular "Napoline" (1833).

In 1831, Delphine married Émile de Girardin, editor of *La Presse.* Taking advantage of her new literary access, she published a series of witty letters under the pseudonym Vicomte de Launay between 1836 and 1848. These letters were published in a collection titled *Lettres parisiennes* in 1843. After her marriage, she established a salon, welcoming such literary stars of the day as Théophile Gautier, Honoré de Balzac, Alfred de Musset, and Victor Hugo.

Girardin was a prolific writer and her skills extended to various genres, including short stories, plays, novels, and poetry. She produced a collection of short stories in 1836 entitled *La Canne de M. Balzac.* Her early poetic work from 1822, "Le Dévouement des médicins français et des souers de Ste Camille dans la peste de Barceloné," was crowned by the Académie Français. Other works include *Le Lorgnon* (1831), *Contes d'une vieille fille à ses neveux* (1832), *Le Marquis de Pontanges* (1835), *Il ne faut pas jouer, avec la douleur* (1853), *C'est la faute du mari* (1851), *La Joie fait peur* (1854), and *Le Chapeau d'un horloger* (1854). *Une Femme qui déteste son mari* appeared after her death in 1855. Her plays include *Judith* (1843), *Cléopâtre* (1847), *Lady Tartufe* (1853) and the banned *L'Ecole des journalistes* (1839).

Judith C. Reveal,
freelance writer, Greensboro, Maryland

Giroud, Françoise (1916—)

French editor, journalist, and government official. Name variations: Francoise Giroud. Born Françoise Gourdji on September 21, 1916, in Geneva, Switzerland; the youngest of two daughters of Salih Gourdji (a journalist) and Elda (Faraji) Gourdji; attended boarding school in Epinay, France, a suburb of Paris; attended the Lycée Molière and the Collège de Groslay; married to M. Eliacheff (marriage dissolved); children: a son born out of wedlock, Alain-Pierre Denis (1941–1972); a daughter, Caroline.

Françoise Giroud, daughter of Salih Gourdji, a well-to-do expatriated Turkish journalist, and **Elda Gourdji**, a Frenchwoman, was born in Geneva, Switzerland, in 1916. She attended boarding school in Epinay, France, and grew up in luxury until her father's death in the early years of the Depression. A bright if reluctant student, Françoise left school at age 15 to learn a marketable trade. After a month of secretarial training, she worked at a bookstore briefly before signing on as a "script girl" for Marcel Pagnol's production of *Fanny.* Over the next five years, she worked in continuity for dozens of films, including Jean Renoir's masterpiece *La grand illusion.* It was Renoir who sensed her flair and allowed her to write some dialogue for the film. In her autobiography, *I Give You My Word*, Giroud discussed her debt to the master director: "What I got from him was the revelation of my possibilities, that anything can happen to you at any time. . . . He would say to me: 'You have gifts. Start off by ruining them.'" By 1938, Giroud had become the first female assistant director in French cinema history. She had a hand in directing several films and continued to write adaptations and dialogue.

In 1939, when the French film industry cut back on production with the onset of World War II, Giroud lost her job. She worked for several months as a private secretary before joining the mass exodus from Paris in June 1940. She settled in Lyon for a time, where she worked for the *Paris-Soir,* then the largest newspaper in France, and also contributed feature articles and short stories to *7 Days,* a small weekly newspaper. When the movie industry revived, she eagerly went back to work, moving unimpeded between sound stages in both the free and occupied zones of France. In 1943, however, she was arrested by the Gestapo in Paris and imprisoned in Fresnes. She was unaccountably freed several months later, shortly before the Allied invasion in June 1944.

After the war, Giroud continued to write movie scripts, but the initial adventure of filmmaking was gone, and she grew increasingly frustrated and bored. She wrote songs and contributed freelance articles to magazines. In 1946, she joined the staff of *Elle,* an innovative women's magazine soon known for its daring subject matter. When editor **Helene Lazaroff** became ill, Giroud took over as editor, staying until 1952, when work on the magazine began to pall for her. "It was because it had become successful," she explained; "we had moved from the artisan stage to the factory level."

After a trip to New York to research a series of articles about women on different economic levels in American society, in 1953, Giroud and Jean-Jacques Servan-Schreiber, the political editor of *Paris-Presse,* founded *L'Express,* a leftist journal of opinion. "Its original mission was to support and nurture a policy of rebuilding France, a policy backed up by solid information," she explained. The magazine, which combined inventive journalistic techniques with political doctrine, attracted some of the best political theorists and writers in France, among them François Mauriac and Albert Camus. In 1956, when Servan-Schreiber, a lieutenant in the military reserves, left to fight in the Algerian War, Giroud took over editorship of the publication. Her ongoing personal relationship with Servan-Schreiber ended completely with his marriage in 1960.

From the time Servan-Schreiber left in 1956 (some believe he was drafted in order to stop his editorials), Giroud became severely depressed, nearly suicidal. "Years went by, during which I was a walking ruin, blacked and burned out like a forest after a fire has swept through it. It took years for me to find another way of living, years before I was able to re-establish a suitable relationship with myself." Psychoanalysis finally brought her back from despair and taught her that her intelligence, on which she had always relied, was powerless against the demons she carried in her soul. "But when you have learned, at your own expense, that intelligence is not what's guiding you, you've really learned a lot. . . . It's not intelligence that rules the world."

Except for a brief stint as the feature editor of *France-Soir* in 1960, Giroud remained editor in chief of *L'Express* until 1974. During her tenure, the magazine metamorphosed into a general news magazine (much like *Time*) and became one of the most widely read and influential

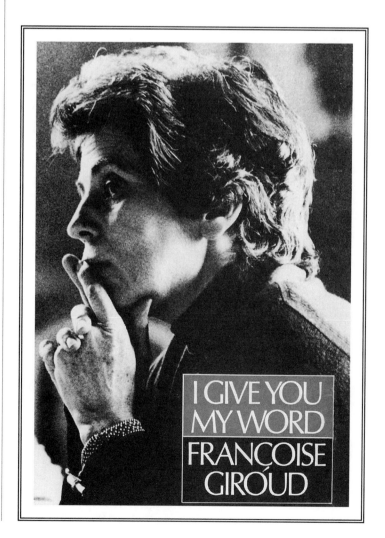

Françoise
Giroud

journals in the country. Giroud not only contributed a weekly editorial, but dozens of longer pieces on a variety of topics from the American space program to the role of women in French society. Especially revealing were her profiles of powerful world leaders such as Charles DeGaulle, Richard Nixon, and Nikita Khrushchev. Giroud had a particular gift for biography, a seemingly effortless ability to capture the essence of her subject. Marcel Archard, who wrote an introduction to *Françoise Giroud vous présent le tout-Paris*, a collection of her anecdotal biographies of celebrities like Jean Anouilh, Jean Renoir, *Colette, and *Edith Piaf, compared her to a painter who skillfully mixes "blood with her paints." During the 1950s, Giroud also published *Nouveaux portraits* (1954) and *La Nouvelle vague: portraits de la jeunesse* (1958).

In May 1974, President Valéry Giscard d'Estaing, honoring a campaign pledge, asked Giroud to become his Secretary of State for the Condition of Women. Initially skeptical (she had supported François Mitterand's candidacy), Giroud wrote in her column that Giscard probably expected her to set up office in the Cabinet's kitchen. Upon further consideration, however, she accepted, with the belief that at age 58 she might be able to learn something new. Giroud immediately set out to change the idealized maternal role that French women had been locked into for centuries. Working with a staff of three and virtually no budget, she announced a series of Cabinet-approved edicts to help equalize the status of women in the work force, education, and public life. They included a call for the elimination of "feminine" jobs, the establishment of free day-care centers, and a revision of the Napoleonic Code, which regarded women as chattel. She proposed maternity and paternity leaves and convinced 800 companies to offer all employees flexible working hours so that workers, male and female, could spend time caring for their families. Her most important message, however, to women throughout the world, was the necessity of achieving economic independence. "Without that," she said, "I don't even know what the word freedom means."

In 1979, after serving an appointment as Secretary of Culture, Giroud returned to journalism, becoming the director of the *Revue du Temps Libre*. In 1993, she co-authored (with philosopher Bernard-Henri Lévy) *Women and Men: A Philosophical Conversation*, which explores the differences between men and women in affairs of the heart.

For a woman so open about her feelings and opinions, Giroud remained remarkably silent about her own personal relationships with men. "Someone once said that you should never tell the story of your life," she wrote in her autobiography, "because it is made up of the lives of others, and you have no right to talk about other people's lives." Just before the German invasion of Paris, Giroud was planning to marry, although in her book the man was not named. Instead, because of the war, they parted, and Giroud, pregnant and unable to obtain an abortion, gave birth to a son in 1941. Always fragile in health, he was killed in a skiing accident in 1972. After the war, Giroud was married for six years to a man described only as a "very seductive Russian." The union produced a daughter, Caroline, and ended around 1952.

SOURCES:

Giroud, Françoise. *I Give You My Word*. Translated from the French by Richard Seaver. Boston, MA: Houghton Mifflin, 1974.

McHarry, Elizabeth. "Journalist takes post in French cabinet," in *The* [Portland, Ore.] *Oregonian*. October 30, 1974.

Moritz, Charles, ed. *Current Biography* 1975. NY: H.W. Wilson, 1975.

Barbara Morgan,
Melrose, Massachusetts

Gisela (c. 753–807)

*Saint. Name variations: Isberge. Born around 753; died about 807; daughter of Bertha (719–783) and Pippin also seen as Pepin III the Short (715–768), mayor of Neustria (r. 741), king of the Franks (r. 747–768); sister of Charlemagne, king of the Franks (r. 768–814), Holy Roman emperor (r. 800–814); aunt of *Gisela of Chelles (b. 781); some sources claim she married; children: some sources cite Rowland.*

The daughter of *Bertha and Pepin the Short, king of the Franks, Gisela was also the goddaughter of Pope Stephen II, who had been a guest of Pepin on a visit to France when Gisela was born in 753. She grew up at Aire in Artois where she met St. Venantius who was living there as a hermit. It was Venantius who advised her to remain chaste as an offering to God. Some sources claim that Gisela turned down all proposals, the first of which came from Constantine Copronyme, whose views ran contrary to those of her father. Another came from a Welsh or Scottish prince. When Pepin died, Bertha urged her daughter to marry a son of the king of the Lombards. Again, Gisela is said to have refused. Instead, she founded a Benedictine abbey at Aire and became a nun. She lived there for 30 years and was visited occasionally by her brother Charlemagne, king of the Franks. Her feast day is May 21.

Gisela (c. 819–c. 874)

Frankish royal in the Carolingian dynasty. Born around 819; died after 874; daughter of *Judith of Bavaria (802–843) and Louis I the Pious, Holy Roman emperor (r. 814–840); married Eberhard, count of Friuli, around 836; children: Uruoch; Adalhard; Rudolf; Berengar I (840–924), Holy Roman emperor (r. 905–924) and king of Italy (r. 888–924); *Judith of Fiuli.

Gisela (1856–1932)

Princess of Bavaria. Name variations: Princess of Austria Habsburg-Lotharingen. Born on July 12, 1856, in Laxenburg; died on July 27, 1932, in Munich; daughter of *Elizabeth of Bavaria (1837–1898) and Franz Joseph also known as Francis Joseph, emperor of Austria (r. 1848–1916); married Prince Leopold of Bavaria (1846–1930), on April 20, 1873.

Gisela Martel (d. 919)

Duchess of Normandy. Name variations: Giselle. Died in 919; daughter of Charles III the Simple (879–929), king of France (r. 893–923), and *Frederona (d. 917); became second wife of Rollo also known as Robert, duke of Normandy (d. 931, the Norse who conquered Normandy), in 912; children: *Adele of Normandy (c. 917–c. 962). Rollo's first wife was *Poppa of Normandy.

Gisela of Bavaria (c. 975–1033)

Queen of Hungary. Name variations: Giselle or Grisela, Princess of Bavaria. Born around 975; died in 1033; daughter of Henry II the Wrangler (951–995), duke of Bavaria (r. 985–995), and Gisela of Burgundy (d. 1006); sister of Henry II (972–1024), Holy Roman emperor (r. 1002–1024); aunt of *Agatha of Hungary; married Stephen I (c. 975–1038), first king of Hungary (r. 1000–1038), in 1008 (some sources cite 995); children: eldest son St. Emeric (also known as Imre) died young (as did all her other children).

A Bavarian princess, Gisela of Bavaria was born around 975, the daughter of Henry II the Wrangler, duke of Bavaria, and ***Gisela of Burgundy**. She married Stephen I, king of Hungary, around 1008, though some sources cite 995. Stephen was faced with great problems as he began the task of organizing, defending, and Christianizing his nation and bringing it into the European fold. One such problem was the revolt of a cousin, Koppàny, who ruled in Transylvania. Koppàny had claimed not only the throne, but the hand of Stephen's widowed mother ***Sarolta**. Immediately moving against him, Stephen eventually defeated Koppàny, executing him in 1003. Then another Magyar—known only by the title Gyula—claimed the rule in Transylvania and usurped it. He, too, was disposed of by the new king Stephen, who was actively supported by German knights in the service of his wife and queen, Gisela.

Their only son Emeric, who enjoyed a reputation for virtue and valor, died in what has been reported as a hunting accident (killed by a "wild boar"). But Stephen Sisa, in his book *The Spirit of Hungary,* alleges that the death was a successful assassination attempt by the Thonuzoba family, who were resisting conversion to Christianity. Because he had led an exemplary life and was well loved by the Hungarian peoples who had accepted Christianity, Emeric was canonized in the late 11th century, at about the same time as his father. Gisela died in 1033.

Gisela of Burgundy (d. 1006)

Duchess of Bavaria. Born before 957; died on July 21, 1006; daughter of Conrad III of Burgundy and Adelaide of Bellay; married Henry II the Wrangler (951–995), duke of Bavaria (r. 985–995); children: Henry II (972–1024), Holy Roman emperor (r. 1002–1024); *Gisela of Bavaria (c. 975–1033); Bruno, bishop of Augsburg; Brigitta (a nun).

Gisela of Burgundy (fl. 1100s)

Countess of Burgundy. Name variations: Gisele of Burgundy. Flourished in early 1100s; died after 1133; daughter of William I, count of Burgundy, and Etienette de Longwy; sister of *Sibylle of Burgundy (1065–1102) and *Bertha of Burgundy (d. 1097); married Humbert also known as Umberto II of Maurienne, count of Savoy; married Rainer, marquess of Montferrat; children: (first marriage) Amadeus II, count of Savoy (d. 1148); *Adelaide of Maurienne (1092–1154); (second marriage) *Joan of Montferrat (who was the second wife of William the Clito, count of Flanders).

Gisela of Chelles (781–814)

Frankish princess and abbess. Name variations: Gisele, Giselle. Born in 781 at Aachen, France; died around 814; daughter of Charles I also known as Charlemagne (742–814), king of the Franks (r. 768–814), Holy Roman emperor (r. 800–814), and Hildegarde of Swabia (c. 757–783); never married; no children.

Gisela of Chelles was the daughter of the Frankish emperor Charlemagne and his empress and third wife *Hildegarde of Swabia. Charlemagne, who believed in the importance of education for women, had his daughters given the same education as his sons. Gisela's instructor was the famous Alcuin of York, one of her father's closest advisors and an extremely learned man. Alcuin wrote that Gisela was an excellent student, with a quick intelligence and a great love of knowledge. She was particularly enthusiastic about astronomy and the other natural sciences. Gisela remained at her father's court for more than 30 years and never married. She entered the convent of Chelles and later became its abbess.

Laura York,
Riverside, California

Gisela of Swabia (d. 1043)

Holy Roman empress. Name variations: Gisele of Schwaben. Born around 1000; died in 1043; married Brunon II, margrave of Saxony; married Conrad II the Salian (990–1039), Holy Roman emperor (r. 1024–1039), in 1016; children: (first marriage) Ludolphe, margrave of Saxony; (second marriage) possibly Emelia (who married Odo II, count of Blois); Henry III (1017–1056), Holy Roman emperor (r. 1039–1056).

Conrad II the Salian began his reign as Holy Roman emperor in 1024. In 1027, he and Gisela of Swabia were crowned in Rome, and they would continue to reign until 1039.

Gisella or Giselle.

Variant of Gisela.

Giselle of Chelles (781–814).

See Gisela of Chelles.

Gish, Dorothy (1898–1968) and Lillian (1893–1993)

American actresses, sisters, and stars of the silent-film era.

Gish, Dorothy. Born Dorothy Elizabeth Gish on March 11, 1898, in Dayton, Ohio; died of bronchial pneumonia in Rapallo, Italy, on June 4, 1968; younger daughter of Mary (McConnell) and James Lee Gish (a struggling grocer and candy merchant); descendant of Zachary Taylor, the 12th president of the U.S.; married James Rennie (an actor), on December 20, 1920 (divorced 1935); no children.

At age five, debuted as the boy "Little Willie," in the play East Lynne; *made New York stage debut as an Irish girl in* Dion O'Dare *(1906); hired as an extra at D.W. Griffith's Biograph Studios (1911); placed under major star contract (1915); revealed great comic gifts in film* Hearts of the World *(1918); made her first talkie,* Wolves, *for Herbert Wilcox in England; made her last professional appearance in the stage play* The Chalk Garden *with her sister (1956).*

Selected films: An Unseen Enemy *(1912); (bit)* The Musketeers of Pig Alley *(1912); (extra)* The New York Hat *(1912);* My Hero *(1912);* The Perfidy of Mary *(1913);* The Lady and the Mouse *(1913);* Almost a Wild Man *(1913);* Her Mother's Oath *(1913);* The Vengeance of Galora *(1913);* The Adopted Brother *(1913);* The Lady in Black *(1913);* The House of Discord *(1913); (bit)* Judith of Bethulia *(1914);* The Mysterious Shot *(1914);* The Floor Above *(1914);* Liberty Belles *(1914);* The Mountain Rat *(1914);* Silent Sandy *(1914);* The Newer Woman *(1914);* Arms and the Gringo *(1914);* The City Beautiful *(1914);* The Painted Lady *(1914);* Home Sweet Home *(1914);* The Tavern of Tragedy *(1914); A Fair Rebel (1914);* The Wife *(1914);* Sands of Fate *(1914);* The Warning *(1914);* The Availing Prayer *(1914);* The Saving Grace *(1914);* The Sisters *(1914);* The Better Way *(1914);* An Old-Fashioned Girl *(1915);* How Hazel Got Even *(1915);* Minerva's Mission *(1915);* Out of Bondage *(1915);* Her Mother's Daughter *(1915);* The Mountain Girl *(1915);* Victorine *(1915);* Bred in the Bone *(1915);* Old Heidelberg *(1915);* Jordan Is a Hard Road *(1915);* Betty of Greystone *(1916);* Little Meena's Romance *(1916);* Susan Rocks the Boat *(1916);* The Little School Ma'am *(1916);* Gretchen the Greenhorn *(1916);* Atta Boy's Last Race *(1916);* Children of the Feud *(1916);* The Little Yank *(1917);* Stage Struck *(1917);* Her Official Fathers *(1917);* Hearts of the World *(1918);* The Hun Within *(1918);* Battling Jane *(1918);* The Hope Chest *(1919);* Boots *(1919);* Peppy Polly *(1919);* I'll Get Him Yet *(1919);* Nugget Nell *(1919);* Out of Luck *(1919);* Turning the Tables *(1919);* Mary Ellen Comes to Town *(1919);* Remodeling Her Husband *(1919);* Little Miss Rebellion *(1919);* Flying Pat *(1920);* The Ghost in the Garret *(1921);* Orphans of the Storm *(1922);* The Country Flapper *(1922);* Fury *(1923);* The Bright Shawl *(1923);* Romola *(1924);* Night Life of New York *(1925);* The Beautiful City *(1925);* Clothes Make the Pirate *(1925); (title role)* Nell Gwynn *(Eng., 1926);* London *(Eng., 1927);* Tip Toes *(Eng., 1927); (title role)* *Madame Pompadour *(Eng., 1927);* Wolves *(Wanted Men, Eng., 1930);* Our Hearts Were Young and Gay *(1944);* Centennial Summer *(1946);* The Whistle at Eaton Falls *(1951);* The Cardinal *(1963).*

Gish, Lillian. Born Lillian Diana Gish on October 14, 1893, in Springfield, Ohio; died at her home in New York City on February 27, 1993; elder daughter of Mary (McConnell) and James Lee Gish; descendant of Zachary Taylor, 12th president of the U.S.; attended various schools including the Ursuline Academy in East St. Louis, Missouri; never married, no children.

Debuted in Convict's Stripes, *starring Walter Huston, around age five; hired as an extra at D.W. Griffith's Biograph Studios (1911); gained attention in* The Mothering Heart *(1913); established stardom in* Broken Blossoms *(1919); made first talkie* One Romantic Night *(U.A., 1930); made television debut in* "The Late Christopher Bean" *(1948); made last film* The Whales of August *(1987). Awards: honorary Academy Award (1970) and American Film Institute's Lifetime Achievement Award (1984). Selected publications: (with Ann Pinchot)* The Movies, Mr. Griffith and Me *(Prentice-Hall, 1969).*

Selected films: An Unseen Enemy *(1912); (bit)* Two Daughters of Eve *(1912); The Aisles of the Wild (1912); The Musketeers of Pig Alley (1912); (bit)* My Baby *(1912); Gold and Glitter (1912); (extra)* The New York Hat *(1912); The Burglar's Dilemma (1912); A Cry for Help (1912); (extra)* Oil and Water *(1912); (bit)* The Unwelcome Guest *(1912); A Misunderstood Boy (1913); The Left-Handed Man (1913); The Lady and the Mouse (1913); The House of Darkness (1913); Just Gold (1913); A Timely Interception (1913); The Mothering Heart (1913); During the Round-Up (1913); An Indian's Loyalty (1913); A Woman in the Ultimate (1913); A Modest Hero (1913); The Madonna of the Storm (1913); Judith of Bethulia (1914); The Battle at Elderbush Gulch (1914); The Green-Eyed Devil (1914); The Battle of the Sexes (1914); Lord Chumley (1914); The Hunchback (1914); The Quicksands (1914); Man's Enemy (1914); Home Sweet Home (1914); The Rebellion of Kitty Belle (1914); The Angel of Contention (1914); The Tear That Burned (1914); The Folly of Anne (1914); The Sisters (1914); (as Elsie Stoneman)* The Birth of a Nation *(1915); The Lost House (1915); Captain Macklin (1915); (as Annie Lee)* Enoch Arden *(1915); Enoch's Wife (1915); The Lily and the Rose (1915); Daphne and the Pirate (1916); Sold for Marriage (1916); An Innocent Magdalene (1916); Intolerance (1916); Diane of the Follies (1916); Pathways of Life (1916); The Children Pay (1916); The House Built Upon Sand (1917); Souls Triumphant (1917); Hearts of the World (1918); The Great Love (1918); The Greatest Thing in Life (1918); A Romance of Happy Valley (1919); Broken Blossoms (1919); True Heart Susie (1919); The Greatest Question (1919);* *(directed only)* Remodeling Her Husband *(1920); Way Down East (1920); Orphans of the Storm (1922); The White Sister (1923); (title role)* Romola *(1924); (Mimi)* La Bohème *(1926); (Hester Prynne)* The Scarlet Letter *(1926); Annie Laurie (1927); The Enemy (1928); The Wind (1928); One Romantic Night (1930); His Double Life (1933); The Commandos Strike at Dawn (1943); Top Man (1943); Miss Susie Slagle's (1946); Duel in the Sun (1947); Portrait of Jennie (1949); The Cobweb (1955); The Night of the Hunter (1955); Orders to Kill (Eng., 1958); The Unforgiven (1960); Follow Me Boys! (1966); Warning Shot (1967); The Comedians (1967); A Wedding (1978); Hambone and Willie (1984); Sweet Liberty (1986); The Whales of August (1987).*

Around 1908, an abandoned wife and mother named **Mary McConnell Gish** used her savings to buy an ice-cream parlor in East St. Louis. While her 10-year-old daughter Dorothy stayed with relatives, her 15-year-old daughter Lillian boarded at the Ursuline Academy, a convent school that she loved for its tranquility and discipline. This prosperity and stability was short-lived, however. A nickelodeon, the precursor of the modern movie theater, that was adjacent to the shop caught fire and destroyed Mary Gish's business. Thus the Gish sisters, who would find wealth and acclaim in films, were forced back on the road and toward their destiny.

Their earlier days were marked by poverty and dislocation. When their father James Lee Gish first disappeared from the family in 1903, Mary had moved with her daughters from Ohio to New York, partly to look for him. There she worked in a department store, but the young actresses she took in as boarders persuaded her to go into the theater. Soon Lillian and Dorothy went on the road in touring companies, where they were featured as needy children in the melodramas of the day. While the younger Dorothy traveled with her mother, Lillian often toured alone, with only friendly troupers to care for her. Of one mishap, where she had to go on stage after a prop misfired and she had been peppered with buckshot, Lillian wrote: "I had already been trained to conceal my private feelings in public. Pride helped me to survive without tears."

While staying at a theatrical boarding house in New York, the Gish sisters attended the theater with a girl named Gladys Smith to learn acting tips from watching child actors in Broadway shows. Lillian managed to land a role as a dancer with *Sarah Bernhardt's French company, which was visiting America. She found the

Europeans brusque compared to American troupes and also found Bernhardt forbidding, though Bernhardt ran her fingers through the girl's long hair. Recalled Lillian, "To my eyes she was an apparition with her dead-white face, frizzed red hair and eyes the color of the sea."

When the Gishes returned to New York after the candy business failed, they sought out their friend Gladys Smith and located her at Biograph Studios, in a Victorian brownstone on East 14th Street. There, Gladys was making "flickers," under the name *Mary Pickford, for D.W. Griffith in between more prestigious stage work. Griffith would later recall his first sight of the Gish sisters:

> They were blondish and were sitting affectionately close together. I am certain that I have never seen a prettier picture. . . . Lillian had an exquisite ethereal beauty. As for Dorothy, she was just as pretty a picture in another manner; pert—saucy—the old mischief seemed to pop right out of her and yet with it all, she had a tender sweet charm.

Griffith offered them parts in *An Unseen Enemy* immediately, but Dorothy was appalled: "Sir, we are of the legitimate theater!" Even so, he convinced them to try a film scene, then chased them around the room, firing a gun. Possibly because they were unaware that he was aiming at the ceiling, they were brilliant as frightened, hunted females, and the munificent ten dollars earned persuaded the sisters and their mother to join his company. While Griffith was impressed with their work, he was unable at first to tell them apart; he pinned a blue ribbon on Lillian and a red one on Dorothy and called them by the color they wore. They and Mary Pickford resisted Griffith's attempts to set up rivalry. Pickford told them, "He thinks we'll all give better performances if we think someone else might get the part." Twelve-hour days passed in a blink, and there was never a script to be memorized. During winters, when Griffith moved his shooting to Los Angeles, the Gish family followed him.

When I go to a party—it stops being a party. On the other hand, Dorothy *is* the party.

—Lillian Gish

In the spring of 1914, Griffith cast Lillian in *Birth of a Nation*, which he shot in nine weeks (a protracted shooting schedule for the time), and spent three more months in cutting, editing and selecting the score. The finished film ran two hours, which was then unheard of, and had a high admission price of two dollars. Lillian played a sweet, virginal girl ravaged by black men after the Civil War. Now considered racist and controversial, the film was seen as a great epic in its day. After critics demanded to know the actors' names, Griffith gave the players credit, which made their names more prominent than his and began the star system.

Lillian truly became a star with *Broken Blossoms* in 1919. Her pure, elusive quality served her well in the tragic story of an abused Chinese girl. That same year in *Way Down East*, she suggested that she could improve a scene in which she fainted on an ice floe by trailing her hand and hair in the water as she drifted toward a waterfall. To capture the moment, she mounted a slab of ice 20 times a day for three weeks of rehearsal. Her hair froze, and she suffered frost bite that flared up even in her old age, but Lillian Gish created an indelible moment in the history of film. Her only frustration was that Griffith insisted her hair be thawed and dried and her numb face be fully made up so that she would look beautiful when rescued.

Intensely loyal to Griffith, with whom she undoubtedly had an affair, Lillian said of him, "David's idea of womanhood was that of the child wife—frail, delicate, compliant, loving. When he married he dreamed of a snug cottage, fresh curtains, spring flowers—even grace before meals. But the dream was in conflict with reality. He idealized womanhood on the screen, but when he had to live with it he could not make the adjustment."

Lillian became one of the world's first great film stars. Except for her insistence on avoiding scandal, which bordered on paranoia, she was the prototype of the Hollywood celebrity. She went to the White House to show both presidents Woodrow Wilson and Warren G. Harding her films and had great faith in the importance of exercise, diet, and quiet personal time each day. She was devoted to self-improvement and studied voice as well as dancing with *Ruth St. Denis and Ted Shawn. "Within a few years my body was to show the effects of all this discipline; it was as trained and responsive as that of a dancer or an athlete," she said. She also knew she had to manage her celebrity and hired a personal press agent to keep her name out of the papers. She feared that if her name was seen too much, the public would tire of her.

As the silent era drew to a close, Dorothy appeared in, among others, *An Unseen Enemy*, *Nell Gwynn*, and *Orphans of the Storm*, a melodrama of the French Revolution which she made

Lillian and
Dorothy
Gish

with Lillian. Her favorite role was The Little Disturber, a vagabond minstrel in war-torn France, in *Hearts of the World* in 1918. Dorothy spotted particular talent in a young Latin extra named Rudolph Valentino, but Griffith dismissed him as "too foreign-looking" and pointed out that he took too long to get ready for his scenes.

Paramount-Artcraft Studios was so impressed with Dorothy's comedic talents that it offered her a million-dollar, two-year contract, but Dorothy said that at her age (20) all that money would ruin her character. Her subsequent films included *Remodeling Her Husband,* which co-starred her future husband, James Rennie, and was directed by Lillian. Dorothy's way with comedy was compared to that of Chaplin and Keaton, but she believed, according to an article she wrote for *Ladies' Home Journal* in 1925, that the public "did not want to see a woman play outright comedy." The loss of most prints of her comedies makes it difficult to evaluate her important early work. In the talkie era, after she

left Griffith, Dorothy made only three films—*Our Hearts Were Young and Gay* (1944), *Centennial Summer* (1946), and *The Whistle at Eaton Falls* (1951). She missed the atmosphere of the early days of film: "To me, there's too much spit 'n' polish about today's film technique," she said in 1951. "When Lillian and I were in silent films, we did everything for ourselves—mother made our costumes, we did our own hair, put on our own make-up. Nowadays you have a couple of people getting you into costume, another couple fussing around on your hair, others with your face. You feel, somehow, like *Marie Antoinette—even with the best will in the world, rather aloof and removed."

In early 1922, shortly after *Orphans of the Storm* was released, Griffith urged Lillian to capitalize on her popularity and go out on her own. Thus the sisters' professional relationship ended after having made 40 films together, including one- and two-reelers.

After Lillian left Griffith, Charles Duell, a lawyer and socialite, handled her business affairs. He acted as her lawyer, producer and financial adviser, and the two developed a romance. She grew skeptical, however, when he gave her a diamond ring and charged it to his production company. He further suggested that she assign her profits to him, move her headquarters to Rome, and that they both enter politics. Lillian changed lawyers, and Duell dragged her into court. To avoid a sensational trial, Gish went to the publishers of leading papers in New York and Los Angeles with her story and with documentation. While all papers covered the trial closely, hints of scandal and speculation were minimized, even when her love letters were read in court. Gish, who started a fad when she was seen munching raw carrots in court, won, but Duell harassed her with nuisance suits for years, and the experience made her wary of romantic and professional relationships.

Lillian then went to MGM, where she did *La Bohème, The Wind,* and *The Enemy.* The studio was able to proceed with *The Scarlet Letter* only after Lillian assured church leaders and women's organizations, who had threatened to boycott such a lurid story, that she would be personally responsible for the film. When Irving Thalberg told her that a scandal would boost the public's interest in her and offered to have his publicity department set something up, she declined. She soon offended MGM's head Louis B. Mayer by refusing to sign contracts without consulting her personal attorney. Knowing such insubordination numbered her days at MGM, she

From the movie Orphans of the Storm, *starring Dorothy Gish, 1922.*

left when her contract expired. The part of Anna Karenina, which she coveted, went to *Greta Garbo, then a rising young star.

Lillian returned to New York and stage work. The writer and critic George Jean Nathan repeatedly proposed to her, but she declined, fearful of his possessiveness and his resentment of her attachment to her mother and sister. Nathan introduced Lillian to all the important writers of the '20s and '30s, including Theodore Dreiser, Scott Fitzgerald, *Willa Cather, Eugene O'Neill, and H.L. Mencken, of whom she was especially fond. Lillian said this intellectual circle fascinated her, but marriage did not. "From the age of nine I was always falling in and out of love. But marriage is a twenty-four-hour a day job, and I have always been much too busy to make a good wife."

In 1948, Lillian made her television debut at the behest of Fred Coe, who produced "Philco Playhouse" on NBC. Excited by the medium and the live performance, she persuaded Dorothy, who was then semi-retired, to do "The Story of Mary Seurat" (*Mary E. Surratt) for Coe. With Coe, Lillian helped create "Silver Glory," a biography of D.W. Griffith, who had recently died, and whose memory she sought all her life to honor.

In a business known for rivalry and competition, particularly between star siblings, the relationship of the Gish sisters was remarkably harmonious. They understood each other very well and marveled at the other's character, in which each found admirable traits she thought missing in herself. In their early 20s, they produced character sketches of each other for *Stage Magazine*. Lillian said of Dorothy:

> Her funny stories, her delight in sitting on men's hats, her ability to interest herself in a hundred and one people in whom she has not the slightest interest, her talent for quick and warm friendships, her philosophy of silver linings—why was I denied these?

Wrote Dorothy in turn:

> How I envy her that singleness of purpose, the indefatigability, the unabating seriousness which have taken her straight to the heights she has reached and will carry her on and on! Nothing really matters to her except her work and career. She has little time or patience for anything or anybody unrelated to her work. Her eyes are fixed on her goal; her ears are attuned only to the voice of her duty. If she misses some of the beautiful shyer souls that require a patient search, of which the reward is only a flash, perhaps, of beauty—why, that is the sacrifice she must make and she makes willingly, almost scornfully.

The emotional and financial insecurity of their childhood affected the sisters in opposite ways. Lillian, the elder, became wise and serious, relying on little but her own resources, more likely to help others than trust others to assist her. Dorothy became more dependent and all her life had trouble making decisions and assuming responsibility. As a newlywed, she expected that she and her husband would move in with her mother, until her mother insisted the couple find a place of their own. Dorothy took no interest in domestic duties, and when she met a strange woman on her staircase, she discovered it was the cook who had been working for her for three months. Dorothy was prone to accidents and often mislaid important things—including Lillian's address book, which for some reason she took to a supermarket and left there. Whenever Dorothy complained that no one would let her do what she wanted to do, Lillian and their mother said she simply did not know what she wanted to do, and tidied up after her. In contrast, Dorothy and their mother teased Lillian

Lillian Gish

about her endless activity and devotion to work. Despite her dependence, Dorothy was fiercely protective of her mother and sister. In 1914, when Biograph was filming its landmark *Birth of a Nation*, Dorothy was struck by a car while crossing the street with the actress *Mae Murray and dragged 40 feet. Griffith carried her to a doctor's office, where she learned the tip of her toe would be amputated. She grabbed Griffith's ears to help her bear the pain and told him: "Don't tell my mother, don't tell my sister!" At a Thanksgiving meal soon afterward, she said, "I'm so glad it didn't happen to my sister. That's what I'm grateful for this Thanksgiving."

The Gish sisters last appeared together in *The Chalk Garden* at Saratoga Springs in 1956, but Dorothy became a recluse soon afterward. Eventually, Lillian placed Dorothy in a sanitarium, where she died in 1968. Lillian Gish continued to work until her death, on February 27, 1993, when she died peacefully at home in her sleep.

SOURCES:

Block, Maxine, ed. *Current Biography*. NY: H.W. Wilson, 1944.

Gish, Lillian, with Ann Pinchot. *Lillian Gish: The Movies, Mr. Griffith and Me*. Englewood Cliffs, NJ: Prentice Hall, 1969.

Moritz, Charles, ed. *Current Biography*. NY: H.W. Wilson, 1978.

The New York Times (obituary). March 1, 1993.

Schickel, Richard. *D.W. Griffith: An American Life*. NY: Simon and Schuster, 1984.

SUGGESTED READING:

Brooks, Louise. *Lulu in Hollywood*. NY: Alfred A. Knopf, 1982.

Paine, Albert Bigelow. *Life and Lillian Gish*. NY: Macmillan, 1932.

Kathleen Brady,
author of *Lucille: The Life of Lucille Ball* and *Ida Tarbell: Portrait of a Muckraker* (University of Pittsburgh Press)

Gisolo, Margaret (1914—)

American pioneer in women's baseball. Born in Blanford, Indiana, on October 21, 1914; attended the University of California and New York University; never married; no children.

Born in the mining community of Blanford, Indiana, in 1914, Margaret Gisolo was taught to play baseball by her older brother, Toney, a semipro and minor-league player. A natural from the start, she pitched for her grade-school team and played sandlot games after classes. In 1928, when the American Legion established a national baseball program for youngsters, she signed up and was accepted on the newly created junior team, the Blanford Cubs, becoming the first female in the national program. By June

18, the start of tournament play, the Cubs were fighting it out with the rival Clinton Baptists in the best-of-three series playoffs to determine the championship of the county. The first game was tied 7-7 and went into extra innings. In the top of the 12th, Gisolo singled to short right and drove in the winning run. When Clinton officials protested the game because a girl had played, Gisolo found herself in the midst of a controversy that would dominate her youthful career. While officials pondered the protest, the Cubs went on to win the second game, after which an Indiana American Legion state athletic officer suspended Gisolo for six days. Ultimately, officials upheld Gisolo's eligibility because there was nothing specifically stated in the rules which would bar girls from playing. The Cubs went on to win the state championship. In the seven games of tournament play, Gisolo, who regularly played second base, had nine hits in 21 at bats and made 10 putouts and 28 assists with no errors. Young girls began signing up for American Legion junior teams throughout the country.

On August 9, 1928, in Comiskey Park, the Blanford Cubs faced the Chicago Marine Post team in the Indiana-Illinois playoff. Although the Cubs lost the first round of interstate play, they were welcomed back to Blanford as heroes. Soon after the celebration, Gisolo was told that the American Legion had written a new rule to exclude girls from junior baseball, and that she would no longer be able to play for the Cubs. Although no one in Blanford supported the rule, it remained on the books until the 1970s.

Gisolo went on the play the game she loved, however, first with **Rose Figg**'s American Athletic Girls (a team started by *Maud Nelson in 1914), and then with the All Star Ranger Girls from 1930 to 1934. (For part of 1931, she also played with the Hollywood Movie Stars Baseball Team.) She put the money she earned toward a college education, which prepared her for a wide and varied career. She was the supervisor of physical education for the public schools of Paris, Indiana, joined the WAVES (earning the rank of lieutenant commander), and taught physical education at the college level. From 1954 until her retirement in 1980, she was an instructor of tennis and dance at Arizona State University. Largely through her vision and efforts, the university developed a nationally recognized department of dance.

After retirement, Gisolo pursued tennis, and she and her partner won gold medals in doubles at the Senior Olympics in both 1989 and 1991.

She still believes that her early experience in baseball helped her achieve her goals. "The sense of achievement and accomplishment was very positive," she recalls, "and that has stayed with me."

SOURCES:

Gregorich, Barbara. *Women at Play: The Story of Women in Baseball*. NY: Harcourt Brace, 1993.

Githa.

Variant of Agatha.

Giulia or Giuliana.

Variant of Julia or Juliana.

Giuranna, Barbara (1902—)

Italian composer, known for her compositions during the fascist period and for editions of old music. Born Elena Barbara in Palermo, Italy, on November 18, 1902; studied with G.A. Fano, C. De Nardis, and A. Savasta; studied at the Naples Conservatory, graduated in 1921; married Mario Giuranna, the conductor.

Was the first Italian woman composer invited to participate in the International Festival of Music (1935) and the Festival of International Music in Brussels (1937).

Barbara Giuranna was born in Palermo, Italy, on November 18, 1902. She studied with G.A. Fano, C. De Nardis and A. Savasta. Composition was her main area of interest during her studies at the Naples Conservatory, from which she graduated in 1921. In Milan, she studied under Giorgio Federico Ghedini, improving her instrumental technique. Giuranna made her piano debut with the Naples Symphonic Orchestra in 1923. During Benito Mussolini's regime, she became known for such pieces as her *X Legio* written in 1936 and *Patria* written in 1938. These pieces have been described as being of a "programmatic-apologetic" character because they were composed to extol the regime. After World War II, Giuranna composed works of various kinds and in 1949 wrote *Tre canti alla Vergine* for soprano, female chorus and small orchestra. *Mayerling,* an opera dealing with the sensational 1889 suicide pact between Habsburg crown prince Rudolf and his mistress *Marie Vetsera, for which the libretto was written by V. Vivani, was staged in Naples in 1960. Barbara Giuranna also taught at the Rome Conservatory where she became known for her editions of old music. A music consultant to the National Radio, she received many prizes and awards.

John Haag,
Athens, Georgia

Giustina or Giustine.

Variant of Justina or Justine.

Gizycka, Eleanor M. (1881–1948).

See Patterson, Eleanor Medill.

Gladney, Edna (1886–1961)

American pioneer in modern adoption practice and legislation who personally oversaw more than 10,000 adoptions. Name variations: "Aunt Edna." Pronunciation: GLAD-nee. Born Edna Browning Kahly on January 22, 1886, in Milwaukee, Wisconsin; died in Fort Worth, Texas, on October 2, 1961, from complications due to diabetes; oldest daughter of Maurice Kahly (a watchmaker) and Minnie Nell (Jones) Kahly; younger sister Dorothy was born in 1895; attended school through seventh grade; attended North Texas Female College (later known as Kidd-Key College); attended Texas Christian University; married Samuel William Gladney, on September 22, 1906 (died, February 14, 1935); no children.

Father died when she was young; at age 17, for respiratory-health reasons, sent to live with an aunt and uncle in Fort Worth, Texas; lived in Havana, Cuba, for part of her first year of marriage; returned to Texas; while living in Sherman, Texas, helped organize an effort to improve conditions in a county poor farm (which also housed orphans and the mentally and physically handicapped); around 1917, started serving as a board member for the Texas Children's Home (later named The Edna Gladney Home), an organization founded to facilitate the adoption of orphans; organized and operated a day-care center for children of working women (1918); due to the loss of her husband's business, moved to Fort Worth (early 1920s); named superintendent of the Texas Children's Home (1927); successfully lobbied Texas legislature to have the label "illegitimate" removed from birth certificates (1933–36); Blossoms in the Dust released (1941); successfully lobbied again for adoption-law revision (1951); featured on television show "This Is Your Life" (1953); retired (1960). Awarded an honorary Doctor of Law degree from Texas Christian University.

In the early 1930s, unmarried girls and women who discovered they were pregnant, faced life as societal outcasts, knowing their children would be labeled "illegitimate," not only by neighbors and acquaintances, but also on birth certificates. Limited support services were available for unwed mothers, who were often forced by their families to marry the father of their children. Abortion was illegal. The other option was to put the child up for adoption. By the 1950s, the situation had improved, much through the efforts of Edna Gladney. **Ruby Lee Piester**, a lifelong professional in the field of adoption who worked with Gladney, wrote, "No one in this country had done more than Edna Gladney to erase the stigma of unwed motherhood. And to promote adoption as a positive option for the child."

Edna Gladney was the head of the Texas Children's Home for almost 30 years. In 1950, the Home was renamed The Edna Gladney Home to honor her for leading the fight in Texas to have the word "illegitimate" removed from children's birth certificates, for modernizing policies in adoption practices (such as early placement of babies), and for providing a wide range of services for birth mothers. Gladney was so committed to the cause that she and her husband used personal resources to help support the Home, even throughout their own long-term financial crisis. Through decades of fund-raising experience, she learned to be tough and demand-

Edna Gladney

ing if necessary. In *For the Love of a Child—The Gladney Story,* Piester illustrates Gladney's resolute approach. Gladney once approached the Home's board of directors to approve an $18,000 expenditure for a recreation building and laundry. When the all-male board refused, she challenged them: "I just wish that all of you men were pregnant! I wish that you had to wear barrel-like clothes over your misshapen figures. I wish that you had to live like this for nine long months—among strangers. Then I wish that you had your babies and had to give them up for adoption. You'd give me that recreation building soon enough!" The board approved that plan and enthusiastically supported many other of Gladney's ideas.

She was born in Milwaukee, Wisconsin, on January 22, 1886. The loss of her father while she was young, in combination with continuing respiratory illness, may have set the stage for her lifelong work to help orphans and those in need. In 1903, her mother **Minnie Kahly** sent Gladney to Texas to live with relatives in the hopes that her health would improve. Three years later, at age 20, Edna married Sam Gladney, who worked in the flour milling industry. For part of their first year of marriage, they lived in Havana, Cuba, where Sam had business. During that time, a tubal pregnancy ended Gladney's chances of ever again becoming pregnant. They returned to Texas in 1909 and, after a few years, settled in Sherman. Sam owned and operated a milling company, while Edna became active in volunteer work. Her efforts to improve conditions in a county poor farm brought her into contact with the Texas Children's Home of Fort Worth.

Orphans who had been sent to the County Poor Farm needed homes, and the Texas Children's Home was their best option. Years earlier, the number of orphans in the area had increased due to the "orphan trains." From the 1850s to the 1920s, there was a nationwide effort to relocate orphans, as well as the poor, from large cities to rural areas throughout the nation. Several organizations were involved. Originally known as "placing out," the movement ended with as many as 200,000 having been relocated. Most of those "placed out" were children (not all of whom were orphans), although adults and even entire families were included. The children were placed on trains that made scheduled stops across the country. At each stop, those who had promised to educate them and care for them as their own would choose from among the youngsters. Most of those making the selections were farmers who needed additional workers. After much controversy, "placing out" stopped during the 1920s. **Belle Morris** and her husband Reverend I(saac) Z(achary) T(aylor) Morris, realizing that unclaimed orphans were arriving in Fort Worth with no one to care for them, took children into their home while the Reverend searched for permanent homes. The Morrises formally established the Texas Children's Home in 1896. By the time of the Reverend's death in 1915, they had found homes for at least 1,000 children and had received national recognition. Belle Morris, who took over the superintendency, recognized Edna Gladney's potential and asked her to serve on the board of the Home. The tradition of finding permanent homes for orphans was shortly to become Gladney's mission.

While living in Sherman, Gladney also saw the need for day care for children of employed women. In 1918, she established the Sherman Nursery and Kindergarten for Working Women. Soon after, the Gladneys lost almost everything due to a crisis in Sam's business caused by wheat speculation. Sam would work for years to pay off debts. Trying to start again, they moved back to Fort Worth in the early 1920s. Edna continued her work for the Texas Children's Home and, three years after Belle Morris died, was named superintendent. She served in that position from 1927 to 1960. Gladney "accepted the position—unpaid—believing she would stay less than a year," writes **Sherrie S. McLeRoy**, "just long enough to help raise money to eliminate the Home's indebtedness." But in 1941, Gladney noted, "I have been here ever since . . . ; still in debt; accepting more children than we ought. This organization was organized in 1892 and has the distinction of never being out of debt.'"

Always able to count on her husband's support, Gladney also involved the rest of her family. Over the years, her mother, who had moved to Fort Worth, as well as her niece, contributed much of their time to the Home. In 1935, Sam Gladney died. Edna almost gave up her work at the Home but struggled through her loss and stayed until her retirement in 1960.

Throughout her more than 30 years as superintendent, Gladney supervised the placement of more than 10,000 children and promoted adoption as a positive option for birth mothers and their babies. She also established one of the model maternity homes in the United States, providing a wide range of services for birth mothers. She established a non-judgmental, supportive environment for birth mothers where they were free to make their own decision as to whether or not to place their children for adoption. Gladney was one of the pioneers in the U.S. to lobby for adoption-law revision. Changes she helped engineer in Texas adoption law included the removal of the label "illegitimate" from birth certificates and the guarantee that a child's adopted status was protected information and not disclosed on the birth certificate. She promoted privacy in the adoption process—protecting the birth parents' privacy as well as the adoptive family's privacy—and helped promote adoption permanence by successfully lobbying to change the then current "guardianship" label to that of "adopted." Additionally, she helped change the laws to ensure inheritance rights for adopted children.

National recognition for Edna Gladney first came in the form of the movie *Blossoms in the Dust*, which was loosely based on her life. ***Greer Garson**, who starred in the film, became a lifelong friend of Gladney's and claimed that playing the role of Edna Gladney had been "the most humanly inspiring experience" in her life as an actress. Other national recognition came from television, magazines, and newspapers.

Edna Gladney retired in 1960 but remained active at the Home until her death in 1961. The adoption tradition she inherited from the Morrises continues at The Gladney Center, still located in Fort Worth, Texas, and still—to a large part—supported by people who volunteer their time, as had Edna Gladney.

SOURCES:

Harris, Eleanor. "I Gave Away 10,000 Babies," in *Woman's Home Companion*. January 1954.

Holt, Marilyn Irvin. *The Orphan Trains*. Lincoln: University of Nebraska Press, 1992.

McLeRoy, Sherrie S. *Red River Women*. Plano, TX: Republic of Texas Press, 1996.

Piester, Ruby Lee. *For the Love of a Child—The Gladney Story: 100 Years of Adoption in America*. Austin, TX: Eakin Press, 1987.

ADDITIONAL SOURCES:

The Gladney Center, Fort Worth, Texas; the National Council for Adoption, Washington, D.C.

Susan Works McCarter, M.Ed.,
freelance writer, Wayne, Pennsylvania

Gladuse.

Variant of Gladys.

Gladys.

Variant of Claudia.

Gladys (fl. 1075)

*Queen of Deheubarth. Married Rhys ap Tewdwr (Tudor), king of Deheubarth; children: three, including ***Nesta Tewdwr** (mistress of King Henry I).*

Gladys (fl. 1100s)

Princess of Gwynedd. Flourished in the 1100s; daughter of Llywarch ap Trahaearn ap Caradog; first wife of Owen Gwynedd, prince of Gwynedd, Wales; children: two, including Iorwerth Drwyndwn, prince of Gwynedd (d. around 1174); grandchildren: Llywelyn II the Great (1173–1240), Ruler of All Wales.

Gladys the Black (d. 1251)

*Welsh princess. Name variations: Gladys de Braose. Died in 1251 in Windsor, Berkshire, England; illegitimate daughter of Llywelyn II the Great (1173–1240), Ruler of All Wales, and his mistress *Tangwystl; sister of *Angharad and *Ellen of Wales (d. 1253); married Reginald de Braose, around 1215; married Ralph Mortimer, in 1230; children: (second marriage) Roger Mortimer (d. 1282).*

Glanville-Hicks, Peggy (1912–1990)

Australian-born composer and critic who was a key figure in the production and promotion of contemporary music in the United States in the years following World War II. Name variations: P.G.-H., P. Glanville-Hicks. Born in Melbourne, Australia, on December 29, 1912; died of a heart attack in Sydney, Australia, on June 25, 1990; daughter of Ernest Glanville-Hicks (an Anglican minister who went on to several other occupations) and Myrtle (Bailey or, possibly King) Glanville-Hicks (a ceramic artist); attended private school in Australia and Royal College of Music, London, 1931–35 (or 1932–36); studied with Nadia Boulanger, 1936–38; married Stanley Bate, on November 7, 1938 (divorced, June 1949); no children.

Left Australia for Britain and received Carlotta Rowe Scholarship for Women at the Royal College (1932, some sources cite 1931); made a visit to India with Indira Gandhi (1933); had compositions broadcast on BBC Empire Service (1934); won Octavia Snow Travelling Scholarship (1936, some sources cite 1935); moved back to Australia (1940); settled in U.S. (1942); hired as a music critic for New York Herald Tribune *and made return visit to Australia (1947); became American citizen (1948); received her first Guggenheim grant for study in Greece (1956); settled in Athens (1959); suffered temporary blindness due to brain tumor (1969); returned to Australia (1976, some sources cite 1975); received Royal Medal from Queen Elizabeth II (1977).*

Major works: (opera) The Transposed Heads (1953), Nausicaa (1960); (ballet) The Masque of the Wild Man *(1958),* Saul and the Witch of Endor *(1959); (orchestral pieces):* Concertina da Camera *(1946),* Letters from Morocco *(1952).*

Of Australian background, Peggy Glanville-Hicks was a distinguished composer who went on to play a major role in the American music scene. The author of five operas and several ballets, Glanville-Hicks was also a skilled composer in numerous other musical genres. She was, in addition, a tireless promoter of modern music. Educated at the Royal College of Music in London and in the Paris studio of *Nadia Boulanger, Glanville-Hicks stands as an innovator whose techniques combined neoclassicism and elements from Greece and the Mediterranean world as well as those from various Asian musical traditions. Although she was temporarily hindered in her rise to prominence by a period of distraction while married to fellow composer Stanley Bate, she gained renown starting in the late 1940s. Distressed by the unwillingness of the music world to accept female composers, throughout her career she signed her works as P. G-H. or P. Glanville-Hicks.

In her last years, the noted composer provided abundant, but apparently contradictory, information to two aspiring biographers. Thus, the works by **Deborah Hayes** and **Wendy Beckett** sometimes present differing versions of some details, especially dates, concerning the life of Peggy Glanville-Hicks. A vibrant and often difficult personality, she readily responded to critics who disliked her work with caustic notes, asking if they had stayed through the entire performance, and she herself was famous as a confident and opinionated commentator on the composition of others. Writes Beckett: "She was usually straightforward, direct and spontaneous, and if this was her least liked side, it was also her most admired quality." Choreographer John Butler found her "always dominating" but "fascinating" and "worth it."

Peggy Glanville-Hicks was born in Melbourne, Australia, on December 29, 1912. She was the daughter or Ernest Glanville-Hicks, an Anglican minister, and **Myrtle Glanville-Hicks**. Peggy's father left the ministry for a variety of other occupations, moving from work as a journalist to become an executive who ran charity operations. Her mother, whom her father met while preaching in New Zealand, was a ceramic artist. Myrtle came from a religious background as well: her father was a minister. She was also, according to members of her family, a talented vocalist and a pianist of professional caliber.

During her piano lessons, the young Glanville-Hicks showed herself to be a gifted musician, and, as early as 12 years of age, she decided to become a composer. She was educated at the local Methodist Ladies College and later at the famous Clyde School, a private academy for girls, in Woodend, Victoria. A teacher at Clyde encouraged Peggy's music ability, though even she failed to grasp the girl's determination to become a composer. A notable temper contributed to Peggy's difficulties at Clyde, and eventually her mother brought her home and permitted

Peggy to study at Melbourne's Albert Street Conservatorium. There she received an intensive grounding in musical fundamentals along with training in languages and proper deportment. According to Beckett, the education she received at the "Melbourne Con" was invaluable as a technical basis for her later achievements.

At the prestigious Royal College of Music in London, which she entered with a scholarship in 1931 or 1932, the young Australian worked with some of the most famous figures in the British musical world. One of them, the composer Cyril Scott, quickly recognized her gift in writing original scores. "She has something very definite to say through her compositions and her piano," he declared. Her years at the Royal College brought her into contact with such luminaries as Igor Stravinsky and the conductors Sir Malcolm Sargent and Sir Thomas Beecham. Beecham sought to recruit her as a conductor, but Peggy stuck to her resolve to compose music.

A lady composer . . . has to be twice as good.

—Peggy Glanville-Hicks

Glanville-Hicks also became a somewhat eccentric figure whom her college friends remembered all their lives. She espoused socialist political views and developed a friendship with *Indira Gandhi, the future prime minister of India, then a student at Oxford. She also smoked a small silver pipe and openly declared her desire to be as famous as the renowned Ralph Vaughan Williams, one of the leading composers of the time. A disturbing note for some of her friends was Peggy's infatuation with a fellow composer, Stanley Bate. While she worked ferociously hard at her studies, she sometimes expressed her affection for Bate by taking time to copy out his scores. "She was mesmerised by Bate," writes Beckett, "and found numerous excuses to be in his company."

As a student composer, Glanville-Hicks produced works ranging from chamber music and brief orchestral pieces to a three-act opera. She continued to take time out to work at copying, but she benefited from the opportunity to do such chores for Vaughan Williams. Her years at the Royal College culminated in notable success. In 1936 (some sources cite 1935), she tied with Bate to receive the prestigious Octavia Snow Travelling Scholarship.

Despite their growing romantic link, Glanville-Hicks and Bate went in separate directions. Bate used his award to work under Paul

Hindemith in Berlin, but Glanville-Hicks' options were limited since many composers were unwilling to work with female students. She studied briefly in Vienna, then found a more congenial musical home in the studio of Nadia Boulanger, a renowned music teacher in Paris. Her year and a half of study with Boulanger constituted a turning point in the young composer's career. Writes Beckett, "Peggy began to feel a stirring of something original within herself," and "she began to create for the first time." She produced a vast quantity of music, ranging from a concerto for flute and small orchestra to a choral suite for women's voices, and she began the synthesis of diverse musical elements that would characterize much of her career. To her training in neoclassicism, she added characteristics of the music of Greece, India, and other parts of Asia. Glanville-Hicks' interest in Indian music went back to a visit she had made to India with her friend Indira Gandhi in 1933.

Her work in Paris culminated in the performance of her music—two movements from her *Choral Suite*—at the International Society for Contemporary Music in London in June 1938. She was the first Australian composer to have a work played at this prestigious gathering of European and American experts in contemporary music.

Also in 1938, Glanville-Hicks and Stanley Bate were married in London. He had joined her shortly before to study with Boulanger in Paris, and the two now settled in London with hopes of moving on to the United States. The marriage required a number of serious adjustments for Glanville-Hicks. Bate was openly homosexual, and he frequently indulged in alcoholic binges. She had the task of bailing Bate out of jail when the British police arrested him for such unsanctioned behavior; homosexuality was then a crime in England. Moreover, the couple's financial needs forced her to put aside much of her work as a composer in order to earn money by copying music and writing free-lance articles on musical topics. In the end, she brought her work as a composer to a complete halt while Bate's career soared.

Bate was exempt from military service in World War II due to an old injury to his leg, but he was showing signs of mental illness. Doctors in Britain advised him to get a prolonged period of rest. Peggy arranged their relocation by secretly soliciting work for Bate with an orchestra in her home country, and the two left for Australia in 1940. The pattern of their recent years in Britain repeated itself: Bate enhanced his reputation as a composer in this new locale, while his wife's work languished. A newspaper headline of the time showed their relative reputations: "Mrs. Bate not as famous as her husband is also a composer." Unfortunately, Bate's professional progress increased his tendency to drink to excess.

A turning point in Glanville-Hicks' life came in 1941 when her husband was offered a teaching position at Harvard. The two settled in the United States, but the strains now evident in the marriage pushed them to live apart. While Stanley settled in Boston, Peggy, hoping to renew her career, set up housekeeping in New York. She worked at a variety of jobs, including writing free-lance articles on a range of topics from women's clothing to modern composers. She also moved to acquire American citizenship.

In her new environment, Glanville-Hicks made a name for herself as a music critic. According to Beckett, she worked at first as a part-time writer at the *New York Herald Tribune,* which needed to fill gaps left by members of the staff who had left for wartime service. On the other hand, Deborah Hayes dates her work as a critic for the *Herald Tribune* as beginning only in 1947 when Glanville-Hicks obtained a regular position on the staff. By the late 1940s, the newspaper printed column after column of her writing, and her critical reviews regularly appeared two or three times a week. She reportedly worked as a ghost composer as well, doing pieces when the individual who had received the original commission turned out to be unable to complete it. Glanville-Hicks continued to present her ideas at even greater length in a number of American magazines devoted to the music scene. She began to obtain an audience for her own music as well, especially after Columbia Studios had recorded her *Concertino da Camera* written in 1946.

In addition to these activities, she took on increasing responsibilities within the New York musical community in organizing concerts. As a key figure in the League of Composers Committee in 1943–44, she helped to organize concerts in Central Park. In the International Music Fund, her efforts helped artists reestablish themselves after their careers had been disrupted by the war. Noted Beckett: "Peggy became very much a person who could make things happen."

While her relationship with Stanley Bate languished, Glanville-Hicks began a love affair with Paul Bowles, an American writer-composer and husband of writer **Jane Bowles**, sometime around 1945. Paul was an expatriate who spent most of his time in Morocco, and he met Glanville-Hicks on one of his visits to New York. Both of them remained married, even though their relationship would extend to the end of the 1950s.

By the last years of the 1940s, Glanville-Hicks' compositions were receiving proper recognition. Twenty of her works had been recorded, and she was soon busy on her second opera. In 1948, her work was performed once again as part of the program of the International Society for Contemporary Music meeting in Amsterdam. This helped spread her reputation to a wide international audience. Moreover, the previous year, she had given a successful series of lectures on modern composers during a visit to her native country. In the next two decades, her career as a composer reached its apex, and her work was now frequently available on records. As her reputation grew, her compositions, notably the *Concertino da Camera,* were performed in such distinguished venues for modern music as the Yaddo Music Group in New York and the Philadelphia Art Alliance. She was sometimes irritated, however, by reviews that called her a "newcomer" and that labeled a recent composition as "a first work."

A notable new work from Glanville-Hicks' pen was *Letters from Morocco.* It grew directly upon her fading relationship with Paul Bowles. Since he was firmly rooted in Tangier while she felt herself tied to New York, they could see each other only from time to time. However, she took his letters, especially those with lyric descriptions of life in Tangier, and used them as the basis for this work for voice and orchestra. It was performed for the first time in early 1953 at the Museum of Modern Art. Another milestone in her career at this time was a commission from the Louisville Philharmonic, supported by a grant from the Rockefeller Foundation, to write an opera. Taken from a novel by Thomas Mann, *The Transposed Heads* was first performed in 1954 in Louisville.

Reviewers found her music, despite its firmly modern character, distinguished by its accessibility. Although she did not work with the harmony that characterized more traditional music, her compositions featured the role of melody and rhythm. As one reviewer put it in 1956, Glanville-Hicks' music is "surprisingly easy to understand once her basic principles or ideas are grasped." That same year, another reviewer stated: "Here is music that is, to my ear, the best of the new."

Continually interested in sponsoring the work of young composers, Glanville-Hicks found an appropriate tool for such efforts in the Composers Forum of New York. She became its director in the early 1950s and set about organizing a series of concerts each year that mixed the work of newcomers with that of established conductors. These performances were often followed by the recording of some of the key works presented. In these same years, she took on the massive task of updating the material on American composers for *Grove's Dictionary of Music and Musicians*. The revised edition, with her material occupying a prominent place, appeared in 1954.

The composer's marriage with Stanley Bate came to an end in 1949. The two had lived separately since their arrival in the United States in the early 1940s. Glanville-Hicks flew to Reno to obtain the divorce, but Beckett suggests that Bate took the initiative in pushing for a formal end to the marriage; he was becoming involved with a wealthy Brazilian woman named **Margarida Nogueora** who was willing to sponsor his work. In October 1959, Glanville-Hicks was devastated to learn of Bate's death from an overdose of sleeping pills. It is likely that he took his life deliberately after Nogueora discovered his homosexuality and terminated their relationship. Glanville-Hicks remained a devotee of Bate's musical accomplishments, and she saw to it that all of his scores still available were gathered and preserved.

In addition to the stimulus she continued to receive from Indian civilization, Glanville-Hicks became increasingly interested in the archaeology of the ancient Mediterranean. She collected Etruscan art, and in 1956 her *Etruscan Concerto* for piano and orchestra was performed for the first time. It tried to capture the moods of Etruscan archaeological sites as described by authors such as D.H. Lawrence. Like much of her work, it was designed to be played by a specific artist, in this case Carlo Bussotti, a talented Florentine pianist.

Seeking to pursue her interest in exotic forms of music, Glanville-Hicks used money she had inherited from her late mother and set off for Greece. She soon bought a house in Athens, and, a few years later, a second home on the island of Mikonos. She took advantage of her residence in Greece to study the country's folk music. Several awards, including two Guggenheim grants in the late 1950s, served as a valuable form of recognition of her status as a composer. They also permitted her extended stretches of time to devote to writing music, and she now wrote only occasional critical pieces for the *Herald Tribune*.

A new turn in Glanville-Hicks' work came in the late 1950s when she concentrated on music for the ballet. *The Masque of the Wild Man* and *Saul and the Witch of Endor* appeared in 1958 and 1959, respectively. Meanwhile, her growing tie to Greece helped foster collaborations with some of the great literary figures of her time. Since the mid-1950s, she had been working on *Nausicaa*, an opera set in Greece and based on Robert Graves' novel *Homer's Daughters*. *Nausicaa* had a triumphal premiere at the Athens Festival of August 1961. Starting in 1963, she became immersed in a similar project, developing a opera entitled *Sappho* from the novel by Lawrence Durrell. Due to artistic disagreements between the two, the finished product never reached the stage.

These years of achievement were accompanied by both mental and physical ailments. In the aftermath of Stanley Bate's death, observers close to her noticed Glanville-Hicks' heavy drinking, and she now suffered from depression and panic attacks. Her eyesight also began to deteriorate noticeably. As early as 1961, both the British and the American press reported that she was going blind. In 1966, her sight worsened to the point that she was taken to a hospital in New York and diagnosed with a brain tumor.

Glanville-Hicks' artistic successes had so far outstripped her financial rewards that a group of her friends had to launch a campaign to raise the money for the surgery she needed. Luminaries of the music world like *Herald Tribune* critic Virgil Thompson and violin virtuoso Yehudi Menuhin took the lead in contributing to the fund. The surgery was successful, and the composer's sight was restored. She was dismayed, however, to learn from her doctor soon afterward that her life expectancy was now only three or four years.

She now retired to her home in Greece. In that inexpensive locale, she was able to live on the royalties from her work. To her happy surprise, her health remained stable. After several years had passed, she announced to a friend: "I've been twiddling my fingers for years and now it hasn't happened. I'm going to live." Typically, she celebrated her revelation with a stiff drink of brandy.

In the early 1970s, she began to think of returning to Australia. Her family had remained in close touch with her, and she heard that her music was becoming increasingly accepted in her home country. Moreover, she was disturbed by many of the new trends in electronic music and had little desire to remain tied to New York, the center of the avant-garde music world.

In 1975 or 1976, Glanville-Hicks began to live in Australia once again. In 1977, she was honored by a medal from Queen *Elizabeth II on the occasion of the monarch's silver jubilee. Tapping her long-standing interest in various areas of Asian music, Glanville-Hicks obtained part-time work at the Australian Music Center as a lecturer on Asian music. In her last years, she was sometimes disturbed to find her own music presented in only mediocre performances in her native country, but she threw herself into a new project, an opera entitled *Becket* based on T.S. Eliot's *Murder in the Cathedral*. Increasingly frail, she was unable to accept an invitation in 1984 to be composer-in-residence at California's Cabrillo Music Festival. Three years later, she was awarded an honorary doctorate from the University of Sydney. She was still at work on *Becket* when she suffered a fatal heart attack at her home in Sydney on June 25, 1990.

SOURCES:

Beckett, Wendy. *Peggy Glanville-Hicks*. Pymble, Australia: Angus and Robertson, 1992.

Ewen, David. *American Composers: A Biographical Dictionary*. NY: Putnam, 1982.

Hayes, Deborah. *Peggy Glanville-Hicks: A Bio-Bibliography*. NY: Greenwood Press, 1990.

Randall, Don Michael, ed. *The Harvard Biographical Dictionary of Music*. Cambridge, MA: Belknap Press, Harvard University Press, 1996.

SUGGESTED READING:

Miller, Jeffrey, ed. *In Touch: The Letters of Paul Bowles*. NY: Farrar, Straus and Giroux, 1994.

Sawyer-Laucanno, Christopher. *An Invisible Spectator: A Biography of Paul Bowles*. NY: Weidenfeld and Nicolson, 1989.

Neil M. Heyman,
Professor of History, San Diego State University, San Diego,
California

Glaser, Elizabeth (1947–1994)

American AIDS activist who founded the nonprofit Pediatric AIDS Foundation (PAF). Name variations: Betsy Meyer. Born Elizabeth Ann Meyer in New York City in 1947; died of complications from AIDS in Santa Monica, California, on December 3, 1994; only daughter of Max (a businessman) and Edith Meyer (an urban renewal planner); graduated from the University of Wisconsin, 1969; received an M.A. from Boston University, 1970; married Hank Koransky, in 1971 (divorced 1973); married Paul Michael Glaser (an actor and director), on August 24, 1980; children: Ariel (August 4, 1981–1988); Jake (b. October 25, 1984).

In 1981, just after giving birth to her daughter **Ariel**, Elizabeth Glaser was administered blood transfusions amounting to seven pints. Four years later, that same daughter became mysteriously ill with stomach cramps and began to tire easily; her lips went white. Though the doctors knew about Glaser's blood transfusions, Ariel underwent a year of tests—for lupus, for leukemia. The diagnosis was not determined until the following May of 1986: Ariel had AIDS, while Elizabeth and son Jake, who had been born in 1984, were both HIV positive. Unknowingly, Glaser had contracted the HIV virus from contaminated blood and had passed the disease to her daughter from her breast milk and to her son in utero. "The prevalent medical thinking at the time was that you needed to have direct contact with blood or semen to catch the virus," said Glaser. "There was nothing about breast milk as a source of transmission."

The doctors warned the Glasers to keep this a closely guarded secret; other families who were dealing openly with AIDS were being treated like social pariahs. It was a time when Ryan White was barred from junior high, when the Ray family, whose three hemophiliac sons had contacted AIDS, returned home to find their house burned to the ground. "From that moment on I had no choice but to become intentionally schizophrenic," said Glaser. "What I felt and what I was thinking were one thing, and what I presented to my children and the rest of the outside world was another."

The Glasers were told they had to follow guidelines from the Center for Disease Control (CDC); they had to notify Ariel's preschool or pull her out. They did as instructed, and Ariel's summer camp refused to take her. When Elizabeth Glaser told close friends, forcing them to join in the "conspiracy," there was sympathy at first, then fear, then restrictions. Her children were not allowed to play with friends' children. Therapists and psychiatrists were unwilling to work with a child with AIDS; even Glaser's yoga teacher asked her to leave the class.

In 1986, though the U.S. Surgeon General C. Everett Koop had debunked these theories, there was still speculation that AIDS could be caused from saliva, kissing, sneezing, and mosquito bites. Koop advocated a massive sex-education campaign in the schools, called for an end to discrimination for those with AIDS, and said that quarantining AIDS victims was ludicrous. But those in power, often led by Senator Jesse Helms, ignored Koop and pushed their own agenda, demanding mandatory testing while opposing any kind of sex education or warnings in schools.

"What could have stopped the fear and hysteria was strong leadership from the Reagan administration," wrote Glaser. "But in those early years of the epidemic, that leadership was absent." The president ignored Koop's report and denied the surgeon general's request to meet with him. Reagan's first speech about AIDS would not come until the middle of 1987, six years after the onset of the epidemic, after over 20,000 Americans had died. By the end of 1987, no one had even begun a study on maternal transmission of AIDS. Scientists knew it happened; they didn't know how it happened.

We had been dealt the worst hand of cards any family could have gotten. I thought about throwing up my hands and giving up. But we decided to play that hand offensively.

—Elizabeth Glaser

Doctors wanted to start Ariel on AZT, which blocks the onset of symptoms and slows deterioration, but the drug had not been approved for pediatric use and no one was doing the testing. When seven-year-old Ariel died in 1988, Glaser felt dead, too. "I could no longer see any beauty in the world." Her second reaction was to help the living. "Different people do different things when they feel vulnerable. I take action so I don't feel helpless." Elizabeth Glaser became an AIDS activist, but gave Ariel most of the credit. "She taught me to love when all I wanted to do was hate; she taught me to help others when all I wanted to do was help myself."

Elizabeth Glaser's life had always revolved around children. She grew up in Hewlett Harbor, a small town on Long Island, along with her younger brother Peter. After Elizabeth and Peter started school, their mother **Edith Meyer** became director of urban renewal for the Town of Hempstead and initiated low-income housing for the poor. Elizabeth's father was vice president for the General Cigar Company. Three years after receiving her M.A. in early childhood education from Boston University in 1970, Glaser moved to Los Angeles to teach at the Center for Early Education in West Hollywood (1973–79); she then helped found the Los Angeles Children's Museum and was its first education and program director.

In 1975, she met actor Paul Michael Glaser who had just been signed for the TV series "Starsky and Hutch." Both the series and the meeting proved successful, and the Glasers were married in August 1980. Elizabeth set about doing what she had always wanted to do, raise a family. But just before Ariel arrived in 1981, Glaser was rushed to Cedars-Sinai Medical Center because of hemorrhaging. Soon after, she was given those seven pints of tainted blood.

During the hours spent in hospital corridors, she had learned to fight back—to question, challenge, and refute doctors. At the moment of Ariel's death, Glaser wanted to hold her, though the doctors tried to dissuade her. "I made them let me pick her up. I sat in the chair and I held her on my lap as I had done so many times before. There were no tubes and the machines had been turned off. I sat there and rocked her and held her. . . . I whispered, 'I love you, Ari,' a hundred times over and over in her ear."

Now, Glaser wanted to learn how to challenge presidents. "I can't keep sitting here in Santa Monica making a cozy little life for my family if we are all going to die," she told a friend. "Something is very wrong." She had been waiting, she said, for an angel to intervene. In the absence of angels, she would have to take up the slack. She had to talk to President Reagan, even if it meant putting the family secret at risk. If she was going to make a dent against AIDS indifference, she knew she needed a bold stroke. So, she set out to save her son.

Glaser taught herself all she could about AIDS, then met with those who could tell her more, including C. Everett Koop. Her aim was to obtain more money for pediatric clinical trial units (PCTUs); at that time, the federal budget for PCTUs was $3.3 million, enough to fund only four or five clinical trials in the entire country. She wanted to find out the reason for the delay in getting AZT to children. On that first trip to Washington, she was amazed at what the experts did not know. She returned home without a presidential meeting but a new awareness: no one was fighting for the children. Families of AIDS children were not speaking out because, like the Glasers, they were in hiding. Said Glaser:

> It seemed that no one really cared about people with AIDS. Our lives were expendable. If AIDS had struck white middle-class and heterosexual Americans, I firmly believe the epidemic would have been handled differently. But gays and drug users, blacks and Chicanos and poor whites? Were they written off as people we would never miss? Whose decision was this?

But a white, heterosexual, middle- to upper-class woman from Hollywood, a peer of those in power, might help change some views. "I felt a mantle of responsibility descend over my shoulders. It was a frightening and unforgettable moment."

With close friends **Susan Zeegen** and **Susan De Laurentis**, Glaser founded the nonprofit Pediatric AIDS Foundation (PAF) in 1988. At first, there was no office and no salary, only a name, home phones, and a kitchen table. Abetted by two $500,000 donations from Steven Spielberg and philanthropist **Vera List**, their goal was to raise $2 to $3 million a year for research. For the

sake of her son, Glaser was still keeping her own illness private; her involvement with the Foundation remained a tightly guarded secret.

On the next trip to Washington, when she finally met with the president and *Nancy Reagan, they listened attentively and seemed deeply moved; Reagan asked what he could do. "I want you to do two things," replied Glaser. "I want you to be a leader in the struggle against AIDS so that my children, and all children, can go to school and continue to live valuable lives, so that no one with AIDS need worry about discrimina-

Elizabeth
Glaser

tion. Secondly, you have commissioned a report on the epidemic. . . . I ask you to pay attention to that report." Though Glaser felt that the Reagans were sincere, the White House shelved the report.

But her efforts were not totally futile. Senator Lowell Weicker began pushing for an added $9 million for pediatric AIDS in the 1989 Congressional budget. Senators Howard Metzenbaum and Orrin Hatch agreed to sponsor a high-powered reception on Capitol Hill in the spring of 1989. Hatch would later join hands with Ted Kennedy to sponsor the bipartisan Kennedy-Hatch Emergency Care Bill for AIDS (subsequently called the Ryan White Bill), though it was hampered by Jesse Helms, who kept attaching amendments to ensure its defeat. Helms "seems to believe AIDS is a curse from God," said Glaser.

But each time Glaser confided in someone, she increased the risk of exposure. After every meeting where she candidly used her story to elicit help, she would beg that it remain out of reach of the press. To protect their children, the Glasers had managed to shield their private life for three years and three months. Then, friends began to get odd phone calls: a man, claiming to be from their insurance company, wanted verification as to Ariel's cause of death; a man called her sister-in-law saying he was a pediatric AIDS researcher from the Centers for Disease Control and wanted to commiserate with her about Ari's death; a man, claiming to be a new neighbor, tried to talk their housesitter into letting him into the Glaser house while they were gone. Then one day, the doorbell rang. When their housekeeper answered the door, the same man was standing there. "Aren't you afraid to work here?" he said. "Don't you know this family has AIDS?" He then went to UCLA and said his father was a rabbi and he was planning a special memorial service for Ariel; he asked the nurse if she would share a few stories about the girl. Unfortunately, the woman did. Shortly after that, the *National Enquirer* telephoned.

The tabloid said it was willing to bargain. If they could get one quote from the Glasers, they would not run the whole story, only the death of Ariel, no mention of Elizabeth or Jake. The Glasers knew it was time to go public. They called a meeting with the parents at Jake's school and met with the *Los Angeles Times*. The *Times*' article came out on Friday, August 25, 1989. Despite her fears, all but two families of Jake's school were supportive. Glaser was now free to be actively and publicly involved with the Foundation. It was a relief, she said.

Glaser's high-profile activism caught the attention of the media. In late 1988, when she convinced the Bush administration to increase funding for AIDS pediatric research, the press was there. The Glasers' February 4, 1990, appearance on "60 Minutes" was seen by millions. But despite the promises, Washington did little. In 1992, a frustrated Glaser appeared before, and galvanized, the Democratic National Convention: "I am here tonight," she began, "because my son and I may not survive another four years of leaders who say they care—but do nothing." (That same year, ❧ **Mary Fisher** spoke at the Republican National Convention.)

By 1994, with its many events, including the annual star-studded picnic in Hollywood, the Pediatric AIDS Foundation had raised over $30 million, 90% of which went to grants for pediatric AIDS research and other programs. In February of that year, scientists discovered that 60% of those HIV-positive pregnant women who were given AZT did not pass the virus on to

❧▶ **Fisher, Mary** (c. 1946—)

American AIDS activist. Born Mary Fisher in Detroit, Michigan, around 1946; daughter of Max Fisher (an industrialist and philanthropist); married Brian Campbell (divorced); children: (adopted) Zachary; Max (b. 1988).

In July 1991, Mary Fisher was in her early 40s when she learned that she had contracted AIDS from her ex-husband who had recently died. A wealthy Republican, Fisher had a great deal of cachet when she spoke before the Republican National Convention in 1992. "Who could forget the demure blonde at the podium," writes **Katie Couric**, "speaking to a sea of delegates who moments earlier were smiling, waving signs, and whooping it up. Suddenly the only sound was Mary's voice, sweet yet strong. Her pain, so raw, her honesty, so riveting—a stark contrast to the dogmatic assertions that often characterize such gatherings." Mary Fisher exhorted the nation to stop stigmatizing those who find themselves HIV positive. They come from all walks of life, she maintained, rich and poor, black and white, gay and straight, old and young. Fisher, who continued to speak across the country, published three books: *Sleep with the Angels*, a compilation of 25 of her speeches, *I'll Not Go Quietly* (1995), and *My Name Is Mary* (1996).

SUGGESTED READING:
Fisher, Mary. *I'll Not Go Quietly: Mary Fisher Speaks Out*. NY: Scribner, 1995.
———. *My Name Is Mary: A Memoir*. NY: Scribner, 1996.
———. *Sleep With the Angels: A Mother Challenges AIDS*. Wakefield, RI: Moyer Bell, 1994.

their babies. They urged that doctors counsel every pregnant woman about AIDS and advise each to be tested for the fatal virus. The research had been partially funded by PAF.

Before she died, many, including **Hillary Rodham Clinton** and Princess *Diana, made the trek to the sunny bedroom of Elizabeth Glaser's home in Santa Monica or to her family vacation home at Martha's Vineyard. Even after she developed a brain infection and her health began to decline in August 1994, Glaser made one last trip to New York City for the September 25th Pediatric Aids Foundation fundraiser. Though the event reaped over $1 million, friends say the trip cost her dearly, and she never recovered her health.

"I have confronted my own fears, the fears of others, social discrimination and lack of education," she told 500 leaders at the Century City Plaza Hotel in L.A. in May 1994. "It has now become a time in my life to learn about and understand death. If I can do that, it will be truly an achievement." Dead at 47, Elizabeth Ann Glaser was buried outside of Boston, Massachusetts, next to her daughter Ariel.

SOURCES:

"The Defiant One," in *People Weekly*. December 19, 1994, pp. 46–53.

Glazer, Elizabeth, with Laura Palmer. *In the Absence of Angels*. NY: Putnam, 1991.

Glasgow, Ellen (1873–1945)

American author. Born Ellen Anderson Gholson Glasgow in Richmond, Virginia, on April 22, 1873; died in Richmond, Virginia, on November 21, 1945; fourth daughter and eighth of ten children of Francis Thomas Glasgow (a managing director of Tredegar Iron Works) and Anne Jane (Gholson) Glasgow; educated at home; never married; no children.

Selected works: The Descendant *(1897);* Phases of an Inferior Planet *(1898);* The Voice of the People *(1900);* The Battle-Ground *(1902);* The Freeman, and Other Poems *(1902);* The Deliverance *(1904);* The Wheel of Life *(1906);* The Ancient Law *(1908);* The Romance of a Plain Man *(1909);* The Miller of Old Church *(1911);* Virginia *(1913);* Life and Gabriella *(1916);* The Builders *(with H.W. Anderson, 1919);* One Man in His Time *(1922);* The Shadowy Third, and Other Stories *(1923);* Barren Ground *(1925);* The Romantic Comedians *(1926);* They Stooped to Folly *(1929);* The Old Dominion Edition of the Works of Ellen Glasgow *(8 vols. 1929–33);* The Sheltered Life *(1932);* Vein of Iron *(1935);* The Virginia Edition of the Works of Ellen Glasgow *(12 vols., 1938);* In This Our Life *(1941);* A Certain Measure: An Interpreta-

tion of Prose Fiction *(1943);* The Woman Within *(1954);* Letters of Ellen Glasgow *(ed. B. Rouse, 1958);* The Collected Stories of Ellen Glasgow *(ed. R. K. Meeker, 1963);* Beyond Defeat: An Epilogue to an Era *(ed. L.Y. Gore, 1966).*

The eighth of ten children, Ellen Glasgow was born in 1873 in Richmond, and raised in a wealthy and socially prominent Virginia family. In her autobiography *The Woman Within*, she described an emotionally confusing childhood overseen by a tyrannical, philandering father and a long-suffering mother with whom she strongly identified. Excused from school because of fragile health, Glasgow educated herself by reading from her father's extensive library of classics. As she entered her teens, her reading encompassed the works of the 19th-century historians and social philosophers, including the British naturalist Charles Darwin, whose books made a particularly lasting impression. At age 17, Glasgow refused a debut into society and set to work on her first novel which she later destroyed. Her second novel, *The Descendant*, published anonymously in 1897, was embraced by advocates of the new realism in American literature, as were the two novels that followed, *Phases of an Inferior Planet* (1900) and *The Wheel of Life* (1906). In these early works, set in New York and populated by uprooted southerners, Glasgow explored the problems of the struggling woman artist.

With *The Voice of the People* (1900), about the Civil War, Glasgow embarked on a series of books about Virginia, which included *The Battleground* (1902), *The Deliverance* (1904), *Virginia* (1913), *Barren Ground* (1925), *Vein of Iron* (1935), and *In This Our Life* (1941), for which she received the Pulitzer Prize. These works explore the social and political history of Virginia from 1850 and represent a break with the sentimental tradition of Southern fiction, what Glasgow called "evasive idealism." She won genuine critical success with *Barren Ground*, a grimly tragic tale set in rural Virginia, which she felt would make or

Ellen Glasgow

break her reputation as a writer. Many consider it her best work.

In three comedies of manners, *The Romantic Comedians* (1926), *They Stooped to Folly* (1929), and *The Sheltered Life* (1932), Glasgow put forth her own ambivalent feelings about the decline of Southern aristocracy in the face of encroaching industrialization. Called an "ironic tragedian" by Henry Seidel Canby, Glasgow was a masterful satirist, particularly in her portrayal of Southern women and their relations to Southern men. "The realism which engages this author," writes **Emily Clark**, "is the penetration of shams, a perpetual rebellion against hypocrisy."

Glasgow never married, although as a young woman she had an intense love affair with a married man, "Gerald B," who died in 1905. She also had an enduring relationship with Henry Watkins Anderson, a successful Richmond lawyer and unsuccessful Republican candidate for governor in 1921, to whom she was once engaged. (Glasgow collaborated with Anderson on the 1919 political novel *The Builders*, for which he also served as a model for the story's hero.)

After the suicide of her brother in 1909 and the death of her beloved sister **Cary Glasgow** in 1911, Ellen exiled herself in New York for a period but returned to Richmond in 1916. Except for travel abroad and summer respites in Massachusetts or Maine, she lived and worked most of her life in a century-old Greek Revival house in the heart of Richmond. "We live," she once said, "where we are born." For many years, she shared her home with her secretary, nurse, and housekeeper, **Anne Virginia Bennett**, and her adored dogs. (Glasgow loved animals and helped found the Richmond Society for the Prevention of Cruelty to Animals.) One of her greatest burdens was her deafness, which came on in adolescence and worsened with age, isolating her and causing bouts of depression. Although she described her life as a "long tragedy," compensated only by her literary pursuits, friends recalled her as charming, with a ready smile and a gift for witty conversation.

Often compared to *Edith Wharton and *Willa Cather, Glasgow was generally recognized during her time as one of America's foremost novelists. In 1932, she was elected to the National Institute of Arts and Letters and, in 1940, received the Howells Medal from the American Academy of Arts and Letters. In 1941, she was given the Southern Authors Award and, in 1942, the Pulitzer Prize for fiction for *In This Our Life*.

Toward the end of her career, Glasgow became disillusioned with modern urban life and grew increasingly nostalgic for the lost agrarian society. Notes Marcelle Thiebaux in *American Women Writers*: "As she grew older she found it difficult to cast aside the values she had once lightheartedly satirized. She saw the modern world as 'distraught, chaotic, grotesque, . . . an age of cruelty without more indignation, of catastrophe without courage.'" In December 1939, after completing the first draft of *In This Our Life*, Glasgow suffered a severe heart attack. Confined to bed for months afterward, she finished the novel with the help of her friend and fellow novelist James Branch Cabell. Through sheer determination, she continued to write, publishing her only nonfiction, *A Certain Measure* (a collection of critical essays), two years before her death in 1945. Her autobiography *The Woman Within* and her final novel *Beyond Defeat* were both published posthumously.

SOURCES:

Glasgow, Ellen. *The Woman Within*. NY: Harcourt, Brace, 1954.

James, Edward T., ed. *Notable American Women 1607–1950*. Cambridge, MA: The Belknap Press of Harvard University Press, 1971.

Mainiero, Lina, ed. *American Women Writers: From Colonial Times to the Present*. NY: Frederick Ungar, 1980.

McHenry, Robert, ed. *Famous American Women*. NY: Dover, 1983.

SUGGESTED READING:

Goodman, Susan. *Ellen Glasgow: A Biography*. MD: Johns Hopkins University, 1998.

Wagner, Linda W. *Ellen Glasgow: Beyond Convention*. University of Texas Press, 1982.

Barbara Morgan,
Melrose, Massachusetts

Glaspell, Susan (1876–1948)

American short-story writer, novelist, and playwright, awarded the Pulitzer Prize for drama in 1931, who was a founding member and major contributor to the acclaimed Provincetown Players. Pronunciation: Glas-pell. Born Susan Keating Glaspell on July 1, 1876, in Davenport, Iowa; died in Provincetown, Massachusetts, of viral pneumonia and a pulmonary embolism, on July 27, 1948; second of three children and the only daughter of Elmer S. and Alice (Keating) Glaspell; attended Davenport public schools; Iowa's Drake University, Ph.B., 1899; graduate study at the University of Chicago, 1903; married George Cram Cook, on April 14, 1913 (died 1924); lived with Norman Matson (a writer), 1925–1931; no children.

Saw publication of first short story (1902); published first novel, The Glory and the Conquered *(1909); published best-known short story, "A Jury of Her Peers," which became the basis of her first play,* Trifles, *produced in the inaugural season of the Provincetown Players (1916); wrote* The Verge, *one of the first expressionistic plays staged in the U.S. (1922); moved with Cook to Greece, where they lived until his death (1922-24); published biography of her husband,* The Road to the Temple *(1926); awarded Pulitzer Prize for drama for* Alison's House *(1931); served as director of Midwest Play Bureau of the Federal Theater Project (1936–38); entered a new period of novel writing, lasting almost to the time of her death (1940–48).*

Selected plays: (with George Cram Cook) Suppressed Desires *(1915);* Trifles *(1916);* The People *(1916);* Close the Book *(1916);* The Outside *(1916);* A Woman's Honor *(1918);* Tickless Time *(1918);* Bernice *(1920);* The Inheritors *(1921);* The Verge *(1921);* Chains of Dew *(1922); (with Norman Matson)* The Comic Artist *(1927);* Alison's House *(1930).*

Fiction: The Glory and the Conquered *(1909);* The Visioning *(1911);* Lifted Masks: Stories *(1912);* Fidelity *(1915); "A Jury of Her Peers," (1916);* Brook Evans *(1928);* Fugitive's Return *(1929);* Ambrose Holt and Family *(1931);* The Morning is Near Us *(1939);* Cherished and Shared of Old *(1940);* Norma Ashe *(1942);* Judd Rankin's Daughter *(1945). Biography:* The Road to the Temple *(1926).*

Susan Glaspell is most often associated with the Provincetown Players, the innovative and experimental theater group that fostered the development of new plays in America and launched the career of one of the country's most acclaimed playwrights, Eugene O'Neill. Until recently, however, Glaspell's own accomplishments as both writer and playwright have been given short shrift. Lost in the shadow of both O'Neill and her husband, George Cram Cook, who was the driving force behind the Provincetown Players, she has been largely overlooked, despite being the author of 11 plays produced by the Players and despite breaking stylistic barriers and using symbolic and expressionistic devices before O'Neill. In 1931, Glaspell was only the second woman in the country to be awarded the Pulitzer Prize for drama. Fortunately, renewed interest has finally placed her in the canon of 20th-century American playwrights.

The Glaspell family was one of the earliest to settle in Davenport, Iowa, in the late 1830s. As farmers, Elmer S. Glaspell and **Alice Keating**

Glaspell were not well-off, but they provided a solid, middle-class foundation for their daughter. Born on July 1, 1876, Susan Keating Glaspell was raised in the Midwestern tradition, with a pioneer spirit and a love of the land that was to figure strongly in much of her writing. After attending public school in Davenport, she entered Drake University in Des Moines, where her interest in writing blossomed. She studied literature and the classics and had several short stories and essays published in the university's paper, *The Delphic.* Following graduation in 1899, she went to work as a house and legislative reporter for the Des Moines *Daily News* and wrote a popular column called "News Girl." In his biography of Glaspell, Arthur Waterman points out, "Although none of this writing gave any opportunity to develop her ability as a creative writer, she did gain a detailed knowledge of Midwestern political life which she used as background in several of her early short stories."

In 1901, encouraged by her success as a columnist, Glaspell quit her reporting job and returned to Davenport to devote herself to writing fiction full-time. According to Waterman, these were mostly "good wholesome endeavors, pleasant tales with chaste heroines who trap their men

Susan Glaspell

within the bounds of propriety." In 1903, Glaspell entered the graduate program in English at the University of Chicago but was soon dissatisfied by the academic approach. Returning again to Davenport, she concentrated on writing short stories. Her first to appear in print was in *Authors Magazine* in 1902; others were accepted in such magazines as *Harper's* and *American.* In 1909, Glaspell saw the publication of her novel, *The Glory and the Conquered,* a sentimental love story between a painter and a scientist.

After less than two years of newspaper reporting, I boldly gave up my job and went home to Davenport to give all my time to my own writing. I say boldly, because I had to earn my living.

—Susan Glaspell

Back in Davenport in 1910, after a year in Paris with a friend, Glaspell had a clearer view of the disparity between the traditional values of her Midwestern heritage and the new thinking that had begun to affect the country. She found support for the new ideas largely through meetings of the Monist Society, a group founded by George Cram Cook, a member of a prominent Davenport family, and his close friend, Floyd Dell. In *Road to the Temple*, Glaspell gives a humorous view of those meetings:

> The Society had a stirring Statement of Belief and attracted to itself all of us who were out of sorts with what we were supposed to believe. Declining to go to church with my parents in the morning, I would ostentatiously set out for the Monist Society in the afternoon. . . . Here were people who had never been together before. A few of the more fearless club women, wanting to know all that should be known about education, even though it involved "certain matters of sex"; a number of free thinking Germans. . . the town atheist . . . disappointed politicians.

Glaspell found herself deeply attracted to the Monist leader, Cook, who was then about to be married for the second time. In 1911, her second novel, *The Visioning,* showed the impact of women's suffrage; it also reflected Cook's influence in its sympathetic portrayal of a socialist. Glaspell's two-year writing sojourn in New York did not end the attraction. Following the failure of his second marriage, Cook and Glaspell moved to Chicago, accompanied by Cook's two children, Nilla and Harl. There, Cook reviewed books for the *Chicago Evening Post*, working with his good friend Dell, and grew intrigued with new trends in theater, stimulated in particular by the 1911–12 tour of the Abbey Players, Ireland's National Theatre.

Theater, like other art forms in the United States, was sadly lagging behind Europe in those years. The ideas of realism and naturalism, fostered by writers like Zola, Ibsen, and Strindberg in the 1880s and 1890s, had already given way in Europe to expressionism, while performances in the U.S. were still tied to the melodramatic standards epitomized by James O'Neill, the father of Eugene O'Neill, who made a lifelong career of repeating the role of Edmond Dantes in a touring version of *The Count of Monte Cristo.*

On April 14, 1913, at age 37, Glaspell married Cook in Weehawken, New Jersey. The following year, she suffered a miscarriage that left her unable to have children. Living in New York by then, the couple divided their time between the bohemian Greenwich Village and the more tranquil Provincetown, Massachusetts. Among their neighbors and friends were such radical "new thinkers" of the day as Jack Reed, Max Eastman, ✥▶ **Neith Boyce** and her husband Hutchins Hapgood, *Louise Bryant, *Mary Heaton Vorse,** and their old friend, Floyd Dell. As an avid follower of the current theater scene, Glaspell assessed the works produced on Broadway as commercially successful but intellectually vapid, as she wryly describes in *The Road to the Temple:*

> We went to the theater and for the most part came away wishing we had gone somewhere else. Those were the days when Broadway flourished almost unchallenged. . . . They didn't ask much of you, those plays. Having paid for your seat, the thing was all done for you, and your mind came out where it went in, only tireder.

At the Liberal Club in the Village, Glaspell and Cook flourished amid stimulating conversations about politics, literature, art, women's rights, and free love. They participated in the formation of the Washington Square Players, New York City's first independent theater, which challenged Broadway for theatrical viability. Glaspell continued to write and sell short stories, and in 1915 she published her third novel, *Fidelity.*

By 1915, according Glaspell, Freudian psychology was so much in the air, "you could not go out to buy a bun without hearing of someone's complex." That year, Glaspell and Cook wrote a short one-act play, *Suppressed Desires,* spoofing the latest psychoanalytical trends in a process described by Glaspell: "Before the grate in Mulligan Place we tossed the lines back and forth at one another, and wondered if any one else would ever have as much fun with it as we were having." After the work was rejected by the Washington Square Players as "too special," the couple decided to stage it themselves that summer in Provincetown.

Their Provincetown neighbor Neith Boyce had also written a play, called *Constancy*. The Hapgoods offered their home for the production, and the two works were staged with the help of Robert Edmond Jones, who was to become a major innovator in scenic design. By merely turning the chairs around, two separate settings were created in the Hapgood living room, and the venture proved such a success that the group came up with a second bill, including Cook's *Change Your Style* and Wilbur Steele's *Contemporaries*. This time the theater was an old converted fish house down on the wharf. At the end of that summer, the couple returned to New York, fired by their success. Cook was now eager to found a theater to foster American playwrights, modeled after the work being done by the Irish at the Abbey Theatre, and the following summer the Provincetown Players became a reality.

The opening season offered four different billings of three one-act plays. Since the group did not as yet have this many scripts, Glaspell asked a Provincetown neighbor, Terry Carlin, if he had any new plays available. He said he didn't, but his friend Eugene O'Neill had a trunk full of scripts. Invited over that night, O'Neill gave a reading of *Bound East for Cardiff*, a short piece about a dying sailor who longs for the firmness of the land under his feet. By the end of the reading, Glaspell recalled, "We knew what we were [there] for."

But to her dismay, Cook had also announced an upcoming play by Susan Glaspell. When she protested that she had no play, he responded, "Then you will have to sit down tomorrow and begin one." The result was *Trifles*, a one-act piece based on one of her short stories, about a murder trial she had covered as a reporter in Iowa. The play centers on Minnie Wright, an Iowa farm wife under investigation for the murder of her husband John. In the course of the play, two women friends of the accused woman, who are apparently concealing evidence of her guilt, win audience sympathy for her by implying that John was a wife-abuser. In addition to using realistic sets and dialogue to help reveal the psychological motivation of the characters, Glaspell employed the device of keeping her main character (Minnie) off stage. *Trifles*, which was to become Glaspell's best-known play, staged nationally and internationally, foreshadowed some of her later works, in

---

☙▸ Boyce, Neith (1872–1951)

American writer. Name variations: Neith Boyce Hapgood; Mrs. Hutchins Hapgood. Pronunciation: Bois. Born Neith Boyce in Mt. Vernon, New York, in 1872; died in 1951; married Hutchins Hapgood (1869–1944, a writer), in June 1899; children: Boyce Hapgood; Charles Hutchins Hapgood; **Miriam Hapgood DeWitt** *(1908–1990);* **Beatrix Hapgood.**

Born in Mt. Vernon, New York, in 1872, Neith Boyce had a tragic childhood. Her four brothers and sisters died during a typhoid epidemic, and, following the deaths of other close relatives, Boyce spent her lonely early years on a ranch in California. At one time the only woman reporter for the *New York Globe*, Boyce was a founding member of the Provincetown Players, along with her husband Hutchins Hapgood and others. Her works, which explore marriage and the conflicts between men and women, include *The Forerunner* (1903), *Eternal Spring* (1906), (with her husband) *Enemies* (1916), *Two Sons* (1917), *Proud Lady* (1923), and *Winter's Night* (1927). Her autobiographical novel, *The Bond*, was published in 1908.

SUGGESTED READING:

DeWitt, Miriam Hapgood. *Taos: A Memory.* Albuquerque, NM: University of New Mexico Press, 1992.

Trimberger, Ellen Kay. *Intimate Warriors: Portraits of a Modern Marriage, 1899–1941: Selected Works by Neith Boyce and Hutchins Hapgood.* NY: Feminist Press at the City University of New York, 1991.

---

which she repeated the device of a protagonist who never appears.

In 1917, Glaspell contributed three more plays to the Provincetown Players repertoire, *The People, Close the Book,* and *The Outside.* The 1918 season saw two new Glaspell comedies, *Woman's Honor* and *Tickless Time.* The following March, she staged her first full-length play, *Bernice.* In the play, Bernice has just died, an event that has brought together her father, her best friend, her sister, and her philandering husband. By then, Glaspell was one of the Players' finest actresses and, along with O'Neill, its leading playwright. (*Edna St. Vincent Millay, Ida Rauh,* and Michael Gold, were also part of this early group. Cook, in addition to his role as producer, also acted and directed.)

Glaspell not only employed innovative theatrical techniques but was one of America's earliest playwrights to present modern female characters, women in search of autonomy and personal fulfillment. In her most controversial play, *The Verge* (1921), the protagonist, Claire Archer, is actually driven over the edge of sanity in her quest for her own freedom, or "other-

---

ness," as she calls it. To reveal Archer's state of mind, Glaspell experimented with symbolism and expressionistic stage settings. The main female character in *The Inheritors* (1921) also sacrifices ease and comfort for her ideals, going to prison for the rights of a Hindu student protesting British domination of India.

While Glaspell's works clearly helped to build the Provincetown Players, they were overshadowed by the group's New York production of O'Neill's *The Emperor Jones*, which became a theatrical milestone. Uptown critics could no longer ignore the work being done at this small Village theater, but success, ironically, began to lure the innovators to Broadway and big salaries. Cook, who may have harbored some jealousy of O'Neill, found the commercial success of the Provincetown Players unnerving, and in 1922 the couple sailed for Greece, where they settled at Delphi on Mount Parnassus. Cook worked to renew interest in drama among the Greek people until his untimely death in 1924.

While still abroad, Glaspell met the writer Norman Matson. After Cook's death, she returned with him to Provincetown, and they lived together for many years. Numerous biographical surveys identify Matson as Glaspell's second husband, but in reality, they never married. In 1926, Glaspell published her biographical tribute to George Cram Cook, *The Road to the Temple*. In 1928, she collaborated with Matson on *The Comic Artist*, which premiered in London, and that same year saw her return to the novel with the publication of *Brook Evans*, followed the next year by *The Fugitive's Return*. Not until 1930 did she return to plays, with her prize-winning drama, *Alison's House*, produced by the Civic Repertory Theater, with *Eva Le Gallienne.

In *Alison's House*, loosely based on the life of *Emily Dickinson, Glaspell returns to the technique of having the protagonist never appear: in this case, Alison has been dead for 18 years. The play takes place on New Year's Eve, 1899, in Iowa. Alison's father, Mr. Stanhope, has decided to sell the family home, and members of the family are in the process of packing up Alison's possessions, each one affected by the unseen protagonist as we learn of her power and beauty through what they say about her. The characters believe that all of Alison's poetry has been previously published, until it is revealed that Aunt Agatha has been hiding a package of poems which show the poet's inner turmoil at a time when she abandoned love for duty, having cut off an affair of the heart. The conflict is between Agatha's belief that the poems should be destroyed, and Alison's

niece, who convinces the family to publish the poems, believing that Alison's anguish shared by many women will be a gift to the new century about to arrive. In what was apparently a controversial decision, Glaspell was awarded the Pulitzer Prize for 1931, although *Alison's House* failed to become a commercial success.

Following Glaspell's winning of the Pulitzer, Matson left her for a much younger woman. Though she published no more plays, Glaspell remained involved in the theater through an appointment as director of the Midwest Play Bureau of the Federal Theater Project, but the work did not afford her much opportunity to write. Eventually she returned to novels, with the publication in 1940 of *Cherished and Shared of Old* and *The Morning Is Near Us*, followed in 1942 by *Norma Ashe* and in 1945 by *Judd Rankin's Daughter*. Glaspell's last years were filled with illness and alcoholism, and she died on July 27, 1948, of a pulmonary embolism and viral pneumonia, at her home in Provincetown. She was cremated in Boston.

Examined today, Glaspell's work reveals a writer who places women at the center of the action, is unafraid of dealing with controversial social and political issues, and is successfully able to experiment with new styles in theatrical presentation.

SOURCES:
Ben-Zvi, Linda, "Susan Glaspell's Contribution to Contemporary Women Playwrights," in *Feminine Focus: The New Women Playwrights*. NY: Oxford University Press, 1989, pp. 147–166.
Bigsby, C.W.E., ed. *Plays by Susan Glaspell*. Cambridge: Cambridge University Press, 1987.
Glaspell, Susan. *Alison's House*. NY: Samuel French, 1930.
———. *Bernice. Theater Arts* Magazine. Vol. 3, 1919, pp. 264–300.
———. *Plays*. Boston: Small, Maynard, 1920.
———. *The Road to the Temple*. NY: Frederick A. Stokes, 1927.
James, Edward T., ed. *Notable American Women 1607–1950*. Cambridge, MA: The Belknap Press of Harvard University Press, 1971.
Mainiero, Lina, ed. *American Women Writers: From Colonial Times to the Present*. NY: Frederick Ungar, 1980.
Makowsky, Veronica. *Susan Glaspell's Century of American Women*. NY: Oxford University Press, 1993.
Waterman, Arthur. *Susan Glaspell*. NY: Twayne, 1966.

SUGGESTED READING:
Heller, Adele, and Lois Rudnick, eds. *1915, The Cultural Moment*. New Brunswick, NJ: Rutgers University Press, 1991.

RELATED MEDIA:
Trifles (16mm, VHS; 21 min.), based on the short story "A Jury of Her Peers" and the play *Trifles*, Phoenix/BFA Films and Video, 1979.

Susan Glaspell Papers are located in the Clifton Waller Barrett Library, University of Virginia, Charlottesville.

Unpublished short stories, essays, drafts, reviews and scrapbooks located in The Henry W. Berg and Albert A. Berg Collection of English and American Literature: Susan Glaspell Papers and George Cram Cook Papers, New York Public Library.

Anita DuPratt,
Professor of Theater, California State University,
Bakersfield, California

Glasse, Hannah (1708–1770)

English cook and author of one of the first British cookbooks. Born Hannah Allgood in London, England, in 1708; died in Newcastle in 1770; married Peter Glasse (a solicitor), before 1725; children: eight, four of whom died in infancy.

Married at a young age and the mother of eight children (four of whom died in infancy), Hannah Glasse won acclaim with *The Art of Cookery made Plain and Easy*, published in 1747, possibly the earliest guide to cookery and meal planning for the English housewife. Remaining in print until 1824, it was considered clear and concise for its day, offering recipes and even some medical advice. The ironical proverb attributed to her, "First catch your hare, then cook it," is not in *The Art of Cookery,* but was probably suggested by her words, "Take your hare when it is cased (skinned)." Other books by Glasse include *The Compleat Confectioner* (c. 1770), and *The Servant's Director or Housekeeper's Companion.* Glasse may have also been a businesswoman; she was known as "Habit Maker" in Covent Garden to *Augusta of Saxe Gotha, princess of Wales, and may have declared bankruptcy in 1754. She died in Newcastle at the age of 62.

Gleason, Kate (1865–1933)

American entrepreneur, engineer, philanthropist, real-estate developer, and innovator of low-cost housing. Born in Rochester, New York, on November 25, 1865; died in Rochester on January 9, 1933; daughter of Ellen McDermont and William Gleason; attended Nazareth Convent, Rochester High School, and Cornell University; never married; no children.

Awards: elected first female member of the Verein Deutscher Ingenieure (1913); elected first female member of the American Society of Mechanical Engineer (1914); admitted to the Rochester Chamber of Commerce (1916); elected first female member the American Concrete Institute (1919).

Enrolled at Cornell University (1884); withdrew from Cornell (1884); enrolled and withdrew from Cornell (1888); served as secretary and treasurer of the Gleason Works (1890–1913); was first female bankruptcy receiver in New York State (1914); was first female president of an American bank, the First National Bank, East Rochester (1917–19); manufactured low-cost housing (1920); developed prefabricated building methods for low-cost housing (1920); left bequest creating the Gleason Fund for educational and charitable causes, which awarded Dr. Howard Kelly of Johns Hopkins University a donation for his pioneering research into cancer (1933); another bequest transformed the Rochester Mechanics Institute into the Rochester Institute of Technology (1933).

Kate Gleason was born in Rochester, New York, on November 25, 1865, the first of four children of Irish immigrants. As her parents were staunch Catholics, she attended parochial schools before enrolling at the local public high school. She was an independent and willful child. She wore her hair short and straight, instead of the long curls popular during the Victorian era, and preferred the company of boys. "They didn't want me," Gleason recalled. "But I earned my right. If we were jumping from the shed roof, I chose the highest spot; if we vaulted fences, I picked the tallest."

During the late 1860s, Kate's father William Gleason, a former machineshop apprentice, opened his own business in Rochester, specializing in toolmaking. He "combined a sympathetic interest in woman's emancipation with an evangelical zeal to acquaint his children—sons and daughters alike—with the marvels of mechanical engineering," writes Christopher Lindley. Kate's mother was a devoted supporter of women's suffrage and a friend of *Susan B. Anthony. Anthony is reputed to have encouraged young Kate with her career ambitions.

After Kate's half-brother Thomas, her father's chosen successor, died during the Civil War, 11-year-old Kate persuaded her father to allow her to work in the shop:

> I walked down to the shop, mounted a stool and demanded work. At the close of the day he handed me one dollar, my first pay. I had no pocket, so I tucked it in my dress, and lost it on the way home. My mother and grandmother made a terrible fuss.

In 1884, Gleason enrolled as a special student at Cornell University, hoping to become its first female graduate in engineering. A downturn in business, however, meant that her family could no longer afford to pay the tuition, and she was forced to return to Rochester. The day the news arrived, recalled Gleason, a male student acquaintance discovered her sitting beneath a tree on campus, crying, as she read the letter from her father.

> He choked up and said brokenly that he was awfully sorry, but that at present he couldn't be more than a brother to me. I tried to convince him that I was crying at leaving college, but he attributed that statement to my maidenly modesty, and in the end I walked off furious if broken-hearted.

In 1888, Gleason once again enrolled at Cornell, but, by the end of the academic year, she had left, this time not to return. Aside from some instruction at the Rochester Mechanics Institute (subsequently the Rochester Institute of Technology), Gleason's education was completed on the shop floor.

William Gleason and his sons were fascinated by the design and manufacture of machine tools. In 1874, William designed an automatic planer for beveled gears, commonly used to transmit power around angles, which had previously been manufactured by hand. Because of William's planer, uniform beveled gears could be mass produced. Thus, when the depression of 1893 decimated the market for machine tools, Kate persuaded her father to focus his efforts on gears, and the Gleason Works soon became known for its specialized gear-cutting machines. Up to this point, beveled gears had been used almost exclusively in the manufacturing of bicycles. Kate, however, recognized their considerable potential.

When William hired his daughter to promote and market his new products, Kate was soon venturing across America and Europe, as the first female seller of machine tools. Her skill lay, not in technical innovation, but in her sales presentation. The quality of the tools made by the Gleason Works, their efficient design, and Kate's obvious knowledge of engineering problems, ensured success, especially with the emerging automobile industry. As **Caroline Bird** noted:

> The early automobile industry was aggressively male. Suppliers selling to big companies entertained them lavishly and sometimes in questionable places. Kate could not, of course, take her prospects to the Everleigh Club. Instead she developed the art of telling amusing stories, and at one point in her selling career affected elaborate hairdos and carried violet garnished muffs to dramatize the advantage she enjoyed on the basis of her sex.

Everleigh Club.
See Everleigh, Aida and Minna.

Over the decades, the automobile industry became the main consumer of the beveled-gear planer and allowed the Gleason Works to monopolize the gear-cutting market. The company became the foremost international manufacturer of specialized gears. Kate Gleason's sales presentations were so technically detailed and thorough that many of her customers believed she had invented the beveled-gear planer herself. Henry Ford once commented that the planer was "the most remarkable machine work ever done by a woman."

By 1913, prompted by disagreements within the family about how the Gleason Works should be run, Kate resigned as secretary and treasurer of the company. She was confident that what she had learned working at Gleason would serve her well in other fields:

> It seemed to me that my experience would make it easier for me to go into a totally different line of business than it would for my brothers, who, up to that time had specialized on the shop end of the work. It was heartbreaking, because it meant leaving father and all the friends I loved.

Her first opportunity came a year later, when she was appointed as receiver in the bankruptcy of a machineshop in Rochester. Not only did Gleason recover the outstanding debt of the company, $140,000, but turned it into a hugely successful enterprise which generated a profit of one million dollars in three years.

In 1914, on the basis of her successful promotion of gear cutters designed by her father, Kate Gleason made engineering history by becoming the first female member of the American Society of Mechanical Engineering. Two years later, she was admitted to the Rochester Chamber of Commerce, as one of its first female members.

The relocation of the Gleason Works to a more spacious and modern location piqued Kate Gleason's interest in construction techniques and architecture. While building a large house of her own in Rochester, she noted that many of the workers on the project lived in East Rochester, where housing was scarce and expensive. In 1917, when Kate Gleason was appointed president of the National Bank in Rochester, she decided to tackle the housing problems of East Rochester. Along with the many properties which the bank held, the National Bank had inherited a semi-completed low-cost housing project.

With her own capital, Gleason took over the project, applying the principles of mass production which she had learned in the automobile industry.

"My particular inspiration for the method came from a visit I made to the Cadillac factory a few years ago, when Mr. Leland showed me the assembly of the eight-cylinder engine," she recalled:

> All this work was done by one man, but he was furnished with a cabinet on wheels, which contained every part he needed and only as many parts as he needed. It is not at all likely that Mr. Leland knew this one assembler out of the 8,000 men in the factory, but in showing me the work, he put his hand on the man's shoulder as though he were his friend and said, as I remember, "This man assembles our engine complete in eight hours, so that it complies with all tests, and it used to take two men four days."

Having experimented with new building materials and designs, Gleason's housing development, Concrest, employed a standardized blueprint and unskilled labor. The 100 houses contained six rooms, at an average cost of $4,000 per unit, and were constructed entirely of poured cement. The innovative design and production methods led to Gleason's election as the first female member of the American Concrete Institute. The Institute was particularly impressed with a system that she designed for employing wet concrete on the building site.

One of the first affordable housing projects in the U.S., Concrest attempted to serve the needs of single families who, until then, were paying an inflated rent of $65 a month for four rooms. The dwellings, though modest, incorporated many novel design features—kitchens came with a gas stove, hot and cold running water, laundry facilities, a refrigerator, cabinets, a built-in ironing board, and a cookbook. Other innovations included built-in bookcases, brass woodboxes, draperies, and so on. But the emphasis was always on the cost savings which mass production brought. Gleason noted:

> We try here to follow Mr. Leland's methods as closely as possible, by having the stock on the job ahead of time, as needed. On very hot days, or to show our appreciation for necessary overtime, we serve occasional cool drinks or ice cream, and on dismal, cold days, we occasionally serve hot coffee and doughnuts. This is done without any idea of being benevolent.

Gleason was aware that many families could scarcely afford a conventional mortgage. Concrest homes were sold for a small down payment and a $40 a month charge which was structured like a rental payment. By taking over the project, Gleason came close to financial ruin, but in the end her business acumen ensured that the project was a financial success.

After World War I, Gleason traveled to France. Intrigued by the 12th-century village of Septmonts, near Soissons, she soon acquired many of its older buildings, including two historic towers, which she renovated. She would visit Septmonts almost every year until her death. She also began a development at Beaufort, South Carolina, where she rejuvenated the local tourist economy by developing a beach, a golf course, and constructing a low-cost artists' colony. Before her death, several of the units would be completed, and the project would eventually be taken over by her sister, **Eleanor Gleason**.

During the late 1920s, Kate Gleason traveled to California, where she studied housing design. As a result, she produced plans for the construction of more concrete suburban houses. In Sausalito, Gleason undertook another low-cost housing project. As with other undertakings, she made an effort to cut costs by buying materials in bulk and warehousing them. She also employed low-cost electrical fittings. The Sausalito project was only partially completed, however, when the State government expropriated a portion of the land for the construction of public-works buildings in 1927.

Gift, like genius, I often think only means an infinite capacity for taking pains.

—*Ellice Hopkins, on Kate Gleason*

For many years, Kate Gleason had suffered from hypertension. In 1933, at age 68, she died from pneumonia in Rochester. She was buried at Riverside Cemetery in Rochester, in a service presided over by a Protestant minister who was a friend of the family. Upon her death, Kate Gleason's estate was valued at $1,250,000. Approximately half of the estate went to create the Kate Gleason Fund for educational and charitable causes. Dr. Howard Kelly of Johns Hopkins University received a bequest for his pioneering research into the uses of radium in the fight against cancer. Another bequest went to the city of Rochester, so that it could construct a local history display in the Rochester Public Library in honor of one of Gleason's former high-school instructors. Finally, Gleason's last endowment transformed the Rochester Mechanics Institute into the Rochester Institute of Technology.

Kate Gleason was a pioneer in several fields. She became the first female student to be admitted to the Sibley College of Engineering at Cornell University. She also developed low-cost housing projects in France, California, South

Carolina, and New York. On several occasions, she represented the American Society of Mechanical Engineering at international conferences. In 1930, Gleason was appointed special representative of the society at the World Power Conference in Germany.

Kate Gleason managed to decouple the contemporary linkages of patriarchy and technology. Her involvement in real-estate development demonstrated her ability to think systematically about engineering problems. Writes Martha Trescott:

> [Women] have displayed not only logical thought but also holistic, or systems thinking. Of course, historically we know of many men in engineering related work, such as George Westinghouse, Thomas Edison, Frederick Becket, Charles Martin Hall, and Benjamin Lamme, who have been excellent systems thinkers. . . . Likewise . . . certain women engineers have also contributed inordinately to concepts of whole, new paradigms, and systems of thought in their fields. Many of these women, such as *Ellen Swallow Richards in sanitary and environmental engineering, Edith Clark in electrical power systems, Kate Gleason in mechanical engineering, *Emily Roebling in civil engineering, and *Lillian Gilbreth in industrial engineering, are familiar names.

But Kate Gleason's forays into the business world also speak of the pioneering role she played as a woman. As with other contemporaries, women such as Gleason sought to break down the barriers which separated the industrial and financial world from women. As Trescott notes, the achievements of such women have too often been ignored or downplayed. Like many of her contemporaries, Gleason was a generalist who sought to apply specialized knowledge to various problems. Writes Lindley:

> For many of her friends and associates, Kate Gleason's captivating energy and enthusiasm obscured the fact that she was neither a gifted engineer nor an exceptionally successful entrepreneur. Her devotion to her career was intense, and excluded marriage. Her importance lay in her experimentation with new techniques rather than in the establishment of flourishing enterprises.

Kate Gleason was a talented businesswoman with a keen eye for niche markets. She demonstrated that quality low-cost housing could be constructed and sold to working-class families with an easy payment plan. But Gleason also recognized a growing trend which had escaped the notice of many of her contemporaries: the suburbanization of the American city.

During the interwar period, the suburb offered a new and healthy alternative for urban dwellers. The allure of green spaces, and individual houses linked by street cars to the industrial heart of the city, contrasted sharply with the crowded and unsanitary conditions of the urban tenement. While this was predominately a middle-class experience, Gleason sought to democratize suburbia, making it accessible and affordable for all.

Whatever Kate Gleason undertook, she did so with determination, attention to detail, and remarkable energy. Her capacity for work was one of her strongest attributes, and partially accounts for her success in the male-dominated world of business. That and her ability to conceptualize and present a vision of what she was selling, marked her out as one of the outstanding American entrepreneurs of her era.

SOURCES:

Bird, Caroline. *Enterprising Women.* NY: W.W. Norton, 1976.

McKelvey, Blake. "Gleason, Kate," in *Dictionary of American Biography.* Edited by Robert L. Schuyler. NY: Scribner, 1944.

O'Neill, Lois Decker. *The Women's Book of World Records and Achievements.* Garden City, NY: Anchor Press, 1979.

Rossiter, Margaret W. *Women Scientists in America: Struggles and Strategies to 1940.* Baltimore, MD: Johns Hopkins University Press, 1982.

Trescott, Martha Moore. "Women Engineers in History: Profiles in Holism and Persistence," in *Women in Scientific and Engineering Professions.* Edited by Violet B. Haas and Carolyn C. Perrucci. Ann Arbor, MI: University of Michigan Press, 1984.

———. "Women in the Intellectual Development of Engineering," in *Women in Science.* G. Kass-Simon and Patricia Farnes, eds. Bloomington: Indiana University Press, 1990.

SUGGESTED READING:

Lindley, Christopher. "Gleason, Kate," in *Notable American Women 1607–1950.* Edited by Edward T. James. Cambridge, MA: The Belknap Press, 1971.

Hugh A. Stewart, M.A.,
University of Guelph, Guelph, Ontario, Canada

Gleditsch, Ellen (1879–1968)

Norwegian president of the International Federation of University Women and the first woman to study at the University of Oslo at which she became professor of chemistry. Born in Mandal, southern Norway, in 1879; died in 1968; awarded licentiate at the Sorbonne, 1912; studied for a year at Yale University; awarded doctorate from Smith College.

Ellen Gleditsch is remembered with pride by the Norwegian branch of the International Federation of University Women, which has established a fund in her name to assist women scholars. She chaired the branch from 1925 to 1928 and was elected president of the International Federation from 1926 to 1929.

Gleditsch was born in 1879 in Mandal, southern Norway, of a distinguished family, whose founder came to Norway from Germany at the end of the 18th century. Ironically, her first cousin Henry, director of Trøndelag Theater during the Nazi Occupation, was shot by the Germans in 1942 for his defense of democratic freedom.

Following in the footsteps of pioneers for women's rights such as *Gina Krog, Gleditsch was able to profit by the action of Cecilie Thoresen (1858–1911), the first woman to matriculate at the University of Kristiania in 1882. After qualifying in pharmacy in 1902, Gleditsch worked on radium research as an assistant at the Paris laboratory of Professor *Marie Curie from 1907 to 1912, the period during which Professor Curie was awarded the Nobel Prize (1911). After passing her licentiate examination at the Sorbonne in 1912, Gleditsch studied for a year at Yale University before taking her doctorate at Smith College. She then returned to Norway to continue her academic career and became professor of inorganic chemistry at the University of Oslo, where she held the chair from 1929 to 1946.

In later years, she researched the history of chemistry, publishing biographies and articles on its practitioners, including Nobel prizewinners Marie Curie and *Irene Joliot-Curie. Honorary doctorates were conferred on Gleditsch by the University of Strasbourg and the Sorbonne.

SOURCES:

Aschehoug & Gyldendal's Store Norske Leksikon. Oslo: Kunnskapsforlaget, 1992.

Lie and Rørslett, eds. *Alma Maters døtre* (Alma Mater's Daughters). Oslo: Pax, 1995.

Elizabeth Rokkan,
translator, formerly Associate Professor,
Department of English, University of Bergen, Norway

Gleichen, Feodora (1861–1922)

English sculptor. Name variations: Lady Gleichen; Countess Gleichen. Born Feodora Georgina Maud Gleichen in London, England, in 1861; died in 1922; daughter of Prince Victor of Hohenlohe-Langenburg, Count Gleichen (1833–1891, an admiral and sculptor) and Laura Williamina (Seymour) Gleichen (daughter of Admiral Sir George Francis Seymour); sister of Lord Edward Gleichen (1863–1937, a British general who organized and ran the nascent intelligence bureau in England during World War I); studied with Alphonse Legros.

Taking over her father's studio in St. James's Palace, Countess Feodora Gleichen became a leading sculptor, exhibiting regularly at the Royal Academy. Members of the art world and visiting royalty frequented the studio, including Faisal I, king of Iraq, whose bust was sculpted. Gleichen's work can be found in many parts of the world. She designed and carved the Queen *Victoria group for the Children's Hospital in Montreal, Canada; the Edward VII Memorial at Windsor, England; the *Florence Nightingale Memorial at Derby, England; and the Kitchener Memorial in Khartoum Cathedral, in the Sudan. Though the award was made posthumously, she was the first woman member of the Royal Society of British Sculptors. Following her death in 1922, a fund was established to award grants to women sculptors.

Glendower, Catherine (d. before 1413).

See Mortimer, Catherine.

Glendower, Margaret (fl. late 1300s)

*Welsh noblewoman. Name variations: Margaret Hanmer; Margaret Hammer; Margaret Glyn Dwr. Born Margaret Hanmer; daughter of Sir David Hanmer (one of the justices of the King's Bench), of Hanmer, Clwyd; married Owen Glendower (c. 1354–1416), around 1383; children: *Catherine Mortimer.*

Between 1400 and 1402, Margaret Glendower's husband, Welsh leader Owen Glendower, waged a guerilla war against Henry IV, king of England. Never captured, Owen Glendower died in obscurity and became a national hero as the father of modern Welsh nationalism. Margaret's daughter Catherine married Edmund Mortimer who also joined in the rebellion.

Glikl of Hameln or Glikl Haml (1646–1724).

See Glückel of Hameln.

Glinskaia, Helen or Elena (c. 1506–1538).

See Glinski, Elena.

Glinski, Elena (c. 1506–1538)

Grand princess of Moscow whose regency saw the creation of a single monetary system for Russia, the obstruction of potential separatist movements, and the restriction of the growth of monastic landholding.

Name variations: Yelena, Helen or Helena Glinskaya, Glinskaia, or Glinsky; Helene of Glinski; Elena Vasil'evna (patronymic). Pronunciation: Ie-LIE-na Va-SIL'-evna GLIN-skee. Born possibly in Lithuania, or in or near Moscow, around 1506; died on April 3, 1538, in Moscow, Russia, possibly of poisoning; regent of Moscow from 1533 to 1538; daughter of Prince Basil (or Vasili) L'vovich Glinskis (also known as Slepyi, meaning the Blind) and Princess Anna Stefanovna Glinskaia; ward of Michael (Mikhail) Glinski, a Lithuanian mercenary; became second wife of Vasili also known as Basil III Ivanovich (1479–1534), grand prince of Moscow (r. 1505–1534), on January 21, 1526 or 1527; children: Ivan IV the Terrible (1530–1584), tsar of Russia (r. 1533–1584); Yuri of Uglitsch (b. 1533).

On the night of December 3, 1533, the grand prince of Moscow, Basil III, died as a result of an illness that had lasted only a few days. While on his death bed, according to some chronicles, the grand prince handed over the crown to his young wife Elena who was supposed to be her son Ivan's guardian and rule the country on his behalf up to the time of his maturity. Basil's decision to make his wife regent (if this actually was the case) apparently had no precedent in the history of the Muscovite dynasty. Thanks to many surviving wills and testaments of princes of Moscow, the traditions of this royal dynasty are relatively well-known. Princes' widows had previously received enough of an estate to support themselves, but they had never been officially appointed rulers of the state.

That story, composed mainly during the reign of Elena's son, Ivan IV the Terrible, who considered his mother the lawful successor to his father, is not the only one told, however. According to opposing chronicles, when Elena asked her dying husband about the future of their children and her own fate, the grand prince bequeathed the throne to his son Ivan. As for Elena, she received only the customary support for a widowed grand princess, "as it had always been from ancient times." Whatever version of the event is correct, less than six months later a released Polish captive, upon returning home from Moscow, reported to his government that great Russian nobles ruling on behalf of the infant sovereign "do everything in accordance with the will and orders of the Grand Princess Elena."

The date of Elena Glinski's birth is unknown. Because she was married in 1526, one may assume she was born around 1506. Her father Prince Basil Slepyi (Basil the Blind) belonged to a large clan of Glinskis and was one of the most powerful nobles in Lithuania in the second half of the 15th century. Elena's mother ❧► **Anna Glinskaia** was the oldest daughter of the Serbian military governor Stefan Yakshich.

According to the legendary information provided by the Russian books of ranks *rodoslovnye knigi*, the Glinskis were descendants of Mamai, ruler of one of the Mongolian Empire's successor states, the Golden Horde, from the 1360s through 1380. The founder of the Glinski family branch, a certain Mongol prince Lekhsada, the legend goes, became a Christian and entered the service of the grand prince of Lithuania, Vitovt. Lekhsada then governed or held the town of Glinski (near the city of Poltava, in the territory of modern Ukraine) and that is the origin of the family name. By the end of the 15th century, the Glinskis had become extremely powerful magnates in Lithuania, the growing political rival to the main powers of Eastern Europe, Russia, and the Crimean Khanate.

Around the time Elena was born, her uncle Michael Glinski, also known as Dorodnyi (Portly), relocated the family to Russia. He, along with his brothers, including Elena's father Basil the Blind, attempted to create a separate state from some eastern territories of the Lithuanian kingdom. Their attempt concluded with a rebellion against the king of Lithuania in 1508. When the failure of the rebellion became clear, the Glinski brothers accepted the offer of the Lithuanian king's enemy, Russian Grand Prince Basil III, to enter his service. The Glinskis were rewarded with lands (given as patrimonial estates, *votchiny*) in the Moscow region. It is possible that Elena was born somewhere in Lithuania shortly before her family moved to Russia. Most likely, however, she was born either in Moscow, where her father was then serving, or somewhere near Moscow, in an estate that the Russian grand prince had granted to her father.

Practically nothing is known about Elena's childhood, except that she spent her teenage years fatherless: her father died before 1522. Elena's mother would outlive her daughter by 15 years, dying in 1553. Elena also had two brothers who survived her, and a brother and two sisters whose dates are not known.

It is supposed that Elena absorbed some features of her family's Western European way of life. Her famous uncle Michael, who was destined to play a significant role in her life, was particularly affiliated with the West. This prominent diplomat was educated at the court of the

German emperor Maximilian I, then was in the service of Albrecht of Saxon, and spent some time in Italy where he accepted the Catholic faith. However, Michael Glinski could hardly have influenced Elena directly during her childhood. In 1514, her flamboyant and ambitious uncle was accused, perhaps not without reason, of plotting treason against the Russian sovereign. As a result, Michael Glinski was arrested and spent a few years in prison. Although the Emperor Maximilian petitioned the Russian grand prince on his behalf, Michael Glinski was released from prison only after Elena's marriage to the grand prince.

Probably Michael Glinski's arrest put Elena's family—a family of newcomers—at a disadvantage among the Muscovite elite. Though the reasons are unknown, the unpopularity of the Glinskis among larger circles of the society is hard to deny. Generally, a foreign noble clan entering the Russian grand prince's service was hardly a rarity, and many Russian nobles of the time could trace their roots to either Western (mainly Lithuanian) or Eastern (mainly Tatar) immigrants. Nonetheless, hostility against the Glinski clan would come to a climax many years after Elena's death.

Years before, however, neither the unpopularity of the Glinskis nor her uncle's political untrustworthiness prevented Elena from winning the love of the Grand Prince Basil III. According to Sigmund von Herberstein, an Austrian envoy in Moscow, when the grand prince began to look for a second wife, he was attracted by Elena's noble origin. At the same time, according to a Muscovite chronicler, the grand prince fell in love with young Elena because of her beauty, youthfulness, and, most of all, purity. For reasons of state, the majority of the Muscovite nobles approved Basil III's decision to divorce his first childless wife *Solomonia and marry again. However, divorce because of a wife's infertility was against the precepts of the Gospel and the habits of the Orthodox Church. The Metropolitan (Patriarch) of Russia, Daniil, authorized the divorce only after significant pressure from the monarch, and Solomonia, despite her explicit protests, was made a nun and sent to a remote nunnery.

Little is known of Elena's personal life during her marriage. Her husband was greatly enamored of her, as their surviving correspondence shows. Apparently to please her predilection for Western ways, he began to shave his beard, which was contrary to the established Muscovite manner and almost unprecedented in the conservative Muscovite society of the 16th century. In the eyes

◆ **Glinskaia, Anna** (d. 1553)

Russian princess. Name variations: Anna Glinskaia; Anna Stefanovna Glinskis. Born Anna Stefanovna; died in 1553; oldest daughter of the Serbian military governor Stefan Yakshich; married Prince Basil (or Vasili) L'vovich; children: *Elena Glinski (c. 1506–1538); as well as sons.

of supporters of the grand prince, Elena fulfilled her function by providing heirs to Basil, and thereby to the major line of the Muscovite house.

However, the birth of an heir in as late as the 52nd year of the grand prince's life provoked a sense of instability at the Muscovite court. As the rebellious Prince Andrei Kurbski, a famous correspondent of Ivan the Terrible claimed, there was a fear that Basil III's brother, Prince Yuri of Dmitrov, would challenge the infant on the throne. The situation was worsened by problems that continued to surround the second marriage of the Grand Prince Basil III. The grand prince's divorce and second marriage aroused the indignation of many Russians. As one of the chroniclers argued, such marriages were adulterous. This opinion found its confirmation in the rumors spread soon after Basil's divorce that virtuous Solomonia gave birth to a son in her exile. Those regarding Solomonia as an innocent victim considered Basil unjust and, therefore, an improper ruler.

In this situation, Elena's young son Ivan's claim to the throne seemed very unstable, as opposed to the claims of his uncles, especially the oldest, Prince Yuri of Dmitrov. Moreover, the idea of a son as the father's successor was relatively new. For centuries, Rurikids, the members of the Russian ruling family, recognized the principle of lateral succession in which seniority passed from the head of the family to his younger brothers, not to sons. Yet the principle of succession was changing: Basil's grandfather, Basil II (1425–1462), successfully fought throughout his reign against his uncle's claims to the throne of Moscow.

On the night of December 3, 1533, the Grand Princess Elena became a widow with two sons aged about three and one. The oldest Ivan was soon crowned as the grand prince of Moscow. The regency was established, comprised of the ruler's younger uncle Prince Andrei of Staritsa, Metropolitan Daniil, Prince Michael Glinski, and some major *boyars* (nobles of the highest rank at the Russian court), including Moscow's Andrei Shuiski. Moreover, both narrative and documentary sources of the time refer to Elena as the main figure in the council. The following four years, until Elena's death, would be filled with events that shocked contemporaries and appeared as a prologue to the bloody reign of Ivan the Terrible. Later chronicles argue about Elena's part in the bloody political executions of the nearest royal relatives. Some claim she was heavily involved; others claim she was just a figurehead for the other regents. Either way, it is significant that these actions were carried out in her name. The major events were as follows.

Almost immediately after Elena's son was announced as the Grand Prince Ivan IV, actions were taken against his oldest uncle, Prince Yuri of Dmitrov, who was accused of plotting against Ivan. The sources contradict each other about whether Prince Yuri planned to usurp the throne or whether he was victimized by the actions of a member of the regent council, the prominent Moscow boyar Andrei Shuiski. In any event, both Yuri and Shuiski were arrested and put in the Kremlin's tower. Though Shuiski remained in detention until the death of Elena Glinski, Yuri died suddenly in confinement in 1536, while in irons; he was buried without any honor and his principality was announced to be the property of Elena's son Ivan, the grand prince.

Soon after Prince Yuri's arrest, his brother Prince Andrei of Staritsa, a member of the regent council and supposedly a major figure in Moscow's government, suddenly left Moscow for his hometown. According to chronicles, Andrei was offended by the failure of his request for new lands, and thus preferred to leave the capital.

Meanwhile the government's boyar appointments strengthened the Glinskis' faction. Thus, Prince Ivan Penkov owed his promotion to boyar rank to his marriage to Elena's sister; another newly appointed boyar, Prince Ivan Fedorovich Belski, was a royal relative. Prince Ivan Obolenski, promoted to ranks of boyar and *konushii*, was openly partial to the Glinskis; there were rumors that he was Elena's lover. (Six days after Elena's death, Obolenski would be arrested and killed by boyars.) Supposedly, Michael Glinski's disapproval of his niece's alleged affair cost him his life. Elena is said to have imprisoned her uncle, put him into irons, and charged him with plotting against the grand prince. Shortly afterward, in the fall of 1534, Michael Glinski suddenly died in the same prison from which he had been liberated after Elena's wedding.

The next three years in Russian history were marked by intense activity by the government. First, it undertook and successfully carried out a monetary reform. By this time, with the growth of Russia's international and domestic trade, a deficit of coins had become increasingly apparent. The old monetary system allowed huge possibilities for counterfeiting. Since the second half of the 14th century, Russian principalities had based their monetary systems on local units of weight. By the end of the 15th century, native coinage of the principalities, now subject to Moscow, was gradually suspended and an increasing quantity of coins issued by the Muscovite princes was in circulation. Silver coins from the largest western Russian trading cities, Novgorod and Pskov, continued to circulate. These cities preserved their mints even after their subjugation to Moscow. In addition, plenty of miscellaneous old coins of varying weights were still in circulation. All this facilitated coin forgery which began spontaneously in the early 1530s and caused a significant monetary crisis. Active searches for the criminals and the imposition of severe punishments, such as cutting off hands and pouring hot tin down throats, proved to be useless.

The remedy for the currency problem was found in the monetary reform of 1534. Elena Glinski's government prohibited usage of any old coins altogether. The government took all old monies out of circulation and monopolized the right to strike new ones. The only legal money for all Russian lands would be coins made in Moscow. However, the Muscovite government decided to keep monetary standards originally used in Novgorod, the most prominent Russian trading town, which profited greatly from of its international trade, especially with German towns of the Hanseatic League. The new coin was referred to as *kopeika*, because it depicted an equestrian with *kop'e* (spear). The word *kopeika* in Russian has remained the name of a small monetary unit, though the coin itself, then the Soviet *kopeika*, was swept away by the inflation following the collapse of the Soviet Union in 1991.

One of other important issues in the Muscovite state of the 16th century was that of ownership of landed property, and in particular, of the monasteries' rights to it. The government of Elena Glinski issued documents to limit the Orthodox Church's landed estates. The state forbade nobles of a secondary rank (*deti boiarskie*), who constituted the majority of potential land sellers, to sell, mortgage, or donate lands to monasteries without the government's permission. Moreover, in the northwestern area, the government took a census of the clergy's meadow lands, announced them to be the state's property, and forced the clergy to pay rent.

The regency, led by Elena Glinski, also focused on the construction of fortifications. The years 1534 to 1537 are marked by work done on the Kremlins of Moscow, Novgorod, and many provincial towns. Not only were old constructions renewed and improved, often with stone or earth walls substituting for wooden ones, but many new fortresses were also built. This provided increasing security for the populations of growing towns against both Tatar and Lithuanian raids, which were common at the time. The method for financing the constructions was unprecedented in Muscovy. While imposing special taxes on the population to provide for the new fortifications, the government disregarded the monasteries' and clergy's traditional tax exemptions and collected money from them.

The foreign policy of Elena Glinski's government was focused on establishing peaceful relations with Lithuania. At this time, Lithuania, Russia's most dangerous and active neighbor, regularly assaulted Russian borders in attempts to enlarge territories subject to Lithuanian kings. After a series of local victories, Moscow concluded a favorable armistice with Lithuania in 1536, allowing the Russians to start preparations for attacking their eastern enemies, the Tatars.

This external activity was paralleled by keeping a watchful eye on internal potential rivals of the sovereign within the royal family. Next in line was Elena's younger brother-in-law, Prince Andrei, residing in his Staritsa principality. By 1537, the government attempted to receive the second written declaration of Andrei's loyalty to the young grand prince. (Prince Andrei signed the first declaration upon Ivan IV's ascension to the throne.) There is no evidence of Andrei's having signed the second document. However, he was soon invited to Moscow and, after some hesitation, forced to go there. Like the older royal uncle, he was accused of plotting against his nephew, arrested, chained and put in prison. Soon after, word came of his sudden death in the Kremlin's tower. Prince Andrei was buried without honor and his principality was added to Ivan IV's lands, just like the principality of Dmitrov, the patrimony of late prince Yuri. Thereby the most important appanage principalities of the 16th century ceased to exist, and Muscovy was well on her way in achieving full control over all Russian lands.

This would be the last power move of Elena Glinski. Some contemporaries, such as Herber-

stein, the Austrian envoy in Moscow, suspected she was poisoned. According to the chronicles, however, during the last months of her life, Elena visited many monasteries around Moscow, donating to them substantial sums of money. This might be an indication of an illness which she may have hoped to overcome by praying in the holy places. Poisoned or not, Elena Glinski died on April 3, 1538.

Hostility towards the Glinski clan would come to a climax many years after Elena's death, when Elena's brothers, counting on their close relationship to their nephew Ivan IV, then a teenage sovereign, tried to regain political power. In the summer of 1547, when extreme heat caused both harvest failure and destructive fires in Moscow, the townspeople revolted. As Ivan IV emphasizes in his letters to Prince Andrei Kurbski, his maternal relatives were subject to the people's anger. One of Elena's brothers barely escaped capture by the mob while another brother was killed by a crowd in the middle of Moscow. And finally, Elena's mother Anna was accused of causing a fire in Moscow. Popular opinion held that she had done so by witchcraft: by cutting out people's hearts, boiling them, and sprinkling the water over houses.

SOURCES:

Akty, otnosiashchiesia k istorii Zapadnoi Rossii. Vol. 2. St. Petersburg, Russia: 1846.

Herberstein, Sigmund von. *Notes upon Russia.* 2 vols. Edited and translated by R.H. Major. *Works issued by the Hakluyt Society,* 1st ser., nos. 10, 12. Reprint of the 1851–52 ed, published by the Hakluyt Society. NY: B. Franklin, 1963(?).

Kurbsky, Prince A.M. *History of Ivan IV.* Edited and translated by J.L.I. Fennel. Cambridge: University Press, 1965.

Lobanov-Rostovskii, A.B. *Russkaia rodoslovnaia kniga.* Vol. 1. St. Petersburg: Izdatel'stvo A.S. Suvorina, 1895.

Perepiska Ivan Groznogo s Andreem Kurbskim. Edited by Ia. S. Lur'e, Ir. D. Rykov. Leningrad: Nauka, 1979.

Polnoe sobranie russkikh letopisei. Vol. 13. Moscow: Nauka, 1965; Vol. 34. Moscow: Nauka, 1978.

Spasskii, I.G. *The Russian Monetary System.* Chicago: Argonaut, 1967.

The Testaments of the Grand Princes of Moscow. Translated and edited by Robert Craig Howers. Ithaca, NY: Cornell University Press, 1967.

Tikhomirov, M.N. "Zapiski o regenstve Eleny Glinskoi i boiarskom pravlenii 1533–1547 gg.," in *Istoricheskie zapiski.* Vol. 46. Moscow, 1954.

SUGGESTED READING:

Alef, Gustaf. "Aristocratic Politics and Royal Policy in Muscovy in the Late Fifteenth and Early Sixteenth Centuries," in *Rulers and Nobles in Fifteenth-Century Muscovy.* London: Variorum Reprints, 1983.

Baron, Samuel. "Herberstein, England and Russia," in *Explorations in Muscovite History.* Hampshire: Variorum, 1991.

Skrynnikov, R.G. *Tsarstvo terrora.* St. Petersburg, Russia: Nauka, 1992.

————. *Ivan the Terrible.* Edited and translated by Hugh F. Graham. Gulf Breeze, FL: Academic International Press, 1981.

Smirnov, I.I. *Ocherki politicheskoi istorii Russkogo gosudarstva 30–50 godov 16 veka.* Moscow-Leningrad: Izdatel'stvo Akademii Nauk SSSR, 1958.

Vernadsky, George. *A History of Russia: Russia at the Dawn of the Modern Age.* Vol. 4. New Haven, CT: Yale University Press, 1959.

Zimin, A.A. *Rossia na poroge novogo vremeni.* Moscow: Mysl', 1972.

Elena Pavlova,
graduate of the Leningrad State University, Russia,
and Ph.D. candidate in Russian history,
University of Chicago, Chicago, Illinois

Glinski or Glinsky, Helen (c. 1506–1538).

See Glinski, Elena.

Gloucester, countess of.

See Fitzhammon, Amabel (d. 1157).

See Beaumont, Hawise (d. 1197).

See Marshall, Isabel (1200–1240).

See Fitzrobert, Amicia (d. 1225).

See Margaret de Burgh (c. 1226–1243).

See Lacey, Maud (fl. 1230–1250).

See Clare, Margaret de (c. 1293–1342).

See Matilda de Burgh (d. 1315).

See Anne of Warwick (1456–1485).

Gloucester, duchess of.

See Joan of Acre (1272–1307).

See Bohun, Eleanor (1366–1399).

See Constance (c. 1374–1416).

See Cobham, Eleanor (d. 1452).

See Walpole, Maria (1736–1807).

See Mary (1776–1857).

See Montagu-Douglas-Scott, Alice (b. 1901).

Glover, Gilman.

See Gilman, Caroline Howard for sidebar on Caroline Howard Jervey.

Glover, Julia (1779–1850)

Irish actress. Born Julia Betterton or Butterton on January 8, 1779, in Newry, County Down; died on July 16, 1850; married Samual Glover, around 1800.

The daughter of an actor, Julia Glover was born in Ireland in 1779 and began her career as a child actress, appearing in the English provinces with her father. After she began securing engagements of her own, her father reputedly demanded all her earnings. He also exercised control over her personal life. After the death of the man she loved, an actor by the name of James Biggs, she was forced by her father to marry the wealthy Samual Glover, who treated her badly. The most positive aspect of Glover's life appeared to be her successful career as the leading comic actress of her day. Praised at the expense of her gender as "a rare thinking actress" by the great tragedian William Macready, she made her last appearance at Drury Lane on July 12, 1850, as Mrs. Malaprop in Sheridan's *The Rivals.* She was so ill during the performance that she could barely speak and died four days later on July 16.

Gluck (1895–1978)

British painter known particularly for her portraits of women. Name variations: Hannah Gluckstein. Born Hannah Gluckstein on August 13, 1895, in West Hampstead, London, England; died in Steyning, Sussex, England, on January 10, 1978; only daughter and first of two children of Joseph Gluckstein (founder of the J. Lyons & Co. catering empire) and his second wife Francesca (Hallé) Gluckstein; tutored at home; attended a Dame School in Swiss Cottage; attended St. Paul's Girls' School in Hammersmith; attended St. John's Wood Art School.

Born into a wealthy Jewish family that founded a catering empire, British artist Hannah Gluckstein rebelled against her conservative upbringing to establish her own unique and controversial life style. Wishing to focus attention on her paintings and not her gender, she chose to be known only as Gluck ("no prefix, no quotes"), a name that distanced her from her family and from society's expectations of women's behavior. She dressed in men's clothing and boots, and had her hair cut at Truefitt gentlemen's hairdressers in Old Bond Street. Her paintings were as unique and arresting as her appearance. She was known for her portraits, particularly those of women, but she also painted haunting landscapes, delicate flower arrangements, and genre scenes. Her biographer **Diana Souhami** calls her striking style "seemingly realistic" but with "a strong inward meaning." Gluck's own view of herself as an artist was as a "conduit open to any unexpected experience, a lightning conductor." Her visions came in a flash and dictated what followed. "The entire composition is received as a whole in scale and in content," she explained. "The Vision once received remains a tyrant. The process of distillation is arduous, the temptations numerous and the discipline needed sometimes hard to endure."

Possessed of a beautiful singing voice, Gluck vacillated between music and art before entering the St. John's Wood Art School, which she later claimed had nothing to teach her. Around 1916, in frustration, she escaped to Lamorna, in Cornwall, where she painted the beautiful landscapes and life in the Cornish countryside and mingled with the painters of the Newlyn School. Later, she divided her time between studios in Cornwall and London, living with "Craig," a woman she had met in art school, then with journalist and author **Sybil Cookson**. It was during this time that Gluck began wearing masculine garb and smoking a pipe, affecting a style her mother attributed to "a kink in her brain." Gluck's father, despite pain over his daughter's self-imposed alienation, provided her with a series of trust funds that supported her throughout her life.

Gluck's first one-woman exhibit was held in 1924, at the Dorien Leigh Gallery in South Kensington. It included 57 pictures, many of them the portraits of sophisticated women, for which she would become known. (Gluck and *Romaine Brooks** did reciprocal portraits of each other in 1926, although Gluck thought Brooks technically and psychologically her inferior and scorned her social circle as "lesbian haute-monde.") Subsequent exhibitions of Gluck's work were held in 1926, 1932, 1937, and then, after a gap of 36 years, in 1973. Her shows were met with excitement and praise from the critics, and her paintings were snatched up by the rich and famous, including Queen *Mary of Teck**, Sir Francis Oppenheimer, Cecil Beaton, interior designer **Syrie Maugham**, and theater impresario C.B. Cochran.

Viewing her paintings as part of an architectural setting, Gluck designed a picture frame to incorporate the artwork into the wall. She described it as consisting of steps, "imitating the costly paneled effect for setting pictures in a wall, but steps of such a character that the usual essence of all frames was reversed and instead of the outer edge dominating, it was made to die away into the wall and cease to be a separate feature." Patented in 1932, the frame was used exclusively in the Gluck Room at The Fine Art Society and was also adopted for other exhibitions in the 1930s. Gluck turned her attention to the quality of artists' materials, abandoning her easel for over a decade (1953–67) to fight what became known as her "paint war," during which she successfully campaigned to formulate a standard among manufacturers for artists' oil paints and the preparation of canvases.

Gluck's numerous love affairs influenced her work. When she lived with Sybil Cookson, she painted all of Cookson's relatives as well as

scenes from the courtroom dramas about which Cookson wrote. When she took up with *Constance Spry**, a genius flower arranger, she painted flower arrangements. Of particular influence was her liaison with **Nesta Obermer**, an international socialite married to an elderly American playwright. (Gluck's painting *Medallion*, the merging profiles of the two women, celebrated Gluck's own "marriage" to Nesta on May 25, 1936.) Coinciding with the onset of her affair with Obermer, Gluck burned the tangible evidence of her past, setting fire to diaries, letters, photographs, her first paintbox and several canvases. "Anything even vaguely smelling of the past stinks in my nostrils," she told Obermer. When their love affair ended in 1945, Gluck suffered a loss of self-esteem that crippled her career. During the last period of her life, from 1945 until her death in 1978, she lived with the journalist **Edith Shackleton Heald** and painted only intermittently. At age 78, claiming she wanted "to go out with a bang," she emerged from near obscurity to present a final one-

Gluck

woman show, a retrospective of 52 paintings held at The Fine Art Society in May 1973. The exhibition, which drew considerable praise from critics, included her last painting, *The Dying of the Light*, the stark likeness of a dead fish's head lying at the edge of the sea. A symbol of decay and death which for Gluck had become "an emblem of resurrection," this final work took her three years to complete, from 1970 to 1973.

A few days after the close of her last show, Gluck slipped in her hotel room and broke her right wrist. She did not paint again but spent her final few years tending to Heald's failing health and getting her own affairs in order. After Heald's death in 1976, Gluck's condition declined further, and in December 1977 she suffered a stroke from which she never recovered. She died on January 10, 1978. Most of her paintings found their way into private collections. Romaine Brooks' portrait of the artist, called *Peter, a Young English Girl* (1926), is held by the Smithsonian Institution.

SOURCES:

Souhami, Diana. *Gluck, 1895–1978: Her Biography*. London: Pandora Press, 1989.

Barbara Morgan, Melrose, Massachusetts

Gluck, Alma (1884–1938)

*Rumanian soprano. Born Reba Fiersohn on May 11, 1884, in Bucharest, Rumania; died on October 27, 1938, in New York; studied with Arturo Buzzi-Peccia, Jean de Rezke, and *Marcella Sembrich; married Bernard Gluck, in 1902 (divorced 1912); married Efrem Zimbalist (the violinist), in 1914; children: (first marriage) Marcia Davenport (music critic and author); (second marriage) Efrem Zimbalist, Jr. (an actor).*

Alma Gluck was the first performer to sell a million records, making RCA Victor Red Seal a household word. To achieve this commercial success, she sang "Carry Me Back to Old Virginny," a megahit which made her a very wealthy woman. She had begun as a performer at the Metropolitan Opera, though after 1918 she appeared there only in concert. Probably her main reason for venturing into recordings was a lack of the dramatic temperament which, along with an excellent voice, is a requirement for opera performers. She decided to devote her energies to recordings, a match for her talents and a well-paying enterprise.

Two years after her daughter *Marcia Davenport's birth (1903), Gluck began her operatic training in New York. When her teacher Arturo

Buzzi-Peccia returned to Europe, Gluck packed up her four-year-old and followed him, intent on furthering her study. "I marvel," wrote Davenport, "at the self-discipline, the strong character of a young and beautiful woman who was working terribly hard at music and yet would let herself be encumbered by a small child and all the annoyances that go with it." In Switzerland, Gluck was discovered by Gatti-Casazza, then director of the Metropolitan Opera House, and was signed for a future engagement.

Alma Gluck was well known for her popular renditions of sentimental songs although she made some excellent recordings of operatic music. Ljuba's aria from Rimsky-Korsakov's *The Tsar's Bride*, for example, demonstrates her excellent musicianship. Her vocal abilities are demonstrated, however, even in songs like "Carry Me Back" which she performed with scrupulous musicianship. Until the 20th century, music lovers often had to create their own music at home. When singers like Alma Gluck offered large listening audiences the opportunity to hear songs they enjoyed, a new world of entertainment opened up. She was one of America's first important recording stars.

SUGGESTED READING:

Davenport, Marcia. *Too Strong for Fantasy*. New York, 1967.

John Haag,
Athens, Georgia

Glück, Barbara Elisabeth (1814–1894).

See Paoli, Betty.

Glückel of Hameln (1646–1724)

Early modern Jewish entrepreneur whose personal memoirs provide historians with information regarding women, commerce, and Jewish family life in her time period. Name variations: Glueckel or Gluckel of Hameln; Glückel von Hameln or Gluckel von Hameln; Glikl of Hameln or Glikl Haml; Glikl bas Judah Leib. Pronunciation: GLOO-kel. Born in 1646 or 1647 in the port city of Hamburg, now in Germany, then part of the Holy Roman Empire; died in 1724 in Metz, now in France; daughter of a man named Loeb (a trader in jewels) and a mother who made lace before her marriage; provided with a Jewish and secular education as evidenced in her references to Torah and Talmud and her capacity for business; married Chayim of Hameln, in 1660 (died 1689); married Hirz Lévy of Metz, in 1700; children: (first marriage) 14, two of whom died before reaching adolescence, including a girl named after her maternal grandmother Mata (Mata lived

about three years between 1666 and 1669); the children who survived were: Zipporah (b. around 1662); Nathan (b. around 1664); Hannah (b. around 1669); Loeb (b. around 1679); Joseph; Mordecai; Esther; Hendele; Samuel; Moses; Freudchen; and Miriam (b. just before her father's death in 1689).

Successfully managed her family's business affairs after the death of her first husband (1689–1700); started writing her memoirs as a testament for her children (1690); recorded her last entry, a reference to the eschatological vision of another woman (1719).

Through personal memoirs dedicated to the moral edification of her children, Glückel of Hameln tells us a great deal about the trials and triumphs of women and Jews in 17th-century Europe. She also demonstrates how an early modern woman could take advantage of the rare opportunities provided women to enter into commercial and financial transactions. To historians, her memoirs offer a rich treasure trove, providing a voice for those women who were not of the wealthiest or most aristocratic families of Europe.

Glückel of Hameln was born in the German city of Hamburg in 1646 or 1647. Her father Loeb traded in jewelry and other assorted items, providing a comfortable enough living for his family. By Glückel's own account, he also provided all his children, male and female, with both religious and secular educations. However, before Glückel turned three, all the Jews of Hamburg were expelled from this important trading port. They moved to the city of Altona, barely a quarter of an hour from Hamburg, but under the control of the king of Denmark, who was willing to provide sanctuary for the Jews.

The expulsion was no surprise, for throughout the medieval and early modern periods, the Jewish minority of Europe served as scapegoat for all sorts of general difficulties. In 1290, all Jews were expelled from England, to be followed by their expulsion from France in 1306, and their expulsion from Spain in 1492. Expulsion generally occurred in the light of increased anti-Semitic rumors in the general populace. One common lie was the claim that Jews required the blood of a slain Christian infant to perform magic rituals and demonic worship. Such rumors circulated among the general populace of places like Hamburg. In addition, very materialistic motivations could intertwine with religious prejudice, and in Hamburg itself, the prime motivation for periodically overtaxing or expelling the Jewish community was tied to the

Opposite page

Alma Gluck

city's dependence on artisanal and commercial activity. Hamburg was a self-ruling German city-state, technically under the sovereignty of the weak Holy Roman emperor, but, in reality, the city's laws were made by the elite masters of its guilds. These merchant and craft guilds self-regulated prices, competition, and quality, much like today's trusts. To be a member, one had to swear certain Christian oaths, and, of course, Jews were therefore excluded from membership. This meant that any Jews engaging in artisanal production or trade to make a living, no matter how meager, were immediately labeled as unregulated, unfair outside competition. Standing in opposition to a free market, the town fathers of Hamburg expelled the Jews to rid themselves of unwanted price competition. In turn, the king of Denmark, like other protective nobles, accepted Jews to stimulate business activity and to create a completely loyal group of subjects who were totally dependent on him for protection and would, for the sake of sanctuary, provide forced loans and loyal bureaucrats.

> The kernel of the Torah is, Thou shalt love thy neighbour as thyself.
>
> —Glückel of Hameln

Glückel describes the Altona Jewish community as consisting of about 40 families, her family being the second richest. Since there was more opportunity in Hamburg than Altona, many of the Hamburg refugees living in Altona purchased four-week passes from Hamburg's government, which allowed them to enter Hamburg for business. Such passes, together with transportation costs from Altona to Hamburg, necessarily increased prices charged by Jewish merchants and artisans. According to Glückel, those traveling between the two towns "often took their life in their hands because of the hatred for the Jews rife among the dockhands, soldiers and others of the meaner classes." When "a poor and needy wretch" tried to slip into Hamburg without a pass, "he was thrust into prison, and then it cost all of us money and trouble to get him out again." This was true since wealthier families, like Glückel's, often paid taxes and extorted fees on behalf of their poorer coreligionists, and Glückel reminisces in her memoirs that "great love and a close community spirit reigned" where the Hamburg exiles were concerned.

When she was ten, war broke out between Sweden and Denmark. At this point, the Hamburg refugees returned home to help defend their native city from Swedish attack. As a result, her father was able to negotiate resettlement for the refugees under a fairly light tax burden. The Hamburg Jews returned "at the mercy and favour of the Town Council," which could always be revoked under merchant or populist pressure. They were allowed no synagogues to worship in any event, and they had to hold prayer meetings in private homes, leading to attacks being made against them by members of the local Lutheran clergy.

Other aspects of Glückel's early life speak a great deal about the bonding of Jewish communities in the face of persecution—a bonding based on an extended definition of family. Glückel's father Loeb married twice, and Glückel was a child of his second marriage, to a poor fatherless woman who made a living by sewing gold and silver lace for textile merchants with her mother Mata. Glückel remembered that, for 17 years, her grandmother Mata was honored with a place at the head of the table, and engaged in such good works as tending sick Jewish refugees from Poland. Therefore, one aspect of Glückel's parents' marriage seems to have been the creation of a type of community-oriented care-taking unit, and when Glückel's sister **Hendele** was honorably married with a substantial dowry, her father provided amply for the poor and needy at the wedding feast.

Part of the early modern Jewish family's definition included a real partnership between husband and wife, but one in which the wife was ascribed the position of junior partner. In synagogues, women were separated from the men in specially partitioned balconies, and were excluded from attendance if menstruating and "unclean." From the very start of a woman's married life, numerous aspects of her future were arranged and managed by men. Glückel casually writes, "My father had me betrothed when I was a girl of barely twelve, and less than two years later I married." Marriages were more family alliances than they were love matches, but Glückel's marriage to Chayim of Hameln seems to have eventually developed the love, respect, and friendship that were hoped for as additional benefits. They spent their first year together in Hameln with Chayim's father Joseph, but, as business opportunities were slim, they moved to Hamburg to live with Glückel's parents at the end of that first year.

Though Glückel describes herself and her husband as inexperienced children, they immediately made some wise business choices. Noting that jewels were not then as fashionable as unadorned gold chains, Chayim bought gold jewelry from house to house and then resold the items to goldsmiths or "merchants about to be married" for a modest but steady profit. By Glückel's own account, though she was young, she became her husband's active business partner, traveling with him on business trips. In her own words, Chayim "took advice from no one else, and did nothing without our talking it over together."

In addition to learning her husband's business, Glückel had her first child, her daughter **Zipporah**, in her parents' house at about the age of 16. She would eventually have a total of 14 children, about one every two years. Twelve of them would survive childhood, though not all of them would live long lives in an age plagued by incurable diseases and other hazards. Despite admitting that her first pregnancy was difficult and that she was, in fact, "a mere child" herself, Glückel clearly appears to have been quite happy in her first marriage. She describes her husband as an ideal Jew, who toiled all day at his business, but who still fasted when required and studied Torah every day. In fact, he prospered so that after only one year in her parents' home, Chayim and Glückel moved to their own rented house with a manservant and a maid. Abraham Cantor, their first manservant, later went on to become a successful merchant in Copenhagen, having been advanced money by Chayim and Glückel.

When Zipporah was two, Glückel had her first son, Nathan, in this home, and the family business continued to thrive, with Chayim dealing in large quantities of goods at various commercial fairs. Glückel even writes that attempts were unsuccessfully made to marry Nathan to the daughter of Samuel Oppenheimer (1635?–1703), one of the most powerful Jews in Europe. A bureaucrat and banker, Oppenheimer managed provisioning for the Austrian Habsburg Holy Roman emperor in his wars with the French and Turks. When Oppenheimer died, the Austrian government owed him millions which were never repaid. Of course, many tried to become in-laws to Oppenheimer, and the attempt made by Chayim and Glückel obviously failed, but Glückel took great pride in the fact that there were at least negotiations toward such an alliance, as she took pride at the successful marriage of Zipporah to the son of wealthy Elias Cleve, and in her husband's work to arrange the marriages of her siblings after the death of her father.

Then, in the midst of success, on January 11, 1689, tragedy struck. Chayim fell over a sharp stone while traveling to another merchant's house. He apparently suffered extreme internal trauma, leading to his death. The last encounters between Glückel and Chayim once again reveal the restrictions placed upon women in early modern Jewish culture. Glückel was prevented by Mosaic law from embracing Chayim one last time since she was "unclean." The great irony is that anti-Semitic claims that Jews desired the blood of Christian children for magic rituals completely ignored the traditional avoidance of contact with blood deeply embedded within Jewish tradition.

Chayim was buried on January 16, 1689, and Glückel writes, "a sad sight it must have been to see me sitting thus with my twelve fatherless children by my side." However, though Glückel mourned profusely, writing, "I truly believe I shall never cease from mourning my dear friend," she did not ignore her very real need to provide for herself and her younger, unmarried children. Always having been privy to Chayim's business dealings, Glückel became an independent merchant. It is also at this time that she began to write her memoirs in order to ease some of the pain caused by Chayim's death and to leave a written record of her advice and counsel for her children.

Throughout the Middle Ages, and well into the 16th and 17th centuries, masters' widows were, on occasion, allowed their husband's status in the guild, though this increasingly became a temporary grant in the post-medieval, early modern centuries. Still, **Elizabeth Baulacre**, widowed in 1641, transformed her husband's small firm into the largest producer of gold thread in Geneva. English widows ran coal mines, sold wool wholesale, and made contracts with the army and navy. In addition, poor women often did piecework for the masters of various guilds, like Glückel's widowed maternal grandmother and mother did. Therefore, there was ample precedent in the whole of early modern society for widows, regardless of religious affiliation, to take on work or take over a deceased husband's business activities in order to support a family.

Being Jewish, Glückel did not have to worry about guild restrictions, and her Judaism actually provided her with some advantages where travel was concerned. Though her husband left behind substantial outstanding debts, upon which the creditors demanded immediate payment, Glückel was able to balance accounts, selling some goods at an auction: "Everything brought a good price, and though I allowed six months for payment, still it all went nicely, and praise God, I suffered no losses." In fact, she cleared her husband's 20,000-Reichsthaler debt within the year, turned a profit on her transactions, and loaned out the profit she made at interest.

At this point, she began to make matches for her unmarried children, listening to their wishes in matters of betrothal as she went about this business. She married her gadabout son Loeb to the daughter of Hirschel Ries of Berlin, on the condition that Ries board her son for three years and provide him with 400 Reichsthalers annually. Unfortunately, Ries would not uphold his part of the bargain where the dowry was concerned, and Loeb, who "knew nothing of business," was allowed, by his father-in-law, to "run like a loose sheep" and to engage in a series of bad business transactions. When Loeb fell thousands of Reichsthalers into debt, Ries was willing to let him rot in prison, according to Glückel, who assumed her son's debts and started paying them. By her own account, Loeb returned to Berlin, "where he ran quacking about and trying to do a little business." Needless to say, he failed at all his ventures, and eventually had to come with his wife and child to live with his mother.

Fortunately for Loeb, Glückel proved to be quite the astute businesswoman. In merchandise, she sold five to six hundred Reichsthalers monthly. She also went to the Brunswick Fair twice a year, turning some several thousands there in profit annually. She bought wares in Holland, and sold goods in her own Hamburg store, while also maintaining "a lively trade in seed pearls. My business prospered," Glückel could observe. "My credit grew by leaps and bounds. If I had wanted 20,000 Reichsthalers [in credit], it would have been mine." She was out on her travels, even in the dead of winter, conducting business, and here, as previously mentioned, her Judaism proved to be of some benefit. Since most inns had restrictions prohibiting the boarding of Jews, Jewish familial networks had established private homes where merchant travelers could stay throughout Europe. Christian merchants failed to establish such extensive networks, and since it was both dangerous and disreputable for a woman traveling alone to stay at an inn, Christian women were at a disadvantage. Glückel, as a Jewish woman, on the other hand, was able to stay with family and friends. Likewise, as noted by the historian Merry Wiesner, since Jewish culture honored the scholar, physician, and rabbi more than the merchant, male business activity was seen more as an evil necessity than something of prestige to be reserved for men. Women could thereby run any number of Jewish businesses, as long as they did not deal with matters of religion, such as kosher butchering.

Still Glückel had to face hardships in the midst of her success. When she sent her 14-year-old son Joseph to learn Talmudic interpretation of Jewish law and scripture, she soon learned that his teacher was fleecing him of both tuition and room and board fees. She promptly had Joseph rescued by another son, Mordecai, and made sure that his new teacher instructed him in her house. Likewise, her travels exposed her to danger, for, in the course of her lifetime, male Jewish merchants traveling as short a distance as the road between Altona and Hamburg were constantly exposed to robbery, and at least two were murdered by her own reckoning during her 11-year career as an independent merchant. Quite literally, Glückel admits to having paid "protection" money on the roads to ensure her safety while traveling.

Then, at about the age of 54, in 1700, she remarried, as she herself wrote, in order to atone for her sins. Hirz Lévy was the leading Jewish banker in Lorraine, so that, on the surface, the match seemed ideal. Glückel had just arranged the marriage of her last son, Moses, and was only caring for a remaining 11-year-old daughter named Miriam, for whom Lévy agreed to care, and whose marriage he agreed to arrange. In turn, Glückel was willing to give all her personal wealth to Lévy as dowry. Though her writing in the memoirs is particularly unclear at this point, it appears that Glückel was lonely, missed Chayim, and was seeking a match that would somehow fill the void. With Miriam, she went to join her new husband in Metz. Her memoirs describe Lévy as a truly good man, but, soon after Glückel's arrival, he began to groan in his sleep and eat poorly.

Within a year of her new marriage, she learned that Lévy was heavily indebted and that his creditors were demanding repayment. With her property now attached to Lévy's estate, Glückel lost all of her personal resources to debt repayment. She proudly writes that she protected the money of her daughter Miriam and made sure that her son Nathan was paid in full by Lévy, who also owed this son-in-law money. She then goes on to remark that the entire economy was suffering in Metz, but that if Lévy had been able to hold off his creditors for two years, he would have benefited from a cyclical upswing. With or without improved business opportunities, the cost of living was periodically quite high in Metz, and Glückel and her husband sometimes lacked bread, and needed to take charitable aid from her son-in-law Moses Krumbach, a local Jewish notable in Metz who was married to Glückel's daughter Esther and who had arranged the marriage to Hirz Lévy in the first place. More important, from her perspective, true tragedy struck as 28-year-old Loeb, her father's namesake, took ill and died during this difficult period.

After a decade of troubles, Hirz Lévy died on July 24, 1712. It appears that some lost ground was regained between 1701 and 1712, however, for Glückel notes that she did get back somewhat less than a third of what she brought to the marriage financially. Though she was not completely penniless, she was evicted from the house she was renting immediately after her husband's death—ironically, the house had once been his. Her son-in-law Moses Krumbach lacked space for his mother-in-law by her account, and Glückel did not have a place to go in Metz until a certain Jacob Marburg allowed her to construct a small room in his house. Her room had no kitchen or hearth, so that she had to make use of his, climbing 22 steps to reach warmth in the wintertime. Glückel writes that, at 66, "It was so hard for me that usually I abandoned the effort."

In 1715, Glückel fell ill and had to keep someone to help care for her—part of that expense being paid for by charitable funds in the Jewish community. Moses Krumbach came at this point and promised his mother-in-law her own room on the ground floor of his house so she would not have to climb any stairs. Glückel, at first, refused his offer, now admitting in her memoirs that she had "long refused" it. Finally, however, she agreed to his plan, though she records that she had many reasons for wishing never to lose her independence and live with her children. Until her death in 1724, Glückel continued to live with Esther and Krumbach. By her own accounts, they treated her to all the honors in the world, letting her travel about the city when she could, and feeding her whenever she arrived home.

Glückel's significance to historians may lie in the insight she gives us concerning the lives of early modern Jewish women, but her own sense of purpose lay in the example she set for her children. At various points in her memoirs she tells her intended audience, her children, to perform acts of charity freely; to be honest in business dealings "with both Jews and Gentiles, lest the name of Heaven be profaned"; and to serve God and Jewish tradition in prayer and sincerity. She freely identifies "righteous gentiles," including monarchs like King Frederick I of Prussia, thereby demonstrating a lack of prejudice not always found in her age. Still, in an era when male dominance was still the rule, it is interesting that this educated woman, who could allude to both Torah and Talmud, felt obliged to open her memoirs by claiming that she, a humble woman, could not hope to present information on morals not already discussed by centuries of male Jewish sages. Then, after opening with such *pro forma* self-abasement, Glückel goes on to cite Talmud and state: "The kernel of the Torah is, Thou shalt love thy neighbor as thyself." From the very start, these memoirs, begun in 1690 to alleviate the pain of losing Chayim of Hameln, promote a sense of the practical, applied communitarianism which guided this woman's life.

SOURCES:

Baron, Salo W., Arcadius Kahan, *et. al. Economic History of the Jews*. Edited by Nachum Gross. NY: Schocken Books, 1975.

Ben-Sasson, H.H., ed. *A History of the Jewish People*. Cambridge, MA: Harvard University Press, 1976.

Finkelstein, Louis, ed. *The Jews: Their History*. 4th ed. NY: Schocken Books, 1970.

Glückel of Hameln. *The Memoirs of Glückel of Hameln*. Translated by Marvin Lowenthal. NY: Schocken Books, 1977.

Hsia, R. Po-chia. *The Myth of Ritual Murder: Jews and Magic in Reformation Germany*. New Haven, CT: Yale University Press, 1988.

Wiesner, Merry E. *Women and Gender in Early Modern Europe*. Cambridge: Cambridge University Press, 1993.

SUGGESTED READING:

Davis, Natalie Zemon. *Women on the Margins: Three Seventeenth-Century Lives*. Cambridge, MA: Harvard University Press, 1995.

Sorkin, David. *The Transformation of German Jewry, 1780–1840*. Oxford: Oxford University Press, 1987.

Abel A. Alves,
Associate Professor of History,
Ball State University, Muncie, Indiana

Gluckstein, Hannah (1895–1978).

See Gluck.

Glueck, Eleanor Touroff

(1898–1972)

American research criminologist. Born Eleanor Touroff in Brooklyn, New York, on April 12, 1898; died in Cambridge, Massachusetts, on September 25, 1972; daughter of Bernard Leo Touroff (a real-estate agent) and Anna (Wodzislawski) Touroff; graduated from Hunter College High School, New York City, 1916; Barnard College, New York, A.B., 1919; diploma in community organization from New York School of Social Work, 1921; Harvard University, M.Ed., 1923, Ed.D., 1925; married Sol Sheldon Glueck (a criminologist and professor of law), on April 16, 1922; children: one daughter, Anitra Joyce Glueck.

Together, Eleanor Glueck and her husband Sheldon distinguished themselves in the field of research criminology, producing numerous volumes dealing with the problems of criminals and juvenile delinquents. Felix Frankfurter, former U.S. Supreme Court associate justice, called them trailblazers, "the most fruitful workers in this resistant vineyard."

Eleanor Glueck came into the field of criminology with an extensive background in social work and education, receiving degrees from Barnard, the New York School of Social Work, and Harvard University, where she was awarded a doctorate in education in 1925. While still a student, she also worked at the Dorchester, Massachusetts, Welfare Center. Having married Sheldon Glueck in 1922, she joined him at Harvard in 1925, working as a research criminologist in the department of social ethics, where he was an instructor. Her first book, *The Community Use of Schools*, was published in 1927, after which she moved to the Harvard Law School as a research assistant in the Crime Survey. In 1930, she obtained a regular faculty appointment as a research assistant.

The Gluecks began their joint research of criminal character and behavior in 1925. With the help of Dr. Richard C. Cabot of the Harvard Medical School and Massachusetts General Hospital, they embarked on a detailed study of the former inmates of the Massachusetts Reformatory, publishing their findings in a groundbreaking work, *500 Criminal Careers* (1930). Follow-up studies of the same group of men were published as *Later Criminal Careers* (1937) and *Criminal Careers in Retrospect* (1943). In these three studies, the Gluecks tackled the problem of scientifically predicting criminal response to penal treatment and identifying treatments most likely to have a positive outcome. A parallel study was conducted at the Massachusetts Reformatory for Women, resulting in the publication *Five Hundred Delinquent Women* (1934). Rounding out their studies was *One Thousand Juvenile Delinquents; Their Treatment by Court and Clinic* (1934), *Juvenile Delinquents Grown Up* (1940), and *Unraveling Juvenile Delinquency* (1950), which concluded that the quality of home life determined whether or not a child would become a juvenile delinquent, and also contained their controversial Social Prediction Tables, by which they claimed that potential delinquents could be identified by the age of six. A series of monographs followed, including *Delinquents in the Making* (1952), *Physique and Delinquency* (1956), *Predicting Delinquency and Crime* (1959), *Family Environment and Delinquency* (1962), *Ventures in*

Criminology (1964), *Delinquents and Nondelinquents in Perspective* (1968), *Toward a Topology of Juvenile Offenders, Implications for Therapy and Prevention* (1970), and *Identification of Predelinquents* (1972).

Eleanor Glueck, who became a research associate in criminology at the Harvard Law School in 1953, was also a trustee of the Judge Baker Guidance Center and the Burroughs Newsboys Foundation in Boston. She was a member of the International Mental Health Conference and of the committee on crime prevention of the American Prison Association. She died in Cambridge, Massachusetts, on September 25, 1972.

SOURCES:

Candee, Marjorie Dent, ed. *Current Biography 1957*. NY: H.W. Wilson, 1957.
McHenry, Robert, ed. *Famous American Women*. NY: Dover, 1983.

Barbara Morgan,
Melrose, Massachusetts

Glueckel of Hameln (1646–1724).

See Glückel of Hameln.

Glyn, Elinor (1864–1943)

Bestselling English novelist, journalist, screenwriter, and social commentator whose romantic fiction critiqued European society in the late 19th and early 20th centuries with famous works such as the novel Three Weeks *and the script for the motion picture* It.

Pronunciation: Glin. Name variations: Nellie Sutherland. Born Elinor Sutherland on October 17, 1864, in Jersey, England; died on September 23, 1943, in London; daughter of Douglas Sutherland (an engineer) and Elinor (Saunders) Sutherland; sister of Lady Lucy Duff Gordon (1862–1935); educated at local schools near Guelph, Ontario, Canada, as well as by governesses and tutors, and self-education in home libraries; married Clayton Glyn, on April 27, 1892 (died 1915); children: two daughters.

With mother and sister, moved to Summer Hill near Guelph after death of father (1865); moved to Scotland after remarriage of mother (1871); presented at British court (1896); published The Visits of Elizabeth *(1900); published* Three Weeks *(1907); lionized on visit to U.S. (1907), plus later visits (1908, 1910); appeared in stage version of* Three Weeks *(1908); conducted affair with Lord Curzon (1908–16); visited Russia (1909–10); served as war correspondent in France, as well as unofficial ambassador to U.S. Army troops (1917); reported on the signing of the Treaty of Versailles (1919); visited Egypt at invitation of Lord*

Milner (1920); worked as screenwriter and consultant in Hollywood (1920–27); returned to England (1929); worked as war correspondent in World War II (1941).

Selected works: (books) The Visits of Elizabeth *(1900),* Three Weeks *(1907),* His Hour *(1910),* "It" and Other Stories *(1927),* Romantic Adventure *(1936); screenplays:* Three Weeks *(1923),* It *(1928).*

"Would you like to sin/ with Elinor Glyn/ on a tiger skin?" went a popular British jingle of the late 19th century. "Or would you prefer/ to err with her/ on another fur?" The object of such attention had gained her reputation as a "scarlet woman" for writing a series of romance novels in the late 19th and early 20th centuries. Set against the backdrop of opulent surroundings and exotic locales, Glyn's books, which were some of the bestselling romance novels of the time, depicted members of European high society engaging in passionate love affairs.

Elinor Glyn intended her novels to portray modern nobility in action. She insisted that the "future happiness of the world" depended on the "elevation of all mankind to the rank of princes and princesses in a fairy kingdom, and not in the abolition of such romantic ideals." Now, however, she is known less for the literary merit of her writings than for her role as a social commentator who chronicled the foibles and hypocrisies of high society in late Victorian and Edwardian Britain.

Although Glyn would be born on October 17, 1864, in Great Britain, her family was Canadian. Her mother **Elinor Saunders Sutherland** was part of a pioneering family, of reduced circumstances, who had shown a talent for survival in rural Canada. As part of his engineering work, Glyn's father Douglas Sutherland had traveled frequently in the company of his wife, even into areas considered hazardous. After completing a Brazilian project, the Sutherlands had gone to New York and eventually to London, where Glyn's older sister Lucy (later Lady *Lucy Duff Gordon) was born in 1862. While Douglas traveled on to Italy to work in a tunnel project, Elinor Sutherland and Lucy went to the British island of Jersey, to stay with a French relative who was spending the winter there. Only five months after Elinor was born in Jersey, word arrived that Douglas Sutherland had contracted typhoid. Leaving the children in the care of relatives, Elinor Sutherland traveled to Italy and returned with her husband to London. He died there in 1865.

Although Glyn's father had made a deathbed wish that his daughters be raised in Europe, money was too short to allow that. A widow at only 24 years of age, Elinor Sutherland chose to return to the protection of her parents' family home, which was located near Guelph, Ontario, Canada. Glyn lived there, with her mother and sister, until she was eight years old.

The imposing family residence, a white house named "Summer Hill," had a large colonnaded front porch and expansive lawn. It was dominated by Glyn's equally imposing grandmother, **Lucy Saunders**. Aloof and proud, Saunders tried to instill into her granddaughters the importance of self-reliance and self-control—in Glyn's words, "molding my character." Each day, Glyn and her sister were required by their grandmother to sit still and be silent for five minutes; when she learned that Glyn was afraid of the dark, Lucy Saunders told Glyn that fear was not shameful but showing fear was. No granddaughter of hers, she declared, would be allowed to show fear.

Although Glyn and her sister Lucy were sent to classes at a local school house, much of their

Elinor Glyn

education came from their grandmother and an aunt. Grandmother Saunders spoke frequently of the glamour and responsibilities of the European nobility, and Glyn later wrote that she gained a sense of *noblesse oblige*. This near reverential attitude toward the European nobility was shared by an unmarried aunt who often cared for the two girls. When Aunt Henrietta read to the sisters from Alfred Tennyson's *Idylls of the King*, Glyn found herself fantasizing about life at court. She believed that it was the source of her preoccupation with the subject, even as an adult.

A visitor to Summer Hill in 1871 changed the family's situation and the girls' lives. Douglas Kennedy, a well-to-do bachelor who was over 60 years old, took a special interest in their mother. Elinor Sutherland showed little interest in marrying Kennedy until she learned that his family owned an estate in Scotland; apparently, the chance to raise the girls in Europe, as her dead husband had wished, was a deciding factor. After their marriage in 1871, the Kennedys crossed the Atlantic ocean to Scotland, accompanied by seven-year-old Elinor and nine-year-old Lucy.

The first months in Scotland were spent in a castle owned by their stepfather's brother near Galloway. Initially, Glyn and Lucy were enthralled with the picturesque castle and the portraits of well-dressed family members lining the walls. The darkness and gloominess of the castle depressed them at night, however, and they noticed the coolness of their new in-laws, who did not approve of the marriage.

In the beginning, the girls were supervised by an English nurse who locked them away in a room while she carried on a tryst with a local gamekeeper. Later, as they stayed in a series of other houses (eventually settling in Jersey because Kennedy thought that the climate benefited his asthma), they were cared for by a series of governesses. None of them stayed for long: Glyn, who had developed a reputation for being rebellious and obstinate, insisted that these silly women could not teach her anything.

The only teacher Glyn accepted was a man of French nationality who was able to teach her writing and the French language, even though, she reported, he had a "ridiculous" moustache and smelled of stale tobacco. She was also enthralled with his stories of Greek gods and goddesses. He failed to convince her of the importance of correct spelling, however, and even as an adult, she relied on editors or printers to correct the many spelling errors in her manuscripts.

A confirmed bachelor who had underestimated the changes that children would bring to his life, Douglas Kennedy was disliked by both sisters. They thought him domineering, especially toward their mother. The houses that they stayed in usually contained sizeable libraries, however, and Glyn sought to escape her stepfather by spending much of her time pouring over the collections. To some degree, she educated herself by reading, among other books, Samuel Pepys' *Diary, Don Quixote,* Gibbon's *Decline and Fall of the Roman Empire*, the *Memoirs* of the Duc de Saint Simon, *The Life of Charles II of England*, and Voltaire's *Zadig*.

When their stepfather died in 1889, their mother decided that they would move to London. Money was tight, and Glyn began to wonder what she should do with her life. Now in her 20s, she discovered, to her surprise, that young men were attracted to her. When she was a child, her red hair had been considered a social handicap, and she had overheard another mother advising her mother to comb her hair with a lead comb "to darken it." Now she found that men were attracted by her red hair and considered her a beauty. Often surrounded by swains who argued over who should be her escort, she remembered, fondly, that at one party the argument became so heated that four young men jumped into a nearby lake, while still shouting at each other. It was the beginning of a lifelong preoccupation with her looks that would cause Glyn, as an adult, to scrub her face daily with a stiff brush and undergo face lifts so painful that her arms had to be strapped down.

Without marriage, women in late Victorian and Edwardian Britain had no social position, and "spinsterhood" was equated with loneliness. The position of governess was open to Glyn, but she believed that her temperament and background made her unsuitable for such work. Although marriage had become important, she did not want to marry a "penniless" youth. She also rejected three marriage proposals from better-off older men, though she wrote in one of her novels, *The Vicissitudes of Evangeline:* "It is wiser to marry the life you like because after a while the man does not matter."

In 1892, Elinor accepted a marriage proposal from Clayton Glyn, who was a neighbor of a family she was visiting. Clayton, in his late 30s, appeared to be economically well-off; his family owned an estate in Scotland. Although qualified to work as a barrister, he had chosen not to do so. They married that same year.

By time of the birth of their second child (and second daughter) in 1898, however, the marriage was foundering. Upset that his wife had not given him a son, Clayton left for several weeks at Monte Carlo, where he gambled away more than £10,000. Relations between Glyn and her husband worsened when she finally told him, after an agonizing self-debate, that a friend, Lord Brooke, had made a pass at her. Her husband's response was to laugh, "No! Did he? Good old Brookie!"

Financial problems also intruded. Elinor did not know that Clayton was in debt when he married her. She gave little thought to their frequent trips to the Continent or the Middle East, where he insisted that they stay in first-class hotels and where she frequently conducted expensive shopping forays. Only later did she learn how often her husband had borrowed money and how little of his debts he could repay. In fact, paying off Clayton's debts would become a major motivation for much of her writings.

Glyn began to record her impressions in her notebooks as she moved through English high society. Many of her comments were both perceptive and critical. When presented at court in 1896, she noticed to her dismay that the clothing and complexions of women did not meet her own high standards. As she learned more about the mores of the upper class in England, she also began to realize that her own marriage was not atypical. In late-19th-century Britain, affairs were not only common but acceptable as long as both parties were discreet. If a husband neglected his wife for others, his wife was free to engage in her own affairs.

By building a career around the hypocrisies and quirks of such a society, Glyn would become a successful novelist. She did not seek to become a writer, however; she entered upon her writing career gradually, and even indirectly. In 1889, an editor of a Scottish magazine asked Glyn to contribute articles on the topic of fashion for future issues. Then, during a long period of convalescence from rheumatic fever, she asked that her mother bring her diaries and notebooks to her. In 1879, Glyn had started a record which she called "The Diary of Miss Nellie Sutherland." She now began to rewrite some of the entries into letter form, producing a manuscript which she titled *The Visits of Elizabeth*. How it came to be published is not clear, although her husband showed it to the editor of a magazine during one of his periodic visits to London. It was serialized in the magazine in 1899 and published as a book in 1900.

The Visits of Elizabeth was centered around Glyn's observations, often humorous, of the atmosphere and social mores of the upper classes, particularly in France and England. Although some reviewers found the book shocking or vulgar, it was a commercial success. Glyn initially decided that her writings would appear anonymously, but she later changed her mind. *Frances Evelyn Greville, countess of Warwick, a local grande dame known as Daisy who had befriended Glyn, urged her to publish under her own name, adding that "Elinor Glyn" sounded like a pseudonym anyway. Glyn's next novel, *The Vicissitudes of Evangeline* (1906), appeared under her real name, despite the fact that it raised a touchy issue: under what conditions might a wife be forgiven for having an affair?

The word "Romance" has been . . . cheapened in modern times.
—Elinor Glyn

Glyn's following book, *Three Weeks* (1907), the story of a woman who initiates a younger man she meets in Switzerland into the art of love, was her most famous. Toward the end of the novel, the heroine is revealed to be the queen of a Balkan country, and is eventually assassinated by an agent of her husband. *Three Weeks* was typical of many of Glyn's writings in its use of an exotic setting (sometimes Eastern Europe or the Middle East); in its description, in voluptuous terms, of passionate love affairs; and in its frequent use of exclamation marks. Daisy Warwick, who had read the novel in manuscript, cautioned Glyn against publication. Not only would others think that Glyn had had an affair with a young man, she warned, but, worse, they would believe that she was boasting of it.

Warwick's prediction came true. Many reviewers assumed it was autobiographical, noting that the heroine shared several characteristics with Glyn, including the use of tiger skins as decorative notes; the love for certain cities, such as Venice; and the mention of certain colors as predominant decorative hues in rooms, such as purple. But the book was a great success, selling more than two million copies throughout Europe and the United States within nine years of its publication; by the early 1930s, sales had reached five million. Glyn was unprepared, however, for public condemnation as a sinful woman. An Eton schoolmaster wrote her about his unhappiness over the book, although he admitted that he had not read it; challenged to read it, he reported that he liked the book but would not allow his students to read it. King Edward

VII, a notorious womanizer, would not even allow the book to be discussed in his presence.

Glyn thought critics missed the point: if she really had been engaged in a number of passionate affairs, it would not have been necessary (or prudent) for her to write such a book. From Glyn's viewpoint, the furor was especially odd because "the Lady" in her book had to "pay" for her failure to observe her marriage vows; she thought that the novel's tragic ending gave the book a "moral" tone.

In 1908, Glyn sought to earn more money by appearing in a stage production of *Three Weeks*, hoping that she would benefit financially when the play moved to the fashionable West End theater district of London. She was extremely disappointed when the Lord Chamberlain's office refused to permit it; only later did she learn that the Foreign Office, alarmed at rumors that the leading female character in *Three Weeks* was copied after Empress *Alexandra Feodorovna of Russia, had asked that such action be taken.

Because of the success of *Three Weeks* in the U.S., Glyn decided to tour America from coast-to-coast in 1908. She took with her a voluminous amount of clothing, including 60 pairs of shoes. Warned that the book might make her a target of the press, she was prepared for the horde of reporters as she arrived in New York City. But she was treated as a celebrity almost everywhere, meeting President Theodore Roosevelt and being invited into the homes of some of America's wealthiest families. At a dinner in her honor, Mark Twain praised *Three Weeks*.

She was overwhelmed by the reception given by a group of miners in Nevada who had champagne shipped to their small community for a dinner in her honor. She later wrote that they "were full of the chivalry, of the abstract respect for honest women, and of the rough sense of justice toward men, which was the heritage of an earlier time." The "magnificent" miners convinced her, she wrote, that manners could be acquired through good character and education and were not exclusively the result of good bloodlines. She gave the episode of the miners a prominent place in her book *Elizabeth Visits America* (1909).

While she was staying in Munich in the summer of 1909, the Russian grand duchess Kiril (*Victoria Melita of Saxe-Coburg) and her mother-in-law the Grand Duchess Vladimir (*Maria of Mecklenburg-Schwerin) invited Elinor to visit Russia. She read the manuscript of her novel *His Hour* (published in 1910 and generally consid-

ered one of her best books) to the Grand Duchess Vladimir. It appears that she did not read all of the manuscript to her Russian hosts, however, since the published novel portrayed Russia as a country 300 years behind the times. Invited to spend parts of 1909 and 1910 in Russia, Glyn did not always reassure her hosts with her behavior. While touring the Winter Palace in St. Petersburg, she was asked how she knew so much about the building. She replied that she felt at home because she believed, at times, that she was the reincarnation of *Catherine II the Great.

Upon her return to Britain, Glyn discovered that her husband was again borrowing and was unable to pay off his debts. Although the Glyns had grown increasingly distant, she felt some responsibility for helping him. He had rescued her from "spinsterhood" and had given her a place in society; in a way, he had even made her career as a novelist possible, since a single woman writing passionate novels would have been an object of ridicule.

For nearly three weeks, she stayed in her bedroom, writing the novel *The Reason Why* (published in 1911) and using the advance money to repay her husband's debtors. The story of a red-haired woman badly in need of money, the book contained several references to Tennyson's *Idylls of the King*. She considered it the worst novel she had written and added that "My only choice on this occasion seemed to lie between the degradation of myself or of my pen." To save money, the family moved into increasingly smaller quarters on her husband's estate. When Glyn placed her husband on an allowance and bought out his holdings in his estate, he never forgave her. Clayton insisted that she was cheating him and that his financial troubles stemmed from her trips and purchases.

Personal distractions during the years 1912 through 1914 slowed Glyn's writing output. She was shaken when news arrived that the luxury liner *Titanic* had sunk, because her sister and brother-in-law, Lady and Lord Duff Gordon, were on board. Thrilled when they turned up among the survivors, Glyn was again taken aback when British newspapers printed charges that the Duff Gordons had bribed crew members in order to be placed in a half-full lifeboat. Although the Gordons were cleared during an official inquiry, Glyn frequently sat in the audience during the hearings.

Glyn was also distracted by the British politician Lord George Curzon, with whom she conducted an eight-year affair. Considering her popular reputation as a "scarlet" woman, Glyn was linked with relatively few men, including Lord Milner and Lord Alastair Innes Ker, a guardsman. Curzon, a widower with three children, had been present at a stage performance of *Three Weeks* and had sent her a congratulatory note. She came to regard him as a high-minded political leader with an "untiring devotion to self-imposed duty" and "little regard for personal advantage in the pursuit of what he believed to be good for the country." He was portrayed as a rising, if egoistic and ambitious, politician in her novel *Halcyone,* which was published in 1912. She presented him with a copy of the book.

Curzon's friends seemed to regard Glyn as a woman of low birth who had gained notoriety by writing a shocking novel—an unsuitable companion for a potential future prime minister. She noticed that she was not invited to his home when others from the highest social levels were present. In the words of one author, he was "compartmentalizing" his friendship with her.

Glyn, who had offered to decorate his home, was in the midst of that project when it was announced that Curzon had been named to Prime Minister David Lloyd-George's war cabinet in 1916. The next day, a notice in the newspapers announced that Curzon, who needed money to refurbish an inherited estate, was engaged to marry ❧▶ **Grace Hinds Duggan (Curzon),** a wealthy widow. Glyn burned all the letters she had received from him and never spoke to him again.

Determined to forget Curzon, she threw herself into her writing, producing *The Career of Katherine Bush,* which was published in 1917. The story of the daughter of an English auctioneer who rises to high society, it was, in a way, a rejection of the aristocracy that her grandmother had worshipped. The message of the novel was that nobility was not a matter of good birth but the result of good character, and that any intelligent person could attain high social standing.

With the advent of World War I, the American newspaper magnate William Randolph Hearst asked her to be a wartime correspondent for his American newspapers. She accepted the offer with enthusiasm, seeing it as a way to forget Curzon. She was disappointed at the response of the "gallant French race" to the war, and she was also horrified that French high society refused to greet newly arriving American troops in 1917. Glyn appointed herself unofficial ambassador to the arriving Americans, visiting troop camps and traveling perilously close to the war front. On more than one occasion, when she had to take

❧▶ **Curzon, Grace Hinds**

Daughter of Joseph Hinds (U.S. minister in Brazil); married Alfred Duggan of Buenos Aires (died); married Lord George Curzon, in 1917.

A beautiful woman of charm and wit, upon her marriage to Lord George Curzon, Grace Hinds Curzon became the center of social gatherings at Carlton House. But she was well aware that she could never successfully compete with the specter of *Mary Leiter Curzon,* her husband's first wife. Lord Curzon was buried beside his first wife; Grace Curzon was buried in a niche nearby.

cover during a bombardment near the fighting, she remembered her grandmother's words about not showing fear. As a reporter at the signing of the Versailles Peace Treaty in 1919, she was one of only two women present.

In 1920, Glyn accepted a contract offer from the Famous-Players-Lasky (later Paramount) studio to travel to Hollywood to work as a screenwriter and consultant. The next seven years in Hollywood would become some of the happiest of her life. As the sole representative of European high society in movie land, she felt a responsibility to correct crude and inaccurate portrayals of Europeans—she called them "travesties"—in Hollywood films.

Glyn tried to add both romance and accuracy to films she worked on, even demonstrating to make-up artists the correct look for powdered wigs. She wrote a historical flashback sequence into the script for *Beyond the Rocks* (1924), so that Rudolph Valentino could wear costumes from the romantic days of European history. At times, she lamented that her efforts failed: despite her complaints, actors were placed in a "Swiss chalet high amidst snow" while wearing evening dress. But she also found occasions to try to improve Hollywood's social graces. Concerning Valentino, she wrote, "Do you know that he had not even thought of kissing the palm, rather than the back, of a woman's hand until I made him do it!"

Although one reason that Hollywood studios hired Glyn was to be able to use her name for publicity and film credits, her screenplays, with their vivid and clear-cut characterizations, were well suited to the silent screen. In 1922, when she went to work for Metro-Goldwyn-Mayer, the studio made every effort to please her, settling her in a five-room suite. Her sister Lucy wrote excitedly that Elinor was "making cinema history in Hollywood." Glyn became a friend of the comedian Charlie Chaplin, an acquaintance of the producer Samuel Goldwyn, and, through a friendship with actress *Marion Davies, a visitor to Hearst's castle at San Simeon, California.

Elinor Glyn's greatest film success came with the motion picture *It* (1928), which made a superstar of its female lead, *Clara Bow. *It* was based on one of Glyn's short stories which was published as a book in 1927. She defined "It" as an "animal magnetism" or a "peculiar fascination possessed by men more often than women" that makes them "immensely attractive to all women and even men." The story of a store clerk who falls in love with the store's owner, *It* earned more than a million dollars for the studio, and the film made Glyn a popular speaker in America on any topic related to love. She lectured in vaudeville theaters in New York City and was asked to contribute articles to magazines on topics such as "How to Hold a Man" and "The Philosophy of Love."

Glyn genuinely liked some of the stars she worked with, but some found her to be far different from anyone they had ever met. *Gloria Swanson termed Glyn's British dignity "devastating," but added that "although she was old enough to be my grandmother, she was the first woman I saw wearing false eyelashes and got away with it." "She talked a blue streak," added Swanson. With her "dyed red hair, green eyes, and mouth of crimson," she seemed like "something from another world."

As with most strong women, Glyn also gained a reputation for difficulty. She selected a British stage actor, Eric Percy, as the best person to play the male lead in the American version of *Three Weeks* (1923). Horrified when a German, Conrad Nagel, was selected instead, she created a scene in the studio commissary. The director King Vidor observed that he had to use all his "diplomatic" ability in dealing with Glyn. Her contract was not renewed in 1927, partly because she had gained a reputation as a meddler who was costing the studios money. For a time, Glyn lived in New York City and then set sail for Britain. Though she planned to return to the States, her daughter and husband intervened, arguing that she had mismanaged her money and would owe a substantial amount of U.S. income tax if she went back.

Agreeing to remain in Britain but feeling trapped, Glyn continued to find projects that interested her. She financed a British film version of *Three Weeks,* thinking that "British critics would be kind to someone spending their own money to make a film," but the movie was a critical and popular flop. Glyn had more success writing. She wrote seven more books and, in 1936, at age 72, published her autobiography *Romantic Adventure.* Well-received by critics, the book also caused some surprise by revealing that the character of "the Lady" in *Three Weeks* was not based on her life.

During the 1930s, Glyn also became a popular "medium" at "spiritualist" parties. Reincarnation appealed to her because it balanced out the fundamental unfairness of life. She did not have fixed opinions about the "possibility of communication with the dead," she wrote, but "could see no reason why this should be impossible." Glyn came to believe that "all supposed communications from the dead are really made by nonhuman sprite-like disembodied entities."

She continued for a time to live in the style to which she had become accustomed, decorating one apartment in an assortment of brocades, silks, and five tiger skins. (An American visitor to one of her apartments quipped, "There wasn't a darned chair in the room you could relax in.") Although she was still in demand as a writer, her finances were less than robust. Her family eventually placed her on an annuity and asked a bank to pay all her bills. She was not allowed to sign a check.

Glyn's last book, *The Third Eye* (1940), was a secret-service thriller. From that point on, most of her writing came as a war correspondent for the Hearst newspapers during World War II. Believing that her "brain has come back more clearly," she reported that she felt "young and spry." Over the next two years, however, she became increasingly ill. She died in a nursing home on September 23, 1943, at 79 years of age.

In her autobiography, Glyn wrote that "The highest essential element in romance is love, but this is love in the highest sense, which becomes self devotion to a spiritual ideal accompanied by disregard of material advantage." One of the great ironies of her life was that, although she never lacked "material advantage," her writing career was partly motivated by her belief that she lacked love in her life.

SOURCES:

Ethrington-Smith, Meredith, and Jeremy Pilcher. *The "It" Girls: Lucy, Lady Duff Gordon, the Couturiere "Lucile," and Elinor Glyn, Romantic Novelist.* NY: Harcourt Brace Jovanovich, 1986.

Glyn, Anthony. *Elinor Glyn: A Biography.* Garden City, NY: Doubleday, 1955.

Glyn, Elinor. *Romantic Adventure: Being the Autobiography of Elinor Glyn.* NY: E.P. Dutton, 1937.

Hardwick, Joan. *Addicted to Romance: The Life and Adventures of Elinor Glyn*. London: Andre Deutsch, 1994.

SUGGESTED READING:

Hamilton, Ian. *Writers in Hollywood*. London: Heinemann, 1990.

Leslie, Anita. *Edwardians in Love*. London: Hutchinson, 1972.

Robinson, David. *Hollywood in the Twenties*. NY: Tantivy Press, 1968.

COLLECTIONS:

Most of the surviving notes and correspondence of Elinor Glyn are privately held by family members, although some letters are contained in the Harry Ransom Humanities Research Center at the University of Texas at Austin.

Niles Holt,
Professor of History, Illinois State University, Normal, Illinois

Goda (c. 1010–c. 1049).

See Godgifu.

Goddard, Arabella (1836–1922)

English concert pianist who was one of the first to play entire concerts by memory and to achieve a world career. Born in St.-Servan, St. Malo, on January 12, 1836; died at Boulogne, France, on April 6, 1922; married the critic J.W. Davison, in 1859.

Born of English parents, Arabella Goddard was the most famous pianist in England during the 1860s and 1870s. Because of Goddard's superb technical skills, George Bernard Shaw felt "nothing seemed to give her any trouble." At age six, she began her studies with Friedrich Kalkbrenner, who was followed by Thalberg and then by her future husband, the critic J.W. Davison. At age 17, Goddard was the first pianist to perform Beethoven's formidable *Hammerklavier Sonata* in London. She played everything from memory, a rare feat at the time. In 1857 and 1858, again in London, she performed the then rarely heard last five piano sonatas of Beethoven. In 1872, she was the soloist at the inauguration of the Royal Albert Hall, playing the *Emperor Concerto* of Beethoven. Goddard was one of the first pianists to achieve a world career. In 1872, she left for a three-year tour, playing in Australia, New Zealand, India, China, and throughout America. Retiring in 1882, she died at Boulogne, France, on April 6, 1922.

John Haag,
Athens, Georgia

Goddard, Mary Katherine

(1738–1816)

*American printer, first woman postmaster in the U.S., and publisher, who is best known for making the Mary-*land Journal *a successful enterprise.* Born Mary Katherine Goddard on August 6, 1738, in either Groton or New London, Connecticut; died in Baltimore, Maryland, on August 12, 1816; daughter of Dr. Giles (a physician and postmaster, c. 1703–January 31, 1757) and Sarah (Updike) Goddard (c. 1700–January 5, 1770); learned at home and on-the-job training at printer's office; never married; no children.

With mother, moved to Providence, Rhode Island, to assist brother in printing business (1763); helped brother publish the Pennsylvania Chronicle (1768–74); joined brother at his new shop in Baltimore (1773); managed the print shop and the publication of the Maryland Journal (1774–84); published books, pamphlets, almanacs, and broadsides; established bookbindery; served as postmaster for Baltimore (1775–89); upon leaving printing business (1784), continued to operate a bookstore to about 1809. Publications: numerous imprints, which includes the first official publication of the Declaration of Independence with the names of the signers.

Arabella Goddard

Women of early America frequently assisted their husbands in their places of business and, during their absences, assumed managerial responsibility. Widows and other single women were proprietors of shops and were represented in most trades. Unmarried, Mary Katherine Goddard assisted her brother in the printing business and, for long periods of time, managed the shop herself. Lawrence C. Wroth writes that Goddard should be thought of as "not simply as a business executive whose part was to direct the labor of others, but as a craftsman whose manual labor was a considerable element in determining the success of her establishment."

Mary Katherine Goddard was one of two surviving children (two died in infancy) of Dr. Giles Goddard, a prosperous physician and postmaster, and **Sarah Updike Goddard**, a woman of Dutch-English ancestry. Soon after their daughter's birth, the Goddards moved from Groton, Connecticut, across the Thames River to New London. Mary Katherine may have attended an elementary school for brief periods as did her brother William (1740–1817). Most likely she was taught chiefly at home. As Isaiah Thomas notes, Goddard's mother "received a good education" and "acquired an acquaintance with several branches of useful and polite learning." Mary Katherine's adult life would be linked with the career of her brother, with whom she acquired on-the-job training as a printer.

M ary
K atherine
G oddard

On July 1, 1762, William Goddard, who served as a journeyman printer in New Haven and New York City, opened a printing shop in Providence, Rhode Island, with £300 borrowed from his mother. On October 20, he began publishing the *Providence Gazette and Country Journal.* Mary Katherine and her mother Sarah moved to Providence the following year, and both women assisted William in the printing business and issuing the newspaper. In 1765, leaving his mother and sister to run the Providence business, William went to work in the printing office of John Holt in New York City while also attempting to establish a press at Woodbridge, New Jersey.

At Providence, the printing firm was reconstituted as Sarah Goddard & Company, with partners including Mary Katherine and several others. The newspaper became a vigorous advocate of the American cause against Great Britain. Besides the newspaper, the printing shop turned out almanacs, broadsides, pamphlets, and legal and business forms; it also engaged in the retail trade of books, stationery, and patent medicines. Topping the list of publications were *The Main Point,* a theological pamphlet by Timothy Allen, and the *New England Almanac* by Benjamin West.

Mary Katherine Goddard diligently learned the printing trade, despite its being physically tasking. Type had to be sorted out and placed on the press. With an apron constantly blackened by printer's ink (made of varnish or linseed oil boiled with resin and lampblack), Goddard had to tug at the lever of a heavy wooden press in order to make each impression; it took ten hours

operation to print 1,000 sheets. To print a four-page, folio newspaper required four days work. Mother and daughter had a rough time trying to make the newspaper a success and never obtained the 800 subscribers that were necessary to make the newspaper profitable.

In November 1766, again with financial support from his mother, William Goddard opened a printing establishment in Philadelphia, in partnership with Joseph Galloway, speaker of the Pennsylvania Assembly, and Thomas Wharton, a Quaker merchant. The *Pennsylvania Chronicle and Universal Advertiser,* which was to be editorially slanted against the Proprietary Party (supporters of the Penn family continuing as the proprietors of the colony), made its appearance on January 6, 1767. It was the fourth English-language newspaper in Philadelphia, and the first to use four columns per page. In November 1768, Sarah and Katherine sold the Providence shop and joined William's Philadelphia firm. Besides assisting in the manual work, Mary Katherine kept the accounts of the shop and also attended to most of the business details.

With her brother spending little time at the Philadelphia shop, Goddard turned the *Chronicle* into one of the most successful newspapers in the colonies, with 2,500 subscribers by 1770. William still set the editorial policy, however, and soon grew tired of taking directions from Galloway and Wharton. A bitter feud erupted, and Galloway and Wharton sold their interest to Benjamin Towne, who, like his predecessors, continued to inject political partisanship into the newspaper. Towne, however, was forced out of the firm in January 1770, undoubtedly due to Mary Katherine's influence; with her mother Sarah dying at that time, Goddard inherited a one-half financial share in the firm.

That year, William published a pamphlet, *The Partnership,* in which he castigated Galloway and Wharton for attempting to ruin the *Chronicle.* According to William, Galloway tried to get Mary Katherine to sell her interest in the printing establishment for a trifle, telling her: "You have no friends here—you would live much happier in New England and may make something for yourself by a sale of this interest." Goddard, however, "Saw his baseness, and that he was a man who could smile with a dagger in his hand," and "told him that she knew the business was very valuable and that she should listen to no such proposals."

On May 12, 1773, William opened a print shop on the corner of South and Baltimore streets in Baltimore, where he inaugurated the *Maryland Journal and Baltimore Advertiser,* the first newspaper in the city, which made its appearance on August 20. Both brother and sister hoped to have a dual publishing venture—in Philadelphia and Baltimore. The Philadelphia *Chronicle,* however, began to experience great competition, and Mary Katherine shut down the Philadelphia shop in February 1774 and joined in her brother's printing venture in Baltimore.

That February 17, the *Maryland Journal* announced that William was "on a very important mission," one that would occupy him throughout the Revolutionary War. Mary Katherine now assumed sole responsibility for the printing shop and the newspaper publication; starting on May 10, 1775, the newspaper's colophon stated: "Published by M.K. Goddard." Meanwhile, William was setting about the task of creating single-handedly an intercolonial postal service that would challenge the British-operated system: "Goddard's Post Office" extended from Casco Bay, Maine, to Williamsburg, Virginia. On July 26, 1775, the Continental Congress took over William's postal network, and, much to William's disappointment, Benjamin Franklin became postmaster general. William received the lowly appointment, at $100 a year, of Surveyor of the Post Office. The position entailed traveling in order to inspect the various components of the postal system. On August 12, 1775, Mary Katherine was named "postmistress" of Baltimore. Among her duties was to print postal schedules and notices of unclaimed letters in the newspaper. Goddard thus became the first female postmaster serving under the U.S. government.

With war inflation, Goddard's newspaper had to raise yearly subscription rates from 10 shillings in 1773 to £10 in 1777. Even so, Mary Katherine's *Maryland Journal* thrived and an issue of November 16, 1779, would declare its circulation was "as extensive as any." Her main competition, John Dunlap's *Maryland Gazette, or Baltimore General Advertiser*, which began in 1775, folded in four years.

A Baltimore citizen could visit the print shop and expect to find a wide assortment of goods for sale at bargain prices. People often paid for subscriptions with commodities. A notice of December 15, 1778, said that payment could be in form of "Beef, Pork, or any Kind of Animal Food, Butter, Hog's Lard, Tallow, Bees-Wax, Flour, Wheat, Rye, Indian Corn, Beans, Buck-Wheat, Barley, Hops, Oats, Vegetables, Flax Seed, Wood Charcoal, tann'd Sheepskins, brown Linen, Linsey Woolsey, Feathers, Linen

and Cotton Rags." In addition, the shop had well-stocked shelves of dry goods, stationery, and books.

On December 11, 1776, Goddard had announced that she was entering into the bookbinding business, and two years later, the shop could boast an addition—"a complete and elegant Bookbinding Room." Mary Katherine was always in need of linen thread to sew the sides of books and vellum to be used for the covers. Not only did the bookbinding help Goddard accomplish an integration of her book publishing under one roof, but it also allowed people from the community to bring in materials to be bound. Goddard had become a versatile entrepreneur: editor, printer, publisher, bookbinder, merchant, and postmaster. Under authorization from Congress, she printed, in January 1777, the first official copy of the Declaration of Independence bearing the names of the signatories. This documents carries the inscription: "Baltimore in Maryland Printed by Mary Katherine Goddard." By November of 1783, the *Maryland Journal* began twice a week publication, and the following year Goddard inaugurated delivery service.

*S*he was an expert and correct compositor of types, and ably conducted the printing house of her brother during the time he was engaged in other concerns.

—Isaiah Thomas

One advantage that Goddard had over any competition was the ready access to paper. On April 8, 1777, she announced that paper would be secured from a new mill at Elkridge Landing, near Baltimore. William Goddard and Eleazer Oswald as partners established this paper mill, which had a monopoly on paper manufacturing in Maryland. Both men published a disclaimer in the *Journal* that the new firm would not interfere with the printing business of Mary Katherine, "who, it must be acknowledged, hath supported her Business with Spirit and Address, amidst a Complication of Difficulties." Frequently Goddard advertised in her newspaper that she would pay cash or commodities for linen rags, which would be used in the production of paper.

Although Goddard's *Journal* had a caption of "Free and of NO PARTY," with brother William occasionally dropping by to lend a hand as to what content was published, it was inevitable that he and Mary Katherine would be involved in heated controversy with segments of the community. William, though brilliant and an able printer, often was given to determined opinions and invective. Mary Katherine, however, was capable herself of offending some local citizens. On June 3, 1776, the Baltimore Committee of Safety considered a complaint from Mary Katherine that George Sommerville "came to her office and abused her with threats and indecent language on account of a late publication in her paper." The Committee, "conceiving it to be their duty to inquire into everything that has a tendency to restrain the liberty of the Press," had Sommerville brought before it, and ordered him "censured" and placed under bond for future good behavior.

On February 26, 1777, the *Journal* had published an anonymous essay (actually written by Samuel Chase), which tongue-in-cheek advised Americans to accept British peace terms. A local super-patriotic body, the Whig Club, failed to see the irony in the essay, and a delegation visited Goddard intent on having her divulge the name of the author. She refused and referred the inquisitors to her brother. Brought forcibly before the Club, William was ordered to leave the town within 24 hours and the state within three days. He complied but went directly to the Maryland Assembly in Annapolis, where he received a legislative denunciation of the Club's highhandedness as "a manifest Violation of the Constitution, directly contrary to the Declaration of Rights." William also responded by writing a pamphlet condemning the Whig Club, which Mary Katherine printed. Ruffians assaulted William, and again he was ordered to leave town. Goddard sought out the town guard to obtain protection for William. This being in vain, the Goddards again appealed to the Maryland government, whereupon the Assembly ordered the culprits punished, and the governor provided protection to William. Both brother and sister were determined to uphold freedom of the press.

Two years later, a publication in the *Journal* caused another confrontation over freedom of the press. Goddard, probably at William's urging, printed Charles Lee's "Some Queries, Political, and Military, Humbly Offered to the Considerations of the Public." Lee had a score to settle with George Washington, whom he blamed for forcing him out of the army after the battle of Monmouth in 1778. The "Queries" denigrated Washington's abilities and his indispensability to the American cause. A mob led by Continental army officers seized William at his home, gave him a drumhead trial out-of-doors, under the threat of lynching, and, therefore, he had no

choice but to print an apology in the *Journal*. This being done, William then followed up in a later issue with a recantation of the apology. Still, with the likelihood of further physical intimidation, William refused to back down. He and Mary Katherine both appealed to the governor and council for protection. No assistance, however, was forthcoming. Meanwhile, Lee submitted even more vitriolic material. This time, Goddard put her foot down and refused publication. The controversy in the community subsided. Lee expressed gratitude for the printing of the first set of queries by giving the Goddards power of attorney to sell his Virginia estate, and when he died in 1782 he left William one-sixth of the property.

Mary Katherine's print shop continued its varied production, which now included regular runs of playbills for the Baltimore theater. As it was for other printers, publication of almanacs was a profitable mainstay. In 1779, she began publication of her own almanac: *The Maryland Almanac for the Year of Our Lord, 1780*, followed by *The Maryland, Delaware, Pennsylvania, Virginia, and North-Carolina Almanack, and Ephemeris, For the Year of our Lord, 1781*. She also sold almanacs printed in German.

The relationship between brother and sister deteriorated. Mary Katherine kept William at arms length, convinced that he would interfere with her printing business. When William Goddard and Eleazer Oswald planned in 1781 to set up shop to print inexpensive editions of European classics, they announced that they did not intend to encroach on Mary Katherine's business and that they wished "the Printress of the MARYLAND JOURNAL, &c. may meet with that Encouragement from the PUBLIC, which her Assiduity and Care shall merit." Nothing came of this proposed venture, and the two men started assisting Goddard in her shop.

Eventually the Goddards decided to go their own ways. He apparently bought out her interest, with an understanding that she continue with some of the book printing. When they each published their own almanacs with the exact same title in 1784, William was resentful of the competition and published an attack on his sister: "Observing a spurious Performance, containing a mean, vulgar and common-place Selection of Articles. . . . I find myself obliged to inform the Public, that the above-mentioned spurious *double-faced* Almanack, is" by "a certain *hypocritical Character*, for the dirty and mean Purpose of FRAUD and DECEPTION." Interestingly, the colophon of the *Maryland Journal* for January 2, 1784, read: "Printed by William and Mary Katherine Goddard, at the Post-Office, in Market Street"; in the next issue, four days later, Mary Katherine's name was dropped. With their estrangement deepening, Goddard became embittered over the terms of her financial settlement with William and instituted five suits against him; the details and outcome of the litigation, however, are unknown.

Leaving the printing business in 1784, Goddard devoted her time to her postmaster duties and to operating a bookstore, which also sold dry goods and stationery. William, at age 45, married **Abigail Angell** in 1786. At that time, John Carter, publisher of the *Providence Gazette*, tried to effect a reconciliation between Mary Katherine and William, but without success. William formed a partnership with Edward Langworthy in 1786 and then in 1789 with his brother-in-law James Angell. In 1792, William sold his interest to Angell and retired from the printing business.

Mary Katherine Goddard had an unexpected jolt in November 1789. Samuel Osgood, postmaster general of the new U.S. government, dismissed her as postmaster of Baltimore on grounds that the office was expanded to include surrounding areas and therefore extensive horseback traveling was required—an activity, he said, that could be better performed by a man; 230 Baltimore citizens unsuccessfully petitioned Osgood to reverse the decision. Goddard wrote President Washington to intervene on her behalf, but he simply replied that the appointment belonged entirely to Osgood to make. She then appealed to the U.S. Senate, emphasizing her 14-year experience and that as postmaster she had endured "her Share of losses and misfortunes." The Senate tabled the request, without taking any further action. When her successor John White died after less than a year as postmaster of Baltimore, Mary Katherine still did not secure reappointment.

Goddard had prospered in the printing business. In a *Journal* notice of March 2, 1783, she had reported the theft of a small trunk belonging to her, "ornamented with Gold-leaf." Among the contents were: "Four Guineas and a Half, Four Half-Johannes (Portuguese coins), Thirty or Forty dollars, and bank notes for fifty, forty, and ten dollars." The 1790 census listed her household with four slaves and one "other free person," probably a boarder.

In 1803, she moved her bookstore from 80 Baltimore Street to a smaller place at 28 Chatham Street. She retired from business about 1809; the census for the following year listed her as "Mary K. Goddard, gentlewoman." During her last years, she made her final residence at 18 Conewago Street in the company of a slave, **Belinda Starling**. Mary Katherine Goddard died at her home on August 12, 1816, at age 78, and was buried in the St. Paul's Parish graveyard. In her will, which does not mention brother William, she gave 26-year-old Belinda her freedom and stipulated that she be the sole heir.

Mary Katherine Goddard had an extraordinary career. She served as printer in Providence, Philadelphia, and Baltimore, and at the latter place, for a decade, oversaw the publishing of a vast amount of work besides issuing one of the most influential newspapers of the time. Her work had a reputation for fine quality, and she never missed a deadline. While in association with her brother, she tempered his excesses, and yet stood by him fully in defending the cause of freedom of the press. Wroth cites a fitting tribute from an "admirer" of Goddard: she was "a woman of extraordinary judgment, energy, nerve and strong good sense."

SOURCES:

Hudak, Leona M. *Early American Women Printers and Publishers, 1639–1820*. Metuchen, NJ: Scarecrow Press, 1978.

Miner, Ward L. *William Goddard, Newspaperman*. Durham: Duke University Press, 1962.

Thomas, Isaiah. *The History of Printing in America*. NY: Weathervane Books, 1970 (originally published 1810).

Wheeler, Joseph T. *The Maryland Press, 1777–1790*. Baltimore, MD: Maryland Historical Society, 1938.

Wroth, Lawrence C. *A History of Printing in Colonial Maryland, 1686–1776*. Baltimore, MD: The Typothetae of Baltimore, 1922.

———. *The Colonial Printer*. Portland, ME: The Southworth-Anthoensen Press, 1938.

SUGGESTED READING:

Bird, Caroline. *Enterprising Women*. NY: W.W. Norton, 1976.

COLLECTIONS:

The Maryland Historical Society, Baltimore, has the *Maryland-Journal*, and the Historical Society of Pennsylvania the *Pennsylvania Chronicle*; both newspapers are available in microfilm editions. Listings of Mary Katherine Goddard's imprints, with locations where they may be found, are published in "Bibliography of Maryland Imprints: An Annotated Bibliography of Books, Newspapers, and Broadsides Printed in Maryland from 1777 to 1790," in Wroth, *Maryland Press*, pp. 77–206 and "Imprints by Mary Katherine Goddard," in Hudak, *Early American Women Printers and Publishers*, pp. 339–392.

RELATED MEDIA:

Mary Kate's War (motion picture, one reel, 25 min.), recreates Goddard's efforts to uphold the freedom of the press by refusing the Baltimore Whig Club's demand that she reveal the author of an unsigned article she had published in the *Maryland Journal*; produced by National Geographic Society, 1975; also on videocassette.

Harry Ward,
Professor of History, University of Richmond,
author of *Colonial America* (Prentice-Hall),
American Revolution—Nationhood Achieved (St. Martin's),
and other books on colonial and Revolutionary America

Goddard, Paulette (1905–1990)

American actress. Born Pauline Marion Levee (also seen as Levy), on June 3, 1905, in Whitestone Land- *ing, Long Island, New York; died of heart failure on April 23, 1990, at her villa in Ronco, Switzerland; married Edgar James (a lumber industrialist), around 1927 (divorced 1931); married Charlie Chaplin (an actor, director, producer), in 1936 (divorced 1942); married Burgess Meredith (an actor), in 1944 (divorced 1950); married Erich Maria Remarque (a novelist), in 1958 (died 1970); no children.*

Filmography: (short) Berth Marks (1929); The Locked Door (1929); City Streets (1931); The Girl Habit (1931); The Mouthpiece (1932); (short) Show Business (1932); (short) Young Ironsides (1932); Pack

*P*aulette
*G*oddard

Up Your Troubles *(1932); (short)* Girl Grief *(1932);* The Kid from Spain *(1932);* Roman Scandals *(1933);* Kid Millions *(1934);* Modern Times *(1936);* The Young in Heart *(1938);* Dramatic School *(1938);* The Women *(1939);* The Cat and the Canary *(1939);* The Ghost Breakers *(1940);* The Great Dictator *(1940);* North West Mounted Police *(1940);* Second Chorus *(1941);* Pot o'Gold *(1941);* Hold Back the Dawn *(1941);* Nothing but the Truth *(1941);* The Lady Has Plans *(1942);* Reap the Wild Wind *(1942);* The Forest Rangers *(1942); (cameo)* Star Spangled Rhythm *(1942);* The Crystal Ball *(1943);* So Proudly We Hail *(1943);* Standing Room Only *(1944);* I Love a Soldier *(1944); (cameo)* Duffy's Tavern *(1945);* Kitty *(1946);* The Diary of a Chambermaid *(1946);* Suddenly It's Spring *(1947); (cameo)* Variety Girl *(1947); (cameo)* Unconquered *(1947);* An Ideal Husband *(UK, 1948);* On Our Merry Way *(A Miracle Can Happen, 1948);* Hazard *(1948);* Bride of Vengeance *(1949);* Anna Lucasta *(1949);* The Torch *(1950);* Babes in Baghdad *(1952);* Vice Squad *(1953);* Paris Model *(1953);* Sins of Jezebel *(1953);* The Charge of the Lancers *(1954);* The Stranger Came Home *(The Unholy Four, UK, 1954);* Gli Indifferenti *(Time of Indifference, It./Fr., 1964).*

Paulette Goddard was born Pauline Marion Levee in Whitestone Landing, Long Island, in 1905, and went to work at age 14, shortly after the breakup of her parents' marriage. Reportedly, an uncle used his influence to get her a job with producer Flo Ziegfeld, who billed her as Peaches Browning (✥▶ **Frances Heenan**) in his 1926 hit *No Fooling.* The next year, while on the road in *Rio Rita,* Goddard met and married her first husband Edward James, president of the Southern States Lumber Company, and retired from the stage to become a housewife. However, by 1931, she had obtained a Reno divorce and was headed for Hollywood to break into the movies. Taking her mother's maiden name, Goddard played a series of bit parts in films until signing as a contract player for Hal Roach. She was let go after six months and returned to the stage, appearing in the choruses of a few musicals of the period, such as *The Kid from Spain* (1932) with Eddie Cantor.

Charlie Chaplin was next in line to impact Goddard's life, but her relationship with him is cloaked in mystery. (Their marriage was not even confirmed until their divorce in 1942.) By some accounts, they met on a yachting excursion, during which he talked her out of investing her alimony in a phony film venture. Captivated by her beauty and her cynical wit, he cast her in the role of the waif in *Modern Times,* which began shooting in 1932 but did not premiere until 1936 (the year they were supposedly secretly married at sea). Goddard appeared in Chaplin's next film *The Great Dictator* (1940), but he worked so slowly that while they were in production, she made some other important films, including *Second Chorus* (1941) in which she briefly danced with Fred Astaire; she also made the acquaintance of Burgess Meredith, whom she married after divorcing Chaplin. Among Goddard's sorrows, at this phase in her career, was the loss of the coveted role of Scarlett O'Hara in *Gone With the Wind,* a part said to have been hers until it was given to ***Vivien Leigh** at the last minute.

Through the 1940s, Goddard was one of Paramount's top stars, usually cast in vixen roles, though she excelled in comedy. She was nominated for an Academy Award as Best Supporting Actress for her performance in *So Proudly We Hail* (1943), a war drama with ***Claudette Colbert** and ***Veronica Lake,** and she starred in top-notch movies such as *Kitty* (1946) and *Unconquered* (1947). By the 1950s, however, like other actresses her age, her star began to fade, and she could only find leads in B pictures with ludicrous titles, movies like *Bride of Vengeance* (1949) and *Babes in Baghdad* (1952).

After divorcing Meredith in 1950, Goddard married the novelist Erich Maria Remarque in 1958 and enjoyed a luxurious retirement shuttling back and forth between Paris and New York. She made one come-back attempt in 1964, as **Claudia Cardinale**'s mother in the Italian film *Time of Indifference.* Her final appearance was in the television movie "The Snoop Sisters" (1972). Goddard died of heart failure in April of 1990; in her final bequest, she left $20 million to New York University.

SOURCES:

Katz, Ephraim. *The Film Encyclopedia.* NY: Harper-Collins, 1994.

Lamparski, Richard. *Whatever Became of . . . ?* 1st and 2nd Series. NY: Crown, 1968.

Shipman, David. *The Great Movie Stars: The Golden Years.* Boston: Little, Brown, 1995.

Barbara Morgan,
Melrose, Massachusetts

Godden, Rumer (1907–1998)

British novelist and children's writer. Name variations: Mrs. Laurence Foster. Born Margaret Rumer Godden on December 10, 1907, in Sussex, England; died at her home in Dumfriesshire, Scotland, on November 8, 1998; second of four daughters of Arthur Leigh Godden (an employee of a steamship company

◀✥
*Heenan,
Frances.* See
*Kuhn, Irene
Corbally for
sidebar.*

in India) and Katherine (Hingley) Godden; sister of Jon Godden (a novelist and painter); attended Moira House, Eastbourne; studied dancing privately; married Laurence S. Foster (a stockbroker), in 1934 (separated 1941, later divorced); married James Haynes-Dixon, on November 11, 1949 (died 1973); children: (first marriage) two daughters, Jane and Paula, and a son who died in infancy.

Awards, honors: commended for Carnegie Medal (1962), for Miss Happiness and Miss Flower; *Children's Book of the Year Awards from the Child Study Association for* Operation Sippacik *(1969),* The Diddakoi *and* The Old Woman Who Lived in a Vinegar Bottle *(1972), and* Mr. McFadden's Hallowe'en *(1975); Whitbread Award (1973), for* The Diddakoi; *Horn Book* Honor List citations for *Miss Happiness and Miss Flower, Little Plum, Home Is the Sailor, The Kitchen Madonna, and* The Old Woman Who Lived in a Vinegar Bottle; *American Library Association Notable Books citations for* The Doll's House, The Mousewife, Impunity Jane: The Story of a Pocket Doll, The Fairy Doll, Miss Happiness and Miss Flower, The Kitchen Madonna, The Old Woman Who Lived in a Vinegar Bottle, A Kindle of Kittens, *and* The Dragon of Og.

Selected writings—novels: Chinese Puzzle *(P. Davies, 1936);* The Lady and the Unicorn *(P. Davies, 1938);* Black Narcissus *(Little, Brown, 1939);* Gypsy, Gypsy *(Little, Brown, 1940);* Breakfast with the Nikolides *(Little, Brown, 1942);* Rungli-Rungliot: Thus Far and No Further *(P. Davies, 1944, published as* Rungli-Rungliot Means in Parharia "Thus Far and No Further," *Little, Brown, 1946);* Take Three Tenses: A Fugue in Time *(Little, Brown, 1945, published in England as* A Fugue in Time, *M. Joseph, 1945);* The River *(Little, Brown, 1946);* A Candle for St. Jude *(Viking, 1948);* A Breath of Air *(M. Joseph, 1950);* Kingfishers Catch Fire *(Viking, 1953);* An Episode of Sparrows *(Viking, 1955);* The Greengage Summer *(Viking, 1958);* China Court: The Hours of a Country House *(St. Martin's, 1961);* The Battle of Villa Fiorita *(Viking, 1963);* In This House of Brede *(Viking, 1969);* The Peacock Spring: A Western Progress *(Macmillan, 1975);* Five for Sorrow, Ten for Joy *(Viking, 1979);* The Dark Horse *(Viking, 1981);* Thursday's Children *(Viking, 1984);* Cromartie v. the God Shiva *(Morrow, 1997).*

Children's books: (illus. by Dana Saintsbury) The Doll's House *(M. Joseph, 1947); (illus. by Saintsbury)* The Mousewife *(Viking, 1951); (illus. by Adrienne Adams)* Impunity Jane: The Story of a Pocket Doll *(Viking, 1954); (illus. by Adams)* The Fairy Doll *(Viking, 1956); (illus. by Adams)* Mouse House *(Viking, 1957); (illus. by Adams)* The Story of Holly and Ivy *(Viking, 1958); (illus. by Adams)* Candy Floss *(Viking, 1960); (poems, illus. by Jean Primrose)* St. Jerome and the Lion *(Viking, 1961); (illus. by Primrose)* Miss Happiness and Miss Flower *(Viking, 1961); (illus. by Primrose)* Little Plum *(Viking, 1963); (illus. by Primrose)* Home Is the Sailor *(Viking, 1964); (illus. by Carol Barker)* The Kitchen Madonna *(Viking, 1967); (illus. by James Bryan)* Operation Sippacik *(Viking, 1969); (illus. by Creina Glegg)* The Diddakoi *(Viking, 1972); (adaptor, illus. by Mairi Hedderwick)* The Old Woman Who Lived in a Vinegar Bottle *(Viking, 1972); (illus. by Ann Strugnell)* Mr. McFadden's Hallowe'en *(Viking, 1975); (illus. by Juliet S. Smith)* The Rocking Horse Secret *(Macmillan, 1977); (illus. by Lynne Byrnes)* A Kindle of Kittens *(Macmillan, 1978); (illus. by Pauline Baynes)* The Dragon of Og *(Viking, 1981); (illus. by Jeroo Roy)* The Valiant Chatti-Maker *(Viking, 1983);* Four Dolls *(includes* Impunity Jane: The Story of a Pocket Doll, The Fairy Doll, The Story of Holly and Ivy *and* Candy Floss, *Greenwillow, 1983);* Fu-dog *(1989);* Coromandel Sea Change *(1991).*

Other: Bengal Journey: A Story of the Part Played by Women in the Province, 1939–1945 *(Longmans, Green, 1945);* In Noah's Ark *(narrative poem, Viking, 1949); (adaptor with Jean Renoir)* "The River" *(screenplay based on her novel of same title, United Artists, 1951); (biography)* Hans Christian Andersen: A Great Life in Brief *(Knopf, 1954);* Mooltiki: Stories and Poems from India *(Viking, 1957); (translator) Carmen de Gasztold,* Prayers from the Ark *(poems, Viking, 1962); (translator) de Gasztold,* The Creatures' Choir *(poems, Viking, 1965, published as* The Beasts' Choir, *Macmillan, 1967); (adaptor) Hans Christian Andersen,* The Feather Duster: A Fairy-Tale Musical *(music by Kai Normann Andersen, Dramatic Publishing, 1964); (autobiography with sister, Jon Godden)* Two Under the Indian Sun *(Knopf, 1966);* Gone: A Thread of Stories *(Viking, 1968, published in England as* Swans and Turtles: Stories, *Macmillan, 1968);* The Tale of the Tales: The Beatrix Potter Ballet *(Warne, 1971); (with J. Godden)* Shiva's Pigeons: An Experience of India *(Viking, 1972);* The Butterfly Lions: The Story of the Pekingese in History, Legend and Art *(Macmillan, 1978); (biography)* Gulbadan, Portrait of a Rose Princess at the Mughal Court *(Viking, 1981); (with Jon Godden)* Indian Dust *(1989); (autobiography)* A Time to Dance, No Time to Weep *(Beech Tree Books, 1988).*

The daughter of a steamship agent, Rumer Godden and her three sisters grew up in East

Bengal, India, where they were educated by their parents who encouraged them to read beyond their age. As children, the girls wrote long books together which were illustrated by Rumer's sister **Jon Godden**, who also became a novelist. (Rumer and Jon's book *Two Under the Indian Sun* [1966], describes their Anglo-Indian childhood.) In 1919, the girls were sent to school in England, where they had a difficult period adjusting to a more disciplined lifestyle. Rumer had a particularly hard time and attended five different schools in a period of six years. She finally settled in at Moira House in Eastbourne, a

more progressive school where she received individualized attention. She was strongly influenced by the vice-principal, **Mona Swann**, whom she credits with giving her a thorough background in English and technique.

After training as a dancing teacher, Godden returned to India and opened a dancing school in Calcutta. (It became large and successful, after which she sold it and happily returned to full-time writing.) In 1934, she married Lawrence Sinclair Foster, a stockbroker, with whom she had two daughters and a son who died in infancy. Her first

Rumer Godden

book, *Chinese Puzzle* (1936), the result of a life-long interest in Chinese culture, was published before the birth of her first daughter. It was followed by *Black Narcissus* (1939), a story about a community of nuns in the Himalayas, which established her as a popular author. In America, the book was a runaway hit, which both pleased and unnerved Godden. "It's not very good for that to happen to you early in your writing career, you really just want a steady climb." Godden also had difficulty with expectations that she would continue to write along the same subject line. "I think the English particularly like you to have a vein and keep to it, so that they know what they're getting. And they are awfully puddingish. . . . Either you write novels with an Indian setting, or you write novels about religious life, or you write about children; you keep to your vein; whereas I don't."

While continuing to write, Godden also ran a day school in Calcutta, ostensibly for the education of her two daughters. In 1941, her husband left her after going bankrupt, and she took the children to stay on a tea estate in Darjeeling. She later published *Rungli-Rungliot*, a diary of the experience, in 1943. In 1947, Godden issued her first children's book, *The Doll's House*, a novel in which adult conflicts and situations are played out through dolls. "I wanted to see if I could write a real novel—it's a murder story—in the tiny compass of a doll's house, and make it acceptable for children." Other doll stories followed, including *Impunity Jane*, *The Fairy Doll*, and *Miss Happiness and Miss Flower*.

In 1949, Godden married James Haynes-Dixon and returned to England, where they lived for several years in Lamb House, in Sussex, once the home of Henry James. She later moved to Dumfriesshire (Scotland), where she continued to write. Extremely versatile, Godden also wrote plays, poems, and translations, and contributed to numerous journals and periodicals. She strongly criticized the practice of categorizing novels for young adults, and of writing children's books with a "limited" vocabulary. "As soon as anyone tries to write a novel with a target," she wrote, "he's bound to fail. A book must spring spontaneously; you can't write with a target. . . . I never try to make my books simple, I never prescribe my words; children adore words." About her own writing habits, she said: "I read all my books aloud when they are finished. To see if they bind. I can't imagine why more writers don't do this . . . how it sounds, the naturalness of the dialogue, is to me very important."

A number of Godden's books were made into films, with varying results. *Black Narcissus*, starring **Deborah Kerr** and adapted by Universal in 1947, was, in Godden's view, disastrous, ill conceived, and even offensive. Some critics, however, now consider it a minor classic. Godden felt that the movie version of her sensitive novel about adolescence, *The River*, fared better in the hands of Jean Renoir, though, having collaborated with the director on the adaptation, she found working on a movie set boring. Also filmed were her adult novel *Greengage Summer* (titled *Loss of Innocence*), for which she co-wrote the film script, *An Episode of Sparrows* (titled *Innocent Sinners*), and "In This House of Brede," which was made for television and starred **Diana Rigg**. Rumer Godden died in 1998, age 91.

SOURCES:

Commire, Anne. *Something About the Author*. Vol 36. Detroit, MI: Gale Research.

Shattock, Joanne. *The Oxford Guide to British Women Writers*. Oxford and NY: Oxford University Press, 1993.

RELATED MEDIA:

The Battle of Villa Fiorita (111 min.), also released as *Affair at the Villa Fiorita*, starring **Maureen O'Hara**, Rossano Brazzi, Richard Todd, **Phyllis Calvert**, **Maxine Audley**, Olivia Hussey, Ursula Jeans, directed by Delmer Daves, produced by Warner Bros., 1965.

Black Narcissus (100 min.), film starring Deborah Kerr, Sabu, **Jean Simmons**, **Flora Robson**, **Kathleen Byron**, David Farrar, directed by Michael Powell and Emeric Pressburger, produced by Universal, 1947.

Enchantment (102 min.) adapted from *Take Three Tenses*, film starring David Niven, **Teresa Wright**, Evelyn Keyes, Farley Granger, **Jayne Meadows**, Leo G. Carroll, **Gigi Perreau**, directed by Irving Reis, set design by **Julia Heron**, produced by Samuel Goldwyn for RKO, 1948.

Innocent Sinners (95 min.), adapted from *An Episode of Sparrows*, film starring **June Archer**, Christopher Hey, Flora Robson, screenplay by Rumer Godden and Neil Paterson, produced by Rank Organisation, 1957.

"In This House of Brede," starring Diana Rigg, produced by Learning Corp of America, televised on CBS, 1975.

Loss of Innocence (99 min.), adapted from *Greengage Summer*, film starring Kenneth More, **Danielle Darrieux**, Susannah York, Jane Asher, directed by Lewis Gilbert, written by Howard Koch, costumes by **Julie Harris**, produced by Columbia, 1961.

Barbara Morgan,
Melrose, Massachusetts

Godgifu (c. 1010–c. 1049)

Anglo-Saxon princess. Name variations: Goda. Born around 1009 or 1010; died before 1049; daughter of *Emma of Normandy (c. 985–1052) and Aethelred or Ethelred II the Unready (r. 979–1016); sister of Edward III the Confessor (c. 1005–1066), king of the English (r. 1042–1066); married Dreux or Drew, *count of Mantes and the Vexin; married Eustache or Eustace II, count of Boulogne (r. 1049–1093), around 1036; children: (first marriage) Ralph the Timid, earl of Hereford (c. 1027–1057); Walter of Mantes, count of Maine (d. around 1063); Fulk of Amiens, bishop of Amiens (b. 1030). Eustace's second wife was *Ida of Lorraine (1040–1113).*

Godgifu (c. 1040–1080).

See Godiva.

Godin des Odonais, Isabel

(1728–d. after 1773)

Peruvian explorer. Born in Riobamba, Peru, in 1728; died in Saint-Amand, France, after 1773; married Jean Godin des Odonais, in 1743.

Isabel Godin des Odonais was born in Riobamba, Peru, in 1728. In 1769, she started out with her brothers and a small company to descend the Napo and Amazon rivers in South America. She was going to join her husband Jean, a French naturalist, as he explored in Cayenne; he had been gone 19 years. The boat was lost, and the rest of the party perished except Madame Godin, who wandered alone in the forest for nine days. When she was finally found by some Indians, her hair is said to have become white. The governor of Omaguas sent her down the river, and she rejoined her husband after nearly two decades of separation.

Godiva (c. 1040–1080)

Anglo-Saxon hero. Name variations: Godgifu; Lady Godiva. Born around 1040; died in 1080; flourished during the reign of Edward the Confessor (1050); sister of Thorold of Bucknall, sheriff of Lincolnshire; married Leofric, earl of Mercia and lord of Coventry, in Warwickshire (died 1057).

According to popular legend, Godiva was a Saxon woman, in the 11th century, who was married to Leofric, the earl of Mercia and lord of Coventry. When the inhabitants of Coventry found themselves so burdened by Leofric's oppressive taxes that they feared starvation, they appealed to Lady Godiva to intercede for them. In sympathy, Godiva petitioned her husband, requesting that—for her sake—the taxes be lowered. Initially, Leofric was unresponsive, but when Godiva persisted in her entreaties, he replied with contempt that he would only agree to reduce the taxes if she rode naked through the town.

Godiva sent word to the people of Coventry of the terms of the agreement and then issued a proclamation that on the designated day no one was to leave their house before noon, that all windows and apertures in houses should be closed, and that no one should look out until past noon. On the day appointed, mounted on a white horse and covered only by her long hair, Godiva rode through the town. Only one person disobeyed her order to remain indoors behind closed shutters, a tailor afterward known as Peeping Tom, who bored a hole in his shutters to look out and was, as the story goes, immediately struck blind. Leofric, in admiration of his wife's heroism, fulfilled his promise and freed the inhabitants from the burdens he had imposed.

The oldest form of the legend is quoted from earlier writers by Roger of Wendover (d. 1236) in *Flores Historiarum.* Roger records that Godiva, attended only by two soldiers, passed through Coventry market while the people were assembled, her long hair preventing her from being seen. It is undecided whether the Godiva of this legend is the historical Godiva (or Godgifu) who lived in the early part of the 11th century. The existence of this name at the time is confirmed by several ancient documents, including the Stow charter, the Spalding charter and the Domesday survey, though there are considerable discrepancies in the spelling of the name. From the *Liber Eliensis* (end of 12th century), it appears that she was a widow when she married Leofric in 1040. Godiva aided in the founding of a monastery at Stow, Lincolnshire, in or about the year of her marriage. She also persuaded Leofric to build and endow a Benedictine monastery at Coventry (1043). A charter given by her brother, Thorold of Bucknall, sheriff of Lincolnshire, to the Benedictine monastery of Spalding (1051) bore her mark: + *Ego Godiva Comitissa diu istud desideravi.* In addition, Godiva is commemorated as benefactor of other monasteries at Leominster, Chester, Wenlock, Worcester and Evesham.

A festival in honor of Godiva was later instituted as a part of the Coventry Fair in 1678 and was celebrated at intervals until 1826; the festival was again revived in 1848 and 1929. A window, with representations of Leofric and Godiva, was said by Sir William Dugdale (1656) to have been placed in Trinity Church, Coventry, around the time of Richard II. Tennyson's short poem "Godiva" deals with her story. A wooden effigy of Peeping Tom, which represents a man in armor, looks out on the world from a house at the northwest corner of Hertford Street, Coventry, and is said to likely be an image of St. George.

See following page for illustration

Godiva

Godolphin, Mary (1781–1864).
See Aikin, Lucy.

Godoy Alcayaga, Lucila (1889–1957).
See Mistral, Gabriela.

Godunova, Irene (d. 1603)

Empress of Russia who was wife of Theodore I and sister of Boris Godunov, both tsars of Russia. Name variations: Irina or Irine Godunov. Pronunciation: Good-un-OV-a. Born Irina Fedorovna Godunova in the 1550s, probably in Moscow; died near Moscow, probably of tuberculosis, in 1603; daughter of Fedor Ivanovich Godunov (a landowner); sister of Boris Godunov, tsar of Russia (r. 1598–1605); had no formal education; married Fedor I also known as Theodore I, tsar of Russia (r. 1584–1598), in 1574 or 1575; children: Theodosia of Russia (1592–1594).

Irene Godunova's place in Russian history has rested primarily on the fact that she failed to produce a male heir for her husband, Tsar Theodore I, and thus contributed to the termination of the Riurik dynasty and indirectly to the beginning of Russia's terrible civil war, the Time of Troubles. Very little is known about Irene's early years. She was born sometime in the 1550s, the daughter of a minor landowner Fedor Ivanovich Godunov who later joined Ivan IV's security police, the Oprichnina. In 1565 or 1566, he died of unknown causes with the result that Irene and her more famous older brother Boris Godunov became the wards of one of the leaders of the Oprichnina and informally were considered part of Ivan's extended household. One of her childhood playmates was Ivan's younger son Theodore who she married in 1574 or 1575. The death of Ivan's older son in 1581 meant that Theodore unexpectedly became tsar of Russia and his wife tsarina when his father died three years later.

Theodore had no interest in his new job. He was gentle, considerate, physically frail and obsessed with religious observances, especially the ringing of church bells. Irene, who one contemporary described as a "beautiful young lady," shared her husband's piety but not his lethargic nature. She exercised considerable influence over him and in part because of her position Boris Godunov became the real power behind the throne. The one problem in an otherwise happy marriage was Irene's inability to produce a son and heir. After more than a decade of marriage and several miscarriages or stillbirths, enemies of Boris sought to solve the problem and also reduce Godunov power by suggesting that Irene be put into a nunnery so that Theodore could remarry. The tsar as well as Boris refused to go along with the scheme. In May 1592, Irene finally had a child, a girl they named Theodosia, but Theodosia died 18 months later. In January 1598, Theodore followed his infant daughter to his grave.

Prior to his death, Theodore had named his wife his co-ruler and had included her in discussions of state matters, an honor rarely bestowed on women in medieval Russia. It appeared to many in the court that it was his intention (or

perhaps Boris') that Irene should succeed to the throne and in this way keep power in the Godunovs' hands. It is also possible that had she done so and then remarried and produced a male heir, a new dynasty would have begun and a succession crisis avoided at Boris' expense. Immediately after Theodore's death, the clergy and many of the Muscovite nobility swore allegiance to the popular tsarina. She reigned by default until Theodore's burial ten days later at which time she renounced any interest in ruling, entered the Novodevichy Monastery outside Moscow, and took the name of Aleksandra. In 1603, after five years as a nun, she died of tuberculosis. Boris, in the meantime, had taken the title of tsar in 1598 basing his claim in part on a rigged election by the Zemskii Sobor and in part on inheritance through his sister. Many contemporaries contested these claims and accused him of all sorts of crimes, including the deaths of Theodosia and Irene. While the new tsar clearly bears some of the responsibility for the Time of Troubles which accompanied his reign, there is no evidence to support the accusation of murder inside his own family.

SOURCES:

Emerson, Caryl. *Boris Godunov: Transpositions of a Russian Theme.* Bloomington: Indiana University Press, 1986.

Grey, Ian. *Boris Godunov: The Tragic Tsar.* London: Hodder and Stoughton, 1973.

Platonov, S.F. *Boris Godunov: Tsar of Russia.* Translated by L. Rex Pyles. Sea Breeze, FL: Academic International Press, 1973.

R.C. Elwood,
Professor of History, Carleton University, Ottawa, Canada

Godunova, Ksenia (1582–1622).

See Godunova, Xenia.

Godunova, Xenia (1582–1622)

Russian daughter of Boris Godunov, tsar from 1598 to 1605. Name variations: Xenia Godunov; Ksenia or Ksenya Godunov; Olga Borisovna. Pronunciation: Good-un-OV-a. Born Ksenia Borisovna Godunova probably in 1582 in Moscow; died in 1622; daughter of Boris Godunov, tsar of Russia (r. 1598–1605), and Maria Skuratova (d. 1605); sister of Theodore II (Feodor), tsar of Russia; had no formal education; never married.

Xenia Godunova appears more often in Russian folklore and fiction than she does in accounts of Russian history. We know only that she was the much-loved daughter of *Maria Skuratova and Boris Godunov, who reigned as tsar of Russia at the beginning of the Time of Troubles. Her father took an interest in her education with the result that she could read and write, skills which few Russian women of the time possessed. She also had some musical training and was fond of singing. Xenia reputedly was very beautiful, modest and decorous in speech. When she approached the age of 20, Boris went to great lengths to find her a suitable husband from among the reigning families of Europe. After failing to convince Prince Gustavus of Sweden to convert to Orthodoxy, Boris was able to attract Duke Johann (Hans) of Denmark to come to Moscow. The couple were duly engaged in 1601 but before the marriage could be celebrated Johann died of disease or perhaps of poisoning by one of Boris' many enemies.

The next decade was a time of misery for Xenia and for Russia. In April 1605, in the midst of a civil war, the tsar himself died. Shortly thereafter, on the orders of the First False Dmitri (Gregory Otrepiev), Xenia's teenage brother

Theodore II, successor to Boris, was strangled along with her mother Maria by members of the Russian nobility in Xenia's presence. Dmitri then usurped both Boris' throne and his daughter. According to legend, Xenia was raped by the new tsar and forced to become his mistress. Bowing to pressure from his father-in-law, Dmitri compelled Xenia to become a nun. Taking the name of Olga Borisovna, she was exiled to a remote convent in Beloozero. Xenia Godunova reappears on the pages of Russian history for the last time in 1607 when the next tsar, Vasilii Shuisky (Basil IV), decided to rebury the body of her father and forced her to march behind Boris' coffin. She joined her father in his new burial place upon her own death in 1622.

SOURCES:

Grey, Ian. *Boris Godunov: The Tragic Tsar*. London: Hodder and Stoughton, 1973.

Skrynnikov, Ruslan G. *Time of Troubles: Russia in Crisis, 1604–1618*. Edited and translated by Hugh F. Graham. Gulf Breeze, FL: Academic International Press, 1988.

R.C. Elwood,
Professor of History, Carleton University, Ottawa, Canada

Magda Goebbels, with two of her children.

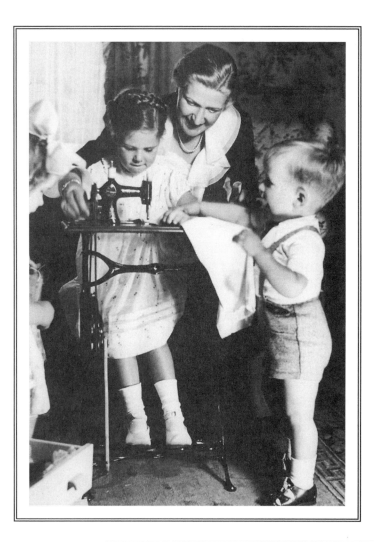

Godwin, Fanny Imlay (1794–1816).
See Wollstonecraft, Mary for sidebar.

Godwin, Mary (1759–1797).
See Wollstonecraft, Mary.

Godwin, Mary (1797–1851).
See Shelley, Mary Godwin.

Goebbels, Magda (d. 1945)

German wife of Joseph Goebbels. Born Johanna Maria Magdalena Quandt; committed suicide on May 1, 1945; married Joseph Goebbels (1897–1945), Reichsminister of propaganda and gauleiter of Berlin, in December 1931; children: Hedda, Heide, Helga, Helmuth, Hilde, Holde.

Magda Goebbels was the wife of Joseph Goebbels, the Nazi *gauleiter* ("district leader") of Berlin-Brandenberg whose skills as an orator earned him the office of Reichsminister of Propaganda after Hitler's ascension to power in 1933. In this position, Joseph enjoyed enormous powers of censorship that touched nearly every segment of life in the Third Reich. His propaganda ministry had a particularly heavy hand when it came to the movie industry, for he had a fondness for beautiful movie stars, especially *Lida Baarova. Although Joseph Goebbels was part of Hitler's inner circle, the details of his extramarital affairs sometimes leaked to the public, erupting into scandals that embarrassed both Hitler and the Nazi party.

Because of this, Magda chose to live apart from her husband and had forbidden him access to their country house in Schwanenwerder. When she learned of the affair with Baarova in 1938, she asked Hitler if she could seek a divorce. Immediately, Hitler summoned Joseph and elicited a promise from him: no divorce and no Baarova for at least one year. Lida Baarova left Berlin, effectively boycotted, and Magda and Joseph reconciled.

Magda, her children, and Joseph stayed with Hitler (and *Eva Braun) in his underground bunker, until Hitler and Braun took their own lives on April 29, 1945. As Russian troops fought toward the Reich Chancellory, Magda, under Joseph's orders, helped an SS doctor poison her six children, of whom the eldest was 12. She then committed suicide with Joseph on May 1, 1945.

Goehr-Oelsner, Marlies (b. 1958).

See Göhr, Marlies.

Goeppert-Mayer, Maria (1906–1972).

See Mayer, Maria Goeppert.

Goethe, Cornelia (c. 1751–c. 1778)

Sister and companion of Goethe. Name variations; *Cornelia Goethe Schlosser. Born around 1751 in Frankfurt am Main, Germany; died in childbirth around 1778; daughter of Elisabeth Goethe (1730–1808) and Johann Caspar Goethe (a jurist); sister of Johann Wolfgang Goethe (1749–1832); married; children: two.*

Cornelia Goethe was born around 1751 in a house on Grosser Hirschgraben, in Frankfurt am Main, Germany, the daughter of *Elisabeth Goethe* and Johann Caspar Goethe, a jurist. Cornelia was the only sibling of poet Johann Wolfgang Goethe who survived infancy, and he was very attached to her. She married a family friend named Schlosser and died at 27, while giving birth to her second child.

Goethe, Elisabeth (1730–1808)

German storyteller and mother of Johann Wolfgang Goethe. Name variations: Elizabeth Göthé. Born Elisabeth Textor in 1730; died on September 13, 1808; one of four daughters of Johann Wolfgang Textor (a fashionable tailor); married Johann Caspar Goethe (a jurist), in 1748; children: Johann Wolfgang Goethe (1749–1832); *Cornelia Goethe (c. 1751–c. 1778), and five boys who did not survive infancy.*

Elisabeth Textor was born in 1730, one of four daughters of Johann Wolfgang Textor, a fashionable tailor, who was mayor of his village and little interested in the education of his daughters. Elisabeth was 18 when she married the 40-year-old Johann Caspar Goethe, a cultured but cold man, who regarded his wife as a child to be educated along with their children. Though she did not have a penny in her dowry, she came from an esteemed family of jurists—a perfect match for a man who had just purchased the title of Imperial Councilor in order to join the upper classes. Their son Johann Wolfgang Goethe was born one year after they married. Elisabeth Goethe, known as both light-hearted and practical, had a gift for storytelling, and loved spoiling her young "Hans." As an adult, Goethe, the renowned author, poet, dramatist, and philosopher, was cold toward his mother, who lived alone during the last 11 years of her life. "Yet it was from Elizabeth that Goethe got his spontaneity, naturalness, and solid, practical sense," wrote Horst Hohendorf, "whereas the marked inclination to systematize, theorize and collect came from his father."

Elisabeth Goethe

SOURCES:
Orlandi, Enzo, ed. *The Life and Times of Goethe.* Italy: Arnoldo Mondadori Editore, 1967.

Gogoberidze, Lana (1928—)

Soviet filmmaker from Georgia. Born in Tbilisi, Georgia, on October 13, 1928; attended VGIK (Moscow Film School), 1959; professor of film at the Tbilisi Film Institute.

Filmography: Gelati (1957); Tbilisi 1500 let (Tbilisi, 1,500 years old, 1959); Pod odnim nebom (Under One Sky, 1961); Ia vizhu solntse (I Can See the Sun, 1965); Rubezhi (Borderlines, 1970); Kogda zatsvel mindal (When Almond Trees Were in Blossom, 1973); Perepolokh (Confusion, 1976); Neskolko interviu po lichnym voprosam (Several Interviews on

Personal Questions, *1979)*; Poslednoe pismo detiam *(*The Last Letter to Children, *1980)*; Den dlinnee nochi *(*Day Longer than Night, *1984)*; Krugovorot *(*Turnover, *1986)*; A Waltz on the Pechora *(1987)*.

Lana Gogoberidze's *Several Interviews on Personal Questions* (1979) was the first of her films to catch the attention of the West. The movie concerns a female journalist who interviews people of varying ages—people whose lives, like her own, are falling apart. Hauntingly autobiographical, the film revolves around a mother and daughter who have been reunited after years of separation. Gogoberidze and her own mother had been separated when her mother was sent to a labor camp in the Arctic Circle during Stalin's Reign of Terror. Gogoberidze's mother had also been a filmmaker prior to her detention. The difficulties of the mother-daughter relationship serve as a recurring theme in Gogoberidze's work.

Gogoberidze's career as a filmmaker was hard won. Because her parents were political exiles (her father was killed by the secret police), Lana was not allowed to become a filmmaker. She attended the University of Tbilisi, studied literature and wrote her doctoral thesis on American poet Walt Whitman. Following Stalin's death, she was finally permitted to attend film school in Moscow, studying at the prestigious VGIK. After graduating, she made her first full-length feature, *Under One Sky*, the story of three women from three different periods in Georgian history.

Gogoberidze is one of the most important filmmakers of the former Soviet Union. Her 1984 film *Turnabout* won the Director's Prize at the Tokyo International Film Festival. A professor of film at the University of Tbilisi, she is politically active and particularly concerned with helping Georgia remain an independent nation. She was the first president of Kino Women International (KIWI), an organization to further the position of women in the film industry, and in 1987 served as president of the International Association of Women Filmmakers. In 1987, she wrote *A Waltz on the Pechora*, a screenplay based on her mother's recollection of her internment.

SOURCES:

Attwood, Lynn, ed. *Red Women of the Silver Screen: Soviet Women and Cinema from the Beginning to the End of the Communist Era.* London: Pandora, 1993.

Foster, Gwendolyn. *Women Film Directors: An International Bio-Critical Dictionary.* Westport, CT: Greenwood Press, 1995.

Galichenko, Nicholas. *Glasnost: Soviet Cinema Responds.* Austin, TX: University of Texas Press, 1991.

Deborah Jones,
Studio City, California

Göhr, Marlies (1958—)

East German runner. Name variations: Marlies Goehr-Oelsner; Marlies Gohr. Born on March 21, 1958, in East Germany; married.

For seven years, from 1977 to 1983, Marlies Göhr was one of the fastest runners in the women's 100-meter race in the world, but she never won an Olympic gold medal in her specialty. Göhr, whose chief rival was *Evelyn Ashford, held the world record in the 100 with a time of 10.81 and beat the 11-second clock nine times. In the Montreal Olympics in 1976, 18-year-old Göhr won a gold medal in the 4x100-meter relay but finished 8th in the 100 meters. In the Moscow Olympics in 1980, minus competitor Ashford, she won a silver medal in the 100 meters (beaten by a hundredth of a second by Russia's *Lyudmila Kondratyeva) and a gold medal in the 4x100-meter relay. In the Seoul Olympics in 1988, Göhr won a silver medal in the 4x100-meter relay. She also took the 100 meters in the European Championships in 1978 and 1982 and placed first in the World Cup in 1977.

Goitschel, Christine and Marielle

French Alpine skiers.

Goitschel, Christine (1944—). Born in June 1944; lived in Val d'Isère.

Winner of an Olympic gold medal in the slalom and a silver in the giant slalom (1964).

Goitschel, Marielle (1945—). Born in Ste. Maxime, France, on September 28, 1945; lived in Val d'Isère.

Won the silver medal in the Women's slalom and a gold medal in the giant slalom at the Winter Olympics in Innsbruck (1964); won the gold medal in the Women's slalom in the Winter Olympics at Grenoble (1968); won the World championship in the giant slalom (1966) and the combined (1962, 1964, and 1966); won the World Cup for the downhill (1967) and slalom (1967, 1968).

Marielle and her sister Christine Goitschel, who was 15 months older, were both world-class skiers from Val d'Isère, home of super-Olympian Jean-Claude Killy. Marielle was only 16 when she won her first world title in the combined in 1962. In 1962, 1964, and 1966, she won the world championship. When the Olympic Winter Games were held in Innsbruck, Austria, in 1964, Christine and Marielle were great rivals, though Marielle was favored. But Christine surprised everyone by winning the slalom with a combined time of 1:29.86, almost a second in front of Marielle at 1:30.77. **Jean Saubert** of the U.S. placed third with 1:31.36. That same day back in France, **Patricia Goitschel**, another sister, won a national junior title.

Two days later, when Marielle stood at the starting line for the giant slalom, Christine and Saubert were tied for the lead at 1:53.11. Fourteenth on the course, Marielle flew down the slopes and took the lead at 1:52.24 and became the youngest athlete to win a gold medal. Christine took the silver, while Saubert again won the bronze. Following her victory, Marielle announced to a gullible press that she had just become engaged to the shy Killy, a practical joke planned by the sisters the previous evening.

In the 1968 Olympics at Grenoble, Christine did not compete, but Marielle did not disappoint, winning a gold medal in the slalom with a combined time of 1:25.86. *Nancy Greene of Canada came in second; **Annie Famose** of France finished third.

Karin Loewen Haag,
Athens, Georgia

Goitschel, Marielle (b. 1945).

See joint entry on Goitschel, Christine and Marielle.

Goldberg, Lea (1911–1970)

German-born Israeli poet, translator, literary critic and scholar who embodied major creative energies within modern Hebrew literature to become one of the best-loved authors in Israel. Name variations: Leah. Born in Königsberg, East Prussia, Germany (now Kaliningrad, Russia), on May 29, 1911; died in Jerusalem on January 15, 1970; daughter of Abraham Goldberg and Cilia (Levin) Goldberg; never married.

Grew up in Kaunas, Lithuania, then Kovno, Russia (until 1918); emigrated from Germany to Palestine (1935), where she worked as a journalist writing literary criticism; taught comparative literature at the Hebrew University, Jerusalem (1952–70); along with Nathan Alterman (1910–1970) and Yehuda Amichai (1924—), remains a representative poetic voice of Israel in the first phase of its cultural as well as political independence.

Selected writings: (poems) three collections, Smoke Rings, Letters from an Imaginary Journey, and Green-Eyed Ear of Corn (1939–40); (for children) The Zoo (1941); From My Old Home (1942); (novel) It Is the Light (1946); (nature poems) Al ha-Perihah (1948,

English translation by Miriam Billig Sivan titled On the Blossoming, NY: Garland, 1992); (translated by Shulamit Nardi) Little Queen of Sheba: A Story About New Immigrant Children in Israel (NY: Union of American Hebrew Congregations, 1959); (for children, with Anna Riwkin-Brick) Eli Lives in Israel (NY: Macmillan, 1966); (for children) Adventure in the Desert (1966); "Certain Aspects of Imitation and Translation in Poetry," in Proceedings of the IVth Congress of the International Comparative Literature Association, Fribourg 1964 (The Hague: Mouton, 1966); Three Stories and The Backpack of Poems (both published 1970); Remnants of Life (1971); (trans. and illus. by Ramah Commanday) Light on the Rim of a Cloud: Fourteen Poems (San Francisco: Didymus Press, 1972); Room for Rent (Los Angeles: Ward Ritchie Press, 1972); "Poems," in Ariel: A Quarterly Review of Arts and Letters in Israel (no. 32, 1973); (translated by T. Carmi) Lady of the Castle: A Dramatic Episode in Three Acts (Tel Aviv: Institute for the Translation of Hebrew Literature, 1974); (translated by Hillel Halkin) Russian Literature in the Nineteenth Century: Essays (Jerusalem: Magnes Press, Hebrew University, 1976); (translated by Robert Friend) Selected Poems (London and San Francisco: Menard Press/Panjandrum Press, 1976).

Although she is considerably less known than the Hebrew writer S.Y. Agnon who in 1966 won the Nobel Prize in literature, Lea Goldberg was a major figure in the literary and intellectual life of Israel for more than three decades. Multitalented, Goldberg was above all else a poet who knew how to create verse that showed sentiment without succumbing to debilitating sentimentality. One critic has argued that whether they are brief lyrics or elegant sonnets, Goldberg's poems often reveal points of resemblance to those of the American *Edna St. Vincent Millay, effortlessly utilizing a conversational tone and an epigrammatic verve that is coupled with elements of satire and surprise. Underlying her poetic creativity was Lea Goldberg's immense erudition. One of the last Jews to be awarded a doctorate by a German university in the Nazi era, she earned it in 1933 at the University of Bonn, her dissertation being an investigation of the manuscript sources of the Old Testament's Samaritan Pentateuch. Ranging far beyond her deep knowledge of the Hebrew Old Testament, Goldberg had an immense knowledge of virtually all epochs and traditions of European literature, be they the works of Dante, Dostoevsky, or James Joyce.

Although born in Königsberg, German East Prussia, Lea Goldberg grew up in Kovno,

Lithuania, then a part of Tsarist Russia. Her family survived World War I after many vicissitudes, and Lea received her primary and secondary education at the Hebrew Gymnasium in Kovno, which after 1918 became Kaunas, the capital of an independent Lithuania. As a teenager, she was already writing Hebrew poetry of considerable literary quality. She continued her education, with a specialization in both philosophy and Semitic languages, at the universities of Kaunas, Berlin, and Bonn. While studying in Germany, Goldberg was an eyewitness to the rapid rise of National Socialism with its violent attacks on Jews, liberals, and other groups demonized by Hitler's followers as being "un-German." These chilling experiences only served to deepen Goldberg's resolve to strengthen her Jewish identity, and she made a decision to adopt Hebrew as her mother tongue.

In 1935, she sailed for Palestine, then under British rule. Life in Palestine's Jewish intellectual community in the 1930s was economically precarious but intellectually exciting. Goldberg was acutely aware that she had chosen to cut herself off from some, but by no means all, aspects of the world of European culture when she moved to Palestine. She was now "coming home" to a Zionist homeland she had never seen before, a situation which inevitably placed her into a complex psychological role whose essence was summed up by her with: "I am here, totally here, in a foreign city in the heart of the great alien motherland." Rather than agonize over how to fit perfectly into her new environment, which included gaining what soon became her mastery of the Hebrew language as a living and flexible instrument of artistic expression, Goldberg chose to put pen to paper to address experiences large and small, thus creating what soon became an acclaimed body of distinguished poetry.

Goldberg was able within a few years to create a niche for herself in her new homeland's literary avant garde as an active member of the Yachdev (Moderna) experimental literary group. This circle of writers, which included Nathan Alterman and Avraham Shlonsky, was strongly influenced by Freudian theories as well as French symbolism. Although Goldberg's writings were enriched by these ideas, she never slavishly embraced literary modernism, always remaining elusive as to categorization. On a more practical plane, her collaboration with Shlonsky brought her work and allowed her to sharpen her skills as both an editor and translator.

Soon after her arrival in Palestine, Goldberg was hired by the Habima Theater School, both as a lecturer on theater history and as a dramatic advisor for the Habima troupe. Besides her Habima affiliation, she was a prolific writer in many genres. She worked for a number of years as drama and literary critic of the newspaper *Davar* (The Word), later joining the staff of another paper, *Ha-Mishmar* (The Observer). In 1952, Goldberg accepted an academic post as lecturer in comparative literature at Jerusalem's Hebrew University. Although she was never drily "academic" in the narrow sense of the word, Goldberg was a success in the academic world, eventually rising to the position of chairing Hebrew University's department of comparative literature. An indefatigable literary worker, she translated into Hebrew such classic authors of the Western tradition as Dante, Ibsen, Petrarch, Pushkin, and Tolstoy, books that all drew encomiums from enthusiastic critics and readers alike. Her translation of Tolstoy's *War and Peace* by itself represented an impressive achievement, and her 1951 anthology of world literature in Hebrew translation represented a first introduction to these treasures of world letters for many young Israelis. Another collection edited by Goldberg that became a popular favorite with Israeli readers was her anthology of classic love poems of the world, first published in 1956.

Lea Goldberg was an enthusiastic teacher who quickly earned an enviable reputation as a university lecturer. Among her most popular presentations were the five introductory lectures on the nature of poetry that became a classic statement for an entire generation of Israeli students, teachers and fledgling poets. Goldberg's lectures on Dante's place in Italian and world literature were faithfully copied down by her students and in time appeared in print with her permission. Besides publishing scholarly essays on the Israeli theater, Goldberg penned a book on the art of the short story and in 1968 published a collection of essays on 19th-century Russian literature and culture (this would appear posthumously in a 1976 English translation).

A special place in Goldberg's prolific literary output was set aside for the entertainment and enlightenment of children. In a fruitful collaboration with photographer **Anna Riwkin-Brick** (1908–1970), Goldberg wrote and published several books for children, including *The Little Queen of Sheba* (1956, English translation 1959), *Adventure in the Desert* (1966), and *Eli Lives in Israel* (published in Sweden and the United States, 1964 and 1966). In *The Zoo* (1941, published 1970), Goldberg used rhyming verses to present animals along with their personalities. But it was in her serious verse, which she wrote throughout her adult life, that Goldberg conveyed her deepest feelings and revealed the full range of her literary virtuosity. Her youthful poems, published from 1935 to 1939–1940 in three collections entitled *Smoke Rings, Letters from an Imaginary Journey,* and *Green-Eyed Ear of Corn,* are all experimental in varying degrees. While the imagery is bold and striking, some critics have viewed these poems as exhibiting little more than considerable technical skill that cannot in the final analysis disguise an "intellectual hardness," whose strategy was to shock readers with no other clear purpose in mind.

By the early 1940s, Goldberg was leaving this approach behind to seek out a more accessible poetic style. The result was her 1942 book of verse, *From My Old Home.* In this clearly autobiographical work, which presents a series of vignettes of life in rural Lithuania before the Holocaust, Goldberg was able to bring to Hebrew verse what literature scholar Robert Alter has described as "a subtle sense of beauty in small words and small things, a gracefulness and even playfulness of style." In "The Alley," one of the most charming poems in *From My Old Home,* she writes how:

> The alley is narrow.
> Pail bumps pail.
> A girl's laughter.
> Scarlet ribbon-tail.
>
> Flitted past,
> Barefoot best.
> Gray stone
> Caressed.

Yehuda Amichai, the major poet of Israel's 1948 War of Independence generation, recalled in a poem that during the 1948 war, everywhere he went, he remembered to take along in his knapsack a battered, taped pamphlet edition of Goldberg's *From My Old Home.*

In her only novel, *It Is the Light* (1946), Goldberg presents another work based on personal experience, this time set in a Lithuanian town in the summer of 1931. Spending the school vacation at home with her parents, the protagonist Nora Krieger, a sensitive and troubled young girl who has returned from her stud-

Israeli postage stamp issued on February 19, 1991, in honor of Lea Goldberg.

ies in Berlin, struggles with her growing realization that she must find ways to live in a world that is filled with both specific terrors as well as evil in general. Having to choose between the escape mechanism represented by madness and the harsh realities of an adult life, the protagonist chooses the latter, having made the decision that "our lives will be life . . . in utter defiance of all the makers of history who torture children and murder their parents." As if it were a talisman, a remembered line from Moses Ibn Ezra serves to guide the protagonist out of her youthful nightmare into the world of light she yearns for. The same themes are dealt with in Goldberg's play, *Lady of the Castle* (1955), where the sensitive girl must choose between the pseudo-escape of madness and the harsh but ultimately necessary world of reality. She is able to find the strength to do so from a long-forgotten children's song.

In the last years of her life, Lea Goldberg became one of the most respected and most beloved Israeli poets. Although she had been associated with the Hebrew literary modernist school in the 1930s, she preferred to use traditional verse forms. The conversational style of her verse was based on a conscious rejection both of the rhetoric of many of her predecessors and the considerable bombast found in the work of her contemporaries. Drawn to simple things, Goldberg consciously limited her symbolic vocabulary to the familiar, and was thus able to endow even everyday words and phrases with often stunningly fresh images and rhythms.

In her book of nature poems, *Al ha-Perihah* (On the Blossoming, 1948, English translation, 1992), Goldberg inhabits a very different world from that of the artifice and intellectual posturing found in some of her youthful verse. Harkening back to the world of feeling and beauty that had fired the imaginations of the 19th century's Romantic artists, she enters into the mysteries of nature. She compares the stone to the stream to point out that, "I am change, its revelation." Accepting the constant transformation that is nature, the poet emphasizes the positive aspect of change, which is a process of renewal in which "every day shall not be like yesterday, and the day before it, and life shall not become trite and habitual." The seductive musicality of Goldberg's best verse has appealed not only to other poets and ordinary readers but to a number of composers as well. Those who have set her poems to music include Yehezkiel Braun, Robert Starer, and Joachim Stutschewsky.

In 1969, Goldberg was honored when she received one of the most prestigious awards in the world of Hebrew letters, the Irving and Bertha Neuman Literary Prize from New York University's Institute of Hebrew Studies. At the end of her life, this important writer remained better known in Israel than elsewhere, despite the profoundly universal themes found in her works. This unsatisfactory situation was remedied only slowly; while English-language translations had appeared from the 1950s onward, it was only in 1971 that a Polish translation of a selection of poetry was published in London, and in 1985 a French translation of her 1957 volume *The Chatelaine* appeared in Tel Aviv. After she died in Jerusalem on January 15, 1970, three posthumous works appeared in print: *Three Stories* and *The Backpack of Poems* (both published 1970) and *Remnants of Life* (1971).

By the end of the 20th century, literary scholars were in the process of rediscovering the rich legacy of Lea Goldberg's poetry and prose. While remaining popular in Israel, her writings also began to take on a genuinely global embrace with the appearance of accessible English translations of important works like *Lady of the Castle*, as well as translations into other foreign languages including French, Korean and Spanish. At the start of a new millennium there were growing signs that one of the most sensitive and distinctive voices of modern Hebrew letters was ready to find her place of honor within the permanent edifice of world literature. Israel honored Lea Goldberg by depicting her on a postage stamp issued on February 19, 1991.

SOURCES:

Aberbach, David. *Revolutionary Hebrew, Empire, and Crisis: Four Peaks in Hebrew Literature and Jewish Survival.* NY: New York University Press, 1998.

Alkalay-Gut, Karen. "Poetry by Women in Israel and the War in Lebanon," in *World Literature Today.* Vol. 63, no. 1. Winter 1989, pp. 19–25.

Alter, Robert. "On Lea Goldberg & S.Y. Agnon," in *Commentary.* Vol. 49, no. 5. May 1970, pp. 83–86.

Bar-Yosef, Hamutal. "Reflections on Hebrew Literature in the Russian Context," in *Prooftexts: A Journal of Jewish Literary History.* Vol. 16, no. 2. May 1996, pp. 127–149.

Burnshaw, Stanley, et al., eds. *The Modern Hebrew Poem Itself, from the Beginnings to the Present.* Cambridge, MA: Harvard University Press, 1989.

Carmi, T., ed. *The Penguin Book of Hebrew Verse.* NY: Viking Press, 1981.

Cohn, James D. "Secret of the Withered Leaf: Perspectives on the Poetry of Leah Goldberg." Rabbinic Thesis, Hebrew Union College—Jewish Institute of Religion, Cincinnati, Ohio, 1978.

Frank, Bernhard. *Modern Hebrew Poetry.* Iowa City: University of Iowa Press, 1980.

———. "Nation in a Mirror: Observations on Modern Hebrew Poetry," in *Judaism.* Vol. 45, no. 1. Winter 1996, pp. 68–78.

Ginsburg, Ruth. "The Jewish Mother turned Monster: Representations of Motherhood by Hebrew Women Novelists 1881–1993," in *Women's Studies International Forum*. Vol. 20, no. 5–6. September–December 1997, pp. 631–638.

Gold, Nili Scharf. "Rereading *It Is the Light*, Lea Goldberg's Only Novel," in *Prooftexts: A Journal of Jewish Literary History*. Vol. 17, no. 3. September 1997, pp. 245–259.

Goldberg, Lea. "Certain Aspects of Imitation and Translation in Poetry," in *Proceedings of the IVth Congress of the International Comparative Literature Association, Fribourg 1964*. The Hague: Mouton, 1966, pp. 839–843.

———. *Lady of the Castle: A Dramatic Episode in Three Acts*. Translated by T. Carmi. Tel Aviv: Institute for the Translation of Hebrew Literature, 1974.

———. *Light on the Rim of a Cloud: Fourteen Poems*. Translated and illustrated by Ramah Commanday. San Francisco, CA: Didymus Press, 1972.

———. *Little Queen of Sheba: A Story About New Immigrant Children in Israel*. Translated by Shulamit Nardi. NY: Union of American Hebrew Congregations, 1959.

———. *On the Blossoming*. Translated by Miriam Billig Sivan. NY: Garland, 1992.

———. "Poems," in *Ariel: A Quarterly Review of Arts and Letters in Israel*. No. 32, 1973, pp. 45–51.

———. *Room for Rent*. Los Angeles, CA: Ward Ritchie Press, 1972.

———. *Russian Literature in the Nineteenth Century: Essays*. Translated by Hillel Halkin. Jerusalem: Magnes Press, Hebrew University, 1976.

———. *Selected Poems*. Translated by Robert Friend. London and San Francisco: Menard Press/Panjandrum Press, 1976.

——— and Anna Riwkin-Brick. *Eli Lives in Israel*. NY: Macmillan, 1966.

Guy, Hanoch. "Themes and Symbols in the Poetry of Leah Goldberg." Ph. D. dissertation, Dropsie University for Hebrew and Cognate Learning, Philadelphia, 1973.

Kaynar, Gad. "National Theatre as Colonized Theatre: The Paradox of Habima," in *Theatre Journal*. Vol. 50, no. 1. March 1998, pp. 1–20.

Lieblich, Amia. *El Leah*. Tel Aviv: ha-Kibuts ha-meuhad, 1995.

Mintz, Ruth Finer, ed. *Modern Hebrew Poetry: A Bilingual Anthology*. Berkeley, CA: University of California Press, 1982.

Patterson, David. "Modern Hebrew Literature Goes on Aliyah," in *Journal of Jewish Studies*. Vol. 29, no. 1. Spring 1978, pp. 75–84.

Penueli, Shemuel Yeshayahu, and Azriel Ukhmani, eds. *Anthology of Modern Hebrew Poetry*. 2 vols. Tel Aviv: Institute for the Translation of Hebrew Literature, 1966.

Ruebner, Tuvia. *Leah Goldberg: Monografyah*. Tel Aviv: Sifriyat poalim, ha-Kibuts ha-meuhad, 1980.

Silberschlag, Eisig. "Redemptive Vision in Hebrew Literature," in *World Literature Today*. Vol. 54, no. 2. Spring 1980, pp. 201–207.

———. "Thirty Years of Hebrew Literature under Independence: 1948–1978," in *Bulletin of the John Rylands University Library of Manchester*. Vol. 63, no. 2. Spring 1981, pp. 485–504.

Taub, Michael. *Israeli Holocaust Drama*. Syracuse, NY: Syracuse University Press, 1996.

Vardi, Dov, ed. *New Hebrew Poetry*. Tel Aviv: Women's International Zionist Organization, 1947.

RELATED MEDIA:

Goldberg, Leah. *Songs of the Jordan River*. Los Angeles: Everest Records 3273, 1969.

———. *Songs of the Land I Love*. Tel Aviv: CBS Records 81240, 1976.

John Haag,
Associate Professor of History,
University of Georgia, Athens, Georgia

Golden, Diana (1963—)

American ski racer who placed 10th out of 39 in a slalom race as the only disabled skier in the competition. Born in Cambridge, Massachusetts, on March 20, 1963; grew up in Lincoln, an affluent suburb of Boston; lost her right leg to cancer at age 12 but continued to ski; attended Dartmouth, graduating in 1984.

Won the World Handicapped championships while a senior in high school; won 4 gold medals and 19 championships; won the Beck Award for being the best American skier in international competition (1986); placed 10th out of 39 in a slalom race as the only disabled skier in the competition (1987); won the gold medal in the giant slalom for disabled skiers at Calgary Olympic Games (1988); named Female Skier of the Year by the U.S. Olympic Committee (1988); named U.S. Female Alpine Skier of the Year by Ski Racing magazine (1988).

From an early age, Diana Golden went to the Cannon Mountain ski resort in Franconia, New Hampshire, near her parents' vacation home; by age five, she was skimming the slopes. In 1975, while walking through snow after a day of skiing, her right leg collapsed. With a diagnosis of bone cancer, the 12-year-old had to have her leg amputated above the knee. "Losing a limb was not something I had to overcome," she said. "I always skied and I intended to keep on skiing. There was never any question in my mind." Golden was back on the slopes in seven months, learning to ski on one leg.

She was spotted by David Livermore, a Sudbury Regional High School ski-team coach, when she was practicing on the slopes of Cannon Mountain. He invited her to try out for the team, and she soon became one of the its best skiers. Her training led her to compete in disabled racing, and at 17 she was a member of the national U.S. Disabled Ski Team (USDST).

Golden studied literature at Dartmouth College and raced with nondisabled skiers at Burke Mountain Academy in Vermont. She placed first

Diana
Golden

in the downhill and second in the giant slalom in the World Handicapped championships held in Norway in 1982. Golden began to tire, however, of her place in the spotlight as "the inspirational girl who overcame cancer." Putting away her skis, she concentrated on completing her English degree and, after graduation in 1984, began selling computer software. But a weekend on the ski slopes in Connecticut rekindled her love of the sport, and she decided to return to racing. Golden rejoined the USDST in March 1985, this time with a scholarship from the Women's Sports Foundation to help with training and travel costs. She also asked for support from companies to assist with full-time training expenses. Rossignol Ski Company became her sponsor, the first company to financially support a disabled skier.

Golden especially disliked being singled out because of her disability, believing that she and others with disabilities could compete with nondisabled athletes. In 1985, she pushed for the passage of the "Golden Rule" by the U.S. Ski Association (USSA), which specified preferential seeding of disabled skiers in sanctioned USSA races. Because places are reserved for disabled skiers after the first 15 racers, the rule allows qualified disabled racers to compete on the course before it becomes too rough from overuse. As a result of this rule, the USDST began to require its athletes to compete in at least five USSA nondisabled races a year.

In the meantime, Golden continued to master the slopes. In 1987, she finished 10th out of 39 in a USSA midseries race, the only disabled skier on the course. She was ranked the 10th-best three-track skier in the world. In 1986, she won the U.S. Ski Association's Beck Award. In 1988, she was named *Ski Racing* magazine's U.S. Female Alpine Skier of the Year. That same year, she was also the U.S. Olympic Committee's Female Skier of the Year. Golden won three gold medals at the World championships in Winter Park, Colorado, in 1990. On one leg, she was clocked at almost 65 miles per hour. In 1991, she won the prestigious *Flo Hyman award for her commitment to excellence.

After her retirement in 1990, Diana Golden continued to work with the USDST promoting sports for the disabled. She was also made a member of the Professional Ski Instructors of America Demonstration Team. Her goal was to teach anyone with a desire to ski. Her prowess convinced public and corporate sponsors to accept disabled athletes on the terms of their ability.

SOURCES:
Johnson, Anne Janette. *Great Women in Sports*. Detroit, MI: Visible Ink, 1998.
Woolum, Janet. *Outstanding Women Athletes: Who They Are and How They Influenced Sports in America*. Phoenix, AZ: Oryx Press, 1992.

Karin L. Haag,
Athens, Georgia

Goldhaber, Gertrude Scharff (b. 1911).

See Scharff-Goldhaber, Gertrude.

Goldman, Emma (1869–1940)

Russian-born labor organizer, leading anarchist writer and lecturer, as well as an early advocate of birth control, who was deported from America for her antiwar activities during World War I. Name variations: (nicknames) Red Emma, Mother of Anarchy. Born on June 27, 1869, in Kovno, Lithuania; died on May 14, 1940, in Toronto, Canada; daughter of Abraham Goldman (an innkeeper and small businessman) and Taube Goldman; married Jacob Kershner, in 1886 (divorced 1889); no children.

Family lived in province of Kurland, part of western Russia, then moved to St. Petersburg; immigrated to the U.S. (1885); became involved with anarchists (1889); was first jailed (1893); studied nursing in Vienna (1895 and 1899); arrested several times for anarchist activities; published Mother Earth, *an anarchist magazine (1906–17); became active in the birth-control movement (1915); arrested for antiwar activities (1917), deported (1919); obtained British passport (1925); wrote her autobiography,* Living My Life *(1931); lectured against Nazi policies (1932–40); moved to Canada and lectured and wrote until her death.*

Emma Goldman was one of the most radical women in the history of the United States; she was also one of the most controversial and, perhaps, one of the most courageous. She was a woman ahead of her time, a fiery advocate of personal freedom, and a supporter of the anarchist movement. Anarchists believe that any government, by its very nature, forces people to conform. Only by doing away with all types of government will people be able to achieve their full potential. As part of a small but active group of anarchists in the late 19th and early 20th centuries, Emma Goldman was viewed as dangerous and subversive. Because anarchists and communists were often linked together, Goldman was labeled "Red Emma."

The American authorities did their best to curtail anarchist activities. As a result, Goldman and her associates were jailed repeatedly and ultimately deported back to Russia which had recently become a communist state. However, she quickly became disillusioned with the new Russian communism, as she had with American capitalism, and before that, with the tsarist government of her childhood. In fact, from her earliest years Goldman rebelled against every authority.

Emma Goldman was born on June 27, 1869, in Kovno, Lithuania, then a province of Russia. Her traditional Russian-Jewish parents struggled to make a living, moving from one city to another throughout Kurland, in western Russia. Her father Abraham Goldman earned a living at various jobs. He ran a stagecoach line, worked as an innkeeper, then owned a grocery store, but failed at every endeavor. Her mother **Taube Goldman** had been born into a more educated family than Abraham. Taube spoke German, considered the language of high culture, and had enjoyed a childhood of relative prosperity. She had already given birth to two daughters, Lena and Helena, and had been widowed and remarried.

By the time Emma was born, Taube was disappointed with her second marriage and disillusioned with her life. She had little interest in yet another daughter, whom the family could hardly support, and Emma always felt unloved. As a little girl, she remembered being subject to her father's fits of temper and violent emotions. He beat her when she disobeyed, but otherwise she was ignored. It was her half-sister Helena, nine years her senior, who gave her the only love she knew in those early years.

In 1875, Emma was sent to Königsberg, capital of Eastern Prussia, to live with her grandmother and an uncle while attending school. But this situation proved disastrous. The small amounts of money sent by her father for her schooling often ended up in her uncle's pocket, while Emma was expected to earn her keep by doing household chores. Rebellion always came easily to Goldman, and, after a few years, a final clash with her uncle ended her stay there. He pushed her down a flight of stairs and left her to be rescued by neighbors, then sent her back to her parents' home.

In 1882, with the Goldman family's move to St. Petersburg, 13-year-old Emma's life changed. She now had two younger brothers, but it was her half-sister Helena, intelligent and well-read, who became her role model and introduced her to revolutionary literature and social activism. Goldman was exposed to all the political movements of a big city in ferment and was especially attracted to nihilism, a form of anarchy popular in Russia at that time.

Emma, like Helena, loved books, music and school, but her independent spirit made it difficult for her to accept authority, and she had many disputes with her teachers. In addition, her father begrudged any time she spent on education. Women only need to know how to cook and produce babies, he insisted. It was good to have a trade, in case she needed to support a scholarly husband, but scholarship, in his opinion, was reserved for men. Partly because of this attitude and partly out of financial necessity, Goldman left school at 15 and went to work in a glove factory in St. Petersburg. But she hated factory work. She felt strangled sitting with 600 other women in a single room all day. She tried her hand at other jobs, at home and in factories, and found each situation too confining for her free spirit.

> True emancipation begins neither at the polls nor in courts. It begins in women's souls.
>
> —Emma Goldman

During those years, important events were occurring in Russia. Tsar Alexander II had been assassinated in 1881 by a few members of a radical terrorist group. This led to the imprisonment of many Russian revolutionaries. A few were executed, including *Sonia Perovskaya, and others were exiled, including *Vera Figner. At the same time, pogroms (anti-Jewish riots) were organized and the May Laws of 1882 were issued by the new tsar, Alexander III. These laws reimposed the restrictive legislation against Jews which Alexander II had lifted.

Many Jews were leaving Russia in the 1880s. Emma's oldest sister, Lena, was already in America, living in Rochester, New York. Helena was preparing to join her, and Emma begged to be allowed to go along. Although her parents wanted Emma to remain in Russia and marry, she finally prevailed and arrived in Rochester at the end of 1885. She was 17 years old.

Despite all her hopes, Goldman was quickly disillusioned. Her job in an overcoat factory subjected her to long hours and oppressive conditions, sometimes even worse than they had been in St. Petersburg. She later wrote about that experience, explaining: "The iron discipline forbade any free movement . . . and the constant surveillance of the foreman weighed like a stone on my heart." Nevertheless, she was earning $2.50 a week and was safe from anti-Jewish riots. Her parents and younger brothers soon joined her and her sisters in Rochester, and Emma finally gave in to their pressures and married.

The man was Jacob Kershner, a young Russian-Jewish immigrant who courted her with talk of books and culture. He seemed to Goldman a better alternative to the pressures of her family and her oppressive father. However, the marriage proved disastrous. Her first disappointment was the wedding night itself. Jacob was impotent. Her new husband imperiously insisted that, like all good American wives at that time, Emma must not work outside the home. Goldman, only 18 years old, soon realized that she had simply exchanged one oppression for another. She demanded a divorce. As soon as it was granted in August of 1889, the young woman picked up her sewing machine and fled, first to New Haven and then to New York City. Though she was 20 years old, with no money and no job, she was independent at last.

Emma Goldman knew no one in New York City, but she knew *about* someone: Johann Most, editor of *Die Freiheit* (Freedom), an anarchist newspaper. While living in Rochester, she had read *Die Freiheit* and followed the anarchist perspective on the Haymarket Affair. The Haymarket Affair began at a workers' rally in May 1886 at Haymarket Square in Chicago. During the rally, a bomb exploded amidst a group of police, killing seven and injuring many more. Anarchists were blamed, and eight prominent members of the group were arrested. The men were tried, found guilty, and a year later four of them were hanged.

Just as she had been in Russia, Goldman was drawn to the anarchists and their cause. She vowed to dedicate herself "to the memory of my martyred comrades." With those memories and commitments to bolster her, Emma's first stop in New York City was Sach's Cafe, a meeting place for the embattled anarchist movement. Young, attractive, and dedicated, Emma did not take long to become part of the inner circle. She met Alexander Berkman, one of the leaders of the anarchists, who took her to hear Johann Most speak.

Both Most and Goldman were impressed with each other. Emma was enthralled by the older man's ability to rouse an audience, while Most quickly discovered Emma's potential as a speaker. He instructed her on his ideas about anarchy, explaining that their goal was not to improve wages and working conditions but to overthrow the entire system. He also coached her in public speaking. Before long, Emma herself was an orator at meetings, urging workers to protest the injustices of their capitalist bosses by overthrowing the government. She spoke mainly to audiences of Jewish immigrant workers and her language was Yiddish, or sometimes German which she spoke with a Yiddish accent. Eventually, she learned English in order to reach more workers. Goldman became known throughout the Northeast as Red Emma, a passionate speaker who encouraged rebellion and inspired large crowds.

Emma
Goldman

Yet she was also a realist. She understood that until the revolution could be accomplished, workers needed some improvements in their working conditions. Goldman was tireless in her attempts to organize female garment workers into unions. She also obtained food for the unemployed and set up distribution centers.

The members of Johann Most's circle were aware that Johann was in love with Emma. However, it was Alexander Berkman, nicknamed

Sasha, who became her lover. Sasha and Emma maintained their relationship for many years, and although they never married, they lived together and worked in the movement until 1892.

In 1892, Berkman conceived a plan to assassinate Henry Clay Frick, a wealthy businessman and owner of a steel mill in Pittsburgh. The purpose of this plan was to protest Frick's oppression of steel workers. Although Emma later insisted that she opposed violence, she raised the money her lover needed to make the train trip to Pittsburgh and to assemble the bomb. Alexander Berkman's plot failed. Frick was wounded but survived the attack, and Berkman was arrested, convicted, and sentenced to prison for 22 years. Throughout the trial and his subsequent incarceration, Goldman kept in contact with Sasha, sending him food, letters, and books in prison while she continued speaking and working for the cause.

After one particularly successful speech, Emma was arrested for inciting a riot. She had not advocated any violence, and none had occurred; nevertheless, she was tried, found guilty, and imprisoned on Roosevelt Island (then called Blackwell's Island) for ten months. Prison proved to be an enlightening experience for Emma Goldman. While in the prison hospital, she met a doctor who took a liking to her. He had her transferred to another part of the prison where she was able to learn the skills of practical nursing. She also had time to read and develop her own ideas, separate from those of Most, her early mentor, or Sasha, her lover. It was during these ten months, from 1893 to 1894, that she first conceived of the idea of studying nursing in order to support herself more easily.

Released from jail, Goldman continued lecturing, with a tour through the Midwest. On her return, she met and fell in love with Edward Brady. Twenty years older than Emma, Brady was an anarchist, a journalist, and an intellectual, and Emma credited him with introducing her to the sexual pleasures of love. However, those pleasures were not enough to keep Goldman home, acting the role of dutiful wife as Brady would have preferred. She continued lecturing and was jailed once again. After her release, she moved into a small apartment with Brady and worked as a practical nurse. The couple also opened a small luncheonette, but this attempt at financial independence failed, and, at age 26, Emma resolved to pursue her old idea and train to be a nurse. With the backing of another male friend, Goldman left for Vienna in 1895, where she not only had the opportunity to take a nursing course but also heard the lectures of Sigmund Freud and the revolutionary philosopher Friedrich Nietzsche, one of her political idols.

Back in New York, Goldman was determined to have a nursing career, continue her anarchist activities, and also maintain her love relationship with Ed Brady. Brady had other ideas. Tired of the life of a revolutionary, he wanted to settle down and have a family. After her first disastrous marriage to Jacob Kershner, however, Emma had resolved never to remarry, convinced that marriage prevented women's emancipation. It was merely an economic arrangement, she believed, in which women traded their sexual favors and domestic labor in return for support. In one of her many essays on the subject, she claimed that "marriage condemns [a woman] to life-long dependency, to parasitism, to complete uselessness." She felt that love, "the freest and most powerful molder of human destiny," had nothing to do with marriage. As a result of their differences, Goldman and Brady separated. He claimed that her desire for a career was simply "her craving for applause," while Goldman bitterly accused Brady of being an egotist with "the man's instinct of possession."

By the turn of the century, Goldman had made a second visit to Europe, touring the Continent and briefly continuing her nursing studies in Vienna. Now the most famous anarchist in the United States, she attracted large crowds wherever she appeared. Her name was so controversial that she had to use a pseudonym in order to rent an apartment.

Emma Goldman began to moderate her activities and support less extreme political causes. She even briefly managed a Russian theater group in 1905. The reason for this, however, was not a desire to improve her disreputable and controversial image, but because the state of New York had passed the New York Criminal Anarchy Act. The legislation made it a felony to advocate overthrow of the government. In 1906, she founded and edited a magazine called *Mother Earth* which included articles by anarchists and other radical authors. This publication continued until her final arrest in 1917. It was in the pages of *Mother Earth* that Goldman first defined her theories about women. Her article, "The Tragedy of Woman's Emancipation," claimed that the working woman merely exchanged the slavery and restrictions of the home for the restrictions of the workplace. True liberation, she claimed, will not come until women are men's spiritual equals.

Emma Goldman had changed and matured since 1892, the year Alexander Berkman went off to prison. When he was released, 14 years later, Berkman found a very different woman than the one he had left. Goldman had a farm in Ossining, New York, given to her by a wealthy activist. She also had a brownstone at 210 East 13th Street in New York City, from where she published *Mother Earth*. Her supporters included important people such as Bill Haywood, leader of the International Workers of the World (IWW), and Hutchins Hapgood, a well-known journalist. Goldman had the security of a nursing degree and considerable education. She was an extremely attractive speaker and, at last, had become financially independent. Berkman criticized her, and they fought. Although he joined her to work on *Mother Earth*, they did not resume their love affair.

Goldman began an affair with Ben Reitman, an interesting and educated man who had once been labeled "King of the Hoboes." With the help of supporters, Reitman had become a physician and then a social activist and protester. Goldman and Reitman traveled together, setting up meetings, arranging publicity, and speaking before large groups. Emma believed that at last she had found someone who would love her as a woman and be able to share her work, too. But Reitman also disappointed her. He had many love affairs with other women, and, despite Emma's espousal of free love, she was hurt by his lack of loyalty to her.

Goldman continued lecturing and working as a nurse, and it was this latter activity which first led to her involvement in the birth-control movement. In the 1900s, it was against the law to distribute any information on birth control to women. Goldman had included this subject in previous lectures, convinced access to birth control was the only way women could begin to be free and to take their proper role as sexual beings. However, she had never dealt with specific methods of birth control until now. Emma herself was not able to have children. She could have corrected this situation with minor surgery but decided in favor of the movement, believing that motherhood and activism were incompatible.

By 1915, she was actively supporting *Margaret Sanger, the only other person working to provide women with actual birth-control material and devices. This decision led to a new spate of arrests for Goldman. Emma was condemned for her views on anarchy, for refusing to marry the men with whom she lived, and for demonstrating how to use the diaphragm. This last activity gained her the most notoriety—even more than her criticism of patriotism, capitalism, government, religion, and marriage.

Goldman's final rebellion in the United States was her opposition to World War I. Insisting that America should not send its sons to war, she wrote articles decrying American policy and spoke out repeatedly against conscription. She was joined in this effort by her ex-lover, Alexander Berkman. This position resulted once more in her arrest, and Emma Goldman, now 46 years old, expected to spend the rest of her life in prison. Instead, she was deported to Russia under the Alien Exclusion Act of 1918. This law, promulgated during the war, provided that any foreigner who advocated the overthrow of the government could be sent back to her or his country of origin. Appeals for Goldman went all the way to the Supreme Court, but there was no reprieve. On December 1, 1919, she was deported together with 247 other aliens.

Emma Goldman received a hero's welcome on her arrival in the Soviet Union, but after a tour of the new communist nation she was bitterly disappointed with the suppression of individual freedom there. She fled Russia in 1921, remaining in Europe where she continued writing and lecturing. She wrote two books on her experiences in the Soviet Union. The first, published in 1923, was entitled *My Disillusionment in Russia,* followed immediately by *My Further Disillusionment in Russia* in 1924.

After many years of effort, during which Goldman remained stateless, she finally managed to obtain a British passport by a sham marriage to a Welsh miner, James Colton, in 1924. Under this new name, she showed up in Montreal, Canada, two years later. She was never allowed to return to the U.S. except for a brief lecture tour. In 1931, living in St. Tropez, France, she wrote her two-volume autobiography, *Living My Life*. Even after 33 years in the United States, as well as sojourns in England and Canada, her first language was still Yiddish and her autobiography was written in that language and translated into English.

By 1932, Goldman recognized the threat of Nazism in Germany and was making speeches throughout Europe and North America denouncing Hitler. However, she never resumed her old involvement in politics except for a brief effort in favor of the anarchist group in the Spanish Civil War. Emma Goldman died on May 14, 1940, in Toronto, Canada, just before her 71st birthday and four years after her friend Sasha Berkman had committed suicide. In her obituary, *The New York Times* called her "an incorrigible revolutionist to the end." Emma Goldman never wavered in her commitments. She continued to believe in the inherent goodness of the working man and the absolute right of women to equality. Above all, she continued to insist on personal freedom.

SOURCES:

"Goldman, Emma," in *Encyclopedia Judaica.* 1972 ed.

Goldman, Emma. *Living My Life: The Autobiography of Emma Goldman.* Laxton, UT: Peregrine Smith Books, 1982.

Hymowitz, Carol, and Michaele Weissman. *A History of Women in America.* NY: Bantam Books, 1978, pp. 235–236, 285–289, 293–295.

The New York Times. May 14, 1940, p. 23.

Taitz, Emily, and Sondra Henry. *Remarkable Jewish Women: Rebels, Rabbis and Other Women from Biblical Times to the Present.* Philadelphia, PA: Jewish Publication Society, 1996.

SUGGESTED READING:

Drinnon, Richard. *Rebel in Paradise: A Biography of Emma Goldman.* Chicago, IL: University of Chicago Press, 1961.

——, and Anna Maria. *Nowhere At Home: Letters from Exile of Emma Goldman and Alexander Berkman.* NY: Schocken Books, 1975.

Morton, Marian J. *Emma Goldman and the American Left: "Nowhere at Home."* Twayne, 1992.

Emily Taitz,
adjunct professor of Women's Studies, Adelphi University, Garden City, New York, co-author of *Written Out of History: Jewish Foremothers* (Biblio Press, 1990), and other writings on women

Goldman, Hetty (1881–1972)

American archaeologist. Born in New York, New York, on December 19, 1881; died in Princeton, New Jersey, on May 4, 1972; one of four children of Julius Goldman (a lawyer) and Sarah (Adler) Goldman; attended Dr. J. Sachs School for Girls, New York (founded by her uncle Julius Sachs); Bryn Mawr College, Bryn Mawr, Pennsylvania, B.A. in Greek and English, 1903; Radcliffe College, M.A., 1911, Ph.D., 1916; attended the American School of Classical Studies, Athens, Greece, 1910–12; never married; no children.

The daughter of a lawyer and granddaughter of the founder of the investment bank Goldman, Sachs and Company, Hetty Goldman grew up in a comfortable home where intellectual and humanitarian pursuits were encouraged. Her uncle, a classicist who also ran the school she attended as a girl, first piqued her interest in archaeology. After graduating from Bryn Mawr in 1903, she worked as a manuscript reader while attending graduate courses in Greek at Columbia University. In 1910, she decided to continue her education at Radcliffe, where she concentrated on classics and archaeology and also became the first woman to receive the Charles Eliot Norton fellowship to attend the American School of Classical Studies at Athens. While in Greece, at a site at the small coastal town of Halae, she undertook her first dig, which in addition to revealing classical remains also uncovered some of the earliest traces of Neolithic village occupation in Greece. The excavation at Halae also provided the basis for Goldman's Ph.D. dissertation, for which Radcliffe awarded her a Ph.D. in 1916. Goldman's work was interrupted by the Balkan war, during which time she served as a volunteer nurse. Later, during World War I, she spent several years with the Red Cross in New York. She was finally able to return to Halae in 1921.

In 1922, Goldman undertook the first of a number of excavations in Asia Minor, at Ionia, under the auspices of Harvard's Fogg Museum. This time her work was cut short by the Graeco-Turkish war. In 1924, she became director of excavations for the Fogg and, for the next three years, led excavations in Turkey and Greece, often at war-ravaged sites that made her work all the more difficult. Her publication *Excavations at Eutresis in Boeotia* (1931) documented her work during this period. Goldman's fourth major excavation was at Tarsus near the southeast coast of Turkey. Hoping to discover prehistoric links between Greece and Anatolia, her team had successfully uncovered levels laid around 3000 BCE, when, once again, the project was interrupted, this time by World War II.

Hetty Goldman passed the war years at Princeton University, having been appointed the first woman professor at its Institute for Advanced Studies in 1936. There, while researching and preparing her findings at Tarsus for publication, she sponsored German refugees who fled the Nazis. In 1947, she was able to return to Tarsus, where two years later her excavations finally reached the deepest level. She retired in 1948 and continued to prepare her Tarsus research, which was published in three volumes: *Excavations at Gözlü Kule Tarsus* (1950, 1956, and 1963). In 1966, Goldman was awarded the gold medal for Distinguished Archaeological Achievement from the Archaeological Institute of America.

Throughout her life, Goldman combined her work and her humanitarian efforts with a wide range of cultural interests and a deep devotion to her family. She died of pulmonary edema in Princeton in May 1972.

SOURCES:

Bailey, Brooke. *The Remarkable Lives of 100 Women Healers and Scientists.* Holbrook, MA: Bob Adams, 1994.

Sicherman, Barbara, and Carol Hurd Green, eds. *Notable American Women: The Modern Period*. Cambridge, MA: The Belknap Press of Harvard University Press, 1980.

Goldmark, Josephine (1877–1950)

American social reformer. Born Josephine Clara Goldmark in Brooklyn, New York, on October 13, 1877; died in Hartsdale, New York, on December 15, 1950; sister of Pauline Dorothea Goldmark, *a welfare worker, and* Alice Goldmark *who married Louis D. Brandeis; graduated from Bryn Mawr College, 1898; studied English at Barnard College.*

While tutoring at Barnard College in 1903, Josephine Goldmark volunteered to assist *Florence Kelley at the National Consumer's League, becoming publication secretary. Goldmark also chaired the League's committee on legal defense of labor laws, resulting in the publication of *Child Labor Legislation Handbook* in 1907. Along with Kelley, Goldmark gathered data for the 1908 Brandeis brief *Muller v. Oregon*. The following year, still content to work behind the scenes, she assisted Felix Frankfurter, then a lawyer, in preparing briefs to support the Illinois ten-hour law. Teaming with her brother-in-law Louis Brandeis, Josephine Goldmark then began a study of fatigue in factory work for the Russell Sage Foundation. Their findings, published as *Fatigue and Efficiency* (1912), were instrumental in reducing excessive labor hours in manufacturing. From 1912 to 1914, Goldmark joined Alfred E. Smith, *Frances Perkins, and Robert Wagner on a committee to investigate the Triangle Shirtwaist Fire which had killed 146 workers. Retiring from public life, Goldmark published *Nursing and Nursing Education in the United States* (1923), *Pilgrims of '48: One Man's Part in the Austrian Revolution of 1848, and a Family's Migration to America* (1930), *Democracy in Denmark* (1936), as well as a biography of her friend Florence Kelley, *Impatient Crusader* (Urbana: University of Illinois, 1953).

Goldring, Winifred (1888–1971)

American paleontologist who was the official state paleontologist of New York from 1939 to 1954. Born in Albany, New York, in 1888; died in Albany, New York, in 1971; fourth of eight daughters of Frederick (a florist) and Mary (Grey) Goldring; granted undergraduate and graduate degrees from Wellesley College, 1909 and 1912, respectively; postgraduate study at Columbia and Johns Hopkins universities; never married; no children.

A pioneering woman in the field of paleontology, Winifred Goldring felt so isolated at times that she once advised young women thinking of going into science to pick a specialty like botany where they would encounter enough other women to make them feel comfortable. However, Goldring, a Phi Beta Kappa and Durant Scholar, knew even as a college student the unusual path she would follow. After graduating from Wellesley in 1909, she stayed on to assist geology professor **Elizabeth F. Fisher**. Goldring subsequently taught geology and petrology at Wellesley and pursued her studies further at Columbia and Johns Hopkins before returning to Albany in 1914. At that time, she was hired as a "scientific expert" in the Hall of Invertebrate Paleontology at the New York State Museum. Under the museum's director, John M. Clarke, she developed exhibits and researched mid-Paleozoic crinoids (small marine animals of the phylum *Echinodermata*).

During her long association with the museum, interrupted only by a year at Johns Hopkins in 1921, Goldring pursued research on a "missing link" between algae and vascular plants and also made Albany's plant collection one of the world's best. Cited for her educational exhibits, Goldring published a textbook on fossils in 1929.

Although she was considered an expert and was well respected among her peers, Goldring endured gender discrimination as well as isolation in her chosen field. Her salary ($2,300) was never on a par with those of her male colleagues at the museum, and she was turned down for a position with the U.S. Geological Survey in 1928, because they wanted to hire a "he-man" type. Determined, however, never to allow her gender to limit her work in the field, Goldring fitted herself with a specially designed walking outfit with bloomers and learned to shoot a revolver. She also compensated by overworking, and once pushed herself to the point of a nervous collapse. Biases aside, Goldring's male colleagues elected her president of the Paleontological Society in 1949 and vice president of the Geological Society in 1950.

At age 67, Goldring retired and withdrew completely from the world of science. She spent her last years within her family circle in Albany. She died there in 1971, two days shy of her 83rd birthday.

SOURCES:

Bailey, Brooke, *The Remarkable Lives of 100 Women Healers and Scientists*. Holbrook, MA: Bob Adams, 1994.

Weatherford, Doris. *American Women's History*. NY: Prentice Hall, 1994.

Goldschmidt, Madame (1820–1887).

See Lind, Jenny.

Goldsmith, Grace Arabell
(1904–1975)

American physician, nutritionist, and public-health educator. Born in St. Paul, Minnesota, on April 8, 1904; died in New Orleans, Louisiana, on April 28, 1975; only child of Arthur William (an accountant) and Arabell (Coleman) Goldsmith; attended the University of Minnesota; University of Wisconsin, B.S., 1925; Tulane University, M.D.; University of Minnesota, M.S. in medicine, 1936; never married; no children.

Grace Arabell Goldsmith, a talented dancer, was the physical education director of the New Orleans YWCA when a friend convinced her to attend medical school. Working her way through Tulane by teaching dance classes, she graduated at the top of her class (edging out Michael DeBakey, the famed cardiovascular surgeon), then worked as an intern at New Orleans' Touro Infirmary. In 1933, she joined the staff of the Mayo Clinic in Rochester, Minnesota, as a fellow in internal medicine. In 1936, after receiving an M.S. in medicine from the University of Minnesota, she returned to Tulane to teach. There, she pursued an interest in vitamin deficiency diseases, establishing tests for vitamin C deficiency and researching pellagra. She was instrumental in recommending dietary allowances for niacin, the vitamin that prevents pellagra, and also conducted studies on riboflavin, folic acid, and vitamin B-12. She then launched a public health campaign on the benefits of nutritionally enriching food.

In 1940, Goldsmith expanded her focus to include worldwide nutrition problems, studying the effects of vitamin enriched foods in Newfoundland. Later, she founded a nutritional training program for medical students at Tulane, the first of its kind. It would gain autonomy as the Tulane School of Public Health and Tropical Medicine, of which she served as dean in the 1960s, thus becoming the first woman dean of a school of public health in the United States. Goldsmith also served as president of the American Institute of Nutrition (1965), the American Board of Nutrition (1966–67), and the American Society for Clinical Nutrition (1972–73). She received the AMA's Goldberger Award in Clinical Nutrition in 1964.

Grace Goldman, an energetic woman who led a rich and varied life, was an excellent gardener and a gourmet cook; she also loved to entertain and had a passion for dancing that was lifelong. She died in New Orleans in 1975, age 71.

SOURCES:

Bailey, Brooke. *The Remarkable Lives of 100 Women Healers and Scientists.* Holbrook, MA: Bob Adams, 1994.

Sicherman, Barbara, and Carol Hurd Green, eds. *Notable American Women: The Modern Period.* Cambridge, MA: The Belknap Press of Harvard University Press, 1980.

Goldstein, Vida (1869–1949)

Australian feminist who was the first woman parliamentary candidate in the British Empire. Born Vida Jane Mary Goldstein on April 13, 1869, in Portland, Victoria; died on April 15, 1949, in South Yarra, Australia; the eldest of five children of Jacob Goldstein (a storekeeper and army officer) and Isabella (Hawkins) Goldstein; graduated with honors from Presbyterian Ladies' College, 1886; attended the University of Melbourne; never married; no children.

Brought up in a progressive household, the well-educated Vida Goldstein spent her early career working with her mother in the anti-sweating movement and in housing and prison-reform campaigns. When the bank crashes of the 1890s threatened the family income, she and her sister **Bella Goldstein**, who married the British socialist H.H. Champion, opened a free, co-educational school in St. Kilda. Meanwhile, Vida continued her political education by reading widely and campaigning for legislative reform. Becoming increasingly involved in women's suffrage, she left her school in 1899 to devote herself full time to the movement. From 1900 to 1905, in addition to working as a paid political organizer, she produced the feminist journal *The Australian Woman's Sphere*, in which she addressed local women's issues and also reprinted material from *Lucy Stone's *Woman's Journal*, thus keeping her readers abreast of the international movement. In 1902, having gained an international reputation for her feminist work, Goldstein was a representative at the Women's Suffrage Conference in Washington, D.C.

In 1903, after the federal vote was gained, Goldstein ran as an independent candidate for the Senate in the federal election, the first woman parliamentary candidate in the British Empire. Although unsuccessful, she polled a large number of votes and drew enormous attention, mostly negative, from the press. Four subsequent attempts to win a parliamentary seat—in 1910, 1913, 1914, and 1917—were also unsuccessful. After state suffrage was won in 1908, Goldstein launched a new journal *The Woman Voter* (1909–11), in which she continued to champion for equal marriage and divorce laws, and equal pay and employment opportunities for women. With *Rose Scott, Goldstein opposed party politics, encouraging women to act independently and lobby every political group. In 1911, she visited Britain, where she enjoyed a successful speaking tour and worked as a political organizer for the Women's Social and Political Union. She also wrote suffrage articles for both British and international distribution.

Goldstein was a staunch feminist and became increasingly socialistic in her views. After returning from Britain, she became more and more involved with anti-militarist activities. In 1915, she helped found the Women's Peace Army, a militant group which organized projects for the relief of women who had experienced unemployment or poverty due to the war. By 1917, the year of her last run for Parliament, her writings were censored and her activities monitored closely. In 1919, Goldstein went to Europe where she represented Australia at a Women's Peace Conference in Zurich. Upon her return to Australia, she gradually withdrew from politics, devoting her last 20 years to Christian Science. She died of cancer on April 15, 1949, at her home in South Yarra.

SOURCES:
Radi, Heather, ed. *200 Australian Women*. NSW, Australia: Women's Redress Press, 1988.

Uglow, Jennifer S., ed. *The International Dictionary of Women's Biography*. NY: Continuum, 1985.

Wilde, William H., Joy Hooton, Barry Andrews. *Oxford Companion to Australian Literature*. Melbourne: Oxford, 1985.

Goldthwaite, Anne Wilson

(1869–1944)

American etcher, lithographer, and modernist painter of the South who helped found the Académie Moderne in Paris. Born in Montgomery, Alabama, on June 28, 1869; died in New York City on January 29, 1944; eldest of four children of Richard Wallach Goldthwaite (a lawyer) and Lucy Boyd (Armistead) Goldthwaite; attended Mrs. Coughanour's "Little Ladies School," a convent school in Dallas, Texas, Hammer Hall, an Episcopal school in Montgomery, and the National Academy of Design, New York; never married; no children.

Destined to be acclaimed one of America's outstanding women artists and a leading regional painter of the South, Anne Wilson Goldth-waite was born into a distinguished Alabama family and raised by relatives after the death of her parents. Seemingly destined for the life of a southern belle, her direction changed abruptly after a devoted beau was killed in a duel. At that time, a visiting uncle interceded, suggesting that she come North to pursue her longtime interest in art. New York eventually became Goldth-waite's adopted city, although she always recalled her early years in the South as golden. "They were filled with love and warmth and ease and approbation. I remember only happy things." Later, she paid regular summertime visits to the rural Alabama of her youth and made it the subject of some of her best work.

At the National Academy of Design, she studied etching with Charles Mielatz and painting with Walter Shirlaw, who was her major influence. In 1906, she went to Paris, where she studied with Charles Guérin and Othon Friesz and was one of a group of students who founded the Académie Moderne. Through her acquaintance with *Gertrude Stein, she discovered the works of Cézanne, Matisse, and Picasso. Goldthwaite later recalled her first meeting with Stein at the Luxemburg Garden. She looked up from her sketching and saw a friend talking to a woman "who looked something like an immense dark brown egg. She wore, wrapped tight around her, a brown kimono-like garment and a large flat black hat, and stood on feet covered with wide sandals." When Stein later invited her home, Goldthwaite wondered if the shabby looking woman could even afford to give her tea. She was amazed to encounter Stein's elegant studio, filled with antique furniture and "the most remarkable pictures I had ever seen."

Returning to New York just before World War I, Goldthwaite exhibited in the 1913 Armory show, which showcased the early modernists. In the ensuing years, in addition to her prolific output, she continued to study, especially etching, and also taught at the Art Students League from 1922 until her death in 1944. She was not only a popular teacher, but an early advocate of women's rights. Never married, Goldthwaite was a member of numerous artists' organizations, including the New York Society of Women Artists, of which she served as president from 1937 to 1938.

Anne Goldthwaite's paintings and prints, which include trenchant portraits of her friends and relatives, are characterized by a relaxed, whimsical style. Although she embraced the modern movement early in her career, her work is more expressionistic than abstract, often remi-

Anne Goldthwaite

niscent of Manet, but "it never resembles the art of his insistently feminine disciples *Berthe Morisot and *Mary Cassatt," writes Harry B. Wehle. Art historian **Adelyn Breeskin**, in discussing Goldthwaite's sympathetic studies of the poor Southern black with his mules, or of the women of the Goldthwaite clan taking an afternoon respite from the oppressive summer heat, writes: "The slow rhythm of lines, the very ease in execution, the sense of hot sun . . . mark these as among the most vivid and eloquent graphic works yet produced of the South."

Goldthwaite's work is exhibited in the Congressional Library and in many American museums, including the Metropolitan Museum of Art, the Art Institute of Chicago, the Brooklyn Museum of Art, the Whitney Museum, and the Worcester (Massachusetts) Museum. Shortly before her death in 1944, she completed two murals on Southern life for the post offices at Atmore and Tuskegee, Alabama. The artist died in New York on January 29, 1944, at age 74. She was buried in Oakwood Cemetery, Montgomery.

SOURCES:

Edgerly, Lois Stiles. *Give Her This Day.*

Petteys, Chris. *Dictionary of Women Artists.* Boston, MA: G.K. Hall, 1985.

Rothe, Anna, ed. *Current Biography 1944.* NY: H.W. Wilson, 1944.

Rubinstein, Charlotte Streifer. *American Women Artists.* NY: Avon, 1982.

Wehle, Harry B. "Anne Wilson Goldthwaite" in Edward T. James' *Notable American Women 1607–1950.* Cambridge, MA: The Belknap Press of Harvard University Press, 1971.

Barbara Morgan,
Melrose, Massachusetts

Golitsin or Golitzyn, Princess
(1748–1806).

See Ney, Elisabet for sidebar on Amalie von Galitzin.

Goll, Claire (1891–1977)

German-French author, best known for her poetry, whose autobiography detailed the literary history of her times, as well as her liaison with the poet Rainer Maria Rilke. Name variations: Claire Studer. Born Clara Aischmann in Nuremberg, Germany, on October 29, 1891; died in Paris, France, on May 30, 1977; had one brother; married Heinrich Studer; married Yvan or Ivan Goll; children: (first marriage) Dorothea Studer.

Selected writings: Eine Deutsche in Paris (Berlin: Martin Wasservogel Verlag, 1927); Der gestohlene Himmel (Munich: List Verlag, 1962); Ich verzeihe keinem: Eine literarische Chronique scandaleuse unserer Zeit (translated by Ava Belcampo. Berne: Scherz Verlag, 1978); Lyrische Films (Basel: Rhein Verlag, 1922); Traumtänzerin: Jahre der Jugend (Munich: List Verlag, 1971).

Although she was born into a wealthy German-Jewish family in Nuremberg, Clara Aischmann did not benefit from the emotional stability and psychological security that affluence can make possible. Instead, she had to endure a horrific childhood of mental humiliation and physical abuse by a mother whose many affairs, which included one with a baron who was Clara's biological father, were intended to wound and crush her husband. Clara endured not only verbal battering from her mother, but physical attacks as well which included violent blows, whipping, denial of meals and incarceration in a darkened room. These brutalities not only left her with mental and physical scars but permanently impaired her health for the rest of her life. Many years later, when her mother was murdered at Auschwitz, Clara Aischmann, by then the writer Claire Goll, recorded that she felt no pain or sense of loss.

When she was 11, Clara's older brother, who was 16 at the time, committed suicide. He had attempted to defend his sister, and when their mother decided to send him to reform school he rented a room and opened the kitchen's gas valve. To escape the horrors of her home life, Clara developed a close friendship with the family cook. Not only did she derive emotional stability from contact with this unsophisticated but warm-hearted woman, Clara was also able to find a place of refuge away from home. The cook's aunt, who worked as a domestic at a nearby parochial school, also befriended Clara, and it was here that she spent countless hours, in an environment that provided her with more security than her affluent home. A more permanent escape from her oppressive home life came when she was enrolled in a Munich progressive school led by Georg and **Julie Kerschensteiner**. Finally given the opportunity to express her feelings, she discovered the possibilities of expressing her deepest fears and hopes through words.

While attending the Munich Opera one night, Clara met and fell in love with a handsome young man, Heinrich Studer. She became pregnant and married him, bringing with her a substantial dowry of 200,000 reichsmarks. After the birth of a daughter **Dorothea Studer**, their marriage began to crumble, and neither she nor her husband remained faithful. Clara began an affair with the publisher Kurt Wolff. After divorcing Studer in 1916, Clara Aischmann went to Switzerland, leaving behind both Wolff and her young daughter. Settled in French-speaking Geneva, she began to call herself Claire and soon became part of an antiwar group of intellectuals. Later, while living in Zurich, she counted as friends such influential creative spirits as Hans Arp, James Joyce, and Stefan Zweig.

Among the antiwar activists Claire met in her Swiss exile were Henri Guilbeaux, editor of the pacifist journal *Demain,* and the famous novelist Romain Rolland. Through Guilbeaux and Rolland, she was introduced to a talented poet, Ivan Goll, author of "Requiem for the Fallen Soldiers of Europe," a poem that had deeply moved Claire. Also born in 1891 into a wealthy Jewish family, Ivan was a native of Alsace, a province of the German Reich that was German-speaking but had largely retained a French spirit. Ivan's father was Alsatian, but his mother was from Lorraine, a German province that had been able to retain stronger French loyalties. His own family resembled Claire's in that they too were dysfunctionally unhappy. His recollection was of an "entire youth [during which] I sat at a family table at which I heard little else but screaming and scolding." It is scarcely surprising that two sensitive young people from such similar—and painful—backgrounds would be strongly attracted to one another.

In 1917, soon after their first encounter, Claire and Ivan "married" symbolically. Ivan had already published some important poetry by the time she met him, but in 1918 Claire too had found her voice as writer, in that year publishing *Die Frauen erwachen* (*The Women Awaken*), a haunting expressionist indictment of the great war still ravaging Europe; this book depicted the horror of the conflict that destroyed not only the lives of soldiers but of their wives and sweethearts as well. *The Women Awaken* uses explosive images and is able to effectively combine emotional visions with bits of crude reality. The work is Romantic in its view of women as providers and keepers of love, and its simple, if not indeed simplistic, pacifist message is that women should activate their power of love to prevent another war.

Despite their strong feelings for one another, neither Claire nor Ivan could long remain faith-

Claire Goll

ful. In 1918 and again in 1920, Claire spent extended periods of time with the Prague-born poet Rainer Maria Rilke. Their relationship was of major significance for Rilke's literary development, because Claire served as an intermediary between him and several French writers. She not only supplied Rilke with books but also introduced him to poets and publishers and drew his attention to selected works by providing him with her German translations of French originals so that he could then make critical comparisons. Claire's intimacy with Rilke concerned Ivan Goll greatly, and in 1921 he and Claire were legally married. By this time, she had permanently separated from Rilke and had aborted an early pregnancy. Rilke would have been the father.

From 1919 to 1939, Claire and Ivan Goll lived in Paris. Often separated and almost never faithful to each other, the couple nevertheless wrote caring letters to each other. Red-haired and provocatively vivacious, Claire attracted countless lovers during these years, including André Malraux. Although she was by no means blind to the turbulent world she lived in, her letters from the 1930s make no mention of the political events in Germany that would soon destroy the lives of millions.

During these years, Claire Goll wrote poetry as well as several novels, including *Der Neger Jupiter raubt Europa* (*The Negro Jupiter robs Europe*, 1926), *Eine Deutsche in Paris* (*A German Woman in Paris*, 1927), *Ein Mensch ertrinkt* (*A Human Being Drowns*, 1931), and *Arsenik* (*Arsenic*, 1933). All of these books are not only works of savage social criticism but are carefully crafted works of literature. Goll also published books of poetry, including *Lyrische Films* (*Lyrical Films*, 1922), a slim but brilliant and verbally extravagant volume that juxtaposed lyrical poems, "sentimentalities" that compared body and facial features with non-human objects, and a third section entitled "Diary of a Horse" that is a prose poem dedicated to "Ivan and all the horses." By the end of the 1920s, Claire Goll was no longer neither exclusively German nor French, but had been able to fuse both Teutonic and Gallic cultural and linguistic traditions into a unique amalgam that was hers and hers alone. Rightfully, she regarded herself as a European rather than a member of either of two nationalities that had set out to destroy each other only a few years previously.

By 1937, Ivan Goll was planning to move to New York, yet kept delaying his departure from an increasingly unstable Europe. In July 1938, Claire tried to end her life because of her rage at her husband's extended affair with the poet **Paula Ludwig** (1900–1974). Claire survived her attempted suicide and then moved to London. The couple arrived in New York in late August 1939, on the last ship to leave France before the start of World War II. While in New York, the Golls continued to write while Ivan also published a literary journal, *Hemisphere,* from 1943 through 1947. By 1947, both were homesick for Europe, and they decided to return to Paris. In his remaining years (he died in 1950 of leukemia, the same affliction that ended Rilke's life), Ivan once again wrote in the German language he had abandoned after World War I, producing what is generally regarded as his finest work. Before his death in February 1950, he asked Claire to promise to destroy all but his last manuscripts.

For the next 27 years, until her own death in Paris on May 30, 1977, Claire Goll wrote her own candid and at times deliberately scandalous autobiography, producing in three volumes a detailed literary history of her times as seen from her own highly subjective vantage point. The rest of her energy went into a veritable crusade to bring her late husband's work to the attention of the literary world. Claire broke her promise to Ivan Goll by not destroying any of his manuscripts. Instead, she saw to it that much of his unpublished work, carefully edited by her, appeared in print in the years after his death. A ferocious defender of Ivan's literary legacy, she was suspicious of those who might unfairly draw upon him for inspiration for their own work; in 1950, soon after she accused the poet Paul Celan of having plagiarized from Ivan Goll, Celan committed suicide in the Seine.

In her last years, old and ill and with virtually all of her generation now dead, Claire Goll lived alone in her Paris apartment, Rue Vaneau 47, in the Saint Germain des Prés district. The walls were covered with paintings by artists who had been friends of the Golls—Chagall, Jawlensky, Delaunay, Kokoschka—and books and manuscripts were everywhere to be seen, tumbling out of drawers and closets. Knowing that her life was drawing to a close, Claire Goll danced alone every night in her apartment while listening to an old tango record, "La Cumbarsita," which she had danced to with Ivan during his last illness. Now, she confided to a visitor, "When I hear the melody, I know that he is with me. And then I dance with him."

SOURCES:

Blumenthal, Bernhardt. "Claire Goll's Prose," in *Monatshefte.* Vol. 75, no. 4. Winter 1983, pp. 358–368.

———. "Rilke and Claire Goll," in *Modern Austrian Literature.* Vol. 15, nos. 3/4, 1982, pp. 169–182.

Brinker-Gabler, Gisela, ed. *Frauen gegen den Krieg.* Frankfurt am Main: Fischer Taschenbuch Verlag, 1980.

Edschmid, Kasimir, ed. *Iwan Goll—Claire Goll: Briefe.* Mainz and Berlin: Florian Kupferberg Verlag, 1966.

Glauert, Barbara. "'Liliane': Rainer Maria Rilke und Claire Studer in ihren Briefen 1918–1925," in *Aus dem Antiquariat I—1976: Beilage zum Börsenblatt für den Deutschen Buchhandel.* No. 7. January 23, 1976, pp. 1–11.

Goldman, Dorothy, ed. *Women and World War I: The Written Response.* NY: St. Martin's Press, 1993.

Goll, Claire. *Eine Deutsche in Paris.* Berlin: Martin Wasservogel Verlag, [1927].

——. *Der gestohlene Himmel.* Munich: List Verlag, 1962.

——. *Ich verzeihe keinem: Eine literarische Chronique scandaleuse unserer Zeit.* Translated by Ava Belcampo. Berne: Scherz Verlag, 1978.

——. *Lyrische Films.* Basel: Rhein Verlag, 1922 (reprint ed., Nendeln, Liechtenstein: Kraus Reprint, 1973).

——. *Traumtänzerin: Jahre der Jugend.* Munich: List Verlag, 1971.

Goll, Yvan. *Dichtungen.* Edited by Claire Goll. Darmstadt: Verlag Hermann Luchterhand, 1960.

Hausdorf, Anna. "Claire Goll und ihr Roman 'Der Neger Jupiter raubt Europa'," in *Neophilologus.* Vol. 74, no. 2, 1990, pp. 265–278.

——. "Der 'Familienroman' im Werk der Claire Goll," in Henk Hillenaar and Walter Schönau, eds., *Fathers and Mothers in Literature.* Amsterdam and Atlanta, GA: Rodopi, 1994, pp. 281–294.

Kübli, Sabine and Doris Stump, eds. *Viel Köpfe, viel Sinn: Texte von Autorinnen aus der deutschsprachigen Schweiz 1795–1945.* Berne: eFeF-Verlag, 1994.

Lorenz, Dagmar C.G. "Jewish Women Authors and the Exile Experience: Claire Goll, Veza Canetti, Else Lasker-Schüler, Nelly Sachs, Cordelia Edvardson," in *German Life and Letters.* Vol. 51, no. 2. April 1998, pp. 225–239.

Serke, Jürgen. *Die verbrannten Dichter: Berichte, Texte, Bilder einer Zeit.* 3rd ed. Weinheim and Basel: Beltz & Gelberg Verlag, 1978.

Studer, Claire. *Die Frauen erwachen: Novellen.* Frauenfeld: Huber & Co. Verlag, 1918.

——. *Der gläserne Garten: Zwei Novellen.* Munich: Roland-Verlag, 1919 (reprint ed., Nendeln, Liechtenstein: Kraus Reprint, 1973).

——. *Mitwelt.* Berlin-Wilmersdorf: Die Akion (Franz Pfemfert), 1918 (reprint ed., Nendeln, Liechtenstein: Kraus Reprint, 1973).

COLLECTIONS:

Claire und Yvan Goll Nachlass. Deutsches Literatur-Archiv im Schiller-Nationalmuseum, Marbach am Neckar.

John Haag,
Associate Professor of History,
University of Georgia, Athens, Georgia

Golofski, Hannah (c. 1923–1974).

See Klein, Anne.

Golubkina, Anna (1864–1927)

Russian sculptor who was a pioneering force in Russian art of the early 20th century. Born Anna Semyonovna Golubkina in Zaraysk, in the region of Ryazan, Russia, in 1864; died on September 7, 1927; studied with sculptor S.M. Volnukhin, 1889; studied with painter Sergei Ivanov at the Moscow School of Painting, Sculpture and Architecture, 1891; worked in studio of V.A. Beklemishev at the Higher Art Institute, part of the St. Petersburg Academy of Fine Art; studied with Italian sculptor Filippo Colarossi, 1895; studied with painter Nikolai Ulyanov, 1901–03; never married; no children.

One of the many children of a market gardener, Russian sculptor Anna Golubkina educated herself with books she borrowed from one of the town's wealthy merchants. Her formal artistic training began at age 25, when she studied with S.M. Volnukhin, one of Russia's best-known 19th-century sculptors. She later attended the Moscow School of Painting, Sculpture and Architecture, and the St. Petersburg Academy of Fine Arts, where she studied with V.A. Beklemishev. Like all young artists, Golubkina struggled under the powerful influence of her teachers to develop her own personal style. "I want to stay independent," she said. "I am sick of all the imitations." In 1897, she traveled to Paris where she studied with Filippo Colarossi and shared lodgings with two other young Russian woman artists, **E.S. Kruglikova** and **E.N. Shevtsova**. Lacking money, Golubkina returned to St. Petersburg within a year. On a second visit to Paris in 1897, she managed to set up her own studio. It was at this time that she made the acquaintance of Auguste Rodin, who became a lifelong friend and confidante. The French sculptor, although a powerful force, did not require Golubkina to sacrifice her creative independence or her Russian spirit.

Golubkina worked in stone, metal, wood, and marble, achieving what she referred to as "the universal" through her use of simple forms and stylization. "[H]er talent, temperament and perception corresponded to her time," notes **Elena Murina**, "which demanded that the artist should transcend the details of daily life and perceive human life on a more general level." In Golubkina's work *Old Age,* form is subordinated to the greater theme of the sorrow caused by the endless suffering of the Russian people. In *Manka* (1898), her marble bust of a child with rickets, Golubkina expresses the tragedy of life through the over-large forehead, swollen eyes, and seemingly trembling lips of the afflicted young girl. Vengeance is another recurring theme, most evident in her sculpture *Walking Man* (1903) as described by M.N. Yablonskaya in *Women Artists of Russia's New Age:* "Her

Walking Man seems to arise, like a primordial creature, out of the very earth itself and, taking its first stumbling steps, it confronts the future threatening revenge for the human condition into which it has been born."

Golubkina's passionate social conscience led her to take an active role in revolutionary events of 1905. That year, upon completion of a bust of Karl Marx, she donated her fee to a fund for homeless workers and even opened her home for use as a temporary hospital and canteen. In 1907, she was arrested and jailed for distributing a document calling for the overthrow of the tsar. After her release from prison, where she staged a hunger strike to protest her arrest, she set up a studio in Moscow where she continued to work for the rest of her life. In the decade before the revolution, she became quite famous for her portraits of leading intellectual and literary figures of the day, which included wooden busts of Alexei Mikhailovich Remizov (1911) and Alexei Nikolaevich Tolstoy (1911), whom she said, "guzzled oysters." Professor Vladimir Ern, who sat for her in 1914, called the artist "coarse in her speech, direct, from a peasant background." In a further description, he said: "She is often hungry but gives away 500 roubles at a time. She mutters rather than speaks. She looks so seriously and deeply that you feel awkward, and then she smiles with a wonderful child-like smile. . . . It seems to me that sculpting is for her a way to perceive people."

During 1914 and 1915, Golubkina arranged a first-of-its-kind exhibition of 150 of her sculptures in Moscow to raise money for the war-wounded. The show was acclaimed for its scope and for its revelations of contemporary life. A contemporary wrote of Golubkina's work: "She has devoted her strength and talent to revealing the abnormal life of the city which forces men to heavy physical toil and drives women to vice. The stamp of want and degeneration is impressed on the faces of children."

In the 1920s, when illness curtailed Golubkina's large-scale work, she produced three delicate cameos, small relief sculptures titled *Borzoi*, *Female Face*, and *Neptune*, which somehow managed to convey the same intensity of her larger works. She also taught for several years and, in 1923, published her book *Some Words on the Sculptor's Craft*, in which she discussed both her professional experience and her social philosophy. As her health deteriorated, her sculpture became more harmonious. In 1927, she produced a powerful and flowing portrait bust of writer Lev Tolstoy. That year, she also created her last and unfinished work, *Little Birch-tree*, an uncharacteristic piece of charm and grace. "It is significant," writes Yablonskaya, "that as her parting statement to the world Golubkina should bequeath an image not of vengeance, old age or sorrow but that of a young girl fanned by a gentle breeze, an image of youth and clarity. Perhaps Golubkina had finally realized that the future did not belong to either the old or the vengeful but to children such as these."

SOURCES:

Yablonskaya, M.N. *Women Artists of Russia's New Age*. Edited by Anthony Parton. London: Thames and Hudson, 1990.

Barbara Morgan,
Melrose, Massachusetts

Gómez, Dolores Ibárruri (1895–1989).

See Ibárruri, Dolores.

Gomez, Sara (1943–1974)

Cuban filmmaker. Name variations; Gómez. Born in Havana, Cuba, in 1943; died on June 2, 1974, in Havana; attended Conservatory of Music, Havana.

Filmography: Ire a Santiago (*I Shall Go to Santiago, 1964*); Excursion a Vueltabajo (*Outing to Vueltabajo, 1965*); Y tenemos sabor (*And We've Got "Sabor," 1967*); En la otra isle (*On the Other Island, 1968*); Isla del tesorel (*Treasure Island, 1969*); Poder local, poder popular (*Local Power, People's Power, 1970*); Un documental a proposito del transito (*A Documentary about Mass Transit, 1971*); Atencion pre-natal ano (*Prenatal Care in the First Year, 1972*); Sobre horas extras y trabajo voluntario (*About Overtime and Voluntary Labor, 1973*); De cierta manera (*One Way or Another, 1975*).

Born into a middle-class black family in Havana, Sara Gomez studied Afro-Cuban ethnography and worked as a journalist on such publications as *Mella* and the Sunday supplement *Hoy Domingo* before turning to filmmaking. In 1961, she was one of two black filmmakers and the only woman to join the newly formed Cuban Film Institute (ICAIC). Subsequently, she worked as an assistant director to Cuban filmmakers Jorge Fraga and Tomas Gutiérrez Alea and to visiting French filmmaker *Agnes Varda.

Gomez made a series of documentary shorts on subjects like mass transit, pre-natal care, and overtime labor before embarking as a director on what would become her first and last feature-length film, an effort that won her renown. *One Way or Another* was originally called *The Mi-raflores Housing Project*. In the film, for which Gomez also wrote the screenplay, the relationship of her two protagonists was loosely based on her relationship with sound man Germinal Hernandez. Gomez examines the difficulties of being both black and female in the Third World. The lovers are Mario, a mulatto worker in a bus assembly plant, and Yolanda, a middle-class schoolteacher who witnesses firsthand the prejudice that exists in their culture. The film is especially noted for Gomez's unconventional choice of intercutting documentary footage that shows the gradual tearing down of colonial Cuba with the traditional narrative. In *Women in Film: Both Sides of the Camera*, E. Ann Kaplan notes that Gomez's intercutting technique "gives the film its power for the juxtaposition provides a commentary on the capabilities of each cinematic form." Although shot in 16mm, *One Way or Another* is the work of an extremely sophisticated filmmaker.

Gomez, as a feminist, a revolutionary, and a black woman offered the world a unique voice. Tragically, she died of an acute asthma attack while her film was in post production. Her colleague, Tomas Gutiérrez Alea, finished the movie for her in 1975; it was released in 1977.

SOURCES:

Foster, Gwendolyn Audrey. *Women Film Directors: An International Bio-Critical Dictionary*. Westport, CT: Greenwood Press, 1995.

Kuhn, Annette, and Susannah Radstone. *The Women's Companion to International Film*. Berkeley, CA: University of California Press, 1990.

SUGGESTED READING:

Burton, Julianne. "Individual Fulfillment and Collective Achievement: An Interview with Tomas Gutiérrez Alea" in *Cineaste*. New York. January 1977.

LeSage, Julia. "One Way or Another: Dialectic, Revolutionary, Feminist," in *Jump Cut*. Vol. 20, 1979, pp. 20–23.

Deborah Jones,
Studio City, California

Gomez-Acebo, Margaret

Spanish heiress who married a Bulgarian royal in exile. Name variations: Margarita Gomez-Acero y Cejuela. Born Margarita Gomez Acebo y Cejuela in Spain; married Simon also known as Simeon II (b. 1937), king of Bulgaria (r. 1943–46), in 1962; children: Kardam of Veliko Turnovo, prince of Bulgaria; Cyril of Preslav, prince of Bulgaria; Kubrat of Panagurishte; Constantine of Vidin, prince of Bulgaria; Kalina of Bulgaria, princess of Bulgaria. Simon II was deposed in 1946, age nine.

*Opposite page
Little Birch-tree,
1927, by Anna
Golubkina.*

Gómez de Avellaneda, Gertrudis

(1814–1873)

Nineteenth-century Spanish dramatist and poet. Name variations: (nicknames) La Avellaneda, Tula; (pseudonym) La Peregrina. Born María Gertrudis de los Dolores Gómez de Avellaneda y Artega or Arteaga on March 23, 1814, at Puerto Príncipe, Cuba; died in Madrid, Spain, on February 1 (some sources cite February 2), 1873; daughter of Francisca de Arteaga y Betancourt and Manuel de Avellaneda (a naval officer); married Pedro Sabater, on May 10, 1846 (died, August 1, 1846); married Colonel Domingo Verdugo y Massieu, on April 26, 1855; children: (with poet Gabriel García Tassara) Brenhilde (b. 1845).

Born in Puerto Príncipe, Cuba, on March 23, 1814, Gertrudis Gómez de Avellaneda was the daughter of **Francisca de Arteaga y Betancourt** and naval officer Manuel de Avellaneda. Early on "Tula," as she was nicknamed, showed signs of literary genius. She read widely and by age 12 was writing poetry, drama, and novels. Meanwhile, her father died in 1823, and Tula's mother quickly remarried, to Isidoro de Escalada. Beautiful and talented, Tula dreamed of visiting Andalusia, her father's homeland. In 1836, the family sailed to Europe, and Tula and her brother Manuel went to Seville. There she published poetry under the pseudonym "La Peregrina" (the Wanderer). She also entertained and rejected several suitors. In 1838, however, she met and fell passionately in love with Ignacio de Cepeda, who sometimes encouraged her affections but ultimately rejected her. Tula's frustration evoked a series of love letters to Cepeda and underlay much of her literary production from 1838 to 1845.

La Avellaneda moved to Madrid in 1840, where she quickly established herself among Spain's literary elite. The following year saw the publication of her first volume of poetry, *Poesías*, and her first novel, *Sab*. Tula wrote prolifically. Several plays, including *Munio Alfonso* and *El Príncipe de Viana*, opened to enthusiastic receptions. Meanwhile, her personal life was turbulent and even scandalous. In 1844, she had an affair with Gabriel García Tassara, a poet, and gave birth to an illegitimate daughter, Brenhilde, a year later. García Tassara rejected the infant, which lived only nine months, and Tula soon began writing Cepeda again. She married Pedro Sabater in 1846 even though he was ill with cancer of the larynx and died four months later. Tula sought refuge in a convent at Bordeaux but soon emerged to resume her career.

Her pen was as prolific as ever: in 1852 five of her plays premiered in Madrid, and another two the next year. In 1853, she applied for membership in the Royal Spanish Academy but was rejected. Academy members acknowledged her literary merit but decided that membership must be restricted to men.

In 1855, La Avellaneda married again. Her second husband was Colonel Domingo Verdugo y Massieu, a Liberal politician. Given his political stature and Tula's friendship with *Isabella II, their wedding took place in the Royal Palace of Madrid on April 26, 1855. Verdugo received a serious but not fatal wound in an attempted assassination in 1858. His appointment as governor-general of Cuba provided Tula a chance to return to her native island. Cubans greeted her return with lavish receptions and great fanfare. Verdugo died in 1863, and Tula left Cuba the following year, visiting the U.S., Great Britain and France on her return to Spain. She lived until 1873, when complications from diabetes claimed her life.

Gertrudis Gómez de Avellaneda achieved lasting renown among Spanish literary critics as a lyric poet. Her plays, while not reaching the stature of the greatest Spanish drama, nonetheless measure up to any written in the 19th century. Tula's novels and shorter prose works add to her fame as one of the chief Spanish literary figures of any gender during the 1800s.

SOURCES:

Bravo Villasante, Carmen. *Una vida romántica, La Avellaneda*. Barcelona: Enrique Granados, 1967.

Harter, Hugh A. *Gertrudis Gómez de Avellaneda*. Boston, MA: Twayne, 1981.

Kendall W. Brown,
Professor of History, Brigham Young University, Provo, Utah

Goncharova, Natalia (1881–1962)

Russian painter and stage designer who drew on a variety of influences from the West but produced her most significant work by tapping the traditions of Russian art. Pronunciation: Na-TAL-ya Gan-CHAR-av-ah. Born on June 4, 1881, in the village of Nechaevo, Russia; died in Paris, France, on October 17, 1962; daughter of Sergei Goncharov (an architect and owner of a linen factory) and Yekaterina Goncharova; attended High School No. 4 in Moscow, 1893–98; studied sculpture at Moscow School of Painting, Sculpture, and Architecture, 1898–1901; married Mikhail Larionov, in 1955; no children.

Met Larionov at art school (1900); won silver medal for sculpture at school graduation (1901); shifted artistic interest to painting (1902); exhibited in Im-

pressionist style at Salon d'Automne, Paris (1906); presented works in folk tradition at Moscow's Jack of Diamonds exhibit and sued newspaper for accusing her of painting pornography (1910); held one-woman exhibit in Moscow's Artistic Salon (1913); created stage designs for production of Coq d'Or *in Paris, then returned to Moscow (1914); joined Ballets Russes in Switzerland (1915); toured Spain and Italy as member of Ballets Russes (1916–17); settled in Paris with Mikhail Larionov (1919); created stage design for* Les Noces *(1923); created stage designs for* Czar Sultan *and* Fair at Sorochinsk *(1932); became French citizen (1938); produced final theatrical designs (1957); sold collection of her works to Victoria and Albert Museum (1961).*

Major works: Haymaking *(Tretyakov Gallery, Moscow, 1910–11);* Landscape No. 47 *(Museum of Modern Art, New York, 1912);* Cats: Rayonist Apprehension in Pink, Black and Yellow *(Solomon R. Guggenheim Museum, New York, 1913);* Scenery and Stage Designs, 1914–1957 *(Victoria and Albert Museum, London).*

Natalia Goncharova, along with her lover and artistic companion Mikhail Larionov, was an important figure in the Russian world of painting in the early 20th century. Women played a significant role within this art world. Both in their numbers and in the prominence they achieved, they far outstripped their counterparts in Western and Central Europe. Fully half of the Russian artists who pioneered the techniques of abstract art at the start of the 20th century were women. M.N. Yablonskaya has referred to Goncharova and her fellow artists, such as *Liubov Popova, *Olga Rozanova, and *Alexandra Exter, as "the Amazons of the Avant-Garde." Some writers believe that the integration of women into the radical political circles of the 19th century paved the way for their acceptance as equals in the art world.

In that exciting environment, young artists found themselves bombarded by the influences of Western European art, such as Cubism, while they were also tempted to explore the rich artistic traditions of their own country. Goncharova stood in the center of such tensions, and thus critics have placed differing emphases on her work. In one assessment of what Goncharova and Larionov accomplished, **Camilla Gray** noted how they "selected and sifted turn by turn the most lively and progressive ideas in Europe and Russia from the beginning of the century up to the First World War." But Yablonskaya has assessed Goncharova's significance very differ-

*N*atalia *G*oncharova

ently: "The essence of Goncharova's art lies in the fact that she was a deeply national painter."

There was a rich artistic tradition in Russian popular culture upon which Goncharova and Larionov drew. Woodcuts (known in Russian as *lubki*) had been a widespread form of popular art since the 17th century. They reflected religious controversies, served as propaganda for Tsar Peter I the Great's effort to bring Western manners to Russia, and, as a primitive teaching device, helped to introduce the alphabet to the country's vast peasant population. *Lubki* were sometimes bound together to tell a story much like a 20th-century American comic book.

The traditional religious paintings of old Russia, known as icons, were also a potent source of inspiration for artists like Goncharova. Both *lubki* and icons featured characters with distorted figures who seemed to float in space. Goncharova also found inspiration in the large stone statues called *babas*. Considered by some a product of the area's prehistoric era, *babas* were more probably constructed in the 11th and 12th centuries. Old embroidery and painted trays offered other traditional techniques.

A member of an impoverished Russian noble family, Natalia Goncharova was born in the village of Nechaevo near the city of Tula, southeast of Moscow. She had numerous hereditary connections with the highest levels of Russian culture. Through her father Sergei Goncharov, the young woman was a descendent of Alexander Pushkin, the greatest Russian poet of the 19th century. Her mother **Yekaterina Goncharova** was a member of the distinguished Beliaev family, publishers and patrons of Russia's 19th-century musical development. Natalia's maternal grandfather had been on the faculty of the Theological Academy in Moscow.

Goncharova's success was to encapsulate the very spirit of Russia in visual form.
—M.N. Yablonskaya

The young girl spent a happy childhood on her grandmother's estate at Ladyzhino near her birthplace. She left the countryside to attend school in Moscow in 1893. In 1898, Goncharova turned to a life of art as she began studying sculpture, from distinguished sculptor Pavel Trubetskoi, at the Moscow School of Painting, Sculpture, and Architecture. But she soon redirected her energies to painting. As she told an interviewer in 1937, she abandoned her early ventures in sculpture for the easel "because I was fascinated by the play of light, the harmonies of colour." Reinforcing this novel direction in her work was a new and lasting personal tie: around 1900, she started her lifelong relationship with Mikhail Larionov, another young Russian artist.

Goncharova had a complex career as a painter, working in a number of different styles. And, rather than abandoning one style for another, she frequently produced works in several styles in the same period. Nonetheless, the most important and lasting theme in her prolific work turned out to be the Russian folk tradition.

Like many young artists at the turn of the century, however, Goncharova began her painting influenced by the French Impressionists. It was in this tradition that she produced her first exhibited works, presented to the Russian public in 1903. She then drew on the innovations of the Post-Impressionists and the Fauve school. Along with Larionov, she displayed paintings done in the Impressionist style at Sergei Diaghilev's Paris exhibition of 1906.

The lessons she learned from these developments in France combined, however, with her basic interest in Russian folk art. Even in these early years, she was attracted to Russian traditions such as icon painting. Moreover, artists like Henri Matisse, who called for the need to look at "primitive" art ranging from medieval woodcuts to Tahitian idols, paved the way for Russians like Goncharova and Larionov to examine their own nation's artistic tradition. Few of her early works in this folk genre have survived, but her *Madonna and Child*, painted

sometime between 1905 and 1907, shows her fascination with her Russian heritage. As **Camilla Gray** has noted, there are "two streams in Goncharova's work" at this time: "her vigorous and independent research in reviving national traditions, and her more timid and academic interpretations of the current European styles."

In 1910, Goncharova painted a series of works on the daily activities of Russian peasants. Here, icon painting, frescoes, and the popular prints of the 19th century guided her efforts. Her pictures were distinguished by brilliant colors and strong emotions. For Anthony Parton, she and Larionov were pioneers in "neo-primitivism," which he defines as an effort "to reinvigorate [Russian] painting by returning to the stylistic principles of native Russian art forms and the pictorial conventions of naive artists and peasant craftspeople."

Ever restless in seeking new inspiration, the young painter also drew heavily on early Cubist artists like Pablo Picasso for a time. This phase in her work, which began after 1910, lasted for several years and overlapped her painting inspired by the Russian tradition. Her illustrations for several books of poetry by Velimir Khlebnikov and Alexei Kruchenykh in 1912 and 1913 showed her devotion to old Russian art forms such as the icon, religious frescoes, and woodcuts. In 1913, she declared dramatically that she was turning away from the West. "It has dried up," she stated in her preface to the catalogue accompanying her exhibit at the Artistic Salon in Moscow, and now "my sympathies lie with the East." At the Salon, in October and November, she presented a remarkable collection of 800 paintings drawn from all phases of her career.

Despite her 1913 declaration rejecting the West, Goncharova drew heavily on Italian Futurism in works she produced just before World War I. Her futurist paintings included *Aeroplane over Train* and *Dynamo Machine*. Reveling in this rebellious Western art form and the conduct associated with it, she and Larionov appeared in public with painted faces. They also organized futurist evenings at a local cabaret, where they painted the faces of patrons and, finally, provoked a riot that led police to close the establishment. She and Larionov even produced and starred in a brief futurist film. Apart from riots, Goncharova found another way to cause a stir in conventional circles. An exhibition of her work in the spring of 1913 in Moscow and St. Petersburg featured pictures of Biblical characters painted in neo-primitive fashion. The government censor stepped in to close part of the ex-

Fragment from
The Fruit
Harvest, *by*
Natalia
Goncharova.

hibit after a newspaper critic called the paintings blasphemous.

In 1914, this eclectic artist made a definitive turn back to the Russian tradition. The stage impresario Sergei Diaghilev was impressed with Goncharova's Futurist paintings. Despite her recent, lurid record of hooliganism, he invited her to design sets for his ballet productions to be presented in Paris starting in the spring of 1914. The work she produced for him was permeated by Russian traditional art. As Parton has put it, from now on Goncharova and Larionov found that "their theatre design began to eclipse their painting" and their reputation outside Russia came to depend upon their work for the ballet stage.

With the start of World War I in 1914, the young artist, who had been in Paris for the premiere of her stage designs, returned to her native country. Larionov was called up for military service at once and wounded during one of the war's first battles. While her companion was recovering from his injuries, Goncharova entered a period of intense work. She did a series of 14 lithographs intended to promote Russian patriotism, *Mythical Images of War.* These combined national symbols with visions and images drawn from the Bible. She also illustrated a book of war poetry. Then, in a decisive step in her variegated career, she left Russia for the last time in 1915 to settle in the West. The impresario Diaghilev was struggling to form a new ballet company in the difficult circumstances of the war and pressed Larionov and Goncharova to help him.

Joining Diaghilev's ballet company as it performed in Switzerland, Goncharova went on to travel in Western Europe. In the spring of 1918, both she and Larionov exhibited a vast collection of their ballet stage designs in Paris. The two Russian emigrés found themselves directly endangered by the course of the war as the Germans began to bombard the city with long range artillery, and they were forced to flee to the countryside. They settled in the French capital at the close of the war. Russia was in the midst of civil war following the Bolshevik Revolution of November 1917, and most of their colleagues from the art world had also left. Their decision to stay in Paris for the time being led to their permanent residence there.

Goncharova spent the remainder of her life in Paris, accepted as an important member of the city's artistic community. She continued to paint, but her most notable work took place in the field of stage design. In this realm, both she and Larionov became international stars. With the death of Diaghilev in 1929, the two of them began to work for a number of ballet and stage companies. Her striking stage designs for *Czar Sultan* and *Fair at Sorochinsk,* both in 1932, reflected her continuing attraction to the themes and techniques of traditional Russian art. But Goncharova increasingly moved to identify her work with France. In 1936, she and Larionov participated in an important international competition in theatrical art held in Milan. They chose to exhibit their work in the French rather than the Soviet Union's section, and, when they

won the silver medal, the honor went to their adopted country.

The darkening international scene in 1938, which raised the possibility of war with Germany over Czechoslovakia, impelled the two Russian refugees to take up French nationality. They could not consider returning to the Soviet Union, now under the dictatorship of Joseph Stalin, and remaining resident aliens in France was equally undesirable. In September 1938, both Goncharova and her longtime companion became French citizens.

Following Adolf Hitler's invasion of France in the spring of 1940, Goncharova and Larionov found themselves under German occupation. During the following difficult years, the two managed to continue their careers in the theater. Then, an exhibition of their nonobjective paintings in Paris in 1948 reminded the public of their prominent role in the growth of modern art at the start of the century. As Parton notes, the two painters deliberately predated some of their work, sometimes by more than a decade, in order to heighten their reputation as path-breaking artists.

In 1950, Larionov suffered a stroke, and the couple's financial circumstances, never very comfortable, became even more precarious. They survived partly by selling off their early paintings. Goncharova also endured a variety of physical ailments, including a severe form of arthritis that made it impossible to paint on an easel. In a continuing display of her devotion to her work, she placed her canvas in a flat position in front of her so that she could continue to manipulate her brush.

Goncharova and Larionov were married in Paris on June 2, 1955, an event that took their circle of acquaintances by surprise. Though they had been intimate companions for more than half a century, the two had shared in the artistic conventions of the early 20th century, rejecting a formal relationship. They decided, however, that a legal ceremony was now appropriate in order to assure that the survivor of the pair could inherit the other's artistic works.

Natalia Goncharova produced her last effort in the field of theatrical design in 1957. This consisted of the costumes and sets for a series of ballets in Monte Carlo. In 1958, she put on a final exhibition of her painting in Paris, showing some 20 canvases inspired by the Russian launch of a space satellite, *Sputnik,* the preceding year. The couple remained beset by financial woes. Only selling a large portion of the couple's library and works to London's Victoria and Albert Museum in 1961 helped to keep them solvent.

Goncharova died of cancer in Paris on October 17, 1962. Her tombstone noted simply that she was an artist and painter. Larionov's death came shortly thereafter, in May 1964. He was buried beside her with an identical statement on his tombstone.

SOURCES:

Chamot, Mary. *Goncharova: Stage Designs and Paintings*. London: Oresko Books, 1979.

Gray, Camilla. *The Great Experiment: Russian Art, 1863–1922*. NY: Harry N. Abrams, 1962.

Harris, Anne Sutherland, and Linda Nochlin. *Women Artists: 1550–1950*. NY: Alfred A. Knopf, 1976.

Parton, Anthony. *Mikhail Larionov and the Russian Avant-Garde*. Princeton, NJ: Princeton University Press, 1993.

Yablonskaya, M.N. *Women Artists of Russia's New Age*. Edited by Anthony Parton. London: Thames and Hudson, 1990.

SUGGESTED READING:

Chadwick, Whitney. *Women, Art, and Society*. London: Thames and Hudson, 1990.

Slatkin, Wendy. *Women Artists in History: From Antiquity to the 20th Century*. Englewood Cliffs, NJ: Prentice-Hall, 1985.

Neil M. Heyman,
Professor of History, San Diego State University,
San Diego, California

Gondwana, Rani of (d. 1564).

See Durgawati.

Gonne, Maud (1866–1953)

Irish activist, journalist and feminist who devoted over 50 years to Irish political, cultural, and social causes. Name variations: Maud Gonne MacBride. Pronunciation: Mawd Gone MAK-bride. Born Maud Gonne on December 21, 1866, near Aldershot, Surrey, England; died at her home Roebuck House in Dublin, Ireland, on April 27, 1953; eldest daughter of Thomas Gonne and Edith (Cook) Gonne; educated at home; married John MacBride, on February 21, 1903; children (with Lucien Millevoye) Georges (1890–1891) and Iseult Gonne Stuart (b. 1894); (with John MacBride) Sean MacBride (b. 1904).

Became involved in Irish nationalist cause (1880s); met with W.B. Yeats (1889); founded L'Irlande Libre, Paris (1897); co-founded Irish Transvaal Committee (1899); founded and served as president of Inghinidhe na hÉireann (Daughters of Ireland, 1900); co-founded Women's Prisoners' Defence League (1922). Publications: Dawn (1904, reprinted, Proscenium Press, 1970); A Servant of the Queen (Gollancz, 1938); Yeats and Ireland (Macmillan, 1940).

Maud Gonne's long public career has been overshadowed by her role as the muse of William Butler Yeats, who immortalized her in his poetry. The process began, to her annoyance, while she was still alive. More than a poetic allusion, Gonne devoted over 50 years of her life to Irish political, cultural, and social causes.

She was born on December 21, 1866, near Aldershot, Surrey, England, into a privileged background. Her mother **Edith Cook Gonne** came from a wealthy family, and her father Thomas Gonne was an officer in the British army. He was an excellent linguist and took a keen interest in the arts, especially music and the theater. The family had no connections with Ireland until the year after Maud's birth, when her father's regiment was sent there. In 1868, her sister **Kathleen Gonne** was born. Edith Gonne died of tuberculosis in 1871, but her husband was determined to rear their daughters himself. He was an unusual father for his time; he was affectionate and easy-going, and his daughters, especially Maud, adored him. Thomas Gonne was one of the greatest influences in her life.

In the 1870s, while Thomas was serving as a British military attache in Eastern Europe, India and Russia, his daughters stayed with their mother's relatives in London and then spent several years in Europe. The family returned to Ireland in 1882 when Thomas was given a senior position in the army. Maud Gonne was presented at the viceregal court in Dublin the following year, and, with her striking height (she was nearly six feet tall) and red-gold hair, her beauty made an immediate impression. She had a busy social life and acted as her father's hostess. But the 1880s also witnessed the Land War in Ireland, a concerted campaign by tenants to reform the system of land tenure. This led to conflict with the landlords, and there were many evictions. It was the sight of these evictions which first interested Maud Gonne in Irish nationalism.

Her life changed with the sudden death of her father in November 1886. She and her sister went to live in London with a guardian, their father's brother William, but they were at odds. William was dismayed when Maud attended demonstrations in Trafalgar Square and horrified when she gave help to her father's mistress, ❧▶ **Margaret Wilson**, who arrived at their door with the news that she had given birth to a daughter Eileen six weeks previous and was now penniless. (Maud's illegitimate half-sister ❧▶ **Eileen Wilson** would later live with Maud for a time.) When William told Maud that her father had left little money, her immediate response was to look

Margaret and **Eileen Wilson** appear in Gonne's memoirs as Eleanor and Daphne Robbins; the name Robbins was also used in Samuel Levenson's 1976 biography, *Maud Gonne*.

for a job as an actress. Gonne performed with a small theatrical company but had to give it up when she fell ill with a lung hemorrhage. She then discovered that her uncle had made up the story about her poverty as a means of exerting control over her.

To recover her health, she journeyed to Royat in France, and it was there she met Lucien Millevoye who was her lover, off and on, for the next 13 years. Millevoye was separated from his wife, but the fact that he could not marry her was of little concern to Maud who was always wary of marriage. A prominent journalist and politician, Millevoye was closely associated with General Georges Boulanger's National Party which was conservative and nationalist in ethos and also had a marked vein of anti-Semitism. In her memoirs *A Servant of the Queen*, Gonne did not reveal her physical relationship with Millevoye and described it instead as an "alliance" against the British Empire. However, her relationship with him, the most important of her life, blinded her to the contradictions between his conservative nationalism and her revolutionary nationalism, although the implications of this were not apparent for some years. For the next 13 years, she divided her time between Ireland, France, and England.

I had made it a rule of life never to ask any man to do a thing I was not ready to do myself or take a risk I was not ready to share.

—**Maud Gonne**

In spring 1888, Gonne went to St. Petersburg on a mission for Millevoye and the Boulangists, carrying a secret document asking for Russian assistance to overthrow the French Third Republic and bring Boulanger to power. On her return, she visited London and met Michael Davitt, the radical Irish member of Parliament, who was skeptical of her wish to work for Ireland, suspecting that she was an agent provocateur. She was more successful in Dublin where she met John O'Leary, a prominent member of the Irish Republican Brotherhood, the painter J.B. Yeats (father of W.B. Yeats), and Arthur Griffith, who was to found Sinn Fein in 1905. Gonne's apartment in Nassau Street became a meeting place for nationalist politicians, writers, and academics. She was invited to do publicity work about evictions in Donegal and helped to organize accommodation for evicted tenants. She also became involved in the campaign for the amnesty of Irish political prisoners and visited some of them in Portland Prison in England.

Gonne met W.B. Yeats in January 1889 when she called to see his father in London. Yeats fell deeply in love with her and so began a long and what he called "perplexed wooing." She had affection for Yeats but regarded him as a friend, never appreciating the misery he suffered in loving her. She did not tell him about her relationship with Millevoye, and it took him years to realize that they were seeking different things. Gonne's "alliance" with Millevoye was also running into trouble. He followed her to Donegal in 1889 where she was again helping evicted tenants and told her she was wasting her time on a group of peasants. She refused to go back to France with him but had no choice when a warrant was issued for her arrest.

In January 1890, she gave birth to their son Georges, and the following summer Yeats proposed to her but was rejected. She was in Ireland in summer 1891 when she was summoned back to Paris where her son was ill with meningitis. His death on August 31 caused her great grief and guilt as she had been away for much of his brief life. She considered leaving Millevoye but decided against this when Boulanger committed suicide just a month after their son's death. Gonne returned to Ireland and became interested in reincarnation, a belief which later attracted her to Buddhism. She had psychic faculties and experimented with marijuana for out-of-body experiences. In her memoirs, Gonne referred to the presence in her dreams of a dark, beautiful woman whom she called the "Grey Lady." Yeats interested her in theosophy and initiated her into an occult society, the Order of the Golden Dawn, which she later left because it smacked too much of freemasonry. She served on the National Literary Society's library committee, of which Yeats was secretary, but they disagreed over literary criteria, a recurring argument between them.

On her return to France in 1892, Gonne persuaded Millevoye, who was still depressed by Boulanger's death, to take up the editorship of *La Patrie*, a move which restored his political fortunes. Although much of the physical feeling had gone from their relationship, Gonne was anxious to have another child, and their daughter Iseult was born in August 1894. Gonne resumed her lecturing and writing career and in 1897 started her own journal *L'Irlande Libre*. She and Yeats dreamed of creating a mystical order for Irish men and women, "the Castle of Heroes." They also worked together on the centennial of Wolfe Tone, the Irish republican leader and thinker who died in 1798, and in Oc-

Maud
Gonne

tober 1897 she spent three months in America raising money for a Wolfe Tone memorial. The tour was a financial success, but she experienced problems with some of the Irish-American leaders. On her return, she became involved in land agitation in the west of Ireland, but the pressures of her life soon caused strain. Her relationship with Millevoye was failing, and in November 1898 she finally told Yeats about him and Iseult. He was stunned, but when she told him of her distaste for physical love they embarked on a "mystical" marriage which lasted until 1903 and which was resumed in 1908.

When the Boer War broke out in 1899, Maud Gonne, with Yeats, Arthur Griffith, James Connolly, and others helped to organize the pro-Boer Irish Transvaal Committee and addressed antiwar meetings in Ireland and Britain. The war also temporarily patched up her relationship with Millevoye, and they organized pro-Boer meetings in France. On her trips to Paris, she organized passports for Irish militants who wanted to fight in South Africa. The peak of her antiwar activities came in April 1900 when Queen *Victoria visited Ireland to rally Irish opinion behind the British war effort. Gonne's article "The Famine Queen," attacking Victoria's neglect of Ireland, caused a sensation and led to copies of the newspaper, Griffith's *United Irishman*, being seized. Pro-British newspapers called for her arrest. To counter a children's treat arranged to celebrate the royal visit, she organized a "Patriotic Children's Treat."

For some years, Gonne had expressed annoyance at the exclusion of Irish women from so many of the political and cultural movements which had sprung up in Ireland since the 1890s. To remedy this she, *Jennie Wyse Power, Annie Egan, *Alice Milligan, *Anna Johnston (Mac-Manus) and others set up Inghinidhe na hÉireann (Daughters of Ireland) in October 1900. Its aims were (1) to reestablish the complete independence of Ireland; (2) to encourage the study of Irish literature, history, and the arts; and (3) to discourage the circulation of English culture in Ireland. The women pledged themselves to mutual help and support and to protect themselves from possible victimization in employment. Drama proved to be one of the most successful activities of the Inghinidhe. They performed tableaux vivants, and the actors included such later luminaries as *Sarah Allgood, *Maire O'Neill, Maire Quinn and *Maire nic Shiubhlaigh. They scored one of their greatest triumphs in *Cathleen Ni Houlihan* (claimed by Yeats although written by Lady *Augusta Gregory) in

which Gonne played the title role (a metaphor for Ireland). Maire nic Shiubhlaigh, who later performed the part, wrote that by watching Gonne it was easy to understand how she had become the inspiration for the Irish revolutionary movement: "Her beauty was *startling*. In her the youth of the country saw all that was magnificent in Ireland." Yeats referred to her "weird power." In 1902, Gonne joined the board of the Irish National Theatre and, as before, argued with Yeats that art should serve propaganda, and should not be art for art's sake. She deprecated Augusta Gregory's influence on Yeats which she thought weakened his interest in the national struggle and finally resigned from the board over Synge's *In the Shadow of the Glen* of which she disapproved because of its portrayal of a loveless Irish marriage.

John MacBride was one of the leaders of the pro-Boer Irish Brigade fighting in South Africa. He first met Maud Gonne in Paris in 1900, and in 1901 she joined him in America where he was on a lecture tour. Her relationship with Millevoye had ended not only because of political differences but also because of his affair with a singer. The English liberal journalist H.W. Nevinson had predicted that Gonne's longing for action would impel her towards a certain kind of marriage: "The first man of resolute action whom she meets will have her at his mercy." She had told Yeats that poets should never marry and that the world would thank her for not marrying him. MacBride was a man of action, but he depended on Gonne for support in a way that Yeats never did. Despite warnings from friends and relations about their mutual incompatibility, Gonne recognized the risks involved in the marriage but wanted stability for herself and Iseult. She converted to Catholicism, although with her eclectic beliefs in mysticism and reincarnation was hardly an orthodox Catholic. She and MacBride were married in February 1903. Their son Sean MacBride was born in January 1904, but by the summer of 1904 the marriage was over. John MacBride was insecure and jealous, and this aggravated his drinking problem. Iseult disliked MacBride, but the final break came when he allegedly assaulted Maud's half-sister Eileen, who was living with them. In February 1905, Gonne filed for a French divorce, citing MacBride's drinking and adultery.

Because of legal difficulties over custody of Sean and MacBride's domicile, the divorce did not go through, but it caused a considerable scandal in Ireland, Britain, France and the U.S. where it was extensively reported and did Gonne much harm. Friends in Dublin took sides, and, when she returned to Dublin in 1906 and accompanied Yeats to the Abbey Theatre, she was hissed. Gonne's visits to Ireland over the next ten years were sporadic because of the reaction to her separation and the fear that MacBride might claim their son. She became close to Yeats again, and it is probable that they finally became lovers in 1908–09, although the relationship was over by the end of 1909.

Despite living in France, Gonne remained president of Inghinidhe na hÉireann and wrote regularly for its journal *Bean na hÉireann* (Irish Woman). She was particularly interested in the provision of school meals for poor children in Dublin which had some of the worst slums in Europe and the highest infant mortality rate in the United Kingdom. The labor leader James Connolly, her friend and colleague from the Boer War, secured trade-union support, and, with the help of *Constance Markievicz, *Helena Molony, *Hanna Sheehy-Skeffington, and **Muriel** and **Grace Gifford**, the first meals were provided in 1910 and the scheme was gradually extended. However, Gonne was regarded with more suspicion in the suffrage movement and was not invited to take part in their meetings; the separation from MacBride still cast long shadows.

When the First World War broke out, Gonne worked as a Red Cross nurse near the Pyrenees. She was appalled by the carnage and told Yeats in November 1914 of her "wild hatred" of the war machine. Her feelings about the war intensified after the death of her sister's son. Gonne returned to Paris in January 1915 and continued to work in hospitals there. The news of the 1916 Easter rebellion in Dublin and the subsequent execution of John MacBride for his part in it came as a shock, but she was moved by reports of his bravery, especially for their son's sake: "He has died for Ireland and his son will bear an honoured name. I remember nothing else." She was also much concerned for the Inghinidhe members who had been arrested after the rebellion, among them Helena Molony, *Kathleen Lynn, the Gifford sisters, and Maire nic Shiubhlaigh, but when she arrived in London she was refused a passport to go to Ireland.

After MacBride's death, Yeats renewed his proposal, but she refused. He was increasingly attracted to 23-year-old Iseult as well, but Iseult also rejected Yeats when he proposed to her in August 1917. Two months later, he married **Georgie Hyde-Lees**. In February 1918, Gonne finally reached Ireland in defiance of the passport ban and rented a house in Dublin. There was criticism of her for wearing widow's weeds, considering the state of her marriage to MacBride, and there was also skepticism that Iseult was, as she claimed, her adopted niece. But she was active in the anti-conscription campaign and was arrested in May 1918 and sent to Holloway prison in London where she shared a cell with Constance Markievicz and *Kathleen Clarke. All three were in poor health, and it was while she was in prison that she learned of the deaths of Millevoye and her sister Kathleen. Gonne was released in November on health grounds and was joined at her house in Dublin by *Charlotte Despard who became a close friend and colleague.

During the Irish war of independence (1919–21), Gonne worked as a judge for the new Irish republican courts. She also did publicity work and served on the American Committee for Relief in Ireland. To her dismay, her son Sean had joined the Irish Republican Army (IRA), and in 1920 Iseult married Francis Stuart who was eight years her junior. When the treaty which ended the war of independence and set up the Irish Free State was signed in December 1921, it caused dissension between Gonne and her son Sean who considered it a betrayal of republican ideals. Gonne thought that the treaty, though imperfect, was a basis for progress. However, when civil war broke out in June 1922, she was horrified. Sean was arrested and narrowly escaped execution while Francis Stuart was interned. Gonne nursed wounded republicans at her house and at the end of 1922, with Charlotte Despard, founded the Women's Prisoners Defence League. The League protested at the treatment meted out to republican prisoners and their families, and its members demonstrated, visited jails, and sought legal aid. Her house was watched constantly by the police, and she and Despard decided to move to a suburb of Dublin, Clonskeagh. In January and April 1923, Maud Gonne was arrested but was released, on the second occasion after 20 days when she went on a hunger strike. In November 1923, during a raid by government forces, many precious papers, including correspondence from Yeats, were burned.

With the gradual release of republican prisoners, Gonne's Roebuck House became a refuge for many of them. To help them secure employment, the outbuildings were turned into small shops for piece work. Gonne also canvassed for the republicans in various elections in the 1920s. In 1926, she and Hanna Sheehy-Skeffington became embroiled in the public debate over Sean O'Casey's *The Plough and the Stars*. Although he disagreed with her, O'Casey respected Sheehy-Skeffington but he was scathing about Maud Gonne in his autobiography: "a sibyl of patriotism from whom no oracle ever came . . . the colonel's daughter still."

Throughout the 1920s and 1930s, Gonne continued to work for the republican cause, especially republican prisoners. When the movement split in 1926, she was skeptical of the new party founded by Eamon de Valera, Fianna Fáil, which came to power in 1932. Her son Sean remained close to the IRA but left in 1937 when the organization was riven by splits. He became a distinguished lawyer and defended republican prisoners in the 1930s and 1940s. He and his family lived at Roebuck House and his wife, **Catalina Bulfin**, was close to Maud. Gonne had not spoken to Yeats for many years because of his decision to accept a seat in the Free State senate. She also deeply disapproved of his support for the quasi-fascist Blueshirt movement, but they met again in the 1930s.

Maud Gonne started writing her memoirs in 1936 and received encouragement from *Dorothy Macardle who put her in touch with the publisher Victor Gollancz. *A Servant of the Queen* was published in 1938 but needs to be treated with some caution. Gonne was over 70; many of the people she was writing about were dead; and she was seriously handicapped by the destruction of her papers during the civil war which meant that a lot of the chronology and details were vague. There were other pressures. Sean did not want her to discuss the more scandalous parts of her private life, including her relationship with Millevoye and her children with him. She was forced to refer to Iseult as "the charming child I had adopted." Only 1,500 copies were sold of the book; the rest were burned in the London Blitz. However, it was reprinted in 1950, 1974, and 1994. Gonne started work on a sequel, *The Tower of Age,* but did not complete it. As with *Servant,* there was much that she could not write about.

Yeats had generously told her to quote what she wanted from his poems for the book, and they met for the last time in August 1938. After his death in January 1939, she wrote a tribute to him in *Scattering the Branches: Tributes to the Memory of W.B. Yeats* (1940). During World War II, she opposed de Valera's crackdown on the IRA and worked for IRA prisoners interned by the government. After the war, she supported her son's new political party, Clann na Poblachta (Followers of the Republic), which took part in the coalition government which won power in 1948. Sean was appointed minister for external affairs. In her last years, Maud Gonne did recordings for Radio Éireann for the 50th anniversary of Inghinidhe na hÉireann and other reminiscences. She died at Roebuck House on April 27, 1953.

SOURCES:
MacBride, Maud Gonne. *A Servant of the Queen: Reminiscences.* London: Victor Gollancz, 1938 (new edition, Gerrard's Cross: Colin Smythe, 1994).
———. "Yeats and Ireland," in *Scattering the Branches: Tributes to the Memory of W.B. Yeats.* Edited by Stephen Gwynn. London: Macmillan, 1940.
White, Anna MacBride, and A. Norman Jeffares. *The Gonne-Yeats Letters, 1893–1938.* London: Hutchinson, 1992.

SUGGESTED READING:
Balliett, Conrad A. "The Lives—and Lies—of Maud Gonne," in *Éire/Ireland.* Vol 14, no. 3, 1979.
Cardozo, Nancy. *Maud Gonne: Lucky Eyes and a High Heart.* London: Gollancz, 1979.
Levenson, Samuel. *Maud Gonne.* London: Cassell, 1976.
Ward, Margaret. *Maud Gonne: A Life.* London: Pandora, 1990.

Deirdre McMahon,
lecturer in History at Mary Immaculate College,
University of Limerick, Limerick, Ireland

Gonwatsijayenni (c. 1736–1796).

See Brant, Molly.

Gonzaga, Agnes (c. 1365–1391).

See Visconti, Agnes.

Gonzaga, Alda (1333–1381).

See Este, Alda d'.

Gonzaga, Anna (1585–1618)

Holy Roman empress. Name variations: Anna of Tyrol. Born on October 4, 1585, in Innsbruck; died on December 14 or 15, 1618, in Vienna; daughter of *Anna Caterina Gonzaga (1566–1621) and Ferdinand II, archduke of Austria; married Matthias (1557–1619), Holy Roman emperor (r. 1612–1619).

Gonzaga, Anna Caterina (1566–1621)

Archduchess of Austria. Name variations: Anna Katharina of Gonzaga-Mantua. Born on January 17, 1566, in Mantua; died on August 3, 1621, in Innsbruck; daughter of *Eleonora of Austria (1534–1594) and Guglielmo Gonzaga (1538–1587), 3rd duke of Mantua (r. 1550–1587), duke of Monferrato; was second wife of Ferdinand II, archduke of Austria; children: **Maria** (1584–1649); *Anna Gonzaga (1585–1618, who married Holy Roman Emperor Matthias). Ferdinand II's first wife was **Philippine Welser**.

Gonzaga, Anne de (1616–1684)

*Countess Palatine. Name variations: Anne Gonzaga; Anne Simmern; princess Palatine. Born in Mantua (Mantova) in 1616 (some sources cite 1624); died in Paris, France, on July 6, 1684; daughter of Charles II Gonzaga, duke of Nevers (r. 1601–1637) and *Catherine of Lorraine (daughter of Charles, duke of Maine); married Edward Simmern (1624–1663), duke of Bavaria and count Palatine of the Rhine (son of Frederick V of Bohemia and *Elizabeth of Bohemia), on April 24 or May 4, 1645; children: Louise-Maria (1646–1679, who married Karl Theodor Otto of Salms); Anne Henriette Louise (1647–1723, who married Henry Julius, prince of Conde); Benedicte Henriette Philippine (1652–1730, who married John Frederick, duke of Brunswick-Luneburg).*

Gonzaga, Antonia (d. 1538)

Noblewoman of Mantua. Name variations: Antonia de Balzo. Died in 1538; married Gianfrancesco Gonzaga (1446–1496), lord of Rodigo; children: Louis also known as Ludovico (d. 1540); Pirro (d. 1529), lord of Bozzolo and S. Martino dall'Argine.

Gonzaga, Barbara (1422–1481).

See Barbara of Brandenburg.

Gonzaga, Barbara (1455–1505)

*Duchess of Wurttemberg. Born in 1455; died in 1505; daughter of *Barbara of Brandenburg (1422–1481) and Louis also known as Ludovico Gonzaga (1412–1478), 2nd marquis of Mantua (r. 1444–1478); married Eberhard, duke of Wurttemberg.*

Gonzaga, Caterina (d. 1501).

See Pico, Caterina.

Gonzaga, Caterina (1593–1629).

See Medici, Caterina de.

Gonzaga, Catherine (1533–1572).

See Catherine of Habsburg.

Gonzaga, Cecilia (1426–1451)

*Noblewoman of Mantua. Born in 1426; died in 1451; daughter of *Paola Gonzaga (1393–1453) and Gianfrancesco Gonzaga (1395–1444), 5th captain general of Mantua (r. 1407–1433), 1st marquis of Mantua (r. 1433–1444).*

Gonzaga, Cecilia (1451–1472)

*Noblewoman of Mantua. Born in 1451; died in 1472; daughter of *Barbara of Brandenburg (1422–1481) and Louis also known as Ludovico Gonzaga (1412–1478), 2nd marquis of Mantua (r. 1444–1478).*

Gonzaga, Chiara (1465–1505)

*Noblewoman of Mantua. Born in 1465; died in 1505 (some sources cite 1503); daughter of *Margaret of Bavaria (1445–1479) and Frederigo also known as Federico Gonzaga (1441–1484), 3rd marquis of Mantua (r. 1478–1484); sister of *Elisabetta Montefeltro (1471–1526) and *Maddalena Sforza (1472–1490); married Gilbert de Bourbon-Montpensier; children: Charles de Bourbon, the Constable, who was killed at the sack of Rome in 1527.*

Gonzaga, Chiquinha (1847–1935)

Brazilian composer. Born Francisca Hedwiges Neves Gonzaga in Rio de Janeiro, Brazil, on October 17, 1847; died in Rio de Janeiro on February 28, 1935; one of Brazil's most popular and prolific composers, Gonzaga wrote over 2,000 works; active in the anti-slave movement.

Few composers, male or female, have written over 2,000 pieces. Chiquinha Gonzaga not only created that many works but she was also one of Brazil's most popular composers. She studied piano under E. Alvares Lobo and Artur Napoleao before writing her first piece of music at age 11. In 1885, she was the first woman in her country to conduct a theater orchestra. From 1885 to 1933, Gonzaga wrote the scores for 77 plays. *Forrobodó* was her most popular and had over 1,500 performances, although *Maria*, a classical work, was considered her best achievement. An opponent of slavery, Gonzaga devoted much effort to the Brazilian abolitionist movement. She used the money from the sale of one of her scores to buy the freedom of José Flauta, a slave musician. From 1902 to 1910, she traveled in Europe and set several Portuguese plays to music. Gonzaga was a founding member of the Sociedade Brasileira de Autores Teatrais and contributed a great deal to the musical life of her country.

John Haag,
Athens, Georgia

Gonzaga, Dorotea (1449–1462)

*Noblewoman of Mantua. Name variations: Dorotea Sforza. Born in 1449; died in 1462 (some sources cite 1469); daughter of *Barbara of Brandenburg*

(1422–1481) and Louis also known as Ludovico Gonzaga (1412–1478), 2nd marquis of Mantua (r. 1444–1478); first wife of Galeazzo Maria Sforza (1444–1476), 5th duke of Milan. Galeazzo's second wife was *Bona of Savoy (c. 1450–c. 1505).

Gonzaga, Eleonora (1493–1543)

Duchess of Urbino. Name variations: Leonora Gonzaga; Eleanora Gonzaga della Rovere; Eleonora della Rovere. Born in December 1493 in Mantua, Italy; died in 1543 in Gubbio, Italy; daughter of Isabella d'Este (1474–1539) and Francesco also known as Gian Francesco Gonzaga (1466–1519), 4th marquis of Mantua (r. 1484–1519); niece of *Elisabetta Montefeltro; married Francesco Maria della Rovere (a nephew of Pope Julius II), duke of Urbino (r. 1508–1538), in March 1509; children: Federico (b. 1511); Guidobaldo (b. 1514), duke of Urbino; Ippolita (c. 1516); Guilia; Elisabetta; Guilio (b. 1535), later Cardinal of San Pietro.

The Italian noblewoman Eleonora Gonzaga was the first child of Marquess Francesco Gonzaga of Mantua and *Isabella d'Este of the ruling house of Ferrara. As was common in a large aristocratic household, Eleonora had little contact with either of her parents during her childhood but spent her time with her many siblings, nurses, and tutors. She received an education typical of Renaissance girls of nobility—reading and writing, some Latin, music, and needlework. These were thought necessary to make her into a suitable wife for the noble with whom her parents contracted a marriage agreement. In Eleonora's case, her parents arranged in 1505 an alliance with the papacy under Pope Julius II, which included the marriage of their eldest daughter to the pope's nephew, along with an impressive dowry of 30,000 ducats. The betrothed was Francesco Maria della Rovere, the young heir to the duchy of Urbino. The wedding was finally celebrated at the Vatican four years later, in March 1509, when Eleonora was just 15 and her new husband 16. By this time, Francesco had succeeded his uncle Guidobaldo as duke of Urbino.

The new duchess left her parents' palaces of Mantua for Urbino, where the dowager duchess, *Elisabetta Montefeltro, still reigned over the court in practice, if not in name. Often such a situation led to rivalry and jealousies between a widowed noblewoman and her younger replacement. But happily for Eleonora, the older woman became a mother figure to her. The two duchesses formed a close and loving bond, much closer than Eleonora's relationship with her own mother would ever be. Most sources agree that Isabella d'Este was distant and rather cold towards Eleonora, communicating with her rarely, although the reason for this is not clear.

Duchess Eleonora had six children with Francesco between 1514 and 1535, three daughters and three sons. Her husband, who was a captain in the papal armies and held other military positions as well, was absent from Urbino much of the time, and thus Eleonora and Elisabetta administered the duchy for many of the years of Francesco's reign. Eleonora suffered most of her married years from ill health, which doctors attributed to epilepsy, gonorrhea (which Francesco suffered from), and from depression linked to her illness. Her poor health is also linked to her numerous miscarriages and stillborn births.

In 1515, the fortunes of Urbino's ruling family changed suddenly. Francesco was nominally allied with the new pope, Leo X, but when Leo ordered Francesco to lead an army in the pope's invasion of France, Francesco unwisely refused. He also dismissed the army organized and paid for by the pope. Leo summoned him to Rome to answer for his refusal, but Francesco fled to the protection of his wife's family in Mantua instead. He was accompanied in his flight by Eleonora, their son Guidobaldo, and the dowager duchess Elisabetta. In response, Pope Leo, who had wanted to get the prosperous duchy of Urbino for his nephew anyway, used Francesco's flight as a pretext for sending an army to take over the duchy. He excommunicated Francesco and stripped him of his titles. Eleonora appealed to her parents to intercede with Leo, but their efforts were in vain. Eleonora and Francesco became rulers in exile; while Eleonora and her son remained in Mantua, Francesco sought to win back his duchy by force. Only in 1521 was he successful, but not through his own efforts. In that year Leo died and the new pope, Hadrian VI, had no argument with Francesco and so restored his rights to Urbino. In the spring of 1523, the duke and duchess returned to their elegant palace. By the agreement restoring the duchy, however, the couple had to leave their son Guidobaldo in Mantua as a sort of guarantee of Francesco's loyalty to the papacy.

Francesco did not stay in Urbino for long. Ever the soldier, he continued to lead armies on one campaign after another, returning to Urbino infrequently. Eleonora (as always, with Elisabetta) returned to her previous obligations of administration, and also undertook the massive rebuilding of Urbino and surrounding towns needed after the destructive wars recently fought there. She also supervised the building of the palatial Villa Imperiale in Pesaro. A Latin inscription on the palace dedicates it to Francesco from Eleonora "as a mark of her love for him." She and Francesco also were liberal patrons of major artists, including Titian, and encouraged the founding of Urbino's majolica industry (decorative enameled pottery). They also continued Elisabetta's patronage of Baldassare Castiglione, author of the influential *Book of the Courtier* (1528), which includes descriptions of the beautiful, intelligent, and gracious duchess, and the elegance and learning celebrated in the court of Urbino under Francesco and Eleonora.

Eleonora was widowed in 1538 when Francesco died suddenly while on campaign, possibly from poison. Her only surviving son Guidobaldo inherited the duchy. *La Bella,* a portrait of her by Titian painted about this time, shows a regal but pale and sickly middle-aged woman. Indeed, her health began to fail rapidly after Francesco's death. The dowager duchess died at age 49 in 1543.

Eleonora
Gonzaga
(1493–1543)

SOURCES:
Dennistoun, James. *Memoirs of the Dukes of Urbino, 1440–1630.* Vol. I. NY: John Lane, 1909.
Olsen, Harald. *Urbino.* Copenhagen: Forlag, 1971.
Simon, Kate. *A Renaissance Tapestry: The Gonzaga of Mantua.* NY: Harper and Row, 1988.

Laura York,
Riverside, California

Gonzaga, Eleonora (1534–1594).

See Eleonora of Austria.

Gonzaga, Eleonora (1567–1611).

See Medici, Eleonora de.

Gonzaga, Eleonora I (1598–1655)

Holy Roman empress and queen of Bohemia. Name variations: Eleanor of Gonzaga; Eleanora I Gonzaga; Eleanore de Mantoue Gonzaque. Born on September 23, 1598, in Mantua; died on June 27, 1655, in Vienna; daughter of Eleonora de Medici (1567–1611) and Vincenzo I (1562–1612), 4th duke of Mantua; sister of *Margherita Gonzaga, duchess of Lorraine (1591–1632); became second wife of Ferdinand II, king of Bohemia and Hungary (r. 1578–1637), Holy Roman emperor (r. 1619–1637), on February 4, 1622.

Eleonora I Gonzaga was born in 1598 in Mantua, daughter of *Eleonora de Medici and Vincenzo I, 4th duke of Mantua. She married Ferdinand II, king of Bohemia and Hungary, on February 4, 1622. Ferdinand's first wife was *Maria Anna of Bavaria (1574–1616). Eleonora I's portrait was painted by *Lucrina Fetti.

Gonzaga, Eleonora II (1628–1686)

Holy Roman empress and queen of Bohemia. Name variations: Eleanor or Eleanora; Eleanora Gonzaga; Eleanor of Gonzaga; Eleonor or Eleonore; Eleonore of Mantua. Born on November 18, 1628 (some sources cite 1630), in Mantua; died on December 6, 1686, in Vienna; daughter of Carlo, count of Rethel (1600–1631) and Maria Gonzaga (1609–1660); third wife of Ferdinand III (1608–1657), king of Bohemia (r. 1627–1646), king of Hungary (r. 1625), Holy Roman emperor (r. 1637–1657); children: Eleanor Habsburg (1653–1697).

Eleonora II Gonzaga was born in 1628 in Mantua, the daughter of Carlo, count of Rethel, and *Maria Gonzaga. Eleonora was the third wife of Ferdinand III, king of Bohemia, Hungary, and Holy Roman emperor. Ferdinand's second wife was *Maria Leopoldine (1632–1649); his first was *Maria Anna of Spain

(1606–1646), daughter of Philip III of Spain, and the mother of three of his children. Thus, Eleonora's stepchildren were Leopold I, Holy Roman emperor, as well as Ferdinand IV, king of Bohemia and Holy Roman emperor, and *Maria Anna of Austria (1634–1696). Eleonora II Gonzaga's portrait was painted by *Lucrina Fetti.

Gonzaga, Elisabetta (1471–1526).

See Montefeltro, Elisabetta.

Gonzaga, Henriette (r. 1564–1601).

See Henrietta of Cleves.

Gonzaga, Ippolita (1503–1570)

Dominican nun. Born in 1503; died in 1570; daughter of *Isabella d'Este (1474–1539) and Francesco also known as Gianfrancesco Gonzaga (1466–1519), 4th marquis of Mantua (r. 1484–1519); never married.

Gonzaga, Ippolita (1535–1563)

Noblewoman of Mantua. Born in 1535; died in 1563; daughter of *Isabella Gonzaga (d. 1559) and Ferrante Gonzaga (1507–1557), prince of Guastalla.

Gonzaga, Isabella (1474–1539).

See joint entry on Este, Beatrice d' and Isabella d'.

Gonzaga, Isabella (d. 1559)

Princess of Guastalla. Name variations: Isabella of Capua; Isabella da Capua. Died in 1559; married Ferrante Gonzaga (1507–1557, son of *Isabella d'Este [1474–1539]), prince of Guastalla; children: Cesare (1533–1575), prince of Guastalla; *Ippolita Gonzaga (1535–1563); Francesco (1538–1566); Giovanni Vincenzo (1540–1591).

Gonzaga, Isabella (1537–1579)

Noblewoman of Mantua. Born in 1537; died in 1579; daughter of *Margherita Gonzaga (1510–1566) and Federigo also known as Federico Gonzaga (1500–1540), 5th marquis of Mantua (r. 1519–1540), 1st duke of Mantua (r. 1530–1540).

Gonzaga, Isabella (fl. 1600s)

Duchess of Mantua. Name variations: Isabella Gonzaga de Novellara. Flourished in the 1600s; married Vincenzo II (1594–1627), 7th duke of Mantua (r. 1626–1627).

Gonzaga, Leonora (1493–1543).
See Gonzaga, Eleonora.

Gonzaga, Lucia (1419–1437).
See Este, Lucia d'.

Gonzaga, Maddalena (1472–1490).
See Sforza, Maddalena.

Gonzaga, Margaret (fl. 1609–1612).
See Margaret of Savoy.

Gonzaga, Margherita (d. 1399)

Noblewoman of Mantua. Name variations: Margherita Malatesta. Born Margherita Malatesta; died in 1399; married Francesco Gonzaga (1366–1407), 4th captain general of Mantua (r. 1382–1407); children: Gianfrancesco Gonzaga (1395–1444), 5th captain general of Mantua (r. 1407–1433), 1st marquis of Mantua (r. 1433–1444).

Gonzaga, Margherita
(1418–1439)

*Marquesa of Ferrara. Name variations: Margherita d'Este. Born in 1418; died in 1439; daughter of *Paola Gonzaga (1393–1453) and Gianfrancesco Gonzaga (1395–1444), 5th captain general of Mantua (r. 1407–1433), 1st marquis of Mantua (r. 1433–1444); married Leonello d'Este (1407–1450), 13th marquis of Ferrara; children: Niccolo d'Este (1438–1476). Leonello's second wife was *Maria of Aragon, marquesa of Ferrara.*

Gonzaga, Margherita (1445–1479).
See Margaret of Bavaria.

Gonzaga, Margherita
(1510–1566)

*Duchess of Mantua. Name variations: Margherita Paleologo of Monferrato or Montferrat; Margaret of Monferrato or Montferrat. Born in 1510; died in 1566; daughter of Guglielmo Paleologo of Montferrat; married Federigo also known as Federico Gonzaga (1500–1540), 5th marquis of Mantua (r. 1519–1540), 1st duke of Mantua (r. 1530–1540); children: Francesco (1533–1550), 2nd duke of Mantua (r. 1540–1550); *Isabella Gonzaga (1537–1579); Guglielmo (1538–1587), 3rd duke of Mantua (r. 1550–1587), duke of Monferrato; Louis also known as Ludovico (1539–1585), duke of Nevers, count of Rethel; Federigo also known as Federico (1540–1565, a cardinal).*

Gonzaga, Margherita (1561–1628)

Duchess of Sabbioneta. Born in 1561; died in 1628; daughter of Cesare Gonzaga (1533–1575), prince of Guastalla, and Camilla Borromeo; second wife of Vespasiano (1531–1591), duke of Sabbioneta. Vespasiano's first wife was Anna of Aragon (d. 1567).

Gonzaga, Margherita (1564–1618)

*Duchess of Ferrara. Name variations: Margherita d'Este. Born in 1564; died in 1618; daughter of *Eleonora of Austria (1534–1594) and Guglielmo Gonzaga (1538–1587), 3rd duke of Mantua (r. 1550–1587), duke of Monferrato; married Alfonso II d'Este (1533–1597), 5th duke of Ferrara and Modena (r. 1559–1597). Alfonso II's first wife was *Lucrezia de Medici (c. 1544–1561).*

Gonzaga, Margherita (1591–1632)

*Duchess of Lorraine. Born in 1591; died in 1632; daughter of *Eleonora de Medici (1567–1611) and Vincenzo I (1562–1612), 4th duke of Mantua (r. 1587–1612); sister of *Eleonora I Gonzaga (1598–1655); niece of *Marie de Medici (1573–1642); married Henry II, duke of Lorraine (r. 1608–1624); children: Nicole (fl. 1624–1625), duchess of Lorraine.*

Gonzaga, Margherita (fl. 1609–1612).
See Margaret of Savoy.

Gonzaga, Maria (1609–1660)

*Countess of Rethel and regent. Born in 1609; died in 1660; daughter of *Margaret of Savoy (fl. 1609–1612) and Frances also known as Francesco Gonzaga (1586–1612), 5th duke of Mantua (r. 1612–1612); married Carlo (1600–1631), count of Rethel; children: Carlo II (1629–1695), 9th duke of Mantua (r. 1637–1665); *Eleonora II Gonzaga (1628–1686).*

Gonzaga, Paola (1393–1453)

*Marquesa of Mantua. Name variations: Paolo Malatesta. Born in 1393; died in 1453; married Gianfrancesco Gonzaga (1395–1444), 5th captain general of Mantua (r. 1407–1433), 1st marquis of Mantua (r. 1433–1444); children: Louis also known as Ludovico Gonzaga (1412–1478), 2nd marquis of Mantua (r. 1444–1478); Carlo (1417–1456); *Margherita Gonzaga (1418–1439); Gianlucido (1423–1448); *Cecilia Gonzaga (1426–1451); Alessandro (1427–1466).*

Gonzaga, Paola (1463–1497)

Countess of Gorizia. Born in 1463; died in 1497; daughter of *Barbara of Brandenburg (1422–1481) and Louis also known as Ludovico Gonzaga (1412–1478), 2nd marquis of Mantua (r. 1444–1478); married Leonhard, count of Gorizia.

Gonzaga, Paola (1508–1569)

Nun from Mantua. Name variations: her name as a nun might have been Livia. Born in 1508; died in 1569; daughter of *Isabella d'Este (1474–1539) and Francesco also known as Gianfrancesco Gonzaga (1466–1519), 4th marquis of Mantua (r. 1484–1519); never married.

Gonzalès, Eva (1849–1883)

French painter who was an early Impressionist. Name variations: Gonzales. Born in Paris, France, in 1849; died in Paris in 1883; daughter of Emmanuel (a novelist) Gonzalès; studied with Charles Chaplin and Edouard Manet; married Henri Guérard (an engraver), in 1879; children: one son, Jean Raimond.

Eva Gonzalès was born into an artistic family in Paris in 1849; her father was a noted novelist and, from 1870, a delegate and honorary president of the Comité de la Société Gens de lettre, and her mother was an accomplished musician. At age 16, Eva began art studies with the fashionable academic painter Charles Chaplin, although her strongest influence was Edouard Manet, whom she met in 1869. She became Manet's model and student, and their friendship would last throughout both of their lives.

In the salon of 1870, Gonzalès exhibited three works, *The Little Soldier* (Villeneuve-sur-Lot, Musée des Beaux-Arts), *The Passer-by*, and a pastel of her sister **Jeanne Gonzalès**. Also exhibited that year was Manet's life-size, full-length portrait of the young Gonzalès at work (*Portrait of Eva Gonzalès*), which invited comparisons among those who criticized Gonzalès for following the principles of Manet more than those of her official teacher, Chaplin. Gonzalès' early efforts reflect the somber palette, the strong contrasts between light and dark, and the disciplined forms that came to dominate her work, and are closely allied to Manet's Spanish period. However, when Manet moved on to the brighter colors and active surfaces of the Impressionists, she retained her neutral color schemes and precise contours. Although generally classified in the premier group of Impressionists, Gon-

zalès seems aligned with the group mostly in her subject matter.

Eva Gonzalès was treated well by the critics and had a small but loyal following in England and Belgium, as well as France. Many of her paintings are now held by the French government as well as private collectors, although the best of her work is in the collection of her son and his heirs. Manet's portrait of the artist is in London's National Gallery.

In 1879, Gonzalès married engraver Henri Guérard, and in 1883, shortly after Manet's death, gave birth to a son. She died just five days later, at the age of 34. Her sister Jeanne became Guérard's second wife.

SOURCES:
Harris, Ann Sutherland, and Linda Nochlin. *Women Artists, 1550–1950*. LA County Museum of Art: Knopf, 1976.
Heller, Nancy G. *Women Artists*. NY: Abbeville Press, 1987.

Barbara Morgan,
Melrose, Massachusetts

Good, Sarah.

See Witchcraft Trials in Salem Village.

Goodall, Jane (1934—)

English ethologist and animal-rights activist responsible for our increased understanding of the chimpanzee. Name variations: Baroness Jane van Lawick-Goodall. Born in London, England, on April 3, 1934; daughter of Mortimer Herbert Morris-Goodall and Vanne Joseph Goodall; received Ph.D. in ethology from Cambridge University, 1965; married Baron Hugo van Lawick (a wildlife photographer), in 1964 (divorced 1974); married Derek Bryceson, in 1975 (died of cancer, 1980); children: (first marriage) Hugo Eric Louis, nicknamed "Grub" (b. 1967)

Raised and educated, mostly in Bournemouth, England (1934–52); worked as a secretary in Oxford and London (1952–57); traveled to Nairobi, Kenya, acquiring position as an assistant secretary to Dr. Louis Leakey (1957–60); commenced research of chimpanzee behavior at Gombe Stream Research Center (1960–71); lectured at Stanford University and Yale University in the U.S. (1970–75); founded Jane Goodall Institute (1977); published The Chimpanzees of Gombe, *her synthesis on chimpanzee behavior (1986); received the National Geographic Society's prestigious Hubbard Medal and was made a Commander of the British Empire (CBE) by Queen Elizabeth II (1995); received honorary doctorates from such schools as Salisbury State University, the University of North Carolina, Munich University, and the University of Utrecht.*

In 1935, a one-year-old English girl was given a stuffed chimpanzee by her mother. Friends of the family complained that little Jane would be horrified by "the ghastly creature," but in 1971 the adult Jane Goodall wrote that she still had Jubilee, the much-adored toy named after the first chimpanzee ever born in the London zoo. As a working scientist, Goodall has revolutionized our thinking concerning animal behavior in general, and chimpanzees and human animals in particular. Since the early 1960s, her meticulous field studies have altered human perceptions of chimpanzees as peaceful vegetarians, and of *Homo sapiens* as the only creature capable of making tools and having learned culture. Her work at the Gombe Stream Chimpanzee Reserve in Tanzania on the shores of Lake Tanganyika has undermined false assumptions that nonhuman animals are mechanisms of instinct without complex feelings or the ability to project conscious goals. Together with Konrad Lorenz, *Dian Fossey, and other early pioneers, Jane Goodall literally created the modern field of ethology, or the study of animal behavior in a natural setting.

Jane Goodall was born in London on April 3, 1934. By her own account, she was "fascinated by live animals" from the time she was an infant. Her father was a businessman and race-car driver named Mortimer Morris-Goodall, but it is her mother, **Vanne Joseph Goodall**, who has remained a focal point in her life. While she was a child, her parents divorced, and she was then raised by her mother in the English town of Bournemouth. Goodall records one of her earliest memories as sitting in a henhouse at the age of four to observe egg laying. Missing for five hours, the youngster frightened her mother into calling the police. Then, at eight, she remembers determining to "go to Africa and live with wild animals." More interested in the animals themselves than the niceties of human academic hierarchies, Jane Goodall achieved her life's goal in a very unconventional way. A childhood reader of the Dr. Dolittle stories, she followed her desire to communicate with other animals like the fictional Dolittle. This was far more important to her than attaining any academic degrees in zoology which might have trapped her in tired paradigms. Such conclusions were usually drawn from observing animals like chimpanzees in artificially created laboratory settings, and they were emphasized at the world's major universities. Later describing

her perspective on formal schooling as a "somewhat truculent attitude," Goodall left school at 18, received vocational training as a secretary, and continued to long for Africa.

While working as a secretary in London, she received an invitation to stay with a school friend at her parents' farm in what was then the British colony of Kenya. Despite the fact that Kenya had just experienced the anti-British Mau Mau insurrection (1952–56), Goodall left her job at a documentary film studio the same day she received the invitation and returned to her hometown of Bournemouth to work as a waitress, serving vacationers and tourists during the busy summer season. By her account, London was too expensive to save any money, and nothing was going to stand in the way of this opportunity to travel to the continent of her dreams. Within a month of arriving in Kenya in 1957, at age 23, she met the mentor who would change her life—the famed anthropologist Dr. Louis S.B. Leakey.

An opinionated and even controversial giant in the field of human evolution, Louis Leakey, together with his brilliant wife *Mary Leakey, founded much of the science of paleoanthropology with their work at Olduvai Gorge. Louis Leakey's legacy also includes finding the initial funds for Jane Goodall to live among the chimpanzees of Gombe and helping the late Dian Fossey to establish her work with the gorillas of the Zaire (now Republic of Congo)-Rwanda border. Of her first encounter with Louis Leakey in 1957, Goodall has written that she had already started a "dreary office job" so as not to overstay her welcome at her friend's farm, when someone told her that she should introduce herself to Leakey if she was interested in nature. She went to see Leakey at Nairobi's natural history museum, where he was curator: "Somehow he must have sensed that my interest in animals was not just a passing phase, but was rooted deep, for on the spot he gave me a job as an assistant secretary."

At the museum, Goodall engaged in enthusiastic conversations with the professional staff, and she was given an opportunity to accompany Louis and Mary Leakey to Olduvai Gorge on the Serengeti Plain, where she participated firsthand in digs uncovering fossils millions of years old. In short, she learned archaeology through field experience and actual digging. Her transformation from secretary to working scientist had already begun under the Leakeys' tutelage. Then, toward the end of the expedition to Olduvai Gorge, Louis Leakey began to talk to Goodall about his conviction that much could be learned about the prehistoric behavior of human ancestors by studying the contemporary chimpanzee.

By the late 1950s, it was already known that chimpanzees and bonobos (i.e., "pygmy chimpanzees") are the living animals most closely related to people. It is now known that the human and chimpanzee lines diverged between five and ten million years ago, and that the chimpanzee and *Homo sapiens* share a little over 98% of their DNA. A study of chimpanzees in their natural environment would therefore point to natural animal traits in humans if any parallels or comparisons could be drawn. Professor Henry W. Nissen had spent two-and-a-half months among the chimpanzees of French Guinea, but Louis Leakey knew that this was too brief a study, and that many years of careful observation would be required. He had already targeted the subspecies of chimpanzee labeled *Pan troglodytes schweinfurthi*. A group of them lived on the shores of Lake Tanganyika, and Leakey was especially interested in this environment since prehistoric human remains were often found on a lakeshore. Leakey surprised Goodall when he asked her if she "would be willing to tackle the job." According to Jane, he felt that university training might be disadvantageous and wanted someone unbiased by prevailing academic theories, "someone with a sympathetic understanding of animals." Goodall enthusiastically volunteered.

Human nature: cunning, selfish, and full of self-righteous intolerance on the one hand; wise, compassionate, and loving on the other. Which side will gain the upper hand? The question is desperately important to those of us who care about the future of the world.

—Jane Goodall

Leakey then went about securing the funding for a Goodall expedition, and he was able to raise enough from the Wilkie Foundation of Des Plaines, Illinois, to cover supplies for a six-month field study, small boat, tent, and air fares. Goodall was visiting her mother in England when she heard that the arrangements had been made with one caveat—British colonial officials insisted that she could not live in the bush alone without a European companion. Her mother, Vanne Goodall, who had already visited Jane in Africa, promptly volunteered.

Jane and Vanne Goodall reached Nairobi, Kenya, in 1960. They were then prevented by British officials from proceeding to the town of Kigoma in what was then the British colony of Tanganyika. (Granted independence on December 9, 1961, Tanganyika merged with Zanzibar on April 26, 1964, to become the United Republic of Tanzania.) The delay was because of growing tensions on the eve of independence between the British imperial administration and the African fishermen of Lake Tanganyika on the periphery of the Gombe Stream Chimpanzee Reserve (now the Gombe National Park). Rather than sit idly by, mother and daughter traveled to Lake Victoria where Jane started a three-week study of Lolui Island's vervet monkeys so as to hone her observational and note-taking skills. Above all else, she began to recognize the marked individuality of different members of a vervet monkey troop. Rather than following the same mechanical program, each vervet exhibited unique personality traits. When Goodall was finally permitted to make the 800-mile journey to Kigoma, the underpinnings of her methodological approach to animal behavior were already clearly set.

Upon arriving at Gombe, however, Goodall had to deal with human territoriality and competition. A game ranger named David Anstey arranged for her to meet with local African notables so as to allay their suspicions that she was a British spy. It was agreed that the son of the chief of Mwamgongo, a fishing village north of the chimpanzee reserve, should accompany her to make sure that she did not unduly inflate the chimpanzee population in her notes and reports. In 1971, Goodall would write, "Later I realized that the Africans were still hoping to reclaim the thirty square miles of reserve for themselves: if I stated that there were more chimpanzees than in fact there were, the Africans felt the government could then make a better case for keeping the area a protected reserve." Just as her scientific work was about to begin, the forces which would lead her to become an animal-rights advocate were also taking shape.

From the very start, in 1960, Jane Goodall insisted on recognizing the individuality of the chimpanzees. This allowed her to realize that the lieutenant of her chosen troop's alpha male, a chimpanzee she named David Greybeard, "was less afraid of me from the start than were any of the other chimps." While the alpha male Goliath maintained his distance, David Greybeard allowed Jane to observe him so that she made two of her most startling discoveries during her first year at Gombe. First, she saw David Greybeard eat a baby bush pig, disproving once and for all

that chimpanzees were strict vegetarians like the gorilla:

> For three hours I watched the chimps feeding. David occasionally let the female bite pieces from the carcass and once he actually detached a small piece of flesh and placed it in her outstretched hand. When he finally climbed down there was still meat left on the carcass; he carried it away in one hand, followed by the others.

Later, Goodall would learn that chimpanzees actually organize hunts as well as eat meat. This pointed to a level of goal-oriented action among the chimpanzees which was reinforced by Jane's observing David Greybeard deliberately trim a wide blade of grass, moisten it, and insert it into a termite nest to extract another important food source. This 1960 discovery has since been joined by numerous other observations of similar activity at Gombe and other sites throughout Africa. Not only do chimpanzees consume meat and termites, in far-West Africa some chimpanzee communities use stones and stumps as hammers and anvils to crack nuts. Until Goodall's initial discoveries, however, humans were considered the only tool-making animals. When she told Louis Leakey of her observation in 1960, he immediately said that it would be necessary to redefine "man" in a more complex manner or accept the chimpanzee as human. He also used the significance of these findings to secure Goodall's first funding from the National Geographic Society in the United States.

Goodall's scientifically significant observations continued to accumulate, though traditionally trained scientists would argue that she was guilty of anthropomorphizing her subjects—among other things, giving them individual names instead of subject numbers (Fossey suffered through similar criticisms). Nearly 40 years later in the 1990s, the refusal to recognize chimpanzees as individuals is no longer dominant—with the preponderance of evidence demonstrating chimpanzees' tool-using capacity, self-recognition in a mirror, and ability to learn and teach each other American Sign Language. This vector of research developed from the boldness of Jane Goodall's sympathetic vision, and the majority of the initial evidence came from Gombe.

In 1964, a male named Figan demonstrated deliberate planning skills. He abducted his sibling Flint to coerce their mother Flo and the entire troop to move to a new location. Likewise, the extent to which Gombe chimpanzee society was influenced by old Flo, who may have been close to 50 years in age (ancient for a chimpanzee), became apparent. Flo, an aggressive female, respected by the males, was the mother of Figan (alpha male in the 1970s) and grandmother of Freud (alpha male in 1995). It was also 1964 that saw Mike usurp leadership from Goliath. This was in fact done by means of intelligence rather than brawn. Goodall had classified Mike as a relatively weak subordinate, but he began to use discarded kerosene cans from her camp to intimidate larger males by banging them together. It has since been learned that alpha males must also demonstrate an ability to settle disputes among subordinates

and to share some surplus food like David Greybeard did. Their rulership must be supported by subordinate coalitions, as Goliath was supported by his David, and they must be much more than mere bullies.

Throughout this period, the Gombe Stream Research Center grew with funding from the National Geographic Society and other sources. In August 1962, Goodall had been joined by Baron Hugo van Lawick, a Dutch photographer and filmmaker who had impressed Louis Leakey. From that day on, Hugo filmed Jane Goodall's interactions with the chimpanzees of Gombe, compiling the footage for her first National Geographic television special, "Miss Goodall and the Wild Chimpanzees" (shown in the U.S. in 1965). In March 1964, Goodall and van Lawick married in London. It was also in 1964 that Goodall's first two research assistants joined her at Gombe. By 1972, there would be as many as 20 students there under her direction—graduate students from around the world and advanced undergraduates from the interdisciplinary human biology program at Stanford and the zoology department of Tanzania's University of Dar es Salaam.

Already a world-renowned authority by 1964, Jane Goodall in fact only earned her doctorate in ethology from Cambridge University in 1965. Her admission to Cambridge was in itself a tribute to the work she had done as early as 1960, for it is extremely rare to be allowed to study for a Ph.D. without having received an undergraduate degree. Due to her continued work at Gombe, which was the subject of her dissertation, her attendance at Cambridge lectures was quite erratic—six terms scattered over four years—and she herself admits to having had little desire to acquire the degree, though she did love learning and felt an obligation to Louis Leakey and others who had written for her admission. Still, her independent spirit could not be enchained by the academic dogmas of her day:

> The editorial comments on the first paper I wrote for publication demanded that every *he* or *she* be replaced with *it*, and every *who* be replaced with *which*. Incensed, I, in my turn, crossed out the *its* and *whichs* and scrawled back the original pronouns. As I had no desire to carve a niche for myself in the world of science, but simply wanted to go on living among and learning about chimpanzees, the possible reaction of the editor of the learned journal did not trouble me. In fact, I won that round: the paper when finally published did confer upon the chimpanzees the dignity of their appropriate genders and properly upgraded them from

the status of mere "things" to essential Being-ness.

Eschewing the careerism and comfortable traditions which so often limit academia, Goodall's desire to live among chimpanzees and learn about their world continued to be the focus of her life. Indeed, this lack of conformity with the academic pack and its methods has assured her status as an innovative and historic investigator rather than as a follower of revealed authority. Until 1975, she continued to direct the daily research efforts at Gombe personally—even while raising her son Hugo, nicknamed "Grub," born in 1967. From the start, Grub accompanied his parents into the bush, and Jane Goodall's work has indeed proved to be a family passion. Her mother Vanne Goodall, who had helped Jane to found the Gombe research center, developed a career as an anthropological writer, coauthoring *Unveiling Man's Origins* with Louis Leakey in 1969 and editing *The Quest for Man*, a collection of essays by her daughter Jane, as well as the German ethologist Irenäus Eibl-Eibesfeldt, and other scholars in 1975. In 1967, the National Geographic Society published Jane Goodall's own book, *My Friends the Wild Chimpanzees*. In 1971, her second book, *In the Shadow of Man*, appeared. Its most captivating passages include an account of the deadly polio epidemic of 1966 which eventually killed six chimpanzees:

> When we realized that the disease was probably polio, we panicked, for Hugo and I and our research assistant **Alice Ford** had not received a full course of polio vaccine. We got through to Nairobi on the radio telephone and spoke to Louis [Leakey]. He arranged for a plane to fly down to Kigoma bringing sufficient vaccine for ourselves, our African staff—and the chimpanzees.

Oral vaccine was administered to the chimpanzees in bananas, and nine afflicted chimpanzees survived this disease which was devastating to both chimpanzees and their human cousins. Another great trial in this period was the death of Flo in 1972. London's *Sunday Times* even published an obituary of Gombe's famed matriarch, citing that "Flo has contributed much to science. . . . But even if no one had studied the chimpanzees at Gombe, Flo's life, rich and full of vigour and love, would still have had a meaning and significance in the pattern of things."

In 1974, Jane Goodall divorced Hugo van Lawick, and in 1975, she married Derek Bryceson, the director of Tanzania's National Park System and a member of that country's Parliament. **Mary Smith**, a long-time friend and former *National Geographic* editor, has described the marriage as "a real love match." Unfortunately, Bryceson would die of cancer in 1980, leaving Jane with her son Grub, her mother Vanne, and the chimpanzees of Gombe.

Like the 1960s, the 1970s proved to be a rich and fruitful time for Goodall's research. With her research assistants, she continued to discover new facets of chimpanzee behavior—and even some individual aberrations. In 1970, chimpanzees were observed to perform spontaneous dance-like displays before a waterfall, leading Goodall to hypothesize that such expressions of wonder may resemble the emotions which led humans to initiate religious observance. In 1974, she witnessed a war break out between the males of her prime study group (the Kasakela community) and the males of a splinter community (Kahama). It lasted four years, with the Kahama community (seven males, three adult females and their young) being annihilated. Single-file patrols and the vicious slaughter of solitary stragglers were observed during this Four Year War—a period of increased tension and violence which also saw cannibalism break out at Kasakela from 1975 to 1977. A female named Passion and her daughter Pom killed and ate ten infants during this time. Finally, the mobility of chimpanzee females, as they migrated from community to community, was noted, and the importance of male coalitions became even more apparent as Figan (alpha male for ten years) proved most formidable with his brother Faben and his protégé Goblin at his side. The chimpanzees of Gombe continue to inform primatology with evidence of intercommunal technology transfer in the use of twigs, and the use of *aspilia* (a medicinal plant which seems to relieve stomachache), coming to the fore. In 1986, Jane Goodall completed a monumental scholarly work, replete with tables, statistics, and graphs. *The Chimpanzees of Gombe: Patterns of Behavior* has been described by the evolutionary biologist Stephen Jay Gould as "one of the Western world's great scientific achievements." It is the current capstone of Goodall's groundbreaking scientific life, even as that state of being recedes into the background, for in recent years, Jane Goodall has spent much of her time as an animal-rights activist.

In 1977, she founded the Jane Goodall Institute, a nonprofit organization which now coordinates her worldwide efforts to save and learn about the threatened chimpanzee. Around 1,900 chimpanzees were found in 25 African countries. By 1990, they had disappeared completely from four countries, while in at least five others the species is so small in numbers that it cannot survive. In 1990, the Committee for Conservation and Care of Chimpanzees, supported by the Jane Goodall Institute, estimated the total African population of chimpanzees to be about 197,150. Zaire had the largest population of *Pan troglodytes*, with some 90,000, and it also had all the world's bonobos, or *Pan paniscus*, at approximately 17,000. Tanzania had 2,000 chimpanzees, while Rwanda, with only 150 individuals, was one of the countries with chimpanzees on the verge of extinction. The small, dwindling populations across Africa all face such a loss in genetic diversity that inbreeding will begin to threaten their sustainability.

Jane Goodall is blunt about the human causes leading to the endangerment of the genus *Pan*. As impoverished human populations grow, she notes, "forests are razed for dwellings and for cultivation." Likewise, the growing cities of an increasingly urban Africa generate the same demands as urbanized areas in Europe and the Americas. Logging and mining threaten chimpanzees' forest habitats, and adults are often killed so as to capture infants for sale to international dealers who deposit them in Europe and the United States to entertain in zoos and circuses, and to be used for experimental purposes in pharmaceutical labs. The Jane Goodall Institute tries to salvage chimpanzee habitat in Africa, care for orphans, and decrease the demand for captive chimpanzees in the Americas, Europe, Australia, and Asia. Where there are laboratory and zoo chimpanzees, pressure is placed upon scientists and zookeepers to improve the quality of life for captives by increasing confinement spaces and allowing for interaction with other chimpanzees. By 1993, the Institute was on the verge of bankruptcy, but Goodall hired a Texas political consultant named Don Buford to supervise its revitalization. As of 1995, the Institute had seen a doubling of contributions and a sevenfold increase in membership.

Since $500,000 alone was required to run the Institute's sanctuaries for chimpanzees, much of Jane Goodall's work in the 1990s was of a fundraising nature. She lectured across North America annually on tours that numbered as many as 15 cities. At the same time, she tried to maintain her ties with Africa and launched an environmental education program for African schoolchildren called Roots and Shoots. Started in 1991, and since then duplicated elsewhere, Roots and Shoots depends on a growing seedbed of environmental awareness among many educated Africans who are struggling to save Africa's biodiversity and introduce environmentalism to its school-age children. Goodall herself notes the heroism of such African efforts, and of researchers like Dr. Geza Teleki, who "got river blindness, an incurable disease, when he worked for the government of Sierra Leone to set up a national park there specifically for chimpanzees."

During the 1990s, Jane Goodall maintained a concrete-block house at Gombe, but her main residence was in Tanzania's capital of Dar es Salaam, 675 miles east of Gombe. There, her son Grub runs a sportfishing business in the house next door. She also sometimes shared a Victorian home in Bournemouth, England, with her Aunt Olly and her mother Vanne, who was nearly 90 in 1995. In actuality, Jane spent much of her time traveling as a goodwill ambassador on behalf of environmentalism, animal rights, and the earth's dwindling population of chimpanzees.

Jane Goodall desperately tries to save chimpanzees, the closest living biological relatives of humanity, from "human arrogance, human greed, and human cruelty," which "have helped create a sick planet and a great deal of suffering, human and nonhuman alike." In the December 1995 issue of *National Geographic*, she wrote:

> We love to point fingers when we try to deal with difficult problems such as the environment, to lay the blame on industry or science or politicians. And there is no question that industrialization has polluted our surroundings. But who buys the products? We do, you and I, the vast amorphous general public. Each of our actions has a global impact.

Struggling as she did against the conventions of science in the 1960s, Jane Goodall argued for the individual initiative of chimpanzees who, by extension, could serve as mirrors of our own behavior. A scientific innovator, Jane Goodall continues to see a role for individual initiative within the human species, even as she has seen it within the genus *Pan*.

SOURCES:

Goodall, Jane. *The Chimpanzees of Gombe: Patterns of Behavior.* Cambridge, MA: Harvard University Press, 1986.

———. *Through a Window: Thirty Years with the Chimpanzees of Gombe.* London: Weidenfeld and Nicolson, 1990.

Green, Timothy. *The Restless Spirit: Profiles in Adventure.* NY: Walker, 1970.

Miller, Peter. "Crusading for Chimps and Humans . . . Jane Goodall," in *National Geographic.* Vol. 188, no. 6. December 1995, pp. 102–129.

Peterson, Dale, and Jane Goodall. *Visions of Caliban: On Chimpanzees and People.* Boston, MA: Houghton Mifflin, 1993.

Van Lawick-Goodall, Jane. *In the Shadow of Man.* Boston, MA: Houghton Mifflin, 1971.

SUGGESTED READING:

Goodall, Jane, with Phillip Berman. *Reason for Hope: A Spiritual Journey.* Warner, 1999.

Abel A. Alves,
Assistant Professor of History, Ball State University, Muncie, Indiana, and author of *Brutality and Benevolence: Human Ethology, Culture, and the Birth of Mexico* (Greenwood Press, 1996)

Goodbody, Buzz (1946–1975)

British visionary theater director and first woman associate director of the Royal Shakespeare Company who pioneered their alternative performance space, The Other Place, hoping to demonstrate that Shakespeare could still communicate intimately, politically, and potently to a 20th-century audience. Name variations: Mary Ann Goodbody. Born Mary Ann Goodbody (known from childhood as "Buzz"), on June 25, 1946, in London, England; committed suicide on April 12 (some sources cite the night of the 11th as time of death), 1975, in London; daughter of Marcelle Yvonne (Raphael) Goodbody and Douglas Maurice Goodbody (a lawyer); educated at Roedean, Sussex, England; Sussex University, 1962-66, B.A.; married Edward Buscombe, in 1967 (divorced 1971).

Showed an early interest in theater and wrote, directed, and performed in university drama while at Sussex; was a founding member of the feminist Women's Street Theatre; won an award for her own adaptation and production of Dostoyevsky's Notes from the Underground *at the National Student Drama Festival (1966) and was invited to become personal assistant to an associate director of the Royal Shakespeare Company (RSC), John Barton; while working for him, presented "in-house" productions and readings (in the Company's corrugated-aluminum rehearsal room), and devised an anthology for the RSC's touring educational program, TheatreGoRound (TGR) entitled* Eve and After *(1967–68); assisted Barton on* Coriolanus *and* All's Well That Ends Well *(1967); was research assistant on* The Merry Wives of Windsor *(1968); appointed assistant director for the RSC season at Stratford Festival Theatre (1968–69)—Henry VIII, Twelfth Night, Women Beware Women, Pericles, The Winter's Tale* and a revival of *The Merry Wives of Windsor—taking the latter two productions on a tour of Japan and Australia; directed* King John *and* Arden of Faversham *for TGR (1970); directed RSC touring production of Trevor Griffiths'* Occupations *and* The Oz Trial *at London's Aldwych Theatre (1971); was assistant to Trevor Nunn for the acclaimed "Romans"*

season (Julius Caesar, Titus Andronicus, Coriolanus and *Antony and Cleopatra)—taking a much more prominent role when Nunn fell ill during the transfer of all four plays from Stratford to the Aldwych (1972); appeared in London's West End in a feminist revue entitled* Top Cats *(1973); directed* As You Like It *for the Festival Theatre, Stratford (1973); became artistic director of The Other Place (1974) where she subsequently produced* King Lear *and* Hamlet *(1975); committed suicide at age 28 (1975).*

When Buzz Goodbody was appointed to the staff of the world-renowned Royal Shakespeare Company, she immediately began to give voice to a new set of concerns within the existing experimental tradition, and as artistic director of their new studio theater space, The Other Place, she sought to change both perceptions and policies. Her untimely death, at age 28, meant that her personal potential was never fully realized, but her legacy of political commitment opened the way to directors, designers, and actors from the fringe, bringing a new vitality and awareness to the company. During her most innovative period, one commentator observed: "Buzz Goodbody doesn't want to burn down the RSC, merely reform it."

Goodbody was born into a relatively privileged family based in North London. Her father was a distinguished barrister, and her mother had been trained as an actress. She was a bright, vivacious child and her brother John nicknamed her Buzz, "probably," he said, "because she was always buzzing about." She read voraciously—anything and everything—instigating the family tradition of having a "Reading Tea" when the children were allowed to bring their books to the table. Showing an early interest in drama, Buzz wrote and performed her first play "The Knave of Hearts" at age six, and when the American playwright Thornton Wilder, a family friend, came to visit she entertained him with a lively puppet show. **Marcelle Goodbody** nurtured her daughter's talent and regularly took the children to see productions of Shakespeare's plays at the Old Vic Theatre in London. By age 12, Buzz had seen much of the Shakespearean repertory and was enthralled by the language and spectacle.

Academically, she was very gifted and, after attending a private junior school, won a scholarship to Roedean, an exclusive girls' boarding school in Sussex. She left at 16 and, eschewing the possibility of going to Oxford or Cambridge, enrolled instead at Sussex University, one of the most avant-garde and politically aware of England's postwar universities. As an undergraduate, her passion for drama and the theater deepened. She rebelled against her background, becoming intensely interested in Communism and increasingly aware of the feminist cause. She directed and acted in a number of productions, including Genet's *The Maids,* a somber piece about two women who plan to murder their oppressive mistress.

Goodbody was intending to acquire a master's degree and had written a dissertation on Shaw when, in 1966, her adaptation and production of Dostoevsky's *Notes from the Underground* was chosen to represent the university at the National Student Drama Festival. As a prizewinner, it was presented the following January (with its companion piece, Gogol's *Diary of a Madman)* at the Garrick Theatre in London. John Barton of the Royal Shakespeare Company was so impressed that he went to the stage door to offer the director a job as his personal assistant for the forthcoming season at Stratford-upon-Avon. However, Barton made it clear that, much as he might value Goodbody's work (which ranged from ironing his shirts to conducting understudy rehearsals for *Coriolanus)* he was not going to promote her as his protégée. So, over the next 18 months, she used any spare moments to develop her own projects which included "in-house" productions of Ben Jonson's *Epicene* and scenes from Shakespeare's *King John* and *Richard III.* These were not for public viewing—they were presented to the company as "work-in-progress" and caught the attention of Terry Hands who had been brought in to take charge of the educational arm of the company, TheatreGoRound (TGR), and was also about to start work on *The Merry Wives of Windsor* for the main stage. He asked Goodbody to do some background research on the play—particularly on class differences and the rise of the bourgeoisie in 17th-century England. While Hands concentrated on the text, Goodbody led improvisation rehearsals based on her investigations. Their work resulted in an acclaimed production enriched with humorous social realism—a lively alternative to the "roly-poly basket farce" the play had become in recent years. This was part of the new perception of Shakespeare: giving his work a context and an immediacy that went beyond the merely entertaining and decorative. The production was revived the following year, and Goodbody was engaged as assistant director for the entire 1969 season.

Gradually, this imaginative and innovative young woman—described in the press as a "leggy brunette in a mini-skirt" who spoke of herself as a "bird" (a rather demeaning word for "girl" popularized in the 1960s)—was beginning to make her voice heard, and she was very much more serious and determined than casual observers might suppose. After all, as she maintained, she loved Shakespeare "because he is saying all the time that politics is people and people politics."

TGR was described at the time as "the most revolutionary activity that the RSC has promoted," and it was therefore something of a natural element for Buzz Goodbody. Her first real opportunity to demonstrate some of her own ideas in a full-length show came when she was asked by Hands to direct *King John* for a TGR tour. She saw the play as a "blistering attack on politicians," one in which "only John's bastard brother dare speak the truth." The staging was simple: a screen-like backdrop, a percussionist and playing-card costumes. Possibly influenced by Karl Marx's observation that "history is played first as tragedy, then as farce," she pushed the performances to the brink of caricature; the king, for instance (played by Patrick Stewart), made his entrances and exits as a toy soldier, marching stiffly to the beat of a drum and wearing a dunce's cap for a crown. One critic wrote enthusiastically, "this is Shakespeare for the masses. This is the sort of adaptation that retains interest and perhaps develops interest in new fields" and RSC chronicler Colin Chambers wrote: "[H]ere was an important voice of the 70s, exploring the choice between the ineffectiveness of self-satisfied political isolation and the compromise of political engagement." Certainly it was this tension which concerned and preoccupied Goodbody both in her work and in her life.

During the 1960s, the directors of the RSC had begun to broaden their theatrical base and were now ready to promote new work which they considered of substantial interest. Goodbody's next major presentation was, in Chambers' words, "the first RSC production to affirm unambiguously a revolutionary commitment to socialism." *Occupations* by Trevor Griffiths was set in Italy during the occupation of the Fiat factories by the workers of Turin in 1920. It was "an exploration of differing philosophies of political action, putting the question of why the workers occupations had not lead to a revolutionary movement." Developing her directing style, Goodbody undertook meticulous study of the period and drew together a tightly knit ensemble of actors committed to extracting de-

tailed characterizations and complex social relationships through argument, improvisation, and research. After a short tour, the play opened at The Place, a fringe venue in London. Although both the director and the play received much attention and praise (though, surprisingly, not much from the left-wing press), Goodbody had realized that, ironically, it was not really modern work that stirred her passion. In Shakespeare's plays, written as they were in as hotly political a climate as any, she saw an opportunity to demonstrate how he explored his own changing society in a concrete and complex way that could be of value to ours.

She was therefore excited to be back in Stratford assisting Trevor Nunn on his *Romans* season—an idea conceived to emphasize the debate about the issues behind the rise and fall of a society. The whole experience (though sometimes gruelling) reconfirmed her belief in Shakespeare's continuing political relevance, but she was equally convinced that it was work seen in studio spaces which could break down the barriers most effectively, allowing a freer exchange of thought and feeling between actors and audience. Thus, despite the enormous popular appeal of her modern dress *As You Like It*—her first production in the main house at Stratford—Goodbody craved the intimacy and immediacy of the smaller stages she had encountered while on tour with TGR and *Occupations*. As 1973 drew to a close, she drew up a report outlining the kind of work a studio theater should and could do as an alternative auditorium to the Royal Shakespeare Theatre. Her clarity of purpose and enthusiasm led Nunn to appoint her as artistic director of The Other Place—housed in the RSC's tin-roofed rehearsal room, minimally converted into a theater. The vision of this enterprise was largely contained in a Goodbody-Nunn memorandum to the company on January 22, 1974, stating that "work in The Other Place will be geared towards sections of the community who, for various reasons, are not regular members of our audience." It was here that Goodbody directed for change, writes **Dympna Callaghan**, weaving "the techniques of marginality into the fabric of mainstream British theatre."

Her first production was her own adaptation of *King Lear*. Using just nine actors and a tiny budget (£150 as opposed to £10,000 for traditional productions) and with tickets selling for a fraction of the price of main house seats, her program notes anticipated the kinds of criticism she would receive for "filleting" the text: "Every area of the production was dictated by the reason for doing it," she said. "The most obvious way in which I was guided was by the purely practical."

Her overriding "reason for doing it" was to awaken young audiences to the excitement and power of Shakespeare's radicalism and the emotional relevance of his story. If she were to present the full version, school audiences coming to an evening show would miss the public transport bus home. Moreover, traditional productions of Shakespeare in traditional theaters had meant that in previous generations a young person's first exposure to the bard had been from a long way off, squeezed against the back wall of a vast auditorium—distanced physically and emotionally from what was happening on the stage far below. She wanted her audience to feel as if they were "inside" the play—so the seating was arranged on three sides and the newly constructed balcony was lit for the soliloquies. After every performance, she and the actors stayed to discuss the play, answer questions or just listen to the audience response. She was praised for distilling the central themes of the play, and the production was internationally acclaimed.

Goodbody continued to generate ideas for subsequent seasons and productions. Her final production, *Hamlet*, is recognized by Callaghan as "the crowning achievement of Goodbody's life" which seemed "to exemplify some of the political principles of her theatre practice" and enabled "a fuller understanding of her earlier work." In contrast to *Lear,* it was performed virtually uncut, and although the action was concentrated, she was careful to retain the philosophical and intellectual impact of the play along with the emotional intensity. The set was minimal, the actors wore modern dress, and the message was bleak. "The bleakest I can recall," wrote *The Times* critic Irving Wardle. "Not only is society poisoned but neither Hamlet nor anyone else has a chance of setting it straight."

It is possible that the interpretation was a grim reflection of a deep malaise that had settled on Goodbody over years of working from the margins of the "Establishment." She had certainly found that, as a director, "being a bird" was sometimes a struggle. "I suppose there are only five women directors in Britain, and there isn't one of my age," she told an interviewer. "Actors simply aren't used to women directors. But all this will change as women come into the theater from universities. Meanwhile one just has to learn to be tactful. Directing is as much handling people as having significant ideas about the theater. You have to be an all-round type—part psychiatrist, part favorite friend, part stool pigeon."

Hamlet opened for previews on April 8, 1975. Buzz Goodbody, exhausted by extensive technical rehearsals and preparations for the first public performance due the following week, returned for the weekend to her London home which she shared with friends. She said she was very tired and going to bed "for a long sleep"; she asked not to be disturbed. The next day, her friend, **Sue Todd**, was worried by her non-appearance and went into her room to find her dead from a large overdose of pills. An annotated copy of T.S. Eliot's "Four Quartets" was found by her bed. Todd told the press that Goodbody had had "problems in her personal life, too." At her cremation, journalist **Bea Campbell** spoke of Buzz Goodbody as "an . . . extraordinary woman—extraordinary for her persistent, stringent and militant application of her intelligence to art and politics, the politics of social relationships and the politics of personal relationships of intimacy." The theatrical community was deeply shaken and mourned the loss of an exceptionally talented young woman who had triumphed over so many obstacles and was on the brink of a spectacular career.

SOURCES:

Callaghan, Dympna. "The aesthetics of marginality" in *Theatre and Feminist Aesthetics.* Edited by Laughlin & Schuler.

———. "Buzz Goodbody: Directing for Change," in *The Appropriation of Shakespeare.* Edited by Jean Marsden.

Chambers, Colin. *Other Spaces.* Eyre/Metheun and TQ Publications.

Interviews with John Goodbody and Anne Daniels from the Stratford-on-Avon Centre.

Pringle, Marian J. *The Theatres of Stratford-Upon-Avon.*

Bonnie Hurren,
freelance director, actor, lecturer, Bristol, England

Goode, Sarah.

See Witchcraft Trials in Salem Village.

Goodenough, Florence Laura

(1886–1959)

American developmental psychologist. Born Florence Laura Goodenough in Honesdale, Pennsylvania, on August 6, 1886; died in Lakeland, Florida, on April 4, 1959; youngest of eight children of Lines Goodenough (a farmer) and Alice (Day) Goodenough; attended rural school in Rileyville, Pennsylvania; Millersville (PA) Normal School, B.Pd., 1908; undergraduate degree from Columbia University, 1920, master's, 1921; Ph.D. from Stanford University; never married; no children.

Florence Goodenough spent a decade teaching in small rural schools in Pennsylvania before earning bachelor's and master's degrees at Columbia during the early 1920s. She then transferred to Stanford University in California, where, for her Ph.D. thesis, she devised the "Draw-a-Man" intelligence test, which could determine the level of development by having a child submit a simple drawing of a man. Her thesis, called *Measurement of Intelligence by Drawings,* was published

in 1926 and widely used. In 1926, after working for two years as chief psychologist at the Minneapolis Child Guidance Clinic, Goodenough joined the faculty at the University of Minnesota. Quickly attaining the rank of research professor, she studied a wide range of problems in the field of child development. Two impressive works, *Experimental Child Study* (with John E. Anderson) and *Anger in Young Children* (both published in 1931), scrutinized the methods used in evaluating children.

During the 1930s and 1940s, her work on intelligence tests put her at the vanguard of psychological research. In 1932, she created the Minnesota Preschool Scale, which estimated intelligence in young children. It was revised in 1940 and 1942, the year she published *The Mental Growth of Children from Two to Fourteen Years,* written in collaboration with **Katherine Mauer.** During World War II, Goodenough created a test used for officer selection in the Women's Army Corps. Unfortunately, her work was cut short by diabetes, which eventually forced her to retire from the University of Minnesota. Although she lost most of her sight to the disease and was virtually deaf, she continued to work with assistance from her niece **Lois M. Rynkiewicz.** In 1956, Goodenough published *Exceptional Children,* followed by yet a third revision of her classic *Developmental Psychology* in 1959, the year of her death.

SOURCES:

Bailey, Brooke. *The Remarkable Lives of 100 Women Healers and Scientists.* Holbrook, MA: Bob Adams, 1994.

Sicherman, Barbara, and Carol Hurd Green, eds. *Notable American Women: The Modern Period.* Cambridge, MA: The Belknap Press of Harvard University Press, 1980.

COLLECTIONS:

Florence Goodenough's papers are in the Archives of the University of Michigan and in the files of the Institute of Child Welfare.

Good Queen Bess (1533–1603).

See Elizabeth I.

Goodrich, Frances (1891–1984)

American screenwriter and playwright who collaborated with her husband Albert Hackett on It's a Wonderful Life. *Name variations: Frances Hackett. Born in Belleville, New Jersey, in 1891; died of lung cancer on January 29, 1984, in New York City; daughter of Henry W. and Madeliene Christie (Lloyd) Goodrich; educated at private school; Vassar College, B.A., 1912; attended the New York School of Social Service; mar-*

ried Henrik Willem van Loon (divorced 1929); married Albert Hackett, on February 7, 1931; no children.

Screenplays (all with Albert Hackett): The Secret of Madame Blanche *(1933);* Fugitive Lovers *(1934);* Hide-Out *(1934);* The Thin Man *(1934);* Ah, Wilderness! *(1935);* Naughty Marietta *(1935);* After the Thin Man *(1936);* Rose Marie *(1936);* Small Town Girl *(1936);* The Firefly *(1937);* Another Thin Man *(1939);* Penthouse *(1939);* Society Lawyer *(1939);* Lady in the Dark *(1944);* The Hitler Gang *(1944);* It's a Wonderful Life *(1946);* The Virginian *(1946);* Easter Parade *(1948);* The Pirate *(1948);* Summer Holiday *(1948);* In the Good Old Summertime *(1949);* Father of the Bride *(1950);* Father's Little Dividend *(1951);* Too Young to Kiss *(1951);* Give a Girl a Break *(1954);* The Long, Long Trailer *(1954);* Seven Brides for Seven Brothers *(1954);* Gaby *(1956);* A Certain Smile *(1958);* The Diary of Anne Frank *(1959);* Five Finger Exercise *(1962).*

Plays (all with Albert Hackett): Up Pops the Devil *(1931);* Bridal Wise *(1932);* Thanks for the Memory *(1938);* The Great Big Doorstep *(1942);* The Diary of Anne Frank *(1955).*

Frances Goodrich with husband Albert Hackett.

The husband and wife writing team of Frances Goodrich and Albert Hackett produced some of the most enduring screenplays of the 20th century, including *The Thin Man* (1934), *Lady in the Dark* (1944), *It's a Wonderful Life* (1946), *Father of the Bride* (1950), and *Seven Brides for Seven Brothers* (1954). They also collaborated on five plays, most notable among them, *The Diary of Anne Frank* (1955), for which they won the Pulitzer Prize, the New York Drama Critics Circle Award, and the American Theater Wing's **Antoinette Perry* ("Tony") Award. In 1959, they turned the award-winning play into a screenplay.

Frances Goodrich was born in Belleville, New Jersey, in 1891 and started an acting career after graduating from Vassar College. In 1924, while appearing in George Kelly's long-running play *The Show Off*, she met Albert Hackett, who was also appearing on Broadway. The two met again doing summer stock and produced their first collaboration, a comedy called *Western Union*, which showcased in Skowhegan, Maine, in the summer of 1930. The partnership flourished, and they enjoyed minor success with two subsequent comedies, *Up Pops the Devil* (1930) and *Bridal Wise* (1932), both of which had respectable runs in New York. Meantime, Goodrich had divorced her husband, the historian Henrik Willem van Loon, to marry Hackett, and in 1931, the couple moved to Hollywood to write for films.

By 1939, they had 13 movies to their credit, many of which were box-office hits. The team was well-known for their ability to produce dialogue and mannerisms suited to the particular actors playing their scripts, a talent that was especially evident in *The Thin Man* (1934), based on a Dashiell Hammett murder mystery, and co-starring William Powell and **Myrna Loy* as the sophisticated Nick and Nora Charles, private eye and wise-cracking wife. The characters proved so popular that Goodrich and Hackett produced several sequels. In 1935, the couple received the first of their five Academy Award nominations for their adaptation of Eugene O'Neill's *Ah, Wilderness!* Their most enduring movie collaboration was *It's a Wonderful Life* (1946), starring Jimmy Stewart, who claimed it was his favorite movie role.

The husband and wife collaboration, according to Goodrich, was fairly confrontational. The two worked in a room with separate desks facing away from each other. After each had written their version of a scene, they exchanged drafts, then mercilessly critiqued each other's effort before undertaking the arduous task of rewriting. "I never knew there could be so many battles about little words," Goodrich said. Only once did she attempt to collaborate with someone else, but found that she spent so much time trying to spare the other person's feelings that little got accomplished.

*The Diary of *Anne Frank*, two years in the writing, was a labor of love for the couple. They wrote eight different versions of the play, which was adapted from Frank's diary, and visited Otto Frank, Anne's father, to share with him the work in progress. With the play's director Garson Kanin, they also visited the garret in Amsterdam, Holland, where the Franks hid from the Nazis. In reviewing the play, which first starred *Susan Strasberg in the role of Anne, *The New York Times*' theater critic Brooks Atkinson called it "a delicate, rueful, moving drama." In a forward to the published version of the play, he wrote: "The reader of the diary is hardly aware of what the Hacketts have done, the craftsmanship and writing are so unobtrusive. . . . Written in a subdued key, without pointing a moral, it chronicles the plain details of a strange adventure. . . . [T]hey have not lost the glow of Anne's character." The couple's last effort was the screenplay for *Five Finger Exercise* (1962), after which they retired from writing. Frances Goodrich died in 1984, at the age of 93.

SOURCES:
Acker, Ally. *Reel Women*. NY: Continuum, 1991.
Candee, Marjorie Dent, ed. *Current Biography 1956*. NY: H.W. Wilson, 1956.

Barbara Morgan,
Melrose, Massachusetts

Goodridge, Sarah (1788–1853)

American painter who produced miniature portraits on ivory of well-known denizens of Boston and Washington, D.C. Born in Templeton, Massachusetts, on February 5, 1788; died in Reading, Massachusetts, in 1853; sixth of nine children of Ebenezer Goodridge (a farmer) and Beulah Goodridge; sister of Beulah Goodridge Appleton and Eliza Goodridge Stone (also a miniaturist); attended local schools; briefly attended David L. Brown's drawing school; never married; no children.

Sarah Goodridge, one of the most distinguished American miniaturists of the 19th century, was one of nine children of **Beulah Goodridge** and Ebenezer Goodridge, a Massachusetts farmer. Sarah's earliest pictures were scratched with a pin on sheets of peeled birch bark or drawn with a stick on the sanded kitchen floor. Largely self-taught, she learned to paint miniatures on ivory by following the written instructions in a booklet. After teaching school in Templeton for two summers, Goodridge took up her

artistic career, selling watercolor and crayon portraits of her friends. In 1820, she opened a studio in Boston and moved in permanently with her brother-in-law and sister, Thomas and **Beulah Appleton**. That same year, she met artist Gilbert Stuart, who, impressed with her talent, took her on as a student. In 1825, after some prodding from his wife **Charlotte Stuart**, Gilbert also let Goodridge paint his portrait, although he hated what he called "having his effigy made." The finished miniature, considered brutally honest and quite unflattering by some, pleased Stuart so much that he preserved it in a bracelet with his own and his wife's hair. The painting was engraved by Asher Durand for the National Portrait Gallery, and Goodridge also painted two replicas which are now in the Metropolitan and Boston Museums.

Goodridge's talent flowered under Stuart's instruction, and she was later commissioned to paint Daniel Webster, General Henry Lee, and many others. A prolific painter, she was able to support her mother for 11 years and also raised an orphaned niece. Sarah Goodridge worked until 1850, when her eyesight failed, then retired to a cottage she was able to purchase for herself in Reading, Massachusetts.

SOURCES:
Petteys, Chris. *Dictionary of Women Artists*. Boston, MA: G.K. Hall, 1985.
Rubinstein, Charlotte Streifer. *American Women Artists*. NY: Avon, 1982.

Barbara Morgan,
Melrose, Massachusetts

Goodson, Katharine (1872–1958)

English pianist who was popular on concert stages throughout Great Britain. Born on June 18, 1872, in Watford, England; died in London on April 14, 1958; married Arthur Hinton (1869–1941).

Katharine Goodson studied at the Royal Academy of Music with Oscar Beringer and in Vienna with Leschetizky. She had a fine reputation and was especially popular with British audiences. Though she played mostly the standard repertory, Goodson ventured to perform novelties like the Delius Concerto and the Concerto by her husband, Arthur Hinton.

John Haag,
Athens, Georgia

Goolagong Cawley, Evonne
(1951—)

Australian Aboriginal tennis champion who ranked among the world's best women players for 15 years.

Name variations: Evonne Cawley; Evonne Goolagong-Cawley. Pronunciation: Eve-on GOO-la-gong CAW-lee. Born Evonne Goolagong on July 31, 1951, in Griffith, New South Wales, Australia; daughter of Melinda Violet Goolagong and Kenny Goolagong (a shearer); completed high school at Willoughby Girl's High and secretarial course at Metropolitan Business College in Sydney; married Roger Cawley, on June 16, 1975; children: Kelly Inala Cawley *(b. May 12, 1977) and Morgan Kyeema Cawley (b. May 28, 1981).*

At age 12, began entering major tennis tournaments (1963); won Under-13 New South Wales (NSW) Hard Court championship (1964); won Under-15 NSW Country championship (1964); received U.S. Sports Illustrated *award of merit (1964); held every tennis title available in her age group in NSW (1965); held 12 age titles (1966); won Queensland Girl, NSW Girl, and Victorian Girl championships (1967); was top-ranked girl in NSW (1968); won Wilson Cup (1969); held 60 age-and-junior titles (1970); was runner-up British Hard Court championship (1970); won Welsh Open, Victorian Open, North England championship, Cumberland Hard Court championship, Midlands Open, Queensland Open, and Bavarian Open (1970); was Australian Hard Court champion in singles, doubles and mixed doubles, and on winning Federation Cup team (1970); won South African Doubles, French Open singles, Wimbledon singles, Dutch Open singles, and Queensland Open singles (1971); awarded MBE by Queen Elizabeth II and named Australian of the Year (1972); won NSW Open, South African Open, and was runner-up at Wimbledon (1972); was U.S. National Indoors champion, and on Federation Cup winning team (1973); won Canadian Open and Italian Open (1973); won Czechoslovakian championship in singles and mixed doubles (1973); won Australian Open and U.S. National Open (1974); named* Sun *Sportsman of the Year (1974); was New Zealand Open champion in singles and doubles, and on winning Federation Cup team (1974); was Wimbledon doubles champion and Virginia Slims champion (1974); won Australian Open and was runner-up at Wimbledon (1975); won NSW Open and Australian Open (1976); was runner-up at Wimbledon (1976); had 15 consecutive victories on Virginia Slims tour (1976); was Sydney Colgate International champion (1977); won NSW Open and Australian Open (1977); was U.S. Indoor champion (1979); won Wimbledon singles (1980).*

By age two, Evonne Goolagong was bashing a tennis ball against a brick chimney with a racquet carved by her father Kenny Goolagong from an old packing case. She also obsessively clutched that old tennis ball she had found behind a car seat like other children hug stuffed toys. But, far from being tennis buffs, Goolagong's parents were itinerant laborers. After her birth in Griffith hospital in the outback of New South Wales (NSW) on July 31, 1951, Evonne was brought home by her mother **Linda Goolagong** to a corrugated iron shack which her father had built on the fringes of tiny Tarbogan.

An Australian Aboriginal, Evonne Goolagong was born into the Wiradjuri people who ranged through a wide area of Southern Central NSW. Though deprived of their traditional lifestyle by the time of her birth, she still had many kin in the area who lived in rough dwellings on the fringes of country towns.

When Evonne was two years old, her family settled down in the small town of Barellan, 400 miles southwest of Sydney. Her father, a hard-working shearer, obtained a permanent position with a local sheep grazier who provided them with an old house in the township. They were the only Aboriginal family in the town and, according to Goolagong, encountered only a minimum of the prejudice and racism so common throughout Australia in that era. Australian Aboriginal people did not have the right to vote, and there was widespread segregation. Linda Goolagong ensured her children were well-cared for and well-dressed on a minimal and erratic income which depended on the availability of work for her husband. Out of shearing season, he sometimes had to travel to find odd jobs.

As the third eldest of seven children, Evonne had a happy childhood. The family often went away on camping trips to a favorite spot on the banks of the Murrumbidgee River so that Kenny could fish and the children swim and play with a freedom reminiscent of their ancestors. Regularly, they traveled further afield to Condobolin, the place from which the Goolagongs originated, to renew the all important ties of family and kin.

Evonne was an active, athletic girl. Together with her older sister and brother, she often roamed the surrounding countryside collecting traditional bush foods. At school, she was protected from racist taunts by her stocky big brother's reputation and participated readily in school sports. She was the champion of her first school sports carnival and often played softball and cricket with the boys. Her opportunity to progress from hitting balls against a chimney came when Bill Kurtzman, a retired local grazier (one who pastures cattle for

Evonne Goolagong Cawley

market), persuaded the Barellan community to build new tennis courts on the grounds of the War Memorial Club in 1956.

By happy chance, these courts backed onto the Goolagong family residence. Only five years

old at the time, Goolagong was too young to join the club but eagerly used the practice wall and watched her older sister and brother play in club games after they joined in 1957. Occasionally allowed to play, her natural talent was soon noticed, and she was given special permission to join the club two years later. A great tennis career, which would bring the small outback town of Barellan to international fame, had begun. Kurtzman took Evonne under his wing in the early days and drove her to tournaments throughout the district. Goolagong's family was so poor she had to borrow a racquet in order to play.

In 1961, on Kurtzman's invitation, two talent scouts from the renowned Victor A. Edwards Tennis School arrived in Barellan to run a coaching clinic. The Goolagong children, especially Evonne, attracted their attention. The following year, the coaches encouraged Victor A. Edwards himself to come to Barellan to see this potential champion. As a result, Evonne, who was already winning district tournaments, was invited to visit Sydney in 1963 and stay with the Edwards family so that she could train and compete in her first big tournament: the Under-13 Grass Court championships. In 1964, she once again traveled to Sydney, sponsored by the Barellan community, and won a number of age competitions, including the Under-15 Country when she was still only 13. She was becoming a media sensation—the new up-and-coming champion.

They didn't want to know about my tennis, they wanted me to speak in Wiradjuri or throw a boomerang or something. I was that year's Wimbledon freak show.

—Evonne Goolagong

By 1965, Goolagong held every title available to her in NSW. Victor Edwards, who was to be her long time coach, persuaded her parents to let Evonne move in permanently with his family so that he could mould and supervise her career. Though she developed a close relationship with the Edwardses and their daughters, Goolagong felt strange and lost in the big city of Sydney and suffered from homesickness. This sometimes affected her performances, but her love of tennis kept her dedicated to the tough routine of training and playing schedules.

Evonne's occasional lapses of concentration—usually attributed to her Aboriginality—occurred throughout her career and became legendary. Sports commentators would almost invariably say "Evonne's gone walkabout." Originally nomadic, the Aboriginal culture required people to fulfil many spiritual and ritual obligations which involved travel to sacred sites and ceremonies. These obligations were not understood by white people who perceived "going walkabout" as an indication of laziness. Evonne Goolagong's lapses of concentration had nothing to do with Aboriginal ancestral obligations.

She had no training in traditional culture. It was simply a personal trait. This tendency to make unfounded and fanciful assumptions dogged Goolagong throughout her tennis career. Even in Australia, she was treated as a great curiosity because so few of her race had managed to emerge from the oppressive conditions they were forced to live under and have successful careers.

In 1970, Goolagong left Australia on her first overseas tour with 60 age-and-junior titles to her credit. Considerable though her talent was, it was her Aboriginality which attracted attention. Her first appearance at Wimbledon, on Court 4 in the opening rounds, drew a large crowd. Consequently, her second round match was scheduled for Centre Court—an unlikely draw for a newcomer. From the first, it was hard to know whether the crowds had come to watch Goolagong's agile tennis talents or to stare at an exotic spectacle. The latter attitude was encouraged by the press who constantly referred to her in terms such as "chocolate coloured piccaninny" which would fall afoul of modern-day anti-discrimination laws.

Through it all, Goolagong usually maintained her serene good nature; even her first appearance on Centre Court did not faze her. "I would like to report that I was so nervous I couldn't sleep a wink," she said, "but losing sleep over tennis was never my style." Though she lost her match against Jane "Peaches" Bartkowicz, Evonne's press conference was jam-packed with reporters eager to ask her inappropriate questions about her Aboriginality. Undaunted, Goolagong went on to win a number of tournaments around Great Britain and Europe before returning to Australia for another series of wins, including the Victorian Open, where she beat the great Australian and Wimbledon champion *Margaret Court for the first time.

In 1971, Goolagong encountered controversy when she toured South Africa while it was under a UN-sanctioned sporting ban to protest the apartheid policy. Though upset by the dispute, Evonne had little knowledge of politics. All decisions, tennis or personal, were made by her coach Vic Edwards. In 1972, she would return to that country and become the first black ever to win the South African Open.

The year 1971 was to be a great one for Goolagong. In the lead up to Wimbledon, she won both the French Open and the British Hard Court championships, thus arriving at Wimbledon as number three seed and the center of attention. "It was an enviable position to be in," she noted, "there comes a point in the career of every major player where you have nothing to lose and everything to gain. At 19, defeat would be seen as heroic, victory a bonus." She was pitted against two of the greatest female players of all time: *Billie Jean King and Margaret Court. The young newcomer beat King in the semifinal and Margaret Court in the final to become the 1971 Wimbledon women's singles champion.

Goolagong returned to a tickertape parade through the streets of Sydney—an honor that had not been accorded to other Australian tennis greats such as John Newcombe or Margaret Court. Evonne would develop a somewhat cynical realism about this disproportionate adulation. All the same, the shy, good-natured, newly acclaimed world champion graciously appeared in processions and shook hands with all the officials who presented her with awards and lauded her in speeches. She became immensely popular. In 1972, she was proclaimed Australian of the Year and made a Member of the Order of the British Empire (MBE) by Queen *Elizabeth II.

Goolagong's success in tennis depended more on her natural ability than a killer instinct which many other tennis stars developed. Early in her career, a sports commentator in the *Daily Telegraph* wrote that her "delicacy of touch, mobility, flexibility and ball sense make her outstanding." Evonne was loved by the public because of her good nature. She did not argue with referees or throw tantrums but approached the game with an infectious smile.

"I rarely felt great pressure to perform," Goolagong admits. This was seen as a failing by some, because it made her performances erratic. Often unbeatable, at other times she seemed to throw games away. One reporter remarked early in her career that she would never become a tennis great "until she gets a little bit more serious about discipline. But maybe, like a wild animal if you tried to discipline her it would destroy the essence that's so great about her." Such racially tinged comments did not seem to bother her. Goolagong's motivation continued to be love of the game rather than fame, fortune, or victory. "Most of the time I played the game with abandon," she once said. "I knew no such thing as safe tennis nor did I understand the percentage game. . . . I only ever knew one way to play tennis and for that I offer no apology."

In an era when women in tennis were finally beginning to win large purses, Goolagong showed little interest in money and went on record as saying she would play at Wimbledon for nothing. She paid scant attention also to the numerous controversies in the tennis world and the many critical comments both true and untrue published about her in the press. In fact, she never read them and only saw herself on television for the first time in 1976, claiming she was so shy she would have been embarrassed to watch herself on the screen.

She approached loss with a similar shrug and was somewhat nonplussed to see how devastated other players were when they lost an important match. As far as she was concerned, "It was only a game." Nonetheless, she continued to win many major championships. In 1972, Vic Edwards signed her up to play for World Team Tennis which ran heavily promoted tours throughout the United States; she also continued to play on the European and Australian circuit.

Goolagong was always happiest when, in the middle of this heavy schedule of promotions and games, she found time to go home to Barellan to catch up with her beloved family and the Barellan locals. Devastated in 1974 when her father Kenny Goolagong was killed by a car while she was overseas, by the following year she was becoming emotionally drained and developing a wrist problem.

There were other sizeable distractions. On her first trip to England in 1970, she had met and was instantly attracted to a young man named Roger Cawley. Over the years, they had written to each other and usually met when she was in England. Though the relationship had been on and off, by 1975 she knew she wanted to marry him. But most of their meetings had been conducted semi-secretly to avoid the wrath of Vic Edwards, who thought of Evonne as his personal protégée. Edwards had opposed her relationship with Cawley from the first.

As she grew older, Evonne was finding Vic's domination more and more inappropriate. In her autobiography, she mentions that he had made two sexual advances, and, though she laughed them off, they left her feeling disturbed. She had always thought of Edwards as a second father, but his behavior was becoming more and more bizarre. When the couple finally announced they were engaged to be married, Vic Edwards refused to speak to them.

On June 16, 1975, Evonne and Roger married in a registry office in England. Vic Edwards declined the invitation to attend and told the press he had not been invited. By July 7, Goolagong had formally severed her contract with her coach. Unfortunately, in the process she became alienated from **Eva Edwards** who had been a second mother to her. After Vic Edwards died in 1976, they were reunited.

Happily married, Goolagong continued her tennis career. In 1976, she won the Australian Open for the third time in a row, reaching No. 1 in the world rankings. On the Virginia Slims tour, she had 15 consecutive victories and was the top prize money winning player. During a match in late 1976 when she was performing badly, Evonne realized she was pregnant and in May 1977 gave birth to her daughter Kelly. Reluctant to stop even before the birth, she took only a few months' break from tennis; later that same year, she won a number of major tournaments, including the Australian Open and the NSW Open.

Despite her will to keep going, Goolagong was experiencing more and more the physical problems which had begun to plague her even before Kelly's birth. Her feet in particular were in bad shape. As a consequence, a tendon snapped in her leg during the Wimbledon semifinal against *Martina Navratilova. Amazingly, though in extreme agony, Goolagong finished the match, but she had to take a break for the rest of the year and from then on played only on grass and clay courts.

In 1979, she was back in action on the tennis circuit and winning matches. All the same, her energy was down, and she started losing again. Goolagong was so weak that she was forced to drop out of a match—something not even a snapped tendon had driven her to do before. She was eventually diagnosed with a rare blood disorder which thankfully was easily cured once identified. Despite all these setbacks, Goolagong battled on, driven by a burning desire to triumph at Wimbledon once more. Since her win in 1971, she had placed runner-up three times, in 1972, 1975 and 1976. Having come so close, so often, she was determined to win again. In 1980, though Goolagong entered the Wimbledon rounds with very little preparation due to her injuries and illness, she achieved her ambition. She took the Wimbledon championship for the second time in a close game against *Chris Evert. Only the second mother to win Wimbledon, Goolagong holds the women's record for the longest interval between titles—nine years. After this penultimate win in her career, Evonne continued playing, but her injury-prone body was getting the better of her. In May 1981, she gave birth to her second child Morgan. Though ranked No. 17 in the world in 1982, her winning streak was over; in 1983, she finally called it quits as a professional player.

Abandoning the career that had been her life for so long, Goolagong was thrown into a depression, but she soon recovered and concentrated on the considerable business interests which had resulted from her widespread fame and popularity. She continued to live in the United States, which had become her home in 1974, until the death of her mother Linda in 1991. Deeply affected by the loss, Goolagong's desire to "immerse myself in the study of what it is to be a Wiradjuri Aborigine" became overwhelming. The Cawley family packed up and moved to Australia to settle at Noosa Heads in Queensland. Goolagong then devoted herself to researching her family and cultural background as well as teaching her children about their heritage.

She made many trips to seek out and talk to her relatives—a labor of love recorded in her autobiography *Home! The Evonne Goolagong Story* which was published in 1993. The most reliable source on Evonne's life, because so much of what was published about her has been inaccurate, distorted and often simply made up, the book speaks strongly of Evonne's pride in her Aboriginality. An earlier "autobiography," published in 1975, was actually written by Vic Edwards and Bud Collins. Far from writing it, Goolagong did not even read it until researching her true autobiography, and she strongly disputes many of the "facts" in it. One of the repeatedly published myths is that the word Goolagong means "still trees by quiet waters." According to Evonne, it actually means "my country" in the Wiradjuri language. Evonne Goolagong Cawley is now applying the passion and dedication she brought to tennis to developing a great pride in her culture of origin, and so continues to be an inspiration to her people and her many admirers.

SOURCES:

Goolagong, Evonne. *Home! The Evonne Goolagong Story*. Sydney: Simon and Schuster, 1993.
———, with Bud Collins and Victor Edwards. *Evonne*. London: Hart-Davis, MacGibbon, 1975.
Robertson, Max. *Wimbledon—Centre Court of the Game*. London: British Broadcasting Corp., 1981.

Chris Sitka,
freelance writer and researcher, Sydney, Australia

Goose, Elizabeth (1665–1757)

American writer, possibly the legendary Mother Goose, who contributed to the first American book of nursery rhymes for children. Born Elizabeth Foster in 1665; died in 1757; married Isaac Goose, in 1682; children: six (two died in infancy); stepmother to ten.

Much in the life of Massachusetts-born Elizabeth Goose establishes her identity as the real

Mother Goose, whose rhymes and stories comprised a book called *Songs for the Nursery, or Mother Goose's Melodies for Children*, published in 1719. Born Elizabeth Foster in 1665, she married the widower Isaac Goose in 1682 and became the stepmother of ten children. The couple added six children of their own, and Elizabeth evidently relied heavily on her memory's store of old rhymes, stories, and fables to keep her brood quiet and entertained. Reportedly, it was Thomas Fleet, a printer and Elizabeth's son-in-law, who assembled her repertoire into the children's book *Songs for the Nursery*. Unfortunately, no copy of the publication is known to have survived, but some scholars believe that Fleet's edition predates by ten years the translation of France's Charles Perrault's *Tales of My Mother Goose* into English. Perrault's work is considered the source of many perennial favorites like "Old King Cole," and "Sing a Song of Sixpence." Elizabeth Goose, who at the very least was probably the first American Mother Goose, died in 1757, and is buried in the Old Granary Burial Grounds near the Park Street Church in Boston.

Goose, Mother (1665–1757).

See Goose, Elizabeth.

Göppert-Mayer, Maria (1906–1972).

See Mayer, Maria Goeppert.

Gorbacheva, Raisa (1932–1999)

Russian sociologist, educator, and wife of the former president of the Soviet Union. Name variations: Raisa Maximovna; Raisa Gorbachev. Pronunciation: Gorba-CHOFF-a. Born Raisa Maksimovna Titarenko in Rubtsovsk, USSR, on January 5, 1932; died of leukemia on September 20, 1999, at the Muenster University Clinic in Muenster, Germany; daughter of Maksim Andreevich Titarenko, sometimes rendered Titorenko (a railway construction engineer) and Aleksandra (or Shura) Petrovna Paradina Titarenko; attended Moscow State University, 1949–54; Lenin Pedagogical Institute (Moscow), 1964–67; married Mikhail Sergeevich Gorbachev (a lawyer and future head of the Communist Party and the Soviet state), on September 25, 1953; children: Irina Gorbacheva Virganskaya (b. 1957).

Was a lecturer (dotsent), Stavropol Agricultural Institute (1959–78) and Moscow State University (1979–85); served as vice-president, Soviet Cultural Foundation (1986–91); granted an honorary degree from Northeastern University in Boston (1989).

Publications: I Hope: Reminiscences and Reflections (New York, 1991); Peasant Life on the Collective Farm: A Social Summary (in Russian; Stavropol, 1969); and numerous articles on academic and cultural topics.

On June 6, 1988, Raisa Gorbacheva appeared on the cover of *Time* magazine—the first Russian woman to be so honored. While this distinction was in part a result of her marriage to the leader of the Soviet Union, she also deserved recognition in her own right. Raised in humble surroundings during the worst period of Soviet history, she had become an articulate, resourceful professional woman with a Ph.D. in sociology and a successful career as a lecturer at two Soviet universities. She also played an important role in her husband's more renowned career. It would be a mistake, however, to view Raisa Gorbacheva, as *Time* did, as Russia's "First Lady" or as a true symbol of the "new Soviet woman."

There are "blank spots" in Gorbacheva's early biography which even her husband's later policy of *glasnost* (openness) failed to illumine. She was born on January 5, 1932, in Rubtsovsk, a remote town in the Altai region of Siberia. Soviet reticence about the background of its political leaders and especially of their wives has led to considerable speculation about Raisa's origins. Some have claimed, perhaps because of her facial features, that she was of Crimean Tatar descent; others have suggested that she was related to key figures in the early Soviet hierarchy. Gorbacheva herself was adamant that she was ethnically Russian and that her parents were of peasant stock. Her father Maksim Titarenko (sometimes rendered Titorenko) was a railway construction engineer who moved from his native Ukraine to Siberia in 1929 in search of work. Her mother **Aleksandra Titarenko** was apparently a Russian brought up in Siberia. The turbulent period of Raisa's childhood witnessed the hardships of forced collectivization, widespread famine and total war. She acknowledged in her reminiscences that her maternal grandfather, who acquired a farm during the more relaxed atmosphere of the 1920s, was arrested under Stalin on charges of being a *kulak* or rich peasant and a follower of Leon Trotsky. He disappeared during the Great Purges of the 1930s. Her only biographer, **Urda Jürgens**, claims the same fate almost befell Maksim Titarenko who allegedly was arrested in 1935 for criticizing collectivization and sentenced to four years in a northern labor camp. Jürgens produces no evidence to support this assertion which may in fact be contradicted by the birth of Raisa's younger sister **Liudmilla Titarenko** in 1938.

Gorbacheva said little about her father other than that she was the favorite of his three children and that he was frequently absent because of his employment. He died in 1986. Aleksandra Titarenko was a more formative influence. Uneducated and religious, she made sure her eldest daughter was christened in the Orthodox faith and that all her children received a good education. To supplement the family's meager income, she often kept a cow or goat for milk, tended a vegetable garden, and made most of her children's clothing. Raisa's abiding memory of these difficult years was of moving "from nest to nest"—sometimes a converted railway car, once a "beautiful large wooden house in the Urals," another time an apartment in a former monastery—as her father was transferred from one place to another in Ukraine and Siberia. She was "always the new girl" in each village school, and she also was always at the top of her class. In 1949, she graduated from tenth grade with a gold medal—an honor given to only one student in every hundred—which allowed her to attend a university of her choice.

Raisa Titarenko chose to go to Moscow State University, the nation's premier institution of higher learning. She enrolled in the Philosophy Faculty and took courses primarily in psychology, sociology and Marxism-Leninism. The subject matter was constrained by the dictates of high Stalinism, but in her words "the teaching and social activities . . . contained more radicalism, more excitement and more creativity." "We were happy. Happy in our youth and in our hopes for the future." At first, she lived in a dormitory room with 11 other young women and existed on a minimal diet cooked in a communal kitchen. Much of her time outside the classroom was spent in Moscow's theaters, museums, and art galleries, experiencing a culture unavailable in Siberia. She spent enough time studying, however, to graduate in 1954 with top marks and an offer of a research fellowship to continue postgraduate studies in Moscow.

After a year of further work, she gave up a prized life in the capital to move to the south of Russia with her new husband, Mikhail Gorbachev. She had met Gorbachev, who was a year older and studying law in Moscow, at a dance in 1951. She was impressed by "his lack of vulgarity" and his willingness to take her ideas seriously. Indeed, she introduced him to the new world of art and culture which she had found in Moscow. They were married in September 1953 and two years later, after he had finished his degree, moved 800 miles to Stavropol which was to be their home for the next 23 years.

Stavropol, with a population of only 100,000, was a world apart from cosmopolitan Moscow. To be sure, it had a temperate climate and an attractive setting on the northern slopes of the Caucasus but, as Raisa acknowledged, it was "excessively provincial." Cultural possibilities were limited to three movie houses, a local history museum, a regional library, and a theater company and orchestra of dubious quality. Few of the streets were paved, and there was little central heating. Their first apartment consisted of one room, no running water, and a paraffin stove in the corridor. What irritated Raisa the most was her inability to find suitable employment which she needed to satisfy her own ambitions as well as to supplement her husband's modest salary as he worked his way up the ladder of the local party organization. At first, she could find no work at all despite her excellent education; then she was hired by a medical institute to do a "job I was not trained for"; and, when she finally found a part-time position which allowed her to teach philosophy, she had "no real rights" and had to accept lower pay than her less qualified male colleagues. These problems, not unknown to female academics elsewhere, were accentuated by the fact that she was seen as a well-educated Muscovite and an outsider. It was only in 1959 that Gorbacheva was able to overcome these obstacles and was given a full-time appointment as *dotsent* or lecturer in philosophy at the Stavropol Agricultural Institute.

In January 1957, with the birth of her daughter **Irina Gorbacheva**, Gorbacheva had to come to grips with another problem common to professional women in the West. Taking care of a child, standing in endless lines to buy supplies, and cooking meals for her family made it difficult to prepare lectures. Sometimes she had to stay home with her sick child or she left Irina in the faculty common room while she met her classes. "It is not easy to combine professional and public obligations with family duties, with the role of mother and wife," she wrote many years later. In 1964, after her daughter had entered school, Gorbacheva decided to resume her graduate training while continuing as a full-time teacher. She was accepted by the Lenin Pedagogical Institute in Moscow to do a *kandidat* degree (roughly equivalent to a North American Ph.D.) in sociology. Her choice of discipline is interesting since sociology was only starting to gain respectability in the Soviet Union after years of abuse and distortion under Stalin. Her dissertation—"The Emergence of New Characteristics in the Daily Lives of the Collective Farmers (Derived from Sociological Investigations in the Stavropol Region)"—was based on 3,000 questionnaires and countless follow-up interviews with farmers. Her methodology, which was virtually unknown in the Soviet Union of the 1960s, is in retrospect more interesting than her somewhat predictable conclusions. She successfully defended her thesis in 1967 and published a popularized summary of it two years later.

It is significant that Gorbacheva's husband, who in 1970 was given the very important position of first secretary of the Communist Party organization in the Stavropol region, was interested in agricultural problems and was later to make his reputation in this field. During their long walks in the surrounding countryside, husband and wife discussed the findings of her research as well as the difficulties of professional women in Soviet society. Raisa also helped her husband entertain party dignitaries who often visited the hot springs near Stavropol. Her self-confidence and wide-ranging interests, which

Raisa
Gorbacheva

rarely were found in party wives of this period, particularly impressed Yuri Andropov, the head of the KGB and future general secretary of the Communist Party, who became Mikhail Gorbachev's mentor and protector in the often cutthroat world of higher Soviet politics. Despite her own early difficulties, this was probably the happiest period of Raisa's marriage. "It was there in the Stavropol region," she later wrote, "that we spent the years of our youth and it was there that our daughter was born and grew up. It was there that we had close friends and family. And it was there, in Stavropol, that we were given the opportunity to realize ourselves."

In November 1978, Gorbachev was called to Moscow to be a member of the party's powerful Secretariat and shortly thereafter of its ruling Politburo. Life in the nation's capital was different for Raisa. She found few friends among the much older and less educated wives of her husband's geriatric associates. To be sure, there were special perquisites that went with his job: a large apartment with servants, a country dacha, access to special stores, and travel abroad. One senses, however, that she derived more satisfaction out of resuming her career at Moscow State University. She started work on a *doktorskii* degree, which is more advanced than a North American Ph.D., and in 1979 was given a lectureship in Marxist philosophy at her alma mater. Six years later, after her husband was named general secretary of the Communist Party and subsequently president of the Soviet Union, she reluctantly gave up her own career to help his.

The "Raisa factor" burst on the Western media when Gorbachev made a state visit to England in December 1984. In the past, wives of Soviet leaders stayed at home. Not this time. Raisa got off the plane at her husband's side, not three steps behind. She was stylishly attired, well coiffured and (unlike her predecessors) thinner than her husband. She confounded her hosts by showing more interest in going to Stratford than in visiting Karl Marx' grave. The tabloids loved it when she pulled out her American Express Gold Card to pay for earrings at Cartier's. It was evident that she was well read in English and willing to try out her few phrases in that language or in French when the occasion presented itself. In public, she expressed her opinions freely to the press; and in private, she was known to correct statements made by her husband. During the next six years, she accompanied Mikhail on over 30 trips abroad. She invariably came informed about museums and galleries she wanted to visit, and she charmed the

media and most of her hosts. The one exception was *Nancy Reagan who was unable to answer Raisa's persistent questions about the history of the White House and perhaps felt upstaged by Russia's version of *Jacqueline Kennedy. It is no wonder that in 1987 a British magazine chose her "woman of the year," and that a year later she was the subject of *Time*'s cover story. In the West at least, she was quite prepared and able to play the role of Russia's "first lady."

The situation was very much different in her homeland where the concept of a "first lady" was foreign and an anathema to a resolutely paternalistic population. It is symptomatic of the difference that when Tom Brokaw's interview with Mikhail Gorbachev was televised in the Soviet Union, the section where the general secretary acknowledged discussing matters of state with his wife was deleted. Raisa, recognizing the difference, declined to give interviews in Moscow and deferred to her husband more than in the West. She still accompanied him on his unusual and well-televised "walk arounds" when he talked to ordinary Russian citizens. She also tried to contribute to his policy of *perestroika* (restructuring) by serving as vice-president of the Soviet Cultural Foundation, a new non-governmental agency which sought to protect, preserve, and promote Russian cultural interests. In private, she remained Gorbachev's alter ego. Despite her own doctrinaire views, there is evidence that she sought to develop his new democratic image. She took it as her personal duty to watch her husband's performances on television or before the Duma (parliament) and to suggest ways in which he might project himself more effectively.

Despite her cautious public approach, jokes were prevalent in Moscow about "the Red tsarina" or about the Napoleonic Gorbachev's "Josephine." She was attacked in the Duma for accepting a salary for her valuable work as vice-president of the Cultural Foundation. Chauvinistic Russian men did not like the idea of any woman, much less a "first lady," advising and shaping state policy. They particularly did not like the widespread rumor that the teetotaling Gorbacheva was behind her husband's much-needed but detested anti-alcohol campaign. Contrary to foreign expectations, few of her own sex saw her as a "new Soviet woman." Her frequent image on television was too remote from their own reality to be credible. Women who owned only two dresses objected when Raisa changed her foreign-designed clothes twice daily when visiting sick children near Chernobyl or wore a fur coat when viewing the devastation caused by the Armenian earthquake. Women who had never visited a hairdresser simply could not relate to the well-combed Raisa. As **Norma Noonan** has noted, "Gorbacheva projected glamour and affluence in an increasingly impoverished Soviet Union." It was commonly believed that she was putting on airs and dipping into the same trough that had kept the Soviet elite well supplied during the Brezhnev years. Raisa Gorbacheva, just like her husband, was far less popular at home than she was abroad and indirectly this contributed to his downfall.

In August 1991, the president of the Soviet Union, his attractive 59-year-old wife, their only daughter and her husband, as well as two grandchildren were vacationing in the Crimea when Gorbachev's opponents in the party struck. The entire family was arrested and for 72 hours held hostage. Raisa, in particular, feared for their lives and thought that an attempt would be made to poison her husband. She apparently suffered a stroke or a nervous breakdown as a result of the ordeal. While the coup itself failed, the Communist Party which Gorbachev headed was outlawed, and in December he resigned as the president of a Soviet Union which no longer existed.

Little is known about Raisa's activity since then. She did not resume her public or academic work, and she still did not grant interviews. While she occasionally accompanied her husband on trips abroad, she adamantly opposed his seeking the presidency again in 1996. That year, when pressed by reporters to comment on her tendency to accompany her husband on trips, she replied, "You all wrote about how I was always by his side when he was in power. But why don't you write that I never left his side after all of you forgot about him."

The story of an intelligent, articulate woman who gave up her own career to help her husband, only to be ridiculed for her efforts, was not dissimilar to that of another first lady—**Hillary Rodham Clinton**. But the Russian climate changed. In August 1999, with her sister as donor, Raisa was to receive a bone marrow transplant for leukemia at the University Clinic in Muenster, Germany. Tens of thousands of letters and telegrams poured into the Gorbachev Foundation office in Moscow from Russian well-wishers. On hearing about it, "Raisa Maximovna even cried," said an aide. But the transplant had to be postponed because of complications caused by chemotherapy and infection. Raisa Gorbacheva died on September 20, 1999, with her husband and her daughter by her side. Only then was the world apprised that Raisa

had donated much of her wealth to charity and had raised more than $8 million for children's leukemia hospitals.

SOURCES:

Gorbachev, Raisa. *I Hope: Reminiscences and Reflections*. Translated from the Russian by David Floyd. NY: HarperCollins. 1991.

Dolgov, Anna. "An Ailing Raisa Gorbachev finally wins affection from Russian public," in *The Day* [New London]. September 11, 1999.

Jürgens, Urda. *Raisa*. Translated from the German by Sylvia Clayton. London: Weidenfeld and Nicolson, 1990.

Noonan, Norma C. "Gorbacheva, Raisa Maksimovna" in *The Gorbachev Encyclopedia*. Salt Lake City: Schlacks, 1993, pp. 186–193.

Whitmore, Brian. "Raisa Gorbachev, who broke mold for Kremlin wives, dies," in *The Boston Globe*. September 21, 1999.

SUGGESTED READING:

"My Wife is a Very Independent Lady," in *Time*. June 6, 1988, pp. 32–35.

Sheehy, Gail. *The Man Who Changed the World: The Lives of Mikhail S. Gorbachev*. NY: HarperCollins, 1990.

R.C. Elwood,
Professor of History, Carleton University, Ottawa, Canada

Gordeeva, Ekaterina (1971—)

Russian ice skater who, paired with husband Sergei Grinkov, won four World championships and two Olympic gold medals. Name variations: Yekaterina Gordeyeva. Born in Russia in 1971; eldest of two daughters of Alexander Alexeyevich Gordeev (a dancer for the Moiseev Dance Company) and Elena (Levovna) Gordeeva (a teletype operator for the Soviet news agency Tass); married Sergei Grinkov (her skating partner), in April 1991 (died on November 20, 1995); children: one daughter, Daria.

On the evening of February 5, 1996, at the Hartford (Connecticut) Civic Center, Ekaterina Gordeeva took to the ice for the first time since the death of her beloved husband and skating partner Sergei Grinkov, who died unexpectedly of a heart attack at a routine practice session on November 20, 1995. The occasion was a tribute to the fallen skater, an exhibition performed by his close colleagues and friends. Gordeeva's solo, created by the couple's long-time choreographer **Marina Zueva** and performed to Mahler's Symphony No. 5, *IV Adagietto*, was the show's closing number followed only by a finale. The performance was not only Gordeeva's first appearance since her husband's death, but the first time the skater had ever performed in front of an audience without a partner. Waiting to go onto the ice, she was overcome with loneliness. "I thought about the words Sergei used to say to me when we were getting ready to skate," she wrote in her autobiography *My Sergei*. "We always kissed each other before we skated, we always hugged and touched each other. Now, in the tunnel, waiting to go on the ice, I didn't have anyone to touch or kiss. It was a terrible feeling to be standing there by myself." But as Gordeeva made her way to the ice, the loneliness disappeared, replaced by a surge of confidence. "I never felt so much power in myself, so much energy. I'd start a movement, and someone would finish it for me. I didn't have a thing in my head. It was all in my heart, all in my soul."

Ekaterina Gordeeva (known as Katia) is the eldest of two daughters of Alexander Gordeev, a dancer with the Moiseev Dance Company, and **Elena Gordeeva**. Since Elena had an important position with the Soviet news agency Tass and worked long hours, Ekaterina and her sister **Maria Gordeeva** were cared for much of the time by their grandmother. The family spent summers at a shared house north of Moscow. There, Gordeeva spent her days outdoors, playing, or hunting mushrooms and fishing with her grandfather. She remembers her childhood as a happy time, filled with pleasant memories.

Gordeeva's father, who wanted her to become a ballet dancer, was extremely disappointed when Ekaterina failed the entrance tests at the central ballet school in Moscow because she was too short. She redeemed herself somewhat by showing considerable promise on the ice, and she trained rigorously throughout her early years at one of the many sports clubs sponsored by the Central Red Army Club. When she was nine, it was determined that her jumps were too weak for her to compete as a singles skater, so her subsequent training was in preparation for pairs competition.

Gordeeva was 11 when she was teamed with Sergei Grinkov, a tall, gawky 15-year-old who exercised a slightly rebellious streak by shunning the mandatory school uniform for more stylish street wear. Despite the fact that Grinkov towered over Gordeeva, whose head barely reached his armpits, the couple learned to move as one and to execute their difficult lifts, jumps, spins, and tosses seemingly without effort. They won their first Junior World championships just two years after they were paired, an event which also encompassed their first trip to the United States. They would go on to win 13 additional events, including a gold medal at the 1988 Olympics in Calgary and a second in Lillehammer in 1994, then turn professional.

Between Olympics, the couple had fallen in love. Gordeeva said it was a natural progression, almost inevitable. "First we were skating partners. Then we were friends. Then we were close friends. Then we were lovers. Then husband and wife. Then parents." They were married in Moscow in April 1991, and their daughter Daria was born 18 months later in the United States. The stunning program to *Moonlight Sonata* that they executed in Lillehammer was actually choreographed to represent the couple's mature relationship. "It expresses what changes love can bring about in people," Gordeeva writes, "how it can made them stronger, make them have more respect for each other. How it can give them the ability to bring a new life into the world." Gordeeva, who remembered little about her first Olympic competition, seemed to have a heightened consciousness during the second try for the gold at Lillehammer. "You cannot describe these four minutes of skating in words, but I was aware of every movement that I was making, conscious of the meaning behind these movements and conscious of what Sergei was doing. It is a clarity that one so seldom finds elsewhere in life, a clarity any athlete can relate to, moments in time that we remember the rest of our lives. I believe it is why we compete."

One year later, on November 20, 1995, the couple were training in Lake Placid, New York, for a tour with Stars on Ice. They arrived at the rink at 10 AM to rehearse some changes in their program made the night before. As Sergei was preparing for an expansive lift, he faltered, lost control, and glided into the boards. Gordeeva thought he might be suffering from his recurring back problem, but when she questioned Sergei, he clutched the boards, unable to speak. Then he bent his knees and lay down on the ice. He lived long enough to make it to the hospital but died shortly thereafter. Just 28, he had suffered a massive heart attack, the result of undiagnosed heart disease.

Following a small wake at Lake Placid, Sergei was taken home to Moscow. "Sergei had a Russian soul," writes Gordeeva. "He was only comfortable there." A huge public service was held at the ice rink of Moscow's Central Red Army Club, followed by a hero's burial in Vagankovsky Cemetery. Afterwards, Gordeeva remained in Moscow, living in the small apartment where she and Sergei had begun their married life. "I felt I was slowly losing myself," she writes of the weeks that followed Sergei's death. "I had no purpose in my life, nothing to strive for. My parents were there to take care of Daria, so I didn't have that to worry about. All I was doing was dealing with my feeling and this was killing me." So Gordeeva sent for her skates and started practicing again at the Central Red Army Club rink. When the call came asking her to make an appearance at Sergei's tribute, she was reluctant, but choreographer Marina Zueva insisted that she should not only make an appearance, but skate, and offered to create a program for her.

Gordeeva continues to skate professionally, although without the confidence she had at Sergei's tribute. She does not want her daughter to be a skater, and is seeing to it that Daria spends more time in school than she did, so that she will have more career options. "I think I'll be learning a lot of things from Daria in the future," she writes. "I already am learning from her. Sergei never taught me things. He protected me; he loved me; he took care of me; he comforted me. But it is only with his death that I start to learn about life. Only now has he started to teach me."

SOURCES:
Gordeeva, Ekaterina, with E.M. Swift. *My Sergei: A Love Story.* NY: Warner Books, 1996.

Barbara Morgan,
Melrose, Massachusetts

*Ekaterina
Gordeeva*

Gordimer, Nadine (1923—)

*Nobel Prize winner in Literature and one of South Africa's leading writers, who has devoted much of her career to exploring the complex personal undercurrents in her country's political and racial history in the second half of the 20th century. Born in Springs, Transvaal, South Africa, on November 20, 1923; daughter of Isidore Gordimer (a Jewish shopkeeper from Lithuania) and Nan (Myers) Gordimer (daughter of a Jewish family from England); attended the University of the Witwatersrand, 1945; married Gerald Gavron (Gavronsky), on March 6, 1949 (divorced 1952); married Reinhold Cassirer, on January 29, 1954; children: (first marriage) one daughter, **Oriane Gavron**; (second marriage) one son, Hugo Cassirer.*

Published first story (1939); published first collection of short stories (1952); published first novel and made first trip abroad (1953); paperback edition of A World of Strangers banned in South Africa (1962); The Late Bourgeois World banned in South Africa (1971); won Booker Prize (1974); The Burger's Daughter banned for several months in South Africa (1979); participated in defense of Alexandra Township (1986); joined African National Congress (1990); won Nobel Prize for Literature (1991); delivered the Charles Eliot Norton Lectures at Harvard University (1994).

Selected works: Face to Face *(1949);* The Soft Voice of the Serpent *(1952);* The Lying Days *(1953);* A World of Strangers *(1958);* Occasion for Loving *(1963);* The Late Bourgeois World *(1966);* Livingston's Companions *(1971);* The Conservationist *(1974);* The Burger's Daughter *(1979);* July's People *(1981);* A Sport of Nature *(1987);* My Son's Story *(1990);* Jump and Other Stories *(1991);* None to Accompany Me *(1994);* The House Gun *(1998); (collection of essays and lectures)* Living in Hope and History: Notes from Our Century *(Farrar, Straus, 1999).*

Nadine Gordimer has been a leading literary figure and a respected and acute observer of South Africa since the early 1950s. The author of 11 novels and more than 200 short stories, she has presented a vivid and profound picture of sensitive members of the white community in South Africa living in a segregated society that does violence to their moral principles. Since early in her career, Gordimer's work has received international acclaim with such awards as the Booker Prize in 1974 and the Nobel Prize for Literature in 1991.

Critics have lauded Gordimer for the delicacy and precision of her writing, notably in her short stories. Robert Haugh, for example, notes her possession of "the quick perceptive glance . . . which sparkles like a gem." And he also has praised how her insight into the human condition presents a skilled combination of "satire and pathos." He is the foremost advocate of the view that the best of her highly regarded fictional works puts aside open advocacy and concentrates instead on exploring the personal world of individuals caught up in a brutal and oppressive system. Indeed, within her large corpus of writing, Gordimer has explored such themes as the psychology of childhood, the human confrontation with death, and middle-class conformity.

But virtually all of Gordimer's works have been set in the South African milieu in which she has lived her entire life; other books, such as *A Guest of Honor,* have been set in different (sometimes imaginary) parts of the African continent. Thus, there is an intriguing, shifting mixture of political awareness and interest in human relations in Gordimer's fiction. She has dealt with a changing South Africa in part by using non-whites as well as whites as her heroes and heroines in order to explore the personal ramifications of South Africa's evolution over the past four decades. Moreover, Gordimer has spoken out candidly in her essays and lectures against the system of apartheid that divided the races until 1992, and she has remained a vocal commentator on political affairs to the present time.

Stephen Clingman has described the combination of the personal and the political in Gordimer's novels by noting that her works contain a "dialectical interplay," marking them with "the exploration of history and character, of external and internal worlds." Gordimer herself noted as early as 1962 that she was trying to write about "private selves" of white and black South Africans while remaining aware that "even in the most private situations, they are what they are because their lives are regulated and their mores formed by the political situation."

Gordimer has never been a popular author in her own country. Moreover, as a privileged white woman in a racist society that she herself criticizes, she has promoted changes that were likely to disrupt her own life. As critic **Kathrin Wagner** has noted, throughout her work stands the paradox of her sympathy for "a historical process whose revolutionary phase must destroy the comfortable contexts within she writes." Gordimer's view of white liberals like herself has featured a scathing criticism of a group that, as

Wagner puts it, "highlights with considerable sharpness their inadequacies and failures as both activists and individuals."

Nadine Gordimer was born to Jewish parents in Springs, a small town located 30 miles east of Johannesburg. Her father Isidore Gordimer, a shopkeeper who had prospered as a jeweler in his adopted country, had immigrated to South Africa from Lithuania. Her mother **Nan Myers Gordimer** was English. Some of the future writer's most successful stories, such as "The Defeated" and "The Umbilical Cord,"

were to be set in Jewish-owned country stores that served a clientele of black customers.

The young girl was a mediocre student. Her education was interrupted at the age of 11 or 12 when her mother, for obscure personal reasons, claimed the girl had heart trouble and insisted on keeping her away from school. For a period of about five years, Nadine was educated at home. Nonetheless, at the age of 15 or so, she was able to attend a local Catholic school, the Convent of Our Lady of Mercy, then studied briefly at the University of the Witwatersrand.

Nadine Gordimer

Her real education came from her prodigious reading program, and, while still a young child of nine, she began to write. Paradoxically, her first piece of writing was a poem praising the hero of South African supporters of apartheid, Paul Krüger, the country's president at the turn of the century. The future Nobel Prize winner published her first works, a number of fables, in the children's section of a Johannesburg newspaper. At the age of 15, however, she placed her first adult short story in print. She then wrote regularly for South African periodicals.

Gordimer received her initial acclaim as the author of carefully constructed and psychologically insightful short stories. Critics like Haugh have compared her skill in this genre to that of such masters as Guy de Maupassant and Anton Chekhov. Her first collection of such works, *Face to Face,* appeared in South Africa in 1949, but soon thereafter she won an international reputation when her stories appeared in England and the United States. She was soon writing regularly for *The New Yorker.*

For her the obverse of a freedom to gaze on everything without fear or favor is clearly an obligation to do so.

—Stephen Clingman

The young writer's sense of human frailty in the face of racial division can be seen in her early story "The Catch." It appeared in *The Soft Voice of the Serpent,* her first collection of short stories to be published outside South Africa. A young white couple befriend an Indian fishermen and share his excitement at catching a huge salmon. Later, accompanied by white friends, they encounter him and his fish once again, but now they are overcome by snobbery and embarrassment. A deeper sense of the depth of racial separation can be seen in "Is There Nowhere Else Where We Can Meet?" In this work, which appeared in 1949, a young white girl is the victim of a purse snatching in the open countryside. Pondering her unsettling experience, she wonders sympathetically about her attacker and their common humanity. Notes Haugh: "Her finest effects are the tangential results, among whites, of a racial encounter."

Gordimer began her longer works at the same time that she was drawing praise for her early short stories. She soon went on to develop a comparably distinguished reputation as a novelist. Her first such work, *The Lying Days,* was published in South Africa in 1953, and in both Britain and the U.S. the following year. It was,

according to Haugh, "an appealing, impressionistic novel of alienation and search" that he considers the best of all her longer works of fiction. The book traces the life of a young South African white woman from her childhood in a mining town though her first encounters with love and on to her years at the university.

Some critics find *The Lying Days* to be Gordimer's most autobiographical work, although her heroine, Nell, is a Christian of Scottish descent. The main Jewish character is a young man, an architecture student with whom Nell has an extended friendship. Clingman attributes the strong depiction of the mining locale and its carefully stratified society in the book to Gordimer's childhood friendship with a girl from a mining official's family. He notes that this early novel is "emblematic of Gordimer's method of writing" as "the product of close observation." It is also, in essence, the story of the heroine's personal education in the ways of her segment of the world.

Nonetheless, the book also features a consideration of the South African political situation at the close of the 1940s, a state of affairs marked by growing division between the races. A Nationalist Party government committed to harsh policies of segregation had just come to power, and black separatism was pushing sympathetic liberal whites away from any common political movement. Meanwhile, as Gordimer notes, individual South Africans involved in long-standing, loving relationships with members of another race found themselves the targets of an increasingly intrusive government.

In her next novel, *A World of Strangers,* published in 1958, Gordimer plunged directly into the political scene. "Virtually seven-eighths," writes Clingman, "is devoted to social observation." By now, Gordimer had become drawn into literary circles that included black writers, and she herself was increasingly interested in the political scene. In the book, the hero is a young Englishman who has come to work in South Africa. Through his eyes, Gordimer examines both the growing racial tension in her native country as well as tentative efforts by blacks and white liberals to encounter one another socially. At the book's conclusion, the hero, Toby Hood, forms a personal bond with one of the story's principal black characters. The bond implies as well the start of a political commitment for Hood. Thus, Gordimer describes the efforts of individuals to challenge the oppressive system around them.

By the early 1960s, Gordimer found herself writing in a rapidly changing political and racial environment. There was, for example, an expanding number of independent African nations. Moreover, within South Africa, the confrontation at Sharpeville in March 1960—in which police killed and wounded over 200 black demonstrators—led to increased police repression. Many of the black writers Gordimer had come to know were forced into exile. In addition, black leaders increasingly rejected an alliance with liberal whites to create a common community as Gordimer had suggested in *A World of Strangers*. Her succession of novels mirrored this changing political reality. Thus, *Occasion for Loving*, published in 1963, shows assertive black protagonists rejecting cooperation with whites as Gordimer, in Clingman's words, "acknowledges for the first time that the ultimate current of history in South Africa . . . is black, and not white."

Her novels now began to offend the censor. In 1962, the paperbound edition of *A World of Strangers* was banned, probably because the government thought the book would circulate too widely in such an inexpensive form. In 1966, *The Late Bourgeois World* ran afoul of South Africa's censorship laws; it too was banned.

In 1970, Gordimer responded to the changing scene in Africa, with its multitude of newly independent states, when she wrote *A Guest of Honor*. It tells the tragic story of a former colonial administrator who returns to the area in which he had worked, now transformed into an independent African state, only to die in a struggle between the various power factions there. The book is notable for being her first work set outside South Africa. Moreover, it introduces new themes in her writing: the conflict between members of the black population, the greed and corruption of black leaders. Some critics have found the book deeply flawed by its focus on the ugly political developments of postindependence Africa, and they consider it most valuable as a sign of Gordimer's personal education in political reality and her compelling desire to share that education with her readers.

In 1974, the prestigious Booker Prize went to Gordimer for her novel *The Conservationist*. In it, she presents a male hero, the industrialist Mehring, who tries to acquire and preserve a vast tract of South African wilderness. The body of an unknown black man found on Mehring's property, writes Clingman, represents how "the peace and serenity he enjoys on his farm are depending upon the institutionalized social violence that keeps the location politically subdued and quiet." In the end, a violent storm arises to drive Mehring from his land. The book's symbolism points to the impending change of power within South Africa that Gordimer perceived. A shift in her own political views likewise took place at this time: she now ceased to call herself a liberal and chose to describe her political position as that of a "white radical."

At times, Gordimer herself expressed a clear understanding that her work would be seen as an important record of changes and changing attitudes in her native country. In the introduction to the 1975 edition of her short stories, for example, she wrote: "The changes in social attitudes unconsciously reflected in the stories represent both that of the people in my society—that is to say, history—and my apprehension of it."

In 1979's *Burger's Daughter*, the heroine is a new type for Gordimer, a young woman who is the daughter of South African radicals. She abandons the political struggle for a time to focus on her personal needs, an action symbolized by her life abroad. But she returns from France to resume political activities. In *July's People*, which appeared in 1981, the author paints a grim picture of whites living in future society that has been transformed by revolution. Fleeing to the home village of their black servant, the adults of the bourgeois Smales family display the impassable gap between them and their hosts.

Dramatic shifts took place in South African life starting in the late 1980s. In 1989, several black leaders from the African National Congress were released after serving long prison terms. In 1990, in an act of vast symbolic significance, Nelson Mandela, the imprisoned hero of the antiapartheid movement, was freed after serving almost 30 years behind bars. As South Africa moved toward historic change in its racial policy, Gordimer's writing reflected the shifting situation in such works as *A Sport of Nature*, published in 1987, and *My Son's Story*, published in 1990.

A Sport of Nature has a white heroine, a Jewish South African, who marries a black revolutionary, then, after his murder, weds a second black leader. It constitutes an imagined history of postapartheid South Africa, and it concludes with the birth of a new, black state in place of the old, white-run Republic. *My Son's Story* likewise takes place in an imagined, postapartheid South Africa. In this work, Gordimer for the first time makes her most important characters neither black nor white but members of South Africa's mixed-race (or "coloured") population. The novel explains how the racial laws that separated whites and nonwhites have now been ended, and it goes on to explore the complex reality of a coloured family in which the father has become entangled in a relationship with a white woman.

Gordimer went well beyond her role as a writer in responding to change. In an act of solidarity with the black majority, she joined several other whites to confront armed police in defense of Alexandra, a black township, in 1986. That same year, she and other South African writers joined in a committee to oppose the government's censorship of literature. Becoming increasingly outspoken, Gordimer stated while testifying at a political trial in 1989 that she now accepted the leadership of the governing circle of the African National Congress. In 1990, she formally joined that organization.

Gordimer was awarded the Nobel Prize for Literature in October 1991. She was the first South African to win the honor; moreover, she was the first female writer to receive the prize in 25 years. The award corresponded in time to the end of the apartheid system in South Africa, the topic that had played so significant a role in her writing. In her acceptance speech at Stockholm, Gordimer concentrated her attention on the plight of persecuted writers. In particular, she defended Salman Rushdie, who had been condemned to death by Islamic militants for his allegedly disrespectful writings concerning the Prophet Muhammed. In the years since, Gordimer has continued to speak out on a variety of political issues.

The complexity of Gordimer's output and the length of her career as a prominent writer have encouraged critics to analyze her work from a number of new angles. For example, in *The Late Fiction of Nadine Gordimer*, Michael Wade has examined the question of Jewish identity in her writing. Gordimer has drawn particular attention in recent years from feminist critics like Wagner, **Karen Lazar**, and **Dorothy Driver**. They have found that, as a writer interested in the political and social world around her, Nadine Gordimer has apparently been firm in her opposition to feminist concerns. Her view of South Africa's long-standing divisions has discounted gender as a crucial factor. In 1975, for example, she wrote that "all writers are androgynous beings." In 1984, reasserting her belief in the primacy of racial over gender issues, she declared: "The white man and the white woman have much more in common than the white woman and the black woman." Nonetheless, much of her work has incorporated material on the growth and psychological changes of women characters in the society of apartheid, and Gordimer has used both male as well as female protagonists.

While the object of increasing scholarly study, Gordimer has remained a productive writer. The year that she received the Nobel Prize, she published *Jump and Other Stories*, her eighth volume of shorter fiction. Gordimer's novel, *None to Accompany Me*, appeared in 1994. Like the bulk of her earlier work, it is set in a changing South Africa in which the old system of apartheid has come to an end. Through her heroine, a liberal attorney named Vera Stark, Gordimer presents a picture of the new South Africa absorbing such changes as the return of imprisoned or exiled political activists. As in most of her work, she balances her picture of political change with an acute examination of her main character's psychological development.

SOURCES:

Clingman, Stephen. *The Novels of Nadine Gordimer: History from the Inside.* 2nd ed. Amherst, MA: University of Massachusetts Press, 1992.

Current Biography. NY: H.W. Wilson, 1980.

Dictionary of Literary Biography Yearbook: 1991. Edited by James W. Hipp. Detroit, MI: Gale Research, 1991.

Haugh, Robert F. *Nadine Gordimer.* NY: Twayne, 1974.

Head, Dominic. *Nadine Gordimer.* Cambridge, England: Cambridge University Press, 1994.

Smith, Rowland. *Critical Essays on Nadine Gordimer.* Boston, MA: G.K. Hall, 1990.

Wagner, Kathrin. *Rereading Nadine Gordimer.* Bloomington, IN: Indiana University Press, 1994.

SUGGESTED READING:

Ettin, Andrew. *Betrayals of the Body Politic: The Literary Commitments of Nadine Gordimer.* Charlottesville: University Press of Virginia, 1993.

Newman, Judie. *Nadine Gordimer.* London: Routledge, 1988.

The Who's Who of Nobel Prize Winners, 1901–1995. 3rd ed. Edited by Bernard S. Schlessinger and June H. Schlessinger. Phoenix, AZ: Oryx Press, 1996.

Neil M. Heyman,
Professor of History, San Diego State University,
San Diego, California

Gordon, Anna Adams (1853–1931).

See Willard, Frances for sidebar.

Gordon, Caroline (1895–1981)

American novelist, short-story writer, critic, and major figure in the Southern Renaissance, whose work described the conflict between industrialism and agrarianism, the tension between the pre-Civil War and post-Civil War South, and humankind's struggle to impose order on an unstable world. Born Caroline Gordon on October 6, 1895, on Merry Mont (or Merimont) farm, Todd County, Kentucky; died on

April 11, 1981, in San Cristobal de las Casas, Mexico; daughter of James Maury Morris Gordon and Nancy (Meriwether) Gordon (both teachers); Bethany College, West Virginia, B.A., 1916; married Allen Tate, in May 1924 (divorced 1945); remarried Allen Tate, in 1946 (divorced 1959); children: Nancy Tate (b. September 1925).

Spent early childhood at Merry Mont farm; at age ten, attended her father's school of classical studies; after graduation from Bethany College, taught high school in Clarksville, Tennessee; moved to Chattanooga, Tennessee (1920) and worked as a reporter for the Chattanooga News; after marriage, moved with husband and child to Paris (1928–29); published first short story in Gyroscope (1929); returned to the South (1930); published first novel, Penhally (1931); began moving frequently (1937) to fill temporary academic positions, including teaching creative writing at the Women's College of the University of North Carolina at Greensboro (1938); moved to Princeton, New Jersey (1939); converted to Catholicism (1947).

Novels: Penhally (1931); Aleck Maury, Sportsman (1934); None Shall Look Back (1937); The Garden of Adonis (1937); Green Centuries (1941); The Women on the Porch (1944); The Strange Children (1951); The Malefactors (1956); The Glory of Hera (1972). Selected short stories: "What Music" (1934); "A Morning's Favor" (1935); "The Women on the Battlefield" (1936–37); "Frankie and Thomas and Bud Asbury" (1939); "The Olive Garden" (1945); The Forest of the South (1945); "The Waterfall" (1950); "The Feast of St. Eustace" (1954); "A Narrow Heart: The Portrait of a Woman" (1960); "The Dragon's Teeth" (1961); Old Red and Other Stories (1963); "Cock-Crow" (1965); "Cloud Nine" (1969); "A Walk With the Accuser (Who is the God of This World)" (1969); "Always Summer" (1971); "The Strangest Day in the Life of Captain Meriwether Lewis as Told to His Eighth Cousin, Once Removed" (1976).

Selected critical works: "Notes on Faulkner and Flaubert" (1948); "A Virginian in Prairie Country" (1953); "How I Learned to Write Novels" (1956); How to Read a Novel (1957); "Flannery O'Connor's Wise Blood" (1958); (with Allen Tate) The House of Fiction (1960); A Good Soldier: A Key to the Novels of Ford Madox Ford (1963). Awards: O. Henry prize (1934); honorary degree from Bethany College (1946).

In her fiction, Caroline Gordon captured the essence of the American South during the first half of the 20th century, when many struggled to maintain a distinct cultural identity as industrialization began to make inroads into the region.

Among the Southern Renaissance intellectuals who emerged to protest the rapid and profound changes brought by industrial development, Caroline Gordon spoke with special eloquence of the bonds of family and tradition. Many of her novels and short stories were based on her Southern childhood, and she remained deeply attached to her heritage. In her fiction as well as in her literary criticism and teaching career, Caroline Gordon was a significant figure in the Southern Renaissance and made valuable contributions to 20th-century American literature.

Caroline Gordon was born on Merry Mont farm, on the southern border of Kentucky, in 1895. Although a number of relatives and extended family peopled the farm, it was Caroline's grandmother, **Caroline Meriwether**, or "Miss Carrie," who dominated the place and for whom Caroline Gordon was named. In her unpublished memoirs, Gordon described Merry Mont as a "golden world," a place that produced "a stirring in my heart which no other name can evoke."

She spent her early years interacting with her brothers, Morris, who was older, and William, who was younger, as well as her two cousins **Mildred ("Mannie") Gordon Meriwether** and **Marion Douglas Meriwether**, who also lived on the property. These two female cousins, though slightly older than Caroline, were "like sisters" to her, and she remained close to them throughout her life. Much of Gordon's later fiction was based on experiences and relationships formed during these years in Kentucky. Her close bond with her cousin Mannie, for example, became the basis for the friendship of Agnes and Daphne in Gordon's 1944 novel, The Women on the Porch.

Yet the person who appears to have had the most influence on Gordon in her youth was her father, James Maury Gordon. A teacher and occasional preacher in the Disciples of Christ Church, James was known for his charm and his restlessness; he moved his young family around the South nearly every two years and, on one occasion, left them to take a solo trip to Europe for a year. Gordon's memories of her father were good ones, and throughout her life she cited the education in the classics and in composition that she received at his college preparatory school in Clarksville, Tennessee, as an important part of her intellectual development. She later immortalized her father in short stories and in her 1934 novel, Aleck Maury, Sportsman, which traced the life of a Southern gentleman whose abiding passion was the outdoors. During her childhood, Gordon did not enjoy such a close bond with her mother, and despite **Nancy Meriwether Gordon**'s reputation as a "passionately intellectual" and devoutly religious teacher, Caroline Gordon never mentions her having any influence on her early education.

I think of a novel, in a way, as a piece of sculpture, I feel that I am molding the material.

—Caroline Gordon

In the early 1910s, Caroline left home to attend Bethany College in Bethany, West Virginia, where her two Meriwether cousins, Marion and Mannie, were also enrolled. Gordon's college years were apparently happy ones. She studied Greek, Latin, and English literature, and joined a sorority and the college literary society. In 1916, after graduating with a bachelor's degree in classical studies and a teaching certificate, she set about finding employment. After a few years of teaching high school in Missouri and Tennessee, Gordon landed a job writing for the Chattanooga *News,* a medium-size daily in Tennessee, in 1920. Despite her lack of journalistic experience, Gordon did well at the paper and was soon given a weekly book-review column. In 1921, she relocated to Wheeling, West Virginia, and began writing for the *Intelligencer,* a smaller paper than the *News.* Although she became the first woman writer to receive a byline in the *Intelligencer* and was given credit for helping to revamp the newspaper's image, Gordon's tenure there was short. A little more than a year later, for reasons that are unclear, she quit her Wheeling post and returned to Chattanooga and her job at the *News.*

Back in Chattanooga, Gordon continued to explore the literary culture of the South through numerous book reviews and essays. In 1923, she published a review essay on the condition of Southern literature that brought her to the attention of some well-known Southern writers. At this time, Southern letters was part of a "Renaissance" that included new work in the fields of sociology, history, and political science. Beginning in the early part of the 20th century, this rebirth produced what some historians have labeled a "literature of revolt" that self-consciously opposed the nostalgic, "moonlight-and-magnolia" yearning for antebellum Southern life that had characterized much of the region's literature. In the vanguard of this movement were members of a philosophical discussion group that called themselves the "Fugitive Poets." The group included, among others, the writers John Crowe Ransom, Stanley Johnson, Merrill

Moore, Robert Penn Warren, and Alan Tate. Ransom, Warren, Tate, and others also identified themselves as "Agrarians," which meant that they were philosophically opposed to the encroachment of industrial society in the South. Their manifesto, entitled *I'll Take My Stand,* was published in 1930.

Caroline Gordon first encountered these writers in the 1920s while reviewing their work, much of which was published in their aptly titled magazine *The Fugitive.* In 1924, while visiting her parents in Kentucky, she met Robert Penn Warren and Alan Tate, who were also visiting the area. Soon thereafter, she and Tate, whom she had pronounced "the most radical member of the group" in her reviews, were deeply involved. That fall, Gordon, who had always found New York City's literary culture appealing, moved there and rejoined Tate. Although she maintained throughout her life that she and Tate married in November of 1924, in fact they were wed at City Hall in May of 1925, after Gordon found out that she was pregnant. Their daughter **Nancy Tate** was born in September.

Gordon plunged into the literary culture of New York and formed friendships with many resident writers, including the English novelist Ford Madox Ford. She worked as Ford's secretary for a short time to make ends meet, and he, along with Tate, encouraged her to pursue a career as a writer. Gordon's association with Ford left an enduring impression. In 1963, she would publish a critical interpretation of his work entitled *A Good Soldier: A Key to the Novels of Ford Madox Ford.*

In 1928, Tate received a Guggenheim fellowship that allowed the small family to move to Paris, where Gordon began to work on a novel. Looking back, she remembered that "in France, where the living was cheaper than in the United States, I was able to hire a nurse for my child. Otherwise I would not have been able to write the novel." Her first published work was a short story called "Summer Dust," which appeared in the magazine *Gyroscope* in 1929. When the fellowship expired, Gordon and the family returned to the States, and in 1930, the year that the Agrarians' manifesto was published, they relocated to a farm in Clarksville, Tennessee, close to Merry Mont. Surrounded by the familiar landscape of the South, Gordon completed the novel. Published in 1931, *Penhally* traced the fortunes of a family through several generations on their Kentucky estate. Drawing on her childhood memories of life at Merry Mont farm, Gordon explored the decline of pre-Civil War

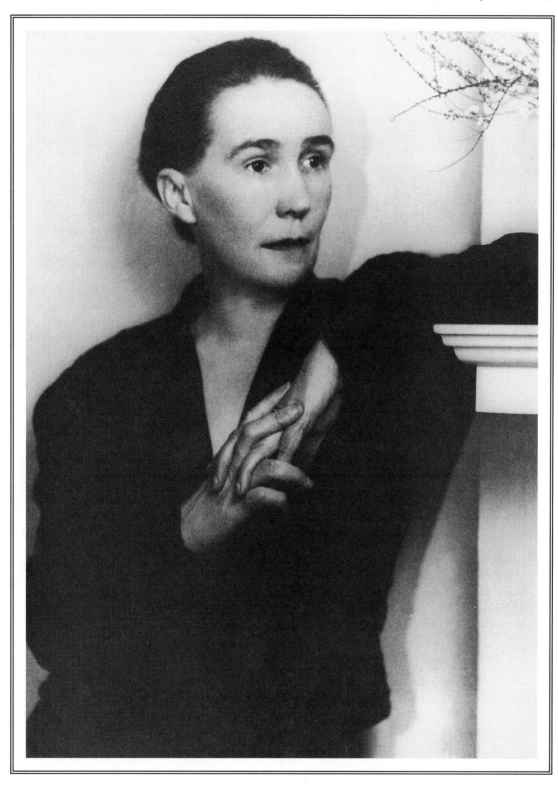

Caroline
Gordon

Southern agrarian life. Many of her fellow writers and some critics considered her debut auspicious and suggested that her work was "far above the ordinary" with a "true feeling for the dramatic" and a unique insight into the South. However other critics found Gordon's plot hectic and confusing, with "much fine feeling . . . but very little judgment." A few even suggested that Gordon's real intent was to air the grievances of the Agrarian movement in her novel. This suggestion upset Gordon a great deal, for her purpose in this work, as in others that followed, was not to promote a particular movement, but to explore a larger dilemma: the possibility of maintaining Southern traditions in a world that seemed hostile to them.

In 1932, Caroline Gordon received a Guggenheim fellowship that allowed the family to travel to Paris once again. Throughout the 1930s, she published a number of short stories as well the novels *None Shall Look Back*, *The Garden of Adonis*, and the work based on the life of her father, *Aleck Maury, Sportsman*. The latter work was "a labor of love" for Gordon, although it painted a portrait of her father that was not entirely uncritical. The novel told the story of a Southern man whose overwhelming passion was the pursuit of sport, namely fishing. Gordon treated the protagonist's zeal as both heroic and selfish, and she alluded throughout the story to the sacrifices his family was forced to make because of his actions. Gordon had high hopes for the novel, which she felt was her best chance for "a popular sale." She was encouraged by the positive responses she received from Ford Madox Ford and other friends, but reviewers offered little praise for the book. Gordon suggested that the "small, inconspicuous review" that appeared in *The New York Times Book Review* had been written "by someone who hadn't read the book."

Although Gordon worried about the absence of critical praise for some of her novels, she never lost her desire to create fiction. In fact, throughout her career she struggled to find enough time to write. In the years following the publication of *Aleck Maury, Sportsman*, Gordon and Tate frequently entertained other writers at their Southern home, and this fact, combined with the close proximity of so many of Caroline's relatives and the commitments involved in raising young Nancy, made writing difficult. By the late 1930s, both Tate and Gordon were ready for a change, and in 1937 they left the farm in Tennessee for the first of many untenured academic appointments. In 1939, they settled temporarily in Princeton, where Tate had received an offer to teach creative writing.

While Gordon's professional success continued in the 1940s, her marriage to Alan Tate began to deteriorate. In 1945, they first separated, then divorced. But this separation was short-lived, for in 1946 they reconciled and decided to remarry. As Gordon biographer **Veronica Makowsky** has noted, they established a new pattern in their married life. "Unable to make a clean break, they were equally unable to live together contentedly for more than a few months at a time." According to speculation, many of their difficulties stemmed from Tate's pattern of infidelity. After their remarriage, they settled again in Princeton, though their relationship continued to be stormy. Furthermore, Gordon took on a full teaching load at Columbia University, which brought added pressures. At this difficult juncture, Gordon found inspiration for her personal life and her fiction in religion.

In 1947, Gordon converted to Catholicism. Robert Brinkmeyer, one of her biographers, has suggested that the horrors of World War II "prompted her to consider more seriously the flawed nature of humanity and the existence of the divine." Two other factors may have influenced her decision as well. First, her husband Alan Tate had flirted with the idea of joining the church for many years; he converted three years after Gordon. Second, several of Gordon's biographers claim that she met the French Catholic philosopher Jacques Maritain while she was at Princeton in the early 1940s and was impressed with his strong beliefs. According to Brinkmeyer, Maritain and others were at the center of a "revival" that was "renewing interest in the Church for many intellectuals," including Gordon.

Gordon's conversion to Catholicism had a significant effect on her work. Indeed, several of her biographers have suggested that although she went through other artistic phases, her decision to join the church produced the most dramatic change in her fiction. Gordon's focus shifted from secular themes to the divine. For example, in her novel *Malefactors*, published in 1956, she envisioned salvation from the destructiveness of life through an embrace of the Catholic faith. Of her beliefs, Gordon once said:

> I have lived most of my life on the evidence of things not seen—what else is writing a novel but that?—and my work has progressed slowly and steadily in one direction. At a certain point I found the Church squarely in the path. I couldn't jump over it and wouldn't go around it, so had to go into it.

Like her literary contemporary *****Flannery O'Connor**, Gordon henceforth included distinctively Catholic themes in her fiction.

Unfortunately, as her biographer **Nancylee Jonza** noted, Gordon's faith became "the only fixed point in her life" in the late 1940s and early 1950s. She continued to have serious problems in her marriage to Tate, and she despaired of finishing her current project, a novel titled *The Strange Children*, because of her teaching responsibilities. In 1959, Gordon found out that Tate was seriously involved with another woman, the poet **Isabella Gardner** (b. 1915), and asked for a divorce. Following the breakup, Gordon remained in Princeton and continued teaching and writing.

She was an active writer and beloved teacher well into her 80s. Through Princeton's University Speakers Bureau, she lectured at many colleges on the East Coast and in the Midwest. Her health eventually began to deteriorate, however, and in 1978, at the urging of her daughter, Caroline Gordon moved to San Cristobal de las Casas, Mexico. It was there that she continued to work on the second of a double-novel project that explored the heroic figures of classical history and mythology, and it was there that she died, after a series of strokes, on April 11, 1981. "I am a novelist by profession," Caroline Gordon asserted in an address before Georgia College in 1974. As reviews of her work demonstrate, her novels were well-regarded. Gordon's short stories also received praise. Contemporary critics have compared her to the writers William Faulkner and *Katherine Anne Porter. As Thomas H. Landess noted in a symposium on Gordon's short fiction, Gordon was able to "crowd into her stories more than their formal limitations would seem to permit: the total experience of a region's history, the hero's archetypal struggle, the complexity of modern aesthetics." Caroline Gordon's lifetime in literature left a legacy beyond her novels and short stories. She produced compelling portraits of the richness of a region and the complexity of human experience. As she noted, "We are moved to imitate our Creator, to do as he did, and create a world."

SOURCES:

Brinkmeyer, Robert H., Jr. *Three Catholic Writers of the Modern South.* Jackson, MS: University Press of Mississippi, 1985.

Gordon, Caroline. *Aleck Maury, Sportsman.* NY: Scribner, 1934.

Jonza, Nancylee Novell. *The Underground Stream: The Life and Art of Caroline Gordon.* Athens, GA: University of Georgia Press, 1995.

Waldron, Ann. *Close Connections: Caroline Gordon and the Southern Renaissance.* NY: Putnam, 1987.

SUGGESTED READING:

Wood, Sally ed. *The Southern Mandarins: Letters of Caroline Gordon to Sally Wood, 1924–1937.* Baton Rouge, LA: Louisiana State University Press, 1984.

COLLECTIONS:

Correspondence and papers located at Princeton University Library, Department of Rare Books and Special Collections.

Christine Stolba,
Ph.D. candidate in American History, Emory University, Atlanta, Georgia

Gordon, Laura de Force (1838–1907)

American lawyer, editor, and reformer. Name variations: Laura D. Gordon. Born Laura de Force on August 17, 1838, in Erie County, Pennsylvania; died on April 5, 1907, in Lodi, California; married Dr. Charles H. Gordon, in 1862 (divorced by 1878).

Laura de Force Gordon skillfully combined her passion for women's suffrage with a successful law and publishing career to enact change in post-Civil War America. She was born in Erie County, Pennsylvania, on August 17, 1838, and received her primary education at local schools. She married Dr. Charles H. Gordon in 1862 and lived in New Orleans before moving to Nevada in 1867. In 1870, they moved again, settling in Mokelumne (later Lodi), California.

Gordon began her activist career in 1868 when she made one of the first public speeches on equal rights for women in the American West. She continued to lecture on suffrage and, in 1870, contributed to the founding of the California Woman Suffrage Society. She served as its president in 1877, and again from 1884 to 1894.

The 1870s proved to be a critical decade for Gordon. In 1873, she became editor of the woman's department of the *Narrow Gauge,* a semi-weekly paper based in Stockton, California. Later that year, she took on the responsibility of publishing and editing the *Stockton Weekly Leader,* and her skills soon brought the paper success. In May of the following year, it became a daily, and in 1875 she moved it to Sacramento as the *Weekly Leader.* Though she sold the paper in 1876, Gordon continued to keep her hand in publishing. In 1878, she edited the Oakland *Daily Democrat,* and in 1879 she published *The Great Geysers of California and How to Reach Them.*

Near the end of the 1870s, Gordon turned her energies to breaking down the barriers for women in the field of law. During the 1877–78 state legislative session, she lobbied to admit women to the practice of law in California. To push the issue, Gordon applied for admission to the Hastings College of Law in San Francisco in 1878. She and *Clara S. Foltz were both denied admission, and they immediately filed suit against the school. They argued their cases jointly in district court and won their case before the state supreme court in the fall of 1879. Gordon's private law studies accelerated her law education, and she was the second woman admitted to the California bar in December of that year. For the next five years, she practiced in San Francisco then moved to Stockton. She developed a strong reputation as a criminal lawyer and in 1885 was admitted to practice before the U.S.

Supreme Court. Laura Gordon died in Lodi, California, on April 5, 1907.

Judith C. Reveal,
freelance writer, Greensboro, Maryland

Gordon, Lucie Duff (1821–1869).

See Duff-Gordon, Lucie.

Gordon, Lucy Duff (1862–1935).

See Duff Gordon, Lucy.

Gordon, Ruth (1896–1985)

American actress and screenwriter who received Academy Award nominations for her screenplays Adam's Rib *and* Pat and Mike *and an Oscar for her performance in* Rosemary's Baby. *Born Ruth Gordon Jones in Wollaston, Massachusetts, on October 30, 1896; died on August 28, 1985, in Edgartown, Massachusetts; daughter of Clinton and Anne Jones; married Gregory Kelly (an actor), in 1921 (died 1927); married Garson Kanin (a director and screenwriter), in 1942; children: (with producer Jed Harris) one son, Jones.*

When a teenager, began appearing in silent films as a bit player and made her Broadway debut at age 19 (1915), followed by several well-received performances in both comedic and dramatic roles on stage and film during the next two decades; during a lull in acting career (1940s), turned to writing for the screen and received Academy Award co-nominations for screenplays of such films as Adam's Rib *and* Pat and Mike; *resumed acting career (1960s), winning a new audience and an Academy Award for work in* Rosemary's Baby *(1968); worked steadily in film and television, along with publishing three volumes of memoirs and one novel, before her death.*

Filmography—as actress: Camille *(1915);* The Whirl of Life *(1915);* Abe Lincoln in Illinois *(1939);* Dr. Erlich's Magic Bullet *(1940);* Two-Faced Woman *(1941);* Edge of Darkness *(1943);* Action in the North Atlantic *(1943);* Inside Daisy Clover *(1966);* Lord Love a Duck *(1966);* Rosemary's Baby *(1968);* Whatever Happened to Aunt Alice? *(1969);* Where's Poppa? *(1970);* Harold and Maude *(1971);* Isn't It Shocking? *(1973);* The Big Bus *(1976);* The Great Houdini *(1976);* Every Which Way But Loose *(1978);* Perfect Gentlemen *(1978);* Boardwalk *(1979);* Scavenger Hunt *(1979);* My Bodyguard *(1980);* Any Which Way You Can *(1980);* Don't Go to Sleep *(1982);* Jimmy the Kid *(1983);* The Trouble with Spies *(1984);* Mugsy's Girls *(also released as* Delta Pi, *1985);* Maxie *(1985).*

Filmography—as screenwriter: Over 21 *(1945);* A Double Life *(1948);* Adam's Rib *(1949);* The Marrying Kind *(1952);* Pat and Mike *(1952);* The Actress *(1953);* Rosie! *(1967).*

The most remarkable thing about Ruth Gordon's 70-year career was the very fact of its existence. It could have come to an abrupt end on any one of several occasions, starting as early as 1915, on the day when the president of New York's American Academy of Dramatic Arts called an 18-year-old Ruth to his office after her first year at the school. "We feel that you are not suited to acting," he bluntly told her. "You show no promise." Gordon was refused admission for a second term and was sent back to her suburban Boston home, only to return to the school in triumph, 53 years later, to receive an award and address the graduating class of 1968. "On that awful day when someone says you're not suited," she told them, "when they say you're too tall, you're not pretty, you're no good, think of me and don't give up!"

No one was more surprised than Ruth Gordon when she was struck by an overpowering desire to take to the stage while watching a performance of a long-forgotten musical called *The Pink Lady* at the old Colonial Theater in Boston during her last year of high school. She never forgot the force of the revelation, and the yellowed program was found among her effects at the time of her death. "I had gone into the Colonial the average human being beset by worry, doubt, questions," she wrote years later. "When I came out, I had taken off for the horse latitudes and have never lit since."

Gordon's parents were equally surprised by their daughter's announcement. "What makes you think you got the stuff it takes?" thundered Clinton Jones, a former sea captain who had settled in Wollaston, Massachusetts, and had found a job as overseer in a local food-processing plant. Ruth did not have a ready answer, for she was pert, rather than pretty, short of stature, and had no stage experience outside of a few school pageants. All she knew was that she had no interest in her father's plans for her to become a physical-education teacher. **Ann Jones**, who supplemented the family income by working as a secretary, was more sympathetic and persuaded her husband to allow Ruth to apply to the Academy in New York, for which Clinton paid the $400 tuition, along with $10 a week for Gordon's board at the genteel Three Arts Club for "young theatrical ladies" on East 85th Street.

The Academy was not what Gordon had been expecting, for she had been attracted by the theater's ebullience, not its discipline. She found the dramatic theories propounded in the class-room elusive; had considerable difficulty remembering lines for student productions, let alone speaking them convincingly; and had no idea how to comport herself gracefully and naturally on the stage. She was back in Wollaston within the year, but she persuaded her parents to let her return to New York in the fall of 1915 to look for work—a task that became even more critical when her mother suffered a stroke and had to be confined to a nursing home, leaving no money for Gordon's support. There followed long, dreary weeks of making the rounds of theatrical managers and agents with no work or offer, her only income being the five dollars a day she received as an extra in silent films then being shot across the Hudson River in Fort Lee, New Jersey. It was her first exposure to the film work that would bring her such a wide audience in later years.

Gordon's luck seemed to change when she landed her first Broadway role, albeit a small one, as one of the Lost Boys in *Maude Adams' 1915 production of *Peter Pan*. Fortunately for Gordon, the role featured little spoken dialogue. But still, *The New York Times* reported that "Miss Gordon is ever so gay as Nibs." Even more encouraging, Gordon successfully auditioned for the lead role in a touring company for a play called *Fair and Warmer*. The play had been successfully mounted on Broadway by the Selwyn Brothers, who proceeded to capitalize on their investment by sending out seven road companies. Gordon toured Ohio and Illinois on a months-long whistlestop journey through small towns with names like Crawfordsville, Hoopestown, and Circleville, during which her performances were universally panned. The Selwyn Brothers' inability to find a replacement was the only thing that saved her from being fired. Her difficulty remembering lines forced the road manager to suggest she remember only the general drift of each scene and improvise her dialogue, much to the confusion of those playing with her. Gordon put the best face on a bad situation in letters she wrote back home to a girlhood friend. "The manager of the company told the stage manager to let me create and ad lib," she burbled back to Wollaston. "That means put in business of my own and little offhand speeches, like stars do!"

Returning to New York late in 1916, Gordon rapidly went through the $60 a week she'd saved on the tour, leaving her desperate for four months before she landed a part in a stage adaptation of Booth Tarkington's *Seventeen,* which

was to open in Columbus, Ohio, and travel eastward to a hoped-for New York run. Gordon was given the role of "the Baby Talk Lady" largely because of the efforts of the actor who would play her leading man, Gregory Kelly. Kelly happened to be at her audition and urged the producer to hire her after the first actress chosen for the role fell ill. Her employment with *Seventeen* lasted only as far as Boston, but it was long enough for Gordon's relationship with Kelly to develop romantically as well as professionally. Kelly, in addition to becoming her lover, gave Gordon her first practical acting lessons during the tour, teaching her badly needed memorization techniques as well as giving her a useful collection of stage mannerisms and line readings to carry her through. By the time the show reached Boston, Gordon was pregnant. Both she and Kelly feared that her condition, when discovered by the theater world, would put an end to her ability to earn a living. She quietly left the theater after one night's performance to have an illegal abortion which left her ill and weak for days afterward. When the tour ended, in the late fall of 1918, Ruth and Gregory Kelly were married.

Their years together were productive ones. Gordon landed her first leading role on Broadway in a play which she and Kelly produced themselves and in which Kelly played opposite her. It was another work from Tarkington, called *Tweedles*, and this time the critics loved her. "One must certainly mention Miss Gordon," wrote Alexander Woolcott in the *New York Herald*, "who has a genuine and forthright actuality which is immensely nourishing to a play like this." Fellow critic Heywood Broun, who just a year before had written, "Anyone who looks like that and acts like that must get off the stage," now viewed Gordon's work with a more sympathetic eye. "Miss Gordon's hands actually seem to blush," he wrote of her demure portrayal of Tarkington's heroine. Next, Gordon played a governess who falls in love with her employer (Gregory again) for the touring company of *Clarence*, also from Tarkington's pen.

By now Gordon was a well-established stage presence and one-half of an acting team that enjoyed a level of recognition rivaling that given to Alfred Lunt and *Lynn Fontanne. There were tours of Europe, friendships with some of New York's most prominent literary and show-business personalities (Woolcott became a good friend, as did *Dorothy Parker, Robert Sherwood, and other members in good standing of the Algonquin Round Table), and summers spent sailing off Nantucket or in Long Island

Sound. But in 1927, just as Gordon was rehearsing a new Maxwell Anderson play called *Saturday's Children*, Gregory Kelly suffered a massive heart attack and died shortly after being admitted to a New York hospital. Perhaps as a tribute to all he had done for her career, Gordon insisted on keeping to the show's rehearsal schedule and out-of-town opening date in Stamford, Connecticut. The show was being directed by Guthrie McClintic, to whom Gordon turned for help. "Gregory taught me how to act so I didn't get fired," she once wrote. "Guthrie taught me the kind of acting you remember." *Saturday's Children* was Gordon's greatest triumph to date, with a sold-out box office well before the show opened on Broadway after a successful run in Stamford. "It was the first real acting I ever did," Gordon said. "Acting in the deep sense. One emotion underneath, one on the surface. Isn't that how it is in real life?"

*A*nyone can be talented. To *want* to be talented is the first step.

—Ruth Gordon

Gordon had now come into her own as a commanding and skillful artist, with nearly unanimous praise for her work in such memorable Broadway productions as Phillip Barry's difficult, mystical *Hotel Universe*, S.N. Behrman's *Serena Blandish*, John Wexley's anti-war polemic *They Shall Not Die,* and a highly original interpretation of Nora in Ibsen's *A Doll's House*. Gordon was especially commended for her versatility and the fresh outlook she gave to every role, in particular for the two diametrically opposed characters she brought to life in 1936. Gordon turned in a highly acclaimed performance as the hilariously scheming Mrs. Pinchwife in Congreve's *The Country Wife,* while in the same year giving a luminous interpretation of the tragic Mattie Silver in a stage adaptation of *Edith Wharton*'s *Ethan Frome*, in which she was again directed by McClintic. Theater historians still enthuse about Jo Mielziner's brooding set and the climactic scene in which Mattie and Ethan, played by Raymond Massey, sped down Mielziner's artificial snow hill on a sled toward their planned double suicide (with six burly stagehands waiting in the wings to stop them from crashing into the theater's exterior wall). Audience reaction to the play was rapturous, and even Edith Wharton wrote to Gordon from Paris that "the human and essential part of Ethan Frome *does* seem to reach your audience. . . . I know how largely your personification of Mattie contributed to their impression." Reviewers who, little more

than ten years before, had dismissed her as a second-rate ingenue, were equally impressed by the startling freshness of each role she played. "There were no echoes of older parts in her performances and no repetitions of her personality," critic Brooks Atkinson wrote of her work. "Miss Gordon created herself as an actress."

As she battled her way with persistence and sheer stubbornness to the top of what once seemed like an ill-chosen profession, Gordon carried on an active romantic life. She reported in her autobiography, *My Side,* that a brief liaison with a producer shortly after Gregory Kelly's death resulted in a second terminated pregnancy; and her long-running affair with producer Jed Harris during the 1930s produced a son, Jones, born in Paris during a discreet European vacation. Harris acknowledged paternity and supported the child. Back in New York just after the outbreak of World War II, Gordon returned to the stage in a production of *The Three Sisters* directed by Elia Kazan, during the rehearsals for which she began appearing in public with writer Garson Kanin.

The two had seen each other socially at parties and theater functions for some years, but there seemed little attraction between them during their first extended conversation, at a dinner party at Sardi's given by director George Cukor, or some months later at the premiere of Gordon's first motion picture in some 20 years, *Abe Lincoln in Illinois,* in which she again played opposite Raymond Massey as Lincoln's wife, *Mary Todd Lincoln*. Two more films followed—*Dr. Erlich's Magic Bullet* (1940) and *Two-Faced Woman* (1941)—before a third encounter with Kanin at which, Gordon recalled, "the sparks began to fly," although she admitted she never thought the relationship could succeed. "I was forty-five, he was twenty-nine. What kind of agony lay in store?" What lay in store was not agony but, following Gordon's marriage to Kanin in 1942, one of the most successful writing partnerships in entertainment history.

Their first collaboration was a play based on an idea of Gordon's, 1944's *Over 21,* the title being Gordon's indignant response to a doctor who asked her age. The pair's story, based loosely on their own relationship, told of the ups and downs of an affair between a young journalist and an older actress, and was adapted for the screen the next year. The first of a string of successful screen comedies was 1948's *A Double Life,* a sly, witty backstage story about an actor playing Othello who finds the role taking over his personal life. The picture was directed by

Ruth
Gordon

George Cukor, who had been responsible for their first encounter that night at Sardi's. Cukor was looking for ideas for two of his favorite actors, *Katharine Hepburn and Spencer Tracy, whose well-known relationship mirrored Gordon's and Kanin's. The first fruits of their collec-

tive labors was 1949's wry *Adam's Rib*, which recounted the rocky history of a decidedly adversarial marriage. The effort brought Gordon and Kanin Academy Award nominations for Best Original Screenplay. *Pat and Mike*, in 1952, cast Hepburn and Tracy as a hard-headed athlete and her small-time manager. That same year, Gordon and Kanin turned out another popular comedy, *The Marrying Kind*, in which *Judy Holliday and Aldo Ray reminisced about their marriage on the eve of their divorce. Gordon turned to her own adolescence as the source for 1953's *The Actress*, which she adapted from a play she had written some years earlier and which told the story of a young woman's struggle to become an actress against her father's wishes.

Although Gordon's successful writing career kept her away from stage or screen, there was a more practical reason for her absence, one which every middle-aged actress faces—the paucity of parts written for women "of a certain age." Although Gordon would not appear again in a major legitimate theater, she returned to films with a vengeance in 1965, when she was 69, with the first in a long series of eccentric, sprightly, sexy, or sometimes malevolent, elderly women. She appeared in director Robert Mulligan's *Inside Daisy Clover*, the dark tale of a childhood actress turned neurotic star, playing opposite *Natalie Wood's Daisy, as "The Dealer" who supplies Daisy's habit (earning an Academy Award nomination for Best Supporting Actress). There followed, the next year, the quirky Stella Bernard in George Axelrod's dark comedy, *Lord Love a Duck*; and in 1968, the role for which Gordon is most famous, the witch Minnie Castevet, in Roman Polanski's eerie *Rosemary's Baby*. Her work in the film won her an Academy Award that year as Best Supporting Actress and another appearance in the same role in a later TV sequel to the film.

From then on, hardly a year passed without an appearance from Gordon in a growing collection of weirdly funny or uncomfortably menacing little old ladies. "She is neither cozy nor sentimental," film reviewer David Thomson once wrote of her. "She has the authority of a woman who knows she has grown perversely sexy and commanding with age." Her usual vehicles were dark comedies like 1970's *Where's Poppa?*, in which George Segal attempts unsuccessfully to induce a heart attack in his nagging, querulous mother; or cheerily offbeat pictures like Clint Eastwood's *Everyone Which Way But Loose* in 1978. She won a whole new, younger audience with her work in what have since become cult films, most notably her performance in Hal Ashby's *Harold and Maude*, the story of a peculiar love affair between an elderly, life-affirming woman and a death-obsessed young man. The film was a commercial disaster and was almost universally panned, but so passionate was Gor-

don about the film's message that she wrote a strongly worded defense of the picture to Vincent Canby, who had delivered one of the more scathing reviews. Nor did Gordon ignore television, a medium that wasn't even imagined during her unpromising early days in the theater. She made notable guest appearances on "The Bob Newhart Show," "Columbo," "Rhoda" (as Carlton the Doorman's mother), and on "Taxi" (as "Sugar Mama"), for which she won an Emmy; she also wrote a television film in 1980, *Hardhat and Legs*.

Gordon spent her time between acting jobs in New York and on Martha's Vineyard, where she and Kanin had purchased a home in Edgartown. It was here that she wrote three volumes of memoirs, starting with 1971's *Myself Among Others*, and a mystery novel, *Shady Lady*, published in 1984. That same year, she accepted the part of Mrs. Lavin in the film *Maxie*, playing a dotty landlord and former vaudeville performer who unwittingly calls forth the spirit of her long-dead stage partner. But before the film was released, Gordon died quietly at home in Edgartown, on August 28, 1985, at the age of 89. (A film she had shot earlier in 1985, *Mugsy's Girls*, was actually Gordon's last released film, reaching theaters in early 1986.)

From that day in 1912, when a young high-school girl gazing down from a dim balcony in a dusty theater decided on her future, Gordon's determination and sheer willpower brought her the success her father once predicted would elude her. "She proved that acting is a craft as well as an art, and not a form of exhibitionism," Brooks Atkinson once wrote of her. "She belongs to no tradition; she founded her own."

SOURCES:
Atkinson, Brooks. *Broadway*. NY: Macmillan, 1970.
Gordon, Ruth. *My Side*. NY: Harper & Row, 1976.
———. *An Open Book*. NY: Doubleday, 1980.
Thomson, David. "Ruth Gordon," in *The Blockbuster Guide to Movies and Videos*. NY: Alfred A. Knopf, 1995.

Norman Powers,
writer-producer, Chelsea Lane Productions, New York

Gordon Low, Juliette (1860–1927).

See Low, Juliette Gordon.

Gore, Catherine (1799–1861)

English novelist and dramatist. Name variations: Catherine Grace Frances Moody; Mrs. Charles Arthur Gore; (pseudonyms) C.D.; C.F.G.; Albany Poyntz. Born Catherine Grace Frances Moody in East Ret-

ford, Nottinghamshire, England, in 1799; died at Lyndhurst, Hampshire, England, on January 29, 1861; daughter of Charles Moody (a wine merchant); married Captain Charles Gore, in 1823; children: ten.

Selected writings: Theresa Marchmont, or the Maid of Honour *(1823);* Lettre de Cachet *(1827);* The Reign of Terror *(1827);* Hungarian Tales *(1829);* Women as They Are; or The Manners of the Day *(1830);* Mothers and Daughters *(1831);* The Fair of May Fair *(1832); (play)* The School for Coquettes *(1832);* The Hamiltons *(1834);* Mrs. Armytage or Female Domination *(1836);* Stokeshill Place; or the Man of Business *(1837);* The Cabinet Minister and The Courtier of the Days of Charles II *(1839);* Preferment *(1840); (play)* Quid Pro Quo, or, The Day of the Dupes *(1843);* Cecil, or The Adventures of a Coxcomb *(1841);* Greville, or a Season in Paris *(1841);* The Banker's Wife *(1843);* Heckington, A Novel *(1858).*

Catherine Moody Gore was a precocious child whose friends nicknamed her "the poetess" because of her early poetic writings. She began her prolific writing career shortly after her marriage to Captain Charles Gore in 1823. Although she had ten children, she found time to write and publish novels, plays, and songs. Her descriptions of the high society of the time made her the undisputed queen of what was known as the "silver-fork" school of fiction. Her first published work, "The Two Broken Hearts" was written in verse, and the following year she published her first novel, *Theresa Marchmont, or The Maid of Honour.* During the 1820s, she saw her popularity rise with *Lettre de Cachet* (1827), *The Reign of Terror* (1827), and *Hungarian Tales* (1829). Her greatest success was *Women as They Are; or The Manners of the Day* (1830), a novel which so entertained King George IV that he remarked it was "the best bred and most amusing novel published in my remembrance."

In 1832, Gore moved to France and continued to support her sick husband and her ten children through her successful writing. She blossomed during the decade of the 1830s, producing *Mothers and Daughters* (1831), *The Fair of May Fair* (1832), *The Hamiltons* (1834), *Mrs. Armytage or Female Domination* (1836), and *Stokeshill Place; or The Man of Business* (1837). During the 1830s, Gore also wrote her first plays. Her most popular comedy, *The School for Coquettes* (1832), was produced at the Haymarket and ran for five weeks. *Lords and Commons,* her next effort, was produced at Drury Lane Theater but ran for only a few nights. A decade later her *Quid Pro Quo, or, The Day of*

the Dupes (1843) won critical acclaim and a £500 prize, but it was not as popular with patrons as her first effort. Other less successful plays included *The King's Seal* and *King O'Neil.*

Gore frequently wrote under pseudonyms and in one instance published two novels during the same week, prompting a deliberate competition. In 1841, she published *Cecil, or The Adventures of a Coxcomb* which was considered to be one of her most revealing novels on the social life of the upper-middle class. In 1843, Gore published *The Banker's Wife,* the plot of which concerned a corrupt banker. Life imitated art when her guardian, Sir John Dean Paul, defrauded her of a £20,000 inheritance in 1850. When he was convicted and imprisoned for the crime, Gore capitalized on the event by reissuing *The Banker's Wife.*

Her talents did not stop with novels and plays. She wrote songs and set poetry to music, including Burns' "And ye shall walk in silk attire." It became one of the most popular songs of the day.

Gore's style was fodder for many critics, chief among them William Thackeray who parodied her style in *Punch* magazine. By modern-day standards, Gore's work is tedious, but its value lies in its view of English society at the time. She was considered a clever writer who had a gift for satire and a keen head for business. Gore is known to have written over 70 novels during her lifetime, but her prolific use of pseudonyms makes it probable that other uncredited works exist.

Toward the end of her life, Gore lost her sight but not her skill. Although her output slowed, she continued to write almost until her death. Her last work, *Heckington, A Novel,* was published in 1858. She had returned to England and purchased a home in Hampshire where she died in 1861.

Judith C. Reveal,
freelance writer, Greensboro, Maryland

Gore-Booth, Constance (1868–1927).

See Markievicz, Constance.

Gore-Booth, Eva (1870–1926)

Irish poet, pacifist, suffragist and labor activist who campaigned to improve the pay and conditions of women workers in Manchester. Born Eva Selena Gore-Booth on May 22, 1870, at Lissadell, County Sligo, Ireland; died in London, England, on June 30, 1926; daughter of Sir Henry Gore-Booth (a landowner and explorer) and Georgina (Hill) Gore-Booth; sister of Constance Markievicz (1868–1927); educated at home; never married; lived with Esther Roper; no children;

Traveled with father to the West Indies and America (1894); diagnosed as having tuberculosis (1895); spent some months in Italy (1895–96), where she met Esther Roper; returned to Lissadell and set up the Sligo branch of the Irish Women's Suffrage and Local Government Association, before settling with Roper in Manchester (1896), where both were associated with the University Settlement, the Manchester and Salford Women's Trade Union Council, the Manchester National Society for Women's Suffrage, the Women's Co-Operative Guild and the Lancashire and Cheshire Women Textile and Other Workers' Representation Committee; published her first collection, Poems (1898); met Christabel Pankhurst (1901); split with Pankhurst on the use of violence in the suffrage campaign (1904); represented the Lancashire Working Women's Societies, the Trade Unions, and Labor Societies in Lancashire in the Women's Franchise Deputation to Prime Minister Campbell-Bannerman (1906); involved in campaigns for barmaids' right to work, for the improvement of florists' assistants' and pit-brow women's working conditions (1908–11); moved to London with Roper (1914); attended trials of conscientious objectors on behalf of the No-Conscription Fellowship (1915–18); was a member of the British organizing committee of the Women's International Congress, held at The Hague (1915); traveled to Dublin following the Easter Rebellion (1916) to visit her sister, Constance Markievicz, one of the rebel leaders, who was condemned to death but reprieved and imprisoned in England; attended the trial in London of Sir Roger Casement and was involved in the unsuccessful campaign for the reprieve of his death sentence (1916); visited Italy (1920–21); diagnosed as having cancer (1924).

Selected writings: Poems *(1898);* New Songs, a Lyric Selection made by AE from poems by Eva Gore-Booth and others *(1904);* The One and the Many *(1904);* The Three Resurrections *and* The Triumph of Maeve *(1905);* The Egyptian Pillar *(1907);* The Sorrowful Princess *(1907);* The Agate Lamp *(1912);* The Perilous Light *(1915);* Broken Glory *(1917);* The Sword of Justice *(1918);* A Psychological and Poetic Approach to the Study of Christ in the Fourth Gospel *(1923);* The Shepherd of Eternity *(1925);* The House of Three Windows *(1926);* The Inner Kingdom *(1926);* The World's Pilgrim *(1927);* Collected Poems of Eva Gore-Booth *(1929);* The Buried Life of Deirdre *(1930).*

In the spring of 1896, two women met on an Italian hillside. Outwardly, they were very different: **Esther Gertrude Roper** was 28 years old, a university educated suffrage and labor activist of working-class stock. The other, Eva Gore-Booth, was an Anglo-Irish gentlewoman of artistic tastes. Introspective and reserved, she had enjoyed a privileged upbringing and had little contact with the world which Roper represented. Nevertheless, the bond between them was immediate, as Gore-Booth eagerly questioned Roper about the campaigns in which she was involved. "What work were we doing for the working women? What was going on in the franchise movement? How did people work and live in an industrial center in Manchester?" As Roper remembered it, in the biographical note which she wrote for Gore-Booth's *Collected Poems,* "We spent the days walking and talking on the hillside by the sea. Each was attracted to the work and thoughts of the other, and we became friends and companions for life—she made up her mind to join me in the work in Manchester." This brisk account conceals the importance which the event held for both of them, and which is more eloquently expressed in Gore-Booth's poem "The Travellers," published in her 1904 collection, *The One and the Many,* and dedicated "to E.G.R":

Was it not strange that by the tideless sea
The jar and hurry of our lives should cease?
That under olive boughs we found our peace,
And all the world's great song in Italy?

Eva Gore-Booth's life story began by another sea, which she remembered with no less affection in poems such as "The little Waves of Breffny."

The great waves of the Atlantic sweep storming
    on their way,
Shining green and silver with the hidden herring
    shoal,
But the Little Waves of Breffny have drenched
    my heart in spray,
And the Little Waves of Breffny go stumbling
    through my soul.

Born on May 22, 1870, at Lissadell, the Gore-Booth family home in County Sligo on Ireland's Atlantic coast, Eva grew up in the landscape which was also to inspire her friend, W.B. Yeats. As one of five children of Sir Henry and Lady **Georgina Gore-Booth,** she was born into the landowning class which still retained most of the land of Ireland, but the Gore-Booths were somewhat unorthodox members of that caste. Sir Henry was an Arctic explorer; at home, at a time when relations between landowners and tenants were generally poor, his reputation as a landlord was high. According to one account, quoted by Roper, during the famine of 1879–80, Sir Henry "kept an open store of food at Lissadell, giving out meal etc. to the starving poor, free to all, at his own cost, and I believe all the members of his family assisted in doing so." Eva, therefore, inherited a strong sense of social obligation, as did her brother, Josslyn, and her sister, *Constance (Markievicz). The former became an exponent of co-operative practices, and the first Irish landlord to sell his estate to his tenants; the latter, as Countess Markievicz, was a feminist and a nationalist, the first woman to be elected to the House of Commons, and the first woman to become a government minister in the independent Irish state.

Gore-Booth left an autobiographical essay, "The Inner Life of a Child," which was found among her papers after her death and published in the *Collected Poems*. According to this account, written in the third person, the most traumatic event of her childhood was the death, when she was nine, of her beloved grandmother, Lady **Emily Hill**, which made her aware both of the fact of death and of "mysteries untouched and unrecognized by one's ordinary outside faculties." The death of the grandmother, she wrote in the essay:

> Did not touch [the child], it seemed vague and unreal. All the same, she realised then for the first time, vividly, that some day she should die herself. . . . The idea of the absence of light and air filled her with unspeakable terror. But a little time afterwards as she lay in bed one evening a new happiness came to her. . . . Without any warning the child became suddenly conscious that a "door had opened in the air," and that her grandmother was standing beside her. . . . The child . . . had no thought of fear, nor did she think it strange, she was simply delighted to be with her again.

Eva told no one of her experience and eventually came to realize that the apparition had no real existence but was "simply a subtler and keener perception of things that are really there." This sensitivity was noted by her former governess in an account written many years later, in which she recalled her as:

> A very fair fragile-looking child, most unselfish and gentle, with the general look of a Burne-Jones or Botticelli angel. As she was two years younger than Constance, and always so delicate, she had been, I think, rather in the background and a little lonely mentally, but music was a great joy to her. The symbolic side of religion had just then a great charm for her, and always of course the mystical side of everything appealed most.

Another who recorded his impressions of Eva at this time was W.B. Yeats, who, in a poem written many years later, remembered a visit to

Eva Gore-Booth (left) with her sister Constance Markievicz.

Lissadell and the two sisters, Constance and Eva, radiantly young and unaware of the disappointments and griefs to come.

> Two girls in silk kimonos, both
> Beautiful, one a gazelle.

Acutely conscious of the beauty around her, Eva was also keenly aware of ugliness and deprivation, and, despite her own sheltered upbringing, she already, in Roper's view, "seems to have been haunted by the suffering of the world, and to have had a curious feeling of responsibility for its inequalities and injustices." Until her meeting with Roper, however, Gore-Booth's life was conventional enough. She and Constance spent a great deal of time together, and, while her sister painted, Eva read or practiced her writing. In 1894, she traveled to the West Indies and America with her father and, in the following year, visited Europe with her mother, going to Bayreuth for the Wagner Festival, and then to Italy. In Venice, she fell ill and was advised to spend the winter on the Mediterranean; it was during that stay, while a guest at the house of the author George MacDonald at Bordighera, that she met Roper and made her decision to live and work with her in Manchester, where Roper was already involved in social work, in the organization of working women and in the women's suffrage campaign.

Before joining Roper, Gore-Booth returned to Sligo and, infected by her friend's enthusiasm for the cause, set up a local branch of the Irish Women's Suffrage and Local Government Association, with herself as secretary, Constance as president, and her other sister, **Mabel Gore-Booth**, as treasurer. By 1897, Roper reports, Eva "was settled in Manchester and was giving the greater part of her time to work for women." She became involved at an early stage with the University Settlement, taking charge of its women's drama group, the Elizabethan Society. As **Louisa Smith**, one of the members who became a friend, remembered:

> We were a class of about sixteen girls . . . all machinists. . . . [W]e had no assets, but we enjoyed every minute of the rehearsals. We were very raw material but keen on acting; she showed such patience and love that we would do anything to please her and she got the best out of us. . . . If any of us were feeling seedy or worried about business or home she would always see, and showed such an understanding sympathy that we came away feeling we had a real friend. . . . She was also very keen on women's rights and trade unions. She persuaded me to join. . . . She was very frail and delicate herself, but full of pluck and determination, and would stand up for people she knew to be unjustly treated, even though the world was against them, and with all so sweet and gentle that one could not help loving her.

"The next ten years," according to Roper, "were full to overflowing with organisation, writing, speaking at large gatherings in all parts of England, deputations to Cabinet Ministers and to Members of Parliament." As joint secretary of the Women's Textile and Other Workers' Representation Committee, of the Manchester and Salford Women's Trade Union Council, and later of the Women's Trades and Labor Council, Gore-Booth played a major part in the struggle for female suffrage, and in campaigns for improved wages and conditions for women in the textile industry. In addition, "on different occasions, women pit-brow workers, barmaids, women acrobats and gymnasts, and women florists were successfully organized in their own defence." While Esther's talent was for organization, it was Eva who was the better communicator and who had a remarkable capacity to overcome barriers of class and culture. According to a colleague, **Sarah Dickenson**:

> The friendly way that she treated all the women Trade Unionists endeared her to them. If she was approached for advice or help she never failed. She is remembered by thousands of working women in Manchester for her untiring efforts to improve their industrial conditions, for awakening and educating their sense of political freedom, and for social intercourse.

Among those whom Gore-Booth inspired was the young *Christabel Pankhurst, who became a member of her Poetry Circle at the University Settlement in 1901. According to *Sylvia Pankhurst, in *The Suffragette Movement*, through her contact with Gore-Booth and Roper, "Christabel was finding the serious interests she had hitherto lacked. She was now an active member of the North of England Women's Suffrage Society Executive, and of the Women's Trade Union Council, and presently her two friends induced her to study law." *Emmeline Pankhurst, however, "was intensely jealous of her daughter's new friendship." Her opposition, together with Christabel's growing militancy, which was the antithesis of Gore-Booth's and Roper's gradualism and pacifism, created a split within the WTUC and ultimately brought the friendship between Eva and Christabel to a close.

During these eventful years, Gore-Booth wrote continuously. Her first collection, *Poems*, appeared in 1898, and was praised by Yeats as being "full of poetic feeling and . . . great promise." Her work also attracted the attention of the author and critic, George Russell, who welcomed her addition to the ranks of writers of the Gaelic Revival, and included some of her poems in a selection by eight young Irish writers, which was published in 1904. Also in 1904, she published her collection, *The One and the Many*, including poems such as "The Soul to the Body," which her biographer Gifford Lewis has speculated, reflect her depression at the failure of her friendship with Christabel. However, the volume also contains her celebration of her relationship with Roper, "The Travellers," together with expressions of her love for her native place, such as "Lis-an-Doill" (Lissadell) and her most famous lyric, "The Little Waves of Breffny," which, wrote *Katherine Tynan, "is a small masterpiece," which "will go singing in the human heart so long as the heart answers to poetry."

Another continuing theme was what George Russell called the "eager adventure of the mind that inspires all Eva Gore-Booth's work." Thus, the Celtic myth which served as the basis of her

1905 play, *The Triumph of Maeve,* symbolized for her "the world-old struggle in the human mind between the forces of dominance and pity, of peace and war." The warrior queen Maeve sees a vision of the crucifixion of Christ, symbolizing the birth of "the new god of pity." As Gore-Booth related in her preface:

> At first the glimpse of the new ideal is not strong enough to make any difference in her life. But Fionavar, her great joy in life, goes down to meet her mother returning in triumph from the fight, suddenly sees the death and pain of the battlefield, and falls dead, crying in bitterness: "Is this the triumph of Maeve?" The effects of these events gradually cause Maeve to lose interest in fighting and ambition. In the end, without force or sovereignty, in loneliness and poverty, she finds the way into faery land—the way to her own soul.

Always delicate, Gore-Booth's health was put under increasing strain by her heavy workload. Nevertheless, she continued her work for trade unionism and, despite her distaste for militant suffragism, for the women's suffrage campaign. In 1906, she was a member of the Women's Franchise Deputation which met the prime minister, Sir Henry Campbell-Bannerman, and in her contribution argued that the low wages currently earned by working women in Lancashire were a direct result of their lack of political power. Disappointment at the failure of this deputation and at her own performance were the themes of "Women's Trades on the Embankment" and "A Lost Opportunity," both published in *The Egyptian Pillar* (1907), but "Women's Rights," in the same collection, concluded with a confident assertion of her belief that the feminist cause would ultimately prevail:

> Oh, whatever men may do
> Ours is the gold air and the blue.
> Men have got their pomp and pride—
> All the green world is on our side.

For Eva, women's right to work and fair pay was inseparable from the right to vote, and she and Roper concerned themselves with the status and conditions of working women who had previously lacked a voice. These included barmaids, whose employment they defended against those who regarded such work as unsuitable for women, florists' assistants, whose conditions they investigated, and pit-brow lasses, whose jobs were threatened by proposed protective legislation. At a meeting in Manchester in 1911, Gore-Booth told how she had herself worked on the pit face with the women, and, at another rally, she declared that "she thought it scandalous that men who sat at Westminster to vote themselves £400 a year should vote away the living of thousands of women."

In 1913, illness forced Eva to leave Lancashire, and she and Esther settled in London. However, she continued to invest a great deal of time and energy in a wide range of causes, including animal welfare and the campaign against capital punishment, while the outbreak of war in 1914 placed a heavy pressure on all those with pacifist opinions. As a member of the Women's Peace Crusade, Gore-Booth traveled the country to speak on its behalf and to attend tribunals and courts martial of conscientious objectors. In 1916, Irish nationalists, among them her sister Constance, launched an unsuccessful rebellion in Dublin. Several of the leaders were executed, and Markievicz was condemned to death, but she was subsequently reprieved and imprisoned in England.

Gore-Booth was deeply affected by these events, and by the trial for treason of Roger Casement, which she attended. *Broken Glory* (1917) included a number of poems on this theme, such as "Easter Week," "To *Dora Sigerson* Shorter" and "Roger Casement," as well as several addressed to Constance who, apart from Esther, was certainly the most important person in Eva's life. "Wild rebels" both, they shared not only the memories of childhood but also a deep hatred of injustice and inequality, and the concept of an ideal world, for which each in her own way was prepared to struggle. During Constance's imprisonment, Eva visited her regularly and experienced the same sense of mystical union with her which she had felt many years before with her grandmother, and which she now recorded in "Comrades."

> The wind is our confederate,
> The night has left her doors ajar,
> We meet beyond earth's barred gate,
> Where all the world's wild Rebels are.

The successive blows of the war years took a severe toll on Gore-Booth, both emotionally and physically. With the end of the Great War in 1918, travel was once more possible, and she and Esther were able to visit their beloved Italy again. Back in London, and now almost retired from active political work, Gore-Booth had more time to devote to her exploration of religious and spiritual matters. She learned Greek and Latin in order to allow her to read the New Testament and classical works in the original languages, and her study of the Gospel of St. John resulted in *The Psychological and Poetic Approach to the Study of Christ in the Fourth Gospel,* published in 1923. Her 1925 collection,

The Shepherd of Eternity, was the last to be published in her lifetime, and many of the poems were reflections on aspects of the life of Christ and of Christian doctrine. As the critic of *The Manchester Guardian* observed, she was "one of the most sensitively clear yet intellectually and imaginatively sure exponents of the mystic faith among modern poets. . . . Though the poems are nearly all of a mystic or religious import, there is a universality and reality about them that widens and strengthens their appeal."

In 1925, Gore-Booth was diagnosed as having cancer. In severe discomfort, she nonetheless retained the serenity which had always characterized her. Throughout her illness, she continued to read widely, to write and to see friends, and to find comfort in her own idiosyncratic religious faith. Not long before her death, on June 30, 1926, she confided to Roper:

> You know, I have always been afraid of death, and I could not get away from the fear of it. Then, quite suddenly . . . I heard the words, "I will come to you." . . . It was absolutely overwhelming. There was a radiance all around and I was filled with an extraordinary feeling of joy, the greatest I have ever known.

For Roper, who took on the task of overseeing the publication of her remaining works, Gore-Booth was an important thinker and an invaluable co-worker in the causes to which both were devoted, but she was above all a lifelong friend and partner. "No words of mine," she wrote in her introduction to the *Collected Poems*:

> could ever tell the beauty of her friendship, but I can say of it truly, "Love never faileth." Through years of difficult and trying work, through periods of terrible strain and grief, through ever-recurring times of intense pain, this was true. To the hard work which we did together for thirty years she brought a spirit of adventure and gaiety which nothing daunted. Of a gallant courage and a gentle courtesy she made life together a gracious thing. Even simple everyday pleasures when shared with her became touched with magic—wandering through the woods of her old home, or seeking the "blue gentians and frail columbines" of a Swiss mountain, or finding "beauty and life and light" in Italy.

In a record of her dreams which she kept during her final illness, Gore-Booth reflected that:

> As in the parable of the Talents, everyone is given a gift. You cannot reach Eternal life till your acorn has grown into an oak-tree. And my own limitations, the rigid walls of my acorn, were shown me clearly. God wants us in heaven—this was the message . . . but the acorn cannot live in heaven, only the oak-tree. Therefore growth is the main object of Life.

But if Gore-Booth looked forward to a heaven after death, she also sought throughout her life to create another heaven for the living. The two concepts were for her inextricably linked, and in "Magna Peccatrix," she links the obligation to serve humanity to what was for her its source.

> What a man does for Christ he does for all,
> Even the least of us; each fair deed done
> Doth on all men in light and gladness fall,
> The whole world's rainbow from the whole
> world's sun.

SOURCES:

Gore-Booth, Eva. *Poems: Complete Edition with a Biographical Introduction by Esther Roper.* London: Longmans, Green, 1929.

Lewis, Gifford. *Eva Gore-Booth and Esther Roper: A Biography.* London: Pandora Press, 1988.

SUGGESTED READING:

Fulford, R. *Votes for Women.* London: Faber and Faber, 1958.

Haverty, Anne. *Constance Markievicz.* London: Pandora Press, 1988.

Markievicz, Constance. *Prison letters of Countess Markievicz.* Edited by Esther Roper. London: Longmans, 1934.

Middleton, L. *Women in the Labor Movement.* London: Croom Helm, 1977.

COLLECTIONS:

Material on English suffrage movement in Fawcett Library, London, and in Manchester Central Library.

Rosemary Raughter,
freelance writer in women's history, Dublin, Ireland

Gorenko, Anna (1889–1966).

See Akhmatova, Anna.

Gorham, Kathleen (1932–1983)

Australian ballerina. Name variations: danced briefly under the name Ann Somers. Born in Sydney, Australia, in 1932; died on April 30, 1983; convent educated; studied ballet with **Lorraine Norton** *and Leon Kellaway; married Robert Pomie (a dancer), around 1958 (divorced); married Barney Marrows; children: (first marriage) one son, Anthony.*

Australian dancer Kathleen Gorham was born in Sydney in 1932 and began ballet lessons at age seven. At 15, she was invited by Edouard Borovansky to join his company in Melbourne. Despite occasional clashes with his pupil, Borovansky had a recurring role in shaping Gorham's career. She, in turn, remained devoted to him, believing that it was her duty to help him build Australian ballet.

Even as a youthful dancer, Gorham possessed a remarkable versatility, dancing dramatic, lyrical, and comic roles with equal success. When the Borovansky Company disbanded in 1948, she joined the Ballet Rambert, which was touring Australia at the time. In 1951, after appearing as a soloist with the Roland Petit Company in Paris and performing with the Sadler's Wells Theatre Ballet, she rejoined Borovansky's new company. During the 1951–52 season, she performed for the first time in *Giselle*, the role for which she is best remembered in Australia. She also created several new roles before the company once again folded. She then danced a season with the Grand Ballet du Marquis de Cuevas in Paris and did another brief stint with Sadler's Wells. From 1954 to 1961, she danced with yet a third Borovansky company, creating new roles and performing principal roles in the classical ballets. After her marriage to Robert Pomie, a French dancer who joined the company in 1957, she retired briefly for the birth of her son. For a short period in 1959, Gorham and her husband worked to establish the Ballet Theatre le Francais in Sydney, but rejoined Borovansky for the 1959–60 season, the final one before his death.

In 1962, after some time in Europe, Gorham became prima ballerina of the newly formed Australian Ballet, where she played a significant role in the artistic development of the fledgling company. With Robert Helpmann (whom she called her favorite director), she created several new roles before retiring in 1966, just after the first overseas tour of the company. She spent her later years teaching in Melbourne and Southport, Queensland, and died in April 1983.

SOURCES:
Radi, Heather, ed. *200 Australian Women*. NSW, Australia: Women's Redress Press, 1988.

Gorizia, countess of.
See Gonzaga, Paola (1463–1497).

Gorka (fl. 920s)
Queen of Poland. Flourished around 920; married Ziemonislaw, king of Poland (r. 913–964); children: Mieczislaw also known as Burislaf or Mieszko I (c. 922–992), duke of Poland (r. 960–992).

Gormfallith.
Variant of Gormflaith.

Gormflaith (c. 870–925)
Irish poet and wife of kings. Name variations: Gormley; Gormfallith; Gormflath; Gormlaith. Born around 870; died in 925; daughter of Flann Sionna, high king of Ireland (r. 879–916); betrothed to Cormac mac Cuilennáin, king-bishop of Cashel; married King Cerball of Leinster; married Niall Glúndubh, high king of Ireland (r. 916–919); children: a son.

Twice married, once betrothed, Gormflaith reputedly wrote poetry about her husbands. Some of her lyrics survive in the Irish annals and in the Scottish manuscript entitled *The Book of the Dean of Lismore*. When her betrothed Cormac mac Cuilennáin was killed in battle by King Cerball of Leinster, Gormflaith married Cerball. Her second husband, Niall Glúndubh was also killed in battle while fighting the Danes in 919. Legend has it that Gormflaith became a beggar and died in poverty.

Gormflaith of Ireland (fl. 980–1015)
Irish queen. Name variations: Gormfallith; Gormflath; Gormlaith; Gormley; Kormlod. Flourished between 980 and 1015 in Ireland; daughter of King Flann of Leister; married Olaf Cuaran of Dublin; married Malachy of Meath (separated 990); married Brian Boru (c. 941–1014), overlord of all Ireland (separated 1000); children: (with Olaf Cuaran) at least one son, Sitric Silkbeard, king of Dublin.

Few facts are certain about this Irish queen. A princess, the daughter of King Flann of Leister, Gormflaith was extremely well educated and had a reputation for great beauty. She married Olaf Cuaran, ruler of Dublin, with whom she had a son, Sitric Silkbeard. When Olaf was defeated in battle by Malachy of Meath, Gormflaith left Olaf and married Malachy who repudiated her around 990. Gormflaith proceeded to take a third husband, this time the celebrated Irish leader Brian Boru. Unfortunately, this marriage too was doomed to failure, and in 1000 the couple separated. Gormflaith then declared war on her last two husbands, Malachy and Brian Boru, and incited rebellion and rioting against their rule. Her rebellion was for the most part unsuccessful, and nothing is known of her life after 1015.

Gormflath.
Variant of Gormflaith.

Gormlaith or Gormley (fl. 980–1015).
See Gormflaith of Ireland.

Gorr, Rita (1926—)
Belgian mezzo-soprano. Born Marguerite Geirnaert on February 18, 1926, in Zelzaete, Belgium.

Sang in Strasbourg Opera (1949–52); made debut at Paris Opéra and Opéra-Comique (1952); debuted at Bayreuth (1958), Covent Garden in Aïda (1959); debuted at Teatro alla Scala debut as Kundry in Parsifal (1960), and Metropolitan Opera (1962).

Belgian mezzo-soprano Rita Gorr, an opera singer of distinction, had an unusually large vocal range which made her equally comfortable as a contralto and mezzo-soprano. Gorr's rich, dark tone made her sound like a natural alto, but her voice had brightness at the top. Many have compared the younger singer **Jessye Norman** to Gorr who performed in the classical French style. Her acting, which combined humanity with epic stature, was ideal, and her enunciation superb. She made several recordings, including Amneris in Verdi's *Aïda* with Georg Solti which may be the finest performance of the part on record. French opera fostered a grand tradition which all but disappeared in the 1960s. Rita Gorr was one of the last operatic stars in this tradition.

John Haag,
Athens, Georgia

Go-Sakuramachi (1740–1814)

Japanese empress who reigned (but did not rule) during the Edo Period (1762–71) and was the tenth woman to sit on the throne of Japan. Name variations: *Princess Toshi-ko or Toshiko; Go-Sakuramachi-tenno. Born in 1740 (some sources cite 1741); died in 1814, at age 74; daughter of Emperor Sakuramachi; sister of Emperor Momosono.*

Go-Sakuramachi was born in 1740 as Princess Toshiko, the daughter of Emperor Sakuramachi. Actual power was held not by her father, however, but by the Shogun Yoshemune. After reigning for 11 years, the emperor abdicated in 1747 in favor of his son and her younger brother, Momosono, then aged 11. During the reign of Momosono, power rested with the Shogun Ieshige. Upon her brother's death in 1762, Princess Toshiko ascended to the imperial throne as the Empress Go-Sakuramachi, but she wielded only ceremonial powers, with Ieshige continuing to actually govern the state. At age 31, in 1771 she abdicated in favor of her nephew Hidehito. Go-Sakuramachi died in 1814, age 74.

SOURCES:
Smith, Robert J. "Divine Kingship in the Formation of the Japanese State, 1868–1945," in John S. Henderson and Patricia J. Netherly, eds., *Configurations of Power: Holistic Anthropology in Theory and Practice.* Ithaca, NY: Cornell University Press, 1993, pp. 51–73.

Webb, Herschel. *The Japanese Imperial Institution in the Tokugawa Period.* NY: Columbia University Press, 1968.

John Haag,
Athens, Georgia

Goslar, Hannah (b. 1928).

See Frank, Anne for sidebar.

Gospel Minnie (1897–1973).

See Douglas, Lizzie.

Gottschalk, Laura Riding (1901–1991).

See Riding, Laura.

Goudge, Elizabeth (1900–1984)

British novelist and children's writer. Born April 24, 1900, in Wells, Somerset, England; died on April 1, 1984, in Peppard Common near Henley-on-Thames, Oxfordshire, England; daughter of Henry Leighton Goudge (Regius Professor of Divinity, Oxford University) and Ida de Beauchamp (Collenette) Goudge; tutored at home; attended boarding school in Southbourne in Hampshire; attended Reading University Art School for two years; never married; no children.

Writings: Island Magic (Coward, 1934); The Middle Window (Duckworth, 1935); A City of Bells (Coward, 1936); (short stories) A Pedlar's Pack (Coward, 1937); Towers in the Mist (Coward, 1938); Three Plays (contains "Suomi," "The Brontës of Haworth," and "Fanny Burney," Duckworth, 1939); (short stories) The Sister of the Angels (Coward, 1939); Smoky House (Coward, 1940); The Bird in the Tree (Coward, 1940); The Well of the Star (Coward, 1941); (juvenile) The Blue Hills (Coward, 1942); The Castle on the Hill (Coward, 1942); Ikon on the Wall (Duckworth, 1943); Green Dolphin Street (Coward, 1944, published in England as Green Dolphin Country, Hodder & Stoughton, 1944); (juvenile) The Little White Horse (University of London Press, 1946); The Elizabeth Goudge Reader (Coward, 1946, published in England as At the Sign of the Dolphin: An Elizabeth Goudge Anthology, Hodder & Stoughton, 1947); Songs and Verses (Duckworth, 1947); (juvenile) Henrietta's House (University of London Press, 1947); Pilgrim's Inn (Coward, 1948, published in England as The Herb of Grace, Hodder & Stoughton, 1948); (short stories) Make Believe (Duckworth, 1949); Gentian Hill (Coward, 1949); The Reward of Faith, and Other Stories (Duckworth, 1950); (juvenile) The Valley of Song (University of London Press, 1951); God So Loved the World (Coward, 1951); White Wings: Collected Short Stories (Duckworth, 1952); The Heart of the Family (Coward 1953); The Rosemary

Tree *(Coward, 1956)*; The Eliots of Damerosehay *(Hodder & Stoughton, 1957)*; The White Witch *(Coward, 1958)*; My God and My All: The Life of St. Francis of Assisi *(Coward, 1959, published in England as* Saint Francis of Assisi, *Duckworth, 1959)*; The Dean's Watch *(Coward, 1960)*; The Scent of Water *(Coward, 1963)*; *(editor)* A Book of Comfort *(Coward, 1964)*; *(juvenile)* Linnets and Valerians *(Coward, 1964)*; Three Cities of Bells: Wells, Oxford, Ely *(Hodder & Stoughton, 1965)*; *(editor)* A Diary of Prayer *(Coward, 1966)*; A Christmas Book *(Coward, 1967)*; *(editor)* A Book of Peace *(M. Joseph, 1967)*; *(illus. by Richard Kennedy)* I Saw Three Ships *(Coward, 1969)*; The Child from the Sea *(Coward, 1970)*; The Lost Angel *(Coward, 1971)*; The Joy of the Snow: An Autobiography *(Coward, 1974)*; *(editor)* A Book of Faith *(Coward, 1976)*; *(anthology, edited by Muriel Grainger)* Pattern of People *(Coward, 1976)*.

Elizabeth Goudge, whose writing career did not bloom until she was well into her 30s, was born in 1900 in Wells, Somerset, England, the only child of the principal of a theological college, who later became a professor of divini-

Elizabeth Goudge

ty at Oxford. As a child, she delighted in the stories told to her by her invalid mother, and also did some storytelling of her own in a magazine she produced monthly with the neighborhood children. Her early education at the hands of a governess was pleasant enough but lacked somewhat in the basics. "When I was fourteen," she later recalled, "my parents suddenly discovered to their horror that their only child knew nothing at all except the dates of the Kings of England and the multiplication table." She was immediately rushed off to boarding school, after which she returned home determined to become a writer. When her first published volume of fairy tales failed to sell, Goudge studied art for two years at Reading College. She returned home and taught art and design before deciding to once more pursue her earlier inclination to become a writer. She began with plays, of which only one was produced; *The Brontës of Haworth* had a single London performance in 1932. At a publisher's suggestion, she tried novels, writing three before a nervous breakdown brought her budding career to a temporary halt.

Following her father's death in 1939, Goudge went to live with her mother in Devon, where she wrote her best-selling *Green Dolphin Street* (1944), a historical romance which won a literary Guild Award and was filmed in 1947. This, and two subsequent novels, *Gentian Hill* (1949) and *The Child from the Sea* (1970), comprise the best of her historical novels. *Child from the Sea* tells the story of *Lucy Walter, mistress and possibly secret wife of Charles II. After her mother's death, Goudge moved to Peppard Common, near Henley-on-Thames, where she remained for over 20 years.

Elizabeth Goudge is also known for her children's fiction, notably *The Little White Horse* (1946), which won the Carnegie Medal, and *The Bird in the Tree* (1940), her own personal favorite. She produced over 40 titles during her career, including novels, short stories, children's books, and nonfiction religious works. Both her children's and adult fiction are marked by a sense of place and history, and her later fiction, such as *The Scent of Water* (1963), and her autobiography *The Joy of the Snow* (1974), reflect her strong Christian faith. The author died on April 1, 1984, just shy of her 84th birthday.

SOURCES:

Commire, Anne. *Something About the Author.* Vol. 2. Detroit, MI: Gale Research.

Shattock, Joanne. *The Oxford Guide to British Women Writers.* Oxford and NY: Oxford University Press, 1993.

RELATED MEDIA:

Green Dolphin Street (140 min. film), starred *Lana Turner, Van Heflin, *Donna Reed, Dame *May Whitty, *Gladys Cooper, Gigi Perreau, directed by Victor Saville, screenplay by Samson Raphaelson, produced by Metro-Goldwyn-Mayer, 1947.

Barbara Morgan,
Melrose, Massachusetts

Gouel, Eva (d. 1915)

Mistress of Pablo Picasso. Name variations: Eve Gouel; Marcelle Humbert. Died in 1915 in Paris.

The French mistress of a sculptor named Marcoussis and a friend of Pablo Picasso's mistress *Fernande Olivier, Eva Gouel went by the name Marcelle Humbert when she first took up with Picasso in 1911, just as his affair with Olivier was coming to an end. Described by Norman Mailer in *Portrait of Picasso as a Young Man*, as "small, sweet, superficially submissive, orderly, thrifty and devoted to Picasso," Gouel ushered in a relatively tranquil period in the artist's life, and she seems to have been one of the few of his mistresses to have escaped his notorious temper. "To look at him, you would think he would be violent, but he is really like a lamb," she used to say. The couple had four years together before Gouel died of cancer in 1915.

Gouel was an orderly housekeeper, keeping the pillows plumped and the furniture polished, and even introducing a tea table and a flowered tea set into Picasso's studio, which was evidently off limits to her cleaning expeditions. She also had a keen eye for business, and was able to tell at a glance which patrons were ready to buy paintings and which were just there for a look. According to Mailer, she encouraged Picasso as he moved into Synthetic Cubism and urged him to bring color back into his palette. During the time she was with him, his paintings fetched better and better prices every year.

Gouel hid the nature of her illness from Picasso as long as possible, although, as Mailer points out, a cruel portrait the artist made of her in the winter of 1913–14, *Woman in a Chemise*, may have anticipated her illness. She was hospitalized in the fall of 1915, during which time Picasso made a long trip each day to visit her, and consoled himself at night with **Gaby Lespinasse,** his beautiful Parisian neighbor.

SOURCES:

Mailer, Norman. *Portrait of Picasso as a Young Man.* NY: The Atlantic Monthly Press, 1995.

Barbara Morgan,
Melrose, Massachusetts

Gouges, Marie Gouze (1748–1793).

See Gouges, Olympe de.

Gouges, Olympe de (1748–1793)

French playwright and political writer who advocated legal and political equality for women during the French Revolution. Name variations: Marie-Olympe de Gouges; Marie Gouze; Marie Gouze Gouges; though she never used her married name Aubry, she was indicted under it in 1793. Pronunciation; OH-lemp de GOOZE. Born Marie Gouze in Montauban, in southwestern France, in 1748; executed for crimes against the state in Paris on November 3, 1793; daughter of Pierre Gouze (a butcher) and Anne-Olympe Mouisset; married Louis-Yves Aubry, in 1765; children: Pierre (b. 1766).

Lived as a courtesan in Paris (1770s); began literary career (1780); anti-slavery play accepted by the Comédie Française (1784); The Loves of Chérubin performed successfully at the Théâtre Italien (1786); Slavery of Negroes (Zamour et Myrza ou l'heureau naufrage) performed by the Comédie Française, causing an uproar (1789); sent Déclaration des droits de la femme et de la citoyenne (Declaration of the Rights of Woman and the Female Citizen) with a cover letter to Marie Antoinette (1791); appeared before the legislature in support of un pauvre ("a poor man") who was voted relief (1792); defended King Louis XVI in a letter to the National Convention (December 1792); wrote The Three Urns, attacking Robespierre; arrested for sedition (July 1793); tried and executed by guillotine, according to her obituary, "for sedition and for having forgotten the virtues which befit her sex" (November 1793).

On October 5, 1789, a crowd of women gathered at the City Hall in Paris. Angered by the rising cost of bread and King Louis XVI's refusal to remedy the situation, they demanded help from the National Guard and, armed with broomsticks, lances, pitchforks, swords, pistols, and muskets, marched 20 miles to the king's palace at Versailles. En route, they were joined by more women, and by the time they reached their destination their numbers had swelled to between eight and ten thousand. At Versailles, they confronted the king with demands for bread and security for Paris. Louis XVI hesitated for some hours until the impatient crowd invaded the palace, killed two royal guards, and demanded that the royal family return with them to Paris. He finally agreed and, accompanied by a joyous throng of women, was taken back to Paris where he and his family took up residence in the royal palace at the Tuileries.

The march to Versailles marked an early turning point in the French Revolution and, more important, signaled the politicization of French women. Traditionally, women were believed to be inferior to men and these ideas were perpetuated by members of the 18th-century French intelligentsia, known as philosophes. The writings of Jean-Jacques Rousseau, in particular, encouraged the belief that women's role in society was dominated by their duty towards men. Rousseau concluded that women were born to please men and, thus, should remain at home to tend their husband's children and his household. In this cozy domestic world there was no need for women to be educated in anything other than traditional female duties. Any woman who dared to relate to men as their intellectual or cultural equal was severely criticized. Above all, women were not supposed to become involved in political affairs. This ideological glorification of women's domesticity was also reflected in law. While women from the aristocratic classes held some legal rights, the vast majority of women were legally subordinate to their husbands. Married women were legal minors under their husband's guardianship, and unmarried women were subject to their father's authority.

The upheavals caused by the French Revolution, however, initiated a new role for women in French society; one which was a direct challenge to Rousseau's ideal of the meek and subservient female. Working-class women met on the streets, in cafes, at the market, and in breadlines where they discussed the latest developments in the revolutionary struggle. They became outspoken, demanding that their concerns be heard. They shouted and disrupted national legislatures and assemblies, circulated petitions, insulted local and national magistrates, and participated in food riots. Educated women made demands for political and legal equality. One of the most outstanding advocates for the rights of women during the French Revolution was Olympe de Gouges.

Born Marie Gouze near Montauban in 1748, she was the daughter of Pierre Gouze, a butcher, and **Anne-Olympe Mouisset**. In later years, Olympe claimed that the man who was her real father was a noble, the Marquis Jean-Jacques Le Franc de Pomignan (d. 1784). Very little is known of her youth except that she was married at age 17 to Louis-Yves Aubry and gave birth to a son, also named Pierre. A few years later, after her husband's death, she changed her name to Olympe de Gouges and moved to Paris where she planned to launch a literary career even though she had little formal education. Exceptionally beautiful, vivacious and intelligent, she soon captured the hearts of many young men and had a series of love affairs. She adored being the center of attention and spent most of the money that she earned as a courtesan on expensive clothes, extravagant entertainment, and numerous pets. She surrounded herself with a menagerie of animals, including monkeys and dogs, all of which were given the names of important figures from the past. De Gouges believed in the transmigration of souls and thus saw her pets as former human beings who were now serving out their time on earth as animals.

> *A woman has the right to mount the scaffold; she must also have the right to mount the rostrum.*
>
> —Olympe de Gouges

Her ambition to become a literary star was punctuated by innumerable attempts throughout the 1780s to have several of her plays produced and performed at the Comédie Française. Although she wrote over 30 plays, only one was ever performed successfully. *Zamour et Myrza ou l'heureau naufrage,* a work which attacked slavery, was produced in 1789 but was canceled after only three performances largely due to protestations from French colonists. After this disaster, de Gouges abandoned the stage and began writing pamphlets and brochures on a variety of social, political, and economic topics.

Between 1790 and 1793, Olympe de Gouges wrote and published more than two dozen pamphlets many of which had feminist overtones. Among the social reforms she advocated were workshops for the unemployed, poor relief, education for women, improved conditions in maternity hospitals, and the creation of a second national theater where only plays written by women would be performed. Unfortunately, many of her pamphlets were poorly written and hastily constructed which, combined with her appalling spelling, led many critics to dismiss her concerns. More important, however, was the fact that she was a woman who was engaged in a traditionally male-dominated activity. De Gouges acknowledged the double standard imposed upon her as a woman writer when she observed: "I put forward a hundred propositions; they are received; but I am a woman; no one pays any attention."

Nonetheless, in 1791, she wrote what became her most famous work, *The Declaration of the Rights of Woman and the Female Citizen.* Divided into four sections (dedication, challenge to the men of the French Revolution, 17 articles, and a postscript), the *Declaration* was a political manifesto which recast the ideals of the revolution so that gender became the central issue.

In the dedication, which is addressed to Louis XVI's queen, *Marie Antoinette, de Gouges encourages her to support the emancipation of women: "This revolution will happen only when all women are aware of their deplorable fate, and of the rights they have lost in society. Madame, support such a beautiful cause; defend this unfortunate sex, and soon you will have half the realm on your side." In the second section, Olympe criticizes her male co-revolutionaries: "Man, are you capable of being just? It is a woman who poses the question; you will not deprive her of that right at least. Tell me, what gives you sovereign empire to oppress my sex?" In nature, she observes, the sexes mingle and "cooperate in harmonious togetherness." Men, however, desire to rule as despots over women.

The third and longest section of the *Declaration* is patterned directly after the 1789 *Declaration of the Rights of Man and of the Citizen* and frequently paraphrases its language. Unlike the earlier manifesto, however, de Gouges' *Declaration* proclaims the incontestable rights of women: "Woman is born free and lives equal to man in her rights. Social distinctions can be based only on the common utility . . . [the] rights of woman and man . . . are liberty, property, security, and especially resistance to oppression." In Article VI, de Gouges demands for women not only the right to vote but that they be admitted to "all honors, positions, and public employment according to their capacity and without other distinctions besides those of their virtues and talents." She states that women are not to be given any special treatment under the law and, in Article X, she proclaims, prophetically, that since women have the right to mount the scaffold, they should be given the right to mount the rostrum. Influenced perhaps by her own claim to noble birth and the taint of illegitimacy, she demanded that women be given the right to name the father of their children. As fully legal citizens, de Gouges concluded that women should pay the same taxes as men and, in return, be given their fair share "in the distribution of positions, employment, offices, honors, and jobs." Likewise, women should have an equal share in public administration and in drafting the constitution. In the fourth and final section, Olympe pleaded for a unified revolutionary struggle. Acknowledging the subordination of women in marriage, she drew up a sample marriage contract which secured property rights for women and children, especially when marriages were dissolved.

Despite its revolutionary potential, the *Declaration* fell on deaf ears. Never being content to remain out of the limelight for long, Olympe de Gouges next attracted public attention when she defended the king at his trial for treason in December 1792. The events leading up to the king's trial began the previous year. In 1791, the Legislative Assembly passed a new Constitution which established a limited monarchy. Louis XVI, however, did not approve of the constraints on his authority, and, in June, he attempted to flee the country. The royal family succeeded in making it to the border but were recognized and forced to return to Paris where virtually all of the king's authority was suspended. In April 1792, the government declared war on Austria in the hopes that the ideals of Revolution would spread throughout Europe as well as be consolidated in France. The war, however, proceeded badly for the French, and the defeats of the army, coupled with economic shortages, led to renewed political demonstrations in which the king became the prime target. This dissatisfaction culminated on August 10, 1792, when an angry mob attacked the royal palace, took the king captive, and forced the Legislative Assembly to suspend the monarchy. Louis XVI's fate was sealed on September 21 when the National Convention, as the new government was now called, abolished the monarchy and established a republic.

Throughout the early years of the Revolution, Olympe de Gouges wavered between royalist sympathies and republican tendencies. Until the king's aborted escape attempt, she had supported the constitutional monarchy, but, after the events of August 10, she welcomed the creation of a republic. Her thirst for notoriety, however, and tendency, as she herself noted, "to range myself on the side of the feeble and oppressed," led her to come to the defense of the king. In a letter submitted to the Convention, she presented her argument in a straightforward manner; a distinction should be made between the man and the king. "He was weak; he let himself be deceived; he deceived us; he deceived himself. That, in a nutshell, is the case against him." She pleaded for his life and warned the government leaders against bringing disgrace upon themselves by making him into a martyr as the English had done 150 years before when they executed Charles I.

Her efforts on the king's behalf were dismissed outright by the Convention, and she was ridiculed in the press. One journalist exclaimed: "Who does she think she is to meddle in such things? Why doesn't she knit trousers for our brave *sans-culottes* instead?" Ridicule turned to violence when an angry mob gathered in front of her house demanding that she come down to face them. Exhibiting a courage which was typical of her personality, she met them coolly even though they began to handle her roughly. When the leader proceeded to stage a mock auction for the price of her head, she kept her composure and diffused the situation by placing the first bid. Laughing, the mob let her return home peacefully.

On January 21, 1793, Louis XVI was executed and most of Europe declared war against France. Once again, the French army suffered defeat abroad which led to fears of foreign invasion and counter-revolution at home. Repressive legislation was increased, and in April 1793 the Convention set up a Committee of Public Safety. The Committee, which was eventually controlled by Maximilien Robespierre, established the "Reign of Terror" in which enemies of the revolutionary Republic were identified as those "who either by their conduct, their contacts, their words or their writings, showed themselves to be supporters of tyranny or enemies of liberty [or] those who have not constantly manifested their attachment to the Revolution." Many royalists, including Queen Marie Antoinette, as well as aristocrats and peasants, were officially executed over the next nine months.

Despite the obvious danger, de Gouges wrote invectives against the Terror throughout the summer of 1793 and against Robespierre whom she called an "insect" and "the egotistical abomination" of the Revolution. She also published a new broadsheet, *Les trois urnes* (The Three Urns), in which she proposed a national referendum to decide the best form of government for France. Three choices were offered: Republican government, Federal government, and a monarchy.

Since the death of Louis XVI, however, a resurrection of the monarchy was hopelessly out of date. Likewise, Federalism was anathema to the majority of government members. Undaunted, de Gouges attempted to have the broadsheet posted around Paris. The billposter, however, alarmed by its contents, refused to post it and instead informed the authorities. Olympe de Gouges was arrested on July 20, 1793, and taken to the prison of L'Abbaye. Even while she was in prison, she maintained her criticism of the government by smuggling out a series of protests in which she denounced her persecutors.

De Gouges was accused of undermining the Republic through seditious writings and was brought to trial before the Revolutionary Tribunal on November 1, 1793. The prosecution was harsh in its indictment: "There can be no mistaking the perfidious intentions of this criminal woman and her hidden motives, when one observes her in all the works to which, at the very least, she lends her name, calumniating and spewing out bile in large doses against the warmest friends of the people." De Gouges conducted her own defense and infuriated the Tribunal by shrugging her shoulders, smiling at the spectators, and raising her eyes towards the ceiling when the charges against her were read out. The eloquence of her defense was preserved in a "Political Testament" which she wrote during her imprisonment and which was tacked on walls throughout Paris. In this broadsheet, she reiterated her patriotism and the disgust she felt towards the proponents of the Terror: "Men deranged by passions, what have you done and what incalculable evils are you perpetrating on Paris and on the whole of France? You are risking everything." Acknowledging that her death was inevitable, she proceeded to list her bequests:

> I will my heart to the nation, my integrity to men (they have need of it). To women, I will my soul; my creative spirit to dramatic artists; my disinterestedness to the ambitious; my philosophy to those who are persecuted; my intelligence to all fanatics; my religion to atheists; my gaiety to women on the decline; and all the poor remains of an honest fortune to my son, if he survives me.

The jury reached a unanimous verdict: "Olympe de Gouges is proven guilty of being the author of these writings and . . . [is] condemned to the punishment of death." In a last attempt to save her life, she declared that she was pregnant. Two doctors and a midwife were brought in to examine her and found her claim to be false. On the night before her execution, she wrote a final letter to her son Pierre. "I die, my son, the victim of my idolatry of my country and of the people. Their enemies, beneath the specious mask of republicanism, have led me remorselessly to the scaffold." On November 3, 1793, sentence of death was confirmed against 45-year-old Olympe de Gouges. Outspoken to the last, as she mounted the platform to the guillotine, she cried out: "Children of the Fatherland, you will avenge my death."

Her forthright behavior and refusal to adopt prescribed feminine behavior led one of the leading revolutionary newspapers to conclude in her obituary that Olympe de Gouges was not only guilty of sedition but also "for having forgotten the virtues which befit her sex." Her death was one of a series of repressive measures which the government adopted in order to curb the political activities of women. By the end of 1793, women's political clubs were outlawed, and in the next year women were banned from attending any public meetings and from assembling in groups. Eleven years later, the Napoleonic Code reasserted women's subordination in marriage and reduced their civil status to that of a minor. The voice of Olympe de Gouges, however, was never silenced, and her vision of equal rights for women has provided inspiration for those working to establish a more just and humane world.

SOURCES:

Kelly, Linda. *Women of the French Revolution*. London: Hamish Hamilton, 1987.

Levy, D.G., H.B. Applewhite, and M.D. Johnson. *Women in Revolutionary Paris, 1789–1795*. Chicago: University of Illinois Press, 1980.

Mannin, Ethel. *Women and the Revolution*. NY: E.P. Dutton, 1939.

SUGGESTED READING:

Gutwirth, Madelyn. *The Twilight of the Goddesses: Women and Representation in the French Revolutionary Era*. New Brunswick, NJ: Rutgers University Press, 1992.

Landes, Joan. *Women and the Public Sphere in the Age of the French Revolution*. Ithaca, NY: Cornell University Press, 1988.

Proctor, Candice. *Women, Equality, and the French Revolution*. NY: Greenwood Press, 1990.

Margaret McIntyre,
Instructor of Women's History, Trent University,
Peterborough, Canada

Gould, Beatrice Blackmar

(c. 1899–1989)

American journalist and magazine editor who, with her husband Bruce Gould, coedited the Ladies' Home Journal *(1936–1962). Born Beatrice Blackmar in Emmetsburg, Iowa, probably in 1899; died in Hopewell, New Jersey, on January 30, 1989; daughter of Harry E. Blackmar (superintendent of public schools) and Mary Kathleen (Fluke) Blackmar; attended public school in Iowa City and Ottumwa; graduated from the University of Iowa; Columbia University, B.S. in journalism, 1923; married Charles Bruce Gould (a writer and editor), on October 4, 1923; children: one daughter Sesaly Gould.*

Journalist and magazine editor Beatrice Blackmar Gould was born in Emmetsburg, Iowa, around 1899. As superintendent of public schools, her father Harry E. Blackmar introduced the first hot-lunch program and "ungraded" classrooms. Her mother **Mary Fluke Black-mar** distinguished herself late in life by receiving her M.A. at Columbia when she was in her 50s and obtaining a driver's license at age 75. Gould later recalled an idyllic childhood, highlighted by family dinners where the children were encouraged to talk and argue "providing it was about books, or the Civil War."

After graduating from the University of Iowa, Gould worked as a reporter before entering the journalism school at Columbia University. Shortly after receiving her degree, she married Bruce Gould, who was also a reporter but dreamed of becoming a playwright. The couple lived in New York, where they worked on newspapers, freelanced for magazines, and wrote plays together, one of which, *Man's Estate*, was produced by the Theater Guild in 1929. (The couple would also write *The Terrible Turk*, produced in 1934, and *Reunion*, a screenplay, released in 1936.) Meanwhile, in 1927, while employed as the woman's editor on the New York *Sunday World*, Beatrice gave birth to the couple's only child, Sesaly. Well established as a writer, Beatrice continued to contribute to magazines like *Collier's*, *Cosmopolitan*, and the *Ladies' Home Journal*, while Bruce joined the staff of *The Saturday Evening Post*. In 1935, the Goulds were appointed coeditors of the *Journal*. It took some persuading for Beatrice to accept the job. "If I could have chosen my own pattern, I would have stayed at home until our daughter was older," she admitted. "But . . . it was then that opportunity offered." It was agreed, however, that she would appear at the office only three days a week, working the rest of the time at home. Although there was equal billing on the masthead, Beatrice, who insisted that Bruce was the boss, received a $5,000 yearly salary while her husband earned $20,000.

Under the Goulds' management, the *Journal* flourished, becoming the most profitable magazine of all time. The October 1946 issue alone established a publishing record by exceeding $2 million in gross advertising revenue. Basing their editorial policy on their high regard for the so-called average American woman, they "edited up," publishing high-quality fiction and in-depth analysis of politics, international relations, and other subjects usually ignored by women's magazines. Despite growing success, Beatrice stuck to her three-day-a-week policy, insisting that a married woman should not let an outside job take too much time away from her home and family. Her particular concern for children was expressed in two wartime editorials

for the *Journal*: "Let's Have No Neglected Children" and "For Forty Million Reason," the latter a proposal for an organization of "Women in National Service," offering community service to children. Beatrice was also a foster mother to two child evacuees from England. The Goulds, who retired from the *Journal* in 1962, wrote about their coeditorship in their joint autobiography, *American Story* (1968).

SOURCES:

Bird, Caroline. *Enterprising Women*. NY: W.W. Norton, 1976.

Moritz, Charles, ed. *Current Biography*. NY: H.W. Wilson, 1989.

Barbara Morgan, Melrose, Massachusetts

Gould, Helen Miller (1868–1938).

See Shepard, Helen Miller.

Gould, Shane (1956—)

Australian swimmer who took five swimming medals at the Munich Olympics. Name variations: Shane Innes. Born Shane Elizabeth Gould on November 23, 1956, in Sydney, New South Wales, Australia; daughter of Shirley Gould (who wrote a book in 1972 called Swimming the Shane Gould Way); married Neil Innes, in 1974.

Won the 100-meter freestyle in the New South Wales championships (1972) as well as 13 other Australian individual championships and three relay championships; won Olympic gold medals in the 200-meter and 400-meter freestyle, and the 200-meter individual medley, a silver medal in the 800-meter freestyle, and a bronze medal in the 100-meter freestyle, all at Munich (1972).

Shane Gould could swim under water with her eyes closed by age three. By age six, she was taking professional lessons and by age 13 began to specialize in freestyle swimming. Shortly after her 15th birthday, Gould held freestyle world records in the 200-meters, 400-meters, 800-meters, and 1,500-meters. She had raised everyone's expectations and that was the problem. In 1972, Australia decided it was time for her to break the 100-meter record of 58.9 set eight years earlier by fellow Aussie *Dawn Fraser. Before the New South Wales championships in Sydney, along with the media buildup, Shane's father tacked a sign on her bedroom door that read "The 58.5 club." People lined the Harbour Bridge to watch Gould race in the North Sydney swimming pool, but she nearly missed the race. "I'd retreated to a room to psych up," she told

Shane
Gould

David Hemery. "The race was called and because of the pumps I didn't hear and everyone else was undressing and the officials came and said, 'Where have you been, everyone's getting on their box!' I raced out crying by that stage and falling apart inside, the adrenalin was pumping so much when I got on the blocks." She won the race in 58.5.

In the 1972 Olympics in Munich, the 15-year-old Gould won the gold in the 200-meter freestyle in a world record time of 2:03.56, a gold in the 400-meter freestyle in a world record time of 4:19.04, a silver in the 800-meter freestyle in a time of 8:56.39 (*Keena Rothhammer** of the U.S. won the gold in a world record time of 8:53.68), a gold in the 200-meter individual medley in a world record time of 2:23.07, and a bronze in the 100-meter freestyle, then went home and said she was tired and just wanted to be an ordinary teenager. Gould had a right to be tired. She had just appeared in 12 races, including heats and finals, more than any other woman swimmer in Olympic history, and had given the Aussies their greatest performance by an individual at a single Olympics.

Weary of the relentless routine, 16-year-old Gould announced her retirement. Two years later, she married a 25-year-old Bible student named Neil Innes at an outdoor wedding. "Instead of saying the formal vows," she said, "we made up our own. It seemed to be in line with what we believe. We like the open air and surfing." She and her husband moved to the Margaret River area of Western Australia.

Gould's retirement allowed other swimmers to breathe again. By the time Montreal rolled around four years later, American swimmers were so intent upon stepping out of her shadow that they wore t-shirts that read: "All that glitters is not Gould." Meanwhile Gould, now Innes, reveled in the ordinariness of her life. Her upbringing had taught that swimming was one of many avenues to success: "At the family meal time we'd have a discussion of what each of us did in the day and if I'd report, 'Well, I'd broken a world record,' my younger sister would say,

'Well, I did this drawing,' and my older sister would say, 'Well, I passed my exams but only with a B+' . . . each of those things was treated as equally terrific."

SOURCES:

Hemery, David. *The Pursuit of Sporting Excellence.* Champaign, IL: Human Kinetics Books, 1986.

Goulue, La (1869–1929)

French cancan dancer at the Moulin Rouge who served as a model for artist Toulouse-Lautrec. Born Louise Weber in 1869; died in Paris in 1929; daughter of a cab driver.

The comely daughter of a cab driver, Louise Weber rose from obscurity to become La Goulue (Greedy Gal), celebrated cancan dancer at the famous Moulin Rouge and one of Paris' last great courtesans. Sadly, her glittering lifestyle was not an easy one to sustain.

In her heyday, La Goulue captured the imagination of Henri de Toulouse-Lautrec, who made her the subject of some of his most famous cabaret posters. He also painted some show curtains for her, which, left in a barn to rot, were later found, cut into salable sections and sold to the Louvre. The museum reassembled and restored them for exhibition. When not performing, La Goulue had rooms at a fashionable private hotel on the Avenue du Bois, once inhabited by her famous predecessor, **Païva**, mistress of Napoleon III. "It was here," writes *Janet Flanner, "that La Goulue was invited to dance before a gentleman who afterward literally covered her with banknotes and turned out to be the Grand Duke Alexis."

La Goulue's downfall began with a jail sentence for some unnamed crime, after which she became a lion-tamer in a street fair. Later, she was a dancer in a traveling show, then a laundress, "then she became nothing," writes Flanner, as her final years were spent in an alcoholic daze on the Paris streets. Her last appearance was in a documentary film about the rag-pickers of Paris, called *The Zone*, in which she danced drunkenly. In a tipsy interview for the weekly *Vu*, she recalled her son who died in a gambling den and her affair with the Grand Duke Alexis. A few weeks later, she died alone and destitute in a city clinic, "murmuring, as if declining a last and eternal invitation," writes Flanner, "'I do not want to go to hell.'"

SOURCES:

Flanner, Janet. *Paris Was Yesterday.* NY: Viking, 1972.

Barbara Morgan,
Melrose, Massachusetts

Gourd, Emilie (1879–1946)

Swiss feminist. Born in Switzerland in 1879; died in 1946.

Emilie Gourd was born in 1879 in Switzerland. She apparently embraced the women's movement in her mid-30s and remained committed to it for the rest of her life. Through the paper *Le movement féministe*, which she founded and edited until her death, she championed suffrage, education, and legal rights for women. Defying the Swiss authorities, she also organized plebiscites asking for support for women's suffrage during cantonal (Switzerland is politically divided into cantons) and national elections. Gourd served as president of the Swiss Woman's Association from 1914 to 1928 and became secretary of the International Alliance of Women in 1923. She also edited a yearbook of Swiss women and wrote a biography of *Susan B. Anthony** (1920).

Gournay, Marie le Jars de (1565–1645)

French philosopher, novelist, translator, and literary critic. Name variations: La Dame de Gournay; Marie de Jars; Marie de Gournay de Jars; "the tenth Muse"; "the French Minerva." Born on October 6, 1565, in Paris, France; died on July 13, 1645; daughter of Jeanne de Hacqueville and Guillaume le Jars, Seigneur de Gournay; had two brothers and three sisters; self-educated.

Selected works: Le Proumenoir de M. de Montaigne *(1594);* Égalite des hommes et des femmes *(1622);* Grief des dames *(1626);* Life of the Demoiselle de Gournay *(1641).*

Destined to be considered the French Minerva, Marie le Jars de Gournay was born in Paris in 1565 into a noble family. Her father, who was Seigneur de Gournay with feudal rights, died in 1577 when she was still quite young. Her mother **Jeanne de Hacqueville** was forced to move with the six children to the estate at Gournay, in Picardy. Jeanne

pushed Marie to learn traditional domestic arts, but her daughter was much more interested in books and spent whatever time she could studying, believing that "to live is to think." She taught herself Latin by comparing Latin and French editions and also worked at Greek, which she found more difficult.

De Gournay read Michel de Montaigne's *Essays* in her late teens and was determined to meet him. In response to her letter, he visited her in 1588 while she was staying in Paris with her mother. Such a close friendship was formed that he regarded her as his *fille d'alliance,* or spiritual daughter, a position she gladly accepted. Devoted to him during his final years, she acted as his assistant, editor and representative. She visited him in Paris, and he went to Picardy for a three-month sojourn. Though Montaigne was frustrated by her devotion, and others found it ridiculous, he made her the editor of a new edition of his *Essays* (1595). The relationship with her "second father" only lasted for four years before Montaigne's death in 1592.

Widely recognized for her honesty and openness, de Gournay believed in kindness and generosity. When her mother died in 1591, as executor of the estate, Marie gave a great deal over to her siblings thus leaving herself in poverty. She was ridiculed for her plainness, impoverishment, and choice of scholarship over marriage, probably in part because others were resentful of her independence. De Gournay argued that women are equal to men in *Égalite des hommes et des femmes* (published in 1622) and despaired of women's situation in *Grief des dames* (published in 1626). In order to receive favor from those with wealth, she spent what she must to dress as their peer. This, and some small expenditures on alchemy and lute lessons, earned her a reputation for frivolity, but she actually lived a frugal private life.

De Gournay also became the subject of ridicule for her defense of Henry IV, king of France, who had promised her financial support just before his assassination. Her essay on the subject was attacked under the title *Anti-Gournay,* and she thenceforth became fair game for tormenters whose tactics included distributing a falsified version of her autobiography.

Some of the jokes revolved in her favor. She chased away the poet Racan, throwing a shoe at him, because she believed him to be an imposter since she had already been visited by two different men claiming to be Racan. But when she discovered the truth, she visited him to explain, and they became good friends. When Cardinal Richelieu greeted her with mockery, she replied: "Laugh, great genius, laugh on—since you should have some amusement." He was so impressed by de Gournay's good nature that he granted her a pension.

Despite social adversity and financial difficulties, de Gournay managed to live a rich intellectual life, corresponding with Cardinal Richelieu, Cardinal du Perron, **Madame de Loges,** Guez de Balzac, the Du Puy brothers, and Justus Lipsius. Although she was thought to be old-fashioned for her allegiance to Renaissance values, her first book, *Le Proumenoir de M. de Montaigne* (1594), was popular and is considered to be the first French psychological novel. She attended the Parisian salons, and her own salon may well have been the place where the French Academy was conceived as a center for intellectual activity. Marie de Gournay is represented in Saint-Évremond's *Comédie des Académistes.*

SOURCES:

Buck, Claire, ed. *Bloomsbury Guide to Women's Literature.* NY: Prentice Hall, 1992.
Kersey, Ethel M. *Women Philosophers: a Bio-critical Source Book.* NY: Greenwood Press, 1989.
Waithe, Mary Ellen, ed. *A History of Women Philosophers.* Boston, MA: Martinus Nijhoff Publications, 1987–1995.

SUGGESTED READING:

Ilsley, Marjorie Henry. *A Daughter of the Renaissance: Marie le Jars de Gournay, her life and works.* The Hague: Mouton, 1963.

Catherine Hundleby, M.A.,
Philosophy, University of Guelph, Guelph, Ontario, Canada

Gouze, Marie (1748–1793).

See Gouges, Olympe de.

Gove, Mary (1810–1884).

See Nichols, Mary Gove.

Gower, Pauline (1910–1947)

British aviator who was a British Air Transport officer during World War II. Name variations: Pauline Fahie. Born Pauline Mary de Peauly Gower in 1910; died soon after childbirth on March 2, 1947; daughter of Sir Robert Vaughan Gower (a politician and member of Parliament); educated by Sacred Heart nuns at a school in Tunbridge Wells; married William Fahie, in the summer of 1945; children: twin boys, including Michael Fahie (b. 1947).

Pauline Gower was born in England in 1910, the daughter of Sir Robert Vaughan Gower, a distinguished member of Parliament for many years and co-owner of an air-taxi service. She attended a Roman Catholic school and, as a teenager, survived a life-threatening illness, an experience which deepened her faith.

Gower started flying at age 18. A licensed pilot before age 20, she wanted very much to fly to India, but her father would not allow it. However, when she turned 21, he presented her with a Spartan two-seater airplane with a Sirrus-3 engine. Shortly afterward, Gower, with another woman pilot, *Dorothy Spicer, established a five-shilling air-taxi service. Gower's safety record was so impressive that she was appointed by Sir Kingsley Wood to serve on the committee investigating flying over populous areas. Meantime, she was actively campaigning for a women's air arm in the national defense, and even wrote a book, *Women with Wings* (1938), which helped prepare the way for women pilots in the ferry pilot service.

At the time England entered the war, Gower was serving as a district commissioner for the London area of the Civil Air Guard. In 1940, she was made commandant of the women's section of the Air Transport Auxiliary (ATA), whose pilots performed many war air services, including flying fighter planes from the factory to frontline defense air stations and ferrying home damaged aircraft. They were dubbed the "ATA-girls," a name that did not sit well with Gower who referred to the 45 crack women pilots in the service not as girls but women. "Women in this service," she said, "are treated exactly like the men. That is one of the things for which I have fought." Gower was enormously proud of the women pilots in her charge. "Every day," she said, "they handle tens of thousands of pounds' worth of Lancasters, Hurricanes, Mosquitoes, Blenheims, Spitfires, and all the rest of our aircraft."

In May 1943, Gower was also appointed to the board of the British Overseas Airways Corporation (BOAC), the first time a woman was appointed to such a position in the United Kingdom and, possibly, the first time a woman served on the board of a state airline anywhere in the world. The assignment meant that in addition to her war job, she served as an advisor to the Air Ministry on the comfort and psychology of women air travelers. In the summer of 1945, Pauline Gower married Bill Fahie at Brompton Oratory. She died on March 2, 1947, at age 37, soon after giving birth to twin boys.

SOURCES:

Block, Maxine, ed. *Current Biography 1943*. NY: H.W. Wilson, 1943.

SUGGESTED READING:

Fahie, Michael. *A Harvest of Memories: The Life of Pauline Gower M.B.E.*, 1999.

Barbara Morgan,
Melrose, Massachusetts

Grable, Betty (1916–1973)

American film actress who was the first "pin-up girl" of note and the highest-paid woman in the country during the mid-1940s. Name variations: acted under the name of Frances Dean; made a recording under the name of Ruth Haag. Born Ruth Elizabeth Grable in South St. Louis, Missouri, on December 18, 1916; died in Las Vegas, Nevada, on July 2, 1973; youngest of two daughters of Leon Grable (an accountant and stockbroker) and Lillian Rose (Hoffman) Grable; attended Mary's Institute, in Missouri, and the Hollywood Profession School; married Jackie Coogan (an actor), on December 20, 1937 (divorced 1940); married Harry James (a bandleader), on July 11, 1943 (divorced 1965); children: (second marriage) two daughters, Victoria James (b. 1944) and Jessica James (b. 1946).

Filmography: Let's Go Places (1930); Whoopee (1930); Kiki (1931); Palmy Days (1931); The Greeks Had a Word for Them (1932); The Kid from Spain (1932); Probation (19132); Hold 'Em Jail (1932); Child of Manhattan (1933); Cavalcade (1933); What Price Innocence? (1933); Student Tour (1934); The Gay Divorcée (1934); The Nitwits (1935); Old Man Rhythm (1935); Collegiate (1935); Follow the Fleet (1936); Pigskin Parade (1936); Don't Turn 'Em Loose (1936); This Way Please (1937); Thrill of a Lifetime (1937); College Swing (1938); Give Me a Sailor (1938); Campus Confessions (1938); Man About Town (1939); Million Dollar Legs (1939); The Day the Bookies Wept (1939); Down Argentine Way (1940); Tin Pan Alley (1940); Moon over Miami (1941); A Yank in the R.A.F. (1941); I Wake Up Screaming (1941); Footlight Serenade (1942); Song of the Islands (1942); Springtime in the Rockies (1942); Coney Island (1943); Sweet Rosie O'Grady (1943); Four Jills in a Jeep (1944); Pin-Up Girl (1944); Billy Rose's Diamond Horseshoe (1945); The Dolly Sisters (1945); All Star Bond Rally (1945); Do You Love Me? (1946); Hollywood Park (1946); The Shocking Miss Pilgrim (1947); Mother Wore Tights (1947); Hollywood Bound (1947); That Lady in Ermine (1948); When My Baby Smiles at Me (1948); The Beautiful Blonde from Bashful Bend (1949); Wabash Avenue (1950); My Blue Heaven (1950); Call Me Mister (1951); Meet Me After the Show (1951); The Farmer Takes a Wife (1953); How to Marry a Millionaire (1953); Three for the Show (1955); How to Be Very, Very Popular (1955).

Legendary Hollywood film actress Betty Grable—the highest-paid woman in the country during the mid-1940s—was hard working, down-to-earth, and quite unaffected by her star status. "As a dancer I couldn't outdance *Ginger Rogers or *Eleanor Powell," she once admitted. "As a singer I'm no rival to *Doris Day. As an actress I don't take myself seriously." Grable, who made 30 films before hitting it big, might not have been in the movies at all had it not been for her mother.

Born in South St. Louis, Missouri, Betty was the younger of two daughters born to Leon Grable, an accountant who later became a stockbroker, and Lillian Hoffman Grable, a frustrated actress who channeled her own desire for a show-business career into her younger daughter. (Grable's older sister successfully rejected her mother's attempt to make her a star.) Betty was dragged to dancing and singing lessons as a child and was a veteran of local talent shows by the age of seven. "Mother was determined not to miss a trick," she later recalled. "I got my start in a children's show playing the saxophone. I was dressed as if I were a piece of coral. Later I did a bit where I played and tapped at the same time. We cut that short but quick; it almost loosened my teeth."

After a visit to Hollywood in 1928, Lillian and Betty moved permanently to the film capital, where after appearing in the chorus line in a film musical called *Let's Go Places*, Grable signed a year's contract with 20th Century-Fox. For the next four years, she made the rounds of the studios, playing small roles and even appearing in some educational shorts. In 1931, she was signed by Sam Goldwyn who changed her name to Frances Dean and cast her in a series of bit parts, then dropped her because he did not feel she was star material. However, her appearance in the Fred Astaire-Ginger Rogers classic *The Gay Divorcée* (1934), performing a zany number called "Let's Knock Knees" with Edward Everett Horton, won her a short-lived contract with RKO under her own name. She then embarked on her "Betty Co-ed" period with Paramount, playing in a string of "B" features with titles like *College Swing* (1938) and *Campus Confessions* (1938). In 1939, when Paramount let Grable go, her career had yet to take off. "Something had to be done," she said, "or I would be a promising youngster until I was a grandmother."

Meantime, on her birthday, December 18, 1937, Grable had married long-time steady Jackie Coogan and was soon in the news when she backed him during his famous court battle. Formerly a child star, Coogan was suing his mother and stepfather to obtain his screen earnings. The couple divorced in 1940, the same year that Grable's parents divorced. After well-publicized romances with Artie Shaw (which ended when he eloped with *Lana Turner), and George Raft (who was married at the time to Grayce Mulrooney, who would not grant him a divorce), Grable would marry bandleader Harry James in 1943. The couple would have two daughters before divorcing in 1965.

In 1939, with her career in a slump, Grable appeared in vaudeville and then accepted the second female lead in the Broadway show *Du Barry Was a Lady*, with *Ethel Merman. Her show-stopping dance number, "Well, Did You Evah," led to a *Life* magazine cover and another contract with 20th Century-Fox. Grable went to work in the lavish Technicolor film *Down Argentine Way*, replacing *Alice Faye who had been stricken with appendicitis. Starring with Faye in another rousing musical, *Tin Pan Alley* (1940), in which she performed a risqué harem number, Grable went on to make a series of splashy musicals during the next decade, among them *Song of the Islands* (1942), *Footlight Serenade* (1942), *Springtime in the Rockies* (1942), and *Four Jills in a Jeep* (1944). Now an unqualified box-office star, Grable's popularity peaked during World War II, when GIs selected her as their number one "pin-up girl." At least three million copies of photographer Frank Powolny's famous pose of the star in a white bathing suit were distributed to servicemen, and Grable's famous legs were insured with Lloyds of London for $1 million.

During the late 1940s and early 1950s, Grable made a series of pictures with Dan Dailey, the first of which, *Mother Wore Tights* (1947), was one of her all-time hits, and also catapulted Dailey to stardom. Delightful complements to each other, the pair charmed audiences again in *My Blue Heaven* (1950) and *Call Me Mister* (1951). During the 1940s, Grable also made appearances on the radio, in shows as "Lux Radio Theater" and "Suspense." Although known as a singer, she made no records, as Darryl F. Zanuck barred his stars from the recording studio. However, she did manage one commercial recording for Columbia Records in 1945, billed as Ruth Haag. The song, "I Can't Begin to Tell You" also featured her husband Harry James.

One of Grable's best known films of the 1950s was not a musical at all, but the comedy

How To Marry a Millionaire (1953), with **Lauren Bacall** and the new Fox star *****Marilyn Monroe**, who received top billing. Grable's portrayal of an over-the-hill showgirl looking for her last big break was one of the best of her career. Although Monroe was stealing her thunder (and would eventually inherit her dressing room), Grable remained good-natured, helping Marilyn when she asked for advice and reportedly telling her at one point, "Honey, I've had it. Go get yours. It's your turn now."

Grable's last film was *How To Be Very, Very Popular* (1955), after which she retired from the movies, claiming that she would only return if the "right" property came along. She performed in a nightclub act with Harry James at the El Rancho in Las Vegas and, in 1958, put together a revue called *Memories*, a pastiche of all her old movie numbers. The show played at Hollywood's Moulin Rouge and also had a successful run at the Latin Quarter in New York. Grable then moved to Las Vegas permanently, concentrating on her beloved horses and her golf game. Growing restless again, however, she and former co-star Dan Dailey put together a condensed version of *Guys and Dolls* (with Grable as Adelaide), which opened in Las Vegas just before Christmas of 1962 and played for 18 weeks to standing-room-only crowds. They repeated that success the following year with a revival of *High Button Shoes*.

In 1965, Grable lost her mother, who for years had served as her secretary. That same year, she was also divorced from James, a staggering blow, although it was said to have been an amicable split with the couple remaining friends. She threw herself into rehearsals for the part of Dolly Levi in a Vegas version of *Hello, Dolly!*, which opened just before New Year's 1966 and enjoyed great success. She later joined the national tour of the show and then, in 1967, replaced *****Martha Raye** on Broadway. After the run of the show, she retired again to Las Vegas, living with Bob Remick, a young dancer she had met while on tour with *Dolly*. In 1969, claiming she could not sit still for long, she embarked for London, to star as a saloon owner in an ill-fated musical called *****Belle Starr***. Although audiences loved her, the critics were cruel, and the play closed after 21 performances. She returned home to a summer tour in *Plaza Suite* and, in 1971, shot a television ad for Geritol with her married daughters and their four children.

Later that year, just before a trip to Australia to star in *No, No, Nanette*, Grable was diagnosed with lung cancer, which she fought

valiantly for several years, even recovering sufficiently to tour briefly in *Born Yesterday*. Her health continued to decline, however, and she died on July 2, 1973, at age 56.

SOURCES:

Agan, Patrick. *The Decline and Fall of the Love Goddesses*. Los Angeles, CA: Pinnacle, 1979.

Parish, James Robert, and Michael R. Pitts. *Hollywood Songsters*. NY: Garland, 1991.

Sicherman, Barbara, and Carol Hurd Green. *Notable American Women: The Modern Period*. Cambridge, MA: The Belknap Press of Harvard University Press, 1980.

Barbara Morgan,
Melrose, Massachusetts

Grace, Princess of Monaco (1928–1982).

See Kelly, Grace.

Graf, Steffi (1969—)

Record-breaking German tennis star and Olympic gold medalist. Born Stephanie Maria Graf on June 14, 1969, in Bruhl, Germany; first of two children of Heidi and Peter Graf (a car salesman).

Under her father's guidance, began taking tennis lessons at the age of four and became the second youngest player to receive a ranking when she turned professional at age thirteen; won her first Grand Slam title at the French Open (1987) and swept all four Grand Slam tournaments the following year, during which she also won a gold medal in the Olympics (1988); became the first woman to win all of the Grand Slam singles titles at least four times (1995); facing stiff competition from younger players and sidelined several times for injuries, saw her game suffer (late 1990s), although victory at the French Open (1999) added a 22nd Grand Slam singles title to her career; announced her retirement from professional tennis (summer 1999).

Visitors to the home of Peter and **Heidi Graf** in the German industrial center of Mannheim were sometimes startled to find a length of string stretched across the living room. It was, as Peter would explain to the uninitiated, the net for the tennis games his daughter Stephanie loved to play. Sometimes, father and daughter would even engage in a brief volley for the amusement of close friends, all of whom had to agree with Herr Graf that his four-year-old daughter did, indeed, love to hit the ball back to him—hard. "I always wanted to hit it hard," Steffi Graf once said. "It's just in you as a child. You pick up the racket and you just play." By picking up the racket and just playing, Steffi rose to the very top of professional

tennis in less than ten years and became the most famous German athlete since World War II, so beloved by her compatriots that she is still referred to as *die Grafen* ("the Countess").

The first of two children, Steffi had been born in suburban Bruhl, Germany, on June 14, 1969. Shortly after the birth of a son Michael three years later, Peter moved the family to nearby Mannheim to take a job as a car salesman. The bond between Steffi and her father was formed early as Peter encouraged and developed his daughter's natural talent for the game, particularly the powerful forehand—a high, chopping downward stroke—that would become her signature on courts around the world. Some said Peter was pushing Steffi too hard and was preventing her from forming the friendships of normal childhood by whisking her off to practice while other children were playing together. Further concerns were voiced when Peter placed ten-year-old Steffi under the tutelage of her first professional coach, Boris Breskvar, at a state-financed tennis program back in Bruhl. "The father was a god for Steffi," Breskvar later said, "and Steffi was for him also everything. She was crazy about tennis, but pleasing him was surely part of it." In 1982, Peter announced that Steffi would be leaving school to play professionally. At 13, she was the second youngest tennis player to receive a ranking, at #124.

For the next three years, Steffi learned the ropes of professional tennis by playing in futures events and in qualifying tournaments. Her mother served as her warmup partner for countless matches on hardwood floors in high school gymnasiums and on cracked concrete courts at small-town tennis clubs throughout Europe. "They were necessary experiences," Graf said years later. "You travel, you learn how to lose and you learn how to win." It seemed perfectly natural to her that Peter should direct her career, choosing her tournaments and her coaches, arranging her travel schedule and managing the prize money. As Steffi neared her 17th birthday, Peter set her on the path that led to her first Grand Slam title at the 1987 French Open, in which she defeated *Martina Navratilova. It would be the first of six French Open victories in coming years. That same year, her relentless advance brought her to the finals at Wimbledon and the U.S. Open, a major win at the Chase championships, and her first million dollars in earnings. By August of 1987, just five years after turning professional with her 124th ranking, Graf had become the #1-ranked player on the professional circuit. She would hold that rank-

ing for 186 consecutive weeks, the longest un-broken #1 ranking in tennis history.

Even at this early stage in her career, the pressure was building. Although Graf was known to close friends as a sensitive and emo-tional young woman, Peter insisted that she keep her emotions in check on the court, in the locker room, and in front of the press, creating the same aloof stoicism that had isolated her from schoolmates back in Mannheim. Steffi's perfec-tionism was almost frightening. "She never appreciated a win as much as she was devastated by a loss," a friend once noted. "She would at times go into a room and not come out for a day." But the wins far outnumbered the losses. With her formidable serve, her powerhouse forehand and her calculating game strategy, *die Grafen* swept all four Grand Slam titles in 1988, made it to the semi-finals of the Chase Championships, and won a gold medal for Germany in that year's Olympics in Seoul, South Korea. Despite the success, Graf remained publicly reticent and showed no outward elation at her good fortune. Her uncommunicativeness won her few fans off the court. "I . . . don't feel comfortable talking a lot, especially in public," Steffi once told a reporter, but Argentina's **Patricia Tarabini** spoke for many when she wondered, "Is 'hello' such a big deal?" Graf seemed able to reach out only in non-verbal ways, as when she ran into the locker room one day at the 1993 Virginia Slims in New York after Martina Navratilova's loss to **Mary Pierce**. Without a word, Graf kissed Navratilova on the cheek, handed her a small bracelet, and then ran out.

> *I*t's great to be a perfectionist, but sometimes being a perfectionist can also stand a little bit in the way.
> —**Steffi Graf**

Complicating matters was her father's increasingly erratic behavior, fueled by alcoholism and an addiction to tranquilizers. Peter's abusive treatment of anyone who criticized his daughter's play or spoke well of her opponents was the talk of the circuit, as was his secretive handling of Steffi's prize money. Peter was known to collect Steffi's appearance fees by stuffing the cash into plastic bags, and his arguments with German tax collectors over late payments were frequent. Further embarrassment was visited on the family when Peter's affair with a 20-year-old model was splashed across the tabloids. Amazingly, Graf's game never seemed to suffer. "I think the only place Steffi is supremely confident is the tennis court," one WTA tour official said at the time, and it was true that her wins grew in number as her personal trials grew more severe. Between 1989 and 1994, she won ten Grand Slam titles; her worst showing in those six years was her loss of the Australian Open in a finals match. By winning the U.S. Open in 1995, Graf became the first woman to win each of the four Grand Slam singles titles at least four times. She finished 1996 as the top ranked player for the fourth straight year, winning all three of the Grand Slams that she entered (withdrawing from the Australian Open because of foot surgery) and ending the year by defeating **Marti-**

na **Hingis** in five sets at the WTA Championships in November.

But the accolades were bittersweet, for not a few critics attributed her remarkable success between 1993 and 1995 to the fact that her chief rival, **Monica Seles**, had been absent from the circuit since being attacked and stabbed during the changeover at a match in Hamburg. Worse, Seles' attacker later proved to be a deranged fan of Graf's who admitted he had wanted to remove Seles from competition so that Steffi could gain the #1 ranking Seles had taken from her in 1991. Graf proved her critics wrong when she faced Seles across the net at the 1995 U.S. Open and walked away with the singles title. But the real challenge came at the post-victory press conference when questions turned from the match she had just played to the fate of Peter Graf, who was by now in a German prison awaiting trial on tax-evasion charges. Unable to face this most difficult of questions, Graf bolted from the press room in tears.

German authorities had become suspicious the year before when a promoter filed a civil suit against Peter for the return of a $300,000 fee for an appearance Steffi failed to make because of an injury. Further inquiries revealed that Peter had not filed tax returns for the previous five years. Early in 1995, tax agents had swept through the Graf home in Bruhl and confiscated $150,000 in cash; and when Steffi arrived for a physical therapy session in Atlanta in August of 1995, just before her U.S. Open match against Seles, she was met by her brother with the news that Peter had been jailed. He warned that she might also be implicated in a scheme that German officials claimed had laundered millions of dollars in prize money through false corporations in Amsterdam, Liechtenstein, and the Netherlands Antilles.

Graf vigorously claimed that she had faithfully heeded her father's repeated advice over the past ten years and had concentrated purely on her game, leaving the finances to him. "Tennis was my part," she said, "and I felt 'OK, you do everything else.' I was fine with it. Maybe also because I didn't know any different." Peter himself was allowed only one public statement on the opening day of his trial, and made sure it was about Steffi's innocence. "I hereby declare unambiguously that until 1995, our daughter was in no way conversant with tax matters," he said. While Peter's trial dragged on and with charges against her still pending, Steffi was forced to face the world outside the tennis court. There were lawyers, accountants, financial brokers to deal with; a staff was needed to do the job her father had done single-handedly for so long. "I needed to do this," Steffi said of her forced entry into the world of deals and planning and bottom lines; but at the same time she was winning her three 1996 Grand Slams and finishing the year with just four losses. Even Graf wondered how she'd gotten through the year. "I wonder how I manage to survive all this," she said at the time. "I am sometimes an enigma to myself."

In January of 1997, Peter Graf was found guilty of evading $7.4 million in taxes and was sentenced to nearly four years in prison. (He was released on some $3 million bail 11 months later.) "He was stubborn and ambitious, and his ambitions misled him," the presiding judge said. But as Steffi took up her racket for the 1997 season, there was still no word on what the authorities intended to do about the charges pending against her. She was still ranked #1, but was overtaken by Martina Hingis after being bounced from both the Australian and French Opens by **Amanda Coetzer** and withdrawing from Wimbledon because of persistent back pain. The strain inevitably broke through her usual aloof manner. "Haven't you had enough?" she snapped at reporters after her loss to Coetzer, most of their questions being about her father and not the game she had just played. She won her only title that year in Strasbourg and was sidelined during much of June with a knee injury that required reconstructive surgery. It was during her recovery that German officials announced all charges against her would be dropped, and that Steffi had agreed to pay $1 million to the government and to charities of her choosing in restitution for taxes still owed. Steffi repeatedly and publicly stated that despite the ordeal, she bore her father no ill will. "I love him dearly," she said. "Nothing in that department will change. He needs help. When you know what alcohol and pills can do to you, it's difficult to be angry."

The press now took note of a new maturity in Steffi's demeanor, while her friends and competitors in the game felt that she had finally begun to open up to them. **Jennifer Capriati**, whose substance abuse had removed her from the court for 14 months for treatment, recalled how Graf was one of the first to welcome her back with a warm embrace. "A very caring person," Capriati said of Steffi, "and more outgoing than I've ever seen her." Steffi herself had been absent from play for nine months because of her knee injury, and only made it to the quarterfinals

in what was to have been her comeback tournament, the 1998 Faber Grand Prix. At 29 years of age, and after 16 years of professional play, Steffi's aging ankles, hamstrings and knees were becoming troublesome, forcing her withdrawal from the WTA tour rankings in June of 1998. It was the first time her name had been absent from the list in 15 years, and Martina Hingis went so far as to venture the opinion that Steffi's reign was finally giving way to younger players.

Graf's subsequent announcement that she would play in the U.S. Open was taken as a retort to Hingis' rash statement, but Steffi denied she was coming back with vengeance in mind. "I don't need to prove to anybody but myself," she said. She played respectably at the Open, but lost in the fourth round to 10th-ranked **Patty Schnyder**. It wasn't until several weeks later, nearly the end of the 1998 season, that Graf reached finals play and captured her first title in 15 months at the Pilot Pen International in New Haven, at least assuring that she would complete 13 consecutive titled years. On her way to the New Haven title, Steffi managed to defeat her old nemesis Amanda Coetzer in the quarterfinals, after losing three times to Coetzer in the previous year, and to make up in the semifinals her two 1998 losses to **Lindsay Davenport**. It was her first win over a top-ten seeded player in more than a year, forcing the gossip mill to change gears and wonder if Steffi was finally getting a second wind.

As the first half of the 1999 season unfolded, Steffi played through to the semifinals at the first Grand Slam event of the year, the Australian Open, where she lost to Monica Seles 5-7, 1-6; and at the Adidas International, the Faber Grand Prix, and the Lipton Championships. She seemed back in top form as she defeated Martina Hingis to capture her 22nd Grand Slam title at the French Open, second only to *****Margaret Smith Court**'s 24, adding to the hush in the press room when Graf announced after her victory that it would be her last appearance in the clay court tournament. She made much the same declaration a month later at Wimbledon, after battling her way to the finals on the grass court only to fall to Lindsay Davenport 6-4, 7-5, missing her seventh Wimbledon championship. "She has clearly grown tired of having to treat every Grand Slam event as a two-week test in pain management," wrote *The New York Times*' George Vecsey, noting the bandage on Steffi's right thigh during the match and her continuing treatments for back pain. She played an uncharacteristically defensive game at Wimbledon, never really recovering after Davenport broke her serve in the first game of the match. "Right now I'm a little sad about everything," Graf said in making her retirement from Wimbledon public, "but in a way I still feel like a winner getting out of this tournament," referring to her defeat of the young and formidable sisters, **Venus** and **Serena Williams**, during semifinals play. Graf could just as easily have pointed in triumph to the 103 singles titles she had won in 17 years of competition, placing her third in that category behind Martina Navratilova and *****Chris Evert**; or the fact that she had held, or shared, the WTA's #1 ranking for a record-breaking 377 weeks during her career.

Going into the U.S. Open, where she had been the #1 seeded player a record nine times, she was still ranked as the world's third best tennis player, behind Davenport and Hingis; but early in August of 1999, several weeks before Open play began, Graf officially announced her retirement from professional tennis. She told a small press conference in Germany that while her recent physical injuries played a part in her decision, her loss of enthusiasm for the game was the primary reason for stepping down. "The weeks after Wimbledon were not easy," she said. "I thought I would carry on playing until the end of the year. But I do not feel like flying to tournaments anymore. That's new. I decided to play a few more tournaments to see if that feeling would go away, but it didn't."

Steffi now splits her time between homes in Florida, New York, and Germany while overseeing her own company, Steffi Graf Sport, which she hopes to expand beyond tennis into live entertainment events. But it's in her private life that she now finds the security only the tennis court could once provide. Her parents' marriage somehow survived Peter's addictions, conviction and imprisonment, and Steffi finds added strength from her long-time relationship with race car driver Michael Bartels. She founded and personally directs Children For Tomorrow, a non-profit organization dedicated to helping children traumatized by war and political persecution. After so many years of competition, she points out, her priorities have begun to change. "When you're seventeen, you win and you win and you just accept it," Graf says. "It's nicer to have these feelings, this joy!"

SOURCES:

Finn, Robin. "Davenport Wins as Graf Says Goodbye," in *The New York Times.* July 5, 1999.

Jenkins, Sally. "Do Not Disturb," in *Sports Illustrated.* Vol. 80, no. 20. May 23, 1994.

Nack, William. "The Trials of Steffi Graf," in *Sports Illustrated.* Vol. 85, no. 21. Nov. 18, 1996.

Vecsey, George. "Graf Takes Next Step in Comeback," in *The New York Times.* September 2, 1998.

Norman Powers,
writer-producer, Chelsea Lane Productions, New York

Graham, Barbara Wood

(1923–1955)

American executed at San Quentin. Born in 1923; executed for murder in San Quentin by cyanide poisoning on June 3 (some sources cite June 5), 1955; married four times; children: one.

Convicted of murder, Barbara Graham was executed by cyanide poisoning in San Quentin in 1955, though some thought she was wrongly implicated by three male companions who were using her in hopes of modifying their own fates. To the final hour, she claimed her innocence, maintaining that she had been home with her husband and newborn son at the time of the killing of **Mabel Monahan**, a wealthy widow, in Burbank. But a troubled past, that included bad checks, drug addiction, and perjury, and her condemnation by a sensationalized press ensured her execution. Graham was the subject of the 1958 movie *I Want to Live!*, for which *****Susan Hayward** won an Academy Award.

SOURCES:

I Want to Live! (120 min. film), based on newspaper articles by Ed Montgomery and letters of Barbara Graham, starring Susan Hayward, directed by Robert Wise, produced by United Artists, 1958.

Graham, Bette Nesmith

(1924–1980)

American entrepreneur who invented Liquid Paper. Born Bette Claire McMurray in Dallas, Texas, in 1924; died in 1980; married Warren Nesmith, in 1942 (divorced); children: Michael Nesmith (an actor).

Bette Nesmith Graham turned her imperfect typing skills into a $47 million fortune. Born in 1924 and raised in Dallas, Texas, she left high school at 17 to marry her high school sweetheart, Warren Nesmith. At 19, she was supporting her son while her husband was fighting in World War II. Divorced soon after her husband's return, she continued to be the sole support of her son.

Despite her lack of training, Graham worked most of her life as a secretary, teaching herself basic office skills along the way, including how to type. She was employed as an executive secretary at Texas Bank & Trust when IBM carbon-film ribbon came into use, making it all but impossible to erase typing errors without smearing the copy. In a flash of ingenuity, Graham brought in some white tempera paint she had been using on holiday windows and began using it to cover her mistakes. Although some of her coworkers thought she was cheating, many of them begged for the formula. In time, she began producing "Mistake Out" in her kitchen, gradually refining the formula with some help from a worker in a paint manufacturing plant and her son's chemistry teacher. When it was perfected into a smooth, opaque, and quick-to-dry fluid, she applied for a patent under the name "Liquid Paper." When IBM refused her proposal to market the product, she produced and sold Liquid Paper out of her garage. Although slow to catch on, it finally took off in 1968, allowing Graham to give up her secretarial job.

In 1970, Graham sold her invention to the Gillette Corporation for $47.5 million, plus royalties, which allowed her to spend her last years happily doing charity work. Upon her death in 1980, her fortune was divided equally between Gillette and her son Michael Nesmith, who in the intervening years made his own mark as a TV star on the sitcom "The Monkees."

Graham, Elizabeth N. (1878–1966).

See Arden, Elizabeth.

Graham, Euphemia (d. 1469)

*Countess of Douglas. Name variations: Euphemia Douglas; Euphemia Hamilton; Lady Hamilton. Died in 1469; daughter of Patrick Graham of Kilpont and *Euphemia Stewart (c. 1375–1415), countess of Strathearn; married Archibald Douglas, 5th earl of Douglas, in 1425; married James Hamilton, 1st Lord Hamilton; children: (first marriage) three, including *Margaret Douglas (b. around 1427).*

Graham, Florence (1878–1966).

See Arden, Elizabeth.

Graham, Isabella (1742–1814)

Scottish-American educator and philanthropist. Born Isabella Marshall on July 29, 1742, in Lanarkshire, Scotland; died in New York City on July 27, 1814; married Dr. John Graham (an army surgeon and local widower), in 1765 (died 1773); children: five, including Joan Graham Bethune.

From the movie I Want to Live!, starring Susan Hayward, based on the life of Barbara Graham.

Isabella Graham was born in 1742 in Lanarkshire, Scotland, and married Dr. John Graham in 1765. In 1767, she accompanied her husband to Canada where he was a physician with a British army regiment. Five years later, the couple moved to Antigua when he was transferred. When her husband died a year later (1773), Graham was left penniless and pregnant with her fifth child. She returned to Scotland to live with her father, opening a school in their home in Paisley which expanded into a girls' boarding school in Edinburgh.

Coming to New York in 1789, Graham established a successful seminary for young ladies. In November 1797, along with *Elizabeth Ann Seton and other women, she organized the Society for the Relief of Poor Widows with Small Children and was its "First Directress." Through her efforts and that of her daughter **Joan Graham Bethune**, the Orphan Asylum Society was founded in March 1806. The Society for Promoting Industry among the Poor and the first Sunday School for Ignorant Adults were also established in New York. Graham systematically visited the inmates of hospitals, as well as the sick female convicts in the state prison, and distributed Bibles to hundreds of families.

Graham, Joyce Maxtone (1901–1953).

See Maxtone Graham, Joyce.

Graham, Katharine (1917—)

American newspaper publisher who guided the Washington Post *through its most turbulent period when it published the "Pentagon Papers" and investigated the Watergate affair. Name variations: Kay Graham; Mrs. Phil Graham; Katharine Meyer. Born Katharine Meyer on June 16, 1917, in New York City; daughter of Eugene Meyer (owner of the* Washington Post*) and Agnes Elizabeth (Ernst) Meyer (1887–1970, a publisher, journalist and social worker); graduated from the University of Chicago, 1938; married attorney Philip Graham (an attorney and publisher), in 1940 (died 1963); children:* Elizabeth "Lally" Graham *(b. 1944);* Donald E. Graham *(b. 1945);* William Graham *(b. 1948);* Stephen Graham *(b. 1952).*

Worked as a journalist in San Francisco before joining the staff of the Washington Post, *which her father had purchased some years earlier; married attorney Philip Graham in 1940, who eventually became publisher of the family's newspaper and greatly expanded its operations and reputation; following husband's suicide (1963), became publisher and guided the* Post *through its most turbulent period during and after its publication of the notorious "Pentagon Papers" and its investigative reporting of the Watergate affair, the revelations of which led to the resignation of President Richard Nixon (1974); elected the first female president of the American Newspaper Publishers Association, and was the first woman to serve on the board of the Associated Press. Although retired from the* Post, *remains active in publishing and in supporting women's advancement in the industry.*

On a spring evening in 1933, some two weeks after pretty young Kay Meyer had returned from her Virginia boarding school to her family's sprawling estate in New York's Westchester County, the dinner conversation between her parents seemed unusually mysterious. They spoke incessantly of Washington D.C. and, in particular, of the capitol city's lively newspaper business. Shy Kay finally found a convenient moment to inquire politely what it was all about. "Oh, didn't we tell you?" Kay's mother *Agnes Meyer casually remarked. "We bought the *Post.*"

Eugene Meyer's purchase of the bankrupt *Washington Post* seemed just the latest event in a shrewd business career that had made him one of America's wealthiest men, a respected adviser to the White House and, at the time of the *Post*

purchase, the chair of the Federal Reserve Board. Twenty years before, when he married Agnes Ernst, a lawyer's daughter and a Barnard graduate, he had already made enough money in investment banking to build his bride a fine townhouse on East 51st Street in Manhattan. By the time his third daughter Katharine was born on June 16, 1917, Eugene had bought an entire building on 5th Avenue, turning the upper floors into his family's residence, along with a mansion in Washington so palatial that it was often mistaken for the nearby Library of Congress; he was completing plans for his country estate, Seven Springs Farm, in Mount Kisco, New York, some 40 miles north of Manhattan. Inspired by the French chateaux that Eugene and Agnes had so admired during their frequent tours of the Continent, Seven Springs was said to have cost more than $2 million by the time of its completion in 1919, an enormous sum in those early years of the century.

The Meyer children—daughters **Florence (Meyer Homolka)**, **Elizabeth (Meyer Lorentz)**, and **Ruth (Meyer)**, in addition to Katharine, and son Eugene, Jr.—saw little of their parents as they grew to maturity, raised by nannies, governesses and private tutors. Agnes, an enthusiastic supporter of women's rights, had little interest in child rearing and housekeeping ("What a horror!," she was said to have exclaimed on being presented with her first baby, Florence, in 1920). Her credo did, however, grant considerable latitude for artistic and intellectual pursuits, for advising Eugene on his business strategies, and for the occasional extramarital affair. One of Agnes' adopted artists, novelist Thomas Mann, was sufficiently impressed with his patron's resourcefulness in dealing with a passport problem that he later wrote to her, "The impression grows that you are running the country." But Agnes showed little inclination to apply the same talents to her home life. "I believe she was often desperately unhappy in her marriage, especially at first," Katharine Graham would later write of her mother. She was "completely self-absorbed."

Her father's financial prowess insulated the family from the Depression, Eugene having taken care well before economic disaster struck the nation to consolidate his vast empire into the giant Allied Chemical Corporation, which he made sure was debt-free by the time of the great stock-market crash of 1929. It was of no great consequence, therefore, for Eugene to make an interest-free loan of $300,000 to Washington's exclusive Madeira School for the construction of a leafy new campus in rural Greenwood, Virginia, completed by the time Kay began her studies there in the footsteps of her older sisters, who had attended the school's original home on Dupont Circle in Washington. Kay excelled in academics and in the school's social life, eventually becoming the editor of the school newspaper. She later described herself as a "Goody Two Shoes" during her years at Madeira, anxious to fit in with her classmates and horrified that her family's immense wealth and influence would be revealed. "What I was trying to figure out was how to adjust to whatever life I found," she later wrote.

Although her father had conceived and set up the Hoover Administration's Reconstruction Finance Board to help keep failing banks afloat during the Depression, Eugene's fiscally conservative advice did not appeal to Hoover's successor, Franklin Roosevelt, who politely but firmly asked for his resignation from both the Finance Board and from the Federal Reserve. Meyer family lore much favors the story of the day Eugene, moping around the house with little to do, picked a fight with Agnes by noting the dust on a bannister. "This house is not properly run!" he complained. "Then you'd better go buy the *Post*!" Agnes is said to have snapped back at him.

Everyone knew that the *Post*, the most disreputable of the capitol's five dailies, had finally gone bankrupt after years of mismanagement and was being put up for auction. Eugene had always been impressed by the power wielded by press barons and decided to bid anonymously for the *Post* through a lawyer, facing stiff competition from Randolph Hearst, who already owned the *Washington Herald*. Eugene's bid of $825,000 won the day, much to Hearst's anger when the identity of his rival became public knowledge once the sale was approved by the courts. Indeed, in his first editorial as publisher of the *Post*, on June 12, 1933, Eugene took a thinly veiled slap at Hearst by promising that the paper's first duty was "to the public . . . and not to the private interests of its owner." It was the paper's editorial independence, in fact, that was to slowly win converts, including Roosevelt himself, who in 1935 admitted his admiration for the *Post*'s editorial quality.

While her father worked at his new business, Kay left Madeira for Vassar in 1934 and soon found herself a job as an apprentice editor on the school paper, although she carefully hid her family's connection to the newspaper business. "She was not an aggressive person at all," a classmate later recalled. "She was very interested in being on a newspaper and very interested in hearing what you had to say." Kay's attrac-

tion to leftist politics was more difficult for her family to digest, but nonetheless of interest to her father. Eugene, now nearing 60 and concerned about the future of his fledgling business, took notice of his daughter's journalistic tendencies and intellectual curiosity, and was especially impressed by Kay's decision to spend a summer in Washington as an apprentice at the *Post* rather than at Mount Kisco with the rest of the family. "She's got a hard mind," he told a friend at the time. "She'd make a great businessman." He followed up on his observations by suggesting to Kay that she leave Vassar and its emphasis on a liberal arts education for the University of Chicago, known for its business school and its liberal politics.

*K*ay's a big shot in the newspaper racket.
—1934 Madeira School yearbook prediction for graduate Katharine Meyer

Arriving there in 1936, Kay was soon being exposed to everything her family background had kept at a distance—workers' rights and union organizing, socialist policymaking and political agitating so suspect that one of Eugene Meyer's contemporaries had withdrawn his daughter from the school because of its possible Communist influences. Kay took up residence in the university's International House where, in another radical departure from staid old Vassar, men and women lived in the same building (although on separate floors) and philosophy and politics were debated late into the night. As usual, Kay never volunteered information about her family or her privileged upbringing, although she was hurt by the fact that neither Eugene nor Agnes attended her graduation in 1938. She received instead a congratulatory telegram from Agnes' secretary which misspelled her first name.

In early 1939, as war loomed in Europe, Kay traveled with her father on a business trip to San Francisco and fell in love with the city. "I chucked my pride and asked my father to help me get a job there," she later remembered, gladly accepting a job covering the waterfront for the *San Francisco News* at $21 a week. The paper dutifully sent Eugene copies of all her stories. At the end of her two months, Eugene insisted she return to Washington to work for the family paper, the *Post* now being the capitol's third-ranked newspaper, behind the Hearst-owned *Times Herald*. "He wants and needs someone who is willing to go through the whole mill, from reporting to circulation management to editorial writing and eventually to be his assistant," Kay wrote home to her sister Elizabeth. "I doubt my ability to carry a load like the Washington Post and . . . damn well think it would be a first class dog's life." But she buckled down to learning everything Eugene laid out for her until December of 1939, when she met and fell in love with the man Eugene would finally choose over her as his newspaper's heir.

Philip Graham was considered one of the most eligible bachelors in Washington at the time Kay was introduced to him at a cocktail party. Handsome and recklessly ambitious, Phil had overcome the disadvantages of genteel poverty growing up in Florida by becoming a brilliant law student and was, at the time he met Kay, a protégé of Felix Frankfurter. He seemed destined for a rewarding law career leading to an eventual judicial appointment. But Eugene Meyer immediately fastened on Kay's new beau as an ideal choice to guide the *Post,* telling friends that Phil Graham was a "winner by nature." On her marriage to Phil in an elaborate ceremony at the Meyer estate in Mount Kisco on June 5, 1940, Kay abandoned any hopes she might have had for a career in journalism and settled down to married life while her husband worked toward his law degree. After a stillbirth and two miscarriages, Kay gave birth to a daughter in 1944, to be followed by three sons between 1945 and 1953. Her only involvement with the *Post* was during her husband's absence for war duty. "I was pregnant and Philip was away and I was just looking for a mindless job to make the time go faster," she later said. Eugene, meanwhile, worried about his son-in-law's plans to practice law in Florida in preparation for a political career. "I've got to know what will happen to this paper when I'm no longer around," he confided to friends.

Eugene's arguments must have been persuasive, for Phil Graham agreed to become an associate publisher of the *Post* on his return from the war in 1946. Two years later, Eugene sold a controlling interest in the business to his daughter and son-in-law, Phil receiving the larger share because, as Eugene explained to Katharine, it wasn't proper for a man to be in the position of working for his wife. "Curiously, I not only concurred but was in complete accord with this idea," Katharine later remembered. "I was the kind of wife that women liberationists talk about," she went on. "I was a second-class citizen and my role was to keep Phil happy, peaceful, calm, and functioning."

This proved to be more difficult as the years passed. Phil, as Kay eventually found out, had a history of depression, his struggles with the disease becoming increasingly desperate. The elusive solace of alcohol only led to abusive public arguments with Kay that became the talk of the Washington social circuit. Said one friend at the time, Graham seemed an "unbelievable, mouse-like woman who didn't move a muscle, who followed behind Phil." Even worse was Phil's years-long affair with Australian journalist **Robin Webb**, with whom Phil would disappear for long stretches. His infatuation was strong enough that, Kay later claimed, he threatened to buy her out of the *Post* and give her share to his mistress. "This was the bottom moment for me," she later said. "Not only had I lost my husband but I was about to lose the *Post.*"

The loss would have been disastrous for more than emotional reasons, for by the early 1960s Phil Graham had turned a respected but financially unrewarding newspaper into a multimedia empire. The Post Companies now owned, besides the *Post* itself, radio and television stations and, most important, *Newsweek* magazine, which Phil Graham had bought in 1961 for $15 million. Competition from the old Hearst-owned *Times Herald* had been eliminated years earlier by Phil's purchase in 1954 of the rival publication for $10 million, using money supplied by Eugene, by then retired and suffering from the cancer that brought his death in 1959. The *Post,* published in a brand new building on state-of-the-art presses, had actually begun turning a profit by the time Phil's illness became so severe that he was forced to run the company through trusted aides. Finally admitting the severity of his disorder, Phil Graham voluntarily committed himself on two separate occasions to a sanitarium outside Washington in 1963.

During these dark years, Kay was much admired for her dedication to her husband, although she herself later admitted that alternatives never occurred to her. "The truth was that I adored him and saw only the positive side of what he was doing for me. I simply didn't connect my lack of self-confidence to his behavior toward me," she said. "I felt as though he had created me and that I was totally dependent on him." Her patience seemed to be rewarded when Phil finally left Robin Webb and convinced his doctors that he was well enough to leave the sanitarium for a weekend with his wife and children at Glen Welby, their Virginia farm, in August of 1963. During lunch after his arrival, he spoke enthusiastically with his sons about a shooting expedition planned for the next day, bird hunting

Katharine
Graham

being one of his chief passions. After the meal, Phil went to his bedroom, loaded one of the 28-gauge shotguns he used for hunting, propped it against a bathtub and shot himself in the head. In her memoirs written more than 30 years later, Kay still found it difficult to describe what she saw when she ran into the bathroom that day or to understand why she had not anticipated her husband's suicide. "It had never occurred to me that he must have planned the whole day at Glen Welby to get to his guns as a way of freeing himself forever from the watchful eyes of his doctors," she wrote. "I believe that Phil came to the sad conclusion that he would never again lead a normal life."

Added to the shock and grief was the inevitable speculation about the future of the *Post*. No one even considered the possibility that Kay would choose to run the company herself. "You're not going to work, are you?" asked one friend after Phil's death. "You mustn't. You're young and attractive, and you'll get remarried." But little more than a week after her husband's suicide, Kay told a meeting of the Post Corporation's executive board that she had no intention of selling the *Post* and intended to look after the business herself until her eldest son, Donald, was old enough to manage the company. She described her role as being that of a "family coordinating hand," a sort of interim silent partner to the exclusively male executive leadership of the firm. "I naively thought the whole business would just go on as it had while I learned by listening," she once recalled. "I didn't realize that nothing stands still—issues arise every day, big and small, and they start coming at you." Her decision was greeted with a great deal of skepticism, for at the time no woman held a leadership position in any business, let alone the rough and tumble world of newspaper publishing. The board room gossip gained more fuel when, as one of her first executive decisions, Kay chose a Friday for a major meeting in New York with the editorial board of *Newsweek*— the day each issue of the magazine closed and the very worst day she could have selected. Then there was the Washington meeting of newspaper publishers at which Kay was the only woman at the table and at which she was stoutly ignored by the meeting's chair when a voice vote was called on the issue under discussion. What few supporters she had were sorely tried when Kay herself told an interviewer from *Women's Wear Daily* in early 1964 that any man could do a better job than she could.

But as her self-styled role of caretaker began to appear hopelessly simplistic and as the realities of the business world settled on her, she began to listen to the advice of such family friends as Robert McNamara, a former chief executive for Ford Motors who had become secretary of defense under Lyndon Johnson, historian Arthur Schlesinger, Jr., and economist John Kenneth Galbraith—all liberal Democrats whom she had met because of her husband's involvement with the party during the 1960 campaign that brought John Kennedy to the White House. (Phil Graham had always claimed that it was his advocacy of Lyndon Johnson as Kennedy's running mate that brought Kennedy the crucial support of southern Democrats.) These advisers and others close to Kay began to notice a strengthening of her self-confidence as 1964 wore on. They noticed that Kay no longer signed herself "Mrs. Phil Graham" but, more boldly, as "Katharine Graham," and that she no longer voiced her usual fervent prayer that her son Donny would finish college soon and come to the rescue. By late 1964, when publisher S.I. Newhouse offered to buy the *Post* from her, Graham firmly told him the paper was not for sale to anyone, at any price.

As the turbulent 1960s swept across a nation divided over the Vietnam War, the editorial pages of the *Post* remained firmly behind the Johnson Administration's pursuit of the conflict, especially after Kay toured Vietnam in 1965; but she scrupulously maintained a hands-off policy when it came to the paper's reporting and did not interfere, for example, with a series of articles revealing the Administration's undercover attempts at overthrowing various South American governments in the late 1960s. When Lyndon Johnson announced his decision not to seek reelection in 1968, Graham threw the paper's support behind Richard Nixon, an editorial decision that would prove troublesome in the near future.

By 1970, she had replaced all of the executives hired by her husband and had named Ben Bradlee, a brash Bostonian who had begun as a reporter for the *Post*, as the paper's executive editor, despite the fact that Bradlee had once ventured the opinion that there was nothing wrong with Phil Graham that a good divorce would not cure. Most significantly, she took the Post Corporation public in 1971 in a shrewd strategy that offered only non-voting shares to the public while she and her children retained the voting shares. The Corporation's balance sheet was thus vastly improved by a stock offering that still left her in firm control. Her prayer of earlier years was answered when her eldest son Donald began working at the paper after a two-year tour of duty as a Washington police officer, which he considered the best way to learn the city his family's paper served.

In 1971, as Kay hosted a cocktail party at her Washington home, an urgent conference call came through from Ben Bradlee and the *Post*'s legal advisers. The Nixon Administration, Bradlee said, had just obtained a restraining order preventing *The New York Times* from further publication of what had come to be called the Pentagon Papers—a collection of classified, leaked documents that laid bare the government's deliberate attempts over the years to cover up its disastrous strategy and appalling losses in Vietnam. Now, Bradlee said over the phone, the *Post* had obtained another 4,000 pages which, if published, could expose the paper to the same legal challenges the *Times* was facing. The decision was hers. "Let's go," Graham was heard to say, even though her paper had editorially supported the war policies of both Johnson and Nixon. "Let's publish." The expected restraining order was soon overturned by higher courts.

Little more than a year later, Kay was told that the June 17, 1973, issue of the *Post* would carry a front-page story about an attempted burglary at the Democratic National Committee's headquarters at the Watergate hotel, reporting that the burglars were intent on installing wiretapping devices. *The New York Times,* the *Boston Globe,* and other nationally prominent papers paid less attention to the story, but Graham supported Bradlee's opinion that there was more to the burglary than met the eye—an opinion that seemed justified when lawyers for the burglars attempted to subpoena her reporters' notes. Kay vowed she would rather go to jail than allow such a thing to happen and prevailed when the court order was overturned. Still, throughout most of 1973, no other paper seemed interested in the story. "Hell, usually if you have a great scoop everyone else is all over it like a wet blanket the next day," Graham later said. "And here we were alone with this . . . cow mess walking down the street and nobody came near it. It was awful. There was always the nagging possibility that we were wrong, being set up, being misled." But the Nixon Administration's reaction to the *Post's* pursuit of the story only seemed to justify the paper's stubborn investigative reporting by Carl Bernstein and Bob Woodward. There were polite, but firm, requests to drop the story from Henry Kissinger, the Administration's secretary of state who was still on friendly terms with her. Then came stronger warnings that the licenses for her company's radio and television stations would not be renewed if she persisted. Graham and her editorial board refused to back down. Finally, to Kay's great relief, CBS News began to support the paper's claims of the White House's covert attempts to illegally obtain and use information about its political enemies. The *Post* was vindicated when two former Nixon Administration aides, James McCord and John Dean, agreed to testify before the House Judiciary Committee. The paper's coverage won a Pulitzer Prize in 1973. The following year, Richard Nixon resigned in disgrace.

By now the first newspaper publisher since William Randolph Hearst to have become a household name, Kay Graham was named the chair and chief executive officer of the Post Companies in 1973. She expanded the firm's interests by buying more broadcasting properties and regional newspapers, and guided the paper through a divisive strike by the pressman's union so effectively that she was charged by labor leaders with deliberately attempting to destroy it. Graham defended herself by pointing out that it had been the union's decision to ransack the press room and destroy thousands of dollars worth of equipment. "Certainly I and everyone else in the building who was interested in putting out an on-time, quality paper were fed up with the tyranny the pressmen's union had imposed on us over the years, but I never dreamed it was possible to re-

place the pressmen, nor did I feel it was desirable. I never wanted a strike." In the wake of the strike and the weakening of the union, the Post Companies' profits rose substantially, tripling to $30 million in the five years between 1975 and 1980. With the future of her father's company now assured, Graham chose to hand control over to her son, who was named publisher in 1979. "Today, as in the rest of my life," Donald Graham said at the ceremony, "my mother has given me everything but an easy act to follow."

Her paper's prominence brought the inevitable broadsides. Graham was horrified, for example, at an unauthorized biography, *Katharine the Great,* that was scheduled for publication in 1976. Author **Deborah Davis** claimed among other things that the *Post* had been used by the CIA to bring down Richard Nixon, whom it considered a threat to national security, and that its operative at the paper was none other than Ben Bradlee. Bradlee, Davis claimed, had worked for the CIA in the 1950s. Graham and Bradlee reacted swiftly to the book, detailing a number of factual errors in its text so egregious that the publisher was eventually obliged to cancel its publication. The incident started Graham thinking seriously for the first time about writing her memoir, a suggestion from friends and family that she had always dismissed. But by 1991, the year she retired and turned the Post Company over to her son, she was ready to begin the writing project that took her five years to complete. She was 79 when *Personal History* finally appeared.

By the time of her retirement, Kay Graham was one of the world's wealthiest women, said to be worth over $500 million, and was one of only two women in the nation leading a Fortune 500 company. More important, she had transformed a newspaper that had once been called "a political hack paper" into one of the world's most respected sources of information, known for its carefully considered editorial opinion. But, Graham admitted at the end of her book, she was glad to have it all behind her. "It's dangerous when you are older to start living in the past," she wrote. "I intend to live in the present, looking forward to the future." Eugene Meyer had kept an eye on the future, too. "Watch my Kay," he had once told a friend. "She's the one."

SOURCES:

Felsenthal, Carol. *Power, Privilege and the* Post: *The Katharine Graham Story.* NY: Putnam, 1993.

Graham, Katharine. *Personal History.* NY: Alfred A. Knopf, 1997.

Norman Powers, writer-producer, Chelsea Lane Productions, New York

Graham, Margaret (d. 1380)

*Countess of Menteith. Name variations: Mary Graham; countess of Albany. Acceded as countess of Menteith on April 29, 1360. Born before 1334; died in 1380; interred at Inchmahome Priory, Perthshire; daughter of Sir John Graham of Abercorn and **Mary de Menteith** (d. 1346), countess of Menteith; married John Murray, lord of Bothwell, after 1348; married Thomas, earl of Mar, around 1354 (divorced 1359); married John Drummond of Concraig, around 1359; married Robert Stewart of Fife (c. 1339–1420), 1st duke of Albany (r. 1398–1420), prime minister to his brother Robert III, king of Scotland, and regent to James I, around September 9, 1361; children: (fourth marriage) Murdoch (b. around 1362), duke of Albany; *Isabel Stewart (fl. 1390–1410, who married Alexander Leslie and Walter of Dirleton); *Joan Stewart (who married Robert Stewart of Lorn, 1st Lord Lorn); *Beatrice Stewart (d. around 1424, who married James Douglas, 7th earl of Douglas); Mary Stewart (who married William Abernethy); Janet Stewart (betrothed as a child on July 20, 1371, to David, infant son of Sir Bartholomew de Loen and Lady Philippa Mowbray but marriage probably did not take place); *Margaret Stewart (who married John Swinton). Following Margaret Graham's death, Robert married *Muriel Keith and had five more children.*

Graham, Martha (1894–1991)

American founder and major leader of the modernist movement in American dance and one of the most famous dancers and choreographers of the 20th century. Born in Allegheny, Pennsylvania, on May 11, 1894; died on April 1, 1991, in New York City; daughter of Dr. George Graham (a physician) and Jane Beers Graham; graduated from Santa Barbara High School, 1913; attended Cumnock School of Expression, 1913–16; married Erick Hawkins, on September 20, 1948 (divorced 1952).

Enrolled in Ruth St. Denis School of Dancing and the Related Arts (the "Denishawn" school of dance, 1916); scored success in title role of Denishawn production of Xochitl (1920); performed in Greenwich Village Follies (1924–25); taught at Milton School of Dance (1925); began teaching at the Neighborhood Playhouse (1928); began teaching dancing at the Eastman School of Music (1925); performed first solo dance recital (1926); premiered Revolt (1927); premiered Lamentations (1930); appeared in performance of Rite of Spring with Leopold Stokowski and the Philadelphia Orchestra (1930); premiered Primitive Mysteries (1931); was first dancer to win a

Guggenheim fellowship (1932); performed at opening gala of Radio City Music Hall (1932); taught at Bennington College Summer Dance Festival (1934–38); began collaboration with designer Isamu Noguchi in Frontier (1935); performed at White House (1937); premiered American Document (1938); premiered Appalachian Spring at the Library of Congress (1944); premiered Judith (1951); opened the Martha Graham Dance Company and School of Contemporary Dance (1952); toured Europe (1954, 1963); toured Asia and Israel (1955); received Dance Magazine award (1957); premiered Episodes in joint dance program with George Balanchine (1959); retired from performing (1970).

Major dances: Revolt (1927); Primitive Mysteries (1931); Frontier (1935); American Document (1938); Appalachian Spring (1944); Judith (1951); Episodes (1950). Published The Notebooks of Martha Graham (NY: Harcourt, Brace, Jovanovich, 1973).

The actress *Katharine Cornell called her the greatest artist that the United States has produced. A critic labeled her work "wholly disarming in its simplicity but curiously profound in its complexity." Another critic insisted that she made special demands on her audiences—she required her audiences to think. The object of their comments was the dancer and choreographer Martha Graham, whose avant-garde work, starting in the 1920s, made her the leader of the modernist movement in dance in the 20th century. The best-known dancer in America, she also became one of the best-known and most-respected choreographers and dancers in the world.

Born in Pennsylvania coal country on May 11, 1894, Graham was descended, on her father's side, from ten generations of New England and New York Dutch; on her mother's side, she was a direct descendant of Miles Standish. The smallest and oldest of three daughters, Graham became aware that she was not the prettiest of the three, and she made no effort to appear so. Instead, she copied her grandmother's severe hair style by parting her hair down the middle and gathering it into a clump on the top of her head. Headstrong, with what one of her adult friends, fellow dancer-choreographer *Agnes de Mille, called a "wicked temper," Graham once recalled that when her mother **Jane Beers Graham** discovered her trying to jump rope while standing in the branch of an oak tree, she was no longer "allowed out for some time without supervision." "They wanted to me to be a good little Presbyterian," she later reminisced. "But good little Presbyterians bored me to death."

Graham was particularly close to her father George Graham, whom she remembered as a "handsome" man notably saddened by the death of an only son William at two years of age. A physician and an avid bettor, George took Martha with him to the track and let her bet on a horse race. She came to adore her father for teaching her many lessons about life. He was sometimes amused by her misbehavior, and he praised her assertiveness, telling her: "If you're going to create a scandal, Martha, be sure to create a good one." When a glass of seemingly "pure" water was revealed, under his microscope, to be full of "wiggles," he warned her: "Just remember this all of your life Martha. . . . You must look for the truth." When he detected her lying, he explained that her body positions gave her away and told her—in words she remembered—that "movement never lies."

George also tried to enlarge his children's imaginations. Martha remembered being taken, at age 6, to a Punch and Judy show: "There was another world. It was a frontier for me that I could enter completely." (*Frontier*, significantly, was the name of one of her later dances.) He also filled his children's minds with stories of Greek myths—stories, she said, "that existed only in history and remembrance." Some of these myths later become the basis of her dances.

Because her sister **Mary Graham** suffered from asthma, the family in 1908 visited the warmer climate of California. That same year, the Grahams moved from Pennsylvania to Santa Barbara. Thus, they left the closed society of eastern Pennsylvania for the more open lifestyles of California. Her father, who retained his physician's practice in Pennsylvania, made periodic trips back to California to be with his family.

For Martha, who was 14 years of age, Santa Barbara, with its mixture of Japanese, Chinese, and Spanish cultures, was an exotic realm totally unlike anything she had seen in Pennsylvania. "No child," she later declared, "can develop as a real Puritan in a semitropic climate." She gained an appreciation for Asian culture, not only because there were "Chinese things in our home" but because "we were surrounded by Chinese people." Taken by her mother to a Catholic mission, she was fascinated by the "Native Americans on horseback" that she saw outside the mission. Neighbors included the family of Alfred Dreyfus, the French army officer whose trial for treason in France had become an anti-Semitic *cause celebre;* she sometimes played with the Dreyfus children. During the visit to the mission, she noticed a poster of the popular "artistic" dancer, *Ruth St. Denis, who occasionally gave performances in nearby Los Angeles. When her father took her to see St. Denis in 1911, it was the first dance performance Martha had ever attended.

In high school at Santa Barbara, Graham was physically short—she eventually grew to 5'2"—and chose activities where determination counted more than beauty, becoming editor of the high-school magazine and captain of the girls' basketball team. When she graduated in 1913, her father wanted her to attend an Eastern school like Vassar. A compromise was struck, and she was sent to the Cumnock School in Los Angeles, which described itself as a school for "boys and girls of 10–20 years of age in their pursuit of learning and expression." Graham's father died from a heart condition during her first year at the school. Although his estate was less than the family anticipated, she chose to return to Cumnock for a second year, using her share of the inheritance.

> The artist is not ahead of his time, the artist is of his time. It is for the audience to catch up.
>
> —Martha Graham

In 1916, Graham enrolled in the dance school of Ruth St. Denis and Ted Shawn. The "Denishawn" dance technique combined stage dancing with ballet skills. Heavily steeped in the costumes and sets of Orientalism, the school promoted an "exoticism" which was part of the Art Nouveau period's revolt against the machine age. Many of the group's performances were in vaudeville theaters.

Graham was a puzzle to some of the school's teachers, who were not sure how to use her in performances. Though she danced with passion and energy—St. Denis wrote that she would move onto the stage "like a tornado"—Graham was convinced that St. Denis and Shawn considered her a "nincompoop." St. Denis, who favored another dancer, *Doris Humphrey, thought Graham too ugly to be cast as a girl; thus initially, Graham's breasts were taped flat, and she performed as a boy. She also did not have the "peachy skin" and blonde hair of many in the troupe. When the company went on tour, unlike many of the other women, she refused to peroxide her hair. Shawn, however, was convinced of her talent and decided that her dark hair and high cheekbones made her suitable for "exotic" roles. Cast as a Mayan-Aztec princess in *Xochitl,* she performed with the same abandon as before, frequently scratching Shawn with her fingernails during a rape scene of the dance. For this, she received favorable critical notices, many of which were more favorable than the ones accorded St. Denis. Graham, worried that she would be fired, began intercepting and destroying local newspapers before the troupe could read them.

In 1924, she began a two-year stint with John Murray Anderson's Greenwich Village Follies while teaching at the Denishawn school. Her dances were Moorish and Oriental in flavor, often in the Denishawn tradition of using veils. "To see that I remained a lady," wrote Graham, her mother temporarily moved to New York City, sleeping in her bedroom. In 1925, Martha began teaching at the Milton School of Dance in New York City. She also accepted a position as dance instructor in the Eastman School of Music in Rochester, New York.

At Rochester, Graham had own her own studio and "all the students I could wish," but she was restless. She was using dances derived from Denishawn techniques in the Rochester and Neighborhood Playhouse courses—because "that was all I knew"—but Shawn threatened to charge her $500 for their use. His demand, intended to convince her to return to Denishawn, had the opposite effect, convincing her to break free of their techniques and begin formulating her own movements.

Her first solo dance recital, in 1926 in New York City, was a financial success and was followed by two more in 1927–28. Reflecting her belief that dance is related to the community from which it comes, her style attempted to portray the vigor and technological orientation of American society. Gradually forsaking the "Oriental" styles of Denishawn, she began to move into percussive movements, using an all-female dance troupe that rejected the style of classical ballet.

Consciously avoiding the five basic positions of arms and feet which were central to ballet and rejecting ballet's leg extensions and leaps as foreign to the "way normal people moved," she sought as a model the "nervous, sharp, zigzag movements of life." Her dancers did not glide across the stage gracefully but appeared propelled across the stage by a series of jerks and spasms. The result has been called "angular, cold, and stylized." It was a mode particularly demanding on an audience, described by one critic as "asymmetrical counterpoint." Deliberately creating dances that were not pretty to look at, Graham was challenging audiences to

devote the kind of attention that they might give to a poem or a complex stage play.

Starting in 1928, Graham taught movement and dance at the Neighborhood Playhouse in New York City, where her students included Gregory Peck, Woody Allen, and **Joanne Woodward**. Woodward was convinced that Graham's breathing exercises helped her to play multiple personalities in her Oscar-winning performance in the film *The Three Faces of Eve.* *Bette Davis** said of Graham: "I worshipped her. She was all tension." With "a single thrust of her body," she could portray either anguish or joy.

Her early choreography and teaching, which emphasized mass group movements, attracted a coterie of devoted women who accepted long (sometimes all night long) rehearsals and little pay (except for the teaching jobs and private lessons she scrounged for them at the Neighborhood Playhouse). Since modern dance in the 1920s and 1930s was not considered socially acceptable, these were dancers whose work was rejected by many of their peers. Yet their devotion to Graham's work went beyond mere enthusiasm. For Graham, these were strong and powerful women to be proud of, who did not do theatrical "creations" but strode boldly across the stage, responding to the earth, pounding the earth instead of leaping. No one dieted; no one wore make up except for dark shadows under the eyes, intended to give every dancer's face a mask-like appearance. She insisted that her dancers not count the music but respond to their own breathing, moving according to a sense of "inner purpose."

From 1926 through 1930, Graham created 64 dances, as she developed the movements and style that would be central to her choreography. Well into the 1930s, she was the company's teacher, choreographer, set designer (generally a simple, dark backdrop), costume designer (she sometimes did the sewing), performance manager (she personally made arrangements for rehearsals and theaters), and business manager.

Her *Revolt* (1927) was an intense work in which she wore a simple, undecorated dress as her costume; whether it represented a personal revolt or a work of social commentary was not clear. In her *Lamentations* (1930), she remained seated for the entire dance, covering herself with a tube of fabric which she manipulated as she rocked and writhed. Her feet remained planted on the stage. Although the style of the dance suggested Greek and Hebraic influences, she intended the dance to be a depiction of what grief feels like. "It was a period that critics called my woolen dances of revolt," wrote Graham. Instead, she added, she was "really casting off Denishawn and its exoticism with a vengeance." In dances like these, she often used breath control to produce special effects, since she had discovered that varying the pace of breathing in and out produced physical changes in her body which were visible even in the rear of the theater.

After she observed Native American dances in Mexico, Graham began to place more emphasis on ritualism and mysticism in her dancing, as reflected in her *Primitive Mysteries* (1931). This dance, in which Graham played the *Mary the Virgin, culminated with the Resurrection of Christ as a symbol of the victory of spirit over death. Her *Primitive Mysteries* was given 23 cheering curtain calls by the opening night audience; 50 years later, some critics were still labeling it as a "masterpiece" and her "signature work." Other dances featured diverse themes, sometimes including social commentary. Her *Ceremonials* (1931–32) was focused on ancient Mayan and Aztec tribal dances. *Deep Song* (1937) highlighted the devastations of war.

With *Revolt*, she began a longterm collaboration with a number of American composers. *Revolt* featured music by Arthur Honegger; *Appalachian Spring* (1944), soon to become a classic, introduced music by Aaron Copland. When she choreographed *Dithyrambic* in 1931, she was the first to use Copland's music for dance. In time, she devised a particular method for working with composers. At the start of a collaboration, she would give the composer a detailed script, comprising notes from her readings and some quotations, plus ideas as to where particular dancers might perform a solo or duet. Only after she received a draft of music did she begin to choreograph, although it was not unusual for her to change her mind, at that point, on how she would adapt a movement to the music. While she insisted that she "never, ever cut a note of music," composer Gian-Carlo Menotti complained to Copland at one point that the dance she had designed bore no rela-

Martha Graham

tionship to what she had planned in her original notes. Copland reportedly responded, "Oh, Gian-Carlo, she does that all the time."

Beginning with *Frontier* (1935), Graham also experimented with set designs, moving away from the stark, black curtain that was typical for her early dances. Her *Panorama* (1935) and *Horizon* (1936) featured designs by Alexander Calder; in the latter dance, the performers moved Calder's mobiles around. After that, most of her scenery and props came from Isamu Noguchi, whose abstract designs frequently functioned as both props and sets. For *Frontier*, which was a dance about distances, Noguchi designed two wooden poles, which could be assumed to be either a barrier or the beginning of a new adventure. Years later, she realized how strongly "American" *Frontier* was, when a European admirer mentioned that many Europeans thought of a frontier as a barrier. To Graham, a frontier was a symbol of hope—"a frontier of exploration, of discovery, and not . . . a limitation."

It was an uphill struggle for acceptance. Ballet was regarded, by dance audiences and critics alike, as serious, elevated, and European. Graham defined her style as "relevant" and "American." Puzzled when an unidentified man told her at a party, "You don't know anything about body movements," she was not at all upset when someone informed her that the man was noted ballet choreographer Michel Fokine. She was not particularly bothered when another representative from the world of ballet, Fredrick Ashton, wrote a hostile article about her style and tersely commented, when asked for a capsule description, that "she is theatrical." Graham did not think of herself as a choreographer. When she received the first award honoring her for her choreography, she reported that it was a "great shock." And she objected to the term "modern dancing," arguing that "modern ages so quickly." She preferred the term "contemporary dance" because "it is of its time."

Graham's work began to garner recognition. In 1930, she was asked to dance in *Rite of Spring* in a performance with the conductor Leopold Stokowski and the Philadelphia Orchestra. In 1932, she was the first dancer to receive a Guggenheim fellowship, which she used to visit Mexico and the American Southwest, two areas where she frequently sought inspiration. In 1933, she was invited to participate in a new dance curriculum at Sarah Lawrence College. She was one of the first dance teachers at the Bennington Summer Dance Festival, in which she participated from 1934 to 1938.

She also began to gain public attention, becoming a celebrity beyond the world of dance. Graham and her troupe were among the performers at the opening-night gala for Radio City Music Hall in New York City in 1932. In fact, the appearance of her troupe backstage—determined-looking women all dressed in a single solid color—drew a great deal of puzzled and bemused attention. The magazine *Vanity Fair* featured Graham in a 1934 issue, along with the "exotic dancer" *Sally Rand. In 1937, Graham performed at the White House for the Roosevelts.

By 1940, she had gained enough prominence that she was asked to participate in the radio broadcasts for the March of Dimes, the national charity which raised funds to conquer polio. Under the name of "Miss Hush," Graham was the mystery voice that listeners could identify to win prizes. The comedian *Fanny Brice, in Broadway appearances, and actor-comedian Danny Kaye, in motion pictures, satirized her dance troupe as "Graham crackers." A football coach offered to pay her if she would share the "secret signals" she used to induce her students to follow her around the stage. Not all of the attention was wanted. Invited by the Nazi government of Germany to perform during the 1936 Olympics in Berlin, she replied that three-quarters of her dancers were Jewish and that she would not visit a country where their coreligionists were treated with such brutality and cruelty. After World War II, she would perform in Germany, but the dance would be *Judith* (1951), the story of a Jewish heroine.

Two men were formative in Graham's work to establish her own distinctive styles. The first was Louis Horst, ten years older than Graham. Horst had been piano accompanist for the Denishawn company when the two had met. Joining Graham when she left to form her own company, he provided the musical scores for many of her early dances and served as teacher and dance master in her troupe. She often relied on his judgment regarding changes that needed to be made in her dances before public performances. They became more than friends, and he encouraged her to read the philosophers Friedrich Nietzsche and Arthur Schopenhauer, whose sense of restlessness sometimes paralleled her moods. Later, in 1934, Horst founded the publication *Dance Observer,* which he used as a forum to promote and defend Graham's style of dance. When Horst died in 1964, Graham, as one of his executors, destroyed all personal correspondence between them.

Equally influential was Erick Hawkins, a Harvard-educated dancer, more than ten years her junior, whom she met at one of the Bennington Summer Dance Festivals. One result of her romance and collaboration with Hawkins was to include more ballet steps in the company's training. Hawkins' ballet background, plus his strong personality, sometimes met with a hostile reception from Graham's regular dancers, who were accustomed to regarding ballet as the enemy. Graham made Hawkins her personal dance consultant, appointing another member of the company as the group's director and teacher.

Hawkins' arrival marked a shift in the membership of the company, as Graham began accepting men into her troupe, though some, including Horst (with whom she maintained a continuing friendship), wanted the group to remain all female. In *American Document* (1938), Hawkins was the sole male dancer, although another male spoke as the interlocutor. During the 1950s, Hawkins would bring some male dancers into her group who later achieved considerable independent success, such as Merce Cunningham and Paul Taylor. The new male-female dichotomy would transform the nature of many of her dances, bringing sexual themes and psychodrama into her performances, as shown in her *Night Journey* (1947), the story of Oedipus and Jocasta, and *Phaedra* (1962), performed in such abbreviated costumes that two members of Congress complained that the State Department should not be sponsoring Graham's tours abroad.

Hawkins assumed the difficult job of fund raiser for the company, scoring some important successes. In 1944, he had convinced the Coolidge Foundation to fund two new dances by Graham, one of which was *Appalachian Spring*. That same year, he observed that among the students in her dance classes was a member of the Rothschild family, **Bethsabée de Rothschild**, who had recently fled from Nazi-occupied Europe. He convinced Rothschild to contribute $500 to Graham's company, the first of many financial contributions she would make over the years.

After Graham and Hawkins made the sudden decision to be married in 1948 in New Mexico, they grew increasingly apart. Some have speculated that, as much as she loved Hawkins, she could not share her company, her creation, with others. Her temper was legendary: she later wrote that she had forgotten slapping Noguchi during a dress rehearsal and hoped he had forgotten it as well. She was known for shouting at Horst during rehearsals, and she and Hawkins sometimes argued in front of the company. Hawkins and Gra-

ham would divorce in 1952, although Graham wrote in her memoirs that she had mentioned the word "divorce" partly to hurt him and wished she could have taken her taunt back.

When she reluctantly agreed to go on a European tour planned by Hawkins in 1950, disaster struck: during a performance in Paris before *Eleanor Roosevelt and other dignitaries, Graham reinjured a knee. By the end of the performance, it had swollen to the "size of a grapefruit," and the tour had to be canceled. Graham rejected the idea of an operation to mend her knee, embarking instead on a regimen of exercise with weights. In 1951, she launched her comeback as a dancer, appearing that year in the premiere of *Judith*. Although 56 years of age, she performed an unusually long 20-minute solo. In 1954, she returned to Europe for a highly successful tour; the following year, she and her troupe were sent by the State Department as dance ambassadors to Asia. In Rangoon, close to 5,000 came to see her.

When a representative of the world of ballet, George Balanchine, asked her to make a joint appearance in 1959, she used her half of the program to present a new dance, *Episodes*, which was based on the historical rivalry between Queen *Elizabeth I of England and *Mary, Queen of Scots. The dance ended with an innovative high-stakes tennis match. Graham appeared as Mary, dancing despite increasing pain from arthritis.

In between a tour of the Middle East and Europe in 1963 and frequent trips to Israel to help create the Batsheva Dance Company for Bethsabée de Rothschild, Graham continued to create new dances. One of the most successful was *Acrobats of God* (1960), which used intricate acrobatic movements to tell the story of a choreographer who hides when dancers turn to her for help. When the first-night audience responded with unexpected laughter, Graham deliberately added comic touches to the dance.

Most of the movements in Graham's classic dances were retained only in her mind, because she resisted the idea of documenting her major dances on film. In the decade of the 1970s, however, she did allow her notebooks to be published. When Connecticut College asked her to recreate *Primitive Mysteries* and *Frontiers* for a memorial concert for Horst, her assistants had to interview former dancers of her troupes to help bring these dances back to life. Now, leaving accurate accounts of her dances for posterity became a real concern to Graham.

The decade of the 1970s was difficult for her. In 1970, she was hospitalized for an intestinal illness. Then, before a planned appearance at the Brooklyn Academy of Music, her company, a nonprofit organization with an independent board, asked her not to dance with the troupe. She reported that she fell into bouts of increasing depression. Her famous feistiness remained: told by an interviewer that her respectability was her best fund-raising tool, she responded, "I wanted to spit. Respectable! Show me an artist who wants to be respectable."

By 1974, at age 80, she was back in control of her (now reorganized) dance company but confined her work to choreography and other company matters; her days as a dancer were over. When a special benefit was held to raise money for her company in 1975—with ticket prices as high as $10,000—the ballet dancer Rudolf Nureyev volunteered to perform. The division between ballet and "modern dance" was disappearing. Modern dance was exerting more influence on ballet than vice versa, and some of her movements were being co-opted by ballet practitioners.

Honors poured in. In 1976, President Gerald Ford awarded her the Presidential Medal of Freedom, the highest civilian honor given to American citizens. Graham was the first dancer and choreographer to be so honored. Among the imposing lists of awards that were given her were the New York Public Library Dance Collection Honors in 1974, the Kennedy Center Honors in 1984, the Knight of the French Legion of Honor in 1984, and the Order of the Precious Butterfly with Diamond from Japan in 1990.

Martha Graham battled health problems throughout the 1980s. Felled by a stroke at the start of the decade, she overheard a young doctor say her chances were not good. She vowed to recover. Graham not only improved but later that year choreographed *Night Chant*, based on Navajo rituals, and *Maple Leaf Rag*, with music by Scott Joplin. She even accompanied her troupe on a 55-day tour of the Far East in late 1990 and then stopped in Hawaii to recuperate. Graham became ill at Diamond Head, Hawaii, and was returned to New York City. She died at a hospital there on April 1, 1991.

In June of the same year, her company presented a memorial concert featuring many of her now-classic dances (out of more than 150 in her career) to a sold-out audience of 2,500. When the performance was over, the curtain was not lowered on the empty stage. It was a gesture to indicate that the spirit of Martha Graham—who had taught and influenced generations of modern dancers, ballet choreographers, and dance directors of musicals—was still present.

SOURCES:

De Mille, Agnes. *Martha: The Life and Work of Martha Graham*. NY: Random House, 1991.

Graham, Martha. *The Notebooks of Martha Graham*. NY: Harcourt, Brace, Jovanovich, 1973.

Horosko, Marian, comp. *Martha Graham: The Evolution of Her Dance Theory and Training, 1926–1991*. Pennington, NJ: A Capella Books, 1991.

Probosz, Kathilyn Solomon. *Martha Graham*. Parsippany, NJ: Dillon Press, 1995.

Stodelle, Ernestine. *Deep Song: The Dance Story of Martha Graham*. NY: Schirmer Books, 1984.

SUGGESTED READING:

McDonagh, Don. *Martha Graham: A Biography*. NY: Praeger, 1973.

Terry, Walter. *Frontiers of Dance: The Life of Martha Graham*. NY: Thomas W. Crowell, 1975.

COLLECTIONS:

Although Graham reportedly destroyed her correspondence with Horst and with her mother after their deaths, material relating to her career, including interviews with some of her associates, is housed in the Dance Collection of the New York Public Library.

Niles Holt,
Professor of History, Illinois State University, Normal, Illinois

Graham, Mrs. Phil (b. 1917).

See Graham, Katharine.

Grahame, Gloria (1924–1981)

American actress who won an Academy Award for her role in The Bad and the Beautiful. *Born Gloria Grahame Hallward on November 28, 1924, in Pasadena, California; died of cancer in New York, New York, on October 5, 1981; daughter of Michael (an industrial designer) and Jean (MacDougall) Hallward (an actress); attended Hollywood High School; married Stanley Clements (an actor), in 1945 (divorced 1948); married Nicholas Ray (a director), in 1948 (divorced 1952); married Cy Howard, in 1954 (divorced 1957); married Tony Ray; children: (second marriage) Tim Ray; (third marriage) Paulette Howard; (fourth marriage) two.*

Filmography: Blonde Fever *(1944);* Without Love *(1945);* It's a Wonderful Life *(1946);* It Happened in Brooklyn *(1947);* Crossfire *(1947);* Song of the Thin Man *(1947);* Merton of the Movies *(1947);* A Woman's Secret *(1949);* Roughshod *(1949);* In a Lonely Place *(1950);* The Greatest Show on Earth *(1952);* Macao *(1952);* Sudden Fear *(1952);* The Bad and the Beautiful *(1952);* The Glass Wall *(1953);* Man on a Tightrope *(1953);* The Big Heat *(1953);* Prisoners of the Casbah *(1953);* Human Desire *(1954);* Naked Alibi *(1954);* The Good Die Young *(1955);* Not as a

Stranger *(1955)*; The Cobweb *(1955)*; Oklahoma! *(1955)*; The Man Who Never Was *(UK, 1956)*; Ride Out for Revenge *(1957)*; Odds Against Tomorrow *(1959)*; Ride Beyond Vengeance *(1966)*; Blood and Lace *(1971)*; The Todd Killings *(1971)*; Chandler *(1971)*; The Loners *(1972)*; Tarot *(1973)*; Mama's Dirty Girls *(1974)*; Mansion of the Doomed *(1976)*; Chilly Scenes of Winter *(1979)*; A Nightingale Sang in Berkeley Square *(UK, 1979)*; Melvin and Howard *(1980)*; The Nesting *(1981)*.

The daughter of an aspiring actress, Gloria Grahame began performing with the Pasadena Community Playhouse at the age of nine. In 1943, after appearing in stage productions at Hollywood High School and in stock, she made her Broadway debut and was signed to an MGM contract within a year. Sensuous in appearance, with a seductive voice and pouty mouth, Grahame played wayward women with enormous success during the 1950s. Winning an Academy Award as Best Supporting Actress for her role in *The Bad and the Beautiful* (1952), Grahame was also memorable in *The Big Heat* (1953) and is often remembered as the "can't-say-no girl" in the musical *Oklahoma!* (1955). Toward the end of the decade, however, good roles diminished, and she retired from films. She later resurfaced, playing mostly in low-budget films of little consequence.

Grahame's personal life was complicated. She had four husbands, including actor Stanley Clements and film directors Nicholas Ray and Cy Howard, and four children. Her last marriage was to her former stepson Tony Ray, the son of her second husband, Nicholas Ray. In 1978, Grahame had a love affair with a young English actor named Peter Turner, which she ended abruptly in 1980. In 1981, when she was ill with cancer, she collapsed on stage while rehearsing a play in Lancaster, England. Alone and frightened, she reconnected with Turner and spent seven days with him and his family in Liverpool, returning to New York on the day of her death, October 5. Turner later wrote a book about this strange interlude called *Film Stars Don't Die in Liverpool.*

SOURCES:

Katz, Ephraim. *The Film Encyclopedia.* NY: HarperCollins, 1994.

Turner, Peter. *Film Stars Don't Die in Liverpool.* NY: Grove Press, 1986.

Barbara Morgan,
Melrose, Massachusetts

Grahn, Lucile (1819–1907)

Danish ballerina of the Romantic period. Born Lucina Alexia Grahn in Copenhagen, Denmark, in 1819; *died in Munich, Germany, in 1907; married Friederich Young (a tenor), in 1856 (died 1884); no children.*

The daughter of a Norwegian officer and his Jutland wife, Lucile Grahn was born in Copenhagen, Denmark, in 1819, and apparently mastered walking and dancing at about the same time. She received ballet instruction as part of her early schooling and, at age ten, became the protégée of dancer, choreographer, and teacher August Bournonville, head of the Royal Ballet School. Thus began a stormy relationship that would endure a decade, during which time Grahn made astonishing progress. At age 16, she danced the starring role in Bournonville's *Waldemar* and a year later appeared in his exquisite version of *La Sylphide*, a performance which so pleased King Frederick VI and ***Marie Sophie of Hesse-Cassel** that they summoned the young dancer to the palace for afternoon chocolate with the princesses, **Caroline** (1793–1881) and ***Wilhelmine**.

After becoming the toast of Copenhagen, Grahn set her sights on Paris, but Bournonville, now infatuated with the young dancer, vetoed her petition for a travel grant in order to keep her with him. Determined to have her way, Grahn bypassed Bournonville and enlisted the support of Princess Wilhelmine who gave her the approval she needed. In May 1837, Grahn set out for France, where she became the student of Jean-Baptiste Barrez, director of the Paris Opéra's ballet school. Unfortunately, her Paris debut was interrupted by instructions to return to Denmark to appear in *Le Postillon de Longjumeau*, which was to be staged for Queen Marie Sophie's 70th birthday. The return to Copenhagen infuriated Grahn, as did her status as solo dancer instead of première danseuse, the highest rank. Her quarrels with Bournonville began to take a violent turn, escalating to the point of involving ministers and even the king, who eventually granted permission for Grahn to leave Copenhagen to perform six guest appearances in Germany. Greeted with enthusiasm by the Germans, Grahn completed her performance schedule and then moved on independently to Paris, ignoring a number of summonses from Copenhagen. In June 1838, she was granted a permanent dismissal from the Danish Royal Ballet without pension, which left her free to pursue her career wherever she saw fit. Grahn never again returned to her homeland.

Back at the Paris Opéra with a three-year contract, Grahn continued to win acclaim from the critics, one of few exceptions being a sour

Lucile
Grahn

critique from Théophile Gautier, in which he nitpicked about the dancer's persistent smile. "[A] smile should hover about a dancer's lips in the way that a bird flutters about a rose," he instructed, "but it does not need to be fixed on those lips under pain of misshaping them."

(Gautier was particularly unkind to dancers, once calling **Louise Fitzjames** as thin as a lizard, and suggesting that *Marie Taglioni, at age 34, had lost much of her lightness and elevation.) Grahn went on to thrill Paris audiences with her performance in *La Sylphide*, a role that came her way at the last minute when *Fanny Elssler was unable to dance because of illness. Unfortunately, Grahn's career at the Opéra ended prematurely in 1840, with a knee injury that sidelined her until 1843, when she turned up in Russia. Now 24, she made her debut in St Petersburg in *Giselle,* then went on to Milan, Italy, where she made some 40 appearances in *Elda assia Il Patto degli Spiriti* by Bernardo Vestris, during the 1844 season.

It was during a five-year period in England, however, that Grahn's career reached its zenith, beginning with her modest debut in *Lady Henrietta,* in 1844. That same year, after a triumph in *Eoline,* she appeared as one of the lovely protagonists in Jules Perrot's famous *Le Pas de Quatre,* considered one of the first "abstract" ballets. As the youngest of the quartet of dancers, which included *Carlotta Grisi, Marie Taglioni, and *Fanny Cerrito, Grahn delighted audiences with her freshness and point work, as well as her considerable acting ability.

Now a star of substantial magnitude, Grahn shunned Paris and returned instead to Germany, which she found so congenial that she purchased a house in Munich, where she also fell in love and married in 1856. Up until then, Grahn had avoided marriage, although she had been engaged years earlier to a Danish count, and her name had later been linked with Benjamin Lumley, director of Her Majesty's Theater. The groom was the English-born tenor Friederich Young who was enjoying a successful career in Germany. The marriage not only signaled the end of Grahn's dancing career but had a tragic outcome. In 1863, Young fell from a stage platform, injuring his spine so severely that he was confined to a wheelchair for the rest of his life. While he took up residence in a nursing home, Grahn rallied courageously to support him and herself. She taught privately for a time and then took a position at the Munich Hoftheatre, where she also choreographed a number of ballets, including the *divertissements* for Richard Wagner operas. After her husband's death in 1884, she remained in Munich, where she became a revered figure. She died in 1907, leaving her sizable estate to her adopted city to be used to help talented young artists. The citizens, in appreciation, named a street Lucile Grahn Strasse in her honor.

SOURCES:
Kirstein, Lincoln. *Four Centuries of Ballet: Fifty Masterworks.* NY: Dover, 1984.

Migel, Parmenia. *The Ballerinas.* NY: Macmillan, 1972.

Barbara Morgan,
Melrose, Massachusetts

Grainé.
Variant of Grace.

Grajales, Mariana (1808–1893)

Afro-Cuban revolutionary who championed rights of both slaves and free blacks during her nation's struggle against Spanish rule and is universally regarded by Cubans as "Madre de la Patria" (Mother of the Nation). Name variations: Mariana Grajales de Maceo; Mariana Grajales y Cuello. Born in Santiago de Cuba, on June 26, 1808; died in exile in Kingston, Jamaica, on November 28, 1893; daughter of José Grajales and Teresa Grajales; married Fructuoso Regüeyferos y Hecheverria; married Marcos Maceo; children: (first marriage) four; (second marriage) nine, including General Antonio Maceo Grajales (1845–1896), the Cuban revolution's "Titan of Bronze."

Throughout the 19th century, sugar dominated the economic life of the Spanish colony of Cuba and its entire social and moral climate as well. As Spain's most prosperous possession in the New World, after the loss of its vast colonial empire in the early 1820s, Cuba experienced an economic boom based on sugar production. To meet the expanding world demand for the commodity, between 1800 and 1865 the Spanish permitted the transport of at least a half-million African slaves to the island. By 1817, the combined black population of Cuba, consisting of slaves and free blacks, was tallied at 54% of the total island population of 630,980. The numerical preponderance of blacks struck fear into the island's rulers as well as their royal lords and masters in faraway Madrid.

White dread of black slave revolts had been a fact of life in the Caribbean since the early 1790s, when Haiti rose up in a bloody insurrection that ended French rule in that part of the island of Santo Domingo. On Cuba, these fears were certainly not without justification, for in 1812 a revolt led by a free black, José Antonio Aponte, "the Cuban Spartacus," was bloodily suppressed. Spanish rule was likely strengthened because of white anxiety, and in 1823 the Spanish Minister Calatrava could boast that the "fear that Cubans have of their blacks is Spain's greatest security in guaranteeing her domination of the island."

It was into this troubled racial situation that Mariana Grajales was born in the eastern Cuban port city of Santiago on June 26, 1808. Her parents, free blacks José and **Teresa Grajales,** had been among the flood of immigrants who had entered Cuba from strife-torn Santo Domingo during the years 1790 through 1804. Like many mulattoes in Santiago, the Grajales quickly took advantage of the relatively benign racial environment in the city to establish themselves economically.

By example, Mariana's parents taught her the virtues of honesty, thrift, and hard work. But daily life in a bustling port city also revealed the world's injustices. Day after day, Mariana saw human suffering that was inherent in a social order based on slavery. Slave ships in the harbor meant that gangs of *bozales,* newly arrived African men, women and children, would customarily be marched naked through the streets of Santiago. Many of the *bozales* died, and when their bodies were hastily and inadequately buried, Mariana and other citizens of Santiago had little choice but to endure the "insupportable stench" caused by their rotting corpses. On other occasions, Mariana watched the wretched *cimarrones,* runaway slaves who had been recaptured, as they gathered around the tiny windows of their prison cells to try to gulp fresh air.

Mariana Grajales' parents could not afford tuition for her to attend school (free blacks were restricted to a primary education, but only if they could afford it), and it is not known if she ever learned to read and write. The events of her later life, however, make it clear that this young girl was an astute observer of human nature from her earliest years, distinguishing between good and evil, right and wrong. As a member of a racial group that was uneasily suspended between the privileged white elite and an increasingly oppressed caste of slaves, Mariana became sensitized to the inhumanities of not only enslavement, but also to the more subtle but nevertheless all-pervasive attitudes of racism on virtually a daily basis.

In 1831, when she was 23, Mariana married Fructuoso Regüeyferos, a man from a similar background. Nine years later, her husband died, and she was forced to move back to her parents' home with her four young boys. Soon, however, she met and became the common-law wife of Marcos Maceo, a Venezuelan immigrant and widower with six children (the couple would legally marry in July 1851). The new and expanded family moved to "La Esperanza" ("Hope"), Maceo's farm in the Majaguabo district of San Luis municipio, north of Santiago. Maceo owned another nearby farm, Las Delicias, and clearly intended to make both properties flourish.

By the time of her second marriage, Mariana Grajales had become an outspoken opponent of slavery, espousing abolitionist sentiments that were common among free blacks and mulattoes. At first, Marcos showed little interest in supporting her beliefs. Indeed, in Venezuela he had been a loyal member of the Royal forces that had fought a losing battle against Simon Bolivar and the armies of independence. After he arrived in Cuba in the 1820s, Marcos swore off war and politics to devote his considerable energies to agricultural and commercial pursuits.

A series of dramatic events in 1843, however, helped to bring Marcos Maceo's beliefs more in line with those of his wife. A major slave revolt in Matanzas province brought savage reprisals from the authorities. Responding to slaveholder panic, Captain-General Leopoldo O'Donnell took measures to crush the spirit of black rebellion once and for all. Convinced he was surrounded by abolitionist conspiracies, he set up a military commission to restore order among the nonwhite Cuban population. Seventy-eight "plotters" were discovered, justifying the unleashing of a reign of terror. The "Conspiracy of the Staircase," named for the scaffold resembling a stairway on which the alleged rebels were flogged to death, was only the most horrific aspect of repressive measures that now convulsed Cuba. On the flimsiest of evidence, more than 1,000 free blacks were thrown into prison, where many hundreds died of disease, torture, and neglect.

Though the terrors did not directly affect the Maceo family, it convinced both Mariana and Marcos that free blacks would never enjoy a guarantee of human rights as long as Cuba was under Spanish rule. Ever fearful of uprisings, the authorities increased their repressions. By the mid-1840s, a series of draconian laws gave slaveowners broad powers to prevent contacts between free blacks, virtually all of whom were now assumed to harbor dangerous abolitionist views. Local authorities were required to deport those free blacks who had moved to Cuba from other countries. This measure presented an immediate threat to Venezuela-born Marcos Maceo, who only avoided deportation by persuading a sympathetic local notary to prepare an affidavit declaring him a native of Santiago de Cuba.

Although the Maceo family remained untouched by the persecutions of the 1840s, they knew only too well that whatever liberties they enjoyed could be arbitrarily taken from them at any time. As free blacks, they were members of a stigmatized group that was under constant surveillance by police and informers. Free blacks who in the opinion of the authorities behaved in what was deemed to be an offensive manner, or displayed "lack of respect," could be fined or punished in other, more drastic ways. Although repressive measures grew dramatically worse in the 1840s, the harsh regime in Cuba in fact dated from a Royal Order of May 29, 1825, a document that would serve as the island colony's de facto constitution until the end of the Spanish regime in 1898. In the 1840s, Cuba was declared to be "a besieged fortress," thus allowing the chief governing official, the captain-general, to govern arbitrarily as if a state of war were the norm. All aspects of public and private life were placed under the scrutiny of military authorities. A harsh system of censorship served to muzzle the press, ban public meetings, and outlaw usage of the "inciting words": *slavery* and *independence*. Public mention of any type of political reform measure was illegal and severely punishable.

In June 1845, Mariana gave birth to a son, Antonio de la Caridad Maceo. Along with four sons she brought into her second marriage, she would give birth to eight additional children, bringing the total to thirteen; the last, Marcos, arrived in 1860, when she was 52. As a result of the hard work of both Mariana and Marcos, they and their large family prospered from the produce of their farms at Las Delicias and La Esperanza. Mariana and her children could be found at either farm, enjoying the bounty which included not only bananas and plantains, but fruit orchards and an herb garden that provided items useful for both food and medicinal purposes. Mariana was affectionate and fair with her family, imposing on them a few basic rules which included showing respect to one's parents, adhering to a reasonable curfew, and, above all, paying strict attention to duty.

This near-idyllic phase of the Maceos' life would be shattered as a result of dramatic changes that began in the 1850s. In 1852–1853, a great epidemic decimated one tenth of Cuba's population, killing at least 70,000 slaves. Then, hopes for political and social reform waxed and waned. Expectations were raised by the appearance on the island of Captain-General Juan de la Pezuela, whose abolitionist sympathies made him take serious steps to halt the importation of slaves into Cuba (treaties signed by Spain and Great Britain in 1817 and 1835 banning the slave trade were never effectively enforced). But the hopes of Cuba's black population and their white liberal supporters were dashed when strong pressure from the slave-owning elite ended this experiment. A world economic depression that began in 1857 diminished the de-

Cuban postage stamp issued on March 8, 1969, in honor of Mariana Grajales.

mand for Cuban exports, bringing about much suffering and triggering serious social unrest. Now, the only path to significant change appeared to be revolution.

In the 1860s many of the white Creole elite in eastern Cuba began to seriously organize revolutionary groups that stood a chance of bringing about a break with Spain. Masonic lodges were formed in the major towns and cities of that part of the island, including Santiago. One of the key leaders in Santiago was a close friend of the Maceo family, the prosperous lawyer Don Ascencio. One day in September 1868, with some hesitation, Marcos Maceo told Mariana that he had been asked to lead the revolutionary forces in the Majaguabo district. Ascencio had made the request, and he had accepted. With the long-desired uprising against the hated Spanish regime about to break out, Marcos feared that his wife might disapprove. After all, neither of them were young, both were in their 60s. To his immense relief, Mariana had no reservations about risking their lives or possessions in order to rid Cuba of the corrupt, ruthless Spanish rulers. Later that same day, when most of her large family had gathered together at the farm, Mariana commanded all of them to solemnly swear "by the blood of the crucified Christ, that you will fight to liberate your country, fight tirelessly, until you see her independent, or until you die achieving it!"

While Marcos and his sons enlisted friends and neighbors for the revolutionary forces, Mariana and several of her daughters-in-law remained behind at Las Delicias, helping to turn that isolated farm into a formidable military encampment and depot. One evening soon after the revolt began, Mariana and the other women were startled by a loud voice calling on them to open the door. Spanish authorities had warned villagers about "bandits" on the loose, so the women were relieved to see Marcos. Behind him was a contingent of about 400 guerrilla fighters now loyal to Marcos and sons Antonio and Miguel. Overwhelmed, Mariana went into the house and returned with her crucifix. The men kneeled while she made them swear "before Christ, who was the first liberal man to appear on earth," that they would all fight to free the nation or give their lives for it. As the men departed, seven of the Maceo boys left with them.

Within months, Mariana Grajales received word that Justo, one of her eldest sons, had been ambushed and shot. Soon after, she learned that her husband Marcos was fatally wounded while fighting under his son Antonio's command. According to Antonio, who cradled his dying father in his arms, Marcos Maceo's last words were: "I've done what Mariana wanted." As the war dragged on, the revolutionary forces eluded capture by living in the jungle. Despite her age, Mariana joined the rebels under Antonio's command, sharing with them their hardships. Whether addressing one of her own sons or another injured soldier, Mariana urged them: "Get well so you can go out and get another!"

Determined to crush the Cuban *mambis* (insurgents), the Spanish troops pursued the rebels into the jungle. Mariana and many women *soldaderas* refused to abandon their men, accompanying them ever deeper into the bush. In September 1871, during one of the bitter battles, Antonio Maceo's unit was surprised by Spanish forces. While engaging in hand-to-hand combat, Antonio was seriously wounded, but he and his fellow rebels were able to halt the enemy assault. While the battle raged around her, 63-year-old Grajales lay quietly crouched in a shallow foxhole. As stories of the courage of Mariana's remarkable family spread throughout Cuba, the Spaniards simply spoke of them as "the terrible Maceos."

Antonio Maceo was quickly promoted to the rank of brigadier general and became a living legend to all Cuban revolutionaries (after his death in battle in 1896, he would be known as the revolution's "Titan of Bronze"), but he was particularly revered by the black and mulatto soldiers. His fame was shared with a mother who was regarded as being equally fearless. To Cuba's rebels, Mariana Grajales became known simply as "the woman who doesn't cry."

Watching young men die in agony after a battle affected Mariana deeply, but she refused to succumb to despair lest it weaken revolutionary morale. In April 1874, after the bloody battle of Cascorro, the usual trickle of wounded and dying men made their way to the nearby rebel encampment. Among the severely wounded, Mariana quickly recognized her son Miguel, whose head wound was obviously mortal. She glanced at her nearby youngest son, 14-year-old Marcos, telling him in a clear voice audible to all in the camp: "And you, stand up straight; now it's time for you to go on campaign." For the cause to succeed, she said, "one son must replace another."

Mariana Grajales and her family fought for not only a Cuba free of Spanish rule but one in which slavery and racism were things of the past. Even among the rebels, racism was by no means extinct. When it was assumed that the post of commander of Oriente province would go to the universally admired Antonio, a Creole was chosen to fill the slot. Maceo had been unfairly accused of desiring the creation of a Black Republic after the end of Spanish rule. Although deeply offended by the racist snub, in his letter of protest Maceo noted that he would continue to fight to bring about a free Cuba. A year later, in August 1877, Maceo was severely wounded by a Spanish attack that left him with eight bullet wounds, five of them in his chest. But Maceo and a dozen or so guerrillas, including his mother, eluded the enemy in the bush, and he was able to make a complete recovery.

Led by an Antonio Maceo whose forces still included his surviving brothers and his mother, the rebels won a dramatic victory in February 1878 over the Spanish at San Quintin, annihilating the enemy and seizing large amounts of much-needed supplies. But this victory proved to be illusory. Ten years of warfare had exhausted both sides, and the rebel leadership decided to make peace. The Spanish regime adopted conciliatory tactics that proved to be highly attractive to war-weary Cubans. Only Antonio and his followers—a minority within revolutionary ranks—wanted to continue the struggle. The stubborn Maceo was finally persuaded to leave Cuba, and after first sending his mother and other family members into exile in Kingston, Jamaica, he joined them there in May 1878. Soon, however, he was off again to start organizing a new rebellion against the Spanish.

Although the Maceos had alienated many members of the Cuban exile community, they soon settled into a new life in Kingston. But by 1880, two of Mariana's sons, José and Rafael, were again in Spanish prisons after having been involved in another unsuccessful Cuban uprising. Rafael died in prison, and, when it became clear from a letter from José that he too would likely not survive his incarceration, Mariana took a remarkable step. In September 1884, she visited the Spanish consul in Kingston to beg for her son's freedom, assuring him that her sons now desired to live in peace with Spain.

Mariana Grajales' swallowed pride was soon redeemed when she received word that José had been able to escape from prison. After following a circuitous route, he was reunited with his mother in January 1885. A year later, Antonio returned to Kingston to visit a now increasingly frail Mariana. Her revolutionary spirit, however, remained as unquenchable as ever. In her final years, Grajales retained the belief that Cuba would one day be free. Although the Spanish had abolished slavery in stages between 1880 and 1886, they would not grant full legal equality to black Cubans until 1893, the year of her death.

In the last phase of Mariana Grajales' life, she became a living legend to all who were willing to offer their lives for Cuba's freedom. José Marti, who visited her in Kingston in 1891 and again shortly before her death, wrote that when he talked of Cuban freedom her tired eyes began to sparkle once more: "She caressed my face and looked on me like a son." The revered woman with the wrinkled face reminisced about the years in which her family had sacrificed so much while fighting for their nation's independence. With pride, she told Marti of one of her sons, who, "although bleeding from every part of his body," had nevertheless been able to lift himself up and, with only ten others, was able to find the strength to fend off 200 of the enemy. Sensing the almost mystical power this frail old woman was still able to exert over a people yearning for freedom, José Marti penned an epitaph that caught the essence of the Mother of the Cuban Nation: "And if one trembled when he came face to face with the enemy of his country, he saw the mother of Maceo, white kerchief on her head, and he ceased trembling!" Mariana Grajales has been honored by Cuba in many ways, including two postage stamps issued on March 8, 1969, and on November 27, 1993.

SOURCES:

Aimes, Hubert H.S. *A History of Slavery in Cuba, 1511 to 1868.* Reprint ed. NY: Octagon Books, 1967.

Corwin, Arthur F. *Spain and the Abolition of Slavery in Cuba, 1817–1886.* Austin: Institute of Latin American Studies/ University of Texas Press, 1967.

Danger, Matilde, and Delfina Rodriguez. *Mariana Grajales.* Santiago de Cuba: Editorial Oriente, 1977.

Garcia Galan, Gabriel. "Mariana Grajales," Marti, Vol. 2, no. 54. December 12, 1931, pp. 6–8.

Henderson, James D. "Mariana Grajales: Black Progenitress of Cuban Independence," in *Journal of Negro History.* Vol. 63, no. 2. April 1978, pp. 135–148.

———, and Linda Roddy Henderson. *Ten Notable Women of Latin America.* Chicago, IL: Nelson-Hall, 1978.

O'Kelly, James J. *The Mambi-Land, or, Adventures of a Herald Correspondent in Cuba.* Philadelphia, PA: J.B. Lippincott, 1874.

Portuondo, José Antonio, ed. *El pensamiento vivo de Maceo.* 3rd ed. Havana: Editorial de Ciencias Sociales, Instituto Cubano del Libro, 1971.

Rodriguez Sarabia, Aida. *Mariana Grajales: Madre de la Patria.* Havana: n. p., 1957.

Sarabia, Nydia. *Historia di una Familia Mambisa: Mariana Grajales.* Havana: Instituto Cubano del Libro/Editorial Orbe, 1975.

Scott, Rebecca J. *Slave Emancipation in Cuba: The Transition to Free Labor, 1860–1899.* Princeton, NJ: Princeton University Press, 1985.

Suchlicki, Jaime. *Cuba: From Columbus to Castro and Beyond.* 4th rev. ed. Washington: Brassey's, 1997.

———. *Historical Dictionary of Cuba.* Metuchen, NJ: Scarecrow Press, 1988.

John Haag,
Associate Professor of History,
University of Georgia, Athens, Georgia

Gramatté, S.C. Eckhardt (1899–1974).

See Eckhardt-Gramatté, S.C.

Gramont, Elizabeth de Clermont-Tonnerre, Duchesse de (fl. 1875–1935).

See Barney, Natalie Clifford for sidebar.

Grammont, countess of.

See Hamilton, Elizabeth (1641–1708).

Grana.

Variant of Grace.

Granahan, Kathryn E. (1894–1979)

U.S. Democratic Congresswoman from Pennsylvania (November 6, 1956–January 3, 1963) who was also U.S. treasurer (1963–66). Born Kathryn Elizabeth O'Hay on December 7, 1894, in Easton, Pennsylvania; died on July 10, 1979, in Norristown, Pennsylvania; interred in Gethsemane Cemetery, Easton, Pennsylvania; daughter of James B. O'Hay and Julia (Reilly) O'Hay; attended public school in Easton, Pennsylvania, and Mount St. Joseph Collegiate Institute in

Chestnut Hill, Philadelphia, Pennsylvania; married William T. Granahan (a politician), on November 20, 1943 (died May 25, 1956).

Kathryn Elizabeth Granahan spent much of her congressional career fighting for tougher pornography laws, but more Americans came to know her as treasurer of the United States, at which time her signature appeared on the country's currency.

Granahan was born in 1894 in Easton, Pennsylvania, and educated in public schools and at Mount St. Joseph Collegiate Institute in Philadelphia. From 1940 to 1943, she worked for the state auditor general, serving as a liaison officer between the auditor's office and the Pennsylvania Department of Public Assistance. In 1943, she married the Democratic leader of Philadelphia's 52nd Ward, William Granahan, who was also the chief disbursing officer for the state treasury. William was elected to Congress in 1944 and served one term before his defeat in

the national Republican sweep of 1946. He was returned to office in 1948 and served four more terms before his death in 1956, shortly after his renomination for a fifth term. Kathryn Granahan succeeded her husband as leader of the 52nd Ward and replaced him as the Democratic candidate for the 84th Congress. In the November 1956 election, she was elected to fill out her husband's term and defeated Robert F. Frankenfield for a full term in the 85th Congress, the first woman to represent a Philadelphia district.

Early in her tenure, Granahan served on the Committee on the District of Columbia, the Committee on Government Operation, and the Committee on Post Office and Civil Service. In 1959, as chair of a subcommittee on postal operations, she called for a crack-down on the pornography trade, introducing legislation requiring mandatory jail sentences for anyone found guilty of using the U.S. mail to distribute pornography. She also sponsored a successful bill which allowed the Post Office to impound the mail of anyone dealing in pornography. In 1961, she consulted the Supreme Court in drafting guidelines to determine obscenity in publications.

Granahan served in the 84th–87th Congresses, but her congressional seat was eliminated in 1963, following the census of 1960, and she was appointed treasurer of the United States as recompense. As treasurer, she served under President John F. Kennedy from 1963 until 1965, when she underwent brain surgery following a fall. Kathryn Granahan formally resigned from office in October 1966. She died on July 10, 1979, in Norristown, Pennsylvania.

SOURCES:

Office of the Historian. *Women in Congress 1917–1990.* Commission on the Bicentenary of the U.S. House of Representatives, 1991.

Kathryn E. Granahan

Granato, Cammi (1971—).

See Team USA: Women's Ice Hockey at Nagano.

Grand, Sarah (1854–1943).

See MacFall, Frances E.

Grand Mademoiselle, The.

See Montpensier, Anne Marie Louise d'Orléans, Duchesse de (1627–1693).

Grande Mademoiselle, La.

See Montpensier, Anne Marie Louise d'Orléans, Duchesse de (1627–1693).

See Dolgorukaia, Alexandra (1836–c. 1914).

Grandison, Katharine.

See Siege Warfare and Women.

Grandma Moses (1860–1961).

See Moses, Anna "Grandma."

Grandval, Marie Felicia

(1830–1907)

French composer. Name variations: Clemence de Reiset; Vicomtesse de Caroline Blangy; Clemence Vaigrand; Maria Felicita de Reiset; Maria Reiset de Tesier. Born at Chateau de la Cour-de-Bois, Saint-Remy des Monts, Sarthe, on January 20, 1830; died in Paris on January 15, 1907; studied under Saint-Saëns and received instruction from Chopin.

One of the foremost woman composers of her era, Marie Felicia Grandval was doomed to amateur status, despite the fact that she was prolific, possessed professional skills and accomplishments, and was well known. Hers was a wealthy aristocratic family, and her composing was not taken as seriously in the musical world as it might have been had she been forced to earn a living in this field. She began studying music at age six and studied composition under Friedrich von Flotow. Later, she received instruction from Chopin and studied two years with Camille Saint-Saëns. As a composer, she used many names, both male and female. A number of her operas were produced in Paris, and by 1869 Grandval began to use her own name. She wrote oratorios, large choral pieces, chamber music, and symphonies. Marie Felicia Grandval's music has been characterized as "essentially French, energetic, vibrant, and melodic."

John Haag,
Athens, Georgia

Grania.

Variant of Grace.

Grant, Anne (1755–1838)

Scottish poet, essayist, and writer. Name variations: Mrs. Grant of Laggan; Anne MacVicar. Born Anne MacVicar in Glasgow, Scotland, on February 21, 1755; died in Edinburgh on November 8, 1838; daughter of Duncan MacVicar (an army officer); married James Grant (an army chaplain), in 1779 (died 1801); children: twelve, eight reached adulthood but only one survived her.

Selected writings: Poems (1802); Letters from the Mountain (1807); Memoirs of an American Lady: Sketches of Manners and Scenery in America as They Existed Previous to the Revolution (1808); Essays on the Superstitions of the Highlanders of Scotland (1811).

Anne Grant was born Anne MacVicar in Scotland in 1755. Two years later in 1757, when her father Duncan MacVicar obtained a commission in a British regiment stationed in America, she found herself uprooted to a foreign country. Settling in Albany, Anne Grant lived among Dutch and British colonists and spent a good deal of time with *Catherine Van Rensselaer Schuyler, the wife of General Philip Schuyler.

On their return to Scotland in 1768, the MacVicars lived at Fort Augustus where Duncan was barrack master. In 1779, Anne married the chaplain of Fort Augustus, Reverend James Grant, and they immediately moved to the nearby town of Laggan, where he was assigned a church. In addition to singlehandedly running the family farm, Anne learned Gaelic and became an expert in Scottish folklore.

The sudden death of her husband in 1801 left Grant without residence or income since the ownership of the farm was connected to her husband's position. To raise money for her eight children, she followed the advice of friends and published a book by subscription. Her earnings from *Poems* allowed her to move to Stirling in 1803. Encouraged by this success, she continued to write and, in 1807, published *Letters from the Mountain.* Its rich descriptions of rural Scottish life brought her acclaim, although the book was less financially successful than her poems. In 1808, Grant published *Memoirs of an American Lady: Sketches of Manners and Scenery in America as They Existed Previous to the Revolution.* This book, which reminisced about her childhood in America, was also a tribute to Catherine Schuyler, her Albany companion.

By 1810, Grant had moved to Edinburgh. While the success of her book placed her well within Scottish literary circles where she cultivated friendships with Sir Walter Scott and Francis Jeffrey, her writing was not sufficiently successful to support her, and she took in boarders to supplement her income. Undaunted by her financial difficulties, Grant continued to write and published *Essays on the Superstitions of the Highlanders of Scotland* in 1811 and "Eighteen Hundred and Thirteen, a Poem" in 1814.

In 1820, a fall crippled Grant for the remainder of her days, and in 1826, with the help of Scott and several other friends, she secured a pension of £100 from the government, easing her life considerably. After her death of the flu in 1838, her son J.P. Grant edited and published *Memoirs and Letters* (1844) which provides additional autobiographical information to her previous works.

Judith C. Reveal,
freelance writer, Greensboro, Maryland

Grant, Julia (1826–1902)

First lady of the United States from 1869 to 1877. Born Julia Boggs Dent on January 26, 1826, in St. Louis, Missouri; died on December 14, 1902, in Washington, D.C.; fifth of eight children of Colonel Frederick Dent (a planter) and Ellen (Wrenshall) Dent; married Ulysses Simpson Grant (1822–1885, president of the United States, 1869–1877), on August 22, 1848, in St. Louis, Missouri; children: Frederick Dent Grant (1850–1912, served as police commissioner of New York City and ambassador to Austria-Hungary); Ulysses Grant, Jr. (1852–1929, became a prominent lawyer in Republican affairs); Jesse Root Grant (1858–1934, became a lawyer and wrote a book about his father); **Ellen Grant**, *known as Nellie (1855–1922, who married Englishman Algernon Charles Frederick Sartoris, son of* ***Adelaide Kemble***, *at the White House in 1874).*

*Julia
Grant*

One of eight children of a wealthy Missouri planter and slaveholder, Julia Dent was born in

St. Louis, Missouri, in 1826. She was raised on a 1,000-acre estate and educated in the classics at a private school. When her brother's West Point roommate, Ulysses S. Grant, visited the Dent estate, Julia captured his heart almost immediately. Three months later, they were engaged, much to the dismay of Julia's father, who saw little promise in Ulysses and could not imagine his favorite daughter living on some barren army outpost. The wedding was postponed for four years while Grant fought in the Mexican War and Julia battled at home to win her father's approval. Vows were finally exchanged in August 1848. A four-month honeymoon included a trip to see Grant's parents in Ohio, who had not attended the wedding ceremony because they disapproved of the Dents for being slaveholders.

Julia followed Ulysses to forlorn army posts in St. Louis, Detroit, and New York, managing her husband's meager wages and attempting to ward off his growing drinking problem. When he left for Pacific Coast duty, she returned to White Haven, Missouri, to care for their young family. Without her influence, Ulysses often slipped off the wagon. After one of his frequent binges, when he was reprimanded by his commanding officer, he abruptly resigned his commission. Returning home, he found it impossible to eke out an adequate living, either from farming or in a job with his father's tanning business. The family was often in despair. At one point, Ulysses was cutting and selling firewood to keep food on the table.

The start of the Civil War probably saved the family from financial disaster and Grant from obscurity. He joined the Union army, and Julia moved the family to City Point to be near his headquarters and to provide Ulysses with the moral support he had come to depend upon. She contributed to the war effort by tending to the wounded and sewing uniforms. There are stories told of her dislike of **Mary Lincoln**, who often accompanied President Abraham Lincoln when he visited the troops. (It may have been Julia who refused Lincoln's invitation to the Grants to attend Ford's Theater on the fateful evening of April 14, 1865, the night Lincoln was shot.) By the end of the war, Ulysses was a general and a national hero, which largely assured him a bid for the presidency. He won the election of 1868.

Julia referred to her eight years in the White House as "a feast of cleverness and wit," but it was a difficult time for her husband. Politically naive, Grant surrounded himself with corrupt appointees. During the first administration, his own brother-in-law was exposed as a participant in Black Friday, when speculators sought to corner the nation's gold market. Later, Grant's private secretary was charged with participation in the Whiskey Ring, and the secretary of war resigned when it was revealed that he had taken kickbacks. Stock-exchange failures and the Custer massacre added further woes. Despite it all, the Grants were popular, and there seemed to be little resentment over the lavish way they spent money.

The Grants undertook the complete remodeling of the White House. In 1873, Grecian columns were added to the facade with an assist by the Army Corps of Engineers. Inside, Julia chose the plush furnishings, gilt wallpapers, and immense chandeliers of the Victorian era. If the setting was formal, Julia's day receptions were known for informality and inclusiveness. "Chambermaids elbowed countesses and all enjoyed themselves." Wives of senators and Cabinet members took particular delight at being included in receiving lines, although Julia may have had a practical reason for pressing them into service. A condition called strabismus—an imbalance of the eye muscles—caused her right eye to wander uncontrollably, affecting her vision, and she needed help to identify visitors who were coming through the line.

For formal state dinners, Julia replaced the army quartermaster in the kitchen with an Italian steward. Weekly state dinners were described as Continental feasts, which included 25 courses and imported French wines. The banquets were followed by 15 minutes of socializing in the Blue Room, after which the Grants retired and guests were free to leave for their own beds, or for a long walk to ward off indigestion.

At the end of her husband's second term, Julia reluctantly left the White House so as not to "prevent others from enjoying the same privilege." The Grants traveled extensively abroad, where there were received like royalty. Returning to New York, Ulysses undertook another disastrous business venture with an unsuccessful brokerage firm which left the couple bankrupt. In his final years, dying of throat cancer and fearing for his wife's well-being, Grant once again turned to the military. Racing to write his memoirs of the Civil War years, he finished just weeks before his death in 1885. The volumes sold well, leaving Julia financially secure.

In her final years, Julia traveled and attended Grand Army of the Republic events honoring her husband. She befriended *Varina Howell Davis, widow of Jefferson Davis, and supported *Susan B. Anthony and the suffragists. She also attempted her own book but did not find a publisher in her lifetime. Julia Grant died in 1902, age 76, and is buried with her husband in Grant's Tomb in New York City. Her book, finally published in 1975, attempts to vindicate her husband of any dishonest dealings during his presidency.

SOURCES:

Healy, Diana Dixon. *America's First Ladies: Private Lives of the Presidential Wives.* NY: Atheneum, 1988.

Melick, Arden David. *Wives of the Presidents.* Maplewood, NJ: Hammond, 1977.

Paletta, LuAnn. *The World Almanac of First Ladies.* NY: World Almanac, 1990.

SUGGESTED READING:

Grant, Julia D. *The Personal Memoirs of Julia Dent Grant (Mrs. Ulysses S. Grant).* Edited by John Y. Simon. IL: Southern Illinois University Press, 1988.

Grant, Zilpah Polly (1794–1874).

See Lyons, Mary for sidebar.

Grant of Laggan, Mrs. (1755–1838).

See Grant, Anne.

Granuaile or Grany.

Variant of Grace.

Granville, Bonita (1923–1988)

American actress and producer. Name variations: Bonita Granville Wrather; (nickname) Bunny. Born on February 2, 1923, in New York City; died of cancer on October 11, 1988; buried in Holy Cross Cemetery; married Jack Wrather, in 1947 (died 1984); children: **Molly Wrather**; **Linda Wrather**; Jack Wrather; Christopher Wrather.

Filmography: Westward Passage (1932); Silver Dollar (1932); Cavalcade (1933); Ah, Wilderness (1935); Maid of Salem (1936); Plough and the Stars (1936); Garden of Allah (1936); These Three (1936); Quality Street (1937); Call It a Day (1937); It's Love I'm After (1937); Merrily We Live (1938); My Bill (1938); Beloved Brat (1938); White Banners (1938); Nancy Drew, Detective (1938); Nancy Drew, Troubleshooter (1939); Nancy Drew, Reporter (1939); Angels Wash Their Faces (1939); Nancy Drew and the Hidden Staircase (1939); Forty Little Mothers (1940); Third Finger, Left Hand (1940); The Mortal Storm (1940); Those Were the Days (1940); Escape (1940); Gallant Sons (1940); Down in San Diego (1941); The People vs. Dr. Kildare (1941); H.M. Pulham, Esq. (1941); Syncopation (1941); The Glass Key (1941); Now Voyager (1942); Andy Hardy's Double Life (1942); Seven Miles from Alcatraz (1942); Hitler's Children (1943); Song of the Open Road (1944);

Youth Runs Wild *(1944)*; Andy Hardy's Blonde Trouble *(1944)*; The Beautiful Cheat *(1945)*; Suspense *(1946)*; The Truth about Murder *(1946)*; Breakfast in Hollywood *(1946)*; Love Laughs at Andy Hardy *(1946)*; The Guilty *(1947)*; Strike It Rich *(1948)*; Guilty of Treason *(1950)*; The Lone Ranger *(1956)*.

As producer: "Lassie" (TV-series on CBS, *1954–71, syndicated 1971–74*) and The Magic of Lassie *(feature film starring James Stewart and *Alice Faye, 1978)*.

Bonita Granville was born in New York City on February 2, 1923, into an acting family. By age nine, she made her film debut in *Westward Passage*. In 1936, at age thirteen, she was nominated for Best Supporting Actress for her work as the spiteful schoolgirl in *These Three*, starring *Miriam Hopkins** and *Merle Oberon**, and based on the play by *Lillian Hellman**. It was the first time an Academy Award was given in this category and the Oscar went to *Gale Sondergaard** for her performance in *Anthony Adverse*. But Granville is best remembered for her portrayal of Nancy Drew, based on the series about the feisty girl detective (*See entries on Harriet Stratemeyer Adams and Mildred Benson*).

In 1947, Granville married Texas oil millionaire Jack Wrather. When she retired from acting in the 1950s, she became an executive in her husband's business empire, the Wrather Corporation. His holdings included oil wells, hotels and entertainment enterprises. It was Wrather's company that produced the "Lassie" television series for which Granville was associate producer, then producer. After her husband died in 1984, Granville succeeded him as chair of the board. She was involved in many cultural affairs and for a time chaired the American Film Institute and was a trustee of the John F. Kennedy Center.

Deborah Jones,
Studio City, California

Granville, Christine (1915–1952)

Polish secret agent during World War II. Name variations: Countess Krystina Skarbek. Born Countess Krystina Skarbek in Poland in 1915; died in London in 1952; married George Gizycki.

One of many women who served as secret agents during World War II, Christine Granville was born in Poland in 1915 as Countess Krystina Skarbek, the daughter of a distinguished Polish family. Known for her beauty and vibrant personality, she was winner of a "Miss Poland" contest during her teens. She was living in Addis Ababa with her second husband when the war broke out, and she went immediately to England to offer her services to British Intelligence. Accepted, she was assigned to Budapest, Hungary, where she undertook the dangerous mission of smuggling Poles and other Allied officers out of Poland. Seemingly without fear and meticulous about security, she made three journeys into Poland and also carried out several missions in the Balkans before being sent to France in 1944. On this assignment, she often parachuted onto the Vercors Plateau in Southern France, where, as a courier for the Hockey network, she maintained contact with the French Resistance and the Italian partisans. Her successes included initiating the surrender of a German garrison of Polish troops located on the Italian frontier and bluffing the Gestapo into freeing two of her captured comrades three hours before they were to be executed. She was awarded the George Medal and an OBE by the British government. Ironically, after surviving so many dangerous missions during the war, she was murdered by a spurned suitor in London in 1952.

Granville, Mary (1700–1788).

See Delany, Mary Granville.

Grasso, Ella (1919–1981)

American politician, U.S. congressional delegate (1971–75), and governor of Connecticut (1974–81). Born Ella Rosa Giovanna Oliva Tambussi in Windsor Locks, Connecticut, on May 10, 1919; died in Hartford, Connecticut, on February 5, 1981; daughter of Giacomo (a baker) and Maria (Oliva) Tambussi; attended St. Mary's in Windsor Locks; graduated from the Chaffee School, Windsor; Mt. Holyoke College, South Hadley, Massachusetts, B.A., magna cum laude, 1940, M.A., 1942; married Thomas A. Grasso (an educator), on August 31, 1942; children: Suzanne Grasso; James Grasso.

The only child of Italian immigrants, Giacomo and **Maria Tambussi**, Ella Grasso was born in 1919 and raised in a modest but comfortable home in Windsor Locks, Connecticut. A bright child, she was encouraged academically by her mother whom she called "a great reader." She received a superior education through a series of scholarships, first to the private Chaffee School in Windsor, and later to Mount Holyoke College, where she graduated with honors in 1940, then went on to earn a master's degree in sociology and economics. She later credited her parents with much of her success. "I suppose I had a

Ella Grasso

compulsion to succeed so my parents could find pride in the sacrifices they made for me," she said. In August 1942, Ella married her longtime sweetheart Thomas Grasso, an educator who spent most of his career as principal of a middle school in East Hartford. The couple had two children, Suzanne and James, and lived in Windsor Locks for their entire married life, leaving only to spend summers at the shore in Old Lyme.

During World War II, Grasso was employed as assistant state director of research for the Federal War Manpower Commission and gained her early political experience on the local level, as a member of the League of Women Voters. After a brief flirtation with the Republican Party, she joined the Democrats and became a protégé of the state party chair John Bailey. After working in the trenches for several local campaigns, Grasso became a candidate herself. In 1952, she was elected to serve in Connecticut's General Assembly, and in 1955, during her second term, she became Democratic floor leader. After four years in the legislature, Grasso was elected secretary of state, a post she held for 12 years. During that time, she became one of the most popular political figures in Connecticut, mainly due to her personal involvement with citizens' concerns. At the same time, she continued to be active in national Democratic politics, serving as a member of the national platform committee in 1960 and as co-chair of the resolutions committee of the Democratic National Convention. In 1968, she proposed a platform plank opposing United States involvement in the Vietnam War.

In 1970, and again in 1972, Grasso was elected to Congress where she compiled a liberal voting record, though the Women's Lobby, a group promoting feminist legislation, ranked her in the bottom third of its Congressional list, largely because of her opposition to abortion and her absence during a child-care vote. She also served on the Education and Labor Committee and the Veterans Affairs Committee, and took part in drafting the Comprehensive Employment and Training Act. Capitol Hill, however, did not engage Grasso the way that Connecticut politics had, partly because of the strain it put on her family life. "I found my four years in Washington most instructive," she later said. "But I would have been happier if they'd moved the capital to Hartford."

In 1974, Grasso entered the Connecticut gubernatorial race, trouncing the other Democratic hopefuls in the primary and winning nomination at the Connecticut Democratic Convention. Running against Republican Robert H. Steele after incumbent Thomas J. Meskill withdrew from the race, Grasso campaigned on accountability for the expenditure of tax dollars and on wooing new industry to the state. The national media, however, often focused on her sex instead of the issues or her qualifications. "The judgment will be made of me as an individual," she countered, "on the basis of what I have accomplished in my career in public life and on the basis of what I'll be saying to the voter." She also distanced herself from the feminist movement,

although she was careful to point out that she had certainly benefited from its efforts. "Whereas four years ago I might have had some difficulty in advancing a viable candidacy as a woman, it's a non-issue at this time. I give silent thanks for that." On election day, Grasso received a plurality of 200,000 votes, becoming the first woman ever to become an American governor elected on her own and not as her husband's successor. As the newly elected state official, however, Grasso remained a reluctant celebrity and only moved to the governor's mansion because security concerns prevented her from operating out of her Windsor Locks home.

Retaining her forthright no-nonsense approach, Grasso attacked the state's precarious financial standing, starting with her own office. "I have turned down a $7,000 raise, and I won't have an official car," she told an interviewer. "I got them to reduce the cost of the Governor's Ball to $30 a couple when I told them I wouldn't go unless they cut the cost." She then imposed a further series of spending cuts in order to ward off the imposition of an income tax, and also increased the authority of the Department of Public Utilities Control so as to restrict the rise in utility rates. Successful in her belt-tightening, Grasso turned the budget deficit into a surplus within four years and was reelected for a second term in 1978. In 1979, she was elected chair of the Democratic Governors' Conference. Ella Grasso's career was cut short by cancer, which forced her to resign as governor on December 31, 1980. She died in Hartford on February 5, 1981.

Grasso, who was unpretentious and down-to-earth, was much-loved by her constituents. At home in Windsor Locks, she would shop downtown, dressed in baggy clothes and comfortable shoes, with her short hair in disarray. **Kay Holmes**, of the *Detroit News*, noted that one of the write-in votes in the gubernatorial election was for Grasso's hairdresser. Although not particularly retiring in speech or manner, Ella had surprisingly few enemies and even political foes eventually became friends. Whether friend or foe, Grasso remained loyal to the home folks, for it was the state of Connecticut that formed the perimeters of her life, politically and personally. "I feel a strong attraction to my state," she once said. "I think my roots are so deep it would be difficult for me to go anywhere else." Following her sojourn in Washington, she never did.

SOURCES:

Bliss, Betty. "Ella Grasso's bid in Connecticut nearing success," in *The Chicago Daily News.* May 20, 1974.

Holmes, Kay. "They Still Call Her Ella," in *The Detroit News, Sunday Magazine.* January 26, 1975.

McHenry, Robert, ed. *Famous American Women*. NY: Dover, 1983.

Moritz, Charles, ed. *Current Biography 1975*. NY: H.W. Wilson, 1975.

Women in Congress 1917–1990. Washington, DC: U.S. Government Printing Office, 1991.

Barbara Morgan,
Melrose, Massachusetts

Gratz, Rebecca (1781–1869)

American founder of five charitable, religious, and educational organizations for needy women and children, who permanently shaped religious education and women's activities in American Jewish life. Born in Philadelphia, Pennsylvania, on March 4, 1781; died on August 27, 1869, in Philadelphia, Pennsylvania, where she lived most of her life; daughter of Michael Gratz (a merchant, originally from Silesia) and Miriam (Simon) Gratz of Lancaster, Pennsylvania; attended the Young Ladies Academy in Philadelphia and possibly another unnamed women's school, but largely educated through her own eager and extensive reading in literature and history; never married.

Founded Female Association (1801), the Philadelphia Orphan Asylum (1815), the Female Hebrew Benevolent Society (1819), the Hebrew Sunday School (1838), and the Jewish Foster Home (1855), all in Philadelphia.

Rebecca Gratz believed that with an "unsubdued spirit" she could overcome all of life's difficulties. A pioneer Jewish charitable worker and religious educator, Gratz established and led important altruistic and religious organizations, including America's first independent Jewish women's charitable society, the first Jewish Sunday school, the Philadelphia Orphan Asylum, and the first American Jewish Foster Home. She surmounted the grief caused her by the deaths of many family members and loved ones, confronted Christian evangelists who tried to convert her from Judaism, and became a leader in education, charity, religion, and cultural life in Philadelphia. Gratz's accomplishments grew out of her own dauntless spirit and her commitments to both Judaism and America.

Born in Philadelphia, Pennsylvania, on March 4, 1781, a middle child among ten children born to Michael Gratz of Silesia and **Miriam Simon Gratz** of Lancaster, Pennsylvania, Gratz grew up in Philadelphia's wealthy society. Her father, her uncle Barnard Gratz, and her grandfather Joseph Simon engaged in Indian trading, land speculation, and coastal shipping. Her brothers Simon, Hyman, Joseph, Jacob, and Benjamin expanded the family financial interest

in the American west. Their far-flung enterprises required a constant flow of letters to maintain communication, and in the Gratz home, letter writing was a serious and constant activity. Family matters mixed with business concerns, and Michael Gratz's daughters, as well as his sons, embraced correspondence. Gratz's letters to her brothers Joseph and Benjamin reveal her deep affection for these men. Joseph's lively wit, taste for adventure, and social ease made him a favorite companion for Gratz, and the pair shared a friendship with literary humorist Washington Irving. Four years younger than Gratz, Joseph often accompanied her on trips to vacation spots like the New Jersey shore, the hot springs in Saratoga, New York, and New York City, where they visited long-time friends. As a young woman, Gratz would also travel with her younger sister, **Rachel**, along with one of her brothers. Accustomed from youth to the highly charged political atmosphere of post-Revolutionary Philadelphia, Gratz became and remained a fervent patriot throughout her life.

In her youth, Rebecca Gratz attended the Assembly Balls, dances that furthered social alliances among Philadelphia's leading families. An intelligent woman who loved literature, she was part of a circle of writers, including Irving and James Kirk Paulding, who contributed to the *Port Folio* literary magazine, although she herself never published. After abandoning her early poetry, Gratz confined her literary talent to an extensive correspondence and to the annual reports of her organizations. Her correspondents included British educator and novelist ***Maria Edgeworth**, American author ***Catherine Sedgwick**, renowned British actress ***Fanny Kemble**, Jewish-British theologian and educator ***Grace Aguilar**, and other less notable and distant friends and family. About 1822, shortly after Edgeworth published *Harrington*, Gratz wrote to the author protesting the book's depiction of a marriage between a Jewish woman and a Christian man. Enormously influenced by the glamour of political heroism, Gratz preferred Sir Walter Scott's *Ivanhoe*, in which a Jewish woman refuses to wed the Christian hero of the tale out of loyalty to her faith and her father. American writer Catherine Sedgwick admired Gratz and sought a more intimate relationship with her, but Gratz, herself a member of Philadelphia's elite society, was hardly pleased with Sedgwick's New England snobbery. Ultimately, the two women shared only a concern for their mutual friend, Fanny Kemble, whose divorce from Georgia plantation owner Pierce Butler scandalized many. When Butler refused to allow Fanny to see her daughters, Gratz and Sedgwick, who both admired Kemble's readings of British classics, rallied to her side and provided a conduit for letters between Kemble and her daughters. Gratz's criticisms of Christian literary women, such as Edgeworth and Sedgwick, contributed to her appreciation of Grace Aguilar, whose work asserted that Jewish spirituality equalled or surpassed that of Christianity and who addressed a primarily female reading public.

There are many kinds of trials in this life, but an unsubdued spirit can overcome them all.

—Rebecca Gratz

Although Gratz argued strenuously for Judaism's equality with Christianity, she argued equally for Jewish social integration. The children of Alexander Hamilton and *Elizabeth Schuyler Hamilton, publisher John Fenno, as well as the Reverend John Ewing, president of the University of Pennsylvania, were among her closest friends. Gratz was so well known in elite Philadelphia circles that Irving asked her to introduce famous portrait painter Thomas Sully to Philadelphia patrons when the artist moved there early in his career. The collected Gratz family portraits include many by Sully, Edward Malbone, and Gilbert Stuart. In addition to important synagogue responsibilities and Gratz's own organizations, the Gratz siblings together promoted the city's Athenaeum, a "Deaf and Dumb" Home, the Academy of Fine Arts, and various libraries.

Well educated for her day, Gratz attended women's academies and utilized her father's extensive library which was stocked with literature, histories, and popular science. To it, she added Judaica, seeking original new works in English, works recently translated into English, as well as requesting new books and early readings of works-in-progress from knowledgeable American Jews like Isaac Leeser and educator Jacob Mordecai.

At 19, Gratz was recruited as a family nurse to help her mother care for her father, who had suffered a stroke. Although Gratz at first found nursing "agonizing," she remained the family nurse throughout her life, sharing duties with her unmarried older sister **Sarah Gratz**, who died in 1817. Gratz's three married sisters, **Frances, Richea**, and Rachel, together had 28 children, and Gratz assisted at most births. As family nurse, she also tended dying relations, including her parents, both of whom died before her 30th year, as well as many of the 19 nieces and nephews whom she outlived.

While nursing her father, Gratz joined her mother, sister, and 20 other women, Jewish and Gentile, to found Philadelphia's non-sectarian Female Association for the Relief of Women and Children in Reduced Circumstances (c. 1801). Gratz was its first secretary and held that office for many years. Established in the wake of a national economic collapse and before married women held the right to own property, this organization served as a mutual-aid society for wealthy women whose husbands or fathers risked financial ruin. In 1815, Gratz helped establish the Philadelphia Orphan Asylum and served as secretary for its first 40 years. In the 1830s, she advised her sister-in-law, **Maria Gist Gratz**, on creating and running the first orphan asylum in Lexington, Kentucky.

Rebecca Gratz sought the post of executive secretary in each of the institutions she founded. As secretary, she not only maintained organizational records but annually addressed the managing boards on policy in each year-end secretary's report. The institutions regularly published her reports as pamphlets or in the popular press in order to raise public support for their work. The secretary's role enhanced Gratz's authority and provided a public forum from which to advance her own ideas about the ways in which her organizations could promote both women's roles and Judaism in Philadelphia and in America. Her Jewish institutions especially reflected her own strong leadership.

Noting that Christian charitable women evangelized while aiding the poor, Gratz became convinced that Philadelphia's Jewish women and children needed their own charitable institution. In 1819, she gathered women of her religious congregation to found the country's first independent Jewish charity, the Female Hebrew Benevolent Society. The FHBS provided food, fuel, shelter, and later an employment bureau and traveler's aid service. During the years of Gratz's leadership, the FHBS served only needy American Jewish women and their children, refusing aid to both emissaries from Jewish settlements in the "Holy Land" and local Jewish women seeking loans for which they could offer substantial collateral. The FHBS also coordinated its efforts with those of sewing and fuel societies serving needy local Jews, organizations to which Gratz also offered significant advice and aid soon after their founding. The FHBS remained an independent society until the late 20th century.

Gratz's religious beliefs reflected her family's membership in Mikveh Israel as well as her

Rebecca
Gratz

own avid readings in Judaism, literature, and popular philosophy, along with lively discussions with Christian friends. Although Gratz, like most Jewish women and some men, knew no Hebrew, her congregation's early use of prayer books imported from England, with English translations on facing pages, allowed her a satisfying and devoted synagogue experience throughout her life. She also found religious insight in Shakespeare's dramas and sonnets and gleaned moral guidance from novelists like Thomas Carlyle. She insisted that her Christian friends respect her own understandings of Biblical texts and frequently argued Judaism's truth. She also insisted on Jews' right to be treated as equals, both as citizens and as pious individuals, under the U.S. Constitution. These lifelong religious discussions shaped her religious ideas and deepened her convictions. While Gratz believed that American religious freedom presaged a new epoch in Jewish history, she also believed that if Jews were to be respected by the Christian majority they must become religiously knowledgeable and observant. Consequently, she was appalled by Judaism's nascent reform movement, which renounced Zion and diminished ritual.

An outspoken woman who thought few marriages happy and few men likely to be an "agreeable domestic companion" for herself, Gratz remained unmarried. She lived with her three bachelor brothers, Hyman, Joseph, and Jacob, and an unmarried sister, Sarah, throughout her life. Despite her skepticism about marriage, Gratz adored children. Around 1818, after Sarah's death, Gratz organized an informal Hebrew school in her home for the children of her extended family, instructed by a young rabbi hoping for employment at her synagogue. When Gratz's sister Rachel died in 1823 leaving six children, Gratz brought the children home with her and raised them. Their father soon purchased the home directly across the street from Gratz. She developed an especially close relationship with her nieces, **Miriam Moses Cohen**, **Sarah Moses Joseph**, and **Rebecca Moses Nathan**. Rachel's youngest child, Horace Moses, who moved into Gratz's home when he was only two years old, continued to live with Gratz and her brothers throughout his youth and eventually became the executor of her estate.

Gratz was the first to apply the Sunday School format to Jewish education. The FHBS women hoped to provide religious education soon after the organization's founding, but they were unable to do so until 1838, when Gratz established the Hebrew Sunday School (HSS), a co-educational institution, with herself as superintendent. She also served as secretary of the managing society and held both offices until she was in her 80s. Her sister congregants, **Simha Peixotto** and **Rachel Peixotto Pyke**, who ran a private school in their home, joined her as teachers, and the Peixotto sisters wrote many of the text books initially used by the school. Gratz wrote morning prayers which she recited to the students each Sunday morning, and which they repeated after her. She also determined the format of the school day, which she adapted from the highly successful schools run by the Protestant American Sunday School Union, headquartered in Philadelphia. As a result, while Philadelphia's synagogues were unable to satisfactorily educate even a small minority of the city's Jewish children, Gratz's school offered instruction in the principals of Judaism and individual attention to students through its large volunteer faculty of women and resulting small classes. Students ranged in age from early childhood to early teens. The HSS soon attracted students and faculty throughout Philadelphia, and it remained an independent, city-wide institution until the close of the 20th century.

The HSS offered Jewish women their first public role in teaching religion and determining curriculum in a Jewish school. Only female graduates were invited to join the faculty and the HSS' teacher-training program furthered the women's religious education. The curriculum focused especially on basic Jewish beliefs, enhancing the role of Jewish women, and training students to refute Christian evangelists. Gratz advised her niece Miriam in Charleston, Savannah, and **Sarah Lopez**, a former teacher in the Philadelphia school who relocated to Baltimore, Maryland, on establishing similar schools there. Their efforts prompted a controversy among the country's leading Jewish educators. Philadelphia's Isaac Leeser, who wrote and translated Jewish catechisms for the school and publicized the HSS, encouraged Jewish women around the country to take similar action. Baltimore's rabbi David Einhorn, on the other hand, railed against the Hebrew Sunday School as offering only a women's religion that distorted Judaism and warped children's minds. Cincinnati's Isaac Mayer Wise believed men ought to appreciate the women's efforts. By the 1840s, Gratz happily noted that Jewish women were "becoming quite literary." She touted books by England's Aguilar, who extolled Judaism and argued its importance to women, and used Aguilar's books in the HSS. Gratz hoped the school would demonstrate that Jewish women equalled Christian women in religious piety, then considered a mark of civility. The school flourished, opened several branches, and served over 4,000 students by the end of the 19th century.

During the 1850s, the plight of an increasing number of Jewish immigrants convinced Gratz of the need for a Jewish Foster Home (JFH). Jewish orphan associations in New York and New Orleans, which relied on foster families, grew inadequate as immigration increased. The first residential homes in those cities were not exclusively for the use of Jewish children. The elderly Gratz, who had served 40 years on the board of the Philadelphia Orphan Asylum, became vice president of the JFH managing society soon after its founding in 1855. Already in her 70s, Gratz at first preferred to limit her activities to committee work, and served on those selecting and overseeing the matron, purchasing the building, and regularly visiting the home. Instead, she guided her niece **Louisa Gratz**, and a young woman of her congregation, both unmarried, to assume leadership while serving as overall advisor to the young institution. But soon after its founding, the board pressed Gratz to take a more formal role, and she agreed to the vice presidency. By then, she had earned a considerable reputation both locally and around the country, and her presence on its board legitimized the new institution in the public mind. The JFH later merged with several other institutions to form Philadelphia's Association for Jewish Children. Largely due to Gratz's influence, Hyman Gratz, her older brother, bequeathed the funds for the founding of the first independent college of Jewish studies in America, Gratz College.

Rebecca Gratz outlived all but her youngest sibling, Benjamin, and many of her nieces and nephews. Despite her grief in her last years, she was relieved that what she believed to be the American experiment in freedom had not ended with the Civil War. She was sure that her lasting monument would be the Hebrew Sunday School, a highly successful institution that most reflected her own unique blend of Judaism and American culture. Gratz died on August 27, 1869, and was buried in Mikveh, a historic cemetery. By the end of her life, a legend claimed Gratz as the prototype for the character of Rebecca of York in Sir Walter Scott's novel, *Ivanhoe*, the first favorable depiction of a Jew in English fiction. Jews pointed to Gratz, an Americanized Jewish woman who retained her Jewish loyalty, to argue the truth of the popular tale. Gratz's own life epitomized the "unsubdued spirit" she admired.

SOURCES:

Ashton, Dianne. "'Souls Have No Sex': Philadelphia Jewish Women and the American Challenge," in Friedman, ed. *When Philadelphia Was the Capitol of Jewish America*. Cranbury, NJ: Associated University Presses, 1993, pp. 34–57.

Bodek, Evelyn. "Making Do: Jewish Women and Philanthropy" in Murray Friedman's *Jewish Life in Philadelphia 1830–1940*. Philadelphia, PA: ISHI Press, 1983, pp. 143–162.

Braude, Ann. "The Jewish Woman's Encounter with American Culture," in Reuther and Keller, eds. *Women and Religion in America*. Vol. 1. NY: Harper & Row, 1981, pp. 150–192.

Cohen, Mary M. *An Old Philadelphia Cemetery: The Resting Place of Rebecca Gratz*. City History Society of Philadelphia, 1920.

Osterweis, Rollin G. *Rebecca Gratz: A Study in Charm.* 1935.

Rosenbloom, Joseph. "Rebecca Gratz and the Jewish Sunday School Movement in Philadelphia," in *Publications of the American Jewish Historical Society*. Vol. 47, no. 2, 1958, pp. 71–75.

———. "Some Conclusions about Rebecca Gratz," in *Essays in American Jewish History*. Cincinnati, OH: American Jewish Archives, 1958, pp. 171–186.

Wolf, Edwin II, and Maxwell Whiteman. *The History of the Jews of Philadelphia from Colonial Times to the Age of Jackson*. Philadelphia, PA: Jewish Publication Society, 1957.

COLLECTIONS:

Gratz Family Papers, Manuscript Collection #236, and the Henry Joseph Collection, American Jewish Archives, Hebrew Union College, Cincinnati, Ohio.

Rebecca Gratz Papers, American Jewish Historical Society, Brandeis University, Waltham, Massachusetts.

Gratz Family Papers, Collection #72, American Philosophical Society, Philadelphia, Pennsylvania.

Miriam Moses Cohen Papers, Southern History Collection University of North Carolina, Chapel Hill, North Carolina.

Philipson, David, ed., *The Letters of Rebecca Gratz*, 1929.

Dianne Ashton,
Professor of Religion, Rowan University, Glassboro, New Jersey, and author of *Unsubdued Spirits: Rebecca Gratz and the Domestication of American Judaism* (Wayne State University Press, 1998)

Graves, Nancy (1940–1995)

American sculptor, painter, and filmmaker. Born Nancy Stevenson Graves on December 23, 1940, in Pittsfield, Massachusetts; died in 1995 in New York City; one of two daughters of Walter L. Graves (an assistant director of a museum) and Mary B. Graves (a secretary and volunteer worker); attended Miss Hall's School, Pittsfield, and the Northfield School for Girls; Vassar College, B.A. in English literature, 1961; Yale University, B.F.A. and M.F.A.; married Richard Serra (a sculptor), in 1965 (divorced 1970); no children.

Was a Fulbright-Hayes fellow in France (1965); lived and worked in Florence, Italy (1966); had solo exhibitions throughout the world (1968–95); partici-

pated in numerous group shows (1970–95); was a resident at the American Academy, Rome, Italy (1979); designed set and costumes for experimental dance Lateral Pass *(1983). Work represented in numerous museums, galleries, and private collections, including Whitney Museum and Museum of Modern Art, New York City; Chicago Art Institute; Museum of Fine Arts, Houston, Texas; Neue Gallerie, Cologne, West Germany; and National Gallery of Canada, Ottawa.*

Selected works—sculptures: Fossils *(1970);* Variability of Similar Forms *(1970);* Inside-Outside *(1970);* Variability and Repetition of Variable Forms *(1970);* Shaman *(1970);* Ceridwen *(1969–77);* Column *(1979);* Bathymet-Topograph *(1978–79);* Archeologue *(1979);* Aves *(1979);* Trace *(1980);* Tarot *(1984). Paintings:* Lion Fish in Grotto *(1971);* Sea Anemone *(1971);* Julius Caesar Quadrangle of the Moon *(1971);* Nearside of the Moon 20° N-S x 70° E-W *(1972);* Bish *(1976);* Yot K Series *(1976);* Moonwater Series *(1977);* Defacta *(1977);* Zitla *(1977);* Lam *(1978);* Calipers, Legs, Lines *(1979). Films:* 200 Stills at 60 Frames *(1970);* Goulimine *(1970);* Izy Boukir *(1971);* Aves: Magnificent Frigate Bird, Great Flamingo *(1973);* Reflections on the Moon *(1974).*

Remembered for the three life-sized Bactrian, or two-humped, camels that comprised her first major solo exhibition at the Whitney Museum in 1969, American artist Nancy Graves also created paleontological sculptures using bones and other parts of animals and, from 1980 until her death in 1995, produced bronze sculptures using directly cast objects. Graves was also a graphic artist, employing a variety of media and working in styles ranging from representational to abstract. She also made several short films and designed sets and costume for a dance production. It is Graves' sculpture, however, that commands the most attention and is the medium by which she made her most lasting contribution. In the introduction to the catalogue *The Sculpture of Nancy Graves*, Robert Hughes characterizes her work as "wonderfully inclusive; formally rigorous, it spreads a wider fan of poetic association than does any sculptor's of her generation."

Graves, who was born in 1940 and raised in Pittsfield, Massachusetts, had an early introduction to art. Her father was the assistant director of the Berkshire Museum of Art and Natural History, and both of her parents made art their hobby. An intelligent and precocious child, Graves was drawing and painting with great precision at an early age and, by the time she was 12, had decided on an artistic career. After

high school, she attended Vassar College, where she majored in English while studying drawing. She then won a scholarship to Yale's School of Art and Architecture, where she earned both a B.F.A. and an M.F.A.

In 1964, Graves received a Fulbright fellowship and went to Paris. It was a period of experimentation and self-discovery for the artist that continued following her marriage to sculptor Richard Serra a year later. (They would divorce in 1970.) The couple moved to Florence, Italy, where Graves became fascinated by the 18th-century anatomist Clemente Susini, who created life-size wax models of animals and humans. She was inspired by both his naturalistic subject matter and his craftsmanship. "I felt as if I were seeing a body of my own work in the future," she said later. Although previously interested only in painting and drawing, she now tackled the problems of three-dimensional art, collaborating with her husband on a series of sculptures, then embarking on what would later be termed her neo-primitive period. Following intense anatomical studies of the Bactrian camel, Graves produced her first life-sized polyurethane sculpture of the animal, supported by a wooden framework and covered with painted animal skin.

Returning to New York in 1966, Graves presented a set of three sculptured camels at her first solo show at New York's Graham Gallery in the spring of 1968, and yet another set of three at the Whitney in 1969. The reviews were interesting and varied. One critic suggested that the camels were "an ingenious put-on" intended to mock abstract expressionism; another viewed them as a statement against the established art world. Grave's objective, as explained by **Brenda Richardson** in *Arts* magazine (April 1972), was neither mockery nor a negative statement, but merely an effort to meld "figuration and abstraction," or, in the words of **Marcia Tucker**, curator of the Whitney show, to establish "sustained tension . . . between the viewer's reaction to the 'real' subject matter and his aesthetic awareness of the camels as sculptural objects."

In her next sculptures, Graves treated the camel as "a prehistoric form from North America," as she explained in an interview for *Artforum* (October 1970). Using wax molded over steel rods, she created forms resembling the bones of ancient camels which she either stood upright on a wooden base, as in *Variability of Similar Forms* (1970), or arranged in abstract patterns on a large expanse of floor, as in a work entitled *Fossils* (1970). In further experiments, Graves created a series of hanging sculptures, inspired by the totems and ceremonial costumes of the North American Indians. *Time* magazine's Robert Hughes called them, a "poignant memorial to dying primitive cultures."

Camels were also the subject of three short films Graves made between 1970 and 1971, which, like the camel structures, focused on the effects of motion on the human perception of form. In the first, an eight-minute film titled *200 Stills at 60 Frames* (1970), she created the illusion of movement by flashing various still images at timed intervals. Another film, *Goulimine* (1970), shot in Morocco, captures the movement of an entire camel herd, and the third, *Izy Boukir* (1971), shows camels running, drinking, and nursing their young. As in her sculptures, Graves was striving to show figuration and abstraction simultaneously. "Carefully directed shots and angles [reveal] patterns of abstraction without obviating the viewer's ability comfortably to recognize and respond to the camel itself," explained Richardson.

Even while she was sculpting and making films, Graves was also producing paintings, etchings, lithographs, and monotypes. In the paintings of this period, which included depictions of snakes, insects, and fish, she utilized a pointillist technique of dots which cause the figures and background to blend in an abstract continuum. Once again, reviewers were baffled. Some identified her brushwork as pointillism, while others called it a "distinctly controlled ascetic gesturalism." Some were disappointed in the paintings; others thought them wildly creative. In a second series of paintings, Graves expanded her vision, employing her dot method to create whole sections of ocean floor. There was an additional series of map paintings and another set based on satellite photographs of lunar topography. Her most ambitious lunar painting, entitled *Nearside of the Moon 20° N-S x 70° E-W*, is comprised of four panels representing different types of 20th-century mapping of the moon. Graves' map paintings were generally better received than her camouflage series. Praised for their complex composition and refined technique, they were hailed as examples of a resurgence in landscape painting. The artist also produced lithographs based on geologic maps of the Lunar Orbiter and Apollo landing sites on the moon.

In conjunction with the map paintings, Graves produced two more films: *Aves: Magnificent Frigate Bird, Great Flamingo* depicts the flight patterns of migratory birds; *Reflections on the Moon* is composed of 200 still photographs taken by the Lunar Orbiter. Like her earlier films

and her paintings, they are abstract, even though the subjects are representational.

In 1977, Graves produced her first bronze piece, the result of a commission from the Museum Ludwig in Cologne, West Germany, to create a more permanent version of a camel bone piece. The resulting sculpture, *Ceridwen* (the medieval Welsh name for death), like the earlier work *Fossils*, consists of Pleistocene-period camel bones arranged to resemble an archaeological dig. (Huge in size, the piece was displayed at the Hammarskjold Plaza Sculpture Garden in New York City in the spring of 1978, before it was sent to Germany.) The sculpture was cast at the Tallix Foundry in Peekskill, New York, where Graves set up an adjunct studio and later worked with artisans there to develop a direct casting technique that allows for more detail than the older lost-wax technique. From 1980 until her death, Graves produced 200 bronze sculptures using the new technique. Expanding her repertory of cast forms, she utilized plants and fish, as well as paper or wooden objects that inspired her. "The possible inventory of forms for her art is endless," wrote **Linda L. Cathcart**, director of the Contemporary Arts Museum in Houston, Texas, in the catalogue essay "Nancy Graves: Sculpture for the Eye and Mind": "She does not fight her materials; rather, she builds with them and allows the process itself to suggest new avenues. Each of her sculptures functions as an energetic abstraction, never remaining merely literal and never giving way to dead weight. She has the ability to amplify forms and to achieve for each individual one many possible readings." Toni Putnam at Tallix also created another new casting and patinating technique that allowed Graves to work in color. *Quipu*, a filigree depiction of an ancient Andean knotted-string counting device, was the first cast sculpture to use the new procedure, which Graves went on to utilize in a number of later works.

In her painting from 1976 on, Graves' images were even more abstract, the result of her concern with process over subject matter. In her pastels and especially in her watercolors, the lines and forms are softer and looser, often the result of stroking the watercolor on wet paper. In a later project, she became involved in semiology, the science of signs, creating a series of painting in which calligraphic lines were drawn on predominantly white canvases, each in a single stroke of the brush. The oil paintings of the late 1970s, including *Defacto*, *Zitla*, *Calipers*, and *Lines*, are composed of dense layers of brushstrokes and relate back to her earlier sculptures, employing forms from her camels and camel-bone pieces. The critics generally reacted favorably to Graves' later paintings, citing their "energy" and their "airy luminosity."

In 1983, Graves collaborated with choreographer **Trisha Brown**, creating the set and costumes for a work called *Lateral Pass*. The complex set, which had to be constructed before the piece was choreographed, consisted of "four scrims of vertically hung Styrofoam boulders (pink or green) and bent silver rods and ultraviolet tubing" which ascended and descended in a constant play of motion and color. The dancers, clad in pastel and white leotards, appeared and disappeared within the maze of the set. The piece, performed by the Judson Dance Theater in Minneapolis and New York in 1985, earned Graves a New York Dance and Performance Bessie Award in 1986.

Graves, described as energetic, articulate, and dedicated, and called by some "a Renaissance woman for the eighties," died young, succumbing to cancer at age 55. Her work is part of the permanent collection at three major museums in New York (the Metropolitan, the Whitney, and the Museum of Modern Art), and other institutions throughout the United States, Europe, and Canada. Thomas Padon's catalogue of a national touring exhibition, *Nancy Graves: Excavations in Print, A Catalogue Raisonné* (1996), provides an illuminating collection of the artist's prints.

SOURCES:

Gareffa, Peter M., ed. *Newsmakers: The People Behind Today's Headlines*. Detroit, MI: Gale Research, 1989.

Moritz, Charles, ed. *Current Biography 1981*. NY: H.W. Wilson, 1981.

Publishers Weekly, February 12, 1996, p. 69.

Rubinstein, Charlotte Streifer. *American Women Artists: From Early Indian Times to the Present*. NY: Avon, 1982.

Barbara Morgan,
Melrose, Massachusetts

Gray, Eileen (1878–1976)

Irish designer, best known in the 1920s for her lacquerwork, and pioneering architect, whose work achieved belated recognition during the final years of her life. Born Kathleen Eileen Moray Smith (her surname was changed to Gray following her mother's inheritance of the Scottish title of Baroness Gray) on August 9, 1878, at Brownswood, Enniscorthy, Ireland; died in Paris, France, on October 31, 1976; daughter of James Maclaren Smith (an artist) and Eveleen (Pounden) Smith; educated at home and at private schools abroad; studied art at the Slade School of Fine Arts, London, and at the École Colarossi and the Académie Julian, Paris; never married; no children.

Settled in Paris (1902); began to study the craft of lacquer under Charles in London and Sougawara in Paris (1907); exhibited at the Salon des Artistes Décorateurs (1913); received her first commissions from Jacques Doucet (1914); commissioned to redecorate and furnish Mme Mathieu-Lévy's Paris apartment, in the process developing her "block" screens (1919); opened the Galerie Jean Désert as a retail outlet for her work (1922); exhibited at the Salon des Artistes Décorateurs (1923); built her first house, E. 1027 (1926–29); was founder member of Union des Artistes Modernes (1929); designed and built second house, Tempe à Pailla (1932–34); invited by Le Corbusier to show at his Pavillon des Temps Nouveaux at the Paris Exposition Internationale (1937); completed her third house, Lou Pérou (1958); appreciation of her work by Joseph Rykwert appeared in Domus (1968); exhibited in Graz and Vienna (1970); her screen, "Le destin," achieved a record price for 20th-century furniture at auction in Paris, and work exhibited at the RIBA Heinz Gallery, London (1972); appointed a Royal Designer for Industry (1972); elected an honorary fellow of the Royal Institute of the Architects of Ireland (1973); work exhibited in New York, Los Angeles, Princeton and Boston (1975); work exhibited at Victoria and Albert Museum, London and at Museum of Modern Art, New York (1979).

Major works: "La voie lactée" (location unknown, 1912); "Le destin" (private collection, 1913); Lotus table (private collection, c. 1917); Pirogue divan (collection Frances and Sydney Lewis, Richmond VA, 1919–20); Block screen (examples in Victoria and Albert Museum [V&A], London, and Virginia Museum of Fine Arts, 1922–25); Transat chair (six known versions, in private collections or location unknown, 1925–26); Bibendum armchair (ten pieces known, one in V&A, London, 1925–26); E. 1027 (1929); Tempe à Pailla (1934); Lou Pérou (1958). A detailed catalogue of her work is included in Peter Adam's Eileen Gray, Architect-Designer: A Biography, pp. 380–395.

In November 1972, the collection of Art Deco furniture which had belonged to the couturier Jacques Doucet was put up for auction at l'hôtel Drouot in Paris. Among the items listed in the catalogue was a four-panel lacquer screen, entitled "Le destin," and "decorated with figures in green and silver on a red background." The designer of the piece was Eileen Gray, then a virtual unknown, who had been celebrated for her lacquerwork and furniture half a century earlier and was later an innovative architect of two houses described by Philippe Garner as "seminal examples of the spirit of the Modern Movement." In any event, the sum fetched by this piece—at $36,000, a world-record price for 20th-century furniture—was to bring Gray out of obscurity. Already over 90 years old, she now found herself celebrated by critics and her work avidly sought by museums and private collectors. Old, ill, and used to neglect as she was, she regarded much of the clamor as "*absurde,*" but some of it, notably the praise from her peers, she accepted with pleasure and with a characteristic modesty. As she told **Evelyne Schlumberger**, who had written on her work for *Connaissance des Arts,* "I am so grateful that you spoke not only about my failures, but also about what I planned to do, as you know what I did realise was so very small, reading it I could hardly believe it was me."

Although she was to spend most of her long life in France, Eileen Gray never lost her affection for Ireland as the place where she had spent her earliest years. Brownswood, her birthplace, an austerely elegant house set in the lush County Wexford countryside, was the family home of her mother, **Eveleen Pounden**, who at the age of 21 had shocked her aristocratic relatives by eloping with an artist, James Maclaren Smith. The couple married in 1864, and over the next 15 years, five children were born to them, of whom Eileen, born on August 9, 1878, and christened Kathleen Eileen Moray, was the last. By the time of Eileen's birth, her parents' marriage was under strain, and within a few years her father had moved to Italy, where he was to live for the rest of his life. Considerably younger than her brothers and sisters and not particularly close to her mother, Eileen was a lonely child with few friends. Intelligent but patchily educated at home and in a variety of schools, she was happiest when traveling with her father in Germany and Italy. However, she also loved Brownswood, keeping a photograph of it by her throughout her life, and she was dismayed when in the 1890s an ambitious brother-in-law dismantled the old house in order to put up what she described as "a horrible brick structure" in its place. This, combined with the death of her father in 1900, and the impression made on her by her first visit to Paris in the same year, determined her to develop her artistic talents and to make an independent life for herself.

In 1901, Gray entered the Slade School in London, where for the next year she attended

Eileen Gray

classes in copying from the antique and in life drawing. Among her friends at the Slade were **Jessie Gavin** and **Kathleen Bruce**, with whom in 1902 she moved to Paris, settling in lodgings in Montparnasse, and enrolling first at the École Colarossi, and later at the Académie Julian. Dissatisfied with her drawing ability, Gray became increasingly interested in the decorative arts, visiting exhibitions such as those of the Société des Artistes Décorateurs, held in Paris from 1906, and the first Paris exhibition of the Deutsche Werkbund, which took place in 1910. While at the Slade, she had frequently visited the Victoria and Albert Museum, which had an impressive collection of oriental lacquer screens, and in 1906, while on a visit to London, she began to work in the medium, taking lessons first from a Mr. Charles, a repairer of antique screens, with a business in Bond Street, and, back in Paris, from a Japanese artisan, Sougawara. At about the same time, she moved into the apartment at 21 Rue Bonaparte, which was to be her main home for the rest of her life.

Over the next few years, under Sougawara's instruction, Eileen Gray set herself to master the craft of lacquerwork, experimenting with surface texture and extending the palette available by mixing natural dye with the lacquer to achieve new colors, including a red, a reddish brown, and a blue. In her designs, she developed a distinctive range of motifs and themes, producing an impression of richness combined with simplicity and restraint; her work at this time, she wrote, was "an attempt to simplify the figurative with almost geometrical designs and to replace those ghastly drapes and curves of Tiffany and Art Nouveau." By 1913, her work was beginning to attract attention, and she was invited to show some of her pieces at the Salon de la Société des Artistes Décorateurs of that year. The exhibition brought her a number of influential clients, most notably the society hostess, ◄❧ **Elizabeth de Gramont** (the duchess of Clermont-Tonnerre), who in 1922 published the first French-language article on Gray's work in *Les feuillets d'art*, and the couturier and connoisseur Jacques Doucet. Visiting Gray in her studio, Doucet found her at work on the large screen, "Le destin," which was to be one of his first purchases from her. Among the many other pieces which she produced for him were the "Lotus" table, in green, brown, and white lacquer, an occasional table in black lacquer, with a later *bilboquet* (cup and ball) design in red on the top, and a display cabinet in red with a blue lacquer interior; these and other works took their place in Doucet's apartment, alongside pieces by artists such as Picasso, Brancusi, Matisse, and Modigliani.

❧►
Elizabeth de Gramont. See Barney, Natalie Clifford for sidebar.

The future projects light, the past only shadows.

—Eileen Gray

The outbreak of war in 1914 put a temporary halt to Gray's designing career. Having served for some months as an ambulance driver at the front, in late 1915 she returned to England, taking Sougawara, her tools and some of her unfinished work with her. In August 1917, she was the subject of an article in British *Vogue*, which carried photographs of some of her designs, including "Le destin," and her first screen, "La voie lactée," and which described her as "an artist of rather an extraordinary sort." "She stands alone, unique, the champion of a singularly free method of expression . . . expressing herself with a terseness which is almost Japanese. . . . She stirs the imagination."

However, despite this favorable publicity, Gray had little commercial success in London. In 1917, she returned to Paris, where, with the end-ing of the war, she found a new patron in **Mme Mathieu-Lévy**, who commissioned her to completely refurbish her apartment on the Rue de Lota. In this project, Gray was able for the first time to create a total environment, thus inaugurating a shift from decoration to architecture. Simpler in line than her previous work, the pieces which she produced for Mathieu-Lévy showed a Cubist influence, seen, for instance, in her brick screens, constructed of panels of lacquer, and regarded by Philippe Garner as being among her "most striking inventions, bridging the gaps between furniture, architecture and sculpture." The Bakst designs for the Ballets Russes were another inspiration, particularly apparent in the Pirogue sofa, a boat-shaped daybed on arched legs in lacquer and tortoiseshell, a form which Garner describes as being "without precedent in the history of furniture design, the essence of extravagant elegance."

Such work, however, was necessarily the preserve of just a few wealthy patrons, and in 1921, in an effort to expand her business, Gray opened a shop, under the name of Jean Désert, in the fashionable Rue du Faubourg Saint-Honoré. The shop, selling furniture, lacquerwork, screens and rugs, attracted a number of celebrated clients, who included the politician Raymond Poincaré, the designer *Elsa Schiaparelli, the singer **Damia**, and the Indian maharaja of Indore, who ordered furniture from her for his new palace. Her reputation had begun to spread beyond France. In July 1922, the *Chicago Tribune* praised her "unusual decorative perception and her rare grasp of detail and art." However, with the exception of the rugs woven by her friend, **Evelyn Wyld**, and her workers, the project was never commercially successful. In 1924, Wyld left to work with another partner, and in 1930, with the Depression further damaging business, Gray finally closed the shop. By now, however, she had moved away from furniture design and decoration to an interest in architecture which was to dominate her later career.

In the spring of 1923, Gray had been invited to create a room for the XIV Salon des Artistes Décorateurs. The "bedroom-boudoir for Monte Carlo" which she produced, while still luxurious, was considerably more austere than the interiors which she had designed for the rue de Lota, and had an extremely mixed reception. Thus, *L'Intransigéant,* May 5, 1923, described it as "maddening with its chrysalid lamps in parchment and wrapping paper. It is the daughter of Caligari in all its horror." On the other hand, the critic René Chavance, writing in *Beaux Arts,* June 1, 1923, while regretting Gray's "experiments with disquieting Cubism," nevertheless found that the room "represents, in its eccentricity, a curious harmony." Praise came too from a number of architects, including Pierre Chareau, Robert Mallet-Stevens and, from Holland, Sybold van Ravesteyn, a member of the De Stijl group, founded a few years earlier with a commitment to freeing art and design from traditional constraints. De Stijl was a profound influence on Gray, whose contacts with members such as Van Ravesteyn, Jan Wils, and Jacobus Oud, and her reading of works such as Van Doesburg's "Toward a plastic architecture," fostered her shift in outlook at this time. Already, as a critic had noted in *Ère nouvelle*, Gray's furniture pieces were "like simple complements to architectural structures," a point which was also made by the young Paris-based Rumanian architect and critic Jean Badovici in an examination of her work in a special 1924 issue of the Dutch magazine *Wendingen*. Badovici went on to place her unequivocally at the center of the modern movement.

> In all her tendencies, visions and expressions she is modern; she rejects the feeling of the old aesthetics and mistrusts old forms. She knows that our time, with its new possibilities of living, necessitates new ways of feeling. The formidable influence of technology has transformed our sensibilities. . . . All her work reflects a lyrical force, an enthusiasm, and the strength of feeling of this new civilization and spirit.

Already in her mid-40s and entirely without architectural training, Gray, under Badovici's guidance, set out to learn the principles of architecture. The first opportunity to put her newly acquired skills into practice came in 1925, when Badovici suggested that she build him a "little refuge," on a rocky, remote site, high above the Mediterranean, near Roquebrune. Completed in 1929, E. 1027 was an L-shaped, flat-roofed structure, on two floors, linked by a central staircase, and with huge floor-to-ceiling windows overlooking the sea; although the house itself was small, Gray created an illusion of spaciousness by, for instance, using the terrace and gardens as an extension of the interior and by installing furniture which could be easily folded away and adapted to various uses. Among her innovations were a bedside table in tubular steel, whose base could be fitted underneath the bed and whose height could be adjusted by the extension of a trombone which supported the top, and the "Bibendum" chair, consisting of three tire-like rolls on a tubular steel base. She made use of other industrial materials, such as perforated sheet-metal and transparent celluloid, but also incorporated elements of comfort, such as

her rugs, and even of humor, in stencilled inscriptions such as "*défense de rire*" (no laughing) and "*entrez lentement*" (enter slowly). According to Peter Adam:

> The house was permeated in every aspect, inside and out, by an intense desire to reconcile the aesthetic principle with human needs. Walking through the rooms, looking at the many personal touches of comfort, wit and romanticism (and some of its minor shortcomings) is like looking into the mind of the person who conceived it. This house on Cap Martin reveals more of Eileen Gray than any object, piece of furniture, or anecdote.

Contemporary acknowledgements of Gray's achievement included the publication of a special issue of *L'Architecture vivante*, entitled "E. 1027: maison en bord de mer," and of a report and photographs of the house in the German magazine *Der Baumeister* (October 1930), as well as an invitation from the Union des Artistes Modernes to display her plans for E. 1027 at its first exhibition, held in Paris in 1930. Gray was particularly touched by the admiration of Le Corbusier, an architect whose ideas had greatly influenced her own development, and who, having visited her house, wrote to her of his appreciation of "the rare spirit which dictated all the organisation inside and outside. A rare spirit which has given the modern furniture and installations such dignified, charming and witty shape."

Gray's next project was the renovation of Badovici's new Paris studio, for which she reproduced much of the furniture which she had designed for E. 1027 and, again, by the use of mirrors and of pieces which could have a variety of uses, managed to obtain an impression of space within a relatively confined area. However, although she spent a number of summers at Roquebrune with Badovici, she was increasingly anxious to have a house which would be hers alone, and in 1932 she obtained permission to build on land which she owned at Castellar, near Menton. On a more difficult site than E. 1027, Gray was nevertheless able to adapt her plans to the terrain, creating in Tempe à Pailla, as she called it, a house which was smaller and more restrained in style than her first attempt, while repeating many of the elements found in E. 1027, such as the flat over-hanging roofs, the terraces and walkways, and the large picture windows. Again, Gray designed all the furniture, integrating it completely into the architecture and crafting it to serve the maximum number of functions and to take up the minimum space: a dining table, on castors for easy movement, could be transformed into a low table; a metal seat became a stepladder, another piece could be used as a towel holder, as steps or as a seat, and her "S" chair, a canvas seat on a wooden frame, could be folded away for storage.

Though the building was finished in 1934, Gray did not complete the furnishing of the house until 1939. During this time, she worked on a number of other projects, among them designs for a "tube house," a prefabricated metal structure, intended as a temporary, emergency or holiday home, which could be easily erected and mass-produced at low cost. Another proposal was a *centre de vacances,* which incorporated a restaurant and cafe, a cinema, an open-air theater and buildings for young people and for children. At the invitation of Le Corbusier, the model for the center was exhibited in his section of the 1937 International Exhibition in Paris. However, neither these, nor any of her other designs were ever built. Disillusioned with the demands of private clients, Gray now preferred to design projects for "the entire people" for which, however, she obtained no commissions. One reason for this was her lack of professional training, with the discipline and organization which that implied. Another was her own preference for working alone: she did not cooperate easily with other architects, belonged to no school, movement or group, and had no agent to promote her work. Moreover, by now her health and, in particular, her eyesight, had begun to deteriorate, affecting her ability to work and tending to distance her even from colleagues and friends.

This alienation was intensified by the outbreak of World War II, which forced her to leave Castellar. Forbidden, as a resident alien, to stay either at Tempe à Pailla or at her flat in St. Tropez, Gray, together with her maid **Louise Dany,** moved further inland to Loumarin, where she lived through the occupation, only to discover at its end that Tempe à Pailla had been looted and vandalized, that most of its contents had been stolen and her drawings and papers burned. The loss was compounded by the destruction of her plans and furniture, when the port of St. Tropez, including her flat, was blown up by the retreating Germans.

With both her homes in the south gone, and with much of her life's work apparently destroyed, Gray returned to Rue Bonaparte, and to the process of reconstruction which preoccupied the architectural world in the aftermath of war. By now, she was all but forgotten by critics and public alike, and her work, when it was photographed or mentioned in exhibitions or publications, was frequently uncredited or wrongly ascribed: E.

1027, for instance, was commonly credited to Badovici alone. Nevertheless, she continued to work as unremittingly as she had always done. In 1946, she reported that she had begun to plan a cultural and social center which, she hoped, would "help solve the problems of the monotony and solitude of those who have to live in provincial towns," and which included a library, theater, exhibition gallery, cinema, restaurant, and conference center. This remained unbuilt, as did a worker's club which she also planned. She also continued to design furniture, experimenting with new materials such as plexiglass, and began the lengthy and difficult process of repairing and refurbishing Tempe à Pailla. When in 1953 the work was finally completed, she put the house up for sale; it was eventually bought by the painter Graham Sutherland, who changed the name and substantially altered and enlarged the house.

In 1956, Badovici died. Although they had parted some years before, Eileen and he were still friends, and it was she who arranged his funeral. Following his death, E. 1027 was bought by his friend, Le Corbusier. However, while he had initially expressed enthusiasm for her work, Gray had been angered by alterations which Le Corbusier had made in the house during Badovici's time there; incensed by his ownership of it and by further changes which he made, she refused to visit her house again. Meanwhile, with Tempe à Pailla gone, she had embarked on the building of her third and last house, on a site near St. Tropez. To a small existing building, she added a wing, which included a bedroom for herself, a bathroom, and a small kitchen. The interior was austere, with the dining and sitting areas bisected by a white brick screen, and furnished with simple wooden benches and a table. On the wall hung a map of Peru, a reminder of the house's Provençal name. Lou Pérou was completed in 1958, and over the next decade Gray spent several months of the year there, living for the rest of the time in Paris, while continuing, despite poor health, to travel and to keep informed on new trends in design and architecture.

After decades of obscurity, Gray's work began to attract renewed attention in the late 1960s. In 1968, an appreciation of her work by Joseph Rykwert appeared in *Domus,* an Italian publication; the article was reprinted in *Architectural Review* in December 1972—by which time the sale of the contents of Doucet's flat had established her reputation as a leading Art Deco designer. In the same year, she was appointed a Royal Designer for Industry, and in the following year was elected an honorary fellow of the Royal

Institute of Architects of Ireland. Her work also began to be included in exhibitions: in 1972, she had her first show in England, organized by the Royal Institute of British Architects, followed by several exhibitions in the United States. Although her furniture was much sought after by collectors, she herself saw her architecture as the most important aspect of her work, writing in 1970 that:

> It seems rather silly to have made these big portfolios giving all the importance to carpets and the early decorations that can interest no-one. Whereas Tempe à Pailla and the Centre de Culture et Loisir and the Maison au Bord de la Mer . . . might still interest students and are much more important to me.

On October 25, 1976, Gray collapsed in her flat at Rue Bonaparte. Taken to hospital, she died the morning of Sunday, October 31. Her ashes were buried a few days later at Père Lachaise cemetery, in the presence of just a few friends, among them Louise Dany, who had served her faithfully throughout the years of ceaseless work, of neglect, and finally of rediscovery and acclaim.

Since her death, Gray's reputation has continued to grow. Working for the most part alone and for a small clientele—in the case of her architecture, largely for herself—her body of work was inevitably small. Nevertheless, in its entirety, it reflects the development of design through the first decades of this century, while also expressing a vision of modernity which is distinctively her own: thus, denying the concept of the house as simply a *machine à habiter,* she outlined her own philosophy of design, a philosophy which consistently took account of human needs and aspirations in a technological age.

> A house is not a machine to live in. It is the shell of man, his extension, his release, his spiritual emanation. Not only its visual harmony but its organisation as a whole, the whole work combined together, make it human in the most profound sense.

SOURCES:

Adam, Peter. *Eileen Gray, Architect-Designer: A Biography.* London: Thames and Hudson, 1987.

Garner, Philippe. *Eileen Gray: Design and Architecture 1878–1976.* Koln: Benedikt Taschen, 1993.

SUGGESTED READING:

Johnson, J. Stewart. *Eileen Gray: Designer, 1879–1976.* London: Debrett's Peerage for Victoria and Albert Museum, 1979.

Loye, Brigitte. *Eileen Gray, 1879–1976: Architecture Design.* Paris: Analeph-J.P. Viguier, 1983.

Rykwert, Joseph. "Eileen Gray: pioneer of design," in *Architectural Review.* Vol. CLII. December 1972, pp. 357–361.

Rosemary Raughter,
freelance writer in women's history, Dublin, Ireland

Gray, Elizabeth Janet (1902–1999).

See Vining, Elizabeth Gray.

Gray, Gilda (1901–1959)

See Bow, Clara for sidebar.

Gray, Hanna Holborn (1930—)

American educator and president of the University of Chicago from 1978 to 1993. Born Hanna Holborn in Heidelberg, Germany, on October 25, 1930; second child and only daughter of Hajo Holborn (a European historian and educator) and Annemarie (Bettmann) Holborn; immigrated to the United States, 1934; naturalized citizen, 1940; Bryn Mawr College, Bryn Mawr, Pennsylvania, A.B., 1950; attended St. Anne's College, Oxford University, as a Fulbright Scholar, 1950–51; Harvard University, Ph.D., 1957; married Charles Montgomery Gray (an educator), on June 19, 1954; no children.

By her own account an "independent, stubborn, and bad-tempered" child, Hanna Holborn Gray was born into a distinguished academic family in Heidelberg, Germany, in 1930. In 1934, after her father was dismissed from his academic post because of his opposition to the Nazi party, the family made their way to the United States, settling in New Haven, Connecticut, where Professor Holborn became a member of the Yale University faculty. As youngsters, Gray and her older brother were strictly disciplined. "We were brought up under all kinds of German theories," she said in an interview with *People* magazine (October 30, 1978). "We weren't allowed to use pillows, and we had to eat rye bread. White American bread was some kind of unhealthy thing." Although much of Gray's life was restricted, her intellectual pursuits were not, and she took full advantage of the educational opportunities that were offered. At age 15, she entered Bryn Mawr, graduating summa cum laude in 1950. After attending Oxford on a Fulbright scholarship, she entered Radcliffe College to work on her Ph.D, which, after a brief hiatus to teach history at Bryn Mawr (1953–54), she received in 1957. Meanwhile on June 19, 1954, she had married Charles Montgomery Gray, a fellow Harvard graduate student.

Gray's teaching career began at Harvard University, where she was a popular history instructor before quickly advancing to the rank of assistant professor. In 1960, she moved with her husband to Chicago, where he was an associate professor at the University of Chicago. After a year as a research fellow at the Newberry Library, she

Hanna
Holborn
Gray

also joined the university faculty as an assistant professor of history. By 1964, she had obtained tenure and been promoted to associate professor. During the latter 1960s, in addition to heading up the history department, Gray worked with her husband editing the *Journal of Modern History*.

In 1972, Gray left the University of Chicago to become the first woman dean of arts and sciences at Northwestern University in Evanston, Illinois, a post she held until July 1974, when she returned to New Haven to become the Provost of Yale. She was not only the first woman in that post, but one of only a handful of non-Yale graduates so appointed. Gray brought the university through a major fiscal deficit by judiciously cutting nonessential programs without sacrificing educational excellence. In 1977, when Yale's president Kingman Brewster, Jr. stepped down to become U.S. ambassador to Great Britain, Gray became acting president, and ultimately one of the prime candidates for the presidency. Quite unexpectedly, however, in July 1977, she withdrew from contention to accept the "irresistible invitation" to succeed John T. Wilson as the tenth president of the University of Chicago. The first woman to serve as chief executive officer of a major American coeducational institution, Gray candidly admitted having some qualms about accepting the position, but also felt that her history with the institution would be an invaluable asset.

Gray's major objective was to maintain the university's academic integrity within the framework of the recession-inflation cycle of the 1970s, a goal she achieved through rigorous belt-tightening and sound planning for the future. Part of her strategy was to make the undergraduate college "more visible" and to revise the student-loan program, allowing students to repay their loans over a longer period of time. During her 15-year tenure, Gray, who called herself an "old-fashioned Bryn Mawr feminist," also expanded teaching and administrative opportunities for women. "I'm interested in the goals of equal opportunity in general," she told Paul Galloway in an interview for the Chicago *Sun-Times* (July 16, 1978). "That includes equal opportunity for women. I'm interested in being sure that people are able, through their own competence, to develop their own independence. These are goals for women, but they are also goals for people. I find it hard to make the distinction."

Gray, who resigned from her position at Chicago in 1993 and returned to a teaching position in the history department, is described by friends and colleagues as a warm and unfailingly cheerful woman who is an avid baseball and football fan. She also has a reputation as an accomplished mimic, and at one time was known for a particularly adept imitation of Henry Kissinger.

SOURCES:

McHenry, Robert, ed. *Famous American Women*. NY: Dover, 1983.

Moritz, Charles, ed. *Current Biography 1978*. NY: H.W. Wilson, 1978.

Gray, Nicolete (1911–1997)

British art historian and designer of lettering who organized the first international exhibition of abstract art held in England and who designed and carved the tombstone of Agatha Christie and the façade lettering of Sotheby's. Born Nicolete Mary Binyon in Stevenage, Hertfordshire, on July 20, 1911; died in London on June 8, 1997; daughter of Laurence Binyon (1869–1943, a poet and literary critic) and Cicely Margaret (Powell) Binyon; had two sisters; married Basil Gray, in 1933; children: two sons, three daughters, including **Camilla Gray Prokofiev** (a Russian art historian, d. 1971).

Selected writings: A History of Lettering: Creative Experiment and Letter Identity *(Boston: D.R. Godine, 1986)*; Rossetti, Dante and Ourselves *(London: Faber and Faber, 1947)*; Jacob's Ladder: A Bible Picture Book from Anglo-Saxon and 12th Century English MSS *(London: Faber and Faber, 1949)*; Lettering as Drawing *(NY: Taplinger Publishing, 1982)*; Lettering on Buildings *(London: Architectural Press, 1960)*; Nineteenth Century Ornamented Typefaces *(rev. ed. London: Faber & Faber, 1976)*; "The Palaeography of Latin Inscriptions in the Eighth, Ninth and Tenth Centuries in Italy," *in* Papers of the British School at Rome *(Vol. 16, 1948)*.

Born in the summer of 1911, during the final years of Edwardian England's unchallenged supremacy of the globe, Nicolete Mary Binyon was the daughter of **Cicely Powell Binyon** and Laurence Binyon, a gifted poet and literary critic who worked at the British Museum as a curator of oriental prints and drawings, and whose broad intellectual interests included William Blake, the English watercolorists, and all aspects of oriental art and culture. She was christened Nicolete after Aucassin's beloved in the medieval French lyric *Aucassin and Nicolete*.

Nicolete grew up in London's Chelsea district, and while she was born too late to encounter Oscar Wilde, who had lived on her street more than a decade earlier, the renowned painter John Singer Sargent was a neighbor of the Binyon family. Even before she began her formal education, Nicolete was exposed to the world of the arts and literature by her father, to whom she would always remain close. Besides being constantly stimulated by a home environment that invariably included many of the leading artists and writers of the day, the precocious girl was able to spend countless happy hours at the British Museum as well as at numerous art galleries and bookshops. Enrolled at London's prestigious St. Paul's School, Nicolete was an excellent student and active in extracurricular activities including taking her classmates to galleries, museums, plays and the ballet. She also had a keen sense of public affairs, running on the Labour Party ticket in the school's mock elections, using as her slogan "Vote for Binyon and a Better Britain."

After graduating with distinction from St. Paul's School in 1929, Nicolete was awarded a scholarship to study history at Lady Margaret Hall, Oxford University. At Oxford, she quickly discovered that she had a deep affinity for the early centuries of medieval history. Her deep interest in the middle ages, an age of belief, was not purely intellectual in that her reading of Christian theologians, particularly the works of St. Augustine, drew her inexorably toward a personal religious faith, and in 1931 she converted to Roman Catholicism. In 1932, Nicolete was awarded a scholarship by the British School at Rome to study post-classical inscriptions in Italy. Traveling throughout Italy on her own, she went from town to town, monastery to monastery, making papier-maché moulds by brushing wet paper into the crevices of ancient inscriptions.

In 1933, Nicolete returned to England one year ahead of schedule in order to marry Basil Gray, who worked as an assistant keeper in her father's department of the British Museum. Nicolete Gray became a loyal partner to her husband, helping him rearrange the museum's Indian Room. Her rapidly growing knowledge of lettering enabled her to write several chapters in her husband's 1937 book *The English Print* (her name does not appear on the title page, given the fact that he was the volume's sole contracted author).

In 1936, Gray revealed a new facet of her many talents when she organized a large-scale art exhibition entitled "Abstract and Concrete," which opened in Oxford and then moved to Cambridge, Liverpool and London. For the first time, many Britishers were exposed to the startling new artistic visions of foreign artists revealed in paintings by Kandinsky, Miro and Mondrian, sculpture by Giacometti, a mobile by Alexander Calder, and constructions by Laszlo Moholy-Nagy and Naum Gabo. To illustrate the universality of these new artistic impulses, the exhibition also provided space for the creations of contemporary British artists including Moore, Nicholson, Piper, and *Barbara Hepworth. The entire exhibit had been organized on a minuscule budget because at that time Christie's declared the art works to have only a minimal market value, thus virtually eliminating problems from insurance or Crown customs officials. Despite—or perhaps because of—Nicolete Gray's love for medieval civilization, she was always responsive to new ideas and stimuli, and was enthusiastic about

contemporary art, which she was convinced marked the fact that they stood "at the beginning of a new civilisation." To show her strong commitment to modern art, she purchased a Mondrian painting. Her first book, published in 1938 under the title *Nineteenth Century Ornamental Types and Title Pages*, quickly became accepted as a classic work of scholarship and appeared in an extensively revised edition in 1976.

By the middle of World War II, Gray had given birth to five children. She spent the war years at Oxford, where she and her family had been evacuated from bomb-threatened London, not only ministering to her large brood but working for the Ministry of Food, where she kept busy "dispensing timber and steel to jam manufacturers." The amount of work taken on by Gray during the war was staggering, including caring for five children with little domestic help, working for the Ministry of Food, and attempting to keep several research projects alive. Soon after the war, she suffered a physical breakdown but fully recovered. Despite all, she was able to publish *Rossetti, Dante and Ourselves* (1947), a concise but brilliant study of romantic love as depicted in art.

In the 1950s, as her children were rapidly maturing, Gray was able to devote ever more time to her investigations of lettering. Sometimes she left library work behind to go on "inscription crawls" in the British Isles and abroad, invariably returning with large number of photographs. In 1953, Nikolaus Pevsner asked her to contribute articles on lettering to the *Architectural Review*. Collected and published in book form in 1960 as *Lettering on Buildings*, these essays were immediately acclaimed as representing another definitive study of an important and hitherto underappreciated topic. At this time, Gray also taught courses in medieval history at Sacred Heart and Sion, local convent schools.

Starting in 1964, she began teaching lettering at the Central School of Art and Design. Until her retirement in 1981, she taught popular courses there, also founding and rapidly building up at the school a major archive, the Central Lettering Record, which collected photographic and other data relating to every aspect of lettering, historic as well as contemporary. If it is clear that many of Gray's students learned an immeasurable amount from her during the years she taught lettering at the Central School of Art and Design, it is also certain that she was able to learn much from them. In particular, her Asian students were able to teach her at firsthand the countless nuances of Oriental scripts.

In 1976, Gray's classic 1938 work on 19th-century ornamented typefaces was published in a new and greatly enhanced format, earning universal acclaim. A decade later, her last book *A History of Lettering: Creative Experiment and Letter Identity* was released to an eager public. Once more, praise came from all corners, noting that the work would not only serve for many years as a superb textbook, but as a deeply felt artistic credo about the artistic quality and communicative function of letters. Refusing to separate academic knowledge from practical skills, Gray mastered the art of letter-cutting in the 1950s. During the next several decades, she created a number of notable works including the wall of writers' names at the Stratford Shakespeare Centre, the facade lettering of Sotheby's, several works for Westminster Cathedral, and the tombstone of *Agatha Christie.

After the retirement of Basil Gray from the British Museum in 1969, both he and Nicolete lived at Long Wittenham on the Thames, where she continued to write and regularly commuted to London to teach. The last decades of her life were full of the rewards of continuing hard work and lifelong friendships, as when Gray was chosen to be the first woman member of the Double Crown, a previously all-male dining club of printers and typographers. Many friends young and old would visit the Gray home, and a fictionalized sketch of the effervescent intellectual life that flourished there is to be found in **Margaret Drabble**'s novel *Jerusalem the Golden*. But there was also tragedy. Gray's eldest daughter Camilla, a brilliant historian of Russian art who was married to Oleg Prokofiev, son of the great composer, died in 1971. And even before her husband's death in 1989, Nicolete Gray's health had begun to decline. Over the next years, she bore the burdens of a failing memory and Parkinson's disease in a spirit of acceptance, dying in London on June 8, 1997.

SOURCES:

Barker, Nicolas. "Nicolete Gray," in *The Independent* [London]. June 13, 1997, p. 20.

Caraman, Philip, ed. *Saints and Ourselves*. Ann Arbor, MI: Servant Books, 1981.

Drabble, Margaret. *Jerusalem the Golden: A Novel*. London: Weidenfeld & Nicolson, 1967.

Gray, Basil. *The English Print*. London: A. & C. Black, 1937.

Gray, Camilla. *The Great Experiment: Russian Art, 1863–1922*. London: Thames and Hudson, 1962.

McQuiston, Liz. *Women in Design: A Contemporary View*. NY: Rizzoli, 1988.

"Nicolete Gray," in *Daily Telegraph* [London]. June 16, 1997, p. 23.

"Nicolete Gray," in *The Times* [London]. June 13, 1997, p. 23.

John Haag,
Associate Professor of History,
University of Georgia, Athens, Georgia

Grayson, Betty Evans (1925–1979)

American softball pitcher. Name variations: Betty Evans. Born Betty Evans in Portland, Oregon, on October 9, 1925; died on July 9, 1979.

Played 17 years as an amateur, with a record of 465 wins and 91 losses, and three as a pro with the Chicago Queens.

Betty Evans Grayson was born in Portland, Oregon, in 1925 and was a softball star in the Portland City League by the time she was 13. Originally an outfielder, she began to excel at pitching under her father's coaching. She was asked to join Erv Lind's Florists, a Portland softball team, and Portland fans began to call her "Bullet Betty" because of her exceptional pitching arm. In her 17 years with the Florists, Grayson had 465 wins and 91 losses, pitching three perfect games and 125 consecutive scoreless innings. In 1943, she led the Florists to the world title and the next year to the national championship. She had an unusual opportunity as a female softball player to become a pro. Grayson signed with the Chicago Queens and played three seasons. In 1950, she had a 35-5 record. In 1944, she was named Oregon Woman Athlete of the Year (1944); she was also named to the National Softball Hall of Fame (1959).

Karin Loewen Haag,
Athens, Georgia

Grayson, Kathryn (1922—)

American actress, singer, and star of many MGM musicals. Born Zelma Kathryn Hedrick on February 9, 1922, in Winston-Salem, North Carolina; attended Manual Arts High School, Hollywood, California; married John Shelton (an actor), in 1940 (divorced 1946); married Johnny Johnston (singer-actor), in 1947 (divorced 1951); children: (second marriage) one daughter, Patricia.

Filmography: Andy Hardy's Private Secretary *(1941);* The Vanishing Virginian *(1942);* Rio Rita *(1942);* Seven Sweethearts *(1942);* Thousands Cheer *(1943);* Anchors Aweigh *(1945);* Ziegfeld Follies *(1946);* Two Sisters from Boston *(1946);* Till the Clouds Roll By *(1946);* It Happened in Brooklyn *(1947);* The Kissing Bandit *(1948);* That Midnight Kiss *(1949);* The Toast of New Orleans *(1950);* Grounds for Marriage *(1951);* Show Boat *(1951)* Lovely to Look At *(1952);* The Desert Song *(1953);* So This Is Love *(1953);* Kiss Me Kate *(1953);* The Vagabond King *(1956).*

A petite brunette, with a heart-shaped face and a coloratura voice, Kathryn Grayson was headed for an operatic career when she was

Kathryn Grayson

During World War II, Grayson left the screen for two years, during which time she entertained for the war effort and made radio appearances. She wanted to pursue an operatic career, but Mayer held her to her contract, and she returned to movie making. Her career continued to founder until 1949, when the studio teamed her in two films with Mario Lanza: *That Midnight Kiss* (1949) and *The Toast of New Orleans* (1950). The two had screen chemistry and formed an off-screen friendship that would endure until Lanza's untimely death in 1959.

The lavish movie operettas of the 1950s added to Grayson's lustre, though by that time the genre was on its way out. In a remake of *Show Boat* (1951), she was cast opposite Howard Keel, with whom she sang the duets "Make Believe," "You Are Love," and "Why Do I Love You?" The movie was such a box-office hit that she was reteamed with Keel in a remake of *Roberta,* titled *Lovely to Look At* (1952). Grayson was then loaned to Warner Bros. for what was to be a quartet of musicals, but only two materialized: *The Desert Song* (1953) and *So This is Love* (1953). Neither had much success. Back at MGM, she was again partnered with Keel in *Kiss Me Kate* (1953), perhaps the best of her brief career. Grayson's final movie was *The Vagabond King* (1956), which had been developed for Grayson and Lanza, but because of his health problems, Lanza was replaced by Oreste, a little-known opera singer.

Unfortunately, Grayson's voice was captured on few recordings, since Mayer refused to allow his stars to make outside recording deals. She did, however, record some of her movie songs for MGM Records, as well as an album, *Kathryn Grayson Sings*.

In the fall of 1955, Grayson had made her dramatic television debut in "Shadows of the Heart" on the "General Electric Theater" series, for which she was nominated for an Emmy. When her movie career ended, she returned to television for roles in "Playhouse 90" and "Lux Playhouse." She also went back to the concert stage and in 1960 appeared in productions of the operas *Madame Butterfly, La Bohème,* and *La Traviata.* As well, she starred in the operettas *The Merry Widow, Rosalinda,* and *Naughty Marietta* and toured in a production of *Camelot.* (A bid to replace **Julie Andrews** in the Broadway production fell through.)

In 1969, Grayson reteamed with Howard Keel for a night-club act that played in Las Vegas to fairly good reviews. She and Keel continued to make club appearances throughout the 1970s

lured into the movies. After studying voice as a child, Grayson was a teenager when she came to the attention of Louis B. Mayer, who heard her sing at a city festival and offered her a contract (with thoughts, perhaps, of grooming her to compete with songbird *Deanna Durbin, then under contract to Universal). Much to the surprise of her vocal coach **Minna Letha White**, Grayson accepted the lucrative offer. To supplement her performance experience, MGM negotiated a regular spot for her on "The Eddie Cantor Show" and encouraged her to take some acting lessons.

Grayson made an auspicious film debut in *Andy Hardy's Private Secretary* (1941), one of a series that starred Mickey Rooney, in which she sang an aria from an opera. In her second movie, *The Vanishing Virginians* (1942), she captured attention with a lilting rendition of "The World Was Made for You." In the middle of launching her film career, Grayson married John Shelton, another MGM player. The marriage was troubled from the beginning and ended in divorce in 1946. In 1947, Grayson would marry actor Johnny Johnston and a year later give birth to her only child, Patricia. After she and Johnston divorced in 1951, the actress never remarried.

and co-starred in a well-received production of *The Man of La Mancha*. During the 1980s, Grayson occasionally appeared on television, notably in an episode of "Murder She Wrote," with **Gloria DeHaven.**

SOURCES:

Parish, James Robert, and Michael R. Pitts. *Hollywood Songsters.* NY: Garland, 1991.

Barbara Morgan,
Melrose, Massachusetts

Greatorex, Eliza (1820–1897)

American artist. Born Eliza Pratt in Ireland on December 25, 1820; died in 1897; married Henry W. Greatorex (a composer and organist), in 1849.

Eliza Greatorex was born Eliza Pratt in Ireland on December 25, 1820, and arrived in New York in 1840. After studying there and in Paris, she produced many landscape paintings but later devoted herself to etching and pen-and-ink work, for which she is chiefly remembered. In 1869, she drew a series of historic buildings and scenes in and around New York. Her publications include *The Homes of Oberammergau, Summer Etchings in Colorado,* and *Old New York from the Battery to Bloomingdale.* In 1868, Greatorex was elected associate of the National Academy.

Gredal, Eva (1927—)

Danish politician and government official. Born in Copenhagen in 1927; married; four children.

An office worker who attended university classes in the evenings, Eva Gredal was a social worker for several years before pursuing her political interests. She served as chair of the National Social Advice Association from 1959 to 1967, and was vice-chair of the National Association of Women from 1967 to 1971. In 1971, she was elected to Parliament by a Copenhagen constituency. She served as Minister for Social Affairs from 1971 to 1973, and again from 1977 to 1978, when a change in government prompted her resignation. Gredal was elected to the European Parliament in 1979.

Greece, queen of.

Green, Alice Stopford (1847–1929)

Historian and nationalist, whose studies of the Irish past justified claims to political independence. Name variations: Mrs. Stopford Green. Born Alice Sophia Amelia Stopford on May 30, 1847, in Kells, Co. Meath, Ireland; died on May 28, 1929, in Dublin; daughter of Edward Stopford (rector of Kells and archdeacon of Meath) and Ann (Duke) Stopford; educated at home and attended lectures at College of Science, Dublin, 1873–74; married John Richard Green, in 1877 (died 1883); no children.

Selected writings: Henry II *(1888);* Town Life in the Fifteenth Century *(1894);* The Making of Ireland and Its Undoing *(1908);* Irish Nationality *(1911);* The Old Irish World *(1912);* Women's Place in the World of Letters *(1913);* The Irish National Tradition *(1917);* Loyalty and Disloyalty: What It Means in Ireland *(1918);* Ourselves Alone in Ulster *(1918);* The Government of Ireland *(1921);* Studies from Irish History *(1926).*

Describing her upbringing to a friend, the adult Alice Stopford Green claimed that she had been "bred up in a remote part of Ireland, in a poverty-stricken home" and had "struggled at self culture in every imaginable adverse circumstance." The account, as her biographer remarks, is "highly colored." Nevertheless, Alice's version of events does convey her dissatisfaction with the options available to her as a middle-class woman at that time, and her wish to put a distance between her past and the career and convictions which she was subsequently to adopt.

Born in 1847, Alice Stopford was the seventh child and third daughter of Archdeacon Edward Stopford and **Anne Duke Stopford.** Alice, educated at home, had access to her father's considerable library, and began to teach herself Greek, German, and metaphysics. When she was about 16, financial difficulties forced a number of changes in the family's way of life, and at around the same time Alice was attacked by an eye ailment which prevented her from reading for a number of years. However, her thirst for learning did not diminish, and when the family moved to Dublin in 1873 she managed to obtain permission from the authorities to attend lectures in physics at the College of Science.

Following Edward Stopford's death in 1874, Alice, her sister, and her mother moved to England, and in 1877 she found a new role with her marriage to the historian John Richard Green. The partnership was to bring her not only great personal happiness but also a profession as her husband's research assistant and collaborator, and when John died in 1883 after a long illness, Alice took on the task of producing a revised edition of his *Short History of the English People*. She followed this with a life of Henry II (1888) and a two-volume study, *Town Life in the Fifteenth Century* (1894). In 1913, she made a brief excursion into the field of women's history with *Women's Place in the World of Letters,* in which she expressed her belief in women's potential to "open new horizons where men's vision has stopped short."

As a celebrated hostess, Stopford Green entertained some of the leading politicians and artists of the day. Her friends included the Fabian reformer *Beatrice Webb and the traveler and anthropologist *Mary Kingsley, who kindled her interest in African affairs. In 1900, she traveled to St. Helena to visit the camps in which Boer prisoners of war were being detained and, in 1901, helped to found the African Society, with which she was closely involved for over a decade.

Stopford Green's African studies left her critical of aspects of colonial policy and impacted on her relationship with her own country. Discarding her family's allegiance to the political union between Britain and Ireland, she became a supporter of the Irish nationalist cause, and this commitment was increasingly reflected in her work. The approved version of Irish history was, she believed, "a political myth," designed to validate English aggression, and she determined to produce a new account which would celebrate the Gaelic inheritance and justify nationalist aspirations. *The Making of Ireland and Its Undoing* appeared in 1908, followed in 1911 by *Irish Nationality*. Though criticized for her partisanship and for romanticization of Gaelic culture and society, she won the admiration of nationalist scholars: as her friend Eoin McNeill declared, she inspired "the people of Ireland with the spirit and hope of a sound future development."

Stopford Green also took an active part in nationalist politics. In 1913, she joined her friend Roger Casement in an unsuccessful effort to rally Protestant support for home rule, and in the following year chaired a committee which raised funds for the importation of arms from Germany into Ireland. Despite her involvement in this affair, she was essentially a constitutionalist, and for that reason disapproved of the republican uprising of 1916. Nevertheless, her nationalist commitment was unshaken: she took a leading part in the campaign for the reprieve of Casement, sentenced to death for treason, and in the following year made the decision to move back to Ireland.

In Dublin, Stopford Green quickly established herself as a central figure in political and cultural life. A supporter of the Anglo-Irish Treaty which ended the War of Independence, she was a member of the pro-Treaty women's organization Cumann na Saoirse (League of Freedom) and a founding member of the political party, Cumann na nGael. Nominated to the first Irish Senate as one of four women members, she served on a committee to establish a scheme for the publication of Irish-language manuscripts, and supported W.B. Yeats' call for the retention of the right to divorce. Meanwhile, she continued her researches in Irish history, her last work, *Studies from Irish History*, appearing in 1926 when she was 79. Three years later, on May 28, 1929, she died in Dublin following a short illness, leaving behind her a body of work which, for good or ill, shaped the version of Irish history which predominated during the formative years of the new state.

SOURCES:

McDowell, R.B. *Alice Stopford Green: A Passionate Historian.* Dublin: Allen Figgis, 1967.

Thirsk, Joan. "The history women," in *Chattel, Servant or Citizen: Women's Status in Church, State and Society.* Edited by Mary O'Dowd and Sabine Wichert. Belfast: Institute of Irish Studies, 1995, pp. 1–11.

COLLECTIONS:

Alice Stopford Green Papers, National Library of Ireland, Dublin.

Rosemary Raughter,
Freelance Writer in Women's History, Dublin, Ireland

Green, Anna Katharine

(1846–1935)

American writer who was called the mother of detective fiction. Name variations: Anna Katharine Green Rohlfs; Mrs. Rohlfs. Born in Brooklyn, New York, on November 11, 1846; died in Buffalo, New York, on April 11, 1935; daughter of James Wilson (a lawyer) and Katharine Ann (Whitney) Green; attended public school in Brooklyn and Buffalo, New York; Ripley Female College (now Green Mountain College), Poultney, Vermont, B.A., 1866; married Charles Rohlfs (an actor turned designer), in November 1884; children: a daughter and two sons.

Selected works: The Leavenworth Case *(1878);* A Strange Disappearance *(1880);* The Defense of the Bride and Other Poems *(1882);* Hand and Ring *(1883);* Marked "Personal" *(1893);* The Doctor, His Wife, and the Clock *(1895);* That Affair Next Door *(1897);* Lost Man's Lane *(1898);* Agatha Webb *(1899);* The Circular Study *(1900);* The Filigree Ball *(1903);* The House in the Mist *(1905);* The Millionaire Baby *(1905);* The Amethyst Box *(1905);* The

Woman in the Alcove *(1906)*; The Chief Legatee *(1906)*; The Mayor's Wife *(1907)*; The House of the Whispering Pines *(1910)*; Initials Only *(1911)*; Masterpieces of Mystery *(1913, reissued in 1919 as* Room Number Three and Other Detective Stories*)*; The Mystery of the Hasty Arrow *(1917)*; The Step on the Stair *(1923)*.

Anna Katharine Green, who is credited with developing the American detective story, had hoped to become a poet and was encouraged in college by a meeting with Ralph Waldo Emerson, who evidently responded favorably to some of her early efforts in verse. Curious, then, was the appearance of her first book, *The Leavenworth Case* (1878), a detective story, which turned out to be a runaway hit, selling over 150,000 copies. Green's only predecessors in the genre were Edgar Allan Poe and Wilkie Collins, and her fictional detective Ebenezer Gryce anticipated the later Sherlock Holmes by nearly a decade. Green's first hit was followed by *A Strange Disappearance* (1880) and *Hand and Ring* (1883). When her two volumes of verse, *The Defense of the Bride and other Poems* (1882) and *Risifi's Daughter* (1887), failed to gain recognition, she returned to detective stories with alacrity. Although Green's novels were not by any means distinguished literature, they were tightly plotted, well-constructed, and extremely popular. Her knowledge of criminal law, which she obtained from her father, kept her stories within the bounds of probability, an absolute necessity in any good mystery, she believed. Also essential, she thought, was an interesting plot with a twist, and a narrative that rises steadily to a climax that surprises the reader. The formula she developed continues to dominate the genre.

Green was described as a shy, mild-mannered woman who enjoyed a quiet life in Buffalo, New York, with her husband and three children. She was married to Charles Rohlfs, an actor turned furniture designer, who later became known for his art nouveau designs. During his acting days, Rohlfs played in a dramatization of *The Leavenworth Case*, a performance that sparked such renewed interest in the book that a second edition was brought out in 1934. Anna Katharine Green died on April 11, 1935, in her 89th year.

Green, Constance McLaughlin

(1897–1975)

American author, teacher, military historian at the Pentagon and winner of the Pulitzer Prize in History.

Born Constance Winsor McLaughlin on August 21, 1897, in Ann Arbor, Michigan; died in 1975; one of six children of Andrew Cunningham McLaughlin (a historian and college professor) and Lois Thompson (Angell) McLaughlin; graduated from University High School, Chicago, Illinois, 1914; attended the University of Chicago; Smith College, B.A., 1919; Mount Holyoke College, M.A. in history, 1925; Yale University, Ph.D., 1937; married Donald Ross Green (a textile manufacturer), on February 14, 1921 (died, November 1946); children: one son and two daughters.

Anna Katharine Green

Constance McLaughlin Green, whose father was a noted historian and college professor, closely followed his career path, even duplicating his Pulitzer Prize in History. She was born in 1897 in Ann Arbor, Michigan, and began her schooling in Chicago, where the family moved after her father joined the faculty of the University of Chicago. After graduating from high school, she attended school in Germany for a term before enrolling at the University of Chicago. After two years there, she transferred to Smith College, receiving her B.A. in 1919. She taught freshman English at the University of Chicago and at Smith before her marriage in 1921 to Donald Ross Green, a textile manufacturer. The couple moved to Holyoke, Massachusetts, where Green enrolled at Mount Holyoke College in nearby South Hadley. She earned her M.A. in 1925, after which she combined a part-time teaching position with growing family responsibility. During the Depression, Green raised three children and studied for her doctorate at Yale University. In 1937, one year after her father won the Pulitzer Prize in History for *The Constitutional History of the United States*, she received her Ph.D. and also won Yale's Edward Eggleston Prize in History. Her dissertation, *Holyoke, Massachusetts: A Case History of the Industrial Revolution in America*, published in 1939, was a pioneering work on urban evolution that presented a well-documented, yet highly readable, study on Holyoke's transformation from an agrarian town to an industrial center.

Green returned to Smith College, this time as a history instructor, a post she held until 1942, when the United States entered World War II. At that time, she left Smith to become an Army Ordinance Department historian at the Springfield Armory in Springfield, Massachusetts. After the death of her husband in 1946, she moved to Washington, D.C., where she worked as a consulting historian for the Red Cross. In 1948, she became chief historian for the Army Ordinance Corps, heading a research team in writing a volume on the technical services. She left her post in 1951, because, as she told the Washington *Sunday Star* (May 20, 1952), "the brass tried repeatedly to speed up the historians."

After a stint as a lecturer at University College in London, Green returned to Washington to work as a historian at the research and development board for the Office of the Secretary of Defense. In 1954, she was named head of the Washington history project, which was funded by a six-year Rockefeller Foundation grant. The project culminated in *Washington, Village and Capital, 1800–1878*, published in 1962, which won critical acclaim. John McKelway, described the book in the Washington *Sunday Star* (May 20, 1962), as an "entertaining narrative of the life of the city and its people, many of whom came up from slavery. More than anything else, perhaps, it is a tale of Washington trying to live up to its name." Arthur Schlesinger, Jr., then special assistant to President John F. Kennedy, called the book "lucid," "authoritative," and "enthralling." For the work, Green was awarded the 1963 Pulitzer Prize in History. Upon hearing the news, she set out to buy her grandson a pair of bright, new red suspenders. "My mother told my father that she certainly hoped he would not invest [his Pulitzer] money, but would spend it for some fun or something he really wanted," Green explained to **Dorothy McCardle** of the Washington *Post* (May 8, 1963). "My father thought a minute, and then he said that yes, he would have some fun with it. He'd go out and buy a new pair of suspenders."

Green produced a second and longer companion volume of Washington history, *Washington, Capital City 1879–1950*, in 1963. Her other books include *History of Naugatuck, Connecticut* (1949), *Eli Whitney and the Birth of American Technology* (1956), and *American Cities in the Growth of the Nation* (1957). She also contributed chapters to a number of other historical works and authored articles for leading American encyclopedias and journals. De-

scribed as a small, bouncy woman with a "tartness in her talk," Green enjoyed camping, gardening, and reading, particularly detective stories, which at one time she tried to write until she discovered that she couldn't come up with a valid plot line. Constance Green died in 1975.

SOURCES:

Moritz, Charles, ed. *Current Biography 1963*. NY: H.W. Wilson, 1963.

Green, Edith Starrett (1910–1987)

American politician who served in the U.S. Congress from 1954 to 1974. Born Edith Starrett in Trent, South Dakota, on January 17, 1910; died in Tulatin, Oregon, on April 21, 1987; daughter of James Vaughn Starrett and Julia (Hunt) Starrett (both schoolteachers); grew up in Oregon; attended Willamette University and University of Oregon, B.S., 1939; graduate studies at Stanford University; married Arthur N. Green (a businessman), on August 19, 1933; children: James S. Green; Richard A. Green.

Edith Starrett Green was born Edith Starrett in Trent, South Dakota, in 1910, the daughter of James Vaughn Starrett and **Julia Hunt Starrett**, both schoolteachers. Six years later, the family moved to Oregon. Early in her career, Edith Green taught in the 1930s and 1940s, enjoyed a stint as radio announcer in Portland, and directed several statewide educational conferences while serving as legislative chair of the Oregon Congress of Parents and Teachers. After an unsuccessful campaign for Oregon's secretary of state in 1952, she entered the race for the U.S. House seat as a Democrat from Oregon's 3rd District (1954), defeating Republican Tom McCall by 6,000 votes.

As a recognized expert on education policy, Green was appointed to the Committee on Education and Labor in her freshman year. During her House tenure (January 3, 1955–December 31, 1974), she served on various committees, including the Committee on Appropriations. She played a central role in the enactment of the National Defense Education Act (1958); authored the Higher Education Facilities Act (1963), Equal Pay Act (1963), and Higher Education Act (1972), which included Title IX, prohibiting institutions receiving federal funds from discriminating on the basis of sex; she was also responsible for the first federal program for undergraduate scholarships.

At successive Democratic National Conventions, Green was chosen to second the presidential nomination for Adlai Stevenson (1956) and

John F. Kennedy (1960). Declining Kennedy's offer of ambassador to Canada, Green was appointed to the Presidential Committee on the Status of Women which allowed her to focus on a pet concern: equal pay. Though she backed most of Lyndon Johnson's Great Society legislation, she incurred his wrath for voting against funding to escalate the Vietnam war. Disillusioned with social legislation, Green began to drift from the Democratic fold and was co-chair of Democrats for Gerald Ford in 1976. Upon her retirement, she taught at Warner Pacific College.

SUGGESTED READING:

Candee, Marjorie Dent, ed. *Current Biography.* NY: H.W. Wilson, 1956.

Green, Elizabeth Shippen

(1871–1954)

American illustrator and watercolorist. Born in Philadelphia, Pennsylvania, in 1871; died in Philadelphia in 1954; studied art at the Pennsylvania Academy; attended Drexel Institute, 1894; married Huger Elliott (an architect and teacher), in 1911; no children.

Known as an excellent draftswoman and a brilliant colorist, illustrator Elizabeth Shippen Green studied at the Pennsylvania Academy with Thomas Eakins, Robert Vonnoh, and Thomas Anshutz. At age 18, she sold her first illustration to the *Philadelphia Times* for 50 cents, after which her work began to pop up in many of the popular journals of the day, including *Ladies' Home Journal*, *Saturday Evening Post*, and *Harper's Weekly*. In 1894, while attending Howard Pyle's class at Drexel Institute, she met *Violet Oakley and *Jessie Willcox Smith, who became her lifelong friends and collaborators. The three women shared a studio-home until Green's marriage in 1911 to architect and teacher Huger Elliott. After her husband's death in 1951, she returned to the Philadelphia area to be near her friends.

Green illustrated over 20 books, most of them after her marriage, and was the first woman staff member of *Harper's* magazine. Strongly influenced by Art Nouveau and the Pre-Raphaelite movement, Green achieved a stained-glass effect in her illustrations through the use of outlines enclosing areas of brilliant color. She was also noted for her pen-and-inks and received numerous awards for her work. The artist died in Philadelphia in 1954.

Green, Henrietta (1834–1916).

See Green, Hetty.

Green, Hetty (1834–1916)

American financier, regarded at the time of her death as the wealthiest woman in the world. Born Henrietta Howland Robinson on November 23, 1834, in New Bedford, Massachusetts; died on July 3, 1916, in New York City; first of two children and only daughter of Edward Mott Robinson (a whaler and foreign trader) and Abby Slocum (Howland) Robinson; attended the Eliza Wing school in Sandwich and a private school in Boston, Massachusetts, run by Reverend Charles Russell Lowell and his wife Anna Cabot (Jackson) Lowell; married Edward Green (a partner in a foreign trade company), on July 11, 1867 (died 1902); children: Edward Henry (b. 1868); Sylvia Ann Green (b. 1871).

Born into wealth in New Bedford, Massachusetts, in 1834, Henrietta Green was the daughter of Edward Mott Robinson and **Abby Howland Robinson**. The Howlands were one of New England's great mercantile families, and Edward became a partner in the venerable firm of Isaac Howland, Jr. & Company upon the death

Edith Starrett Green

of Abby's father. Henrietta then became the sole heir of the Howland fortune with the death of her brother in infancy. Despite the family's wealth, Hetty was raised according to Quaker values: thrift and simplicity. From her father, a strict, strong-willed man, she acquired a keen business sense and an independence and aloofness which she carried into her adult life. Upon his death in 1865, and that of her maternal aunt **Sylvia Ann Howland** the same year, she inherited a fortune of about $10 million in outright bequests and trust funds. She would later file a law suit to obtain her aunt's entire estate based on a second deathbed will. The celebrated case would drag on for five years until an eminent handwriting expert testified that the second will was a forgery.

In July 1867, Hetty married Edward Green, a silk merchant who was a millionaire in his own right. The couple spent the first years of their marriage in England, where Edward served as director of three London banks. There, Hetty gave birth to two children: son Edward, called Ned (1868), and daughter Sylvia (1871). It was to be the only period of domesticity in Hetty's life, for upon their return to New York in 1874, she devoted herself to the management of her fortune. Aided by her husband and a legion of financial advisors, she purchased government bonds and railroad stocks, also maintaining a liquid fund for lending purposes. She purchased real estate or mortgages in Chicago, New York, Kansas City, St. Louis, and San Francisco. In 1885, Edward, who apparently was less conservative in his speculations than his wife, went bankrupt. Hetty refused to underwrite his debts, and the two separated, although they remained on good terms until his death in 1902. Contrary to later gossip, Hetty provided well for her children, who attended parochial schools. Sylvia lived with her mother until her marriage in 1909. Ned attended Fordham College and studied law in Chicago. He then went to work for his mother, first managing her real-estate holdings in Chicago, and then going to Texas, where he acted as his mother's agent in the purchase of a portion of the Texas & Midland Railroad. He eventually became president of the line and moved to Texas permanently.

Hetty became quite eccentric during her later years, and it is her strange behavior rather than her financial genius that dominates much of what has been written about her. For whatever reasons, she became distrustful and tight-fisted, dressing in rags and carrying bits of food around in her pockets. She reputedly lived in a series of run-down boardinghouses outside New

York City (some say for tax purposes), sought health care in free clinics, and haggled with shopkeepers over small purchases. Newspapers found her good copy, publishing apocryphal anecdotes about her behavior and dubbing her "the Witch of Wall Street." Of many stories that circulated about her miserliness was one about her supposed negligence in treating her son's knee injury. She tried to have it treated without charge at a number of public clinics, reportedly resulting in the eventual loss of his leg.

In 1910, when her financial affairs became overwhelming, Hetty called in her son, who organized the Westminster Company to take over the management of her fortune. When she died in 1916, at 81, she left her son and daughter an estate worth $100 million; over the years, she had increased her inheritance 20 times over. At the end, however, she was bitter about her reputation, which she said was determined by people who didn't really care to know anything about the real Hetty Green. "I am in earnest," she said, "therefore they picture me heartless. I go my own way, take no partners, risk nobody else's fortune, therefore I am Madame Ishmael, set against every man."

Following Hetty's death, her son ran through his inheritance at the rate of 5 million a year, with most of it spent on jewels, rare stamps and coins. When Ned died in 1936, Sylvia was the sole beneficiary. She died in 1951, bequeathing her fortune to schools, hospitals, churches, and the bookkeeper who had served the Green family for 36 years.

SOURCES:

James, Edward T., ed. *Notable American Women 1607–1950*. Cambridge, MA: The Belknap Press of Harvard University Press, 1971.

Ketchum, Richard M. "Faces from the Past—VI," *American Heritage*. April 1962.

McHenry, Robert. *Famous American Women*. NY: Dover, 1983.

SUGGESTED READING:

Sparkes, Boyden, and Samuel Taylor Moore. *The Witch of Wall Street: Hetty Green*. NY: Doubleday, 1935.

Barbara Morgan,
Melrose, Massachusetts

Green, Lucinda (1953—)

British equestrian, winner of World and European championships. Name variations: Lucinda Prior-Palmer. Born Lucinda Prior-Palmer in London, England, on November 7, 1953; daughter of a cavalry general; married David Green (an Australian Olympic rider), in 1981; children: two.

Won team gold in the European Junior Championships (1971); won Badminton Horse Trials on six different horses: Be Fair (1973), Wideawake (1976), George (1977), Killaire (1979), Regal Realm (1983), and Beagle Bay (1984); was runner up at the Badminton Horse Trials (1978 and 1980); won individual on Be Fair and team runner up in European championships (1975); won individual on George and team winner in European championships (1977); won individual on Regal Realm and was team winner at World championships (1982); was Olympic team captain and won team silver on Regal Realm (1984); won team gold in Burghley's European championships (1985) on Regal Realm.

A specialist in three-day eventing, Lucinda Green took Britain's prestigious Badminton Horse Trials six times on six different horses. "To win it six times against the sort of opposition that exists there suggests a great partnership between an outstanding rider and one or two wonder horses," writes Guy Wathen in *Great Horsemen of the World*. "To win six times on six different horses implies a truly great rider." Three-day eventing consists of dressage on the first day, cross country which includes steeplechase on the second, and show jumping on the third.

Daughter of a cavalry general, Lucinda Green started riding at age four. On her 15th birthday, she was given her horse Be Fair (whose sire was Fair and Square, winner at Burghley with **Sheila Willcox** in 1968). Be Fair was a brilliant horse, says Green, responsible for getting her into the world of eventing: she won a team gold at the Junior European championships at Wesel, Germany, in 1971, finished 5th at Badminton in 1972, and was victorious at Badminton in 1973. She also won a team bronze in the European championships at Kiev in 1973. Along with Princess *Anne, Janet Hodgson, Sue Hatherly, Green was on the first all-woman team ever selected to represent Britain in the European championships at Lumuhlen, West Germany, in 1975. (In equestrian events, men and women compete against each other and together.) It was also one of Britain's best performances. Green took the individual gold, Princess Anne the silver, and both won team silver. But in the Montreal Olympics in 1976, while jumping over the last fence, with a medal in sight, Be Fair pulled a tendon and spent his last years happily roaming a hunting field.

In 1973, Green had begun working with a tough, workmanlike horse named Wideawake, who had a propensity for skimming the fences or

Opposite page
Hetty
Green

Lucinda
Green

In 1982, on Regal Realm, Green was the individual winner and team winner at the World championships. She was also chosen Olympic team captain at the summer Olympics in Los Angeles in 1984, where she and her team—**Virginia Holgate**, Ian Stark, **Diana Clapham**—won the silver in the Team Three-Day Event. Green was also the winner of team gold in Burghley's European championships (1985) on Regal Realm.

SOURCES:
Wathen, Guy. *Great Horsemen of the World.* London: Trafalgar Square, 1990.

Green, Mrs. (d. 1791).
See Hippisley, Jane.

Green, Mrs. Stopford (1847–1929).
See Green, Alice Stopford.

Greenaway, Kate (1846–1901)

English illustrator of children's books whose particular style proved widely influential, making her a household name at home and abroad and spawning a host of imitators. Born on March 17, 1846, in Hoxton, London, England; died on November 6, 1901, in Frognal, Hampstead, London, of breast cancer; daughter of John Greenaway (an engraver and woodcut maker) and Elizabeth (Jones) Greenaway; studied at the Finsbury School of Art, the National Art Training School, Heatherley's School of Art, and Slade School of Art; never married; no children.

Published first book illustration (1867); established herself as a freelance illustrator (c. 1872); achieved independent success with Under the Window *(1879); published* Kate Greenaway's Birthday Book *(1880).*

Writings—all self-illustrated: Under the Window: Pictures and Rhymes for Children *(Routledge, 1878); (verses by Mrs. Sale Barker)* Kate Greenaway's Birthday Book for Children *(Routledge, 1880);* Art Hours: After Kate Greenaway *(McLoughlin, 1882);* Steps to Art: After Kate Greenaway *(McLoughlin, 1882);* Kate Greenaway's Almanack for 1883–95, 1897 *(14 volumes, Routledge, 1882–96);* Language of Flowers *(Routledge, 1884, featured in* The Complete Kate Greenaway, *Century House, 1967);* Kate Greenaway's Alphabet *(Routledge, 1885);* Marigold Garden: Pictures and Rhymes *(Routledge, 1885);* A Apple Pie *(Routledge, 1886);* Kate Greenaway's Book of Games *(Routledge, 1889);* Kate Greenaway's Pictures from Originals Presented by Her to John Ruskin and Other Personal Friends *(F. Warne, 1921); (ed. by Edward Ernest and Patricia Tracy Lowe)* The Kate Greenaway Treasury: An Anthology of the Illustrations and Writ-

taking them with him. Atop Wideawake, she won her second Badminton in 1976, but, writes Wathen, as Queen *Elizabeth II was presenting Green with her trophy, the horse "stopped in his tracks, reared up, and died." The reason for his sudden death has never been discovered. Then George arrived, but his past preceded him; the horse had fallen five times at major events. Though George clouted several fences on the steeplechase in 1977, he made no mistakes on the cross country. Green had taken her third Badminton.

Though Green had twice broken her collar bone, she was not prepared for a rugged ride in the European championships at Burghley in 1977. During the steeplechase, George began to hang to the left and became entangled in ropes. Green went flying over his head and was dragged by the reins under her horse's legs while he "thundered" on. Somehow Green managed to halt the horse, vault back into the saddle, and finish the course. Amazingly, she had picked up no time penalties. She and George went on to win the championship; then the 12-year-old George retired.

ings of Kate Greenaway *(World Publishing, 1967); (ed. by Bryan Holme)* The Kate Greenaway Book *(Viking, 1976).*

Illustrator: Diamonds and Toads, *in the "Aunt Louisa's London Toy Books" series (F. Warne, 1871); Marie Aulnoy,* Madame d'Aulnoy's Fairy Tales *(9 vols., Gall & Inglis, 1871); Aunt Cae (pseudonym of Henry Courtney Selous),* The Children of the Parsonage *(Griffith & Farran, 1874); Kathleen Knox,* Fairy Gifts; Or, A Wallet of Wonders *(Griffith & Farran, 1874); Knox,* Seven Birthdays; Or, The Children of Fortune *([London], 1875); (with Walter Crane)* Quiver of Love: A Collection of Valentines, M. Ward *(1876); Fanny LaBlanche,* Starlight Stories Told to Bright Eyes *(Griffith & Farran, 1877); Lady Colin Campbell (pseudonym of G.E. Brunefille),* Topo *(M. Ward, 1878); Charlotte Mary Yonge,* Heir of Redclyffe *(Macmillan, 1879); Yonge,* Heartsease *(Macmillan, 1879); George Weatherly,* The "Little Folks" Painting Book *(Cassell, 1879);* Mother Goose; Or, The Old Nursery Rhymes *(Routledge, 1881); Myles Birket Foster,* Day in a Child's Life *(Routledge, 1881); Ann and Jane Taylor,* Little Ann and Other Poems *(Routledge, 1882); Montgomerie Ranking and Thomas K. Tully,* Flowers and Fancies: Valentines Ancient and Modern *(M. Ward, 1882); Helen Zimmern,* Tales from the Edda *(Sonnenschein, 1883); (with others) Robert Ellice, compiler,* Songs for the Nursery: A Collection of Children's Poems, Old and New *(W. Mack, 1884); William Mavor,* English Spelling Book *(Routledge, 1884); John Ruskin, ed.,* Dame Wiggins of Lee and Her Seven Wonderful Cats *(G. Allen, 1885); Bret Harte,* The Queen of the Pirate Isle *(Chatto & Windus, 1886); William Allingham,* Rhymes for the Young Folk *(Cassell, 1887); Robert Browning,* The Pied Piper of Hamelin *(Routledge, 1888); Beatrice F. Cresswell,* Royal Progress of King Pepito *(Society for Promoting Christian Knowledge, 1889); Mary Annette Arnim,* April Baby's Book of Tunes *(Macmillan, 1900); Mabel H. Speilmann,* Littledom Castle and Other Tales *(Dutton, 1903). Contributor to various magazines, including* Little Folks *and* Illustrated London News.

The early years of Kate Greenaway's life could not have been further removed from the idyllic depictions of childhood for which she would achieve fame. Her father John Greenaway, a respected woodcut maker and engraver, had established his own business shortly before her birth, having been offered the job of engraving plates for a series of illustrations for Charles Dickens' *Pickwick Papers.* To avoid distracting her husband from his task, **Elizabeth Greenaway** took the infant Kate and her elder sister to stay with relatives in a village some 200 miles away. It was two years before they were reunited, by which time John's business was beginning to fail, forcing him to take any work he could find and to move the family into less salubrious surroundings in a new working-class district of London. The Greenaway fortunes began to improve only when Elizabeth opened a millinery shop, where, despite two further children, she proved to be an astute and capable businesswoman who became the breadwinner.

By all accounts, Kate was an imaginative and sensitive child, given to inventing games with her older sister as they played near their home along streets busy with shoppers, vendors, and colorful entertainers. Tenacious enough to save her farthing pocket-money for 24 weeks to buy a piece of furniture for her dolls' house, she could be strong willed, stubborn, and given to displays of emotion. Though she enjoyed her visits to the theater with her father, she was often unable to separate events on stage from real life, embarrassing her siblings by her unrestrained reactions. Despite life's early hardships, Kate would later write: "I had such a very happy time when I was a child, and curiously, was so very much happier than my brother and sisters, with exactly the same surroundings."

A religious and puritanical woman, Elizabeth Greenaway wanted a better life for her children and used some of the profits of her success to pay for private French and piano lessons. Kate, however, was more fascinated with her father's craft and persuaded her mother to pay for evening classes in art. Such was her talent that, at the age of 12, she was accepted as a full-time pupil in the Finsbury School of Art where she began the National Course of Art Instruction. This was a program dedicated to the production, not of fine artists or sculptors, but of men and women with the design skills to work with industry in ensuring good taste in the panoply of manufactured goods essential to the ornamentation of a Victorian home. Through a rigorously structured curriculum, the students engaged in the repetitive copying of geometric shapes and architectural features, produced clay ornaments, and painted watercolors of stuffed animals. Kate thrived on this disciplined restrictiveness, winning medals which included a national award for tile designs at the end of her six-year studies.

In 1865, Greenaway elected to continue her studies at the National Art Training School, a more fashionable center committed to the promotion of design skills above fine art training.

Though her class, shyness, and general lack of glamour meant exclusion from the dominant social cliques of well-born young ladies there, Kate proceeded to win another national award, this time for a watercolor of a young boy's head. This daytime training she supplemented with evening classes in life-study at Heatherley's School of Art, one of the few progressive institutions which allowed women to study from the nude in the same room as the male students. But the heavy emphasis on individualistic style confused Kate after her years of regimented design training. She left to enroll at the Slade School of Art.

Throughout these years of study, Kate spent many vacations with her family in Rolleston Village, where the heavy influence of the English countryside, combined with her training in design, formed the basis for the popular Greenaway style. By the time her studies were completed, she had already published her first book illustration in the 1867 *Infant Amusements, or How to Make a Nursery Happy* and had exhibited drawings of fairies and gnomes at the Dudley Gallery in London. With sufficient commissions to establish herself as an illustrator by the early 1870s, she began to work freelance from her parents' home.

Her treatment of quaint early nineteenth-century costume, prim gardens, and the child-like spirit of her designs in an old-world atmosphere . . . captivated the public in a remarkable way.

—Walter Crane

The greeting-card industry had seen phenomenal growth over the previous few years as the Victorian public clamored for cards at Christmas, Valentine's Day and other holidays. Kate soon established a successful collaboration with the leading manufacturer, Ward, after her first design for a Valentine achieved sales of 25,000 within a few weeks. A shrewd instinct for popular taste led to the development of a successful style which depicted a romantic vision of children in historical dress, set against a plain background with an ornate border. From her alliance with Ward, Greenaway gained valuable experience, not just in the creation of workable, mass-market designs, but also in the business skills she would require as a young woman working alone. As workload and income increased, Kate and her father jointly rented a large house in a more sedate area where a small studio was established. Guided by him, her work began to focus upon illustrations for children's books.

In 1877, Greenaway's fortunes changed dramatically. For years, she had dreamed of illustrating a book of simple verse which she had written since childhood. Despite misgivings, John Greenaway was enchanted when he saw Kate's efforts and introduced his daughter to Edmund Evans, a printer who had achieved renown for his color publications and who was familiar with the children's book market. He had previously produced works by Walter Crane and Randolph Caldecott, the leading children's artists of the day. After some debate with his associate, George Routledge, Evans undertook to publish Greenaway's book, once the verses had been "tidied up" by another, more respected poet, Frederick Locker. Meanwhile Kate, by now experienced in such matters, ensured a contract of lucrative terms. *Under the Window*, published just in time for Christmas 1879, was an instant success. Evans' gamble in a large print run of 20,000 copies paid off when the first edition sold out within a few weeks, establishing Kate Greenaway as a household name. The commendatory reviews in fashionable journals ensured a broader purchasing market by inspiring belief in the collectability of the book and its future status as a children's classic. Within Greenaway's lifetime, over 100,000 copies were sold in English, French, and German.

The great success of *Under the Window* with its clean, pastel illustrations and sparse design "suggests that Kate had judged her public shrewdly," writes Rodney Engen. "Her book appealed to children as well as to fashion-struck aesthetes of the burgeoning Aesthetic Movement." With its nonsensical verse, cherubic, archaically dressed children, and evident intent to amuse, not inform, the book provided a contrast to the plethora of gaudily colored, instructive texts on the shelves. But it was not without its critics, primary amongst them Henry Stacy Marks, a renowned book illustrator, who lost no time in criticizing Greenaway's "naive defiance of all rules of composition." Kate accepted his comments humbly and in future sent him copies of her work for review.

Throughout her life, Greenaway sought the guidance and approbation of older males, beginning with her father, the primary guide for her career; the Reverend W.J. Loftie who purchased her works; Stacy Marks; and, most important of all—the art critic, John Ruskin. Though evidently capable of managing her own business relations, she often deferred to her mentors—financially secure men who did not understand the realities of life for a working woman. On many

occasions, they implored Greenaway not to work so hard, to take rests and breaks and to treat her work more like a dilettante. Yet Kate cultivated these pupil-master relationships, at the heart of which was her firmly held belief in the lower status of women. As she grew older, she became exasperated by the women's suffrage movement—"I don't want a vote myself. . . . For my part I do feel the men can do it better and so hope it may remain," she wrote. Almost more infuriating was the idea of being classed a "lady artist"—a group whose ranks she refused to join when an exhibition of women's art was held to mark "Victoria year," 1897. She wrote to a friend, "Now why can't we just take our places fairly—get just our right amount of credit and no more. Of course we shouldn't get the first places—for the very simple and just reason—that we don't deserve them."

It was Stacy Marks who provided an introduction to Ruskin, whose critical voice continued to wield great power, even though he was now in self-imposed semi-retirement. From his house in the picturesque Lake District, Ruskin

managed an incredible number of epistolary relationships, mainly with unattached women, upon whom he lavished his advice and guidance in tones ranging from the paternal to the overtly flirtatious. In January 1880, Greenaway became a new beneficiary of his patronism when she received a gushingly appreciative letter, thus beginning the association which would dominate her life. With her burgeoning fame, she was swept into a different world from the beginning of the decade, finding herself at dinners with such literary greats as Robert Browning, or artists like Edward Burne-Jones, as she was inundated with requests for her presence at society events. The publication of *Kate Greenaway's Birthday Book* in the autumn of 1880 reassured her position as a leading illustrator when sales reflected its critical and popular acclaim.

But Kate was soon to experience the less enjoyable effect of fame: imitation. By the early 1880s, the shop windows were full of plagiarized Greenaway children, often engaged in activities—like pipe-smoking—which would curl the hair of their angelic prototypes. "It feels so

*Illustration
by Kate
Greenaway.*

queer, somehow, to see your ideas taken by someone else and put forth as theirs," wrote Kate to a friend. The loose, light Regency costumes of her figures provided a refreshing contrast to current, formal fashions, and this inspired another market. In England and in France, fashionable types began to dress their offspring "a la mode Greenaway," a vogue which continued into the 20th century. But the supreme accolade and acknowledgment of her fame came with the invitation, in 1881, to bring her sketchbook to Buckingham Palace, where she entertained the young princes and princesses with her skills.

Mother Goose, or the Old Nursery Rhymes, published at Christmas of that year, signified the first small decline in Greenaway's popularity. Evans' haste to ensure that the book would arrive on time for the holiday, coupled with Kate's lack of control over the production of her work, resulted in poorly printed copies. And though the press received the book with enthusiasm, Greenaway and her mentor, Locker, were disappointed by the results. *A Day in a Child's Life*, a book of piano music, bordered by Greenaway illustrations, was less well received. "Miss Greenaway seems to be lapsing into a rather lackadaisical prettiness of style. Her little people are somewhat deficient in vitality" was the response of *The Times*.

The relationship with Ruskin was by now Greenaway's primary obsession outside of her work. With only infrequent meetings, he insinuated himself as her dominant critic through a voluminous correspondence. Kate wrote to him almost daily from the notepad she kept on her desk to jot down thoughts or observations she believed would interest or amuse him. Ruskin, in return, became one of her keenest champions. He went so far as to claim, in an 1883 lecture at Oxford, that she was one of the great artists of all time who could be a savior from the prevailing industrial grimness. In private, he encouraged Kate to return to drawing from nature, suggesting that she improve her technique with drawings of her "girlies" without their Greenaway garb. Undoubtedly Kate's devotion was inspired by romance—the only such attachment of her life. Ruskin solicited her affections with demands for "love letters" and the instigation of postal "kissing games." But this was to be the extent of Kate's romantic life—she never married and had no other suitors.

From 1883 to 1897, with the exception of one year, the Kate Greenaway *Almanack* became an institution with collectors and the general public alike. American sales had now expanded, French and German copies were immediately available, and Kate's publishers continued to capitalize on her widespread popularity. By the end of 1884, her early card designs had been reissued in the *Baby's Birthday Book*, the Kate Greenaway *Painting Book* had been published using earlier illustrations, and her new works, *The Language of Flowers* and *The English Spelling Book*, were on the shelves. A move to a house on the edge of Hampstead Heath brought new financial burdens for Greenaway, by now the breadwinner of the family. Her brother de-

scribed her monotonous routine of work: long days spent alone in her studio, struggling for the inspiration to produce original ideas for her latest projects. By now, Kate was becoming disillusioned with her role as illustrator, depressed by the imitations she saw everywhere, and keen to move onto other work. *The Marigold Garden*, a book of her own verse, and illustrations inspired by Gainsborough, took nearly two years of her time, and was published in 1885. The book was not a commercial success, and the lukewarm reception of the following year's *Almanack* were evidence that her career was in decline.

By the end of the decade, Greenaway was searching for new sources of income and had even resorted to the sale of one of her pictures as an advertisement for Pears soap. Further financial burdens were placed upon the artist following the death of her father in 1891. Her income provided from royalties could no longer cover the costs of keeping a large house and family. Guided by a sense of artistic mission and hoping to make money, Kate focused her attention on watercolor painting. She spent days in the countryside working alongside her friend, the successful watercolorist, ✥▶ Helen Allingham, where the two depicted romantic images of English cottages and idealized country life. But an 1891 sale of Greenaway's works proved disappointing when the watercolors were largely overlooked in favor of her earlier designs. In a sale three years later, the older works from her studio were again

---

✥▶ **Allingham, Helen Patterson** (1848–1926)
English watercolorist and illustrator. Born Helen Patterson on September 26, 1848; died at Haslemere in 1926; daughter of A.H. Paterson (a doctor); attended the Birmingham School of Design and the Royal Academy Schools; married William Allingham (the Irish poet), in 1874.

Influenced by the work of Fred Walker, Helen Allingham devoted her illustrations to domestic and rural life. She achieved her first success at age 26 by illustrating the serialization of Thomas Hardy's *Far from the Madding Crowd* for *The Cornhill Magazine* (1874). A rarity among woman artists in Victorian England, Allingham was extremely popular and was frequently given one-woman shows by the Fine Art Society in the 1880s and 1890s. She also illustrated books of *Juliana Horatia Ewing, including *A Flat Iron for a Farthing* (1872) and *Jan of the Windmill* (1876). Her *Angelika Kauffmann in the Studio of Joshua Reynolds* was painted in 1875.

SUGGESTED READING:
Huish, H.B. *Happy England as Painted by H.A.* 1903.

---

snapped up, while more recent pieces were criticized for being excessively influenced by (though inferior to) Allingham's. The loneliness of Kate's later years was eased by the friendship of **Violet Dickinson**, lively and 20 years younger, who encouraged her to venture out of the seclusion of her studio. Later to be known as the lover of *Virginia Woolf, Violet replaced Ruskin in Kate's affections, to become the recipient of her frequent illustrated notes and letters.

In 1899, Kate was told that she had breast cancer for which immediate surgery was needed. Informing her friends that she had a "bad cold," Greenaway continued to work, especially writing introspective and somber poetry while the cancer spread and eventually reached her lungs, causing her eventual death on November 6, 1901. For all of her deficiencies in skill—her poorly drawn animals, her skewed attempts at perspective—Kate Greenaway was one of the primary influences on children's illustration and children's publishing in general. The whimsical innocence of her little figures engaged in childish activities have inspired many. This singular and much-copied style retains its attraction for children today, while her original works have continued to attract high prices among collectors.

SOURCES AND SUGGESTED READING:

Alderson, Brian. *Sing a Song of Sixpence: The English Picture Book Tradition and Randolph Caldecott.* Cambridge, 1986.

Engen, Rodney. *Kate Greenaway: A Biography.* London: MacDonald Futura, 1981.

Spielmann, M.H., and G.S. Layard. *Kate Greenaway.* London: Adam and Charles Black, 1905.

Viguers, Ruth Hill. *The Kate Greenaway Treasury.* London: Collins, 1968.

Diane Moody,
freelance writer, London, England

Greenaway, Margaret (fl. 15th c.)

English merchant. *Flourished in England in the 15th century.*

Although few records remain of Margaret Greenaway's life, it is clear that she was an active entrepreneur in England, during its emergence as a nascent industrial nation. She established herself as a businesswoman in the highly competitive area of international commerce. Her husband had been a dealer in biscuits and baked goods with the newly established East India Company; after his death, Margaret maintained the business and supported herself well for many years.

Laura York,
Riverside, California

Greenbaum, Dorothea Schwarcz
(1893–1986)

American sculptor and activist for artists' rights and opportunities. Born Dorothea Schwarcz in Brooklyn, New York, on June 17, 1893; died in 1986; daughter of Maximilian Schwarcz (an importer); attended New York School of Design for Women and the Art Students League; married Edward Greenbaum (a lawyer), in 1926; children: two sons.

Dorothea Greenbaum, the daughter of a well-to-do New York importer who died in the sinking of the *Lusitania* in 1915, started out as a painter, a member of Kenneth Hayes Miller's class at the Art Students League during the 1920s. Greenbaum (who was known as "Dots") became one of the Fourteenth Street School painters along with Alexander Brook, Reginald Marsh, *Isabel Bishop, and *Peggy Bacon, with whom she shared a Union Square studio. Following her marriage to lawyer Edward Greenbaum and the birth of her two sons, Greenbaum abandoned painting and took up sculpture. Beginning with clay modeling, she gradually expanded to stone carving and, finally, hammered lead, the medium she found most alive and responsive. Some of her work carries political undertones. *Fascist* (c. 1938), an enormous, brutal-looking head, conveys her attitude toward the movement founded by Mussolini in 1919. Other works, however, like *Girl With Fawn* (1936) and *Drowned Girl* (1950), evoke a sense of peacefulness. The latter work, carved from Tennessee marble, is marked by a play of textures: the smooth contours of the face are contrasted by the roughly textured hair. In a catalogue commemorating a two-person exhibit with Isabel Bishop in 1970, Greenbaum was called a "romantic realist" whose works "radiate serenity."

Although financially secure herself, Greenbaum worked throughout her career to help her fellow artists. In 1938, she aligned herself with the Sculptors Guild, an avant-garde group founded in opposition to the traditional National Sculpture Society. The group was so non-conformist that it could hardly agree on its own policies. In a 1940 interview with the (Martha's) *Vineyard Gazette*, Greenbaum joked about her role as secretary and peacemaker and described the Guild as "an organization so radical . . . that it even refuses to have a president. That means I'm the boss." After World War II, a particularly lean period for many artists, Greenbaum helped found Artist's Equity, an organization concerned with improving rights and economic opportunities for artists. She and her husband also came to the aid of sculptor William Zorach (husband of *Marguerite Zorach), when he was threatened with deportation during the McCarthy era.

Greenbaum's sculpture *Sleeping Girl* (1928) had been in the 1933 Chicago Century of Progress Exposition, and her first one-woman exhibition had been held at the Weyhe Gallery in Manhattan. Later, during the war, she held a solo show in Washington D.C., where her husband, then a brigadier general, was stationed. The *Washington Post*'s announcement of the exhibit was typical of the 1940s: "General's Wife To Have One Man Art Exhibit." In 1947, Greenbaum was honored by the American Academy of Arts and Letters with a $1,000 grant "in recognition of sculpture of a high order replete with a warm and sensitive appreciation of the human spirit." Dorothea Greenbaum died in 1986, age 93.

SOURCES:

Bailey, Brooke. *The Remarkable Lives of 100 Women Artists*. Holbrook, MA; Bob Adams, 1994.

Rubinstein, Charlotte Streifer. *American Women Artists*. Boston, MA: G.K. Hall, 1982.

Barbara Morgan,
Melrose, Massachusetts

Greene, Belle da Costa (1883–1950)

American librarian and bibliographer. Born in Alexandria, Virginia, on December 13, 1883; died in New York, New York, on May 10, 1950; second daughter and third of five children of Richard and Genevieve (Van Vliet) Greene; attended local schools in Princeton, New Jersey; never married; no children.

Although born in Virginia in 1883, Belle Greene grew up and attended school in Princeton, New Jersey, where her mother moved after the breakup of her marriage. Unable to afford college, Greene went directly from school to her first job at the Princeton University library. It was there that she mastered the cataloguing system and gained experience at the reference desk. She also developed an interest in the rare book department, which brought her to the attention of Junius Spencer Morgan, a collector and the nephew of banker J. Pierpont Morgan, who was looking for someone to oversee his collection of rare books and manuscripts. On the recommendation of his nephew, J. Pierpont hired Greene in 1905, thus beginning her long association with the Morgan family.

Although just 21 years old, Greene hit it off splendidly with her boss whom she called "chief." From 1905 to 1907, she labored to bring order to Morgan's large and diverse collection, which at the time had just been moved to a library building on 36th Street in New York City. To help her sort, catalogue, and shelve the collection, Morgan had also hired **Ada Thurston**, an experienced bibliographer with whom Greene worked for the next 30 years.

Greene's receptive mind and forthright personality impressed Morgan, who put more and more trust in his young assistant. By 1908, she was traveling regularly to Europe as his agent, to seek out and purchase additions to the Morgan library. While abroad, Greene also worked diligently to increase her own knowledge of rare books and manuscripts, a pursuit in which she was assisted by her associations with Sydney Cockrell of the Fitzwilliam Museum in Cambridge, England, and later with Bernard Berenson in Italy.

Morgan's death in 1913 not only devastated Greene but left her career in limbo, as J.P. Morgan, Jr., showed little interest in his father's collection. As America entered the war in 1917, she threw herself into war work, and in 1919, when her brother-in-law was killed in action, Greene provided a home for her sister and her infant nephew. Upon her sister's remarriage, Greene legally adopted the boy and provided for his education. In 1920, when the younger Morgan became interested in the library, Greene once again resumed her research abroad.

In 1924, Morgan converted the library into an incorporated and endowed educational institution and named Greene its director. For the next 24 years, she worked to establish the library as a center for scholarly research. Publication and lecture programs were arranged and, in 1928, an annex was added for exhibitions. To those she deemed serious of purpose, Greene offered her valued assistance and enduring friendship.

Greene also continued her European trips, often accompanied by her nephew, until 1936, when her health began to fail. She retired from the library in November 1948. The following year, the staff and the library's new director, Frederick H. Adams, Jr., honored her with an exhibition recognizing the growth of the library and its collections under her directorship. At that time, a group of scholars and collectors began a *festschrift* ("a publication in her honor") which, unfortunately, was not completed before her death in May 1950. The volume, entitled *Studies in Art and Literature for Belle da Costa Greene*, was published by Princeton University Press in 1954.

SOURCES:

James, Edward T., ed. *Notable American Women 1607–1950*. Cambridge, MA: The Belknap Press of Harvard University Press, 1971.

McHenry, Robert, ed. *Famous American Women*. NY: Dover, 1983.

Barbara Morgan,
Melrose, Massachusetts

Greene, Catharine Littlefield

(1755–1814)

Renowned participant in the political society of Revolutionary America who, with Eli Whitney and Phineas Miller, invented the cotton gin. Name variations: Katherine or Catherine, and Caty (KAY-tee). Born Catharine Littlefield, possibly with "Ray" as a middle name, on December 17, 1755, on Block Island, off the coast of Newport, Rhode Island; died on Cumberland Island, Georgia, on September 2, 1814; daughter of John Littlefield (a landowner and deputy of the General Assembly) and Phebe (Ray) Littlefield; tutored sporadically from age 10 to 18; mostly self-taught through reading; learned French as a young woman; married Nathanael Greene (later a leading general in the Revolutionary army), on July 20, 1774 (died 1786); married Phineas Miller, in 1796 (died 1803); children: (first marriage) George Washington Greene (1776–1793); Martha Greene (Patty, b. 1777); Cornelia Lott Green (b. 1778); Nathanael Ray Greene (b. 1780); Louisa Catharine Greene (b. 1784); Catharine Greene (1785–1785).

Left home at age ten to live with Greenes of East Greenwich, Rhode Island (1764); married Nathanael Greene, set up housekeeping in Coventry (1774); began a series of journeys from Coventry to join husband in the Continental Army (1775), to Jamaica Plain (1775), to Cambridge, Massachusetts (1775), to New York City (1776), to Fort Lee, New Jersey (1777), to Valley Forge (1778), to Middlebrook, New Jersey (1778), to Morristown and Philadelphia (1779), to Charlestown, South Carolina (1781), to Philadelphia (1783); returned home with husband to Coventry (1783); hired Phineas Miller as tutor, family moved to Mulberry Grove, Georgia (1785); premature baby born and died (1786); filed a claim of indemnity on husband's behalf versus Federal government (1787); granted plea by Congress with cash award (1792); Eli Whitney arrived at Mulberry Grove (1792); with Whitney and Miller, invented the cotton gin (1793); involved in Yazoo Land Fraud (1795); moved to Cumberland Island after Mulberry Grove auctioned (1800); patent rights of gin sold to South Carolina legislature (1802).

In her own time, Catharine Littlefield Greene became famous, with good reason, in her role as the wife of a famous man, Nathanael Greene, a leading general in the American Revolution. Somewhat ironically, however, her contribution to an invention made a decade after the end of that war was to have far greater impact in shaping the future of the country that the revolution gave birth to. In conventional history books, it is the young Eli Whitney who is usually given sole credit for the invention of the cotton gin. If the name of Catharine Greene appears at all in this connection, it is usually as nothing more than a sexually beguiling social butterfly. But in 1793, her contribution to this basically simple, but revolutionary, machine was to provide the impetus for bringing it into being. She also made effective contributions, along with Whitney and Phineas Miller, to its design, actions that inadvertently helped to precipitate the paradox of slave power as the underpinning of prosperity in the South, which became the torment of the country throughout the next century. But if Caty Greene deserves her place in the annals of American inventors, the fullness of her life also bears examination for what it reveals about the experience of women at the intersection of politics and society in the earliest years of America as a nation.

Born on December 17, 1755, in New Shoreham, on Block Island, 12 miles off the Rhode Island coast, Catharine Littlefield has been identified as the second or third child of **Phebe Ray Littlefield** and John Littlefield. Her parents came from two old island families; John was landed gentry and served as deputy of the general assembly, and Phebe Ray was a direct descendant of Roger Williams. When Phebe died, in May 1761, at age 28, she left her husband with five young children.

Catharine, called "Caty," enjoyed childhood in an almost idyllic setting. Block Island had only 50 white families and a small number of friendly Native Americans and free blacks. Without schools, markets or roads, and with only one public gathering place, it allowed her to roam free, walking or riding the entire island from a young age.

Shortly after her mother's death, ten-year-old Caty was sent to live in Greenwich, Rhode Island, with her mother's sister, for whom she had been named. A beautiful, captivating woman, **Catherine Ray** won her place in history as an object of Benjamin Franklin's ardent wooing, though he was much older and married to

Deborah Read at the time. His chagrined letters suggest she did not capitulate entirely—he complained of her "virgin innocence"—but they corresponded for years and even exchanged family visits. By the time Caty came to live with her, Catharine Ray was married to William Greene, a fervent patriot and later a governor of Rhode Island.

In the Greenes' home, Caty began to study with tutors, who were impressed by her intelligence. The household, meanwhile, was becoming a center for pre-revolutionary political activity, where Caty, at age 18, met a distant relative, Nathanael Greene. The fourth son of a prosperous Rhode Island Quaker minister and farmer who owned grist mills and forges, Nathanael was a sophisticated young man of 30 who had begun to question his family's faith. His favorite pastime was dancing, which had widened the rift, and his enrollment in a local militia, the Kentish guards, had finally caused his expulsion from the pacifist church. After the death of his father, Nathanael and his brothers invested some of their inheritance in merchant ships. At 28, he had built a house in nearby Coventry, allowing frequent visits to the Greene home for both political and personal reasons.

Family legends relate that Nathanael met Caty while recovering from a broken romance with her cousin, Anna Ward, whom she resembled. True or not, Catharine did not have to rely on family resemblance to enchant the young man from Coventry. She is described as having black hair, violet or gray eyes, clear-cut features and a transparent complexion, and possessed a "power of fascination" that observers noted as "absolutely irresistible," even as a young woman.

On July 20, 1774, Catharine and Nathanael were married in the home of her aunt and uncle, and they set up housekeeping in Coventry. From the start, the young couple's life was played out against the dramatic backdrop of the American crisis. During their courtship, Nathanael had clashed with British authorities over the burning of a royal schooner, the *Gaspee*, and on April 19, 1775, a knock on the newlyweds' door caused Nathanael to march off with his regiment to the battles at Lexington and Concord. By the time these troops reached Massachusetts, the British had retreated, but the couple knew that war had come. Shortly afterward, Nathanael left for military duty as a private but, in an army badly in need of officers, was soon given the post of brigadier general.

Nathanael was stationed with the rest of the provincial brigades in Jamaica Plains, Massa-

chusetts, when Caty discovered she was with child. To the astonishment of her relatives, she soon left to join Nathanael at his headquarters, establishing a pattern that was to characterize their marriage. During the eight years of the war, she would remain with her husband whenever she could, often traveling while pregnant, with or without her children. As military or reproductive developments dictated, she would return to the home of her husband's family or to Coventry, then quit the household as soon as circumstances permitted a return to camp life, often leaving behind one or more of the children.

Awaiting the birth of her first child, she returned to Coventry and spent some months improving herself with the help of her husband's library of 300 books, while also carrying out the duties of a general's wife by visiting the families of recently killed soldiers. Growing bored in the late stages of her confinement, she returned to her husband's camp at Cambridge and helped to nurse soldiers through a smallpox epidemic, safe from the disease because of her earlier inoculation. There she began a lifelong friendship with *Martha Washington, known as "Lady Washington." In the command echelon, the atmosphere of the camp was that of an extended family, and Caty shone there, as a skilled card player, a wonderful dancer, not above indulging in flirting and risqué humor, charming to all the officers and a favorite, in particular, of George Washington.

[My mother had] the most remarkable combination of intellectual power and physical beauty I have personally encountered in womanhood.

—Cornelia Greene

Observers of the time describe Caty Greene as possessing a great deal of "charm"; undoubtedly, a large measure of her attractiveness lay in her intelligence. According to *Elizabeth Ellet, a 19th-century writer who interviewed friends of the young general's wife, Catharine possessed "the capacity for quick perception and the faculty of comprehending a subject with surprising readiness." An excellent listener and observer, she once astonished a group by conversing intelligently on botany after merely turning over the pages of a book. Other comments about her gifts—a retentive memory, an ability to apply what she read to practical matters, fluent speech, and a lively imagination—all suggest a formidable mind. "When to all these gifts was added the charm of rare beauty," Ellet concluded, "it cannot excite wonder that the possessor of such attractions should fascinate all who approached her."

Read, Deborah.
See Bache,
Sarah for
sidebar.

These endowments are all the more remarkable given that the young Catharine was not well-educated—a lack she felt keenly, according to her husband's letters. Unfortunately, historians have only his side of the exchange since Caty burned her correspondence, perhaps because it was too revelatory, or perhaps because she was ashamed of her spelling. She wished to be regarded as a cultivated lady and felt insecure with some officers' wives. Nathanael's letters, though affectionate and indulgent, could also be scolding and full of admonitions about her personal deportment. When advising her to write to **Lucy Knox**, another general's wife, he cautioned her about her spelling. "You are defective in this matter, my love," he wrote, "a little attention will soon correct it. . . . [P]eople are often laughed at for not spelling well but never for not writing well."

Some observers pictured Caty as superficial and frivolous, if not downright promiscuous. Her ability to excite deep feelings in men has caused more romantic biographers to depict her as a vamp or mere flirt, a characterization belied by the lifelong friendships she enjoyed with several admirers. From this period of her life onward, rumors surrounded her, and Lady Washington aside, she apparently had few female friends. She obviously preferred the company of men, and evidence exists that when some of the young military men fell in love with her, she did not discourage their attentions. Her husband appears to have taken pride in her power to attract other men, and the passionate and tender affirmations of his correspondence with her—"My heart pants for you" and "I hope to meet you again in the pleasure of Wedlocke"—seem more than merely conventional. On the other hand, he often mentioned other women in a way that was calculated to make her jealous.

Historians must tread cautiously in assessing the reactions of the day to her behavior. Her laughter upon learning that Lady Washington had, in all innocence, named a tomcat after Alexander Hamilton may have signaled lightness of character to some late 18th-century folk, but to a modern scholar it may suggest a sense of humor and quick mind. Also, such talk could be highly gendered. Part of the gossipers' indictments named her indifference to religion, which she shared with her husband. An excommunicated Quaker, Nathanael was seldom seen at services, but when he missed a sermon during Caty's visits, she took the blame. Apparently sexual gossip was the cause of a lifelong rift that developed between Caty and her Aunt Catharine Ray, who was horrified by reports of her niece's behavior.

Catharine has also had her defenders. Those who believe the gossip cite letters from her husband reminding her that modesty and delicacy were the foundation of all female charms, and to a letter from Caty herself, relating a proposition by a French officer. But a Georgia politician, Isaac Briggs, tracked down a rumor that Nathanael, motivated by her infidelity, had petitioned for divorce, only to discover it "was all a lie." Briggs attributed the talk to envy and her free and direct manner. "She has an infinite fund of vivacity, the world calls it levity," hazarded Briggs. "She possesses an unbounded benevolence . . . the world calls it imprudence." Perhaps the final say belongs to Catharine, who admitted that she had "passions and propensities," and "if she had any virtue 'tis in resisting and keeping them within bounds," and to her husband, who wrote, "Altho I have been absent from you I have not been inconstant in love, unfaithful to my vows or unjust to your bed. [I consider] myself equally secure in your affections and fidelity."

It is not clear whether Caty's first child, George Washington Greene, born in February 1776, was delivered in camp or in Rhode Island. In late spring, she left her new son with Nathanael's family to rejoin her husband, then encamped in the Battery section of Manhattan, where she socialized with Lucy Knox and others. During this time, she made a good friend of Captain Alexander Hamilton and heard the Declaration of Independence read on the green before assorted civilians and the Continental troops. As the British pressed closer, she returned to Coventry, and soon discovered she was pregnant again. Conditions of war now prevented her traveling, and she lived for months in a state of fear, longing to join her husband, and worried about his safety, as well as her own. Ensconced in nearby Newport, the British undoubtedly considered the home of a leading Continental Army general an attractive target.

Finally, astonishing news arrived from New Jersey: General Washington, with Nathanael by his side, had crossed the Delaware River at McKonkee's Ferry and defeated a sleeping Hessian force at Trenton. In January, the Continental Army routed the last of the redcoats from Princeton before settling down for the rest of the winter in Morristown.

In March 1777, Caty gave birth to a girl **Martha Greene**, whom she named after Martha Washington. In February of the following year, she left her babies to join her husband at Valley Forge, in Pennsylvania. This winter of encampment has become famous as the low point in the fortunes of the revolutionary force, when morale had plunged, and cold, hungry soldiers scavenged the countryside to survive while officers felt forced to imposed severe penalties on their ragged troops to keep military discipline. It was against this background that Catharine Greene earned lasting fame, and the gratitude of many, including George Washington. Statements by Washington and others have led historians to credit her with holding the despairing officers' corps together, tipping the balance toward survival in a situation on the verge of disintegration. Making close friends that winter among the revolutionary notables, including the Marquis de Lafayette, Casimir Pulaski, Baron von Steuben, Tadeuscz Kosciusko and especially "Mad Anthony" Wayne, she undoubtedly raised the spirits of the officers with her vivacity. Pierre Duponceau, a 17-year-old aide that winter, recalled her as a "handsome, elegant and accomplished woman [who] spoke the French language and was well versed in French literature," a bright spot "in the middle of our distress."

Only recently have historians begun to uncover the underlying assumptions behind the judgment that women's presences affected the outcome at Valley Forge. They focus on a school of thought that profoundly influenced the revolutionary generation—the Scottish Common Sense School, whose major proponents included David Hume and Adam Smith. These thinkers insisted that while men made the laws that controlled behavior, women made manners which shaped the individual and thus insured a virtuous citizen for the new republic. Though the women lacked legal equality with the men, their social equality was therefore as important as any political power, because their activities pushed forward the progress of civilization. To Washington and others, these ideas became crucial as they believed that the future of the young republic lay in the virtue of its citizenry. When Nathanael wrote to Caty of the "sweet influence of female charms" as an "an antidote to wicked men and their ambitions," he was not merely commenting on a woman's decorative or recreational function, but on her political and social duty.

Caty conceived at Valley Forge and gave birth to a girl, **Cornelia Lott Greene,** on September 23, 1778, in Coventry. (Though a sickly baby, this child was to outlive all her family and leave the clearest embodiment of her mother's essence in her writings.) That same year, at General Washington's express request, Caty met the army at their encampment at Middlebrook, New Jersey, taking all of her children. On the last day of January 1780, Nathanael Ray was born in Morristown, and the crude gifts made for him by the soldiers touched Catharine's heart.

Catharine and her family were back in Rhode Island when troubles arose concerning Nathanael's promotion to quartermaster. Accused of extravagant spending and incurring debt, Nathanael was outraged and tried to resign. Washington would not hear of it and appointed him instead to command the Southern Army. Forced to content herself with the company of French soldiers at Newport, Caty aroused further whispers and gossip.

In December 1781, six weeks after news of the Yorktown surrender had reached Rhode Island, Caty set off for South Carolina, accompanied only by her six-year-old son, George. She left the boy in Philadelphia with the Washingtons, who persuaded her it was time for him to be sent to school. Upon arriving at her husband's headquarters, she discovered that he had acquired landholdings in Georgia, but it soon became clear that the Greenes could not expect a leisurely postwar life. Nathanael was found responsible for debts he had contracted on behalf of the U.S. government, and only the land grants stood between the growing family and utter ruin.

For the next several years, Caty and Nathanael traveled between Newport and Georgia. In March 1784, **Louisa Catharine Greene** was born; the following year, another girl was born but lived only a short time, and the death left Caty bereft and depressed. The following autumn, as the family prepared to move to Georgia, she discovered she was pregnant again and suffered a nervous collapse. To help with the children, Nathanael hired Phineas Miller, a 21-year-old graduate of Yale, as a tutor. Before the entourage sailed, Caty and Phineas had become fast friends.

The Greene family settled into their plantation at Mulberry Grove, Georgia, and entered into the local social life. But any contentment was to be short-lived. In the spring of 1786, a pregnant Caty fell, injuring her ankle and hip, and brought on the premature birth of another child who died. In June, after a long afternoon in the sun, Nathanael complained of a headache, the pain quickly worsened, and on June 19th he suddenly died, at the age of 44.

At age 32, Catharine Greene was a widow with five children, who had lived no more than a year or so with her husband uninterrupted. But after her initial confusion and despair, she began to adjust, and then to thrive. Having handled much responsibility during the war, she was now legally and financially her own agent. Along with Phineas Miller, she supervised the plantation, where slaves were producing bumper crops of rice and corn; she also prepared a claim of indemnity against the federal government on behalf of her husband's estate, for recovery of funds Nathanael had spent in the service of the army. Eventually, she was awarded $47,000. She put her children in northern schools and sent her eldest son off to France, where his education was supervised by the Marquis de Lafayette. Dividing her time between Georgia and New England, she traveled sometimes with Miller and sometimes alone. Her widowed state allowed her to enjoy other freedoms, and she had at least one lengthy sexual liaison, with a business partner of her late husband. Over several years, as her infatuations ceased, she turned increasingly to Miller, who was ten years her junior.

In the fall of 1792, Catharine and Phineas were in the North when she approached Ezra Stiles, the president of Yale, about a tutor for the children of neighbors in Mulberry Grove. Stiles recommended Eli Whitney, 27 years old and a recent Yale graduate. A Massachusetts native, raised in a Puritan atmosphere, Whitney had been burdened with family responsibilities from an early age, but his talent for tinkering had brought in extra money through the manufacture of ladies' hatpins, tools, and walking sticks. He also earned money as a schoolmaster before entering Yale.

By the time the Greene party reached Georgia, Whitney was yet another conquest of the 38-year-old beauty. With no real appetite for teaching and charmed by Caty, who was clearly by this point an accomplished lady, he agreed to stay on at Mulberry Grove, to construct useful items while studying law. Wondering at the tender, almost conjugal relationship between Caty and Phineas, he wrote to his brother, "I find myself in a new natural world and as for the moral world I believe it does not extend so far south." Caty had good reasons for not marrying again—propertied widows exercised more power over their own legal and financial lives than any other women in the culture.

Soon after his arrival, Eli and Catharine began to discuss with others the need for a machine to automate the tedious handwork of removing the stubborn seeds from the tangled fibers of cotton bolls before they could be combed and made into thread and cloth. Caty converted a room into a workshop into which only she, Phineas, and Eli were admitted, and

Whitney created a model for such a machine. A partnership was then drawn up between Miller and Whitney, with Caty as the primary investor.

When people collaborate, it is often hard to separate out their individual contributions. In the case of teams of male inventors, "who did what" is usually not an issue. But historians of women have a different burden of proof and have taken pains in the case of Catharine to determine that she was not merely an inspiration or a patron in this invention. Two specific modifications, significant to the machine's operation, are credited to her: the addition of wire teeth, made from an old birdcage, and the suggestion that a brush could be employed to remove the cotton fibers from the teeth.

At Mulberry Grove, the spring of 1793 started as a happy time. The cotton "gin" (for "engine") was in the model stage, and looked promising; and Caty's son George was back home from France, after a narrow escape from the Reign of Terror, so that she had all five of her children with her for the first time in five years. George held a special place in his mother's heart. He was the child who had traveled most with her on her journeys, and he had been her comfort in the darkest days of the war. Home only a few weeks, George drowned while canoeing in the swollen Savannah river, and Caty would never again be able to regard the river without grief; according to her children, she was never the same.

Things also began to go wrong with the cotton gin. Whitney had gone to New England, looking to sell the patent rights, which took far longer than he imagined. Production was further delayed by a fire which required Eli to reproduce all his drawings and plans, in an amazing feat of memory. Caty and Phineas, looking for ways to raise capital to produce the invention, became involved in a land investment that turned into one of the biggest scandals of the day—the Yazoo Land Fraud. There was nothing technically illegal about the plan to buy cheap land from the state of Georgia and sell it to farmers for a profit, but when the public found out that members of the Georgia legislature had received free shares, a cry of corruption went up. Caty and Phineas, along with many others, found their investment lost and further capital tied up in a prolonged legal battle. As a result of the scandal, the patent rights for the gin were also set aside and competitors played on the public uproar, calling Phineas and Eli greedy monopolists. While Eli launched into the long legal fight to secure the patent, others were able to copy the relatively simple machine.

But all these troubles also brought Phineas and Caty closer together, and in the spring of 1796, with George and Martha Washington at their sides, they married in Philadelphia. The news so stunned Eli that it was months before he could bring himself to speak of it, and his love for Caty was slow to fade. In a bizarre twist, both he and Caty tried on two occasions to shift his affections to two of her daughters, but Louisa and Cornelia would have none of it. By 1800, despairing of ever making a living from the gins, Eli turned to manufacturing firearms, thus setting aside their collective dreams. That same year, news reached Caty that her friend George Washington had died in 1799. To satisfy unpaid taxes, Mulberry Grove was finally auctioned off for $15,000. Caty and Phineas moved with her children to one of Nathanael's remaining properties, on Georgia's Cumberland Island.

Life on the island could be warm and balmy, and was abundant with natural delicacies. The family changed residence, settling on a location they called "Dungeness." Cornelia and Louisa, both married, lived on the mainland nearby. In the spring of 1802, news came that the South Carolina legislature had agreed to buy the patent rights to the gin for $50,000, finally rendering the old partnership solvent. Under Phineas' management, the plantation prospered, but on a trip to procure tropical garden plants, he pricked his finger on a thorn and died of blood poisoning on December 7, 1802, at age 39. The death of her second husband left Caty both emotionally wrenched and financially embarrassed, with much of her property still tied up in the negotiations surrounding the Yazoo scandal, and Phineas' partnership with Whitney effectively dissolved by his death. Catharine's support had been *sub rosa* (confidential), so she had no legal right to the profits from the gin and had to rely on Eli's good faith. Though their correspondence reveals misunderstandings and tension at this time, all evidence suggests that he did not fail her.

In 1802, Caty's grief was compounded by the loss of several friends to dueling, including the handsome captain of her past, Alexander Hamilton. His murderer, Aaron Burr, was also her friend, and asked to stay at her house while on the run from the law. Caty solved this grisly social dilemma by permitting him to stay while removing her family to another part of the island; Burr took the hint and left after one night.

Her last days on Cumberland Island were marred by accusations of ill-treatment by Cornelia and Martha and their husbands. Though Catharine eventually settled with her two elder daughters, she did not speak of them in her letters and excluded them from her will. In the spring of 1814, a bill passed in Congress for the relief of the Yazoo investors, giving Caty a measure of financial security. That summer, struck by an island fever, she tossed and turned for a week while Nat and Louisa watched at her side. On September 2, 1814, near the end of her 60th year, she drifted into death.

A study of Caty Greene's life presents many challenges to generalizations about her times. Though historians are hampered by the lack of her own papers, a serious consideration of her life, constructed by surrounding documents, would surely shed light on the current debate about whether or not the American Revolution was a liberating experience for women. Wartime provided wide experience and freedom for Caty, as did widowhood and her own taste for adventure. But autonomy also entails responsibility. She grew, sometimes reluctantly when forced by circumstance, sometimes eagerly on her own initiative. And she flourished.

SOURCES:

Booth, Sally Smith. *The Women of '76.* NY: Hastings House, 1973.

Engle, Paul. *Women in the American Revolution.* Chicago: Follett, 1976.

The Papers of Nathanael Greene. Vols. 1–7. University of North Carolina Press, 1976–1994.

Stegeman, John F., and Janet. *Caty: A Biography of Catharine Littlefield Greene.* Athens, GA: University of Georgia Press, 1985.

SUGGESTED READING:

There has not been any recent scholarly study of Catharine Greene's life. Shirley Seifert's *Let My Name Stand Fair* (NY: J.B. Lippincott, 1956) is not historically accurate, though it is highly colored. John and Janet Stegeman's book provides an interpretive narrative account. *The Papers of Nathanael Greene,* which are being published by the Rhode Island Historical Society, are the best source for the scholar.

COLLECTIONS:

The largest collection of Greene family papers is at the Clements Library at the University of Michigan; the National Archives, Library of Congress and American Philosophical Society Library also possess sizable holdings. The Rhode Island Historical Society, which sponsors the ongoing publication of Nathanael Greene's papers, should be the first stop on any journey to recreate Catharine Greene's life. Yale University has a good collection of Eli Whitney's papers.

Catherine A. Allgor,
Assistant Professor of History, Simmons College,
Boston, Massachusetts

Greene, Gertrude Glass (1904–1956)

American painter and sculptor. Born Gertrude Glass in Brooklyn, New York, in 1904; died in 1956; attend-

ed the Leonardo da Vinci Art School, New York; married Balcomb Greene, in 1926; no children.

Described as a free spirit, Gertrude Glass was born in 1904 and grew up in Brooklyn; she studied art at the Leonardo da Vinci Art School in New York City. When she was 22, she married painter Balcomb Greene and for the next five years traveled in Europe with her husband exploring the new art movements. In 1931, they returned to New York where Gertrude set up a studio. For the next 15 years, she sculpted in abstract, non-representative forms. **Paula Charmonte** deemed her "a link between 1930s constructivism in Paris and post World War II abstraction in New York." Greene was also active in bringing together other experimental artists and helped organize the American Abstract Artists Association, the Artists Union, and the Sculptors Guild.

One of her non-representative forms was wood reliefs, wall-hung sculptures that were pieced together from carefully shaped, sometimes painted, wood forms. These works, which include *Construction in Blue* (1935), *Construction in Grey* (1939), and *White Anxiety* (1943–44), may have been influenced by the Cubism movement which the artist encountered in Europe. Later, Greene created abstract sculptured painting, using a palette knife to give them a textured, dimensional look. Gertrude Greene's promising career was cut short by her death in 1956, age 52.

SOURCES:

Bailey, Brooke. *The Remarkable Lives of 100 Women Artists.* Holbrook, MA; Bob Adams, 1994.

Charmonte, Paula. *Women Artists in the U.S., 1750–1986.* Boston, MA: G.K. Hall, 1990.

Greene, Katherine (1755–1814).

See Greene, Catherine Littlefield.

Greene, Nancy (1943—)

Canadian skier. Born Nancy Catherine Greene on May 11, 1943, in Ottawa, Ontario, Canada; grew up in Rossland, British Columbia; married Al Raine, in 1969 (a skier).

Won the Olympic gold medal in giant slalom and the silver in slalom in Grenoble (1968); won 14 World Cup races; won the World Cup overall (1967 and 1968); named Canada's Athlete of the Year (1967 and 1968).

Nancy Greene won the World Cup in the first two years it was offered in competition, beating out the remarkable racers of her time—**Annie Famose** of France, the *****Goitschel** sisters (**Marielle** and **Christine**) of France, **Jean Saubert** of the U.S., and **Christl Haas** of Austria. The wildly popular Greene was a Canadian superstar, who would eventually sign endorsement contracts with General Motors, Mars candy bars, Jergens Hand Lotion, and the British Columbia Telephone Company.

At 16, Greene finished 31st in the slalom while her roommate *****Anne Heggtveit** won the gold medal in that event at Squaw Valley in 1960. Awed by the ceremony, Greene later reported: "The Canadian flag was flying and everyone cheered and I think most of the girls were crying. I was anyway." But Greene was a slow start. Beaten twice by **Linda Crutchfield** of St. Sauveur, Quebec (who would later become a champion waterskier), for the Canadian women's title (1962 and 1964), Greene's best placement in the 1964 Olympics was a sluggish 7th.

In the early 1960s, Canada's National Team lacked funds, discipline, training, and organization. "The skiers who toured Europe, carrying the Team's banner, weren't necessarily the best racers to be found in Canada—they were merely the skiers who could spare the time and raise the capital to make the trip," wrote Greene in her autobiography. "Deserving racers without the money stayed home, and, on the other side of the coin, well-heeled skiers were able to join the Team and use it simply as a pleasant and exciting way to tour the continent."

Things began to change. Canadian skiers took over the coaching from Europeans; ski-minded businessmen began to provide adequate financing. By February 1965, when a new National Team journeyed to Aspen, Colorado, for their first meet, Nancy Greene took 1st in the downhill and slalom. From the middle 1960s, she racked up an impressive series of victories in European and North American championships, but she was still not winning the important races.

In July 1966, in the World championships at Portillo, Chile, Greene flipped in the downhill competition at 40 mph and crashed into a retaining wall, tearing ligaments in her arm. Sick of failing in the big ones, she came away from Portillo "plain blazing mad" and was determined to win in 1967, the first year of the World Cup tour. And win she did. She took 1sts in the slalom and giant slalom at Oberstaufen in Germany, 1sts in the downhill and giant slalom at Grindelwald in Switzerland, and 1sts in the slalom and two giant slaloms at Jackson Hole, Wyoming. She also took the first World Cup.

In the 1968 Olympic games at Grenoble, Greene won a silver medal in the slalom and a gold medal in the giant slalom, crossing the finish line with a whopping 2.64 margin. Following the games, she embarked on another run of nine consecutive victories, more than any racer had ever achieved. "I was skiing against the greatest racers in the world," she commented, "and I was beating them consistently. I couldn't ask for anything more." That year, she won her second World Cup.

After her retirement in the spring of 1968, Greene pushed hard to benefit her sport. She served on a federal task force for Canada's physical-fitness program and amateur sport; she demanded from her endorsing companies that they also contribute to the coffers of the National Team. The Nancy Greene Ski League, established in 1968 to train children (8–13) for competition, began to turn out 6,000 junior racers across Canada. Nancy Greene, who, with her husband, operates Nancy Greene's Cahilty Lodge in Sun Peaks, British Columbia, is one of the most well-known sport stars in Canada.

SOURCES:
Batten, Jack. *Champions: Great Figures in Canadian Sport.* Toronto: New Press, 1971.

SUGGESTED READING:
Greene, Nancy. *Nancy Greene's Pocket Guide to Skiing.*

Greenfield, Elizabeth Taylor

(c. 1819–1876)

Black concert artist and teacher, who became the first American singer to win critical acclaim for her performances both in the U.S. and in Europe. Name variations: The Black Swan. Born Elizabeth Taylor around 1819 in Natchez, Mississippi; died on March 31, 1876, in Philadelphia, Pennsylvania; daughter of slaves; her father's surname was Taylor and her mother's name was given as Anna Greenfield; taught herself to play guitar, harp and piano; studied voice briefly in Philadelphia and in England; never married; no children.

Born into slavery; freed in infancy; taken by former owner to Philadelphia; traveled to Buffalo, New York (1851); made professional debut in Buffalo (October 1851); toured extensively (1851–53); traveled to England for further study and concertizing (1853); returned to U.S. (summer 1854); concertized extensively and taught (1854–74); directed Opera Troupe in Philadelphia (1860s).

While prestigious performances and enthusiastic reviews were commonplace for singer Elizabeth Taylor Greenfield, her celebrated tour of Great Britain stands out as the major accomplishment of her career. In 1853, Greenfield received one of the highest honors possible for any musician—a command performance before Queen *Victoria. The queen's organist, composer and musical advisor, Sir George Smart, served as Greenfield's accompanist. It was an unprecedented event, and Greenfield went on to become the first African-American performer to win praise from British audiences and the press.

Born Elizabeth Taylor in Natchez, Mississippi, to slave parents, Greenfield's birth took place in the home of her family's owner, **Mrs. Holliday Greenfield**, an elderly widow. The exact year of birth remains uncertain, though Greenfield's biographer Arthur R. La Brew places it between 1819 and 1820. Her death certificate lists her age at time of death as 57.

Not much is known about Greenfield's parents or family. Her father's surname was Taylor and her mother's name was given as **Anna Greenfield**. In her will, Greenfield mentioned a sister, **Mary Parker**, and several nieces and nephews. No evidence of a marriage between Greenfield's parents has been found, and the exact relationship of Greenfield to the persons she listed in her will may never be clarified. Surviving accounts of Greenfield's lineage conflict in details, but all concur that she was of racially mixed heritage. Most likely her father was African while her mother was of African, caucasian, and Native American descent.

Sometime around 1821, Mrs. Holliday Greenfield freed her slaves and moved to Philadelphia, Pennsylvania, where she joined the Society of Friends and, in keeping with the antislavery sentiment of the Quakers, provided her former slaves with financial assistance and transportation to Liberia. Elizabeth Greenfield's father was among those who requested to emigrate, but there is no indication of whether he was accompanied by her mother. The young Elizabeth remained with Mrs. Holliday Greenfield until she was about seven or eight years of age, and then presumably went to live with Mary Parker. Around 1835, Elizabeth Greenfield moved back to Mrs. Holliday Greenfield's residence and would serve as nurse and housekeeper until the elderly widow's death.

It became apparent early in Greenfield's childhood that she possessed unusual musical gifts. She taught herself accompaniments to simple songs on both piano and guitar. Formal music lessons were begun without the knowledge of Mrs. Holliday Greenfield, as Elizabeth feared that her affiliation with the Quakers would preclude any participation in music. She began to study voice, guitar, piano and music rudiments with a neighbor, a musician and teacher known only as Miss Price. Owing to the rapid progress Elizabeth made, an informal recital was planned, to take place in Price's home. With Price providing piano and guitar accompaniment, Greenfield's first performance met with favorable response. Historian James M. Trotter recalled:

> [B]efore she had finished she was surrounded by the astonished inmates of the house, who, attracted by the remarkable compass and sweetness of her voice, stealthily entered the room, and now unperceived stood gathered behind her. The applause which followed the first trial before this small but intelligent audience gratified as much as it embarrassed her, from the unexpected and sudden surprise.

Mrs. Holliday Greenfield learned of Elizabeth's clandestine music lessons and performances, and, rather than voicing immediate disapproval, she invited her to sing. Even though the Quakers disapproved of secular music, Mrs. Holliday Greenfield was so favorably impressed with Elizabeth's talent that she provided financial support for continued instruction.

Greenfield had a voice the likes of which the American public had seldom heard from any singer, white or black.

—Rosalyn M. Story

On July 9, 1845, Mrs. Holliday Greenfield died, leaving a substantial portion of her estate to Elizabeth. Mrs. Holliday Greenfield's relatives contested the will on racial grounds and the intended recipient never received her bequest. Nonetheless, in honor of her benefactor's generosity, Elizabeth assumed her surname. Shortly after, Elizabeth Taylor Greenfield began to see students and to perform in public. Her singing drew the attention of William Appo, one of Philadelphia's prominent musicians, who engaged her to participate in a concert in Baltimore, Maryland, sometime during 1849. By 1850, Greenfield had gained sufficient notoriety to justify a listing in the Philadelphia City Directory as "E.T. Greenfield, music teacher."

In 1851, Greenfield left Philadelphia on a trip to Buffalo, New York, to visit friends and to attend a performance of renowned soprano *Jenny Lind, the "Swedish Nightingale." While crossing Seneca Lake, she entertained passengers on board the boat with her singing. Members of her audience included the wealthy philanthropist Mrs. H.B. Potter (✤➤ **Electa Potter**), who invited Greenfield to her residence in Buffalo to perform. Shortly after her arrival in Buffalo, Greenfield presented a recital at a large reception arranged for her benefit by Potter. Many of Buffalo's elite were in attendance, one of whom suggested that Greenfield give a series of public recitals.

Elizabeth Greenfield made her stage debut in Buffalo on October 22, 1851, in a performance sponsored by the Buffalo Musical Association. Numerous newspapers and periodicals carried reviews of the event, including Frederick Douglass' *North Star*. Trotter offered this appraisal by a Buffalo resident:

> The concert got up for [Greenfield] was unsolicited on her part, and entirely the result of admiration of her vocal powers by a number of our most respectable citizens, who had heard her at the residence of Gen. Potter, with whose family she had become somewhat familiar. The concert was attended by an audience not second in point of numbers to any given here before, except by Jenny Lind; and not second to any point of respectability and fashion. The performance of Miss Greenfield was received with great applause; and the expression since, among our citizens generally, is a strong desire to hear her again.

A notice of Greenfield's debut in the Buffalo *Daily Express*, quoted by La Brew, earned her the sobriquet "Black Swan": "Give the 'Black Swan' the cultivation and experience of the fair Swede [Jenny Lind] and Mlle [**Theresa**] **Parodi**, and she will rank favorably with those popular singers who have carried the nation into captivity by their rare musical abilities."

While the sobriquet remained with Greenfield throughout her career, its irony was not lost on critics. A reviewer in the *New York Tribune* commented: "The person who does the ornithology for her musical renown should remember that, though a black swan is a rara avis . . . it does not sing. Its song when dying is the fancy of a poet when lying." And similarly, an article in the *Carpet Bag* of February 14, 1852, described the "Black Swan" as "absurdly cognominated. We say absurdly—for swans are never black, neither do they sing. Their modulations are anything but melodious, and their inflections are absolute inflictions." The Albany (NY) *Evening Journal* of January 19, 1852, printed this observation:

> It has become so customary lately, to call concert triumphs and songstresses by the name of some bird to which they bear a real or fancied resemblance, instead of their Christian and proper names, that if we were to say that Miss Greenfield's concert on Sat-

urday evening was well attended and successful, probably most of our readers would not know what we meant. So we will adopt the usual formula, and say that "the Black Swan" was enthusiastically received.

After Greenfield's success in Buffalo, she was invited to appear in other western New York communities, including Rochester and Lockport. Her performances intrigued the impresario Colonel J.H. Wood, a former museum owner, whom she subsequently engaged as her promoter and manager. Wood arranged a lengthy concert tour for Greenfield that lasted well into 1852 and covered major metropolitan areas in the northeastern and upper midwestern United States. Nearly all of her recitals received press coverage and positive reviews. Critics marveled at her vocal ease, flexibility, and sweetness, and her amazing range of at least three octaves.

As Greenfield rose to prominence, the Swedish soprano Jenny Lind was touring the United States. Despite Lind's success and critical acclaim, the American public longed for a singer of its own who could rival the prestige and enthusiastic following generated by Lind and, to a lesser extent, other European singers. Almost immediately after Greenfield began to draw notice from the press, critics succumbed to the temptation of comparing her performances to those of Lind. Greenfield unwittingly contributed to the debate by choosing many of the same pieces for her recital that were, by now, Lind standards. For example, the Rochester (NY) *Daily American* reported on December 13, 1851: "It was a bold attempt for the Black Swan to sing 'Do Not Mingle,' after Jenny Lind." The Buffalo *Daily Courier* mentioned, according to La Brew, a Greenfield program "consisting of some of Jenny Lind's most popular songs." Even Greenfield's vocal range was compared to that of Lind. "The compass of [Greenfield's] marvelous voice embraces twenty-seven notes, reaching from the sonorous bass of a barytone [sic], to a few notes above Jenny Lind's highest," the Albany *State Register* reported on January 19, 1852.

In February 1853, an unnamed promoter engaged Greenfield to sing in various locations in New England, New York, and Canada, and to perform a New York City debut recital. Intended to coincide with the opening of the World's Fair, the debut was scheduled at Metropolitan Hall for March 31, 1853. In the only autobiographical account of her career, *The Black Swan at Home and Abroad*, Greenfield alluded to the racial oppression that marred her stay in New York. Shortly after arriving, she attempted to attend a recital of the celebrated Italian contralto

❧➤ Potter, Electa (1790–1854)

American philanthropist. Name variations: Mrs. H.B. Potter. Born Electa Miller on March 16, 1790; died on October 13, 1854; second daughter of Frederick and Elizabeth (Babcock) Miller; married Heman B. Potter (a judge), on July 12, 1812 (died, October 7, 1854); children: Mary Eliza Potter (1813–1814); Mary Bradley Babcock (1815–1877, who married George Reed Babcock); Frederick Miller Potter (1817–1818); Elizabeth Miller Potter (1819–1854); Heman Bradley Potter (1824–1859).

Electa Potter, a prominent philanthropist in Buffalo, New York, died on October 13, 1854, six days after the death of her husband, judge Heman B. Potter.

*Marietta Alboni at the Italian Opera House but was refused a ticket. Blacks were also excluded from Greenfield's debut, and unrest was threatened if she went through with the performance. Her recital took place as planned, however, though police were posted throughout the hall to control a rather restless audience numbering nearly 4,000.

In April 1853, Greenfield sailed for England to begin a concert tour. Upon arrival in London, a dispute over back pay forced Greenfield to seek another promoter. Left completely on her own, she appealed to Lord Shaftsbury, a member of a prominent antislavery society, for assistance. He referred her to *Harriet Beecher Stowe, who was in England at the time promoting her first novel, *Uncle Tom's Cabin*. Stowe recorded her recollections of Greenfield in her diary, later published as *Sunny Memories of Foreign Lands*. In an entry dated May 6, 1853, Stowe described Greenfield as "a gentle, amiable and interesting young person." Greenfield must have been requested to perform for Stowe at their initial meeting as the author included observations about her singing: "She has a most astonishing voice . . . [that] runs through a compass of three octaves and a fourth. . . . She sings a most magnificent tenor, with such breadth and volume of sound, that, with your back turned, you could not imagine it to be a woman." Stowe was so impressed with Greenfield's gifts that she made arrangements for Greenfield to be introduced to Sir George Smart, organist and composer to Her Majesty Queen Victoria's Chapel Royal.

Stowe's diary contained a brief but important description of Greenfield's physical appearance, and also revealed the more enlightened racial attitudes among those closest to Queen Victoria. "I never realized so much that there really is no natural prejudice against colour in the human mind," Stowe recorded in *Sunny Memories.*

> Miss Greenfield is a dark mulattress, of a pleasing and gentle face, though by no means handsome. She is short and thickset, with a chest of great amplitude, as one would think on hearing her tenor. I have never seen in any of the persons to whom I have presented her the least indications of suppressed surprise or disgust.

During the remainder of Greenfield's stay in Great Britain, Smart served as her accompanist and mentor, and, with his assistance, she participated in several prestigious concerts. In 1853, she performed at Stafford House, Exeter Hall, and at Hanover Square Rooms. Stowe, who was present at the Stafford House performance, wrote again of Greenfield's voice, "with its keen, searching fire, its penetrating, vibrant quality, its timbre, as the French have it, cuts its way like a Damascus blade to the heart." On May 10, Greenfield received a royal command from Queen Victoria to sing at Buckingham Palace—an invitation reserved for only the most celebrated of musicians.

In July of 1854, Greenfield returned to the United States and began a second extensive concert tour, traveling throughout the northeast and into Canada. Advertisements for her appearances referred to her success in Great Britain, her vocal range, and her musical maturity acquired through study with Sir George Smart. After completing this second tour, Greenfield began to teach students in her place of residence in Philadelphia. A third tour was undertaken in 1856, lasting approximately one year, and a final concert tour took place in 1863.

In addition to concertizing and teaching, Greenfield participated in numerous charity causes, including benefits to assist orphanages in Buffalo, Detroit, Philadelphia, and New York. She organized the Black Swan Opera Troupe, one of the earliest efforts to involve African-Americans in the performance of standard operatic literature. Her troupe became well-known throughout the northeast and opened up new opportunities for black singers.

Throughout her later years, Greenfield became increasingly active in her church, Shiloh Baptist, where she directed the choir. An illness in 1874 forced her to curtail nearly all her activities. She never recovered and on March 31, 1876, she died of apoplexy. Her death was widely reported and received at least some mention in nearly every major newspaper.

SOURCES:

Austin, William W. "Greenfield, Elizabeth Taylor," in *The New Grove Dictionary of American Music.* Vol. II. Edited by H. Wiley Hitchcock and Stanley Sadie. NY: Macmillan, 1986.

Carpet Bag. February 14, 1852.

Daily American [Rochester, NY]. December 13, 1851.

Daily Express [Buffalo, NY]. October 23, 1851.

Dwight's Journal of Music. Vol. 3, no. 1. April 9, 1853, pp. 2–3.

Evening Journal [Albany, NY]. January 19, 1852.

Greenfield, Elizabeth Taylor. *The Black Swan.* Detroit, MI: self-published, 1869.

La Brew, Arthur R. "Elizabeth Taylor Greenfield," in *Notable Black American Women.* Edited by Jessie Carney Smith. Detroit, MI: Gale Research, 1992.

Southern, Eileen. *Biographical Dictionary of Afro-American and African Musicians.* Westport, CT: Greenwood Press, 1982.

Spencer, Samuel R., Jr. "Greenfield, Elizabeth Taylor," in *Notable American Women, 1607-1950.* Vol. II. Edited by Edward T. James. New Haven, CT: Belknap Press of Harvard University Press, 1971.

State Register [Albany, NY]. January 19, 1852.

Story, Rosalyn M. *And So I Sing: African-American Divas of Opera and Concert.* NY: Warner Books, 1990.

Stowe, Harriet Elizabeth Beecher. *Sunny Memories of Foreign Lands.* London: England: T. Nelson and Sons, 1854.

Thompson, Kathleen. "Greenfield, Elizabeth Taylor," in *Black Women in America.* Edited by Darlene Clark Hine. Vol. I. Brooklyn, NY: Carlson, 1993.

Trotter, James M. *Music and Some Highly Musical People.* NY: Charles Dillingham, 1880 (reprint, Chicago: Afro-Am Press, 1969).

Young, William S., ed. *The Black Swan at Home and Abroad, or a Biographical Sketch of Miss Elizabeth Taylor Greenfield, the American Vocalist.* Philadelphia: self-published, 1855.

SUGGESTED READING:

Clift, Virgil A., and W. Augustus Low, eds. *Encyclopedia of Black America.* NY: McGraw-Hill, 1981.

Cuney-Hare, Maud. *Negro Musicians and Their Music.* Washington, DC: Associated Publishers, 1936 (reprint, NY: Da Capo, 1974).

Delany, Martin Robinson. *The Condition, Elevation, Emigration, and Destiny of the Colored People of the United States.* Philadelphia: self-published, 1852 (reprint, NY: Arno Press and The New York Times, 1968).

Lemieux, Raymond. "Greenfield, Elizabeth Taylor," in *Dictionary of American Negro Biography.* Edited by Raymond W. Logan and Michael R. Winston. NY: W.W. Norton, 1982.

Majors, Monroe A. *Noted Negro Women: Their Triumphs and Activities.* Chicago, IL: Donohue and Henneberry, 1893 (reprint, Freeport, NY: Books for Libraries Press, 1971).

McGinty, Doris Evans. "The Black Presence in the Music of Washington, D.C.: 1843–1904," in *More Than Dancing.* Edited by Irene V. Jackson. Westport, CT: Greenwood Press, 1985.

Robinson, Wilhelmena S. *Historical Negro Biographies.* NY: Publishers Company, 1969.

Rywell, Martin, ed. *Afro-American Encyclopedia*. Vol. IV. North Miami, FL: Educational Book Publishers, 1974.

Scruggs, Lawson Andrew. *Women of Distinction*. Raleigh, NC: self-published, 1893.

Southern, Eileen. *The Music of Black Americans*. 2nd ed. NY: W.W. Norton, 1983.

Juanita Karpf,
Assistant Professor of Music and Women's Studies,
University of Georgia, Athens, Georgia

Greenfield, Meg (1930–1999)

American journalist and editor who was a longtime columnist for The Washington Post *and* Newsweek. *Born on December 27, 1930, in Seattle, Washington; died on May 13, 1999, in Washington, D.C.; daughter of Lewis and Lorraine (Nathan) Greenfield; Smith College, B.A., 1952; Fulbright Scholar, Newnham College, Cambridge (England) University, 1952–53; never married; no children.*

A Pulitzer Prize-winning editor and writer, and the editorial voice of *The Washington Post* from 1979 until her death in 1999, Meg Greenfield not only raised the bar for women journalists, but set a new standard for the editorial pages of American newspapers. "She shaped the editorial page of the *Post* in a highly personal way—independent and strong but respectful of others' opinions," said publisher Donald E. Graham. "On the ethics of our business she was the Supreme Court, as far as I was concerned."

Meg Greenfield was born in Seattle, Washington, in 1930, and graduated summa cum laude from Smith College in 1952, after which she spent a year at Cambridge University in England as a Fulbright Scholar. Greenfield worked for 11 years on the old *Reporter* magazine before joining the *Post* in 1968 as an editorial writer. She worked her way steadily through the ranks, serving as deputy editor of the editorial page from 1970 to 1979, then moving up to editor. From 1974 to 1999, Greenfield was also a columnist for *Newsweek* magazine. She won a Pulitzer Prize in 1978 for her editorials on social policy.

Greenfield voiced opinions on some of the great turmoils and scandals of her time, from Watergate to Monicagate, never once losing sight of the frailties of the human condition. "I am to this day, even given the uncountable number of scuzzy public betrayals and lies, much more comfortable when a scoundrel eludes us or we miss the scent, than when we are pursuing someone who shouldn't be charged," she wrote in a *Newsweek* column in November 1998. In a style that was called "textured" and "elabo-

rate," Greenfield urged her readers to look at the facts for answers to any debate. "The principal occupational hazard of editorial writer," she once said, "is 'Mussolini-ism': censorious tone; circular logic; and an instruction that is probably entirely unrealistic and impractical."

Greenfield remained on the job even while battling the lung cancer that took her life on May 13, 1999. "She called on those of us who work in government to pursue far-sighted public policy and bipartisan solutions," said President Clinton following her death. "Her voice of eloquence and reason will be sorely missed."

SOURCES:

"Obituaries." *The Boston Globe*. May 14, 1999.

"Obituaries." *The Day* [New London]. May 14, 1999.

"People in the News," *U.S. News & World Report*. Vol. 126, no. 20. May 24, 1999, p. 16.

Greenhow, Rose O'Neal

(c. 1817–1864)

Washington socialite, confidante of Senator John C. Calhoun and President James Buchanan, who was a daring Confederate spy during the Civil War. Name variations: Wild Rose, Rebel Rose. Born around 1817 in Port Tobacco, Maryland; drowned on October 1, 1864, in the Cape Fear River near Wilmington, North Carolina; daughter of John O'Neal (a Maryland planter); had little formal education, but was tutored by South Carolina Senator John C. Calhoun; married Robert Greenhow (a Virginia doctor, lawyer and linguist), in 1835; children: four daughters, Florence Greenhow; Gertrude Greenhow; Leila Greenhow; Rose Greenhow.

Moved as an infant to Montgomery County, Maryland, after the murder of her father; moved to Washington, D.C., and lived in the boarding house of her aunt, Mrs. H.V. Hill (c. 1830); married Robert Greenhow (1835); widowed while living in California (1854); established herself as the most influential woman in Washington during James Buchanan's presidency (1857–61); organized an effective spy ring and supplied military information to the Confederate government (June 1861); arrested for espionage and imprisoned (August 1861); released from prison and deported to the South (June 1862); sent by President Jefferson Davis on a diplomatic and intelligence mission to England and France (August 1863); published her memoirs, My Imprisonment and the First Year of Abolition Rule in Washington (November 1863); became engaged to the 2nd Earl of Granville in London (1864); boarded the blockade runner Condor, carrying secret dispatches and gold for the Confederacy

(August 1964); drowned in a storm off Wilmington, North Carolina (October 1864).

On the eve of the Civil War, in the District of Columbia, Rose Greenhow had a reputation for witty repartee and political intrigue. Her intelligence and vivacity, in addition to her carefully nurtured connections to men of power, made her easily the most influential and persuasive woman in the capital. Wild Rose, as she was called by friends and detractors alike, had a gregarious charm and a striking appearance which made it easy for the men of Washington to overlook her Southern secessionist sympathies. For almost 30 years, Greenhow had cultivated the friendship of political greats and military rising stars. She moved with ease in the highest social circles and counted among her intimates many of the city's elite, including diplomats, senators, congressional representatives, cabinet secretaries, generals, and U.S. presidents.

I employed every capacity with which God has endowed me, and the result was far more successful than my hopes could have flattered me to expect.

—Rose O'Neal Greenhow

After the secession of the Southern states, Greenhow remained in Washington to begin a career as one of the most successful spies of the Civil War. An outspoken Southern sympathizer, she was happy to capitalize on her access to information carelessly spoken by friends in high places. Furthermore, she was quite willing to exploit the affections and indiscretions of her numerous male admirers. At the outbreak of hostilities, Greenhow organized an efficient spy ring, complete with couriers and a secret coded cipher. Her very first attempts at espionage provided the Confederate Army with information which assured an overwhelming Southern victory at the Battle of Bull Run (also known as Manassas).

Rose O'Neal was born into a family with ancestral ties to the Calverts and other original holders of the Maryland colony. Her father, John O'Neale (who dropped the final "e" in his name before Rose's birth) was not a wealthy man, but as a planter he was able to provide a comfortable living for his family. Rose's life took a drastic turn during her infancy when her father was killed by one of his slaves. The family moved to Rockville, Maryland, about 15 miles from Washington, where Rose and her sisters spent the remainder of their childhood. By the time Rose had reached her early teens, she and her older sister **Ellen Elizabeth O'Neal** were sent to live with their aunt, **Mrs. H.V. Hill**, who ran the Congressional Boarding House in the old U.S. Capitol building. A popular residence for members of Congress, the boarding house afforded Rose her first exposure to the people and issues which would preoccupy her for the rest of her life.

Life at the boarding house, in the company of men like Henry Clay and Daniel Webster, was truly educational for young Rose. Preeminent among her tutors, however, was John C. Calhoun, the fiery senator from South Carolina, who became her mentor. She listened with rapt attention as Calhoun fulminated about Southern rights and grievances, and his convictions became her own. "I am a Southern woman, born with revolutionary blood in my veins," she wrote, "and my first crude ideas on State and Federal matters received consistency and shape from the best and wisest man of this century." Though many years separated them, Calhoun and Greenhow grew quite close. After a friendship of 20 years, it was Rose who nursed the aged Calhoun as he died in the boarding house in 1850.

Rose's first serious romantic interest was Cave Johnson, a somewhat dour congressional representative from Tennessee, who would ultimately serve as postmaster general under President James Knox Polk. Johnson noticed Rose while he was residing at the Congressional Boarding House and began to court her even though she was only 16 years old at the time. Though she eventually came to feel that Johnson was somber and uninteresting, Rose was for a time his constant companion, and it was he who initiated her into the Washington society which so fascinated her. A short time later, she met Virginian Robert Greenhow, geographer, linguist and historian, who also had background in medicine and the law. Rose's senior by 17 years, Robert was working as a translator for the State Department and was considered an authority on Mexico and the West. They married in 1835 and spent the next 15 years in Washington where three of their four daughters were born.

Greenhow enjoyed the life of a State Department official's spouse and took advantage of every opportunity to learn more of political affairs and to make friends of those in power. There is no indication of unhappiness in the Greenhows' marriage, although the quiet scholar and his wife were of entirely different temperaments. Her counsel was sought by many men in Washington, but it was James Buchanan upon whom she exercised the greatest influence. She became one of the most ardent supporters of his political

Rose O'Neal Greenhow in the Old Capitol Prison with one of her visiting daughters.

aspirations, and he would not forget their friendship when he was elected president in 1856.

In 1850, the same year that Greenhow's mentor John C. Calhoun died, she and her family left Washington. Robert resigned his position with the State Department and became an officer with the U.S. Land Commission in San Francisco. During this time, California became a state, and Greenhow continued to be politically active on behalf of Southern interests and those of James Buchanan, with whom she kept up a lively correspondence. Greenhow returned to Washington in the winter of 1853 pregnant with her fourth child. In February or March of 1854, while still in San Francisco, Robert suffered a serious accident, falling six feet from a plankway down an embankment to the street. Robert had no idea of the critical nature of his injuries, so he did not send for his wife. He died after six weeks of acute pain and partial paralysis. By the time Rose was notified of his death, she found it impossible to make the long journey to California with a newborn infant in tow.

When Greenhow brought suit against the city of San Francisco, she won a judgment large enough to enable her to purchase a fashionable house on Washington's 16th Street. Having no intentions of playing the withdrawn widow, she soon reestablished herself as the leading host of the Democratic regime, and her house became a mecca for political powerbrokers of both parties, from the North as well as the South.

Numerous aspiring politicos became indebted to Greenhow for their appointments, thanks to her skill at parlor diplomacy. When her friend James Buchanan was elected president in 1856, Greenhow's relationship to the old bachelor became the subject of endless gossip. Her neighbors on 16th Street, and indeed speculators all over Washington, were scandalized by the fact that Buchanan's easily identifiable carriage stopped at Greenhow's home frequently and stayed so late. As Major William E. Doster, provost marshall of Washington, wrote, "There was much gossip at this time arising from the intimacy between Mrs. Greenhow and the President."

By the late 1850s, political storm clouds were gathering in Washington. By 1861, the secession crisis was forcing Southern politicians and military leaders to leave Washington in a steady stream, in preparation for the coming conflagration. Colonel Thomas Jordan, who resigned his commission in the U.S. Army to serve with Confederate General Pierre Beauregard as adjutant, suggested that Greenhow remain in Washington in order to supply information to the Confederate military. Rose was eager to use her numerous friendships in Washington to help the Confederate cause.

Jordan gave her a secret cipher with which to encode her messages and set up for her use a string of couriers charged with moving information out of Washington and into Confederate territory. Almost immediately, Greenhow found herself in a perfect position to spy for the Confederates. In July, she learned from her Union contacts that General Irving McDowell was moving south from Washington with a large force toward Manassas Junction, Virginia, with the intention of crushing the rebellion with one mighty blow. Greenhow quickly penned a message to Beauregard, "In a day or two twelve hundred cavalry plus four batteries of artillery will cross Bull Run . . . for God's sake heed this, it is positive."

When Beauregard received this message from a courier, he lacked specific information regarding the time and place of the planned assault. Another dispatch from Greenhow on July 10 was smuggled through Union lines by her close friend, **Betty Duvall**, who hid the message inside the curls of her hair. It was more specific: "McDowell has certainly been ordered to advance on the sixteenth." Thanks to Greenhow's timely intelligence, Beauregard was able to mass together several scattered divisions at Manassas in time to confront McDowell's green recruits with sufficient strength to accomplish a complete rout of the Northern army. Greenhow soon received the following grateful dispatch, which she proudly carried with her for the rest of her life, "Our President and our general direct me to thank you. We rely upon you for further information. The Confederacy owes you a debt."

Greenhow was almost certainly receiving this sensitive military information from her most ardent admirer, Senator Henry Wilson of Massachusetts. There exists a group of passionate love letters among Rose Greenhow's papers in the National Archives. These letters, written on Senate stationery and signed simply "H," were undoubtedly written by Wilson and are anything but platonic. "H" vows: "You well know that I love you and will sacrifice anything. Tonight, whatever the cost, I will see you, and then I will tell you again and again that I love you." How fortunate for a Confederate spy that these sentiments were written by the chair of the Senate Military Affairs Committee; through Wilson, Greenhow was privy to classified information from the war department, the White House, and the staffs of generals McDowell and McClellan. She bragged openly in Washington that she knew what McDowell was going to do before he knew it. McClellan complained, "She knew my plans, and has four times compelled me to change them."

During her brief but successful spying career in the summer of 1861, Greenhow gathered information on Lincoln's personal guards, the strength of Washington's defenses, and other data which would have been useful had the Confederates successfully invaded the Union capital.

After Greenhow plied Secretary of State William Henry Seward with generous amounts of wine until he was "properly attuned with the gifts the gods provide," he let slip several compromising tidbits regarding the state of the Union navy. Soon, Greenhow was sending daily reports from Washington to Richmond.

Within weeks, suspicious Union leaders began regarding Greenhow as a potential leak in their security; the defeat at Bull Run was widely blamed on the existence of an espionage ring. All of Washington knew of her open advocacy of the Confederate cause and of her close relationships with several Union officials. Thomas A. Scott, assistant secretary of war, hired the famous detective Allan Pinkerton to stake out Greenhow's house, convinced she was actively engaged in spying for the South. On the night of August 22, 1861, Pinkerton and two other detectives arrived at her house on 16th Street in a pouring rainstorm. Frustrated in his attempts to see into her parlor windows, which were situated half a story above ground level, Pinkerton took off his shoes and stood on the shoulders of his subordinates to give himself a clear view.

Inside Greenhow's parlor Pinkerton saw a Union officer, who appeared to be showing her a map of Washington fortifications. After several minutes, Greenhow and her companion left the room for a longer period, after which the couple emerged holding hands. Soon thereafter, the man left the house to the sound of a vigorous goodnight kiss.

The next day, Pinkerton and his entourage were waiting at her door as Greenhow approached with a diplomatic acquaintance. Greenhow was arrested, and the men set about ransacking her house for evidence. While Pinkerton's men tore apart pictures, bed frames, closets, and drawers looking for evidence, Greenhow remained inside. Bits of paper with messages written in cipher were found in the fireplace, shredded but unburnt. When the searchers reached her liquor cabinet, she opened a bottle of brandy and passed it around. Then, while the search turned into revelry, Greenhow quietly stole upstairs, removed her secret papers from a top shelf, and slipped them into her maid's stocking. As the officers continued their search, the maid spotted a blotter, on which was a perfect mirror image of Greenhow's last message. She quickly destroyed it. Later, her maid was allowed to leave, taking the most incriminating evidence with her. Greenhow's daughter, Little Rose, ran to an upstairs window, where she yelled repeatedly to passersby: "Mother's been arrested! Mother's been arrested!"

All Washington was buzzing the next day with news of the arrests, which eventually included many prominent figures. For the next several months, Greenhow was kept under house arrest. Her spying continued, however, as she was able to send messages through her maid and her daughter Rose. She once used a carrier pigeon to dispatch crucial information to Confederate President Jefferson Davis. She boasted at her ability to carry on her espionage activities under the noses of her captors. Frustrated law enforcement officers eventually confined Greenhow to the Old Capitol Prison, formerly the boarding house where she had grown up. She was assigned to the very room where she had nursed the dying John C. Calhoun in 1850.

Although possessed of sufficient evidence to try her for treason, Union officials feared a trial would implicate high-ranking officers and prominent politicians in her activities should they be made public. Wanting nothing more than to be rid of the pesky widow, Union officials offered her a safe conduct to Confederate territory. On the day of her release, Greenhow emerged, wearing a heavy shawl, to a curious throng of spectators. Just before boarding the carriage that was to take her to Baltimore, Maryland, she lifted the edge of her shawl to reveal a full-sized Confederate flag.

Rose Greenhow became the toast of the town upon her arrival in Richmond on June 4, 1862. President Jefferson Davis assured her, "But for you there would have been no Battle of Bull Run," and paid her a bounty of $2,500 for her "valuable and patriotic service." In August 1863, Davis sent Greenhow to Europe to act as a propagandist and courier. She was charged with gathering intelligence and spreading good will regarding the Confederate cause. She was received warmly in Britain, where she found strong sympathy for the Southern effort. She was less warmly received, however, in France at the court of Napoleon III. In 1863 London, Greenhow published her memoirs, entitled *My Imprisonment and the First Year of Abolition Rule in Washington*. Her book sold well in Britain and brought her generous royalties. While in England, she met and dazzled the second earl of Granville, recently widowed, who asked for her hand in marriage. Though she agreed to marry the earl, she felt that the information she had gathered was too sensitive to be entrusted to a courier; so she insisted on delivering the news to Davis personally back in the States.

In August 1864, Greenhow boarded the blockade runner *Condor* and proceeded across the Atlantic without incident. But when the ship reached the Cape Fear River, above Wilmington, North Carolina, a fierce storm blew up. In his haste to reach the protection of the guns of Fort Fisher, the captain stranded the vessel atop a sandbar. Fearing capture by a pursuing Federal gunboat, Greenhow insisted that the captain provide her with a rowboat to take her to shore. The captain hesitated, fearing the raging storm, but he was no match for the insistent Greenhow. As she entered the shaky boat, around her neck she wore a heavy bag filled with $2,000 worth of gold coins she had received as royalties from her book, which she intended to donate to the Confederate cause. Within yards of the ship, the rowboat capsized. Greenhow was immediately swept under the waves with the weight of the gold and her own voluminous skirts. Her body was discovered the next morning by a Confederate soldier, who stole the money and pushed her corpse back into the surf. Later, search parties found her body, and when news of her death was published in the local newspaper, the guilt-stricken soldier turned himself in, along with the money he had taken. Rose Greenhow was buried with full military honors in Oakdale Cemetery in Wilmington, North Carolina.

A daring and courageous woman, Rose Greenhow was one of the most successful spies of the Civil War, prompting Senator Charles Sumner of Massachusetts to claim: "Mrs. Greenhow is worth any six of Jeff Davis' best regiments." There is no doubt that her efforts contributed strongly to the early victories of the Confederate Army.

SOURCES:

Bakeless, John. *Spies of the Confederacy.* Philadelphia, PA: J.B. Lippincott, 1907.

Kane, Harnett T. *Spies for the Blue and Gray.* NY: Doubleday, 1954.

Kinchen, Oscar A. *Women who Spied for the Blue and the Gray.* Philadelphia, PA: Dorrance, 1972.

Ross, Ishbel. *Rebel Rose: Life of Rose O'Neal Greenhow, Confederate Spy.* NY: Harper & Brothers, 1954.

SUGGESTED READING:

Garrison, Webb. *A Treasury of Civil War Tales.* Nashville, TN: Rutledge Hill Press, 1988.

Stern, Philip Van Doren. *Secret Missions of the Civil War.* NY: Bonanza Books, 1959.

Peter Harrison Branum, Ph.D.,
Philosophy, Auburn University, Auburn, Alabama

Greenough, Alice (d. 1995).

See Orr, Alice Greenough.

Greenway, Isabella Selmes
(1886–1953)

American congresswoman, frontier homesteader, cattle rancher, airline operator, hotel owner, and community activist. Name variations: Isabella Selmes Ferguson Greenway King. Born Isabella Selmes on March 22, 1886; died on December 18, 1953, at her home at the Arizona Inn, of congestive heart failure; daughter of Tilden Russell Selmes (a rancher and lawyer) and Martha Macomb (Flandrau) Selmes; attended Miss Chapin's and Miss Spence's schools, New York City; married Robert H. Munro Ferguson, on July 15, 1905 (died 1922); married John Campbell Greenway, on November 4, 1923 (died 1926); married Harry Orland King, on April 22, 1939; children (first marriage) Robert and Martha; (second marriage) John Selmes.

Father ranched in South Dakota, lost ranch in blizzards (1886–87); moved to St. Paul, Minnesota; spent summers on mother's family farm in Boone County, Kentucky; father died (1895); moved to New York City to attend high school (1901); husband Bob diagnosed with tuberculosis (1908); lived at sanitarium near Saranac Lake, New York (1908–10); homesteaded in New Mexico, served on local school board and, during World War I, on local National Defense Council and as chair of Women's Land Army of New Mexico (1911–21); moved to Santa Barbara, California (1921–22); bought ranch near Williams, Arizona, then moved to Tucson and opened the Arizona Hut, a rehabilitation workshop for veterans, among other community activities (1927); appointed national Democratic committeewoman from Arizona (1928–32); campaigned for Al Smith (1928); co-founded G & G commuter airline (1929–30); founded Arizona Inn, resort hotel (1930); seconded nomination of Franklin Roosevelt at Democratic national convention and campaigned for him (1932); elected congresswoman-at-large in special election (1933–37); was active in the Democrats for Willkie movement (1940); served as chair of American Women's Voluntary Services (1941).

Isabella Selmes Greenway led a highly textured life. Her infancy was spent on a snow-swept ranch in South Dakota, where young Theodore Roosevelt was a neighbor. Her adolescence was spent in New York where a wealthy uncle enabled her to attend an exclusive girls' school. A bridesmaid at the wedding of Franklin and *Eleanor Roosevelt, she also became involved in mining, ranching, and aviation; founded a furniture cooperative for disabled veterans; established an inn; achieved national prominence when she seconded Franklin Roosevelt's nomination at the Democratic convention; and was elected to Congress. Remarkably good-looking, at home in Southern tobacco country, on Western ranches, or in New York salons, shrewd, energetic and idealistic, she was, as her obituary in *The New York Times* claimed in something of an understatement, "one of the more colorful personalities who flashed into prominence in the political upheaval that brought Franklin Delano Roosevelt to the presidency."

Isabella Selmes was born in 1886 on Dinsmore Farm in Boone County, Kentucky, the home of **Julia Stockton Dinsmore**, her mother's great-aunt, who both ran the farm and published poetry. Shortly after Isabella's birth, her mother **Martha Selmes**, with Isabella in arms, rejoined her husband Tilden on his cattle ranch near Mandan, South Dakota, where Theodore Roosevelt also had a ranch. Roosevelt and Tilden Selmes lost most of their livestock in the blizzards of 1886–87, as did many, and Tilden quit ranching and moved to St. Paul, where his mother's father lived, to practice law. He died of cancer when Isabella was nine.

Isabella Selmes Greenway

For the next few years, Greenway spent winters with her grandparents in St. Paul and summers at Dinsmore Farm, where her mother supported them from the sale of bacon and ham. In 1901, her mother's brother-in-law and sister, Franklin and **Sarah Cutcheon**, invited Isabella and her mother to live with them in New York. Cutcheon, a corporate lawyer, helped with the cost of clothes and tuition so Isabella could attend Miss Chapin's and Miss Spence's schools, where she became friends with Eleanor Roosevelt.

Don't you ever tell me I can't do anything.

—Isabella Greenway

During her debutante season, Isabella met Bob Ferguson, a Scot who had served with Theodore Roosevelt's Rough Riders in the Spanish-American War. They were married in 1905 and had two children. In 1908, Ferguson was diagnosed with tuberculosis. For two years, the Fergusons lived at a sanitarium near Saranac Lake, New York. From 1910 to 1913, when Ferguson was advised to move to the dry climate of the southwest, the family lived in tents in Cat Canyon, near Silver City, New Mexico. At that time, a tuberculosis patient like Ferguson would have been warned to have separate eating utensils and bedding, and not to touch his wife or children. Isabella, with the help of her mother, was able to run the unorthodox household, nurse her husband, educate the children, manage the cattle ranch, and even entertain guests like Franklin and Eleanor Roosevelt, who made several visits. Eventually, the Fergusons built a large sprawling house with gardens and a pool.

Isabella Greenway was active in the community, serving as chair of the local school board 1914–16; she began by closing the schools because the taxes for their support had not been paid. During World War I, she was chair of the Grant County National Defense Council, and she organized and headed the Women's Land Army of New Mexico, which raised and harvested crops and took over other work in place of the men who were away in the army. During the epidemic of influenza which followed the war, she worked to help former Land Army families.

When Bob Ferguson's condition worsened in 1921, the family moved to Santa Barbara, California, where the children could attend school. Ferguson died in October 1922. During his illness, the family had been assisted by Bob's friend and fellow Rough Rider John Campbell Greenway. Jack, 14 years Isabella's senior, had been a star athlete at Yale, a resourceful mining engineer, and a decorated soldier during World War I who was promoted to brigadier-general in 1922. He and Isabella were married in 1923, and their son John Selmes was born a year later. Jack Greenway was at the height of a successful career, and the couple traveled throughout the country in his private railroad car, visiting his mining interests in the West, going East to lobby for development projects, or to California for vacation. During one of his trips, Jack experienced a gall bladder attack; as a preventative measure, he allowed his doctors to remove the gall bladder before a planned expedition to southern Africa where he had mining interests. He died of a blood clot a week later.

After his death, Isabella Greenway continued many of their intended projects. She bought a ranch outside of Williams, Arizona, near the Grand Canyon, where they had planned to raise cattle. She invested in a commuter airline with Charles W. Gilpin, a pilot who had been Jack Greenway's chauffeur. Both Greenways had been concerned with the plight of soldiers wounded in World War I, and in 1927 Isabella Greenway moved to Tucson and opened the Arizona Hut, a workshop where disabled veterans or their families could earn a living by making furniture. By the end of 1928, 40 people were working, and Greenway found outlets at large retail stores in major cities. In 1930, Isabella Greenway, who by that time had built or completely renovated six houses, began construction on a resort hotel, the Arizona Inn, where furniture from the Hut could be used. The Depression finally put the Hut out of business, but the Inn prospered. The ambiance Greenway created, comfortable and private, attracted celebrities from the very beginning.

Jack Greenway had also entertained political ambitions, seeking the Democratic gubernatorial nomination in 1922, and attending the Democratic national convention as a delegate in 1924, where he received a nomination for vice-president. As his wife, Isabella had met many Arizona politicians. Later, her work with the veterans brought her national attention. In addition, she was active in the Tucson community, fund-raising and serving on the boards of local charitable organizations. In 1928, she was elected Democratic national committeewoman, a position which she expanded into a full-time job, campaigning vigorously for Al Smith. After the election, she reorganized the Democratic Party, integrating the men's and women's divisions for greater unity and efficiency. She was re-elected to the post in 1930. The Depression created political issues for which the Democrats offered solutions. By 1932, Greenway was credited with having won the commitment of the Arizona delegation to Franklin Roosevelt's nomination, and she traveled with them to the Democratic convention in Chicago to second that nomination herself.

Roosevelt visited her ranch in Williams during his September campaign tour through the West; his visit there, and in Phoenix, marked the first time a national candidate had visited Arizona in 20 years. Isabella Greenway organized the Democratic Party in Arizona to support his candidacy, the only woman among Roosevelt's state leaders, and toured the state on his behalf. When Roosevelt nominated Arizona's sole congressman, Lewis W. Douglas, as director of the budget, Isabella Greenway was well-placed to run for a statewide office.

She had been mentioned as a potential gubernatorial candidate in prior years, but considered that it would be unfair to her young son. By 1933, however, Jack was nearly nine years old, and she declared her intention to run. She used an airplane to make stops on her speaking tour; the novelty gained her publicity as well as convenience in a state where roads were often poor. There was little difference between Greenway and her two principal opponents for the Democratic nomination. Isabella stood out because of her ability to project her empathy for people through her experiences on the Boone County farm, her mining contacts, her role as the widow of a war veteran. Her opponents made an issue of her gender indirectly; one spoke of himself as a "real he man," and of Congress as a place where "men meet men." Several congresswomen had been serving since the 1920s, however, so the argument, according to Avan Probst's 1994 study of Greenway's campaign, persuaded no one who was not already convinced that women should not be in politics. Greenway downplayed her position as a longtime friend of the president: "A great deal has been said about my being a friend of the Roosevelts," she was quoted as saying in *The New York Times*. "The Roosevelts have thousands of friends not qualified to be congressmen. I am not asking for votes on that basis, but on the basis that I feel qualified to do the work." She won easily in both the primary and the general elections.

The Depression had closed down the copper mines, and more than 140,000 men and women were on relief. Ten days after the election, Greenway visited Secretary of the Interior Harold Ickes, the Public Works Administrator, who promised money for irrigation and flood control projects, as well as a new post office in Phoenix.

Greenway, in her maiden speech, surprised those who had expected her to be a creature of the administration by criticizing Roosevelt for his opposition to a veterans' benefits bill. In her second term (she was easily re-elected in 1934), the bill became law. In 1935, she again took issue with Roosevelt, this time over the social security bill. Roosevelt insisted that the entire package be passed, but Greenway, fearing agreement impossible, urged separate consideration of the old-age pension, its least controversial aspect. She also worked effectively to secure bills which helped re-establish Arizona's cotton and copper industries, and to revise the tax code to give people economic security to enjoy the "liberty of living" which she believed was every citizen's right. Her tenure in Congress was not without its light-hearted moments. Her son Jack, who had a pass to the gallery, would come after school to wait for his mother to finish work. Sometimes he would bring his roller skates, and his mother would join him in skating through the halls of Congress.

The energetic lobbying for her constituents Greenway exhibited during her first week on the job was characteristic of her entire three years in Congress. At the end of 1936, she announced her intention to retire, saying she wanted to spend more time with her family. Many speculated that she was leaving because of her well-publicized disagreements with Roosevelt. Jack Greenway believed, however, that, as Arizona's only representative in the lower House, his conscientious mother was simply overworked and exhausted: "Everybody who wanted somebody to go and trace out . . . their lost veteran's pension, they spread the word how good she was and she got thirty referrals." She also declined suggestions that she run for governor.

Two years later, Isabella Greenway married Harry O. King, a New York and Bridgeport industrialist who had been the copper code administrator of the National Recovery Administration during the time she was in Congress. She divided her time between the East Coast and Arizona, where her Arizona Inn continued to flourish.

In 1940, convinced that presidents should not serve more than two terms, Greenway refused to support Franklin Roosevelt, and she adamantly opposed America's entry into the European war. She joined Democrats for Wendell Willkie, the Republican candidate. Roosevelt, seldom tolerant of what he perceived as disloyalty, pointedly invited her children to dinner at the White House without including Greenway. After America went to war following Pearl Harbor, she was named chair of the board of directors of the American Women's Voluntary Services, which gave women defense training in case of invasion. The Arizona Inn was classified as an "essential industry," due to the need for accommodations near the air base and naval training schools in the area. Isabella Greenway died in her home at the Arizona Inn on December 18, 1953, the 23rd anniversary of the opening of the Inn, of a heart attack, and was buried at her childhood home in Boone County, Kentucky.

SOURCES:

Brophy, Blake. "Tucson's Arizona Inn: The Continuum of Style," in *The Journal of Arizona History.* Vol. 24, no. 3. Autumn 1983, pp. 255–282.

Chamberlin, Hope. *A Minority of Members: Women in the U.S. Congress.* NY: Praeger, 1973.

Probst, Avan S. "Isabella Greenway: Arizona's 1933 Congresswoman." M.A. Thesis, Northern Arizona University, 1994.

COLLECTIONS:

Correspondence and papers at the Arizona Historical Society, Tucson, Arizona; papers and memorabilia at the Dinsmore Foundation, Boone County, Kentucky.

Kristie Miller,
author of *Ruth Hanna McCormick: A Life in Politics 1880–1944*
(University of New Mexico Press, 1992)

Greenwood, Grace (1823–1904).

See Lippincott, Sara Clarke.

Greenwood, Joan (1921–1987)

British actress. Born in London, England, on March 4, 1921; died in London in February 1987; daughter of Sydney Barnshaw (an artist) and Ida (Waller) Greenwood; attended St. Catherine's, Bramley, Surrey; attended the Royal Academy of Dramatic Arts; married André Morell (an actor), on May 16, 1960 (died 1978); children: one son.

Theater: made London debut as Louisa in The Robust Invalid *(Apollo, 1938); appeared as Timpson in* Little Ladyship *(Strand, 1939),* Little Mary *in* The Women *(Strand, 1940),* Pamela Brent *in* Dr. Brent's Household *(Richmond, 1940),* Wendy *in* Peter Pan *(Adelphi, 1941),* Henriette *in* Damaged Goods *(Whitehall, 1943); succeeded Deborah Kerr as Ellie Dunn in* Heartbreak House *(Cambridge, 1943); appeared as Ophelia in* Hamlet *(on tour, 1944),* Lady Teazle *in* School for Scandal, *Cleopatra in* Antony and Cleopatra, *and Nora in* A Doll's House *(Oxford Playhouse, Feb.–Nov., 1945),* Bertha *in* Frenzy *(St. Martin's, 1948),* Sabina Pennant *in* Young Wives' Tale *(Savoy, 1949); portrayed the title role in* Peter Pan *(Scala, 1951); appeared as* Noel Thorne *in* The Uninvited Guest *(St. James, 1953); made New York debut as* Lucasta Angel *in* The Confidential Clerk *(Morosco,*

1954); was a Visitor in The Moon and the Chimney *(Lyceum, Edinburgh, Scotland, 1955),* Gillian Holroyd *in* Bell, Book, and Candle *(Phoenix, 1954),* Mrs. Mallett *in* Cord of Identity *(Royal Court, 1957); portrayed the title role in* Lysistrata *(Royal Court, 1957),* Hattie *in* The Grass is Greener *(St. Martin's, 1958), the title role in* Hedda Gabler *(Oxford Playhouse, 1960),* Hedda *in* The Irregular Verb To Love *(Criterion, 1961); played in* The Broken Heart *and* Ilyena *in* Uncle Vanya *(Chichester Festival Theater, 1962); had the title role in* Hedda Gabler *(St. Martin's, 1964); appeared as* Olga Sergeyevna Ilyinska *in* Oblomov *(New Lyric, 1964); repeated that role in revised* Son of Oblomov *(Comedy, 1964); appeared as* Valentina Ponti *in* Those That Play the Clowns *(New York, ANTA, 1966),* Julia Sterroll *in a revival of* Fallen Angels *(Vaudeville, 1967); had the title role in a revival of* Candida *(Richmond Theater, 1968); appeared as* Mrs. Rogers *in* The Au Pair Man *(Duchess, 1969),* Lady Kitty *in a revival of* The Circle *(New Bromley, 1970), and* Miss Madrigal *in* The Chalk Garden *(Yvonne Arnaud, 1970).*

Selected films: John Smith Wakes Up *(1940);* The Gentle Sex *(1942);* Latin Quarter *(Frenzy, 1945);* A Girl in a Million *(1946);* The Man Within *(The Smugglers, 1947);* The October Man *(1947);* The White Unicorn *(Bad Sister, 1947);* Saraband for Dead Lovers *(Saraband, 1948);* The Bad Lord Byron *(1948);* Whisky Galore *(Tight Little Island, 1949);* Kind Hearts and Coronets *(1949);* Flesh and Blood *(1950);* The Man in the White Suit *(1951);* Le Passe-Muraille *(Mr. Peek-A-Boo, Fr., 1951);* Young Wives' Tale *(1951);* The Importance of Being Earnest *(1952);* Monsieur Ripois *(Knave of Hearts or Lovers Happy Lovers, Fr./UK, 1954);* Father Brown *(The Detective, 1954);* Moonfleet *(US, 1955);* Stage Struck *(US, 1958);* Mysterious Island *(US/UK, 1961);* The Amorous Prawn *(The Playgirl and the War Minister, 1962);* Tom Jones *(1963);* The Moon-Spinners *(US/UK, 1964);* Girl Stroke Boy *(1971);* The Hound of the Baskervilles *(1978);* The Water Babies *(1979);* Wagner *(1983);* Little Dorritt *(1987).*

Elfin in stature and distinguished by a voice that columnist William Hawkins said sounded like "Lynn Fontanne imitating Carol Channing," British actress Joan Greenwood was born in London, England, on March 4, 1921, and enjoyed a career that embraced stage, screen, and television. The daughter of **Ida Greenwood** and artist Sydney Barnshaw Greenwood, she studied ballet at the age of eight and entered the Royal Academy of Dramatic Art at the age of 14. She made her first London stage appearance as

Louisa in *The Robust Invalid* in 1938 and, close on the heels of that performance, made her film debut in *John Smith Wakes Up* (1940). After a two-year stage tour as Wendy in *Peter Pan* (1941), Greenwood gave up juvenile roles, graduating to more adult portrayals.

Greenwood was well established on the British stage and screen before her New York stage debut as the ingenue in T.S. Eliot's play *The Confidential Clerk*, in 1954. Audiences found her bewitching as did the critics. Columnist George Freedley of the *New York Morning Telegraph* called her "an out-of-this world comedienne," and John Beaufort of the *Christian Science Monitor* wrote: "Her presence is electric and her movements are marvelously graceful." Unfortunately, Greenwood made very few return trips to Broadway, and the most that American audiences saw of her was in films, notably *Kind Hearts and Coronets* (1950) and *The Man in the White Suit* (1951), both with Alec Guinness.

Greenwood married actor André Morell in 1960 and had a son. She once confided to being something of a rebel. Once during the filming of *Saraband*, she gave into a childish fantasy and ran off for a week to perform as an acrobat with a circus troupe. The actress made her final stage appearance in *The Chalk Garden* in 1970. She died in 1987.

SOURCES:

Candee, Marjorie Dent, ed. *Current Biography 1954.* NY: H.W. Wilson, 1954.

Greenwood, Marion (1909–1980)

American-born Mexican muralist, easel painter and printmaker. Born in Brooklyn, New York, in 1909; died in Woodstock, New York, in 1980; left high school at age 15 to study at the Art Students League, New York; studied at the Académie Colarossi, Paris, France; married Robert Plate; no children.

Known primarily for her powerful murals, Marion Greenwood's career reflects an interesting progression of styles, beginning with the revolutionary fervor of her early work in Mexico, through the restrained and classical murals commissioned by the Federal Art Project during the 1930s, and culminating in her later independent murals which represent a freer, almost expressionistic, quality.

Born in Brooklyn, New York, in 1909, Greenwood was a child prodigy who quit high school at the age of 15 to accept a scholarship at the Art Students League where she studied with John Sloan and George Bridgman. At 18, she

Joan Greenwood

made the first of several trips to Yaddo, a retreat for artists and writers in Saratoga Springs, New York. There, she painted portraits of artists-in-residence, like composer Aaron Copland and writer Waldo Frank. Still in her teens, Greenwood used the money she earned from painting the portrait of a wealthy financier to pay her way to Europe, where she studied at the Académie Colarossi in Paris.

Returning to New York in 1930, she sketched theater portraits for *The New York Times* for a year before embarking on a trip to the Southwest to paint the Navajo Indians. Crossing the border to Mexico, Greenwood met the expatriate American artist Pablo O'Higgins, who encouraged her to try mural painting. Her initial mural of native life, painted on the wall of the Hotel Taxqueno, resulted in a commission from the Mexican government, the first ever granted to a woman. As her interest in the Mexican people deepened, Greenwood undertook an exhaustive study of the Tarascan Indians, which culminated in a 700-square-foot mural depicting

Indian life for the University of San Hidalgo in Morelia. The authenticity of the work captured the attention of the head of the government mural program, who in 1934, hired her and her sister **Grace Greenwood** to work on a portion of a group mural at the central market and civic center in Mexico City (the Mercado Rodriguez). On the strength of this huge mural portraying peasant life, Greenwood, still in her 20s, became a legend in that country. "She could have been the queen of Mexico," said Mexican muralist David Alfaro Siqueiros.

Back in the United States in 1936, Greenwood and her sister Grace were hired by the Treasury Relief Art Project to create wall painting for a housing project that architect Oscar Stonorov was designing in Camden, New Jersey. Greenwood chose a labor theme for her subject, producing an oil-on-canvas mural depicting the collective bargaining agreement between the Camden shipyard workers under the New Deal. Unfortunately, the mural, like many works of its type from the period, is now covered over. Other government commissions of this period included an oil mural for the post office at Crossville, Tennessee, and frescoes commissioned by the Federal Art Project for the Red Hook housing project in Brooklyn. Entitled *Blueprint for Living* (1940), the Red Hook work expressed an idealistic view of a harmonious future when everyone's basic needs would be met. Sadly, this mural was also painted over, though existing photographs show it to be an impressive work.

In 1937, Marion and Grace Greenwood joined the Architect, Painters and Sculptors Collaborative, whose membership included artists **Concetta Scaravaglione**, José de Rivera, Isamu Noguchi, and William Zorach, among others. The Collaborative, writes **Charlotte Rubinstein**, was "a group devoted, as were many such organizations in the thirties, to the idea of improving the lives of common people by providing them with a harmonious architectural environment." They designed a community center which they hoped to build for the 1939 World's Fair. Although the design was never executed, it was hailed as an advanced environmental concept.

During the war, Greenwood, together with **Anne Poor**, worked for the U.S. Army Medical Corps to produce a series of paintings depicting the rehabilitation of wounded soldiers. After the war, Greenwood concentrated on easel painting and prints, enjoying a period of self-expression free from the supervision and censorship of government agencies. Her continuing interest in different ethnic groups took her to Hong Kong, the West Indies, North Africa, and India, where she created a series of sketches and paintings.

In 1954, while a visiting professor at the University of Tennessee in Knoxville, Greenwood was commissioned to paint a large mural for the student center auditorium. Using the theme of Tennessee music, Greenwood created a rhythmic work interweaving black jazz, spiritual, country mountain music, banjo guitar, bull fiddle, and folk dance. Her last mural, created at Syracuse University in 1965, was dedicated to the women of the world, and combined studies from the drawing and paintings Greenwood made during her travels.

Greenwood was described as a high-spirited, adventuresome woman with a keen sense of humor. She spent her later years in an art colony in Woodstock, New York, with her husband Robert Plate. She died in 1980, while recovering from injuries incurred in an automobile accident.

SOURCES:

Rubinstein, Charlotte Streifer. *American Women Artists: From Early Indian Times to the Present.* NY: Avon, 1982.

SUGGESTED READING:

Henkes, Robert. *American Women Painters of the 1930s and 1940s: The Lives and Work of Ten Artists.* Jefferson, NC: McFarland, 1991.

Greevy, Bernadette (1939—)

Irish mezzo-soprano. Born in Dublin, Ireland, on August 29, 1939; sixth of seven children of Josephine (Miller) and Patrick Joseph Greevy; educated at Holy Faith Convent, Clontarf, Dublin and at Guildhall School of Music, London; married Peter A. Tattan, in 1965 (died March 1983); children: one son (b. 1967).

Awards: Harriet Cohen Award (1964); honorary doctorates of music from University College Dublin and Trinity College Dublin; life member Royal Dublin Society; Order of Merit (Order of Malta); Pro Ecclesia et Pontifice (Vatican).

Bernadette Greevy, born in Dublin, Ireland, in 1939, came from a musical family who consistently supported her musical career. She was educated at a school which also had a strong musical tradition. She later paid tribute to this. "We got a marvelous general education and a wonderful musical education. We were encouraged to think and do things for ourselves and to be creative and imaginative." She performed in school operas and musical plays and regularly took part in local musical competitions in Dublin, and in choral groups and trios. When she was 16, she took lessons from the Dublin teacher Jean Nolan. She then went to London to study at the Guildhall School which she found somewhat restricting; she also studied privately with **Helene Isepp** and later with *****Nadia Boulanger** in Paris which she found particularly valuable for her later performances of French songs. She made her professional debut in Dublin in 1961 and the following year she performed at the Wexford Festival in Mascagni's *L'Amico Fritz*. In 1964, she made her London debut at the Wigmore Hall.

Greevy later recalled the pressures she faced after her successful debut. "I was being shoved all over the place with contracts to join here and there. That never appealed to me. . . . I knew from the first day that I was going to be free to make my mistakes or to be successful. It would be my choice." She turned down offers to sing with Scottish and Welsh Opera, and at Covent Garden. "I'm a very disciplined person," she later said, "but I can't bear the constraints of an opera house or something where I'd have to go in every day and be told what to do. I liked my independence." She also described herself as a perfectionist. "Every avenue has to be explored, you have to go into every area. I really do want to know every dot around me. I want everything to be perfect and then there'll be a good show." As her career developed, Greevy did comparatively little opera. She was offered the role of Carmen early on but declined it as she felt her voice was not ready. She returned to Wexford in Massenet's *Hérodiade* and also sang Laura in Ponchielli's *La Gioconda* in Dublin and Geneviève in Debussy's *Pelléas et Melisande* at Covent Garden. Greevy's marriage in 1965 and the birth of her son Hugh in 1967 also made her less willing to embark on a peripatetic career around the opera houses of Europe. She based herself in Dublin where she had strong family support which enabled her to undertake engagements abroad.

Instead of embarking on an operatic career, she forged fruitful working relationships in the 1960s with the Hungarian conductor Tibor Paul and the Radio Eireann Symphony Orchestra in Dublin, and with Sir John Barbirolli and the Hallé Orchestra in Manchester. "It was a crucial, very interesting time in my life, working with these two powerful but different men." With Barbirolli, she performed works with which she became particularly associated, notably Mahler's *Lieder eines fahrenden Gesellen* and the Angel in Elgar's *Dream of Gerontius*. Greevy greatly regretted that Barbirolli's death in 1970 cut short their work together. Other conductors with whom she enjoyed working included Franz-Paul Decker, Janos Fürst and Paul Hamburger.

Greevy was best known for her recordings of Elgar and Mahler but she also made several recordings of French songs, including Berlioz and Duparc. She performed with the chamber group Musica Antica e Nuova and said later that she had learned a great deal from working with instrumentalists, especially cellists. On the concert platform, she sang most of the major requiems and oratorios. She considered Bach and Schubert to be particularly demanding but regretted that Mozart composed so little for the mezzo repertory. She also created roles in works by leading Irish composers: Seoirse Bodley's *Meditations on lines from Patrick Kavanagh* (1971), *A Girl* (1978) and *The Naked Flame* (1987); Brian Boydell's *A Terrible Beauty is Born* (1965); and Gerard Victory's requiem cantata *Ultima Rerum* (1984).

In 1984, she gave the first in what was to be a regular series of master classes at the National Concert Hall in Dublin. She stipulated that "the only emotion that I want to see is healthy competition. I don't want to see any jealousy or petty rivalry. The fact that one person has a better voice than another is something that we have no control over. It's what we do with our hundred per cent that matters. Don't be envious of someone's better instrument, learn from them. That's the attitude I look for." Greevy emphasized the importance of carefully maintaining the voice, citing her own experience. "If anyone tries to make you do something that causes stress or strain, just walk away. Otherwise you'll be sung out. . . . I've seen it with my own contemporaries. I've seen it with people years younger than me." As her performances became less frequent, she concentrated more on teaching both in Ireland and abroad.

SOURCES:
Interview with Yvonne Healy, in *Irish Times*. September 26, 1995.
Music Ireland. Vols 1–6, 1986–1991.
"Pursuing Perfection: Robert O'Byrne talks to Bernadette Greevy," in *Music Ireland*. February 1988.

Deirdre McMahon,
lecturer in History at Mary Immaculate College,
University of Limerick, Limerick, Ireland

Gregoria-Anastasia (fl. 640s)

Byzantine empress. Flourished around 640s. Married Heraclonas-Constantine, Byzantine emperor (r. 641).

Gregory, Augusta (1852–1932)

Irish patron, author, playwright, and folklorist who co-founded the Abbey Theater in Dublin. Name variations: Lady Gregory. Born Isabella Augusta Persse on March 15, 1852, at Roxborough, County Galway, Ireland; died at Coole Park, County Galway, Ireland, on May 23, 1932; daughter of Dudley Persse (a landowner) and Frances (Barry) Persse; educated at home; married Sir William Gregory, on March 4, 1880 (died 1892); children: Robert (1881–1918).

Published her first writing (1882); had meeting with W.B. Yeats (1894); responsible for first performances of Irish Literary Theater (1899); wrote plays with Yeats (1901); served as director, Abbey Theater (1904); was manager for the first U.S. tour of Abbey (1911–12); beginning of Lane Pictures controversy (1915); death of son (1918); had friendship with Sean O'Casey (1924); saw the sale and lease-back of Coole (1927).

Selected publications: The Coole Edition of the Works of Lady Gregory: Collected Plays *(4 vols, Gerrards Cross, Colin Smythe, 1970);* Cuchulain of Muirthemne *(Gerrards Cross, Colin Smythe, 1972, first published 1902);* Gods and Fighting Men *(Gerrards Cross, Colin Smythe, 1970, first published 1904);* The Kiltartan Books *(Gerrards Cross, Colin Smythe, 1971, first published 1909–18);* Our Irish Theater *(Gerrards Cross, Colin Smythe, 1972, first published 1913);* Visions and Beliefs in the West of Ireland *(Gerrards Cross, Colin Smythe, 1970, first published 1920);* Sir Hugh Lane *(Gerrards Cross, Colin Smythe, 1973, first published 1921).*

Augusta Gregory's family, the Persses, had been established at their County Galway estate, Roxborough, for nearly 200 years by the time of her birth in 1852. The Persses were Protestant landowners of English origin, part of a close-knit network of families who dominated local government in Galway until the end of the 19th century. However, her maternal grandparents, the O'Gradys and the Barrys, were descended from native Irish and Norman families who had converted to Protestantism to escape the penal legislation imposed on Catholics. Augusta's father had three children during his first marriage and thirteen with his second wife, **Frances Barry Persse**, Augusta's mother. Frances Persse was a fervent evangelical Protestant and, with her eldest daughter and two stepdaughters, actively proselytized among the local Catholic peasantry around Roxborough. This caused much resentment, especially during the Great Famine, and remained an issue of political sensitivity for the family. In later life, Gregory was accused by some detractors (notably the writer George Moore) of having participated in her family's proselytizing activities.

Augusta, who was 12th in the family, had a distant relationship with her mother whom she referred to in her autobiography as "the Mistress." Frances Persse preferred her sons to her daughters and, in any event, had little in common with her quiet, studious daughter. Augusta, though devoted to her four younger brothers, lacked the wildness and instability which drove several of them to alcoholism. One of the formative influences of her early life was her nurse **Mary Sheridan**, a Catholic, who worked for the family for over 40 years. Sheridan remembered the Irish rebellion of 1798 and had a fund of stories, legends, and folklore for the receptive Augusta. There was no library at Roxborough and novels were forbidden, but Gregory read extensively in essays and poetry.

In the mid-1870s, Augusta accompanied her brother Richard, who was suffering from tuberculosis, to France and Italy. In 1877 at Roxborough, she met Sir William Gregory, who owned Coole Park, a neighboring estate. William, who was 61, had been a member of Parliament, first as a Conservative from 1842 to 1847 then as a Liberal from 1852 to 1871. In 1872, he was appointed governor of Ceylon and was successful in this post, doing much to stimulate the production of tea and coffee. C. Litton Falkiner, in his entry on Sir William for the *Dictionary of National Biography,* described him as a man of "great natural abilities, real political talent, and marked personal charm" who, but for a certain instability, would have achieved high political office. His first wife **Elizabeth Clay Bowdoin** died in 1873, and he had just returned from Ceylon when he met Augusta Persse. Their relationship, though not a passionate one, was based on mutual affection and respect. Sir William was attracted by her intelligence, good sense, and culture which marked her out from her contemporaries. Augusta admired William and, despite initial reservations, realized that marriage to him offered wider social and intellectual horizons denied to her as the "spinster" daughter who was at the beck and call of her large family. This was particularly true after the death of her father in 1878. He left only £10,000 to be divided among the 13 children of his second marriage. Her brother Richard died in 1879 and when Sir William proposed to her early in 1880, she accepted. They were married in Dublin in March 1880.

Over the next 12 years, the Gregorys spent most of their time either at their house in London or traveling abroad, spending only summers at Coole. In the first year of their marriage, they went to Rome, Athens, and Constantinople where they were guests of the ambassador, Sir Henry Layard, and his wife **Enid Layard** who became Augusta's closest friend. Henry Layard and William Gregory were both trustees of the National Gallery in London and many of the Gregorys' continental visits were to the great European galleries and museums. Sir William also knew some of the most distinguished literary celebrities in London and Lady Gregory met Robert Browning, Henry James, and the historians W.E.H. Lecky and J.A. Froude. She was also involved in charitable work. Her only child Robert was born in May 1881.

The Gregorys spent the winter of 1881–82 in Egypt where they met Lady ❧➤ **Anne Blunt** and her husband Wilfrid Scawen Blunt. Wilfrid was one of the most remarkable men of his age: a Catholic who flirted with Islam, writer, traveler, great landowner, horse-breeder and notorious womanizer. He was sympathetic to Egyptian nationalism and impressed the Gregorys with his views. Together, they supported the cause of Arabi Bey, an Egyptian officer who was put on trial for his opposition to Egypt's Turkish rulers. The case was the subject of Gregory's first published writing, *Arabi and his Household* (1882).

➤❧
Blunt, Anne.
See Lovelace,
Ada Byron for
sidebar.

Augusta
Gregory

However, for all her sympathy with Egyptian nationalism, she was hostile to Irish nationalism and especially to the campaign for land reform which was bound to affect the Gregorys and the Persses.

In summer 1882, Lady Gregory and Wilfrid Blunt began a passionate year-long affair which remained a well-kept secret until the publication of Wilfrid's official biography in 1979. The relationship ended in 1883 by mutual consent, but they remained friends for 40 years and Wilfrid had great affection and respect for her. She was, he wrote in 1913, "the only woman I have known of real intellectual power equal to men." She was also "an entirely practical business woman." Over the following years, Gregory's life settled into a routine of summer at Coole and winter and spring in London with more far-flung travels to India. She wrote articles about her travels and in 1891 published her first fiction in *The Argosy*. She was devoted to her son but was increasingly concerned by her husband's failing health. He died on March 6, 1892, just before her 40th birthday.

It is the visionary who is the really practical worker, for he works with the faith that moves mountains.

—Augusta Gregory

Coole was the most pressing problem she faced after William Gregory's death. Two-thirds of the estate had been sold to pay off debts, and the rest was mortgaged. Augusta was determined that her son would inherit the estate unencumbered by debt. Her own attitude to Coole was ambivalent: compared to Roxborough, the exterior was undistinguished but its contents reflected the more cosmopolitan lives of the Gregorys. It was not until after her husband's death that she came to love the house. She kept a London base and edited and published her husband's autobiography and the letters of his grandfather. But the early 1890s witnessed the beginning of the Irish cultural renaissance. In 1893, the Gaelic League was founded to promote the Irish language, and that year also saw the publication of W.B. Yeats' *The Celtic Twilight* and Douglas Hyde's *Love Songs of Connacht*. These and other works made a considerable impression on Gregory, and she became increasingly interested in history and folklore. She also learned the Irish language.

She first met "Yates," as she called him, in 1894, but their friendship became established in 1896–97 when she invited him to stay at Coole. He was in the throes of his unhappy affair with *Maud Gonne, and his two-month stay at Coole in 1897 provided him with much needed rest

and peace. They discussed plays, poetry, and folklore and gave each other valuable intellectual stimulus. In 1898, Gregory visited the Aran Islands, off the west coast of Ireland, one of the last outposts of Irish peasant culture. By the end of the 1890s, her political views had shifted radically, and she now supported self-government for Ireland. Her refusal to light a bonfire to celebrate Queen *Victoria's jubilee in 1897 led to disapproving comments, but she was aware that time was running out for her class. Roxborough had been beset by a succession of problems, and in March 1898 her brother Gerald had died, the third of her brothers to die from alcoholism. The 1898 Local Government Act finally broke the power base of the Persses, the Gregorys, and the other Anglo-Irish families in Galway.

Gregory, Yeats, and Edward Martyn, a wealthy Galway neighbor who was interested in the literary revival, drew up a prospectus for an Irish literary theater, proposing a season of Irish and Celtic plays. Augusta solicited subscriptions and the first performances took place in Dublin in May 1899. They were a success and a second season took place in February 1900. In the summer of 1900, Yeats suggested that Gregory take over a projected book about the ancient Irish epics which he had no time to complete. Over the next four years, she researched in British and Irish libraries and the results of her work were seen in *Cuchulain of Muirthemne* (1902) and *Gods and Fighting Men* (1904), the first books to render Irish mythology into an Irish idiom. They attracted admiring tributes from, among others, Mark Twain and Theodore Roosevelt.

Gregory's playwrighting career started tentatively in 1901–02. She and Yeats collaborated on *Cathleen ni Houlihan* and *The Pot of Broth*. In both cases the ideas had been Yeats' but were put into dramatic form by Gregory, though she allowed Yeats' name to appear as author. *Cathleen ni Houlihan* was performed in April 1902 with Maud Gonne in the title role and created a sensation, becoming one of the most popular plays in the repertory. In 1904, thanks to a gift from *Annie Horniman, the wealthy English patron, the Abbey Theater was founded with Gregory, Yeats, and the playwright John Millington Synge as directors. The next ten years were the most active and prolific of Gregory's life. She wrote over 20 plays—comedies, historical dramas, adaptations from Molière—of which the most successful were *Spreading the News* (1904), *Kincora* (1905), *Hyacinth Halvey* (1906), *The Rising of the Moon* (1907), *The Workhouse Ward* (1908), and *MacDonogh's Wife* (1912).

In January 1907, the Abbey had its first major scandal with the premiere of Synge's *The Playboy of the Western World* which caused a riot. Gregory was staunch in her public support for Synge and the play, though privately she disliked it. In Gort, the town nearest to Coole, the council expressed its disapproval, and the local children were forbidden to attend her treats at Coole which distressed her. In fact, the riots were short-lived and when the play returned to the repertory in 1909 there was little opposition. Synge's death in 1909 was a great blow to the theater, although she and Yeats had often found Synge a difficult collaborator. *The Playboy* was not the only problem play. George Bernard Shaw had been a supporter of the Abbey from its early days, and in 1909 the theater agreed to stage his play *The Shewing-Up of Blanco Posnet* which had been banned in Britain. The authorities threatened the Abbey with fines and the loss of its license if it proceeded with the play, but Gregory and Yeats ignored them. To their relief, nothing happened, and Shaw remained a friend and admirer for the rest of Gregory's life. This could not be said for James Joyce whom she helped with money and a job reviewing books. Her reward was the description of her folklore as "bagses of trash" and the lampoon in the National Library section of *Ulysses*.

In October 1911, Gregory took the Abbey company on its first American tour, a tour which tested to the full not only her administrative and promotional skills but also her resolve. *The Playboy* had been requested by the tour's promoters and during the first weeks of the circuit was well received. However, the Irish-American press in New York was hostile both to the play and the company, and there were disturbances on the first night in New York. The presence of Theodore Roosevelt in the audience on the second night gave Gregory valuable moral support. The tour was a considerable financial success for the company and a personal success for Gregory who was much in demand for lectures and interviews. There were further U.S. tours in 1912–13 and 1914–15.

The outbreak of the First World War in 1914 brought Gregory personal anxiety. Her son Robert joined the British army and then transferred to the Royal Flying Corps which was more dangerous. Robert was a well-known painter and had designed several plays for his mother and Yeats. He married **Margaret Graham (Gregory)** in 1907 and Augusta was devoted to her three grandchildren who spent much of their childhood at Coole. Gregory was also close

to her nephew Sir Hugh Lane, the art dealer and connoisseur, who died in the sinking of the *Lusitania* in 1915. Augusta was the trustee of his will but soon found it a poisoned chalice. Lane's efforts to establish a gallery of modern art in Dublin had been the subject of contentious debate. In his will, he left his collection of pictures to the National Gallery in London but changed his mind and left them to the National Gallery in Dublin. Unfortunately, the codicil containing the change was not witnessed, and thus began a long and exhausting battle for the pictures which was not finally resolved until nearly 30 years after Gregory's death. In January 1918, Robert Gregory was killed in action, and it was a measure of the depth of her grief that she rarely referred to his death in her published writings. Yeats wrote one of his most famous poems about the event: "An Irish Airman Foresees his Death." Robert's death meant that the future of Coole was uncertain as his widow Margaret was now the owner and was anxious to sell the estate.

The years 1919–23 saw major political unrest in Ireland. Coole and its neighborhood were not immune from the troubles, as Gregory's journals testified. Her sympathies were with the republicans although her family was the subject of their attacks. Her nephew was murdered by the Irish Republican Army and her daughter-in-law narrowly escaped death in an IRA ambush. Roxborough was burned in 1922 although Coole escaped. Following the turmoil of the war of independence and the civil war, the Abbey was rescued from the doldrums by Sean O'Casey whose plays were a huge critical and financial success. As with Synge's *Playboy,* Gregory staunchly supported *The Plough and the Stars* which provoked disturbances in 1926 although this time she had no doubts about the play. O'Casey was notoriously difficult and touchy but respected her more than he did the other Abbey directors, Yeats and Lennox Robinson. O'Casey and Gregory developed a deep friendship which was broken off in 1928 when the Abbey rejected his play *The Silver Tassie.* To his subsequent remorse, O'Casey rejected overtures from Gregory to heal the rift but made some amends in his autobiography *Inishfallen Fare Thee Well* (1949). His touching and respectful portrait of her came at a time when her contribution to the Abbey was gradually being forgotten, if not actively dismissed.

In 1923 and 1926, Gregory had two operations for breast cancer, and in 1927 Coole was finally sold to the Irish Land Commission with the proviso that she could rent it back annually for a small sum until her death. Her essay *Coole,* published in 1931, was her elegy for the house, and in it she thanked her husband for bringing her to Coole 48 years before. Her health failed, and she told Yeats in February 1932 that she was grateful for her full life: "I do think I have been of use to the country & for that in great part I thank you." She died on May 23, 1932. Coole was demolished in 1941.

Despite the many tributes paid to her after her death, Augusta Gregory's reputation went into eclipse until **Elizabeth Coxhead**'s biography in 1961. Coxhead attacked Yeats and a group of "Dublin literary gossips," notably Oliver St. John Gogarty, for minimizing and denigrating her contribution to the literary revival and to the Abbey. Their efforts, Coxhead wrote, "passed pretty well unchallenged in an anti-feminist country" and were "an injustice as outrageous as any that literary history can show." After this, the balance began to be redressed, and in 1970 the first volumes of the *Coole Edition of the Works of Lady Gregory* were published. Later volumes included the first publication of her autobiography *Seventy Years*.

SOURCES:

Murphy, Daniel, ed. *Journals 1916–32*. 2 vols. Gerrards Cross: Colin Smythe, 1978–87.

Pethica, James, ed. *Lady Gregory's Diaries 1892–1902*. Gerrard's Cross: Colin Smythe, 1996.

Smythe, Colin, ed. *Seventy Years: Being the Autobiography of Lady Gregory. The Coole Edition of the Works of Lady Gregory*. Gerrards Cross: Colin Smythe, 1974.

SUGGESTED READING:

Coxhead, Elizabeth. *Lady Gregory: A Literary Portrait*. 2nd ed. London: Secker and Warburg, 1966.

Kohfeldt, Mary Lou. *Lady Gregory: The Woman Behind the Irish Renaissance*. London: Andre Deutsch, 1985.

Saddlemyer, Ann, and Colin Smythe, eds. *Lady Gregory: Fifty Years After*. NY: Barnes and Noble, 1987.

COLLECTIONS:

Gregory archives in the Berg Collection, New York Public Library.

Deirdre McMahon,
lecturer in History at Mary Immaculate College,
University of Limerick, Limerick, Ireland

Gregory, Cynthia (1946—)

American ballerina. Born Cynthia Kathleen Gregory on July 8, 1946, in Los Angeles, California; only child of Konstantin Gregory (a dress manufacturer) and Marcelle (Tremblay) Gregory; attended Catholic schools until 1961; later received high school diploma through a correspondence course; married Terrence S. Orr (a dancer), on May 14, 1966 (divorced 1975); married John Hemminger (a rock-music manager and promoter), in 1976 (died 1984); married Hilary B. Miller (an investment banker), in December 1985: children: a stepdaughter, Amanda Hemminger, and a son, Lloyd Miller.

Acclaimed for her technical virtuosity and dramatic appeal, Cynthia Gregory gained international stardom as a principal dancer with New York's American Ballet Theater (ABT), where she was best known for her individualized interpretations of the leading roles in classical ballets, particularly *Swan Lake*. Mikhail Baryshnikov, one time artistic director and dancer with the prestigious company, called Gregory one of the great dancers in the ABT's history. "The range of her repertory and brilliance of her dancing have been a standard for many."

Gregory was born in Los Angeles, California, in 1946, and began ballet lessons at age five with **Eva Lorraine** at the California Children's Ballet Company. Within a year, she was dancing on point in children's versions of *Swan Lake* and *The Sleeping Beauty*. Her training continued in classes with Michel Panaieff, Robert Rossellat, and *Carmelita Maracci*, to whom she credits her technical ability. "She would give you very technical things to do," Gregory told John Gruen in an interview for his book, *The Private World of Ballet*. "I did them all, but I never understood *how* I did them. Actually, I *still* don't understand. I do things naturally, without knowing how I do them." At 13, Gregory took special classes with Jacques D'Amboise, a principal dancer with the New York City Ballet. Impressed with her ability, he recommended her to Lew Christensen, the head of the San Francisco Ballet School. Christensen, in turn, offered her a Ford Foundation grant, and Gregory enrolled in the San Francisco Ballet School and danced as an apprentice with the company's corps de ballet. In late 1961, she became an official member of the company, dancing her first solo in *The Nutcracker*. Promoted to soloist within a few months, she spent the next two years expanding her repertory of classical roles as well as branching out into more experimental works.

Looking for more challenges than the small regional company could offer, Gregory and a fellow dancer, Terry Orr (whom she married in 1966), moved to New York City, where they hoped to join George Balanchine's New York City Ballet. However, after attending a number of performances of the American Ballet Theater, they decided to audition there instead. Although Orr was immediately taken into the company, Gregory had to audition three times before being accepted, because the directors were worried that at 6'1" on point, she might not fit in with the rest of the corps. Gregory was elevated to soloist in 1966 and, nine months later, became a principal dancer. In 1967, she first appeared as Odette/Odile in *Swan Lake*, the ballet with which she would come to be identified. Alternating in the role with more experienced dancers, Gregory completely mesmerized the critics. "Already she dances Odette/Odile as if she had the accumulated tradition of a young Russian or British dancer behind her," wrote Clive Barnes of *The New York Times* (May 24, 1967). "She dances as if she had dreamed of the ballet from her cradle." Walter Terry, in the *Saturday Review* (June 3, 1967) also recognized Gregory's innate talent. "She had . . . that ballet 'line,' that definition of the body in space, which distinguished a ballerina from a mere dancer. No one could have taught it to her. It was instinctive, this placement of arms, this extension of the legs, this tilt of the head."

Through the mid-1970s, Gregory continued to distinguish herself in the classical interpretations as well as modern dramatic roles in works like Antony Tudor's *Undertow*, *Birgit Cullberg's *Miss Julie*, and Eliot Feld's *Intermezzo*. In December 1975, suffering through a painful divorce and disagreements with ABT's management, Gregory quite suddenly announced her retirement and moved to California with rock-music promoter John Hemminger to live a "normal" life. (The couple married in 1976.) After a year, however, she became bored and returned to ABT on a limited schedule. "Before I quit I had just been killing myself, working so hard I wasn't enjoying it," she told Joe Butkiewicz of the Wilkes-Barre, Pennsylvania *Times Leader*. "When I came back I decided I would only perform three times a week. Every performance would be special."

New York fans greeted her with a standing ovation when she made her first entrance as Swanilda in *Coppélia* on January 5, 1977, and, despite her ten-month absence, critics found her in splendid form. "She radiates joy as she never has," reported **Frances Herridge** in the *New York Post* (January 6, 1977). "She spins into her turns with free leg extended exceptionally high. She held her balances longer than necessary. . . . We are accustomed to technical perfection from her, but this technical daring made her even more exciting." Once again, Gregory reigned as one of the most popular dancers in the company, rivaling even the Soviet dancers who were favored at the time by artistic director *Lucia Chase. Gregory often used her box-office draw as leverage

in management disputes. In 1977, she quit in protest over their refusal to hire a Rumanian dancer as her partner, and in 1979, she left again during an impasse over salary negotiations. That same year, Chase retired and Mikhail Baryshnikov took over as artistic director of the ABT. Because of his preference for experimental works over the classics, Gregory's performance schedule was further cut, and she used the opportunity to perform as a guest artist with other companies, among them the Stuttgart Ballet and the state opera ballets of Zurich, Vienna, and Munich.

In June 1985, the ABT mounted a gala performance to celebrate Gregory's 20 years with the company. In an evening dedicated to her husband John Hemminger, who died of a heart attack in 1984, Gregory was seen in slides of her childhood and excepts from 20 of the 70 ballets in which she had danced over the years. Looking back at her career with the company, Gregory told Gruen in an interview for *Dance* magazine, "maturing with ABT was a fabulous experience. Although there were some rough spots along the way, it's really been my whole life."

In 1985, Gregory married Hilary Miller, an investment banker with a daughter of his own, Amanda. A year later, despite a foot operation, a hip injury, and recurring tendinitis, Gregory signed a two-year contract as a permanent guest artist with the Cleveland San Jose Ballet. She subsequently organized and toured 32 cities with her own troupe of nine dancers in "Cynthia Gregory: A Celebration of Twenty-Five Years of Dancing," a show to benefit drug-abuse programs. She also appeared in a television commercial and published a book *Ballet is the Best Exercise*, geared toward the non-dancer. In 1988, the dancer gave birth to a son, Lloyd, and three months later was back on stage in *Romeo and Juliet*. "I'd love to do videos, or try my hand at acting," she said in an interview with the *Nashville Banner*. "I'd like to go to art school and learn to draw. I'd like to write a book other than an exercise book. I want to still be as creative as I can and keep learning."

SOURCES:
McHenry, Robert, ed. *Famous American Women*. NY: Dover, 1983.

Mooney, Louise, ed. *Newsmakers: The People Behind Today's Headlines*. Detroit, MI: Gale Research, 1990.

Moritz, Charles, ed. *Current Biography 1977*. NY: H.W. Wilson, 1977.

Barbara Morgan,
Melrose, Massachusetts

Gregory, Lady (1815–1895).

See Stirling, Mary Anne.

Gregory, Lady (1852–1932).

See Gregory, Augusta.

Greig, Teresa Billington (1877–1964).

See Billington-Greig, Teresa.

Grenfell, Helen L. (b. 1868)

American educator and penologist. Born Helen Loring in Valparaiso, Chile, in 1868; married Edwin I. Grenfell, in 1889.

Helen L. Grenfell was born Helen Loring in Valparaiso, Chile, in 1868. After serving as superintendent of schools, she was made state superintendent of public instruction in Colorado; during her three terms from 1899 to 1905, she greatly increased the school revenues and revised and annotated school laws. From 1909 to 1914, Grenfell was commissioner of the Colorado State Penitentiary and Reformatory, with full control of the penal institutions of the state, the only woman at the time to hold such an office.

Grenfell, Joyce (1910–1979)

British actress and writer, known for her impersonations of somewhat daffy aristocratic women. Born

Joyce Irene Phipps in London, England, on February 10, 1910; died on November 30, 1979, in London; only daughter and one of two children of Paul Phipps (an architect) and Nora (Langhorne) Phipps (the sister of Nancy Astor); attended schools in Claremont, Esher, and Surrey, England; attended the Royal Academy of Dramatic Art, London; married Reginald Pascoe Grenfell (a chartered accountant), on December 12, 1928; no children.

Theater: The Little Revue *(Little Theater, 1939);* Diversion *(Wyndham's, 1940);* Diversions No. 2 *(Ambassadors', 1941);* Light and Shade *(Ambassadors', 1942);* Sigh No More *(Piccadilly, 1945);* Tuppence Coloured *(Lyric, Hammersmith, 1947);* Penny Plain *(St. Martin's, 1951);* Joyce Grenfell Requests the Pleasure *(Fortune, 1954); New York debut in same (Bijou, 1955).*

Selected films: The Demi-Paradise *(Adventure for Two, 1943);* The Lamp Still Burns *(1948);* While the Sun Shines *(1948);* The Happiest Days of Your Life *(1949);* A Run for Your Money *(1949);* Stage Fright *(1950);* Laughter in Paradise *(1951);* The Galloping Major *(1951);* The Pickwick Papers *(1952);* Genevieve *(1953);* The Million Pound Note *(*Man With a Million, *1954);* The Belles of St. Trinian's *(1954);* The Pure Hell of St. Trinian's *(1960);* The Old Dark House *(US/UK, 1963);* The Americanization of Emily *(US, 1964);* The Yellow Rolls-Royce *(1964).*

Joyce Grenfell

Joyce Grenfell, who described herself as "three-fourths American," was born in London in 1910 to an American-born architect, Paul Phipps, and **Nora Langhorne Phipps** of Virginia. One of Nora's sisters was Lady *Nancy Astor; another, *Irene Langhorne Gibson, married artist Charles Dana Gibson. Nora and Irene were models for his "Gibson Girl" series. As a child, Grenfell adored the theater and was strongly influenced by *Ruth Draper, who was a distant cousin of her father. After completing her education at a finishing school in Paris, Joyce spent one term at the Royal Academy of Dramatic Art before marrying Reginald Grenfell, whom she had known for many years.

As a young married woman Grenfell began contributing light verse to the British humor magazine *Punch* and, in 1935, became a radio critic for the London Sunday *Observer*. All the while, she had been entertaining friends and family with her off-beat but witty monologues. Producer Herbert Farjeon heard Grenfell's piece, "How to Make a Boutonniere out of Empty Beech Nut Husk Clusters" (one of her "Women's Institute lectures"), at a dinner party and invited her to join his show *The Little Revue*. She made her professional debut in April 1939 and went on to play in three subsequent editions of the revue. Appearing next in *Diversion* in 1940, she shared the bill with *Edith Evans, Peter Ustinov, and a young Dirk Bogarde. That revue also went on to a second edition, *Diversions No. 2.*

During the war, Grenfell joined a troupe of entertainers touring the battlefields and traveled to British military, naval, and air force hospitals in 14 countries. (She would be awarded the OBE in 1946 for her war work.) Back in London in 1945, she appeared in Noel Coward's revue *Sigh No More*. Critic James Agate found her performance of "Backfischerei" one of the high points of an otherwise lackluster evening. "Lewis Carroll is the father of that grin with which the maddening child greets misfortune," he wrote, "a grin which grows and Grows and GROWS." Grenfell then appeared in two new revues, *Tuppence Coloured* (1947) and *Penny Plain* (1953). She supplemented her stage work with appearances on the BBC radio, and also appeared regularly in films, usually in brief but memorable roles.

In June 1954, Grenfell opened in an intimate revue called *Joyce Grenfell Requests the Pleasure*. Consisting of songs and monologues of her own composition, the show was well received by British critics and ran for a year. Grenfell brought the show to New York in 1954, opening with mixed reviews from the American critics. Brooks Atkinson of *The New York Times* found that he was "not tuned in to Miss Grenfell's brand of humor," and Henry Hewes, in the *Saturday Review* (October 29, 1955), was somewhat ambiguous, calling Grenfell "more gently and reasonably funny, and less preposterously zany than the incomparable *Beatrice Lillie." Walter Kerr, writing for the *New York Herald Tribune* (November 13, 1955), provided an enlightening definition of the Grenfell genre. "Miss Grenfell seems to me to have built for herself a small but quite valid theater of her own. What she does is to take a familiar, sometimes almost routine little snapshot of overheard life, define the comment she wants to make on it, and then expand the picture to the precisely controlled, severely stylized dimensions of the musical stage—without losing the comment."

Joyce Grenfell eventually evolved into a solo performer, touring extensively in the U.S., Canada, Australia, New Zealand, and other countries with great success. She continued to appear on television (including the "Ed Sullivan Show" in the States), and wrote light verse and humorous essays for British and American periodicals. Grenfell's last performance was on June 21, 1963, at a command performance for Queen *Elizabeth II at Windsor Castle. She then retired to write her autobiography. The actress died in 1979.

SOURCES:

Candee, Marjorie Dent, ed. *Current Biography.* NY: H.W. Wilson, 1958.
Morley, Sheridan. *The Great Stage Stars.* London: Angus & Robertson, 1986.

Barbara Morgan,
Melrose, Massachusetts

Grès, Alix (1910–1993)

French fashion designer. Name variations: Germaine Krebs; Alix Barton; Madame Alix Gres. Born Germaine Barton in 1910; died in obscurity at a nursing home in southern France on November 24, 1993, though her death was not disclosed until December 1994; married M. Krebs; children: daughter Ann Grès.

Madame Grès, the professional name of Germaine Krebs (née Barton), was prominent on the French fashion scene for 50 years. Known for her independent approach to design and her respect for the figure of the wearer, Grès created well-cut clothes that pleased clients as well as fashion commentators and columnists. Despite her celebrity, Grès shunned the spotlight. Thus, it is not surprising that 13 months passed before anyone was aware of her death: the announcement made the front page of France's *Le Monde* on December 13, 1994. Her daughter Ann, angry at an industry that had neglected—in her view—one of its greatest creators, had deliberately kept the press uninformed when her mother died in a nursing home on November 24, 1993.

Educated in the arts, Germaine Barton apprenticed at the Paris couture house of Premet. In 1937, she started a shop with a partner on the fashionable Rue du Faubourg St. Honore under the name Alix Barton, specializing in day dresses made of jersey. The boutique was an instant success. In 1942, she made a fresh start taking her husband's pseudonym of Grès and was still designing in 1985, when she introduced a ready-to-wear line and licensed scarves, neckties, and design jewelry for Cartier. For many years, Grès was president of the Federation Française de la Couture, the fashion syndicate. Her original training as a sculptor influenced her trademark Grecian draped gowns that clothed such clients as *Grace Kelly, *Marlene Dietrich, and *Jacqueline Kennedy.

Grese, Irma (1923–1945)

German Nazi who was supervisor of females at Auschwitz and Bergen Belsen and a convicted war criminal. Name variations: Griese. Born in 1923; executed in Hamelin, Germany, on December 13, 1945.

Epitomizing Adolf Hitler's blonde, blue-eyed Aryan ideal, Irma Grese developed into one of Germany's most notorious war criminals, performing some of the most brutal and sadistic murders committed by any woman in this century. Born to a hardworking family, she was employed on a farm and later as a nurse before becoming involved with the Nazi youth groups, against her father's wishes. Like so many other well-intentioned but naive German youths, Grese believed that Adolf Hitler would bring a sound moral leadership to her country. She soon became obsessed with the military supremacy of Germany and the Nazi ideology.

During World War II, Grese was a supervisor at the concentration camps at Ravensbrück and later at Auschwitz. Fanatical in her dedication to the Nazi commitment to eradicate the Jews, she was particularly cruel to the female prisoners in her charge. Dressed in an SS uniform, wearing heavy hobnailed boots, and carrying a pistol and whip, she was frequently accompanied by two half-starved Alsatian hounds. When prisoners displeased her, the dogs were ordered to attack and kill. Grese not only murdered at will, but she seemed to enjoy inflicting mental and physical torture. She would mock those scheduled for the gas chambers with such taunts as: "Your turn comes Friday."

In 1945, Grese was transferred briefly to the Bergen Belsen camp where she was captured by Allied troops at the end of the war; by then, she was known as the "beast of Belsen." At her war crimes trial, the 22-year-old Grese sat stone-faced as survivors came forward with shocking testimony against her, details that nauseated members of the British court. Irma Grese, who claimed until the end, like Hermann Göring, that she had no conscience, that her conscience was that of Adolf Hitler, was eventually condemned to death. She was hanged on December 13, 1945, in Hamelin, Germany.

Grétry, Lucile (1772–1790)

French composer of opera. Name variations: Lucile Gretry. Born Angélique-Dorothée-Louise Grétry in Paris, France, on July 15, 1772; died in Paris in March

1790; daughter of André Ernest Modeste Grétry (a composer); had two sisters.

The composer Angélique-Dorothée-Louise Grétry, who would be known as Lucile Grétry, was born in Paris on July 15, 1772, and named after the heroine in an opera written by her father, the composer André Grétry. He would teach her counterpoint and declamation, while Jean-François Tapray would teach her harmony. At age 13, Lucile composed the vocal parts, as well as the bass and a harp accompaniment for *Le mariage d'Antonio* which her father later orchestrated. The full score, published in 1786, was performed 47 times between 1786 and 1791, during the tumultuous French Revolution, and many music critics commented on the work's freshness. She also composed *Toinette et Louis* which had only a single performance. Both Lucile and her two sisters had contracted tuberculosis in childhood, the disease which was responsible for her early death.

John Haag,
Athens, Georgia

Greuter, Helen Wright (1914–1997).

See Wright, Helen.

Greville, Frances Evelyn

(1861–1938)

Countess of Warwick, British philanthropist, and social leader. Name variations: Daisy Warwick. Born Frances Evelyn Maynard in 1861; died in 1938; married Charles Greville, Lord Brooke (who became 5th earl of Warwick in 1893), in 1881 (died 1923).

A celebrated beauty and a woman of enormous wealth, Frances Evelyn Greville inherited the estates of her grandfather, Viscount Maynard, who died when she was just a child. Following her marriage in 1881, to Charles Greville, Lord Brooke, heir to the fourth earl of Warwick, she became a member of the "Marlborough House Set," the prominent social circle of the prince of Wales (the future King Edward VII), with whom she reportedly had a long affair during the 1890s.

Apparently inspired by reforming journalist W.T. Stead, Greville founded various organizations for the welfare of the poor, as well as a home for crippled children in Warwick. In 1895, following criticism of an extravagant ball she gave at Warwick Castle in the socialist paper *The Clarion*, she went to meet the editor, Robert Blatchford. Under his influence, she gradually turned into an active socialist, establishing schools for rural children in the late 1890s, and eventually founding the Lady Warwick College, an agricultural institution located at Studely Castle, Warwickshire, for training young women in horticulture, dairy, bee, and poultry keeping. From 1899, she served as editor of the *Women's Agricultural Times* and also published pamphlets and several books, including *Warwick Castle and its Earls* (1903) and *William Morris, his Home and Haunts* (1912).

Under the aegis of the Social Democratic Federation, which she joined in 1904, Greville lectured on Socialism in London and the United States. In opposition to World War I (although she worked for the Red Cross), she published her views in *A Woman and the War* (1916). Following the war, she joined the Labor Party and made an unsuccessful bid as a candidate for Warwick and Leamington in the 1923 election, losing to her relative, Sir Anthony Eden. After the death of her husband in 1923, she was forced to rely exclusively on her writing for income. Her later works include two autobiographies, *Life's Ebb and Flow* (1929) and *Afterthoughts* (1931), a novel, *Branch Line* (1932), and a natural history book, *Nature's Quest* (1934). Remembered as somewhat eccentric but essentially warm-hearted and generous, Frances Greville died in 1938.

Grey, Anne (d. 1474).

See Holland, Anne.

Grey, Beryl (1927—)

*English ballerina. Born Beryl Elizabeth Groom in Highgate, London, England, in 1927; attended theater schools; early dance training with Madeline Sharp in Bromley; studied at the Sadler's Wells Ballet school under Nicholas Sergeyev, *Ninette de Valois and *Vera Volkova; married Sven Svenson (a Swedish osteopath), in 1950; children: one son, Ingvar.*

One of Britain's most admired ballerinas, Beryl Grey entered the Sadler's Wells Ballet School at age nine and joined the Sadler's Wells (which became the Royal Ballet at Covent Garden), in 1941. Her career break came in 1942, when, due to illnesses in the company while on tour, she danced leading roles in *Les Sylphides*, *Comus*, *The Gods Go a'Beggin*, and the second act of *Swan Lake*. Months later, on her 15th birthday, Grey appeared as Odette/Odile in the full-length *Swan Lake*. She subsequently danced nearly every major ballet role, including most all of the classical and

Opposite page

Irma

Grese

Beryl
Grey

modern ballets from *Giselle* to *Ballet Imperial*. Grey also created many new roles, including the memorable Winter Fairy in Frederick Ashton's *Cinderella*. She has danced with the Royal Ballet in countries all over the world.

Grey resigned from the Royal Ballet in 1957 to become a free-lance artist. That year, she became the first foreign ballerina to be a guest artist with the Bolshoi Ballet in Moscow. In 1964, she became the first Western dancer to appear with the Beijing (Peking) and Shanghai ballets. She recorded her experiences in two books: *Red Curtain Up* (1958) and *Through the Bamboo Curtain* (1965). In 1966, Grey was appointed director of the Arts Educational School in London. From 1968 to 1980, she served as the artistic director of the London Festival Ballet.

Grey, who was married in 1950 to Dr. Sven Svenson, a Swedish osteopath, also became a great favorite in Sweden, where she made regular guest appearances with the Royal Swedish Ballet. She has one son, Ingvar.

SUGGESTED READING:
Grey, Beryl. *Through the Bamboo Curtain*. NY: Reynal, 1966.

Grey, Catherine (c. 1540–1568)

Countess of Hertford. Name variations: Katherine Grey; Lady Catherine Seymour. Born around 1540 or 1541 in England; died on January 22, 1568, in Cockfield, Suffolk, England; daughter of Henry Grey, marquis of Dorset (later duke of Suffolk) and *Frances Brandon (1517–1559, granddaughter of King Henry VII); younger sister of Lady Jane Grey (1537–1554); married Henry Herbert, 2nd earl of Pembroke, on May 21, 1553 (divorced before 1554); married Edward Seymour, 2nd earl of Hertford, in November 1560; children: (second marriage) Edward Seymour (b. 1561, Viscount Beauchamp); Thomas Seymour (b. 1563).

At 17, Lady Catherine Grey was in line for the throne of England but was excluded because of the actions of her sister, Lady ***Jane Grey**. In 1558, their cousin ***Elizabeth I** was crowned queen. When it became known at the English court that French and Spanish intriguers were scheming to have one of their own kidnap and marry an unwitting Catherine to usurp the crown, Elizabeth began to grow wary. And Catherine Grey's behavior did not help. She seemed incapable of comprehending that, because of her importance in the line of succession, all her youthful actions would have grievous consequence.

In the first week of 1560, Lady Catherine Grey married Edward Seymour, secretly and without royal approval, her mother having died before a letter of permission could be sent to the queen. When Catherine became pregnant and Elizabeth was apprised of the marriage, she had Catherine sent to the Tower of London. Edward Seymour was also imprisoned. Elizabeth, who had long been convinced that Edward would lend his name to foreign rivals, now saw a double threat. The queen's inability to produce an heir was also an important consideration. In September of 1561, Catherine gave birth to a son while in prison, and Elizabeth allowed him to be baptized as Edward Seymour, Viscount Beauchamp. Then, England's Privy Council set out to prove that the marriage was illegal and that Catherine's child, another claimant to the throne, was illegitimate.

On May 12, 1562, the marriage of Catherine and Edward was declared invalid by the archbishop of Canterbury, and the couple were both sentenced to prison for life for "carnal copulation." Each time Elizabeth's stance began to soften, events intervened. The sympathy of the public was on the side of the young lovers, and while in prison Edward and Catherine were allowed by their jailers to reunite from time to time. By July 1562, Catherine was once again pregnant, and the following year gave birth to another son. Then, two English rebels, without Catherine's assent, took up her cause for succession, further jeopardizing Elizabeth's position as queen.

Elizabeth had Catherine removed from the Tower and put under arrest in Essex at the home of Lord John Grey, an uncle who had always disliked Catherine. There, Catherine could not eat and wept continuously. She began to waste away, a victim of her fate and tuberculosis. By 1566, in advanced stages of consumption, Catherine Grey was in custody at the home of Sir Owen Hopton at Cockfield Hall in Yoxford. She died there, on January 22, 1568, age 28.

SUGGESTED READING:

Chapman, Hester W. *Two Tudor Portraits*. Boston, MA: Little, Brown, 1960.

Grey, Denise (1897–1996)

French actress of stage and film. Born in 1897; died on January 13, 1996, in Paris, France.

Born in 1897, Denise Grey's remarkable show-business career spanned nine decades. She began as a leading can-can dancer in the famous Follies Bergères. By the time she retired, just four years before her death at age 99, she was an actress playing grandmother roles. "I love life," she said shortly after leaving her profession. "I am very happy God has let me stay awhile on Earth."

SOURCES:

Obituaries. *The Boston Globe*. January 14, 1996.

Grey, Elizabeth (1437–1492).

See Woodville, Elizabeth.

Grey, Elizabeth (fl. 1482–1530)

*6th Baroness Lisle. Born around 1482; some sources cite death in 1525; daughter of Edward Grey (b. 1462), 1st viscount L'Isle or Lisle, and *Elizabeth Talbot (d. 1487); married Edmund Dudley (c. 1462–1510), chancellor of the Exchequer; married Arthur Plantagenet (d. 1541), Viscount L'Isle or Lisle (son of King Edward IV and his mistress *Elizabeth Lucy), before April 1533; children: (first marriage) John Dudley (c. 1502–1553), duke of Northumberland; Andrew Dudley; Jerome Dudley; Elizabeth Dudley (who married William, 7th baron Stourton); (second marriage) Frances Plantagenet; Elizabeth Plantagenet; Bridget Plantagenet.*

Grey, Elizabeth (1505–1526)

5th Baroness Lisle. Name variations: Baroness L'Isle. Born in 1505; died in 1526 (some sources cite 1519); daughter of John Grey, 4th viscount Lisle, and Muriel Howard (d. 1512); married Charles Brandon, later duke of Suffolk (annulled); married Henry Courtenay, marquis of Exeter, after June 11, 1515; children: Edward Courtenay, earl of Devon.

Elizabeth Grey was the only child of John Grey, 4th viscount Lisle, and *Muriel Howard. As heir, she was betrothed to Charles Brandon (later duke of Suffolk), who was given the title Viscount Lisle. When Elizabeth came of age, however, she refused to marry him, and Charles had to give up the title.

Grey, Elizabeth (1581–1651)

Countess of Kent. Name variations: Elizabeth Talbot. Born Elizabeth Talbot in 1581; died on December 7, 1651; daughter of Gilbert Talbot (b. 1552), 7th earl of Shrewsbury, and Mary Cavendish; married Henry Grey, 7th earl of Kent.

Elizabeth Grey was rumored to be secretly married to the jurist John Selden, who had been a steward to her deceased husband Henry Grey. Elizabeth published a collection of culinary recipes as well as *A Choice Manuall, or Rare and Select Secrets in Physick and Chyrurgery* (2nd ed., 1653).

Grey, Elizabeth (d. 1818)

Countess of Gainsborough. Died on September 20, 1818; daughter of George Grey (b. 1767) and Mary Whitbread; married Charles Noel, 1st earl of Gainsborough, on May 13, 1817; children: Charles George Noel, 2nd earl of Gainsborough (b. on September 5, 1818).

Grey, Elizabeth (d. 1822)

Countess Grey. Died on May 26, 1822; daughter of George Grey; married Charles Grey, 1st earl Grey, on June 8, 1762; children: Charles Grey, 2nd earl Grey (b. 1764); Henry George Grey (b. 1766); George Grey (b. 1767).

Grey, Frances (1517–1559).

See Grey, Lady Jane for sidebar on Frances Brandon.

Grey, Lady Jane (1537–1554)

Teenaged usurper of the English throne who reigned for nine days before being executed in the Tower of

London. Name variations: Lady Jane Dudley. Born in October of 1537 at Bradgate, Leicestershire, England; executed on February 12, 1554, in the Tower of London; eldest surviving daughter of Henry Grey (d. 1554), marquis of Dorset (later duke of Suffolk), and Frances Brandon (1517–1559, granddaughter of King Henry VII); sister of Lady *Catherine Grey (c. 1540–1568) and ◄❧ Mary Grey (1545–1578); married Lord Guildford Dudley, on May 21, 1553; no children.

Entered the service of Queen Catherine Parr (1546); coerced into marrying Lord Dudley by his father, the duke of Northumberland (1553); convicted of high treason against Queen Mary and executed (1554).

On a brisk February morning in 1554, a petite, black-garbed figure emerged from the gentleman-jailer's lodgings in the Tower of London. As she proceeded slowly toward the scaffold erected on Tower Green, Lady Jane Grey passed a handcart bearing the headless corpse of her husband, Lord Dudley. Clutching her Prayer Book, she mounted the scaffold and addressed the spectators:

Good people—I am come hither to die, and by a law I am condemned to the same. My offence against the Queen's Highness was only in consent to the devices of others, which is deemed treason; but it was never my seeking, but by counsel of those who should seem to have further understanding of things than I . . . . I pray you all, good Christian people, to bear witness that I die a true Christian woman.

After a few moments spent in prayer, the 16-year-old made her way to the block—and the piles of straw which surrounded it. All too familiar with the tales of botched beheadings, she implored the executioner, "I pray you—dispatch me quickly." The straw rustled as she knelt in it. Blindfolded, she reached out for the block she could no longer see. Finally placing her neck across its curved aperture, she stretched out her arms. The masked executioner performed his grisly task with one blow of the axe. Then, holding up the severed head by its blood-soaked hair, he proclaimed: "Behold the head of a traitor! So perish all the Queen's enemies!"

Born in 1537, during the reign of King Henry VIII, Jane Grey lived out her brief life as a pawn of her ambitious parents and their political connections at court. Her mother ◄❧ **Frances Brandon** was the daughter of Charles Brandon, duke of Suffolk, and *Mary Tudor (1496–1533), younger sister of Henry VIII. Jane and her mother stood next in line to the throne after Henry VIII's three children, Edward [VI], *Mary [I] and *Elizabeth [I]. This fact—and the use made of it by her ruthless kith and kin—largely determined the course of Jane Grey's tragic life.

A highly intelligent as well as unusually beautiful child, Lady Jane Grey acquired an exceptional humanistic education. Tutored primarily by Cambridge-educated John Aylmer (later bishop of London under Elizabeth I), she became proficient in Latin, Greek, French, and Italian, and in her teens added Hebrew in order to augment her study of the Scriptures. That she loved learning, and found in Aylmer an inspiring school master, is apparent from her lifelong preference for reading, writing, and music over the more ostentatious pastimes of the Tudor aristocracy. At age 14, she began corresponding in Latin with continental reformers (including the learned pastor of Zurich, Heinrich Bullinger), a clear indication that her training and up-bringing had drawn her into Protestant circles.

While scholars and religious reformers lauded young Lady Jane's character and intellect, her

❧► Grey, Mary (1545–1578)

English noblewoman. Name variations: Lady Mary Keys or Keyes. Born in 1545 (some sources cite 1540); died on April 20, 1578, in London, England; daughter of Henry Grey, marquis of Dorset (later duke of Suffolk) and *Frances Brandon (1517–1559, granddaughter of King Henry VII); sister of *Catherine Grey (c. 1540–1568) and Lady *Jane Grey (1537–1554); married Thomas Keyes, on August 10, 1565.

Born a dwarf, Mary Grey retained her position at court, despite the behavior of her sisters, until she too married in secret in the summer of 1565. A month after the wedding, Mary was placed in the custody of a married couple in Buckinghamshire while her husband Thomas Keyes was incarcerated until his death in 1571. Mary Grey died penniless in 1578, age 33.

❧► Brandon, Frances (1517–1559)

Duchess of Suffolk. Name variations: Frances Grey. Born on July 16, 1517, in Hatfield, Hertfordshire, England; died on November 21, 1559, in London, England; daughter of Charles Brandon (1484–1545), duke of Suffolk, and *Mary Tudor (1496–1533, younger sister of Henry VIII); married Henry Grey, marquis of Dorset (later duke of Suffolk), in 1535 (d. 1554); married Adrian Stokes, on March 9, 1554; children: (first marriage) *Jane Grey (1537–1554); *Catherine Grey (c. 1540–1568, later Catherine Seymour); *Mary Grey (1545–1578, who married Thomas Keyes); (second marriage) Elizabeth Stokes (1554–1554, died at birth).

parents held an entirely different view. Severe and demanding, Henry Grey and Frances Brandon took every opportunity to chastise their daughter. In 1550, in a rare private conversation recorded by Roger Ascham (Princess Elizabeth's tutor), Lady Jane spoke of the nightmarish home life she endured:

> When I am in the presence either of father or mother, whether I speak, keep silence, sit, stand or go, eat, drink, be merry or sad, be sewing, playing, dancing, or doing anything else, I must do it, as it were, in such weight, measure, and number, even so perfectly as God made the world, else I am so sharply taunted, so cruelly threatened, yea presently sometimes with pinches, nips and bobs [blows], and some ways I will not name for the honour I bear them, so without measure misordered that I think myself in Hell.

No wonder she waited anxiously each day "till the time comes when I must go to Master Aylmer, who teacheth me so gently."

Though clearly more vicious than most parents, the Greys' behavior reflected standard 16th-century child-rearing practices. Sons and daugh-

The execution of Lady Jane Grey.

ters of the English nobility and gentry could expect harsh discipline—even physical abuse—at the hands of their parents, guardians, and teachers. Viewed as miniature adults, youngsters experienced little freedom of action or expression. Children were frequently beaten or flogged in order to crush their wills and teach them absolute obedience to authority. Lady Jane was not a rebellious child, but like so many of her class, she came to fear and loathe her parents.

At age nine, Lady Jane entered the service of Queen ❧ Catherine Parr, who treated her with kindness and affection. Here, Lady Jane became acquainted with her royal cousins, including the future King Edward VI who was exactly her own age and much impressed by her. Following the death of Henry VIII in 1547, the widow Parr married Thomas Seymour, Lord High Admiral and uncle of the new king. Seymour, a charming but unprincipled schemer, purchased Lady Jane's wardship from her father, promising to arrange a marriage between Lady Jane and King Edward. Parr's death in childbirth in 1548, and Seymour's political downfall a year later, forced Lady Jane to return home; thus ended the only happy years of her life.

❧▶

*Catherine Parr
(1512–1548).*

*See Six Wives of
Henry VIII.*

𝒢reat pity was it for the casting away of that fair lady, whom nature had not only so beautified but God also had endowed with singular gifts and graces.

—John Foxe, martyrologist

Nine-year-old Edward's accession to the throne in 1547 unleashed the inevitable power struggle among the regents who ruled England in his name. The first half of the reign was dominated by King Edward's older uncle, Edward Seymour, duke of Somerset and Lord Protector. While Somerset's younger brother connived at a Lady Jane-Edward VI match, the Protector made very different plans to marry his own daughter to the king, and his son, the earl of Hertford, to Lady Jane. Soon after Thomas Seymour's execution for treason in 1549, Lady Jane's parents agreed to a marriage contract between their daughter and young Hertford, whom Jane knew and liked. But Somerset's grip on King and Council slipped badly in 1550; his enemies at court engineered his arrest, trial for treason, and ultimately, his beheading in 1552. Henry Grey, now duke of Suffolk, quickly allied his family with the new ruling faction led by John Dudley, duke of Northumberland. Radical Protestantism and personal greed characterized the Northumberland government. Lady Jane's destiny henceforth lay in the hands of utterly unscrupulous men.

By early 1553, it was obvious to both Northumberland and Suffolk that the frail young king's days were numbered. In an effort to exclude Edward's sisters from the succession and secure the throne for his roguish teenaged son, Northumberland proposed a marriage between Lady Jane and Guildford Dudley. Now 15 and pledged (or so she thought) to Hertford, Jane vehemently refused. Her enraged parents physically beat her into submission, and the marriage to Dudley took place on May 21. Forced to reside with her hated in-laws, Lady Jane suffered a collapse and soon withdrew from public life. Most authorities agree that she knew nothing of the plot Northumberland had hatched, or the role in it she was expected to play.

Having given his assent to the altered succession, a consumption-ridden Edward VI died on July 6, 1553. Three days later, Northumberland and the Council proclaimed Lady Jane queen of England. When informed of her new status, she fainted. Over the next nine days, a reluctant "Queen Jane" resided in the Tower of London, far more a prisoner of Northumberland's attempted coup than a willing participant in it. In a singular act of courage—and royal prerogative—Jane adamantly refused the violent demands of the Dudley family that she make her husband, Guildford, king. Meanwhile, the English people—Catholic and Protestant alike—declared for the Princess Mary. By July 19, Jane knew the plot had failed and bitterly informed her father, "Out of obedience to you and my mother, I have grievously sinned. Now I willingly relinquish the crown."

Lady Jane Grey remained a prisoner in the Tower until her trial on November 14, 1553, at which time she pleaded guilty to treason and was sentenced to death. Queen Mary seemed inclined to spare her cousin, despite pressure from her advisors to execute this heretical rival forthwith. An ardent Catholic, Mary nonetheless pardoned the Suffolks, and probably would have released Jane in due course had not Henry, duke of Suffolk, rashly joined in Wyatt's Rebellion in January 1554. In so doing, Suffolk sealed his daughter's doom. Writing to him on the eve of her execution, Jane expressed her abiding religious faith, but also acknowledged her sense of injury at his hands:

> Although it hath pleased God to hasten my death by you, by whom my life should rather have been lengthened, yet can I so pa-

tiently take it that I yield God more hearty thanks for shortening my woeful days than if all the world had been given into my possession.

She refused to see her husband who faced similar punishment. On February 12, 1554, 16-year-old Lady Jane was beheaded on Tower Green. She was buried, along with Lord Dudley, in the church of St. Peter ad Vincula within the Tower of London.

Lady Jane Grey was only one of many female casualties of the turbulent Tudor age. Yet she remains perhaps its most pitied aristocratic victim, in part because of her unhappy life and youthful innocence. Had she been less pious and scholarly and more clever and worldly—like her wily cousin Elizabeth—she might have developed some much-needed survival skills. Later chroniclers capitalized on her steadfast adherence to the Reformed Faith and transformed Lady Jane into a Protestant martyr. Her staunch Protestant views certainly contributed to her downfall, but they mattered far less than her gender and family ties. Patriarchal authority and dynastic ambition inevitably placed high-born Tudor women at risk. It should be remembered that Lady Jane Grey's remains shared their final resting place in St. Peter's Church with two other headless queens: Protestant *Anne Boleyn and Catholic ❧➤ Catherine Howard.

SOURCES:

Plowden, Alison. *Lady Jane Grey and the House of Suffolk.* NY: Franklin Watts, 1986.

Routh, C.R. *Who's Who in Tudor England.* London: Shepheard-Walwyn, 1990.

Stephen, Leslie, and Sidney Lee, eds. *Dictionary of National Biography.* Rev. ed. 22 vols. London: Oxford University Press, 1937–38.

Stone, Lawrence. *The Family, Sex and Marriage in England, 1500–1800.* NY: Harper and Row, 1979.

SUGGESTED READING:

Chapman, Hester. *Lady Jane Grey: The Nine Days Queen.* Boston, MA: Little, Brown, 1962.

Luke, Mary. *The Nine Days Queen: A Portrait of Lady Jane Grey.* NY: William Morrow, 1986.

Mathew, David. *Lady Jane Grey: The Setting of the Reign.* London: Eyre Methuen, 1972.

COLLECTIONS:

Calendar of State Papers (Domestic Series) of the Reigns of Edward VI, Mary Elizabeth (1547–1603). Edited by R. Lemon, Mary Everett Green, *et al.* London, 1856–70; *The Chronicle of Queen Jane and Two Years of Queen Mary.* Edited by J.G. Nichols for the Camden Society. London, 1850.

RELATED MEDIA:

Lady Jane Grey (also titled *Nine Days a Queen*), produced in England by Gainsborough-Gaumont, starring Sir Cedric Hardwicke, John Mills, **Gwen Ffrangcon-Davies** as Mary Tudor, and **Nova Pilbeam** as Lady Jane Grey, 1936.

Lady Jane (VHS, 140 min.), fictionalized costume epic, starring **Helena Bonham Carter**, Paramount Pictures, 1985.

Constance B. Rynder,
Professor of History, The University of Tampa, Tampa, Florida

ℒady ℐane 𝒢rey

Grey, Josephine (1828–1906).

See Butler, Josephine.

Grey, Mary (1545–1578).

See Grey, Lady Jane for sidebar.

Catherine Howard (1520/22–1542).

See Six Wives of Henry VIII.

Grieg, Nina (1845–1935)

Norwegian singer who was best known for performances of her husband's compositions. Born Nina Hagerup on November 24, 1845, in Bergen, Norway; died on December 9, 1935, in Copenhagen; daughter of Herman Hagerup and Madame Werligh (a Danish actress); studied with Carl Helsted; married Edvard Grieg (the composer), on June 11, 1867 (died 1907).

Nina Grieg was born Nina Hagerup on November 24, 1845, in Bergen, Norway, the daughter of Herman Hagerup and **Madame Werligh**, a Danish actress. When Nina was eight, the family moved to Denmark and settled near Elsinore where she studied with Carl Helsted. Her vocal power was slight, but her artistry compensated for this defect.

Nina married her cousin, Edvard Grieg, on June 11, 1867 (her father and Edvard's mother were brother and sister). In highly successful joint concerts the couple gave throughout Europe, she performed her husband's work many times and became the most sensitive interpreter of his songs. Her talented singing inspired the composer Delius to dedicate two sets of songs to her in 1888 and 1890.

John Haag,
Athens, Georgia

Griese, Irma (1923–1945).

See Grese, Irma.

Griffin, Marion Mahony (1871–1961).

See Mahony, Marion.

Griffith, Corinne (1896–1979)

American actress and film star of the silent era. Born in Texarkana, Texas, on November 24, 1896; died in 1979; attended Sacred Heart Academy, New Orleans; married Webster Campbell (an actor-director), in

Corinne Griffith

1920 (divorced 1923); married Walter Morosco (a producer), in 1933 (divorced 1934); married George Preston Marshall (owner of the Washington Redskins and a laundry empire), in 1936 (divorced 1958); married Danny Scholl (marriage dissolved after 33 days).

Selected filmography: The Last Man *(1916);* The Love Doctor *(1917);* The Menace *(1918);* Miss Ambition *(1918);* The Girl of Today *(1918);* Adventure Shop *(1919);* Thin Ice *(1919);* The Bramble Bush *(1919);* Human Collateral *(1920);* The Garter Girl *(1920);* The Tower of Jewels *(1920);* The Whisper Market *(1920);* What's Your Reputation Worth? *(1921);* Moral Fibre *(1921);* The Single Track *(1921);* Island Wives *(1922);* A Virgin's Sacrifice *(A Woman's Sacrifice, 1922);* Divorce Coupons *(1922);* The Common Law *(1923);* Six Days *(1923);* Black Oxen *(1924); (also executive producer)* Lilies of the Field *(1924); (also executive producer)* Single Wives *(1924); (also executive producer)* Love's Wilderness *(1924); (also executive producer)* Déclassé *(The Social Exile, 1925); (also executive producer)* The Marriage Whirl *(1925); (also executive producer)* Classified *(1925); (also executive producer)* Infatuation *(1925); (also executive producer)* Mademoiselle Modiste *(1926); (also executive producer)* Into Her Kingdom *(1926); (also executive producer)* Syncopating Sue *(1926); (also executive producer)* The Lady in Ermine *(1927); (also executive producer)* Three Hours *(1927);* The Garden of Eden *(1928);* Outcast *(1928);* The Divine Lady *(1929);* Saturday's Children *(1929);* Prisoners *(1929); (remake)* Lilies of the Field *(1930);* Back Pay *(1930);* Lily Christine *(UK, 1932).*

Called "The Orchid Lady of the Screen" because of her delicate beauty, Corinne Griffith was signed to a contract with New York-based Vitagraph Pictures in 1916; by the time she reached Hollywood in the 1920s, Griffith was already a star. She made numerous silent films and, during her heyday, was voted "The Most Beautiful Woman in the World" in a poll of 500 movie editors throughout the country. Griffith's career ended abruptly with the talkies. She attempted several sound movies, one in England titled *Lily Christine* (1932), but none were successful.

Griffith's first two marriages, to actor Webster Campbell and producer Walter Morosco, were short-lived. In 1936, she married George "Wet Wash" Preston Marshall, the owner of a laundry empire and the Washington Redskins. They were together for six years, during which time Griffith wrote six books, the two most popular being *My Life with the Redskins* (1944) and *Papa's Delicate Condition* (1952), which was adapted for the screen in 1963. A fourth marriage to a much younger man ended in divorce court after only 33 days. During the trial, in response to her husband's claims that she had tricked him into marriage by telling him she was only 52, Griffith reputedly took the stand and claimed that she was not Corinne Griffith at all, but a stand-in who took over when the real Corinne Griffith died in the mid-30s.

Griffith made some wise investments in California real estate, and at one time was one of the largest landowners in Beverly Hills. Late in life, she devoted her energies to the repeal of the personal income tax, which she regarded as "legalized thievery."

Barbara Morgan,
Melrose, Massachusetts

Griffith, Elizabeth (c. 1720–1793).

See Clive, Kitty for sidebar.

Griffith, Florence (1959–1998).

See Joyner, Florence Griffith.

Griffith, Linda (1884–1949).

See Arvidson, Linda.

Griffith-Joyner, Florence (1959–1998).

See Joyner, Florence Griffith.

Griffiths, Ann (1776–1805)

Welsh hymn-writer and mystic. Born Ann Thomas in 1776; died in 1805; daughter of John Thomas (a country poet); married Thomas Griffiths, in 1804; children: one died in infancy.

Ann Griffiths spent her short life in the parish of Llanfihangel-yng-Ngwynfa, Montgomery, Wales. At age 17, she lost her mother, and in 1804 married Thomas Griffiths, but lost her baby daughter the following year and died shortly thereafter. Her father John Thomas was a *bardd gwlad* (country poet) who mastered the traditional metres of Welsh poetry and recorded local occasions in verse. He was an ardent adherent of the Anglican Church, but he and four of his children were converted to Methodism during the religious revival that took place in that part of Wales. Ann, too, converted to the Methodist Fellowship in 1796, and her home became a center for Methodist preaching.

Her few extant letters are considered to be sublime examples of religious prose. Most of her hymns were never written down but have survived because they were recorded from the memory of **Ruth Evans**, her maidservant, and published in *Casgliad o Hymnau* (A Collection of Hymns) the year after her death (1806). These expressed "the peculiar depth and intensity of her spiritual experience and a firm grasp of the essential truths of her faith," influenced by folk songs and carols. Despite her small body of work, it has been the subject of much study in Welsh and English, and English translations have been made of her hymns. She is described as "a central figure in the European tradition of Christian poetry."

SOURCES:

Evans, Gwynfor. *Welsh Nation Builders.* Llandyssul: Gomer, 1988.

Stephens, Meic, ed. The *Oxford Companion to the Literature of Wales.* Oxford University Press, Oxford & New York, 1986.

Elizabeth Rokkan,
translator, formerly Associate Professor, Department of English,
University of Bergen, Norway

Griffiths, Martha Wright (1912—)

U.S. congressional representative (D-Michigan) who sponsored the Equal Rights Amendment and worked for more equitable laws in the areas of welfare, pensions, credit, and health care. Born Martha Edna Wright on January 29, 1912, in Pierce City, Missouri; daughter of Charles Elbridge (a mail carrier) and Nelle (Sullinger) Wright; attended Pierce City public schools; University of Missouri at Columbia, B.A., 1934; University of Michigan Law School at Ann Arbor, LL.B., 1940; married Hicks George Griffiths of Schenectady, N.Y., on December 28, 1933; no children.

Family moved to Pierce City (1921) when farmhouse just outside city limits burned to ground; taught school in Pierce City between sophomore and junior years of college; admitted to Michigan Bar (1941); joined legal department of American Automobile Insurance Company (1941–42); served as contract negotiator for Army Ordnance in Detroit during World War II; went into law partnership with husband Hicks and G. Mennen Williams (1946); served as state representative (1949–52); served as recorder and judge, Recorder's Court, Detroit (1953–54); was a member of the U.S. House of Representatives (1955–74); was lieutenant governor of Michigan (1982–90); was scholar-in-residence, University of Missouri (1990–91). Awarded 29 honorary degrees; received Alice Paul Award, National Women's Party (1983); named Michigan Woman of the Year (1990); inducted into the National Women's Hall of Fame (1993).

The Equal Rights Amendment (ERA) was introduced in Congress in 1923, and again in every session thereafter for almost 50 years. Although the measure had passed twice in the Senate, it had never come before the full House of Representatives. In 1970, Martha Wright Griffiths broke the barrier, through a combination of political savvy and persistence.

The ERA bill had been bottled up in the House Judiciary Committee for 20 years. In an attempt to get the bill out of committee and onto the floor for a vote, Griffiths took the unusual step of petitioning to discharge the amendment from committee. In order to pull this off, she needed a majority of House members, 218, to sign the petition. Many of her colleagues owed her for supporting their measures when she served on the powerful Ways and Means Committee. She was relentless in making sure that members signed, sometimes literally dragging them by the arm to the signing desk. "Louisiana's Hale Boggs, Democratic whip [husband of *Lindy Boggs and father of ABC newscaster **Cokie Roberts**], was opposed to the amendment," said Griffiths. "But he promised to sign as number 200, convinced that I would never make it. You may be sure when I had Number 199 signed up, I rushed to his office, and Hale Boggs became Number 200." When she saw that three times more Democrats had signed than Republicans, she persuaded House Minority Leader Gerald Ford that it would look bad to have so few Republicans. Ford delivered 17 Republican votes in addition to his own, and on August 10, 1970, the ERA passed the House. The victory was one of many in Griffiths' long battle for legal equity for women.

> *I* chased fellow Congressmen ruthlessly. I'd even listen to roll call for names of any who hadn't signed. Having spotted the face, I'd promptly corner him for his autograph.
>
> —Martha Wright Griffiths

Martha Edna Wright was born in the Missouri Ozarks on January 29, 1912. Both sides of her family, the Wrights and the Sullingers, had lived in the region since the 1850s. Pierce City, at the time of her birth, boasted a post office, hotel, electric lights and telephone system, churches and schools, a lyceum where philosophy and Greek were taught, even an opera house. There was, however, no public library, much to the dismay of Martha Wright. She was an ambitious girl who dreamed of a career as a journalist, and wrote in her diary the day before she turned 15: "One more year of life has gone. What have I accomplished? . . . I must be, I will be successful in something, if it is merely washing dishes." She resolved to sleep less and not "end up in the poor house due to a wasted youth."

The women in her family had always had ambitions. Her father's mother, **Jeanettie Hinds Wright**, a widow with three sons, had become a seamstress, clerked, and managed a hotel to put her boys through high school at a time when few children attended school beyond eighth grade. Martha's mother **Nelle Sullinger Wright**, an imposing woman, 5'10" tall, worked as a substitute letter carrier during World War I and often raised money for the sick and poor.

Martha's father Elbridge, a postal carrier, had hoped his children would have more opportunities than he had. His daughter was valedictorian of her graduating class, but the Great Depression had begun by the time she finished high school. The Wrights wanted to send both their children to college, but Elbridge believed Martha's opportunity would have to be sacrificed for that of her brother Orville, four years older. Nelle disagreed and took in boarders to help her daughter attend the University of Missouri. Martha herself took out a loan, of which she proudly repaid "every cent," and taught school in Pierce City between her sophomore and junior years.

In college, Martha worked as hard as ever, as a volunteer on the campus radio and captain of the debate team. She read prodigiously, often three books in a weekend. During her sophomore year, Hicks Griffiths arrived from Union College in New York to study political science at the University of Missouri, and the two were paired on the debate team. A deepening attachment led to marriage during Martha's senior year, on December 28, 1933.

The couple moved to Ann Arbor, Michigan, to attend the University of Michigan Law School. Hicks had been accepted at Harvard, but chose Michigan because it admitted women. He had persuaded Martha to study law also, so that she could have a professional career for financial security. After graduation, both were hired by the American Automobile Insurance Company, Martha at $10 a week less than Hicks. After America entered World War II, Martha became the first woman contract negotiator with the Army Ordnance Department in Detroit, working with munitions and vehicle manufacturers and gaining valuable knowledge of the world of big business.

In 1946, the couple started a law practice and were joined early the next year by law school classmate G. Mennen ("Soapy")

Martha
Wright
Griffiths

Williams, who would later be governor of Michigan. Griffiths had already made her first bid for public office. An advocate of women's political rights, at a gathering of women lawyers, had urged her to run for the legislature. At first Martha Griffiths declined, but Hicks convinced her to try. She admitted that she did like to picture herself "swaying vast audiences, doing great good, changing the whole course of the world." She finished 80 in a field of 92 competing for 27 seats, but the experience and exposure led to her election the following year to the

Michigan State Central Committee as 17th District representative.

The Democratic Party was in need of fresh leadership. Both Martha and Hicks worked hard to reorganize it, and then to nominate their partner, "Soapy" Williams, as the Democratic candidate for governor. Martha, who wanted to help Williams, was told she could do it best by becoming a candidate for the legislature and running with him. Although Michigan went for the Republican presidential candidate, Thomas Dewey, Williams was elected in November. Martha Griffiths was elected too, but she modestly insisted that the only possible explanation was "that all of Ordnance must have voted for me." Hicks became state chair of the Democratic Party.

Griffiths' work in the legislature was not easy. She was 37 years old, one of two women in a 100-member body. The 61 Republicans blocked in committee many of the reform measures Williams proposed, and she learned the use of the discharge petition to force legislation onto the floor for a vote. State representatives were poorly paid, and she and Hicks, himself busy with the continuing reform of the Democratic Party, had to keep up their law practice. Still, she was named by the Capitol Press Corps as one of Michigan's ten best legislators.

Martha Griffiths made her first run for the U.S. House of Representatives in 1952, with Hicks managing her campaign. During her 1950 campaign for re-election to the state legislature, she had begun attending block parties to explain election issues to women, appearing at 200 during the last month of the campaign. In 1952, she traveled throughout the district in a trailer, where constituents, especially women, would come by to drink a glass of juice and discuss topics of concern to them. She lost by just 3% of the vote, in a year when the election of Republican Dwight Eisenhower made it hard for Democrats to be elected. The following year, Governor Williams appointed her recorder and judge of Detroit's Recorder Court, the first woman in the court's 127-year history.

Martha Griffiths' work on the bench impressed the men of her party, and in her second run for Congress, in November 1954, she defeated her Republican opponent. Sixteen women were elected to the House that year, a new record.

As the representative from an urban district, Griffiths was interested in housing—she supported the creation of a Cabinet position on urban affairs—and schools, which became crowded as the baby boom hit and 70% of Americans were living in cities. True to her roots, she also sponsored bills to increase the pay of postal workers and to promote library service in rural areas. She was concerned about many other issues, including consumer protection, the nation's water supply, tobacco advertising, and the humane slaughter of meat animals.

By 1958, unemployment in Detroit had reached 17%, and Representative Griffiths became an ardent supporter of the food-stamp program. In part due to her strenuous efforts, the bill passed Congress, but Eisenhower's Secretary of Agriculture, Ezra Taft Benson, failed to implement the plan. In 1961, a new Democratic administration designated Detroit for a pilot food-stamp project.

As a junior legislator in a conservative administration, Griffiths often felt frustrated. She had been named to the Banking and Currency Committee, but the 80-year-old chair seldom called a meeting. Northern liberals were at a disadvantage because southern conservatives from safe districts dominated the committees where legislation originated. As one of 17 women in the House, she sometimes felt "like a fragile little goldfish among the barracuda." One of her colleagues expressed his dismay at the "influx" of women (five in 1955–56) and was horrified to think that soon half the House would be women.

Fortunately, Griffiths had also been assigned to the Government Operations Committee, which met almost daily, and she worked on the Military Operations Subcommittee on civil defense in case of nuclear attack and mismanagement of defense spending. Mail and visitors kept her busy, and she tried to travel home every weekend. She and Hicks were able to endure separation when she was in Congress, because each believed that what the other was doing was vitally important. At first, she insisted on cooking a week's supply of food before she left on Sunday, until he assured her he could fend for himself. She would later say that if every man were like her husband, there would be no need for an Equal Rights Amendment.

At the beginning of her fourth term in February 1961, Martha Griffiths was the first woman appointed to the Joint Economic Committee (JEC) of the House and the Senate, which influenced the all-important congressional budget. She would use the unique forum of the JEC to work for revenue sharing, pension reform, and welfare reform.

A vacancy on the Ways and Means Committee opened up in 1961. Griffiths persuaded the

Michigan delegation to support her, and in January 1962 she became the first woman member of that influential committee. Griffiths thought her appointment significant because "a feminine voice removes a proverbial blind spot in the thinking of male lawmakers. Men think of women as wives or widows, but never as workers."

On the Ways and Means Committee, Griffiths spent more time on the tax code than on any other issue, and she quickly saw that it discriminated against women. Tax law showed, she said, "that the work of women has never meant anything." A married couple paid more in taxes than two single people with the same total income, and the law allowed deductions for business entertainment but not for domestic help.

National health insurance was another important topic covered by the Ways and Means Committee. Lyndon Johnson's Medicare plan was passed after a lengthy struggle. Griffiths supported the idea of universal health care coverage, and sponsored a bill in 1970. It, too, faced an uphill fight, and work ground to a halt in 1974 when the Congress focused on the possible impeachment of Richard Nixon.

More successful were her efforts to eliminate legal sex bias. Inequities in the Social Security law particularly troubled her, such as the rule that men could not claim a wife's retirement or survivor benefits unless he proved financial dependence on her; "surviving spouse" replaced the term "widow" in legislative terminology. In the 1960s, Congress passed two bills to improve women's situation, the Equal Pay Act of 1963 and the Civil Rights Act of 1964. Although the Equal Pay Act was, according to President John F. Kennedy, "a significant step forward," women were still earning about 60% of what men were paid. Title VII of the Civil Rights bill was a comprehensive equal opportunity statute and established the Equal Employment Opportunity Commission (EEOC) to hear grievances.

Before the bill passed the House, 18 amendments were suggested, including the addition of "sex" to race, color, religion, and national origin as categories protected from discrimination. Although the idea originated with Martha Griffiths, the amendment was actually offered by Howard W. Smith of Virginia, some think in an effort to sabotage the passage of the entire Civil Rights bill. Many women also protested that the gender classification would jeopardize the act, among them Assistant Secretary of Labor **Esther Peterson** and civil-rights champion **Edith Starrett Green.** Griffiths had no such doubts and let Smith

offer the amendment, because she knew that as Rules Committee chair, he would bring in votes.

In proposing the amendment, Smith, 80, joked with the 75-year-old Emmanuel Celler, chair of the Judiciary Committee, about his desire to redress "the imbalance of spinsters." Griffiths stopped their bantering with the observation that without a sex clause, white women would not be protected by the law, while black women would be. The bill passed the House, and she continued to follow its progress in the Senate, threatening that if the word "sex" were deleted, she would send her remarks to the constituents of every opponent.

After the bill passed, she continued to work hard to make it effective, urging women to bring suits before the EEOC. It was partly to support such initiatives that NOW, the National Organization of Women, was founded. One of Griffiths' special targets was sex-segregated help-wanted ads. "I have never entered a door labeled 'Men,' and I doubt that Mr. Holcomb [acting chair of the EEOC] has frequently entered the women's room," she argued. "The same principle operates in the job-seeking process."

The policy of airlines to dismiss flight attendants who were married or beyond their late 30s also drew Griffiths' ire, and she challenged the tradition by asking the vice president of United Airlines: "What are you running, Mr. Mason, an airline or a whorehouse?" She urged President Johnson to have the EEOC issue guidelines bringing age and marital status under the anti-discrimination ban.

Martha Griffiths was not only concerned about continuing sex discrimination in the workplace, she wanted gender-based distinctions eliminated everywhere. Women still did not have equal educational opportunities. In the area of criminal law, women were tried as adults at an earlier age than men, and were given longer sentences for the same crimes on the grounds that they would benefit more than men from rehabilitation. Griffiths denounced such practices as "pure witchcraft, a belief that women—like Eve—are responsible for any evil that befalls." Women could be excluded from serving on juries. Discrimination was widespread in credit and insurance.

At first, Martha Griffiths had hoped the courts would be the route for women to legal equality, but progress was so slow that she began to consider another avenue. In 1970, the 50th anniversary of the 19th Amendment granting all women the right to vote contributed to new interest in the Equal Rights Amendment. There was also a dramatic philosophical shift in the Department of Labor at the same time. The Women's Bureau had traditionally opposed any measure that would do away with protective legislation for women. Martha Griffiths stressed the need for the ERA: "So-called protective legislation never did protect women," because weight-lifting laws didn't apply in mercantile establishments or hospitals where many women worked, and child-support payments were largely ignored. The Bureau reversed its stand and persuaded Labor Secretary George Schultz to support the ERA.

Both political parties had endorsed the idea as early as 1945. In 1950 and 1953, the measure passed the Senate, and again in 1960. In February of 1970, members of NOW had disrupted Senate Judiciary Committee hearings on votes for 18-year-olds to demand hearings be scheduled on the ERA. Senator Birch Bayh, chair of the Subcommittee on Constitutional Amendments, promised to sponsor the ERA in the Senate and hearings began in May. His example did nothing to inspire Representative Emmanuel Cellar, House Judiciary Committee chair, forcing Griffiths to use the previously mentioned discharge petition to get the amendment to the floor of the House for a vote. She succeeded, according to **Hope Chamberlin**, author of *A Minority of Members*, with "a handful of political IOUs and a good pair of track shoes."

The fight had just begun. A vigorous debate followed in the Senate. Senator Sam Ervin objected to the House ERA on the grounds that it would not exempt women from military service, it would nullify state protective labor legislation, and it would undermine laws guaranteeing privacy to women. (Griffiths called this the "potty argument.") Congress adjourned at the end of 1970 with no ERA.

The bill was re-introduced in January 1971 with minor technical changes: a seven-year ratification period and a two-year extension after ratification before implementation. In March, the Senate began the first hearings on the ERA since 1948. Griffiths was an important witness. During the spring and summer, she toured the country making several speeches a week to urge audiences to flood their representatives with mail. In the fall, the House passed the bill a second time, but it did not get to the floor of the Senate that year.

For 15 months, organizations all along the political spectrum had been lobbying Congress. On the last day of February 1972, the Senate Judiciary Committee reported the original bill to the floor. Three weeks later, President Nixon endorsed the ERA, and it passed 84 to 8, with Griffiths sitting in a back-row desk keeping score on the roll call.

Twenty-two states ratified the amendment before the end of 1972, and eight more before a year had passed. Rapid approval was expected; Martha Griffiths predicted in the spring of 1973 that "the ERA will be part of the Constitution long before the year is out." By then, however, a strong counter-offensive had been launched. The anti-ERA movement, spearheaded by conservative leader ❧▶ **Phyllis Schlafly**'s Stop-ERA organization, took the amendment's supporters by surprise. In 1967, Schlafly, a well-educated, influential activist in the Republican Party, had lost a bitter fight for president of the National Federation of Republican Women, who thought her too right-wing and too hard to control. She had begun a newsletter at that time, which was quickly expanded when she began to oppose the ERA on the grounds that it would undermine the special privileges that women enjoyed, such as the right to be supported by a man if she chose to stay home with her children. Her argument that the second section of the amendment gave Congress broad powers of enforcement which would encroach on the powers of state legislatures convinced many legislators to vote against ratification. Emotional scenarios about women in the military, lesbian schoolteachers, and abortion had powerful influence not only on women but on the growing ranks of conservatives in the late 1970s who opposed other liberal programs like school busing. By the end of 1978, only 35 states had ratified, three short of the two-thirds needed, and the ratification period expired.

Although she was best known for her work on the ERA, Martha Griffiths' three-year welfare reform study was one of her top personal achievements. She believed that the welfare system undermined the work ethic and weakened family stability. She called for a plan to eliminate female dependency by recognizing men's equal responsibility for their children and requiring all recipients of Aid to Families with Dependent Children (AFDC) to work or take job training. She wanted to coordinate AFDC with Social Security, housing, health and food benefits. In the summer of 1971, she began to gather data for a comprehensive bill. By the time the study was completed, and legislation based upon it could have been written, Richard Nixon was embroiled in the Watergate scandal. When he stepped down in 1974, his successor, Gerald Ford, was unwilling to take on the challenge of welfare legislation.

In February of 1974, Martha Griffiths had announced her intention to retire in December. At age 63, she was tired of the constant campaigning that, with redistricting, had become harder, and she wanted to spend more time with her husband. Perhaps, too, she was motivated by the realization that she was not likely to become chair of the Ways and Means Committee. "I've sent for my seed catalogs and bought a sewing machine," she announced. A quiet retirement was not yet in store for the energetic congresswoman. She was quickly named to a number of boards of prestigious companies, including Burroughs, Chrysler, and the American Automobile Association. "I am a token Democrat, not a token woman," she laughed.

In 1982, Michigan gubernatorial candidate James Blanchard, anticipating a close race, talked the still-popular Martha Griffiths into joining him on the ticket as lieutenant-governor. In 1984, she was considered by *Time* magazine to be one of the Democratic vice-presidential possibilities (*Geraldine Ferraro was chosen). In 1990, Governor Blanchard dropped her from the ticket, citing her age, then 78. "That's the biggest problem in politics," said Griffiths, whom age had not mellowed. "You help some S.O.B. get elected and then he throws you off the train." That same year, **Wendy Reid Crisp**, writing in *Executive Female*, applauded Martha Wright Griffiths and the growing number of other older women in politics, who provided leadership on issues like public transportation, children's welfare, and the defeat of sports stadiums built at the expense of health and education programs. "It will mean," she predicted, "a decrease in mealy-mouthing."

SOURCES:

Boneparth, Ellen, ed. *Women, Power & Policy.* NY: Pergamon Press, 1982.

Chamberlin, Hope. *A Minority of Members: Women in the U.S. Congress.* NY: Praeger, 1973.

Crisp, Wendy Reid. "What It Takes," in *Executive Female.* November–December 1980, p. 80.

Forbes. May 1976, p. 115.

George, Emily. *Martha W. Griffiths.* Lanham, MD: University Press of America, 1982.

The New York Times Magazine. June 24, 1973, pp. 8–9.

Sochen, June. *Movers and Shakers: American Women Thinkers & Activists 1900–1970.* NY: Quadrangle, 1973.

Time. September 17, 1990, p. 53.

Wandersee, Winifred D. *On the Move: American Women in the 1970s.* Boston, MA: Twayne, 1985.

COLLECTIONS:

Papers located in the Bentley Historical Library, University of Michigan.

Kristie Miller,
author of *Ruth Hanna McCormick: A Life in Politics 1880–1944*
(University of New Mexico, 1992)

Schlafly, Phyllis (1924—)

American author, lecturer, and anti-feminist campaigner. Name variations: Mrs. John Fred Schlafly. Born Phyllis Stewart in Port Stewart, Missouri; grew up in St. Louis; Washington University, A.B., 1944; Radcliffe, M.A. in government, 1945; married John Fred Schlafly, in 1949; children: six. Worked as research librarian, First National Bank, St. Louis (1946–49); was research director Cardinal Mindszenty Foundation (1958–63); was a commentator for "America Wake Up" radio program (1962–66); served as a delegate to Republican National Convention, several years; was president of the Illinois Federation of Republican Women (1960–64); was first vice-president, National Federation of Republican Women (1965–67).

Phyllis Schlafly caused a stir in 1964 with her ultra-conservative book *A Choice not an Echo* in support of Barry Goldwater. A second book, *The Power of the Positive Woman*, maintains that women are essentially different from men and should not compete. Schlafly worked tirelessly, crisscrossing the United States, while building a powerful lobby to defeat the ERA. She advocated that women stay at home rather than have careers and argued that the ERA was redundant since women were already protected by legislation. Schlafly has also attacked homosexuality, abortion, divorce, extra-marital sex, and socialism. In 1993, there was another national stir when one of her sons broached the subject of his homosexuality.

Grignan, Françoise Marguerite de Sévigné, Comtesse de (1646–1705).

See Sévigné, Marie de for sidebar.

Grimké, Angelina E. (1805–1879)

Southern-born American abolitionist, writer and lecturer who campaigned for the extinction of slavery and worked toward resolution of the question of woman's rights. Name variations: Angelina Emily Grimké or Grimke; Nina; Angelina Grimké Weld. Pronunciation: GRIM-kay. Born Angelina Emily Grimké on February 20, 1805, in Charleston, South Carolina; died in Hyde Park, Massachusetts, on October 26, 1879; daughter and youngest child of the Honorable John Faucheraud (a judge of the Supreme Court of South Carolina) and Mary (Smith) Grimké; sister of Sarah Moore Grimké (1792–1873); attended Charleston Academy for Girls; married Theodore Dwight Weld, on May 14, 1838; children: Charles Stuart Weld (b. 1839); Theodore Weld (b. 1841); Sarah Grimké Weld (b. 1844).

Entered Charleston Academy for Girls (1819); expelled from Charleston Presbyterian Church (May 1829); accepted into Philadelphia Society of Friends (March 1831); published first antislavery writings (1835); attended Antislavery Convention of American Women in Philadelphia (May 1837); undertook New England speaking tour against slavery (1837–38); addressed legislative committee of Massachusetts Assembly (February 1838); elected to central committee of Women's Rights Convention, Worcester, Massachusetts (1850); retired from schoolteaching (1867).

Selected publications: "Slavery and the Boston Riot: A Letter to Wm. L. Garrison" (broadside, Philadelphia, August 30, 1835); (with Sarah Moore Grimké) "A Sketch of Thomas Grimké's Life written by his sisters in Philadelphia and sent to his Friends in Charleston for their Approbation," in The Calumet, *magazine of the American Peace Society (1835);* Appeal to the Christian Women of the Southern States *(New York, 1836);* An Appeal to the Women of the Nominally-Free States *(1837);* Letters to Catherine E. Beecher, in Reply to an Essay on Slavery and Aboli-*tionism, Addressed to A.E. Grimké (1838);* Letters from Angelina Grimké Weld, to the Woman's Rights Convention, held at Syracuse, September 1852 *(Syracuse, 1852).* Published speeches: before the Legislative Committee of the Massachusetts Legislature, printed in* The Liberator *(May 2, 1838); in Pennsylvania Hall (May 16, 1838); before the Women's Loyal League (May 14, 1863); "Address to the Soldiers of our Second Revolution," resolution read and adopted by the business meeting of the Women's Loyal League (May 15, 1863).*

*A*ngelina *E. G*rimké (1805–1879)

On May 16, 1838, two days after her marriage to abolitionist Theodore Dwight Weld, Angelina Grimké attended an antislavery convention in Philadelphia, Pennsylvania, where she was one of several women and men scheduled to speak. Over 3,000 reformers were assembled in the recently dedicated Pennsylvania Hall, and a noisy and hostile crowd had gathered outside the building. Following the opening address by William Lloyd Garrison, some of the mob managed to break inside, but they retreated when the first speaker, ☙➤ **Maria Chapman**, began her oration. Grimké was next, and when she rose she was greeted by bricks crashing through the windows and pieces of glass falling to the floor. As the listening audience grew uneasy, Grimké raised her voice:

> Men, brethren and fathers—mothers, daughter and sisters, what came ye out for to see? A reed shaken with the wind? Is it curiosity merely, or a deep sympathy with the perishing slave, that has brought this large audience together? . . . As a Southerner I feel it is my duty to stand up here tonight and bear testimony against slavery. I have seen it—I have seen it. I know it has horrors that can never be described. . . . I have *never* seen a happy slave. . . . I have exiled myself from my native land because I could no longer endure to hear the wailing of the slave.

The speech went on for over an hour, while the crowd outside the hall continued to throw stones. Finally Grimké closed by urging the women in the audience, particularly, to exercise their right to petition their state legislatures. It was to be her last formal, public speech for the cause of abolition.

Angelina Emily Grimké, called Nina, was born February 20, 1805, in Charleston, South Carolina, the 14th and youngest child of John Faucheraud Grimké, a judge of the South Carolina Supreme Court, and **Mary Smith Grimké**. A sister, *****Sarah Moore Grimké**, who was 13 years her senior, stood as godmother at her christening. The family were slaveowners of wealth and high social standing; the stature of the judge made them part of the ruling elite. Growing up, the Grimké children received the majority of their care and personal attention from house slaves, modified in Angelina's case by the loving attention of her godmother-sister, whom she addressed as "mother" from an early age. Since most of her siblings were many years her senior, she effectively grew up as an only child, and displayed the strong and outgoing personality of a highly self-assured and active person.

Though some of her older siblings had been tutored at home, Angelina was sent to the Charleston Academy for Girls at age 14, beginning a gradual separation from her family that took some years to complete. Her first year at the academy coincided with the departure of her father and sister Sarah for Pennsylvania and New Jersey, as the judge sought treatment for what proved to be a fatal illness. Meanwhile, Angelina was confronted at the academy for the first time with physical evidence of the evils of slavery when she witnessed the scars on the body of a young slave boy. The effect was so distressing that the young girl fainted.

By 1824, when Angelina Grimké experienced the social rituals of "coming-of-age" in Charleston society, her sister Sarah had been living in Philadelphia for three years. In April 1826, Angelina exchanged the Episcopalianism of her family for Presbyterianism, and became an active member of the congregation in her new church. As a teacher of large Sunday School classes and an organizer of interfaith prayer meetings for women in Charleston, she was regarded by the society around her as somewhat unorthodox, but tolerable, as she operated within the 19th-century ideology of separate spheres of activity and influence for women and men.

When she initiated daily prayer meetings for her family's plantation slaves, however, her behavior was considered far less acceptable. It was a threat to the society to put her questioning of the morality of slavery into action. Then Grimké approached the Presbyterian minister in Charleston. Though a Northerner, who readily admitted that slavery was evil, he argued that its abolition would only foster worse evils in its place. Dissatisfied by his advice that she pursue prayer and work, Grimké chose instead to challenge the slave-owning church elders at one of their meetings. After they, too, refused to speak out against slavery, her regular attendance at church began to decline.

In the winter of 1827, after a visit from her sister Sarah who had joined the Society of

◆ Chapman, Maria (1806–1885)

American abolitionist. Born Maria Weston in Weymouth, Massachusetts, on July 25, 1806; died on July 12, 1885, in Weymouth; educated in Europe; married Henry G. Chapman (a liberal merchant), in October 1830 (died 1842); lived in Paris, 1844–55; children: three.

Maria Chapman was a proper Bostonian and principal of the Young Ladies' High School until she married into a rogue family of abolitionists in 1830. Within two years, she was helping to found the Boston Female Anti-Slavery Society, editing its annual report *Right and Wrong in Boston*, and occasionally editing William Lloyd Garrison's *Liberator*. As Garrison's principal assistant, Maria was ostracized by Boston society and often physically threatened. The proper Mrs. Chapman, disregarding a Philadelphia mob, spoke before the Anti-Slavery Convention of American Women at Philadelphia Hall. The hall was burned down the following day, along with the Shelter for Colored Orphans. Maria Chapman was a supporter of the Grimké sisters and wrote the biography of her good friend *Harriet Martineau (1877).

Friends, Grimké began irregular attendance at Quaker meetings in Charleston. By February 1828, she had adopted the Quaker style of noting calendar dates, and, in May 1829, she was called before the Charleston Presbyterian Church Session for neglect of her public worship. Though the issue of slavery and her opposition to it was not mentioned during the proceedings, Grimké eventually received a letter expelling her from the church.

We Abolition Women are turning the world upside down.
—Angelina Grimké

Disappointed with both the limited liberalism of the Presbyterians and the smallness of the local Quaker assembly, Grimké began to recognize the overwhelming futility of conducting a solitary struggle against slavery in Charleston. By now she also wanted to become a Quaker and to play a useful part in securing personal freedom for black slaves. In April 1829, she wrote in her diary, "How long, oh Lord, wilt thou suffer the foot of the oppressor to stand on the neck of the slave!" Two years later, with the consent and blessing of her mother, she had accepted her sister's invitation to move to Philadelphia, where she could enter into the political fray, making her self-imposed exile a mark of protest against the Southern practice and institution of slavery.

In Philadelphia, Grimké underwent the evaluation process of approval for her membership in the Society of Friends, granted in March 1831. For a while, she continued the same kind of charitable work she had performed in Charleston. She visited the poor, led weekly prayer meetings for prison inmates, and established centers for private poor relief, but remained effectively isolated from political events. Within a couple of years, she was dissatisfied with her philanthropic work, despite its acceptability by the larger community as an appropriate extension of women's domestic role. Approached by *Catharine Beecher who was seeking a teacher for the female seminary she had established in Hartford, Connecticut, Grimké was effectively discouraged by the Philadelphia Quaker assembly from taking the position; through this contact, however, she became friends with Catharine's younger sister, *Harriet Beecher (Stowe).

Grimké taught for a while at an infant school in Philadelphia but did not enjoy it. Meanwhile she was receiving the attentions of a young man named Edward Bettle, and her thoughts on how to respond were central to many of her diary entries during this period. In the early autumn of 1832, Bettle died in the cholera epidemic then sweeping through the eastern United States, and Grimké found herself shunned by Bettle's family, and her life irrevocably changed. Biographer *Gerda Lerner says the youngest Grimké now joined "the army of disappointed spinsters, cut off from love and clutching at religion, trying to bury their unhappiness in uplifting work."

When the American Anti-Slavery Society was formed in Philadelphia in December 1833, Grimké's interest was still largely theoretical. In October 1834, the death of her older brother Thomas left the two sisters alone, unmarried, aged 30 and 43. "By the standards of their day," wrote Lerner, "their lives were over." By the end of 1834, Grimké had turned her life energies to abolitionism. Compared to the majority of Northern reformers, the concept of slavery for her was no abstraction. She began attending meetings and lectures held by abolitionists and established friendships with members of some of the black families who attended the Quaker meetings, especially ❧➤ Sarah Douglass. She also met the revivalist preacher-reformer Theodore Dwight Weld.

When Grimké became a member of the Philadelphia Female Anti-Slavery Society, which was predominantly concerned with educational activities, she found a renewed focus to her life, but she lacked the wholehearted support of her sister Sarah. By 1835, Angelina was ready to declare her stance in favor of immediate abolition when she wrote a letter in support of fellow abolitionist and publisher William Lloyd Garrison who had recently had a narrow escape from an angry mob while speaking in Boston. Wrote Grimké:

> If persecution is the means which God has ordained for the accomplishment of this great end, EMANCIPATION; then . . . I feel as if I could say, LET IT COME; for it is my deep, solemn, deliberate conviction, that this is a cause worth dying for.

Garrison was so struck by the clarity and sincerity of the letter that he published it, without securing her permission, in his weekly paper *The Liberator*. The publication was not well received by the Philadelphia Quaker assembly, which tended to avoid speaking out on the subject of slavery. Once past the initial shock, Grimké refused to retract or alter what she had written, and later that year the letter was reprinted as a one-page broadside, securing her position in the eyes of the public as an active abolitionist. In September 1835, when she was accused of being too absorbed in the topic of abolition, she reportedly replied: "If thou wert a slave, toiling in the fields of Carolina, I apprehend thou wouldst think the time had *fully* come." Her involvement also took the form of support for the Free Produce Movement, committed to buying only those items as had been produced without the labor of slaves, rather than following the more accepted practice of buying slaves in order to manumit them. In Grimké's view, this method still demonstrated acceptance of the enslavement of "a poor and friendless race."

While visiting a friend in New Jersey in 1836, Grimké was inspired to write an entreaty, entitled *Appeal to the Christian Women of the Southern States*, condemning slavery as a violation of human, natural, and Biblical laws, and calling on Southern women to work toward the abolition of the slave system. When copies of the *Appeal* reached Charleston, the Charleston postmaster had copies publicly burned, and the mayor declared that Angelina Grimké would not be permitted to enter the city, ending her tentative plans to visit her mother. Instead, she accepted a speaking engagement in Shrewsbury, New Jersey, for September, accompanied by her sister, and then the sisters went on to New York City to be trained by Theodore Weld in abolitionist oratory. Thus the two became among the first female antislavery agents in the United States.

Grimké was an abolitionist before she was a feminist, but she held that women had a right and a responsibility, as citizens, to speak on political issues like slavery. She saw no conflict between the fight for abolition and for women's rights: "Whatever it is morally right for a man to do, it is morally right for a woman to do. I recognize no rights but human rights. I know nothing of men's rights and women's rights. For in Christ Jesus there is neither male nor female."

On the return of the sisters to Philadelphia, their behavior was found disturbing by the Quaker assembly. For one thing, they chose to sit on the side of the racially segregated meeting-house designated for free blacks, and in May 1837 Angelina Grimké attended the Antislavery Convention of American Women, insisting that race prejudice had to be fought in both Northern and Southern states. In the Amesbury debate, 14 months later, she declared to two Southern men, who were not opposed to slavery, that she "had seen too much of slavery to be a gradualist."

In June 1837, Angelina and Sarah Grimké undertook an antislavery speaking tour of New England; Angelina was considered by most who heard them to be the better speaker of the two. Toward the end of the tour, they were exhausted; Sarah was ill with bronchitis, and both found themselves increasingly attacked, not so much for being abolitionists but for being women out of their appropriate place. The tour continued into October, with Grimké giving all the lectures until she also became ill, with typhoid fever. By this time, she was labeled a "notorious abolitionist," and there was no theory of guidance to help the two women cope with such hostility and accusation.

Prior to the speaking tour, Grimké had become a "devoted disciple" of Theodore Weld. Still in New York, while Angelina was ill in New Jersey and Massachusetts, Weld was deeply worried for her health. Eventually he wrote a letter, not meant to be shared with Sarah, confirming her hopes that his brotherly feelings had developed into more romantic ones, and also fretting that she would not consider him personally or spiritually worthy, especially since he was not a Quaker. After she wrote begging Weld to re-evaluate these perceptions, he visited her in Boston, and the two began to make plans to marry.

The wedding occurred in May, after Angelina Grimké's speech in February before the Legislative Committee of the Massachusetts Assembly. The offer had originally been made as a joke by Henry Stanton, but Angelina had accepted the

✿➤ Douglass, Sarah Mapps (1806–1882)

African-American educator and abolitionist. Born Sarah Mapps Douglass in Philadelphia, Pennsylvania, on September 9, 1806; died in 1882; daughter of Robert and Grace (Bustill) Douglass; privately tutored; attended the "colored" school founded by her mother and James Forten; married William Douglass (a rector of St. Thomas Protestant Episcopal Church), on July 23, 1855 (died 1861).

Sarah Mapps Douglass was a leading light in the Philadelphia Female Anti-Slavery Society which was founded by her mother **Grace Douglass** in 1833. Sarah also taught in the Philadelphia area most of her life. Through the cause, she came to be lifelong friends with *Angelina E. Grimké and *Sarah Moore Grimké.

opportunity and undertook it seriously, speaking on the subject of slavery and the slave trade:

> I stand before you as a repentant slaveholder. I stand before you as a moral being, endowed with precious and inalienable rights, which are correlative with solemn duties and high responsibilities; and as a moral being feel that I owe it to the suffering slave, and to the deluded master, to my country and the world, to do all that I can to overturn a system of complicated crimes, built upon the broken hearts and prostrate bodies of my countrymen in chains, and cemented by the blood and sweat and tears of my sisters in bonds.

Following the wedding, in mid-May 1838, with an interracial company of guests, both Grimké and her husband began to experience physical ailments that barred them from public speaking. The couple, along with Sarah, moved to a home in Fort Lee, New Jersey, and Grimké began to assist Weld in the research for a book to indict and debunk the myth of the happy slave. *American Slavery As It Is: Testimony of a Thousand Witnesses* was published in 1839 and contained Angelina Grimké's own testimony and narrative based on her knowledge of slavery:

> While I live, and slavery lives, I *must* testify against it. . . . And yet [when living in South Carolina] I saw *nothing* of slavery in its most vulgar and repulsive forms. I saw it in the *city*, among the fashionable and the honourable, where it was garnished by refinement, and decked out for show.

Speaking publicly, Angelina had always been clear that she did not, and could not, make any accurate comments on the practice of plantation slavery. This in no way diminished the impact of her statements.

The first son born to the marriage was Charles Stuart Weld, in 1839. After a move to Belleville, New Jersey, a second son, Theodore, was born. Grimké was a loving and affectionate mother, but not sentimental, and found child-rearing something of a trial, probably aggravated by her own experience as the youngest in a family where children were in the care of nurse-maid slaves. Through the 1840s, she experienced a number of health problems, as well as an increasing sense of failure as a mother, which coincided with her children's apparent preference for their Aunt Sarah.

Poor health kept Angelina from attending the World Anti-Slavery Convention in London, England, in June 1840. In 1843, after a miscarriage which preyed upon her spirit, she began forming the opinion that women's health and well-being could best be protected through conscientious practice of birth control. Into the late 1840s, Grimké wrestled with a strong need to reclaim her family without hurting her sister's feelings, and Sarah moved away temporarily, but within a year had been asked by her sister to return to the Weld household.

By the early 1850s, Grimké had realized that she was not suited to "an existence limited to domestic duties and self-effacement." Her concern with the rights and status of women developed much later than did her interest in abolition, but, by 1850, she was elected, *in absentia,* to the central committee of the women's rights convention held in Worcester, Massachusetts. The following year, she managed to attend the next conference, in Rochester, New York, but had to participate in the 1852 Syracuse convention by letter. For a brief time, she also adopted the costume of pants made famous by *Amelia Bloomer, but Angelina soon decided that it was inappropriate for her as a means of effecting reform. She continued to link the abolition and women's rights causes well into the early 1860s, despite her husband's assertion that abolition was the more important issue of the two; this included attending the 1863 women's rights convention in New York.

Grimké—and her sister—had always been part of a minority among antislavery-minded reformers in their belief that abolition should be brought about without violence. By the 1850s, though, a sense of "righteous violence" began to seep into Grimké's abolitionism. This came largely as a response to the "legally sanctioned slave catchers," whom she saw operating within Northern communities.

Over the years, Grimké taught school to help keep the household financially intact. When the family moved to Hyde Park, Massachusetts, in the mid-1860s, she was hired at a girls' boarding school in nearby Lexington, where she taught modern history until the school closed in 1867. In this community, she lived a quiet life of household duties and neighborhood charities.

Grimké had retired from teaching when she learned that her brother Henry had fathered three sons with his slave **Nancy Weston.** The discovery became "the acid test of the sisters' convictions." Weston's young sons—Frank, Archibald Henry, and Francis James—had been freed by then, by the Emancipation Proclamation, but Henry had made no provision for them in the event of his death, other than to have bequeathed them to his white, legitimate son to provide them with their full heritage as his children. The son did not honor his father's wishes and the biracial sons were sold into slavery. Ashamed of their family's racism, Angelina and Sarah felt it their responsibility to assist these nephews in completing their college educations and sought the necessary help through soliciting financial contributions from other abolitionists. In 1868, Angelina attended the commencement of her nephew Frank Grimké at Lincoln University; the second nephew, Archibald Henry Grimké, graduated in 1874 from Harvard Law School and practiced law in Boston, and the third, Francis James Grimké, attended Princeton Theological Seminary and became a Presbyterian pastor in Washington, D.C.

Beginning in the early 1870s, Angelina suffered a series of small strokes which left her partially paralyzed. Near the very end of her life, she lost the use of her voice, the symbol of her fame for decades. On October 26, 1879, Angelina Grimké died at age 74, in Hyde Park, Massachusetts. Among the reformers who spoke at the funeral service were John H. Morison, abolitionist Elizur Wright, and feminist campaigner *Lucy Stone, who succinctly addressed the impact of Angelina's life:

> To those around her she seemed a quiet, gentle woman, devoted to her home, her husband, and her children. And such she was. But those whose memory goes back to the time of fiery trials, in the early anti-slavery days, know that the world never held a nobler woman. The slaves' cause was her cause. . . . She never stopped to think of herself.

SOURCES:

Evans, Sara M. *Born for Liberty: A History of Women in America.* NY: The Free Press, 1989.

Lerner, Gerda. "The Grimké Sisters and the Struggle Against Race Prejudice," in *Journal of Negro History*. Vol. XLVIII, no. 4. October 1963, pp. 277–291.

——. *The Grimké Sisters from South Carolina: Rebels Against Slavery*. Boston, MA: Houghton-Mifflin, 1967.

——. *The Woman in American History*. Menlo Park, CA: Addison-Wesley, 1971.

Lumpkin, Katharine Du Pre. *The Emancipation of Angelina Grimké*. Chapel Hill, NC: University of North Carolina Press, 1974.

SUGGESTED READING:

Barnes, Gilbert H., and Dwight L. Dumond, eds. *Letters of Theodore Dwight Weld, Angelina Grimké Weld and Sarah Grimké, 1822–1844*. 2 vols. Gloucester, MA: Peter Smith, 1965.

Birney, Catherine H. *The Grimké Sisters. Sarah and Angelina Grimké: The First American Women Advocates of Abolition and Woman's Rights* (1885). NY: Haskell House, 1970.

Dumond, Dwight L. *Antislavery: The Crusade for Freedom in America*. Ann Arbor, MI: University of Michigan Press, 1961.

Filler, Louis. *The Crusade Against Slavery, 1830–1860*. NY: Harper, 1960.

Koch, Adrienne. "The Significance of the Grimké Family," in *Maryland Historian*. Vol. 3, no. 1. Spring 1972, pp. 59–84.

Welter, Barbara. "The Cult of True Womanhood: 1820–1860," in *American Quarterly*. Vol. XVIII, 1966, pp. 151–174.

Donna Beaudin,
freelance writer in history, Guelph, Ontario, Canada

Grimké, Angelina Weld

(1880–1958)

African-American poet and writer. Name variations: Angela Weld Grimke. Born on February 20, 1880, in Boston, Massachusetts; died on June 10, 1958, in New York, New York; daughter of Archibald Henry Grimké (nephew of *Sarah Moore Grimké and Angelina E. Grimké) and Sarah (Stanley) Grimké; never married; no children.

Selected writings: Rachel (1920); Mara (unpublished); "The Grave in the Corner"; "To Theodore Weld on His Ninetieth Birthday"; "Street Echoes"; "Longing"; "El Beso"; "To Keep the Memory of Charlotte Forten Grimké"; "To Dunbar High School."

Angelina Weld Grimké, a child of a biracial marriage between Archibald Henry Grimké and **Sarah Stanley Grimké**, grew up in prominent Bostonian society. Her maternal grandparents opposed the biracial marriage of their daughter, even though Archibald Grimké had a long and distinguished pedigree. His father Henry Grimké was a white plantation owner who entered into a relationship with one of his slaves, **Nancy Weston**, after the death of his wife. When Grimké

died he asked one of his white sons to provide Weston and his children by her with their full heritage as his children. The son did not honor his father's wishes and the biracial sons were sold into slavery. Angelina's father escaped to the North; one of Henry's sisters, ***Angelina E. Grimké**, discovered Archibald and his brother at Lincoln University in Pennsylvania and openly acknowledged them as her nephews.

Archibald continued his studies at Harvard Law School and earned his LL.B. in 1874, setting up practice in Boston. In 1879, he married Sarah E. Stanley, and in 1880, when their daughter was born, they named her Angelina in honor of his aunt.

The marriage between Archibald and Sarah did not last, and in 1883 she returned to her parents, taking Angelina with her. After seven years, Angelina returned to her father and had no further contact with her mother. Although abandoned by her mother, Grimké had a sheltered childhood. Being in the upper class, she did not

Angelina
Weld
Grimké
(1880–1958)

experience the same prejudices that most African-Americans experienced. Her first drama, *Rachel* (1920), however, reflects her growing awareness of, and anger at, the racial problems of the times.

Grimké received an excellent education at upper-class schools, including Carlton Academy in Northfield, Minnesota, and Cushing Academy in Ashburnham, Massachusetts. In 1902, she graduated from Boston Normal School of Gymnastics and took a teaching position in Washington D.C. Between 1906 and 1910, she spent her summers as a student at Harvard. It was during her time in Washington that she wrote her better-known pieces. She retired from teaching in 1926 due to ill health from a back injury sustained in a railway accident in July of 1911.

Grimké's work reflects the deep frustrations and unhappiness that were always present within her. Her poetic form is focused and orderly, while the internal meanings are seen as distorted, reflecting back on her sad life. In many poems, she accepts death as the only solution to agonizing problems. This point is brought home in her most radical work, a short story entitled "The Closing Door," where she expresses her belief that black women should not bring children into such a painful world.

Part of her mental anguish may be attributed to the inner turmoil she experienced regarding her love for women. In a letter to **Mamie Burrill** in 1896, she refers to such a loving relationship and asks Mamie to be her "wife," signing the letter "Your passionate lover." It is not known if she had other relationships similar to this one, but the tone of her poetry indicates that she may have suppressed her desires, since many of her poems concern unconsummated, unrequited love.

Grimké counted among her friends many important writers of the Harlem Renaissance, but her relationship with her father had the strongest impact on her. Her devotion to him was such that one person termed their relationship as "almost incestuous." His illness from 1928 until 1930, and his subsequent death, were a turning point in her life. She moved to New York to work on her writing, but produced nothing. Her last years were spent as a recluse in her New York apartment.

Most critics agree that Grimké's finest works were her two plays, *Rachel* and *Mara*. *Rachel* was staged at the *Myrtilla Miner Normal School in Washington D.C. in 1916, the Neighborhood Theater in New York City in

1917, and in Cambridge, Massachusetts in 1917. It was finally published in 1920 and received mixed reviews. The play analyzes the effects of prejudice on a respectable black family and while it effectively presents the problems of racism, it offers no solutions. Most critics agree that her second play, *Mara*—also with racial themes—is the better of the two. There is no record that Grimké ever published the play. The final version is a handwritten copy of 190 pages.

Angelina Weld Grimké lived at a time when the literary world was beginning to pay attention to black writers, but attention and publishing opportunities were given more to male than female authors. She did, however, receive many offers to write articles and for speaking engagements, but there is little indication that she took advantage of these opportunities, perhaps due to her retiring personality and preference for solitude.

In addition to her dramas, Grimké wrote short stories and articles, but her many poems represent her best creative efforts. Only a few of her works were published during her lifetime. Her poetry appeared in the Norfolk *Country Gazette*, *The Boston Globe*, the *Boston Transcript*, and *Opportunity*. Among her published works are "The Grave in the Corner" (1893), "To Theodore Weld on His Ninetieth Birthday" (1893), "Street Echoes" (1894), "Longing" (1901), "El Beso" (1909), "To Keep the Memory of Charlotte Forten Grimké" (1915), and "To Dunbar High School" (1923). Her works also appear in various anthologies, including Alain Locke's *The New Negro* (1925), Otelia Cromwell's *Readings from Negro Authors* (1931), and Robert T. Kerlin's *Negro Poets and Their Poems* (1935).

SOURCES:

Smith, Jessie Carney. *Notable Black American Women*. Detroit, MI: Gale Research, 1992.

Judith C. Reveal,
freelance writer, Greensboro, Maryland

Grimké, Charlotte L. Forten
(1837–1914)

African-American abolitionist, teacher, poet, and intellectual, from the well-known, politically active Forten family of Philadelphia, whose Journal, *published after her death, is a rare account of a free and educated black woman's response to the racist culture which she hoped to change. Name variations: Charlotte L. Forten; also wrote as Miss C.L.F. and Lottie. Born Charlotte Lottie Forten on August 17, 1837, in Philadelphia, Pennsylvania; died on July 22, 1914, in Washington, D.C., of a cerebral embolism; daughter of Mary Virginia (Woods) Forten, who died when*

Charlotte was only three years old, and Robert Bridges Forten, who was a sailmaker and a political activist; was tutored at home until age 16, enrolled in Higginson Grammar School in 1854, graduated in 1855; prepared for teaching career at Salem Normal School, graduated in 1856; married Reverend Francis James Grimké (nephew of Sarah Moore Grimké and Angelina E. Grimké), on December 19, 1878; children: Theodora Cornelia (born January 1, 1880 and died six months later).

Death of her mother, Mary Virginia Woods Forten (August 1840); moved to Salem, Massachusetts to attend integrated public schools, Higginson Grammar School and Salem Normal School (1853–56); accepted an offer, the first ever to a black person, to teach at Epes Grammar School in Salem (June 1856); returned to Philadelphia to recover from a respiratory ailment, the first of many such efforts to maintain her fragile health (June 1857); returned to Salem to teach at Epes and then later at Higginson Grammar School, several times being forced to resign from teaching posts and move back to Philadelphia due to ill health (July 1857–summer 1862); applied for and acquired a teaching position in Port Royal, South Carolina, to teach contraband slaves held by Northern troops (August 1862–May 1864); moved to Boston and worked as secretary of the Teachers Committee of the New England Branch of the Freedmen's Union Commission (October 1865); taught at the Shaw Memorial School in Charleston, South Carolina (1871–72); taught at the M Street School, a preparatory high school in Washington, D.C. (1872–73); worked as first-class clerk in Fourth Auditor's Office of the U.S. Treasury in Washington, D.C. (1873–78); moved with husband Francis to Jacksonville, Florida, where he was pastor of the Laura Street Presbyterian Church (1885–89); moved back to Washington, D.C., when Francis took over pastorship of the Fifteenth Street Presbyterian Church (1889); became a founding member of the National Association of Colored Women (1896); after spending 13 months confined to bed, died in her home (1914), age 76.

Selected publications: "To W.L.G. on Reading His 'Chosen Queen,'" in Liberator (March 16, 1850); "Glimpses of New England," in National Anti-Slavery Standard (April 2, 1859); "The Two Voices," in National Anti-Slavery Standard (January 15, 1859); "The Wind Among the Poplars," in National Anti-Slavery Standard (April 2, 1859); "The Slave Girl's Prayer," in Liberator (February 3, 1860); "Letter," in Liberator (December 12, 1862); "Interesting Letter from Miss Charlotte L. Forten," in Liberator (December 19, 1862); "Life on the Sea Islands," in Atlantic Monthly (Vol. 8, May 1864, pp. 587–596, and Vol. 8, June 1864); "Personal Recollections of Whittier," in New England Magazine (Vol. 8, June 1893, pp. 468–476); "A Parting Hymn," in The Black Man, His Antecedents, His Genius, and His Achievements, by William Wells Brown (NY: Hamilton, 1863); (translated by Charlotte Forten) Émile Erckmann and Alexandre Chatrian, Madame Thérèse; or, The Volunteers of '92 (NY: Scribners, 1869); (edited by Ray Allen Billington) The Journal of Charlotte L. Forten (NY: Dryden, 1953, London: Collier-Macmillan, 1961); (edited by Brenda Stevenson) The Journals of Charlotte Forten Grimké (New York, Oxford: Oxford University Press, 1988).

At age 16 when she moved away from her family in Philadelphia to attend integrated public schools in Salem, Massachusetts, Charlotte Lottie Forten began a diary. Not published until after her death, the diary would reveal an introspective nature that paved the way for an invaluable record of her life as a significant member of the activist community in the 19th century. The mention of friends, daily events, studies, and her own self-scrutiny are emblematic of concerns that would occupy Grimké throughout life. Her diary opens:

> A wish to record the passing events of my life, which, even if quite unimportant to others, naturally possess great interest to myself, and of which it will be pleasant to have some remembrance, has induced me to commence this journal. I feel that keeping a diary will be a pleasant and profitable employment of my leisure hours, and will afford me much pleasure in other years, by recalling to my mind the memories of other days, thoughts of much-loved friends from whom I may then be separated, with whom I now pass many happy hours, in taking delightful walks, and holding "sweet converse"; the interesting books that I read; and the different people, places and things that I am permitted to see. . . . Besides this, it will doubtless enable me to judge correctly of the growth and improvement of my mind from year to year.

The family names "Forten" and "Grimké" have a place of honor in the American abolitionist movement because both families have long, distinguished histories of fighting oppression, especially slavery, in the United States. Charlotte Forten Grimké was a connecting link between these two aristocratic and socially-active families, both of which were influential in the anti-slavery movements of the 19th century. Born on August 17, 1837, in Philadelphia, Pennsylvania, she belonged to the fifth generation of free Fortens in the United States. Her lifetime of devotion to the eradication of both slavery and racism reflect her family's devotion to these causes. Beginning with her grandfather James Forten, Sr., who was born free in Philadelphia in 1766 and was chiefly responsible for creating the family fortune in the sailmaking business, the Fortens produced a long line of reformists and abolitionists who took an active role in the political and cultural life of their community. Among his many public responses to slavery in the South and discrimination against free blacks in the North, Forten's participation in the petitioning of the U.S. Congress to establish guidelines for the abolition of slavery and to weaken the Fugitive Slave Act of 1793 is probably among the most well known. He not only financially supported William Lloyd Garrison's publication of the *Liberator*—on occasion, Forten financed the publication and distribution of an entire issue when funds were low—but he also garnered support for a variety of antislavery organizations by hosting meetings in his home at 92 Lombard Street in Philadelphia.

James Forten's generous support and advocacy of liberal causes, from abolition to women's rights and world peace, had a great impact on his children, who also became politically active members of the antislavery community. Charlotte's father, Robert Bridges Forten, followed in her grandfather's footsteps both in the sailmaking industry and also in the abolitionist cause, as did her aunts **Sarah, Harriet,** and ***Margaretta Forten.** The three sisters and their mother, Charlotte's grandmother and namesake, played a significant part in Charlotte Forten's early life. They served as caretakers for her after 1840, when her mother **Mary Woods Forten** died at 26, and as role models of politically active, intelligent, and strong women. Grandmother Charlotte Forten and her three daughters, as well as Charlotte's mother Mary, were all feminists as well as founding members of the Philadelphia Female Anti-Slavery Society in 1833. The extended family, including brothers-in-law Robert and Joseph Purvis, were involved at all levels of the antislavery fight, including Robert Purvis' active participation in the Underground Railroad (there was a trap door to hide fugitive slaves in his home in Bucks County, Pennsylvania, a place Forten often spent time as a child).

In conjunction with her family's active role in the abolitionist movement, which also included her father's participation in the Union army during the Civil War—for which he received the first military funeral for a black person in Philadelphia—came the presence of other influential advocates in the movement. Even after her father remarried and Charlotte moved from the home at 92 Lombard, she continued to exist in a social circle that included some of the most famous political activists of the day. Charlotte continued to live amidst leading intellectuals after she moved to Salem at age 16 to study in the public schools there. Moving into the home of Forten family friends, abolitionist Charles Lenox Remond and his wife **Amy Matilda (Williams Cassey) Remond,** Charlotte attended lectures by and visited with famous speakers in support of abolition, including William Lloyd Garrison, Wendell Phillips, John Wittier, ***Abby Kelley** and her husband Stephen Symonds Foster, ***Lydia Maria Child,** ◄ **Maria Chapman,** William C. Nell, and William Wells Brown. The Remond home was similar to Forten's in its centrality to the abolitionist movement. Charles Remond, in fact, represented the American Anti-Slavery Society at the 1840 World Anti-Slavery Convention in London, where he stirred up excitement when he refused to tolerate gender-biased seating arrangements and sat in the gallery seats designated for women.

Charlotte Forten arrived at Salem in 1853 to attend the Higginson Grammar School. The only black student among the 200 women students, she was highly conscious of racial tensions and sensitive to racist behavior on the part of her classmates. She also felt pressure as a representative of a minority culture to perform in an exemplary way, which, combined with an already heightened sense of social duty, led her to work extremely hard. A lengthy entry from early in the first volume of her diary reveals the depth of her racial sensitivity as well as her desire to emulate the highly romanticized writing style popular in her day:

> Wednesday, Sept. 12 [1855]. To-day school commenced.—Most happy am I to return to the companionship of my studies,—ever my most valued friends. It is pleasant to meet the scholars again; most of them greeted me cordially, and were it not for the thought that will intrude, of the want of *entire sympathy* even of those I know and like best, I should greatly enjoy their society. . . . I wonder that every colored person is not a misanthrope. Surely we have everything to make us hate mankind. I have met girls in the schoolroom [—] they have been thoroughly kind and cordial to me,—perhaps the next day met them in the street—they feared to recognize me; these I can but regard now with scorn and contempt. . . . These are but trifles, certainly, to the great, public wrongs which we as a people are obliged to endure. But to those who experience them, these ap-

Chapman, Maria. *See Grimké, Angelina E. for sidebar.*

parent trifles are most wearing and discouraging; even to the child's mind they reveal volumes of deceit and heartlessness, and early teach a lesson of suspicion and distrust. . . . In the bitter, passionate feelings of my soul again and again there rises the questions "When, oh! when shall this cease?" "Is there no help?" "How long oh! how long must we continue to suffer—to endure?" Conscience answers it is wrong, it is ignoble to despair; let us labor earnestly and faithfully to acquire knowledge, to break down the barriers of prejudice and oppression. Let us take courage; never ceasing to work,— hoping and believing that if not for us, for

another generation there is a better, brighter day in store,—when slavery and prejudice shall vanish before the glorious light of Liberty and Truth; when the rights of every colored man shall everywhere be acknowledged and respected, and he shall be treated as a *man* and a *brother*.

Forten read extensively, well beyond the scope of her requirements; a loose leaf sheet in her journal registered over 100 titles she had read in one year. She also became close lifelong friends with the principal of the Higginson School, **Mary Shephard**, with whom she often

Charlotte L. Forten Grimké (seated holding book).

traveled to antislavery lectures and other intellectual programs. She graduated from Higginson with "decided éclat" in 1855; her poem "A Parting Hymn" was selected by her classmates to be sung during her graduation ceremony. Forten enrolled in Salem Normal School in order to prepare herself for a teaching career, which she began upon her graduation in 1856. Her joy upon graduation was muted by the death of her hostess, Amy Remond, with whom Charlotte had established a close, almost mother-daughter bond. Charlotte was proud to be the first black woman to hold a teaching post in the city of Salem at Epes Grammar School. Another poem, "Poem for Normal School Graduation," was published in the *Liberator* in 1856.

I am hated and oppressed because God gave me *dark skin*. How did this cruel, this absurd prejudice ever come to exist? When I think of it, a feeling of indignation rises in my soul too deep for utterance.

—Charlotte L. Forten

The time between first assuming her teaching post at Epes in 1856 and leaving for a new position in South Carolina were years of alternating activity and recuperation for Forten. She enjoyed living in New England and participating in the intellectual climate of the Boston-Salem area. Although sources are less clear on exactly how much she enjoyed teaching, the occupation obviously served her deeply ingrained philosophy of service to her race and gave her the opportunity to continue her own scholarly pursuits. These included learning French, German, Latin and continual participation in local lectures on art, literature, and social problems. An excerpt from her June 15, 1858, journal entry reveals how seriously she took the responsibility of self-education as well as how critical she was of herself:

> Have been under-going a thorough self-examination. The result is a mingled feeling of sorrow, shame and self-contempt. Have realized more deeply and bitterly than ever in my life my own ignorance and folly. Not only am I without the gifts of Nature,—wit, beauty and talent; without the accomplishments which nearly every one of my age, whom I know, possesses; but I am not even *intelligent*. And for *this* there is not the *shadow* of an excuse. Have had many advantages of late years; and it is entirely owning to my own want of energy, perseverance and application, that I have not improved them. It grieves me deeply to think of this.

Always introspective and sometimes self-critical, Forten was equally capable of turning her critical eye inward as she was of perceiving and commenting on society. One particular cultural practice which drew her ire as well as a critical comment in her journal was the patriotic celebration of "Independence Day" in the United States: "*Saturday, July 4* [1858]. The celebration of this day! What a mockery it is! My soul sickens of it. Am glad to see that the people are much less demonstrative in their mock patriotism than of old."

Forten returned to Philadelphia to recuperate from headaches and general weakness for the first time in May of 1857. She was back in Salem teaching at Higginson Grammar School with her friend Mary Shephard in September of 1859, but relapsed and returned again to Philadelphia in 1860. Missing New England, Forten regretted that her ill health kept her from more direct activism. The work of caring for her health and that of active participation in her cause were in recurrent conflict:

> Wednesday, March 3 [1858]. Announced my determination of leaving; to everybody's astonishment. I am sorely disturbed in mind. Constantly I ask myself "Am I doing right?" Yet I *believe* that I am. If I entirely lose my health *now* of what use will my life be to me? None. I shall only be dependent, miserably dependent on others. I would ten thousand times rather die than that.

It was during a return to Salem to teach summer school with Mary Shephard in 1862 that John Whittier suggested that Forten might contribute to the abolition movement and the black community by moving to the South to teach in schools established on former slaveowners' lands which had been captured by Northern troops. After being turned down by the Boston Educational Commission for such a post on the basis of her sex, Forten was accepted by the Philadelphia Port Royal Relief Association and gained a teaching post on Saint Helena Island, just off the South Carolina coast, which had been captured by Union troops in 1861. She traveled to Port Royal in October of 1862 and spent two challenging years there teaching basics to the contraband slaves, who were, in effect, freed as the result of Northern occupation of their "owners'" lands. The now-famous Port Royal experiment was a perfect match of Forten's ideas of racial equality and her interest in promoting opportunities for blacks.

But along with the strain of her still faltering health, she found herself an outsider among the almost exclusively white teachers and the distrusting ex-slaves. Forten revealed herself a product of her own upper-class upbringing in her delight in what she at first termed the island blacks' "wild" and "strange" singing. Though she eventually grew to appreciate the culture of the black ex-slaves, she remained most closely identified with the society of the more highly educated, mostly military presence on the island. She also spent a great deal of time with her dear friend Dr. Seth Rogers, whom she had met a few years earlier when she tried a water cure under his care.

In South Carolina, Forten continued to interact with influential people in the abolitionist cause. On January 31, 1863, she recorded a visit to Beaufort and a meeting with *Harriet Tubman, the famous "conductor" of the Underground Railroad:

> In Beaufort we spent nearly all our time at Harriet Tubman's otherwise [sic] "Moses." She is a wonderful woman—a real heroine. Has helped off a large number of slaves, after taking her own freedom. She told us that she used to hide them in the woods during the day and go around to get provisions for them. Once she had with her a man named Joe, for whom a reward of $1,500 was offered. Frequently, in different places she found handbills exactly describing him, but at last they reached in safety the Suspension Bridge over the Falls and found themselves in Canada. Until then, she said, Joe had been very silent. In vain had she called his attention to the glory of the Falls. He sat perfectly still—moody, it seemed, and w'ld not even glance at them. But when she said, "Now we are in Can[ada]" he sprang to his feet—with a great shout and sang and clapped his hands in a perfect delirium of joy. So when they got out, and he first touched *free* soil, he shouted an hurrahed "as if he were crazy"—she said. "How exciting it was to hear her tell the story. . . . My own eyes were full as I listened to her—the heroic woman!"

Forten had the opportunity to hear other harrowing stories from the ex-slaves on Saint Helena Island, including that of a woman—whom Forten thought must have been over a hundred years old—who recounted her capture from Africa. During her tenure on St. Helena, two letters to William Lloyd Garrison describing her experiences were published in the *Liberator* in 1862, and the *Atlantic Monthly* published her two-part essay "Life on the Sea Islands" in 1864.

It is unclear whether ill health, her father's death in April 1864, or other factors caused Forten to resign in May of 1864 and return to Philadelphia. Her relationship with her father appears to have been somewhat strained, both by his desire to have her return from Salem earlier in her career and by his inability to help support her

financially. Despite the wealth of her family, Forten at times struggled to support herself, though refuge in Philadelphia was most probably always guaranteed. In October of 1865, she took a position as secretary of the Teacher Committee of the New England Branch of the Freedmen's Union Commission in Boston and acted as a liaison between the Northern fund raisers and the teachers of freed slaves in the South.

In October 1871, she returned to South Carolina to teach at the Robert Gould Shaw Memorial School. Undoubtedly, this teaching experience in Charleston held special significance to her since the school was committed to the memory of a man she had befriended during her time in Port Royal. Forten had been very disturbed by the news of his death in battle. After moving back North to Washington, D.C., in 1872, she held a one-year post at the now-famous Paul Laurence Dunbar High School, then known as the M Street School, before accepting the position of first-class clerk in the Fourth Auditor's Office of the U.S. Treasury Department in 1873, a position which she held until 1878.

During her time in the Treasury Department, Forten met and, on December 19, 1878, married Reverend Francis James Grimké when she was 41 years old. Although he was 13 years her junior and, having once been enslaved, did not have the privileged background Charlotte did, they were united in their intellectualism and deep commitment to racial issues. After the Civil War, Francis attended Lincoln University, graduating as valedictorian in 1870; earned a master's degree; and began a law degree at Howard University before finally settling on his vocation. He graduated from Princeton Theological Seminary in 1878, the year of his marriage, and took over the ministry at the Fifteenth Street Presbyterian Church in Washington, D.C. His education at both Lincoln and Princeton was partially funded by *Angelina E. Grimké, a famous feminist and abolitionist who accepted Francis and his brother into her family when she found out that they were her nephews, the illegitimate sons of her brother Henry Grimké and his slave, **Nancy Weston**.

Charlotte stopped teaching after her marriage but continued to work, writing anti-racism essays both alone and with Francis and also continuing her lifelong interest in writing poetry. Their daughter, Theodora Cornelia, was born on January 1, 1880, but died six months later. Charlotte's poor health and advancing age—she was 43—made it unlikely that they would have another child. She did forge a special relationship with her niece, the poet *Angelina Weld Grimké, who was born just two years after Theodora died and who lived with Charlotte and Francis while her parents were out of the country. Angelina and her father, Francis' brother Archibald Henry Grimké, eventually moved into Charlotte's home when Archibald separated from his wife, and Charlotte's relationship with Angelina was cemented.

Charlotte Forten Grimké's fourth journal ends in May of 1864 and her final one does not begin until November of 1885; she offers no explanation for the missing time. It may be possible that ill health, headaches and poor eyesight kept her from her journal. Except for a five-year period from 1885 to 1890, in which Charlotte and Francis lived in Jacksonville, Florida, and Francis was pastor of the Laura Street Presbyterian Church, the Grimkés remained in Washington, D.C., throughout the rest of Charlotte's life. She continued to concern herself with political and intellectual activism despite her health difficulties. Bedridden for her last 13 months, she nonetheless appeared to be happy to have her family around her and to discuss the defining matters of her life. She died in her home on July 22, 1914, at 76 years of age. Her clear vision and voice had a major impact on the antislavery community in which she participated, and her journals serve as lasting documentation of a time of American oppression and change.

SOURCES:

Braxton, Joanne M. *Black Women Writing Autobiography: A Tradition Within a Tradition.* Philadelphia, PA: Temple University Press, 1989.

Draper, James P., ed. *Black Literature Criticism: Excerpts from Criticism of the most Significant Works of Black Authors over the Past 200 Years.* Detroit, MI: Gale Research, 1992.

Grimké, Charlotte L. Forten. *The Journal of Charlotte L. Forten: A Free Negro in the Slave Era.* Ed. & introd. by Ray Allen Billington. NY: Collier Books, 1953.

———. *The Journals of Charlotte Forten Grimké.* Ed. & introd. by Brenda Stevenson. NY, Oxford: Oxford UP, 1988.

Harris, Trudier. "Charlotte L. Forten" in *Afro-American Writers Before the Harlem Renaissance.* (Vol. 50 in the *Dictionary of Literary Biography* series.) Detroit, MI: Gale Research, 1986.

McKay, Nellie Y. "Charlotte L. Forten Grimké" in *Notable Black American Women.* Detroit, MI: Gale Research, 1992.

Sumler-Edmond, Janice. "Charlotte L. Forten Grimké," in *Black Women in America: An Historical Encyclopedia, Vol. 1: A-L.* Ed. by Darlene Clark Hine. Brooklyn, NY: Carlson, 1993.

SUGGESTED READING:

Braxton, Joanne M. "Charlotte Forten Grimké and the Search for a Public Voice," in *The Private Self: Theory and Practice of Women's Autobiographical Writings*, edited by Shari Benstock. NC: University of North Carolina Press, 1988, pp. 254–271.

Grimké, Charlotte L. Forten. *The Journals of Charlotte Forten Grimké.* Ed. & introd. by Brenda Stevenson. NY, Oxford: Oxford University Press, 1988. [Stevenson's is the most thorough of the biographies and this edition of the *Journals* is the only one to include the fifth volume. Unlike the edition by Billington, the Stevenson edition is unedited and therefore contains a broader sense of Forten's daily life.]

RELATED MEDIA:

"Black Pioneers in American History," Educational Record Sales, New York.

"Charlotte Forten's Mission: Experiment in Freedom," starring **Melba Moore**, American Playhouse, PBS, 1985.

COLLECTIONS:

The manuscript collection of Charlotte Forten Grimké's journals and typescripts by her friend, *Anna J. Cooper, are located at the Moorland-Springarn Research Center at Howard University.

Sharon L. Barnes,
Ph.D. candidate, University of Toledo, Toledo, Ohio

Grimké, Sarah Moore (1792–1873)

Southern-born American feminist and schoolteacher who lectured, wrote, and campaigned on the issues of women's rights and abolition. Name variations: Sally Grimke. Pronunciation: GRIM-kay. Born Sarah Moore Grimké on November 26, 1792, in Charleston, South Carolina; died in Hyde Park (now in Boston), Massachusetts, on December 23, 1873; daughter of the Honorable John Faucheraud Grimké (1752–1819, judge of Supreme Court of South Carolina) and Mary (Smith) Grimké; sister of Angelina E. Grimké (1805–1879); received education at home, attending brother Thomas Grimké's tutored lessons; never married; no children.

Made godmother to youngest sister (1805); accompanied father to Philadelphia and New Jersey, nursing him through a fatal illness (1819); moved to Philadelphia (1821); accepted into Philadelphia Society of Friends (1823); underwent training as abolitionist agent in New York City (1836); attended Anti-Slavery Convention of American Women (1837); engaged in antislavery speaking tour throughout New England (1837–38); moved to New Jersey and retired to private life (1839); concluded teaching career (1867).

Selected publications: Epistle to the Clergy of the Southern States (1836); Letters on the Equality of the Sexes and the Condition of Woman (1838); Address to Free Colored Americans (1837). Translation: Alphonse M.L. de Prat de Lamartine's Joan of Arc: A Biography (1867). (With Angelina Emily Grimké) "A Sketch of Thomas Grimké's Life written by his Sisters in Philadelphia and sent to his Friends in Charleston for their Approbation," in The Calumet, magazine of the American Peace Society (1835).

The ideology of republican motherhood that had taken root in America during the Revolutionary War transformed the boundaries of the domestic world as experienced by respectable middle-class and elite women. The 19th-century American woman, portrayed in her role of mother and housewife, existed largely in a child-centered, private sphere. This prescription underscored the position of ascribed moral superiority occupied by respectable women within a society which considered them inferior in every other respect. A woman's usefulness and duty precluded both a political existence and the articulation of her legal rights, and the situation was exacerbated in the American South by an ideology which positioned respectable white women on a pedestal of inactivity.

In the closing decades of the 18th century, the Grimkés were respected elites within the Southern plantation society, in Charleston, South Carolina. Sarah Moore Grimké, born November 26, 1792, was the sixth child, and second daughter, of Judge John Faucheraud Grimké and **Mary Smith Grimké**. Sarah's father epitomized the masculine South Carolina elite in that he had fought in the Revolutionary War against British tyranny and then established himself as a planter, slaveholder, lawyer, politician and, eventually, an assistant judge of the South Carolina Supreme Court. Sarah's mother came from an Anglo-Irish Puritan background and was counted as a direct descendant of the colonial founder in South Carolina. In a society which valued wealth, family, and status, all these factors had daily significance.

After her christening at age four, Sarah grew up securely within the Charleston planter aristocracy, surrounded by a large number of household servants. The family's place of residence was largely dependent upon crops and seasons: from November until mid-May of each year (except carnival week, in February, spent in Charleston), they lived out at their plantation house; otherwise they were in town. As a matron of elevated social status, Sarah's mother spent little time with her children, leaving them under the supervision of house slaves; Sarah was like other children of her class in discovering quickly that even young daughters of the master could order these slaves around and expect to be obeyed. She also learned to fill the vacuum left by her mother's absence by attaching herself to her older brother Thomas, six years her senior. Their closeness evolved into inseparability, and, until the age of 12, Sarah spent as much time as she could manage in the boy's company.

Sarah
Moore
Grimké

Never regarded as pretty, even by her own family, Sarah was a healthy child, possessed of a quick intelligence, an outgoing spirit, and a generous disposition. In a society that placed considerable emphasis on the face and accomplishments of its young women, she received the stereotypical "polite education." Most of the lessons considered appropriate (reading, writing, arithmetic geared to household management, needlework styles, a bit of French meant to be sprinkled throughout her conversation, and the drawing, singing, piano, and manners suitable to her social status) were neither stimulating to her, nor mentally taxing. Years later, she would address the superficiality and anti-intellectuality of this approach in her *Letters on the Equality of the Sexes and the Condition of Woman.*

Sarah did have the good fortune to be allowed to share most of Thomas' lessons with his tutor. She thus gained exposure to some mathematics, history, geography, botany, natural science, and Greek, although her father refused to allow her to study Latin, which he considered unsuitable for an elite woman in Southern society. Judge Grimké did require that all his children be exposed to useful skills, however, and, as a result, Sarah learned how to spin and weave the coarse cloth used for slave clothing, to shuck corn, and even to pick cotton from the bushes in the field. At these tasks, she demonstrated an eagerness to be useful, as well as to be loved for her usefulness, while learning the role of the plantation woman.

The most perfect social system can only be attained where the laws which govern the sexes are based on justice and equality.

—Sarah Grimké

Because of her ability and "unusual interest," Sarah was included in the debates and discussions that Judge Grimké encouraged among his sons. According to biographer *Gerda Lerner, the judge is alleged to have commented that "if Sarah had only been a boy, she would have made the greatest jurist in this country." In her late teens, when Sarah revealed her dream of becoming a lawyer, such an ambition was held too improper and too unfeminine for a 19th-century woman to be encouraged.

In later life, Sarah often recalled times she had cried as a child because of punishments inflicted on slaves at her family's plantation. She was also disturbed that the slaves were kept illiterate, and thus unable to read a Bible. By the time she was 13, she had reached a state of despondency that she later attributed to a resigned acceptance of her inability to help the slaves, combined with the limitations she encountered as a woman. In an attempt to "cure" her unhappiness at this time, she was made godmother to her youngest sister, *Angelina E. Grimké, born in February 1805. Sarah called the baby Nina, and focused her love and energy on raising the child 13 years her junior, who in return called her "mother"; meanwhile, the older girl struggled to accept the situations she perceived she could not change.

Following the usual course of young women of her class, Sarah made her debut into Charleston society at age 16 and joined in the whirl of fashionable events surrounding the typical "Southern belle." She refused an early offer of marriage, and rather than shock her family and friends, she kept the majority of her dissenting opinions to herself. By 1816, she was regarded in Charleston as "an over-aged social butterfly," who held eccentric opinions and was likely to die an "old maid." Sarah herself was less disturbed by this possibility than were her family and the local society.

In the spring of 1819, Sarah left the Charleston area for the first time in her life, to travel with her father by boat to Philadelphia to consult a surgeon. When the judge was led to believe that his illness could be cured with rest and a change of climate, Sarah accompanied him to a New Jersey resort, where she became nurse to her dying father. In August 1819, she was the only family member present at his death and saw to his burial in the cemetery of a Methodist church.

The period of barely four months away from Charleston had served to liberate Sarah. Before going home, she returned to Philadelphia and stayed with a Quaker family for two months, leading to a correspondence, after she reached home, with Israel Morris, a Philadelphia merchant. Her own health appears to have deteriorated while caring for her father, and she spent a period of recuperation at the home of a maternal uncle in North Carolina, identifying her symptoms in predominantly religious terms.

A few years earlier, Sarah had left the Episcopal Church to become a Presbyterian, but this had not eased her spiritual malaise. She began to explore other denominations, particularly Catholicism and the Society of Friends, whose members are known as Quakers. Upon her second return to South Carolina, she attended Quaker meetings in an effort to redress her loneliness and sense of alienation. When she announced that she felt a "religious call" to go to the Northern states, the action was considered shocking for a woman of her status; nevertheless, she sailed for Philadelphia on May 15, 1821, with the intention of becoming a Quaker, and within two years she had been accepted into the Society of Friends.

In the years following her conversion, her sense of loneliness was not greatly eased. Sarah was not eager to undertake any type of mission activity, although the Quakers put considerable emphasis on doing useful work. At Quaker meetings, she initially felt pulled toward inspirational speaking, especially after hearing *Lucretia Mott, but she was naturally shy around people she did not know well; also she tended to receive criticisms made in open discussion as personal condemnation. Twice, in September 1826, she refused offers of marriage from her former correspondent, Israel Morris, who was now widowed, possibly because of self-renunciation, or perhaps the potential domestic tyranny that marriage implied. In the depths of loneliness, she made a visit to her family in the winter of 1827 and found her views about the Society of Friends well received by her youngest sister, Angelina, who was also spiritually dissatisfied. Back in Philadelphia, Sarah Grimké encouraged her sister to visit for the summer and become acquainted with other Quakers; by 1831, Angelina had moved to Philadelphia and begun the evaluation process required for acceptance into the Society of Friends.

Despite the reunion with her beloved Nina, Grimké continued to be unhappy through the early 1830s. She was a regular reader of *The Friend*, a Quaker weekly publication, and took particular interest in its ongoing discussion of the position of women within society. In 1828–1829, the Englishwoman *Frances Wright had made a speaking tour in the United States, during which she asserted the equality of women and men, but her position had been deemed radical and inappropriate to be voiced by a woman. Grimké did not read Wright's published writings; Quakers at this time did not always encourage free intellectual inquiry and debate. She did meet the educator *Catharine Beecher, who ran a female seminary in Hartford, Connecticut, and Beecher's arguments for improved standards of education for women, primarily because of their role as mothers, helped to rekindle her interest in women's socio-legal position.

In the years 1832–1834, cholera swept through the eastern United States. In November 1834, when Grimké received the news that her beloved brother Thomas had died of the disease, the loss marked the severance of her last real link with her family in South Carolina. In her grief, Grimké stopped making daily entries in her diary and burned all her letters; in her mourning, she and Angelina wrote a sketch of Thomas' life and accomplishments which appeared in *The Calumet* magazine in 1835.

At age 43, Sarah found herself emotionally stagnant—disillusioned, intellectually stifled, and desperate to be useful, but unsure of her true purpose. Then, much to her concern, her sister Angelina began to speak out against the practice of slavery, a topic that was rarely discussed in Philadelphia's Quaker community. Although she viewed Angelina's growing interest in abolitionism as "taking a temptation of the devil," she did go with her to a lecture given by the English abolitionist George Thompson in March 1835, and when she became an enthusiastic supporter of the Free Produce Movement, which boycotted all goods produced through the labor of any (not just American) slaves, the action set the tone, in effect, of her abolitionism: Angelina became the example that her sister followed.

By October 1836, Grimké was willing to go with her sister to New York City, to take a "training course" as antislavery agents. Though normally quiet in groups, Grimké felt compelled to relate her firsthand experience of slavery in the South, and after the training, the sisters began to speak together at antislavery meetings. Grimké preferred to address the moral and theological implications of the issue. In 1836, she wrote a pamphlet, *Epistle to the Clergy of the Southern States*, that was grounded in Biblical and legal arguments, urging the clergy of the South to assume a position of moral leadership in the crusade against the institution. Her fascination with law and its workings since adolescence was evident in her reliance on Southern slave codes and debates from the Virginia House of Delegates in her arguments. Grimké also began teaching a free black Sunday School class and joined the Temperance Society in New York City.

During a return visit to Philadelphia, Sarah and Angelina were disowned by the local Quaker assembly on a technicality. Shortly afterward, in May 1837, Grimké attended the Antislavery Convention of American Women in New York City. Among the 71 women who came as delegates from eight states, she saw her longtime friend Lucretia Mott, and met **Ann Warren Weston**, **Maria Chapman**, and *Lydia Maria Child. The objectives of these conventioneers included a campaign for one million signatures to an antislavery petition, and development of a fight against "race prejudice" in both the South and the North. Following this time, both Grimké and her sister began to compare the condition of white women with enslaved blacks, but this "new and bold reasoning" did not dominate Sarah's *Address to Free Colored Americans*, published by the convention. Two weeks later, the Grimké sisters went to Boston to prepare for a speaking tour throughout New England, supported by the belief of organizers for the antislavery movement that their combined effort would be "a unifying force" for abolitionism.

The New England speaking tour quickly changed from a novelty to very hard work. Neither meals nor rest were available with any semblance of regularity, and the sisters met with increasing hostility from their audiences, some of whom opposed them as abolitionists while others were critical of them as women speaking publicly, and in such a decidedly political fashion. While on tour, Grimké still worried over, and mothered her "baby sister," while lecturing, researching,

Chapman, Maria. See Grimké, Angelina E. for sidebar.

and writing for the antislavery cause. While self-pity and a tendency toward martyrdom caused Grimké to disparage her own contributions to the campaign, she found a new concern gaining primacy within the realm of her interest in reform. Throughout New England, she was repeatedly struck by the plight of women and children who labored in Northern mills and factories under conditions as oppressive as Southern slavery. The journey became the beginning of a period of remarkable, though erratic, intellectual growth, as Grimké came to see the "woman question" as an issue separate from abolition. According to biographer Gerda Lerner, throughout 1837–1838 Grimké was "gradually developing a theory of woman's right to equality before the law and a concern with the abuses to which women, as a group, were subjected," which would draw such issues as the legal disabilities faced by American women into her focus.

While still on the New England speaking tour, Grimké wrote 12 "letters" which appeared in the *New England Spectator* in 1837. They were reprinted in *The Liberator*, the abolitionist paper of William Lloyd Garrison, and published collectively the following year as *Letters on the Equality of the Sexes and the Condition of Woman*, making their author one of the first Americans to be published in support of women's rights. In these epistles, Grimké refuted Biblical arguments as proof of women's inferiority, interpreted "man" as a generic term for woman and man in the creation story, criticized women's education as superficial and "marriage-centered," argued that women doing the same work as men should receive the same amount of wages, and stressed the dignity and worth that was inherent in all women. Grimké continued to compare woman-as-slave with slavewomen, and her arguments for improving the rights and status of women were both legally and theoretically sound, as well as far more original than any of the antislavery work she had done. Originally addressed to **Mary S. Parker,** president of the Boston Female Anti-Slavery Society, the letters eloquently but urgently declared:

> I ask no favours for my sex. I surrender not our claim to equality. All I ask of our brethren is, that they will take their feet from off our necks and permit us to stand upright on that ground which God designed us to occupy.

Elsewhere in the essays, Grimké questioned the accuracy of the translations and interpretations of the New Testament, while urging women to learn Greek and Hebrew to be able to read the original material for themselves.

Abolition organizer Theodore D. Weld viewed the women's rights cause as a lesser issue, compared to the eradication of slavery, and one which Grimké should leave to others to pursue so as not to dilute the impact the sisters' speaking tour was having on support for antislavery. Near the end of the tour, it was decided that both sisters would address the Massachusetts State Legislature, but Sarah Grimké became too ill with bronchitis to speak. Her formal speaking in public ended soon afterward, largely at the suggestion of her new brother-in-law, Weld, who married Angelina in May 1838. Grimké lived with the couple in their first home, in Fort Lee, New Jersey, and moved with them to Belleville, New Jersey, in March 1840. By this time, *American Slavery As It Is: Testimony of a Thousand Witnesses* had been published under the assigned authorship of Theodore Weld. Grimké's last public comment of any significance on the subject of slavery was her testimony for the work:

> As I left my native state on account of slavery, and deserted the home of my fathers to escape the sound of the lash and the shrieks of tortured victims, I would gladly bury in oblivion the recollection of those scenes with which I have been familiar; but this may not, cannot be; they come over my memory like gory spectres, and implore me with resistless power, in the name of a God of mercy, in the name of a crucified Savior, in the name of humanity; for the sake of the slaveholder, as well as the slave, to bear witness to the horrors of the Southern prison house.

Effectively retired from both antislavery and women's rights work, and trying to adjust to "the daily lives of common women," Grimké turned down an invitation to the World Anti-Slavery Convention in London, England, scheduled for June 1840. Throughout the 1840s, the sisters essentially reversed roles in their shared home, as Sarah again became the stronger and healthier of the two. Living on a farm, they took in student boarders to help meet expenses, and when the Welds were invited to join Rarity Bay Union, a utopian community, Grimké began, at age 60, to plan her separation from her sister's family in favor of an independent life. Part of her independent work involved compiling laws concerning women in the various states, with the aim of revealing their unfairness and rousing the nation's conscience. Her approach was systematic, done in consultative correspondence with lawyers, and included research trips to Boston and Washington, D.C. In 1848, Grimké did not attend the famous Seneca Falls Convention in New York state, but her concern for women's rights did not diminish. Although her stance on divorce was morally conservative, she was clear and emphatic in her support of female suffrage and the need to remedy the economic plight which most working women faced, one that she interpreted as an "enormous evil." She subscribed to *The Una* and *The Lily*, two early feminist papers, and briefly wore the Bloomer costume before deciding that physical freedom was less of an issue than "mental bondage."

Sarah's second attempt at an independent life ceased with her acceptance in 1854 of Angelina's invitation to return to the Weld home and join them in teaching at Eagleswood School. Throughout the mid-1850s, although war was wholly at odds with her pacifist position, Sarah became increasingly convinced that slavery would not be abolished peacefully in the United States. Near the end of the Civil War, Grimké moved with the Welds again, to Hyde Park, Massachusetts, near Boston. All three taught at a girls' boarding school in nearby Lexington, where Grimké's subject was French, until the school closed in 1867.

Grimké's last years were occupied with increased management of the Weld household after her sister was partially paralyzed by strokes in the early 1870s. On December 23, 1873, Sarah Moore Grimké died in Hyde Park, Massachusetts, at 81. At her funeral service, abolitionist William Lloyd Garrison called her a "venerated and saintly woman" and summed up her life:

> Here there is nothing to depress or deplore, nothing premature or startling, nothing to be supplemented or finished. It is the consummation of a long life, well rounded with charitable deeds, active sympathies, serviceable toils, loving ministrations, grand testimonies, and nobly self-sacrificing endeavors. For one, I feel this occasion to be one of exultation rather than of sorrow.

SOURCES:
Koch, Adrienne. "The Significance of the Grimké Family," in *Maryland Historian*. Vol. 3, no. 1. Spring 1972, pp. 59–84.
Lerner, Gerda. *The Grimké Sisters from South Carolina: Rebels Against Slavery*. Boston, MA: Houghton Mifflin, 1967.
———. *The Woman in American History*. Menlo Park, CA: Addison-Wesley, 1971.
Weld, Theodore Dwight. *In Memory: Angelina Grimké Weld*. Boston, MA: George H. Ellis, 1880.

SUGGESTED READING:
Barnes, G.H., and D.L. Dumond, eds. *Letters of Theodore Dwight Weld, Angelina Grimké Weld and Sarah Grimké, 1822–1844*, 2 vols. Gloucester, MA: Peter Smith, 1965.
Birney, Catherine H. *The Grimké Sisters. Sarah and Angelina Grimké: The First American Women Advocates of Abolition and Women's Rights*, 1885 (reprinted NY: Haskell House, 1970).

Smith-Rosenberg, Carroll. "The Hysterical Women: Sex Roles and Role Conflict in Nineteenth-Century America," in *Social Research*. Vol. XXXIX, 1972, pp. 652–678.

Donna Beaudin,
freelance writer in history, Guelph, Ontario, Canada

Grimshaw, Beatrice (c. 1870–1953)

Irish writer. Born in Cloonagh, County Antrim, Ireland, in 1870 (some sources cite 1871); died in Bathurst, New South Wales, in 1953; educated at Margaret Byers' Ladies' Collegiate College, Belfast, and in Caen and London.

Beatrice Grimshaw was born in Cloonagh, County Antrim, Ireland, around 1870, and began her writing career in 1891 as a journalist in Dublin. From 1895 to 1899, she edited the *Social Review*. Succumbing to a growing ennui, she went to the Pacific in 1903, working as a tour promoter and eventually settling in New Guinea, where she was commissioned by the Australian government to publicize the region. The results were several travel books: *In the Strange South Seas* (1907), which was illustrated with her own photographs, *From Fiji to the Cannibal Islands* (1907), and *The New New Guinea* (1910). The South Seas also inspired some 40 romance and adventure novels, among which *When the Red Gods Call* (1911) is perhaps the best known. She also produced ten volumes of short stories and contributed articles to the *National Geographic*.

In her early years, Grimshaw was an avid cyclist and surpassed the women's world 24-hour record by five hours. She was also mistakenly credited in a British *Who's Who* entry (1928), as "the first white woman to ascend the notorious Sepic and the Fly River." She later disavowed the claim, saying, "I have no new range of rivers to my credit, though I have mapped a few odd corners here and there, and often met natives who had never seen a white person—that is easy in Papua." Grimshaw died in Bathurst, New South Wales, in 1953.

Grinberg, Maria (1908–1979)

Soviet pianist who recorded Beethoven's 32 sonatas and was famous for her interpretation of Romantic works. Born in Odessa, Crimea, on September 6, 1908; died in 1979.

One of the most respected pianists of the Soviet era, Maria Grinberg was born in Odessa, Crimea, in 1908, and studied with Konstantin

Igumnov and Felix Blumenfeld. She was a powerful pianist who was able to rein in her energies when necessary. Essentially a Romantic performer, she was equally at ease in the rhetoric of César Franck's *Symphonic Variations* or the acerbic modernity of Dmitry Shostakovich's First Piano Concerto. She presented Brahms with warmth, the French school (particularly Ravel) with elegance and flair, and the high Romanticism of Schumann with passion and *Innigkeit* ("intimacy"). A celebrated Beethoven performer, Grinberg fortunately recorded for posterity all of his 32 sonatas. Her Beethoven style was unadorned, spiky and sincere.

John Haag,
Athens, Georgia

Grinham, Judith (1939—)

British athlete who was the first English woman to win an Olympic gold medal for swimming in 32 years. Born Judith Brenda Grinham in England on March 6, 1939.

In 1956, at the Olympic Games in Melbourne, Australia, British teenager Judith Grinham won a gold medal for the 100-meter backstroke. During the event, the 17-year-old got off to a poor start and was only fifth at the turn. With ten meters to go, she caught up with America's ◄ **Carin Cone** and outtouched her at the finish; both had turned in a time of 1:12.9 seconds, setting an Olympic record. Grimshaw's teammate ◄ **Margaret Edwards** took the bronze with 1:13.1.

The victory marked the first time in 32 years that an English woman had won an Olympic gold medal for swimming. Britain's *Lucy Morton had previously won a gold in the 200-meter breaststroke in 1924. Grinham later added the Empire (1958) and European (1958) backstroke

---

◄ **Cone, Carin** (1940—)

American swimmer. Born Carin Alice Cone on April 18, 1940.

America's Carin Cone won the silver medal in the backstroke at the Melbourne Olympics in 1956.

◄ **Edwards, Margaret** (1939—)

English swimmer. Born on March 28, 1939.

In 1956, England's Margaret Edwards took the bronze medal in the backstroke at the Melbourne Olympics.

---

titles to her Olympic success, becoming the first competitor ever to accomplish the feat. On the eve of her 20th birthday, she retired from swimming to pursue a career in journalism. Grinham documented her years in swimming in her autobiography *Water Babe* (1960).

SOURCES:

Arlott, John, ed. *The Oxford Companion to World Sports and Games.* London: Oxford University Press, 1975.
Grinham, Judy. *Water Babe.* London: Oldbourne Book, 1960.

Grisela.

Variant of Gisela.

Griselda (fl. 11th c.)

Marquise of Saluzzo. Name variations: Griseldis; Griselidis, marquise de Saluses; Grissel. Flourished in the 11th century; married Walter, marquis of Saluces or Saluzzo; children: a son and a daughter.

Griselda is said to have been the wife of Walter, marquis of Saluzzo, in the 11th century, and her misfortunes were considered to belong to history when they were handled by Boccaccio and Petrarch, although the probability is that Boccaccio borrowed his narrative from a Provençal *fabliau*. He included it in the recitations of the tenth day (*Decameron*) and must have written it about 1350. Petrarch related the story in a Latin letter in 1373, and his translation formed the basis of much of the literature to come. The letter, printed by Ulrich Zel about 1470 and many times thereafter, was translated into French as *La Patience de Griselidis* and printed at Bréhan-Loudéac in 1484. The story was dramatized in 1395, and a *Mystére de Griselidis, marquise de Saluses par personnaiges* was printed by Jehan Bonfons. Chaucer followed Petrarch's version, assigning it to the Clerk of Oxenforde in his *Canterbury Tales*. Not surprisingly, the narrative of Griselda continued to attract many male writers. Ralph Radcliffe, who flourished under Henry VIII, is said to have written a play on the subject, and the story was dramatized by Thomas Dekker, Henry Chettle and W. Haughton in 1603.

Griselda was noted for the patience with which she submitted to the most cruel ordeals as a wife and mother. In the *Decameron*, she is the poor Griselda who married Gualtieri, eldest son of the marquess of Saluzzo. Prodded into marriage by his subjects, Gualtieri had Griselda promise that she would be obedient, never angry, and always try to please him. When she agreed, he had her exchange her rags for finery. In an instant, she appeared to be a true noble-woman and all were pleased.

Griselda had two children: a son and a daughter. To test her devotion, Gualtieri said he intended to have them put to death. Even so, Griselda sent them off with him, since that was what he wished. The children did not return. Years later, Gualtieri set out to test his wife once more: he sent her home, clad only in a ragged dress, informing her that he intended to remarry. Even so, Griselda remained calm. Soon after, Gualtieri had her return to his house, ordering her to prepare it for his wedding. No one, he said, could arrange the house quite so well. Griselda prepared the wedding feast, welcomed the guests, and cheerfully tended to the wishes of the new bride who was accompanied by a young boy. Deciding that Griselda had passed all his trials, Gualtieri introduced the supposed bride as Griselda's daughter. The young boy was Griselda's son. Then, Gualtieri had Griselda don her best clothes, resume her station as his wife, and all rejoiced.

Griseldis or Grizzell.

Variant of Griselda.

Grisi, Carlotta (1819–1899)

*Italian ballerina of the Romantic period who created the role of Giselle. Born on June 28, 1819, in Visinada, Italy; sister of Ernesta Grisi; died in 1899; cousin of *Giulia Grisi (1811–1869) and *Giuditta Grisi (1805–1840); children: (with Jules Perrot) one daughter, Marie-Julie; (with Prince Léon Radziwill) one daughter Ernestine.*

Born into the celebrated Italian theatrical family, Carlotta Grisi began studying ballet and singing at Milan's school of La Scala as a child and joined the corps de ballet at the age of ten. At age 14, while performing in Naples, she met the celebrated dancer and choreographer Jules Perrot who became her teacher and later her lover. In 1840, they made their debut together at the Renaissance Theater in Paris, in a gypsy comedy-ballet called *Le Zingaro*, in which Grisi both sang and danced. The following year, she was contracted by the Paris Opéra where she first appeared in Donizetti's *La Favorita* with Lucien Petipa. Her talent, as well as her stunning red hair and violet eyes, enchanted poet and critic Théophile Gautier, who sang her praises in the press and also became her ardent admirer.

Although Gautier's passion for Grisi was not reciprocated (he later had two children with Grisi's sister **Ernesta Grisi**), his love for her was by all accounts ongoing. She inspired the ballet *Giselle*, which he wrote for her in 1841, in collaboration with Vernoy de Saint-Georges (libretto) and Adolphe Adam (music). It became her most famous role, although she was notable in *La Péri* (1843), *La Esmeralda* (1844), and *Paquita* (1846). Grisi was also one of the celebrated quartet in Perrot's *Pas de Quatre* (1845), appearing with *Marie Taglioni, *Fanny Cerrito, and *Lucile Grahn. Known for her versatility, Grisi made several triumphant tours throughout Europe and made her debut at Saint Petersburg Imperial Theater in *Giselle* in 1850.

Grisi's personal life was complicated by the attentions of many men. She was Perrot's mistress (never his wife), and the mother of his daughter, **Marie-Julie Perrot**. (Confusion about the status of Grisi's relationship to Perrot may have arisen from the fact that when they initially danced together, she was billed as Mme Perrot. As a result, critics often referred to them as man and wife.) By 1842, she had left Perrot for a romantic interlude with her new dancing partner Lucien Petipa. At age 34, Grisi retired from danc-

Carlotta
Grisi

ing to have a second child, Ernestine, by yet another longtime admirer, Prince Léon Radziwill, a Polish noble who provided her with a lovely home in Switzerland. Grisi remained friends with Gautier until his death in 1872, and he often visited her bringing news of Paris and the ballet. Carlotta Grisi died in 1899, a month short of her 80th birthday. Remembered primarily for her triumph in the first Paris performance of *Giselle*, Grisi may have been the first ballerina to have used a boxed slipper for dancing on point.

SOURCES:
Migel, Parmenia. *The Ballerinas.* NY: Macmillan, 1972.
Richardson, Joanna. *Judith Gautier.* NY: Franklin Watts, 1987.

Barbara Morgan,
Melrose, Massachusetts

Grisi, Giuditta (1805–1840)

Italian mezzo-soprano. Born on July 28, 1805, in Milan, Italy; died on May 1, 1840, in Robecco d'Oglio near Cremona; daughter of Gaetano Grisi, one of Napoleon's Italian officers, and a mother who was also a singer; sister of soprano Giulia Grisi (1811–1869); cousin of ballerina *Carlotta Grisi (1819–1899); studied with Josephina Grassini (1773–1850), the contralto, who was also her aunt, and at the Milan Conservatory; married Count Barni, in 1833.

Debuted in Rossini's Bianca e Faliero *in Vienna (1825); sang in Florence, Parma, Turin and Venice as well as in London and Paris (1832); retired (1839).*

Giuditta Grisi was a second-ranked singer who was the sister of the better-known *Giulia Grisi. Although Giuditta's career was brief, it was consequential, taking her to Europe's major cities. She created roles in a number of operas, the most important being Romeo in Bellini's *I Capuleti ed i Montecchi*. She primarily sang mezzo roles early in her career and is thought of as a mezzo, essentially because of her creation of Romeo. In reality, Grisi sang soprano almost as often, but she never earned her reputation for her work as a soprano. Grisi and her sister sang together during the 1830 autumn season at the Teatro all Scala and during the 1832–33 Paris season. Giuditta's voice began to decline toward the end of her brief career, and she sang in smaller houses in the provinces. Known for the power of her voice, it was neither particularly beautiful nor sweet.

John Haag,
Athens, Georgia

Grisi, Giulia (1811–1869)

Italian soprano who was one of the great prima donnas of her time. Born on May 22, 1811, in Milan,

Italy; died on November 25 (some sources cite the 29th), 1869, in Berlin, Germany; daughter of Gaetano Grisi, one of Napoleon's Italian officers, and a mother who was also a singer; niece of Josephina Grassini (1773–1850), a contralto; cousin of ballerina Carlotta Grisi (1819–1899); sister of mezzo-soprano Giuditta Grisi (1805–1840); studied with Giuditta as well as Filippo Celli and Pietro Guglielmi; also studied with Marliani in Milan and Giacomelli in Bologna; married Count de Melcy, on April 24, 1836 (divorced); lived with her singing associate, the tenor Mario, Marchese di Candia (some sources say they were married in 1856); children: (with Mario) three daughters.

Made debut in Bologna (1828); created the role of Adalgisa in Norma *in Milan (1831); made Paris debut (1832), London debut (1834).*

Giulia Grisi was born into a family of gifted musicians, her maternal aunt **Josephina Grassini** (1773–1850) was a popular opera-singer both on the Continent and in London; her mother had also been a singer, and her elder sister *Giuditta Grisi* and her cousin *Carlotta Grisi* were both exceedingly talented. Giulia was trained to a musical career and made her stage début in 1828 as Emma in Rossini's *Zelmira*. Rossini and Bellini both took an interest in her, and at Milan she was the first Adalgisa in Bellini's *Norma*, in which *Giuditta Pasta* took the title part. On opening night, the first act was a fiasco, and it was not until the second act, with the duet of Norma and Adalgisa, that the audience began to applaud. Grisi appeared in Paris in 1832 as Semiramide in Rossini's opera and had a great success; in 1834, she appeared in London as Ninetta in *La Gazza Ladra*. Her first great London success, however, was in Donizetti's *Anna Bolena*. Grisi would appear in London each season from 1834 to 1861, missing only one year, 1842.

Giulia Grisi was the reigning Italian prima donna of the mid-19th century who is all too often remembered for a feud with her arch-rival, *Pauline Viardot*. The rivalry began when Grisi was chosen to replace Viardot's half-sister, *Maria Malibran*, in Paris and London. The feud grew when the tenor known as Mario, Giulia Grisi's companion, could not perform with Viardot in Covent Garden in 1848 due to illness. Later that year, illness forced him to cancel a second time. Although there was substantial evidence that Mario was truly ill, Viardot refused to believe it. In order to smooth things over, Grisi offered to sing *Norma* in Pauline Viardot's honor. Viardot agreed if she could perform the title role with Grisi singing Adalgisa. The opera was a huge success but did not smooth over the relationship. When Mario canceled an appearance with Viardot in *La Juive* in 1852, she was outraged. Matters were not helped when Grisi took over the role of Fidès in Meyerbeer's *Le prophète* at Covent Garden which Viardot thought she should be given.

Grisi was a talented performer despite a tumultuous life on stage. "She was known for her great beauty," said a contemporary, "although she was never known to be a coquette on stage. Her soprano voice was rich, sweet, equal throughout its compass of two octaves (from C to C) without a break, or a note which had to be managed. Nor has any woman ever more thoroughly commanded every gradation of force than she." Grisi was famous for her roles as Norma, *Lucrezia Borgia, Donna Anna, and Anna Bolena. She was a particularly fine actress, and in London opera her association with such singers as Lablache, Rubini, Tamburini and Mario was long remembered as the palmy days of Italian opera.

Some considered Giulia Grisi a neurotic but these stories seem to come from her rival, Viardot. A major presence on the opera stage who was revered by an adoring public, including a young Queen *Victoria, Grisi performed in Paris for 18 seasons and London for 26. She was the first in line of great dramatic coloraturas which began with her and continued with *Rosa Ponselle, *Maria Callas, *Joan Sutherland, and *Monserrat Caballé. While on tour in 1869, Giulia Grisi was felled by a severe cold; she died in Berlin of inflammation of the lungs at the Hotel du Nord on November 25.

John Haag,
Athens, Georgia

Grizodubova, Valentina, Polina Osipenko, and Marina Raskova

Three Soviet aviators who flew 3,717 miles nonstop from Moscow to the Soviet east coast near Japan in 1938, a journey one third longer than Amelia Earhart's 1932 solo flight, and crash landed, spending ten days in the Siberian taiga until rescued.

Grizodubova, Valentina (1910–1993). Born Valentina Stepanovna Grizodubova on January 18, 1910, in Kharkov; died on April 28, 1993, in Moscow; daughter of aviator and aircraft designer S.V. Grizodubov.

Completed flying-club training and began work in the civil air fleet (1929); assumed command of the 101st Long-Range Air Group (later the 31st Guards Bomber Group) which lent support to partisan detach-

ments (1942); awarded the Order of Lenin, the Order of the Red Banner of Labor, the Order of the Patriotic War First class, and the Order of the Red Star.

Osipenko, Polina (1907–1939). Name variations: Paulina. Born Polina Denisovna Osipenko on October 8, 1907, in the village of Osipenko, Berdansk; died in an air crash on military duty, on May 11, 1939; buried near the Kremlin Wall in Red Square; graduated from the Kacha Aviation School, 1932.

Set five world flight records for women; awarded Two Orders of Lenin and the Order of the Red Banner of Labor.

Raskova, Marina (1912–1943). Born Marina Mikhailovna Raskova on March 28, 1912, in Moscow, Russia; died on January 4, 1943, in military combat, near Saratov; buried in the Kremlin Wall in Red Square; daughter of teachers; married with children.

Author of Notes of a Navigator (1939); began work at the air navigation laboratory of the N.E. Zhukovski Air Force Academy (1932); graduated from the Central Training Center of the Civil Air Fleet (1934); joined the Red Army (1938); commanded an air detachment for the formation of air regiments and was made commander of a women's bombardment aviation regiment (1942); awarded two Orders of Lenin and Order of the Patriotic War First Class (posthumously).

Following the Russian Revolution of 1917, the founding of the Soviet Union opened up many opportunities for women under the new regime. The value of aviation was meanwhile being proven across Europe during World War I, and, after the war ended in 1918, there were flyers of both sexes eager to conquer the skies. The next two decades became a notable era for aeronautical record-setting as Americans Charles Lindbergh flew from Long Island to Paris in 1927 and *Amelia Earhart flew from Newfoundland to Ireland in 1932. Pilots inside the Soviet Union were showing a similar penchant for encroaching on new frontiers, as competitive in the air as the next generation would be in space decades later. Soviet flyers V.K. Kokkinaki set the record for altitude with a gross weight of 500 kg. in 1936; V.P. Chkalov, G.F. Baidukov, and Alexander Beliakov flew nonstop from Moscow to North America across the North Pole in 1937; and M.M. Gromov, A.B. Iumashev, and S.A. Danilin set the world distance record over a straight course in 1937. These were all men, however, and given the number of women making their way through the ranks of Soviet flyers, it is not surprising that the Soviet government was ready to sponsor a long distance flight by three women, Valentina Grizodubova, Polina Osipenko, and Marina Raskova, by September 1938. Although their flight of 3,717 miles set new records for distance flown by women, one-third longer than Earhart's had been, what grabbed the headlines at the time was the crash of their plane and the massive effort to rescue them.

$\mathcal{W}$omen in our . . . land have long ago shattered the chains of their age-old slavery and the old perverted theories of their inequality and lack of ability to do great deeds.

—Lazar Kaganovich

In the 1930s, aviation was still such a new field that almost everyone began flying in some roundabout way; the most important characteristic for gaining entrance to the cockpit appeared to be determination. Valentina Stepanovna Grizodubova was the exception to this rule, in that she grew up around planes. She was the daughter of a peasant who became an aviator after he built his own plane, inspired by a movie about the Wright brothers. A pilot at 19, Grizodubova became a member of the famous "Maxim Gorky" squadron which flew to remote areas of the USSR on educational missions. She had ten years experience by the time she was selected to pilot the historic flight of the three women. By comparison, Polina Osipenko's entry into the field was almost whimsical. Born into a poor peasant family in South Russia, she left school because of poverty, became a nurse, a weaver, and then a farm laborer. On a hot day in July 1927, she was working in a field with her family on a collective farm when an airplane made a forced landing nearby. Entranced by what she had witnessed, Osipenko began to read everything she could in the hope of being admitted to flying school. She was a waitress at an airport when her eagerness attracted the attention of pilots who helped her study; within a year, she was a full-fledged military pilot. In yet another contrast, Marina Raskova was born into the family of an opera singer and studied music before she became interested in aerial navigation. In preparation for flying, she had taught herself astronomy, meteorology, topology, and other related studies when she met a transpolar flyer, Alexander Beliakov, who helped her become a pilot.

The long-distance flight for the three women was to be nonstop from Moscow to the Soviet east coast. Grizodubova was chosen to pilot, Osipenko to co-pilot, and Raskova to navigate. Their twin-engine plane was christened *Rodina* or Motherland, and the flight was to symbolize the adventuresome spirit of the new Soviet nation. On the morning of September 24, 1938, the *Rodina* took off at 8:12 AM, from the Shelkovo airport near Moscow. The crew was well rested after seven hours of sleep and had eaten enormous breakfasts. Though they took off into a mist, the *Rodina* was soon flying above the clouds, rising effortlessly despite a 12.5 ton load. Skies were at first clear as far as Kazan, but then the crew ran into stormy weather. Grizodubova simply took the plane higher to get above the storm, and when dusk fell that evening the plane was flying over Sverdlovsk at an altitude of 5,000 meters. The pilot had dipped over the Irtysh River so that Raskova could take exact bearings when Osipenko took the controls, and for a while the flying was smooth. As night fell, however, the flight became bumpy. Seeing ice form, Osipenko took the plane still higher, to 7,500 meters, where the air was so cold that the lubricating oil froze in the electric transformer, cutting off radio transmission, and leaving the crew with only the stars to guide them.

All night, the flying remained rough, with the three women using oxygen tanks to get air necessary at such high altitudes. Each of the crew was in a separate compartment, communicating with the others by handwritten notes sent through pneumatic tubes. When dawn broke, they watched the sun's rise reflected on snowy mountain peaks as they passed over Rukhlovo. But thick clouds lay ahead. At 7 AM. Moscow time on September 25, they approached the Okhotsk Sea to the north of Japan and turned inland, setting their course for Khabarovsk. They had been in the air about 23 hours, and Grizodubova and Osipenko calculated that they had enough fuel to fly three hours more. Soon after, they noticed the confluence of the Amur and Amgun rivers, although visibility was almost down to zero with mists covering most of the terrain below. Shortly after passing over Kameka, a red light flared on the dash, signaling that fuel was running low, and the plane began to lose altitude. Over a region that was forested and swampy, with few, if any, safe landing places, it soon became clear that they would have to make an emergency landing.

The crew was familiar with emergency plans for just such an eventuality. As navigator, Raskova flew forward in a glass-covered cockpit, and was in most danger of being killed on impact. At this point, Grizodubova sent her a note, "Can you jump?" Raskova looked back at her colleague through the glass and shook her head no. But as the plane dipped lower, Grizodubova sent a second note, "Jump, jump, don't hold us up!" As a military pilot accustomed to obeying orders, Raskova grabbed some chocolate, looked out at the ground below her in search of a landing place, opened the cockpit, and jumped when the plane was at an altitude of 2,000 meters. She fell for three seconds before opening her parachute. Grizodubova nosed upward, looking to see where she had landed. Then the pilot and co-pilot retracted the landing gear,

to help prevent the *Rodina* from sinking in a swamp, and prepared to crash land. The plane was brought down so skillfully on the soft marsh surface that the body of the plane and all its instruments remained intact. The time was 10:41 AM on September 25; thus, the crew had flown for 26 hours and 29 minutes, breaking the women's long distance record in international flying. In terms of testing their endurance, however, their adventure had hardly begun.

Before launching herself out over the vast, forested, subarctic *taiga* below, Raskova careful-

Three Soviet flyers with their airplane, Rodina.

Valentina
Grizodubova

ly returned the maps to a safe place and noted that the altimeter read 2,000 meters. She took very little with her when she jumped, only matches, a hunter's compass, a revolver, and a piece of chocolate. Manipulating her parachute in a high wind, she tried to note the plane's distant landing place while she looked for an open spot in the trees. As she glided toward a meadow, her parachute caught in a fir, leaving her hanging five meters above the ground; she cut herself free. In the distance, she heard the *Rodina*'s motors roar and then fall silent. Next came the sound of a shot, and she took out her compass to note the direction. A second shot confirmed that the sound was from the southeast. But the distance was great enough that she decided to rest before setting off toward the plane.

With the plane on the ground, Grizodubova and Osipenko's primary concern was for their colleague. Jumping from the cockpit, Grizodubova fired three shots to indicate their whereabouts, but no reply came. The women then tried to establish radio contact and discovered that their transmitter was not working. Following their emergency plan, the women prepared then to wait for Raskova to locate them. At one point, they thought they heard voices, then saw a figure approaching the plane; it turned out to be a large bear. They climbed back into the plane where they spent the night. Awakened by clawing, they peered out at a lynx trying to get in. Grizodubova fired a shot to frighten it away, but more rubbing sounds indicated other animal visitors, attracted by the smell of food. Osipenko

released a rocket to frighten them off. "We were in a distant, unexplored wilderness," said Grizodubova. "But we were not alone. We felt the whole people was with us, thinking of us."

Raskova, in the meantime, after hearing the shots fired and determining the direction of the plane, had fallen into an exhausted sleep. When she woke, she set off to traverse the swampy ground covered with fallen trees. Dressed in heavy fur clothes to ward off the cold, she did not find the going easy. For food, aside from the chocolate, she began to pick berries, mushrooms, and soft birch leaves. On the third morning, she was traversing a marsh covered in tall grass when it began to rain, and she suddenly sank up to her waist and then to her neck. Seizing a stick, she gradually and with great effort worked her way out of the bog, and most of that day was spent trying to dry her clothes. The next day, she spotted a snow-capped mountain that she had observed while leaping from the plane, reassuring her that she was headed in the right direction.

At the plane site, Grizodubova and Osipenko had food, and felt the main threat was a possible attack by wild animals. On the third night, however, there was a violent storm, and they began to fear that the plane might sink into the subarctic marsh. To pass the time, the women sang songs and told stories. The nights were full of sounds, and they took turns sleeping. In an attempt to keep other creatures at bay, they set off another rocket, which set off a fire in the dry grass, and leaping flames were soon moving toward the *Rodina*. The fliers put out the blaze with their hands and feet.

While the downed flyers spent hours over the radio trying to establish contact, a massive search had been launched to locate them. Six thousand people and 50 planes took part in the rescue mission that covered land, air, and sea. Horse, reindeer, motor boat, and parachute parties joined the search, and local hunters, familiar with the area, fanned out to locate the *Rodina*. Radio news bulletins and newspapers brought the Soviets news of the search. In Moscow, Marina Raskova's 12-year-old daughter Tanya went to school, where she told people confidently, "Don't worry, Mama is safe. She told me just what they would do if they were forced to land."

On the morning of October 3, Mikhail Sakharov was flying the plane that located the *Rodina*. Far below, he saw two small figures standing on the wing of the downed aircraft. Though he could not land, he dropped them much-needed supplies. That same day, another flyer located Raskova and tried dropping supplies, but they were out of her reach. But the good news that the women had been located was relayed to millions of waiting Soviets. Parachutists, headed by Captain Polozhayev, landed near the *Rodina,* and more food, medicines, clothing, and warm boots were dropped in. Osipenko cooked up a dinner with the new supplies and all seemed well except that they had not been reunited with Raskova.

Word reached the downed plane that Raskova had been spotted, and shortly afterwards Raskova and her rescuers appeared. A doctor in the party wanted to examine her, but the navigator insisted first on checking her cockpit for what had survived the crash. Ten days in the Siberian wilderness had left Raskova badly weakened, and she was carried out by stretcher on an eight-hour trek up the Amgun River. Nevertheless, Raskova wrote later about the end of her ordeal, "That evening we cooked fresh salmon chowder on the shores of the Amgun. Such delicious chowder I have never tasted in my life, and I doubt whether I ever will again."

A fleet of boats awaited the flyers carrying them to the little town of Kerbi. From there, they went to Komsomolsk, where they embarked on a triumphant journey back to Moscow, across the Siberian *taiga* by train. All the way back, admirers waited to cover the train with flowers, exulting in the new flying record and in the aviators' safe homecoming. On October 27, a reception was held at the Kremlin, attended by leaders of government as well as other aviators, explorers, scientists, artists, writers, and workers. "Your threshold, comrades, proved to be the Pacific Ocean," said a government leader, "and your path turned out to be 6,000 kilometers long. You have demonstrated what great things Soviet women are fitted for."

The celebration was short lived. World War II was on the horizon, and millions of Soviet women and men would soon be drawn into the struggle against Germany and its allies, with women aviators playing a crucial role. Although women were officially supposed to fly only supply routes, many in fact engaged in combat and downed Nazi planes. Throughout the war, their exploits were greatly publicized. Grizodubova commanded an air regiment of long-ranging planes, flew bombing missions, and survived attacks by German fighters. Speaking of women in combat in 1942, she said, "In my experience, girls make just as good pilots as men. You cannot judge by appearance. I know girls so quiet and apparently timid that they blush when spo-

Marina Raskova

ken to, yet they pilot bombers over Germany without qualm. No country at war today can afford to ignore the tremendous reservoir of woman power."

On May 11, 1939, shortly before the start of the war, Osipenko was killed in an airplane crash while on military duty. She was buried with honors in Red Square near the Kremlin wall. When Raskova was killed in action on January 4, 1943, there was a tremendous national outpouring of grief over the loss of this much-beloved figure, who was given the first state funeral of the war. Crowds passed by the coffin, paying their respects in the domed hall of the Civil Aviation Club, and the funeral oration given by General Scherbakoff was broadcast throughout Russia. While Chopin's *Funeral March* and the *Internationale* were played, banners were dipped and officers saluted, and a lone plane flew over Moscow in tribute.

Grizodubova alone survived the war. She lived until 1993, a symbol of the accomplishments of the Soviet Union's women aviators. Given how well women had proved their skill and endurance in flight, it is not surprising that the Soviet Union was quick to send them into space. And while countries in the West still debate combat roles for women in the military that threshold was crossed by Soviet women decades ago.

SOURCES:

Campbell, D'Ann. "Women in Combat: The World War II Experience in the United States, Great Britain, Germany, and the Soviet Union," in *The Journal of Military History.* Vol. 57, April 1993, pp. 301–323.

"Many Nazi Planes Are the Victims of Russian Women Fighter Pilots," in *The New York Times*. January 17, 1944, p. 16.

Myles, Bruce. *Night Witches: The Untold Story of Soviet Women in Combat*. Novato, CA: Presidio Press, 1981.

"Noted Soviet Aviatrix and Officer Are Killed," in *The New York Times*. May 12, 1939, p. 13.

"Russians to the Pole," in *Time*. June 28, 1937, pp. 45–46.

"Russian Woman Flier Killed on Active Duty," in *The New York Times*. January 10, 1943, p. 7.

Smith, Jessica. "The *Rodina* Flies East," in *Soviet Russia Today*. Vol. 7, no. 9. December 1938, pp. 16–21, 32.

"State Funeral Held for Major Raskova," in *The New York Times*. January 13, 1943, p. 4.

"Valentina S. Grizodubova, 83, A Pioneer Aviator for the Soviets," in *The New York Times*. Obituaries, May 1, 1993, p. 31.

"Woman Heads Soviet Airlines," *The New York Times*. March 9, 1939, p. 13.

John Haag,
Associate Professor of History,
University of Georgia, Athens, Georgia

Grizzel.

Variant of Griselda.

Grog, Carven (b. 1909).

See Carven.

Grosman, Haika (1919–1996).

See Grossman, Haika.

Grossinger, Jennie (1892–1972)

American hotel executive and philanthropist. Born in Baligrod, Austria, on June 16, 1892; died in Ferndale, New York, on November 20, 1972; eldest daughter and oldest of three children of Asher Selig (an estate overseer) and Malka (Grumet) Grossinger; attended public school in New York City; married Harry Grossinger (a laborer in a garment factory), on May 25, 1912 (died 1964); children: one child (b. 1913, died in infancy); Paul Grossinger (b. around 1915); Elaine Grossinger (b. 1927).

Called "one of the world's great hostesses," Jennie Grossinger was a guiding force behind America's premiere resort, the opulent Grossinger's Hotel, located on 700 acres in New York's Catskill Mountains and catering to a largely Jewish clientele. At the height of its success, Grossinger's hosted over 150,000 guests a year, including numerous world celebrities. Featuring strictly kosher cuisine, the resort had its own airport, post office, newspaper, ski slope, Olympic-size swimming pool, golf course, and riding academy. Night life at Grossinger's featured some of world's top entertainers, many of whom received their first big break performing at the hotel. (Jerry Lewis, Sid Caesar, Sam Levenson, Morey Amsterdam, Red Buttons, and Eddie Fisher all launched their careers from the Grossinger's stage.) Joel Pomerantz, author of *Jennie and the Story of Grossinger's*, calls Grossinger's a Jewish institution, a "symbolic representation of an affluent life style for an entire ethnic class that rose from the ghettoes to positions of wealth, power, and importance during the first half of the 20th Century." For many, he added, "coming to Grossinger's was indisputable evidence of having 'arrived'—of having 'made it!'" Canadian novelist, Mordecai Richler defined the resort in less erudite terms, calling it, "Disneyland with knishes."

Jennie Grossinger was born in Austria in 1892 but migrated with her family to America in 1900. Her education was cut short at age 13, when she quit school to take a job as a buttonhole maker. Working 11 hours a day while attending night school, she helped support her sister and father, and sent money to her mother who had returned to Europe to find medical help for her brother, who was profoundly deaf. In 1912, Jennie married her cousin Harry Grossinger, a production man in a garment factory, and went to work as the cashier in the family's new enterprise, a small restaurant. The business was abandoned in 1914, when her father suffered a physical and mental breakdown. At the doctor's suggestion, he moved the family to a run-down farmhouse in the Catskill Mountains, where they hoped to make a living by growing crops. When that failed, they began to take in summer boarders, most of whom were fellow Jewish immigrants from New York City who were looking for low-cost vacations in the country. A small hotel emerged, with Jennie's mother **Malka Grossinger** overseeing the kosher kitchen, and Jennie acting as chambermaid, bookkeeper, and host. Jennie's husband Harry remained at his job in New York, but assisted by doing the marketing in the city and also recruiting guests from his acquaintances. During the summer of 1914, their first season, the Grossingers hosted nine boarders who paid a total of $81. A year later, they built a new wing, adding six rooms and providing for 20 guests.

Despite its modest facilities, the hotel, called Longbrook House, soon became known for its wonderful food and inexpensive rates. In 1916, Harry Grossinger quit his job in New York to join the growing enterprise. Meantime, Jennie balanced her long hours on the job with caring for her son Paul, who was often put in the care of the hotel guests while she worked. (Jennie's first child, born in 1913, died in infancy. Her daughter Elaine was born in 1927. By then, Jennie could afford a governess.) In 1919, the family sold the original farmhouse and bought a larger property nearby with a better equipped hotel building. That same year, they also purchased a lake and 63 acres of woodlands, so as to provide their guests with fishing and other sporting facilities.

Over the next decade, the business steadily expanded and, by 1929, had a guest capacity of 500. That year, Milton Blackstone was hired to promote the hotel. It was he who originated the

idea of offering a free honeymoon to couples who met at the facility and came up with the slogan "Grossinger's has everything." Jennie Grossinger, however, remained the hotel's greatest asset, serving as host and business manager and somehow managing to retain the hotel's family-run ambiance even as it expanded into a year-round luxury resort.

Throughout her career, Jennie was plagued by ill health, suffering severe headaches, chronic high blood pressure, back problems, and bouts of depression. In 1941, and again in 1946, she

Jennie Grossinger

underwent major surgery. Beginning in the 1930s, she began to delegate many of her former responsibilities and to devote more of her energy to philanthropic causes, both Jewish and non-sectarian. Much of her charity work focused on the Jewish homeland of Israel, where she helped to build a convalescent home and a medical center. The Hebrew University in Jerusalem also benefited from her charity, reflecting her lifelong interest in education. Jennie also contributed to the National Association to Help Mentally Retarded Children, the Deborah Tuberculosis Hospital, and the Leo N. Levi Memorial Hospital for Arthritic Patients. During her lifetime, she received many awards and honors for her philanthropy, including honorary degrees from Wilberforce College in Ohio and New England College. In 1954, she was the subject of the popular television show "This Is Your Life."

After World War II, Jennie presided over the resort's further expansion into a more diversified clientele. Now catering to guests who were not Orthodox Jews, the resort, in 1948, began to provide entertainment on the Jewish Sabbath. In 1964, following the death of her husband, Jennie turned the business over to her children, who had long been involved in its management. She died of a stroke in her cottage at Grossinger's on November 20, 1972.

Grossinger's remained a family-run enterprise until 1986, when it was sold to Servico, Inc., who razed the old buildings to make way for a more up-to-date facility, with a gourmet dining room, a spa, and an 8,000-square-foot "action lounge," targeted to a young clientele. Several old-timers were on hand to watch the implosion of the old Grossinger Playhouse, where so many young entertainers had broken in their acts. "If Jennie were here, she'd cry," remarked comedian Mal Z. Lawrence, who had often played the "G." Lou Goldstein, the director of daytime social and athletic activities at the old resort for 37 years, tried to keep his sense of humor. "I look at it with mixed emotions," he said. "It's like watching your mother-in-law drive over a cliff—in your new Cadillac."

SOURCES:

Current Biography 1956. NY: H.W. Wilson, 1956.

Kanfer, Stefan. "NY: Bulldozers Have the Last Laugh," in *Time.* October 27, 1986.

Pomerantz, Joel. *Jennie and the Story of Grossinger's.* NY: Grosset & Dunlap, 1970.

Sicherman, Barbara, and Carol Hurd Green. *Notable American Women: The Modern Period.* Cambridge, MA: The Belknap Press of Harvard University Press, 1980.

SUGGESTED READING:

Grossinger, Richard. *Out of Babylon: Ghosts of Grossinger's.* Berkeley, CA: Frog, Ltd., 1997.

Grossinger, Tania. *Growing up at Grossinger's.* NY: D. McKay, 1975.

Barbara Morgan,
Melrose, Massachusetts

Grossman, Haika (1919–1996)

Polish-born Israeli who became a leader of the Jewish resistance in Bialystok and Vilna during WWII, then served in the Knesset from 1968 to 1988, often identifying with highly controversial causes. Name variations: Chaika or Chaike Grosman or Grossman; Chayke; Haikah; Haike; Haykah; Jaika; Khaya. Born in Bialystok, Poland, on November 20, 1919; died at Kibbutz Evron, Israel, May 26, 1996; had two sisters and one brother; married Meir Orkin; children: two daughters.

Born in Bialystok, Poland, in 1919, Haika Grossman was a Zionist from her earliest years, at the age of ten becoming a member of the Marxist-oriented Hashomer Hatzair movement. Immediately after the German occupation of Poland began in September 1939, she went to German-occupied Warsaw to help reorganize the Hashomer Hatzair for future underground work on a national basis. Although barely 20, she was quickly recognized as a leader and accepted an assignment to work in Vilna, a formerly Polish city which first became part of Lithuania in the fall of 1939 and was then annexed into the Soviet Union in the summer of 1940. At this point, Grossman could have escaped from Europe. On the eve of the war, she had been issued an exit visa for emigration to Palestine. Ignoring the dangers, she turned down the opportunity, convinced that she could achieve more for the Zionist cause in Europe rather than in the Middle East.

Grossman arrived in a Vilna (Vilno or Vilnius) that had long enjoyed an almost fabled reputation as the Jerusalem of Lithuania. With a Jewish population of more than 55,000, an invigorating cultural and political life flourished there despite poverty and anti-Semitism. Even before the war, Grossman had developed strong political beliefs based on left-wing Zionist Marxist (but never Communist) ideals. In her view, the Jewish national agenda must include not only the creation of a Jewish state in Palestine but also fight for conditions of social justice for everyone suffering from oppression. Politically astute as well as persuasive, Grossman became an important part of Vilna's Zionist youth landscape. Besides her own Hashomer Hatzair group, another

Zionist youth unit, the Dror (Freedom) Halutz Organization, was active in Vilna, and the two organizations struggled to coordinate policies for the future. The onset of Soviet rule in mid-1940 brought the official suppression of Zionist and Jewish-nationalist activities, but Grossman and her colleagues succeeded in keeping their group functioning on an informal basis.

The German invasion of the Soviet Union on June 22, 1941, led to the occupation of Vilna by Nazi forces two days later. While about 3,000 Jews were able to flee into Soviet territory to escape the Germans, Grossman decided to remain in Vilna, soon making plans to return to her German-occupied hometown of Bialystok. During her final months in Vilna, she experienced firsthand the savagery of Nazi rule as many thousands of Jews lost their lives at the nearby Ponary killing site.

With the German master plan for the total destruction of European Jews at this point still not finalized, many of Vilna's Jews believed they could somehow survive Nazi rule. The city's Jewish underground movement was, however, composed of realists, able to intuit that an entire people now stood on the brink of mass destruction. Having finally overcome its factionalism in which a persuasive Haika Grossman played an important role, the Vilna Jewish resistance coalition (Fareynegte Partizaner Organizatsye—United Partisan Organization) celebrated its birth on January 21, 1942. To mark the occasion, a warning was issued to the Jews of the world that "Hitler is plotting to annihilate all the Jews of Europe. It is the fate of the Jews of Lithuania to be the first in line. . . . It is true that we are weak and defenseless, but the only answer to the murder is self-defense."

Arriving back in Bialystok in early 1942, Grossman became the leader of Bialystok's small but enthusiastic Jewish underground organization, the "Antifascist Bialystok" cell. On many occasions she volunteered for dangerous courier missions to ghettoes in other cities, there to gather information, help raise morale, and bring precious weapons and other military supplies. A particularly perilous but important mission was her trip to Warsaw in April 1942. Here she reported to leaders of the Warsaw Jewish underground on developments in Vilna and Bialystok. Grossman returned to Bialystok satisfied with her achievements, which included the receipt of funds to purchase weapons. Taking great risks, she was able to purchase weapons not only from the Polish underground but even from corrupt German soldiers.

Contacts between the Bialystok and Vilna underground organizations, and the outside world in general, were made possible not only because of the courageous acts of members of both groups, but also because of the remarkable assistance rendered to these groups by Anton Schmid (1900–1942), a Wehrmacht sergeant who not only rescued Jews but became an active member of the Jewish underground; Schmid's activities were eventually discovered, and he was executed on April 13, 1942. Overcoming numerous obstacles, by August 1942 Haika Grossman and Commander Adek Boraks had finally been able to establish a united Jewish resistance front in the ghetto of Bialystok.

With blonde hair and blue eyes, Grossman relied on forged papers to pose as a Polish woman. Along with five other young women of Bialystok's Jewish resistance, **Marila Ruziecka, Liza Czapnik, Hasya Bielicka-Borenstein, Ana Rud,** and **Bronka Winicki** (Klibanski), Grossman was able to build up a small but determined resistance movement both within the city of Bialystok and in the nearby forests where bands of armed Jewish partisans were growing in both numbers and determination.

Diminutive in stature but fearless and well-versed in underground work, Grossman had to deal not only with the Germans, but with a Polish population that was concerned with its own real sufferings and thus largely indifferent or even hostile to the Jewish community's plight. She was also deeply frustrated by the majority of Jews who continued to hold onto illusions about their chances for survival. Many dismissed stories of death camps and a general Nazi plan of genocide almost to the very end. Even when this was no longer possible, some still found solace in a rumor that German forces intended to destroy every remnant of Jewry except for a dozen selected individuals who would then be bussed from place to place as examples of the exotic species that had once existed in plentiful numbers. Decades later, Grossman noted, "We all thought we would get on that bus."

The year 1943 was to be tragic for the Jews of Bialystok. From February 5 to 12, the Nazis initiated an *Aktion* in the ghetto that resulted in 2,000 Jews being shot on the spot and five times that number being deported to the Treblinka extermination camp. During this period, Grossman's colleague, Adek Boraks, was captured and sent to Treblinka. In April 1943, the resistance forces of the Warsaw ghetto rose in revolt, a doomed but glorious page of Jewish defiance against the Nazis. In Bialystok, many continued to hope that they might survive by not offering resistance to the German forces, but on the night of August 15–16, 1943, the Bialystok ghetto, which still contained about 30,000 frightened and malnourished Jews, was surrounded by heavily armed German soldiers, SS men and Ukrainian auxiliary forces.

On the morning of August 16, the Jewish Council posted wall announcements ordering the entire ghetto population to report immediately for "evacuation." For months, the Jewish underground had been preparing for this day with a detailed plan as well as the creation of arms caches in strategic locations. At eight that morning, the underground's messengers appeared on every corner of the ghetto, exhorting the population not to follow the orders of the Jewish Council and the Germans: "Jews, don't go of your own will. This is not an evacuation to Lublin. Every time they take anyone from the Ghetto it means death. Don't go! Hide yourself! Fight with everything that comes to hand!"

Now the moment the underground had long prepared for was finally at hand. Following their predetermined plans, the fighters began their revolt precisely at 10:00 AM on August 16. Surprised and enraged, the Germans soon brought in heavily armed units that included armored cars and tanks. The Jewish fighters of Bialystok had only a small number of weapons at their disposal, but still they fought for five days, from August 16 through August 20. Each day, more than 300 Jewish women and men died. The fighters knew from the start that their struggle was doomed, but their deepest disappointment stemmed from the fact that they were able to mobilize only a small fraction of the ghetto population to engage in acts of resistance or even make systematic attempts to flee the ghetto. "Our fighters and our positions were only isolated islands in a desolated, lonely Ghetto," wrote Grossman. "We didn't have the masses behind us."

On August 20, the Germans and their Ukrainian allies celebrated their "victory" over the Bialystok ghetto. Miraculously, a handful of Jewish partisans, including Grossman, were able to live through an inferno of death. At the end of the uprising, having seen bullets hit walls only a few millimeters away, she found herself covered "[f]rom head to foot . . . with blood and mud." As part of a pitifully small group of fellow survivors, she managed to elude the enemy and was able to join up with a Jewish partisan unit operating in the nearby forest. For a time Grossman and her group maintained contact with the few remaining Jews in the town, supplying them with weapons and medical supplies. Her partisan group grew in size and experience, and even attracted a handful of Germans grown hostile to Nazism. Grossman and her colleagues re-entered Bialystok in August 1944 as part of the liberating Soviet forces, but virtually all of the Jewish population had vanished forever; the "sad victors" could only find eerily empty houses in what had been the ghetto.

The end of the war in the spring of 1945 revealed the full extent of Jewish losses in Poland. More than 90% of the prewar Jewish population of three million had perished, murdered by the Nazis and their allies. Many of the survivors wished to leave bloodstained Europe behind, but their path was blocked by the British who controlled Palestine, and other nations which felt uneasy when faced with the prospects of absorbing refugees. The personal losses suffered by Haika Grossman were staggering but typical of her generation: her father had been shot, while her mother had died at the Maidanek death camp; her brother had lost his life in combat while on active duty in a unit of the Soviet armed forces. Determined to move on, Grossman took various jobs in Jewish survivor organizations. Much of her work was involved in coordinating the departure of Poland's rapidly dwindling Jewish population. Only when it was clear

Haika Grossman

that the most pressing needs had been met did she finally decide to immigrate to Israel in 1948.

Soon after her arrival in Israel in May 1948, Grossman became a member of Kibbutz Evron, a settlement affiliated to the Hashomer Hatzair movement. She married Meir Orkin, a childhood friend from Bialystok, and had two daughters. As independent in spirit as ever, Grossman took the almost unheard-of step of retaining her maiden name, not so much to assert her feminism as to accept the fact that her resistance exploits had already earned her a place in Jewish history. In 1968, after many years of local political activities, she was elected to the Israeli Knesset (parliament) as a representative of the far-left Mapam Party. She was re-elected several times, serving from 1968 to 1981 and again from 1984 through 1988. Grossman served in the social affairs committee and was known to both her political friends and foes as a fiery orator (speaking in her Yiddish-accented Hebrew), always prepared to defend the rights of the poor and weak. In the last two years of her Knesset tenure, she served as that body's deputy speaker.

Never one to hide behind diplomatic language, Grossman chose to disagree on countless occasions with those she believed were in the wrong. Although as a Holocaust survivor and heroine from wartime Poland who played a central role in annual commemorations of the Shoa and the Warsaw ghetto uprising, she made no attempt to hide her resentment of the tendency of politicians, including Prime Minister Menachem Begin, to evoke memories of those horrors to justify current Israeli policies, including the 1982 invasion of Lebanon. On that occasion, she told the prime minister, who believed the invasion had saved Israel from Arab annihilation: "Return to reality! We are not in the Warsaw ghetto, we are in the State of Israel."

Responding in 1992 to a question posed by her German friend **Ingrid Strobl** if she did not sometimes yearn to forget what she had seen and experienced during the Holocaust, Grossman noted: "It is not a matter of artificially keeping memories of those days alive within myself, or that I always find myself living in the past. I have been very active in my nation's public life and have been deeply involved in all aspects of the people's problems here. But what happened in the past will always remain there in the background, it cannot be extinguished. It makes no sense to try to suppress it—and I have no desire to do so."

An energetic supporter of Arab rights, she spoke out in favor of a Palestinian state in the West Bank and Gaza at a time when such an idea was less than popular even among some of her ideological friends on the Zionist Left. Maintaining her global perspective on matters of right and justice and unconcerned about the controversial aspects of the trip, she was a member of an Israeli delegation that visited beleaguered Sandinista-ruled Nicaragua in December 1984. Always alert to the threat of anti-Semitism around the world, she responded in June 1985 to stories that passengers with Jewish-sounding names had been separated from others aboard a hijacked TWA jetliner by saying that these reports had served to "send shivers through me."

In 1993, while a guest of honor at an Arab village, Grossman tripped and fell down a steep staircase. She slipped into a coma, never recovering consciousness, and died in the retirement home at Kibbutz Evron on May 26, 1996. In his message of sympathy to her family, Prime Minister Shimon Peres noted that Grossman's remarkable life "symbolized the strength and rebirth of the Jewish people." At a memorial service held in Tel Aviv on July 2, hundreds paid their respects. Those on hand included her political allies from the Mapam Party, historians including Holocaust scholar Israel Gutman, and close friends and fellow survivors from the war years including Hasya Bielicka-Borenstein. At Haika Grossman's funeral, held at Kibbutz Evron, a broad spectrum of Israeli life could be seen including young people she befriended over the years, Israeli president Ezer Weizman, her trusted chauffeur, the Palestinian mayor of the neighboring Arab village, as well as a representative of the Likud Party, who had differed sharply with Grossman on many political issues but respected her. At the conclusion, those present sang the anthem of the Jewish resistance both in Yiddish and Hebrew, symbolically linking the "old" and "new" lives of Haika Grossman in Poland and Israel.

SOURCES:

Ainsztein, Reuben. *Jewish Resistance in Nazi-Occupied Eastern Europe: With a Historical Survey of the Jew as Fighter and Soldier in the Diaspora.* NY: Barnes & Noble Books, 1975.

Bender, Sarah. "From Underground to Armed Stuggle— The Resistance Movement in the Bialystok Ghetto," in *Yad Vashem Studies.* Vol. 23, 1993, pp. 145–171.

Freedland, Michael. "The Faith of a Ghetto Fighter: Haika Grossman," in *The Guardian* [London]. June 14, 1996, p. 18.

Grossman, Chaika. *The Underground Army: Fighters of the Bialystok Ghetto.* Translated by Shmuel Beeri. NY: Holocaust Library, 1988.

Gutman, Israel. *Resistance: The Warsaw Ghetto Uprising.* Boston: Houghton Mifflin, 1994.

Gutman, Yisrael. *The Jews of Warsaw, 1939–1943: Ghetto, Underground, Revolt*. Translated by Ina Friedman. Bloomington: Indiana University Press, 1989.

"Haike Grossman," in *Daily Telegraph* [London]. June 27, 1996, p. 17.

"An Israeli Delegation Has Visited Nicaragua," in *Latin American Weekly Report*. December 14, 1984.

Kowalski, Isaac, ed. *Anthology on Armed Jewish Resistance*. 2nd rev. ed. 3 vols. Brooklyn, NY: Jewish Combatants Publishers House, 1986–1987.

Strobl, Ingrid. "'Mir zeynen do': Partisanin, Pionierin, Politikerin: Israel nahm Abschied von Chaika Grossman," in *Allgemeine jüdische Wochenzeitung*. No. 14. July 11, 1996, p. 3.

———. "*Sag nie, du gehst den lezten Weg*": *Frauen im bewaffneten Widerstand gegen Faschismus und deutsche Besatzung*. Frankfurt am Main: Fischer Taschenbuch Verlag, 1989.

Syrkin, Marie. *Blessed is the Match: The Story of Jewish Resistance*. Philadelphia, PA: Jewish Publication Society of America, 1976.

RELATED MEDIA:

Strobl, Ingrid. "*Mir zeynen do!*" *Der Ghettoaufstand und die Partisaninnen von Bialystok*, German documentary film, Cologne, 1992.

John Haag,
Associate Professor of History,
University of Georgia, Athens, Georgia

Grote, Harriet (1792–1878)

English writer and biographer. Born Harriet Lewin near Southampton, England, on July 1, 1792; died at Shiere, near Guildford, Surrey, on December 29, 1878; married George Grote (1794–1871, an English historian, who wrote a History of Greece, *and member of Parliament from 1831 to 1841), in 1820.*

Harriet Lewin was born near Southampton, England, on July 1, 1792. She married George Grote, a celebrated English historian and member of Parliament, in 1820. Two years after his death in 1871, she published his biography, *The Personal Life of George Grote*; she had also written *The Life of Ary Scheffer* (1860).

Grouchy, Mlle de (1764–1822).

See Condorcet, Sophie Marie Louise, Marquise de.

Gruaidh

*Countess of Moray. Daughter of Aedh, mormaer (ruler) of Moray; maternal granddaughter of *Gruoch (Lady MacBeth); married William Dunkeld, earl of Moray (son of Duncan II, king of Scots); children: six, including William Dunkeld, Lord of Egremont.*

Gruberová, Edita (1946—)

Czechoslovakian soprano. Name variations: Edita Gruberova. Born in Bratislava, Czechoslovakia, 1946.

Considered one of the finest coloratura singers of her generation, Czechoslovakian soprano Edita Gruberová studied in Prague and Vienna before making her debut with the Slovak National Theater. She has performed at the Vienna State Opera, Bayreuth, Frankfurt Opera, and, in America, at the Chicago Lyric Opera.

Grundig, Lea (1906–1977)

German-Jewish graphic artist of the later years of the Weimar Republic who became one of the most honored artists of the German Democratic Republic. Born Lea Langer in Dresden, Germany, on March 23, 1906; died while on a Mediterranean cruise on October 10, 1977; daughter of Moses Baer Langer and Juditta (Händzel) Langer; had sisters Marie and Klara; married Hans Grundig; no children.

Lea Langer was born in 1906 in Dresden, Germany, into a prosperous Jewish family that was considerably more traditional in its religious orthodoxy than the majority of German Jews, who regarded themselves as "German citizens of the Jewish faith" (both of her parents had been born in Polish territory). Lea's upbringing at first provided few of the stimuli that would one day propel her into the world of revolutionary art. While she did show an early interest in drawing, and even as a child often spoke of her determination to grow up be an artist, the essential elements of her environment were typical of Germany's Jewish urban middle class.

In her teens, the popular and attractive Lea was a member of Dresden's militantly Zionist youth organization Blau-weiss (Blue-White). In 1922, drifting from her orthodox roots, she embarked on a serious study of art. At first, she was a student at the municipal school of arts and crafts, but by 1924 she had set her sights much higher by enrolling in the Dresden Academy of Fine Arts. Here she met and fell in love with Hans Grundig, a talented fellow artist who was also a militant Communist.

Having become convinced that only the creation of a Marxist society could assure Germany and the world a future of social justice without the scourge of war, in 1926 Lea joined the German Communist Party (KPD). She further alienated herself from her conservative family in 1928 by marrying Hans Grundig, who was not only a Communist but a non-Jew as well. To signal her break with her comfortable bourgeois background, and rebelling as well against the "commercial spirit" (*Händlertum*) of her family, Lea moved with Hans to a small apartment in the working-class Ostbahnstrasse district of Dresden. As was customary among many leftist couples of the day in Weimar Germany, the Grundigs looked upon their marriage as a *Kameradschaftsehe*—a companionate union of fully equal partners.

Lea Grundig and her husband regarded themselves not as artistic individualists but rather as members of a revolutionary collective body, the German Communist Party. Rejecting the middle-class ideals of aesthetic subjectivity, both Grundigs accepted the discipline of a highly regimented (eventually Stalinist and totalitarian) mass movement committed to social revolution. In their artistic lives, in 1929 they became members of the Communist-oriented Asso (Assoziation Revolutionärer Bildender Künstler Deutschlands—German Association of Revolutionary Artists). As active Asso members, the Grundigs chose to harness their developing artistic talents to the cause of Marxist social revolution. They regarded their art as a weapon in the class struggle, believing that if it could not be disseminated among the masses, there was little point in creating it. To enhance the effectiveness of KPD agitation and propaganda (agitprop) among Dresden's workers, Lea and Hans often produced flyers, posters, and inexpensive drawings that could be sold to poor workers for a few pfennigs.

The early 1930s were years of social distress and political instability in Germany. The collapse of world trade cost millions of industrial workers their jobs, and while many of the unemployed were now sympathetic to the appeals of Communism, many more Germans of all backgrounds found themselves listening seriously to the Nazi movement led by Adolf Hitler. For Lea and Hans Grundig, the Nazis, who preached violent hatred of Jews and Marxists, had to be fought with every means at their disposal. As militant anti-Fascists, they attended countless meetings and rallies. As artists, they were determined to create paintings and prints that could serve as weapons in the struggle against Hitlerism. In one of her earliest series of prints on topical subject matter, "Harzburger Front," Lea was able to capture with savage irony the faces of the Nazis and their conservative allies who claimed to represent "the German spirit" but in reality embodied the poisonous frustrations of a sick society.

By early 1933, the battle to save Germany from the Nazis had been lost. Hitler came to power in January of that year in an alliance with gullible conservatives and nationalists fearful of chaos and social upheaval. Within weeks, the

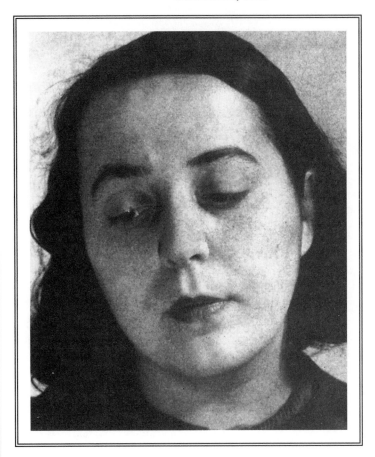

Lea
Grundig

KPD was destroyed. Only small secret cells of determined party members like the Grundigs now kept the flame of working-class resistance against the Nazis alive. Although Hans Grundig was "of pure Aryan blood" and thus presumably acceptable to the new rulers of Germany, his outspokenly Marxist affiliations in the past and his refusal to divorce his Jewish wife led to his expulsion from the Reich Culture Chamber, thus making it impossible for him to find legal employment. As a Jew, Lea Grundig was banned from earning a living as an artist.

Subsidized by Lea's family, the Grundigs concentrated on their art as well as their anti-Nazi underground activities. In the spring of 1933, when the Nazis had barely begun to consolidate their dictatorship, the Grundigs purchased a copper-plate etching press. Over the next five years, Lea and Hans printed about 230 engravings, many of which were treasonous in their commentary on the Nazi political regime. Lea Grundig, who produced the majority (approximately 150) of these engravings during the years 1933–38, emerged during this difficult period not only as a courageous member of Germany's anti-Nazi underground but as a powerful artistic personality as well.

Although she had mastered various forms of printmaking by the 1930s, Lea was particularly fond of drypoint, a process in which she used a diamond-sharp needle to incise her drawings into copper plates. Of the prints (*Kaltnadelradierungen*) she made during these years, 114 copies survived Gestapo raids and searches, her and her husband's imprisonment, and the destruction of Dresden in 1945. In most instances, only from one to five copies were pulled from their small press, to be given to trusted colleagues. A number of unique prints were smuggled out of Nazi Germany at great risk. In one case, the Grundigs' poet friend Auguste Lazar took some copies to Denmark, where they were given to Bertolt Brecht's wife, actress *Helene Weigel, who in turn took the precious prints to France. In another instance, some of the engravings were sent to Switzerland for safekeeping.

The works of art produced in Nazi Germany in the 1930s by Lea and Hans Grundig are remarkable both aesthetically and in a broader sense. These pictures both defined and defied a fascist regime that was preparing for war and genocide while many Germans were its enthusiastic supporters and the outside world remained indifferent. In series after series created between 1933 and her arrest and imprisonment in the spring of 1938, Lea depicted the harsh realities of working-class life in Nazi Germany. Entitled "Women's Lives," "Under the Swastika," "The Jew is to Blame," "War Threatens!" and "On the Spanish War," these sets of engravings represent a powerful indictment of fascism, even though they were produced within Nazi Germany by an artist whose life was under constant threat for both political and racial reasons.

In her "Women's Lives" series, Grundig depicts the daily existence of working-class women, boxed in their tenement rooms. One of the most moving in the series is *The Dying Child* (1935), which shows a near-skeletal girl on a bed, with her mother facing her, but her father turned away. In *The Laundry Room*, an exhausted woman bends over a washbowl, while a small, neglected child stands in the back of the room. Another print, *The Kitchen*, portrays a pregnant woman whose youth has vanished, sitting dejectedly in her ancient, suffocating kitchen. Yet not all of Grundig's art from these years is despairing. In *Comrade Else Frölich and Sonia* (1935), a working-class mother and child, though obviously impoverished, radiate dignity. After her parents were imprisoned by the Nazis, Sonia, aged ten, undertook dangerous courier tasks for the resistance cell of which the Grundigs were members.

In her "Under the Swastika" ("Unterm Hakenkreuz") series, Grundig captures the continual fear of arrest of anti-Nazis like herself and her husband Hans. Her depictions of those of the working-class are compassionate but not idealized. They are shown to be both weak and strong. In *Gestapo in the House*, the palpable fear of a lower-class family of three is presented in the instant they realize the Nazi authorities suspect them of involvement in resistance activity. The print *Sleeping Prisoners* shows five emaciated prisoners in a cell, each self-contained in their only escape from daily fear and pain. *The Hunted One* shows a solitary man running from wolves, with witnesses in the background unable or unwilling to offer help. The etching *Christl Beham* is a haunting portrait of a colleague in the Communist underground who was not only the Grundigs' closest friend, but a man destined to die in a Nazi concentration camp.

As a Jew, Lea Grundig had particular cause to both fear and hate the National Socialist regime. Although she ceased to think of herself as being Jewish in religious terms, she was fully cognizant of a Nazi racial regime that defined her as being a member of an element that must be driven from German soil. Her response, not surprisingly, was an artistic one. In her etching series, "The Jew is to Blame," she portrays Jews both as individuals and a community, victimized but clinging to their humanity and retaining dignity in the face of relentless persecution. In *Pogrom* (1935), a small group of Jews shriek in terror while their unseen tormentors continue to attack. The composition and lighting of this stark work was possibly inspired by Goya's classic painting of heroic Spaniards' deaths in the Napoleonic Wars, *The Third of May, 1808*. In *The Scream* (1937), another work in this series that anticipates art inspired by the Holocaust, a man's open mouth summons up a scream that is at once a testament of defiance and a warning to a still indifferent world. In *The Jewish Burial* (1935), of which only five were initially printed (sixty additional copies were drawn from the plate in 1972), a group of grieving and still-proud Jews, led by their rabbi, proceed to the cemetery past an ugly, indifferent industrial landscape.

Although only a handful of trusted friends saw their art, the Grundigs continued to etch, draw and paint. In her 1936 print *Mothers, War Threatens!*, Grundig captured the same spirit of compassion and anguish that had earlier inspired another great German artist, *Käthe Kollwitz. The anticipated terrors of a new, infinitely more destructive conflict are summed up in *Gas*

Masks, in which science and technology are unleashed to snuff out lives. *The Children,* another in the "War Threatens!" series, shows abandoned children holding hands in a nightmare landscape of generalized destruction. In her "On the Spanish War" etchings, Grundig depicts despair in the print *As Madrid fell* and defiance in *We Will Liberate Ourselves,* which shows a bound man about to break his fetters.

Despite almost constant surveillance by the Gestapo, the Grundigs continued to produce large numbers of art works which they showed and in some cases presented to colleagues they could trust. But over a period of several years, many of their friends were arrested and sent to concentration camps, and their small circle kept being reduced in size. On several occasions, trusted individuals turned out to be Nazi agents or simply lost their faith in the cause and defected to the enemy.

In 1936, soon after her return from a trip to Switzerland, Lea was arrested (Hans would also be arrested several times during these years). After each arrest, the Grundigs would return to their increasingly risky activities even though they realized their prospects for keeping intact a successful underground network were precarious. In May 1938, Lea once again found herself under arrest, but this time she received a long prison sentence—a grim prospect for a Jewish Communist in Nazi Germany, but still a somewhat more hopeful situation than being sent to a concentration camp.

In December 1939, a ray of hope appeared for the imprisoned Lea. Her parents and sister, who had already immigrated to Palestine, were able to secure exit papers for her. Hans approved of her plans, and after several brushes with calamity, including the sinking of her ship, she arrived in Palestine in 1941. Life in the British Mandate of Palestine in the early years of World War II was tension-ridden and uncertain. For a number of months, Grundig was kept by British authorities as an illegal immigrant in the Athlit internment camp. Here, she produced a new series of graphics, "Anti-Fascist Primer," as powerful an indictment of Nazism as the works she had produced in Dresden. Outspoken in her rejection of Zionist ideology, and daring to continue to converse in a now-hated German language, Lea established a number of deep friendships while in Palestine but also managed to attract enemies. Within the Betar movement of Zionist extremists, some came to regard her as being little better than a crypto-Nazi. The fact that she also advocated peaceful coexistence with the Arabs was

for Betar the last straw. As a result of her "treason," Grundig was the recipient of death threats.

Her reunion in Palestine with the Langer family, who had long had mixed feelings about her lifestyle, was in many ways bittersweet. But just as her parents had offered support to Lea and Hans in Dresden, once more they offered their help. After staying for a time with her sister in Haifa, Grundig found employment in her father's Tel Aviv restaurant. In her precious leisure time, while the Holocaust raged in Europe, and millions of Jews went to their deaths in Nazi death camps, in 1942–43 she created another series of graphics entitled "In the Valley of Death." This bone-chilling representation of the Holocaust, perhaps the first major artistic statement on this central tragedy of our era, was initially published in Palestine as reproductions in 1944, and would be her first postwar publication in Germany, appearing in print in Dresden in 1947 as *Im Tal des Todes,* with poems by Kurt Liebmann. In view of the fact that details on the death camps had been only reported in the press in a highly fragmentary fashion, Grundig's depictions of gas chambers and Holocaust victims are truly astonishing. Still haunted by the Holocaust even after the defeat of Hitler, from 1945 through 1948 the exiled artist refused to turn away from this painful subject. She created several new etching series, including "Never Again!," "Ghetto," and "Ghetto Revolt."

Undeterred by the hostility to some of her political views, Grundig was extremely active during her years in Palestine as an artist and citizen. Supported by a German-Jewish emigré circle led by Joseph Kastein, she was able to produce sufficient art works to mount exhibits in Haifa, Jerusalem, and Tel Aviv as well as at several art-starved kibbutzim. Her large circle of German refugee friends included the venerable poet *Else Lasker-Schüler, the artist Hermann Struck, and the novelist Arnold Zweig, but Lea did not live in the past as did some emigrés, preferring instead to enter into contemporary political struggles, which included the contribution of drawings to *Kol Haam* (Voice of the People), the local Communist newspaper, as well as forging ties to the Palestinian Communist Party and the Society for Arab-Jewish Understanding. Concerned that her life as an urban intellectual would cut her off from ordinary people's concerns, she lived for several months on a kibbutz, a visit that inspired artistic creations she believed would be of permanent value.

For more than five years, Lea Grundig did not know what had happened to her husband, sometimes losing hope that he had remained alive. Arrested in 1940, Hans Grundig was taken to the infamous Sachsenhausen concentration camp near Berlin. Dragooned into the Wehrmacht in 1944 to fight on the Russian front, Hans was able to desert to the Soviets. He returned to Dresden in 1946, but his health had been shattered (he would suffer for the rest of his life from severe pulmonary disorders). Until she received a letter from him, Lea did not know until July 9, 1946, that Hans had survived Sachsenhausen, the war, and captivity in a Soviet POW camp. "Lea, once again it is springtime for us," he wrote. But the couple's reunion was to be delayed, not for weeks or months, but for years.

Since Hans had returned to Dresden, a devastated city since the Allied bombing raids of February 1945, he lived in what was now the Soviet Zone of Occupied Germany. By 1946, when he and Lea were reunited if only by mail, it was clear that a new conflict, the east-west Cold War, would tear apart not only defeated Germany but most of Europe and the rest of the globe as well. The fates of individuals were now to be decided on the basis of strategic national interests. In Palestine, as British rule was waning, movement of Jews both in and out of the territory was subject to countless bureaucratic restrictions. Lea Grundig, as a German-Jewish Communist, found herself facing a particularly precarious situation. Not until 1948, some months after Israel had declared its independence but with a war with its Arab neighbors still raging, was Lea able to finally depart for Germany. Even then, roadblocks remained, and she found herself stranded in Prague from November 1948 until February 1949, when she finally returned to her hometown of Dresden.

Soon after her arrival, Lea was finally reunited with a husband that she had not seen since May 1938. Because of his poor health, Hans was once again confined to the sanatorium at Sülzhayn which specialized in treating patients with pulmonary illnesses. "And then he stands before me, my old gray Hans," she wrote in her memoirs. "He is ill, and in his small face one can still see the frightful tensions of those terrible years. His hair has gone totally white—but his straight mouth is laughing, as before."

Hans Grundig had served as rector of the denazified Dresden Academy of Fine Arts from 1946 to 1948, but by the time he was reunited with his wife in 1949 he had already resigned that position. Although poor health was a major factor in Hans' resignation, he and Lea would soon find themselves enmeshed in the Byzantine cultural-political conflicts of the newly constituted East German state. In October 1949, the Soviet Union had orchestrated the creation of the German Democratic Republic (GDR). With their sterling anti-Fascist pedigrees, the Grundigs appeared at this juncture to be destined for nothing but smooth sailing. In 1949, Lea Grundig was appointed the first female chaired professor of graphics and drawing at the Dresden Academy of Fine Arts, a post she held until her retirement in 1967.

By 1950, Cold War fears were spiralling out of control. Many in both east and west believed a nuclear war was all but inevitable. While loyalty oaths, the search for "un-American activities" and a spirit of anti-Communist hysteria plagued America's public life, in the Soviet Union and its satellite states, including the GDR, general paranoia was the order of the day, and many feared that in the Kremlin an aging Joseph Stalin would unleash a purge matching the savage bloodletting of the 1930s.

Throughout the Soviet bloc, the arts were by no means immune from a mounting pressure to achieve a state of absolute Marxist orthodoxy. The anti-Fascist art of the Grundigs, while respected in the immediate postwar years, now was seen as being too pessimistic for a society engaged in the tasks of "socialist reconstruction." Lea Grundig was also suspect in the eyes of some Socialist Unity Party ideologues, being potentially too "Western-oriented" not only because of her Jewish origins but because she had spent the war years neither in Germany nor the Soviet Union, but in British-ruled Palestine.

The expected bombshell against the Grundigs and other artists suspected of displaying insufficient orthodoxy burst on January 20, 1951, when a pseudonymous article signed "N. Orlow" appeared in the Soviet-controlled East Berlin newspaper *Tägliche Rundschau*. Entitled "Right and Wrong Paths in Modern Art," the article did not mention the Grundigs by name but clearly linked their work to a "formalist" art that did not serve the needs of a socialist society. Hans and Lea responded in an article that appeared a month later in the same newspaper, asserting that new concepts of what is beautiful or ugly would have to evolve, and that their art, which had served as weapons in the war against fascism, should now serve to advance the cause of social progress, even if it did not appear to meet standards of conventional beauty or "socialist realism."

Although neither she nor her husband suffered legal sanctions for their assertiveness on this and other occasions, the GDR cultural bureaucracy regarded their claims of artistic integrity with great suspicion. Measures were taken to restrict the influence of the Grundigs largely to the Dresden region, but even here they were forced for years to endure what was clearly a centrally orchestrated boycott of their art. Only with the start of a timid de-Stalinization process in the GDR in 1956 (which in no way matched the much more sweeping cultural "thaw" in neighboring Poland) was it possible for the Grundigs to exhibit their works in public. One such exhibition took place in 1956 in the Saxon town of Zwickau. In June 1958, Lea and Hans had the satisfaction of seeing a large number of their works exhibited in East Berlin's Pavillion of Art. A few months later, the same works were shown in Moscow.

Unfortunately, this belated sign of recognition came too late for Hans Grundig, who died in Dresden on September 11, 1958. Within weeks of his death, both Hans and Lea were named recipients of the National Prize of the GDR, Second Class. Lea Grundig never remarried and remained strongly influenced by her husband's example. She gave expression to these feelings in her 1964 self-portrait, which shows her own face, marked by grief, wisdom, and a lifetime of painful events, merging with that of Hans. From the late 1950s to the end of her life, Lea Grundig's reputation in the GDR was secure. As a living embodiment of the Marxist republic's anti-Fascist traditions dating back to the pre-Hitler epoch, she was now celebrated as a Grand Old Lady of the GDR cultural scene. With the end of a blatantly Stalinist regime in the arts, her work could now be studied and praised.

Starting in the early 1950s, Grundig produced graphics that positively portrayed the building of socialism in the GDR and looked critically at the "imperialist" societies of the West. Unambiguous in their support of socialism, these works are generally less convincing than her anti-Fascist works of the 1930s. Grundig once suggested that she hoped to be remembered not as an artist, but rather as "an agitator" for the noble cause of socialism. Perhaps this is a key to understanding the totality of her work, both in its strengths and weaknesses.

No longer an outsider, in 1958 Grundig published her autobiography, *Gesichte und Geschichte (Faces and History)*, which became a GDR bestseller, going through ten printings between 1958 and 1984. In 1961, she was elected a member of the prestigious German Academy of the Arts, followed in 1964 by her election as president of the League of German Artists (Verband Bildender Künstler Deutschlands). In 1967, she received the GDR National Prize, First Class, and in the same year was elected a member of the Socialist Unity Party's Central Committee. A number of additional awards came her way during the next decade, including the granting in 1972 of an honorary doctoral degree by the University of Greifswald.

In 1973, an ambitious exhibition of many aspects of her life's work took place in West Berlin's Ladengalerie, a gallery that had been showing her art on a more modest scale since the early 1960s. It was this show that broke the ice jam that had kept Grundig's graphic oeuvre largely hidden behind the Iron Curtain and, in her own case, the Berlin Wall as well. In the crisis-ridden GDR's last decade, the 1980s, there was an "organized lack of interest" in Grundig's achievements, a situation that changed dramatically in 1996–97 when a one-woman show brought her work to the attention of art lovers in both Berlin (Ladengalerie) and New York (Galerie St. Etienne).

In her final years, Grundig enjoyed maintaining and deepening her contacts with friends and students. She also looked forward to her foreign travels and was able to visit a number of countries she had dreamed of exploring when young, including several socialist societies: Cuba, Chile, and the People's Republic of China. It was during another such trip, a Mediterranean cruise, that Lea Grundig died suddenly, on October 10, 1977. She is buried in Dresden, next to her beloved husband Hans.

SOURCES:

Amishai-Maisels, Ziva. *Depiction and Interpretation: The Influence of the Holocaust on the Visual Arts.* NY: Pergamon Press, 1993.

B., C. "'Ich bin eine Agitatorin': Lea Grundig siebzig," in *Frankfurter Allgemeine Zeitung.* March 24, 1976.

Badstübner-Peters, Evemarie. "Kulturdebatten im Vorfeld des Zweijahrplans 1948," in *Zeitschrift für Geschichtswissenschaft.* Vol. 30, no. 4, 1982, pp. 304–321.

Birnbaum, Brigitte. *Die Maler aus der Ostbahnstrasse: Aus dem Leben von Hans und Lea Grundig.* Berlin: Der Kinderbuchverlag, 1990.

Domesticity and Dissent: The Role of Women Artists in Germany 1918–1938. Leicester: Leicester Museum and Art Gallery, 1992.

Feist, Günter. *Hans Grundig.* 2nd ed. Dresden: VEB Verlag der Kunst, 1984.

Frommhold, Erhard. "Eine Künstlerin zwischen Glaube und Illusion: Zum 85 Geburtstag der Malerin Lea Grundig," in *Sächsische Zeitung.* March 23–24, 1991.

———. *Hans und Lea Grundig.* Dresden: Verlag der Kunst, [1958].

————. *Kunst im Widerstand: Malerei, Graphik, Plastik 1922 bis 1945.* Dresden: Verlag der Kunst, 1968.

Gesellschaft für Christlich-Jüdische Zusammenarbeit Dresden. Juden in Sachsen: Ihr Leben und Leiden. Leipzig: Evangelische Verlagsanstalt, 1994.

Grundig, Hans. *Zwischen Karneval und Aschermittwoch: Erinnerungen eines Malers.* 9th ed. Berlin: Dietz Verlag, 1969.

————. *Künstlerbriefe aus den Jahren 1926 bis 1957.* Edited by Bernhard Wächter. Rudolstadt: VEB Greifenverlag, 1966.

———— and Lea. "Schön ist, was dem Fortschritt dient: Ein Beitrag zur freien Kunstdiskussion," in *Tägliche Rundschau* [Berlin]. February 21, 1951.

Grundig, Lea. *Blätter gegen den Imperialismus.* Leipzig: E.A. Seemann Verlag, 1975.

————. *Das Gesicht der deutschen Arbeiterklasse.* Berlin: Volk und Wissen Volkseigener Verlag, 1978.

————. *Gesichte und Geschichte.* 10th ed. Berlin: Dietz Verlag, 1984.

————. *Im Tal des Todes: Zeichnungen. Einleitung und Text von Kurt Liebmann.* Dresden: Sachsenverlag, 1947.

————. *Zeitgenossen: Bildnisse aus drei Jahrzehnten.* Dresden: Verlag der Kunst, 1963.

Hütt, Wolfgang. *Deutsche Malerei und Grafik im 20. Jahrhundert.* Berlin: Henschelverlag Kunst und Gesellschaft, 1969.

————. *Lea Grundig.* 2nd ed. Dresden: Verlag der Kunst, 1971.

Jakobs, Monika. "Die grösste lebende deutsche Malerin, Lea Grundig, über: Form und Inhalt der Kunst," in *Montrealer Nachrichten.* June 23, 1973.

Junghanns, Kurt. "Lea Grundig und der Faschismus," in *Bildende Kunst.* Vol. 4, no. 4, 1956, pp. 193–196.

Jürgens-Kirchhoff, Annegret. *Schreckensbilder: Krieg und Kunst im 20. Jahrhundert.* Berlin: Dietrich Reimer Verlag, 1993.

Kober, K.M. "Kunstzentrum Dresden: Erlebnis und moralische Landschaft," in *Die Kunst.* No. 11. November 1987, pp. 892–897.

Lea Grundig: Jüdin, Kommunistin, Graphikerin. Ladengalerie, Berlin vom 27. September bis 23. November 1996/Galerie St. Etienne, New York City März bis Mai 1997. Berlin: Ladengalerie, 1996.

Lixl-Purcell, Andreas, ed. *Women of Exile: German-Jewish Autobiographies since 1933.* NY: Greenwood Press, 1988.

Meskimmon, Marsha. "Grundig, Lea," in Delia Gaze, ed. *Dictionary of Women Artists.* Vol. I of 2 vols. London and Chicago: Fitzroy Dearborn Publishers, 1997, pp. 620–621.

Schmidt, Walter. "Jüdisches Erbe deutscher Geschichte im Erbe- und Traditionsverständnis der DDR," in *Zeitschrift für Geschichtswissenschaft.* Vol. 37, no. 8, 1989, pp. 692–714.

Vieregg, Hildegard. "Künstler und bildende Kunst im Widerstand gegen das NS-Regime," in Hinrich Siefken and Hildegard Vieregg, eds. *Resistance to National Socialism: Kunst und Widerstand: Forschungsergebnisse und Erfahrungsberichte.* Munich: Iudicium Verlag, 1995, pp. 13–65.

John Haag,
Associate Professor of History,
University of Georgia, Athens, Georgia

Gruoch (fl. 1020–1054)

*Queen of Scotland. Name variations: Lady Macbeth or Lady MacBeth. Born around 1015; flourished around 1020 to 1054; daughter of Beoedhe also known as Bodhe or Boite (who was probably the son of King Kenneth II or Kenneth III); granddaughter of either King Kenneth II (971–995) or Kenneth III (997–1005); married Gillacomgain or Gillacomgan, mormaer (ruler) of Moray; married Macbeth or Mac-Beth also known as Machethad, Machetad, Macbethad, and often confused with MacHeth in later sources (c. 1005–1057), king of Scotland (r. 1040–1057), after 1032; children: (first marriage) Lulach (1032–1058, known as the Fool or the Simple), mormaer of Moray and king of Scots (r. 1057–1058, who married **Finnghuala of Angus**).*

Gruoch, the historical "Lady Macbeth" (though she would not have been called this), was the daughter of Bodhe and probably the granddaughter of King Kenneth III. Gruoch married Gillacomgain, who, in 1020, had been involved in the murder of his uncle Findlaech MacRuaridh, mormaer of Moray. As a result, Gillacomgain was mormaer of Moray at the time of the marriage.

Consisting of a large territory centered on modern Inverness, Moray extended west to the coast, east to the river Spey, and south along Loch Ness while being separated from the rest of Scotland by a rugged ridge of mountains called the Mounth. Strategically, Moray was important because it acted as a buffer zone between the attacks of the Norsemen in the north and the remainder of the kingdom of Scots in the south.

The rulers of this province had a special importance attached to them. Although often referred to as *mormaers* like the rulers of the other provinces, in many Irish sources the rulers of Moray are called "kings," and sometimes even "king of Scots," suggesting their high status. Modern genealogical research, moreover, has demonstrated that they were descended from one of the three families which first settled on the western coast of Scotland from Ireland in the early 6th century. Since the kings of Scots were regularly drawn from the other two of these families, the rulers of Moray had a legitimate claim to royal status in the 11th century.

In 1032, the same year that Gruoch and Gillacomgain had a son Lulach, Gillacomgain was "burned, along with fifty of his men," according to the *Annals of Ulster*, possibly by his cousin Macbeth for killing Findlaech—for Findlaech was Macbeth's father. On the death of her first husband, Gruoch married Macbeth, the new mormaer of Moray. By this marriage, Macbeth merged several claims to the kingship of Scots: his own, as the son of Findlaech, and those of Gruoch, since she was granddaughter of Kenneth. At the same time, Macbeth adopted Gruoch's son Lulach. Although marrying the killer of one's spouse may seem strange, it is found quite frequently in Irish and Scandinavian literature.

Duncan I, king of Scotland, died in 1040, after a brief reign of six years. Having come to the throne in 1034, aged about 33, he had spent much of his reign raiding south into England; these raids proved largely unproductive, and in 1040 he was forced to turn his attention northward to Moray. One source says that Duncan was killed "by his own subjects" near Elgin. However, Marianus Scottus recorded that "Duncan, the king of Scotland, was killed in autumn, by his earl, Macbeth." His account is the only contemporary evidence implicating Macbeth in the murder of Duncan, suggesting that all future accounts of Macbeth's involvement were derived from it. Regardless of whether or not Macbeth was personally involved in Duncan's death, as mormaer of Moray he would still have been held partly responsible for the murder that took place within his province. Yet even so, Macbeth did not murder a kindly old man in his sleep, urged on, as he was in Shakespeare's play, by "vaulting ambition, which o'erleaps itself," and by an equally ambitious Lady Macbeth.

Macbeth was inaugurated as king of Scots, and Gruoch was queen. In the year 1050, Macbeth next appears on the record, on a pilgrimage to Rome, possibly with Gruoch. Sometime during his reign, likely after he returned from the pilgrimage, Macbeth and Gruoch made a grant of land to the Culdees or Celtic monks of Lochleven in return for prayers for their souls.

In 1054, Macbeth was driven from southern Scotland by Malcolm (III), son of Duncan, and Siward, the earl of Northumbria. Macbeth and Gruoch fled to Moray. In 1057, Macbeth was killed by Malcolm at Lumphanan. Because Macbeth had no children of his own, Gruoch's son Lulach was able to gather enough support to rule briefly over part of Scotland. In 1058, Lulach was killed, and Malcolm III's reign formally began. Both Macbeth and Lulach, and possibly Gruoch, were buried on the tiny island of Iona, situated off Scotland's west coast.

Much of Macbeth's evil reputation has been derived from chroniclers writing long after his

Julia Marlowe as Lady Macbeth.

death, who often had dramatic or moral obligations to fulfill. Although accounts of the historical King Macbeth are scarce, it is apparent that his contemporaries found him more deserving of praise then condemnation. As for Gruoch, she has suffered severely from the pen of William Shakespeare.

SUGGESTED READING:

Anderson, A.O. *Scottish Annals from English Chroniclers, A.D. 500–1286.* David Nutt, 1908.
———. *Early Sources of Scottish History, A.D. 500–1286.* 2 vols. Oliver & Boyd, 1922. Vol. 1, pp. 550–604.
Barrow, G.W.S. *Kingship and Unity: Scotland, 1000–1306.* Edward Arnold, 1981.
Dickinson, W.C. *Scotland from the Earliest Times to 1603.* 3rd ed. Revised and edited by A.A.M. Duncan. Clarendon Press, 1977.
Dunbar, Sir A.H. *Scottish Kings. A Revised Chronology of Scottish History, 1005–1625.* David Douglas, 1899.
Dunnett, D. "The Real MacBeth," in *The Sunday Mail Story of Scotland.* Vol. 1, pt. 4. R. Maxwell, 1988.
Ellis, P.B. *MacBeth High King of Scotland, 1040–1057.* Frederick Muller, 1980.

McDonald, Russell Andrew. "MacBeth," in Anne Commire, ed. *Historic World Leaders*. Detroit, MI: Gale Research, 1992.

Shakespeare, William. *Macbeth*. Edited by S. Barnet. Penguin, 1987.

Skene, W.F. *Celtic Scotland*. 3 vols. David Douglas, 1876–1880.

Grushevski, Agraphia (1662–1681)

Russian empress. Born Agraphia Simeonova Grushevski in 1662; died on July 14, 1681; daughter of Simeon Grushevski; married Feodor also known as Theodore III (1661–1682), tsar of Russia (r. 1676–1682); children: Ilya Feodorovich Romanov (1681–1681).

Guan Daosheng (1262–1319)

Chinese artist and poet, generally regarded as the greatest woman painter and calligrapher in the history of China. Name variations: the Lady Guan; Lady Kuan; the Lady Kuan Tao-sheng; the Lady Kuan Tao-jen; Kuan Fu-jen; Wu Hsing Chün fu-jen; Wei Kuo fu-jen; Zi Zhongji. Born in 1262 in Wuxing (Wu Hsing), Zhejiang (Chekiang) province, in Central China; died of beriberi near Linqing (Lin Ch'ung), Shandong (Shantung) province, on May 29, 1319; daughter of Guan Shen (Kuan Shen); mother was a member of the Zhou clan; had two sisters; married the artist Songxue also seen as Chao Meng-fu, Zhao Mengfu, or Zhao Meng (1254–1322); children, two sons, including Zhao Yong, and two daughters (some sources cite nine children).

Despite the restrictions placed on women of the elite classes in a traditional Chinese Confucian society based on hierarchy and inequality, over the centuries a remarkable number of them displayed extraordinary creativity. One of the most brilliant was the artist known as the Lady Guan (Lady Kuan). Born into a landed family in 1262 in the fertile province of Zhejiang (Chekiang), she was regarded by her father from birth as being an exceptional child, a parental attitude attested to in her name, Guan Daosheng ("Way of Righteousness Rising as the Sun"). It was hoped by her family that she would one day attract an equally exceptional husband. In 1289, at the advanced age (for matrimony) of 27, Guan Daosheng married Zhao Mengfu (Chao Meng-fu), an ambitious and artistically talented young man who could boast of descent from the imperial Song (Sung) family and who had by this time begun a promising career in the state bureaucracy. Zhao was regarded by Guan's father as a suitable husband because he appeared to possess the talent and energy to one day "attain wealth and rank."

Although the marriage of Guan Daosheng and Zhao Mengfu was doubtless an arranged one that brought with it financial and social advantages to each partner's families and clans, their union soon blossomed into both a love match and a magnificent artistic collaboration. The couple's bliss was, however, overshadowed by the dramatic changes that had taken place in all of China in recent years. In 1279, Kublai Khan had founded the Yuan Dynasty (1279–1368), thus finalizing the Mongol conquest—and reunification—of China begun by his grandfather Genghis Khan.

Determined to win over the Chinese spiritually as well as militarily, in 1286 Kublai had ordered his officials to bring him the most talented Chinese scholars to fill the highest offices of state. Realizing that acceptance of the offer would open him to accusations of collaboration with the hated conquerors, at first Zhao had begged off, claiming poor health. The next year, however, he relented and began a career in the War Ministry. Until his death 35 years later, Zhao would loyally serve the Emperor Kublai and four of his successors.

Soon after the start of his career as a high state official, Zhao Mengfu was honored not only as a great painter and calligrapher but also as a versatile man of letters appointed to maintain a permanent record of the emperor's activities. Although she gave birth to four children, two sons and two daughters, Guan Daosheng, Zhao's beloved wife, quickly matched, and perhaps even excelled, his level of brilliance. The couple's fame extended throughout the vast Yuan realm. Both Guan and her husband would always be welcome at the imperial court, and the Emperor Renzong (Jen-tsung, r. 1312–1321) would honor her entire family when he ordered calligraphies from not only her husband and son Zhao Yong, but from herself as well. At this time, she created an extended calligraphic work, the Thousand Character Classic, which so pleased the ruler that he predicted, "Later generations can know that my reign not only had an expert female calligrapher, but a whole family capable in calligraphy, which is an extraordinary circumstance."

In 1289, soon after their marriage, Guan Daosheng and her husband had moved to the capital of the new Yuan state, Dadu (now Beijing). Then, Dadu was a small and primitive frontier town in the north of the freshly con-

Fragment of a painting by Guan Daosheng.

quered realm and quite unlike the metropolis of imperial palaces that the Ming rulers would transform it into more than a century later. Guan and her husband's bittersweet memories of their previous home in the heart of China, with its lush vegetation, canals, rice fields, and bamboo clumps, were often reflected in their art. Besides his depictions of landscapes and bamboo, Zhao became a master painter of a subject matter very much favored by the formerly nomadic Mongol conquerors, namely horses.

The depiction of bamboo was an important theme in Chinese art, both before and after the Yuan Dynasty. Philosophers and poets believed the plant symbolized "the perfect gentleman" and embodied many virtues, including strength and flexibility, because of its ability to bend without breaking. Under Mongol rule, many painters looked upon the bamboo plant, bent but still unbroken under the overwhelmingly superior force of the barbarian Yuan rulers, as a symbol of their nation's current state of humiliation and despair.

Although Guan Daosheng had produced many highly praised works of calligraphy, as well as paintings of landscape, birds, plum blossoms, orchids, rocks, and Buddhist figures done in the traditional Song style, she dared to venture into creating important works depicting bamboo. Because of its associations with the ideal of the gentleman, bamboo was clearly a masculine preserve. An indicator of her artistic and social confidence in this regard is to be found in a bamboo handscroll done in her husband's studio in 1310, in which she wrote: "To play with brush and ink is masculine sort of thing to do, yet I made this painting. Wouldn't someone say that I have transgressed? How despicable; how despicable."

By the time Guan wrote this, her fame as a bamboo artist had spread throughout China. Her sovereign mastery of the art of monochrome black-ink (*mozhu*) resulted in her treatise, *The Bamboo in Monochrome,* which after almost seven centuries remains venerated as a classic account of artistic philosophy and technique. One of Guan Daosheng's most important artistic innovations was the reintegration of bamboo into a landscape setting. Equally significant for future generations of painters were her depictions of bamboo clumps, particularly groves of the plant enveloped in mist after fresh rain. Artists were inspired by Lady Guan's scenes of bamboo groves highlighted at the base of a series of staggered mountains in mist. Others were influenced by her novel views of bamboo panoramas, as well as by her format of low-level views of groves of tall bamboo with short, sharp leaves densely arranged over the top half of the stalks. Some art historians have suggested that she chose to paint bamboo along waterways in order to bring feminine associations to the plant's image. What is undisputed is the stunning sensitivity of the several masterpieces attributed to her brush that have survived the centuries. These include the ink on paper hanging scroll, "Bamboo Groves in Mist and Rain" (dated 1308, National Palace Museum, Taipei, Taiwan), a work that is regarded by some critics as one of the supreme masterpieces of traditional Chinese art.

Both Guan Daosheng's contemporaries and later generations esteemed her work as "a jewel" and large sums were offered for even an inch or two of silk or paper containing a specimen of her art. Both she and her husband were among the most respected artist-intellectuals of the Yuan Dynasty. In 1318, she was granted the most exalted of several titles that the emperor would bestow on her, that of Wei Kuo fu-jen, the Lady of the Wei Principality—giving the beloved artist a position approximating that of a feudal lord (some years earlier, she had been designated Wu Hsing Chün fu-jen, the Lady of the Wu Hsing Region).

When Guan became seriously ill with a recurrence of "foot-anger illness," probably beriberi, the best physicians of the imperial court attempted to prescribe cures but to no avail and her condition deteriorated from day to day. In early May 1319, a solicitous emperor gave his permission for her to return to her home in the south. Accompanied by her husband and a son, the gravely ill Lady Guan was placed on a boat for the journey via the Grand Canal. Fifteen days later, on May 29, 1319, having still not arrived home, she died. Her husband was inconsolable, and the character used on her gravestone to mark her death was the one used to announce the death of a prince or feudal lord. Zhao Mengfu, who never would return to Dadu, died in 1322 still longing for the wife whose "manner was winning . . . [and] . . . intelligence clear as moonlight." After her death, the multitalented Guan Daosheng quickly entered the pantheon of China's greatest artistic masters, the only woman in this cultural elite. Down through the centuries, her paintings, calligraphy and poems have continued to be revered. She remains the first lady of painting in China's artistic Golden Age.

SOURCES:

Ayscough, Florence Wheelock. *Chinese Women, Yesterday & To-Day.* Boston, MA: Houghton Mifflin, 1937.

Burling, Judith, and Arthur Hart Burling. *Chinese Art.* NY: Studio Publications, 1953.

Cahill, James. *Hills Beyond a River: Chinese Painting of the Yuan Dynasty, 1279–1368.* NY: Weatherhill, 1976.

———. *The Painter's Practice: How Artists Lived and Worked in Traditional China.* NY: Columbia University Press, 1994.

Carter, Dagny Olsen. *Four Thousand Years of China's Art.* Rev. ed. NY: Ronald Press, 1951.

Chang, Leon Long-yien, and Peter Miller. *Four Thousand Years of Chinese Calligraphy.* Chicago, IL: University of Chicago Press, 1990.

Fong, Mary H. "Views from Jade Terrace," in *Woman's Art Journal.* Vol. 17, no. 1. Spring–Summer, 1996, pp. 41–43.

Fong, Wen C. *Beyond Representation: Chinese Painting and Calligraphy, 8th–14th Century.* New Haven, CT: Metropolitan Museum of Art and Yale University Press, 1992.

———, and James C.Y. Watt. *Possessing the Past: Treasures from the National Palace Museum, Taipei.* NY: Metropolitan Museum of Art, 1996.

Fu, Shen C.Y. *et al. Traces of the Brush: Studies in Chinese Calligraphy.* New Haven, CT: Yale University Art Gallery, 1977.

Hackney, Louise W. "Chinese Women Painters," in *International Studio.* Vol. 78, no. 317. October 1923, pp. 74–77.

Hearn, Maxwell K. *Splendors of Imperial China: Treasures from the National Palace Museum, Taipei.* New York and Taipei: Metropolitan Museum of Art, National Palace Museum, and Rizzoli International Publications, 1996.

Lee, Sherman E., and Wai-kam Ho. *Chinese Art under the Mongols: The Yuan Dynasty, 1279–1368.* Cleveland, OH: Cleveland Museum of Art, 1968.

Lee Yu-min. "Chinese Painting in the Imperial Age: The National Palace Museum and Its Collection—Part 2: The Yuan Dynasty," in *Arts of Asia.* Vol. 16. November–December 1986, pp. 85–95.

Li Chu-tsing. *The Autumn Colors on the Ch'iao and Hua Mountains: A Landscape by Chao Meng-fu.* Ascona, Switzerland: Artibus Asiae Publishers, 1965.

———. "Recent Studies on Zhao-Mengfu Painting in China," in *Artibus Asiae.* Vol. 53, no. 1/2, 1993, pp. 195–210.

Lin Yutang. *The Chinese Theory of Art: Translations from the Masters of Chinese Art.* NY: Putnam, 1967.

Nelson, Susan E. "Intimations of Immortality in Chinese Landscape Painting of the Fourteenth Century," in *Oriental Art.* Vol. 33, no. 3. Autumn 1987, pp. 275–292.

Petersen, Karen, and J.J. Wilson. *Women Artists: Recognition and Reappraisal from the Early Middle Ages to the Twentieth Century.* NY: New York University Press, 1976.

Shaw, Miranda. "Buddhist and Taoist Influences on Chinese Landscape Painting," in *Journal of the History of Ideas.* Vol. 49, no. 2. April–June, 1988, pp. 183–206.

Soong, May-ling [Madame Chiang Kai-shek]. *Chinese Bamboo.* [Taipei]: Chung yang yueh kan she, min kuo 61, [1972].

Vinograd, Richard Ellis. "'River Village—The Pleasures of Fishing': A Blue-and-Green Landscape by Chao Meng-fu." M. A. Thesis, Department of History of Art, University of California, Berkeley, 1972.

Weidner, Marsha. "Views from Jade Terrace," in *Free China Review.* Vol. 39, no. 9. September 1989, pp. 58–71.

———, et al., eds. *Views from Jade Terrace: Chinese Women Artists, 1300–1912.* Indianapolis, IN: Indianapolis Museum of Art, 1988.

———, ed. *Flowering in the Shadows: Women in the History of Chinese and Japanese Painting.* Honolulu: University of Hawaii Press, 1990.

John Haag,
Associate Professor of History,
University of Georgia, Athens, Georgia

Guanhumar or Guanhumara

(d. 470 or 542).

See Guinevere.

Guastalla, duchess of.

See Bonaparte, Pauline (1780–1825).

Gubaidulina, Sofia (1931—)

Russian composer, considered by some critics to be the most important woman composer of the 20th century and perhaps of all time, who chose her own course in creating music that is unique and increasingly appreciated. Name variations: Sofiya or Sofia Gubaydulina. Pronunciation: Goo-BUY-doo-LEEN-ah. Born Sofia Asgatovna Gubaidulina in Chsistopol, Tatar Soviet Socialist Republic, USSR, on October 24, 1931; daughter of a Tatar and a mother of mixed Russian, Polish and Jewish blood; studied at the Kazan Music Academy, Kazan Conservatory, and Moscow Conservatory; never married; no children.

Studied piano under Maria Piatnitskaya and theory under Nazib Zhiganov at the Kazan Music Academy (1946–49); studied composition at the Kazan Conservatory with Albert Leman and piano with Leopold Lukomsky and Grigory Kogan (1949–54); studied at the Moscow Conservatory with Nikolai Peiko and Vissarion Shebalin, beginning 1954; composed more than 20 film scores in order to support herself; after years of working in obscurity, began to gain international attention in the 1980s and to have her works played by major orchestras outside the Soviet Union.

Principal works: (orchestra) "Fazelija" (1956); Piano Quintet (1957); Piano Sonata; (harp, double bass, percussion) Five Studies (1965); (mezzo-soprano, male chorus, orchestra) "Night in Memphis" (1968); (piano) "Musical Tog"; (B, small orchestra) "Rubaiyant" (1969); String Quartet No. 1; (orchestra) "Fairy Tale"; (small orchestra) "Concordanza" (1971); "Music for Harpsichord and Instruments from the Collection of Mark Pekarsky"; (orchestra) "Intervals"; (cello, small orchestra) "Detto II"; (soprano, piano) "Roses" (1972); (cello) 10 Preludes; (percussion, harpsichord-cello) "Humore e silenzio" (1974); (double bass, piano) Sonata; (cello, double bass) Concerto; (soprano, alto, tenor, bass, two choirs, orchestra) "Laudatio pacis" (1975); (percussion, orchestra) "Percussio per Pekarsky"; (orchestra, jazz band) Concerto (1976); (7 percussion) "Misterioso" (1977); (organ, percussion) "Detto I" (1978); (piano, small orchestra) "Introitus"; (4 percussion) "Jubilatio"; (cello, organ) "In croce" (1979); (violin, orchestra) "Offertorium" (1980); (violin, cello) Sonata (1981); (3 trombone, 3 percussion, harp, harpsichord-cello, cello-piano) "Descensio"; (cello, accordion, string orchestra) "The Seven Words" (1982); (soprano, bass, 2 violin, 2 viola, 2 cello, double bass, tape) "Perception" (1983); (viola, bassoon, piano) "Quasi Hoquetus"; (7 percussion) "In the Beginning was Rhythm"; (unaccompanied chorus) "Homage to *Marina Tsvetaeva" (1984); (accordion) Sonata (1985); (orchestra) Stimmen . . . verstummen (1986); String Quartet no. 2; String Quartet no. 3; (8 instruments) "Homage to T.S. Eliot" (1987).

Considered by her peers to be the world's most important woman composer of the 20th century, Sofia Gubaidulina was born on October 24, 1931, in Chsistopol, a town on the banks of the Volga River. Her heritage reflects the complex history of Russia, part of an ancient empire composed of many different peoples who were conquered and brought under the rule of the former tsars. Sofia's father was pure Tatar, Muslim by birth, and Sofia's paternal grandfather was a religious mullah. Her mother's family was of mixed Russian, Polish, and Jewish heritage, her maternal grandparents were practicing members of the Russian Orthodox faith, but descended from practicing Catholics and Jews. As proponents of the Revolution of 1917, Sofia's parents had forsaken religion, derided at the time as the "opiate of the people"; they had little sympathy for faith of any kind. Their daughter, however, had a spiritual bent, and throughout her life Sofia would reflect the many religions embodied in her heritage. When she decided to be a composer as a young girl, she went out into the fields near Chsistopol where she knelt and prayed, "Lord, make me a composer and I will endure whatever you might want me to suffer."

Sofia's musical talent was apparent from her early years, but her childhood was seriously disrupted by World War II, which killed tens of millions of Soviet citizens. In 1946, when she was 15, she went to Kazan, the capital of the Tatar Republic where she studied at the Kazan Music Academy from 1946 to 1949. After graduating from her studies of piano under **Maria Piatnitskaya** and theory under Nazib Zhiganov,

Gubaidulina went to the Kazan Conservatory where she studied composition with Albert Leman and piano with Leopold Lukomsky and Grigory Kogan, from 1949 to 1954. Bright and talented, Sofia Gubaidulina became one of the select few students given the opportunity to study at the Moscow Conservatory, where she arrived in 1954 and remained until 1963.

I am the place where East and West meet.

—Sofia Gubaidulina

During those nine years, composition was her main focus. Nikolai Peiko and Vissarion Shebalin were her principal teachers. Her background and the fact that she was a woman made her a unique student in several respects. "Nobody took much notice of me," she said. "They could always dismiss what I did as simply female eccentricity."

During Gubaidulina's early musical career, the arts, like all aspects of life, were strictly controlled. Joseph Stalin, the ruler of the USSR as Communist Party secretary, mistrusted artists as potential troublemakers, and as a result many perished in the Soviet prison camps known as the Gulag. Although it was never an easy task, performers, composers, and teachers toed the party line in order to survive. As a student in Moscow, Gubaidulina experienced surveillance by musical bureaucrats, but her teacher there was Nikolai Peiko, a broad-minded liberal. An assistant to Dimitri Shostakovich, the modern composer much admired in the Soviet Union and throughout the world, Peiko invited Shostakovich to hear some of Gubaidulina's pieces. Shostakovich listened to her compositions, along with several other musical bureaucrats who admonished the young composer for taking a "mistaken" path. Later, Shostakovich came up to Gubaidulina, shook her hand, and told her, "I want you to continue along your mistaken path," advice she continued to follow for the rest of her life.

After the death of Stalin in 1953, a new spirit of freedom swept through the Russian musical world. Gubaidulina entered the Moscow Conservatory at a time when many restrictions had been lifted, and the prejudice she now faced generally centered more on her gender than her political ideas. Even in the West, after all, music has never been an easy field for women, despite the fact that St. *Cecilia was the patron saint of music. For centuries, the discrimination that women faced was due in part to the influence of the church, where they were prohibited from performing in public—a prohibition taken to extreme lengths. In 17th-century Europe, young boys were castrated before their voices changed in order sustain their roles as male sopranos. For two-and-a-half centuries, the sexual mutilation of thousands of young boys, known as castrati, was considered preferable to having women fill the soprano roles. Although this prejudice in the vocal world was extreme, women also had an equally difficult time in the instrumental field and were prohibited in some countries from playing certain instruments. Until the late 19th century, for example, Swedish law forbade women to play the pipe organ, and no major orchestras included women as players or conductors until the 20th century. It is not surprising, therefore, that although women have always composed music, few major female composers emerged in such an atmosphere.

Faced with discrimination as a woman, isolation as a modern composer, and lack of opportunities as a Soviet musician, Gubaidulina nevertheless managed to turn these limitations to her own advantage. Ignored as she was, she could write what she pleased, rather than compose the patriotic drivel so many Soviet composers wrote in order to gain recognition. She also ignored the tortuous path of the *refusenik,* which some termed the "burden of Shostakovich" because the subject of his compositions was always dictated by his suffering under the repressive Soviet system, a theme which some felt limited his art. Instead, Gubaidulina devised a uniquely new music, returning to themes popular in tsarist Russia but expressing them in a more modern way. Her spiritual nature also asserted itself, producing works which have "eclectic mysticism" as a central theme. Titles of her compositions—"Introitus," "Offertorium," "De profundis," "In croce," "In the Beginning Was Rhythm," and "The Seven Words" among them—often have a religious theme.

Some have felt that Gubaidulina's work reflected music written by Alexander Scriabin, the Russian composer who experimented with quarter-tone music with mystical themes. "Rejoice!" typifies Gubaidulina's work. It consists of five titled movements inspired by the "spiritual lessons" of Grigory Skovoroda, the 18th-century Ukrainian philosopher. This work, which features the violin and cello, calls for utter mastery of these instruments. At times, the listener has the impression that two works are being played simultaneously. Although spirituality is a constant theme of Gubaidulina's work, she did not express herself as a traditionally religious person. "For me," she said, "composition is an intuitive, meditative type of existence. Music in itself is a spiritual art form."

Sofia Gubaidulina chose not to teach, a traditional occupation for composers. In search of work to support the practice of her art, she wrote the musical scores for more than 20 films produced by the Russian film industry, work she considered totally separate from her classical compositions. "Working for films is a nerve-wracking job, better suited to a man or for thick-skinned people," she said. "When I write for films, I feel very different from a man; yet when I write my own music, there is no sense of gender involved."

Sofia Gubaidulina's compositions were often inspired by other musicians and composers. Mark Pekarsky, the brilliantly wayward percussionist who also lived in Moscow, was an especially strong influence. The compositions "Music for Harpsichord and Instruments from the Collection of Mark Pekarsky," written in 1972, "Percussio per Pekarsky," written in 1976, and "Jubilatio," written in 1979, all reflect their close association. Pekarsky collected musical instruments from Africa, India, and China as well as from the Asiatic and Caucasian republics in the Soviet Union. Using these instruments, he created a percussion ensemble which inspired Gubaidulina's compositions. During the same time, she began a close association with the composers Viktor Suslin and Viacheslav Artiomov, and the three founded the improvisational group, Asteria. Although Asteria gave occasional concerts, its main purpose was to provide its three collaborators with the opportunity for private experiment, playing their own compositions using rare Russian, Caucasian and Central Asian folk instruments. Around the same time, Gubaidulina made forays into jazz, writing a score backing the scat singing of the gypsy (Rom) singer **Valentina Ponomareva**. The influence of Pekarsky, Suslin, Artiomov, and Ponomareva brought more graphic imagery and syntax to Gubaidulina's music. When she returned to classical symphonic composition, she brought this diverse experience to "Offertorium," written in 1980 and her first work to find an international public.

By the mid-1970s, years of non-recognition, composing movie music, and struggling to have her music performed were taking their toll on Sofia Gubaidulina. No modern music was taken seriously in Moscow, making reception of her work more difficult still, although she had worked outside the establishment and remained uninfluenced by current trends. "Up until about 1975, things were very negative," she said. "I became depressed and disturbed. Finally I went

to the Composers' Union and explained my position. For some reason—I'm not sure why—things got a little better."

The mid-1970s were a turning point in Gubaidulina's musical career and over the next 15 years, she would cease to be viewed as a minor musician, moving into the front ranks of the world's composers. In 1979, some of her pieces were included in the Moscow Autumn Festival, and not long afterwards La Maison de Radio in Paris gave a performance of her violin concerto. In 1984, the New York Philharmonic performed her "Offertorium." As major orchestras began to play her compositions, others followed suit. Unfortunately, travel restrictions and lack of funds still prevented the composer from leaving the Soviet Union. Under ordinary circumstances, the exposure of her works would have led her to be a featured speaker at international music conferences which would have further advertised her work. Asked if she would come to the United States to hear her music performed in the mid-1980s, she replied, "It is doubtful that I would be allowed to come to the USA, but still, an official invitation would be most welcome."

Four years later, in 1988, at a time when Mikhail Gorbachev's administration had lessened travel restrictions, the official invitation arrived. The American conductor *Sarah Caldwell, sponsored a festival called "Making Music Together" which featured Gubaidulina's work, and the Russian composer was invited to hear her work performed at Boston's Symphony Hall in April. Caldwell's introduction of Gubaidulina led to recording contracts, making her music available to classical radio stations as well as numbers of music lovers throughout the world.

Hearing the music of Sofia Gubaidulina, international music audiences recognized an important new talent. Wrote Alfred Schnittke:

> From her first pieces, Sofia Gubaidulina revealed in her music an unusual stylistic unity, a highly original spiritual world and an unbending composer's will. The stylistic evolution she has undergone since then has merely enhanced the expressiveness of her music without in the least affecting its character. Her extreme self-criticism compels her to spend much time on polishing the most minute details—which, however, leads not to superficial elegance but to strict asceticism. Her music is well integrated and devoid of all compromise. Such is the composer herself.

When young Sofia knelt in the field to pray that she might become a composer, she took on a greater burden than she knew. Nevertheless, her career marks an important turning point in the history of music. When audiences listen to her works, they do not hear the gender of the composer. They hear only her marvelous creation.

SOURCES:
Jacobs, Arthur. "Eclectic Mysticism," in *The Listener.* Vol. 123, no. 3168. June 7, 1990, pp. 36–37.
McBurney, Gerard. "Encountering Gubaydulina," in *The Musical Times.* Vol. 129, no. 1741. March 1988, pp. 120–123, 125.
Polin, Claire. "Interviews with Soviet Composers," in *Tempo.* No. 151. December 1984, pp. 10–16.
Rockwell, John. "Sofia Gubaidulina. A Soviet Composer Awaiting Discovery," in *The New York Times Biographical Service.* January 1988, pp. 110–111.
Steinitz, Richard. "Gubaidulina, Sofia," in *Contemporary Composers.* Edited by Brian Morton and Pamela Collins. Chicago. IL: St. James Press, 1992.

John Haag,
Associate Professor of History,
University of Georgia, Athens, Georgia

Guda (fl. late 12th c.)

German nun and artist. Flourished in the late 12th century in Westphalia, Germany; never married; no children.

A German nun, Guda worked in the *scriptoria* of her convent at Westphalia. Few of her works have been identified, but she left her mark on one particular manuscript. It is a homiliary (book of sermons) for which she prepared the miniatures and decorated the ornate capital letters. Eager to be remembered by the book's readers, Guda painted a charming portrait of herself standing within a capital D. It is a simple image of a woman in a nun's habit, solemnly holding up one hand in the traditional gesture of an oath. With her other hand, Guda grasps a curve in the middle of the letter, along which she painted the words *Guda peccatrix mulier scripsit et pinxit hunc librum* ("The sinful woman Guda wrote and painted this book"). Nothing else is known about Sister Guda.

Laura York,
Riverside, California

Gudula of Brussels (d. 712?)

*Patron saint of Brussels. Flourished in Brussels; died around 712; daughter of Count Witgar and Amalberga of Brussels; greatniece of Pepin I of Landen, king of the Franks; goddaughter and disciple of *Gertrude of Nivelles (626–659); never married; no children.*

A Frankish noblewoman, Gudula became the patron saint of Brussels. She was the daughter of Count Witgar and **Amalberga of Brussels**, and was sent to the Belgian convent at Nivelles for her education. She then returned to her father's court. Gudula took a vow of virginity and refused to marry. As part of her religious service, she gave her fortune to the poor and lived an ascetic lifestyle. Her devotion to helping the poor and her deep piety led to a reputation for holiness. She was thought to be able to effect miracles, even of curing lepers, and influenced many others by her self-mortification and humility. Popular worship led to her canonization some years after her death. Her feast day is January 8th.

Laura York,
Riverside, California

Guebhard, Caroline Rémy (1855–1929).

See Séverine.

Gueden, Hilde (1915–1988)

Austrian soprano. Name variations: Hilde Güden. Born Hilde Geiringer on September 15, 1915, in Vienna, Austria; died on September 17, 1988, in Klosterneuburg, Austria; daughter of Fritz Geiringer and Frida (Brammer) Geiringer (both musicians); studied with Wetzelsberger at the Vienna Conservatory.

Made debut in Zurich (1939); Bavarian Staatsoper in Munich (1941); Rome (1942); appeared in Salzburg as Zerlina (1947); Covent Garden debut (1947); Metropolitan Opera debut (1951), associate of the Vienna Staatsoper until 1972; made an Austrian Kammersängerin (1951).

Light lyric sopranos face many obstacles on the operatic stage. While pleasing, their voices are not especially distinctive, so they rarely achieve genuine star status. Hilde Gueden was one of the few lyric sopranos to achieve this rank. She was born Hilde Geiringer on September 15, 1915, in Vienna, Austria, the daughter of Fritz Geiringer and **Frida Brammer Geiringer**, both musicians. Her father belonged to a well-known Italian-Austrian industrial banking family, while her mother attended the Vienna State Academy of Drama. Gueden began studying piano at age seven, vocals at fourteen. She then studied dramatics at the Max Reinhardt School and ballet at the Vienna State Opera.

Hilde Gueden was a charmeuse rather than one of the most accomplished vocalists. Her sustained notes were often flattened and her intonation was not always true. Combined with imprecision, rhythmic laziness, and a tendency to lag behind the beat, her singing left something to be desired. Yet, she was a marvelous vocalist. Gueden's tendency to trail behind actually enhanced some performances, giving them a dreamy rapture which eludes many singers. Hilde Gueden was an accomplished actress who was quite good looking and these qualities did much to enhance her career. The light music of Johann Strauss and Franz Léhar seems to have been written for her. Many records preserve examples of her great talent.

John Haag,
Athens, Georgia

Guelders, countess of.

See Marguerite de Brabant (c. 1192–?).
See Katherine of Holland (d. 1401).

Guelders, duchess of.

See Sophia of Malines (d. 1329).
See Eleanor of Woodstock (1318–1355).
See Marie of Guelders (1325–1399).
See Catherine of Bourbon (d. 1469).
See Catherine of Cleves (1417–1479).

Guenevere (d. 470 or 542).

See Guinevere.

Guenhumare (d. 470 or 542).

See Guinevere.

Guenièvre (d. 470 or 542).

See Guinevere.

Guérin, Eugénie de (1805–1848)

French poet and diarist. Name variations: Eugenie Guerin. Born on January 11(?), 1805, at Château du Cayla, near Albi, in southern France; died on May 31, 1848, in Languedoc; sister of Georges Maurice de Guérin (1810–1839, a poet); never married; no children.

Diarist Eugénie de Guérin was born in 1805 at the Château du Cayla, near Albi, in southern France, into an old family of high standing. Despite their distinguished pedigree, Eugénie and her three siblings were poor and lived a simple life. Although Eugénie enjoyed close relationships with her sister and older brother, she was intensely devoted to her younger brother, Maurice de Guérin, who showed a great deal of poetic promise and encouraged Eugénie in her own writing. After the death of their mother, Eugénie took on the role of mother to Maurice, being especially concerned about his salvation. Her own life was so consumed by his that her diary addressed him as the intended audience; although Maurice had a great deal of affection for his sister, he did not return her love with the same zeal.

Hilde
Gueden

When Maurice left Château du Cayla to embark on a religious and, later, a literary vocation, Eugénie spent long hours praying for him. He married in 1837, but by then was near death due to tuberculosis. He returned to his boyhood home with his wife, where he died at age 29. Maurice was a talented and creative poet, but published nothing during his lifetime. He may be best known for a prose poem "Le Centaure" he wrote in 1835, which was published after he died. For the nine years between Maurice's death and Eugénie's, she labored constantly to see his work published and continued writing her journal to him well after his death. Her own work, *Reliquiae d'Eugénie de Guérin,* was published in 1855 for private circulation and G.S. Trébutien edited *Journal et Fragments d'Eugénie de Guérin* in 1862.

Eugénie de Guérin never married, although there is a hint of desire in her writings for home and family. After Maurice's death, when his child was about to be born, Eugénie expressed a longing to have a child to mother and nurse. On the whole, she shunned society, preferring to remain at one with nature and God. Her sense of the world was one of disdain, feeling it was frivolous and unproductive. She did, however, have a weakness for literature. She said that writing was almost a necessity to her, and she used her creative talents as an outlet for her trials and passions. However, she came into conflict with her own religious ideals over her desire to write and publish. On one occasion, she consulted her priest, fearing it was unseemly to want to write, and he assured her it would do no harm. When she consulted Maurice on the subject, he told her to worry less about her conscience and just write. Her writing is creative, showing a natural talent as a poet; Saint-Beuve considered her to have superior talent to her brother. Eugénie de Guérin died in Languedoc in 1848, several years before her journals were published.

SOURCES:

Bradford, Gamaliel. *Portraits of Women*. Boston, MA: Houghton Mifflin, 1916.

Judith C. Reveal,
freelance writer, Greensboro, Maryland

Guerin, Veronica (1960–1996)

Irish journalist whose articles on organized crime resulted in her assassination. Born in Dublin, Ireland, in 1960; killed in Dublin on June 26, 1996; attended parochial schools in Dublin; married Graham Turley (a builder), in 1985; children: one son, Cathal.

Veronica Guerin, Ireland's leading investigative reporter, was in the middle of an ongoing crusade against the nation's crime lords when she was gunned down, gangland-style, on the afternoon of June 26, 1996, while stopped at a traffic light in the outskirts of Dublin. One of the few Western European journalists ever murdered for her reporting, Guerin was 36 when she died, leaving behind an attentive husband and a cherished seven-year-old son. Police had little doubt that she was killed in retribution for her revealing articles. Sixty detectives were assigned to the case, and Guerin's newspaper offered a large reward for the killers' conviction. Prime minister John Bruton declared the assassination "sinister in the extreme" and recalled members of Parliament from their summer holiday for a special session on organized crime. Police responded with the most comprehensive murder investigation in the history of the country.

Guerin, one of five children, was born in 1960 and raised in Dublin's North Side. Educated in parochial schools, where she excelled in soccer, basketball, and a game called camogie

(similar to lacrosse), she ran her own public relations firm for several years before moving into journalism in 1990. She began as a freelancer for Dublin's *Sunday Business Post* and the *Sunday Tribune,* then, in 1994, joined the *Sunday Independent* as an investigative reporter. Almost immediately, her articles on organized crime put her in harm's way. In the fall of 1994, four weeks after her report on the life and death of Dublin godfather Martin Cahill, who was shot in his car, someone fired a bullet into a room of Guerin's house where she was playing with her son. The following January, after she wrote an article implicating a mobster in Cahill's murder, she was confronted at her front door by a masked man who, after first aiming a gun at her head, shot her in the thigh. After the attack, which hospitalized the reporter for several days, the paper provided her with a security system in her home and round-the-clock police protection, but Guerin felt hampered by her constant security escort and dismissed him. Less than a year before her murder, an ex-convict she had met for an interview beat her and later, on the phone, threatened to injure her son and kill her if she wrote about him. Though worried about Cathal, she would not give in. "That's what they want," she said. "Then they'll think that they can just continue doing it to everybody else." Alan Byrne, who was Guerin's news editor at the *Tribune,* called her a brilliant reporter. "I've never met anybody with a greater ability to get people to talk," he said.

In December 1995, Guerin was in New York for a week to participate in meetings and to receive an International Press Freedom Award from the Committee to Protect Journalists. William A. Orme, executive director of the committee, remembered that she hated the spotlight and couldn't understand why she was singled out for this recognition. "In interviews and editorial meetings," he recalled, "she was acutely uncomfortable, though always gracious. A born reporter, she was much more interested in quizzing her fellow award winners about their home countries—Guatemala, Zambia, Russia—than she was in discussing her own case." Orme also said that Guerin's assassination should serve as a reminder of the threats against a free press even in nations that are not undergoing political or civil conflict.

In November 1998, Paul "Hippo" Ward, the man who disposed of the .357 Magnum used to kill Guerin, was sentenced to life in prison. Ward, a former heroin addict, was thought to be a bit player in the slaying. Indictments were expected for others, including Patrick "Dutchy" Holland, Brian "The Tosser" Meehan, and gang leader John Gilligan. Gilligan, a career criminal who tried to pose as a country squire, was the subject of a Guerin exposé.

SOURCES:

Orme, William A., Jr. "Irish journalist really was a heroine," in *The* [New London] *Day.* July 15, 1996.

Rosen, Marjorie. "Death of a Reporter," in *People Weekly.* July 22, 1996.

SUGGESTED READING:

O'Reilly, Emily. *Veronica Guerin: The Life and Death of a Crime Reporter.* UK: Vintage, 1999.

Barbara Morgan,
Melrose, Massachusetts

Guerre, Elisabeth-Claude Jacquet de la (c. 1666–1729).

See Jacquet de la Guerre, Elisabeth-Claude.

Guerrero, Maria (1867–1928)

Spanish actress and theatrical impresario. Name variations: María Ana de Jesús Guerrero. Born on April 17, 1867; died on January 23, 1928; eldest child of Ramón Guerrero (a prosperous merchant) and Casilda Torrijo; married Fernando Díaz de Mendoza (an actor), on January 10, 1896; children: Luis Fernando, Carlos.

Born in Madrid on April 17, 1867, Maria Guerrero was the eldest child of a prosperous merchant, Ramón Guerrero, and **Casilda Torrijo**. Her father provided furniture and other scenery for Madrid's theaters, and Maria showed a dramatic interest from an early age. She learned French fluently in her youth and studied with Teodora Lamadrid, a famous Spanish actress. Maria made her debut in 1885 under the direction of Emilio Mario at the Teatro de la Princesa and later moved with him to the Teatro de Comedia. Her early roles were frivolous comedies.

She soon insisted on appearing in important dramatic parts, both in classical Spanish plays and new works written by José Echegaray, Benito Pérez Galdós, Jacinto Benavente, and Juan Eduardo Marquina. Guerrero and her father formed a company and remodeled Madrid's Teatro Español. They hired aristocratic playboy-turned-actor Fernando Díaz de Mendoza as a male lead. He and Maria married on January 10, 1896. When the company struggled financially in Madrid, Guerrero toured Spain and in 1897 spent a season in Buenos Aires. She was at her apogee as actress and theatrical impresario in the early 20th century. An attempt at filmmaking in 1916 failed, in part because she appeared affected and also because her impressive voice was use-

less in a silent movie. She and Fernando built the huge Teatro Cervantes in Buenos Aires. Still active as an actress, she died on January 23, 1928.

SOURCES:

Manzano, Rafael. *Maria Guerrero.* Barcelona: Ediciones G.P., 1959.

Kendall W. Brown,
Professor of History, Brigham Young University, Provo, Utah

Veronica Guerin

Guest, Lady Charlotte (1812–1895)

Welsh industrialist, educator, translator of Welsh medieval tales, The Mabinogion, *and renowned collector of ceramics and fans. Name variations: Lady Charlotte Bertie; Lady Charlotte Schreiber. Pronunciation: Bartie. Born Lady Charlotte Elizabeth Bertie on May 19, 1812, at Uffington House, near Stamford, Lincolnshire, England; died at Canford Manor, Dorset, England, on January 15, 1895; daughter of Albermarle Bertie, 9th earl of Lindsey (a former army general and member of Parliament for Stamford, 1801–09) and Charlotte Susanna Elizabeth (Layard), Lady Lindsey; no formal schooling, educated at home by governesses;*

married Josiah John Guest, on July 29, 1833 (he became Sir John Guest in 1838; died 1852); married Charles Schreiber, on April 10, 1855; children: (first marriage) **Charlotte Maria Guest** *(b. 1834); Ivor Bertie Guest (b. 1835);* **Katherine Gwladys Guest** *(b. 1837); Thomas Merthyr Guest (b. 1838); Montague John Guest (b. 1841); Augustus Frederick Guest (b. 1840); Arthur Edward Guest (b. 1841);* **Mary Enid Evelyn Guest** *(b. 1843);* **Constance Rhiannon Guest** *(b. 1844);* **Blanche Vere Guest** *(b. 1847).*

Moved to South Wales on marriage (1833), living next to the Dowlais ironworks run by her husband; taught herself Welsh; published English translation of 12 medieval Welsh tales (1849); produced a lavish 3-volume illustrated edition of the tales which she called The Mabinogion; *developed works schools; took over the running of the Dowlais Iron Company, largest ironworks in the world (1852); became (with second husband) a leading collector of 18th-century china and fans.*

Selected works: The Mabinogion *(published under titles of individual tales from 1838 on, then in collected 3-volume edition in 1849, printed by Rees of Llandovery, published by Longmans of London); (as Lady Charlotte Schreiber)* Fans and Fan Leaves: English *(London: John Murray, 1888);* Fans and Fan Leaves: Foreign *(London: John Murray, 1890);* Playing Cards of Various Ages and Countries *(3 vols. London: John Murray, 1892, 1893, 1895).*

In mid-19th-century Britain it was especially tough for any woman in the overwhelmingly male world of business. Yet on her husband's death in 1852, Lady Charlotte Guest began running the world's largest ironworks. The Dowlais Iron Company, situated above the town of Merthyr Tydfil, the largest and most unhealthy town in Wales, supplied much of the bar iron for railroads as far away as America and Russia. Here was a classic example of the devastating effects of the industrial revolution on both landscape and lives. Within a year of taking charge, Lady Charlotte had a strike on her hands and was forced to negotiate with both her workforce and the other employers. The Masters, as the employers were known, formed an obdurate oligarchy and were unaccustomed to having a woman as a business partner. Why, they must have wondered, was an English aristocrat from a sleepy, rural village in such an unlikely place and position?

Born at Uffington House in Lincolnshire in 1812, Lady Charlotte Bertie was the first child of the elderly 9th earl of Lindsey and his wife Charlotte Susanna (**Lady Lindsey**). She had two younger brothers, one of whom was recognized to be as dull-witted as she was intelligent. Yet, as the eldest son, he inherited the family title and sat in the House of Lords. Lady Charlotte's father died when she was six, and her mother soon remarried. She now gained two half-sisters. Charlotte cast the Reverend Peter Pegus as the classic wicked stepfather. Yet it was he who, unknowingly, set in train one of the great consolations of her life, the keeping of a journal. From the age of nine, when he gave her a diary, until she was 79, Lady Charlotte Guest recorded and reflected on her thoughts in what she called the "Depository of my dreams," filling thousands of pages. Her journal became "my old friend."

Charlotte was an introspective youngster, uninterested in social chit-chat and, although taught the accomplishments thought proper for a young lady, far more interested in tales of Persia or Petra. She described the "great object of my existence" as "improvement in my studies," schooling herself into habits of disciplined application. In addition to acquiring languages such as French, Italian, Latin, and Greek, she taught herself Arabic, Hebrew, and Persian. She revelled in things medieval.

After a brief flirtation with a future prime minister, the young Benjamin Disraeli (whose novel *Sybil* contains an oblique reference to her), she married, aged 21, the wealthy, middle-aged, widowed John Guest. He was the town of Merthyr Tydfil's first member of Parliament (representing the Whig Party) and was an iron manufacturer. Marriage appeared as a providential escape from the stultifying atmosphere of Uffington House and, as ironmasters went, John Guest seemed singularly enlightened. His young wife had never before seen mountains. Now she was to live in Merthyr, a raw, industrial mountainous and potentially mutinous community of 20,000 ironworkers. Lady Lindsey saw this as somewhat alarming, particularly in its social implications. As Lady Charlotte wrote, "in this aristocratic nation the word Trade conveys a taint." She now resolved to make society accept her husband while her children must "never feel that there live any on the earth who do or who dare look down upon them." In 1838, just one year after the young Queen *Victoria came to the throne, John Guest was made a baronet. This was not enough for Lady Charlotte. To aid her husband's acceptance in society, a vast estate was purchased in Dorset called Canford Manor. Lady Charlotte's hopes were realized when, in 1880, her eldest son Ivor was elevated to the Peerage and became Lord Wimborne.

From her initial arrival in Wales, Lady Charlotte wasted no time in immersing herself in her new community; she eagerly learned about her husband's business. On her first day, she toured the furnaces and forges. After dinner, she watched the casting of iron. This set the pattern for almost daily trips to the works. She inverted the usual gendered demarcation of daily life ("He for the public, She for the private") by writing of the works, "I always feel here in my proper sphere." In a telling comment, she wrote: "I am *iron* now—and my life is altered into one of action, not of sentiment." Her journal brims with details of blast furnaces, mines, and rails. She translated and published a French pamphlet on the advantages of using hot air in the manufacture of iron. By the early 1840s, she was declaring that she found it "more congenial to calculate the advantage of half percent commission on a cargo of iron than to go to the finest ball in the world." She accompanied her husband on business trips, discussed matters with leading scientists such as Charles Babbage, worked as her husband's secretary and did bookkeeping. She had her own room in the company's offices in the City of London and became adept at han-

Lady Charlotte Guest

dling aggrieved employees. In a number of capacities therefore, she was well equipped to shoulder responsibility when her husband died, particularly since (even though he was not always happy with this), she had increasingly deputized for him during his last months of illness.

Whatever I undertake, I must reach an eminence in.

—Lady Charlotte Guest

Lady Charlotte also involved herself in social welfare. There already existed an educational system instigated by her husband. Between the 1830s and 1850s, she developed this, giving Dowlais a reputation for progressive approaches. Teachers were properly trained and a ladder of education stretched from infancy into adulthood for boys, girls, men, and women (not until 1870 did England and Wales possess a national system of even elementary schooling). She even occasionally taught in the schools herself. In 1855, new and impressive school buildings were opened, designed by the leading British architect Sir Charles Barry (who also designed the rebuilding of the Houses of Parliament and remodeled the Canford estate). Although, like all women of her time, she could not vote in elections, Lady Charlotte had played an active part in canvassing and promoting her husband's cause during elections. She had also supported the (relatively) radical views he expounded in the newly reformed House of Commons. At the same time, she understood that "one cannot make people good and religious by Act of Parliament. The first step is to make them comfortable and happy."

Though the Guests' record on housing for their workers leaves much to be desired, Lady Charlotte did attempt to provide recreation for the workforce. In this, she was aided by her cousin Henry Layard, famed for his archaeological discoveries at Nineveh. Attempts to provide sport, musical evenings, and workers' outings need, however, to be viewed in the context of threats from Chartism, the movement which sought to give parliamentary democracy to all adult men. Chartism found strong support in Wales, and paternalistic efforts to provide "rational recreation" and education were in part seen as conducive to harmony, valuable antidotes to working people taking affairs into their own hands.

Yet despite her efforts at Dowlais (where there is even a public house named after her), Lady Charlotte is probably best remembered for her translation work. To her love of languages, romance literature, and the medieval was added her new-found devotion to Wales. She began studying Middle Welsh as soon as she came to Dowlais. This task was as significant as it was unusual. It set her apart from most of the English ruling class who had settled in industrial Wales and ignored the Welsh language. Lady Charlotte was not the first to attempt to translate these tales, neither did she work in isolation (collaborating, more than she actually acknowledged, with leading Welsh clerical scholars) but, from the first publication in 1838 to the collected edition 11 years later, it was she who was responsible for the overall production. Her detailed annotated notes were instructive and very well informed. One later Celtic expert has argued that her range of knowledge and breadth of English, Welsh, and "Continental" scholarship made her "one of the most remarkable women of that Victorian age." Dr. **Rachel Bromwich** sees her as probably the first person to make the connection between the three Arthurian Romances which form part of *The Mabinogion* and their European analogues.

Her powers of application were immense. Before translating, it was necessary to do transcriptions. For one tale alone this involved copying 2,288 lines of a medieval manuscript. This painstaking work took her six days. In 1911, an Arthurian scholar took one month to complete the same task. Alfred Tennyson praised Lady Charlotte's translation. It was "the finest English he knew," and he compared it to Malory's *Le Morte d'Arthur*. Part of Tennyson's *The Idylls of the King* (the most popular poetic work of the Victorian period) was based on Lady Charlotte's tale "Geraint the Son of Erbin." Matthew Arnold, like many others, acknowledged the debt which Celtic scholars owed to Lady Charlotte. Her "happy entry into the world of letters" enabled contemporaries to appreciate medieval Welsh literature, and it inspired successors. Yet so influential was her translation that not until over 90 years after her first tale had been published did a new translation appear. *The Mabinogion* remains part of the canon of Celtic literature. It (though no longer Lady Charlotte's version) is reprinted in Britain almost yearly, has been translated into many languages, and the tales have appeared in numerous forms, including a Disney film.

Lady Charlotte's achievement is all the more remarkable when it is recognized that during the period that she was engaged on this work and immersing herself in the ironworks and fortunes of its workforce, she was almost continually pregnant. She had ten children in thirteen years (plus a miscarriage). Her five girls and five boys all survived into adulthood though one died as a young man. Most were born in Merthyr where there was no hospital, and infant mortality rates were among the highest in Britain. Although her journal suggests that childbirth was one more facet of a busy and literally productive life, it can also be suggested that her consciously matter-of-fact entries at such times (written a few days after the event) contain more than a hint of bravado. Perhaps she was trying to convince herself (let alone any possible reader), of the ease with which she took to motherhood, and the ways in which this could be reconciled with her other roles. It is also the case that the complete journals reveal her to have been ill, depressed, and frustrated during the many months she was pregnant.

Lady Charlotte was ambitious for her children though this was largely couched in hopes (well realized) of "good" matches. Her eldest son married Lady **Cornelia Churchill**, eldest daughter of the 7th duke of Marlborough, and the next son married Lady **Theodora Grosvenor**, sister of the 1st duke of Westminster. Yet she did not encourage her daughters to emulate her own achievements or even develop their own, though unlike their mother they were born at the height of Victorian domesticity. One of her many grandchildren did, however, become a militant suffragist who was arrested for breaking windows in support of women's suffrage.

Lady Charlotte's journal reveals her own ambivalence about women's roles and rights. Her class, acquired wealth (and tolerant husbands) permitted her to enjoy a qualified freedom unknown to most Victorian women. Yet even so, there were times when she protested against the legal constraints and ways in which men, unlike women, had "field for action." She acknowledged that John Guest saw women as "rational beings" and on the whole encouraged her, but she was still acutely aware of her disadvantages as a woman. She wrote:

> I have given myself almost a man's education from the age of twelve when I first began to follow my own devices—and since I married I have taken up such pursuits as in this country of business and ironmaking would render me conversant with what occupies the male part of the population. Sometimes I think I have succeeded pretty well—but every now and then I am painfully reminded that, toil as I may, I can never succeed beyond a certain point and by a very large portion of the community my acquire-

ments and judgements must always be looked upon as those of a mere woman.

Yet, despite her personal example of female capability, her misgivings tended to be confined to her journal.

Within three years after Sir John Guest's death, Lady Charlotte was married again, this time to a much younger man. The 28-year-old Charles Schreiber, 14 years younger than Lady Charlotte, was also an employee who was tutoring her eldest son for Cambridge University. Partly because they were aware of how society could view such a *mésalliance,* the couple now began traveling extensively on the Continent. Lady Charlotte left the world of Dowlais behind her (though it remained in family hands) and began a new "career" collecting ceramics. Her collection of 18th-century English china, displayed at the Victoria and Albert Museum in the Schreiber Room, is still reckoned to be among the finest in the world. Lady Charlotte wrote a comprehensive catalogue to accompany the 1,800 or so pieces she bequeathed in memory of Schreiber who died in 1884. The couple had scoured the Continent in their search for china, finding wonderful bargains just before the craze for china collecting truly developed.

Lady Charlotte is also well represented in the British Museum by her vast collections of fans, playing cards, and even board games. She produced five illustrated folio volumes depicting and describing her fans and cards. Her fan collection, like her china, focused on the 18th century. For example, she possessed some rare French Revolutionary fans, depicting scenes such as the fall of the Bastille. In 1891, she received a unique honor, becoming the first woman to receive the Freedom of the Worshipful Fan Makers' Company. At this time only one other woman, the philanthropist Baroness *Angela Burdett-Coutts**, was a "Freewoman" of a City of London Guild.

Lady Charlotte's three folio volumes on European and English playing cards again demonstrate her interest in political history. Her rare collection included packs on events such as the Popish Plot of 1678 to murder King Charles II. The catalogue of her cards (in the British Museum) itemizes 1,066 packs, many of them French, German, and Italian.

Lady Charlotte Guest died in 1895. She had stopped keeping her journal four years earlier due to her deteriorating eyesight. Throughout her life, she had set herself extremely high standards. Despite the strictures on women's lives, she excelled in a number of markedly different pursuits and over a long timespan, remaining active into her old age. Her journal resonates with a determination born of her own undoubted skills and intellect. Its tone is also shaped by the uneasy combination of being both extremely privileged and yet at one and the same time circumscribed as a woman of the Victorian period. All of this made it imperative for her to prove that she could persevere and triumph: "But whatever I undertake, I must reach an eminence in. I cannot endure anything in a second grade."

SOURCES:

Bessborough, Earl of. *The Diaries of Lady Charlotte Guest.* London: John Murray, 1950.

———. *Lady Charlotte Schreiber 1853–1891.* London: John Murray, 1952.

Bromwich, Rachel. "*The Mabinogion* and Lady Charlotte Guest," in *Transactions of the Honourable Society of Cymmrodorion.* 1986, pp. 127–141,

Evans, Leslie Wynne. "Sir John and Lady Charlotte Guest's Educational Scheme at Dowlais in the mid-nineteenth century," in *National Library of Wales Journal.* Vol. ix, no. 3, pp. 265–283.

Guest, Lady Charlotte. *The Mabinogion.* Ruthin: Spread Eagle Publications, Facsimile, 1977.

Guest, Montague, ed. *Lady Charlotte Schreiber's Journal: Confidences of a Collector of Ceramics and Antiques.* London: Bodley Head, 1911.

Havill, Elizabeth. "The Respectful Strike," in *Morgannwg.* Vol. xxiv, 1980, pp. 61–81.

SUGGESTED READING:

Guest, Revel, and Angela V. John. *Lady Charlotte: A Biography of the Nineteenth Century.* London: Weidenfeld and Nicolson, 1989.

COLLECTIONS:

The original journals remain in family hands, but Lady Charlotte's Deed Box is in the National Library of Wales, Aberystwyth, Wales; her china collection is in the Victoria and Albert Museum, London, and fans and playing cards are in Prints and Drawings in the British Museum, London. The Dowlais Iron Company Records are in the Glamorgan Record Office, Cardiff, Wales.

Angela V. John,
Professor of History, University of Greenwich,
Woolwich, London, England

Guest, Irene (1900–1979).

See Bleibtrey, Ethelda for sidebar.

Guggenheim, Mrs. Daniel (1863–1944).

See Guggenheim, Florence Shloss.

Guggenheim, Florence Shloss (1863–1944)

American philanthropist. Name variations: Mrs. Daniel Guggenheim. Born Florence Shloss on September 3, 1863; died on May 13, 1944; married Daniel Guggenheim (1856–1930); sister-in-law of *Irene and

Olga Guggenheim; children: M. Robert Guggenheim (1885–1959); Harry Frank Guggenheim (1890–1971); Gladys Eleanor Guggenheim (1895–1980, who married Roger W. Straus, founder of Farrar, Straus & Giroux; she would serve as president of the Daniel and Florence Guggenheim Foundation)

During World War I, Florence Shloss Guggenheim personally sold $4 million worth of war bonds. In 1924, with her husband, she established the Daniel and Florence Guggenheim Foundation for "the promotion, through charitable and benevolent activities, of the well-being of man throughout the world," an enterprise close to her heart. She became its president on the death of her husband in 1930. In 1940, she opened her mansion, Hempstead House, to war orphans, then deeded the place to the Institute of Aeronautical Sciences. By 1975, the Daniel and Florence Guggenheim Foundation had given over 400 grants to 98 organizations which included hospitals and medical institutes. Florence Guggenheim was also sponsor of the Guggenheim Concerts in New York City and treasurer of the Women's National Republican Club from 1921 to 1938.

SUGGESTED READING:

Davis, John H. *The Guggenheims: (1848–1988) An American Epic.* NY: Shapolsky, 1988.

The New York Times (obituary). May 14, 1944.

Guggenheim, Irene (1868–1954)

American art collector and philanthropist. Name variations: Mrs. Solomon Guggenheim; Irene Rothschild. Born Irene Rothschild in New York City on December 16, 1868; died in New York City on November 25, 1954; daughter of Henry Rothschild (a merchant and broker); married Solomon R. Guggenheim (1861–1949), in 1895; sister-in-law of *Olga H. and *Florence S. Guggenheim; children: Eleanor May Guggenheim (b. 1896, who married Arthur Stuart, earl of Castle Stewart); Gertrude R. Guggenheim (1898–1966); Barbara Josephine Guggenheim (1904, who married John R. Lawson-Johnston, Fred E. Wettach, Jr., and Henry Obre).

Guggenheim, Olga H. (1877–1970)

American philanthropist and organization executive. Name variations: Mrs. Simon Guggenheim. Born Olga H. Hirsh on September 23, 1877; died in 1970; daughter of Barbara (Steiner) Hirsh and Henry Hirsh (a New York realtor and diamond merchant); educated at private schools in America and Europe; married Simon Guggenheim (1867–1941, U.S. senator and *philanthropist), on November 24, 1898; sister-in-law of *Irene and *Florence S. Guggenheim; children: John Simon Guggenheim (1905–1922); George Denver Guggenheim (1907–1939, committed suicide with a hunting rifle).*

Olga Guggenheim was an early member of the board of The Museum of Modern Art and benefactor of the museum collections. With her husband Simon Guggenheim, an erstwhile U.S. senator from Colorado, Olga Guggenheim established the John Simon Guggenheim Memorial Foundation in February 1925, in memory of their deceased son who had suddenly died of pneumonia and mastoiditis at age 17 while at Phillips Exeter Academy in New Hampshire. The purpose of the Foundation was to bestow scholarships "to promote the advancement and diffusion of knowledge and understanding, and the appreciation of beauty by aiding—without distinction on account of race, color, or creed—scholars, scientists, and artists of either sex in the prosecution of their labors." The couple made a preliminary gift of $3 million, later supplemented by an additional gift of $1 million to include Latin-American scholarships.

When Simon died in 1941, the foundation was the residuary legatee of his estate, now worth $28 million. Olga succeeded him as president of the foundation and remained in that position for many years; at the time of her death in 1970, she was president emeritus and also left the bulk of her estate, $40 million, to her foundation.

Through the years, there have been two attempts by Congress to limit the use of the Foundation's monies. An attempt was made during the Nixon years to curb the rights of any foundation to make individual grants. In 1951, during Joseph McCarthy's anti-Communist crusade, the Foundation's existence had also been threatened when some in Congress learned that Aaron Copland, a Guggenheim Fellow, had written for the left-leaning *New Worker* and *New Masses.* During a congressional probe, Harry Allen Moe, in defense of the Foundation, told a Congressional committee:

> I hold fast to what Mr. Justice Jackson of the U.S. Supreme Court wrote: "If there is any fixed star in our constitutional constellation, it is that no official, high or petty, can prescribe what shall be orthodox in politics, nationalism, religion, or other matters of opinion." I believe that if this Foundation . . . should attempt to prescribe "what shall be orthodox in politics, nationalism, religion," natural science, social science, or in any other manifestations of the mind or spirit, it had better not exist.

In 1952, when Olga Guggenheim was honored by the National Institute of Arts and Letters, it was noted at the award ceremonies that she kept an atrocious third-rate tapestry on the wall of the foyer of her lavish Fifth Avenue apartment to "remind her continuously of her mistakes." By 1976, nearly 10,000 scholars, artists, and scientists had benefited from the generosity of the Guggenheims, and the foundation's assets were over $100 million; by 1986, 57 Guggenheim Fellows had received the Nobel Prize.

SOURCES:
Davis, John H. *The Guggenheims: (1848–1988) An American Epic.* NY: Shapolsky, 1988.

Guggenheim, Peggy (1898–1979)

*American art patron and collector. Born Marguerite Guggenheim in 1898 in New York City; died on December 23, 1979, in Venice, Italy; middle child and one of three daughters of Benjamin Guggenheim (partner in family-owned American Smelting and Refining Company) and Florette (Seligman) Guggenheim; niece of *Irene Guggenheim and Solomon R. Guggenheim of the Guggenheim Museum in New York City; educated by private tutors until age 15; graduated from the Jacobi School, New York City, 1915; married Laurence Vail (a writer), in May 1922 (divorced July 1930); married Max Ernst (an artist), in December 1941 (divorced 1946); children: (first marriage) Sindbad Vail (1923–1986); Pegeen Vail (1925–1967, who married Jean Helion and Ralph Rumney).*

Celebrated for amassing one of the world's foremost collections of 20th-century art and for subsidizing artists Jackson Pollock and Robert Motherwell, among others, Peggy Guggenheim was also renowned for her flamboyant and colorful lifestyle. Born into wealth in 1898 in New York City (her father made his fortune in the family-owned American Smelting and Refining Company), she described her "gilt-edged childhood" as lonely and unhappy despite the company of an older and younger sister. "I have no pleasant memories of any kind," she wrote of her early years, "and it seems that it was one long-protracted agony." She was tutored at home until the age of 15, when she was enrolled in the Jacobi School, a private school for Jewish girls on New York's West Side. Each summer, the family traveled to Europe, and Guggenheim later credited her father with initiating her interest in art. Upon his death aboard the ill-fated *Titanic* in 1912, Peggy Guggenheim inherited $450,000. A similar amount left to her by her mother in 1939 made her a wealthy woman, though her fortune was often reported to be much larger than it really was.

After graduating in 1915, Guggenheim set out to liberate herself from what she considered a stifling Jewish bourgeois background. In 1919, after working in her cousin's radical bookshop, she traveled to Paris where she stayed for the next 21 years. There, she met the writer Laurence Vail, who introduced her to the bohemian group of writers and artists that would become her circle of friends. In 1922, she married Vail and had two children, Sindbad and Pegeen. Their troubled relationship ended in divorce in 1930, after which Guggenheim embarked on a long series of tumultuous and mostly unhappy love affairs, including a liaison that gained her a stepdaughter whom she raised with her other children.

By 1937, Guggenheim was living in England and searching for something useful to do. Inspired by her earlier readings of Bernard Berenson's books on Italian Renaissance art and the paintings she had seen on her travels, she decided to open a modern-art gallery. By her own admission, she knew frightfully little about modern art at the time, but with encouragement from Samuel Beckett, her latest paramour, and guidance from the surrealist painter Marcel Duchamp, she opened the Guggenheim-Jeune Gallery in London, on January 24, 1938. Focusing as she did on the avant-garde work of her friends, her exhibition paintings rarely sold, so Guggenheim bought a piece from each show so that the artists, which included the likes of Kandinsky, Klee, and Miro, would not be disappointed. Thus, her collection began.

In March 1939, with an expanded dream of establishing a museum of modern art, Guggenheim enlisted the help of literary and art critic Herbert Read, then editor of *Burlington Magazine* and one of England's leading proponents of modern art. He agreed to serve as director of the museum and also drew up a list of painters whose representative work would cover all the important art movements since 1910. With the onset of the war, Guggenheim put the museum project on hold and, after closing the gallery, went back to Paris where, following Read's list, she began purchasing pictures at the amazing rate of one a day. As the Germans approached Paris, Guggenheim asked the Louvre to help her hide her collection, but the museum did not deem the collection worth saving, so she brought it to the United States (shipped as "household goods"). Now involved in a stormy relationship with artist Max Ernst, whom she married in 1941, Guggenheim set up housekeeping in a mansion by the East River and set out to complete her purchase of pictures by the painters on Read's list. With Ernst and surrealist painter Andre Breton, she also prepared a detailed catalogue of the artists she collected. The document, called *Art of This Century*, became an important source for students of the modern-art movement.

"Art of This Century" was also the name Guggenheim selected for her posh new gallery on New York's West 57th Street, which she opened in October 1942. Designed by Frederick J. Kiesler, of the Columbia School of Architecture, the setting was as sensational as the art treasures housed within. (The Cubist Gallery, for example, had blue canvas walls, with unframed paintings suspended in mid-air on strings. Even the pedestals holding the sculptures were suspended, giving them the appearance of floating mid-air.) In addition to exhibiting her collection, Guggenheim also presented solo shows of Jackson Pollock, Robert Motherwell, Mark Rothko, Hans Hoffmann, and other artists that later be-

Peggy Guggenheim

came part of the influential group known as "The New York School." She was particularly devoted to Pollock who became "the central point" of her gallery. As Pollock's patron, Guggenheim also acquired a sizeable number of his paintings, but later gave many of them away, unaware of the large sums of money the works would bring after his death.

In 1946, after her divorce from Ernst, Guggenheim closed the gallery and moved to Europe once again, where she showed her collection in a special pavilion at the 24th Venice Biennale. The collection was subsequently exhibited in museums in Brussels, Zurich, Amsterdam, Florence and Milan. Guggenheim eventually settled in Venice, purchasing Palazzo Venier dei' Leoni, an 18th-century palace on the Grand Canal, where visitors were invited to view her collection three days a week. *Aline B. Saarinen, in *The Proud Possessors*, called Guggenheim's collection one of the best in Europe. "Nowhere else in Europe is there a similar historic survey of modern art, nor one that exhibits the Americans—like Pollock and Rothko—who are major figures in the international world of art." In later years, Guggenheim felt that the modern-art movement had fallen into decline, and she turned her attention to pre-Columbian art as well as her seven Lhasa terriers. Guggenheim, who was made an honorary citizen of Venice in 1962, was known there as "L'Ultima Dogaress" (The Last Duchess). She died in 1979, leaving her art collection to her adopted city.

Guggenheim chronicled her life in two provocative tell-all autobiographies, *Out of This Century* (1946) and *Confessions of an Art Addict* (1960).

SOURCES:

Jenkins, Alan. *The Rich Rich: The Story of the Big Spenders*. NY: Putnam, 1978.

Moritz, Charles, ed. *Current Biography 1962*. NY: H.W. Wilson, 1962.

———. *Current Biography 1980*. NY: H.W. Wilson, 1980.

Roosevelt, Felicia Warburg. *Doers & Dowagers*. Garden City, NY: Doubleday, 1975.

Saarinen, Aline B. *The Proud Possessors*. NY: Random House, 1958.

Barbara Morgan,
Melrose, Massachusetts

Guggenheim, Mrs. Simon (1877–1970).

See Guggenheim, Olga H.

Guggenheim, Mrs. Solomon.

See Guggenheim, Irene.

Guggenheimer, Mrs. Charles S.
(b. 1882).

See Guggenheimer, Minnie.

Guggenheimer, Minnie (1882–1966)

American music patron and philanthropist. Name variations: Minna Schafer; Minna Guggenheimer; Mrs. Charles S. Guggenheimer. Born Minna Schafer in New York City on October 22, 1882; died on May 23, 1966; daughter of Samuel and Sophie (Schwab) Schafer; educated at private schools in New York City; married Charles S. Guggenheimer, on April 22, 1903 (died 1953); children: son (born 1904, died four months later); Elizabeth (1905–1912); Sophie Guggenheimer Untermeyer; Randolph Guggenheimer (who married Elinor Coleman [Guggenheimer]).

Minna Schafer Guggenheimer, the seventh of eight children, was born into wealth in New York City in 1882. Her father, a stockbroker, was the son of a Bavarian entrepreneur who made his fortune in the gold mines of California. "Minnie" received her education at a series of fashionable private schools, learning piano at an early age and maintaining a love of music throughout her life. She was raised in a house she described as monstrous and cluttered with dust-collecting antiques, but her family also spent time at their summer house in West End, New Jersey.

At the West End house Minnie met Charles S. Guggenheimer, a family friend. She and Charles married in 1903 and settled in with her mother-in-law, **Eliza Katzenberg Guggenheimer**. Her relationship with her in-laws was cool, with both mother-in-law and sister-in-law controlling the young bride's activities. The women made it clear that Minnie's primary purpose was to have children, and limited her to this sphere alone. The monotony of this life was broken only by the afternoon concerts arranged by Eliza Guggenheimer, who was well acquainted with artists and musicians of the day. In this environment Minnie met such notable performers as Rachmaninoff, Prokofieff, and Enrico Caruso.

Guggenheimer faced tragedy early in her marriage when a son born in 1904 died when he was only four months old. A daughter born in 1905 died of a mastoid infection when she was just seven. During this time, Guggenheimer became the patron of the outdoor concerts at the Lewisohn Stadium on the campus of New York's City College, raising the initial $10,000 needed to fund the symphony concerts. On June 23,

1918, Arnold Volpe conducted the first open-air concert with Sir Edward Elgar's "Pomp and Circumstance."

The two-week series had a modest beginning and over the next 50 years more than tripled in size. The first season cost approximately $41,000, with that figure mounting to over $300,000 by the mid-1960s. Guggenheimer's fund-raising efforts covered any deficit experienced by the concert series. She maintained a select list of donors which she carefully guarded, but she was not beyond approaching total strangers and soliciting donations if she thought they looked like they had money to spare.

The Lewisohn Stadium concerts frequently suffered from failure in acoustics, noisy audiences, and the greatest plague of all—uncooperative weather—but on the whole the concerts were brilliant. The series was a showcase for both established and new performers. In 1925, *Marian Anderson made her debut performing an aria from *La Favorita* by Donizetti. Nelson Eddy's first major solo appearance occurred when he sang a solo part from Verdi's *Requiem* and in 1927 George Gershwin performed his piano concerto, *Rhapsody in Blue,* for the first time.

Minnie Guggenheimer generally remained behind the scenes, but eventually began to appear during intermissions to address the audiences. As a result of these off-the-cuff discussions, she became known as the "Mrs. Malaprop of 20th-century America," for her amusing mispronunciations of names and unique sense of humor. Her announcements came to be anticipated with as much enthusiasm as the music; a reporter commented after one of her appearances, "Minnie Guggenheimer was a disappointment at last night's Stadium opening. She made sense. . . . The crowd was perfectly able to follow her comments and felt it just hadn't gotten its usual money's worth."

Guggenheimer's support of musical endeavors did not go unrewarded. She sat on the board of directors of the New York Philharmonic Symphony Orchestra; received the ribbon of the French Legion d'Honneur (1951); the National Arts Club annual award (1959); the Annual Music Award of New York City presented by Mayor Robert F. Wagner (1960); and the annual Gold Medal of the 100 Year Association (1961).

Minnie Guggenheimer had other passions besides music, including mushroom hunting, which she pursued during the late summer and fall with total disregard for the property of others. Her outgoing personality and inimitable style endeared her to audiences and she particularly enjoyed being interviewed on television. She chain-smoked, vowing to give up the habit one week and starting anew the next. Guggenheimer's daughter, **Sophie Guggenheimer Untermeyer**, wrote in her biography about Minnie that she suspected her mother's "compulsive dedication" to the stadium concerts was self-indulgent. She felt her mother did not want to see the concert series succeed without her.

SOURCES:

Brody, Seymour. *Jewish Heroes and Heroines of America.* Lifetime Books, 1996.
Current Biography. NY: H.W. Wilson, 1962.

Judith C. Reveal, freelance writer, Greensboro, Maryland

Guglielma of Milan (d. 1282)

Leader of a heretical Italian sect. Died around 1282 in Milan; never married; no children.

Guglielma was born and raised in Milan, and as a young woman became the center of a new heretical religious movement about 1271. She was a mystic as well as a prophet, and found numerous supporters for her special calling, especially Mayfreda de Pirovano, who was to become her pope in the new church they wanted to create. Guglielma and her followers believed that she was the embodiment of the Holy Spirit, and her supporters held that only through a woman's intervention, and thus through all women, would humanity be saved. Only women held the position of priest in this sect, whose practitioners came to be known as the Guglielmites. Guglielma was accused by Milanese authorities of heresy and other crimes, but she managed to survive over a decade, gaining more followers every year. The circumstances of her death are unclear.

Laura York, Riverside, California

Guglielminetti, Amalia (1881–1941)

Italian author whose erotic poetry and novels created a sensation in the first four decades of the 20th century. Born in Turin, Italy, on April 4, 1881; died in Turin on December 4, 1941; daughter of Pietro Guglielminetti and Felicita (Lavezzato) Guglielminetti; had a brother Ernesto and sisters Emma and Erminia; never married.

Born into a wealthy family in the Northern Italian industrial city of Turin, Amalia Guglielminetti experienced several tragedies in her early years. She lost her beloved father when she was still a child, and in 1909, after years of lingering illness, her sister Emma died. In both instances, Amalia's response was to write verse expressing her feelings. In 1903, she published *Voci di giovinezza* (Voices of Youth), poems that received enthusiastic reviews. Four years later, in 1907, she published another volume of verse entitled *Le vergini folli* (Mad Virgins). In part reflecting her experiences from a girls' school run by Roman Catholic nuns, this book solidified the already substantial literary reputation she enjoyed while still in her early 20s.

A woman who was both aware of and unafraid of displaying her physical attractions, Guglielminetti was tall and slender with a mass of dark hair (the critic G.A. Borgese called her "Sappho with violet hair"). A famous painting of Amalia, by the artist Raviglione, depicts her half-reclining on a divan, wearing a dark form-fitting dress that contrasts with her bare arms and neck; Amalia's face reflects an ambiguous mix of melancholy and assertiveness. Dressed in the latest Parisian fashion, she was a striking figure in Turin's world of elite parties and literary coffeehouses.

Choosing never to marry, Guglielminetti was romantically involved with many men, but her most important love affair took place while she was in her early 20s, with the poet Guido Gozzano. Their relationship evolved from mutual admiration to passion and tumult. Their letters to each other, published in 1951, document not only the emotional intensity of young lovers but also provide details of both writers' daily lives as they intersected with the tensions of European intellectual culture on the eve of World War I. In one letter, Guglielminetti responds with amusement to the prejudices of male writers and critics toward female authors like herself, simply exclaiming: "Oh, how wonderful to be a woman and write verses!" The lovers' correspondence also serves to document Gozzano's apprehensiveness, whose patriarchal stereotypes were directly challenged as he entered into a relationship with a woman who was not only physically beautiful but whose intellectual talents made her his artistic equal, if not indeed his superior.

With the publication of her third volume of verse in 1909, entitled *Le seduzioni* (Seduction), Amalia Guglielminetti continued to enhance her image as "a woman dominated by Eros." Many critics saw her work as the female counterpart to the exhibitionistic eroticism of the notorious playwright Gabriele D'Annunzio. While her erotic experiences are clearly reflected in this volume, the literary historian **Barbara Turoff** has pointed out that other seductive aspects of existence are

Amalia Guglielminetti

exposed here as well, including an exquisite gemstone or a perfectly formed, ripe fruit.

Guglielminetti wrote only two novels, both of them brimming over with irony and sarcasm, but it was the second of these, *La rivincita del maschio* (The Male's Return-Match), that became the center of a public scandal after its publication in 1923. Charges of obscenity and immorality were hurled at the novel's author by a local morality league. The trial, in Turin, became a local event with Amalia's friends and literary colleagues in constant attendance. She felt vindicated when the defendants were acquitted of all charges.

Although Guglielminetti was highly regarded by feminists as a woman who had succeeded in leaving her mark in a largely male domain, she did not regard herself as a feminist. After attending some sessions of one of the first feminist congresses to be held in Italy, she informed her lover Gozzano of having been deeply disappointed by witnessing an "assembly of people without any grace or elegance of spirit . . . Women . . . so unwelcoming, so lacking in fraternal feelings . . . that they awaken in me a dull sense of disdainful aversion." While she found it difficult to warm up to assembled feminists or their abstract agendas, in practice Guglielminetti often urged Italian women to speak out for themselves, praising both ancient and modern women such as *Sappho and *Karin Michaëlis as examples of writers who had revealed female voices that were strong and confidently assertive.

Encouraged by early successes as a poet, Guglielminetti turned her attention to the novel and other literary forms. She quickly mastered the short-story format, publishing prolifically in popular periodicals such as *Il secolo XX* (*The Twentieth Century*). In 1913, she published her first collection of short stories, *I volti dell'amore* (The Faces of Love), followed by four subsequent collections that appeared in print between 1915 and 1924. Attracted to the theater, she wrote a tragedy that was not a success, then turned to creating comedies. Her comedies, particularly one entitled *Nei e cicisbei* (Beauty Marks and Gallants), were both frothy and thought-provoking. Premiering in 1920, the play shows two statues of the 17th century coming to life at a masked ball early in the 20th century. With this device, Guglielminetti points out the many changes brought by the passage of time to relationships between men and women, noting all the while her own preference for a more romantic past that can still give lessons in love to an ostensibly "progressive" modern epoch.

Amalia Guglielminetti was in many ways a private and, as she grew older, solitude-seeking artist. Yet at the same time she was capable of intense relationships, not only with her many lovers but with countless friends as well. Although she never married or became a mother, Guglielminetti both appreciated and understood children, publishing four children's books between 1916 and 1925. She also was drawn to the dissemination of ideas on a mass basis, often lecturing throughout Italy on such topics as "Napoleon and His Women" and "Talismans of Beauty," which provided audiences with an overview of cosmetics that was as amusing as it was historically accurate.

Confident of her literary skills, Guglielminetti became editor of a new literary journal, *Le Seduzioni* (Seduction), in 1926. Making its debut in August, this bimonthly was such a sensation that its first issue sold out in three days. She celebrated her success proclaiming: "To found a literary review is, for a woman, a more momentous event than that of taking a husband." Despite the journal's success—it was able to attract as contributors such literary stars as Luigi Pirandello—Guglielminetti chose to cease its publication after only two years, most likely because she simply grew tired of the tedious routine that is part of the life of any editor.

In the final decade or so of her life, Amalia Guglielminetti was no longer the center of literary attention. Nevertheless, she continued to write and publish. Her last book, *I serpenti di Medusa* (*Medusa's Serpents*), appeared in print in 1934, and she remained active as a respected journalist. Countless Italian readers looked forward to the appearance of her short stories and essays on the *terza pagina* of their newspaper; the third page was customarily reserved for articles by noted intellectuals on topics of general cultural interest. Although Guglielminetti continued to live for her writing, life increasingly became a struggle as she suffered from bouts of depression. She was more and more reclusive, and when she died in December 1941, at age 56, from complications following a fall suffered during an air-raid alarm, many younger Italian intellectuals needed to be reminded how famous she had been at the turn of the century.

Amalia Guglielminetti's reputation was in eclipse for a generation after her death, but by the 1980s it had begun to rebound as a result of scholarly reevaluations of her work. Her poetry and other writings were now seen by some critics as not only being spectacular celebrations of sensuality but as often subtle insights into other facets of the human condition. Guglielminetti's deep awareness of the "tedium of life," and her art of uncovering the precise words for describing humanity's painful and perennial search for love (which she called "the beautiful deception"), has come to be regarded as her single most important contribution to modern Italian literature.

SOURCES:

Amoia, Alba della Fazia. *Twentieth Century Italian Women Writers: The Feminine Experience.* Carbondale, IL: Southern Illinois University Press, 1996.

Asciamprener, Spartaco, ed. *Lettere d'amore di Guido Gozzano e Amalia Guglielminetti.* Milan: Garzanti, 1951.

Curti, Daniela. "Le Paure di Guido: Il Carteggio Guglielminetti-Gozzano," in *Memoria: Rivista di Storia delle Donne.* Vol. 8, 1983, pp. 114–120.

De Toma, Aldo. "Lo sconosciuto unico incontro d'amore di Guido Gozzano e Amalia Guglielminetti," in *Lettere Italiane.* Vol. 38, no. 4. October–December, 1986, pp. 527–541.

Gastaldi, Mario. *Amalia Guglielminetti.* 2nd rev. ed. Milan: Gastoldi, [1957].

Goldberg, Isaac, ed. *Italian Lyric Poetry: An Anthology.* Girard, KS: Haldeman-Julius Company, 1925.

Guglielminetti, Marziano. *Amalia: La rivincita della femmina.* Genova: Costa & Nolan, 1987.

Pickering-Iazzi, Robin Wynette. *Politics of the Visible: Writing Women, Culture, and Fascism.* Minneapolis, MN: University of Minnesota Press, 1997.

——. *Unspeakable Women: Selected Short Stories Written by Italian Women during Fascism.* NY: Feminist Press at the City University of New York, 1993.

Piromalli, Antonio. "Le non godute di Guido Gozzano," in *Il Lettore di Provincia.* Vol. 16, no. 61–62. June–September 1985, pp. 14–21.

Russell, Rinalda, ed. *The Feminist Encyclopedia of Italian Literature.* Westport, CT: Greenwood Press, 1997.

Russo, Luigi. *I narratori.* Edited by Giulio Ferroni. Palermo: Sellerio editore, 1987.

Shepard Phelps, Ruth. *Italian Silhouettes.* NY: Alfred A. Knopf, 1924.

Spaziani, Maria Luisa. *Donne in poesia: Interviste immaginarie.* Venice: Marsilio, 1992.

Turoff, Barbara. "Amalia Guglielminetti (1885–1941)," in Rinalda Russell, ed., *Italian Women Writers: A Bio-Bibliographical Sourcebook.* Westport, CT: Greenwood Press, 1994, pp. 163–170.

Wood, Sharon. *Italian Women's Writing, 1860–1994.* London and Atlantic Highlands, NJ: The Athlone Press, 1995.

John Haag,
Associate Professor of History,
University of Georgia, Athens, Georgia

Guicciardini, Isabella (fl. 16th c.)

Florentine townswoman. Flourished early 16th century in Florence, Italy.

Isabella Guicciardini represents the life of wealthy townswomen in the last years of the Middle Ages. Her husband, a local governor, was usually away from their home in Florence, Italy, on business; to Isabella was left the responsibility of maintaining the family's large estates, and managing their agricultural business. Allowed to live practically independent of male guardianship, Isabella revealed her business acumen and her administrative abilities. She supervised every function of her extensive household, acted as an accountant, planned the seasonal harvest and marketing of the produce, and arranged loans from creditors when needed, as well as providing her absent husband with any supplies he required.

Laura York,
Riverside, California

Guiccioli, Teresa (c. 1801–1873).

See Blessington, Marguerite for sidebar.

Guidi, Rachele (1891–1979)

Italian wife of Benito Mussolini. Name variations: Rachele Mussolini. Born Rachele Guidi in Romagnol, Italy, in 1891; died in October 1979; daughter of peasants; attended school to second grade; married Benito Mussolini (1883–1945, Fascist dictator and prime minister of Italy), around 1916; children: *Edda Ciano (1910–1995); Vittorio Mussolini (b. 1916); Bruno Mussolini (b. 1918); Romano Mussolini (b. 1927, who with his first wife had daughters Rachele Mussolini and Alessandra Mussolini, an Italian politician); Anna Maria Mussolini (b. 1929).

"I was already a revolutionary when I was six," Rachele Guidi told **Kay Withers**. "I wanted to go to school and my parents didn't want to send me. Finally my mother let me go, and I finished the second grade. But then my father died and I had to go to work. I earned a plate of spaghetti a day minding two sheep."

Guidi was tiny and tough, with a wealth of energy, and only 19 when she began living with the promising Socialist writer Benito Mussolini in 1910. She was also seven years his junior. She doted on the writer, having looked up to him ever since she had attended his mother's elementary school at age seven.

Still, Rachele was not interested in marriage. Their first child Edda was born out of wedlock in 1910. During World War I, while serving in the Italian army, a grenade thrower exploded during a practice session, wounding Mussolini with 40 fragments. A shaken Benito felt it was time to marry. Besides, Rachele was expecting Vittorio. Though Rachele was unconvinced, she reluctantly agreed, and they were married by proxy. But she never used her husband's name, preferring to call herself Rachele Guidi. She also had to share him with journalist *Margherita Sarfatti for a number of years. (He would later be machine-gunned to death with another lover, *Clara Petacci.)

During the early 1920s, while the family lived in the north on a farm, Benito lived in Rome as prime minister and would visit them three or four times a year. He moved his wife and family to Rome in 1927, when family life became a litmus test for fascist convictions. By then, there was still some affection between Rachele and Benito but also a great distance. "Rachele was made out to be the ideal fascist woman," writes Denis Mack Smith, "a hardworking, dutiful stay-at-home."

Throughout the turbulent years, though indifferent to ideology, Rachele was loyal to her husband, in power and out of power, though she never deigned to interfere in matters of state. During his entire 20-year political tenure, she did not set foot in his office. Instead, she stayed home and raised the children. "But I was sorry that he went into the government," she told Withers in 1975,

Rachele Guidi (far left) with her family, 1931.

"He had a newspaper, he was the owner. You can't be happy in politics, never. Because one day things go well, another day they go badly."

After Benito's death in Como at the hands of partisans, Rachele spent three days in jail, and her children Anna and Romano were taken from her and handed over to the partisans. Following the war, Rachele lived out her years in solitude and silence at their Villa Carpena, near the Adriatic city of Forli. There, she could view the tall pines she had planted in the early years, one for each of her five children. There, she could enter the library, filled with photographs and books by and about her husband. Her husband, Il Duce, was buried 12 miles away.

SOURCES:
Smith, Denis Mack. *Mussolini.* NY: Alfred A. Knopf, 1982.
Withers, Kay. "Donna Rachele Mussolini," in *Miami Herald* [Florida]. April 27, 1975.

Guidosalvi, Sancia (fl. early 12th c.)

Spanish sculptor. Name variation: Sancha. Flourished in the early 12th century in Spain.

Sancia Guidosalvi was a Spanish sculptor of great talent. The only known work of hers to survive is a large silver cross with figures carved in relief. Her origins are unclear; she was probably a nun, although she may have been a professional artist commissioned to create the cross for an altar. Sancia seems to have been a pious and dedicated worker, while at the same time a woman proud of her accomplishments. She carved her own personal statement onto a cross, spelling out her name as the creator of the piece and attesting that she did it to further the glory of God; this is rather unusual for a piece of medieval art, for most artists of the time chose to remain anonymous.

Laura York,
Riverside, California

Guilbert, Yvette (1865–1944)

Noted French cabaret singer who developed into a collector, scholar, and performer of historic French folk songs. Nicknames: Queen of Paris; The Lean Witch. Pronunciation: Eve-ETT Geel-BEAR. Born

Emma Laure Guilbert on January 29, 1865, in Paris, France; died on February 3, 1944, at Aix-en-Provence, of heart failure; daughter of Hippolyte Guilbert (a shopkeeper) and Albine (Lubrez) Guilbert (a seamstress); attended private school in Paris, 1873–77; married Max Schiller (an impresario), on June 22, 1897; children: none.

Family bankrupted when her mother's hat business failed, and father deserted the family (1878); began employment as model and saleswoman (1881); death of her father (1882); became protégé of circus impresario Charles Zidler (1885); made theatrical debut in Paris (1887); began career in concert cafés (1889); album of pictures of her published by Toulouse-Lautrec; gave her first performance in London (1894); went on American tour (1895–96); met Max Schiller (1896); toured Europe (1897–99); had surgery for kidney ailment (1899); began concert career, and published first novel (1901); published Struggles and Victories, *and founded school for working class children (1910); was a wartime resident in U.S. (1915–18); opened "School of the Theater" in New York (1919); returned to France (1922); demanded Legion of Honor from Aristide Briand (1926); began newspaper column (1930); awarded Legion of Honor (1932); fled Paris for Aix-en-Provence in face of German invasion (1940).*

Yvette Guilbert, who survived an impoverished childhood to become France's most famous cabaret singer in the 1890s, delivered her melodies in a half-sung, half-spoken fashion that led critics to describe her as a *diseuse* (reciter, or teller of songs) rather than as a pure singer. Guilbert's fame arose from her prominent role in the *café concert* (or cabaret) world of late 19th-century Montmartre. There in cafes, where the audience enjoyed popular singers while they were able to drink alcohol, she became one of the leading performers of the *chanson* or traditional French song. Like other cabaret performers of the time, she presented songs that reflected the dark side of Parisian life with themes like poverty, prostitution, and crime. Such songs often had a sharp anti-bourgeois and anti-establishment tone. Her most important venues in this phase of her artistic career were the famous cafes Le Chat Noir and the Moulin Rouge. There, she drew especially on the witty songs of Léon Xanrof. Famous for the dramatic costume that had distinguished her performances in the 1890s—especially her long black gloves—she came to despise such popular artifices in favor of her role as a practitioner of high culture.

At age 35, she redirected her formidable energies, and this self-educated woman turned into a scholarly caretaker and performer of France's historic folk songs. Her collection of original texts grew to the proportions of a scholarly treasure trove, containing more than 80,000 songs. In later life, her performances often took the form of song recitals in conjunction with scholarly lectures given by authorities on historic French literature. Her energetic life also included friendship with such intellectual luminaries as Sigmund Freud and George Bernard Shaw, while she plunged into new roles as a writer, stage and screen actress, and unofficial ambassador of French culture. Nonetheless, Yvette Guilbert is still largely remembered in the words of Harold Segel as "the great chanteuse of turn-of-the-century Paris."

The future cabaret star was born in Paris on January 29, 1865, the daughter of an ambitious but feckless merchant, Hippolyte Guilbert, and **Albine Lubrez Guilbert**, a former farm girl from Normandy. Shortly before their daughter's birth, Albine and Hippolyte had moved to the French capital to realize Hippolyte's hopes for a brilliant career in business; instead, he experienced a series of devastating failures. Despite a period of prosperity for the family in the mid-1870s when Albine was a successful hat designer, Albine and Yvette spent the following years in poverty. After Hippolyte Guilbert deserted the family in 1878, mother and daughter sometimes found themselves in outright destitution.

In 1881, Yvette began work as a model and shopwoman. In a story derived from her memoirs—and which her biographers **Bettina Knapp** and **Myra Chipman** have accepted at face value—the turning point in her life came in 1885 in a chance meeting with Charles Zidler, the great circus impresario. Guilbert claimed that Zidler offered her a chance to become a circus equestrian, and even though she rejected the offer because her mother thought the work too dangerous, Zidler remained her friend and patron. It seems more likely that he continued his tie with Yvette because she offered him sexual favors. Her romanticized account of the years after 1885 also included a similar story of a chance meeting and allegedly platonic relationship with Edmond Stoullig, a noted theater critic. She gave credit to Stoullig, along with Zidler, for encouraging her to train for the stage and to begin a career as an actress in 1887.

Demonstrating a significant musical talent that may have come from her ne'er-do-well father, Guilbert was attracted to the thriving world of the *café concert*. These cabarets ranged from those aimed at artists and intellectuals to others that attracted a working-class audience, and they offered a variety of inexpensive entertainment to crowds that ate and drank while watching the performances. Guilbert was strongly tempted by the greater earnings available to her as a cabaret performer compared to what she could earn on the legitimate stage.

At first, her performances were unimpressive, even disastrous. A tall, thin woman with a restrained manner, she did not meet the expectations audiences had for a buxom and shapely female entertainer who would present them with ribald ditties. In a set of early performances in the provincial city of Lyons in late 1889, she was shouted off the stage night after night by audiences that mocked her flat-chested figure.

No nation has, nor will have, another Yvette Guilbert, for the simple reason that the art of Yvette Guilbert is her own creation.

—José Granier

Undiscouraged, this tough product of a poor Parisian childhood turned herself into a unique and compelling performer. She accentuated her physical features by whitening her face, dying her hair a striking shade of red, and wearing shoulder-length black gloves. The gloves became her signature garment and featured prominently in the cartoon images that the painter Henry Toulouse-Lautrec produced of her after her fame was established. Guilbert searched Paris for appropriate songs, finding raucous, pathetic, and dramatic tunes that mesmerized audiences. The superior diction she had learned as a stage actress set her off from other cabaret performers as she presented the half-spoken lyrics of such songs with unforgettable effect. One that had particular appeal was "My Head," in which she played the role of a pimp sentenced to die for murder. She ended the song by suddenly tipping her head to drop her hat which had been weighted with lead to fall quickly. This action jolted audiences with the simulated sound of a head dropping after the guillotine had done its work.

Yvette Guilbert became one of the leading stage personalities in Paris during the 1890s, commanding huge sums of money for her memorable appearances. In 1891, an American reporter in Paris caught the flavor of her sudden success. "A year ago Yvette Guilbert was practically unknown," he wrote, but now "the whole gay capital is at her feet." She is "indisputably the most talked of and, by all odds, the most popular woman in Paris." By the middle years of the decade, she had become an international star as well. Her tour of the United States was followed by triumphal visits to the capitals of Europe.

As the rage of Paris, the fashionable cabaret singer soon found herself with a range of acquaintances stretching from the prince of Wales (the future Edward VII) to the French artist Toulouse-Lautrec. She came to know the heir to the British throne when she agreed to sing at a private party in 1894, and he turned out to be the guest of honor. She was a favorite subject for the drawings of Toulouse-Lautrec. The bitter, talented, and physically misshapen noble at first observed the singer shyly from a distance when he made his initial sketch of her in 1892. He was soon following Guilbert avidly from theater to theater, and she became the subject of an entire book of sketches that he published in 1894. His images of her were not flattering. The singer was so shocked to find that Toulouse-Lautrec was presenting her in a distorted and distasteful manner that she considered legal action against him. In time, however, the two became warm friends.

In 1896, her life took a new turn when she met Max Schiller during another tour of the United States. A member of a Jewish family from Rumania that had fled persecution to settle in Berlin, he had been educated as a scientist but subsequently took up a career as a theatrical producer. It is uncertain exactly how they became acquainted, but the relationship quickly took the form of a passionate romance. They were married in Paris in June 1897. Max took on the role of her manager, and they began a life together that lasted for almost half a century.

A new turn of a different sort came two years later when Guilbert nearly died as a result of surgery. In her efforts to present a striking figure on stage, she had for years appeared in a tightly laced corset that produced a 19-inch waistline. The price she paid for this was the development of a severe kidney ailment. Although the operation to remove a kidney was life-threatening, the singer survived and gradually regained her health. Her lean figure, however, was gone forever. And her brush with death turned her artistic interests in a new direction.

Although without much formal education, Guilbert had plunged into an enthusiastic study of French language and cultural history as far back as the mid-1880s when she trained for a career in the legitimate theater. From the time she took up the role of cabaret singer, she be-

𝒴vette
𝒢uilbert

came seriously interested in historic antecedents of French popular music. Her appearances after her operation came to include examples of French historic music dating back as far as the Middle Ages. In time, such music emerged as the most prominent component in her repertoire. In another departure from her earlier career, she now began a career as a writer, producing a number of novels and several sets of autobiographical works starting with *Struggles and Victories,* which she wrote in collaboration with Harold Simpson in 1910.

The outbreak of war in August 1914 brought turmoil to all citizens of France, but Yvette Guilbert found herself in a particularly painful situation. The imminent declaration of war found Yvette and Max in Berlin, and they had to endure a crowded express train filled with other French citizens in order to escape to Belgium. Moreover, she was married to a German, and she had developed a longstanding identification with Germany due to her frequent appearances there. Thus, the great singer's loyalty soon came into question. Complimentary remarks she had made publicly about Germany added to the cloud of suspicion. Public distrust of the famous singer took the form of rumors that her house, located near the city's fortifications, had been transformed into a base for German agents.

In response, Yvette and Max left in 1915 for an extended stay in the United States. Already committed to a tour there, they now saw the neutral country across the Atlantic as a refuge. As Guilbert wrote to her manager, "America to me is like unto the divine grace of entrance into the Promised Land." She failed to get the French government to help her case by awarding her some kind of official title, but she transformed herself, nonetheless, into a public spokeswoman for the French cause.

Her reception was often more than enthusiastic. Critics praised the unique nature of her performance, one noting that "it is not acting, it is not singing, it is not recitation; yet it combines the finest beauties of all three." Guilbert presented the historic songs of France, ranging from religious ballads to the coarse songs of the French people in past centuries. She accompanied her performances with pleas to Americans to support France in the war, not merely with money but with recruits for the French armed forces.

For years, Yvette Guilbert had enlivened her foreign tours with quotable remarks about the superiority of French culture and the relative inferiority of English and American taste. Even in wartime circumstances, she retained her characteristic candor. Her inability to restrain herself when criticizing American culture was combined with her increasingly vocal enthusiasm for the cause of women's suffrage. Thus, remarks about American materialism and proclamations about the moral superiority of women over men tempered the favorable reception she was getting in the States. Her remarks about why a foreign artist would come to America were particularly sharp. It was "for the sake of making money. Honestly, for what other reason can you Ameri-

cans suppose that an artist would come?" Nonetheless, she was still able to draw audiences even when her performances included such stodgy elements as formal lectures on the history of the French song, recitations of French poetry, and discussions of stage technique. Her appearances also took place on college and university campuses, beginning with an invitation to perform at Bryn Mawr in 1916. The woman who had once shocked Parisian cabaret audiences with pornographic songs had now become a respected authority on France's musical history.

Following a brief trip to Paris in 1919, Yvette and Max returned to the United States. After long efforts and little success, she had managed to find a wealthy American sponsor for her longstanding dream of a theater school. It opened in the Hotel Majestic. Though she tapped specialists, such as leading academic and newspaper critics, she made herself the main instructor. Her biographers attribute her passion for this project in part to "her early educational deprivations" and "the instinctive deference the self-educated always pay to organizational trappings." In the end, however, the school could not survive financially. In 1922, Guilbert returned reluctantly to France.

Parisian crowds again flocked to see her, even though some critics carped that her recitation of medieval religious songs now seemed tedious. She succeeded in establishing a French theater school like the one she had offered to American students. But, once again, financial problems led to the project's collapse. Her sense of impending mortality grew, as old friends and associates—the author Pierre Loti, the actresses *Sarah Bernhardt and *Eleonora Duse—died within months of one another in the early 1920s.

Guilbert revived her spirits—and her shaky finances—by returning to her longstanding style of bawdy performances in 1924. Wearing her old costume—including the long black gloves she had come to despise—she delighted music-hall audiences with the songs that had made her famous. Nonetheless, she continued her presentations of French historical songs to smaller, but equally devoted, audiences. In a daring move given the prevailing postwar bitterness between her country and Germany, she even appeared in Berlin in 1925, ending her performance with a plea for Franco-German friendship. Soon she was touring the German and Austrian cities where she had appeared in prewar days.

In 1927, she completed her most ambitious attempt to tell her own story. *La Chanson de ma vie* (soon published in English as *The Song of My Life*) was a more extensive book than *Struggles and Victories*. Moreover, this dramatic account of her life from impoverished childhood to professional glory was purely the product of her own pen. The famed singer continued her literary efforts with the publication of another book that tapped her life's experiences. Entitled *The Astonished Passer-by*, it appeared in 1929. The book stressed her foreign travels, but it now showed, in the words of her biographers, "the voice . . . of an embittered woman." Guilbert devoted much of her writing in *Passer-by* to a sharp condemnation of America and the Americans, taking special aim at the American financiers who had long frustrated her ambitions to set up a school for the theater. A year later, her literary career moved in still another direction; she began a column of personal opinion and observation, with the title of *Guilbertinages*, that appeared at irregular intervals for years in the newspaper *Paris Soir*. "Whatever caught her imagination," according to Knapp and Chipman, "her quick pen flung on paper."

Contact with the world of European high culture came through a series of remarkable friendships. She had known George Bernard Shaw from the days before World War I, and she maintained their personal tie by visiting him in London during her tours. In the 1930s, she initiated an extensive correspondence with Sigmund Freud.

In 1932, Yvette Guilbert was awarded the Legion of Honor, the decoration that signified distinguished accomplishment in the interests of France. Ironically, only a few years earlier in 1926, she had scandalized France's elite by baiting the renowned political leader Aristide Briand for the government's failure to give her such a mark of distinction. Accosting Briand at a luncheon for the French and foreign press, she had vocally demanded the award.

Her tours of Europe continued throughout the 1930s, although the spread of Nazism made it difficult, then impossible for Guilbert and her Jewish husband to travel to Germany and Austria. Burdened by arthritis, the singer found it increasingly arduous to perform. At times, it appeared she no longer had the drawing power of earlier years, and empty seats became common during both her appearances abroad and in France. Nonetheless, she had a nostalgic triumph in 1937 when a committee led by France's minister of education, Jean Zay, organized a mammoth jubilee celebration at Paris' Salle Pleyel to mark her 50 years on the stage.

When World War II brought the German invasion of France in the spring of 1940, Yvette and Max fled southward and set up housekeeping in Aix-en-Province. Here, in the part of France not under direct German occupation, the country's Vichy government conducted its own program of persecuting Jews, and the singer and her husband led a precarious existence for the next several years. An official investigation established that Guilbert was not Jewish, but her husband's life remained in danger. The strain brought on a near fatal heart attack for Guilbert in December 1942, but she kept busy writing a new volume of memoirs. Her life ended on February 3, 1944, when her heart failed following an attack of bronchial pneumonia. Her husband survived the war and brought Guilbert's body back to Paris where she was reburied in the Père Lachaise Cemetery.

SOURCES:

Frey, Julia. *Toulouse-Lautrec: A Life*. NY: Viking, 1994.

Guilbert, Yvette. *The Song of My Life*. Translated by Béatrice de Holthoir. London: G.G. Harrap, 1929.

Knapp, Bettina, and Myra Chipman. *That Was Yvette: The Biography of Yvette Guilbert, The Great Diseuse*. NY: Holt, Rinehart and Winston, 1964.

Segel, Harold B. *Turn-of-the-Century Cabaret: Paris, Barcelona, Berlin, Munich, Vienna, Cracrow, Moscow, St. Petersburg, Zurich*. NY: Columbia University Press, 1987.

Sorel, Nancy Caldwell. "Yvette Guilbert and Henri de Toulouse-Lautrec," in *Atlantic Monthly*. November 1986, p. 125.

SUGGESTED READING:

Geffroy, Gustave. *Yvette Guilbert*. Translated by Barbara Sessions. Illustrated by Henri de Toulouse-Lautrec. NY: Walker, 1968.

Oberthur, Mariel. *Cafes and Cabarets of Montmartre*. Salt Lake City, UT: Gibbs M. Smith, 1984.

Rearick, Charles. *Pleasures of the Belle Epoque: Entertainment and Festivity in Turn-of-the-Century France*. New Haven, CT: Yale University Press, 1985.

Neil M. Heyman,
Professor of History, San Diego State University,
San Diego, California

Guillelma de Rosers (fl. 1240–1260)

Provençal troubadour. Name variations: Guillelma of Rougiers. Flourished between 1240 and 1260 in southern France.

Guillelma was a Provençal troubadour who maintained a long-term love relationship with a lawyer-troubadour from Genoa. Her identity is unclear, but she was probably from the town of Rougiers on the Cote d'Azur. She apparently met her lover, Lanfrancs Cigala, when Lanfrancs visited Provence. Later, Guillelma spent a good deal of time in Genoa, causing one troubadour to write a poem honoring her and asking her to return to Provence. Whether she was married or not is not known; presumably she would not have been, at least at the time of her stay in Genoa with Lanfrancs. The couple exchanged at least one tenson which still survives, in which they debate the loyalty a lover owes his lady.

Laura York,
Riverside, California

Guillemete, Mary (d. 1262).

See Guzman, Mayor de.

Guillemete du Luys (fl. 1479)

French physician. Flourished in 1479 in Paris.

Very few facts are known about Guillemete du Luys' life. She was a surgeon of Paris who gained widespread admiration and respect for her skills. She was not, however, university trained, for the masters of medicine at the University of Paris did not allow women to study or take degrees there. Guillemete managed to succeed despite the restrictions placed on women healers, and eventually her fame won her the position of royal surgeon in the household of King Louis XI. She also owned a bathhouse featuring medicinal baths which was frequented by many members of the French court.

Laura York,
Riverside, California

Guillet, Pernette du (c. 1520–1545).

See Labe, Louise for sidebar.

Guimard, Marie Madeleine

(1743–1816)

French dancer. Born in Paris, France, on October 10, 1743; died in Paris on May 4, 1816; married Jean Etienne Despréaux (a choreographer and poet), in August 1789; children: (with Benjamin de Laborde) a daughter, also named Marie-Madeleine Guimard (1763–1779).

Star of the Paris Opéra for 25 years and known as much for her love affairs as her dancing, Marie Madeleine Guimard was the illegitimate daughter of an inspector of a Paris cloth factory. When she was 15, she secured a place in the corps de ballet of the Comédie-Française. She first appeared at the Paris Opéra in May 1762, as Terpsichore in *Les Fêtes Grecque et Romaines*, replacing her friend *Marie Allard.* Guimard became première danseuse the follow-

ing year and went on to perform in many ballets, including *Le Premier Navigateur, Ninette à la Cour, La Fête de Mirza, Le Déserteur,* and *Les Caprices de Galatée,* perhaps her best work. Despite her less than perfect technique and her slim stature, for which she was often criticized, Guimard was a superb actress, a skill that served her particularly well as she grew older. In 1778, during her 16th year with the ballet, her performance as the simple farm girl Nicette in *La Chercheuse d'Esprit* was praised by the critics as a masterpiece of coy innocence and naiveté.

Of Guimard's numerous paramours, the most significant was a ten-year liaison with Benjamin de Laborde, first gentleman-in-waiting to Louis XV. (Guimard had a daughter with Laborde, also named Marie-Madeleine, who died at age 16.) In 1772, Laborde oversaw the building of a lavish house on the Chaussée d'Antin that boasted a winter garden and a private theater, the Temple of Terpsichore, where Guimard staged many performances and supposedly held wild parties. In defiance of the archbishop of Paris but to the delight of Paris society, she presented some of the most scandalous plays of the day, including *Les Fêtes d'Adam* and Colle's *Partie de chasse de Henri IV.* So many of the best actors from the Opéra and the Comédie-Française began turning up in Guimard's productions that the minister finally issued an order forbidding the actors to appear anywhere except in their own theater without special permission from the king. Guimard also had a country estate in Pantin, with yet another attached theater.

When Laborde's money began to dwindle, Guimard also became the mistress of the Prince de Soubise and, for at least five years, managed to keep both relationships humming along without incident. However, even the treasury of the prince could not withstand her expenditures, and Guimard moved on to a liaison with the bishop of Orléans, who provided yet a new store of revenue from the dioceses. For all her extravagance, however, Guimard was also known for her kind heart and contributed generously to the poor. When the House of Soubise came upon hard times, she voluntarily returned a pension the prince had given her.

In 1786, Guimard evidently ran out of rich lovers and was compelled to sell the Temple of Terpsichore. It was disposed of by lottery for the sum of 300,000 francs, although the winner sold the property almost immediately for nearly double the sum. Guimard's career at the Opéra, which survived a bout of smallpox in 1783 and a subsequent knee injury, endured until 1789,

Marie
Madeleine
Guimard,
visiting the
poor.

when at age 46 she retired to marry Jean Etienne Despréaux (1748–1829), a choreographer and poet who was 15 years her junior. During the long years of the Revolution, the couple lived in a small apartment at the top of Montmartre. Although their dancers' pension allowed few luxuries, Guimard appeared truly content for the first time in her life. After eight years, they moved back to Paris, where the dancer died on May 4, 1816. At the time of her death, the public had forgotten her, though her grieving husband noted that along with Marie Guimard "the divine century" of ballet had also died.

SOURCES:

Migel, Parmenia. *The Ballerinas*. NY: Macmillan, 1972.

Barbara Morgan,
Melrose, Massachusetts

Guinan, Texas (1884–1933)

American star of vaudeville and silent films until the Roaring '20s, when Prohibition cast her as reigning queen of New York City nightclubs, where her outsized personality and heart took in everyone within reach. Name variations: Mary Louise Cecelia Guinan; Mayme Guinan; Marie Guinan. Pronunciation: GUY-nan. Born Mary Louise Cecelia Guinan on January 12, 1884, in Waco, Texas; died on November 5, 1933, after intestinal surgery, in Vancouver, British Columbia; daughter of Michael Guinan and Bridget "Bessie" Duffy Guinan; married John J. Moynahan, on December 2, 1904; no children.

Appeared on the Broadway stage and in vaudeville (1909–17, 1929–33); appeared in at least 37 films (1917–33); hosted several New York City nightclubs (1923–29).

Filmography: Fuel of Life *(1917);* The Gun Woman *(1918);* The Heart of Texas *(1919);* Little Miss Deputy *(1919);* South of Santa Fe *(1919);* Girl of the Rancho *(1920);* The Lady of the Law *(1920);* Outwitted *(1920);* The Code of the West *(1921);* Queen of the Night Clubs *(1929);* Broadway Thru a Keyhole *(1933).*

"Hello, Suckers!" The excitement was palpable. It was one o'clock in the morning, and the restless crowd had been waiting for hours. Now,

Texas Guinan, the loud, brassy, maternal (and always sober) queen of the night clubs, took her seat on the stage; the real party was about to start.

Texas Guinan's life in New York City—breakfast at midnight, up until dawn in the Prohibition-era night spots—could hardly have been imagined by her forebears. Both her grandfathers had left Ireland during the potato famine of the late 1840s and settled on farms in Ontario, Canada. Her father Michael Guinan seemed to have shared his daughter's penchant for adventure: he left home at age 20, crossing the border into the United States at Detroit on May 2, 1877. By 1881, he was living in Georgetown, Colorado, where he met and married **Bessie Duffy** (**Guinan**), who had also come to the U.S. from Canada. The couple set out for Waco, Texas, a booming trade town with electricity, phone service, 44 churches, and almost as many saloons (though it was the 1885 invention of Dr. Pepper, the soft drink, that brought Waco its lasting fame). In this climate, Mike's hard work paid off: he soon was co-owner of a wholesale grocery.

My big kick in life is crowds of humanity. When I can get them with me, rooting for me, I am drunk with the joy of it.

—**Texas Guinan**

In 1882, Mike and Bessie's first child, William, was born, followed two years later by Mary Louise Cecelia, then called Mayme, later called Texas. Bessie had five more children, but only two (Pearl, b. 1887, and Tommy, b. 1891) survived. Mayme was the liveliest of the lot. She adored her mother, sharing her strong will and devotion to the Roman Catholic Church, and would do anything for her attention. Writes biographer **Louise Berliner**: "She was constantly being ousted as new characters joined the Guinan cast. Poor Mayme would do anything to regain the spotlight. . . . [She] had a wild laughing streak in her, a prankster side, and Bessie didn't seem to mind." But Guinan's hometown found her hard to take. Waco, home to Texas Christian University, was a Baptist stronghold. Even though Catholics were a small minority in the South, the town took pride in the Convent School of Sacred Heart. It is probably the only school Mayme Guinan ever attended, although she repeatedly told stories of her higher education. She was popular but full of imagination; parents, if not their daughters, were wary.

From their staid perspective, parents had every reason to worry. Once, after reading one too many girls' adventure books, Guinan decided to reenact a scene wherein a brave young wife escaped her villainous husband by taking their baby and crossing river rapids in a leaking boat. Borrowing a neighbor's baby and another neighbor's leaky, wooden tub, she set out in the swollen spring waters of the Brazos river, which ran close to her own backyard. Guinan might have needed a real rescue had she not been caught by a suspicious Bessie and the baby's mother. Guinan got a whipping, but, instead of remorse, she was furious at them for spoiling her scene and refused to speak to either woman for days.

In 1900, when Guinan was 16, the family moved back to Colorado. Guinan later claimed that while her family went to Denver, she headed East, to attend the prestigious Hollins Institute, a finishing school in Virginia. In reality, she spent four years in Denver, where she blossomed into a beautiful young woman with a sense of style and many suitors. The *Denver Post* took note on its social pages: Mayme Guinan, "fortified by a beauty of the fresh brunette type, a strong personality, charm and a decidedly friendly nature, stormed the social fort and gained admission."

She was nearing the age when most young women settled down with a husband, and, indeed, it may have appeared to be the best adventure around. At any rate, evidence suggests that she truly loved the man she chose: John J. "Moy" Moynahan, a Denver journalist she had known for several years. Married in December 1904, they moved to Chicago, where Moy took a job as a cartoonist for a newspaper, and Marie, as Mayme had decided to call herself, put all of her housekeeping skills to work. Later, she would maintain that she had studied voice at the Chicago Conservatory, after winning a scholarship sponsored by Marshall Field, the Chicago department store magnate. "Exaggerate the world," Guinan wrote in 1931. "Dress up your lives with imagination. . . . [D]on't lose that purple mantle of illusion." In reality, the Moynahans had moved to Cleveland in 1906, the year Marie claimed she attended the Conservatory.

Keeping house in Cleveland was even more tedious than keeping house in Chicago, and Guinan was apparently getting restless. The Moynahans' separation was relatively amicable. They remained friends, as well as husband and wife, for the rest of her life. (He was to remarry several years after her death.) In 1907, age 22, Guinan headed for New York City. "Better a square foot of New York than all the rest of the world in a lump—better a lamppost on Broadway than the brightest star in the sky," she was to say. "Texas" had come home: to the bright lights of Broadway, the throngs on the sidewalks, the congestion of double-decker buses, hansom cabs, and trolleys.

Struggling actresses have never had it easy, and the early days of show business were particularly difficult. Competition was keen, and, once cast, actors and actresses were expected to spend from three to ten weeks in unpaid rehearsals, with no guarantee of their show's success. Despite these daunting obstacles, Guinan arrived on Broadway at one of its finest hours. There were 41 legitimate theaters, more than anywhere else in the world, and owners were scrambling month after month to top each other with bigger and more lavish shows. The most extravagant of them all, the Ziegfeld Follies, was born that year.

One of Guinan's favorite tales concerned her emergence in New York, though no one knows how much of it is embellished, or simply fiction. She claimed to have met the composer Reginald De Koven enroute who had offered her a job on Broadway. Upon her arrival at the New York train station, she hailed a cab to his house

and found him in the middle of a dinner party, which was made up of artists from the Metropolitan Opera. She pulled up a chair, enjoyed the dinner, and, after a brief consultation with her host, was told to report to his operetta, *The Snowman*, the following morning.

Guinan found a room in Greenwich Village for $2 a week, indulged in bright, flashy clothes, fake jewelry, and frequent escorts, and lived on rye bread and milk. But the life of *The Snowman*, which opened on Broadway as *The Girls of Holland*, was brief. She then turned to vaudeville, where W.C. Fields, *Mae West, Charlie Chaplin, and Fred Astaire were also getting their show-business starts. The medium allowed entertainers to develop their own style, and Guinan was becoming a spirited soprano and promising actress. She was handsome, though plump, and intent on attracting notice.

Guinan was a hard worker, much like her Irish immigrant parents. Less than two years after her arrival in New York, before her 25th birthday, that hard work began to pay off in tangible ways. A prominent producer of the day, John P. Slocum, cast her as the lead in *The Gay Musician*, with a four-year, $500-a-week contract. After two years, the two became partners. Guinan replaced her fake jewels with the real thing and bought a seven-room apartment in her beloved, bohemian Greenwich Village. She would soon move her parents and younger brother to New York.

Slocum treated her like a star, showered her with gifts, and spoiled her. "Don't let anybody get away with the impression that you're not the greatest thing in show business," he told her. "Talk big, think big—be big. Remember nobody is as important as you—keep thinking that way and you'll be important." But the *Los Angeles Times* of November 24, 1909, notes: "Miss Texas Guinan is in the budding prima donna stage. Her whimsical little egotisms are calling loudly for a strong stage manager to put an end to them. A pretty and vivacious girl, she loves the spotlight too much." She loved the spotlight, and she hated that review, so much so that months later, at a luncheon in Los Angeles, she complained about it to the handsome man seated next to her. At dinner that night, he confessed to being Julian Johnson, *L.A. Times* drama critic and author of the review. It was the beginning of a solid, eight-year relationship; Johnson was a kind, cultured man who taught Guinan much about literature, art, and managing her finances.

Though she spent more time in Los Angeles, New York was always home. Her career contin-

ued to flourish there: she had starring roles on Broadway every season and changed roles almost as often as she changed costumes. "Tex knew she was not the great operatic star she had set out to be, nor was she a great dramatic actress," writes Berliner. "However, she knew how to entertain, how to make people laugh. Her critics declared her a good singer and clever actress and noted her enthusiasm."

All the qualities that made Guinan a good entertainer made her an asset to the country in 1917 when the United States entered World War I. Box-office receipts fell drastically, since much of the money spent on theater tickets went into Liberty Bonds. The "stage-door Johnnies" who had habitually haunted the theaters were either working overtime in factories or enlisting in the armed forces. By December 1917, the government had ordered a Broadway blackout. Entertainers threw themselves into benefits, fostering patriotism around the country with songs such as "Over There" and "I'm in the Army Now." Texas Guinan was an ideal antidote for the European conflict.

Despite the war, the pace of popular culture had been quickening for several years. It was the beginning of the Jazz Age; Americans were dancing to a faster beat. The film industry, based in Hollywood, was attracting more interest, and in 1917, shortly after the U.S. joined the war, Guinan made her first silent film, *The Fuel of Life*. Her second, *The Gun Woman*, the following year, began a five-year journey that would make Guinan a true pioneer: she created a new role for women: a self-reliant heroine, a gunslinger who, as Berliner writes, "had feelings like a woman, but shot like a man. . . . [A] bad woman with a good heart."

By 1922, Texas Guinan was 38. Prohibition, as the 18th Amendment was called, had been in effect since January 16, 1920. Prohibiting the manufacture and sale of all beer, wine, and liquor, the law had reduced only the quality, not the quantity, and had contributed to the giddy tenor of the times. People were frequenting speakeasies, clandestine night clubs that were made more mysterious and inviting by secret passwords and peepholes. New York had more than 5,000 speaks: almost every basement in the theater district had one. In the early days of Prohibition, drinking was the main event, but as the years went on, with no repeal of the law, the quality of entertainment became more important.

No one knows where Texas Guinan first took the stage, probably at Gypsyland, a club on

West 45th Street, but she had no act other than her own persona. She laughed, told silly stories and bawdy jokes, and called out to patrons, many of whom were friends, introducing them to each other and indulging in matchmaking. Wrote journalist Colgate Baker: "It was self-expression, a thing she did unconsciously by force of breeding, training, environment and heritage." Notes Berliner: "Hostessing allowed Tex to be a friendly, talkative arranger of others' destinies; a meddler, a nosy (and noisy) 'old' lady; and someone who liked to see others enjoy themselves . . . someone who knew how to read audiences and give them what they wanted."

Entertaining all night at top speed proved to be difficult, but it so suited Guinan that she made it work, using young dancers in scanty costumes, celebrity guests of honor, and other tricks to get the audience involved. But she was the center of the show, and soon became an owner, rather than an employee, of her succession of clubs. One of the first was the El Fey, also on 45th Street, opened by a rumrunner named Larry Fay who was looking to polish his image. The club was relatively elegant, more nightclub than speakeasy, and Guinan perfected her act there. But all of the clubs were illegal, of course, and after ten months, the El Fey was padlocked. Somewhere else, another would open: the Texas Guinan Club, the Del Fey, the 300 Club, Club Intime, and the Salon Royale. This became a familiar ritual.

Guinan would leave work at dawn, return to her apartment at 17 West Eighth Street, walk her dog, and go to bed. Even her home could be said to resemble a club: dimly lit, it was furnished with exotic tapestries from the Far East and filled with photos of herself and other celebrities. It was also filled with an odd collection of bottles, hotel towels and china. One thing her home lacked was people. Her family had lived with her only briefly, and, though she had a series of mostly younger escorts during her 30s and 40s, the relationships were not serious. So she slept most of the day, rising at 11 PM for breakfast in bed and paperwork. She was back on stage by midnight, smoking and drinking coffee but never liquor. By all accounts, she never had a drop of liquor in her life.

But the federal agents were becoming increasingly tough on New York's clubs. Guinan's nightspot had endured many raids, some dramatic and some not, and she made occasional trips to the police station. After one widespread raid in June 1928, she was charged with being a public nuisance. Although the long, well-publicized trial ended with a widely celebrated verdict of not guilty, her legal troubles—much as she made light of them—marked the end of her reign as queen of the clubs. Organized crime had become increasingly active in the clubs, and although Guinan had long looked the other way at mob involvement, she did not approve. Turning her attentions elsewhere, she opened a club in Valley Stream, Long Island, made the first of her three "talkies," and began to take her troupe on tours around the country and in Europe.

Then she opened a club in Chicago, called the Green Mill, where she spent much of the next four years. She was also a major attraction at the 1933 World's Fair. Though she missed New York City, the climate was still not right for her return. There was a somber mood after the stock-market crash of 1929. There was also the potential for legal troubles and the unfriendly gangsters. Instead, she toured the Northwest in the fall of 1933. Despite severe abdominal pain, she played four shows in one day at the Beacon Theater in Vancouver, British Columbia, and did not stop until the third show of the following day. She was forced to enter a hospital, where abdominal surgery revealed an advanced state of peritonitis. Guinan never recovered from the anesthetic and died on November 5, 1933, two months shy of her 50th birthday.

At last she was back in New York. More than 12,000 mourners walked past her casket at Campbell's Funeral Home on Broadway at 66th. Wrote Heywood Broun in the New York *World Telegram*: "It would be a fearful error in taste if by any stipulation Tex were barred from the knowledge that the police had to fight back the thousands." One month after Texas Guinan died, Prohibition was repealed, and her "suckers" were free to drink in the daylight. Several years earlier, Guinan had chosen her own epitaph from an Oscar Wilde poem, "The Harlot House":

And down the long and silent street
The dawn with silver sandeled feet,
crept like a frightened girl.

SOURCES:
Berliner, Louise. *Texas Guinan: Queen of the Nightclubs.* Austin, TX: University of Texas Press, 1993.

James, Edward T., ed. *Notable American Women 1607-1950.* Cambridge, MA: The Belknap Press of Harvard University Press, 1971.

Elizabeth L. Bland,
reporter, *Time* magazine

Guinevere (d. 470 or 542)

Queen of Britain and wife of King Arthur. Name variations: Ganor, Ganora or Ganore; Ganeura, Ginevra,

Genievre, Guenever, Guanhumara, Guanhumar, Guenevere, Guenhumare, Guenièvre, Gwenhwyfar (modern: Jennifer). Pronunciation of Guinevere in Modern English is, roughly, "Gwineveer." Born either as a member of a noble Roman family in post-Roman Britain, or as a Pictish princess during the period of the Saxon invasions in the 400s; died in either 470 or 542; married King Arthur, or Arthur, war leader of the British, and according to some traditions had from one to three sons, sometimes referred to as Lohot and/or Amhar or Amr; many other traditions leave her childless.

Became Arthur's archivist, administered his lands during his absence, and may have assumed the role of high priestess; died not long after Arthur's death in battle either in 470 or 542 CE, after having either retired to an abbey or after having returned to her people in Scotland; she may have been buried either in Glastonbury, England, or at Meigle, Scotland.

The legendary Queen Guinevere is a familiar figure throughout the modern world: young Guinevere, reportedly the fairest maiden of the land, married King Arthur, hero of the fabled Knights of the Round Table. Sir Lancelot became the champion of the queen, they fell in love, and because of their adultery the Round Table was riven with faction, dissent, and war. Arthur, his house divided, fell in battle on the fatal field of Camlann and with him, the realm of Britain.

This storyline has descended to the modern reader through the pen of Sir Thomas Malory who published *Le Morte d'Arthur* in England in 1485. The splendid Victorian romanticist, Alfred Tennyson, adopted these themes and immortalized them further in his 19th-century work, *The Idylls of the King*. Thereafter, 20th-century film and literature embellished the ever-growing corpus of Arthurian lore, virtually transmitting them throughout the world.

Most legends contain a kernel of truth, as does the legend of Guinevere. However, the pursuit of the truth behind Arthur's queen is particularly vexing and even controversial, often not unlike following the proverbial will-o'-the-wisp. There really was a Guinevere: to find her, one must search in the period of Dark Ages Britain. Far from being a medieval queen, Guinevere is more appropriately positioned in history as one of the last of the great figures of the ancient world. She was born in the 5th century, after the Romans—the frontiers of their empire increasingly beset by a myriad of foes—had abandoned the province of Britain and sailed for home. By the time of her birth, Britain had faced invasions

for over a hundred years by the Scots from Ireland, by the Picts from the Highlands, and by the Saxons, Angles, and Jutes from the Continent.

The search for Guinevere must first inevitably involve locating in history her larger-than-life husband and king, Arthur. Unfortunately, the historical Guinevere had no biographer, and she is only mentioned in documents and oral tradition when she directly affected either Arthur or his realm, and even here she has had scant mention. Arthur himself is exceedingly hard to trace and is perennially the subject of scholarly, but acrimonious, debates.

Much of the trouble lies in the exceptionally meager documentation of the Dark Ages when very few records were kept, and still fewer survived. Those that did surmount the ravages of time are, for the most part, translations—some crude indeed—or copies of copies, which through the centuries suffered many human errors when transcribed. In the words of archaeologist Leslie Alcock: "Thus, we may have a twelfth century copy of a tenth century compilation which includes annals written down in the fifth century; or a thirteenth century copy of a poem composed orally in the sixth but not written down before the ninth century." Other manuscripts passed through appreciative but careless hands, such as the mysterious Arthurian romance lost in a gambling debt by King Richard the Lionheart of England when on crusade in the Holy Land.

Throughout the ages, Arthur and Queen Guinevere have had many powerful admirers, including King Edward III of England (who flirted with the idea of establishing a Knights of the Round Table) and King Henry VII (who created a remarkable if wholly fictional Round Table tapestry which has hung in the town of Winchester, England, since the late 15th or early 16th centuries). Few took the quest for the historical Arthur seriously until the early 20th century.

By 1993, however, several schools of thought emerged, each school championed by exacting scholars. One of the first was proposed by Leslie Alcock who conducted the famous archaeological digs at Cadbury hill fort in Somerset, England, a location which is arguably a candidate for the legendary Camelot:

> In our examination of the most reliable Arthurian documents we have discovered acceptable evidence that Arthur was a renowned British soldier, more probably a great commander than a king. His battles were fought principally in the first part of the sixth century AD or perhaps around the

turn of the fifth and sixth centuries. It is difficult to overthrow the traditional view that his military activities extended very widely over Britain, perhaps from the southern uplands of Scotland down to Somerset or Dorset. And since no cogent case can be made for dismissing as fable Arthur's connection with the battle of Badon, we should see his major enemy, the one against whom he won his most signal victory, as the Anglo-Saxon invaders. This, then, provides the focal point for any description of the historical background to Arthur, or any discussion of the Arthurian situation.

Historian Geoffrey Ashe has placed Arthur firmly in the 5th century and contends that he was none other than the documented figure Riothamus, which in the ancient British language was "Rigotamos," a title meaning "king-most," or "supreme king." In Ashe's words:

> In the High King called Riothamus we have, at last, a documented person as the starting point of the legend. He is the only such person on record who does anything Arthurian. Or, to put it more precisely, he is the only one to whom any large part of the story can be related.

Ashe extracts three references regarding the Roman Emperor Leo I, who ruled at Constantinople from 457 to 474, from Geoffrey of Monmouth's 12th-century work, *The History of the Kings of Britain*, and thereby achieves a chronological "fix" for the historical Arthur. Based on this and other clues, Ashe places the royal accession of Arthur-Riothamus in 454 CE and has postulated that his death probably occurred, after several years of victorious battles against the Saxons in Britain, in 470 while campaigning against the Saxons on the Continent. Ashe asserts that instead of being buried in "Avalon" in Glastonbury, England, Arthur was probably put to rest in "Avallon" in Burgundy, which is in modern France. Ashe suggests: "Arthur's legend began as a memory of a *Restitutor*, of civilization endangered and beset, and of Britons headed by their King staging a brave, temporarily successful renewal."

Author **Norma Lorre Goodrich** views Arthur and Guinevere as personages from the north of Britain. Arthur, son of a noble Roman or Roman of senatorial rank who claimed descent from Constantine (possibly the emperor), and son of a noble British mother, may have been born at the Dark Ages hill fort which is located at the site Caerlaverock Castle in southwestern Scotland, near Carlisle. Goodrich speculates that the Arthurian base of operations was probably between the Roman walls of Hadrian and Antonine, a Celtic area which included Stir-

ling in the northeast to Dumbarton in the northwest to Carlisle and the Lake District in the southwest, then along Hadrian's Wall to Berwick in the southeast. Indeed, Stirling is the most probable place for Camelot and the birthplace of Guinevere. Goodrich asserts that Arthur, a contemporary and equal to King Clovis I of the Franks who carved out territory later known as France, could have launched raids on Ireland and the Continent after halting the Anglo-Saxon invasions from this northern base. Indeed, this historical High King may be "one of the greatest military thinkers of all time."

> *W*hen Arthur learned of their coming, he handed over the task of defending Britain to his nephew Mordred and to his Queen, Guinevere. He himself set off with his army for Southampton, and embarked there with a following wind.
>
> —**Geoffrey of Monmouth**

But what of the wife of this historical though elusive king? Geoffrey of Monmouth, who finished *The History of the Kings of Britain* in 1136, claimed to have translated an ancient source from the British language directly into Latin. Whatever truth lies in this allegation, thus far, Geoffrey's account represents the earliest known written mention of Guinevere:

> Finally, when [Arthur] had restored the whole country to its earlier dignity, he himself married a woman called Guinevere. She was descended from a noble Roman family and had been brought up in the household of Duke Cador. She was the most beautiful woman in the entire island.

At their joint coronation, Guinevere sported "her own regalia," and "four white doves." Thereafter, she took charge of the administration of Britain along with Arthur's nephew, "Mordred," when the king went on campaign on the Continent. According to Geoffrey, while adventuring against a legion of foes who otherwise would have invaded Britain, Arthur was betrayed by Mordred who "had placed the crown upon his own head." Moreover, "this treacherous tyrant was living adulterously and out of wedlock with Queen Guinevere, who had broken the vows of her earlier marriage." Mordred had arranged an alliance with the pagan Saxon leader Chelric as well as with the Scots, Picts, and Irish against his uncle and the Britons.

Returning with his troops, Arthur fought a bloody battle on the seashore and drove Mordred's host inland. Meanwhile, Guinevere "fled from York to the City of the Legions and there, in the church of Julius the Martyr, she took her vows among the nuns, promising to lead a chaste life." During the final battle in 542 CE at the River Camblam (often referred to as "Camlann"), Mordred was killed and his forces overthrown, while Arthur "was mortally wounded and was carried off to the Isle of Avalon."

Within a generation, Geoffrey's mixture of history and fictional literature had inspired a host of British, French, and even German writers who drew on and embellished the growing Arthurian corpus. Chrétien de Troyes, who dedicated the prose work *Lancelot* to Countess *Marie de Champagne* in 1177, was particularly damaging to the reputation of Guinevere by elaborating on the theme of adultery with the renowned warrior-knight, Lancelot. This theme was elevated to the pinnacle of courtly love by the pen of Sir Thomas Malory in *La Morte d'Arthur* and subsequently was handed down through the word of Alfred Tennyson, who, writing from the position of Victorian England, condemned the queen as a fallen woman.

Yet, as Norma Lorre Goodrich has proposed, there may have been more slander than truth in the allegations. Geoffrey of Monmouth made no mention of Lancelot and Guinevere as lovers (and, indeed, the queen may not have been a willing participant in the supposed affair with Mordred). Certainly, the French had a stake in representing a British queen in a less than favorable light. Chrétien de Troyes, in embellishing the theme of adultery, may have only been following the bidding and pleasure of his patron, Countess Marie de Champagne. In the words of Goodrich: "Lancelot was certainly Guinevere's love. It is far from certain that he ever became her lover."

Goodrich, who believes Guinevere was actually a Pictish noble, has pointed to traditions quite acceptable to the ancient Picts as well as to Roman society which were socially abhorrent by the period of the Middle Ages, when the Arthurian literature began to flower. Medieval chroniclers often assumed the worst, sometimes took meanings out of context, and all too occasionally translated words incorrectly. Geoffrey Ashe, who believes Guinevere was of Romanized Celtic extraction, says much the same with regard to Arthur's queen.

In any case, Guinevere was obviously a prize sought by various contenders, such as King Urien of Rheged who abducted her on at least one occa-sion. Guinevere came with the splendid dowry, the "Round Table," a legend which blossomed soon after Geoffrey of Monmouth's work became fashionable. Medieval writers explained the Table was round so that no knight would have precedence over the other, or said that the wizard Merlin designed the Table to emulate the universe. Whatever the intent, legend ascribes that Merlin created the Table for Uther Pendragon, Arthur's father, and upon his death the Table was transferred to Guinevere's father, who is sometimes referred to as Duke Cador or King Lodegreaunce. From there, the Round Table passed to Arthur through his marriage to Guinevere.

Increasingly, however, scholars have come to view the Round Table not as a cumbersome wooden construction purporting to seat over 150 knights, but as a stone rotunda or even circle wherein Arthur's warriors, and perhaps the notables of Britain, held session. Goodrich, as a proponent of the "Northern" school of thought, sees Guinevere's dowry, the Round Table, in more general terms: "Guinevere was heir to that one prime section of real estate that could sink or crown King Arthur and, if acquired, immortalize both him and Merlin." This dowry was the modern Scottish district of Stirlingshire, which was called the "Round Table" because it was "the most strategic property in Britain."

This property, according to Pictish (and even Celtic) laws of inheritance, would have made Guinevere powerful in her own right, with lands and warriors of her own. Indeed, Goodrich views Guinevere as a noble "warrior" in the footsteps of *Boudica, the 1st-century British queen of the Iceni tribe, and points to accounts which suggest Guinevere occasionally led expeditions when disputes involved her properties. Further, Guinevere may have been a Pictish high priestess along with the enchanting Lady of the Lake, and both figures may have been intimately connected with the Isle of Man (set in the "Lake" or Irish Sea). Arthur may have sought betrothal to Guinevere because, in this capacity, she could have countered the influence of his enemies, the Saxons, and their own high priestess called **Camille**.

Goodrich adds additional dimension to Arthur's wife by gleaning records which suggest Guinevere was the archivist of the realm: these archives were probably destroyed by Arthur's enemies after the fatal battle of Camlann. Both of the Dark Ages chroniclers, Gildas and Nennius, admitted that older British works known as the *Northern Annals* were lost before they came to write their own histories.

Thus, Guinevere resides in the realm of historical and archaeological speculation even though nearly all scholars have come to accept her existence. Likewise, her unsurpassed beauty remains unchallenged even though posterity has no exact physical description. Monks, who claimed to have uncovered the grave site of Arthur and Guinevere at Glastonbury in the west country of Britain in the 12th century, reportedly discovered among the smaller bones believed to be those of the queen a larger skeleton of impressive size, believed to have been Arthur, which was holding a lock of golden hair. If Goodrich's theory is correct concerning Guinevere's Pictish origins, however, the queen's hair would probably have been dark.

Available records also are controversial regarding the question of children. Many sources, possibly inspired by political malice, have insisted Guinevere was barren. Some have said she gave birth to a son with Arthur called Lohot and possibly one named Amhar or Amr, while the possibility of a third son cannot be ruled out.

Her death, whether in legend or in fact, was certainly one of high drama. Malory and Tennyson recounted the final episodes of Guinevere's life as ones of slander, as the queen's "treasonous" acts with Lancelot were uncovered. Lancelot successfully championed Guinevere's honor in repeated trials-by-combat, but eventually was forced to rescue her from burning at the stake, after which he carried her away to his castle. Thereafter, the Knights of the Round Table chose sides between their king and the most renowned warrior of their brotherhood.

Civil war ensued. Arthur's nephew, Mordred, then staked his claim for the throne, allying himself with a coalition of Arthur's enemies. As Guinevere was conducted out of harm's way to the Abbey of Amesbury, King Arthur faced his final challenge and rode with the remainder of his loyal knights to fall in battle and to live in legend. Guinevere survived Arthur by three years, and became the abbess of Amesbury before her passing. If there is truth to the claim the monks made in the 12th century, Guinevere lies buried with Arthur in Glastonbury.

Goodrich contends that Guinevere had another fate. After Camlann, the queen was either taken prisoner or was escorted to the fortress at Barry Hill in Scotland, and later was buried nearby at Meigle where an ancient stone, called the Guinevere Monument, still stands. Although locals say the stone marks the grave of Arthur's queen and insist that this knowledge has been handed down through the centuries, the monument is still controversial among Arthurian scholars. Goodrich notes that before the bold, equestrian engraving of Arthur stands:

> A slim but little angel . . . Guinevere's wings show clearly in the picture. They strain to form a halo around her face. . . . Thereabouts popular memory treasures her still as King Arthur's queen and theirs. To them she is forever his Guardian Angel, and their Stone Flower.

The once and future queen.

SOURCES:

Alcock, Leslie. *Arthur's Britain: History and Archaeology, AD 367–634*. London: Penguin Press, 1971.

Ashe, Geoffrey (in association with Debrett's Peerage). *The Discovery of King Arthur*. Garden City, NY: Anchor Press, 1985.

Geoffrey of Monmouth. *The History of the Kings of Britain*. London: Penguin Books, 1966.

Goodrich, Norma Lorre. *Guinevere*. NY: HarperCollins, 1991.

———. *King Arthur*. NY: Harper & Row, 1986.

Malory, Sir Thomas. *Le Morte d'Arthur*. NY: Bramhall House, 1962.

Tennyson, Alfred, Lord. *Idylls of the King*. Edited by J.M. Gray. Penguin Books, 1983.

Troyes, Chrétien de. *Arthurian Romances*. Translated by D.D.R. Owen. London: J.M. Dent, 1987.

David L. Bullock, Ph.D.,
author of *Allenby's War: the Palestine-Arabian Campaigns, 1916–1918* (London: the Blandford Press, 1988).

Guiney, Louise Imogen (1861–1920)

American poet, known as the "Laureate of the Lost," who wrote over 30 books. Name variations: often signed poetry L.I.G. Born on January 7, 1861, in Roxbury, Massachusetts; died in Chipping Camden, England, on November 2, 1920; daughter of General Patrick Robert Guiney (a Union army general) and Jenny Guiney; never married; no children.

A scholar when mankind had no use for women scholars, Louise Imogen Guiney was brilliant, inquisitive, and had a keen wit. "Her tastes were severely classical," wrote her biographer Henry Fairbanks, "while her spirit was vibrantly romantic." As a talented classicist, Guiney would have been comfortable teaching at an ivy-covered hall. Instead, she spent her days, like many women in the 19th century, trying to find a way to make a living.

Guiney's predilection for scholarship was not always thus; initially, her need for independence took precedence. She wrote of her first school experience:

> I did not like the looks of the teacher; I disliked the room. I looked the children over,

and made up my mind I did not like them either, and that if I ever got out of the place no mortal power should get me back again. I remember that the teacher tried to make me take part in the exercises, but I was mute; the sphinx herself was not more obstinately dumb than I was.

I made no demonstration at home, but waited until next morning when preparations were made to send me up to school again. Then I quietly informed them that I was not going anymore. . . . I did not cry: I simply stood still and refused to budge. I only yielded to superior force, for my mother took my head and the nurse my heels, and I was ignominiously lugged to school. But I did not give in. As fast as they put me in the room, I dashed out; and finally I was tied in my chair. That was the way I went to school every day, until convinced that I was conquered.

At age 11, Guiney entered boarding school at the Convent of the Sacred Heart in Providence, Rhode Island, where she would remain for seven years, leaving in 1879. While there, her beloved father died. General Patrick Guiney had been a commanding officer of the 9th Massachusetts Volunteers. Wounded in the Civil War at the Battle of the Wilderness, he wore an eyepatch over his eyeless socket. In 1877, at age 42, "while crossing Franklin Square Park on his way home," wrote Fairbanks, "the veteran felt a spurt of blood to his lips. Instinctively, with the composure that marked his conduct under fire at Gaines' Mill and the Wilderness (thirty engagements in all), he removed his hat, knelt down beside a tree and crossed himself. Within seconds, he was dead, still propped against the tree in this attitude of reverence." Louise would one day write an essay about the incident, titled "On Dying Considered as a Dramatic Consideration." At his death, the general left Louise and her mother **Jenny Guiney** "more glory than dollars." Louise turned to writing to help support the household which consisted of her mother, her Aunt Betty, and sundry dogs and cats. A lover of nature, Guiney could be seen striding briskly beside the Charles River with her beloved St. Bernards. Throughout her life, she was never without a pet, mostly dogs.

In 1884, with the successful publication of her poetry collection *Songs at the Start,* Guiney became a recognized poet at age 23. She had articles published in *The Atlantic,* was a frequent contributor to the juvenile magazine *Wide Awake,* and became a popular member of the literati; one of her many admirers was Oliver Wendell Holmes. She was also a salon attendee at the home of *Louise Chandler Moulton, a lifelong friend of *Alice Brown, and a prodi-

gious correspondent who had many epistolary friendships. Her letters to Herbert E. Clarke, Clement Shorter, Reverend William H. van Allen, and Charles Knowles Bolton (librarian of the Boston Athenaeum) all contain thoughts on religion, literature, public and daily life, and the movement to restore John Keats to his rightful place in the literary pantheon. Nine hundred of her letters to her good friend Fred Holland Day reside in the Library of Congress.

In May 1889, Guiney traveled to England with her mother for an extended stay. Residing mostly in London, she also journeyed to Ireland, made friends with the Sigerson sisters, *Dora and **Hester,** and wrote a short biography of Irish patriot Robert Emmet (1904), before returning to Auburndale in 1891. Two years later, she published another collection of poetry, *A Roadside Harp.* Guiney's scholarly pursuits led her to little known heroes. Count Henri de La Rochejaquelin, leader of France's provincial rebellion of 1793–95, could be found in the pages of her *Monsieur Henry* (1892); she also wrote of Thomas William Parsons, translator and first American publisher of Dante's *Divine Comedy.*

"We are poor but honest, and have been growing poorer and no honester," she wrote a friend. Since she could not profit by her erudition, she was encouraged by friends to seek the vacant postmaster position at Auburndale in 1893. To Guiney's alarm, her application to President Grover Cleveland caused a stir throughout the nation. Wisecracks abounded in the national dailies about the woman of letters becoming a woman of letters. Wrote Henry Sherman Wyer in the *Transcript:*

> What's this I read of thee, Louise . . .
> That thou a poet in thy prime
> A princess in the realm of rhyme,
> Art fettered to old Father Time,
> His last Postmistress!
>
> Is't possible those dainty lays
> That all the world delights to praise
> No more enable thee to raise
> The needful shilling?
>
> Our times, indeed, are out of joint,
> When one whom critics all anoint
> Must needs ask Grover to appoint
> Her Queen of Letters.

In answer to an inquiry of Charles E.L. Wingate, a columnist for *The Critic,* Guiney wrote:

> It is no eccentricity or ambition (!) or restlessness that makes me willing to accept (should it be given me) an office flung at my door. I must arise and hew my way. Like all

*ℒouise
ℐmogen
𝒢uiney*

rational folk, I had much rather loaf. Post-mistressing, luckily, is a thing I can do; that is, until the fatal day when the Public shall command me to hand through the grating sixteen five-cent stamps, eighty-seven fours, twenty twos, and nine ones, and make change for them out of a ten-dollar bill. When that hour strikes, pray for me.

In January 1894, Guiney was appointed to fill the vacancy. For the next three and a half years, she lived behind the grate, 11 hours a day. "My bread-winning began in 1894, and my poetry ended," she wrote. "The Muse, poor lass, is scared off utterly." Though she did not write a line of poetry in those years, Guiney managed to publish a few scholarly books. "Quick to champion slighted worth," wrote Fairbanks, she wrote of those who had been shunted aside historically. *A Little English Gallery* (1894) contained studies of ✥▶ **Lady Danvers**, Henry Vaughan, George Farquhar, Topham Beauclerk, and Bennet Langton; she also wrote of Irish poet James Clarence Mangan. *Patrins,* a compilation of her essays, received a large printing and went into a second edition, while her preface to Prosper Mérimée's *Carmen* was much lauded.

But there were those in the town of Auburndale who were extremely unhappy with the ap-

✥▶

See sidebar on the following page

❦▸ **Danvers, Lady Magdalene** (1561–1627)

English patron of the arts. Name variations: Magdalene Danvers; Magdalene Herbert. Born in 1561; died in 1627; buried at Chelsey church on July 1, 1627; married Richard Herbert (died); married Sir John Danvers of Wilts (1588–1655); children: (first marriage) Lord Edward Herbert of Cherbury (1583–1648, a philosopher and historian); George Herbert (1593–1633, an orator).

Lady Magdalene Danvers was born in 1561. The mother of George Herbert and close friend of John Donne, Lady Danvers was a generous patron of letters. On her death, she was buried at Chelsey church; John Donne preached her funeral sermon.

pointment of an Irish Catholic as postmaster. When pressure groups tried to have her expelled, friends and admirers throughout the United States came to her side. Wrote Arlo Bates, a professor at the Massachusetts Institute of Technology (MIT): "A lady of highest character, of rich and unusual gifts, of perfect official rectitude,—the daughter of a brave and patriotic officer in the Union army,—is being hounded out of her means of livelihood by a company of narrow-minded and violent fanatics, simply on account of her faith. The thing would be incredible were it not actual."

Guiney wrote to Dora Sigerson:

The fuss about my office, I regret to say, absurd as it seems, was no myth, and gave me great worry. Auburndale is a town populated with retired missionaries, and bigots of small intellectual calibre. . . . I had some rather rough sailing, thanks purely to my being a Catholic, i.e., one likely at any given moment to give over the government mail, and the safe keys, to the Pope! . . . I am somewhat broken in, now, and somewhat broken up, too!

Accompanied by her friend Alice Brown, Guiney took a short sabbatical to England in the spring of 1895. In 1897, after spending six weeks recovering from a physical breakdown due to overwork, which had been misdiagnosed as meningitis, she resigned her post on July 5, looking forward to freedom, she said, and the almshouse. A consolidation of six post offices had brought a reduction in salary.

Though solicited to join the *Atlantic*'s "Men and Letters" department, she could not live on the proceeds. Instead, she sought an interview, with the help of *Sarah Orne Jewett, at the Boston Public Library. On her application,

Guiney made no mention of 12 books published and her long list of scholarly essays: "Know something of typewriting and a couple of foreign languages. Can read proof expertly."

"After January 1st, 1899, I am to do chores of cataloguing at the Boston Public Library," she wrote Herbert E. Clarke, "probably until I get pneumonia or cerebrospinal paralysis. Regular work always makes me come down with sickness. . . . It is really ludicrous. Gimme Liberty, or gimme death, seem to be my nature's motto." With her mother, she moved to Pinckney Street in Boston, within walking distance of the library; they took in boarders, and she reluctantly began work.

During her two year tenure at the BPL (January 1899–December 1900), she published *Matthew Arnold's Sohrab and Rustum and Other Poems* (1899) and *The Martyrs' Idyl and Shorter Poems* (1899); in the latter, she turned to religion for solace. Guiney gamely chafed once again under the 9-to-5 prison. "Some day, when I am free," she wrote Dora Sigerson, "I am going to emigrate to some hamlet that smells strong of the Middle Ages, and put cotton-wool in my ears, and swing out clear from this very smart century altogether."

Help came in the form of sculptor *Anne Whitney who offered Guiney $5,000 to finance a long-held wish, to live in or near Oxford, England. On February 1901, with her Aunt Betty in tow, Guiney sailed to England on a boat named the *Devonian,* along with five passengers and 700 head of cattle. Though her aunt died there the following year and the medical bills were staggering, Guiney remained, reading proofs for a New York publisher and often taking up residence in the British Museum Reading Room or the Bodleian Library, increasingly interested in Catholic subjects. Except for two minor trips back to America, one of them to attend her dying mother in 1909–10, Louise Guiney would live in England until her death in 1920.

Though she was proud of her heritage, she was running from celebrity and appreciated the right of seclusion not deigned her in America. The artist "will not be asked by an interviewer at 4 a.m., and at the point of a moral bayonet, for his impressions concerning problems fiscal or forensic. If he is understood to have exhibited in the Salon, or to have published a sonnet, not a living British creature will think any the better of him for it."

With her orphaned cousins **Grace** and **Ruth Guiney**, as well as **Louise Mary Martin**, a granddaughter of her uncle, Guiney lived in a small cottage throughout World War I. Eventually, in 1916, she had to abandon the cottage for lack of funds, renting rooms or staying with friends. Just getting by continued to hamper her writing.

For her last seven years, though a touch deaf, Guiney worked on *Recusant Poets 1535–1745,* concerning poets of the Catholic underground hiding from parliamentary persecution. Completed by Grace Guiney, the book would be published posthumously in 1939. Wrote Fairbanks: "Besides preserving the authentic voice of catacombed Catholicism, *Recusant Poets* is a stirring record of independence in the face of oppression." During Guiney's stay in England, her poetry was also published in *Harper's Monthly, Atlantic Monthly, Current Literature, Nation, Century, Dublin Review, Catholic World,* and *McClure's.* A collection entitled *Happy Ending* appeared in 1909. Her prose again revived forgotten figures: essayist Lionel Johnson, the Oxford Movement's J.A. Froude and William Cartwright, and poets *Katherine Philips and Thomas Stanley.

On September 8, 1920, Louise Guiney suffered a stroke, losing her ability to speak. She never recovered and died on November 2, All Souls' Day, at Chipping Camden. Wrote her cousin Grace: "In the final 5½ hours she was entirely unconscious. Her last conscious act, at 11 o'clock Monday night, was to put her arm over my shoulders & draw my head down beside hers." Louise Guiney was buried in Wolvercote Cemetery, Oxford; the inscription on the Celtic cross was *Delassata* (very tired).

SOURCES:

Fairbanks, Henry G. *Laureate of the Lost: Louise Imogen Guiney.* Albany, NY: Magi Books, 1972.

Tenison, Eva Mabel. *Louise Imogen Guiney, Her Life and Works, 1861–1920.* Macmillan, 1923.

COLLECTIONS:

Guiney-Norton Letters, Holy Cross College, Worcester, Massachusetts

Guion, Connie M. (1882–1971)

American physician and clinical educator in New York City for 50 years, who broke many barriers for women in medicine, becoming the first woman to be appointed professor of clinical medicine in the United States (1946) and the first female physician to have a hospital building named for her in her lifetime (1958). Pronunciation: GUY-on. Born Connie Myers Guion on August 29, 1882, on a farm near the small town of Lincolnton, North Carolina; died at the New York Hospital-Cornell Medical Center on April 29,

1971; daughter of Benjamin Simmons Guion (a civil engineer and farmer) and Catherine Coatesworth (Caldwell) Guion; attended public school in Charlotte, North Carolina; graduated from Piedmont Seminary in Lincolnton, 1900; studied at Northfield Seminary in Massachusetts, 1900–02; graduated from Wellesley College, 1906, and Cornell University Medical College, 1917; never married; no children.

Awards: Elizabeth Blackwell citation from New York Infirmary for Women and Children (1949); first woman to receive the Award of Distinction, Cornell University Medical College Alumni Association (1951); Northfield Award for significant service from the Northfield Schools (1951); first woman elected honorary governor of the Society of the New York Hospital (1952); named Medical Woman of the Year by the American Medical Women's Association (1954); honorary doctorates from Wellesley College (1950), Women's Medical College of Pennsylvania (1953), Queens College (1957), and University of North Carolina (1965); Jane Addams Medal from Rockford College (1963).

Family moved to Charlotte, North Carolina (1892); taught chemistry at Vassar College (1906–08) and Sweet Briar College (1908–13); interned and assisted attending physician at Bellevue Hospital (1917–20); entered medical practice as assistant to Dr. Frank Meara (1919); served as attending physician at Booth Memorial Hospital (1920–26); was consulting physician at the New York Infirmary for Women and Children (1929–40s); served as chief of the medical clinic, Cornell University Medical College (1929–32); served as chief of the general medical clinic, New York Hospital-Cornell Medical Center (1932–52); was professor of clinical medicine, Cornell University Medical College (1946–51); was professor emeritus, Cornell University Medical College (1951–67); served as attending physician, New York Hospital-Cornell Medical Center (1943–49); was consultant in medicine, New York Hospital-Cornell Medical Center (1949–68); served as member of the medical board, New York Hospital-Cornell Medical Center (1947–66), member of the Sweet Briar College Board of Overseers (1950–69), chair of the Development Committee of the Board of Overseers at Sweet Briar College (1954–62), member of the Sweet Briar College Board of Directors (1956–69); saw the dedication of the Dr. Connie Guion Building at the New York Hospital-Cornell Medical Center (1963). Published in various medical journals (1914–50).

As the women of the South struggled to rebuild their lives after the Civil War, many opportunities for employment and higher education opened for them that had previously been closed. New obligations also arose, including the need for women to help provide for extended families. In many respects, Connie Guion's family was typical of those in the postwar South that took advantage of these new trends. Her older sisters were employed—two as nurses and one as a clerk in the post office—and helped finance the college education of the younger siblings, including Connie. As the ninth of twelve children on a North Carolina farm that produced only enough for the Guions and a few tenant farmers, Connie's prospects might otherwise have been quite limited.

Connie Guion's parents, Benjamin Simmons Guion and **Kate Caldwell Guion**, were married in the small town of Lincolnton, North Carolina, in 1864 at the height of the Civil War. Benjamin Guion was a graduate of the University of North Carolina who worked as a civil engineer with the railroad, helping to keep the railroads open in Virginia, North Carolina, and South Carolina during the war. Kate, the daughter of a prominent physician in Charlotte, was a high-spirited, independent 18-year-old at the time of their wedding. For the next ten years, they lived in Lincolnton where the first four daughters were born. In 1873, feeling the need to provide for their growing family, they bought a large farm three miles away where Connie was born in 1882.

𝒩obody would treat Connie Guion in a haphazard fashion, at least not in my time.

—Benjamin H. Kean, M.D.

Connie's ten years on the farm were a joy to her. Her experiences there engendered a lifelong love of nature, and she always felt refreshed by activities that renewed her contact with the earth, especially fishing. In her later years, she often mentioned how beautiful the land had been, and how loved, protected, and secure she felt as one of such a large family. Each child had the responsibility for certain farm chores, and each understood the need to work for the well-being of the entire family. This shared sense of purpose was typical of many Southern families during that era and was a factor in the later achievements of countless young Southerners.

As soon as Guion was old enough to run free on the farm, she delighted in following her three older brothers around, doing chores they disliked, such as picking tomato and tobacco worms from plants. In exchange, her brothers would let her hitch up the wagons and ride the mules. As she grew older, her responsibilities increased, and she occasionally drove the mule wagon into Lincolnton with a load of fruit to be exchanged for sugar and other commodities. By age nine, though Guion could hitch up and drive any wagon on the farm and could hang onto the neck of even the wildest colt or calf, she could neither read nor write. Although she was familiar with literature from listening as the adults read aloud from the works of Sir Walter Scott, Dickens, and Shakespeare, she had never been to school. There were few public schools in rural areas of North Carolina; opportunities for the Guion children's education were limited to a small private academy in Lincolnton, run by two of Kate's cousins, **Daisy** and **Mary Wood**. The older children had gone there, but nine-year-old Connie had managed to avoid formal education.

After attending the Mary Wood School, the two oldest Guion girls left home in 1883 to study nursing, one of the new career opportunities opening for women. Their work helped support the family and also provided Connie with appealing stories of medical life. Connie's mother, however, was her most significant medical role model. Kate Guion regaled her daughter with stories of her paternal grandmother, who was a doctor in the fashion of the early 19th century, traveling around the North Carolina countryside with her herbs and salves whenever she was summoned, with one of her 11 sons perched on the back of her horse. Kate's father often went with his mother and later went to medical school. Kate apparently had the natural healing ability of her grandmother and some of her father's medical skills. Every morning, she would make the rounds of the Guion farm, tending to sick tenants and animals, usually with Connie at her heels. Connie gathered the white mud used for poultices and helped her mother pour castor oil into sick cows and mules. From watching Kate, Connie learned much about the art and practice of medicine and was soon convinced that she, too, would be a doctor.

Although her mother provided the medical inspiration, Connie's older sister **Laura Guion (Haskell)** was the one who enabled Connie to embark on the arduous road to medical school. In 1890, 19-year-old Laura left home to take a job in Charlotte at the post office; two years later, she had Connie come live with her at a boarding house to begin her education at the public school. The efforts of older women to encourage the advancement of daughters and younger siblings was common at this time in the South, as educator A.D. Mayo discovered during his southern sojourn in 1880–92. He was struck by "the push to the front of the better sort of Southern young, everywhere encouraged by the sympathy, support, sacrifice, toils, and prayers of the superior women of the elder generation at home." In Connie's case, Laura's resolve, financial support, and unwavering faith enabled Connie's own determination and intelligence to blossom. Laura's fiancé, Alexander Haskell, had to wait 13 years for Laura to set a wedding date, because she refused to consider marriage until she had seen to the education of her younger brothers and sisters. Alex Haskell said later that he thought there would never be an end to little Guions.

Alex, whose sister Mary had graduated from Wellesley College in the class of 1897, never ceased talking about the college, and Laura decided that Connie would go there. However, after attending a newly established private high school in Lincolnton for two years on a scholarship offered by a family friend, Connie was still unprepared for Wellesley. The secretary of Wellesley suggested that Connie undertake the necessary preparatory work at Northfield Seminary in Northfield, Massachusetts. The tuition was $110 per year while Laura's salary was $100 a month, but she was undaunted.

Connie
M.
Guion

As she was the first to admit, Connie was never a brilliant student, just tenacious. She graduated from Wellesley in 1906, after four years of financial support from Laura, as well as a generous scholarship from the college. Just as Laura had postponed marriage, Connie delayed medical school to finance the college education of her two younger sisters. For seven years, Connie taught chemistry—at Vassar and newly founded Sweet Briar College—and worked on a master's degree in chemistry at Cornell University during the summers. By the time she entered Cornell University Medical College in 1913 on a full-tuition scholarship, she had just celebrated her 31st birthday and was more qualified for medical school than most of her male classmates.

During the years of Guion's medical career, the number of women admitted to medical schools was limited to about five percent. At many schools, such as Harvard, women were simply not admitted. Guion was one of three women in a class of twenty-four men at Cornell. In her later life, she often maintained that she had rarely experienced discrimination in her attempts to become a doctor or in her medical practice, except where biases against women were so ingrained that all women were affected. In those situations, she had to prove that she was as capable as any man, and she never hesitated to stand up for herself. On one occasion during medical school, when the urology professor attempted to bar the women students from the class, Guion responded that this was absolutely ridiculous since she expected to treat men as well as women in her medical practice. As usual, she prevailed.

After graduating first in her class in 1917, Guion spent two years of residency at Bellevue Hospital, one of the few hospitals that offered internships to women. Her start in private practice came when Frank Meara, a prominent consulting physician and one of Guion's professors at Cornell, invited her to become his associate. With the backing of Meara, one of New York's most respected physicians, Guion was able to overcome any reservations his patients may have had over being treated by a woman doctor. Soon she was attracting her own patients. At the same time, she began teaching clinical medicine at Cornell University Medical College, a career she continued for almost 50 years at the New York Hospital-Cornell Medical Center.

In 1929, Guion was appointed chief of the new Cornell Medical Clinic. This was a major achievement for a woman physician, the first of her many trailblazing accomplishments for

women in medicine. *The New York Times* called her appointment "a landmark in the professional progress of her sex." Guion's work in outpatient clinical medicine, as a physician, administrator, and teacher, culminated in the medical center's decision in 1958 to name the new clinic building for her. Acknowledged in medical circles as "the Dean of women doctors," Guion was the first woman in the United States to receive this kind of honor.

Although Guion achieved much in the hierarchy of medicine, her private patients were equally important to her, and she had one of the largest practices in Manhattan. In an age when there were few practicing internists, and men, when given a choice, would usually choose a male physician, Guion had many male patients who felt comfortable with her. Among her patients were some of New York's most prominent citizens, including many associated with the theater: Vincent Astor, *Pamela Churchill Harriman, John Hay Whitney and ◄❧ Betsey Cushing Whitney, ◄❧ Babe Paley, *Mary Martin, *Greta Garbo, *Greer Garson, *Jennifer Jones, and David O. Selznick. Her practice also included the grocer across the street and many of her patients' servants, all of whom received the same attention.

Like many career women of her generation, Guion preferred to avoid the kinds of restrictions that marriage and childbearing had imposed on her mother and older sisters. She liked men and enjoyed their company, but her life was devoted to medicine. Her sisters, brothers, nephews, nieces, friends, colleagues, and patients were her extended family. After putting her niece, **Parkie McCombs**, through medical school, Guion brought McCombs into her medical practice in 1930. They worked together until Guion's retirement in 1968 at age 86.

Throughout her life Guion lived modestly, giving much of her time and resources to causes that were important to her, especially the education of women. Inspired by Laura's example and grateful for her sacrifices, Guion in turn helped educate her nephews and nieces into the third generation. She encouraged many of her wealthy friends and patients to give to her favorite educational and medical causes. Guion's legacy endures in the scholarships, professorships, and awards that have been endowed in her name.

In the 1960s, Guion often remarked how rewarding her long life had been. Twenty years after her death, one of her younger colleagues, Dr. **Marjorie Lewisohn**, captured the essence of Guion's spirit:

❧► *Whitney, Betsey Cushing.* See *Cushing Sisters.*

❧► *Paley, Babe.* See *Cushing Sisters.*

Connie had this wonderful way of never feeling that being a woman was in any way inferior. She never gave you the feeling that being a woman was anything but a joy. And I think there are very few people, men or women, who have that quality of full investment of themselves in what they're doing. She really liked being Connie Guion.

SOURCES:

Connie M. Guion Collection, and the Guion-McCombs Papers, Medical Archives, New York Hospital-Cornell Medical Center, New York City.

Mayo, Amory Dwight. *Southern Women in the Recent Educational Movement in the South.* Edited by Dan T. Carter and Amy Friedlander. Baton Rouge, LA: Louisiana State University Press, 1978.

"The Reminiscences of Connie Guion," Oral History Research Office, Columbia University, New York City, 1958.

SUGGESTED READING:

Morantz-Sanchez, Regina Markell. *Sympathy and Science: Women Physicians in American Medicine.* NY: Oxford University Press, 1985.

Walsh, Mary Roth. *Doctors Wanted: No Women Need Apply: Sexual Barriers in the Medical Profession, 1835–1975.* New Haven, CT: Yale University Press, 1979.

Katherine G. Haskell,
freelance writer and medical editor,
Jeffersonville, Pennsylvania

Guion, Madame (1648–1717).

See Guyon, Jeanne Marie Bouviéres de la Mothe.

Guirande de Lavaur (d. 1211)

French noblewoman and warrior. Name variations: *Giralda de Laurac. Died in 1211 in Lavaur, France; sister of Aimery de Montréal.*

Bitter fighting took place in 13th-century France during the crusade against the Cathars, who were considered heretics. Guirande de Lavaur was a Cathar known as an educated, gentle and charitable lady. A valiant defender of her estates, Guirande was a French noblewoman of substantial wealth. Although it is not clear from surviving records, she was either widowed or her husband was absent during the year 1211, for his name is not mentioned with hers. In that year, Guirande defended her castles against attacks by the armies of three bishops; eventually, however, she had to give in to the superior military forces of Simon de Montfort, one of England's most famous rebel soldiers.

When Montfort attacked the town of Lavaur to cleanse it of heresy, the Castle of Lavaur was defended by Guirande, assisted by her brother, Aimery de Montréal. The castle held out for two months. When Montfort finally prevailed, Aimery and some 80 knights were hanged, 400 Cathars burned alive, and Guirande was flung into a well and pelted to death with stones.

Laura York,
Riverside, California

Guise, countess of.

See Marie of Guise (d. 1404).

Guise, duchess of.

See Isabelle of Lorraine (1410–1453).

See Jeanne de Laval (d. 1498).

See Mary of Guise for sidebar on Antoinette of Bourbon (1494–1583).

See Morata, Fulvia for sidebar on Anne of Ferrara (1531–1607).

See Catherine de Cleves (fl. 1550s).

See Isabella of Orleans (b. 1878).

Gülabahar (fl. 1521)

Ottoman sultana. Name variations: *Gulabahar or Gulbehar; Gülfem or Gulfem. Flourished in 1521; born a Montenegrin or Albanian or Crimean; consort of Suleiman also seen as Suleyman, Ottoman sultan (r. 1520–1566); children: (with Suleiman) Mustafa or Mustapha (governor of Mansia).*

Gulbehar (fl. 1521).

See Gülabahar.

Gulbranson, Ellen (1863–1947)

Swedish soprano. Born Ellen Nordgren on March 4, 1863, in Stockholm, Sweden; died in Oslo, Norway, on January 2, 1947; trained in Stockholm and in Paris under *Mathilde Marchesi and *Blanche Marchesi.

Ellen Gulbranson was born Ellen Nordgren in Stockholm, Sweden, in 1863. Known for her interpretation of Wagnerian roles, Gulbranson made her debut in Stockholm in 1889 as Amneris in *Aïda;* she would eventually play Ortrud and Aïda. She first sang Brunnhilde at Bayreuth in 1896 and was reengaged for the part from 1897 to 1914. Gulbranson, whose favorite roles were Kundry and Brunnhilde, also performed in Paris, Moscow, Berlin, Vienna, St. Petersburg, Amsterdam, and other European cities, as well as Covent Garden. She retired in 1915.

Gulfem or Gülfem (fl. 1521).

See Gülabahar.

Gulliver, Julia Henrietta (1856–1940)

American scholar. Born July 30, 1856; died on July 25, 1940; graduated B.A. Smith College, 1879, Ph.D., 1888; postgraduate study at the University of Leipzig, 1892–1893. President of Rockford College (1902–1919).

Selected works: Studies in Democracy (1917); many papers in academic journals.

At a time when very few women were able to have academic careers, Julia Henrietta Gulliver's career flourished with the study of philosophy and psychology. She entered Smith College in its inaugural year (1875) and was granted a B.A. in 1879 and a Ph.D. in 1888. In the 1890s, Gulliver went to Rockford Female Seminary, where she was head of the department of philosophy and Biblical literature. For two years, she resumed her own studies in Europe at the University of Leipzig with Wilhelm Wundt, and then returned to Rockford. The seminary was now a college, and she acted as its president from 1902 to 1919.

Catherine Hundleby, M.A.,
Philosophy, University of Guelph, Guelph, Ontario, Canada

Gullvåg, Harriet (b. 1922).

See Holter, Harriet.

Gund, Agnes (1938—)

American art historian, collector, philanthropist, educator, and administrator. Born in 1938 in Cleveland, Ohio; daughter of George Gund; married Albrecht Saalfield, around 1966 (divorced); married Daniel Shapiro, in 1987; children: (first marriage) David Saalfield; Catherine Saalfield; Anna Saalfield; Jessica Saalfield.

Agnes Gund was born in 1938 in Cleveland, Ohio, and developed her appreciation for art while surrounded by her father's eclectic collection. One of six children of George Gund, a banking executive, Agnes learned responsibility at age 15, when her mother died. Agnes took on the job of maintaining the family. Her father made his fortune in a variety of industries, including real estate and investments, and when he died in 1966 Agnes became a millionaire. Around that same time, she married a private-school teacher, Albrecht Saalfield. The couple had four children, a son David and three daughters, Catherine, Anna and Jessica.

Gund attended the Fogg Museum at Harvard University where she earned a master's de-gree, and in 1976 she was elected to the Museum of Modern Art's (MOMA) board of trustees. In 1977, Gund discovered an unusual outlet for her love of art when she founded her Studio in a School project, which brought artists into public schools to teach art. Although the program has met with some criticism, many agreed that it built confidence and allowed children the pleasure of creative expression.

In 1981, Gund divorced, relocated to New York City, and became hostess to artists and art lovers alike. Six years later, she married David Shapiro, an attorney who specialized in art and cultural- and intellectual-property law.

Gund won admiration for her sharp eye for both the beautiful and the unique. In 1991, she became president of MOMA, responsible for directing the board of trustees and managing the institution. Many praised her fresh approach to fundraising and her ability to foster a sense of trust and inspiration as she took on the problems of the institution, including its lack of space and aging contemporary collection. In 1998, Agnes Gund was one of several honorees receiving National Medal of Arts awards, presented by President Bill Clinton and **Hillary Rodham Clinton** at the White House.

SOURCES:
Newsmakers 93. Issue 2. Detroit, MI: Gale Research.

Judith C. Reveal,
freelance writer, Greensboro, Maryland

Günderode, Karoline von (1780–1806).

See Arnim, Bettine von for sidebar.

Gunderson, JoAnne (b. 1939).

See Carner, JoAnne.

Gunhild (c. 1020–1038)

Norman princess. Name variations: Gunhilda or Gunnhildr. Born around 1020; died on July 18, 1038, on the Adriatic Coast; daughter of *Emma of Normandy (c. 985–1052) and Cnut also known as Canute the Great (c. 994–1035), king of England (r. 1016–1035), king of Denmark (r. 1019–1035), king of Norway (r. 1028–1035); married Henry III (1017–1056), king of Germany (r. 1039–1056), Holy Roman emperor (r. 1039–1056), on June 10, 1036. Henry III's second wife was *Agnes of Poitou (1024–1077), whom he married in 1043.

Gunhild of Norway (d. 1054)

Queen of Denmark. Name variations: Gunnhild Sveinsdottir. Died in 1054; daughter of Svein, earl of

Ladir, and Holmfrid Ericsdottir; married Anund Jakob of Sweden, king of Sweden (r. 1022–1050); first wife of Svend II Estridsen (d. 1076) also known as Sweyn Estridsen, king of Denmark (r. 1047–1074).

There are 16 children attributed to Svend II who had four wives or paramours (Gunhild of Norway, *Gyde, *Elizabeth of Kiev, and **Thora Johnsdottir**). Any one of the four could be the mother of Svend's royal offspring: Harald Hén, king of Denmark (r. 1074–1080); St. Knud or Canute the Holy, king of Denmark (r. 1080–1086); Oluf or Olaf Hunger, king of Denmark (r. 1086–1095).

Gunhilda of Denmark (d. 1002)

Danish princess. Name variations: Gunhild Haraldsdottir. Killed on November 13, 1002; daughter of Harald Bluetooth (c. 910–985), king of Denmark (r. 940–985) and *Gyrid; sister of *Thyra of Denmark (d. 1000) and Sven or Sweyn I Forkbeard, king of Denmark (r. 985–1014), king of England (r. 1014); married Jarl Pallig or Palig, ealdorman in Devon.

Gunhilda of Poland (d. around 1015)

Polish princess. Name variations: Gunhild of Poland; Sygryda Swietoslawa. Died around 1015; daughter of Mieszko I, duke of Poland, and *Dobravy of Bohemia (d. 977); married and was first wife of Sven or Sweyn I Forkbeard (b. 965), king of Denmark (r. 985–1014), around 990 (divorced in 1000); children: (second marriage) Canute the Great (c. 994–1035), king of England (r. 1016–1035), king of Denmark (r. 1019–1035), king of Norway (r. 1028–1035); *Thyra (d. 1018); possibly Harald (d. 1019), king of Denmark (r. 1014–1018).

Gunhilda of Poland, a Polish princess and sister to Duke (later King) Boleslav Chrobry, became consort and mistress of Sweyn I Forkbeard, king of Denmark. Though they had no formal marriage arrangement, King Sweyn made their infant son Canute one of his heirs. When Sweyn married *Sigrid the Haughty (the widow of King Eric of Sweden) in order to cement an alliance with Sweden, Gunhilda had to leave Sweyn's court. Evidently, she took her son Canute—then no more than two or three years old—to the court of her brother Boleslav.

Gunnell, Sally (1966—)

British runner. Born in Chigwell, England, on July 29, 1966; married Jonathan Bigg (a runner).

Immensely popular in England, Sally Gunnell placed first in the 400 meters at the Commonwealth Games in 1986 and the European Indoor championships in 1989. In the 400-meter hurdles, she placed first in the Commonwealth Games (1990, 1994), European Cup (1993, 1994, 1996, 1997), Goodwill Games (1994), European championships (1994), World Cup (1994), and took the World championship in 1993 with a world-record time of 52.74. In the 4x400-meter relay, Gunnell placed first in the Commonwealth Games (1990, 1994) and the European Cup (1994). She also won the gold medal in the 400-meter hurdles, with a time of 53.23, and the bronze in the 4x400 relay at the Barcelona Olympics in 1992. Her personal best times include an 11.83 in the 100 meters in a race in Auckland on January 20, 1990; a 23.30 in the 200 meters in London on June 13, 1993; a 51.04 in the 400 meters on July 20, 1994 at Gateshead; a 12.82 in the 100-meter hurdles on August 17, 1988, at Zurich; and a 52.74 in the 400-meter hurdles on August 19, 1993 in Stuttgart. Gunnell was #1 in *Track & Field News World* rankings in 1993 and 1994.

Gunness, Belle (1860–c. 1908)

American murderer. Born in 1860; may have died in a house fire in 1908; married Mr. Gunness (a farmer); three children.

A Norwegian immigrant who settled with her husband on a farm outside of La Porte, Indiana, Belle Gunness was involved in a grisly series of murders beginning with her husband, whose skull she crushed with a hatchet. Telling the coroner's jury that the hatchet "slipped from the shelf" and killed her husband accidentally, she was believed and acquitted. Later, Gunness began to advertise for a husband in the lovelorn columns, luring dozens of men to her farm, supposedly drugging and strangling them, then chopping their bodies up for hog feed and burying their bones in her pigsty. On April 28, 1908, her deeds came to light when a fire devastated her farm house. Along with her body and those of her children, searchers inadvertently found the remains of 13 victims, although there may have been more. There was later speculation that Belle set the fire herself, substituting the corpse of a female friend for her own, then absconding with the money from her victims to live out her life in San Francisco.

Gunnhild.

Variant of Gunhild.

Gunnhild (fl. 1150s)

Norwegian consort. Flourished around 1150s; had liaison with Sigurd II Mund also known as Sigurd II Mouth (1133–1155), king of Norway (r. 1136–1155); children: Sverre also known as Sverri (c. 1152–1202), king of Norway (r. 1177–1202); **Cecilia Sigurdsdottir** (who married Folkvid and Baard of Rein and was the mother of Inge II, king of Norway); Eric.

Gunnhildr.

Variant of Gunhild.

Gunning, Elizabeth (1734–1790)

Duchess of Hamilton and Argyll. Name variations: Elizabeth Hamilton. Born in 1734; died on May 20, 1790; daughter of John Gunning of Castle Coote, County Roscommon, Ireland; sister of *Maria Gunning (1733–1760); married James, 6th duke of Hamilton, 1752; married John Campbell, marquis of Lorne, afterward 5th duke of Argyll, in 1759; children: Lady *Charlotte Bury (1775–1861).

Gunning, Elizabeth (1769–1823)

English author. Name variations: Elizabeth Gunning Plunkett. Born in 1769; died in Suffolk, England, on July 20, 1823; daughter of John and *Susannah Minifie Gunning (c. 1740–1800); married Major James Plunkett.

Gunning, Maria (1733–1760)

Countess of Coventry. Name variations: Maria, Countess of Coventry. Born in 1733; died on October 1, 1760; daughter of John Gunning of Castle Coote, County Roscommon, Ireland, a poor Irish squire; sister of Elizabeth Gunning (1734–1790); married George William, 6th earl of Coventry, in 1752.

Maria Gunning and her sister *Elizabeth Gunning went to London in 1751 and were at once pronounced "the handsomest women alive." They were followed by crowds wherever they went, and Maria, who was considered the better looking by those who deigned to compare, was mobbed one evening in Hyde Park. The king, George II, gave her a guard to protect her, and she once walked in the park for two hours with two sergeants of the guard before her and twelve soldiers following. In 1752, she married George William, 6th earl of Coventry. "The beautiful Misses Gunning" were painted a number of times, and there are many engravings of these portraits in existence.

Gunning, Susannah Minifie (c. 1740–1800)

English author. Name variations: Susannah Minifie; Mrs. Gunning. Born Susannah Minifie around 1740; died in London, England, on August 28, 1800; daughter of James Minifie; married John Gunning (a colonel of the 65th regiment of foot and lieutenant-general), in 1768; sister of Margaret Minifie; sister-in-law of *Elizabeth Gunning (1734–1790) and *Maria Gunning (1733–1760); children: Elizabeth Gunning Plunkett (1769–1823).

Details on Susannah Gunning's early life are sketchy. She was the daughter of the Reverend Dr. James Minifie of Fairwater in Somerset, and, by age 23, she published *Histories of Lady Frances S . . . and Lady Caroline S . . .* (1763), a collaboration with her sister, **Margaret Minifie**. This work was followed by three more, *Family Pictures* (1764), *The Picture* (1766), also written with her sister, and *The Hermit* (1770), a story with conventional plots of love and marriage in the nobility.

In 1768, with her marriage to Captain John Gunning, her writing stopped. Her husband has been described as a morally corrupt individual who may have had his brother-in-law, the duke of Argyll, to thank for his advancement in the military. Gunning and her husband had one daughter, *Elizabeth Gunning** (Plunkett), and when she reached adulthood, a family breach occurred over a marriage partner for the girl. When Elizabeth embraced her mother's preference for a suitor over her father's, both Susannah and Elizabeth were turned out of the house. Susannah issued a public letter to the duke of Argyll stating her innocence of any deception (there was an intrigue involving a forged letter). The situation grew to such proportions that it became public fodder for the press, with English writer Horace Walpole referring to the incident as 'Gunninghiad.' John Gunning was soon involved in an adulterous affair with his tailor's wife and moved to Italy with her.

In the early 1790s, Susannah Gunning returned to writing. She took advantage of the scandal in the novels, *Anecdotes of the Delborough Family* (1792) and *Memoirs of Mary* (1793), in which the heroine suffers as the result of a forged letter, and a poem "Virginius and Virginia" (1792). Her novel *Delves* (1796) was set in Wales, and her last works, *Love at First Sight* (1797) and *Fashionable Involvements* (1800), were novels of manners. Gunning's daughter, Elizabeth Gunning Plunkett, also wrote novels, and one of her works, *Combe Wood* (1783), was thought to have been written by Susannah Gunning. On the day before he died in 1797, John Gunning changed his will leaving his wife and daughter provided for, with Susannah receiving his Irish estate. Susannah Gunning died in London three years later.

Judith C. Reveal,
freelance writer, Greensboro, Maryland

Gunnor of Crêpon (d. 1031).

See Gunnor of Denmark.

Gunnor of Denmark (d. 1031)

Duchess of Normandy. Name variations: Gunnor of Crêpon; Gunnora of Crepon; sometimes referred to as Gunhilda. Birth date unknown; died in 1031; second wife of Richard I the Fearless (d. 996), duke of Normandy (r. 942–996); children: Richard II (d. 1027), duke of Normandy (r. 996–1027); Robert, archbishop of Rouen (d. 1037); Mauger, earl of Corbeil; *Emma of Normandy (c. 985–1052); *Hawise of Normandy (d. 1034, who married Geoffrey I, duke of Brittany); *Maud of Normandy (d. 1017, who married Odo I, count of Blois, Champagne, and Chartres). Richard I the Fearless' first wife was *Emma of Paris (d. 968).

Gunnora of Crepon (d. 1031).

See Gunnor of Denmark.

Guntheuca (fl. 525)

Queen of the Franks. Flourished around 525; married Chlodomer, Clodomir, also known as Clotimir (495–524), king of Orléans (r. 511–524); married his brother Chlothar, Clothaire, Clotar or Lothair I (497–561), king of Soissons (r. 511), king of the Franks (r. 558–561); no children. Lothair's second wife was *Chunsina; his third was *Ingunde; his fourth was *Aregunde (sister of Ingunde); his fifth was *Radegund (518–587); his seventh was *Vuldetrade.

Guntrud of Bavaria (fl. 715)

Queen of the Lombards. Flourished around 715; daughter of Theodebert, duke of Bavaria, and *Folcheid; sister of *Sunnichild (d. 741, who married Charles Martel, king of the Franks); married Liutprand, king of the Lombards, in 715.

Guraieb Kuri, Rosa (1931—)

Mexican composer. Born in Matias Romero (Oaxaca), Mexico, on May 20, 1931; has composed many works performed in her native country of Mexico; most of her works have been composed for various chamber ensembles.

Rosa Guraieb Kuri was born in Matias Romero, Mexico, in 1931, into a Lebanese family who had settled in Mexico. She began her musical studies at the age of four, and by eighteen had achieved sufficient musical mastery to become a piano teacher; a year later, she continued her studies of piano, theory, and harmony under Michel Cheskinoff at the National Conservatory in Beirut. Kuri Guraieb then did advanced work at the Conservatory of Mexico under Juan Pablo Moncayo and Salvador Ordones Ochoa. Afterwards, she went to the United States where she studied with Professor Simmonds at the Yale University School of Music, returning to Mexico to study advanced composition techniques with Carlos Chavez at the National Conservatory of Mexico. Guraieb Kuri composed chamber, vocal, and piano works which were performed at music forums and festivals throughout Mexico. Some of her works, including her Second String Quartet, *Hommage a Gibran* (1982), represent her personal perspective on her Lebanese heritage.

John Haag,
Athens, Georgia

Gurley, Elizabeth (1890–1964).

See Flynn, Elizabeth Gurley.

Gurney, Nella Hooper (1838–1887).

See Adams, Clover for sidebar.

Gurrah, rani of (d. 1564).

See Durgawati.

Gusenbauer, Ilona (b. 1947).

See Balas, Iolande for sidebar.

Gushington, Impulsia (1807–1867).

See Blackwood, Helen Selina.

Gushterova, Vangelia (1911–1996)

Bulgarian prophet. Name variations: Aunt Vanya; Vanya Gushterova. Born in Macedonia in 1911; died in Rupite, Bulgaria, on August 11, 1996.

Blinded in a windstorm when she was 12, Vangelia Gushterova, by her own account, was a visionary who drew her powers from an ancient city buried under her village in southwestern Bulgaria. Many believed in her ability, and by the time she was a teenager, her reputation had spread across the impoverished Balkan country. "Aunt Vanya," as she was called, ministered to politicians and peasants, reputedly diagnosing the sick and even locating missing persons. In 1941, she dreamed of an "ancient horseman" who foretold the Nazi march into the Balkans.

Gushterova consulted from her modest house in Rupite, where hundreds stood in line outside her door almost daily. Upon her death in 1996, at age 84, she was estimated to have administered to over one million believers. "She lived not for herself but for the people. That made her a living saint for us," said Prime Minister Zhan Videnov.

SOURCES:
"Milestones," in *Time*. August 26, 1996.
"Obituaries." *The Day* [New London]. August 13, 1996.

Gusmao, Luisa de (1613–1666).

See Luisa de Guzman.

Marie Gutheil-Schoder

Guta or Gutta.

Variant of Judith and Jutta.

Gutheil-Schoder, Marie (1874–1935)

German soprano. Born in Weimar, Germany, on February 16, 1874; died in Bad Ilmenau, Thuringia, on October 4, 1935; engaged by Gustav Mahler at the Vienna Staatsoper where she performed for over 25 years.

There was never agreement over Marie Gutheil-Schoder's voice. Some called her "the singer without the voice" while critic Erwin Stein contended that her voice was "the perfect instrument of a great artist." She had a long and successful vocal career, and her singing was famous for its refinement. Unfortunately, recordings do not reveal how her voice actually sounded. What *is* known is that Gustav Mahler, Richard Strauss, Bruno Walter, and *Lotte Lehmann* held Gutheil-Schoder in very high regard. She made her debut in Weimar in 1891. After appearing elsewhere in Germany, she was engaged by Mahler at the Vienna Staatsoper where she appeared from 1900 until 1926. Richard Strauss coached her in roles for *Elektra* and *Der Rosenkavalier* which was a great honor. Gutheil-Schoder was also known for her many roles in Mozart operas.

Despite her success in traditional operatic roles, she was an adventurous singer who performed in Arnold Schoenberg's avant-garde vocal work *Erwartung* when it premiered in Prague in 1924. This was a particularly difficult role, as *Erwartung* or *Expectation* is a psychological drama consisting of three brief scenes followed by a long final scene. It begins with a road disappearing into a dark wood; a woman searches for her lover, fearful of the dark. In the next scene, she gropes through the wood in terror. In the final scene, she emerges exhausted and battered. A shuttered house is visible in the distance. She stumbles and discovers her lover's murdered body. This dream-like work was extremely difficult to perform and Schoenberg always preferred Gutheil-Schoder's interpretation of it. After her retirement, Marie Gutheil-Schoder continued her career as a teacher and director in Vienna and Salzburg.

John Haag,
Athens, Georgia

Guthrie, Janet (1938—)

American auto racer and first woman to qualify for, and race in, the Indianapolis 500. Pronunciation: GUTH-ree. Born Janet Guthrie on March 7, 1938, in Iowa City, Iowa; daughter of Jean Ruth (Midkiff) Guthrie and William Lain Guthrie; attended Miss

Harris' Florida School for Girls; graduated, University of Michigan, B.Sc. in physics, 1960.

Moved from Iowa City to New York, Atlanta, and then Miami (1941); attended private school in Florida; started flying at 13, soloed at 16, and had her commercial pilot's license by 19; worked at Republic Aviation in the aerospace division, Long Island, New York; granted her competition license from the Long Island Sports Car Club (1962); granted her license from the Sports Car Club of America (1963); applied to be one of the first scientist-astronauts (1965); worked as a physicist and non-professional auto racer; participated in the 24-hour International Manufacturer's Championship at Daytona (1966); successfully finished in nine consecutive runnings of the Daytona 24-hour, Sebring 12-hour, and Watkins Glen 500 endurance races (1964–70); was second in class at the Watkins Glen race (1965); was second in class at the Sebring race (1967); won the Governor of Florida's Award at Sebring (1968); took a job as a technical editor for Sperry Rand (1968); was first in class at the Sebring 12-hour race (1970); participated in the North Atlantic Road Racing Championship (1973); did public relations work for Toyota (1975); became the first woman to enter and pass the rookie test at the Indianapolis 500 trials (1976); was first woman to compete in a NASCAR (National Association for Stock Car Auto Racing) superspeedway race (1976); competed in four Indy-car races at other tracks; was the first woman to qualify for, and race in, the Indianapolis 500 (May 1977); finished ninth in the Indianapolis 500 (1978).

Janet Guthrie worked her way up the ranks of auto racing to gain national recognition on several levels, but the climb was not easy. The Indy-car and stock-car racing establishments were dominated by men, and they were in no hurry to open the circuit to women. Until 1972, when the gender ban was lifted by lawsuit, women had not even been allowed in the garage area or the pits at Indianapolis. After that, a few women had publicly announced their intention to race at Indy but then faded away.

On May 29, 1977, Janet Guthrie skillfully drove through the barrier. But long after she had proved that a woman could qualify and drive in the Indy 500, long after she had demonstrated that auto racing depends on skill, coordination, and courage, Guthrie would still be asked, "Can you physically compete with men?" A tall, elegant woman, with light brown hair and hazel eyes, Guthrie's response was always polite, acknowledging a remark first made by Belgian driver **Christine Beckers:** "I drive the car, I don't carry it."

Janet Guthrie was born in Iowa City, Iowa, on March 7, 1938, to William Lain Guthrie and **Jean Midkiff Guthrie**. The oldest of five children, she came from what she has described as a bookish, eccentric family. Her father, whom she regarded as a crusader, operated the Iowa City airport and exposed the airlines' practice of dumping jet fuel from aloft after takeoff, a disclosure which quickly brought reform within the industry. When he was hired as a pilot for Eastern Airlines, he moved his family to Miami where Janet attended Miss Harris' Florida School, a private school for girls, from 1944 to 1955.

"I don't know what it was about the way my parents brought us up," said Guthrie, "but I never had the feeling that I couldn't be this or that because I was a girl. I was never pressured toward the idea that the best thing was to marry and raise children . . . that there was no other option." At 13, she began flying lessons, instructed by her father; at 16, she made her first parachute jump. She earned her pilot's license at age 17 and her instructor's license at 21. Grown into a slender, articulate, but softspoken woman who intended to make a career in physics, she sometimes wondered herself about her affinity for so-called men's pursuits. Eventually, she concluded that it was the challenges she liked, and that all her interests were intrinsically exciting.

After high school, Guthrie attended the University of Michigan where she received a B.Sc. in physics in 1960. That year, she became an aerospace research and development engineer for Republic Aviation Corporation, Long Island, New York, bought her first sports car, a used Jaguar XK 120, and joined local sports-car clubs. From 1961 to 1966, while at Republic, she entered gymkhana competitions, low-speed events which stress precision driving, such as contests on zigzag courses marked with pylons. In 1962, she was named the women's gymkhana champion of Long Island. By then, Guthrie had discovered sports-car racing and bought a used Jaguar XK 140 prepared expressly for racing. She passed tests for competition licenses from the Long Island Sports Car Club and the Sports Car Club of America (SCCA) and finished third in her driver-school race against faster Corvettes. (In 1965, she also passed the first round of testing by the National Aeronautics and Space Administration to become an astronaut, one of only four women to pass, but she lacked the required doctorate or experience to advance further with NASA.)

From 1964 to 1970, Guthrie finished nine consecutive times at the Big Three American sports-car endurance races: the Watkins Glen 6-hour, the Sebring 12-hour, and the Daytona 24-hour. At Watkins Glen, New York, in 1964 and 1965, she finished second in her class, and in 1964 she was sixth overall in the country's top endurance events. Only about half the drivers who start in those events finish. Her awards included the Sebring Reye Dreyfus Twin Cup, the Falstaff Team Trophy, the KLG Trophy, and the Governor of Florida Award. For five years, she drove for a team sponsored by the Macmillan Ring-Free Oil Company.

A driver is a driver—whether male or female is irrelevant. The essentials are in the mind: concentration, judgment, emotional detachment, and desire.

—Janet Guthrie

In 1967, she had quit Republic Aviation Corporation in order to race full-time; the following year, she signed on as a technical editor for the Sperry Rand Corporation, a part-time job that allowed more time for racing. By then, Guthrie had become known to race fans, but she preferred to be viewed as an auto-racing driver who happened to be a woman rather than as a woman auto-racing driver. Severely depleting her funds, Guthrie bought a new Toyota Celica and rebuilt it as her own race car. It took a year, one she describes as the nadir of her life, as she took the vehicle apart and put it back together, in preparation for the 1972 2.5 Challenge Series racing program. Then, at the end of 1971, the SCCA canceled the competition.

For the next three years, Guthrie worked part-time and raced her Toyota in amateur and professional events. She won the North Atlantic Road Racing Championship in 1973. By 1975, she had competed in 120 races, in which she was usually the only woman entered. It was an outstanding record by any account, but the male racing-car establishment was still not anxious to let her in. She approached racing team owners, factory representatives, and other drivers, searching for sponsors and owners with cars willing to let her race. She was frustrated, in debt, and the Toyota Celica was now obsolete, forcing her to think about ending her racing.

In October of 1975, Guthrie went to work for Toyota as a consumer information specialist, demonstrating safe-driving techniques. Four months later, when the proposal finally came from an established Indianapolis team that opened the way to the Indianapolis 500, Guthrie insisted on a private test. "Unless the car went fast enough," she said, "and I could make it go fast enough, so that we had a viable situation, we'd shake hands and that would be the end of it." She had been approached by Rolla Vollstedt, a championship auto designer and builder from Oregon, who wanted her as a driver for one of his cars at Indianapolis. Though Guthrie had been racing for over 13 years, handling a championship Indy car was different. To see if she was up to it, Vollstedt rented the Ontario Speedway in California, a track almost identical to the one at Indianapolis for her to test drive.

Two weeks before Guthrie was to fly to California, she landed badly while doing jumping exercises, breaking a bone in her left foot. As the test date approached, her foot was still swollen and painful and sealed inside a cast that doctors refused to remove. On the advice of a friend, she soaked the cast off in the bathtub and limped to the airport with her leg wrapped in an Ace bandage. In California, she left the plane with a steady walk, in case the man who had recruited her was watching.

The Ontario track was rented for three days. Watching with Vollstedt from the pits was Dick Simon, the senior driver on his team, who wanted to see what kind of feel this new driver had for racing. By the third day, Guthrie was averaging 172.5 miles an hour on the two-and-a-half-mile track. A minor example of the preparation required for the Indianapolis 500 was learning to "ride the wall." To see how close she could get to the wall on the turns, Guthrie attached a four-inch metal rod to her car and drove nearer and nearer to the banked wall until she could hear the screech of the metal.

At one point, after making some adjustments to the car without Guthrie's knowledge, Vollstedt and Simon waited for her reaction. Her immediate recognition of the changes left both men impressed, as well as the representatives of Bryant Heating and Cooling, the company sponsoring the car. Still nobody knew yet that she was driving with a broken foot. A month later, Rolla Vollstedt filed his entry form for the Indianapolis 500, listing Janet Guthrie as one of his two drivers.

Her first race on the Indy-car circuit was the Trenton (NJ) 200 on May 2, 1976, in the Bryant Special. At a press conference before the race, she had her photograph taken with Indy champion, Johnny Rutherford, a welcome surprise after months of hostility and problems from those still talking about "women drivers." Some drivers claimed a woman could not handle a race car at 200 miles per hour. Though Guthrie was also welcomed by A.J. Foyt, Bobby Unser called her presence a publicity stunt, saying he would apologize if she qualified at Indianapolis. (She did; he didn't.) Unser, a driver who had never seen her drive, claimed he could "take a hitchhiker" and teach him how to drive better than Janet Guthrie.

The following day, *The New York Times* printed an account of her race against Foyt, Rutherford and Gordon Johncock. Unser's car had broken down in the morning trials.

In the pit area of Trenton International Speedway, mechanics in fireproof clothes tinkered with the empty blue race car. Above the seat, a white driver's helmet had "JAN" marked with tape on each side. On the back of the helmet were four small identification strips: Janet Guthrie. Blood Type O Plus, Last Tetanus 2–75, No allergies. After competing in sports car events for 13 years, the 38-year-old physicist was about to become a "debutante in asbestos." With a roar, the cars moved down the gray straightaway in front of the grandstand. . . . Lap after lap, Janet Guthrie streaked along. Shortly after her first pit stop to refuel, one of her pit

Janet Guthrie

crew began shouting. "She's coming back in," he was yelling. "I couldn't hear why but she's coming back in." The chinstrap of her helmet had loosened.

"Of all the dumb things that I never had happen to me before in my life," she said later. "That sip of Gatorade at the pit was just enough to loosen the buckle."

Guthrie finished 15th in a field of 22 at Trenton, forced out by a gearbox break; but it was good enough to attempt the Indy 500. Though she passed the rookie test in the trials at Indianapolis, Vollstedt's car was not fast enough to qualify. When A.J. Foyt let her drive his back-up car in practice, she proved she was fast enough to qualify, but he thought better of letting her use it.

Making up for her disappointment at Indianapolis was the opportunity to become the first woman to race in a Grand National superspeedway event sponsored by the National Association for Stock Car Auto Racing (NASCAR). Only a few women had competed on the quarter and half-mile tracks in the 1940s, before the construction of the first superspeedway at Darlington. Admirers of Guthrie in North Carolina saw to it that she could race in the Charlotte World 600 on May 30, 1976. In a 1975 Chevrolet Laguna provided by Lynda Ferreri, a bank executive, and tuned up by veteran mechanic Ralph Moody, Guthrie came from the 27th position to finish 15th. For completing all 600 miles without a relief driver, she won the Curtis Turner award. Moving on to five other NASCAR events in 1976, Guthrie finished 15th twice and earned $8,179 in prize money. At the Daytona 500 stock-car race in February 1977, she was Top Rookie.

In 1977, Vollstedt provided Guthrie with a new and faster car, the Lightning, for another assault on the Indy 500. On a practice run at the Indianapolis Speedway on May 10, she crashed into a wall seconds after she was clocked at 191 mph. Even so, she recuperated and had her car repaired in time for the Indy qualifications, which she passed with a four-lap average of 188.403 miles per hour.

On May 29, 1977, the president of the Indianapolis Motor Speedway, in his last call to the drivers beginning the 500, made the now famous statement: "In company with the first lady ever to qualify for the Indianapolis 500—gentlemen, start your engines." During the historic race, engine trouble forced Guthrie to make eight pit stops for repairs. She completed 27 laps out of

200 to finish in 29th place. But though no one could dispute her record behind the wheel, though she had demonstrated that she could drive with the best, skeptics were not to be silenced until 1978.

For the remainder of 1977, she competed for Rookie of the Year in NASCAR, taking the Top Rookie position in five races. In Vollstedt's car, she competed in the U.S. Auto Club's (USAC) other two 500-mile races, running as high as eighth at Ontario. "There is no question about her ability to race with us," said Cale Yarborough, the reigning NASCAR champion. "She has made it in what is the most competitive racing circuit in the world." But Guthrie was still without a sponsor. Discouraged, in March 1978, she admitted in a television interview that she probably would not be at Indianapolis that year. That same day, Texaco agreed to sponsor her, a mere month before the 1978 Indianapolis race. This time, her car was more reliable. Guthrie formed her own team and qualified for the race in 15th place, with a four-lap average of 190.325.

On May 28, 1978, in the Texaco Star, a "Wildcat" built by George Bignotti, Guthrie raced at Indianapolis with a broken right wrist. Her strategy was to maintain a conservative pace at the outset and finish strong. She gradually improved her position, a move that went unnoticed by radio and television announcers. While many drivers dropped out with car problems, more than 400,000 saw Al Unser's first-place finish and Janet Guthrie's completion of what was described as an intelligent, well-planned race. She finished ninth, in the top ten, the first woman to complete the Indianapolis 500, again defeating some of the world's best drivers. The prize was nearly $25,000.

"I hope this ends the nonsense once and for all that a woman can't compete in these cars," she told the press:

> Nobody would pay any attention to the fact that I had been running 500 miles in stock cars, a much tougher job than this physically—although these cars demand total precision, which is mentally grueling. Just remember, too, that the driver is the most visible part of the team. But the crew is most important. I had, I believe, the best crew in Gasoline Alley.

Janet Guthrie's 1978 Indianapolis 500 driver's suit and helmet are in the Smithsonian Institution in Washington, and she is a member of the International Women's Sports Hall of Fame. There is "very little in civilized life that demands everything you've got intellectually, physically, and emotionally," said Guthrie. "Auto racing demands all of this and more. Driving is living. It's aggressive instead of passive living."

SOURCES:

Correspondence with Janet Guthrie, 1995.

Current Biography. NY: H.W. Wilson, 1978, p. 183.

Davidson, Judith A. *Biographical Dictionary of American Sports.* Edited by David L. Porter. Westport, CT: Greenwood Press, 1988.

Eskenazi, Gerald. "It's One Woman Against 70 Men For Indy Berths," in *The New York Times Biographical Service.* March 10, 1976, p. 353.

"Janet and Gentlemen, Start Your Engines," in *The New York Times Biographical Service.* May 3, 1976, p. 697.

Olney, Ross R. *Janet Guthrie, First Woman to Race at Indy.* NY: Harvey House, 1978.

SUGGESTED READING:

Fox, Mary Virginia. *Janet Guthrie: Foot to the Floor.* Minneapolis, MN: Dillon Press, 1991.

Hahn, James, and Lynn Hahn. *Janet Guthrie: Champion Racer.* St. Paul, MN: EMC Corp, 1978.

Robison, Nancy. *Janet Guthrie: Race Car Driver.* Chicago, IL: Children's Press, 1979.

Susan Slosberg,
Adjunct Professor of Public Relations at Baruch College and
freelance writer, New Rochelle, New York

Gutiérrez de Mendoza, Juana Belén (1875–1942)

Mexican revolutionary, journalist and feminist who never abandoned her belief in the need for the sweeping agrarian reforms that had been fundamental to the political agenda of Emiliano Zapata. Born in Durango state in 1875; died in Mexico City on July 13, 1942; daughter of Santiago Gutierrez; children: two daughters.

Born in the arid region of Durango in 1875, Juana Belén Gutiérrez de Mendoza grew up in a world in which poverty was the norm but the human spirit was not crushed. Indeed, her family was proud that her grandfather, a poor workingman, had been executed by firing squad because of his beliefs. Juana's father earned meager wages as a blacksmith, horse-tamer, and farm laborer. Racially, the Gutiérrez family was typical of the Mexican masses, with Juana's father being of *mestizo* background, and her mother of pure Indian descent. Juana was trained to be a typographer, and since printers were often political freethinkers, by 1901 she had become a teacher and was an active member of the Precursor movement, a small but committed group throughout Mexico who spoke out against the increasingly oppressive regime of President Porfirio Diaz (1830–1915).

In 1901, Gutiérrez was living in the town of Guanajuato, and it was there that she and fellow schoolteacher **Elisa Acuña y Rossetti** founded the weekly newspaper, *Vésper.* Gutiérrez had sold some of her goats in order to raise sufficient cash to buy a small printing press. From its first issue, *Vésper* was militant in its defense of the rights of the poor and oppressed. In her articles, Gutiérrez called for sweeping social reforms that would improve the lot of local miners, who worked in deplorable conditions for pathetically low wages. She linked the servile state of an ignorant peasantry to the teachings of a Roman Catholic Church which claimed that it only held the keys to heavenly salvation. Besides attacking the Diaz presidency for its arrogance and indifference to the sufferings of Mexico's masses, *Vésper* laid some of the blame on the same masses, who would not rise up and demand change. Gutiérrez's journalism infuriated conservatives, but one male editor characterized the content and style of her writing as nothing less than "virile."

Within a short time, *Vésper* had become famous beyond the confines of Guanajuato. In 1903, one of the leading anti-Diaz newspapers, *Regeneración,* paid tribute to a brave dissident journal edited by two provincial women: "Now, when many men have lost heart and, out of cowardice, retired from the fight . . . . now that many men, without vigor, retreat . . . there appears a spirited and brave woman, ready to fight for our principles, when the weakness of many men has permitted them to be trampled and spit upon." When Gutiérrez began publishing some of her essays in *Excélsior,* one of Mexico City's leading opposition newspapers, it was a sign of the growing esteem in which she was now held in anti-government circles.

By 1904, the Diaz regime had reached the limits of its ability to tolerate sharp dissents like those customarily found in *Vésper.* Both Gutiérrez and Acuña y Rossetti were arrested and thrown into the women's prison at Belén. Gutiérrez remained incarcerated for three years and was then exiled. In 1910, Camilo and **Juana Arriaga**, respected veterans of the anti-Diaz struggle, reestablished *Vésper* and began to publish it in exile in San Antonio, Texas.

The resignation of Porfirio Diaz in May 1911 did not end Gutiérrez's militant journalism. She soon concluded that both of the men who had succeeded Diaz, Francisco Madero and Venustiano Carranza, were either too politically inept or cynically Machiavellian to deal decisively with Mexico's immense social and cultural burdens. In 1911, at the beginning of Mexico's turbulent and bloody decade of revolution, Juana Gutiérrez became an enthusiastic supporter of Emiliano Zapata, the fiery champion of Mexico's oppressed peasants and Indians. By 1914, she was serving as a colonel in Zapata's "Victoria" regiment, a military unit she not only commanded but had organized from scratch. During this time, she also served as editor of a journal, *La Reforma*, advocating liberation of the Indian masses. For her outspoken writings, she served another prison term, after having been captured by government forces.

In June 1919, Juana Gutiérrez began publishing *El Desmonte*, a lively journal that enabled her to offer commentary on Mexico's increasingly chaotic political landscape. Her publication was based on the notion that "one must dismount" from the "old logs" (e.g., it was imperative that Mexico's newly emancipated citizenry cut through all the conflicting claims to political leadership). Although only a few issues of *El Desmonte* appeared, it remains one of the most interesting documentations of women's concerns in the final phase of the Mexican revolution.

Disillusioned by the military men and politicians who offered little more than flowery rhetoric or ceaseless bloodshed to a war-weary people, the only national figure Gutiérrez continued to have faith in was Emiliano Zapata. Even when Zapata was assassinated in April 1919, Gutiérrez refused to abandon her belief that one day, perhaps in the distant future, Mexico's peasants would possess the land they labored on, and Mexico's women would be liberated from their ancient burdens and discriminations.

In the 1920s and 1930s, she made a precarious living as a journalist, also spending much of her time in the struggle for an effective system of rural education. Having grown up in a world influenced by Indian traditions, she also alerted the public to the need for preserving indigenous cultural values. In November 1935, Gutiérrez began publishing a biweekly magazine entitled *Alma Mexicana: Por la Tierra y Por la Raza*, which more than ever embodied her radical and independent spirit. She did not hesitate to criticize by name those feminists she believed to be "un-Mexican" because of their inability to understand the needs of ordinary women. She also was disillusioned by what she believed to be pointless ideological dogmatism and infighting within the women's movement, and decided to break off her contacts with a number of leading feminists and Communists.

Although she was no longer young, Juana Gutiérrez refused to accept the limitations imposed by her advancing years. Extreme poverty did not break her, even when she was forced to burn many of her papers in order to heat beans that she sold on the street. Choosing to ignore her own destitution, she continued to speak out for the cause of social and economic justice for women. Towards the end of her life, Juana told an interviewer that she could never abdicate her responsibilities and simply retreat into a peaceful corner: "I don't have a corner. In all the world's corners lives a pain; in all the world's corners is coiled a treachery with open jaws, ready to swallow; and I don't have the indifference necessary to ignore it, nor the cowardice to flee it, nor the gentility to accommodate it." Shortly before her death, she spoke to friends of her plans for building a girls' school in the state of Morelia. An uncompromising foe of injustice and a dreamer of dreams to the very end, Juana Belén Gutiérrez de Mendoza died forgotten by most of her compatriots in Mexico City on July 13, 1942.

SOURCES:

Adams, Jerome R. *Latin American Heroes: Liberators and Patriots from 1500 to the Present.* NY: Ballantine, 1993.

———. *Liberators and Patriots of Latin America: Biographies of 23 Leaders from Doña Marina (1505–1530) to Bishop Romero (1917–1980).* Jefferson, NC: McFarland, 1991.

Cano, Gabriela. "Feminism," in Michael S. Werner, ed. *Encyclopedia of Mexico.* Vol. I. 2 vols. Chicago, IL: Fitzroy Dearborn Publishers, 1997, pp. 480–486.

Macias, Anna. *Against all Odds: The Feminist Movement in Mexico to 1940.* Westport, CT: Greenwood Press, 1982.

Mendieta Alatorre, Angeles. *La mujer en la Revolucion Mexicana.* Mexico City: Instituto Nacional de Estudios Historicos de la Revolucion Mexicana, 1961.

———, ed. *Juana Belén Gutiérrez de Mendoza (1875–1942): Extraordinaria precursora de la Revolucion Mexicana.* Mexico City: Universidad México, 1982.

Salas, Elizabeth. "The Soldadera in the Mexican Revolution: War and Men's Illusions," in Heather Fowler-Salamini and Mary Kay Vaughan, eds. *Women of the Mexican Countryside, 1850–1990: Creating Spaces, Shaping Transitions.* Tucson: University of Arizona Press, 1994, pp. 93–105.

Soto, Shirlene Ann. *Emergence of the Modern Mexican Woman: Her Participation in Revolution and the Struggle for Equality, 1910–1940.* Denver, Colorado: Arden Press, 1990.

———. *The Mexican Woman: A Study of Her Participation in the Revolution, 1910–1940.* Palo Alto, CA: R & E Research Associates, 1979.

Villaneda, Alicia. *Justicia y Libertad: Juana Belén Gutiérrez de Mendoza, 1875–1942.* Mexico City: Documentacion y Estudios de Mujeres, 1994.

Womack, John. *Zapata and the Mexican Revolution.* NY: Alfred A. Knopf, 1969.

John Haag,
Associate Professor of History,
University of Georgia, Athens, Georgia

Gutsu, Tatyana (1976—)

Russian gymnast. Name variations: Tatiana. Born Tatiana Constantinovna Gutsu on September 5, 1976, in Odessa, Ukraine; coached by Victor Sergeevich Dikii.

Representing the Soviet Union, Tatyana Gutsu won two Olympic gold medals in the all-around individual and all-around team in Barcelona in 1992; she was also awarded a bronze in the floor exercises and a silver in the uneven parallel bars. One of four sisters, Gutsu began her career in 1982. In 1988, she participated in the USSR Jr. national championships. She was first all-around at the European championships (1990), the USSR national championships (1991), the Europa Cup (1991), the CIS cup (1992), and the European championships (1992). She was also first all-around at the Moscow Stars (1991 and 1992).

Gutteridge, Helena Rose

(1879–1960)

British-born suffragist, trade-union activist, and politician who championed women's rights in British Columbia and was influential in securing mother's pensions and the minimum wage for women. Name variations: Nell. Born Helen Rose Gutteridge on April 8, 1879 (some sources cite 1880, but 1879 is documented), in Chelsea, London, England; died of cancer on October 1, 1960, in Vancouver, British Columbia, Canada; daughter of Charles Henry Gutteridge (a blacksmith) and Sophia (Richardsson) Gutteridge; attended Holy Trinity Church School and Regent Street Polytechnic School; also Royal Sanitary Institute, earning a South Kensington Department of Education certificate for teaching and sanitary science; married Oliver Fearn, on October 11, 1919 (divorced, December 21, 1928); no children.

Left home at 14; began career as tailor; was a London suffragist (1908–11); immigrated to Vancouver, British Columbia, Canada (1911); founded the radical British Columbia Woman's Suffrage League; co-edited the woman-suffrage page in the B.C. Federationist *(1913–15); served as secretary of the United Suffrage Societies (1915 and 1916); served as secretary of the Vancouver City Central Woman's Suffrage Referendum Campaign Committee (1916); was a member of the Pioneer political Equality League and the Vancouver Council of Women; served the Vancouver Trades and Labor Council as first woman Council executive and as organizer, secretary-treasurer, business agent, statistician, vice-chair and trustee; helped to organize women laundry and garment workers; was a member of tailor's union; correspondent for the Labor Gazette (1913–21); served as chair of the Women's Minimum Wage League (1917); was an active supporter of the Mother's Pension Act; was the first woman "alderman" for Vancouver (1937), re-elected (1939), defeated (1940); served as chair of the Vancouver Town Planning and Parks Committee (1937); was an active campaigner for improved housing, revision of tax laws and assistance for destitute women; worked as a poultry farmer (1921–32); served as supervisor of the welfare office of Japanese internment camp at Slocan City during World War II; served as chair of the Women's International League for Peace; was active in the Socialist Party of Canada as chair of the Economic Planning Commission.*

Trained under the watchful eye of the militant British suffragist *Sylvia Pankhurst, Helena Gutteridge had taken the stump at Hyde Park corner, participated in hundreds of parades for the suffrage cause, been thrown out of meetings, and waved banners in the British House of Commons. Once she was arrested but escaped imprisonment because there was not enough room in the jail for all 260 suffragists taken into custody that day. On September 8, 1911, when Gutteridge set sail for Canada, 32 years old and unmarried, her deeply ingrained sense of justice for women, especially working-class women, was honed and ready for advancement in a new land. In Canada's British Columbia, politics were never to be the same.

Born in Victorian England on April 8, 1879, to working-class parents, Helena Gutteridge was one of seven children. As London's Chelsea underwent redevelopment, the Gutteridges were one of the many families who endured constant threats of eviction, along with fetid air filled with sulphurous smoke from coal fires, the stench of animal and human waste running in the streets, and the fumes from gas lighting in poorly ventilated rooms. Helena, known to her family as Nell, was never to forget these hardships.

She attended the local Holy Trinity Church School with other working-class children until age 13. Arithmetic, spelling, reading, reciting poetry, needlework, some geography, history and grammar were crammed in, with the admonition that three mistakes and "the child was failed." In this humble setting, Gutteridge's strong sense of class difference was born, as students were constantly reminded of the donation of the school's land by the earl of Cadogan, while the countess of Cadogan occasionally sailed through to remind the students of their indebtedness to their benefactors. Class privilege also determined that her schooling ended at age 13. Beyond this age, education was dependent upon access to private schools, rarely available financially to the working-class child. In Helena's family, the money was found for her brothers to continue; when she left home at age 14, it was because she was denied the same privilege. It marked the beginning of her lifelong feminist sympathies.

Growing up in working-class Chelsea, Gutteridge was surrounded by the ferment of the trade-union movement, forming her first notions of workers' rights. The extent of her early labor activities is not fully known, but she was a member of England's Labor Party until she immigrated to Canada.

The need of political power for working women is greater than that of any other class because only when she is able to influence industrial legislation will she cease to be exploited and forced into starvation and shame.

—Helena Gutteridge

At 14, Helena went to work as an apprentice in a draper's shop. From running errands and sorting buttons, she moved up to sewer, cutter, fitter, and eventually tailor, an unusually high position for a working woman in the late 1890s. The work was 12 hours a day, Monday to Friday, and half a day on Saturday, and wages were extremely low. At the same time, Gutteridge managed to attend Regent Street Polytechnic School and the Royal Sanitary Institute, where she earned a certificate in teaching and sanitary science, a background that was to stand her in good stead when she dealt with the city politics of Vancouver. But women's suffrage was the cause that drew her into a lifetime of politics and social reform.

Turn-of-the-century London was a hotbed of suffrage activity. Young Helena became an effective public speaker and took part in a parade of 250,000 women marching to Albert Hall. She gradually became recognized as a leader in suffrage. By 1911, England's women had not yet won the vote when she decided to immigrate with several other British suffragists to Canada. Her plan to stay for four years stretched to 49, and she never returned to England.

Upon reaching Vancouver, Gutteridge joined the Pioneer Political Equality League (PPEL) but soon found it too conservatively middle class for her taste. Within weeks, she founded the British Columbia Woman's Suffrage League (BCWSL), whose aim was to "deal with all matters connected with the interests of women, particularly those things that affect women out in the labor market." In her mind, to organize working-class women to attain the vote would improve their lot in a myriad of ways, by "securing significant changes in industrial legislation, governing working conditions and pay rates, thereby eliminating sweated labor, the undervaluing of women's work and poverty-induced prostitution."

In 1913, Gutteridge also formed the United Suffrage Societies of Vancouver. From 1913 to 1915, as co-editor of the woman suffrage page in the *B.C. Federationist*, she received much attention for her wit and spirited determination to win women the vote on the grounds of the collective power it would bring to women of the working class. In her words, "The economic value of the ballot is one of the strongest arguments in favour of votes for women."

By 1913, as a member of the Vancouver Council of Women, Helena had also appeared before the Royal Commission on Labor Conditions in British Columbia. To present an accurate picture of the hardships of working women, she investigated many local factory workrooms where women were employed. Under the guise of a woman seeking a job, she found women working as glovemakers, cigarmakers, and canvas- and awning-makers. Biscuit factory employees were working up to fifty hours a week for less than six dollars. Once her findings were presented to the commission, a minimum wage for women began to receive its first serious consideration.

A woman member of the tailor's union and the Vancouver Trades and Labor Council (VTLC) was unheard of in the early 1900s. In 1914, however, Helena was elected secretary treasurer of the VTLC and became the first woman to sit on the council's executive committee. She held many positions with the VTLC, eventually, including vice chair and trustee, and was a delegate to provincial and national labor conventions. From 1913 to 1921, she was also the B.C. correspondent on women's labor issues for the *Labor Gazette,* the paper of the Federal Department of Labor. In the summer of 1913, in order to present the truth of women's working conditions to the VTLC, she had spent three weeks employed as a fish cannery worker.

Helena Gutteridge

"Women's lack of interest in her economic future as a wage earner," Helena once wrote, "is shown by her lack of interest in trade unions."

In 1917, she was chair of the Women's Minimum Wage League, leading an intense effort to ensure that women's pay was based on the cost of living and their work time limited to eight hours a day. In the spring of 1918, she headed a deputation to the provincial legislature requesting minimum-wage legislation. Only six months after the campaign was launched, on July 19,

1918, a Minimum Wage for Women Bill was passed by the B.C. government. That same year, she organized women laundry and garment workers, and in September she led them on a strike that finally won their demand to be included under the minimum wage.

During this same period, Gutteridge also worked in active support of a Mother's Pension, to provide financial aid to destitute women for the care for their children. The Mother's Pension Act was passed, finally, in 1920. Workers' compensation was another area of legislative reform she supported. According to Gutteridge, "We finally did succeed in 1918 in establishing the principle that injury or death on the job must be compensated by industry, it was a model piece of legislation for North America."

Following her marriage to Oliver Fearn in October 1919, the couple settled outside of Vancouver, and Helena Gutteridge spent several years as Mrs. Fearn, poultry farmer. From 1921 to 1932, her involvement in social reform came to a standstill. The couple remained childless and were divorced in 1928, after which Gutteridge moved back to Vancouver. Though she took up work again as a tailor, she became increasingly engaged in municipal politics.

As a member of the Cooperative Commonwealth Federation (CCF), a newly formed socialist party, she held prominent positions on the CCF executive board, including chair of its Economic Planning Commission. In the fall 1933 provincial election, she campaigned avidly for the new party. In face of the economic devastation of the Great Depression, Gutteridge and her allies in the CCF found hope in the party's philosophy of cooperation and brotherhood.

Sponsored by the CCF, Helena ran for Vancouver City Council alderman in 1937 and won, becoming Vancouver's first woman ever elected to the office. As chair of the Vancouver Town Planning and Parks Committee, she promoted government-subsidized social housing, an idea just being introduced in British Columbia. As alderman, she worked ceaselessly on this issue, through her reelection in 1939 and until her defeat in 1940. It was not until 1954, six years before her death, that she saw the beginnings of public housing in Vancouver. According to the *Province*, Vancouver's premiere newspaper, "No council member has been more faithful or more zealous than she. She has been consistently in the van of every movement of social conditions among the underprivileged."

With the outbreak of the Second World War, and its impact on city politics, Helena's career as a municipal politician ended. Packing up her belongings, she headed for British Columbia's interior, where from 1942 to 1945 she was supervisor of the welfare office at the Japanese internment camp at Slocan City. Officially declared enemy aliens by the Canadian government and stripped of all rights and belongings, thousands of Japanese were then being relocated to work camps across Canada for the duration of the war, though many were Canadian citizens. As a welfare officer, Helena oversaw the housing and personal needs of these internees, managing to carry out the job with exceptional humaneness for the time.

In retirement, Gutteridge was active in the Women's International League for Peace and Freedom, founded in 1915, and she remained on the Vancouver Town Planning Commission as late as 1957. By the time she died of cancer on October 1, 1960, at age 79, she was well aware that much of the social reform legislation she helped to introduce was firmly in place.

SOURCES:

Howard, Irene. *The Struggle for Social Justice in British Columbia.* Vancouver: UBC Press, 1992.

Wade, Susan. "Helena Gutteridge: Votes for Women and Trade Unions," in *In Her Own Right: Selected Essays on Women's History in B.C.* Victoria: Camosun College, 1980.

SUGGESTED READING:

Prentice, Alison, *et al. Canadian Women: A History.* Toronto: Harcourt Brace Jovanovich Canada, 1988.

COLLECTIONS:

Helena Gutteridge File MSS. 285, City Archives of Vancouver.

Natania T. East,
historian, Valemount, British Columbia, Canada

Guy, Alice (1875–1968).

See Guy-Blaché, Alice.

Guy-Blaché, Alice (1875–1968)

First woman film director and probably the first director to produce a story film, who was a pioneer in motion-picture production in France and the U.S. Name variations: Alice Guy; Alice Guy Blache; Alice Guy Blaché. Pronunciation: blah-SHAY. Born Alice Guy on July 1, 1875 (some give the year as 1873 but her daughter maintained that 1875 was correct) at Saint-Mondé, France; died on March 24, 1968, in a nursing home in New Jersey; daughter of Emile Guy (a bookshop owner) and Madame Guy; attended convent schools at Viry and Ferney, France; studied briefly in Paris; studied typing and stenography; mar-

ried Herbert Blaché-Bolton (known as Herbert Blaché after moving to the United States), in 1907 (divorced 1922); children: daughter Simone Blaché (b. 1908), son Reginald (b. 1912).

Spent early years with her family in Chile; sent to France for schooling; family later returned to live in France; after father's death, found employment as secretary to Léon Gaumont in a company that sold film and photographic equipment; directed her first story film La Fée aux choux (1896); promoted to head of film production for Gaumont where she directed some 400 films, including the first sound films using Gaumont's Chronophone; married (1907) and accompanied her husband to U.S. when he was transferred to Gaumont's New York operation; resumed film directing after birth of her daughter; was president and director-in-chief of Solax Company (1910–14) where she directed or supervised production of more than 300 films; was vice-president of Blaché Features founded in 1913; was director of U.S. Amusement Corporation founded in 1914; directed several films for Popular Plays and Players; lectured on film at Columbia University (1917); returned to France following her divorce; honored with the award of the Legion of Honor for pioneer work in the French film industry (1955); spent final years with daughter Simone in U.S.

Films directed by Alice Guy for Gaumont: Le Fée aux choux (later retitled Sage-femme de première classe, 1896); Le Pêcheur dans le torrent; Leçon de danse; Baignade dans le torrent; Une nuit agitée; Coucher d'Yvette; Danse fleur de lotus; Ballet Libella; Le Planton du colonel; Idylle; L'Aveugle (1897); L'Arroseur arrosé; Au réfectoire; En classe; Les Cambrioleurs; Le Cocher de fiacre endormi; Idylle interrompue; Chez le magnétiseur; Les Farces de Jocko; Scène d'escamotage; Déménagement à la cloche de bois; Je vous y prrrrends! (1897–98); Leçons de boxe; La Vie de Christ (11 tableaux) (1898–99); Le Tondeur de chiens; Le Déjeuner des enfants; Au cabaret; La Mauvaise Soupe; Un Lunch; Erreur judiciaire; L'Aveugle; La Bonne Absinthe; Danse serpentine par Mme Bob Walter; Mésaventure d'un charbonnier; Monnaie de lapin; Les Dangers de l'alcoolisme; Le Tonnelier; Transformations; Le Chiffonnier; Retour des champs; Chez le Maréchal-Ferrant; Marché à la volaille; Courte échelle; L'Angélus; Bataille d'oreillers; Bataille de boules de neige; Le marchand de coco (1899–1900); Avenue de l'Opéra; La petite magicienne; Leçon de danse; Chez le photographe; Sidney's Joujoux (series); Dans les coulisses; Au Bal de Flore (series); Ballet Japonais (series); Danse serpentine; Danse du pas des foulards par des almées; Dance de l'ivresse; Coucher d'une Parisienne; Les Fredaines de Pierette (series); Vénus et Adonis (series); La Tarentelle; Danse des Saisons (series); La Source; Danse du papillon; La Concierge; Danses (series); Chirurgie fin de siècle; Und Rage de dents; Saut humidifié de M. Plick (1900); La Danse du ventre; Lavatory moderne; Lecture quotidienne (1900–01); Folies Masquées (series); Frivolité; Les Vagues; Danses basques; Hussards et grisettes; Charmant Froufrou; Tel est pris qui croyait prendre (1901); La fiole enchantée; L'Equilibriste; En faction; La Première Gamelle; La Dent récalcitrante; Le Marchand de ballons; Les Chiens savants; Miss Lina Esbrard Danseuse Cosmopolite et Serpentine (series); Les Clowns; Quadrille réaliste; Und Scène en cabinet particulier vue à travers le trou de la serrure; Farces de cuisinière; Danse mauresque; Le Lion savant; Le Pommier; La Cour des miracles; La Gavotte; Trompé mais content; Fruits de saison; Pour secouer la salade (1902); Potage indigeste; Illusionniste renversant; Le Fiancé ensorcelé; Les apaches pas veinards; Les Aventures d'un voyageur trop pressé; Ne bougeons plus; Comment monsieur prend son bain; Le Main du professeur Hamilton ou le Roi des dollars; Service précipité; La Poule fantaisiste; Modelage express; Faust et Méphistophélès; Lutteurs américains; La Valise enchantée; Compagnons de voyage encombrants; Cake-Walk de la pendule; Répétition dans un cirque; Jocko musicien; Les Braconniers; La Liqueur du couvent; Le voleur Sacrilège; Enlèvement en automobile et mariage precipite (1903); Secours aux naufrages; La Mouche; La Chasse au cambrioleur; Nos Bons Etudiants; Les Surprises de l'affichage; Comme on fait son lit on se couche; Le Pompon malencontreux; Comment on disperse les foules; Les Enfants du miracle; Pierrot assassin; Les Deux Rivaux (1903–04); L'Assassinat du Courrier de Lyon; Vieilles Estampes (series); Mauvais coeur puni; Magie noire; Rafle de chiens; Cambrioleur et agent; Scènes Directoire (series); Duel tragique; L'Attaque d'une diligence; Culture intensive ou Le Vieux Mari; Cible humaine; Transformations; Le Jour du terme; Robert Macaire et Bertrand; Electrocutée; Le Rêve du chasseur; Le Monolutteur; Les Petits Coupeurs de bois vert; Clown en sac; Triste Fin d'un vieux savant; Le Testament de Pierrot; Les Secrets de la prestidigitation dévoilés; La Faim . . . L'occasion . . . L'herbe tendre; Militaire et nourrice; La Première Cigarette; Depart pour les vacances; Tentative d'assassinat en chemin de fer; Paris la nuit ou Exploits d'apaches à Mont-Martre; Concours de bébés; Erreur de poivrot; Volée par les bohémiens; Les Bienfaits du cinématographe; Patissier et ramoneur; Gage d'amour; L'Assassinat de la rue du Temple; Le Réveil du jardinier; Les Cambrioleurs de Paris (1904); Réhabilitation; Douaniers et contrebandiers; Le Bébé embarrassant; Comment on dort à Paris!; Le Lorgnon accusateur; La Charité du Prestidigitateur; Une Noce au lac Saint-Fargeau; Le Képi; Le Pantalon coupé; Le Plateau; Roméo pris au piége; Chien jouant à la Balle; Le Fantassin Guignard; La Statue; Villa dévalisée; Mort de Robert Macaire et Bertrand; Le Pavé; Les Maçons; La Esmeralda; Peintre et ivrogne; On est poivrot, mais on a du coeur; Au Poulailler! *(1905)*; La Fée printemps; La Vie du marin; La Chaussette; La Messe de minuit; Pauvre pompier; Le Régiment moderne; Les Druides; Voyage en Espagne *(series)*; La Vie du Christ (25 tableaux); Conscience de prêtre; L'Honneur du corse; J'Ai un hanneton dans mon pantalon; Le Fils du garde-chasse; Course de taureaux à Nimes; La Pègre de Paris; Lèvres closes; La Crinoline; La Voiture cellulaire; La Marâtre; Le Matelas alcoolique; A la recherche d'un appartement *(1906)*; La vérité sur l'homme-singe; Déménagement à la cloche de bois; Les Gendarmes; Sur la barricade *(1907)*. *Sound films:* Carmen *(opera series)*; Mireille *(opera series)*; Carmen *(suite series)*; Les Dragons de Villars *(opera series)*; Mignon *(opera series)*; Faust *(opera series)*; Polin *(series)*; Mayol *(series)*; Dranem *(comic song series)*; *music series recorded in Spain:* La Prière de Gounod *(1900–07)*.

Films directed or supervised by Alice Guy-Blaché for Solax: A Child's Sacrifice; The Sergeant's Daughter; A Fateful Gift; A Widow and her Child; Her Father's Sin; One Touch of Nature; What Is To Be, Will be; Lady Betty's Strategy; Two Suits; The Pawnshop; Mrs. Richard Dare *(1910)*; The Nightcap; Salmon Fishing in Canada; The Girl and the Burglar; A Reporter's Romance; His Best Friend; Ring of Love; Mixed Pets; Corinne in Dollyland; Love's Test; A Costly Pledge; Out of the Arctic; Put Out; Caribou Hunting; A Midnight Visitor; Highlands of New Brunswick, Canada; A Hindu Prince; Cupid's Victory; Out of the Depths; A Package of Trouble; She Was Not Afraid; The Mill of the Gods; A Maid's Revenge; The Rose of the Circus; Tramp Strategy; The Scheme that Failed; The Little Flower Girl; The Old Excuse; The Voice of his Conscience; The Count of No Account; Across the Mexican Line; Sensible Dad; The Somnambulist; Nearly a Hero; Beneath the Moon; Between Life and Duty; His Dumb Wife; In the Nick of Time; The Devil in a Tin Cup; An Officer and a Gentleman; A Marvelous Cow; Never Too Late to Mend; Bridget the Flirt; A Mexican Girl's Love; A Bad Egg; A Daughter of the Navajo; Cupid and the Comet; Johnnie Waters the Garden; Marked for Life; The Fascinating Widow; A Terrible Catastrophe; Greater Love Hath No Man; Starting Something; The Silent Signal; Baby's Rattle; That June Bug; The Girl and the Bron-

cho Buster; All Aboard for Reno; Sergeant Dillon's Bravery; The Double Elopement; Outwitted by Horse and Lariat; When Reuben Came to Town; The Mascot of Troop "C"; His Wife's Insurance; A Bum and a Bomb; An Enlisted Man's Honor; The Phoney Ring; Let No Man Put Asunder; A Gay Bachelor; The Stampede; The Patched Shoe; The Hold-up; Hector's Inheritance; The Best Policy; Her Uncle's Will; The Altered Message; Oh! You Stenographer!; Nellie's Soldier; How Hopkins Raised the Rent; An Italian's Gratitude; A Breezy Morning; His Sister's Sweetheart; He Was a Millionaire; His Mother's Hymn; A Corner in Criminals; A Lover's Ruse; His Better Self; Percy and His Squaw; For Big Brother's Sake; Following Cousin's Footsteps; A Heroine of the Revolution; An Interrupted Elopement; Grandmother Love; Baby Needs Medicine; Only a Squaw; Husbands Wanted; The Will of Providence; A Troublesome Picture; Life on Board a Battleship; A Revolutionary Romance; Baby's Choice; The Paper Making Industry; The Little Shoe; Fickle Bridget; The Little Kiddie Mine; Love, Whiskers, and Letters; The Violin Maker of Nuremberg; When Marian was Married; The Divided Ring; Christmas Presents; His Musical Soul *(1911)*; Our Poor Relation; Economical Brown; Black Sheep; By the Hand of a Child; Parson Sue; A Man's Man; The Legend of the Balanced Rock; The Little Soldier; Memories of '49; Frozen on Love's Trail; The Wonderful Oswego Falls; The Fixer Fixed; Mignon; The Snowman; A Guilty Conscience; Mrs. Cranston's Jewels; Lend Me Your Wife; Bessie's Suitors; A Terrible Lesson; The Wise Witch of Fairyland; Hubby Does the Washing; God Disposes; His Lordship's White Feather; Algie the Miner; Blighted Lives; Sealed Lips; The Animated Bathtub; The Boarding House Heiress; Falling Leaves; Count Henri, the Hunter; The Bachelor's Club; The Child of the Tenements; Billy's Shoes; Handle with Care; The Witch's Necklace; Billy's Troublesome Grip; The Detective's Dog; Billy's Nurse; Saved by a Cat; Billy, the Detective; The Sewer; Billy's Insomnia; The Reformation of Mary; A Question of Hair; The Wooing of Alice; Auto Suggestion; Souls in the Shadow; In the Year 2000; The Glory of Light; The Knight in Armor; A Message from Beyond; Just a Boy; The Old Violin; The Dog-gone Question; Billy Boy; Mickey's Pal; The Great Discovery; Four Friends; Indian Summer; Planting Time; Love's Railroad; The Call of the Rose; Father and the Boys; Between Two Fires; Winsome but Wise; Fra Diavolo; Hotel Honeymoon; Slippery Jim; The Four Flush Actor; Broken Hearts; The Requital; Bottles; Imagination; Buddy and his Dog; Two Little Rangers; The Pink Garters; The Blood Stain; The Strike; The Equine Spy; Phantom Paradise;

Playing Trumps; The Fight in the Dark; Open to Proposals; Treasures on the Wing; The Soul of the Violin; The Spry Spinsters; The Life of a Rose; The Love of the Flag; The Fugitive; Si's Surprise Party; The Retreat from Eden; Dublin Dan; Canned Harmony; A Fool and his Money; The Gold Brick; The Maverick; The High Cost of Living; The Idol Worshipper; Making an American Citizen; At the Phone; The New Love and the Old; Just Hats; The Prodigal Wife; Flesh and Blood; A Comedy of Errors; The Power of Money; The Paralytic; The Jenkins-Perkins War; The Raffle; The Face at the Window; The Hater of Women; The Girl in the Armchair; Hearts Unknown; Five Evenings; The Finger Prints; The Woman Behind the Man *(1912)*; Cousins of Sherlock Holmes; Canine Rivals; A Million Dollars; Beasts of the Jungle; The Mutiny of Mr. Henpeck; Mother and Daughter; The Quarrellers; The Coming of Sunbeam; The Roads that Lead Home; The Wrong Box; The Scheming Woman; Overcoats; The Monkey Accomplice; The Eyes of Satan; The Thief; Burstop Holmes, Detective; Till the Day Breaks; The Bashful Boy; The Veteran's Mascot; Dick Whittington and his Cat; Napoleon; The Kiss of Judas; What Happened to Officer Henderson; The Plans of the House; In the Wrong Flat; The Way of the Transgressor; Burstop Holmes' Murder Case; The Climax; The Bachelor's Housekeeper; The Ogres; The Lady Doctor; His Son-in-law; The Mystery of the Lost Cat; Where Love Dwells; His Wife's Affinity; A Severe Test; The Silver Cross; A House Divided; The Case of the Missing Girl; The Past Forgiven; Dad's Orders; The Man in the Sick Room; Kelly from the Emerald Isle; The Amateur Highwayman; The Man Who Failed; The Henpecked Burglar; The King's Messenger; The Hopes of Belinda; Blood and Water; Gregory's Shadow; Matrimony's Speed Limit; Her Mother's Pictures; Romeo in Pajamas; Strangers from Nowhere; The Merry Widow; The Dynamited Dog; The Message to Heaven; An Unexpected Meeting; True Hearts; The Flea Circus; As the Bell Rings; Cooking for Trouble; Brennan of the Moor; The Intruder; That Dog; As Ye Sow; The Coat that Came Back; When the Tide Turns; The Heavenly Widow; Falsely Accused; Four Fools and a Maid; A Drop of Blood; The Pit and the Pendulum; The Smuggler's Child; A Terrible Night; A Child's Intuition; Men and Muslin; Retribution; Dooley and his Dog; Gratitude; Invisible Ink; Western Love; The Quality of Mercy; The Soul of Man; Tale of a Cat; The Lame Man; Blood and Water; The Little Hunchback; Handcuffed for Life; Ish Ga Bibble; Fisherman's Luck; The Rogues of Paris; Ben Bolt; Shadows of the Moulin Rouge *(1913)*; Beneath the Czar; The Monster and the Girl *(1914)*.

Films directed by Alice Guy-Blaché for Blaché Features, Popular Plays and Players, U.S. Amusement Corporation, and other companies: Hook and Hand *(may have been directed by Herbert Blaché)*; The Dream Woman; The Million Dollar Robbery; The Woman of Mystery; The Yellow Traffic; The Lure; The Tigress *(1914)*; The Heart of a Painted Woman; Greater Love Hath No Man; The Vampire; My Madonna *(1915)*; What Will People Say?; The Ocean Waif *(1916)*; The Adventurer; The Empress; A Man and the Woman; House of Cards; When You and I Were Young; Behind the Mask *(1917)*; The Great Adventure *(1918)*; Tarnished Reputations *(1920)*.

The painted backdrop of a garden fence was in place. Against this view were arranged large wooden cutouts of cabbages. A few friends dressed in rental costumes waited to act out their parts. Alice Guy was about to direct *La Fée aux Choux* (*The Cabbage Fairy*), the short film that would earn her an undisputed place in film histo-

Alice Guy-Blaché

ry as the first woman film director and probably the first film director to produce narrative films.

Alice Guy was born at Saint-Mondé on the outskirts of Paris on July 1, 1875, because her mother (whose name has been lost to history) was determined that her fifth child be born in France. Alice's father Emile Guy owned bookshops in Valparaiso and Santiago, Chile. Within a few months of her birth, her parents returned to Chile, leaving her in the care of her maternal grandmother. Three-year-old Alice rejoined her parents in South America, but when she reached school age, she was returned to France and enrolled in the same school her three sisters attended at the Convent of the Sacred Heart at Viry. Then a series of disasters, including an earthquake, left the family bankrupt, and Alice was sent to a less expensive convent in the château of Voltaire at Ferney. Following the death of their only son, the Guys returned to France, settled in Paris, and Alice completed her education there.

There is nothing connected with the staging of a motion picture that a woman cannot do as easily as a man, and there is no reason why she cannot completely master every technicality of the art.

—Alice Guy-Blaché

When Emile Guy died at age 51, his wife was poorly prepared to support the two daughters who remained at home. A family friend suggested that Alice take typing and stenography lessons. Noting her rapid progress, her instructor recommended her for a secretarial position at Comptoir général de Photographie. This company, which made and sold film and equipment for still photography, was soon acquired by Alice Guy's employer, Léon Gaumont, and renamed the Société des établissements Gaumont.

In 1895, Louis Lumière brought Gaumont his new invention, a camera that filmed moving objects. Though Gaumont soon developed his own version of the camera, he saw little practical use for it. Alice, however, was intrigued by the possibilities. To demonstrate the new cameras, Lumière and Gaumont both shot short films of actual events: parades, trains arriving at railroad stations, and portraits of laboratory personnel. Alice was convinced that there would be more interest in films that told stories. Gaumont, thinking the camera was little more than a toy, agreed to her making a film as long as it did not interfere with her secretarial duties.

Guy was in the office every morning at eight to open, record, and distribute the mail. Then she would commute to the Buttes Chaumont to work on her films. She returned to the office by 4:30 and often worked until 10 or 11 at night handling correspondence and other details. To help shorten her commute, Gaumont arranged for her to rent a house behind the photographic studio and granted the use of a paved terrace covered by a glass roof next to the studios.

In 1896, she directed *La Fée aux choux,* based on an old French tale about a fairy who raises children in a cabbage patch. Whether this was the first story film is still unsettled. Most film histories, which make no mention at all of Alice Guy-Blaché, credit French filmmaker Georges Méliès (known as "father of the fiction film") with making the first narrative films. Anthony Slide, Charles Ford, and others believe that *La Fée aux Choux* preceded Méliès' first effort by a few months. According to Guy-Blaché's daughter **Simone Blaché**, this film was shown in 1896 at the International Exhibition in Paris. Regardless, Alice Guy and Méliès, working independently, were discovering and using similar story-telling techniques at about the same time.

Guy describes some of those techniques in her memoirs. By reversing the film, a house that fell down could be magically reconstructed. Slowing down or speeding up the turn of the handle on the camera could produce frenzied movement or slow motion. Stopping the camera allowed objects to be moved, creating the impression they were animated by a supernatural life. Fade outs could be used for visions and dreams. Double exposures and masks allowed other special effects.

These early films were short, about 75 feet in length. The titles suggest the story lines: *Leçon de danse* (*Dance Lesson,* 1897), *Le Déjeuner des enfants* (*The Children's Lunch,* 1899–1900), *Les Dangers de l'alcoolisme* (*The Dangers of Alcohol,* 1899–1900). They were so successful that Gaumont named Alice Guy head of production and in 1901 built a studio for her use. There she began to produce more sophisticated films, many painstakingly tinted by hand by artisans working in the laboratory. As film quality improved and mechanical methods of film development replaced tedious hand developing, longer films were possible. These often ran 150 feet, while one, *La Vie du Christ* (1906), ran almost 2,000 feet.

When Gaumont bought the rights to the newly invented Chronophone, a device that synchronized sound, recorded on a wax cylinder, with the projector, Guy directed a series of talking pictures between 1900 and 1907. Some featured popular singers, others were scenes from operas including *Carmen, Mignon, Manon, Faust,* and *Les Dragons de Villars.* The work was demanding. The role of the director included responsibility for the scenario and choice of actors, working with the decorators and costumers, overseeing lighting, rehearsals and stage direction, editing and cutting the final film. It was also filled with unexpected problems. In one instance, Guy decided to use a gypsy (Rom) camp as the location for *Volée par les bohémiens* (1904). The scenario included a bear which the animal trainer had tied under a wagon. Startled by the screams of the actress whose foot he sniffed, the bear escaped and jumped on a goat. As the trainer tugged and the gypsies rushed to save the goat, the bear turned to a donkey which fled, braying wildly. The camera captured the melee and, according to Alice Guy, this "added greatly to the interest of the film."

As demand for films grew, Guy worked with several assistants, including Victorin Jasset. (Early film historians often erroneously credited direction of Guy's films to these assistants.) Jasset helped her manage the 250–300 extras and the outdoor scenes in *La Vie du Christ* (1906). The film, based on illustrations by James Tissot, was lavish by the standards of the time: 25 solid sets were constructed, costumes were carefully matched to Tissot's documents, and two Jesuits were brought in as consultants. *La Vie du Christ* was undoubtedly one of the first large spectacle films, with superimpositions used to depict Jesus rising from the sepulchre.

In 1906, Herbert Blaché-Bolton arrived at Gaumont headquarters from the company's English office to work with the camera. Intent on learning film directing, he accompanied Guy to film the bullfights at Saintes-Maries-de-la-Mer. By Christmastime, they were engaged; they were married in 1907.

Meanwhile, Gaumont had the sold rights to the Chronophone to a Cleveland entrepreneur, and the newlyweds were sent to the United States to represent Gaumont's interests. (Once in the U.S., the couple dropped Bolton from their name and were known as Herbert Blaché and Alice Guy-Blaché.) When the Cleveland company went bankrupt, the Blachés moved to Flushing, New York, to head up Gaumont's manufacturing and film-production activities. In 1908, Alice Guy-Blaché gave birth to a daughter Simone, but she was soon restless with domestic life and decided to return to films.

On September 7, 1910, Guy-Blaché—along with her husband and George A. Magie—founded the Solax Company. Alice was president and director-in-chief. (Herbert was still under contract to Gaumont.) That same year, Solax released its first film, *A Child's Sacrifice.* **Magda Foy,** later known as the "Solax Kid," played an eight-year-old girl who tries to aid her starving family. With her father out on strike and her mother ill, the child sells her doll to a junk dealer who then gives it back as a present. The girl goes on to intervene in a bitter quarrel provoked by the strike.

At first, the new company rented the Gaumont's Flushing studio. But Solax prospered and, in 1912, moved production to a new studio complex in Fort Lee, New Jersey. News reports described the size and complexity of the nascent operation. The studio had south-facing windows two stories high. There were also shops for building sets and storing props, large dressing rooms for the actors, laboratories and darkrooms for processing the film, and projection rooms for viewing.

Madame Guy-Blaché directed or actively supervised all the films produced by Solax. Anthony Slide lists well over 300 films that were produced there. Since most of these films were lost and few carried director credits, it is difficult to ascertain which were directed by Guy-Blaché and which by Edward Warren who joined Solax in 1911.

Guy-Blaché attracted considerable interest from the press. Reporters, who often attended filmings, sought interviews frequently. When she could not comply, they wrote articles anyway, in which she learned, she said, "some absolutely unsuspected details about my beginnings, my family, my ancestors." At the time, a woman managing such complex activities was viewed as unique. If, to reassure an actor, Alice had to be the first to stroke the tiger or drape the snake around her neck, she did it. At times when the physical risks were obvious, her husband stepped in, as he would in setting off the explosion to sink the pirate ship in *Dick Whittington and His Cat* (1913).

In addition to the technical expertise she had developed, Guy-Blaché had a keen sense of the beauty of a photographic image. She took advantage of the most favorable hour for the best light, noted how the setting sun lengthened shadows, captured the reflections in a rippling pond, and was aware of the waves made by the wind blowing across a field of wheat.

At Solax, she directed a variety of films. An advertisement in the November 18, 1911, issue of

The Moving Picture World listed several Solax releases. In the ad, *An Interrupted Elopement* was announced as a clever comedy in which a couple, held up and detained by thieves, escape as love triumphs. *Grandmother Love* was promoted as a small, simple drama of the heart, while *Only a Squaw* boasted beautiful photography. It also heralded a special release: the "Big Naval Review" with 102 naval vessels reviewed by President William Howard Taft in New York Harbor. Next to Solax's blazing sun logo was the reminder that "all our films are tinted and toned."

In 1912, Guy-Blaché gave birth to her second child, a son Reginald. Noting the number of films produced at Solax that year, it is reasonable to assume she was quickly back at the studio. Then, Herbert Blaché left Gaumont and established Blaché Features in October 1913, with himself as president and his wife as vice-president. He persuaded her to join in directing films for the new company, and Solax soon ceased production. The following year, Herbert was involved in another production company, U.S. Amusement Corporation.

While Guy-Blaché continued to work for the companies started by her husband, she also directed several films for a New York company, Popular Plays and Players. These included the first two films featuring the dramatic actress ◄⁂ Olga Petrova: *The Tigress* (1914) and *The Heart of a Painted Woman* (1915). Petrova was impressed by Guy-Blaché's courtesy to artists; by earning their respect, she got the results she sought. Reporters writing for *The Moving Picture World* also had praise for her directing style. One who visited the location where *Fra Diavolo*

(1912) was being filmed found Guy-Blaché conducting rehearsals on the elevated camera platform. She was never ruffled, never agitated, never annoyed, he wrote. "With a few simple directions, uttered without apparent emotion, she handles the interweaving movements like a military leader might [handle] the maneuvers of an army." Another who visited the set of *Dick Whittington and His Cat* (1913) commented on "how sharp and clear-cut is her visualizing power and how thoroughly she knows just what she wants." Yet, he observed, she was also quick to find the humor in situations, helping to ease the nervous strain of production.

In 1917, Guy-Blaché was invited to lecture on film at Columbia University. But small independent filmmakers like the Blachés were finding it more difficult to compete with large, well-financed companies. The last two films Alice directed, *The Great Adventure* (1918) and *Tarnished Reputations* (1920), were released through the Pathé Exchange. Lured by the sunny climate, many film companies were moving to California, and the Blachés joined the migration. Herbert was hired to direct several films, but Alice was restricted to a position as his assistant. By this time, the marriage was foundering, and, following a divorce, Guy-Blaché and her two children returned to France in 1922.

When Alice Guy-Blaché tried to reestablish herself in the French film industry, she found no one willing to hire her. Since she had left all of her work behind in America, she had no films to show as evidence of her ability. The only offers she received would have required her to make large financial investments in the projects. This she was in no position to do. From time to time, she earned some income by writing summaries of scenarios, short stories, and children's stories.

The difficulties Alice Guy-Blaché encountered in trying to continue working in film had been foreshadowed in an interview that had appeared in the November 6, 1912, issue of *The New York Dramatic Mirror*. Talking about her work as a filmmaker, she maintained that she "would not have been able to accomplish so much in any other country, particularly in France." In the United States, she felt, "the fight and victory is to the strong, irrespective of sex." In France, women are "commonly in a state of dependence, and are not likely to exercise their reason with freedom."

For the rest of her life, Guy-Blaché tried to reclaim her place in film history. She lived with her daughter Simone who, from about 1941,

⁂► **Petrova, Olga** (1886–1977)

English actress. Born Muriel Harding in England in 1886; died in 1977.

Billed by studio publicists as the daughter of a Russian noble from Warsaw, Poland, Olga Petrova was born Muriel Harding in England in 1886. She played femmes fatales in Hollywood silents for Metro, including *The Tigress* (1914), *The Soul Market* (1916), *The Undying Flame* (1917), *The Soul of a Magdalene* (1917), *Daughter of Destiny* (1918), and *Panther Woman* (1918), and produced and wrote several of her own films. After retiring from the screen in 1918, Petrova returned to the stage, starring in many plays, including three that she had also written.

SUGGESTED READING:

Petrova, Olga. *Butter with my Bread* (autobiography), 1942.

worked with the American foreign service, first in France, then in Switzerland. In 1952, when Simone was transferred to Washington, D.C., Alice came with her and began a search for her films but was unsuccessful. All had disappeared. Finally, in 1955, her work as a pioneer in France's motion picture industry was recognized by the award of the French Legion of Honor. Simone Blaché retired to live in the United States, accompanied by her mother. Alice Guy-Blaché died in New Jersey on March 24, 1968.

To date, film historians have uncovered a few of Guy-Blaché's films. A positive negative of *La Fée aux choux* exists at the Cinémathèque Française. Anthony Slide lists six one-reelers produced at Solax that are in the National Film Collection at the Library of Congress: *Greater Love Hath No Man* (1911), *The Detective's Dog* (1912), *Canned Harmony* (1912), *The Girl in the Armchair* (1912), *A House Divided* (1913) and *Matrimony's Speed Limit* (1913). A few other films may exist in private collections.

In trying to reach conclusions about Alice Guy-Blaché's contribution to film history, one fact is obvious. She was prolific. Film historian Francis Lacassin compiled a list of 403 films directed by Alice Guy for Gaumont alone. Anthony Slide asserts that of the 331 films produced by the Solax Company through 1913, she was involved in the production of all of them as supervising director and producer. He credits her with directing 23 more films that were released between 1914 and 1920. Her choice of subject matter ranged widely: comedy, fantasy, religious themes, drama, military and cowboy adventures, adaptations of plays and stories, dance, opera—the list goes on. In addition, she was inventive. While many of the techniques such as running film in reverse or masking or varying the speed of the film may have been discovered by trial and error, the ways in which she used these techniques as story-telling devices was truly creative. As Slide comments about the films in the National Film Collection, they demonstrate "a remarkable sophistication in story-telling." Whether or not historians reach agreement about who was first in producing a narrative film, Alice Guy-Blaché will retain her place as the first woman film director and a remarkably successful one.

SOURCES:
Blaché, Alice Guy. *The Memoirs of Alice Guy Blaché*. Translated by Roberta and Simone Blaché and edited by Anthony Slide. Metuchen, NJ: Scarecrow Press, 1986.
Lacassin, Francis. "Out of Oblivion: Alice Guy Blaché," in *Sight and Sound*. Summer 1971, pp. 151–154.

Slide, Anthony. *Early Women Directors*. NY: A.S. Barnes, 1977.

SUGGESTED READING:
Acker, Ally. *Reel Women: Pioneers of the Cinema*. NY: Continuum, 1991.
Guy-Blaché, Alice. "Woman's Place in Photoplay Production," in *Moving Picture World*. July 11, 1914.
Heck-Rabi, Louise. *Women Filmmakers: A Critical Reception*. Metuchen, NJ: Scarecrow Press, 1984.
Kay, Karyn, and Gerald Perry, eds. *Women and the Cinema*. NY: E.P. Dutton, 1977.
Smith, Sharon. *Women Who Make Movies*. NY: Hopkinson and Blake, 1975.

Lucy A. Liggett,
Professor of Telecommunications and Film,
Eastern Michigan University, Ypsilanti, Michigan

Guyard or Guyart, Marie (1599–1672).

See Marie de l'Incarnation.

Guyon, Jeanne Marie Bouviéres de la Mothe (1648–1717)

French Catholic aristocrat who, despite rigorous opposition and persecution, devoted her life to the pursuit of spiritual union with God through faith and prayer. Name variations: Jean Marie Guyon; Jeanne Marie Bouviéres de la Mothe; Jeanne-Marie Bouvier de la Mothe; Jeanne Marie de la Motte-Guyon; Madame Guion or Madame Guyon. Born on April 13, 1648, in the town of Montargis, 50 miles south of Paris, France; died on June 9, 1717, age 69; daughter of Claude Bouviéres de la Mothe, Seigneur de la Mothe Vergonville (a widower whose first wife was **Marie Ozon**) and Jeanne le Maistre de la Maisonfort (widow of Etienne Ravault); married Jacques Guyon (1625–1676), on March 21, 1664; children: Armand-Jacques Guyon (b. May 21, 1665); Armand-Claude Guyon (b. January 8, 1668, d. October 20, 1670); Marie-Anne Guyon (b. 1669, d. June 4, 1672); Jean-Baptiste-Denys Guyon (b. May 31, 1674); Jeanne-Marie Guyon, later countess of Vaux (b. March 21, 1676).

Spent most of early years in convents where she received a rudimentary education; lived at home until marriage at age 15 (1659–1663), did not meet her wealthy, 38-year-old husband, who had been selected by her father, until three days before the wedding; despite her long cherished ambition to become a nun, was attracted by the idea of comfort and independence; found herself a virtual prisoner, however, of her husband and mother-in-law; became increasingly spiritual and, after the birth of her first two children, underwent a religious "conversion" (1668), from which time she dedicated her life to God;, widowed at age 28 (1676); though two of her children had died in infancy, was left with three others; felt called to go on a *mission to Geneva, to convert the Protestants there and left Paris (July 1681), renouncing her possessions and giving up her sons to the care of her stepmother; thwarted in plans to get to Geneva, traveled with her little daughter and a maid to Gex, Thonon, Turin and Grenoble, speaking to small groups and individuals about religion, particularly the importance of faith and prayer; also began to write devotional works; because her doctrines were regarded with increasing suspicion by church and state authorities, was confined in the Convent of the Visitation for most of the year under suspicion of Quietism (1688); was rearrested (December 1695) and imprisoned in the castle of Vincennes for nine months; was then transferred to a convent near Paris where she was kept for two years; was sent to the fortress prison of the Bastille (June 1698), where she spent more than four years in solitary confinement; released (March 1703) and was banished to Blois, in the custody of her son, Armand-Jacques.*

Madame Guyon had been imprisoned before. She had spent most of 1688 confined in a convent, and in December 1695 she had been held in the royal prison at Vincennes for almost a year before being transferred to close captivity in another convent. But on June 4, 1698, she entered the Bastille and began the harshest and most isolated confinement of all. When she was eventually released, almost five years later, although she was only 54 years old, her active life was over. Madame Guyon's health had been broken but her ardent spirit burned on.

𝒩othing is greater than God: nothing more little than I. He is rich: I am very poor. I do not want for anything. I do not feel need of anything. Death, life, all is alike. Eternity, time: all is eternity, all is God.

—Madame Guyon, *Autobiography.*

Jeanne Marie Bouviéres de la Mothe was born on April 13, 1648, in the town of Montargis, 50 miles from Paris. Her father, Claude Bouviéres de la Mothe, lord of la Mothe-Vergonville, and a legal officer of the king, was a widower with a son and a daughter from his first marriage. Her mother, **Jeanne le Maistre de la Maisonfort**, was a widow with a daughter from her first marriage. Both parents came from wealthy and influential families and both, especially Jeanne Marie's father, seem to have been deeply religious, unswerving, during this century following the Reformation, in their adherence to the Catholic faith. Born a month premature, the

little girl was weak and sickly and neither parent seems to have had much concern for her. At the age of only two and a half, Jeanne was sent to stay at an Ursuline convent; she returned home briefly, placed mostly in the care of servants, only to be sent to live at three different convents in turn before she reached the age of 11. Following her First Communion on April 14, 1659, she returned home to live with her parents.

With such an early upbringing, it would have been surprising if Jeanne Marie had not become religious; in her autobiography, she describes having nightmares as a small child in which she had vivid visions of Hell. It was perhaps the nightmares which helped shape her early decision to become a nun. "Young as I was," she recalled in her autobiography, "I loved to hear of God, to be at church, and to be dressed in the habit of a little nun." But the child felt her parents' neglect keenly, particularly missing her mother's affection. Her half-brother was her mother's favorite, and the boy, who was later to become a priest and cause endless trouble for his sister, started to plague Jeanne Marie early. According to her own account, he persuaded her to climb to the highest point on the carriage, then threw her down, almost killing her. She was convinced that only divine protection saved her.

As she grew into a beautiful young woman, Jeanne Marie felt torn between the religious life to which she was sure she had been called and the allure of the rich and elegant world into which she had been born. In 1661, the visit of a pious cousin, about to depart as a missionary to China, moved her towards religious life again and induced her to read the biographies of *Jeanne de Chantal* (1572–1641) and St. Francis de Sales, bishop of Geneva. Jeanne Marie "loved reading madly" and would read day and night, so that "for several months I had completely lost the habit of sleeping." However, rather than the lives of missionary saints, she was soon reading romances; "I was not prevented; on the contrary, people have the foolish idea that they teach one to speak correctly." At last, her mother began to take some interest in her: "My mother, seeing that I was very tall for my age and more to her taste than usual, only thought of bringing me out, making me see company and dressing me well." In her autobiography, written almost 30 years later, Jeanne Marie judged her younger self harshly: "I began to seek in the creature what I had found in God. . . . I readily gave way to sallies of passion. I failed in being strictly conscientious and careful in the utterance of the truth. I became not only vain, but corrupt in heart."

In 1663, the family moved from Montargis to Paris, at that time the most magnificent capital in Europe, reflecting the splendor of the absolutist "Sun King," Louis XIV. According to Madame Guyon's biographer, Thomas Uppham, the glittering city was "equally characterized by its unfounded pretensions, its vanity and its voluptuousness." Paris charmed the young Jeanne Marie, and her tall good looks, keen intelligence, good manners and engaging conversation soon captivated a bevy of suitors. She seems to have developed some affection for a cousin but refused his offer of marriage. Instead, on January 28, 1664, her father arranged her engagement to Jacques Guyon. The chosen suitor was a man of great wealth whose father had been given his patent of nobility by Cardinal Richelieu. Jeanne Marie's ambivalence about her future life was clear in the period leading up to the marriage: she accepted her father's choice, even though there were other suitors she would have preferred; she says that she signed the articles of marriage without knowing what they were; and she saw her husband only three days before marriage.

The wedding probably took place on March 21, 1664; Jeanne Marie was almost 16, her husband 38. Although she wept after the ceremony, remembering her plans to become a nun, "I was well-pleased to be married, because I imagined thereby I should have full liberty." The young Madame Guyon's dreams of liberty were dashed immediately. She was taken to live in her husband's house which was firmly under the direction of his widowed mother; it became "a house of mourning" for Jeanne. If she dared to speak, she was contradicted and reproved. She was lodged in her mother-in-law's room: "I had no place into which I could retire as my own; and if it had been otherwise, I could not have remained alone in it for any length of time without offence." Even the maid treated Jeanne Marie like a governess. "For the most part I bore with patience these evils, which I had no way to avoid; but sometimes I let some hasty answer escape me, which was to me a source of grievous crosses and violent reproaches for a long time together." Her movements were watched and reported. "My proud spirit broke under her system of coercion. Married to a person of rank and wealth, I found myself a slave in my own dwelling rather than a free person." Unwilling to sadden her parents with reports of her misery, "I was alone and helpless in my grief."

The birth of her first child, Armand Jacques Guyon, on May 21, 1665, seems not to have

ameliorated her miserable situation. Jeanne Marie tried to revive her spirits by going for walks. Her pregnancy had improved her appearance, and she tells of removing her mask and gloves when out walking so as to show off her beauty. At the same time, she attempted to curb her vanity: "I did not curl my hair, or very little; I did not even put anything on my face, yet I was not the less vain of it." She rarely looked into a mirror so as not to encourage her vanity, and she read pious books, such as the *Imitation of Christ* and the works of St. Francis de Sales while her hair was being combed so that "the servants profited by it." She wore no make up but "other women, who were jealous of me, maintained that I painted, and said so to my confessor, who reproved me for it, although I assured him to the contrary." But still, according to her autobiography, she was vain and proud and told lies.

Madame Guyon dates her "conversion" from the feast day of the Biblical sinner *Mary Magdalene, July 22, 1668. She was 20 and had given birth to her second son earlier that year. Visiting her father during his illness, she was introduced to a Franciscan friar, and she described to him her futile efforts to become closer to God. She quotes his response in her autobiography: "Your efforts have been unsuccessful, Madame, because you seek outside what you have within. Accustom yourself to seek God in your heart, and you will find him there." From that moment, she records, "my heart was quite changed. . . . God was there; for from that moment he had given me an experience of his presence in my soul. . . . I slept not all that night, because thy love, oh my God, flowed in me like a delicious oil, and burned as a fire which was going to destroy all that was left of self in an instant."

Madame Guyon's earlier sporadic efforts to become more spiritual were completely eclipsed by this conversion experience; "Through an inconceivable goodness, O my God, you introduced me into a state very pure, very firm, and very solid." Her new state meant a change in her behavior: "I bade farewell, forever, to assemblies which I had visited, to plays and diversions, to dancing, to unprofitable walks, and to parties of pleasure." All such entertainments "now appeared to me dull and insipid." She replaced worldly distractions with rigorous bodily mortification; she whipped herself for long periods with a lash tipped with nails, and although the beatings drew much blood, they failed to satisfy her. She wore tight girdles made of hair and nails and, she writes, "I tore myself with brambles, thorns and nettles, which I kept on me." The resulting pain "entirely deprived me of sleep." In order to mortify her appetite, she kept bitter tasting herbs in her mouth and mixed her food with a purgative. "All that could flatter my taste was refused to it. All that was most disagreeable to it was given to it" with the result that her taste was soon unable to distinguish. She lost all sense of disgust by dressing wounds and nursing the sick. Although she continued with these austerities for many years, "in less than a year my senses were reduced to subjection."

She describes her new relationship with God as being like a "devouring fire," a kind of purgatory in which "you [God] purified me from all that was contrary to your divine will." She was active in giving charity, donating money, food and clothing to the poor, and arranging for young beautiful women to be taught a trade so that they might not be tempted to prostitution; "I went to visit the sick, to comfort them, to make their beds. I made ointments, aided in dressing wounds, and paid the funeral expenses incurred in the interment of those who died." Yet despite her bodily penances and good works, as a young married woman of the nobility, Madame Guyon was expected to conform to the role imposed by society. While she gave up all social activity and refused to curl her hair, she continued to be well dressed "for my husband wished it so." She took care not to let anything appear on the outside, but her "occupation by God" gave her such a "gentleness, modesty, and majesty that people of the world perceived it." However much she might have attempted concealment, her new spirituality encountered opposition: "When the world saw that I had quitted it, it persecuted me, and turned me into ridicule." Her husband and mother-in-law were particularly unhappy with the change: "My husband was out of humour with my devotion; it became insupportable to him. 'What!' says he, 'you love God so much that you love me no longer.'" He objected to her praying even when he was away from home, and he and his mother watched her constantly.

Madame Guyon asked God to send her more suffering to test and purify her devotion and, as if in answer to her prayers, in 1670, she was infected with smallpox and almost died. She describes her body as being covered in sores, like a leper, "but as for my soul, she was in a contentment I cannot express." Both sons also contracted the disease, and the younger one, aged two, died. Two years later a third child, Marie-Anne, her much-loved daughter, died at the age of three, and Madame Guyon's father and her dearest friend died the same year. Her friend, **Geneviève Granger**, had been prioress of a house of Benedictine nuns: "I concealed from her none of my sins nor of my troubles. I would not have done the least thing without telling it to her. I practiced no austerities but those she permitted me." Mother Granger must have permitted a great deal, for Madame Guyon's physical self-punishment intensified: "I often had my teeth pulled out, although they did not pain me. It was a refreshment for me, and when my teeth pained me I did not think of having them pulled out. . . . I once poured molten lead on my naked flesh, but it did not cause any pain, because it flowed off and did not stick. In sealing letters I let Spanish wax fall on me, and this causes more pain, because it sticks. When I held a candle, I let it come to an end and burn me for a long time."

She was to have two more children, a son in 1674 and another daughter, **Jeanne-Marie Guyon**, in 1676, just four months before the death of her husband. Madame Guyon reconciled with her husband before his death; he had come to value her piety and realized that others, especially his mother, had conspired to turn him against her. She was left a widow at the age of 28 with three small children to care for. If it had not been for the children, she recounts in her autobiography, she would have finally fulfilled her childhood ambition and become a nun. As it was, she resisted invitations to remarry and attempted to reconcile with her mother-in-law. She was becoming increasingly close to Father La Combe, a priest whom she had first met in 1671; he had immediately seen "an extraordinary presence of God on my countenance" and had experienced his own "conversion" as a result of their meeting. She began to feel that God was calling her to be a missionary to the Protestant city of Geneva, and La Combe sensed that he was being called to assist with the task.

Since it was brave to the point of folly to aspire to be a Catholic missionary in the city which was at the heart of the Protestant Reformation, Madame Guyon left Paris in secret during the summer of 1681, heading first for the Catholic city of Gex, just 12 miles from Geneva. Leaving her sons in the care of her mother-in-law and accompanied only by her five-year-old daughter and a maid, she established a convent for Protestant converts, the "New Catholics" as they were called, at Gex. There she found Father La Combe, who had been assigned by the local bishop to be her confessor. After a fall from a horse which forced her to return briefly to Paris, she left the capital again, renouncing all her possessions in return for a small pension and settling, in April 1682, at Thonon, close to Geneva. Having spent two years at the convent of the Ursulines, she moved, with her daughter and faithful maid, to a small cottage. "Never did I enjoy a greater content, than in this hovel" she wrote. Her daughter and maid had the larger room—she had only a small chamber, reached by ladder. It was at Thonon that she spent some of the most contented months of her turbulent life. It was there that she received "the most pure, penetrating, and powerful communication of grace that I had ever experienced," and there that she wrote the first of her devotional works, *The Torrents*. Eventually her collected works were to fill 40 volumes, and her vast correspondence was to be collected into 5 thick volumes.

With her attention focused on the conversion of Protestants, Madame Guyon seems not to have been aware of her growing notoriety in Paris. King Louis XIV, determined to keep France Catholic and united under his uncompro-

misingly authoritarian rule, was unwilling to tolerate forms of worship which appeared to deviate in any way from conventional Catholicism. In 1685, signalling the new religious conservatism, the king had revoked the Edict of Nantes, the 1598 legislation which had given Protestants the right to worship in France. Paradoxically, some of those most concerned with converting the Protestants, fell under suspicion also.

Madame Guyon's writings and her meetings with those seeking spiritual enlightenment centered around a single question; she asked those who were searching for God "were they willing to be NOTHING? That is to say, *nothing in themselves*, in order that the Lord might be ALL IN ALL." Hers was not an ecstatic, empowering spirituality of visions and revelations. Rather, Madame Guyon felt herself becoming more and more childlike, as she advanced in spirituality towards the ideal state of complete self-negation, or "pure love," a state sustained by the simplicity of prayer. Such a private, interior means of seeking salvation was clearly a source of suspicion for the established church, which it could, potentially, render redundant. Nor did it help that this fervent spirit was a woman; her gender further accentuated the negative reaction of the religious and state establishment.

Madame Guyon's own experiences paralleled those of the poor laundress whose story she tells in her autobiography. The woman had five children and a sick husband and was sustained in her hard life only by her prayer. When two devout tradespeople came to assist her by reading from religious books, they found that God "had taught her inwardly. . . . So much was this the case, that they were willing to receive instruction from her." The conservative church authorities reproved her, telling her, "it was very bold in her to practice prayer in the manner she did. They said it was the business of priests to pray, and not of women." Like the laundress, Madame Guyon remained steadfast in the face of threats, enduring the burning of all her books on spirituality in the public square. Opposition to her mounted following the official condemnation of the Spanish preacher, Michael de Molinos, by the Papal Inquisition in July 1685. Although Madame Guyon had never heard of him, her ideas and his were seen to be similar and were both branded as "Quietism." In October 1687, Father La Combe was arrested. Scurrilous stories were spread about Madame Guyon's relationship with the priest: they were alleged to have ridden together on horseback on their return to Paris the previous summer; one rumor even claimed that she had become pregnant by him. She reports that her half-brother, Dominique de la Mothe, who had introduced her to La Combe, intrigued with her enemies against them both.

La Combe was imprisoned in the Bastille, and his book, *An Analysis of Mental Prayer,* was condemned by the Inquisition. He died, still in custody, 27 years later. But Madame Guyon was quite undaunted. She had no fear for her friend: "I know by the spirit communication that he is very content and abandoned to God." Nor was she afraid for herself, although she must have known that her turn would come next. On January 29, 1688, she was taken into custody and confined to the Convent of the Visitation. She was held in solitary confinement for eight months by devout nuns who had been instructed to regard her as a dangerous heretic. During this period, cut off from her beloved daughter and refused any news of her, she stubbornly refused to admit that she had been in error, nor would she condemn Father La Combe. So far was she from repentance that on her release in October 1688, she met and soon won over an even more distinguished disciple, the Abbé Fénelon, archbishop of Cambray, missionary to the Protestants, tutor to the royal household, and one of the most brilliant men of his day. Fénelon's conversion to the "new spirituality," as Madame Guyon's religious practice was sometimes called, soon brought his chief rival, Bossuet, the bishop of Meux, into the dispute. Bossuet was the effective head of the Catholic Church in France, and he resolved to eradicate the heretical teachings of Madame Guyon and her new adherent. After interviewing her several times, Bossuet succeeded in obtaining an official condemnation of her doctrine of "pure love" in March 1694. Later that year, a royal commission, headed by Bossuet, was set up to examine the whole body of her writings. Although the other members of the committee were inclined towards leniency, Bossuet remained in resolute opposition, and in December 1695 Madame Guyon was arrested and shut up in the castle of Vincennes, "accused of having maintained, both by word of mouth and by her writings, a very dangerous doctrine, and one which nearly approaches to heresy."

Fénelon attempted to explain and justify Madame Guyon's views in his own published works; he claimed that her concept of "pure love" was not a rejection of the Catholic faith but was, rather, a rejection of self, an advanced spiritual state of "holy indifference." Despite the unremitting opposition of Bossuet, he stoutly defended her piety by incorporating significant aspects of her theology into his own. But not even Fénelon could withstand the pope. Pressured by Bossuet and other conservatives at the French court, the pope finally issued a decree on March 12, 1699, condemning 23 propositions extracted from Fénelon's book. Fénelon was submissive; he withdrew from all doctrinal controversy, left Versailles forever, and spent the rest of his life serving the people of his diocese.

After nine months in custody at Vincennes, Madame Guyon was transferred, probably in August 1696, to Vaugirard near Paris, remaining there for two years, all the while refusing to admit culpability in any aspect of her thought or behavior. Doubtless as a result of her stubbornness, in September 1698 she was moved once more, this time to the most dreaded of all the royal prisons, the Bastille. It was here that Madame Guyon was held for four years in solitary confinement. Her autobiographer records the irony of the situation: "It was thought necessary, by those who knew her influence and thought it unfavorable, that twelve feet of thick wall, built up on every side, should guard her against making any exertions in the cause of Christ." This pious, middle-aged woman was incarcerated at the same time and in the same terrifying place as the legendary Man in the Iron Mask, rumored to be the twin brother of the king and a dangerous threat to royal power. Yet Madame Guyon's spirit remained strong: "So long as God is with me, neither imprisonment nor death will have any terrors." Her imprisonment was the talk of Versailles, and a memoir of the period records that although she was interrogated by the chief of police, "She is said to defend herself with great ability and firmness."

Released in 1702, Madame Guyon was permitted only a brief visit to her daughter Jeanne-Marie, now the countess of Vaux, in Paris, and was then banished for life to Blois, 100 miles from the capital, given into the custody of her eldest son, Armand Jacques. She lived for another 15 years, but her health, never robust, had been broken by the harsh conditions of her imprisonment. Although she was ill most of the time, she continued to write letters and conduct private conversations on spiritual matters. It was during her enforced retirement that she resumed writing the autobiography she had begun during her first imprisonment in 1688. In a passage dated December 1709, she asks for forgiveness of those who have treated her unkindly. They had done their worst but their efforts had served merely to bring her to the state of "profound annihilation" for which she had always striven. As she records in her closing pages, her state had become "simple and invariable. . . . There is neither clamor nor pain, nor trouble, nor pleasure, nor uncertainty; but a perfect peace."

Jeanne Marie Bouviéres de la Mothe Guyon died at 11:30 PM on June 9, 1717, age 69. It must be said that, according to her own terms, her life ended in triumph. It had been a life completely dedicated to God from the time of her "conversion" at the age of 20. While she felt herself to be in almost constant communication with God, she did not become an ecstatic in the visionary sense; she distrusted "illumination" and all other spectacular evidence of holiness. Rather, neglecting her beauty, abandoning her wealth, and giving up her children, she devoted herself to prayer and self-imposed suffering. Consumed with a sense of mission, she endured constant harassment, ill treatment and accusations of heresy from political and religious leaders as a result of her efforts to spread God's word. For her, there was no choice. She had received a Divine calling and, in response, she gave all she had and all she was.

SOURCES:

Allen, Thomas Taylor, trans. *Autobiography of Madame Guyon.* 2 vols. London: Kegan Paul, Trench, Trubner, 1898.

Guion, Madame. *Poems, Translated from the French of Madame de la Mothe Guion by the late William Cowper.* Newport-Pagnel: J. Wakefield, 1801.

Lillie, Arthur. *Modern Mystics and Modern Magic.* NY: Scribner, 1894.

Sahler, Benjamin. *Madame Guyon et Fénelon; La Correspondance secrète.* Paris: Dervy-Livres, 1982.

Upham, Thomas C. *Life and Religious Opinions and Experience of Madame de la Mothe Guyon.* 2 vols. NY: Harper & Brothers, 1862.

Dr. Kathy Garay,
Acting Director of the Women's Studies Program at
McMaster University, Hamilton, Canada

Guzman, Eleonore de (d. 1512)

Duchess of Braganza. Died on November 2, 1512; daughter of Isabel de Velasco and Juan Alfonso de Guzman, duke of Medina Sidonia; married Jaime or James (1479–1532), duke of Braganza, in 1502; children: Toeodosio or Theodosius (1510–1563), duke of Braganza. James second wife was *Joana de Mendoza.

Guzman, Leonora de (1310–1351)

Countess of Clermont, mistress of Castilian king Alphonso XI, and mother of Henry II of Trastamara. Name variations: Leonor de Guzmán; La Favorita. Born in 1310; died in 1351; daughter of Pedro Martínez de Guzmán and Beatriz Ponce de León; married Juan de Velasco (died 1328); mistress of Alphonso XI (1311–1350), king of Castile (r. 1312–1350); children: (with Alphonso XI) Pedro (b. 1330); Sancho (b. 1331); Enrique II also known as Henry II Trastamara (1333–1379), king of Castile (r. 1369–1379); Fadrique (b. 1333); Fernando (1336–c. 1342); Tello (1337–1370), count of Castaneda; Juan (1341–1359); Pedro (1345–1359); Juana (who married Fernando de Castro and Felipe de Castro).

Born into one of the chief Castilian noble families in 1310, Leonora de Guzmán was the daughter of Pedro Martínez de Guzmán and **Beatriz Ponce de León.** As a youth her parents married her to Juan de Velasco, whose death left her a widow by 1328. Attracted by her beauty and bearing, Alphonso XI, king of Castile, became enamored of her when they met during his visit to Sevilla. Meanwhile, in 1328 Alphonso married ❧▶ **Maria of Portugal,** the daughter of ***Beatrice of Castile and Leon** and Alphonso IV, king of Portugal, but did not immediately succeed in having any children with her.

Only in 1334 did Maria finally give birth to a son, Peter (I the Cruel), who survived to become Alphonso's heir to the throne. In contrast, Leonora and Alphonso had ten children. Following Peter's baptism, Alphonso spent no further time with Queen Maria, preferring instead to be with Leonora de Guzmán. Maria passed the rest of her husband's life, humiliated by his snub and resenting his obvious preference, both public and private, for Leonora. By flaunting his relationship with Leonora, Alphonso angered the king of Portugal, Maria's father, and war erupted between the two realms. Aside from her wealth and physical attractions, Leonora was apparently bright and able. She participated energetically in Alphonso's rule, and the king often sought her advice on political matters.

❧▶ **Maria of Portugal (1313–1357)**

Queen of Castile and Leon. Name variations: Mary Henriques, Enriques or Enriquez. Born in 1313; died on January 18, 1357, in Evora; interred in Seville, Spain; daughter of *Beatrice of Castile and Leon (1293–1359) and Alphonso IV, king of Portugal (r. 1325–1357); married Alphonso XI (1311–1350), king of Castile and Leon (r. 1312–1350), in September 1328; children: Fernando (1332–1333); Pedro el Cruel also known as Peter I the Cruel (1334–1369), king of Castile (r. 1350–1369).

Although most of the court accepted the liaison between Leonora and Alphonso, the superficial peace lasted only as long as the king lived. When he died during the siege of Gibraltar on March 27, 1350, from the Black Death, the tensions between the partisans of Maria and Leonora broke into violence. Leonora accompanied her lover's body toward Sevilla, performing the role of grieving widow. She refused to enter Sevilla, however, rightly fearing for her own safety. Peter, Alphonso's only surviving legitimate child, was king, and his mother, the long-humiliated Maria, maneuvered to arrest and imprison Leonora. Initially Leonora received protection from Alphonso Fernández Coronel, but he later switched allegiance to Maria and Peter, giving Leonora over to their custody. In the royal fortress of Sevilla, Leonora's conditions were initially mild. She received friends and relatives and her son Henry II Trastamara was allowed to visit frequently. Eventually, however, the chance for revenge against Alphonso's favorite, and fear that Leonora's partisans might endanger the crown on her own son's head, caused Maria to transfer Leonora to Talavera de la Reina and shortly thereafter have her executed. She died in 1351. Some have credited her execution to Maria's spite. For others, it resulted from Leonora's complicity in her son Henry's secret marriage and Henry and Tello's rebellion against Peter.

Leonora's life was symptomatic of the turmoil that afflicted Castile during the 14th century. Ambitious aristocratic families divided the kingdom, conspiring against the monarchy. The Black Death that killed Alphonso and indirectly brought on Leonora's premature demise caused havoc and consternation throughout the peninsula. From the enmity between Leonora and Maria sprang two sons, Henry and Peter, who over the following two decades fought to the death. In the end Leonora triumphed when Henry murdered Peter the Cruel in 1369 and claimed the crown of Castile for himself as Henry II.

SOURCES:

Estow, Clara. *Peter the Cruel of Castile, 1350–1369*. NY: Brill, 1995.

Sánchez-Arcilla Bernal, José. *Alfonso XI, 1312–1350*. Palencia: Editorial La Olmeda, 1995.

Kendall W. Brown,
Professor of History, Brigham Young University, Provo, Utah

Guzman, Luisa de (1613–1666).

See Luisa de Guzman.

Guzman, Mayor de (d. 1262)

Mistress of Alphonso X. Name variations: Mary de Guzman; Mary Guillemete or Guillemette. Born Mayor Guillen de Guzman; died in 1262; daughter of Guillen Prez de Guzman and **Maria Gonsalez Giron***; mistress of Alphonso X the Wise (1221–1284), king of Castile and Leon (r. 1252–1284); children:* ***Beatrice of Castile and Leon** (1242–1303). (One source also places Sancho IV, king of Castile and Leon, as a son of de Guzman.)*

Gwen.

Variant of Winne.

Gwenddolen or Gwendolen.

Variant of Winifred.

Gwenddyd.

Variant of Winnie.

Gwenfrewi.

Variant of Winifred.

Gwenhwyfar or Gwenhwyfer (d. 470 or 542).

See Guinevere.

Gwenllian of Wales (fl. 1137)

Welsh princess and heroine. Flourished around 1137 in Gwynedd, Wales; daughter of Gruffydd ap Cynan, king of Gwynedd; married Gruffydd ap Rhys, king of Deheubarth; children: Maredudd and Rhys.

Gwenllian, the daughter of King Gruffydd ap Cynan, of Gwynedd, was a Welsh patriot and warrior. She married the Welsh warrior Gruffydd ap Rhys, king of Deheubarth. In the 1130s, England and Wales were involved in constant warfare, with King Henry III's English forces determined to gain the submission of the Welsh princes and make Wales part of their kingdom, and the Welsh people equally determined to create their own autonomous state. Gwenllian served as a link between her royal brothers and Gruffydd, leading to their alliance against England. Gwenllian was by no means a passive witness to this conflict; she led her own army into battle in southern Wales. Eventually, Gwenllian was killed on the battlefield. Her sons Maredudd and Rhys both became Welsh kings. Gwenllian's name lived on as a symbol of Welsh spirit and patriotism in legends for many years.

Laura York,
Riverside, California

Gwent, Gwenynen (1802–1896).

See Hall, Augusta.

Gwynedd, princess of (fl. 1173).

See Marared.

Gwyneth.

Variant of Wenefrid or Winifred.

Gwynn, Nell (1650–1687)

English comedy actress, mistress of Charles II, who was one of the most popular figures of Restoration England. Name variations: Gwyn or Gwynne. Born Eleanor Gwynn on February 2, 1650, in England (authorities are unsure whether in London, Oxford, or Hereford); died on November 14, 1687; daughter of Helena and Thomas or James Gwynn (a common soldier); children: (with Charles II) Charles Beauclerk (1670–1726, later duke of St. Albans); James Beauclerk, earl of Plymouth (d. 1680).

As one of England's best-known royal mistresses, Nell Gwynn's remarkable popularity has endured into modern times. She arose from lowly origins to become a favorite of Charles II and held his affections from about 1669 until his death in 1685, bearing him two sons who were eventually raised to the English peerage.

She was born Eleanor Gwynn (in typical 17th-century fashion, her name is spelled with countless variations) and came from obscure origins. The cities of London, Oxford, and Hereford all claim to be her birthplace. Because Gwynn was a common surname, tracing her origins becomes an even more daunting task, but it is known that she was born on February 2, 1650, to **Helena Gwynn**. Her father Thomas Gwynn was a shadowy figure, reputedly a soldier who was said to have died in an Oxford prison when Nell was a young girl. She had one sister, **Rose Gwynn**, who was about two years her senior.

Left to her own devices, Gwynn's mother had a difficult time making ends meet. In a filthy tenement in Coal Yard Alley in London, she and her daughters eked out a marginal living selling vegetables, fish and oysters, and, as Gwynn later admitted, "serving strong waters to the gentlemen" at a brothel. At that time, the driving ambition of many girls brought up on the streets of London was to escape the drudgery of street selling and prostitution by attracting the attention of a man with wealth and status who would set them up with a home and a small income.

Gwynn's looks and personality worked in her favor. So did political circumstance: in 1660, when she was only ten years old, Lord Protector Oliver Cromwell died leaving the protectorship to his son Richard. Richard was not the leader his father had been, and England had already begun to chafe under the somber yoke of Puritan rule.

Within weeks, a group of Parliamentarians led by George Monck hatched a conspiracy to bring the son of Charles I back to the throne. (Charles I had been executed by Parliament in 1649.) Upon hearing of the scheme, Richard fled the country. Within weeks, Charles II was crowned king of England amidst great celebration.

The Restoration brought about a relaxation of public morality and new opportunities for young girls like Gwynn. Charles II immediately reopened the theaters and even decreed that women's parts would be played by women (instead of by men dressed as women, as in the earlier days of the 17th century). In 1663, one of the new theaters, the King's House, opened on Nell Gwynn's very doorstep. She was already becoming a lovely woman, with fair hair, large blue eyes, and a disarming smile. She soon secured her first theater job, as an "orange-girl," selling oranges and other fruit to playgoers.

> *And once Nell Gwynn, a frail young sprite,*
> *Look'd kindly when I met her;*
> *I shook my head perhaps—but quite*
> *Forgot to quite forget her.*
>
> —Fred Locker, *London Lyrics*

Gwynn quickly caught the eye of a merchant, John Duncan, who set her up in a small room at the Cock and Pie tavern and kept her as his mistress. In late 1663, her sister Rose was arrested for burglary and sent to Newgate prison, a filthy cesspool from which few emerged except aboard the executioner's tumbrel. In desperation, their mother sent Gwynn to plead with Thomas Killigrew, whose son Harry had been Rose's lover, to intercede on Rose's behalf. As chance would have it, Killigrew was manager of the King's House Theater. With his help, Rose was released from Newgate. Gwynn, who had impressed Killigrew with her looks and frank conversation, soon made her first appearance on stage.

As an actress, she excelled in comedy, and with her good voice and ready wit she quickly endeared herself to her London audiences. Her ascendancy to stardom, however, was temporarily halted in the summer of 1665 with the outbreak of the Great Plague of London. Everyone with the means to do so fled the city as death tolls rose to 1,000 per day. The taverns and the theaters were closed for a year. Soon after they reopened in August 1666, the city was ravaged by the Great Fire, which destroyed most of Old London, including St. Paul's Cathedral, and the theaters were closed once again. When the King's House finally put on a play called *The English Monsieur* in December, Gwynn stole the show, becoming one of the most popular actors in London before her 17th birthday.

As she earned more leading roles, it was inevitable that she would catch the eye of Charles II who had developed a ferocious appetite for both theater and women during his long exile in France. Even before his marriage in 1662 to *Catherine of Braganza, Charles had surrounded himself with beautiful mistresses. Within a few weeks of his marriage, he had resumed his passionate affair with *Barbara Villiers (later Lady Castlemaine and duchess of Cleveland). Charles had acknowledged several of Barbara's children as his own and also had other illegitimate off-

❧▶ **Killigrew, Elizabeth** (c. 1622–?)
Mistress of Charles II. Name variations: Betty Killigrew. Born around 1622; daughter of Sir Robert Killigrew; sister of the duke of York's chaplin (the duke of York later became James II, king of England); married Francis Boyle, later 1st Viscount Shannon; mistress of Charles II (1630–1685), king of England (r. 1661–1685); children: (with Charles II) Charlotte Jemima Henrietta Maria Fitzroy or Fitzcharles (1651–1684, who married James Howard, earl of Suffolk, and William Paston, 2nd earl of Yarmouth).

❧▶ **Pegge, Catherine** (fl. 1657)
Mistress of Charles II. Name variations: Katherine Pegg. Daughter of Thomas Pegge, a Derbyshire squire; mistress of Charles II (1630–1685), king of England (r. 1661–1685); children: (with Charles II) Charles Fitzcharles, earl of Plymouth (b. 1657); Catherine Fitzcharles (1658–1759, a nun at Dunkirk); possibly had another daughter who died in infancy.

❧▶ **Davies, Moll** (fl. 1673)
English actress and dancer. Name variations: Mary Davies; Moll Davis. Flourished around 1673; mistress of Charles II (1630–1685), king of England (r. 1661–1685); children: (with Charles) illegitimate daughter known as Mary Tudor (1673–1726, who married Edward Radclyffe, 2nd earl of Derwentwater, Henry Graham of Levens, and James Rooke).

Moll Davies was a member of Sir William Davenant's troupe at Lincoln's Inn, when she caught the eye of Charles II, king of England. In keeping with the fashion of comparing the king's mistresses, Samuel Pepys proclaimed her a better actress than *Nell Gwynn. Davies' relationship with Charles was short lived, though they had one daughter together.

spring from previous mistresses, ◄❧ **Elizabeth Killigrew,** ◄❧ **Catherine Pegge,** ◄❧ **Moll Davies,** and *Lucy Walter. The king was known to occasionally indulge in dalliances with the actresses at the theaters, and by 1668 Gwynn's performance of a merry jig while attired in men's clothing induced Charles to add her to his retinue of occasional companions.

Her quick wit and lively personality endeared her to the inconstant monarch, and, as his ardor for Barbara Villiers began to cool, he spent an increasing amount of time with the spirited actress. They shared a love of gambling, horse racing, and country life, and often were together in the king's residence at Newmarket. By the autumn of 1669, she was quite obviously pregnant. Delighted at the newest proof of his virility, Charles openly acknowledged his paternity and moved Gwynn into a comfortable house while showering her with gifts. He ate at least one meal a day with her and whiled away the hours regaling her with gossip and playing card games.

Charles' solicitude did not blind him to the charm of others, however. While Gwynn was pregnant, he developed an interest in *Louise de Kéroüalle, one of his sister's (*Henrietta Anne) ladies-in-waiting. The daughter of an old but impoverished French noble family, Louise was considered beautiful, although her face was called "simple and babyish." Though Gwynn quickly returned to the stage after the birth of a son, whom she named Charles Beauclerk, Charles continued to see her and gave her a larger house at 79 Pall Mall, closer to Whitehall. By 1671, she was pregnant again and gave birth to another son on Christmas Day. She named him James Beauclerk, in honor of Charles' brother James. By this time, Louise de Kéroüalle was also pregnant, and she gave birth to a son during the following summer.

By 1672, Nell Gwynn and Louise de Kéroüalle had become firmly established as Charles II's primary mistresses. He divided his time fairly evenly between them, although de Kéroüalle's grasping nature guaranteed her the majority of the king's bounty. Gwynn, however, was unquestionably the most popular of all his mistresses. The public preferred Gwynn to her rival, whom they referred to as "Mrs. Carwell" or "Mrs. Cartwheel," in a simplified version of her French surname. In fact, Nell Gwynn was different from Charles' other mistresses in many ways. She was the only favorite without an aristocratic pedigree, and she took every opportunity to ridicule the noble pretensions of her rivals.

Nell
Gwynn

When Barbara Villiers acquired a luxurious coach-and-six, Gwynn rigged up an old wagon with six oxen and drove around outside Villiers' window cracking an enormous whip and yelling "Whores to market, Ho!" Mocking Louise de Kéroüalle's habit of dressing in mourning garb for the death of members of European royalty to whom she claimed kinship, Gwynn began to dress herself in mourning for an assortment of unlikely potentates; when asked why she was dressed in mourning for the recently deceased Cham of Tartary, she quickly claimed that she was related to him "in exactly the same way as is Louise de Kéroüalle [to] the Prince of Rohan," for whom Louise had recently donned mourning garb. When confronted by Louise for her disrespect, Gwynn jokingly proposed, "Let us agree to divide the world: you shall have the Kings of the North, and I the Kings of the South."

Gwynn's lack of pretension contributed to her popularity, as did her indifference to the melee of politics and the struggle for noble titles. Barbara Villiers had baited the king incessantly until he ennobled all of her children and made her duchess of Cleveland. Louise de Kéroüalle persuaded Charles to make her son duke of Richmond. Not satisfied when Charles made her duchess of Portsmouth, Louise pushed Charles to intervene with Louis XIV to secure for her a French title as well. Soon after her ennoblement, Louise remarked to Gwynn, "Why Nelly, you 'ave such beautiful clothes. You could be queen." Nonplussed, Gwynn replied, "And you, Cartwheel, look whore enough to be a duchess."

Although she had many powerful and influential friends, Nell Gwynn never stooped to playing games of petty politics. Charles' other mistresses, by virtue of their proximity to the king's ear, built up large factions of ambitious office-seekers and badgered Charles constantly to give them preferment. Gwynn, by contrast, attended plays and horse races with the king and took him fishing. When Charles came to her after a particularly difficult day of struggling with the factions of Council and Parliament, he exclaimed, "Nelly, what shall I do to please the People of England? I am torn to pieces by their clamours." Without skipping a beat, Gwynn frankly replied, "If it please your Majesty, there is but one way left, which expedient I am afraid it will be difficult to persuade you to embrace. . . . Dismiss your ladies and mind your business, the People of England will soon be pleased." On another occasion, she was said to have advised the king to "lock up his codpiece."

By 1673, Gwynn had retired from the stage, although she attended performances frequently in the private box Charles had provided. Her house became a kind of political turf, where representatives of all the contending camps could meet to discuss their differences, and where Charles could often gain valuable information. Foreign dignitaries visited often, bringing expensive gifts for Nell and her children. During 1674 and 1675, Louise de Kéroüalle was often out of the picture, bedridden with the pox which she had contracted from Charles or some other suitor. Although Charles' lax sexual morality caused him to be plagued with a wide spectrum of venereal diseases, Gwynn seems to have been mercifully spared from ill health.

In Louise's absence, Nell encountered a new rival for the king's affections. In 1675, *Hortense Mancini, Duchess Mazarin, rode into London on horseback dressed as a cavalier in boots and spurs. Following a brief marriage to a religious fanatic, Hortense had fled to a convent and petitioned for a separation. When the nuns tired of her antics, she fled to Savoy, where she began her existence as a famous courtesan. While her welcome in Savoy was beginning to wear thin, Hortense was persuaded by an out-of-favor British ambassador to travel to London to try to oust de Kéroüalle and Gwynn from the king's favor. Hortense, already 30, was still strikingly beautiful. Her black hair and eyes, together with her creamy white skin, gave her an exotic loveliness that provided a stark contrast to Gwynn's fairer coloring.

Hortense Mancini's arrival wreaked havoc on the royal household. When the king showed every evidence of falling under Hortense's charm, de Kéroüalle beat her head against the bedpost and gave herself a black eye. Gwynn accepted the new arrival more philosophically. She even organized entertainments for both Louise and Hortense in her home, where the three spent many long afternoons playing cards, often losing thousands of pounds to each other and appealing to Charles to satisfy their debts. Despite Hortense's undeniable charms, Charles still seems to have enjoyed Gwynn's company above all. She traveled with him whenever he left town. During one of their absences to the country, Hortense took up with the prince of Monaco. Charles did not accept this public humiliation well; he revoked her allowance, and her star fell as quickly as it had risen.

As Gwynn reached her late 20s, she became more conscious of the need for security and responsibility for herself and her two sons. Although Charles expressed his intention to make her a countess, his ministers flatly refused to grant a noble title to a former orange-girl without a drop of noble blood in her veins. Her children, however, were half-royal, and so in 1676 Charles was able to procure for her older son the titles Baron Huddington and earl of Burford. In 1684, Charles also made him duke of St. Albans. Her younger son was raised to the peerage as Lord James Beauclerk.

In addition to her many charms, Gwynn's religious preference also contributed to her popularity. She was a good Anglican. De Kéroüalle and Queen Catherine of Braganza were openly Catholic. In that age, Roman Catholics were notoriously unpopular in England and usually considered to be less than patriotic. Louise, as a French noblewoman who kept up a close correspondence with Louis XIV, was universally believed to be a foreign spy. When Gwynn's coach was mistaken for de Kéroüalle's, a crowd of detractors gathered to shout insults. Gwynn bravely stuck her head out of the window and called out: "Be still, friends; I am the Protestant whore," whereupon she left amidst universal cheers.

Until age 30, Gwynn enjoyed impeccable health, but in 1680 she fell ill and was confined through the spring. In a worse turn of events, in June her younger son James died of a "bad leg" while visiting Paris. She blamed herself for allowing him to go abroad and for not being with him when he was on his deathbed. She shut herself up in her house until Charles was finally able to persuade her to reemerge in the fall.

Widely praised by contemporaries for her generosity, Gwynn was actually a poor manager of her own money but was willing to give what she had to those in distress. Sincerely moved by the plight of Civil War veterans, many of whom had been injured or maimed and then left without a cent, she persuaded Charles in 1682 to build a Royal Hospital.

As the king neared middle age, he spent increasingly more time in her company, and several encounters with the pox and the clap put a damper on his sexual exploits. Charles yearned for refuge from the never-ending squabbles of court. With each passing year, de Kéroüalle became more politically minded and finally grew too fat to engage in any strenuous activity. Meanwhile, Catherine of Braganza, always the retiring type, was easily satisfied with an occasional game of cards with her husband. Gwynn, however, continued to accompany the king on his travels, hunting, hawking and riding together whenever he could escape the duties of state.

By the end of 1684, Charles' health was noticeably in decline. He developed a painful ulcer in his left leg which prevented him from taking exercise outdoors. On the morning of Gwynn's 35th birthday, February 2, 1685, the king rose early with the intention of acquiring a proper gift for her. While being dressed, he suffered a severe seizure, was immediately put to bed, and a cadre of doctors was called to his bedside. Gwynn and the other mistresses were barred from his rooms, and only the queen was allowed to attend him. Charles lingered for several days, but it was clear that his end was near. His brother James procured for him a Roman Catholic priest, who gave Charles absolution and extreme unction. After calling all his sons to him, including Gwynn's son Charles, and apologizing to his doctors for "being such an unconscionable time dying," Charles passed away on February 5th. His last words to his brother were "to be kind to the Duchess of Cleveland and especially Portsmouth, and that Nelly might not starve."

Nell Gwynn did not long outlive her royal paramour. She fell on economic hard times, as did all of Charles' mistresses. Since Charles and Catherine of Braganza never produced a legitimate heir, the throne passed to Charles' brother James II. As a Roman Catholic, James was very unpopular (he would be deposed in 1688), but despite his personal struggles with Parliament he found enough money to help Gwynn pay her debts. By March 1687, she fell ill with apoplexy, which was blamed by some of her doctors on syphilis transferred to her by Charles II. By June, she was told she was dying. Her first concern was for her son. Charles Beauclerk, duke of St. Albans, had been well provided for by his father. He had a modest income from several houses and a few annuities; more important, as a child he had been betrothed to Lady **Diana de Vere**, the only child of the earl of Oxford. She eventually married him, bringing with her a substantial fortune, and they had five children, through whom Gwynn's line was continued into the 20th century.

During the fall of 1687, Gwynn revised her will, leaving gifts to all her servants and making generous bequests to be used to aid the poor. She died on November 14, 1687. The Anglican minister Dr. Thomas Tenison preached her funeral sermon before a crowded church. Tenison praised Gwynn for her charity, her goodness of heart, and her pious and repentant end. Her popularity in life did not dim with her death. In the 18th, 19th and 20th centuries, several biographies of her were produced, all of which attempted to describe her giving spirit and lively personality. Nell Gwynn's fame has followed her into modern times, and she remains the most beloved mistress of the English Royal Family.

SOURCES:

Cunningham, Peter. *Nell Gwyn*. London: The Grolier Society, 1892.

MacGregor-Hastie, Roy. *Nell Gwyn*. London: Robert Hale, 1987.

Melville, Lewis. *Nell Gwyn*. NY: George H. Doran, 1926.

SUGGESTED READING:

Bevan, B. *Nell Gwyn*. London: 1969.

Fraser, Antonia. *Royal Charles: Charles II and the Restoration.* NY: Alfqed A. Knopf, 1979.

Gramont, Count de. *Memoirs of the Court of Charles II.* NY: P.F. Collier & Son, 1910.

Wilson, John H. *Nell Gwyn: Royal Mistress.* Pellegrini & Cudahy, 1952.

Kimberly Estep Spangler,
Assistant Professor of History and Chair of the Division of Religion
and Humanities at Friends University, Wichita, Kansas

Gwynne-Vaughan, Helen

(1879–1967)

British botanist who was the head of women's services in both world wars. Name variations: Dame Helen Gwynne-Vaughan. Born Helen Charlotte Isabella Fraser in England in 1879; died in 1967; attended Cheltenham Ladies' College and King's College, London; B.S. in Botany, 1904; D.S., 1907; married D.T. Gwynne-Vaughan, in 1911 (died 1915).

British botanist and college professor Dame Helen Gwynne-Vaughan combined an academic career with distinguished military service in two wars. Receiving her degree in botany in 1904, Gwynne-Vaughan taught at various London colleges while studying for her doctorate, which she received in 1907. In 1909, she became the head of the botany department at Birkbeck College in London. Early in her career, she was active in the University of London Suffrage Society, which she founded with **Louisa Garrett Anderson**. During World War I, Gwynne-Vaughan served as joint chief controller of the Women's Army Auxiliary Corps in France, and then as a commandant in the Women's Royal Air Force (1918–19). Returning to Birkbeck College in 1921, she served as a member of the Royal Commission on Food Prices in 1924. At the onset of World War II in 1939, she was appointed the first director of the Auxiliary Territorial Service, although disagreements with senior officers brought about her forced resignation in 1942. She returned to Birkbeck College, where she remained until 1944. Gwynne-Vaughan published many scientific studies, two textbooks on fungi, and authored an autobiography, *Service with the Army* (1942). She was created Dame of the British Empire (DBE) in 1919 and Dame Grand Cross of the Order of the British Empire (GBE) in 1926.

Gyde (fl. 1054)

Queen of Denmark. Name variations: Guda Anundsdottir. Daughter of Anund Jakob, king of Sweden (r. 1022–1050); became third wife of Svend II or Sweyn Estridsen, king of Denmark (r. 1047–1074), around 1054 (divorced).

There are 16 children attributed to Svend II who had four wives or paramours (***Gunhild of Norway**, Gyde, ***Elizabeth of Kiev**, and **Thora Johnsdottir**). Any one of the four could be the mother of Svend's royal offspring: Harald Hén, king of Denmark (r. 1074–1080); St. Knud or Canute the Holy, king of Denmark (r. 1080–1086); Oluf or Olaf Hunger, king of Denmark (r. 1086–1095).

Gyllembourg-Ehrensvärd, Thomasine

(1773–1856).

See Heiberg, Johanne for sidebar.

Gyp (1850–1932).

See Martel de Janville, Comtesse de.

Gyrid (fl. 950s)

*Queen of Denmark. Name variations: Gyrid Olafsdottir. Flourished in the 950s; married Harald Bluetooth (c. 910–985), king of Denmark (r. 940–985); children: Haakon; ***Gunhilda of Denmark** (d. 1002); ***Thyra of Denmark** (d. 1000); Sven or Sweyn I Forkbeard, king of Denmark (r. 985–1014), king of England (r. 1014).*

Gyring, Elizabeth (1906–1970)

Austrian composer. Born in Vienna, Austria, in 1906; died in New York City, 1970; received her musical education in Vienna.

Elizabeth Gyring was one of several thousand musicians who arrived in the United States in the late 1930s as refugees from Nazi racial and political persecution. Like most of them, she arrived without money, connections, or even a working knowledge of the English language. As a young composer in a Vienna beset by immense economic problems and political tensions, not to mention deeply embedded gender prejudice against female composers in a city that prided itself on being the "Musical Capital of Europe," Gyring had been able to assert herself as an artist. By the mid-1930s, a number of her compositions had received public performances, including concert premieres played by virtuoso members of both the Vienna and Berlin Philharmonic orchestras. Nazi ideology demanded that Jewish, female, and progressive composers be eliminated from the "Greater German" cultural landscape that was created with the annexation of Austria in March 1938.

Gyring had to flee her home and create a new artistic home for herself in a United States that was itself reeling from the immense economic and social problems of the Depression. By the end of her life in 1970, Elizabeth Gyring had become a productive American composer, one who had seen many of her works performed by American soloists and ensembles and been fortunate enough to have several works recorded. She composed in virtually all forms, including a symphony, military marches (a genre rarely practiced by contemporary women composers), organ works, and several cantatas set to patriotic texts.

John Haag,
Athens, Georgia

Gyseth (fl. 1070)

*English princess. Name variations: Gytha. Flourished in 1070; daughter of Harold II Godwineson, king of England (r. 1066), and ***Eadgyth Swanneshals***; married Vladimir II Monomakh or Monomach, grand prince of Kiev (r. 1113–1125), around 1070; children: Mstislav I, grand prince of Kiev (r. 1125–1132); Yaropolk I, grand prince of Kiev (r. 1132–1139); **Maria of Kiev** (d. 1146, who married Leo Diogenes of Byzantium); Yuri Dolgoruki, grand prince of Kiev (r. 1154–1157).*

Gytha.

Variant of Agatha.

Gytha (fl. 1022–1042)

*Countess of Wessex. Name variations: Agatha. Born in Denmark; flourished around 1022 to 1042; died after 1069 in Flanders; daughter of Thorgils Sprakalegg; granddaughter of *Thyra of Denmark (d. 1000); great-granddaughter of Harald Bluetooth, king of Denmark (r. around 940–985); married Godwin (b. around 987), earl of Wessex, before 1042 (died 1053); children: Harald or Harold II Godwineson (c. 1022–1066), king of the English (r. 1066); Tostig (c. 1026–1066), earl of Northumberland; *Edith (c. 1025–1075), queen of England; Sveyn, earl of Mercia; Gyrth (d. 1066), earl of East Anglia; Leofwine (d. 1066), earl of Kent; Alfgar (monk at Rheims); Wulfnoth; Edgiva; Elgiva (d. around 1066); Gunhilda (d. 1087, a nun at Bruges or St. Omer in France); and possibly Driella (who married Donnchad, king of Munster).*

posers, including Florent Schmitt and Darius Milhaud, dedicated piano works to her.

John Haag,
Athens, Georgia

Habbaba (d. 724)

Arabian songstress who was influential in the court of Yazid II. Birth date unknown; died in 724; exerted great influence in the court of Yazid II (r. 720–724) of the Eastern Caliphate (whose capital was modern-day Baghdad in Iraq).

The future caliph Yazid II met Habbaba when he made the journey to Mecca as a young man, and he became enamored of her. A slave and a talented singer, Habbaba had been taught her art by Azza al-Maila, Jamila, Ibn Muhriz, Ibn Suraij, Ma'bad and Malik, which set her apart from the average slave. Yazid could not forget the singer, though as a mere prince he could ill afford to purchase her. As soon as he ascended the throne in 720, he paid 4,000 gold pieces to acquire Hababba, a bargain at the time. At his court, Hababba mounted large productions, often performing with an orchestra of 50 singing women accompanied by lutes hidden behind a curtain. Charming and beautiful, she was the sole recipient of the caliph's affections and consequently exercised considerable political influence. When she died suddenly, Yazid kept her body for three days, weeping and kissing her. He died of a broken heart 15 days after her burial. Habbaba typifies the power of the Arabian songstress throughout the centuries.

John Haag,
Athens, Georgia

Haag, Ruth (1916–1973).

See Grable, Betty.

Haakulou (c. 1798–1853).

See Kapule, Deborah.

Haas, Christl (b. 1944).

See Greene, Nancy for sidebar.

Haas, Monique (1906–1987)

French composer and pianist known for her fine recordings of major works. Born in Paris, France, on October 20, 1906; died in Paris on June 9, 1987; won the coveted Grand Prix du Disque award in 1954.

Monique Haas studied piano with Lazare-Lévy, receiving a first prize in his class in 1927. She continued her education with lessons from Robert Casadesus and Rudolf Serkin. Her excellent Debussy and Ravel recordings revealed a sharp intellect conquering the technical problems created by the composers. Her recordings of Chopin, Schumann, Bartok, Hindemith and Stravinsky are a testimony to her skill in creating order in often complex musical pathways. During her career, Haas performed and recorded with such stellar musicians as Igor Stravinsky, Paul Hindemith, Georges Enesco, Pierre Fournier, Paul Paray, Ferenc Fricsay and Eugen Jochum. Her recording of Debussy's *Etudes* won the coveted Grand Prix du Disque award in 1954. She made her New York debut in 1960 with Charles Munch and the Boston Symphony Orchestra. A number of distinguished com-

Habets, Marie Louise (1905–1986).

See Hepburn, Audrey for sidebar.

Habsburg, Elisabeth von (1837–1898).

See Elizabeth of Bavaria.

Hachette, Jeanne (c. 1454–?)

French military hero. Name variations: Jeanne Laisne, Lainé, Laine; Jeanne Fourquet. Born Jeanne Laisne, Lainé, or Fourquet on November 14, around 1454, in Beauvais, France; flourished in 1472; date of death unknown; there is no precise information about her family or origin; married Colin Pilon, a French bourgeois.

A townswoman of Beauvais, Jeanne Laisne gained the sobriquet "Hachette" when, on June 27, 1472, she led a troop of French women armed with hatchets and swords against the Burgundian soldiers of Charles the Bold, duke of Burgundy, who were besieging Beauvais. The town was being defended by only 300 soldiers commanded by Louise de Balagny, when the women surprised the enemy. As the Burgundians made their assault, one of them planted a flag upon the battlements, when Jeanne, axe in hand, attacked him, hurled him into the moat, tore down the flag, and revived the garrison's faltering courage. For this act of bravery, Jeanne was rewarded by the grateful King Louis XI. He married her to her chosen lover Colin Pilon, and in compensation the couple was exempt from paying taxes. Jeanne gained national fame for her exploit. For the next 400 years, the town of Beauvais remembered the brave "Hachette" by holding an annual march, the Procession of the Assault, in her honor.

SUGGESTED READING:

Vallat, Georges. *Jeanne Hachette*. Abbeville, 1898.

Laura York,
Riverside, California

Hack, Maria (1777–1844)

English author of children's books. Born Maria Barton on November 10, 1777, in Carlisle, Cumberland, England; died on January 4, 1844; daughter of Quakers; sister of Bernard Barton (a poet and friend of Charles Lamb); married Stephen Hack (a Chichester merchant), in 1800; children: several.

The daughter of Quakers, Maria Hack was born in Carlisle, England, in 1777. She married when she was 23 and had many children. Following her husband's death, Hack moved to Southampton where she joined the Church of England. Her then-popular books, which were morally instructional, included *Winter Evenings* (1818), *Grecian Stories* (1819), and *English Stories* (1820, 1825), the last of which ranged from Alfred's accession to the English throne to the time of the Tudors.

Hackett, Frances (1891–1984).

See Goodrich, Frances.

Hackett, Joan (1942–1983)

American actress and activist. Born Joan Ann Hackett on May 1, 1942, in New York City; died of cancer on October 8, 1983, in Encino, California; daughter of John (a postal clerk) and Mary (Esposito) Hackett; graduated from St. Jean Baptiste School, New York City; married Richard Mulligan (an actor), on January 3, 1966 (divorced 1973).

From the movie Treasure of Matecumbe, *starring Joan Hackett and Peter Ustinov.*

Theater: New York debut in A Clearing in the Woods *(Sheridan Square Playhouse, February 12, 1959); in stock, appeared in* The Play's the Thing *(Princeton University Playhouse, Princeton, NJ, June 1959); understudy for Hero in* Much Ado About Nothing *(Lunt-Fontanne, New York City, September 1959); Marguerite in a pre-Broadway tryout of* Laurette *(Shubert Theater, New Haven, CT, September 1960); Chris in* Call Me by My Rightful Name *(One Sheridan Square, NYC, January 1961); appeared in stock productions of* Two Queens of Love and Beauty *(Bucks County Playhouse, New Hope, PA, July 1961), and* Journey to the Day *(Westport County Playhouse, CT, August 1961); Pat in* Peterpat *(Longacre, NYC, January 1965); appeared in* Young Woman in the Park *(Center Stage, Baltimore, MD, February 1970, and John Golden Theater, NYC, April 1970); Elaine Wheeler in* Night Watch *(Morosco Theater, NYC, February 1972).*

Filmography: The Group *(1966);* Will Penny *(1968);* Assignment to Kill *(1968);* Support Your Local Sheriff *(1969);* Rivals *(1972);* The Last of Sheila

(1973); The Terminal Man (1974); Mackintosh and T.J. (1975); Treasure of Matecumbe (1976); Mr. Mike's Mondo Video (1978); One Trick Pony (1980); Only When I Laugh (1981); The Escape Artist (1982); Flicks (release delayed from 1981 to 1987).

Admired for her intelligence and versatility, Joan Hackett studied acting with **Mary Welch** and was also an alumna of Lee Strasberg's Actors' Studio. She worked in stock and held a variety of jobs before making her New York debut in *A Clearing in the Woods* (1958). She later distinguished herself on stage with her portrayal of Chris in *Call Me by My Rightful Name* (1961), for which she received an Obie and the Vernon Rice Award, and in film as Dottie Renfrew in the movie adaptation of *Mary McCarthy's The Group*. Hackett successfully combined her stage career with films, numerous television appearances, and political activism, especially in regard to the women's rights movement of the 1960s and '70s. She received an Academy Award nomination for her work in the movie *Only When I Laugh* (1981) and was also nominated for an Emmy for an episode of "Ben Casey" (1962). Hackett was married to actor Richard Mulligan from 1966 to 1973. Her career was cut short when she died of cancer in 1983, at the age of 41.

SOURCES:

Katz, Ephraim. *The Film Encyclopedia*. NY: HarperCollins, 1994.

McGill, Raymond D., ed. *Notable Names in the American Theatre*. Clifton, NJ: James T. White, 1976.

Barbara Morgan,
Melrose, Massachusetts

Hackley, E. Azalia Smith

(1867–1922)

African-American singer, choir director, and advocate of African-American music and musicians. Born Emma Azalia Smith in Murfreesboro, Tennessee, on June 29, 1867; died in Detroit, Michigan, on December 13, 1922; elder of two daughters of Henry Smith (a blacksmith) and Corilla (Beard) Smith (a teacher); attended the Miami Avenue School, Detroit, Michigan; graduated with honors from Central High School, Detroit, in 1883; graduated from Washington Normal School, 1886; received a Bachelor of Music degree from the University of Denver, 1900; married Edwin Henry Hackley (a lawyer and newspaper editor), on January 29, 1894 (separated 1909); no children.

Born in Murfreesboro, Tennessee, Emma Hackley was the eldest of two daughters of a blacksmith and a schoolteacher. Her mother **Corilla Beard Smith**, the daughter of a freed slave who established a successful laundry business in Detroit, had founded a school in Murfreesboro for former slaves and their children, but was forced by the hostile white community around her to close the facility in 1870. The family relocated to Detroit, where Hackley became the first black student at the Miami Avenue Public School. Precocious both academically and musically, she took piano, violin, and voice lessons as a child, and later helped with the family income by singing and playing the piano at high school dances. After graduating from high school with honors, Hackley worked her way through Washington Normal School by giving piano lessons. She then taught grade school for eight years, while she continued with her music studies and sang with the Detroit Musical Society, the finest choral group in the city.

In 1894, against her mother's wishes, Emma eloped with attorney Edwin Henry Hackley and moved with him to Denver. While earning a bachelor's degree in music from the University of Denver, she served as choir director at her church and as the assistant director of a large Denver choir. She also devoted time to various black organizations, including a local branch of the Colored Women's League which she founded and publicized through the woman's page of her husband's struggling newspaper, the *Denver Statesman*. With her husband, she helped organize the Imperial Order of Libyans, a fraternal group whose mission was to combat racial prejudice and promote equality. In 1901, with her marriage faltering, Hackley left her husband and moved to Philadelphia, where she became the music director of the Episcopal Church of the Crucifixion, a black congregation. (The couple permanently separated in 1909.) Earning a reputation as a skilled choral director, in 1904 Hackley organized the 100-member People's Chorus (later known as the Hackley Choral). The chorus not only contributed to community spirit but helped launch the careers of a number of talented black performers, including contralto *Marian Anderson* and tenor Roland Hayes. Hackley also helped organize a series of highly acclaimed recitals featuring herself and talented members of the chorus, the proceeds from which enabled her to study for a year in Paris with Jean de Reszke, a well-known opera singer and vocal coach.

In 1907, upon her return to the United States, Hackley began to look beyond her own career and to focus more on the advancement of black music and musicians. Keenly aware of the barriers facing them (she herself had scorned concert managers who asked her to "pass" as white), Hackley raised money through concerts and private solicitations to establish a fund to aid African-American musicians who wanted to study abroad. Around 1910, she began a series of lecture tours designed to further advance black music and to raise self-esteem among her people. She published a selection of her lectures in a book called *The Colored Girl Beautiful* (1916). Later lectures focused on traditional Negro folk music, a form she hoped to keep alive even though many young black musicians were moving to newer musical styles.

Although stricken in 1916 by a recurring ear ailment which impaired her hearing and caused episodes of dizziness, Hackley produced a series of community folk concerts in black churches and schools across the United States. In the fall of 1920, she introduced black folk music at an international Sunday school convention in Tokyo, after which she embarked on a California tour. When a San Diego concert date fell through, however, Hackley, who was said to be high strung, suffered an emotional collapse and was forced to return to Detroit. She died there in 1922, of a cerebral hemorrhage.

In recognition of Hackley's contributions to the cause of racial equality, the E. Azalia Hackley Memorial Collection of Negro Music, Dance, and Drama was established in the Detroit Public Library in 1943.

SOURCES:

James, Edward T., ed. *Notable American Women 1607–1950*. Cambridge, MA: The Belknap Press of Harvard University Press, 1971.

McHenry, Robert, ed. *Famous American Women*. NY: Dover, 1983.

Smith, Jessie Carney, ed. *Notable Black American Women*. Detroit, MI: Gale Research, 1992.

COLLECTIONS:

Hackley's papers are located at the E. Azalia Hackley Collection of the Detroit Public Library.

Barbara Morgan,
Melrose, Massachusetts

Hadewijch (fl. 13th c.)

Flemish Christian beguine, mystic and writer-poet. Name variations: Hadewijch of Brabant; Hadewijch or Hadewych of Antwerp; Suster Hadewych; Adelwip. Pronunciation: HAD-e-vitch. Born around 1200 in or near Antwerp in the duchy of Brabant (Belgium); died around 1260.

Became the mistress of a group of young beguines and wrote a series of letters, poems, and accounts of her visions for their instruction; had her authority called into question and her pupils sent away; possibly exiled from the community for her teachings, scholars speculate, and spent the rest of her life caring for others in a hospital or other service-oriented institution.

Writings: 31 Letters, 14 visions, 45 poems in stanzas, and 16 couplet poems were published together in one volume entitled The Complete Works of Hadewijch.

On a Sunday after Pentecost, a young woman lay in bed, too overcome with spiritual yearning to go to church. There, she received communion and experienced a vision of a meadow filled with trees. In the center of the pastoral was an uprooted tree of many branches. "O mistress," she heard an angel say, "you climb this tree from beginning to the end, all the way to the profound roots of the incomprehensible God!" As she turned from the tree, she saw Christ, who warned her that the cost of being one with him was to be poor, miserable, and despised by all, but the reward was the knowledge of his will and the experience of Love. He left her with these words, "Give all, for all is yours."

Like all of Hadewijch's writings, this narrative tells much about her character but nothing about the date or place of her first vision. Similarly, no other accounts can confirm information about her life. We know that she was one of one-hundred pious women who lived in the 12th and 13th centuries because a "list of the perfect," a listing of eighty people known to her, can be found at the end of her visions. Among the perfect is the name of a woman condemned to death by Robert le Bougre who was in Flanders from 1235 to 1238. From this, we surmise that Hadewijch lived in the middle of the 13th century.

Therefore, information about her background and education is conjecture based on her writings. In her letters, Hadewijch quotes a wide range of sources. She is well versed in Scripture, quotes Christian writers such as Augustine, is familiar with Latin and French, and writes in Dutch. Her poems incorporate rules of writing and versification taught at the schools of her day and are filled with references to courtly life, suggesting that she belonged to the higher class and had access to schooling.

Likewise, the tone of her letters implies an air of self-confidence and authority that could be attributed to a noble upbringing. She writes to Gilbertus, the abbot of nearby St. James' Abbey, as if he were her equal, freely chastising him for his lack of support and citing a wide range of scholarly sources that would impress him to elicit his aid. This emphasis on learning appears significant to Hadewijch, for she advocates the importance of intellectual progress. She writes of the "beautiful faculty of reason" given by God for enlightenment and instruction. She does not, however, see herself as a scholar, warning that scholastic theologians who put intellect before love will not reach the summit of spiritual life.

We know from her letters that she was mistress of a group of young beguines, women who lived a semi-religious life (*religious* because they lived a life of devotion to God; *semi* because they took no permanent vows of chastity, poverty, or obedience). They did not live a cloistered life like nuns but lived in communal houses that were usually in urban areas. There, they engaged in trades to support themselves and cared for the sick and orphaned. Because of their independence, they were often criticized by ecclesiastical authorities and were eventually outlawed.

The history of the beguine movement receives much scholarly attention as an early example of a women's emancipation movement. Likewise, the writing of beguines is seen as a new type of literature: one of the first examples of writing by women, for women, in the language of the common people. As all but one of Hadewijch's letters are written to young beguines for their care and instruction, they give us insight into their days. She charges them to a life of virtue and good works: "Be good," she writes, "toward those who have need of you, devoted toward the sick, generous with the poor, and recollected in spirit beyond the reach of all creatures."

I can will as highly as I wish, and seize and receive from God all that He is, without objection or anger on His part—what no saint can do.

—Hadewijch

To be "recollected in spirit," Hadewijch advises a life of humble service and personal dignity. While she suggests being docile and prompt, she also warns that a person must only satisfy everyone "as far as you can manage it without debasing yourself." She advises beguines not to dwell on conflicts that arise among themselves, adding that the one who fails in faithfulness or justice is harmed more than the one wronged. She is, however, quick to chastise a beguine who is not living up to the ideal of service and love. To one such, she writes: "You not [loving God] is hurtful to us both; it is hurtful to you and too difficult for me."

The main point of all her instruction, as noted by Nicholas Watson, was "refusing any-thing less than everything for herself, [and] demanding the same of others." But such a leadership style eventually got Hadewijch into trouble both among her followers and from outside sources. In one letter, she laments: "our adversaries are many." She writes of the pain of knowing that some of the beguines in her group are trying to disband and desert her. In another letter, she writes to Gilbertus and accuses him of projecting the shortcomings of his group onto hers. "To all of us it seems pitiable that people should be leading one another astray," she writes, "so as to charge us with their errors instead of helping us to love our Beloved." She appeals to him to act out of love and use his position in the community to see that her group is treated fairly.

We do not know if Gilbertus responded to Hadewijch's appeal, but her letters suggest that eventually her companions were either taken away from her or left her, and she was exiled. In one letter, she writes of her exile from the beguines named Sara, Emma, and Margriet. The pain of this separation is particularly poignant in regards to Hadewijch's references to Sara who was the beguine closest to her and yet most critical of her leadership. Her final letters struggle with finding solace in the midst of this separation. She ponders why God allows her to serve him and yet holds her apart from those he loves. She speculates that others abhor her because she shares little in common with them, and they do not know the experience of love as she does.

What actually became of Hadewijch remains a mystery. She speculates that, in the future, she may be imprisoned or left to wander alone. We have no evidence that either was the case. Because she urged others to care for the sick, it is possible that she may have spent the rest of her life working in a hospital or another typical beguine institution of service. Whatever her fate, scholars speculate that she remained true to these words of encouragement written to a faithful companion: "But you must still labor at the works of Love. . . . For my part I am devoted to these works at any hour and still perform them at all times, to seek after nothing but Love, work nothing but Love, protect nothing but Love, and advance nothing but Love."

There is, however, no mystery about Hadewijch's writing, the earliest original prose written in the Flemish language (c. 1230–50). She composed in a variety of forms, including letters, visions, and poetry, to instruct the beguines under her care. Her 14 visions describe not only the visions and their messages but the turmoil beforehand and return to consciousness afterward that marks visionary experience. Ulrike Wiethaus proposes that these accounts were challenges to authority in worship, empowering beguines to trust their own religious experience. Hadewijch's 31 letters clarify ideas about God's love and human response implicit in the visions. Her 16 poems in couplets, addressed to young beguines, cover such topics as the nature and names of love. Considered by many to be her greatest works are the 45 poems in stanzas. By fusing ideas about love found in courtly literature, Latin liturgy, and Christian mysticism, Hadewijch created a new genre of religious poetry. Columba Hart suggests that these poems served the function of reclaiming young beguines to their early fervor by poetically conveying the uncertainty, isolation, yet deep companionship and spiritual ecstasy of their life.

Central to all her writings is Hadewijch's view of the beguine life as a life of love. She writes, "If [God] is yours in love, you must live for Him, by yourself being love." She understood this life of love to be a spiritual pilgrimage to God, a long and arduous journey that required the same hard work and dedication as a physical pilgrimage. Just as any pilgrim needed good company and an eye for thieves, so too did beguines need a spiritual community of love and an awareness of those who would steal their spirits. Just as a pilgrim must bend into the wind and endure pain en route, the beguine must endure the heavy burden of Love with its terrible and implacable essence, its devouring and consuming shadow. Hadewijch showed that in order to reach the journey's end, unity with God, the beguine must become as God in Christ, one in his power to love and help others unto suffering and death. Summing up Hadewijch's ideas, Don Christopher Nugent observes, "Love is fire, and, as with so many great mystics, Hadewijch is a pyromaniac."

Not only does she declare herself a free creature, but Hadewijch asserts that she is closer to God than the saints, that, indeed, she is God's closest friend. She struggles with reconciling the unreasonableness of this idea with the certain knowledge of her spiritual experience. It is this self-knowledge which both inspired her followers and incited their anger. Refusing to compromise knowledge for reason or comfort, she writes, "In the end, I cannot believe that I have loved Him best, and yet I cannot believe that there is any living man who loves God as I love Him."

It has been left to her readers to decide if her certain knowledge reflects a truth or a self-obsessed fantasy. Her writing has never been popular or well-known. Only four copies of her work survive: three copies of her complete works from the 14th century written in Dutch, another containing her poetry from the 16th century. Her writings were known to Jan Van Ruysbroeck (1293–1381) who was the prior of a hermit group called the Canons Regular of Groenendael. Hadewijch's ideas about unity with God are found in his book *The Kingdom of the Lovers of God*. Her image of the upside-down tree of knowledge appears as the tree of faith in another of his books, *The Spiritual Espousals*.

Hadewijch's writings were evidently passed on to Ruysbroeck's disciples, then lost. The reason for their disappearance may be suggested in remarks made by one of these disciples, John of Leeuwen. Leeuwen testified to the validity of Hadewijch and her work, calling her a "true mistress of spirituality" and her writing "good, and just, born of God and revealed by Him." Yet he admitted that her teachings were not profitable to all, for there are "many who cannot understand them: those whose inner eyes are too dimmed, not yet opened by the love that adheres to God in the nakedness and silence of fruition."

Evidently few people were opened to the profitability of her ideas. Her work was known by the Canons Regular of Windesheim and the Carthusians of Diest, and a few of her letters were known in Bavaria where she was named Adelwip. By the mid-16th century, her writings were unknown. They were rediscovered in 1838 by the medieval specialist Maeterlinck and reintroduced to the scholarly community in the critical edition published by J. Van Mierlo in 1920. Her writing has become accessible to the general population with the 1980 *Classics of Western Spirituality* edition by Columba Hart.

At the end of the 20th century, Hadewijch enjoyed a revival of interest among scholars indicated by a number of scholarly articles and conference papers about aspects of her work. Hart argues that Hadewijch is "undoubtedly, the most important exponent of love mysticism and one of the loftiest figures in the Western mystical tradition," noting that Van Mierlo called Hadewijch, "universally human, her art is for all times." However, unless these scholarly investigations find new information about the writer of these works, the facts of Hadewijch's life will forever remain a mystery. Hadewijch realized the likeliness of her anonymity and the frustration inherent to those who would wish to study her in the future. "Since you wish to know all that concerns me," she wrote, "I am very sorry that you do not know everything you wish to know."

SOURCES:

Hadewijch. *The Complete Works.* Translated and introduction by Columba Hart. NY: Paulist Press, 1980.

Nugent, Don Christopher. "Harvest of Hadewijch: Brautmystik and Wesenmystik," in *Mystics Quarterly.* Vol. 12, no. 3. September 1986, pp. 119–126.

Watson, Nicholas. "Classics of Western Spirituality, II: Three Medieval Women Theologians and Their Background," in *King's Theological Review.* Vol. 12, no. 2. Autumn 1989, pp. 56–64.

Wiethaus, Ulrike. "Learning as Experiencing Hadewijch's Model of Spiritual Growth," in *Faith Seeking Understanding: Learning and the Catholic Tradition.* Edited by George C. Berthold. Manchester, NH: Saint Anselm Press, 1991, pp. 89–106.

SUGGESTED READING:

Brunn, Emilie Zum, and George Epiney-Burgard. *Women Mystics in Medieval Europe.* NY: Paragon Publishers, 1989.

Dreyer, Elizabeth. *Passionate Women: Two Medieval Mystics.* NY: Paulist Press, 1989.

Milhaven, John Giles. *Hadewijch and Her Sisters: Other Ways of Loving and Knowing.* NY: SUNY, 1993.

Jane McAvoy,
Associate Professor of Theology, Lexington
Theological Seminary, Lexington, Kentucky

Hadewych of Antwerp or Brabant

(fl. 13th c.).

See Hadewijch.

Hadice Turhan (1627–1683).

See Reign of Women, The.

Hading, Jane (1859–1941)

French actress. Born Jeanne Alfrédine Tréfouret on November (some sources cite March) 25, 1859, at Marseilles, France; died in 1941 (some sources cite December 31, 1933); daughter of an actor; married Victor Koning (1842–1894, the manager of the Gymnase theater), in 1884 (divorced 1887).

Jane Hading was born Jeanne Alfrédine Tréfouret on November 25, 1859, in Marseilles, where her father was an actor at the Gymnase. She made her first appearance at age three, as Little Blanche in *Le bossu,* a part usually represented by a doll. She was trained at the local conservatoire and in 1873 performed with a theater in Algiers. Later appearing with the Khedivial Theater in Cairo, she took on coquette, soubrette, and ingenue roles. Hading had an excellent voice, and when she returned to Marseilles she sang in operetta and acted in *Ruy Blas.* Her Paris debut was in *La Chaste Suzanne* at the Palais Royal, and she again appeared in an operetta at the Renaissance. In 1883, she enjoyed a great success at the Gymnase in *Le Maitre de forges.* In 1884, she married Victor Koning, manager of the Gymnase, but di-

vorced him three years later. Hading toured America with Benoît Coquelin in 1888 and on her return abetted the success of Henri Lavedan's *Le Prince d'Aurec* at the Vaudeville. By then, she was known as one of the leading actresses of her day in France, America, and England. Her later repertoire included Alexandre Dumas *fils' Le Demi-monde* and *La Princesse Georges,* Alfred Capus' *La Châtelaine* (1902), and Maurice Donnay's *Retour de Jerusalem.*

Hadwig.

Variant of Hedwig.

Hadwisa.

Variant of Avisa, Hadwig, or Hedwig.

Hadwisa of Gloucester (c. 1167–1217).

See Isabella of Angoulême for sidebar on Avisa of Gloucester.

Hadwisa of Normandy (d. 1034).

See Hawise of Normandy.

Haebler, Ingrid (1926—)

Austrian pianist known as a champion of neglected Schubert piano sonatas. Born in Vienna, Austria, on June 20, 1926.

Ingrid Haebler's artistry reveals many subtle touches. A specialist in the Austrian classical and Romantic school, she has long been admired both by professional musicians and the public for her interpretations of Mozart and Haydn. Haebler has championed the often neglected Schubert piano sonatas for decades. She is also a respected Schumann performer. Many critics have commented on her unique tone quality, and most of her recordings have received the highest critical praise. She has won several prizes, including the *Harriet Cohen Beethoven medal in 1957. In 1969, Haebler became a member of the faculty of the Salzburg Mozarteum.

John Haag,
Athens, Georgia

Haffenden, Elizabeth (1906–1976)

British costume designer. Born in Croydon, England, in 1906; died in 1976.

Selected films: Wedding Group *(*Wrath of Jealousy, *1936);* The Young Mr. Pitt *(1942);* Fanny by Gaslight *(1944);* The Wicked Lady *(1945);* The Magic Bow *(1946);* The Man Within *(*The Smugglers, *1947);* The Bad Lord Byron *(1949);* Christopher Columbus *(1949);* Beau Brummel *(1954);* Invitation to the Dance

(1956); Bhowani Junction *(1956);* Moby Dick *(1956);* The Barretts of Wimpole Street *(1956);* Ben Hur *(1959);* The Amorous Adventures of Moll Flanders *(1965);* A Man for All Seasons *(1966);* Half a Sixpence *(1967);* Chitty Chitty Bang Bang *(1968);* The Prime of Miss Jean Brodie *(1969);* Fiddler on the Roof *(1971);* Pope Joan *(1972);* The Day of the Jackal *(1973);* Luther *(1974).*

Elizabeth Haffenden began designing costumes for British films in 1933 and eventually became head of the costume department at Gainsborough Studios, where she mentored designer *Julie Harris. Haffenden designed for both American and British films, and won Academy Awards for *Ben Hur* (1959) and *A Man for All Seasons* (1966).

Hafsa (d. 1534)

*Ottoman sultana. Name variations: Hafsa Sultana; Hafsa Hatun. Died in March 1534; possibly a Tatar princess from the Crimea, or a Circassian or Georgian woman from the Caucasus; consort of Selim I the Grim, Ottoman sultan (r. 1512–1520); children: Suleyman or Suleiman I the Magnificent (1494/95-1566), Ottoman sultan (r. 1520–1566); and daughters *Sah and *Hatice.*

Hafsa was possibly a Tatar princess from the Crimea, or a Circassian or Georgian woman from the Caucasus, before she married the sultan, Selim I the Grim. The new paradigm for women's public buildings in the Ottoman Empire commenced during the reign of her son Suleiman I the Magnificent (r. 1520–1566). The precedent for imperial buildings was set by Hafsa Sultana. Mothers of sultans had enormous influence, ranking second only to their sons in power. Shortly after Suleiman's accession to the throne, Hafsa built the largest mosque complex ever constructed. It included a mosque, soup kitchen, religious college, primary school, and dervish hostel. Baths were added later. Hafsa's work set another precedent in that her mosque had two minarets, an honor which had heretofore been reserved only for the sultan. From this point forward, members of the sultan's family, especially female members, were allowed to give their mosques the same status as the ruler's.

Hagan, Ellen (1873–1958)

Swedish feminist, journalist and speaker. Born in 1873; died in 1958; married to the governor of Gävleborg County.

Devoting her life to feminist causes, Ellen Hagan founded the Uppsala Suffrage Society (1903) and served on the Central Board of the Federation for Women's Suffrage (1903–22). After World War I, she became president of the Federation of Liberal Women in Sweden. During the 1920s, she was the editor of the women's journal *Tiderarvet* and for ten years, beginning in 1922, was a member of the International Alliance Committee. During World War II, she worked as an executive with "Help for Norway." Hagan, who was married to the governor of Gävleborg County, was awarded the Order of the Star of the North in 1953.

Hagar.

See Sarah (fl. 3rd, 2nd, or 1st century BCE) for sidebar.

Hagen, Uta (1919—)

German-born actress and teacher whose books, Respect for Acting *(1973) and* A Challenge for the Actor *(1991), have become standard references for professionals. Pronunciation: OO-ta; Hagen rhymes with noggin. Born Uta Thyra Hagen on June 12, 1919, in Göttingen, Germany; only daughter and one of two children of Oskar Fran Leonard Hagen (a professor of art history) and Thyra A. (Leisner) Hagen; graduated from Wisconsin High School, 1936; attended the Royal Academy of Dramatic Art, London; attended the University of Wisconsin, 1936–1937; married José Ferrer (an actor), on December 8, 1938 (divorced 1948); married Herbert Berghof (an actor, director, and teacher), on January 25, 1951 (died 1990); children: one daughter,* Leticia Ferrer, *an actress.*

Selected theater: stage debut as Sorrel in Hay Fever *(Bascom Hall, University of Wisconsin, July 1935); Ophelia in* Hamlet *(Cape Playhouse, Dennis, Massachusetts, August 1937); New York debut as Nina in* The Seagull *(Shubert Theatre, March 1938); Louka in* Arms and the Man *and the Ingenue in* Mr. Pim Passes By *(Ridgefield Summer Theatre, Connecticut, July 1938); Suzanne in* Suzanna and the Elders *(Westport Country Playhouse, Connecticut; Mt. Kisco Playhouse, New York, August 1938); toured as Nina in the national company of* The Seagull *(October 1938–January 1939); Edith in* The Happiest Days *(Vanderbilt Theatre, New York City, April 1939); a Chinese Girl in* Flight into China *and a Nurse in* Men in White *(Paper Mill Playhouse, Milburn, New Jersey, August 1939); Secretary in* Topaze *(Mt. Kisco Playhouse, New York, July 1940); Ella in* Charley's Aunt *(Ann Arbor Drama Festival, Michigan, May 1941);*

Ellen Turner in The Male Animal *and the Woman in* The Guardsman *(Suffern County Playhouse, New York, July–August 1941); Wife in the pre-Broadway tryout of* The Admiral Had a Wife *(December 1941); toured as Desdemona in the Theatre Guild's production of* Othello *(July–August 1942); title role in* Vicki *(Plymouth, New York City, September 1942); Desdemona in Paul Robeson's* Othello *(Shubert Theatre, New York City, October 1943); Olga Vorontsov in* The Whole World Over *(Biltmore Theatre, New York City, March 1947); Mr. Manningham in* Angel Street *(Yardley Theatre, Pennsylvania, July 1947); toured as the leading lady in* Dark Eyes *(July–August 1947), and at the Barbizon Plaza Theatre, New York City; Gretchen in* Faust *(October 1947); Hilda in* The Master Builder *(January 1948); Mrs. Manningham in* Angel Street *(New York City Center, January 1948); succeeded (June 1948) Jessica Tandy as Blanche DuBois in* A Streetcar Named Desire *(Ethel Barrymore Theatre, New York City, 1947); Georgie in* The Country Girl *(Lyceum Theatre, New York City, November 1950); title role in* Saint Joan *(Cort Theatre, New York City, 1951); Tatiana in* Tovarich *(New York City Center, May 1952); toured in a summer production of* The Play's the Thing *(July–August 1952); Hannah King in* In Any Language *(Cort Theatre, New York City, October 1952); toured as Jennet Jourdemayne in* The Lady's Not for Burning *and Georgie in* The Country Girl *(June–August 1953); Grace Wilson in* The Magic and the Loss *(Booth Theatre, New York City, April 1954); toured summer theaters in title role of* Cyprienne *(June–August 1954); played all the female characters in* The Affairs of Anatol *(Ann Arbor Drama Festival, Michigan, May 1955; Edgewater Beach Hotel, Chicago, Illinois, July 1955); Agata in* Island of Goats *(Fulton Theatre, New York City, October 1955); Natalie Petrovna in* A Month in the Country *(Phoenix Theatre, New York City, April 1956); Shen Te in* The Good Woman of Setzuan *(Phoenix Theatre, New York City, December 1956); Argia in* The Queen and the Rebels *(Bucks County Playhouse, New Hope, Pennsylvania, August 1959); Angelique in the American premiere of* Port Royal *(Grace Church Theatre, New York City, May 1960); Leah in* Sodom and Gomorrah *(Vancouver International Festival, Canada, August 1961); Martha in* Who's Afraid of Virginia Woolf? *(Billy Rose Theatre, New York City, October 1962), and also played this role in London (Piccadilly Theatre, February 1964); Madame Ranevskaya in* The Cherry Orchard *(Lyceum Theatre, New York City, March 1968); Melanie Klein in* Mrs. Klein *(1995); appeared in David Margulies'* Collected Stories *(off-Broadway, Lucille Lortel Theater, 1998).*

One of America's first ladies of the theater and an inspired and devoted acting teacher, Uta Hagen was born in 1919 in Göttingen, Germany, where her father was an art history professor and her mother an opera singer. "In my parents' home, creative instincts and expression were considered worthy and noble," Hagen wrote in the introduction to *Respect for Acting*. When she was six, her father accepted a position at the University of Wisconsin and moved the family to Madison. While growing up, Hagen attended the theater regularly with her parents, both in the United States and on frequent trips to Europe. She made up her mind to become an actress at the age of nine after seeing **Elisabeth Bergner* in *Saint Joan*. At 16, newly graduated from high school, she enrolled at London's Royal Academy of Dramatic Art, but left after one term because she found the classes too academic. Following a semester at the University of Wisconsin, she wrote to **Eva Le Gallienne*, asking to join her prestigious Civic Repertory Theatre company. She not only won an audition but, in 1937, played Ophelia in Le Gallienne's production of *Hamlet* at the Cape Playhouse in Dennis, Massachusetts. Bypassing the usual progression of bit parts, Hagen made her Broadway debut at age 19, in the role of Nina in the Theatre Guild's production of *The Seagull*. According to at least one New York critic, the fledgling actress stole a few scenes from her formidable co-stars Alfred Lunt and **Lynn Fontanne*.

In December 1938, Hagen married actor José Ferrer, whom she met in summer stock. (According to one story, she knocked him unconscious one night during a fight scene.) Their daughter Letty was born when Hagen was just 20. "That's my excuse for what a rotten mother I was," she later told *People* magazine. "I was selfish with my career and expected too much of her." Hagen's marriage to Ferrer lasted ten years, during which time the couple co-starred in several successful plays, including the comedy *Vickie* (1942) and Shakespeare's *Othello* (1943), with Paul Robeson as Othello, Ferrer as Iago, and Hagen as Desdemona. The production, directed by **Margaret Webster*, had a run of 295 performances, a record at the time for a Shakespearean play. Burton Rascoe of the New York *World-Telegram* praised Hagen's performance as "glorious and heart-gripping," and Lewis Nichols of *The New York Times* called her death scene "the most moving of the play." After its Broadway run, the production enjoyed a successful tour.

In 1947, shortly after her separation from Ferrer (they divorced in 1948), Hagen was cast in

The Whole World Over, directed by Harold Clurman, whom she credits with introducing her to a new way of acting, a method that challenged the "tricks" that had come to shape her performances. "He never allowed the setting of line readings, mechanizing of stage positions or pieces of 'business,'" she writes in *A Challenge for the Actor*, "exploring instead the existence of the characters and their behavior as they came into conflict with each other in the action of the play. I was asked to work subjectively, to give birth to the new person I was to become rather than to present a preconceived, theatrical illustration of

her on the stage." Hagen's co-star was actor Herbert Berghof, who had fled Vienna during World War II. The two fell in love during the run of the play although they did not marry until 1951. "He was something," she told *People* magazine. "He was the miracle of my life." Berghof helped Hagen to understand and apply the new acting technique she was testing and also recruited her to teach in his acting school, the HB Studio, which she has been associated with ever since.

The late 1940s also brought Hagen one of her juiciest roles, that of Blanche DuBois in Ten-

Uta Hagen

nessee Williams' *A Streetcar Named Desire* (1947). After receiving glowing reviews while touring the play with the National Company, she was called upon to replace *Jessica Tandy in the original Broadway cast. On the heels of *Streetcar* came the role of Georgie, the dowdy wife of an alcoholic in Clifford Odets' stinging drama *The Country Girl* (1950), for which she won her first Tony Award as well as the Donaldson Award and the New York Drama Critics Award. With her career now in high gear, Hagen starred in a Theatre Guild production of *Saint Joan* (1951), directed again by Margaret Webster. Critics were particularly taken with her intensely controlled performance. Wrote William Hawkins, in the New York *World-Telegram and Sun* (October 5, 1951): "Miss Hagen has that rare gift of creating spiritual energy in the theater, then controlling it at will. She has the authority to compel an audience into silent attention like suspended animation. Unquestionably she is among the theater's greatest in her day."

During the 1950s, because of her liberal views and her earlier relationship with Paul Robeson, Hagen was blacklisted, making it impossible for her to work in movies or television. She wryly commented later that it might indeed have been for the best. "It was a time when I might've been tempted to do movies," she said. "The blacklist saved my integrity." Some 20 years later, Hagen finally did venture into films (only for the money, she insists), appearing in the thriller *The Other* (1972), followed by *The Boys from Brazil* (1978) and *Reversal of Fortune* (1990).

Hagen won a second Tony for her memorable portrayal of Martha, the embittered, vulnerable wife of a college professor in Edward Albee's first full-length play, *Who's Afraid of Virginia Woolf?* (1962). Although critics expressed reservations about the play, particularly Albee's exploitation of obscenity, they were overwhelming in their praise of Hagen. "As the vulgar, scornful, desperate Martha, Miss Hagen makes a tormented harridan horrifyingly believable," reported Harold Taubman in *The New York Times*. Hagen made her London debut as Martha in February 1964, receiving the London Critics Award for Best Female Performance. "Martha is a superb creation," wrote British critic Hugh Leonard, "honey tongued, bawdy, obtuse, perceptive, tender, lustful, and—at any given moment—lethal. Miss Hagen and Mr. [Arthur] Hill wage total war on each other with the most exquisitely refined playing one could ever hope to see."

Hagen's personal integrity and her preference for roles of quality have led her to seek fulfillment in venues other than Broadway. "This whole standard of not being anything unless you're on Broadway is rotten," she said in a 1963 *New York Post* interview. Teaching has been an important component of her career since 1947, and the alumni list from the HB Studio (which she took over following her husband's death on November 5, 1990), reads like a who's who of American theater: *Geraldine Page, Fritz Weaver, Jason Robards, Jack Lemmon, **Whoopi Goldberg**, and Matthew Broderick have all studied with Hagen. "I try to teach actors to bring a human being onstage," she says, "not an actor." Her method is derived from Constantin Stanislavsky, although she is strongly opposed to the use of emotional memory, which she believes is self-indulgent and self-destructive. Her teaching style is marked by brevity; she uses technical code words, an actor's shorthand, which her students learn to interpret. Hagen set forth her theories in two books, *Respect for Acting* (1973) and *A Challenge for the Actor* (1991), both of which have become standard references for students and professionals. She also wrote *Love for Cooking* in 1976, and an autobiography, *Sources,* in 1983.

In 1995, at age 76, the now-legendary Hagen appeared off-Broadway, in Nicholas Wright's *Mrs. Klein,* a biographical drama about the Austrian-born pioneering child psychologist *Melanie Klein, which also starred **Laila Robins** in the role of Klein's daughter. The play traces Klein's slow realization that the death of her son in a mysterious climbing accident, may indeed have been a suicide. "Pitiable and monstrous by turns," wrote Brad Leithauser, in *Time* (November 20, 1995), "Hagen brings to each new revelation a miraculous range of responses." For the actress, who has no intention of retiring and "sitting around," the role of *Mrs. Klein* was like a dream come true. "If I had my way, I'd be onstage all the time."

SOURCES:

Hagen, Uta. *A Challenge for the Actor.* NY: Scribner, 1991.

———, with Haskel Frankel. *Respect for Acting.* NY: Macmillan, 1973.

Leithauser, Brad. "Legends of the Fall," in *Time.* November 20, 1995, p. 121.

Moritz, Charles. *Current Biography 1963.* NY: H.W. Wilson, 1963.

Morley, Sheridan. *The Great Stage Stars.* London: Angus & Robertson, 1986.

Rosen, Marjorie, and Toby Kahn. "The Indomitable Miss Hagen," in *People.* February 5, 1996, pp. 93–94.

Wilmeth, Don B., and Tice L. Miller. *Cambridge Guide to American Theatre*. NY: Cambridge University Press, 1993.

Barbara Morgan,
Melrose, Massachusetts

Hagerup, Inger (1905–1985)

Norwegian poet, playwright, prose writer and children's author. Born in Bergen, Norway, in 1905; died in 1985; married Anders Hagerup; children: two sons, Helge and Klaus (both writers).

Inger Hagerup was born in Bergen in 1905 and brought up in West Norway. After taking her university entrance examination, she worked for a year as a governess in the far north of Norway, but then moved to Oslo, where she earned her living as a secretary, proof-reader, and left-wing journalist.

The German occupation of Norway caused her to write the patriotic poem for which she is best remembered, "Aust-Vågøy, March 1941"; it concerns German reprisals on the local inhabitants after an Allied raid on the Lofoten Islands. Such poetry was circulated illegally among Resistance supporters. Hagerup spent the latter years of World War II in exile in Sweden, where she came into contact with other Norwegian writers. For a few years after her return to Oslo, she worked on the short-lived newspaper *Friheten* (Freedom), then the second-largest newspaper in Norway, and on the women's periodical *Kvinnen og Tiden* (Women and Current Affairs, 1945–55), edited by *Kristen Hansteen.

Much of Hagerup's poetry is politically inspired, but in her love poetry she emphasizes the struggle between the demands of life and the isolation of women, split between their feelings of dependency and their feelings of distance in relation to men. Her tone is frequently that of the melancholy inherent in memories and desire. The individual is always central to her concerns, and her ability to write simply and directly gives her poems their force.

Hagerup's radio plays are extensions of the themes of her poetry: the gulf between dream and reality, the transitory nature of love, and the gap between lovers. The motifs are treated with amusement and irony, but also with tragic undertones. As a writer of children's poetry, Hagerup followed the tradition of English nonsense verse, playing with words, sounds and rhythms. Her collaboration with the Norwegian artist and illustrator Paul René Gaugin (grandson of the French painter Paul Gaugin) produced what have become three classics of children's lit-

erature. Hagerup also published three volumes of autobiography in the 1960s.

SOURCES:

Beyer, E., ed. *Norges Litteraturhistorie* (A History of Norwegian Literature). Cappelen, Oslo, 1975.
Hagerup, Inger. *Samlede dikt* (Collected Poems). Aschehoug, Oslo, 1976.

Elizabeth Rokkan,
retired Associate Professor of the Department of English
at the University of Bergen, Norway

Haggard, Lilias Rider.

See Rider Haggard, Lilias.

Hagge, Marlene Bauer (1934—)

American golfer and winner of seven LPGA titles who finished among the top ten in earnings for eight seasons. Name variations: Marlene Bauer. Born Marlene Bauer in Eureka, South Dakota, on February 16, 1934; younger sister of golfer Alice Bauer who was the first woman to win the L.A. Open; married.

Professional women's golf was a growing sport when Marlene Bauer, and her older sister **Alice Bauer**, began playing. In 1944, the ten-year-old Marlene won the Long Beach Boys' Junior championship at a time when few young women were playing golf. In 1949, at age 15, Bauer won the first USGA Junior Girls' championship, the Western Junior Girls' championship, and the Helms Award; she was also named Associated Press Athlete of the Year. Bauer and her 18-year-old sister chose to turn pro that year. The Bauer sisters, considered by the press to be the first "glamour girls" of the Tour, were also the youngest. In 1952, Marlene won her first LPGA tournament, the Sarasota Open, in what was to be the beginning of her 25 official career victories. Married by 1956 and now appearing as Marlene Bauer Hagge, she won the LPGA championship in a sudden-death playoff with *Patty Berg. Hagge's powerful swing was exceptionally compact and had a great deal to do with her success on the course. There have been few 29-stroke scores for nine holes in LPGA history. Hagge shot a 29 in Columbus, Ohio, in 1971.

Karin Loewen Haag,
Athens, Georgia

Haggith (fl. 1000 BCE)

Biblical woman. The fifth wife of David, Israelite king (r. 1010–970 BCE); children: Absalom and Adonijah.

Hagman, Lucina (1853–1946)

Finnish educator. Born in 1853; died in 1946.

Ahead of her time as a feminist and a champion of the co-educational movement, Lucina Hagman was the head of a co-educational school in Finland from 1886 to 1899. She founded the Finnish New School in Helsinki in 1899, remaining its director until 1938. Hagman also founded and was the chair of Finland's Women's Association and served in Parliament from 1907 to 1914. She became an honorary professor in 1928. Her writings include bio-bibliographies of *Fredrika Bremer and *Minna Canth (*Minna Canthin elämänkerta*, 1906–11).

Hahn, Madame (1814–1842).

See Blavatsky, Helena for sidebar on Elena Gan.

Hahn, Emily (1905–1997)

American writer and traveler whose unconventional adventures were chronicled in over 50 books and nearly 200 articles. Name variations: Mickey Hahn. Born in St. Louis, Missouri, on January 14, 1905; died in New York City on February 18, 1997; daughter of Isaac Newton Hahn and Hannah (Schoen) Hahn; had four sisters and a brother; married Charles Boxer; children: Carola Boxer Vecchio (b. 1941); Amanda Boxer.

Selected writings: Seductio Ad Absurdum: The Principles and Practices of Seduction—A Beginner's Handbook *(1930);* Beginner's Luck *(1931);* Congo Solo *(1933);* The Soong Sisters *(1941);* Mr. Pan *(1942);* Diamond: The Spectacular Story of Earth's Rarest Treasure and Man's Greatest Greed *(1956); (juvenile)* Around the World with Nellie Bly *(1959);* China Only Yesterday *(1963);* Animal Gardens *(1967, published as* Zoos in England, *1968);* Times and Places *(Crowell, 1970);* On the Side of the Apes *(1971);* Once Upon a Pedestal: An Informal History of Women's Lib *(1974);* Look Who's Talking! *(1978);* The Islands: America's Imperial Adventures in the Philippines *(1981);* Eve and the Apes *(1988); and autobiography* China to Me.

Born in America's heartland at the beginning of the 20th century, Emily Hahn grew up in a large German-Jewish family that prized intellectual independence. Her father Isaac Newton Hahn was a self-made businessman who had once been attracted to Methodism but chose atheism. The highly assimilated Hahn family even celebrated Christmas. At the same time, Isaac was stubborn in his opposition to all organized religions, going so far as to read passages from the Bible to his children in order to point out its inconsistencies. All of the Hahn children were encouraged by their parents to write and

think critically. Emily's mother **Hannah Schoen Hahn** was a militant suffragist who wore bloomers while riding a bicycle and could be quite demanding of Emily and her four sisters (two siblings had died in infancy). Called "Mickey" by her mother (a nickname that stuck), Emily became an independent young woman, unafraid of taking risks and defying conventions. In 1924, despite the poor roads of the day, she and her sister **Dorothy** drove their Model T Ford from Wisconsin to California, 2,400 miles. Years later, the Hahns noted that the adventure transformed Emily, making her a lifelong thrill-seeker.

Emily Hahn decided to study engineering at the University of Wisconsin, despite the fact that women had traditionally been barred from applying for a degree in this field. University administrators attempted to keep Emily from enrolling in what had until then been an all-male program, but she was able to bring the matter before the Wisconsin legislature and, in due course, graduated as the first woman at the University of Wisconsin with a degree in mining engineering. Hahn's first job with Deko Oil, a mining company in St. Louis, introduced her to the monotony of office routine. "The last thing in the world I wanted was a future," she later recalled. "I merely wanted to live, without aiming for anything." When a low-paying job as a Fred Harvey tour guide in New Mexico turned up, Hahn jumped at the opportunity.

Although she had been inspired by Charles Lindbergh's successful transatlantic flight to embark on a life of adventure, Hahn settled down briefly in 1929 by accepting a teaching post in geology at Hunter College in New York City. Soon after arriving in New York, she met Harold Ross, editor of *The New Yorker*, and before long she had become a regular contributor; her first article was based on letters she had written her brother-in-law during her cross-country trip by Model T. Over the next 68 years, the great majority of her 181 articles would initially appear in *The New Yorker*. In 1930, Hahn was sufficiently confident to publish her first book, *Seductio Ad Absurdum*, a tongue-in-cheek guide to "the principles and practices of seduction."

As determined as ever to explore the world, she sailed from London for equatorial Africa on Christmas Day, 1930. Her destination was a remote Red Cross clinic in a Pygmy region of the Belgian Congo (now Republic of Congo) run by an American, Patrick Putnam. As a solo white woman in Africa in the early 1930s, Hahn was a rarity and regarded by most as odd, mad, or perhaps a prostitute. To reach her destination, Hahn traveled up the Congo River on the steamboat *Micheline,* trying to adapt to the climate as well as the mosquitoes, tsetse flies and other biting insects. The heat and humidity were oppressive, even after dark, and she would recall being "so hot that I thought I would rather die than lie there any longer, but even my desire for death was languid and unpassionate. It's the first time in my life that I grew slippery with perspiration just lying in bed." As the *Micheline* steamed upstream, the Congolese jungle, mysterious and lush, hugged the river on both sides, fully measuring up to Hahn's childhood reading about a Dark Continent.

On March 3, 1931, Hahn arrived at her destination, the remote settlement of Penge located 200 miles northeast of Stanleyville on the Aruwimi, a tributary of the mighty Congo River. She and her party arrived at Penge after several hours' paddling in a pirogue (a native canoe fashioned from a hollowed-out tree trunk), where she was greeted by Patrick Putnam. Settling into a routine, Hahn befriended Putnam's chimpanzee Chimpo. For the remainder of her life, Emily would be fascinated by primates.

As Putnam's assistant, she acquired medical skills including the ability to give injections, wrap bandages, take blood, and remove "jiggers"—chigoes or small fleas that burrow painfully under a victim's toenails, where they then lay their eggs. She learned Swahili, first mastering basic medical terminology and swear words. Hahn's immense curiosity was never disappointed while she lived in Penge, and her diary and notes would appear in print as *Congo Solo* in the summer of 1933. In August 1931, while she was still in Africa, her first novel was published. Entitled *Beginner's Luck,* it tells the story of three young Americans who run away to Mexico after becoming disillusioned while living in an artist's commune in Santa Fe.

In Penge, Hahn worked, observed, and wrote. She was at first shocked by, but soon came to accept, the fact that Patrick Putnam had three native women as his wives. He would often punish "the natives" harshly, arguing that in Penge the law of the jungle prevailed and "the strong should dominate the weak." Quite suddenly, after 20 months, Hahn no longer felt comfortable living in the village. The immediate cause of her growing sense of unease was Putnam's chaining of one of his wives to a tree, her punishment for having been unfaithful to him. Exhibiting her "usual sublime self-confidence," Hahn set off with her pet baboon Angélique, as

Emily Hahn

well as a Pygmy guide, a cook, and a dozen porters carrying luggage and food. After a grueling and dangerous trek from Penge to Lake Kivu that would cover about 800 miles, her party arrived at a mining camp. She was able to depart Africa in excellent health and spirits and ready for more adventures.

Her experiences in the Congo turned Hahn into a confirmed world traveler and cosmopolitan writer. "I had long given up the struggle against being a writer," she said. "There is really nothing else to be, if you like traveling." The opportunity for new excitement presented itself in 1935, when Emily and her sister **Helen Hahn** visited Shanghai. Although her books, including her novel *Affair,* had probed youthful alienation and the question of abortion, and had mostly received good and even enthusiastic reviews, Emily had yet to publish a bestseller. Restless as always, Hahn was taken with China, even though that nation now found itself locked in a war with an aggressive Japanese Empire.

Settling in Shanghai as the permanent China correspondent of *The New Yorker*, Hahn soon scandalized the European community in that cosmopolitan city by becoming the lover of Sinmay Zau, a married Chinese poet and artist. Through Zau, she was able to meet some of China's leading intellectuals and political luminaries including Communist revolutionary leaders Mao Zedong and Zhou Enlai, men who would change the course of Chinese, and world, history. On a more personal level, living in China changed Hahn's perspectives when she discovered that after a year or so of frequenting opium dens she had become addicted to the drug (she found a cure through hypnosis). "I was young and I thought it was romantic to smoke opium," she told *The Washington Post*. "I was quite determined. It took me a year or so to become addicted, but I kept at it." Hahn further scandalized the expatriate community in China when she fell in love with Major Charles Boxer, a married man who was in charge of British Army Intelligence in Hong Kong. A few weeks before Pearl Harbor, Hahn gave birth to a daughter, **Carola Boxer (Vecchio)**, fathered by Boxer. When Boxer was wounded during the Japanese attack on Hong Kong in December 1941, becoming a prisoner of war, Emily was on her own. She convinced Japanese occupation officials that she was Eurasian, thus enabling her to remain free and bring needed food and medicines to Boxer and other starving prisoners.

In September 1943, Hahn made a difficult choice by accepting an offer of repatriation for herself and her infant daughter as part of a prisoner swap negotiated between the Allies and the Japanese, though it meant leaving Boxer behind to an uncertain fate. Along with 1,400 American and Canadian repatriates, Emily and Carola set sail on the ship *Teia Maru*. Major Charles Boxer survived imprisonment, and with the end of the war he and Hahn married, soon adding another daughter, **Amanda Boxer**, to their family. Boxer went on to become a distinguished historian of the Portuguese colonial empire. Although their marriage endured, it was by no means a conventional one. While he remained in England, living at their house named Ringshall End, at Little Gaddesden in Hertfordshire, she settled down to life in New York, where she continued to contribute articles to *The New Yorker* and freelanced as a book author. Their successful relationship was based on "an intimacy built around absence" as well as the tax laws that limited her sojourns to the United Kingdom to no more than 91 days a year.

Although she was at times regarded by the public as little more than an exhibitionist (one of her more controversial publications was her 1944 article in the *Chicago Sun* entitled "I was the concubine of a Chinese!"), Emily Hahn was in reality a hardworking researcher and writer. Although her prose could at times be superficial, her books were knowledgeable and insightful. Adept at living by her wits in Africa and China, she helped to inform an American public curious about the larger world.

Her books on China—there would be ten in all, including two children's books and two cookbooks (these by a woman who was rarely found in a kitchen)—served to introduce readers to a great civilization that remained largely mysterious and even at times ominous to even educated men and women. With *The Soong Sisters* (1941), Hahn produced an entertaining bestseller, an informative composite biography of the three sisters—*Song Ailing, *Song Qingling (*see The Song Sisters*), and *Song Meiling—who had married three of the most important men in China in the first half of the 20th century, H.H. Kung, Sun Yat-sen, and Chiang Kai-shek. In Hahn's *Mr. Pan* (1942), the turbulent intellectual and political life of Shanghai in the late 1930s is revealed through conversations between the author and "Pan Heh-ven," a thinly disguised version of her Chinese lover of those days, Sinmay Zau. In *China Only Yesterday* (1963), she presented a critical picture of white Europeans' arrogance in their dealings with China in the 19th and early 20th century, while also pointing out that the Chinese contributed to mutual misunderstandings with their ignorance of the outside world and xenophobia.

Enjoying good health to the end of her long life, Emily Hahn worked as a *New Yorker* correspondent, turning out entertaining pieces on various subjects. She was one of a handful of writers who worked for the first four editors of the magazine, Harold Ross, William Shawn, Robert Gottlieb, and **Tina Brown**. A master of many literary genres, Hahn published 54 books ranging from novels (five in all), histories (of love, bohemianism in America, and the Philippines), biographies (including studies of *Fanny Burney and *Mabel Dodge Luhan), and children's books (11 in all, including *Around the World with Nellie Bly*, 1959).

In the last decades of her life, Hahn became increasingly interested in zoology. Long fascinated by apes, she kept pet gibbons during her years in Shanghai and Hong Kong and often visited zoos and primate research facilities. Her fascination produced a number of books, including *Animal Gardens* (1967, published as *Zoos* in its 1968 British edition) and *On the Side of the Apes* (a 1971 volume on primate research). Her 1978 *Look Who's Talking!* presented new discoveries in animal communication, followed a decade later by *Eve and the Apes*, which told of remarkable women who owned or worked with apes, including *Belle Benchley, Penny Patterson, and Augusta Hoyt, all of whom were on the scene long before *Jane Goodall and *Dian Fossey.

Emily Hahn remained active to the end, publishing a poem, "Wind Blowing," in *The New Yorker* only a few weeks before her death in New York City on February 18, 1997. The deepest motivations of Hahn's long and productive life were perhaps best described in her first travel book, *Congo Solo,* where she spoke of the "old euphoria of the traveler . . . that keen expectation of something happening soon, something fascinating." "My younger daughter once rebuked me for not being the kind of mother one reads about," Hahn told an interviewer. "I asked her what kind that was, and she said, the kind who sits home and bakes cakes. I told her to go and find anybody who sits at home and bakes cakes."

SOURCES:

Alsop, Joseph W., and Adam Platt. *"I've Seen the Best of It": A Memoir.* NY: Norton, 1992.

Angell, Roger. "Ms. Ulysses," in *The New Yorker.* Vol. 73, no. 3. March 10, 1997, pp. 52, 54–55.

Cuthbertson, Ken. *Nobody Said Not to Go: The Life, Loves, and Adventures of Emily Hahn.* Boston: Faber and Faber, 1998.

"Emily Hahn," in *The Times* [London]. February 25, 1997, p. 19.

Foskett, Maggie. "A Scandal in Rio," in *The New Yorker.* Vol. 73, no. 7. April 7, 1997, p. 10.

Hahn, Emily. *China Only Yesterday, 1850–1950: A Century of Change.* Garden City, NY: Doubleday, 1963.

——. *China to Me: A Partial Autobiography.* Reprint ed. Boston, MA: Beacon Press, 1988.

——. *Congo Solo: Misadventures Two Degrees North.* NY: Bobbs-Merrill, 1933.

——. *The Emily Hahn Reader.* NY: Alfred A. Knopf, 1989.

——. *Eve and the Apes.* London: Weidenfeld & Nicolson, 1988.

——. *The Soong Sisters.* Reprint ed. NY: Greenwood Press, 1970.

——. *Times and Places.* NY: Crowell, 1970.

Rose, Phyllis, ed. *The Norton Book of Women's Lives.* NY: W.W. Norton, 1993.

Sherman, Geraldine. "Remember me . . . ?," in *Ottawa Citizen.* March 7, 1999, p. C16.

Smith, Dinitia. "Emily Hahn, Chronicler of Her Own Exploits, Dies at 92," in *The New York Times.* February 19, 1997, p. B7.

John Haag,
Associate Professor,
University of Georgia, Athens, Georgia

Bly, Nellie.

See Seaman, Elizabeth Cochrane.

Hahn, Helen or Helena Andreyevna Fadeyev (1814–1842).

See Blavatsky, Helena for sidebar on Elena Gan.

Hahn, Yelena Andreyevna Fadeyev (1814–1842).

See Blavatsky, Helena for sidebar on Elena Gan.

Hahn-Hahn, Ida, Countess von

(1805–1880)

German author. Name variations: Gräfin Hahn-Hahn; Countess Hahn-Hahn. Born Ida Marie Luise Sophie Friederike Gustave von Hahn at Tressow, in Mecklenburg-Schwerin, Germany, on June 22, 1805; died in Mainz, Germany, on January 12, 1880; daughter of Graf (Count) Karl Friedrich von Hahn (1782–1857); married Count Adolf von Hahn, in 1826.

Selected writings: Aus der Gesellschaft (1838); Gräfin Faustine (Countess Faustine, 1840); Ulrich (1841); Orientalische Briefe (Oriental Letters, 1844); Sigismund Forster (1843); Cecil (1844); Sibylle (1846); (autobiography) Von Babylon nach Jerusalem (From Babylon to Jerusalem, 1851); Maria Regina (1860).

Ida von Hahn was born in Tressow, in Mecklenburg-Schwerin, Germany, in 1805, the daughter of Count Karl Friedrich von Hahn, who was well known for his love of the stage, upon which he squandered a substantial amount of his fortune. In 1826, Ida married her wealthy cousin Count Adolf von Hahn. The marriage was extremely unhappy and led to a divorce three years later, in 1829. The countess traveled, produced some volumes of poetry, and in 1838 published the novel *Aus der Gesellschaft.* Since the title was appropriate for her subsequent novels, it was retained for the series, while the book was renamed *Ida Schönholm.* For several years, Ida continued to produce novels on subjects similar to those being chosen by her contemporary *George Sand, but they were less critical of social institutions and involved the aristocracy.

The countess' patrician airs were parodied by *Fanny Lewald in *Diogena* (1847). This mockery, the death of her lover, Count von Bystram, and the revolution of 1848 seems to have induced Ida to turn to Catholicism in 1850. She justified her conversion in the polemical work *Von Babylon nach Jerusalem (From Babylon to Jerusalem,* 1851). In 1852, the countess retired to a convent at Angers, but soon left, taking up residence at Mainz where she founded a nunnery. She lived there without joining the order and continued to write. For many years, her novels were the most popular works of fiction among the aristocracy. Though many of her later publications went unnoticed, *Sigismund Forster* (1843), *Cecil* (1844), *Sibylle* (1846) and *Maria Regina* (1860) enjoyed considerable popularity. Ida von Hahn-Hahn died at Mainz on January 12, 1880.

SUGGESTED READING:

Haffner, P. *Gräfin Ida Hahn-Hahn, eine psychologische Studie*. Frankfort, 1880.

Jacoby, A. *Ida Gräfin Hahn-Hahn*. Mainz, 1894.

Keiter, H. *Gräfin Hahn-Hahn*. Würzburg, n.d.

COLLECTIONS:

Her collected works, *Gesammelte Werke*, with an introduction by O. von Schaching, were published in two series, 45 volumes in all (Regensburg, 1903–1904).

CORRESPONDENCE:

Contained in collections at university libraries at Bonn and Leipzig, and at the Schiller Nationalmuseum at Marbach.

Haig, Margaret (1883–1958).

See Rhondda, Margaret.

Hainault, countess of.

See Margaret of Alsace (c. 1135–1194).
See Maria of Champagne (c. 1180–1203).

Hainault and Holland, countess of.

See Philippine of Luxemburg (d. 1311).
See Jeanne of Valois (c. 1294–1342).
See Joanna of Brabant (1322–1406).
See Margaret of Holland (d. 1356).
See Maud Plantagenet (1335–1362).
See Margaret of Burgundy (c. 1376–1441).
See Jacqueline of Hainault (1401–1436).

Hainisch, Marianne (1839–1936)

Austrian feminist, founder and doyenne of the Austrian women's movement, who was a champion of higher education for women and a leader of the world peace movement. Born Marianne Perger in Baden bei Wien, Lower Austria, on March 25, 1839; died in Vienna on May 5, 1936; daughter of Josef Perger; married Michael Hainisch; children: **Marie Hainisch;** *Michael Hainisch (1858–1940, who served as the first president of the Republic of Austria, 1920–28); Wolfgang Hainisch.*

Marianne Perger was born in 1839 into a financially comfortable middle-class family in Baden bei Wien, a town from which one could visit nearby Vienna by rail. First tutored at home, in 1855 she completed her education at a finishing school for elite young women, Vienna's Institut Betty Fröhlich. In September 1857, Marianne married Michael Hainisch, a successful textile factory owner. Few clouds appeared on her horizon in the early years of her marriage. Shielded from material worries, she was able to concentrate on the domestic sphere, giving birth to three children. By the early 1860s, however, Marianne Hainisch became involved in concerns beyond her home and family. As a result of the Civil War in the United States, the import of cotton into Austria virtually ceased and a deep economic depression hit the textile industry. As a result, factory workers and their families found themselves thrown into conditions of extreme poverty. Hainisch organized charitable activities that enabled a significant number of working-class families to survive the immediate economic crisis, which ended in the mid-1860s. Now sensitive to working-class conditions, she began to view the issue of the economic and social advancement of women in terms of more basic reforms, particularly in the area of women's education.

In an address delivered on March 12, 1870, to the Women's Employment Association of Vienna (Wiener Frauenerwerbsverein), Hainisch called for the creation of grammar schools for girls. Such a reform, she argued, would profoundly change the role of women by enabling them to break down barriers that had until that time kept them from entering professions traditionally reserved for males. Although seen as radical by many contemporary observers, Hainisch's reform proposals were meant to stabilize society, not destroy it. Just as the aim of vocational schools for women of the lower-middle class was to train them for the skilled professions to prevent them from slipping into the proletariat, so too the aim of girls' grammar schools would be to prevent women of the upper-middle class from falling into the lower-middle class.

Hainisch's campaign to create equal opportunities for Austrian women in both secondary and higher education met with vehement opposition from the start. Determined to achieve her goals, she emphasized their apolitical nature. With secondary educations, she noted, women would not only become more economically independent, but would also become more intellectually autonomous. They would then reject the vacuous lifestyles prevalent in the upper-middle class.

Hainisch believed that the new era of higher moral ideals would be inaugurated by women but that its spirit would in time be diffused throughout society. Positive signs of change for Austrian women began to appear before the end of the 19th century, including the inauguration in 1892 of Vienna's Gymnasiale Mädchenschule, a girls' secondary school in all but official designation, located in the Rahlgasse. By 1897, a major victory was won for Austrian women when the philosophical faculty of the flagship University of Vienna admitted them on a basis of unrestricted matriculation, a reform which was also conceded in 1900 by the same institution's medical faculty. In 1899, as Hainisch represented Austrian women at the international women's conference in London, she could report significant progress in her homeland.

By the dawn of the 20th century, Hainisch was the acknowledged leader of the Austrian women's movement. Always a political moderate, she rejected radical feminism as well as the class warfare ideology and Marxist militancy of the emerging Social Democratic movement. Radicals within the women's movement called for a fundamental restructuring of societal and gender relations, but Hainisch remained convinced that the goal of the movement should continue to be the transformation of women as individuals. In May 1902, she became president of the League of Austrian Women's Associations (Bund österreichischer Frauenvereine), an umbrella organization that by 1914 could boast of 90 constituent groups with 40,000 members. The League's goals, which remained moderate because of Hainisch's guiding hand, included the achievement of equal educational opportunities and enhanced employment opportunities.

As a pacifist and friend of *Bertha von Suttner, Hainisch saw World War I as a failure of civilization. She called on the members of the League's constituent organizations to render humanitarian assistance on all levels. "We women cannot change the war," she said, "but nonetheless we can make contributions to ameliorate at least some of the misery and suffering of this conflict." As head of the peace commission of the League, she worked tirelessly to further the agenda of its previous chair, Bertha von Suttner.

The end of the war in November 1918 led to the dissolution of Austria-Hungary and the emergence of an unstable Austrian Republic. Many of Vienna's citizens were close to starvation in the immediate postwar years; Hainisch organized relief work, appealing to the outside world for humanitarian assistance. In 1918, she retired from full-time leadership of the League of Austrian Women's Associations, accepting a less demanding role.

Despite the immense upheavals, there were also victories to celebrate after 1918, including

the granting of suffrage to Austria's women. Her son Michael Hainisch (1858–1940) was the first president of the Republic of Austria (1920–28). In 1926, Marianne was rewarded when Mother's Day, another of her advocacies, became an official holiday in Austria. In 1929, still active at age of 90, Hainisch announced the founding of the Austrian Women's Party (Österreichische Frauenpartei). The universally respected Grand Old Lady of the Austrian women's movement died in Vienna on May 5, 1936. Austria honored Marianne Hainisch by depicting her on a commemorative postage stamp issued on March 24, 1989.

Austrian postage stamp issued on March 24, 1989, in honor of Marianne Hainisch.

SOURCES:

Anderson, Harriet. *Utopian Feminism: Women's Movements in fin-de-siecle Vienna.* New Haven, CT: Yale University Press, 1992.

Eltz-Hoffmann, Lieselotte. "Bedeutende Vorkämpferin für die Sache der Frau: 150. Geburtstag von Marianne Hainisch am 25. März," in *Salzburger Nachrichten.* March 25, 1989.

Fellner, Günter. "Athenäum: Die Geschichte einer Frauenhochschule in Wien," in *Zeitgeschichte.* Vol. 14, no. 3. December 1986, pp. 99–115.

Hacker, Hanna. "Frauenbiografien: Eine Annäherung an vier Lebensläufe 'prominenter' Österreicherinnen," in *Mitteilungen des Instituts für Wissenschaft und Kunst.* Vol. 38, no. 4, 1983, pp. 90–94.

Hainisch, Marianne. "Geschichte der österreichischen Frauenbewegung," in Marianne Hainisch, ed., *Frauenbewegung, Frauenbildung und Frauenarbeit in Österreich*. Vienna: Selbstverlag des Bundes österreichischer Frauenvereine, 1930, pp. 13–24.

Kern, Elga, ed. *Führende Frauen Europas: Neue Folge, in fünfundzwanzig Selbstschilderungen*. Munich: Ernst Reinhardt Verlag, 1930.

Richter, Elise. "Marianne Hainisch und das akademische Studium der Frauen," in *Die Österreicherin*. No. 3. March 1, 1929, pp. 4–5.

Wagner, Renate. *Heimat bist Du grosser Töchter: Österreicherinnen im Laufe der Jahrhunderte*. Vienna: Edition S/Verlag der Österreichischen Staatsdruckerei, 1992.

———. "Marianne Hainisch: Eine Pionierin der Frauenbewegung," in *Volksblatt-Magazin* [Vienna]. May 12, 1989, pp. 2–3.

John Haag,
Associate Professor,
University of Georgia, Athens, Georgia

Halaby, Lisa (b. 1951).

See Noor al-Hussein.

Haldane, Charlotte (1894–1969)

British novelist and journalist, who, despite a varied career as a woman of letters, remains best known for her first novel, the dystopia Man's World *(1926).*

Name variations: (pseudonym) Charlotte Franklyn. Born Charlotte Franken in Sydenham, London, England, on April 27, 1894; died in London on March 16, 1969; daughter of Joseph Franken and Mathilde (Saarbach) Franken; had a sister Elizabeth; niece-in-law of *Elizabeth Sanderson Haldane (1862–1937); married Jack Burghes, in 1918; married J(ohn) B(urdon) S(anderson) Haldane (1892–1964, a geneticist and biochemist), in 1926; children: (first marriage) Ronald John McLeod Burghes (b. January 1919).*

Charlotte Franken was born in 1894 in the south London suburb of Sydenham into a wealthy German-Jewish family. Her father Joseph Franken was a successful fur merchant, while her New York-born mother **Mathilde Saarbach Franken** remained culturally more German than British, having spent her formative years with relatives in Frankfurt am Main. Besides the complexities of her family background, young Charlotte had to endure the opposition of her parents when it became clear during her teens that she had literary ambitions. Gifted in foreign languages (she had spent almost five years at a school in Antwerp, Belgium), Charlotte was a voracious reader, but plans for her to study languages at the Bedford College for Women had to be abandoned in 1910 when her father suffered serious business reverses. After a brief course at a secretarial school, Charlotte found work at a concert manager's office, where her duties included translating ballet synopses of *Anna Pavlova from French into English. Soon she was working for a music publisher, ghostwriting articles under the names of music-hall stars for women's pulp magazines.

The start of World War I unleashed anti-German sentiment throughout the United Kingdom, and Joseph Franken, as a British subject, was declared an enemy alien. To avoid internment, he sought refuge in a still-neutral United States. Charlotte chose to remain in London, keeping a low profile because of her family's German background. In 1916, using the pseudonym Charlotte Franklyn to disguise her Teutonic surname, she published her first short story in *The Bystander* magazine. In 1918, Charlotte married Jack Burghes, a war veteran who had returned from the front suffering from shellshock. After the couple's son Ronald was born in January 1919, Charlotte supported her family by working as social editor and freelance reporter for the *Daily Express* and *Sunday Express*. One of the first newswomen on Fleet Street, she was soon known throughout the British Isles for her well-argued articles championing married women who like herself carried the burden of supporting war-wounded husbands and young children. Convinced that the divorce laws were unfair to women, Charlotte relied on current court cases to reinforce her claims. Although regarded by many of her readers as a militant feminist, she in fact believed that while women needed to break the shackles of traditional female roles they should not embrace society's definition of male roles. In time, her idealistic assessment of motherhood and marriage resulted in strong criticism of her views from radical feminist quarters.

In "The Sex of Your Child," an article she published in the *Daily Express* in July 1924, Charlotte forecast the issues to be raised by a technique for prenatal sex determination and predicted that such a scientific advance would bring about major changes in the social organization of race and gender. Only months earlier, the geneticist and biochemist J.B.S. Haldane had published *Daedalus; or, Science and the Future*, a novel in which he predicted the possibility of one day successfully carrying out extrauterine gestation. Fascinated, Charlotte sought out J.B.S. for advice on a novel she was planning. Although both were married, they quickly fell in love. The affair became an open scandal and nearly cost J.B.S. his readership at Cambridge

University. Only in 1926, after Jack Burghes had divorced Charlotte, was it possible for her to finally marry J.B.S. Haldane.

That same year, Charlotte resigned from the *Daily Express* and published her first novel, *Man's World*. She writes of a dystopia (a place that advocates a malevolent social order) in which the state advances its goals, namely the progressive development of the white race, by highjacking scientific advances for its patriarchal, nationalist, and racist imperatives. In this community, which foreshadows Aldous Huxley's *Brave New World* (1932), women who do not wish to have children must accept sterilization, after which they can behave "promiscuously" and are free to be artists or serve as administrators. The other women, much more highly regarded by the community, serve as "vocational mothers" and determine the sex of their children by performing "Perrier exercises" during pregnancy. As members of "motherhood councils," they control the genetic stock of the state and regulate the proportion of male and female babies.

Although most critics have interpreted *Man's World* as a dystopian novel, some scholars have suggested that the work may have been intended to depict a feminist utopia. Whatever its intent, it was enthusiastically reviewed at the time of its publication and remains Charlotte Haldane's best-known work. Her next book, *Motherhood and Its Enemies* (1928), surprised and angered a majority of feminists, because its essential argument was that only after having mated and borne children could a woman be regarded as "normal." The book's controversial nature made it the center of an intellectual storm. Although it was clearly a strongly pronatalist work, *Motherhood and Its Enemies* was not merely a polemic for traditional marriage and procreation patterns. Many of her suggestions in this work were in fact progressive if not radical in nature, including her strong advocacy of the use of contraceptives by married women, the regular use of anesthesia in childbirth, and a systematic investigation of the most effective methods of child-rearing and primary education.

Within a year of their marriage, Charlotte and J.B.S. found themselves settled into a hectic but exhilarating routine of lecturing, writing and travel. In 1927 and 1928, they attended academic conferences in Geneva and Berlin, selling copies of *Motherhood and Its Enemies*. After a trip to the Soviet Union in 1928, the Haldanes became increasingly convinced that the Soviet model of social reconstruction was the ideal for a capitalist world in disarray. Their faith in

Communism was strengthened in the early 1930s, when the great Depression brought immense suffering to millions. Throughout the 1930s, Charlotte published novels, including the essentially autobiographical *Youth Is a Crime* (1934). Although she had revealed her skepticism about the automatic benefits of science and technology in *Man's World,* Charlotte followed her husband's trailblazing work in biochemistry and genetics with great interest. Her journalistic experience, as well as an ability to present the essential facts of complex scientific experiments in clear prose, led to the founding of the Science News Service, a successful enterprise that sold scientific articles to the popular press. For a decade, Charlotte Haldane ran this agency, writing most of the articles herself.

After the appearance of Nazi Germany in 1933, the Haldanes became increasingly active in the British Communist Party. Because of her Jewish origins, Charlotte regarded the Hitler regime as a personal as well as ideological threat. With the eruption of a Fascist-initiated civil war in Spain in the summer of 1936, Charlotte played an important role in recruiting British volunteers for the International Brigade that fought the Franco forces, spending a number of months in Paris to help bring the volunteers to the border where they illegally entered Spain. Troubled by the struggles of the Spanish Republic, in 1938 she returned to that country to serve as guide and interpreter for Paul Robeson, the American singer, actor and political activist. In May 1938, Haldane spoke eloquently on behalf of Spain at the Second World Congress Against Fascism held in Marseilles. With Japanese aggression in China, in 1938 Charlotte Haldane went to China on a special assignment for the *Daily Herald.* Her reportage from the Orient made it clear that a war in Europe was all but inevitable.

As a Communist, Haldane was shocked by the German-Soviet Nonaggression Pact signed in late August 1939. She suffered "mental discomfort" from the Soviet Union's dramatic about-face, but did not rebel against party discipline, still trusting the Stalin regime. Soon after Nazi Germany attacked the USSR in June 1941, Haldane became the first British woman war correspondent to be assigned to the Russian front. Writing for the *Daily Sketch,* she witnessed an epic struggle that would eventually cost tens of millions of lives and incalculable destruction of factories, cities, towns, villages and cultural monuments. Although Haldane would publish a book in 1942 documenting in positive terms the heroic spirit of resistance of the Soviet peoples,

Russian Newsreel: An Eye-Witness Account of the Soviet Union at War, her stay in the USSR proved disillusioning. What she witnessed with her own eyes—a population living with disease, poverty, and fear—made it impossible for her to continue to swallow the Stalinist propaganda that this was a nation that had succeeded in creating a socialist commonwealth. On visits to collective farms, Haldane was shocked by the overwhelming passivity. She was particularly shaken by the image of a young mother carrying her starved infant to its grave.

On her return to England, Charlotte Haldane severed her ties to the British Communist Party. As she would explain in her autobiography *Truth Will Out,* unlike her husband, who remained a committed Communist to the end of his life, she could no longer respond to the party's propaganda, blindly follow its discipline, or believe in "the sacred text of Communism, the works of Marx, Engels, Lenin and Stalin." This ideological break marked the end of her marriage. Since 1939, she and J.B.S. had seriously considered divorcing, but pressure from party officials (who argued it would bring negative publicity down on the British Communist movement) had delayed their final decision.

Even before her divorce in 1945, Charlotte Haldane paid a heavy price for having broken with the Communist movement. Held in contempt as a defector by Communist intellectuals and most of their sympathizers, she became "a political leper" and was shunned by her former friends. A faction of journalists on Fleet Street sympathetic to Communism kept her from getting assignments as a war correspondent. Haldane was also considered suspect by British Intelligence, which assembled a dossier on her because of her many years as a Communist. At first, she earned a modest living writing articles for *Everywoman,* a journal aimed at low-income housewives. Rescue from her predicament, and an assured source of income, came from the BBC which in August 1943 hired her to work in its Eastern Service. When George Orwell gave up his BBC post as "talks producer" in the Indian Section of the BBC Eastern Service, Haldane succeeded him. She would work for the BBC well into the 1950s, at the same time continuing to write novels. Starting in 1951, when she published a life of Marcel Proust, Haldane wrote a number of finely crafted biographical studies, including well-received volumes on ◄◊ **Marie d'Agoult,** Mozart, Alfred de Musset, and *****Madame de Maintenon.**

In her final years, Charlotte Haldane struggled with health problems, including failing eye-

sight, but she continued to write and remained active. Recent studies of Haldane make a persuasive argument that she is a significant personality in modern Britain's intellectual and cultural history. As **Susan Squier** has noted, Haldane was a woman of deep contradictions who, although she was a self-declared lifelong feminist, also created in *Man's World* an "antifeminist classic" that appears to support the idea of vocational motherhood while blaming suffragists and "spinsters" for devaluing motherhood. Her denunciations of anti-Semitism are contradicted by the same novel's white-only social order run by eugenicists whose leader is a "particularly Jewish" visionary named Mensch. In some of her writings, Haldane championed the beneficence of the modern scientific enterprise, while in others, including *Man's World,* she sounds the alarm bell over the dangers of scientists in control of a repressive state apparatus.

SOURCES:

Adamson, Judith. *Charlotte Haldane: Woman Writer in a Man's World.* Basingstoke, England: Macmillan, 1998.

Armitt, Lucie, ed. *Where No Man Has Gone Before.* London: Routledge, 1991.

Bowker, Gordon. *Pursued by Furies.* London: HarperCollins, 1993.

Clark, Ronald William. *J.B.S.: The Life and Work of J.B.S. Haldane.* NY: Oxford University Press, 1984.

Clute, John, and Peter Nicholls, eds. *The Encyclopedia of Science Fiction.* NY: St. Martin's Press, 1993.

Ferguson, Neal A. "Women's Work: Employment Opportunities and Economic Roles, 1918–1939," in *Albion.* Vol. 7, no. 1. Spring 1975, pp. 55–68.

Gates, Barbara T., and Ann B. Shteir, eds. *Natural Eloquence: Women Reinscribe Science.* Madison: University of Wisconsin Press, 1997.

Haldane, Charlotte. "Passionaria," in *Left Review.* Vol. 3, no. 15. April 1938, p. 926.

———. *Truth Will Out.* NY: Vanguard Press, 1951.

Hartley, Jenny, ed. *Hearts Undefeated: Women's Writing of the Second World War.* London: Virago Press, 1995.

Ingram, Angela J. C., and Daphne Patai, eds. *Rediscovering Forgotten Radicals: British Women Writers, 1889–1939.* Chapel Hill, NC: University of North Carolina Press, 1993.

Kent, Susan Kingsley. "The Politics of Sexual Difference: World War I and the Demise of British Feminism," in *Journal of British Studies.* Vol. 27, no. 3. July 1988, pp. 232–253.

John Haag,
Associate Professor,
University of Georgia, Athens, Georgia

Haldane, Elizabeth S. (1862–1937)

Scottish philosopher and social worker. Born Elizabeth Sanderson Haldane on May 27, 1862; died on December 24, 1937; daughter of Robert Haldane and Mary Elizabeth Burdon-Sanderson; granddaughter of

❧►

d'Agoult, Marie.

See Wagner, Cosima for sidebar.

James Alexander Haldane (1768–1851, a religious writer); sister of J(ohn) S(cott) Haldane (1860–1936, a physiologist and philosopher) and Richard Burdon, Viscount Haldane (1856–1928, a diplomat, lawyer, and philosopher); aunt of J(ohn) B(urdon) S(anderson) Haldane (1892–1964, a geneticist), *Charlotte Haldane (1894–1969), and novelist *Naomi Mitchison (1897–1999); educated by tutors at home; various appointments in social welfare and nursing; founded the Auchterarder Institute and Library; first woman to receive an honorary LL.D. from St. Andrew's University (1911).

Selected works: (trans. with Frances Simon) Hegel's Lectures on the History of Philosophy *(3 vols.: 1892, 1894, 1896); (ed.)* The Wisdom and Religion of a German Philosopher *(1897);* James Frederick Ferrier *(1899);* Descartes: His Life and Times *(1905); (trans. with G.T.T. Ross)* The Philosophical Works of Descartes *(2 vols.: 1911–12); "Notes on a Criticism" in* Mind *(Vol. 22, 1913);* British Nurse in Peace and War *(1920);* George Eliot and her Times *(1927);* Mrs. Gaskell and Her Friends *(1930);* From One Century to Another: the Reminiscences of Elizabeth S. Haldane *(1937).*

Elizabeth Haldane is unusual among contemporary women philosophers because she received her education from tutoring at home and through her own studies. Born to a wealthy Scottish family in 1862, Haldane grew to love the philosophy she learned from the tutors who educated her and her brothers. After studying nursing and working under *Octavia Hill, she became vice-chair of territorial nursing service and was manager, for some years, of the Edinburgh Royal Infirmary. Politically active as a lifelong liberal, she became the first woman justice of the peace in Scotland in 1920. While she is known for her nursing work and for having advanced the field of social welfare (she established and supported the Auchterarder Institute and Library), Haldane is particularly known for her contributions to philosophy. Despite her lack of university training, she published several biographies and translations of philosophy. Her translation with **Frances Simon** of *Hegel's Lectures on the History of Philosophy* is still the standard. Her biography of Rene Descartes (*Descartes: His Life and Times* [1905]), the 17th-century mathematician also known as the father of modern philosophy, was probably responsible for her receiving, in 1911, the first honorary LL.D. given to a woman by St. Andrew's University.

SOURCES:
Haldane, Elizabeth S. *From One Century to Another: The Reminiscences of Elizabeth S. Haldane.* London: A. Maclehose, 1937.

Kersey, Ethel M. *Women Philosophers: a Bio-critical Source Book.* NY: Greenwood Press, 1989.
Waithe, Mary Ellen, ed. *A History of Women Philosophers.* Boston: Martinus Nijhoff Publications, 1987–1995.

Catherine Hundleby, M.A.,
Philosophy, University of Guelph

Haldimand or Haldimond, Jane (1769–1858).

See Marcet, Jane.

Hale, Clara (1905–1992)

American social activist and child-care worker who founded Hale House, a group home for babies born addicted to drugs and alcohol and, later, those born HIV-positive. Name variations: Mother Hale; Clara McBride. Born Clara McBride on April 1, 1905, in Philadelphia, Pennsylvania; died on December 18, 1992, in New York City; graduated from high school in Philadelphia; married Thomas Hale (d. 1932); children: Lorraine Hale (Ph.D., executive director of Hale House); Nathan Hale; Kenneth Hale.

"Mother" Clara Hale devoted most of her life to the disenfranchised mothers and children of New York City's Harlem, first as the foster mother of 40, and then as the founder of Hale House, a home for babies, many born to drug-addicted mothers or HIV-positive.

The youngest of four children, Hale was born in 1905 and raised in Philadelphia. Her father died when she was just a baby and her mother supported the family by taking in boarders. After graduating from high school, Hale married and moved to New York, where her husband ran a floor-waxing business. Besides caring for her three young babies, she supplemented the family income by cleaning theaters. When she was 27, her husband died of cancer, leaving her to raise the children alone. At first she doubled her domestic jobs, cleaning houses during the day and theaters at night. However, she hated leaving her children without supervision, so she began offering day care from her home. In addition to caring for the children of women who worked as live-in maids, Hale began to take in foster children, for which she was paid two dollars a week per child. For the next 27 years, in a five-room walk-up in Harlem, Hale cared for seven or eight foster children at a time along with her own three. Her daughter **Lorraine Hale** was almost 16 before she realized that all the other children were not her real brothers and sisters. "Everyone called me 'Mommy,'" Clara Hale told Tom Seligson of *Parade* (November 18, 1984). "I took care of forty of them like that. They're now all grown up. They're doctors, lawyers, everything. Almost all of them stay in touch. I have about sixty grandchildren."

In 1968, Hale retired from foster care, quite unaware that her greatest challenge lay ahead. The following year, her daughter Lorraine encountered a young woman heroin addict half asleep on a bench in a Harlem park with a young baby girl dangling from her arms. Rousing the woman, Lorraine told her to take the baby to her mother, then get herself into treatment. The next day, the young woman arrived on Hale's doorstep, baby in arms. "Before I knew it," Hale later told **Irene Verag** of *Newsday* (January 29, 1985), "every pregnant addict in Harlem knew about the crazy lady who would give her baby a home." Within two months, Hale was caring for 22 drug-addicted babies lined up in wall-to-wall cribs in her apartment. It was exhausting work for the 67-year-old. For weeks, the tiny infants cried inconsolably with withdrawal symptoms that included leg and back stiffness, diarrhea, and vomiting. Hale's treatment, simple hands-on loving at-

Clara Hale

tention round-the-clock, was 90% effective, surprising doctors and health-care workers who had long-since despaired of finding effective treatment for these babies.

For a year and a half, Lorraine and Hale's two sons, Nathan and Kenneth, provided financial support for the operation. In the early 1970s, New York City began funding the project through the New York City Department of Social Services. In 1975, aided by a federal grant, the not-for-profit Hale House was founded in a five-story reclaimed brownstone on West 122nd Street. One of only two programs at the time addressing the problem of New York's alarming number of chemically dependent newborns (the other was the state-funded New York Medical College Pregnant Addicts and Addicted Mothers Program), Hale House was unique in its approach, as pointed out by **Mary Ann Giordano** in the *New York Daily News* (November 14, 1983). "Only Hale House takes these children in after birth, cares for them through the withdrawal process, and raises them until their mothers complete a drug-treatment program— or simply decide they are ready to take their children back." Hale often reminded people that the house was "not an orphanage," and that only rarely was it necessary for a child to be put up for adoption. Lorraine Hale (who earned doctorates in child development and developmental psychology in order to function as the executive director of Hale House) told a reporter for *The New York Times* (March 12, 1984): "When we can send a child back to his family, that's a precious moment for me."

By 1985, annual funding for Hale House was $190,000, with an additional $30,000 coming in from private gifts. When the city withdrew funds in 1989, claiming the drug-addicted baby epidemic had passed, Hale and her daughter Lorraine turned to fundraising in order to stay in operation. With the help of generous celebrities as well as ordinary citizens, Hale expanded the operation to include treatment programs for HIV-infected babies, troubled teens, and young drug-addicted mothers.

In 1985, Hale was honored with an invitation to attend President Ronald Reagan's State of the Union address before Congress. "When the President called, I was sick, but I went anyway," she later said. "I wanted the kids to see it and know it." Cited by the president as "a true American hero," Hale received a standing ovation from the spectators, including members of Congress, the Supreme Court, and the Cabinet. In 1985, Hale also received an honorary doctorate in humane letters from the John Jay College of Criminal Justice.

Clara Hale's charity was not limited to Hale House. "Anyone can come to my mother for a handout, and she'll give it," Lorraine once said. "She gets paid a salary and she gives it all away. . . . Every month, I write thirty envelopes to different causes she supports." Although Hale trained several child-care workers and sleep-in aides to help her, and was also assisted by the rest of the Hale House staff, she continued to personally care for her little patients until her failing health made it impossible. After a series of strokes confined her mother to bed, Lorraine would still bring one of the babies into her from time to time for a cuddle. "I tell [the baby] about my past—he is the only one who will listen to me anymore—and about his future," said Hale. Mother Clara Hale died on December 18, 1992, at age 87.

SOURCES:

Graham, Judith, ed. *Current Biography Yearbook 1993.* NY: H.W. Wilson, 1993.

Mooney, Louise, ed. *Newsmakers: The People Behind Today's Headlines.* Detroit, MI: Gale Research, 1993.

Moritz, Charles, ed. *Current Biography Yearbook 1985.* NY: H.W. Wilson, 1985.

Smith, Jessie Carney, ed. *Notable Black American Women.* Detroit, MI: Gale Research, 1992.

Barbara Morgan,
Melrose, Massachusetts

Hale, Lucretia Peabody

(1820–1900)

American author of **The Peterkin Papers**. *Born on September 2, 1820, in Boston, Massachusetts; died on June 12, 1900, in Belmont, Massachusetts; second daughter and third of the 11 children (7 of whom survived infancy) of Nathan Hale (a lawyer and owner-editor of the* Boston Daily Advertiser*) and Sarah Preston (Everett) Hale (a writer); sister of writer Edward Everett Hale (1822–1909) and artist Susan Hale (1833–1910); attended Susan Whitney's dame school; attended Elizabeth Peabody's school; graduated from the George B. Emerson School for Young Ladies; never married; no children.*

Selected works: (with E.E. Hale) Margaret Percival in America *(1850);* Seven Stormy Sundays *(1959);* Struggle for Life *(1861);* The Lord's Supper and Its observance *(1866);* The Service of Sorrow *(1967);* Six of One by Half a Dozen of the Other *(with E.E. Hale et al., 1872);* The Wolf at the Door *(1877);* Designs in Outline for Art-Needlework *(1879);* More Stitches for Decorative Embroidery *(1879);* Point-Lace: A Guide to Lace-Work *(1879);* The Peterkin Papers *(1880);* The Art of Knitting *(1881);* The Last of the Peterkins, with Others of Their Kin *(1886);* Fagots for the Fireside *(1888);* An Uncloseted Skeleton *(with E.L. Bynner, 1888);* Stories for Children *(1892); (with B. Whitman)* Sunday School Stories *(n.d.).*

ℒucretia
𝒫eabody
ℋale

A descendent of the famous American patriot Nathan Hale on her father's side, Lucretia Peabody Hale grew up in a distinguished literary family Her mother **Sarah Preston Hale** was a writer, and her father Nathan was owner-editor of the Boston *Daily Advertiser*. Privately educated at ***Elizabeth Palmer Peabody**'s school, among other institutions, Hale also spent much time at home due to ill health. In addition to numerous family-oriented activities, which included printing two family newspapers, she collaborated with her brother Edward Everett Hale on her first novel, *Margaret Percival in America*, a religious story which they published in 1850. That same year, the family fell upon hard times and Hale's father was forced to move his wife and unmarried daughters, Lucretia and **Susan Hale**, to a small house in Brookline. To help the family through mounting financial hardship, Hale turned to writing in earnest. She began publishing articles in the *Atlantic Monthly* in 1858, the first of which was a fanciful tale called "The Queen of the Red Chessman," in which a willful red chess queen comes to life. In the course of the next several years, Hale produced a novel, *Struggle for Life* (1961), and several books of devotional readings.

Hale gained her reputation, however, with her whimsical sketches about the Peterkins, beginning with "That Lady Who Put Salt in Her Coffee," which was published in *Our Young Folks* in April 1868. Subsequent stories eventually filled two books, *The Peterkin Papers* (1880) and *The Last of the Peterkins* (1886), both of which became extremely popular with children and adults and still enjoy a following. The amusing tales center on a family of proper Bostonians named Peterkin, a well-meaning albeit scatterbrained clan who is rescued from a variety of exaggerated disasters by "the lady from Philadelphia," a summer visitor who offers common sense solutions to their endless difficulties. Hale created the first Peterkin stories while vacationing, to entertain a friend's small daughter. The later stories were often inspired by her own family experiences.

In 1866, after the death of her parents, Hale and her sister Susan spent a year in Egypt, where her brother Charles was the American consul general, and then spent another two years with friends in Keene, New Hampshire. Upon her return to Boston, Hale lived alone for the first time in a succession of small apartments. In addition to assisting Edward in editing his journal, *Old and New Magazine*, she became involved in various educational and charitable causes. In 1874, she was one of the first six women, including **Lucretia Crocker** (1829–1886) and **Abby W. May** (1829–1888), elected to the Boston School Committee. She served two terms, until 1876, during which time she advocated the establishment of kindergartens and vacation schools. She also occasionally took students into her home for instruction.

Hale's later writings included a series of game and sewing books, and a story called *An Uncloseted Skeleton* (1888), written in collaboration with Edwin L. Bynner. One of her last works, *The New Harry and Lucy* (1892), a novel that traces the adventures of a couple who meet and marry during a tour of Boston in the fall of 1891, was written with her brother Edward. Hale spent her last years in ill health and died at the age of 80 in the McLean Hospital in Belmont, Massachusetts.

SOURCES:

James, Edward T., ed. *Notable American Women 1607–1950*. Cambridge, MA: The Belknap Press of Harvard University Press, 1971.

Mainiero, Lina, ed. *American Women Writers*. NY: Frederick Ungar, 1980.

McHenry, Robert. *Famous American Women*. NY: Dover, 1983.

Barbara Morgan,
Melrose, Massachusetts

Hale, Mother (1905–1992).

See Hale, Clara.

Hale, Sarah Josepha (1788–1879)

Novelist, poet, advocate of women's education, and editor of Godey's Lady's Book, *the most popular American magazine of the mid-19th century. Name variations: Used "Cornelia" as a pseudonym very early in her publishing career; sometimes signed arti-* cles "S.J.H." or "The Lady Editor." *Born Sarah Josepha Buell on October 24, 1788, in Newport, New Hampshire; died on April 30, 1879, in Philadelphia, Pennsylvania; daughter of Gordon and Martha (Whittlesey) Buell (farmers and innkeepers); married David Hale, on October 23, 1813 (died 1822); children: David (b. 1815); Horatio (b. 1817); Frances Ann (b. 1819); Sarah Josepha (called Josepha, b. 1820); William (b. 1822).*

Became editor of The Ladies' Magazine *(1828); published children's poem "Mary's Lamb" (1830); became editor of* Godey's Lady's Book *(1837); began Thanksgiving holiday campaign (1846); published 900-page women's biographical dictionary (1853).*

Edited: The Ladies' Magazine *(Boston, 1828–36);* Juvenile Miscellany *(Boston, 1834–36);* Godey's Lady's Book *(Philadelphia, 1837–87).*

Novels: Northwood: A Tale of New England *(1827);* The Lecturess; or, Woman's Sphere *(1839);* Keeping House and Housekeeping *(1845);* Boarding Out: A Tale of Domestic Life *(1846);* Harry Guy, the Widow's Son: A Story of the Sea *(1848);* The Judge: A Drama of American Life *(1850);* Northwood; or, Life North and South, Showing the Character of Both *(1852);* Liberia, or Mr. Peyton's Experiments *(1853).* Nonfiction: Sketches of American Character *(1829);* Traits of American Life *(1835);* The Good Housekeeper; or, The Way to Live Well and to Be Well While We Live *(1839);* Manners; or, Happy Homes and Good Society All the Year Round *(1867).*

Poetry collections: The Genius of Oblivion and Other Original Poems *(1823);* Poems for Our Children *(including "Mary's Lamb," 1830);* Alice Ray: A Romance in Rhyme *(1845);* Three Hours; or, The Vigil of Love, and Other Poems *(1848);* Love; or, Woman's Destiny: A Poem in Two Parts, with Other Poems *(1870).*

Wrote lyrics for two children's songbooks, The School Song Book *(1834) and* My Little Song Book *(1841). Edited more than 30 children's books, household advice manuals, and volumes of verse, including* Flora's Interpreter; or, The American Book of Flowers and Sentiments *(1832) and* The Ladies' Wreath: A Selection from the Female Poetic Writers of England and America *(1837). Edited a 900-page women's biographical dictionary,* Woman's Record; or, Sketches of All Distinguished Women, from "The Beginning" Till A.D. 1850 *(1853, revised and reissued in 1855 and 1870). Wrote thousands of articles, many of them unsigned, for* Godey's Lady's Book *(1837–77).*

The life and career of Sarah Josepha Hale, a prolific editor and author, represents one model of womanhood and female achievement in 19th-century America. A widow forced to work to support her five children, she rose to national fame and influence while maintaining her belief in a separate sphere for women in American life, a philosophy evident in the books she wrote and the magazines she edited. Yet the woman who signed her articles "The Lady Editor" staunchly supported women's education and property rights, and her varied accomplishments during her 50-year career in publishing opened doors for other women journalists.

Sarah was the third of four children born to Gordon and **Martha Buell,** a rural New Hampshire couple who valued education and patriotism—Gordon had fought in the American Revolution. Martha Buell was a positive role model for Sarah, who later explained, "I owe my early predilection for literary pursuits to the teaching and example of my mother. She had enjoyed uncommon advantages of education for a female of her times—possessed a mind clear as rock water, and a most happy talent of communicating knowledge." At home, the teenaged Sarah read classical literature, including all of Shakespeare's plays, and studied Latin, Greek, geography, and philosophy. She also was tutored by her older brother Horatio, who attended Dartmouth College and believed it was unfair that women were denied higher education. In 1806, the 18-year-old Sarah began a private school for children, where she taught reading, writing, math, and Latin to girls as well as boys for the next seven years.

In 1813, Sarah married David Hale, a New Hampshire attorney. Though she stopped teaching, she continued her own education at home, with David's encouragement. Every evening the couple spent two hours together studying literature, French, and botany. David's devotion to Sarah and appreciation of her intellectual abilities may well have been reasons for her later editorial view that women's first priorities should be their husbands and children. Hale began writing prose and poetry, publishing some verse in a local newspaper, though most of her time was spent caring for their four children. She struggled with her health, coming close to death in 1819 but ultimately surviving tuberculosis, the disease that had killed her mother and sister eight years earlier.

It was David who succumbed to illness, dying of pneumonia on September 25, 1822, two weeks before Sarah gave birth to their fifth child. Hale suddenly found herself sole provider for the family. After working briefly in her sister-in-law's millinery shop, she turned to writing to earn a living. She was quickly successful, pub-

lishing a book of poetry in 1823 and a novel, *Northwood: A Tale of New England,* in 1827. During the intervening years, she contributed regularly to the *Boston Spectator* and *Ladies' Album,* work that attracted the attention of Boston publisher John Lauris Blake. In 1828, Blake offered the 39-year-old Hale the editorship of his new *Ladies' Magazine.*

She filled the pages of the *Ladies' Magazine* with works by American writers—in contrast to the common practice of reprinting articles from English periodicals—and included not only fiction, but also articles about women's education, employment opportunities, and civic obligations. Among the contributors were ****Lydia Maria Child** and ****Lydia Sigourney.** Hale herself wrote much of the text, republishing her articles in two collections, *Sketches of American Character* (1829) and *Traits of American Life* (1835).

> *The Lady's Book* was the first avowed advocate of the holy cause of woman's intellectual progress. . . . We intend to go on . . . till female education shall receive the same careful attention and liberal support from public legislation as are bestowed on that of the other sex.
>
> —Sarah Josepha Hale, 1850

During these years, she also published the volume of children's verse, *Poems for Our Children* (1830), that contained the poem for which she is best-remembered, "Mary's Lamb" ("Mary had a little lamb . . ."). In addition to the two books of children's poetry she wrote in the early part of her career, Hale had a hand in the production of several other works for children. She served as editor of a ten-volume children's library series and as lyricist for two books of children's songs written by music-education pioneer Lowell Mason. From 1834 to 1836, she briefly took the helm of *Juvenile Miscellany,* a children's magazine previously edited by Lydia Maria Child. Many of Hale's verses for children were reprinted, most without attribution, in McGuffy's *Readers.*

During the 13 years she lived in Boston, Hale began her long involvement in civic projects. Her own experience of widowhood led her to found the Seaman's Aid Society, a women's group that raised funds for the support of the families of men who were away at sea or had died at sea. This organization provided day-care for children and vocational training for women and girls. Hale spearheaded a campaign to complete the American Revolution monument at Bunker Hill, organizing an 1840 "women's fair" at Boston's Quincy Hall where women sold homemade food, clothing, quilts, and decorations, raising more than $30,000 and ensuring the monument's completion. She also led a literary club, as she had in New Hampshire, and encouraged a young doctor, Oliver Wendell Holmes, in his early attempts at writing.

The *Ladies' Magazine,* which was briefly rechristened the *American Ladies' Magazine,* failed in 1836 but was absorbed by Philadelphia publisher Louis Godey's seven-year-old fashion magazine, the *Lady's Book,* which would be retitled *Godey's Lady's Book* four years later. Offered the top position on the combined publication, Hale accepted on the condition that she work from her home in Boston until her youngest child graduated from Harvard in 1841. That year, she moved to Philadelphia.

While she had little personal interest in fashion, Hale made no attempt—nor would Godey have allowed her—to change the magazine's focus. The *Lady's Book* had already attracted considerable attention because of its fashion illustrations, which pioneered sophisticated woodcut (plus some copper and steel) engraving techniques and color printing in American magazines. The new editor contained her remarks on women's clothing to repeated editorials about the pain and ill health caused by the tight lacing of corsets (she instead urged women to get out in the fresh air and exercise in order to stay thin). The bulk of Hale's editorial work lay in procuring non-fashion editorial for the magazine. During the 1840s, she bolstered the magazine's literary reputation by commissioning the work of major American writers, including Ralph Waldo Emerson, Henry Wadsworth Longfellow, William Cullen Bryant, and Nathaniel Hawthorne.

Hale herself wrote a great deal of the magazine, contributing fiction, poetry, editorials, features, and book reviews. Some of her articles dealt with issues such as physical fitness, parenting, and homemaking—a set of skills to which she assigned the label "domestic science." While maintaining that women's greatest achievement lay in marriage and motherhood, she defended women's rights within that sphere, particularly their property rights. In 1837, she wrote:

> The barbarous custom of wresting from woman whatever she possesses, whether by inheritance, donation or her own industry, and conferring it all upon the man she marries, to be used at his discretion and will,

perhaps wasted on his wicked indulgences, without allowing her any control or redress, is such a monstrous perversion of *justice* by *law,* that we might well marvel how it could obtain in a Christian community.

Hale's primary editorial theme, however, was the importance of women's education, a position partly attributable to her own upbringing but also greatly influenced by her friendship with education pioneer *Emma Willard. In the pages of the *Lady's Book,* Hale supported Dr. *Elizabeth Blackwell, the first American woman to earn a medical degree, and endorsed the idea of medical schools for women. She believed in the establishment of separate colleges for women in all fields, and during the early 1860s she served as an advisor to Matthew Vassar as he planned his new women's college, not only supporting the project but insisting on the hiring of women faculty. In her magazine, she wrote about the many women entering the field of teaching in elementary and secondary schools, especially as the country expanded westward, and argued that they deserved college-level training and adequate pay. For her editorial support of these positions, Hale was named an honorary vice president of Emma Willard's Association for the Mutual Improvement of Female Teachers.

Hale defended women's education not as a challenge to conventional femininity, but rather as a natural responsibility dictated by women's role within the home and by their moral superiority within society. In 1837, she wrote that rather than "there being any danger that the intellectual and moral progress of woman will make her, what is termed, masculine, we hold that her enlightened influence . . . will, by making men better Christians, make them more like women." Consistent with her belief in a separate, domestic sphere for women, however, Hale criticized women's involvement in politics and opposed the idea of women's suffrage.

Nevertheless, she provided a new national forum that advanced discussion of women's social issues. She also provided a new forum in which American writers could advance their careers. She continued to publish only original material, copyrighted those works in an effort to prevent unauthorized republication elsewhere, and *paid* her writers—not yet a standard practice in the periodical business. She provided steady work for authors in the early stages of their careers, including Edgar Allan Poe and *Harriet Beecher Stowe. Stowe wrote almost exclusively for the *Lady's Book* before the 1852 publication of her bestselling novel, *Uncle Tom's Cabin.* She was only one of many women writers

whose work Hale bought and published; others included *Catherine Sedgwick, *Ann Stephens, Grace Greenwood (*Sara Clarke Lippincott), and the sisters *Alice and *Phoebe Cary. Hale also staffed her magazine largely with women editors and artists.

Even during the peak years of the magazine's success, Hale continued to produce books, all targeted toward women. In the mid-1850s, she edited two volumes of household-management advice and two cookbooks. At the same time, she was compiling and editing a 900-page reference book titled *Woman's Record; or, Sketches of All Distinguished Women from "the Beginning" till A.D. 1850*. Published in 1853 and updated in 1855 and 1870, this biographical dictionary included entries on more than 1,600 women. Looking back on this work in the December 1877 issue of the *Lady's Book*—her final issue as its editor—she explained that "My object was to prepare a comprehensive and accurate record of what women have accomplished, in spite of the disadvantages of their position, and to illustrate the great truth that woman's mission is to educate and ameliorate humanity."

Hale probably also had a female audience in mind when she published her 1852 novel *Northwood; or, Life North and South, Showing the Character of Both*, an expanded version of her 1827 novel; its anti-slavery (yet pacifist) theme was directed at essentially the same women's readership that made Stowe's *Uncle Tom's Cabin* a bestseller the same year. In both *Northwood* and *Liberia*, the novel she published in 1853, Hale warned that economic differences in the American North and South needed resolution and that slavery was morally wrong. Unlike Stowe and other abolitionists, however, Hale believed that the solution to the problem of slavery was the education of Southern slaveowners, who in turn would educate their slaves, free them, and encourage their colonization in Africa. Hale's opinions about slavery and the Southern economic system were expressed only in her fiction, however, and never in the magazine. Louis Godey feared that any mention of the conflicts leading to the Civil War—indeed, any mention of the war itself once it was underway—would offend his Southern readers.

During her 40-year tenure at *Godey's Lady's Book*, Hale was involved in several prominent philanthropic, educational, and civic projects. She helped to organize the Ladies' Medical Missionary Society of Philadelphia and lent her support to the establishment of the Women's Medical College of Philadelphia. She endorsed the founding of the Philadelphia School of Design for Women. She used the *Lady's Book* as a platform for publicizing ***Ann Pamela Cunningham**'s campaign to preserve Mount Vernon. But her best-known project was her drive to make Thanksgiving—an idea that had originated with George Washington—a formally recognized holiday celebrated across America. For nearly two decades, she wrote hundreds of editorials on the subject and mounted a letter-writing campaign to public officials. Largely due to her efforts, Abraham Lincoln

proclaimed Thanksgiving a national holiday in 1863 (though it did not become a legal holiday until 1941).

Under Hale's editorship, *Godey's Lady's Book* prospered during the mid-century, becoming the most widely read magazine in America. By 1860, its paid readership totalled 150,000—six times what it had been when Hale first arrived, and more than 20 times the average magazine circulation of the day. Hale remained at its helm until December 1877, when she retired at age 89. She died a little more than a year later, on April 30, 1879.

SOURCES:

Beasley, Maurine H., and Sheila J. Gibbons. *Taking their Place: A Documentary History of Women and Journalism*. Washington, DC: American University Press, 1993, pp. 77–90.

Finley, Ruth E. *The Lady of Godey's: Sarah Josepha Hale*. Philadelphia, PA: J.B. Lippincott, 1931.

Hale, Sarah Josepha. *Northwood; or, Life North and South*. 1852 (NY: Johnson Reprint, introduction by Rita K. Gollin, 1970).

Mott, Frank Luther. *A History of American Magazines, 1741–1850*. Vol. 1. Cambridge, MA: Harvard University Press, 1966, pp. 580–594.

Okker, Patricia. *Our Sister Editors: Sarah J. Hale and the Tradition of Nineteenth-Century American Women Editors*. Athens, GA: University of Georgia Press, 1995.

Rogers, Sherbrooke. *Sarah Josepha Hale: A New England Pioneer, 1788–1879*. Grantham, NH: Tompson & Rutter, 1985.

Woodward, Helen. *The Lady Persuaders*. NY: Ivan Obolensky, 1960.

SUGGESTED READING:

Entrikin, Isabelle. *Sarah Josepha Hale and Godey's Lady's Book*. Lancaster, PA: Lancaster Press, 1946.

Fryatt, Norma R. *Sarah Josepha Hale: The Life and Times of a Nineteenth Century Career Woman*. NY: Hawthorn Books, 1975.

Tarbell, Ida. "The American Woman: Those Who Did Not Fight," in *American Magazine*. Vol. 69, March 1910, pp. 656–669.

Carolyn Kitch,
Assistant Professor at the Medill School of Journalism at Northwestern University, Evanston, Illinois, and former editor for *Good Housekeeping* and *McCall's*

Haley, Margaret A. (1861–1939)

American educator. Born Margaret Angela Haley in Joliet, Illinois, on November 15, 1861; died in Chicago, Illinois, on January 5, 1939; attended public and convent schools.

A prominent figure in Chicago politics from 1900 to the mid-1930s, Margaret A. Haley was a dynamic leader and vice-president of the Chicago Teacher's Federation. She was president of the National Federation of Teachers in 1902 and instrumental in securing election of *Ella Flagg Young as superintendent of Chicago schools (1910). Her autobiography *Battleground* (edited by Robert L. Reid, University of Illinois Press) was published in 1982.

Halicarnassus, queen of.
See Artemisia I (c. 520–? BCE).

Halicarnassus, queen of.
See Artemisia II (c. 395–351 BCE).

Halide Edib (c. 1884–1964).
See Adivar, Halide Edib.

Halimi, Gisèle (1927—)

French lawyer and feminist. Name variations: Gisele Halimi. Born Gisèle Zeiza Elisa Taieb in La Goulette, Tunisia, in 1927; attended a lycée in Tunis: obtained a degree in law and philosophy from the University of Paris, 1948; married Paul Halimi; married Charles Faux; children: three sons.

A practicing lawyer since 1956, Gisèle Halimi gained recognition as the lawyer for the Algerian National Liberation Front (FLN) and as counsel for Algerian nationalist *Djamila Boupacha, in 1960. She also served as representative on many cases involving women's issues, and attracted national publicity for her part in the Bobigny abortion trial in 1972. In 1971, Halimi had founded Choisir, a feminist group organized to protect the women who had signed the *Manifeste des 343*, admitting to receiving illegal abortions. Transforming itself into a reformist body in 1972, Choisir campaigned for passage of the contraception and abortion laws that were eventually framed by *Simone Veil in 1974.

Halimi authored *La cause des femmes* (1973) and initiated and contributed to the collective work *Le Programme commun des femmes* (1978), which addressed women's medical, educational, and professional problems and also suggested solutions that woman voters should demand. In 1981, Halimi was elected as an Independent Socialist to the National Assembly.

Halket, Elizabeth (1677–1727).
See Wardlaw, Elizabeth.

Halkett, Anne (1622–1699)

English royalist and author. Name variations: Lady Halkett; Anna Halkett. Born Anne Murray on January 4, 1622 (some sources cite 1623), in London, England; *died on April 22, 1699; daughter of Thomas Murray and Jane (Drummond) Murray; married Sir James Halkett, in 1656; children: one survived infancy.*

Anne Murray was born into London's high society in 1622. Her father Thomas Murray, a member of Scottish nobility, died when Anne was three years old. Her mother **Jane Drummond Murray** provided Anne with a scholastic and religious education, teaching her French, dancing, music, and needlework, as well as physic and surgery to facilitate her work with the poor. Her religious education included daily prayers, Bible readings, and church attendance.

Anne was first engaged to Thomas Howard, a suitor of small financial prospects, but her mother forbade the marriage as being below her station. In 1647, Anne became involved with royalist Colonel Joseph Bampfield and assisted him in 1648 with the plan to aid the escape of James, duke of York, second son of Charles I, from prison. When James later became king as James II, he gave her a pension as a reward for her part in the escape. Anne continued her royalist activity by nursing soldiers after the battle of Dunbar in 1650.

Anne's relationship with Bampfield ended after she discovered that he had misrepresented himself as a widower, and that his wife, in fact, was very much alive. In 1656, she married Sir James Halkett, a genuine widower with two young daughters. The couple had four children together, three of whom died in infancy. Before the birth of her first child, Anne wrote "The Mother's Will to her Unborn Child." Her husband died in 1676, and she began teaching children of the nobility.

Anne left several volumes after her death, mostly religious works written between 1644 and 1699. She also wrote an autobiography in 1677–78, which records political events of the time along with her own experiences and her deep religious and political beliefs. *The Life of Lady Halkett*, published posthumously in 1701, contains various religious works as well as "Instructions for Youth" and "Life" derived from her autobiography.

Judith C. Reveal,
freelance writer, Greensboro, Maryland

Hall, Adelaide (1904–1993)

African-American jazz singer and actress. Born on October 20, 1904, in Brooklyn, New York; died on November 7, 1993, in London, England; married Bert Hicks, in 1925 (died 1962).

Adelaide Hall was the daughter of a music teacher and began her own enduring singing and acting career after the death of her father in the early 1920s. Hall was one of the few African-American performers of the mid-20th century to earn success both in the United States and in Europe. Her illustrious singing career included collaborations with such stars as Duke Ellington, Art Tatum, Fats Waller, and Joe Loss. Hall may be best known for her rendition of "Digga Digga Do" from *Blackbirds*, and for her collaboration with Duke Ellington on the song "Creole Love Call," in which she sang a wordless instrumental solo.

Hall's theater credits on both sides of the Atlantic include *Shuffle Along* (1922), *Runnin' Wild* (1923), *Chocolate Kiddies* (1925), *Desires of 1927* (1927), *Blackbirds of 1928* (1928), *Brown Buddies* (1930), *The Sun Never Sets* (1938), *Keep Shufflin'* (1938), *Kiss Me Kate* (1951), *Love from Judy* (1952), *Someone to Talk To* (1956), *Jamaica* (1957), and *Janie Jackson* (1958). She also appeared in the films *Dancers in the Dark* (1932), *All-Colored Vaudeville Show* (1935), *Dixieland Jamboree* (1935), *The Thief of Bagdad* (1940), and *Night and the City* (1950).

Adelaide Hall

Although she had stopped acting by the 1950s, Hall continued touring as a singer into the 1960s. She was a popular performer and frequently appeared at the top nightclubs in the United States and Europe such as the Alhambra, Les Ambassadeurs, the Cotton Club, and the Savoy. She and her husband-manager Bert Hicks settled in England in 1938 and ran several successful nightclubs there until his death in 1962.

Hall was an energetic performer and maintained a strong pace even as she aged. In 1979, she appeared at the Newport Jazz Festival with other stars of the 1920s and 1930s, including *Edith Wilson and John W. Bubbles. They performed songs reminiscent of "Black Broadway" shows from the first half of the century and repeated the performance in May of 1980 at Town Hall in New York City. Adelaide Hall passed away on November 7, 1993, at her home in London.

SOURCES:

Smith, Jessie Carney, ed. *Notable Black American Women*. Detroit, MI: Gale Research, 1992.

Judith C. Reveal,
freelance writer, Greensboro, Maryland

Hall, Anna Maria (1800–1881)

Irish author. Name variations: Mrs. S.C. Hall. Born Anna Maria Fielding on January 6, 1800, in Dublin, Ireland; died on January 30, 1881, in East Moulsey, Surrey, England; married Samuel Carter Hall, in 1824.

Anna Maria Hall was born in Dublin in 1800. Her father died while she was still young, and she moved to England with her mother when she was 15. At 24, Anna married Samuel Carter Hall, a journalist and editor. She published her first short story when she was 29 and followed that with a collection of stories, *Sketches of Irish Character* (1829). Her themes consistently focused on Irish life, yet her work was not popular in her native land because she refused to take political sides. Hall wrote a total of nine novels, including *The Buccaneer* (1832), *Marian: or A Young Maid's Fortunes* (1840), *Light and Shadows of Irish Character* (1838), *The White Boy* (1845), and *Can Wrong be Right?* (1862). She also published two plays, *Tales of the Irish Peasantry* (1840) and *Midsummer Eve, a Fairy Tale of Love* (1848). Hall collaborated with her husband on several works, and she contributed to *New Monthly Magazine* and the *Art Union Journal*, both edited by her husband. She also edited *Sharpe's London Magazine* and *St. James's Magazine* from 1862 to 1863.

Hall was an industrious worker and a philanthropist, helping to found several benevolent institutions including the Brompton Consumption Hospital, The Governesses' Institution, the Home for Decayed Gentlewomen and the Nightingale Fund. She was also active in temperance and women's rights movements. In 1868, she received a civil pension in the amount of £100 a year. She died on January 30, 1881, in East Moulsey, Surrey, at age 81.

Judith C. Reveal,
freelance writer, Greensboro, Maryland

Hall, Anne (1792–1863)

American painter of miniature portraits and figures on ivory. Born in Pomfret, Connecticut, on May 26, 1792; died in New York City, on December 11, 1863; the third daughter and sixth of eleven children of Dr. Jonathan (a physician) and Bathsheba (Mumford) Hall; received art instruction from Samuel King; studied oil painting with Alexander Robertson; never married; no children.

A respected painter of miniatures on ivory, and the first woman to become a full member of the National Academy of Design, Anne Hall was born in Connecticut in 1792, one of 11 children of a prominent and cultured Connecticut physician who had encouraged his daughter's early artistic efforts. At age five, Hall was cutting paper figures and modeling in wax, a common medium of the period. She was aided in her childhood endeavors by a family friend, who supplied her with watercolors and pencils. Within a short time, she was painting and drawing birds, flowers, and insects. Although she gradually gravitated to portraiture, she never lost her love of flowers, and often incorporated bouquets into her later figure paintings.

During a visit to Newport, Rhode Island, Hall met Samuel King, the teacher of Gilbert Stuart, Washington Allston, and miniaturist Edward Green Malbone. King gave Hall her first lessons in the technique of painting miniatures on ivory, which she later supplemented by studying oil painting with Alexander Robertson, a miniaturist and landscape painter and one of the first art teachers in America. Hall's brother, a successful businessman in New York, also supported her art instruction by sending paintings from Europe for her to copy. The "old master" color of her later miniatures was attributed to these early copies.

Hall had her first exhibitions at the American Academy of Fine Arts in New York in 1817 and 1818. She moved to the city in the mid-

1820s and was the first woman admitted to the newly formed National Academy of Design in 1827. She was elected to full membership in 1833 and exhibited regularly in the Academy's annual shows, although, as a proper lady, she did not attend regular meetings. (The one exception was in 1846, when she was summoned to fill out a quorum for an important vote.)

Specializing in portraits of women and children, which she painted as single figures or groups, Hall received numerous commissions from prominent New York families; her group portraits reportedly fetched as much as $500. Her work was admired for its delicacy and was often compared to the paintings of portraitists Sir Joshua Reynolds and Thomas Lawrence. In 1859, historian *Elizabeth Ellet wrote that Hall's "soft colors seemed breathed on the ivory, rather than applied with a brush." By modern-day standards, however, Hall's portraits might be considered overly "pretty" or sentimental, reminiscent of the religious works of Guido Reni, who strongly influenced her early years.

Little is known of Hall's private life. She never married and remained close to her family, many of whom were the subjects of her paintings. She died of heart disease in December 1863, at the home of her sister in New York City.

SOURCES:

James, Edward T., ed. *Notable American Women 1607–1950*. Cambridge, MA: The Belknap Press of Harvard University Press, 1971.

Rubinstein, Charlotte Streifer. *American Women Artists*. Boston, MA: G.K. Hall, 1982.

Barbara Morgan,
Melrose, Massachusetts

Hall, Augusta (1802–1896)

Patron of Welsh culture. Name variations: Lady Llanover; (pseudonym) Gwenynen Gwent. Born Augusta Waddington on March 21, 1802; died on January 17, 1896; married Benjamin Hall (1802–67, member of Parliament, 1832–37), in 1823; children: one daughter, Augusta.

In 1823, Augusta Waddington married Benjamin Hall, a member of Parliament from 1832 to 1837 and commissioner for works, after whom "Big Ben," the clock at the Palace of Westminster, was named. They had one daughter, Augusta. Hall took the title of Lady Llanover in 1859, when her husband was raised to the peerage as Baron Llanover.

Her activities during the period of the Romantic revival of interest in indigenous, and therefore in Celtic, history were of considerable importance to posterity and to Welsh culture. Although not a Welsh speaker, she organized her household in a "Welsh" manner, giving her servants Welsh titles. She won a prize at the Cardiff *eisteddfod* of 1834 for an essay on the Welsh language, and became patron of the Welsh Manuscripts Society, acquiring the manuscripts of Iolo Morgannwg (1747–1826), founder of the Welsh Gorsedd of Bards, from Iolo Morgannwg's son. These papers are now deposited at the National Library of Wales, Aberystwyth. Hall collaborated on the collection of Welsh melodies; established a factory to make the triple harp; assisted D. Silvan Evans in producing his famous Welsh dictionary; edited *The Autobiography & Correspondence of Mary Granville, Mrs. Delany* (*Mary Granville Delany) in six volumes (1861–62); and wrote and illustrated a recipe book containing color plates of traditional Welsh female costumes (1867).

Augusta Hall's sister was married to a German, who was for a time German ambassador to the Court of St. James, and who belonged to a circle interested in Celtic studies. Hall survived her husband by almost 30 years, and died on January 17, 1896. It has been written that "No aristocratic house had for centuries given such patronage to the national language and culture." A further example of this activity is Lady Llanover's patronage of *Y Gymraes* (The Welshwoman), the first women's periodical in the Welsh language.

SOURCES:

Dictionary of Welsh Biography—1940. London: Honourable Society of Cymrodorion, 1959.

Evans, Gwynfor, *Welsh Nation Builders*. Llandyssul: Gomer, 1988.

Stephens, Meic, ed. The *Oxford Companion to the Literature of Wales*. Oxford: Oxford University Press, 1986.

Elizabeth Rokkan,
translator, formerly Associate Professor,
Department of English, University of Bergen, Norway

Hall, Cara (b. 1922).

See Women POW's of Sumatra for sidebar.

Hall, Dorothy Gladys (b. 1927).

See Blankers-Koen, Fanny for sidebar on Dorothy Manley.

Hall, Elsie (1877–1976)

Australian composer who won the Mendelssohn Prize. Born in Toowoomba, Australia, on June 22, 1877; died in Wynberg, South Africa, on June 27, 1976.

Elsie Hall, a prodigy who played the piano before her third birthday, was born in Toowoomba, Australia, in 1877. Though she won a scholarship to the Royal Academy of Music in London, her parents turned it down. Her first recital took place in 1884, and by age of nine she had performed Beethoven's Third Concerto in public. On her first trip to Europe, her playing was praised by Johannes Brahms, and her performances in London attracted the attention of George Bernard Shaw. In Berlin, she studied with Ernst Rudorff (1840–1916) and won the prestigious Mendelssohn Prize. An excellent teacher, Elsie Hall gave lessons to members of the British royal family (especially Princess *Mary [1897–1965]), and to the brilliant composer-conductor Constant Lambert. A veteran of many world tours, Hall finally settled down in South Africa, where she performed concertos until she was in her 90s. At age 93, she traveled to the United States, and while there gave a number of enthusiastically received recitals. During World War II, Hall had entertained Allied troops in North Africa and Italy. On one wartime flight taking her from South Africa to a concert in Cairo in a Royal Air Force plane, the pilot's cargo invoice simply read: "8,000 gallons of brandy; Elsie Hall."

SOURCES:

Burgis, Peter. "Hall, Elsie Maude Stanley (1877–1976)," in *Australian Dictionary of Biography*. Vol. 9, pp. 162–163.

P.E.H. "Elsie Hall," in *The Times* [London], July 28, 1976, p. 16.

John Haag,
Athens, Georgia

Hall, Juanita (1901–1968)

African-American singer and actress. Born Juanita Long on November 6, 1901, in Keyport, New Jersey; died on February 29, 1968, in Bayshore, New York; one of three children, two girls and a boy, of Abram and Mary (Richardson) Long; attended schools in Keyport and Bordentown, New Jersey; attended Juilliard School of Music, New York; married Clement Hall (an actor, d. 1920s); no children.

Selected theater: chorus member in Show Boat *(1928); chorus member in* Green Pastures *(1930); appeared in* The Pirates *(1942),* Sing Out Sweet Land *(1944),* The Secret Room *(1944),* Deep Are the Roots *(1945),* Mr. Peebles and Mr. Hooker *(1946),* Street Scene *(1947),* S. S. Glencairn *(1948), and* Moon of the Caribees *(1948); appeared as Bloody Mary in* South Pacific *(1949),* Madame Tango *in* House of Flowers *(1954), and Madame Liang in* Flower Drum Song *(1958).*

Selected films: South Pacific *(1958);* Flower Drum Song *(1961).*

Remembered for her portrayal of Bloody Mary in the 1949 Pulitzer Prize-winning Rodgers and Hammerstein musical *South Pacific,* Juanita Hall set her sights on a singing career at age 12, after hearing her first spirituals at a revival meeting in New Jersey. "The whole quality of the singing grabbed hold of me," she said. By age 14, she was teaching singing at Lincoln House in East Orange, New Jersey. After studying at Juilliard and with private teachers, Hall made her first professional stage appearance in the chorus of the Ziegfeld production of *Edna Ferber's *Show Boat* in 1928, but it was not until 20 years later, at age 49, that the plum role of Bloody Mary came her way. In the interim, Hall made concert appearances and played countless small roles in dramatic and musical productions both on and off-Broadway. In 1935, she formed her own group, the Juanita Hall Choir, which was together for five years under the Works Progress Administration (WPA). The choir made public appearances and was also heard three times a week on the radio. In October 1939, it was one of several groups that participated in the ASCAP Silver Jubilee at Carnegie Hall in New York City. Choir members, many of whom went on to Broadway, remembered Hall's high standards of musicianship and discipline.

Juanita Hall won a Tony Award for *South Pacific,* in which her songs "Bali H'ai" and "Happy Talk" contributed largely to the show's success. She went on to play Madame Tango in the 1954 musical *House of Flowers,* and in 1958 she played Madame Liang in a second Rodgers and Hammerstein collaboration, *Flower Drum Song.* She also performed in the film versions of *South Pacific* and *Flower Drum Song.*

During the 1950s, Hall appeared in major night clubs across the country and on television, in shows like "Philco Television Playhouse," "The Ed Sullivan Show," and "Mike Wallace P.M. East." In 1966, two years before her death, she gave a successful blues recital at the East 74th Street Theatre. Following her death, Richard Rodgers remembered her as an extraordinarily kind woman and a joy to work with. "Everything she did on stage came across with such zestful spontaneity that many were surprised to learn of her classical voice training at Juilliard or her career as a concert singer," he wrote. "Juanita was also highly emotional. I recall that when I first played her song 'Bali H'ai,'

Juanita Hall

she was so overcome that she wept. For a composer, there's no nicer compliment."

SOURCES:

Smith, Jessie Carney, ed. *Notable Black American Women.* Detroit, MI: Gale Research, 1992.

Barbara Morgan,
Melrose, Massachusetts

Hall, Katie Beatrice (1938—)

U.S. Democratic Congresswoman from Indiana (November 2, 1982–January 3, 1985). Born Katie Beatrice Green on April 3, 1938, in Mound Bayou, Mississippi; daughter of Jeff Louis Greene and Bessie Mae (Hooper) Greene; Mississippi Valley State University, B.S., 1960; Indiana University, M.S., 1968, postgraduate, 1972; married John H. Hall, on August 12, 1957; children: Jacqueline Hall; Junifer Hall.

Serving only one full term in the House of Representatives, Katie Beatrice Hall introduced the bill that made the birthday of Martin Luther

King, Jr. a federal holiday. The bill was signed into law in November 1983.

Hall was born in 1938 in Mound Bayou, Mississippi, where she attended public school. She received a B.A. from Mississippi Valley State University in 1960 and an M.S. from Indiana University in 1968, after which she settled in Gary, Indiana, and became a teacher. She gained her early political experience working in the mayoral campaigns of Richard Hatcher and entered the political arena herself in 1974, becoming a member of the State House of Representatives. She was elected to the Indiana State Senate in 1976 and served until 1982. She also chaired the Lake County Democratic Committee from 1978 to 1980.

In September 1982, Hall made a successful bid for the congressional vacancy left by the death of Adam Benjamin, Jr., defeating Republican Thomas Krieger in the election and serving for the remainder of the 97th Congress and for the succeeding term. During her tenure, she was a member of the Committee on Post Office and Civil Service and the Committee on Public Works and Transportation. Concerned with the high rate of unemployment among her con-

Katie
Beatrice
Hall

stituents and the resultant erosion of family life, she supported the Fair Trade in Steel Act and the Humphrey-Hawkins bill, both aimed at increasing job opportunities. The latter also addressed child abuse and family violence issues.

Unsuccessful in her bid for renomination in 1984, Hall remained active in Democratic politics, serving as a state senator. She failed in two subsequent efforts to win nomination to Congress, in 1986 and 1990.

SOURCES:
Office of the Historian. *Women in Congress 1917–1990.* Commission on the Bicentenary of the U.S. House of Representatives, 1991.

Hall, Marguerite Radclyffe (1880–1943).
See Hall, Radclyffe.

Hall, Radclyffe (1880–1943)

English novelist, poet, and champion of lesbian rights. Name variations: Radclyffe Hall; John or Johnny Hall. Born Marguerite Antonia Radclyffe-Hall on August 12, 1880, in Bournemouth, England; died on October 7, 1943, in London; daughter of Radclyffe Radclyffe-Hall and Mary Jane (Marie) Diehl Sager; educated by governesses; never married; no children; lived with Una Troubridge for 28 years.

Wrote first book of poems (1906); met Mabel Veronica (Ladye) Batten (1907); converted to Catholicism (1912); met Margot Elena Gertrude (Una) Taylor Troubridge (1915); sued St. George Lane Fox-Pitt for slander (1920); published first novel, The Forge *(1924); won the Prix Femina and James Tait Black Prize for* Adam's Breed *(1926); published* The Well of Loneliness *(1928); figured in obscenity trial against her publisher, London (1928); met Evguenia Souline (1934); diagnosed with cancer (1943); death of Una Troubridge, Rome (1963).*

Instantly banned on two continents upon its publication in 1928, Radclyffe Hall's *The Well of Loneliness,* arguably the most famous novel about love between women ever written, sold over 1 million copies and saw translation into 11 languages by the time of the author's death. Radclyffe Hall, who termed herself in accordance with the language of her day a "congenital invert," regarded herself as neither male nor female but rather as one of a third sex, or "other." Both her work and life were influenced by the medical community of her era, a time which witnessed a rush toward classification of everything imaginable, including sexuality.

As the sexologists of this period began to categorize "normal" and "abnormal" sexual behavior, romantic relationships between women—often tolerated until the latter half of the 19th century—were increasingly regarded with suspicion. Women who loved other women and possessed traditionally masculine attributes were often categorized as men whose unfortunate lot it was to be born into the bodies of women. For Radclyffe Hall, who recalled wanting to be known by the masculine name of Peter or John from her youth, the view of masculine lesbians as such "inverts" provided a scientific explanation for both her masculinity and her love of women. Declaring inversion a "part of nature, in harmony with it, rather than against it," she posed the question: "if it occurs in and is a part of nature, how can it be unnatural?"

Known as unconventional, humorless, restless, poorly educated, and unapologetically a lover of women, Hall was condemned and vilified for her outspoken defense of lesbianism. Publication of *The Well of Loneliness,* a largely autobiographical work in which the main character Stephen is a sexual invert, sparked historic controversy over issues of lesbianism and obscenity. The enormous success of the novel was directly responsible for bringing the sexologists' views, consciously incorporated into the novel, to the reading public. For better or worse (the arguments still rage), Radclyffe Hall had set the standard for what became the predominant portrayal of lesbians in literature of the first half of the 20th century: men trapped in women's bodies, members of the third sex.

On August 12, 1880, she was born Marguerite Antonia Radclyffe-Hall, an unwanted child destined for an unhappy childhood. Her father, the only child and heir of a wealthy physician, attended Eton and St. John's College, Oxford, but never graduated. Rejecting a career in law, the flamboyant, indolent philanderer married **Marie Sager**, an American widow, in 1878 and settled in Bournemouth, England. Four years later, Marie filed for divorce, charging cruelty. Abandoned by her father who provided an adequate trust fund for her maintenance, Hall saw him no more than a dozen times before "Rat" died when she was 18. She was neglected and rejected by her mother because the child was a constant reminder of the Radclyffes. When Hall was nine, her mother married Albert Visetti, a music teacher; they maintained a comfortable lifestyle in London by plundering the child's trust funds. Hall seldom alluded to her childhood, even to friends and lovers, leaving little record of her

early days. There is evidence to suggest that in later life she would regard her youth with a revisionary eye, altering a feminine picture of her young self by blacking out the long hair and creating a masculine image that could then be traced to her earliest beginnings. Until age 40, however, Hall's hair was waist length and worn in a chignon. A solitary child, she had a musical talent that was ignored, as was her education in general. Governesses and a few fashionable dayschools in London were considered adequate for the solemn, insular youth.

By her late teens, Hall realized she was different from other girls; she evinced no interest in men or marriage, an attitude likely lent support by her own family experience. In her later fiction, she would characterize "men as a breed [that] had little to recommend them," almost invariably portraying them as weak, untrustworthy, insensitive, and complacent. Though this was an apt portrait of her father, Hall idealized and romanticized him, justifying his absence by reasoning that he had been disappointed that she was not a boy.

At age 21, she inherited a fortune from her paternal grandfather and took control of her trust. When she learned that her mother and Visetti had squandered the trust, she confronted them and left home with her "warm-hearted [but] weak and foolish" Grandmother Diehl. "Thus being freed of economic need to marry," writes historian **Lillian Faderman**, "she was able to eschew traditionally feminine pursuits and indulge her love of hunting, fast horses, and fast cars." Hall's inheritance precluded the need for her ever to have to earn a living, but she was unsure of what to do with her life. A year at King's College in London and another year of study in Germany were inadequate preparation for any career that demanded an advanced degree. But there was no urgent need to make a decision; writing poetry, traveling, and numerous affairs with young women occupied her unstructured life. During her 20s, Hall wrote, and received, few letters and kept no diary or journal, leaving only a sketchy portrait of this period. However, we know that she traveled extensively; it satisfied her restless nature and assuaged her aimlessness. In 1906, she financed the publication of her first book of poems, *Twixt Earth and Stars,* 80 short lyrics depicting "unfulfilled love." But Radclyffe Hall, the writer whose life and work would help lead the lesbian cause, had not yet come into being.

Unattached and drifting, Hall made a trip to Homburg in 1907, where she met the first love of her life, **Mabel (Ladye) Batten,** a 50-year-old married grandmother who had ties to aristocratic society and was rumored to have had an affair with King Edward VII; witty, elegant, cultured, beautiful, and worldly, Batten was all that Hall admired and hoped to become. The following year on a trip to Brussels, they became lovers. Hall's book of poems, *A Sheaf of Verses,* published in 1908, reveals her first, tentative references to homosexuality. Batten proved to be a good influence on Hall, encouraging her to read classic literature. Batten was politically conservative and outspokenly a monarchist, and Hall adopted similar loyalties. Hall was acquiring direction and purpose from this passionate attachment, which included a spiritual awakening. Ladye was a Catholic convert, and Hall had been seeking "a scheme, an order that gave meaning to the apparent misery and chaos of existence." Catholicism provided her with a means of sharing an afterlife with her lover. On February 5, 1912, Hall joined the Church and in December had an audience with the pope in Rome. The refined Ladye was both a maternal and wife-like figure for Hall; in public, Batten was sophisticated and stately, and in private she was "girlish, lazy, impractical, accident-prone, and rather helpless." Meanwhile, Hall—calling herself John as she would for the rest of her life—was the tutelary husband, the masculine element, attired in severely tailored clothes. She smoked and swore, even though Batten thoroughly disapproved of these coarse habits, and credited her companion with making her take herself seriously as a writer.

Hall continued to write poetry, securing her reputation as a poet with her *Songs of Three Counties and Other Poems.* The volume received good reviews, and the poem "The Blind Ploughman" was widely popular when set to music. The ploughman was afflicted with blindness, and Hall was homosexual; both endured suffering from their "handicaps" which were "a part of God's scheme," a means of testing the individual. Certainly Hall was giving more thought to her sexuality, and through Batten she met other lesbians such as **Winnaretta Singer,** a cultured patron of the arts in Paris who was heiress of the Singer sewing machine company and widow of Prince Edmond de Polignac. Though Batten and Hall were interested in promoting women's rights and publicly endorsed divorce, Hall's feminist support was ambiguous; seeing herself as a man in a woman's body, she identified strongly with men and maintained many traditionally male views about women's incompetence. She was convinced that few women were capable of

accomplishing great things and that they would be happier as wives and mothers. Both in her world view and physicality, Hall inhabited a man's world, reinforced by her reactionary politics and class consciousness. Regarding herself as a man, she actively pursued women and would struggle with issues of monogamy, torn by her desire to live up to her own image of a dutiful husband and her desire to love more than one woman at a time. Hall had a brief affair with **Phoebe Hoare** which may have served as a respite from Batten's dependency.

When war engulfed Europe in August 1914, Hall wanted to join the women's ambulance corps in order to be actively engaged in this horrific conflict, but she could not leave Batten who was now a semi-invalid. Frustrated at being forced to remain at home in the village of Malvern, Hall converted two rooms into a care facility for wounded soldiers while deeply resenting the ties that prevented her from being more engaged in the war effort. In 1915, Hall's last anthology of poems, *The Forgotten Island,* was published. They reveal her increasing dissatisfaction with her relations with Batten and allude to her affair with Hoare. But poetry was not her forte. Hall's short stories were never published (they would be destroyed, at her request, after her death), but upon reading some of them her publisher, William Heinemann, encouraged her to write a novel. By this time, Hall in fact had attempted a prose work but failed to complete it.

On Sunday, August 1, 1915, Hall met **Una Troubridge** at a tea party in London. Troubridge was impressed with Hall whom she described as "a very handsome young man," fully realizing Hall was a woman. And Hall was attracted to the young, intelligent, talented, well-read, cosmopolitan woman. Troubridge was a wife and mother who was married to a career naval officer 25 years her senior. She was Batten's cousin and also a Catholic convert, tying her to Hall in two important ways. Fluent in French and an artist of some repute, Troubridge was in London taking singing lessons and seeing a therapist about her "nerves," while her husband Jack was in Malta. Her relationship with Hall progressed cautiously, but in November 1915 they became lovers. After eight years of marriage to Jack Troubridge, Una would spend 28 years with Hall. Despite the matched gender of their bodies, Hall's identity was shaped by what she saw as the man in her, and as such she was attracted to the "eternal feminine" that Una symbolized. Hall and Batten now lived in London. In May 1916, Batten suffered a cerebral hemorrhage after a quarrel with Hall

Radclyffe
Hall

over Troubridge and died ten days later. Distraught over Batten's death, Hall tried to break off her relationship with Troubridge, but Una's persistence kept them together. Troubridge got a legal separation from her husband in 1918, with Jack agreeing in order to avoid public scandal.

From the summer of 1917 to 1943, Hall and Troubridge lived together as a married couple. There is no doubt that Hall would have legally married Troubridge had that been possible. In their adaptation of married life, Hall in practice served as the husband and a kind of "enlightened despot" while Troubridge was relegated to coping with household affairs. "Each of their lives would have been the less without each other," Troubridge's biographer noted. Reflecting the notion that the husband should be the property owner, Hall bought a house near Windsor in her name only. Troubridge's daughter **Andrea** was sent off to a boarding school because Hall did not like children. For Troubridge, life was not always easy with Hall, who could lapse into black moods and use sexual abstinence to "punish." However, the two established a comfortable home and lived well, employing numerous servants. They began taking more interest in the subject of lesbianism which would serve as a theme in Hall's future novels.

Hall and Batten had shared an interest in spiritualism, and after Batten's death Hall and Troubridge attended spiritual séances with a Mrs. Leonard, trying to contact Batten, and they joined the Society for Psychical Research. Hall delivered a paper to the Society in 1918, based on their sittings with Leonard. Because the Catholic Church condemned spiritualism, Hall, but not Troubridge, confessed that she had attended séances.

In 1919, Hall began writing *Octopi*, based on a scene she had witnessed of a middle-aged, unmarried daughter caring for her elderly mother. Such caretakers were "unpaid servants," Hall declared, and the elderly were "sucking the very life out of them like octopi." The novel likely reflects Hall's perceptions of her own sacrifice in caring for Ladye Batten. Rooted in the real-life relationship of Batten, Hall, and Troubridge, the book reveals Hall's sense of guilt in being unfaithful to Batten while also expressing her sense of being trapped by Batten's dependence and love. Writing was an ordeal since Hall had no routine or inspiration to focus her thoughts. During her "blackout periods," words failed her, which brought on bouts of insomnia, ill-temper, and depression. *Octopi* underwent frequent revisions and took two years to complete. Hall wrote in longhand, and Troubridge read the finished pages aloud to Hall who corrected and rewrote each section. Troubridge corrected the spelling, and the revision was dictated to a typist. Later Hall's habit of working all night undermined her health. Her biographer claimed she had "a positive lust for suffering—which affected her writing for the worse."

Una Troubridge was a mainstay in Hall's personal life and her literary career. Jack Troubridge, however, still had an affect on their lives. At the time Hall was being considered as a council member of the Society of Psychical Research, Jack confided to Fox-Pitt, a member of the council, that the paper Hall had delivered before the Society was "immoral," and he intimated that Hall was responsible for the breakup of his marriage. Fox-Pitt relayed this to the council, and Hall's nomination was withdrawn. She and Una contacted their solicitor and sued Fox-Pitt for slander. At the trial in November 1920, Fox-Pitt stated that he characterized the paper as immoral, not Hall personally. The jury, nevertheless, awarded Hall £500. This unfortunate incident increased Hall's consciousness of the roadblocks barring the way for "inverts," but she did not let it alter her lifestyle. In fact, Hall and Troubridge adopted more masculine attire, including starkly tailored clothes (not trousers yet). Una wore a monocle, and Hall cut her hair short and tried smoking a pipe. Both donned long capes and tricorn hats. Despite the eccentricities wealth affords, there is no overstating the degree to which this framed them apart from the majority of other women of their time. When in 1922 Hall no longer menstruated, she felt her manhood had commenced, making her and Una unequivocally man and wife. They lived in a fashionable section of London, and their social circle expanded to include many artistic and literary lovers of women who influenced Hall's career. *Violet Hunt and *May Sinclair, founders of PEN (the international writers' club), and *Ida Wylie often accompanied Hall and Troubridge to gay clubs such as the Orange Tree club, where they dined and danced. Through these women Hall met the artist *Romaine Brooks and her lover *Natalie Clifford Barney, the well-known American whose Paris salon was frequented by the intellectual elite.

Hall joined PEN and the Women Writers' Club and made efforts to improve her writing. She was contemptuous of "modern" literature which she labeled "experimentalist," thus dismissing such writers as James Joyce, D.H. Lawrence, and *Virginia Woolf. More "middlebrow," traditional writing appealed to her, especially romantic historical novels. Hall's first novels are largely autobiographical and deal with love and feminism. *Octopi*, judged too long and not commercial enough, did not attract a publisher. Undeterred, Hall began another novel, *Chains* (published as *The Forge* in 1924 and dedicated to Troubridge), again autobiographical and dealing with the subject of love. The characters of Hilary (the husband) and Susan (the wife) are models of Hall and Troubridge, and the plot reflects their life together since 1918. Hall completed *The Forge* in five months, and it appeared under the name Radclyffe Hall, with no hyphen and no feminine identity attached to the author. **Audrey Heath,** Hall's literary agent, finally found a publisher for *Octopi,* renamed by Troubridge *The Unlit Lamp,* which appeared in September 1924, received good reviews and sold well. Many critics consider it her best book.

As Hall gained recognition as a writer, her self-confidence grew and her circle of friends became a bit more eclectic; Princess **Violette Murat** and the American actress *****Tallulah Bankhead** were among the most unorthodox. *A Saturday Life* was published in 1925, and Hall's female character Frances Reide became the archetype of the masculine woman, similar to those in *The Unlit Lamp* and to Stephen in *The Well of Loneliness.* Created by Hall, this type of character is a 20th-century phenomenon, which biographer Richard Ormrod claims is perhaps Radclyffe Hall's "main contribution to literature as an extension of human understanding." In her novels, plot takes a backseat to characterization, and her plots, considered her weakest feature as a writer, reveal what has been called "a tendency to be platitudinous, pompous, to over-state, sentimentalize, and over-employ the pathetic fallacy." *A Saturday Life*—the last of Hall's novels to deal with the Batten-Troubridge-Hall love triangle—was well received.

Hall approached each new work with trepidation, fearing that she might lose the ability to write, and each recounted her increasing sense of isolation. In a world that judged difference harshly, Hall was ever conscious of the ways in which her homosexuality set her apart; in being true to herself, she became dislocated from the world at large. Troubridge, however, provided a stable, orderly work environment for Hall, willingly sacrificing her own artistic talents to serve as Hall's "amanuensis, housekeeper, and social secretary." Radclyffe Hall's success brought public acclaim and invitations to speak at women's clubs. In 1926, with the publication of *Adam's Breed,* she reached the pinnacle of her career when she was awarded the Prix Femina Vie Heureuse and the James Tait Black Prize for best novel of the year.

Radclyffe Hall had achieved the recognition she had coveted so long; with her next novel, she would also acquire notoriety for her outspoken defense of homosexuality. Knowing it could damage her career and bring public condemnation to both her and Troubridge, she was determined "to speak on behalf of a misunderstood and misjudged minority." Hall had been thinking of writing about "sexual inversion" for a long time, and her work would rely heavily on *Studies in the Psychology of Sex,* by the sexologist Havelock Ellis, which asserted that homosexuality was "congenital" and urged toleration. *The Well of Loneliness* (originally titled *Stephen*) would create a furor and be castigated as harmful to public morality. This 500-page novel is largely autobiographical and covers a period of 35 years, from the late Victorian era to the early 1920s. Stephen Gordon, a female, is forced to leave home when her mother discovers she is a lesbian. Stephen is a composite figure, and Hall largely based the character's life on Troubridge's childhood and her own adult experiences. "What have I done to be so cursed," Stephen asks, and she pleads, "Give us the right to our existence." Like other proponents of "inversion theory," Radclyffe Hall argues that homosexuality is inborn, not acquired, an "affliction" which proscribes the lesbian as a social pariah. Writes historian Faderman:

> Autobiographical writings of the first half of the twentieth century suggest how useful the sexologists' pronouncements were to lesbians in identifying their differences, explaining their sexual drives, and denying moral culpability for who they were and what they did. The sexologists' work gave them ammunition to argue against moralists who condemned lesbian sexuality. If lesbians were born men trapped in women's bodies then they could not help their sexual urges, and they had as much right to sexual expression as men fortunate enough to be born into the right bodies.

Nevertheless, as expected, publishers hesitated to commit to a book they were certain would arouse adverse public reaction to the subject of homosexuality. Hall explained that she had approached the subject "as a fact of nature—a simple, though at present tragic, fact." Finally, the publishing house of Jonathan Cape accepted the challenge; Hall insisted that not a word, not a comma, be changed. She was also eager for the book to be published in America. Houghton Mifflin, in "Puritan Boston," declined the offer; *****Blanche Knopf,** however, accepted the book, but only if Hall would accept all legal responsibility for any action undertaken by American authorities. Hall's irritation with Knopf prompted her to remark, "I put it down to the fact that she is a woman, and that in many cases, it is better for women to keep out of business negotiations."

The Well of Loneliness appeared in July 1928, and, despite mixed reviews, the first printing sold out in a week. One powerful reviewer, James Douglas, editor of the *Sunday Express,* voiced moral outrage and demanded that Jonathan Cape withdraw the book; if the publisher refused, he wrote, the authorities should suppress it by law. Cape, attempting to be conciliatory, offered to request approval for the book from the Home Office, without consulting Radclyffe Hall. She was furious. The Home Secretary, a Christian fundamentalist known as "The Policeman of the Lord," demanded repression of *The Well* or Cape would be legally culpable of obscenity. This was, in fact, beyond the purview of the Home Office, but Cape capitulated and halted production; however, he had a contingency plan to undermine the Home Office censure. He would ship the type-molds to an English-language publisher in Paris who would print *The Well* and send copies to English booksellers. When a shipment was seized at the port of Dover, it was eventually released and sent to Leopold Hill, an English book distributor. But the books were confiscated, and Hill was now liable to be tried under the Obscene Publications Act of 1857. Hall hired a lawyer, Harold Rubinstein. In an interview, she had stated that banning the book "can only insult the public intelligence." The issue was larger than suppressing a work on homosexuality; the issue was freedom of expression. In fact, lesbianism was not a crime in England, though many considered it "disgusting" and persecuted lesbians, but male homosexuality was still a criminal offense.

The trial opened in London on November 9, 1928, and Hill and Cape were ordered to show why *The Well* should not be destroyed. Several eminent writers, such as E.M. Forster and *Virginia Woolf, appeared as defense witnesses; George Bernard Shaw declined, explaining that "he was too immoral to stand as a credible witness for the defense." Hall contributed to the defense's legal costs (she sold her house in London), but she did not testify. She, as author, was not on trial. The publisher and book distributor were found guilty and paid a modest fine. Meanwhile, the book sold well in Paris, but in New York 800 copies were seized by police. Knopf was found guilty of selling an obscene book which would "debauch public morals." The verdict was overturned by an Appeals Court. Over 50,000 copies of *The Well* were sold by the end of February 1929. Translated into 11 languages, it sold over one million copies by the time Radclyffe Hall died in 1943. The obscenity trials revived interest in Radclyffe Hall's other works which were reprinted and sold well.

Hall was disappointed in the limited support she had received from her fellow writers.

Regarding herself as a member of a third sex, "neither man nor woman, but uniting the best qualities of both (and, therefore, implicitly superior to either)," she saw herself as the defender of a "defenseless minority." Response to the book made Hall ever more mindful of her sexuality; publicly, it brought the subject of lesbianism "into the forefront of public consciousness," while reinforcing an image of the lesbian as a masculine woman.

With increased royalties from her books, Hall bought Troubridge a house—in her own name—in Rye, a small town favored by artists and writers. Despite the success of her new novel, *The Master of the House* (1931), Hall and Troubridge began to isolate themselves, and Hall became increasingly convinced that she was a failure, that everyone was against her, everyone except Una, whose support was constant during the obscenity trials. Wrote Hall in a later letter: "When all the world seemed against me at the time of the 'Well of Loneliness' persecutions, Una stood shoulder to shoulder with me, fighting every inch of the terrific battle. She has given me all of her interest and indeed all of her life ever since we made common cause."

While writing *The Master of the House,* a bizarre occurrence took place when Hall experienced a pain in the palm of her right hand and then "livid red stains" appeared on the palms of both hands. This phenomenon is particularly arresting since *The Master* dealt with a carpenter's son and had a religious theme. Five short stories, published in 1934, did not do well; in the midst of the Great Depression, the "bleak vision" and obvious despair that permeated the stories had little appeal. Despite her drop in sales, Hall remained a notable literary figure and was invited to lecture at Oxford University and London University. However, increased isolation and restlessness marked Hall and Troubridge's lives. They frequently traveled abroad and divided their time between their house in Rye and their apartment in London. As Hall turned inward, Troubridge remained loyal, never doubting the "insoluble bond, spiritual as well as physical," that united them. They had, she believed, made a "sacred commitment" to each other, which she took for granted. But Hall—never demonstrative, often morose and dissatisfied—withdrew even more from Troubridge. It became evident that her irascibility was a product of her attitude towards the confining "domestic bliss" represented by Troubridge and her efficient household management. Hall's idea of self has been characterized as "the anguished loner," and one can infer that she felt trapped in a "marriage" that lacked passion and expression. Troubridge suffered from a variety of ailments and bouts of "nerves" and was aging noticeably faster than Hall. Perhaps Hall viewed Troubridge as a potential burden, a dependent invalid as Batten had been.

In 1934, Hall injured her leg in a hunting accident, and Troubridge suggested they go to Bagnoles, France, one of their favorite places, where Hall could recuperate. While there, Troubridge developed enteritis, and Hall cared for her. Troubridge, however, insisted they hire a nurse, a decision that would change their lives forever. **Evguenia Souline** was a White Russian who had fled Russia in 1922; manipulative, exploitative, uncultured, selfish, and plain, Souline was the antithesis of all Hall admired in Una. The 54-year-old Hall fell passionately in love with the 32-year-old Souline, and the stable, monogamous relations that had sustained Troubridge and Hall since 1915 became displaced by Hall's open admissions to Una that she loved Souline. Troubridge asked only that Hall remain faithful to her "in the fullest and ultimate meaning of the word." For the last nine years of her life, Hall poured out her longings to Souline in hundreds of letters. To Troubridge's great dismay, Hall's creative energies diminished, and she abandoned her writing. Hall and Souline became lovers, despite Hall's promise to Troubridge. How could Hall be so smitten with a woman of "inferior intellect," Una wondered, to which Hall replied that she "could never tolerate a woman with brains." Wrote Hall to Souline:

> Then [Una] has reminded me over and over again until I have nearly gone mad, that I have always stood for fidelity in the case of inverted unions, that the eyes of the inverted all over the world are turned towards me, that they have respected me because for many years my union has been faithful and open. And when she says that I can find no answer, because she is only telling the truth—I have tried to help my own poor lot by setting an example, especially of courage, and thousands have turned to me for help and found it, if I may believe their letters, and she says that I want to betray my inverts who look upon me almost as their leader.

Indeed, Hall did not want to leave her long-time devoted partner. "Remain with me for ever and ever. . . . You are permanent," she wrote to Una. Nonetheless, Hall's obsession with Souline outweighed Troubridge's obvious distress, and it ignored Souline's avaricious nature. This was to be the scenario followed by the three women to the close of their triangular relationship.

Through it all, Troubridge comforted her distraught companion and clung to the hope that Hall would realize the futility of her painful infatuation for an unworthy woman. The ill-sorted triangle survived despite quarrels and the undisguised hostility Troubridge felt towards Souline.

In October 1935, Hall and Troubridge returned to Rye from a lengthy visit to France and Italy. In Italy, Troubridge had arranged for Hall to meet the Italian poet and patriot Gabriele d'Annunzio. They shared a love of Italy, an admiration of Fascism (as did Troubridge), and the rejection of modern values. On their return to Rye, Troubridge was encouraged by Hall's completion of *The Sixth Beatitude* (1936), which was set in Rye and contained portraits of many local inhabitants. The novel received mixed reviews and sales were sluggish. Restlessness drove Hall and Troubridge back to France and Italy, and back to Souline who often traveled with them, though she adamantly refused to share an apartment with them. The ever accommodating Troubridge was responsible for finding lodging and hiring a maid for Souline. Hall and Troubridge particularly loved Florence and its marvelous cultural offerings, and they began to think of settling in Italy.

After a year abroad, Hall and Troubridge returned to Rye in July 1937. A month later, Hall broke her ankle which was slow to heal, forcing her to use two canes; she had problems with her eyes, contracted influenza, and suffered from insomnia. Troubridge patiently nursed her and accompanied Hall to consult doctors and specialty clinics in London. Unhappy with the changes modernization had brought to Rye, Hall and Troubridge decided to move permanently to Italy. They sold their house, but the outbreak of war in 1939 altered their plans. Hall blamed the Jews and the Treaty of Versailles for Europe's problems, maintaining her regard for Fascism.

From 1940 to 1942, as Hall's health deteriorated rapidly, Troubridge grew more robust; she was indispensable now. Unlike Hall in her caretaking role with Batten, Troubridge willingly, almost happily, took over the direction of Hall's life. But for Hall, ill health and her turbulent relations with Souline made her sadly aware of her age and "the hollowness of her own cherished values, of fidelity in particular." In March 1943, Hall was diagnosed with inoperable cancer. Troubridge located an apartment with ready access to medical treatment and stayed with Hall until she died at 8:07 PM on October 7, 1943. Only Una was present, and she later recalled that as she looked at Hall she detected "not a trace of femininity; no one in their senses could have suspected that anything but a young man had died." In her will, Hall left everything to Troubridge who was directed to provide for Souline "at her own discretion." Hall had asked Una to destroy her unfinished novel; too much of her pain from loving Souline had gone into it. Troubridge kept her promise. Seven hundred letters from Hall to Souline survive. Only one letter from Souline to Hall survives; Troubridge may have destroyed the others.

Radclyffe Hall was buried in a vault next to Ladye Batten in Highgate Cemetery in London. Troubridge, now a wealthy woman, moved to Italy and died of cancer in Rome in September 1963, at age 76. Shortly before Troubridge died, a woman asker her how she and Hall reconciled their relationship with their Catholic religion. What did they do about confession? Answered Una, "There was nothing to confess."

SOURCES:
Baker, Michael. *Our Three Selves: A Life of Radclyffe Hall*. London: GMP Publishers, 1985.
Faderman, Lillian. *Chloe Plus Olivia*. NY: Viking Penguin, 1994.
Ormrod, Richard. *Una Troubridge: The Friend of Radclyffe Hall*. NY: Carroll & Graf Publishers, 1985.

SUGGESTED READING:
Brittain, Vera. *Radclyffe Hall: A Case of Obscenity?* UK: Femina Books, 1968.
Dickson, R. Lovat. *Radclyffe Hall at the Well of Loneliness: A Sapphic Chronicle*. London: Collins, 1975.
Franks, Claudia Stillman. *Beyond the Well of Loneliness*. UK: Aveburg Publishing, 1982.
Troubridge, Una. *The Life and Death of Radclyffe Hall*. London: Hammond, 1961.

COLLECTIONS:
Papers and letters are located in the Lovat Dickson Collection, National Archive, Ottowa, Canada, and in the Radclyffe Hall Collection, Humanities Research Center, University of Texas, Austin.

Jeanne A. Ojala,
Professor of History, University of Utah, Salt Lake City, Utah

Hall, Ruby Bridges (b. 1954).

See Bridges, Ruby.

Hall, Mrs. S.C. (1800–1881).

See Hall, Anna Maria.

Hall-Mills.

See Mills, Eleanor (1888–1922).

Hallé, Lady (c. 1838–1911).

See Neruda, Wilma.

Halliday, Margaret (1956—)

New Zealand-born Australian racer who, in April 1984, became the first woman in the world to win a national motor sport Grand Prix. Born in 1956 in New Zealand.

On April 22, 1984, Margaret Halliday, a Sydney secretary, became the first woman to win an Australian national motor sport Grand Prix when she partnered her boyfriend, Doug Chivas, to win the Grand Prix of the Mount Panorama circuit for 1000cc motorcycle sidecars. Held at Bathurst, 100 miles west of Sydney, the race saw Halliday, who was the passenger in the motorcycle driven by Chivas, sharing the victory in a six-lap, 23 mile contest in which Halliday and Chivas led the pack from start to finish. With this victory, Halliday also became the first woman in the world to win a national motor sport Grand Prix.

SOURCES:
"Sports News," in United Press International, April 22, 1984.
Stell, Marion K. *Half the Race: A History of Australian Women in Sport*. North Ryde, New South Wales: Angus & Robertson, 1991.

John Haag,
Athens, Georgia

Hallowell, Anna (1831–1905)

American welfare worker and educational reformer who was the first woman to be chosen as a member of the Board of Public Education in Philadelphia. Born on November 1, 1831, in Philadelphia, Pennsylvania; died on April 6, 1905, in Philadelphia, Pennsylvania; daughter of Morris Longstreth and Hannah Smith (Penrose) Hallowell.

Anna Hallowell was born in Philadelphia in 1831, the eldest child of Quakers, Morris Longstreth Hallowell and **Hannah Penrose Hallowell**. Anna and her six brothers and sisters learned to hate the institution of slavery from the example of their parents; Anna's father was a silk importer who risked financial ruin at the hands of his Southern business associates to speak out against slavery. Anna's personal activism at first focused on abolishing the institution of slavery, and later included the eradication of poverty through education reform. At 15, Anna Hallowell began her work with the poor by bringing black children to her parents' yard to play. By the time she reached her 20s, she was serving on the board of the Home for Destitute Colored Children, where she also worked as its secretary.

In 1859, Hallowell further delved into the abolitionist cause by attending the trial of fugitive slave Daniel Dangerfield to protest the Fugitive Slave Act. With the onset of the Civil War, Hallowell's brothers served in the Union army, and Hallowell converted the family home into a hospital where she nursed her injured brothers and their comrades.

In the late 1870s, Hallowell did relief work with the many freed slaves who had fled to Philadelphia after the war. In 1878, she joined others to establish the Society for Organizing Charitable Relief and Repressing Mendicancy which later became the Society for Organizing Charity. She served on the Society's Committee on the Care and Education of Dependent Children. In 1883, when the group was reorganized as the Children's Aid Society, Hallowell became a member of its first board of directors.

Through her work Hallowell soon came to believe that the solution to the problems of poverty was in the education of the city's children. In 1879, she began a personal project to establish free kindergartens in poor neighborhoods. With the aid of several friends, she enrolled 60 children in kindergarten. Two years later, she organized the Sub-Primary School Society with partial funding of the kindergartens by the city. By January of 1887, the Board of Public Education took control of all 27 kindergartens. Hallowell continued to work toward improving education for children and was instrumental in introducing both manual training and domestic science into the classroom. She eventually became the first woman to be chosen as a member of the board of public education. While in this role, she introduced training courses for kindergarten teachers into the Philadelphia Normal School for Girls. She remained on the board for 14 years where she continued to introduce innovative courses of study.

Hallowell focused attention on the importance of appointing women as inspectors for state prisons, asylums, and hospitals for women and children, and in 1882 was appointed by the president of the State Board of Charities to the position of chair of a committee of women visitors for Philadelphia County. She remained in this position for 17 years.

In 1890, she undertook one of her most challenging projects: the rehabilitation of the James Forten School, a run-down building with an unsavory reputation. Hallowell oversaw the remodeling of the building, hired trained teachers, and added such courses as carpentry, sewing and cooking, and art and music to the curriculum. Within ten years, the student enrollment more than doubled.

In 1893, with **Mary E. Mumford** (1824–1935), Hallowell founded the Civic Club, an or-

ganization of upper-class women working for social reform. She chaired discussion programs as head of the club's education department. Anna Hallowell died on April 6, 1905, in Philadelphia of heart disease and chronic bronchitis. She was cremated and her ashes were buried in Laurel Hill Cemetery.

SOURCES:

James, Edward T., ed. *Notable American Women 1607–1950*. Cambridge, MA: The Belknap Press of Harvard University Press, 1971.

Judith C. Reveal,
freelance writer, Greensboro, Maryland

Hallowes, Odette (1912–1995).

See Sansom, Odette.

Halpert, Edith Gregor

(c. 1900–1970)

Russian-American art collector and dealer who introduced contemporary American art and American folk art to the realm of commercial galleries. Born on April 25, around 1900, in Odessa, Russia; died on October 6, 1970, in New York City; daughter of Gregor and Frances (Lucom) Fivoosiovitch; married Samuel Halpert, in 1918 (divorced 1930); married Raymond Davis, in 1939 (divorced).

Edith Gregor Halpert was born around 1900 in Odessa, Russia, but moved to America with her widowed mother and older sister in 1906. They settled in New York, where Edith attended Wadleigh High School in Manhattan. She enrolled in the National Academy of Design when she was only 14 by convincing the instructors that she was 16. Sometime between 1914 and 1918, Edith stumbled upon modern art for the first time at the galleries of Alfred Stieglitz and Newman Montross. Although discouraged from studying modernism by the instructors at the academy, she developed a strong attraction to the style.

While at the academy, Edith met Samuel Halpert, and they were married in 1918. Edith did not pursue a career in art after her marriage, feeling that one artist in the family was enough. In 1917, she began work in the advertising department of Stern Brothers department store. By 1918, she had moved into a management position with the firm of Cohen Goldman where she worked as an efficiency expert. Halpert remained with Goldman until 1920 when S.W. Straus & Co. hired her as a personnel manager. She eventually became a member of the board, earning $6,000 a year plus bonuses. With this unheard-of salary, she was able to turn her attention back to her first love: art.

In 1925, Halpert moved to France to reorganize the Galeries Lilloises, a department store in Lille. There she observed the vast difference between the freedoms and appreciation given French artists by their public and that of American artists. Upon her return to the States, Halpert was determined to open a gallery that would give modern American artists a much-needed outlet. Though she fought an uphill battle against public opinion, Halpert proceeded with her plans and, on November 6, 1926, opened the Downtown Gallery of Contemporary Art in Greenwich Village. The first gallery of its type, the Downtown featured artists who were otherwise ignored by most dealers. Among those she showcased were Stuart Davis, Charles Demuth, Arthur Dove, Yasuo Kuniyoshi, John Marin, Ben Shahn, Charles Sheeler, Niles Spencer, Max Weber and William Zorach.

During the 1920s, Halpert spent time at the Perkins Cove art colony in Ogunquit, Maine, where she was introduced to American folk art. A shrewd businesswoman, she realized that there would be a market for the furniture, portraits, and various other artifacts that currently resided in the barns, attics and cellars of America. With Holger Cahill, the future director of the Federal Arts Project, she began to collect these forgotten pieces of Americana and introduced American folk art to the Downtown Gallery. She was likewise instrumental in collecting artifacts for other exhibits and collections. *Abby Aldrich Rockefeller approached her for assistance in assembling the collection of American artifacts instilled in Williamsburg in 1940. Halpert also assisted *Electra Havemeyer Webb in gathering works of American art for the Shelburne Museum in Vermont.

Taking her artistic insight a step further, Halpert introduced the concept of municipal art exhibits to many of America's larger cities. She organized the first municipal art exhibit in Atlantic City, New Jersey, in 1929, and in 1934 she convinced New York Mayor Fiorello La Guardia to endorse a municipal exhibition at the Rockefeller Center. She also worked with the Works Progress Administration (WPA) to promote shows by project artists.

Halpert's desire to erase the color boundaries in the artistic community resulted in the Downtown Gallery being the first commercial gallery in the United States to present an exhibition of black artists. La Guardia and *Eleanor Roosevelt were among the show's sponsors. In 1952, Halpert took another innovative step when she established the Edith Gregor Halpert Foundation. The organization lobbied for the rights of the artists to control their own work and published a code of relations between museums and living artists. The foundation also endowed universities with paintings they could sell to raise money for scholarships for art students.

A tireless worker for her cause, Halpert was honored in 1959 with the curatorship of the Moscow-bound National Art Exhibition, a show of American artists from Thomas Hart Benton to Marca-Relli, sponsored by the State Department. The show was extremely successful, and during its run Halpert often delivered lectures in Russian.

Edith Halpert's first marriage ended in divorce in 1930 after a long separation. She married for a second time in 1939, but that union was also terminated a short time later. In the late 1960s, her health began to fail, and she had difficulty promoting her artists, resulting in some deserting for other galleries. Halpert died on October 6, 1970 of cancer at New York Hospital. Her art collection was auctioned at a value of $3 million.

SOURCES:

James, Edward T., ed. *Notable American Women 1607–1950*. Cambridge, MA: The Belknap Press of Harvard University Press, 1971.

Judith C. Reveal,
freelance writer, Greensboro, Maryland

Halsingland, duchess of.

See Madeleine (b. 1982).

Hamer, Fannie Lou (1917–1977)

African-American civil-rights activist whose challenges to racist codes in the Deep South hastened political reforms and the enfranchisement of black citizens during the 1960s. Name variations: Fannie Hamer. Born Fannie Lou Townsend on October 6, 1917, in central Mississippi, probably Montgomery County; moved to Sunflower County near the town of Ruleville at age two, where she remained; died on March 14, 1977, after suffering from breast cancer, heart disease, and diabetes, in Mound Bayou, Mississippi; daughter and 20th child of Jim and Ella Townsend (cotton sharecroppers); formal education limited to completion of sixth grade, due to field labor as a child; later taught basic literacy to adults in SNCC's "freedom school" project; taught black studies classes at Shaw University, Raleigh, North Caroli-

na; married Perry "Pap" Hamer, in 1944; children: (adopted in 1950s) **Dorothy Jean Hamer** (d. 1967) and **Vergie Hamer**; (adopted granddaughters) Lenora and Jacqueline.

Awards and honorary degrees: LLD from Shaw University. Also, honorary degrees from Columbia College in Chicago, Tougaloo College (1969), Howard University (1972); George W. Collins Award for Community Service, from Congressional Black Caucus (1976); "Fannie Lou Hamer Day" recognition from Ruleville, Mississippi; Alpha Phi fraternity Paul Robeson Award for humanitarian service.

Started working in cotton fields at age six (c. 1924); her father died (1939); attended civil-rights meeting and attempted to register to vote (August 1962); lost job and home, began fugitive existence (autumn 1962); returned to Ruleville for second registration bid which was successful (December 1962); became SNCC fieldworker (1963); arrested in Winona, Mississippi, when co-workers tried to integrate bus terminal (June 1963); severely beaten in Winona jail; entered primary election contest against incumbent Jamie Whitten (March 20, 1964); helped establish Mississippi Freedom Democratic Party (April 16, 1964); defeated in primary election by Whitten (June 2, 1964); SNCC Freedom Summer voter registration campaign began in Mississippi; Hamer residence served as home and headquarters for white SNCC workers (June 1964); elected delegate to Democratic National Convention at MFDP state convention (August 6, 1964); led MFDP delegation in challenge to white Mississippi delegation at Democratic National Convention (August 22, 1964); testified before credentials committee at Democratic convention nationally televised in prime time; joined in filing challenge to seating of Mississippi congressional delegation (December 4, 1964); eventual vote in House of Representatives is 228 to seat white delegation, 143 to seat challengers; spoke out against war in Vietnam (1965); participated with Martin Luther King, Stokely Carmichael, and other leaders in Meredith March through Mississippi (June 1966); her daughter Dorothy Jean denied admission to local hospital, died en route to Memphis hospital due to internal hemorrhaging (1967); adopted granddaughters, Lenora and Jacqueline; attended Democratic National Convention in Chicago as a member of the integrated Loyalist democratic party delegation (August 1968); criticized that delegation for its domination by male delegates; started "pig bank" and bought land for Freedom Farm with help from outside contributors (1969); Fannie Lou Hamer Day proclaimed in Ruleville (March 1970); Freedom Farm helped local poor ac-

quire loans and build new homes (1970–71), 70 homes built by 1972; helped found National Women's Political Caucus (July 1971); ran unsuccessful campaign for Mississippi senate (fall 1971); appointed delegate to Democratic national convention in Miami Beach (July 1972); several bad harvests caused Freedom Farm to lose most of its land acreage to creditors (January 1974); at second Fannie Lou Hamer Day in Ruleville (October 1976), Charles Evers led fundraising effort to pay her medical bills; UN Ambassador Andrew Young delivered eulogy at her funeral in Ruleville (March 20, 1977).

Fannie Lou Hamer had never heard of the civil-rights movement until the summer of 1962; she had certainly never heard of Martin Luther King, Jr. Her days were spent in the cotton fields. Long, hard days, and the nearly complete lack of television sets in the poor homes of Delta blacks, created an isolated existence. When King was making headlines in Montgomery, Alabama, less than 300 miles away, Hamer was oblivious. "Even if you had a radio," she told Leo and **Miriam Selby**, "you was too tired to play it. So we didn't know anything about no civil rights."

Then "the movement" came to the Mississippi Delta. Fannie Lou Hamer's first encounter with civil-rights workers was on the fourth Sunday of August, 1962. Bob Moses, James Forman, James Bevel, and other leaders of the Student Nonviolent Coordinating Committee (SNCC) had called a mass meeting for that evening at the Williams Chapel Baptist Church in Ruleville. The 44-year-old Hamer, married for 18 years, listened closely as Forman told the audience that they had a constitutional right to vote; if they used that right, he said, they could clean up Mississippi politics. This idea both surprised and appealed to Hamer. In school, she had been taught nothing about her political rights; she was unaware, she said later, that Mississippi even *had* a constitution. Though blacks constituted over 40% of the state's population, only about 5% were registered to vote in 1960. When Forman asked for a show of hands of those willing to travel to Indianola to apply at the registrar's office for Sunflower County, "I raised mine," said Hamer:

> Had it high up as I could get it. I guess if I'd had any sense I'd a-been a little scared, but what was the point of being scared. The only thing they could do to me was kill me and it seemed like they'd been trying to do that a little bit at a time ever since I could remember.

Early on the morning of August 31, 1962, Hamer and 17 other blacks rode to Indianola in a private, yellow bus that normally shuttled workers to the cotton fields. At the county seat, white men circled the bus with hostile stares, menacing. At the registrar's office, the group found that the application process would take hours because the registrar would allow only two persons at a time to take the lengthy literacy tests then required in Mississippi of prospective voters. When all had finally finished and they had begun the trip home, their bus was stopped by the police because it was "the wrong color." (It was "too yellow," the officer said, presumably meaning that it resembled a school bus.) The police arrested the driver and took him back to Indianola. Meanwhile, the would-be voters sat on the bus and waited. As time passed, people became fearful, wondering whether they might end up in jail or worse. Then came a voice in song, as **Kay Mills** tells it, a gospel-singers voice, strong and clear, singing "This Little Light of Mine," "Down By the Riverside," and "Ain't Gonna Let Nobody Turn Me Around." Hamer's singing calmed the other riders and made a deep impression on the young SNCC activist Charles McLaurin, who had accompanied the group to Indianola. In her voice, Hamer had found an instrument of leadership and inspiration. It was a voice that many people were to hear and remember.

To tell the truth today is to run the risk of being killed. But if I fall, I'll fall five-feet four-inches forward in the fight for freedom.

—Fannie Lou Hamer

Fannie Lou Townsend was born on October 6, 1917, the 20th child of poor sharecropping cotton farmers in Montgomery County, or perhaps in an adjacent county; the record is not clear. Her parents took her to a new home in Sunflower County near Ruleville, Mississippi, when she was two years old, and she was to live there for the remainder of her life. Her first four decades were lived in the unpleasant certainty of labor and hardship. All she had ever known was the exploitative Mississippi Delta plantation system, a system that put her in the cotton fields when she was six years old. At that time, the plantation owner gave her gingerbread and candy to coax her into picking cotton with the grown-ups. As Hamer related to George Sewell and **Margaret Dwight**, "So I picked thirty pounds of cotton that week, but I found out what actually happened was he was trapping me into beginning the work I was to keep doing; and I never did get out of his debt again!"

The sharecropping system was rigged in favor of the landowners. The most common arrangement was for the land tenant to give the owner a 50% share of the profits from the cotton fields. However, the tenants had to purchase their seeds, tools, mules, etc., from the "commissary" store owned by the plantation owners. Often, they borrowed from the landowner to do this. Sharecroppers took their cotton to gin mills owned by the plantations as well, so they had little recourse if they were cheated on price or poundage. The Townsend family often picked about 50 or 60 of the 500 pound bales of cotton each year, but still had trouble making ends meet. Sometimes, they would end the year in debt to the plantation owners. Terror enforced the system. If people of the black community resisted, they could be fired from their jobs or evicted from their homes. More serious defiance of white authority might result in torture or lynchings.

Her father eventually saved enough money to buy three mules and two cows, but a white neighbor poisoned the family's well water, killing the livestock and forcing the family to return to sharecropping. Aware that black families lived lives of hardship while white landowners enjoyed leisure and wealth, Fannie Lou once remarked to her mother that she wished she was white. **Ella Townsend** quickly challenged her thinking and worked to instill a pride in her African-American heritage. "Through her," Hamer told the Selbys, "I learned very early that black power and dignity was self respect."

The Townsend family had a deep faith in God, which proved to be a force in shaping Hamer's idealism. At church on Sundays, Hamer listened attentively and memorized many Biblical passages. For her, God and Jesus Christ were synonymous with freedom, a belief she expressed in her civil-rights speeches and "freedom songs." And when the movement turned toward black radicalism in the middle 1960s, Hamer worked to counter that trend with an appeal to the universality of the Christian message.

"I just loved school," Hamer told the Selbys, yet she completed only the sixth grade. When there was work to do in the fields, the school was closed. That meant that school for Delta blacks lasted for about four months, between November and March. And when the school was in session, Fannie Lou frequently missed classes because firewood needed chopping or cornstalks needed cutting, but she did learn to read and write.

Hamer's father died in 1939. In 1944, Fannie married Perry Hamer, a tractor driver on W.D. Marlow's plantation, near Ruleville; un-

able to have children, they adopted two girls. Starting on the Marlow farm as a sharecropper, Fannie later became a plantation timekeeper. During those years, her mother was gradually going blind from an eye injury received while chopping down trees, clearing land for planting.

Ella Townsend moved in with her daughter and son-in-law in 1953.

The political awakening of Fannie Lou Hamer occurred when she returned home on that yellow bus in 1962. The voting registrar had informed her employer, cotton plantation owner W.D. Marlow, III, about her attempt to register. Marlow gave her a choice, said Hamer, either to withdraw her registration or to move off the plantation property immediately. She chose the latter, leaving her family and moving in with her friends, the Tuckers, in Ruleville. But Marlow ejected the rest of her family from his plantation and there were threats on Fannie's life, so the Hamers soon departed the area for a cousin's home in a neighboring county. On September 10, shortly after Fannie Hamer left the Tucker residence, white segregationist snipers fired into the house; bullets entered the bedroom where she had slept.

By late December, Hamer decided that events had cooled enough for her to return home. Since she had not successfully passed the literacy test which required takers to interpret a portion of Mississippi's Constitution, she made another trip to Indianola. With no job to lose, Fannie Lou declared to the official that she would be back every month to retake the exam until she was registered. On January 10, 1963, after three attempts, she learned that she had passed, but she was not allowed to vote because she did not have poll tax receipts for the previous two years.

Hamer's persistence again caught the attention of SNCC workers McLaurin and Moses. Signing her on as a SNCC volunteer, they paid her a small stipend which she sorely needed; she and her husband were both without jobs. SNCC sent Hamer to a civil-rights conference in Nashville that fall, where she made her speaking debut, telling of her experiences since August 31st. Then she joined the SNCC Freedom Singers as they toured the South to raise money.

In 1963, Hamer attended a training program for teachers of the "citizenship schools" set up by SNCC and the Southern Christian Leadership Conference. The main purpose of citizenship schools was to enable uneducated voters to read and write well enough to pass voter registration exams. Traveling back home from the program held in Dorchester, Georgia, Hamer and other civil-rights workers were arrested at a restaurant in Winona, Mississippi, for attempting to get served in the "whites only" section. (Another account claims that Hamer tried to use a white restroom in a bus station in Winona.) While in jail, they were treated brutally when the officers learned that were civil-rights workers. Hamer later told audiences that she heard the screams of other prisoners as they were beaten and tortured, and overheard her

guards considering the possibility of killing them all and dumping the bodies. When it was Hamer's turn, two other prisoners, black men, were ordered to beat her mercilessly with a blackjack (or suffer worse for disobeying). Hamer lay face down on the prison cot as they hit her, the second man taking over when the first became exhausted. At one point, she told the Selbys, a police officer pulled her dress up around her head. Though civil-rights leaders James Bevel and Andrew Young managed to secure her release, the beating caused a blood clot in the artery to an eye and damaged her kidneys. Hamer never fully recovered from her injuries.

The Justice Department eventually filed civil and criminal charges against the Winona authorities, but the civil charges were later dropped. On the criminal charges, the officers were found not guilty by an all-white jury. Despite this, Hamer continued to stand firm for civil rights. Her courage in the face of danger revealed her leadership. "She would sing 'Nobody's Going to Turn Me Around' better than anybody else," **Annie Devine** told Kay Mills. "Why not follow somebody like that? Why not just reach out with one hand and say, just take me along?"

In March 1964, Hamer campaigned for the Democratic nomination for the U.S. House of Representatives seat for District Two, against long-term incumbent (and segregationist) Jamie Whitten. The electorate was nearly all white, so she had little chance of winning, but her candidacy served notice that African-Americans could also run for office and would someday win elections.

The summer of 1964 had been earmarked by the Student Nonviolent Coordinating Committee for a strong voter registration drive. SNCC leaders decided to bring in white student volunteers from the North to enroll unregistered African-American Mississippians. Volunteers, trained in Oxford, Ohio, were sent to Mississippi to work with the SNCC people already there. Perry and Fannie Lou Hamer lodged some white students in their home, as did their friends and neighbors. Called the "Freedom Summer" campaign, activities began in June.

But Freedom Summer had a horrifying beginning. Two white volunteers, Andrew Goodman and Mickey Schwerner, and a black student from Mississippi, James Chaney, arrived from the Ohio training center on June 21, the first day of summer. Immediately, they disappeared and were presumed to have been the victims of violence. It took weeks to verify this. Their bodies were found on August 4, 1964.

A more positive occurrence that summer was the creation of the Mississippi Freedom Democratic Party (MFDP), which Hamer helped organize. On August 6, 2,500 black activists and white liberals met in Jackson to select a delegation of four whites and 64 blacks, including Hamer, to represent the MFDP at the Democratic National Convention. Since Mississippi's regular Democratic Party excluded blacks, and could not be trusted to support the Democratic presidential ticket in the fall, the MFDP planned to challenge the seating of the regular delegation at the national convention to be held in Atlantic City, New Jersey, that August. They hoped to earn the right to sit as the legitimate Mississippi delegation.

Testifying before the party's credentials committee, Hamer made a powerful witness, describing her own beating as well as the violence and intimidation other civil-rights workers had endured in Mississippi. Tearfully, she concluded her testimony with the words:

> If the Freedom Democratic Party is not seated now, I question America, is this America, the land of the free and the home of the brave where we have to sleep with our telephones off the hooks because our lives be threatened daily because we want to live as decent human beings, in America?

Hamer's appearance before the committee had a profound impact because the networks replayed her testimony during prime time, on Saturday, August 22, 1964. The result was a deluge of telegrams and telephone calls to the convention and to President Lyndon Johnson from people in support of the MFDP.

As it was a presidential election year, the convention's main task was to endorse Johnson in his campaign against Republican candidate Barry Goldwater. Johnson, fearful of alienating white Southerners, gave Minnesota Senator Hubert Humphrey, favored candidate for vice president, the task of forging a compromise. He offered the MFDP a modest concession: the all-white regular faction would be seated, providing they would swear loyalty to the party's presidential candidate, but two members of the MFDP would also be seated as "delegates-at-large." The final element in the agreement would be to require that all future delegations would be integrated. The MFDP delegation, and most of the white Mississippi Democrats, rejected the proposal. Disappointed and disillusioned, Hamer told television reporters that "we didn't come all this way" for token representation; then she led

a demonstration on the floor of the convention to protest the exclusion of the MFDP; the group then occupied the seats of the Mississippi regulars, most of whom had left the convention in protest over the loyalty requirement. Republican Barry Goldwater carried Mississippi that year.

For the November elections, Hamer, Annie Devine, and **Virginia Gray** attempted to put their names on the ballot for the U.S. House of Representatives as independents, but were unable to get the voting registrars to certify the names on their petitions. Consequently, SNCC and the MFDP conducted an election so that the disenfranchised black population could express its choices. In the mock election, Hamer received over 33,000 votes, compared to a mere 49 votes for incumbent Representative Whitten, proving that blacks could elect their own candidates to office, if they were permitted to vote.

The result prompted another seating challenge. At the start of the new U.S. congressional session in January 1965, the MFDP candidates asked that they be seated in place of the all-white Mississippi delegation on the grounds that the state wrongfully excluded blacks from the political process in violation of the 14th Amendment to the U.S. Constitution. When the House vote on the challenge came to the floor on September 17, Hamer and the others were invited to witness the vote; she became the first black woman to sit with an assembly in the U.S. House of Representatives. Again, however, they lost the challenge, with 143 members voting in favor of seating the MFDP candidates, to 228 voting against.

That year marked another civil-rights milestone. In August, President Johnson signed into law the Voting Rights Act of 1965, which guaranteed that the federal government would come to the aid of citizens who were being denied the opportunity to vote. The voting bill was a major success for the civil-rights movement, and its effectiveness moved Hamer's activism in other directions. Because she was a powerful speaker, she traveled the country to speak at rallies and public lectures, and appeared on many college campuses. After reflecting upon America's efforts in Vietnam, she also became an outspoken critic of the war. As usual, her position was several years ahead of that of the American public. In 1967, Hamer's daughter Dorothy Jean died en route to Memphis hospital due to internal hemorrhaging, having been denied admission to a local hospital.

The Freedom Party of Mississippi was active until about 1968, when a number of its members decided to join forces with white liberals in order to broaden their voter appeal. The result was the Loyalist Party. Hamer was selected as a delegate to the 1968 Democratic nominating convention in Chicago as a member of the Loyalist delegation, which again challenged the seating of the white regulars. This time, an integrated delegation from Mississippi successfully challenged the seating of the traditional all-white faction, and Hamer was named to the Democratic National Committee. The event was overshadowed, however, by protests in the streets of Chicago and the repressive police responses.

In her travels and speaking tours, Hamer sought donations to help provide food for the children and jobs for the people of rural Mississippi who had been displaced by the mechanization of farm operations. After the 1968 convention, she turned her attention to found the Freedom Farms Corporation, an agricultural co-operative project based in Sunflower County. The organization apparently began with the donation of fifty female and five male pigs, arranged by **Dorothy Haight** of the National Council of Negro Women. This became the "pig bank," which enabled the poor to put meat in their diet. In February 1969, Hamer's organization received enough money to acquire 40 acres of land, which they leased to local needy people for a minimal fee. With access to land and livestock, people could raise their own food and eventually become self-sufficient. The farm soon grew to 680 acres, with 70 homes built, including a new brick home which Hamer and her family moved into in late 1969 or early 1970; it was her first home with an indoor bathroom and hot running water. Unfortunately, Freedom Farms was fraught with problems, including inexperienced management, successive seasons of bad weather, and an apathy on the part of individuals and government agencies who might have helped the struggling co-op survive. It failed in 1976.

By the mid-1970s, Hamer's health was failing. In the spring of 1976, she underwent surgery for breast cancer, after which she seldom left home. Suffering from hypertension, diabetes, and cancer, Hamer died of heart failure on March 14, 1977, at the hospital in Mound Bayou, Mississippi. Andrew Young, formerly of the Southern Christian Leadership Conference, future mayor of Atlanta, and at that time, U.S. ambassador to the United Nations, delivered the eulogy at her funeral on March 20th. Fannie Lou Hamer was buried in Ruleville on the Freedom Farm land.

SOURCES:

Branch, Taylor. *Parting the Waters: America in the King Years, 1954–1964.* NY: Simon and Schuster, 1988.

Fairclough, Adam. *To Redeem the Soul of America: The Southern Christian Leadership Conference and Martin Luther King, Jr.* Athens, GA: University of Georgia Press, 1987.

Garland, Phyl. "Builders of the South: Negro Heroines of Dixie Play Major Role in Challenging Racist Traditions," in *Ebony.* Vol. XXI, no. 10. August 1966, p. 27–37.

Grant, Jacquelyn. "Fannie Lou Hamer." *Notable Black American Women.* Edited by Jessie Carney Smith. Detroit, MI: Gale Research, 1992.

Hamer, Fannie Lou. "It's in Your Hands." Speech to the NAACP, May 7, 1971. Reprinted in Gerda Lerner, ed. *Black Women in White America: A Documentary History.* NY: Vintage Books, 1992.

———. "To Praise our Bridges," in Clayborne Carson, et al, eds., *The Eyes on the Prize Civil Rights Reader.* NY: Penguin, 1991.

Hine, Darlene Clark, ed. *Black Women in United States History: Trailblazers and Torchbearers, 1941–1965.* Brooklyn, NY: Carlson, 1990.

Lee, Chana Kai. "A Passionate Pursuit of Justice: the Life and Leadership of Fannie Lou Hamer, 1917–1967." Ph.D. thesis. University of California at Los Angeles, 1993.

Lerner, Gerda. "Developing Community Leadership," in *Black Women in White America: A Documentary History.* NY: Vintage Books, 1992.

McAdam, Doug. *Freedom Summer.* NY: Oxford University Press, 1988.

McMillen, Neil. *An Oral History with Mrs. Fannie Lou Hamer, Native Mississippian and Civil Rights Leader.* Hattiesburg, MS: University of Southern Mississippi, 1977.

Mills, Kay. *This Little Light of Mine: The Life of Fannie Lou Hamer.* NY: Dutton, 1993.

The New York Times. August 23, 1964; August 24, 1964; June 7, 1965; March 21, 1977.

Selby, Miriam, and Earl Selby. *Odyssey: Journey Through Black America.* NY: Putnam, 1971.

Sewell, George A., and Margaret L. Dwight. *Mississippi Black History Makers.* Jackson, MS: University Press of Mississippi, 1984.

Stoper, Emily. *The Student Nonviolent Coordinating Committee: The Growth of Radicalism in a Civil Rights Organization.* Brooklyn, NY: Carlson, 1989.

Williams, Juan. *Eyes on the Prize: Americas Civil Rights Years, 1954–1965.* NY: Viking Penguin, 1987.

COLLECTIONS:

Fannie Lou Hamer papers (1966–1978), Amistad Research Center, Tulane University, New Orleans, Louisiana.

RELATED MEDIA:

"Fannie Lou Hamer" (song), on *B'lieve I'll run on . . . See What the End's Gonna Be* album, played by Sweet Honey in the Rock (Musical Group), Redwood Records, 1978.

"Mississippi: Is This America? (1962–1964)," *Eyes On The Prize: The American Civil Rights Struggle, 1954–1965,* Television Documentary Series, funded by the Corporation for Public Broadcasting, Blackside, 1986.

Portrait in Black: Fannie Lou Hamer (16mm; 10 min.), directed by Bill Buckley, written by **Tracy Sugarman**, Rediscovery Productions 1972.

Michael Cary,
Chair, Department of History and Political Science,
Seton Hill College, Greensburg, Pennsylvania

Hamill, Dorothy (1956—)

Charismatic figure skater and one of only three American women to win the U.S. National championship, the World championship, and an Olympic gold medal in the same year. Name variations: (nickname) Squint (because of her nearsightedness) and Dot. Born Dorothy Stuart Hamill, July 26, 1956, in Chicago, Illinois; third child of Chalmers (an executive at Pitney Bowes) and Carolyn Hamill; married Dean Paul Martin, on January 8, 1982 (divorced); married Dr. Kenneth Forsythe, in 1987 (separated 1995); children: one daughter, Alexandra (b. 1988).

Won the U.S. National championship (1974, 1975, 1976); won Olympic gold medal, Innsbruck, Austria, XII Winter Games, as well as World championship (1976); was World Professional Figure Skating champion (1984–87); was a product spokesperson, an Ice Capades headliner, a television performer-producer, president of Dorothy Hamill Enterprises, and executive producer of Cinderella . . . Frozen in Time. Publications: Dorothy Hamill, On and Off the Ice (Alfred Knopf, 1983).

The moment she pushed off and began to glide across Morse's Pond, a span of ice behind her grandparents house in Wellesley, Massachusetts, writes Dorothy Hamill, something inside her "surged." She had no way of knowing that those eight-year-old wobbly legs were setting in motion a skating career that would continue for over three decades. Despite the limited resources of her parents and her relentless stage fright, Hamill's ability to balance and move gracefully upon a set of metal blades took her to nearby arenas, competitions around the country, and ultimately around the world. She circled endlessly, sped forward, turned, twisted, jumped, and lifted herself to the pinnacles of skating. Before she had a chance to pause during her pursuit, she was smiling back at herself from the cover of *Time* magazine. After earning three U.S. National championships, a World championship, an Olympic gold medal, and, finally, a chance to relax, her childhood was essentially over.

Dorothy Hamill, who grew up in a comfortable two-story house in Riverside, an upper-middle-class section of Greenwich, Connecticut, had an older brother Sandy and shared a room with her older sister **Marcia**. Blue-eyed, with dark brown hair, Hamill was small but athletically built: she would eventually compete at 5'3", 115 pounds. As a young girl, Hamill liked to swim, collect stuffed animals, listen to music, and play the violin.

When she first skated on that frozen pond, Hamill was wearing an old, borrowed set of skates. Back home in Riverside, she continued the activity at Binney Park on new $6.95 skates with her sister Marcia. Fascinated with others ability to skate backwards, she asked her parents to let her take lessons. She was soon among the best beginners, though she joined the Binney Park class midcourse. It was, however, during her first lessons at the Rye Playland Ice Rink in New York that she learned to skate backwards. The ten-minute trip to Rye was the beginning of a long journey to find instruction and ice time. She moved on to **Shirley Ayre**'s Ice Studio in the Stamford Shopping Mall and up to $25 skates, purchased by her grandmother. The more she skated, the more she learned; the more she learned, the more she enjoyed her increasingly expensive hobby.

Her first private teacher was **Barbara Taplan** at Rye. "The technique Barbara taught me in that first year was an excellent underpinning for my years of free skating" writes Hamill. Her next tutor, Otto Gold, who trained the 1948 Olympic champion *Barbara Ann Scott, introduced Hamill to school figures. Beginning musicians learn scales, beginning skaters learn school figures—skated circles that require concentration, balance, and tedious, repetitive practice. Going around a complete circle on one stroke, a skater glides backwards, forwards, and changes feet. The U.S. Figure Skating Association (USFSA) uses figures as an official test to measure a skater's progress. Figures are also a required component in competitions, called compulsories. During competitions, each skater traces three circles, later examined by the judges. Graded on a scale of 2.0 to 5.0, figures count for 30% of a skater's total. A short program, made up of seven set moves, makes up 20% of the score, and the free skating program makes up the remaining 50%. Hamill, a natural free skater, had to work hardest on her figures.

She was nine when she passed her preliminary USFSA test. The following year, she passed her first and second tests and entered her first competition at Wollman rink in Central Park in New York City. The USFSA groups ladies (even young girls are called ladies) into Juvenile, Intermediate, Novice, Junior, and Senior divisions. Hamill placed a surprise second in the Juvenile division. "I felt my head float away from my body," she wrote. "I was so happy. I couldn't believe it."

Encouraged by her success, Hamill and her mother **Carolyn Hamill** drove to rinks in Connecticut, New York, and New Jersey in search of "patch time," a section of ice large enough for practice. "It was a rough time and I felt bad that I could never get to my friends' slumber parties," Hamill wrote, "but I never skipped a lesson, ice time was too hard to come by in those days." Hamill often ate, slept, and studied in the car, sometimes reading by flashlight. So dedicated was the young skater that one morning when her mother overslept, Hamill reportedly set out to walk to the rink. When Hamill's parents asked if she was serious about pursuing skating, Dorothy assured them she was willing to put in the hard work. From then on, said her mother, "it was just like having a child who was good in school. You sacrifice."

I won the Olympics . . . for all those Americans whose love and good wishes carried me through those last few days at Innsbruck. But I won the World championship for myself, and for all those people who had believed in me since I first put on skates down by Morse's pond.

—Dorothy Hamill

In Hamill's day, it was not unusual to spend ten years and $10,000 on a promising skater. In addition to the financial burden, Dorothy's schooling had to be adjusted and her social life limited by early morning practices. Her mother became a full-time chaperon, seamstress, chauffeur, personal cook, and manager. Her father Chalmers, who worked to provide the extra income, did not see much of his daughter or wife. Chalmers helped Dorothy select and edit her skating music and attended competitions.

One summer, Dorothy moved to Lake Placid and lived with Coach Gold and his wife. At the training center there, she watched many great skaters and developed a crush on Gordie McKellen, a future U.S. champion, who became a close friend and source of encouragement. Hamill returned to Lake Placid the following year and began to work with Gustave Lussi, trainer of two-time gold medalist Dick Button. Although most of her time went to skating, Hamill attempted to maintain friendships and live like a normal teenager.

In January of 1969, she won the Eastern Sectional championships in Wilmington, Delaware. Next, despite poor figures, a terrific free-style performance pulled her to third place in the Novice division in her first Regional competition at Lake Placid. The result earned Hamill a trip to Seattle, Washington, where she became National Novice champion at age 12. There, she watched *Janet Lynn win one of her five National Seniors championships. Though Hamill admired Lynn, her skating hero was John Misha Petkevich, the National Senior Men's gold medalist. Because of her own innate leg strength and superior jumping ability, Hamill idolized the male skaters, especially the great jumpers.

After Seattle, Hamill switched to Coach **Sonya Klopfer** (Dunfield), the 1951 Ladies' National Figure Skating champion and former captain of the 1952 U.S. Olympics team. Hamill lived with Dunfield and her husband in the Catskill Mountains. The Dunfields introduced Dorothy to ballet as well as the great bootmaker Stanzione in New York, when they flew her down for custom-fitted skates. They also took her to Toronto where she worked with choreographer Bob Paul, a 1960 gold-medal winner. Despite her success, Hamill suffered from uncontrollable stage fright. "Before any competition I used to sit in the dressing room and just want to die. Just die. It's like well, it's like going to an execution. Every year, I would swear—This is my last competition." Dunfield convinced Hamill to accept the anxiety and channel it into useful energy.

Returning to Lake Placid for a reunion with Coach Lussi, Dorothy made great strides. Lussi, who helped center her spins, increase her speed, and improve the height of her jumps, encouraged more artistic interaction with the music. He also planted the seeds for a different type of move; he had Hamill work on a new combination that started with a flying camel layover, and, after she bent her skating knee, dropped into a sit spin. Dunfield helped refine the move after Hamill's season with Lussi ended.

A freak accident forced Hamill to withdraw during competition at the Junior Ladies level in Buffalo, New York. She was third after the compulsories but while attempting to practice on a dimly lit rink early in the morning she skated into a rope and suffered a concussion. A somewhat controversial ruling by the USFSA allowed her to compete in the Regionals despite not finishing in Buffalo.

All facets of Hamill's skating continued to improve. In January of 1970, she became the Eastern Junior Ladies champ. In February at the Nationals, she won her first school figures and performed her first double axle in public. Finishing second overall, Hamill also thrilled the audience with her new move, which became know as the Hamill Camel. That same year, she passed her "gold" figure test and was officially ready to compete as a senior.

In 1971, after skating to a fifth place finish at her first senior level Nationals competition, Hamill was asked to compete in the pre-Olympic invitational in Sapporo, Japan. At age 14, she became one of the youngest women to represent the U.S. in international competition. In Sapporo, she took third and met Coach Carlo Fassi whose resumé listed several famous students, including two-time World champion and 1968 Olympic gold medalist *Peggy Fleming. In her autobiography, Hamill praises all her coaches, but she credits Fassi for putting it all together.

International competition meant increased media exposure, more pressure, and more travel. Luckily, the USFSA began to absorb some of the financial burden. A 1972 fourth place finish at the Nationals kept Hamill one spot away from making the U.S. Olympic team. Dejected, she watched the games on television as Janet Lynn settled for a bronze medal after a fall during a flying sit spin.

When **Julie Lynn Holmes** announced her retirement, Hamill moved up to take her spot on the U.S. team and took seventh in her first World's competition. Touring with the team, Hamill went on to win the International Grand Prix championship at St. Gervais, France, and the Nebelhorn Trophy at Obersdorf, West Germany. Upon her return, Fassi discovered Hamill was nearsighted and had her fitted for glasses. The glasses, with wide lenses so she could see her figure patterns on the ice, later set a fashion trend. Fassi also sent Hamill to work in Toronto with **Ellen Burka**, the 1945–46 Dutch champion. Burka worked on Dorothy's stroking technique, her performing, and her "acting" on ice.

When Hamill joined Fassi at his new rink in Denver, Colorado, she attended school at the Colorado Academy in Englewood. There, she made friends and maintained good grades de-

Dorothy Hamill

spite the long hours of skating practice, weight training, and ballet classes. Carolyn Hamill was a constant companion with little to do except return to the hotel while her daughter practiced. It was a hard, sometimes lonely life. During one stretch, Dorothy did not see her sister or brother for an entire year, but her schedule kept her preoccupied. Fassi, who enforced a nine o'clock curfew, kept up the pressure with grueling training sessions for his nearly three dozen students.

In 1973, at the Nationals in Bloomington, Indiana, Hamill stood on the second place riser as Janet Lynn won her fifth consecutive title. A month later, Dorothy took fourth at the World championships in Bratislava, Czechoslovakia. Lynn then retired from amateur competition prior to the 1974 Nationals competition in Providence, Rhode Island. Despite a shaky final program, as heir apparent to the U.S. throne, Hamill seized the opportunity by winning her first National championship.

A month later, at the World championships at Olympia Halle in Munich, when Hamill began her free-skating performance, she faced a stage-fright nightmare. A chorus of boos from the audience greeted her as she took to the ice. Unaware that the crowd was booing the scoring for hometown favorite **Gerti Schanderl**, Hamill burst into tears and skated off. After learning that the crowd wasn't against her, noted *Time* magazine, she composed herself and skated "back out on the ice, head and shoulders set in grim determination. Her music started and suddenly came the smile like a flash of sunlight. Surely, evenly, she started to skate, and soon was sweeping through her routine as if gravity did not exist. The crowd was caught up in the moment, and in four minutes Dorothy turned the entire, week-long championship into her show." It was one of her best performances ever. She received enough total points to finish second overall.

Hamill graduated from the Colorado Academy but continued to spend five hours a day, or more, on the ice. While performing double axles, she caught a skate in a rut, fell and felt terrific pain in her leg and ankle. There was no break or torn tendons or strained ligaments, just pain. After consulting specialists, she wore a walking cast for several weeks. Despite this, she managed to reclaim the National Senior's title, her third, in January of 1975, but afterwards the pain returned. Finally, a sports physiotherapist in Denver used ultrasound treatments to restore her ankle.

At the 1975 World championships, a fall during a flying sit spin cost her first place. Hamill finished second to **Diane de Leeuw**, an American who skated for the Netherlands. The loss built up the pressure heading into the '76 Olympics. As a two-time second place finisher, Hamill's ability to perform under stress began to be questioned. She was inconsistent. On the one hand, said Dick Buttons, there were no seams in her skating; "every move is right, every line is clean." On the other hand, he said, "she can blow it." The pressure forced her to focus on her Olympic preparations. She made a final trip to Toronto to work on her free-style routine with choreographers Ellen Burka and Brian Foley. When coach Fassi left to supervise John Curry, Hamill turned to Peter Burrows. The New York area coach agreed to assist in any way he could. She later wrote, "Peter pulled my head together, helped me to focus, inspired me and motivated me."

A few years earlier, while on tour with the USFSA, Hamill had had her hair cut by a stylist in London who had reportedly done **Julie Andrews**' hair for Hamill's favorite film, *The Sound of Music*. What worked for Julie, failed Hamill. She hated the way she looked while performing an exhibition before Queen *Elizabeth II in London. Still flinching from her disastrous haircut, she sought assistance. Fellow skater, **Melissa Militano**, recommended a Japanese stylist named Suga because he understood that a skater's hair had to fall back in place easily as they whirled around the rink. After repeated requests to find time in his schedule, Suga agreed to see Hamill. Soon after, they both became famous for the "Hamill Wedge."

On February 4, 1976, the entire Hamill family was together in Innsbruck to watch the Opening ceremonies of the XII Winter Games. At the time, Dorothy told a reporter, "I owe so much to so many wonderful people that I'm determined to overcome anything for the Olympics." She had to overcome a great deal. The media attention was relentless and ice time for practice was limited. Because Carlo Fassi was her coach of record, neither Foley nor Burrows were allowed to accompany her to Innsbruck. One evening a car forced her to jump out of the way as she walked with Fassi. A deliberate attempt, she thought, to psyche her out.

Despite the distractions, Hamill placed second in the school figures. A fall during a routine sit spin in her final warm up alarmed the crowd but probably helped ease some of the tension and reminded Hamill to maintain focus. A nearly perfect short program placed her ahead of the pack. Afterwards, a trip with her family out to Salzburg to see the locations for *The Sound of*

Music proved to be the perfect distraction for the upcoming free-style competition.

Hamill returned from the outing to find her hotel room filled with correspondence. "I sat in my room by myself, reading 300 telegrams and letters from people I did not know. It was nice to have so many people rooting for me but I realized I had to live up to their high expectations. . . . I felt in a sense I was no longer Dorothy Hamill—I was the United States. The medal was not mine to lose—I was representing the hopes and dreams of thousands of people I had never met."

Carolyn Hamill, who had devoted more than a decade of her life to her daughter's career, stayed back in the hotel room, too nervous even to watch the televised finals on February the 13th. She missed one of Innsbruck's most memorable television shots: a close up of Hamill, short of breath, smiling, hugging her coach, and squinting to read her scores. The television audience became aware of Dorothy Hamill's nearsightedness, and, as the 5.8s for technical ability and 5.9s for artistic merit were posted, they also learned she had won the gold medal.

After Innsbruck, several advisors urged Hamill to retire, to cash in, to go out a winner. Dorothy wasn't sure. She wanted a World championship, even though anything less than a first place finish at the World's might undermine her stature and earnings potential. "I thought if I didn't compete, I would always regret it. It had been a goal," wrote Hamill. "I was so close at that point that I would have been crazy not to. So many people were involved besides me; my parents, my coach, my sponsors. I couldn't let them down."

When she arrived at Göteborg, Sweden, she was pleased to find her good friend John Curry, the men's Olympic gold medalist. Both took top honors at the 1976 World championships. (Only two other U.S. women have won a National championship, an Olympic gold medal, and a World championship in the same year—*Peggy Fleming* and *Kristi Yamaguchi*. Norway's *Sonja Henie* won the Grand Slam twice.)

Hamill returned home to a parade in Riverside and an invitation to visit the White House for a state dinner in Queen Elizabeth's honor. Her new mega-agent Jerry Weintraub allowed the Ideal Toy Company to produce Barbie-like, Dorothy Hamill dolls, and wangled a three-year iceshow deal for a reported $1 million. Hamill chose the Ice Capades, she said, because they "had a family way about them." That same year, Desi Arnaz, Jr., invited the world champion to dinner and introduced her to Dean Paul Martin,

a professional tennis player, pilot for the Air National Guard Flyer, and son of actor Dean Martin. Hamill and Martin courted on and off for five years, in between hectic schedules, and married at a celebrity wedding in 1981.

With the Ice Capades, Hamill found a grueling 13-show week, 18-to-23-weeks-per-year schedule, and a return to the loneliness of life on the road. There were endless interviews, hassles with demented fans, and Hamill suffered from a difficult relationship with the press. Money became a problem. A $100,000 lawsuit, initiated by Fassi, was settled out of court. Loans she had made to friends were never repaid. Hamill felt exploited. "I was such a baby then," she told a reporter. "And I probably still am. It's all happened so quickly. It just all happened so quickly. The contract with Ice Capades and Clairol and the TV specials. It's just all happened so fast."

Hamill moved from Riverside, Connecticut, to Hollywood and appeared in TV specials with Gene Kelly, Bruce Jenner, Hal Linden, and **Sally Kellerman**, which were not perceived as well produced, or wise career moves. Eventually, Hamill developed a bleeding ulcer, and her marriage to Martin ended after two years. They remained good friends until his death in a plane crash in 1987.

After 1982, Hamill's career and personal life rebounded. In 1983, she performed in *Romeo and Juliet* on CBS to good ratings. In 1984, she skated with the John Curry Skating Company, a small artistic troupe. Hamill won four straight World Professional Figure Skating championships from 1984 to 1987. In 1986, she met Ken Forsythe, a sport's physician and former member of the Canadian ski team. They married and moved to Indian Wells, California. A daughter, Alexandra, was born in 1988. That same year, Hamill and Forsythe co-produced the well-received *Nutcracker on Ice*.

By the end of the 1980s, the Ice Capades, once the standard of excellence for a skating show, was in decline, damaged by competitors such as Walt Disney's "World of Ice." The brunt of sitcom jokes, in 1991 the Ice Capades filed for bankruptcy. Hamill and her husband, in partnership with Alaskan businessman Ben Tisdale took over the Ice Capades on June 24, 1993. "This is my second dream come true," Hamill said. "My first dream came true when I was 19, which is a little early to start asking, What next? So I had to find another dream and this is it."

The first show staged by the revamped Ice Capades was called *Cinderella . . . Frozen in*

Time. Hamill improved the caliber of skaters after first convincing **Catherine Foulks** to leave her prestigious law firm to play the fairy godmother. Hamill brought in choreographers Tim Murphy and Nathan Birch from *The Next Ice Age* in Baltimore, had Desmond Heeley, who had dressed Richard Burton for *Camelot,* design the set and costumes, and Michael Conway compose the score. New equipment, 30 skaters, 15 crew members, and several tractor trailers were assembled for concurrent East and West tours.

Skaters loved working for Hamill. Audiences and critics enjoyed the new show. An ABC special and a home-video release took the event into people's homes. Unfortunately, it wasn't enough. At the end of March 1996, after a series of financial set backs, Dorothy Hamill once again made prime-time news by declaring bankruptcy. "I am confident that with the assistance of my current, competent and qualified business advisers and counsel that I will be able to satisfactorily resolve my financial difficulties, thereby allowing me to focus on my skating," she communicated in a statement released to the press. Twenty years after the Olympics, Dorothy Hamill was still competing and winning, against skaters who had not yet been born when she won her gold medal.

SOURCES:

Bachrach, Judy. "The Ice Princess Comes of Age," in *The Washington Post.* February 1, 1978, Section B, Page 1.

Current Biography. NY: H.W. Wilson, 1979.

Dolan, Edward F., Jr., and Richard B. Lyttle. *Dorothy Hamill: Olympic Skating Champion.* NY: Doubleday, 1979.

Hamill, Dorothy. *Dorothy Hamill: On and Off the Ice.* NY: Alfred E. Knopf, 1983.

Philips, Betty Lou. *The Picture Story of Dorothy Hamill.* NY: Julian Messner, 1978.

"Stealing the Show in Innsbruck," in *Time.* February 23, 1976, p. 57.

"Test of the Best on Snow and Ice," in *Time.* February 2, 1976, p. 56–65.

Van Steenwyk, Elizabeth. *Dorothy Hamill: Olympic Champion.* NY: Harvey House, 1976.

Wulf, Steve. "Cinderella Story," in *Sports Illustrated.* March 7, 1994, pp. 48–57.

Jesse T. Raiford,
President of Raiford Communications, Inc., New York, New York

Hamilton, Mrs. Alexander (1757–c. 1854).

See Hamilton, Elizabeth Schuyler.

Hamilton, Alice (1869–1970)

Groundbreaking practitioner of industrial toxicology and leading American social reformer of the 19th and 20th centuries. Pronunciation: Ham-il-tun. Born on February 27, 1869 in New York City; died at age 101
on September 22, 1970, in Hadlyme, Connecticut; daughter of Gertrude Pond Hamilton (1840–1917) and Montgomery Hamilton (1843–1909, a businessman); sister of classical scholar Edith Hamilton (1867–1963) and artist **Norah Hamilton** (b. 1873); attended Fort Wayne College of Medicine, 1890–1891, University of Michigan Medical School, 1892–93, University of Leipzig, Germany, 1895–96, and Johns Hopkins Medical School, 1896–97; never married; no children.

Took position teaching at the Woman's Medical School of Northwestern University in Chicago (summer 1896); joined the settlement at Jane Addams' Hull House (1897); was appointed to the Illinois Occupation Disease Commission and became a special agent for the U.S. Bureau of Labor, for whom she would conduct various surveys of American industries (1910); joined Jane Addams' Women's Peace Party (1915) and attended, with 50 other American women, the International Congress of Women at The Hague; began an appointment as assistant professor of industrial medicine at Harvard Medical School (1919); commenced a ten-year career as medical consultant to the General Electric Company (1923); served on the Health Committee of Council of the League of Nations (1924–28); served on President Hoover's Research Committee on Social Trends (1930–32); retired from Harvard (1935); worked on her last major study of the dangerous trades, in this case, a survey of the viscose rayon industry (1937–38); gave annual lectures about industrial toxicology at the Women's Medical College of Pennsylvania (1937–43); traveled to Frankfurt, Germany, as a representative of the Department of Labor at the Eighth International Congress on Occupational Accidents and Diseases (1938); published her autobiography, Exploring the Dangerous Trades *(1943); became president of the National Consumers' League (1944); received the Lasker Award for contributions to workers' health (1947); was awarded an honorary doctorate by the University of Michigan (1948); received the Knudsen Award of the Industrial Medical Association (1953); was given the Elizabeth Blackwell Citation of the New York Infirmary (1954); was named New England Medical Woman of the Year (1956); was honored on the occasion of her 90th birthday with the establishment of the Alice Hamilton Fund for Occupation Medicine at the Harvard School of Public Health (1959).*

Major publications on public health and industrial medicine—all published by the U.S. Government Printing Office, unless otherwise noted: Lead Poisoning in Potteries, Tile Works, and Porcelain Enameled Sanitary Ware Factories *(1912);* Hygiene of the Painters' Trade *(1913);* Lead Poisoning in the Smelting and Refining of Lead *(1914)*; Industrial Poisons Used in the Rubber Industry *(1915)*; Lead Poisoning in the Manufacture of Storage Batteries *(1915)*; *(with Charles H. Verrill)* Hygiene of the Printing Trade *(1917)*; Industrial Poisons Used or Produced in the Manufacture of Explosives *(1917)*; Women in the Lead Industries *(1919)*; Industrial Poisoning in Making Coal-tar Dyes and Dye Intermediates *(1921)*; Poverty and Birth Control *(NY: American Birth Control League, 1921)*; Carbon-Monoxide Poisoning *(1922)*; Women Workers and Industrial Poisons *(1926)*; Industrial Poisons of the United States *(NY: Macmillan, 1929)*; Industrial Toxicology *(NY: Harper, 1934)*; Occupational Poisoning in the Viscose Rayon Industry *(1940)*.

In the early 20th century, Dr. Alice Hamilton began an unprecedented exploration of what she termed "the dangerous trades." By studying the environments of lead workers, miners, painters, enamelers, printers, and munitions makers, Hamilton became the first American scientist to demonstrate the dangers of working with industrial toxins. The occupational safety requirements now standard in the United States are in large part a result of Hamilton's early efforts as an agent of the U.S. Bureau of Labor. By bringing her scientific training to bear on the social problems of the laboring poor, Hamilton uncovered important links between poverty and disease, elevating issues of class and industrial reform to the forefront of American public health policy.

Born to Montgomery and **Gertrude Pond Hamilton** in New York City in 1869, Alice Hamilton was the second of five children—four girls and one boy—and grew up in Fort Wayne, Indiana. Her early years were profoundly shaped by the insular world in which she lived, which was almost solely populated by relatives. A well-to-do family when Alice was a child, the Hamiltons lived in three houses on an estate which covered three city blocks. The relationships between Hamilton, her siblings, and cousins were especially strong and close, and the children rarely felt a need to move beyond their circle for entertainment or friendship.

The education of the Hamilton children was directed by their parents, who disapproved of both the curriculum and the stifling quality of public education. Montgomery Hamilton instructed his children in Latin, hired a tutor to teach them French, and sent them to a Lutheran schoolteacher to learn German. Otherwise, Alice and her siblings were encouraged to read litera-

ture and history on their own, which they did with fervor. Montgomery was a strict schoolmaster and demanded rigorous thinking from his daughters. "We were not allowed to make a statement which could be challenged unless we were prepared to defend it. One of my father's favorite quotations was, 'Be ready always to give a reason of the hope that is in you.'" He encouraged a scientific, logical approach to problems, although he never encouraged his children to study science itself. Alice believed that such self-directed learning had been "valuable," but she regretted the lapses in her education as well. She considered herself, at age 17, "completely ignorant" of the natural sciences, and too limited in philosophy and literature.

Alice remembered her mother as "less intellectual but more original and independent" than her father. In particular, Alice admired her mother's pragmatic sensibility, her fiery sense of justice, and her advocacy that women engage the world outside their homes. "She made us feel that whatever went wrong in our society was a personal concern for her and for us. . . . Something she said once gives a picture of her quality and of the atmosphere in which we girls grew up:—'There are two kinds of people, the ones who say "Somebody ought to do something about it, but why should it be I?" and those who say "Somebody must do something about it, then why not I?"'" Alice's public health career and her general interest in the well-being of the less fortunate had their roots in this guiding principle of her early development.

At age 17, Hamilton and her cousin and friend **Agnes Hamilton**, following in older female relatives' footsteps, entered Miss Porter's School for Young Ladies in Farmington, Connecticut. Although Alice disparaged the school's teaching as "the world's worst," while there she experienced a measure of independence that thrilled her. She met people who had utterly different backgrounds and "passionately admired" them, treasuring the friendships she made there for years to come.

When her short tenure at Farmington ended, Alice returned to Fort Wayne to confront, as did her older sister *Edith Hamilton, the reality that the family fortune had dwindled rather substantially. Montgomery Hamilton, although a devoted intellectual, had failed at business and thereby depleted his family's resources. The elder Hamilton women decided to prepare themselves to "earn our living" and chose from the few careers that seemed attainable: "teaching, nursing, and the practice of medicine." Alice determined to become a doctor, but not, as she readily admitted, from any devotion to scientific pursuits. In fact, throughout her education, she had avoided the sciences, first because her father had not deemed it important and later because, without some basic training, mathematics and the natural sciences appeared daunting. Instead, Alice chose to become a doctor because "I could go anywhere I pleased—to far-off lands or to city slums—and be quite sure that I could be of use anywhere." To this end, she set about remedying her deficient scientific knowledge with the help of a local high school teacher. Within a year, she was able to begin anatomy training at the provincial Fort Wayne Medical College, and in 1892 she entered the Medical School of the University of Michigan for what she termed "a real course."

Although the road Hamilton chose was not an easy one for women of her era, she was not alone. One historian has called the late 19th century "a golden age for women in medicine," pointing out that when Hamilton began her career, there were more than 4,500 registered female physicians in the United States. Even so, great challenges faced a woman who chose to enter medicine in those days, and for Alice, the first great opposition came from her own family. Her older sister Edith vociferously opposed the choice, as did a former teacher, who viewed "the whole affair as if it were an amusing childish whim." In her closest family relation and dear friend, Agnes, however, Hamilton found unwavering support; Agnes confessed in her journal that she hoped Alice would become a doctor rather than anything else.

When Hamilton arrived in Ann Arbor, Michigan, she was both excited and discomfited by the latitude accorded young women in the liberal world of a large university. She was also struck by the lonesome reality of the independent life she had longed for, so different from Fort Wayne society. As she wrote to Agnes, "It is so queer to be one of so many and of such very little importance. I am absolutely nobody, for the first time in my life, with no family name or reputation to fall back on, just one of the multitude with no more deference shown me than any of the others." Quickly, though, her initial misgivings gave way to an eager exploration of the new horizons offered her by the fast-paced, intellectually stimulating environment. In the course of her studies, Hamilton impressed both her peers and her professors. She performed so well, in fact, that during her senior year the Medical School voted to allow her to graduate early, obviating the usual routine transfer to the Woman's Medical College of Pennsylvania for post-graduate studies.

During her final year at Michigan, Hamilton decided to become a bacteriologist and pathologist, rather than a physician. After graduating, she traveled to Germany to study under leading scientists there, and after returning to the U.S. in 1896, undertook another semester of work in pathological anatomy—"really pure enjoyment"—at Johns Hopkins Medical School. The following summer, the Women's Medical School of Northwestern University offered her a teaching position, which she happily accepted. While she desperately needed an income, she also wanted the job for another, more idealistic, reason. "At last I could realize the dream I had had for years, of going to live in Hull-House." Although Hamilton's sheltered life in Indiana had not introduced her to the problems of poverty and disease that late-19th century social reformers hoped to conquer, she and her cousin Agnes learned about the settlement movement in books and by hearing *Jane Addams speak at a Methodist church in Fort Wayne. From that time on, they had determined to spend at least some of their adult lives at a settlement.

Jane Addams had been inspired to found her own settlement after visiting the famed Toynbee House in London. Like her predecessors, Addams had adopted the philosophy that reform-minded individuals should "settle" destitute urban neighborhoods and set up houses as staffed centers for community improvement. Addams moved to Chicago, where she and fellow reformers purchased an old mansion (Hull House) in the slum-ridden West Side, and in 1889 they established a complex of services which included a day-care nursery, adult-education and worker-training classes, and cultural activities like theater and musical concerts. Addams staffed her settlement (the third in the United States) with interested young men and women who served for no pay other than the opportunity to participate in the revolutionary experiment. By 1900, the movement had spawned over 100 settlements across the country.

Alice's years at Hull House were truly transformative for her. In Jane Addams, she found a mentor, hero, and source of inspiration, and in the settlement she found a purpose and lifelong commitment. Later she recalled, "To me, the life there satisfied every longing, for companionship, for the excitement of new experiences, for constant intellectual stimulation, and for the sense of being caught up in a big movement which enlisted my enthusiastic loyalty." This place where

Hamilton had found total satisfaction lay in the midst of the 19th Ward, one of the poorest and most squalid immigrant neighborhoods in Chicago. People from at least 18 nations lived in the community, including Irish, Poles, Greeks, Italians, Jews, Russians, and Bohemians. Hamilton felt renewed by her daily contact with those in need, and engaged with fellow reformers in debates about the meanings and solutions to poverty and degradation. As she worked in the well-baby clinic and confronted teenage boys addicted to cocaine, Hamilton lost her small-town naiveté; in its place grew a handy pragma-

tism and a rapidly growing liberal sensibility toward the poor. "Life in a settlement does several things to you. Among others, it teaches you that education and culture have little to do with real wisdom, the wisdom that comes from life experience. You can never, thereafter, hear people speak of the 'masses,' the 'ignorant voters,' without feeling that if it were put up to you whether you would trust the fate of the country to 'the classes' or to 'the masses,' you would decide for the latter." At the same time, during her early years with the settlement, Hamilton approached the problems she saw primarily from the stand-

Alice
Hamilton

point of a scientist who could, simply by applying the knowledge she had, remedy the ills that beset those around her. In 1902, she received a life-changing, bittersweet lesson about the limits of this approach when she saw the search for scientific truth undermined by class prejudices and political injustice.

That year, typhoid fever had become epidemic throughout Chicago's poorer neighborhoods. The tenements surrounding Hull House were especially hard hit by the plague, but no one on the city's ineffective Board of Health could determine the reason. Hamilton, however, had made some observations on her own. "As I prowled about the streets and the ramshackle wooden tenement houses I saw the outdoor privies (forbidden by law but flourishing nevertheless), some of them in backyards below the level of the street and overflowing in heavy rains; the wretched water closets indoors, one for four or more families, filthy and with the plumbing out of order because nobody was responsible for cleaning or repairs; and swarms of flies everywhere." The flies instantly riveted her attention, bringing to mind a case she had studied in medical school, in which scientists had argued that there was a link between poor sanitation, flies, and the spread of typhoid fever.

Hamilton, with fellow Hull House residents **Maude Gernon** and **Gertrude Howe**, commenced her own study of flies along the back alleys of the 19th Ward's tenements by collecting the insects and submitting them to microscopic study in the lab, which revealed that they did carry typhoid. Hamilton was fully satisfied that the questionable sanitation in her poor neighborhood led to the presence of typhoid-bearing insects. Moreover, this conformed to her general idea that poverty was the root cause of the epidemic because in well-screened middle-class homes with safe plumbing, such epidemics did not occur.

Hamilton's solid investigation of the problem garnered her great acclaim and prompted a major reorganization of the Board of Health. However, it was at this moment that Hamilton learned the most valuable lesson from the episode: the extreme concentration of typhoid in the 19th Ward had not been caused solely by the causes she had identified. Although typhoid was endemic in poorer neighborhoods because of poor sanitation and disease-bearing insects (as she assumed), the cause of the great outbreak in the neighborhood had a political, as well as a scientific, source. The local pumping station had a break in its pipes, which caused raw sewage to leak into the drinking water. For three days, the people in the 19th Ward had drunk the contaminated water, but the Board of Health refused to reveal that fact to the public. Hamilton never ceased to be mortified by both the city government's treatment of the poor and by the way her work was used to hide the truth from the people she cared for so much. From this episode, Hamilton learned that although scientific inquiry was vital to the protection of public health, social and political realities could have an equal, if not greater, impact on social welfare. It was a lesson she never forgot.

It was not until 1908 that Hamilton found a way to put her talents as a scientist and her sense of social compassion to best effect. During that year, she began the work for which she is best known today: an exploration of the "dangerous trades." The term was coined by Britain's Thomas Oliver, who wrote a book with the same title which Hamilton read with great interest. She began researching the subject of toxins in the workplace but quickly discovered that virtually nothing had been written about the subject in regard to American industry. "Everyone with whom I talked assured me that the foreign writings could not apply to American conditions, for our workmen were so much better paid, their standard of living was so much higher, and the factories they worked in so much finer in every way than the European, that they did not suffer from the evils to which the poor foreigner was subject. That sort of talk left me skeptical." Hamilton's doubt arose from the bald contradiction between the experts' assertions and what she had learned through daily contact with her neighbors in the 19th Ward. "I could not fail to hear tales of the dangers that workingmen faced, of cases of carbon-monoxide gassing in the great steel mills, of painters disabled by lead palsy, of pneumonia and rheumatism among the men in the stockyards."

Hamilton soon had an opportunity to put her suspicions to the test. Charles Henderson, a professor of sociology at the University of Chicago, had encouraged the governor of Illinois to appoint an Occupational Disease Commission to establish the extent of sickness caused by industrial hazards in the state. Henderson knew that Hamilton had been keenly interested in the subject and arranged to have her appointed to the board. In 1910, they began their work by taking up one facet of the larger problem of industrial disease, that of occupational poisons. Because no official body in the state actually knew which trades used poisons in the first place, the commission had to investigate in a rather haphazard fashion. Using cases from local hospitals as a guide, the scientists sought out sick laborers and then worked backward to target particular factories. Although daunting, the work gave Hamilton great satisfaction. "It was pioneering exploration of an unknown field. . . . Everything I discovered was new and most of it was really valuable."

In the course of the Illinois Survey, Hamilton came into contact with hundreds of sick workers, from whom she elicited disturbing stories of sickness and suffering. She credited her successful interviewing techniques to the years she had spent at Hull House, which had made her quite comfortable "going straight to the homes of people about whom I wished to learn something and talking to them in their own surroundings, where they have courage to speak out what is in their minds." Almost all the men with whom she spoke were immigrants; Hamilton felt sure that many factory managers, bent on getting the cheapest labor possible, took advantage of immigrants' inability to communicate and their desperate poverty. With no family nor means, a man took whatever job he could find, no matter what the dangers. Hamilton argued that the employers viewed the situation with cold indifference: if the job "proved to be one that weakened and crippled them—well, that was their bad luck!"

Within a year, Hamilton presented her findings to the commission. Her first investigation had examined the hazards of lead manufacturing. She quickly determined that lead poisoning occurred when workers inhaled lead fumes and dust, not when they handled their food with unwashed hands as had always been assumed by employers. Moreover, it soon became clear that lead poisoning had a number of different symptoms, not all of which were easily identified, but all of which eventually led to utter debilitation. She later described one of the poisoned men she met in this way:

> A Hungarian, thirty-six years old, worked for seven years grinding lead paint. During this time he had three attacks of colic, with vomiting and headache. I saw him in the hospital, a skeleton of a man, looking almost twice his age, his limbs soft and flabby, his muscles wasted. He was extremely emaciated, his color was a dirty grayish yellow, his eyes dull and expressionless.

At the end of the survey, Hamilton had documented at least 578 cases of lead poisoning like this, a conservative number in her estimation. In light of the commission's findings, Illinois passed a law requiring employers to adequately protect those employees who worked with certain toxins, including lead and arsenic. Moreover, the new law mandated strict rules for the reporting of work-related diseases to the state's factory inspection department.

During her time with the Illinois survey, Hamilton had been invited to attend the International Congress on Occupational Accidents and Diseases which had convened in Brussels, Belgium. While there, she met Charles O'Neill, commissioner of the Bureau of Labor for the U.S. government (the Department of Labor did not exist until 1912), and a kindred spirit on the subject of "the deplorable impression our country made" in regard to industrial safety. After returning to the United States, Hamilton received a letter from O'Neill, in which he asked her to officially become an agent of the Bureau of Labor and begin a federal survey like the one she was performing for Illinois. She would have no supervisor and no salary; instead, she would work on her own terms and once she had written a report on each investigation, the government would simply purchase it from her.

The federal survey required that she give up her pathology work at Northwestern, but she saw this as a great opportunity. As she recalled later in her autobiography:

> I had long been convinced that it was not in me to be anything more than a fourth-rate bacteriologist. Interesting as I found the subject, and pleasant as I found the life, I was never absorbed in it. . . . I never have doubted the wisdom of my decision to give it up and devote myself to work which has been scientific only in part, but human and practical in greater measure.

After many years, Hamilton had finally found her vocation in a pursuit which allowed her to use her scientific training to further the social ends so close to her heart. Just as she had in the Illinois survey, Hamilton began her federal work with an investigation of white-lead and lead-oxide production. In her travels to Omaha, St. Louis, Cincinnati, Pittsburgh, Philadelphia, and New York, Hamilton repeatedly encountered industries that employed men on the lowest rung of the social ladder, subjected them to profound physical hazards, and then blamed their diseases on perceived ethnic or racial failings. Lack of cleanliness, general laziness, stupidity, or inborn weaknesses were repeatedly blamed for the occurrence of "lead fits" or "lead palsy." One of the biggest challenges that Hamilton faced was to convince employers that their work endangered the laborers and that with little trouble, the risks could be significantly lessened. Although she met with stubborn resistance from some, Hamilton believed that by spreading the word, publishing her reports, and personally encouraging employers to change their practices, she would be able to enlighten them and thereby alter their point of view.

Hamilton's first federal survey was published by the Bureau of Labor in 1911. In it, she documented conditions at 22 of the 25 lead factories in the country, isolated 358 cases of lead poisoning, and established herself as an expert on the subject. By the time the report was published, at least half of the factories she visited had already made improvements in their facilities. Impressed with her initial efforts, the government next asked Hamilton to investigate lead poisoning in ancillary trades which used lead in the production of other items, rather than the making of lead itself. She published extensive reports on the pottery, tile, and porcelain enameled sanitary ware (i.e. bathtub) industries; the painters' trade; the printers trades; the production of storage batteries; and the manufacture of rubber.

Hamilton's carefully documented studies undermined the long-held belief that American factories were safer than European industry simply by virtue of their being American. Moreover, by refusing to limit herself to mere analysis, she was able to advocate change to factory owners. As **Barbara Sicherman** has noted, "Convinced that any man of goodwill would do the right thing once he knew the truth, she had an uncanny ability to appeal to the best instincts of others." Using a combination of persistence, persuasion, and publicity, Hamilton successfully brought the attention of Americans to the problem of occupational safety and the disproportionate risk industrial diseases posed to the working classes. Her assiduous research was matched only by her commitment to social justice; she did everything with a sense of solemn responsibility for the welfare of the poorest and least represented in American society.

While she continued to investigate the dangerous trades throughout the 1910s and 1920s, Hamilton expanded her professional life beyond the survey work. In 1919, she became the first woman ever appointed to a professorship at Harvard University, where she taught industrial toxicology, the scientific study of the effects of industrial poisons on humans. In 1923, she began a ten-year stint as a medical consultant to the General Electric Company. During the late 1920s and early 1930s, she published two well-received books on industrial poisons and served on President Herbert Hoover's Research Committee on Social Trends. After retiring from Harvard (upon being asked to do so) in 1935, she found work with the Department of Labor as a consultant to the Division of Labor Standards. During 1937, she embarked on her last detailed and original investigation of the dangerous trades, a survey of the viscose rayon industry, and began giving annual lectures on toxicology at the Women's Medical College of Pennsylvania.

Throughout her busy professional career, Hamilton had also embraced a wide range of social causes, including Jane Addams' Women's International League for Peace and Freedom and *Margaret Sanger's campaign for birth control, for which she wrote *Poverty and Birth Control* in 1921. Even as she moved into her 70s and 80s, Hamilton remained actively engaged in the prominent social issues of the day, writing and speaking on subjects ranging from trade unions to McCarthyism.

In 1943, while living with her younger sister, **Margaret Hamilton**, at Hadlyme, Connecticut, Hamilton wrote her autobiography, *Exploring the Dangerous Trades*. In 1947, she became the first woman to receive the Lasker Award in public health, which was followed by numerous distinctions and prizes over the next two decades. At age 88, she wrote to a friend that "life is still as interesting as ever," and, as she predicted to another correspondent, she lived longer than any of her contemporaries. In 1970, Hamilton died in Hadlyme at the age of 101, having changed the face of industry and radicalized the cause of public health in America.

SOURCES:

Hamilton, Alice. *Exploring the Dangerous Trades.* Boston, MA: Little, Brown, 1943.

Sicherman, Barbara. *Alice Hamilton: A Life in Letters.* Cambridge, MA: Harvard University Press, 1984.

SUGGESTED READING:

Addams, Jane. *Twenty Years at Hull House with autobiographical notes.* Illustrated by Norah Hamilton, with an introduction and notes by James Hurt. Urbana: University of Illinois Press, 1990.

———, Emily G. Balch, and Alice Hamilton. *Women at the Hague: The International Congress of Women and Its Results.* NY: Garland Publishers, 1972 (reprint of 1915 edition).

COLLECTIONS:

Correspondence and papers located at the Schlesinger Library of Radcliffe College in Cambridge, Massachusetts; also see relevant material in collection of Radcliffe College's "Women in Science Exhibit" of 1936, similarly located in the Schlesinger Library.

Margaret M. Storey,
Assistant Professor of History,
DePaul University, Chicago, Illinois

Hamilton, Anne (1636–1716)

Duchess of Hamilton. Born on December 24, 1636 (some sources cite 1634); died on October 17, 1716; daughter of James Hamilton (b. 1606), 1st duke of Hamilton, and *Mary Hamilton (1613–1638); married William Douglas (1635–1694), 1st earl of Selkirk, 3rd duke of Hamilton (r. 1660–1694), on April 29, 1656; children: James Douglas-Hamilton (1658–1712), 4th duke of Hamilton; William Hamilton; Charles Hamilton (1662–1739), 2nd earl of Selkirk; John Hamilton (1665–1744), 3rd earl of Selkirk; Archibald Douglas-Hamilton (1673–1754, governor of Jamaica); George Hamilton, 1st earl of Orkney (r. 1696–1737); Basil Hamilton (1671–1701); Mary Hamilton (1657–died before 1683); Catherine Hamilton (d. 1707, who married John Murray, 1st duke of Atholl); Susannah Hamilton (d. 1736, who married Charles Hay, 3rd marquess of Tweeddale); Margaret Hamilton (d. 1731).

Anne Hamilton was born in 1636, the daughter of Mary Hamilton and James Hamilton, the first duke of Hamilton. It was because of her petition that her husband William Douglas, royal commissioner under William III, became the third duke of Hamilton.

Hamilton, Anne (1766–1846)

Lady-in-waiting to Queen Caroline of Brunswick. Name variations: Lady Anne Hamilton. Born in 1766; died in 1846; daughter of Archibald, 9th duke of Hamilton; sister of Lord Archibald Hamilton (1770–1827).

As lady-in-waiting, Lady Anne Hamilton accompanied *Caroline of Brunswick on the queen's return to England from exile in 1820. Lady Hamilton's book, *Secret History of the Court*, was published under her name without her consent.

Hamilton, Betsey (1757–c. 1854).

See Hamilton, Elizabeth Schuyler.

Hamilton, Catherine (1738–1782).

See Hamilton, Emma for sidebar.

Hamilton, Cicely (1872–1952)

English author, playwright, actress, and suffragist. Name variations: Cicely Hammill. Born on June 15, 1872, in Kensington, London, England; died on December 5, 1952, in London, England; daughter of Captain Denzil Hammill and Maude Piers Hammill (Irish); educated at private schools in England and Germany; never married.

Cicely Hammill, who was born in Kensington, London, in 1872, to **Maude Piers Hammill** and Captain Denzil Hammill, a commander of a Highland regiment, turned to writing and acting to help support the family when their finances declined. She worked for a short time as a teacher in the Midlands but soon took to writing and acting, assuming Hamilton as a stage name.

Hamilton began her writing career with novels and detective mysteries but found her calling when she produced three one-act plays for an all-women performing company, the Pioneer Players. Developing feminist themes, she wrote *Just to Get Married* and *The Cutting of the Knot* (later published as the novel *A Matter of Money*) in 1906. She experienced her first major success with the production of *Diana of Dobson's* (1908), a comedy with a more serious underlying theme about the inequities of wealth and the exploitation of working women. In 1908, her interest in feminism blossomed when she co-founded, with **Bessie Hatton**, the Women Writers' Suffrage League, an arm of the National Union of Suffrage Societies. She produced two plays in quick succession, *How the Vote was Won* (1909) and *The Pageant of Great Women* (1909). Both plays dealt with the achievements of women. That same year, she produced *Marriage as a Trade* where she argued that women do not marry so much by choice as by economic requirement. *The Child in Flanders* (1917), a modern nativity play, and *The Old Adam* (1925), about the spirit of men in war, both played to critical acclaim.

Throughout World War I, Hamilton lived in France, working as a military hospital administrator and helping to arrange for entertainment for the patients. During this time, her pacifist views took hold. She wrote *Senlis* (1917), the story of the destruction of a French village and its population by the German army. She followed this with *William: An Englishman* (1919), an anti-war novel that won the Femina Vie Heureuse Prize in 1919. After the war, she continued to promote pacifism, writing *Theodore Savage* (1922), a story of a society destroyed by scientific warfare.

In the 1920s, Hamilton returned to her feminist views as a journalist and commentator. She also began to expand on her topics, writing a history of the Old Vic in 1926 and writing a series of travel books, beginning with Germany in 1931 and continuing with many European countries throughout the 1930s. Although she continued to write plays and novels, she turned to politics in the 1930s and 1940s, writing her treatise *Lament for Democracy* in 1940. In 1935, she published her autobiography *Life Errant*.

Early in life, Hamilton's talents traveled beyond writing to acting. Her best-known performances were in George Bernard Shaw's *Fanny's First Play* (1911) and J.M. Barrie's *The Twelve-Pound Look* (1913). She was awarded a civil-list pension in 1938, and died in London on December 5, 1952.

Judith C. Reveal,
freelance writer, Greensboro, Maryland

Hamilton, Clara Decima (1909–1983).

See Norman, Decima.

Hamilton, duchess of.

See Hamilton, Mary (1613–1638).
See Hamilton, Anne (1636–1716).
See Gunning, Elizabeth (1734–1790).
See Marie of Baden (1817–1888).

Hamilton, Edith (1867–1963)

Scholar of the ancient classical world who communicated her passion to her students as well as readers of **The Greek Way.** *Born Edith Hamilton on August 12, 1867, in Dresden, Germany, of American parents; died on May 31, 1963, in Washington, D.C; daughter of Montgomery Hamilton and* **Gertrude Pond Hamilton;** *sister of industrial reformer Alice Hamilton (1869–1979) and artist Norah Hamilton (b. 1873); was home schooled until 16; attended Miss Porter's School in Connecticut for two years; Bryn Mawr College, B.A., M.A., 1894; studied classics in Germany at the University of Leipzig, 1895; first female classics student at the University of Munich; never married; lived with Doris Reid; children: adopted Dorian Reid in later life.*

Took over administration of Bryn Mawr School in Baltimore (1896); served as headmistress (1906–22); after retirement, began second career as essayist on the classics, first in New York City (1924–43), then Washington, D.C. (1943–63); actively involved in the arts until her death at age 95.

Selected writings: The Greek Way *(1930, revised, 1942, 1948);* The Roman Way *(1932);* Three Greek Plays *(1937);* Mythology *(1942);* Witnesses to the Truth: Christ and His Interpreters *(1948, revised, 1957);* Spokesmen for God *(1949);* The Echo of Greece *(1957); (coedited with Huntington Cairns)*

Collected Dialogues of Plato *(1961). Reviews and essays collected in* The Ever Present Past *(1964).*

Edith Hamilton achieved fame as an essayist on the ancient world, but only her closest friends realized that writing was actually her second successful career, launched after her retirement as headmistress of the Bryn Mawr School in Baltimore. In every activity she undertook during her long life, however, Hamilton stressed the importance of intellectual excellence and clear thinking. She was as familiar with the literature of ancient Greece as she was with the Nobel winners of the 20th century, and as quick to point out the dangers of ignorance in the atomic age as well as the Biblical era. As educator, commentator, and author, she encouraged all to be "caught up in the world of thought."

Edith Hamilton's commitment to promoting education was spurred by her own mental gifts as well as by her uneven experiences as a young woman seeking quality education. Hamilton never actually attended school until the age of 17. In many families, this would have left a severe academic handicap, but the Hamilton family was not ordinary. In the closing years of the American Civil War, Montgomery Hamilton of Indiana had been sent abroad by his family to recuperate from his military service. While in Germany, he met and married Gertrude Pond, a New Yorker, whose family had moved abroad to manage their sugar business during the war years. Shortly before the couple returned to the Hamilton farm in Fort Wayne, Indiana, their first child, Edith, was born in Dresden.

In Indiana, the young Hamiltons lived in the shadow of Montgomery's father, an Irish immigrant who had become a successful farmer and entrepreneur, and Montgomery's mother, an avid reader and fan of *Susan B. Anthony. Montgomery never inherited his father's commercial talents, but he shared his mother's reverence for books and her insistence that women as well as men deserved a superior education. The Hamilton children had no formal lessons but were pressed to read history and literature by their parents. They were taught French by Gertrude, German by the servants, and Latin and Greek by Montgomery. Edith remembered sitting down to study Latin with her father at age seven.

Edith thrived during her years of home schooling. She was a "natural storyteller" who would entertain her siblings and cousins by reciting poems and retelling favorite stories. Often she would leave off the endings to make the younger ones read the works themselves. Although Edith was considered by her siblings to be the star pupil, all the Hamilton's later enjoyed active intellectual lives. *Alice Hamilton, the second child, became a physician specializing in industrial medicine and the first female to serve on the faculty of Harvard Medical School. Quint and Margaret Hamilton became teachers, while Norah Hamilton pursued a career as an artist associated with Hull House in Chicago.

As each turned 17, the young women of the family were sent to Miss Porter's School in Connecticut for two years. Miss Porter's, one of the most famous finishing schools for young women in the nation, exposed Edith to students from different backgrounds but did little for her academics. The school was typical of the schools of the era in that it emphasized social preparation rather than intellectual training. Students were allowed to avoid the subjects they disliked, and even the subjects which Edith enjoyed were taught with little enthusiasm. Alice Hamilton remembered the classics professor staring at the ceiling while his charges recited passages from the text. There was little opportunity for discussion, and few teachers expected the young women to take an interest in the material.

The flaws of their secondary education became more apparent when Edith and Alice returned home to Indiana. The two sisters quickly assessed the diminished family financial situation and decided to prepare themselves for professional careers. Alice chose to enter medicine, while Edith decided to seek a teaching career. Miss Porter's had done nothing to prepare the two for college entrance exams. For example, Edith, who had never studied mathematics in her life, would now have to pass an exam in trigonometry. After a year of home study in Indiana, she passed the entrance exam to Bryn Mawr College and left for Pennsylvania.

Bryn Mawr was decidedly different from Miss Porter's. When Edith arrived in the early 1890s, the school had been open barely ten years. *M. Carey Thomas, a tireless champion of women's education, had recently assumed the presidency. Thomas' insistence that women should prepare themselves to be self-supporting was highly controversial. More typical was the opinion of G. Stanley Hall, the president of Clark University, who insisted in 1904 that education led to "mental strain" in women and promoted a "slow evolution of fertility" that ruined the institutions of marriage and the family. Even some of the Bryn Mawr faculty, chosen from the most promising young scholars of their fields, had reservations about the college. Woodrow

Wilson, who joined the staff as a young professor of political science in the 1880s, worried that teaching women would harm his professional reputation. For Edith Hamilton, however, Bryn Mawr provided not controversy but the intellectual challenges she craved.

Greece never lost sight of the individual, and I'm afraid we have; that frightens me much more than the Sputniks and the atomic bombs.

—Edith Hamilton

After only two years of study, Edith graduated from Bryn Mawr in 1894 with a B.A. and an M.A. in Classics. She was awarded a fellowship to study in Europe, and she and Alice (who had recently completed medical school) decided to spend a year in Germany, first at the University of Leipzig, then at the University of Munich. The two soon found that the prejudice against women in academics was not confined to the United States. Edith's request to study Latin and Greek literature at the University of Munich stunned the classics department. No women had ever enrolled in the lectures, and, because many of the students were divinity students, it was assumed that the presence of a woman would be offensive and disruptive. After intense debate, Edith was accepted, but the question of her seating still provoked concern. Some faculty proposed that she be seated in a specially constructed, curtained cubicle where she could listen but would not be seen. In the end, Edith was seated on the stage behind the lecturer, in full view of the students, but safely away from physical contact with the divinity students. Alice's experience in the laboratories of the university was less dramatic, but both sisters noted that they were only tolerated at the universities because they were foreign women. German women would have faced far greater opposition.

In 1896, M. Carey Thomas wrote Edith and asked her if she would consider taking over the administration of the Bryn Mawr School in Baltimore. An extension of Bryn Mawr College, it was the only women's private high school in the nation which aimed strictly at college preparation. Although a few other public and private women's high schools were capable of preparing students for college entrance exams, the Bryn Mawr School was the only school which did not offer an easier, non-college prep track. All students were required to pass the entrance exam for Bryn Mawr College in order to graduate.

Thomas, who was from Baltimore, understood that few Baltimore families felt comfortable with the intellectual and physical demands made of their daughters at the school. Thomas knew that any administrator would face a difficult time maintaining the high standards of the school, and her invitation to Edith Hamilton was a mark of great respect. Although Edith had once considered completing a Ph.D. while in Germany, she was unimpressed with the education she was receiving in Munich and ready to return to the States. In 1896, she settled in Baltimore.

Although Hamilton remembered feeling "terrified" and unqualified initially, she became a successful administrator. She maintained the high intellectual tone of the school, despite frequent parental requests to simplify the curriculum, and was revered by her students. One recalled that Hamilton brought with her the "air of having come from some high center of civilization." She was not afraid to branch out from traditional academic concerns; her proposal that the Bryn Mawr basketball team play a match against another nearby girls' school was regarded as scandalous because the girls' names would be reported in the newspapers. Hamilton met with the editors of the Baltimore press to request their cooperation, and the match was played without news coverage. In 1906, Hamilton's talents were recognized when M. Carey Thomas appointed her first headmistress of the school. There had been no headmistress during the early years of the high school. Thomas felt that teachers had an easier time resisting the opposition of the parents if complaints had to travel the 125 miles to Thomas' office in Pennsylvania.

In 1922, after 26 years with the Bryn Mawr School, Edith Hamilton retired. Though only 54 years old, she was physically and emotionally exhausted and anxious to leave behind both the responsibilities of headmistress and the social circles of Baltimore which had never fully understood her commitment to education for women. The one exception was the family of a former student, **Doris Reid**. Doris' parents had formed a close friendship with Edith and invited her to vacation with them for several summers on Mount Desert Isle, Maine. The year of her retirement, Edith had the vacation cottage winterized and remained on the nearly deserted island with Doris, and Doris' five-year-old nephew Dorian Reid. Years later, Edith spoke of this year as a dark period of her life when she battled depression and feelings of failure. During the winter, however, she gradually recovered her health and enthusiasm. She alternated her time between reading her much-loved British detective stories and tutoring Dorian. By 1924, when Doris ac-

cepted a job in New York City, Edith was ready to move on as well.

During her first years in New York, Hamilton considered herself a retiree whose prime responsibility was in providing a safe and happy home for Doris, Dorian, and Dorian's siblings, who, for family reasons, soon joined the household. Throughout their lives, the Reid children remained close to Hamilton. Many of them lived with Doris and Edith until they left for college and joined them for summers in Maine even after they had spouses and children of their own.

Gradually, Hamilton's circle began to grow beyond her new family, and within a few years she had established what one friend, John Mason Brown, recalled as the "Edith Hamilton Club." Her circle included publishers, editors, and writers who listened attentively as Hamilton explained the virtues of classical literature. One remembered that she spoke of the ancient authors as if they were her own children, anxious that all her listeners would befriend them. Another, who worked for *Theatre Arts Monthly*, encouraged Hamilton to write up her discussions. Hamilton protested but eventually published several essays on Greek literature in the magazine. The essays caught the eye of an editor at Norton, who began pressuring Hamilton to produce a book. Again, Hamilton protested. The editor continued to pursue her, and years later, when Hamilton was asked how she began her writing career, she insisted, "I was bullied into it."

The Greek Way, a collection of essays on the esthetics of Greek literature published in 1930, launched Hamilton in a new career at the age of 62. She had worried that libraries were filled with books on the classical world, and that yet another book (especially one by an unknown and uncredentialed author) would pass unnoticed. Initially, her fears seemed justified, the book received favorable reviews but inspired no dramatic sales. Over time, however, interest in the book increased rather than declined. *The Greek Way* went through several reprintings and in 1957, 27 years after its publication, remained so popular that it was chosen as a Book-of-the-Month-Club selection. Hamilton followed the first work with *The Roman Way* (1932), *Three Greek Plays* (1937), *Mythology* (1942), *Witnesses to the Truth* (1948), *Spokesmen for God* (1949), *The Echo of Greece* (1957), and *The Collected Dialogues of Plato* (1961).

Hamilton's popularity was not due to her subject matter so much as her understandable and intriguing writing style. She did not offer her readers finished judgments on the literature of the ancient world but invited them to join with her in exploring the mental worlds of the past. Hamilton used the same techniques she had used on her siblings as a child: she teased the reader with the implications of the literature but left out any plot synopsis. Her work had to be read as a companion to the literature, not a substitute. Finally, Hamilton avoided the techniques of the professors she endured in Leipzig and Munich, who seemed more interested in the grammar of the ancient Greek and Latin than in the ideas conveyed. Her words in the preface to *The Roman Way* easily explain Hamilton's approach to all literature, "What the Romans did has always interested me much less than what they were, and what historians have said they were is beyond all comparison less interesting to me than what they themselves said."

Hamilton was always quick to point out the relevance of ancient literature to contemporary debates, but she did not restrict her energy to studies of Greece and Rome. *Witnesses to the Truth* explored the world of the early Christian writers, while *Spokesmen for God* examined the Old Testament prophets. Nor did Hamilton shy away from discussing 20th-century literature. In 1929, her essay "Sad Young Men" lambasted Joseph Wood Krutch, Aldous Huxley, and their brethren for their attitude of fashionable despair with modern life. Hamilton found nothing original in their lamentations. She encouraged them to read a bit more widely in order to see that their assumption of "decay" was nothing new; hopelessness, she said, was a perennial cry of humankind. Ironically, it was Hamilton, the 60-year-old classicist, who encouraged the young modernists to concentrate on the advantages of the present. What, she wondered, would Mr. Huxley do if "confronted with a sabre-toothed tiger, when he cannot face a Victrola and can hardly endure a motor car?" In 1952, she penned a similarly controversial critique of William Faulkner, who had recently won a Nobel Prize. While admitting his gifts as a writer, she questioned his "puritanical" discomfort with women's sexuality and his insistence

Edith Hamilton

on a reverse romanticism that tainted all with moral filth. John Mason Brown noted that every work of Hamilton's reflected her preoccupation with the "moral and intellectual foundations of modern civilization."

In 1943, the Hamilton-Reid household moved to Washington, D.C., where Doris had accepted a new job. Edith was 75 at the time, but her writing energy was undiminished. Her writing habits, however, drove publishers crazy. She wrote on scraps of paper and the backs of envelopes; an editor once called her about a fragment of a soup recipe that appeared in the middle of a poetry translation.

During these years, Hamilton became a respected commentator on education. Just as she had at Bryn Mawr, she maintained her insistence on quality education as a fundamental condition for civilization. She reminded Americans that the Greeks and Romans were important not only for what they had done, but for how they had failed. In 1932, she compared American technological achievements to the advances of the Roman empire, but reminded her readers that the Roman "failure of mind and spirit" occurred when material development outstripped human development. In 1958, during the debate over the National Defense in Education Act (a Cold War initiative to preserve American superiority through specific education programs), she noted that "beating the Russians" was not a healthy rationale for education. More pointedly, she stressed that the Greek democracies had collapsed due to the decay of domestic civic culture, not foreign threats.

During her final years, Edith Hamilton was honored at home and abroad. In Washington, she was sought out by writers such as Robert Lowell, Stephen Spender, and Robert Frost, as well as by cultural representatives of President John F. Kennedy, who sought her opinion on the construction of a new cultural center (later known as the Kennedy Center) on the Potomac. She was granted honorary degrees by the University of Rochester, the University of Pennsylvania, and Yale University, and offered the Women's National Press Club Award and the Jane Addams Medal for Distinguished Service. In 1957, Hamilton journeyed to Athens at the invitation of the Greek government where King Paul I presented her with the Gold Cross of the Legion of Benefaction and the mayor of Athens made her an honorary citizen. During her final years, she recorded programs for network television and the Voice of America, and made several pleasure trips to Europe with Doris. When Hamilton was 92, an editor asked if she would consider translating the *Oresteia*. "No," she responded, "I am saving translating for my old age." In 1963, Edith Hamilton died at home in Washington of natural causes.

SOURCES:

Brown, John Mason. "The Heritage of Edith Hamilton: 1867–1963," in *Saturday Review*. June 22, 1963, p. 16–17.

"Edith Hamilton," in *The New York Times*. June 1, 1963, p. 22.

Hamilton, Alice. *Exploring the Dangerous Trades: The Autobiography of Alice Hamilton, MD*. Boston, MA: Little, Brown, 1943.

Knight, Edgar. ed. *Readings in American Educational History*. Appleton, 1951.

Reid, Doris. *Edith Hamilton: An Intimate Portrait*. NY: W.W. Norton, 1967.

RELATED MEDIA:

"A Conversation with Edith Hamilton" (Broadcast) Wisdom Series, NBC, 1959.

"Echoes of Greece" (sound recording), Recorded live at the Institute of Contemporary Arts in Washington, D.C., January 31, 1958, Spoken Arts, c. 1966.

COLLECTIONS:

Hamilton Family Papers and Edith Hamilton Papers filed at Schlesinger Library, Radcliffe College. (Most early family papers were destroyed by a flood in 1938.)

Janice Lee Jayes,
Department of History, The American University, Washington, D.C.

Hamilton, Elizabeth (c. 1480–?)

*Countess of Lennox. Born around 1480; daughter of James Hamilton, 1st Lord Hamilton (d. 1479), and *Mary Stewart (d. 1488, daughter of James II of Scotland and *Mary of Guelders); married Matthew Stewart, 2nd earl of Lennox; children: John Stewart, 3rd earl of Lennox (murdered by royal architect James Hamilton of Finnart in 1536).*

Hamilton, Elizabeth (1641–1708)

*Countess of Grammont. Name variations: La Belle Hamilton. Born in 1641, probably in County Tyrone, Ireland; died in 1708; daughter of Sir George Hamilton, 1st baronet and governor of Nenagh (d. 1679); sister of Anthony Hamilton (c. 1646–c. 1720, author of *Mémoires du Comte de Grammont*); married Philibert, comte de Grammont, in 1663 (died 1707).*

Elizabeth Hamilton was known as one of the most brilliant and beautiful women at the court of Charles II. She married the gambler and libertine Philibert, count of Grammont in 1663, at the instigation of her Royalist brother Anthony Hamilton, and moved to France the following year. Her husband's memoirs (*Mémoires du*

Comte de Grammont), a French classic, concerned the amorous intrigues at the court of Charles II. The first half of the book was supposedly dictated to Anthony Hamilton by the count; the second half was presumed to be the creation of Anthony Hamilton. The book appeared anonymously in 1713. It was edited by Horace Walpole in 1772, Sir Walter Scott in 1811, and M. de Lescure in 1876. Elizabeth Hamilton's portrait was painted by Lely.

Hamilton, Elizabeth (c. 1657–1733).

See Villiers, Elizabeth.

Hamilton, Elizabeth (1734–1790).

See Gunning, Elizabeth.

Hamilton, Elizabeth (1758–1816)

Reformist writer in early 19th-century Britain who argued for the education of women and for charity toward the needy. Name variations: (pseudonym) Almeria. Born on July 21, 1758, in Belfast, Ireland; died on July 23, 1816, in Harrogate, Yorkshire, England; daughter of Charles Hamilton and Katherine Mackay Hamilton; never married.

Moved to Scotland (1772); began to collaborate with scholar brother (1766); published first novel (1796); granted royal pension (1804); tutored in Edinburgh (c. 1805); wrote popular "domestic" novel (1808).

Selected writings: Translation of the Letters of a Hindoo Rajah *(1796);* Memoirs of Modern Philosophers *(1800);* Letters on the Elementary Principles of Education *(1801);* Memoirs of the Life of Agrippina, Wife of Germanicus *(1804);* Letters Addressed to the Daughter of a Nobleman *(1806);* The Cottagers of Glenburnie *(1808);* Exercises in Religious Knowledge *(1809);* Popular Essays on the Elementary Principles of the Human Mind *(1812);* Hints Addressed to Patrons and Directors of Schools *(1815); (edited by Elizabeth Ogilvy Benger and published posthumously)* Memoirs of the Late Mrs. Elizabeth Hamilton with a Selection from Her Correspondence and Other Unpublished Writings *(1818).*

Elizabeth Hamilton was a reform-minded British author whose writings espouse a moderate feminism, and were infused with a decidedly Episcopalian sense of charity. Never married, Hamilton supported herself through her writing.

She was born in Belfast, Ireland, in 1758 to Charles Hamilton, a merchant, and **Katherine Mackay Hamilton**. The family was of Scottish descent but had been grounded in Ireland since the emigration of an ancestor the century prior. Charles Hamilton died of typhus when Elizabeth was still an infant, and Katherine Hamilton was forced to place all three of her children into homes of relatives or acquaintances, because she knew that as a widow she could not adequately provide for them or their education. Elizabeth, the youngest, was sent to live with an aunt and uncle, the Marshalls. She was fortunate to attend a coeducational primary school, then as a teenager moved with them to Scotland. Later Hamilton recalled her childhood as a happy one, because her guardians had encouraged her to read. She tried to hide her interest in books on philosophy and theology, however, since such topics were considered inappropriate for young women.

In 1772, Hamilton renewed contact with her older brother Charles, not long before he departed to serve in the British colonial forces in India. They corresponded, and he also encouraged her pursuit of further learning and exposed her to progressive ideas and political strains. He was an "Orientalist," a scholar of the Asian subcontinent and pro-Indian, and before his death in 1792 he worked actively to reform British attitudes toward its lucrative colonial possession. At one point, Charles wanted Elizabeth to visit him in India, in the hope that she would find a husband from among his colleagues, but she declined. Yet she did keep her passion for writing and her modest success with published articles a secret to those outside her family for many years, lest she be deemed a poor candidate for a wife.

Hamilton lived with her aunt and uncle well into her adulthood, and after her brother returned from India in 1786 she and her sister Katherine moved to London with him. She also began to help him with his scholarly work, including translations. After his death in 1792, she and Katherine, greatly saddened, relocated to the Suffolk countryside and later to Berkshire. In 1796, Hamilton's first novel, *Translation of the Letters of a Hindoo Rajah,* appeared in print. The work was a homage to her brother, the fictional account of an Enlightenment-minded British army captain who tutors a Hindu prince. Her character of Captain Percy is modeled on her brother, and the character Charlotte, his sister, upon herself. In the book, through the writings of the Indian prince, Hamilton is able to offer a critical view of English society, exposing its foibles and the decadence of the era. Other passages skewer the colonial bureaucracy in India.

By the turn of the century, Hamilton and her sister had moved to Bath and she saw her second novel published. In *Memoirs of Modern Philosophers* (1800), she lampoons the more radical feminists of her era, such as *Mary Hays and *Mary Wollstonecraft. More of a moderate feminist who believed in the "women's sphere"—in other words, that women could achieve the highest form of success at home and in raising a family—Hamilton believed in a Christian ideology in perspective while still progressive in spirit. *Memoirs of Modern Philosophers*, published anonymously, offered a counterargument to what was known as the "Godwin" group, the intellectual circle centered around William Godwin, who was the husband of Wollstonecraft, and his anarchistic beliefs. With this satire, Hamilton directed criticism against some of her fellow Britons, especially in the upper classes, who displayed little sense of charity to the poor.

Yet Hamilton also gained renown for her writings on education, and in some ways shared many of the same views as Wollstonecraft, who argued for equal access to learning for women in her groundbreaking *On the Vindication of the Rights of Women* (1792). In Hamilton's 1801 work, *Letters on the Elementary Principles of Education,* she penned a series of interrelated essays on philosophy and the education of women that would help women play a greater social and political role in Britain. She returned to the novel format with the 1804 opus *Memoirs of the Life of Agrippina, Wife of Germanicus,* which was essentially a fictionalized account of *Agrippina the Elder. This work was rather progressive in its day for its sheer presence as a biography of a female historical figure—a topic of scarcity at the start of the 19th century. Agrippina was the mother of the notorious Caligula, the Roman emperor of the 1st century CE, as well as the adoptive grandmother of Nero, the first emperor to persecute Europe's new Christians on a systematic scale. With Hamilton's Episcopalian outlook, her work does not romanticize classical culture, but instead shows how decadence caused a mighty empire to fall from within. The Roman era and its decline were topics of intellectual pursuit in the England of Hamilton's day, and similarities between the two civilizations were analyzed by many others. Most notably in her *Memoirs of the Life of Agrippina,* Hamilton attempted to show how a mother—by remaining within the feminine sphere—might influence her child, and in turn could shape political destinies and indeed the world.

For her achievements, Hamilton was granted a royal pension in 1804, and from that year on she resided with her sister in Edinburgh.

There she became a tutor to a lord's daughters, which inspired her 1806 book *Letters Addressed to the Daughter of a Nobleman.* She also became involved in the Edinburgh House of Industry, a charitable establishment that helped impoverished women gain work skills. Far from a dour do-gooder, however, the unmarried Hamilton was known for her great parties and held a Monday evening salon at her Edinburgh home. She also lent support and encouragement to other women writers.

Her most lasting contribution was perhaps her 1808 novel *The Cottagers of Glenburnie.* It chronicles the efforts of Betty Mason, a virtuous yet practical-minded woman who has greatly bettered her station in life through hard work and common sense. Mason retires to a Scottish village notorious for its poverty and amorality, and predictably succeeds in cleaning Glenburnie up house by house. This work became a commercial success in the social-realism vein, a genre later popularized by Charles Dickens. Hamilton also wrote two other nonfiction works, *Exercises in Religious Knowledge* (1809) and *Hints Addressed to Patrons and Directors of Schools.* The latter work, published in 1815, echoed many of the themes espoused by Swiss educational reformer Johann Pestalozzi, who also supported the idea of women having equal access to learning. In this book, Hamilton writes of the way in which young boys from impoverished backgrounds seem more intelligent than girls of their age from the same class, but points out that this is probably the result of the common practice of confining girls to the home; boys, on the other hand, are set free to play and roam about, and thus gain needed stimulation and interaction.

Hamilton, who had long suffered from gout, traveled to Harrogate in Yorkshire for the treatment of an eye condition. She died there on July 23, 1816, just two days after her 58th birthday. *Memoirs of the Late Mrs. Elizabeth Hamilton with a Selection from Her Correspondence and Other Unpublished Writings,* edited by **Elizabeth Ogilvy Benger,** appeared in 1818. Both *Jane Austen and Sir Walter Scott were familiar with Hamilton's work and gave it praise.

SOURCES:

British Authors of the Nineteenth Century. Edited by Stanley J. Kunitz. NY: H.W. Wilson, 1936.

Dictionary of Ulster Biography. Compiled by Kate Newmann. Belfast: The Institute of Irish Studies Queens's University of Belfast, 1993.

Kelly, Gary. "Elizabeth Hamilton," in *Dictionary of Literary Biography,* Vol. 158: *British Reform Writers, 1789–1832.* Edited by Gary Kelly. Detroit, MI: Gale Research, 1996, pp. 119–123.

The Oxford Guide to British Women Writers. Edited by Joanne Shattock. Oxford: Oxford University Press, 1993.

Rich, Myra L. "Elizabeth Hamilton," in *Dictionary of Literary Biography*, Vol. 116: *British Romantic Novelists, 1789–1832*. Edited by Bradford K. Mudge. Detroit, MI: Gale Research, 1992, pp. 130–137.

Carol Brennan,
Grosse Pointe, Michigan

Hamilton, Elizabeth Schuyler

(1757–c. 1854)

American promoter of her husband Alexander Hamilton. Name variations: Betsey Hamilton; Mrs. Alexander Hamilton. Born Elizabeth Schuyler in 1757; died around 1854; daughter of General Philip Schuyler; married Alexander Hamilton (1755-1804, American statesman and U.S. secretary of the treasury), on December 14, 1780; children: Philip (d. 1801); Angelica Hamilton; Alexander Hamilton; James Alexander Hamilton; John Church Hamilton; William Stephen Hamilton; Eliza Hamilton; Philip Hamilton (named for the first child who was killed in a duel in 1801).

The wife of American statesman Alexander Hamilton, controversial leader of the Federalist party, Elizabeth Schuyler Hamilton remained a shadowy figure until her husband's death in 1804, when she emerged as one of his most ardent champions. Described as a sickly woman, given to nervous attacks, Hamilton was beleaguered by a long succession of pregnancies, during which she gave birth to eight children and suffered numerous miscarriages. Her marriage was further strained by Alexander's infidelities, one of the most notable being a liaison with **Maria Reynolds**, the wife of a disreputable man with whom Alexander had financial dealings. More troubling to Betsey Hamilton, no doubt, was her husband's close relationship with her attractive sister **Angelica Schuyler**, who wrote to Betsey in 1794, "I love him very much and, if you were as generous as the old Romans, you would lend him to me for a little while." Angelica went on to assure Betsey that she need not "be jealous," since all she wanted was to "promote his glory" and engage in "a little chit-chat." Even so, the Hamilton marriage was said to be comprised of genuine love and mutual respect.

With Alexander's death, Betsey Hamilton's health improved, indeed flourished, and she lived to be 97. During her 50 years of widowhood, she busied herself with elevating her husband's reputation, interviewing and rejecting le-

gions of biographers who refused to write what she dictated. She even initiated a lawsuit with one of Alexander's closest colleagues to obtain papers which she believed would help enhance her husband's reputation. In the end, it was her son John C. Hamilton who finally prepared a biography that met her approval, although it was criticized as overly reverent and exaggerated in claims. The book did not appear until 1840, by which time Betsey Hamilton was an elderly woman.

SOURCES:

Flexner, James. "The American World Was Not Made for Me," in *American Heritage*. December 1977, p. 75–76.

Barbara Morgan,
Melrose, Massachusetts

Elizabeth Schuyler Hamilton

Hamilton, Emma (1765–1815)

Mistress and subsequently wife to the British ambassador to the court of Naples at the close of the 18th century, who became involved in a passionate and scandalous love affair with Admiral Lord Horatio Nelson, the greatest naval leader in British history. Name variations: Emily or Emma Hart; Amy, Emy, Emma, or Emily Lyon. Born Amy Lyon in the spring of 1765 (some sources cite April 26), in the village of Denhall, county of Cheshire, in northwestern England; died in Calais, France, on January 15, 1815; daughter of Henry Lyon (a blacksmith) and Mary Kidd Lyon (a domestic servant); no formal schooling, tutored from 1782 onward in subjects like singing and languages under the auspices of her lovers, Charles Greville and Sir William Hamilton; married Sir William Hamilton, in 1791; had liaison with Lord Horatio Nelson, 1799–1805; children: (father unknown) Emily (b. 1782); (with Nelson) Horatia Nelson (b. 1801); Emma Nelson (died in infancy, 1804).

Started work as domestic servant in Cheshire (1777); moved to London (1778); was mistress of Sir Harry Featherstonhaugh (1781); was mistress of Charles Greville (1782–86); moved to Italy (1786); was mistress of Sir William Hamilton (1786–91); married Hamilton (1791); had first meeting with Nelson (1796); began love affair with Nelson (1799); re-

turned to England (1800); saw the purchase of Merton (1801); death of Hamilton (1803); death of Nelson (1805); left Merton (1808); imprisoned for debt (1813); fled to France (1814).

As actress and rich man's mistress, Emma Hamilton was a product of the dark side of English society in the second half of the 18th century. She later took on a more public role in the turbulent world of Mediterranean politics and military conflict in the era of Napoleon. Finally, she was the scandalous figure who both humanized the great hero Lord Horatio Nelson and placed his reputation under a cloud.

Her simplicity, her courage and her vital beauty have ensured that with all her faults it is not her enemies but Emma who has been remembered.

—Colin Simpson

Eighteenth-century England displayed a society of sharp contrasts. Its landed gentlemen lived in a world of culture and luxury, supported by inherited wealth of substantial, sometimes vast, proportions. To such individuals, a fleeting relationship with a young servant woman or a professional actress was part of their normal quota of pleasures. To women of modest background, especially those in vulnerable positions such as domestic service, only their wits and their sexual attractiveness provided them with tools to use in their own interest. A particularly lucky or talented female might convert a transitory relationship into a marriage that brought stability and a measure of respectability.

Meanwhile, great changes were at work in the public world. By the close of the century, the vast upheaval of the French Revolution had led to dramatic shifts in the entire political order of Europe. France's mobilized military strength, energized by revolutionary fervor, spread outward into neighboring countries where it often found support in the native population. Old forms of government were threatened and often overturned when the French moved in. At the close of the 1790s and in the first decade of the next century, the most effective military instrument in holding back the spread of French power was the British navy. Its most successful and charismatic leader was the young admiral Horatio Nelson, whose life was intertwined with Emma Hamilton over a dramatic, historically crucial period from 1798 to his death in 1805.

Nelson's future mistress and one of the most famous women in British history was born sometime in the spring of 1765. The date some biographers give, in the absence of more precise information, is April 26, 1765. She was the daughter of Henry Lyon, an illiterate blacksmith. Her mother was **Mary Kidd Lyon**, a domestic servant who also worked as a dressmaker. Some writers in Victorian England portrayed Henry as the son of a noble who became involved with the young servant girl and married her against his father's wishes. While some biographers like Colin Simpson still take this account seriously, most authorities reject it as a romantic fabrication. Christened Amy Lyon, the infant soon found herself an orphan: her father died only two months after her birth.

Amy grew up with her mother and grandmother in the family's longtime home region of Flintshire in the northeastern corner of Wales. At age 12 or 13, she followed a family tradition and went to work as a maid in the home of a local doctor and landowner. Soon afterward, she and her mother moved to London where the young girl continued to work as a domestic servant.

Over the next few years, Amy Lyon's life took a variety of turns and many of her activities remain uncertain and poorly documented. She remained a domestic servant in a London doctor's home for only a short time, moving on to become a fringe figure in the London theater as a dresser to an actress at the Drury Lane. Using a variety of names such as Emy Lyon and Emy Hart, she became romantically involved with a number of men. One of the uncertain aspects of her life at this time is the question of whether or not she became pregnant and underwent an abortion. For a time, she worked in Dr. James Graham's "Temple of Health." Graham's Temple was a shady theatrical enterprise that mixed demonstrations of popular science, displays of scantily clad young women, and, reportedly, sexual favors for sale.

A series of romantic liaisons soon pointed her toward Naples and her eventual encounter with Horatio Nelson. In 1781, she had a yearlong affair with a fabulously wealthy country gentleman, Sir Harry Featherstonhaugh. While living at his estate near Portsmouth, she met Charles Greville, a member of Parliament and minor government official. When Featherstonhaugh abruptly threw her out of his home at the close of 1781 because she was pregnant, she turned to Greville for help. One of the unanswered questions about her early life is whether Featherstonhaugh or Greville was the father of her first child, a girl born in 1782 and named Emma. Changing her own name from Amy to the more elegant "Emily" and the still more sophisticated "Emma," Nelson's future

Emma Hamilton

mistress now began a liaison with Greville that lasted
until he broke it off in 1786.

Emma's chief asset as she made her way
among her aristocratic patrons was her physical
beauty: she was a tall young woman with a lovely face, a slim figure, and long auburn hair.
While she was Greville's mistress, the artist
George Romney painted her more than 20 times.
As biographer Jack Russell put it, the infatuated
Romney "recorded her as one of the most beautiful creatures of that, or any other, age."

The man who became the dominant influence in the elder Emma's life for most of the
next two decades was Greville's uncle, Sir

William Hamilton. A
former soldier, thought by
some to be an illegitimate son
of the British royal family, William
had entered the diplomatic service in 1764.
He never rose beyond his initial post, that of
British representative at the court of King Ferdinand of Naples. Because of his first wife
Lady ❧▶ **Catherine Hamilton**'s dowry he lived
in comfort, becoming a passionate collector
of Italian art and immersing himself in scientific observations of the volcano of Mount
Vesuvius, just outside Naples. Catherine died
in 1782, the year before his first encounter
with Emma; he had been in Naples for almost
20 years.

❧▶
*See sidebar
on the
following page*

Emma passed only reluctantly from Greville's side to that of William Hamilton. Greville, who saw clearly the advantage of keeping his widowed uncle, from whom he expected a substantial legacy, from remarrying, took the initiative in carrying out the transfer. Emma seemed likely to appeal to William as a mistress; it seemed impossible he would ever marry her, especially since an ambassador's marriage required the approval of the British monarch. Greville shipped Emma, along with her mother, to Naples in the spring of 1786. William's efforts led to her seduction by the close of the year.

The young Englishwoman kept her strong Cheshire accent, but she soon became a sophisticated companion for the elderly ambassador. She learned Italian, improved her natural singing voice with music lessons, and joined William in his enthusiastic study of volcanoes. Emma also became the confidante of Queen *Maria Carolina of Naples (1752–1814), formerly an Austrian princess and the sister of Queen *Marie Antoinette of France. Emma's efforts at attaining respectability ended with success: in September 1791, while on leave in London, William received the consent of King George III and made Emma his legal wife.

☙❧ Hamilton, Catherine (1738–1782)

English harpsichordist and composer. Name variations: Lady Catherine Hamilton. Born Catherine Barlow in 1738 in Wales; died outside Naples of febbre biliare, *or bilious fever, on August 25, 1782; buried in Pembrokeshire; married Sir William Hamilton (envoy to Naples), in 1758; no children.*

Lady Catherine Hamilton was highly esteemed in her own time for her proficiency on the pianoforte and the harpsichord, but only one of her works as a composer, a minuet in C major, is extant. She was born in Wales in 1738. By her 20th birthday, she was a rich woman, who owned estates in Pembrokeshire and other areas in Wales. Though Sir William Hamilton, envoy to Naples, married her for her wealth, she soon became, he told others, his "bosom friend and companion." His love was returned. Said her niece **Mary Hamilton**: "She had no object in life but him & only regretted dying because she left him behind." Catherine disliked Neapolitan court life, preferring to give concerts, "at which all the best musicians, herself included, performed," writes **Flora Fraser**. Catherine had a deep understanding of music and even played before a young Mozart.

SOURCES:

Fraser, Flora. *Emma: Lady Hamilton*. NY: Alfred A. Knopf, 1986.

By the time of the Hamiltons' marriage, great historical currents were moving Emma toward her first encounter with Horatio Nelson. The French Revolution had begun two years earlier, and the French king Louis XVI and Marie Antoinette were already at odds with the government of the new limited monarchy that controlled France. In 1793, the French king and queen were executed by their own people, and France declared war against Britain. The Mediterranean became a war zone.

That September, Captain Nelson, a talented but still relatively obscure British naval officer, visited Naples. His mission was to secure Neapolitan help in defending the French port of Toulon. There, conservative French leaders had allowed the British to occupy the city, but Italian troops were needed urgently to help stop French revolutionary armies from closing in, bent on recapturing Toulon.

The initial meeting between 28-year-old Emma Hamilton and 35-year-old Horatio Nelson, who had been married since 1787, was not a memorable one. Nelson was frantically busy arranging for the transfer of Neapolitan forces to the French coast. He and Emma had little contact; he was far more concerned with her husband, and the elderly ambassador expressed his admiration for the energetic young naval officer. Nelson sailed off, the Neapolitan troops at Toulon suffered heavy losses when the French revolutionary armies retook the city, and Emma had no contact with her future lover for five years.

The lives of Emma Hamilton and Horatio Nelson touched a second time in the midst of a greater European crisis. By the spring of 1798, the brilliant French general Napoleon Bonaparte had conquered northern and central Italy and gathered a massive fleet and army at the port of Toulon. In May, the French forces sailed out into the Mediterranean. The French leader's exact intentions were uncertain, but he posed a threat to British interests and Britain's allies from Italy to Egypt. Nelson had the mission of hunting down the French fleet and opposing Napoleon's next moves.

Naples, facing French forces only 60 miles away, clung to a status of political neutrality. Nonetheless, in an episode that remains a source of controversy, Emma may have played a key role in setting the stage for British success: some historians believe she interceded decisively with Queen Maria Carolina to provide crucial supplies in Sicily for Nelson's vessels.

In September 1798, Nelson returned to Naples as a conquering hero after destroying the French fleet at Aboukir Bay near the Egyptian port of Alexandria. In the dramatic aftermath of this triumph at the Battle of the Nile, he and Emma Hamilton began their close personal relationship. Emma nursed Nelson's battle wounds and wrote cheerful letters to his wife ❧▶ **Frances** about his health.

When French forces advanced against Naples in December 1798, Emma and William Hamilton, along with the monarchs of Naples and the royal court, made a dramatic escape on Nelson's battle fleet to Sicily. The voyage was marked by a terrifying storm during which the youngest son of the Neapolitan monarchs suddenly died. Emma was the hero of the hour, comforting the Neapolitan rulers in the midst of the chaos and family tragedy.

In Sicily during the first months of 1799, Hamilton and Nelson began their love affair. At this time, as wife of the British ambassador, Emma played a political role as well. With her fluent Italian, she served as Nelson's interpreter and wrote propaganda leaflets to bolster support for King Ferdinand and Queen Maria Carolina from their subjects under French occupation in Naples. She also became pregnant for the first time with Nelson's child but ended the pregnancy with an abortion.

By the close of 1799, Ferdinand and Maria Carolina were back in Naples largely as a result of the military support they had received from the British. In the ensuing bloodbath, in which the Neapolitan monarchs struck at their subjects who had supported the French invasion, Emma tried with some success to shield several of the targets of royal vengeance. Meanwhile, she was becoming an object of hostility in her own country. Some senior naval officers held her responsible for keeping Nelson at port in Naples when he was obligated to join in British efforts to take the island of Minorca in the western Mediterranean. As rumors of Nelson's liaison with Hamilton reached home, satirical pamphlets and cartoons made her the object of public ridicule.

In November 1800, after a trip by land from Italy through central Europe to Hamburg and then by sea to Great Yarmouth, Emma, her husband, and Lord Nelson returned to England. Hamilton was again pregnant with Nelson's child, and the impact of their virtually open relationship now struck Nelson's public. After being presented to King George III at St. James's Palace, Nelson found the monarch willing to give

❧▶ Nelson, Frances Herbert (1761–1831)

Viscountess Nelson. Name variations: Frances Nisbet. Born Frances Woodward in 1761; died in 1831; married Josiah Nisbet (died); married Lord Horatio Nelson, on March 12, 1787 (separated 1801).

Fanny Nisbet was a widow, living at Nevis in the West Indies, when she met Lord Horatio Nelson in 1784. Three years later, they were married there, then returned to England that summer to live at Burnham Thorpe. Fanny was said to be a "good and faithful wife" but "unappreciative" of her unpredictable husband. While Nelson was intermittently away at sea, Fanny corresponded affectionately with him, until she learned of his liaison with Lady *Emma Hamilton in 1798. When Lord Nelson eventually returned to England in 1800, he brought the Hamiltons with him, causing a breach in the Nelson marriage. In London and elsewhere, the affair was the topic of conversation and speculation on every side. After many quarrels with her husband, Fanny Nelson could no longer endure the humiliation of the estranged wife and finally separated in 1801. At the time of his death, Nelson left her £1,200 per annum.

him only a few brief words and a nod, a seemingly deliberate public rebuff to Britain's heroic young fighting admiral. Meanwhile, Hamilton was the target of jibes in the press which exaggerated her age, called attention to her swelling figure, and reminded readers of her May–December marriage with William Hamilton. One newspaper article noted that after William's 38 years in Italy, she was "the chief curiosity" with which he had returned to his country.

On January 12, 1801, Nelson broke off relations with his wife Frances. At the close of the month, Emma presented him with his only surviving child, a daughter whom she named Horatia. Nelson and Hamilton maintained the fiction that they had adopted the girl. In the last years of Emma's life, she would tell Horatia that she was Nelson's daughter. But Emma would hold back the information that Horatia was her daughter. It was not until **Horatia Nelson-Ward** was an adult, with a family of her own, that she learned all the facts about her parentage.

The admiral soon left for the Baltic, where he added to his reputation as his country's greatest naval hero with a victory over the Danes at Copenhagen in April. When he returned to England, he asked Hamilton to find him a country house. The farm house at Merton in Surrey that she discovered and Nelson purchased was the scene of the two interludes of happiness they were able to enjoy.

Peace with France, signed at Amiens in March 1802, brought Emma and her lover together at Merton for nearly a year. Accompanying them was Emma's husband, William Hamilton, now past 70 and retired from the diplomatic service. William had been present throughout the relationship between Emma and Nelson. Long reconciled to the possibility that his wife might take up with a lover younger than he, William had not been surprised when Nelson and Emma had begun their affair in Sicily. He had accompanied them in the long journey across Europe and now seemed more or less content to spend his last years in the shadow of their love affair. When he died at Merton in the spring of 1803, his will contained a specific statement of his regard for Nelson.

The final phase of Hamilton's love affair with Nelson began when Britain renewed its war with Napoleon in May 1803. The young admiral left to take command of British forces in the

Mediterranean. For the next two years, he never touched shore, and the two could contact each other only by letter. Tragedy struck in early 1804 when Emma gave birth to a daughter who soon died from smallpox. Hamilton found herself increasingly plagued by financial problems; Nelson's income had to support his estranged wife Frances as well Emma. Moreover, at his request, Emma was expanding and developing the property at Merton where they hoped to live out their lives. Her debts were manageable mainly because her creditors understood that Nelson was the real debtor. So long as he was at sea, it was pointless and possibly even unpatriotic to press for payment.

Nelson chased the French fleet from the Mediterranean to the Caribbean and back. A combined fleet of these French vessels and their Spanish allies was now reportedly hiding in the Spanish port of Cadiz. Nelson had to wait until his navy had been refitted before he could sail southward to engage them. While he tarried at home, Emma Hamilton spent her last moments

From the movie That Hamilton Woman, *starring Laurence Olivier and Vivien Leigh.*

with her lover in late August 1805. Three weeks later, he left her for the last time.

Emma Hamilton learned of Nelson's death on November 6, more than two weeks after he fell at the head of his victorious fleet at the Battle of Trafalgar on October 21. The first sign of momentous news came when she and **Sarah Nelson**, Nelson's sister, heard celebration guns being fired off in London. In short order, a representative of the British Admiralty arrived. When Emma asked him for her latest letters from the admiral, his silence made Nelson's death clear to her. She fainted from shock.

Shortly before the start of the battle, as his forces awaited the French and Spanish off the Spanish coast, Nelson had added a codicil to his will. His original will gave Emma the estate at Merton, a modest yearly allowance, and £4,000 in trust for Horatia's education. In the codicil, Nelson went much further to secure his family's future. He named Emma "a Legacy to my King and Country," and he asked the government to provide her with funds appropriate to "her Rank in Life." He justified his request in part by citing her help in supplying his fleet in 1798 prior to the Battle of the Nile. In thinly disguised acknowledgement of his role as Horatia's father, he asked that she, "my adopted daughter," also receive financial aid, and he expressed his hope she would henceforth use the name "Horatia Nelson."

The last decade of Emma Hamilton's life was marked by a descent into poverty and illness. Her effort to keep possession of Merton, despite its heavy costs, proved a severe burden. While her generosity to Nelson's servants, members of his family and her own, and numerous old sailors who visited her for help, put her deeply in debt. After she was forced to sell Merton in 1809, she was already weakened by illness and lacked the energy to pursue her right to the yearly sums she was entitled to from the estates of William Hamilton and Nelson. Sinking into poverty, hounded by her creditors, and finally arrested for debt in 1813, she used her meager resources to provide Horatia with a first-class education.

Emma Hamilton died in Calais on January 15, 1815. Friends had arranged her release from confinement and provided her and Horatia with the funds to escape to France. The woman who had stood beside Britain's legendary naval leader died in the same country whose ambitions Nelson had effectively stymied. The graveyard in which she was buried was relocated in the course of the 19th century, and the spot where her remains now rest is unknown.

SOURCES:

Fraser, Flora. *Beloved Emma: The Life of Emma, Lady Hamilton*. London: Weidenfeld and Nicolson, 1986.

Russell, Jack. *Nelson and the Hamiltons*. NY: Simon and Schuster, 1969.

Simpson, Colin. *Emma: The Life of Lady Hamilton*. London: Bodley Head, 1983.

SUGGESTED READING:

Hibbert, Christopher. *Nelson: A Personal History*. Reading, MA: Addison-Wesley, 1994.

Lofts, Nora. *Emma Hamilton*. NY: Coward, McCann & Geoghegan, 1978.

Pocock, Tom. *Nelson and his World*. NY: Viking Press, 1968.

Rattigan, Terence. *A Bequest to the Nation*. Chicago, IL: The Dramatic Publishing, 1971.

Sontag, Susan. *The Volcano Lover: A Romance*. NY: Farrar, Straus, and Giroux, 1992.

RELATED MEDIA:

That Hamilton Woman, film with *Vivien Leigh and Laurence Olivier, directed by Alexander Korda, 1941.

The Nelson Affair (titled in England *Bequest to the Nation*), film with Peter Finch and *Glenda Jackson, directed by James Cellan Jones, 1973.

Neil M. Heyman,
Professor of History, San Diego State University,
San Diego, California

Hamilton, Frances (d. 1730).

See Jennings, Frances.

Hamilton, Gail (1833–1896).

See Dodge, Mary Abigail.

Hamilton, Hariot (fl. 1845–1891).

See Blackwood, Helen Selina for sidebar on Hariot Blackwood.

Hamilton, Lady (1765–1815).

See Hamilton, Emma.

Hamilton, Margaret (1902–1985)

American actress best known for her role as the **Wicked Witch of the West** *in* The Wizard of Oz. *Born Margaret Brainard Hamilton on September 12, 1902, in Cleveland, Ohio; died on May 16, 1985, in Salisbury, Connecticut; youngest of the four children (three girls and one boy) of Walter Jones Hamilton (an attorney) and Jennie (Adams) Hamilton; graduated from Hathaway-Brown High School, Cleveland, 1921; obtained teaching certificate from Wheelock Kindergarten Training School (now Wheelock College), Boston, 1923; studied voice with Grace Probert, Cleveland; studied acting and pantomime with *Maria Ouspenskaya and Joseph Moon; married Paul Boynton Meserve (a landscape architect), on June 13, 1931 (divorced 1938); children: one son, Hamilton.*

Selected theater: New York debut as Helen Hallam in Another Language *(Booth Theater, April 25,*

1932); *Hattie in* The Dark Tower *(Morosco Theater, 1933); Lucy Gurget in* The Farmer Takes a Wife *(46th Street Theater, 1934); Gertrude in* Outrageous Fortune *(48th Street Theater, New York City, 1943); the Aunt in* On Borrowed Time *(Patio Theater, Los Angeles, California, 1946); Gwennie in* The Men We Marry *(Mansfield Theater, New York City, January 1948); Lucy Bascombe in* Fancy Meeting You Again *(Royale Theater, New York City, 1952); Mrs. Zero in* The Adding Machine *(Phoenix Theater, New York City, 1956); Madame Kleopatra Mamaeva in* Diary of a Scoundrel *(Phoenix Theater, New York City, 1956); Parthy Ann in* Show Boat *and the Wicked Witch in* The Wizard of Oz *(St. Louis Municipal Opera, summer 1957); Bessie in* Goldilocks *(Lunt-Fontanne Theater, New York City, 1958); Dolly Tate in* Annie Get Your Gun *(New York City Center, 1958); Grandma in* The American Dream *(Civic Theater, Los Angeles, 1962); Clara in* Save Me a Place at Forest Lawn *(Pocket Theater, New York City, 1963); Connie Tufford in* UTBU *(Helen Hayes Theater, New York City, 1966); Madame Arcati in* Blithe Spirit *(Seattle Repertory Theater, 1966); Mrs. Malaprop in* The Rivals *(Seattle Repertory Theater, 1967–68 season); Dorinda Pratt in* Come Summer *(Lunt-Fontanne Theater, New York City, 1969); Mrs. Dudgeon in* The Devil's Disciple *(American Shakespeare Festival, Stratford, Connecticut, summer 1970); Madame Desmermortes in* Ring Round the Moon *(Seattle Repertory Theater, fall 1971); Madame Armfeldt in national tour of* A Little Night Music *(1974).*

Selected films: Another Language *(1933);* Broadway Bill *(1934)* The Farmer Takes a Wife *(1935);* Way Down East *(1935);* These Three *(1936);* The Moon's Our Home *(1936);* You Only Live Once *(1937);* Mountain Justice *(1937);* Nothing Sacred *(1937);* A Slight Case of Murder *(1938);* The Adventures of Tom Sawyer *(1938);* Stablemates *(1938);* Four's a Crowd *(1938);* The Wizard of Oz *(1939);* Angels Wash Their Faces *(1939);* Babes in Arms *(1939);* The Villain Still Pursued Her *(1940);* My Little Chickadee *(1940);* The Invisible Woman *(1941);* Meet the Stewarts *(1942);* The Ox-Bow Incident *(1943);* Johnny Come Lately *(1943);* George White's Scandals *(1945);* Janie Gets Married *(1946);* Mad Wednesday *(1947);* State of the Union *(1948);* The Red Pony *(1949);* The Beautiful Blonde from Bashful Bend *(1949);* Riding High *(1950);* Wabash Avenue *(1950);* People Will Talk *(1951);* Comin' Round the Mountain *(1951);* 13 Ghosts *(1960);* Paradise Alley *(1962);* The Daydreamer *(1966);* Rosie! *(1967);* Brewster McCloud *(1970);* The Anderson Tapes *(1971); (voice only)* Journey Back to Oz *(1974).*

Although her career spanned more than 50 years, and included 75 films and as many stage plays, Margaret Hamilton will forever be identified with the dual role of the detestable Mrs. Gulch and the cackling, green-skinned Wicked Witch of the West in the 1939 film version of L. Frank Baum's *The Wizard of Oz.* Aired on American television at least once a year since 1956, the movie has introduced Hamilton to generations of children who otherwise would never have had the opportunity to see her perform.

Ironically, the woman who terrorized Dorothy and her companions on the road to Oz wanted nothing more than to be a kindergarten teacher. "I was born loving devotedly—first my dolls, then babies and children (little ones)," she once said. At the age of 12, she served as a kindergarten aide at Hathaway-Brown School, a private school near her home in Cleveland, Ohio. Hamilton studied voice for four years and had her first stage experience in high school, playing an elderly Englishman, Sir Peter Antrobus, in *Pomander Walk,* the senior-class play. With the encouraging applause of her friends and relatives, she decided that she might prefer acting to teaching, a change of mind that did not sit well with her mother, who insisted that Hamilton attend Wheelock Kindergarten Training School as planned. "When you know how to earn your living, you can fool around with the theater all you want," she told her stage-struck daughter.

In retrospect, Hamilton had few regrets about her education, feeling that her better understanding of children enriched her life. She received her teaching certificate in 1923 and returned to Cleveland where she ran a nursery school for several years before going to New York to teach kindergarten in the Rye Country Day School. After the death of her mother, however, she went back to Cleveland once again and opened her own private nursery school. In 1927, still harboring a desire to act, she embarked on a three-year apprenticeship at the Cleveland Playhouse where she appeared in some 25 different roles. She had never been happier. "At last I experienced the indescribable joy of doing what I longed to do," she recalled.

Hamilton spent a year making the rounds of Broadway casting agents before she finally landed a role in *Another Language* (1932), playing Helen Hallam, a warm-hearted though acerbic wife who is victimized by a possessive mother-in-law. The play was a surprising hit, and Hamilton repeated the role in the film adaptation in 1933. From then on, she divided her time between the stage and screen, although she always remained partial to live theater. "Only in the theater do you have the opportunity to experiment, to change, to grow, to better each performance," she wrote in an article for *Junior League News*. Hamilton's roles were not widely diversified, limited somewhat by her tiny stature and sharp features. For the most part, she was relegated to hard-bitten domestics and gossipy "spinsters," or, as she said, "women with a corset of steel and a heart of gold."

Hamilton made 25 films before being cast in the dual role of Mrs. Gulch and the Wicked Witch in *The Wizard of Oz*. Although it was her most memorable role, it was not her favorite. "I don't look on it as any great shakes of acting," she told Al Cohn in an interview for *Newsday* (March 19, 1978). "It's not subtle or restrained. It isn't any of the things you like to think might apply to your acting." From the first telecast of the movie, Hamilton received hundreds of letters, mostly from children. She always advised parents that children under seven might be truly upset by the Wicked Witch, and she turned down offers to resurrect the character in a sequel to the movie, although she often appeared in less formidable stage versions of the musical. "Little children's minds can't cope with seeing a mean witch alive again," she explained. "It's as though they think maybe I'm going to go back and cause trouble for Dorothy again."

During the early days of television, Hamilton, who had previously been heard on the radio, performed in dozens of live dramatic productions, including "The Man Who Came to Dinner" (1954), "The Devil's Disciple" (1955), "The Trial of Lizzie Borden" (1957), and "The Silver Whistle" (1959). She had on-going roles in the soap operas "Secret Storm" and "As the World Turns," and often made guest appearances on sit-coms and variety programs such as "Johnny Carson," "David Frost," and "Dick Cavett." Hamilton also made her mark in television commercials, as a harassed homemaker for Jello, and as the voice of Emily Tipp, the cartoon character in ads for Tiptop Bread. During the 1970s, Hamilton became known in households across America as Cora, the New England storekeeper who stocked and sold only Maxwell House coffee.

Hamilton's stage credits encompassed comedy, drama, and musicals and included performances on Broadway, off-Broadway, stock, and regional theater. Some of her more notable portrayals included Mrs. Zero in *The Adding Machine* (1956) and Clara in the two-character play

Save Me a Place at Forest Lawn (1963). One of her own favorites was the Grandma in Edward Albee's *The American Dream* (1962). Of her musical roles, she was memorable as Dolly Tate in *Annie Get Your Gun*, Aunt Eller in *Oklahoma!*, and Parthy Ann Hawks in *Show Boat*. In 1974–75, she toured for 51 weeks as Madame Armfeldt in Stephen Sondheim's *A Little Night Music*, winning accolades from the critics, some of whom thought she stole the show.

In 1931, Hamilton had married Paul Boynton Meserve, a landscape architect, with whom she had a son, Hamilton. The couple divorced in 1938, after which Hamilton stayed in Los Angeles where she raised her son as a single parent. Active in the community, she taught Sunday school, was in the PTA, and served for a time as president of the Beverly Hills board of education. In 1951, she moved to New York City, where she was a member of the Veterans Hospital Radio and TV Guild and was active in the Bedside Network, an organization that entertained hospital patients. In 1969, she was a co-founder of AMAS, a repertory theater and school in New York City. Of her numerous honors was the Governor's Award of the State of Ohio (1977) and an honorary degree from her alma mater, Wheelock College (1970). Margaret Hamilton died following a heart attack on May 16, 1985.

SOURCES:

Evory, Ann, and Peter M. Garaffa, eds. *Contemporary Newsmakers*. Detroit, MI: Gale Research, 1985.

Katz, Ephraim. *The Film Encyclopedia*. NY: HarperCollins, 1994.

McGill, Raymond D., ed. *Notable Names in the American Theater*. Clifton, NJ: James T. White, 1976.

Moritz, Charles, ed. *Current Biography 1979*. NY: H.W. Wilson, 1979.

Barbara Morgan,
Melrose, Massachusetts

Hamilton, Mary (1613–1638)

*Duchess of Hamilton. Name variations: Margaret Fielding; Mary Fielding. Born Mary Fielding in 1613; died on May 10, 1638; daughter of William Fielding, 1st earl of Denbigh, and *Susan Villiers; married James Hamilton (1606–1648), 1st duke of Hamilton, in 1630; children: *Anne Hamilton (1636–1716); Charles Hamilton, earl of Arran; Susannah Hamilton.*

Mary, duchess of Hamilton, was lady-of-the-bedchamber to Queen *Henrietta Maria. Poet Edmund Waller praised her in "Thyrsis Galatea." Her husband James Hamilton was beheaded in 1648 for leading a Scottish army into England.

Hamilton, Mary (1739–1816)

British novelist. Name variations: Lady Mary Hamilton. Born Mary Leslie in 1739; died in 1816.

Lady Mary Hamilton, who published four novels, lived with her second husband in France. She was a friend of Sir Herbert Croft, an English scholar and linguist, and the French writer Charles Nodier.

Hamilton, Mary (1882–1966)

British feminist, politician, journalist, and author. Born Mary Adamson in 1882; died in 1966; one of six children of Robert (a professor) and Daisy (Duncan) Adamson; honors degree from Newnham College, Cambridge University; married Charles Hamilton (an educator), in 1905.

Raised by enlightened parents who believed strongly in women's rights, Mary Hamilton attended Newnham College, where her mother had been among the first female students. There she befriended *Margery Corbett-Ashby and together they joined the Cambridge branch of the National Union of Women Suffrage Societies. After receiving a first class honors degree from Newnham College, Hamilton took a position as a history teacher at the University College of South Wales. In 1905, she resigned to marry a university colleague, Charles Hamilton.

After a conversion to socialism, Hamilton joined the Independent Labor Party. Following World War I, she began writing for *Time and Tide*, a feminist journal, and was later employed as a journalist for *The Economist*. In 1929, Hamilton was elected as Labor MP for Blackburn. During her term, she served as parliamentary private secretary to Clement Attlee, the postmaster general under Ramsey MacDonald. She also served on the Royal Commission on the Civil Service, where she supported equal pay for men and women. During this time, she was part of a campaign to eliminate the marriage ban for teachers.

Though Hamilton was defeated in the 1931 General Election, she remained in the public eye, serving as a governor of the BBC (1932–36), and as a member of the London County Council (1937–40). During World War II, she headed the American Division of the Ministry of Information. Hamilton also wrote several biographies of Labor figures, including *Margaret Bondfield and Arthur Henderson.

SUGGESTED READING:

Hamilton, Mary. *Remembering My Good Friends,* 1944.
———. *Uphill all the Way,* 1953.

Roberts, Marie, ed. *The Reformers: Socialist Feminism,* 1995.

Hamiltrude (fl. 700s).

See Himiltrude.

Hamm, Margherita (1867–1907)

Canadian journalist and author. Name variations: Margaret Hamm. Born Margaret Hamm on April 29, 1867, in St. Stephen, New Brunswick, Canada; died on December 17, 1907, in New York City; daughter of Rufus La Fayette Hamm (owner of a lumber business) and Martha Almenia (Spencer) Hamm; educated at the Convent of the Sacred Heart in Carleton, New Brunswick; attended Emerson College of Oratory, 1889–90; married William E.S. Fales (a vice-consul), on October 14, 1893 (divorced 1902); married John Robert McMahon (a journalist), on August 1, 1902; children: one daughter, Arlina Douglas McMahon (b. 1903).

Margherita Arlina Hamm was born in St. Stephen, New Brunswick, Canada, on April 29, 1867, one of six children of **Martha Spencer Hamm** and Rufus La Fayette Hamm. She was raised in the Episcopalian Church but educated at the Convent of the Sacred Heart in Carleton, New Brunswick. While still young, her family moved to Bangor, Maine, where her father established a successful lumber business.

In her 20s, Hamm moved to Boston where she worked for the *Boston Herald* as a reporter before moving to New York City. Her journalism work at this time did not provide her with a secure income, and she took numerous special assignments from daily newspapers. She is said to have established her reputation by conducting interviews with the likes of Grover Cleveland and James G. Blaine. She traveled throughout the United States as a correspondent for several New York newspapers.

Hamm married William E.S. Fales, then the U.S. vice-consul in Amoy, China, on October 14, 1893, and the couple traveled throughout Asia. When the Sino-Japanese war broke out in June of 1894 while they were in Korea, Hamm scored a journalistic coup by presenting her firsthand accounts of events to a variety of newspapers in America. Her stories included the attack on the palace at Seoul, the assassination of Queen *Min of Korea, and the declaration of war. During this struggle, she also assisted with nursing activities and was commended by *Clara Barton.

After the war, Hamm and her husband returned to America and made their home in Brooklyn, New York. Drawing on her vast travel experiences, Hamm delivered a series of lectures in various American cities on topics such as "Chinese Jurisprudence" and "Irrigation in the Far East." Continuing with her writing, Hamm contributed many magazine articles on Asia. She edited *Journalist*, a trade weekly from 1894 to 1895, and acted as assistant editor of *Peterson's Magazine* in 1898. She also headed the women's department of the New York *Evening Mail and Express*.

Like most Americans, Hamm's sympathies turned toward the insurgents in the Cuban uprising against Spanish domination after a visit to the West Indies in 1895, and in 1898 she left the *Evening Mail* to cover the Spanish-American war. During the conflict, she also volunteered on the nurses' staff of the women's auxiliary of the National Guard. She was recognized for her contributions by Cuban president Tomás Estrada Palma. After the war, she returned to journalism and traveled to England in 1901 to report on the coronation of King Edward VII. Hamm wrote several books, including three works relating to the Spanish-American War: *Manila and the Philippines* (1898), *Puerto Rico and the West Indies* (1899) and *Dewey, the Defender* (1899). Two of her more popular works were *Eminent Actors in Their Homes* (1902) and the two-volume *Famous Families of New York* (1902).

Hamm's marriage to Fales ended in divorce in 1902 and two days after the final decree, on August 1, 1902, she married John Robert McMahon, a fellow journalist. She died five years later, on December 17, 1907, at Woman's Hospital in New York City of pneumonia. She was survived by her second husband and her four-year-old daughter, **Arlina Douglas McMahon**.

SOURCES:

James, Edward T., ed. *Notable American Women 1607–1950*. Cambridge, MA: The Belknap Press of Harvard University Press, 1971.

Judith C. Reveal,
freelance writer, Greensboro, Maryland

Hamm, Mia.

See Soccer: Women's World Cup, 1999.

Hammer, Barbara (1930–1994).

See Avedon, Barbara Hammer.

Hammond, Joan (1912—)

New Zealand-born soprano. Name variations: Dame Joan Hammond. Born on May 24, 1912, in Christchurch, New Zealand; studied at the Sydney Conservatory.

Debuted in Sydney (1929) before going to London to study with Dino Borgioli; made her operatic debut in Vienna (1939); was a member of the Carl Rosa Opera Company (1942–45); made Covent Garden debut (1949); received the Sir Charles Santley award (for musician of the year) from the Worshipful Company of Musicians in London (1970); retired from singing (1971); became artistic director of the Victoria Opera and head of vocal studies at the Victorian College of the Arts; made a Dame of the British Empire (DBE, 1974).

Joan Hammond did much to popularize opera, and her career paved the way for such international opera stars as Luciano Pavarotti and Placido Domingo. As a child, Hammond's first love was the violin, which she studied at the Sydney Conservatorium of Music and played with the Symphony Orchestra. She also took on golf, winning the New South Wales (NSW) junior championship in 1929 and 1930. She then went on to win the NSW Champion of Champions twice, represented Australia in contests in Britain and New Zealand, was runner-up in the Australian amateur in 1933, and won the NSW ladies' championship in 1932, 1934, and 1935. When an accident left her with a two-inch differential in arm lengths, forcing her to give up the violin, women golfers raised funds to send Hammond to Italy to study singing.

Hammond's record of "O, my beloved father" from Puccini's *Gianni Schicchi* sold over a million copies by 1969 as audiences loved her warm, expansive style. She came from a long line of important Australasian opera singers which includes *Nellie Melba, *Frances Alda, and *Joan Sutherland. After training and performing in Sydney, she went to Europe and began her international career at the Vienna Staatsoper in 1938. Her warm and vibrant voice was a hit with audiences everywhere. In 1947, Hammond returned to Sydney and gave concerts to raise funds to send a women's golf team to England for the 1950 tournament year. Her voice was not powerful enough for Wagner, and, though too mature for Mozart, she performed creditably in *Madame Butterfly*, *Tosca*, and *La Bohème*. Hammond understood her abilities, and huge audiences enjoyed her voice in recordings as well as on stage.

John Haag,
Athens, Georgia

Hammond, Kay (1909–1980)

British actress who originated the role of Elvira in **Blithe Spirit**. *Born Dorothy Katherine Standing in*

London, England, on February 18, 1909; died on May 5, 1980; daughter of Guy Standing (an actor) and Dorothy Standing; attended Banstead in Surrey; studied at the Royal Academy of Dramatic Art; married John Selby Clements (an actor-manager), around 1945; no children.

Theater: stage debut as Amelia in Tilly of Bloomsbury *(Regent Theatre, June 25, 1927); Ellen in* Plus Hours *(Regent, July, 1927); Valerie Hildegard in* 77 Park Lane *(St. Martin's, October 1928); Beatrice in* Nine Till Six *(Arts and Apollo, January 1930); "Foxey" Dennison in* The Last Chapter *(New, May 1930); Babs in* Dance with No Music *(Arts, July 1930); Diana Lake in* French Without Tears *(Criterion, November 1936); Adeline Rawlinson in* Sugar Plum *(Criterion, March 1939); Elvira in* Blithe Spirit *(Picadilly, St. James, and Duchess, July–February 1941); Amanda in* Private Lives *(Apollo, November 1944); Lady Elizabeth Gray in* The Kingmaker *(St. James's, May 1946); Melantha in* Marriage á la Mode *(St. James's, July 1946); Mrs. Sullen in* The Beaux' Stratagem *(Phoenix, May 1949); Ann Whitefield and Dona Ana de Ulloa in* Man and Superman *(New, February 1951); Helen Mansell-Smith in* The Happy Marriage *(Duke of York's, August 1952); Eliza Doolittle in* Pygmalion *(St. James's, November 1953); Gabrielle in* The Little Glass Clock *(Aldwych, December 1954); Lydia Languish in* The Rivals *(Saville, February 1956); Mrs. Millamant in* The Way of the World *(Saville, December 1956); Hippolyte in* The Rape of the Belt *(Picadilly, December 1957); Louise Yeyder in* Gilt and Gingerbread *(Duke of York's, April 1959);* The Marriage-Go-Round *(Picadilly, October 1959).*

Born in 1909, the daughter of actors, Britain's Kay Hammond was raised in the theater and coached in elocution by *Mrs. Patrick Campbell, a close family friend. After studying at the Royal Academy, Hammond made her debut in 1927 as Amelia in *Tilly of Bloomsbury*. Distinguished by her elegant beauty and what one critic called "a funny voice," she played a progression of bit parts until her first starring role in Terence Rattigan's *French Without Tears* (1936), which ran for two years. She had a second two-year run as Elvira in Noel Coward's *Blithe Spirit*, which she also filmed in 1945. In a revival of Coward's *Private Lives* in 1944, Hammond played opposite John Clements, whom she married during a tour of the play. It was a personal and professional partnership that lasted many years. (After her marriage, Hammond more often than not performed with her husband.)

Under her husband's management, Hammond appeared in *The Kingmaker* (1946) and *Marriage à la Mode* (1946), before the health problems that would plague her for the rest of her life. Forced to retire from the stage for two years, she made a triumphant return in May 1949, appearing as Mrs. Sullen opposite her husband in *The Beaux' Stratagem*, which enjoyed a record run. Critic **Audrey Williamson** found the actress in fine form, calling her "particularly exquisite—a pouting period beauty with a sidelong glance and a perfection of wit in the pointing of her lines. Despite her famous 'plummy' yet attractive drawl, she has a style and intelligence in dialogue surpassed only by *Edith Evans among modern actresses of Restoration Comedy." Hammond's later appearance in Shaw's *Man and Superman* (1951) was not nearly so well received. T.C Worsley found her speech pattern unsuitable for Shaw. "Her particular trick of speech, by which in modern comedy she gets all her characteristic effects, is a slow over-articulated drawl, insinuating an innuendo," he wrote. "For most of Shaw an opposite technique is required. Miss Hammond doesn't just lack speed, which it might be possible to get away with; she completely holds things up."

For the role of Eliza in a revival of Shaw's *Pygmalion* (1953), Hammond successfully subdued her distinguishing drawl with a series of voice lessons, but it returned to haunt her performance as Lydia Languish opposite her husband in *The Rivals* (1956). Reviewing the play, Frank Granville-Barker called her "always charming but unhappily not so invariably audible." With her husband again, she had a less than successful run in Congreve's *The Way of the World* (1956). As the comic Mrs. Millamant, she seemed, according to most of the critics, unable to find the wit and humor in her role. (She also often missed performances due repeated attacks of bronchitis.) She was back in form, however, for Benn Levy's *The Rape of the Belt* (1957) and won raves as Louise Yeyder in *Gilt and Gingerbread* (1959), a modern comedy by Lionel Hale.

Kay Hammond's last performance was in *The Marriage Go Round* (1959), after which she retired from the stage. She remained in fragile health until her death on May 5, 1980.

SOURCES

Hartnoll, Phyllis, and Peter Found. *The Concise Oxford Companion to the Theatre.* Oxford and NY: Oxford University Press, 1993.

Morley, Sheridan. *The Great Stage Stars.* London: Angus & Robertson, 1986.

Barbara Morgan,
Melrose, Massachusetts

Hamnett, Nina (1890–1956)

British artist of portraits, still lifes, landscapes, and illustrations. Born in Tenby, South Wales, on February 14, 1890; died in 1956; eldest daughter of George (an army officer) and Mary Hamnett; attended boarding school at Portsmouth; attended Dublin School of Art; attended Pelham School of Art, London; attended London School of Art; married Roald Kristian (an artist), on October 12, 1914 (separated, but never divorced); children: one son who died shortly after his birth in 1915.

Selected works: The Landlady (oil on canvas, 1913); Zadkine (oil on canvas, 1914); Still Life No. 1 (oil on canvas, c. 1915); Der Sturm (oil on canvas, c. 1915); Three Figures in a Cafe (pen and wash, 1916); The Student (oil on canvas, 1917); The Ring Master (oil on canvas, c. 1918); Major General Bethune Lindsay (oil on canvas, 1919); Colliure (oil on canvas, 1921); Gentleman with a Top Hat (oil on canvas, c. 1921); Rupert Doone (oil on canvas, 1922–23); James Hepburn (oil on canvas, 1922); Landscape in Provence (oil on canvas, 1926); A Bench in Regent's Park (watercolor, 1930); Delores (oil on canvas, 1931).

Rebelling against her Victorian upbringing and her family's opposition to her artistic career, Nina Hamnett was one of London's most promising avant-garde painters from 1915 to about 1928. However, her flamboyant personality and bohemian lifestyle, documented in two autobiographies, *Laughing Torso* (1932) and *Is She a Lady?* (1955), eventually eclipsed her standing as a significant contributor to the modern art movement.

The eldest daughter of an army officer, Hamnett's schooling and art training were sporadic, interrupted by her father's military postings which took the family from city to city. At the age of 13, she left boarding school to begin art lessons at the School of Art in Portsmouth, where she was excluded from life classes because of her gender. (At the time, Hamnett resorted to taking off her clothes and drawing her reflection in the mirror, a practice that horrified her prudish family.) She attended a year each at the Dublin School of Art and the Pelham School of Art, South Kensington, and then wound up her formal training at the London School of Art under artists Frank Brangwyn, John Swan, and William Nicholson. Hamnett received little encouragement from her family, and at the age of 21, aided financially by her grandmother and two sympathetic aunts, she left home and took a rented room in Bloomsbury, the heart of London's artistic community. She en-

joyed a close association with artists Roger Fry, who hired her in 1913 to work in his Omega Workshop, and Walter Sickert, who wrote the preface for her first solo exhibition of paintings and drawings in 1918.

On a trip to Paris in 1914, Hamnett met and fell in love with a struggling Norwegian artist Roald Kristian, whom she convinced to come live with her in London. They were married in October 1914, but Hamnett soon realized that the marriage was a mistake and the two parted. A son born of the union in March 1915 died in infancy, and Hamnett lost contact with Kristian around 1917, when he was arrested as an alien agent and sent to France to fight in the Belgian army. Hamnett never obtained a divorce and remained legally married for the rest of her life. She later had a long-term relationship with Polish artist Waclow Zawadowski (known as "Zawado"), but for the most part she preferred her independence. Monogamy, however, did not preclude a series of lovers and a lifestyle which

Nina Hamnett

gained her the title "Queen of Bohemia." Her social life and drinking absorbed her for a period of ten years beginning in 1932, during which time she virtually abandoned her art. In the 1940s and 1950s, however, Hamnett returned to work, producing some of her most poignant drawings.

Hamnett was fascinated by people, and she is best known for her illuminating portraits, although she also painted still lifes and landscapes. Her work is dominated by a straightforward simplicity and lack of detail, which is particularly apparent in the spatial and volumetric aspects of her still lifes. Influenced strongly by her association with Fry (a champion of Impressionist Paul Cézanne) and the Bloomsbury painters, she liked to paint everyday domestic objects viewed from a slightly tilted perspective, so that the viewer could see the interior space of the object as well as the shape of the outside contours. In her still life *Der Sturm*, not only does Hamnett incorporate the use of domestic objects in her composition (a two-handled cup and pitcher), but also paints in the foreground a copy of the timely journal *Der Sturm*, a radical weekly arts magazine published in Berlin which advocated the avant-garde movements in art.

Hamnett's portraits represent the greatest body of her paintings, and include likenesses of some of the better-known personalities in London and Paris between 1910 and 1940: Walter Sickert, Osbert and *Edith Sitwell, Ossip Zadkine, Amedeo Modigliani, Frank Dobson, Henri Gaudier-Brzeska, Rupert Doone, Anthony Powell, and Lytton Strachey. In *Five Women Painters*, authors **Teresa Grimes**, **Judith Collins**, and **Oriana Baddeley** elaborate on the artist's portraits. "Hamnett was gifted with the capacity to grasp the essential in both the form and the character of her sitters," they write, "and to set this down with subtlety and strength. This was helped by the use of a subdued yet quietly rich range of colours, in which she could well have been encouraged by both Sickert and Fry." In a 1928 interview, Hamnett singled out as her best work a commissioned portrait of Major General William Bethune Lindsay, painted in 1919, for the Canadian War Memorials Fund, which was set up to provide a visual record of World War I. Many of Hamnett's portraits, as well as other works, were destroyed in a fire in 1947. Fortunately, she had many of her paintings professionally photographed, and saved the pictures along with her volumes of press-clippings.

Hamnett also explored various areas of English life through her drawings. Whenever an amusing person or social scene captured her attention, she would record it in a deftly-drawn pen or pencil sketch, often as small as two-inches square. Some of her most witty and highly praised line illustrations appeared in Osbert Sitwell's book *The People's Album of London Statues* (1928). Sickert, who said that Hamnett "drew like a born sculptor," also helped her obtain a part-time job teaching drawing at the Westminster Technical Institute for two terms in the winter of 1919. It was one of only two paying jobs Hamnett ever held, the other being her brief employment with the Omega Workshop. Money always posed a problem for the artist, prompting Basil Bunting to comment: "Nina Hamnett subsists miraculously by rare falls of manna on the stormy coast of Bohemia." Indeed, when the artist died in 1956, after falling from the window of her flat, she was alone and in severe poverty, her reputation as an artist already forgotten.

SOURCES:

Grimes, Teresa, Judith Collins, and Oriana Baddeley, *Five Women Painters*. Oxford: Lennard Publishing, 1989.

Petteys, Chris. *Dictionary of Women Artists*. Boston, MA: G.K. Hall, 1985.

Barbara Morgan,
Melrose, Massachusetts

Han, Suyin (1917—).

See Han Suyin.

Hanaford, Phebe Ann (1829–1921)

American Universalist minister, author, and feminist. Born Phebe Ann Coffin on May 6, 1829, in Siasconset, Nantucket Island, Massachusetts; died on June 2, 1921, in Rochester, New York; daughter of George W. Coffin and Phebe Ann (Barnard) Coffin; married Dr. Joseph Hibbard Hanaford, on December 2, 1849 (separated 1870); lived with Ellen E. Miles (a Universalist author); children: Howard Hanaford; **Florence Hanaford**.

Phebe Ann Coffin's ancestors established and maintained a strong presence in New England. Tristram Coffin founded the first settlement on Nantucket Island in 1659 and Phebe's mother and namesake traced her heritage to Gregory Priest, pilot of the *Mayflower*, and Peter Folger, grandfather of Benjamin Franklin. Phebe's mother died shortly after Phebe's birth and her father entered into a second marriage to **Emmeline Barnard Cartwright**. Early in her life, Phebe showed an interest in both social reform and literature. At eight, she signed a temperance pledge and by thirteen she was writing for the local press. In her native town of Siasconset, she attended both public and private schools where she studied Latin and mathematics.

On December 2, 1849, Phebe married Dr. Joseph Hibbard Hanaford, a homeopathic physician, teacher and writer. The couple taught for a year in Newton, Massachusetts, before returning to Nantucket. The Hanafords had two children, Howard and Florence. Although Hanaford dedicated the early years of her marriage to her family, she soon started writing to help support them.

Hanaford wrote 14 books including *Lucretia the Quakeress* (1853) and a collection of poems *From Shore to Shore* (1870). She also contributed to numerous periodicals and published small volumes for children. Although her book sales were not large, her biographies of Abraham Lincoln (1865) and George Peabody (1870) sold 20,000 and 16,000 copies respectively. Between 1866 and 1868, she edited a monthly Universalist magazine, the *Ladies' Repository,* and a Sunday-school paper, the *Myrtle.*

Hanaford had been raised a Quaker and joined the Baptist Church with her husband, but with the death of a brother and sister she looked more deeply into her faith and soon turned to Universalism. She began preaching in 1865 and a year later substituted for the Reverend *Olympia Brown in South Canton, Massachusetts. Hanaford entered the ministry and was ordained in Hingham, Massachusetts, in 1868. She took charge of the parish at Waltham, Massachusetts, and in 1870, after separating from her husband, she began her service at the First Universalist Church of New Haven, Connecticut, at a salary of $2,000 a year. During this time, she served as chaplain of the Connecticut house and senate. Her busy schedule as a minister all but ended her career as a writer.

In 1874, Hanaford moved to the Church of the Good Shepherd in Jersey City, New Jersey. In 1877, a rift occurred within the congregation regarding the question of women's rights, and, as a result, Hanaford spent the next seven years preaching in a public hall. In 1884, she assumed the role of pastor of the Second Church in New Haven. She spent this time lecturing through the Middle Atlantic and Western states, closing her active pastoral career in 1891. She settled in New York, making her home with fellow Universalist author, **Ellen E. Miles**.

Throughout her life, Hanaford was active in women's rights issues. In 1869, she participated in the convention of the American Equal Rights Association. Later that same year, she helped develop the American Woman Suffrage Association. She sat as vice-president of the Association for the Advancement of Women in 1874 and conducted services at the International Council of Women (1888). In 1876, she published *Women of the Century,* which was revised in 1882 as *Daughters of America.* Hanaford died in Rochester, New York, on June 2, 1921, and was buried in Orleans, New York.

SOURCES:

James, Edward T., ed. *Notable American Women 1607–1950.* Cambridge, MA: The Belknap Press of Harvard University Press, 1971.

Judith C. Reveal,
freelance writer, Greensboro, Maryland

Hanau, Marthe (c. 1884–1935)

French confidence woman who was extremely intelligent and just as notorious. Born in Paris, France, around 1884; died in Paris on July 19, 1935; married Lazare Bloch (a businessman), in 1908 (divorced); no children.

France's notorious Marthe Hanau was said to have been outdone only by the prince of swindlers, Serge Alexandre Stavisky, who stole close to ten billion francs and caused the February riots of 1934, in which 14 people lost their lives. By comparison, Hanau only bilked 150 million francs from her victims, seven of whom quietly took their own lives because of their losses.

Marthe Hanau was born in Paris around 1884. Little is known of her father; her mother was the proprietor of a small but profitable baby-clothes shop in Montmartre. Well educated, Hanau showed an early propensity for mathematics. At 24, she married Lazare Bloch; "the kind of fellow," she noted, "who could sell peanuts to the Pope." Within the course of the next 20 years, he managed to go through her dowry of 300,000 francs, forcing the couple into bankruptcy. Divorcing Bloch, Hanau opened a perfume and soap shop but was soon bored by the beauty business. Hatching a scheme to capitalize on France's postwar money woes, in 1925 she opened a so-called investment house, where she employed her ex-husband, with whom she remained on friendly terms. In addition to brokering, Hanau published the famous *Gazette du Franc,* a tipster's sheet in which she promoted herself as a staunch supporter of the French franc and French investments, as opposed to her competitors who marketed English and American enterprises. As her stature grew, Hanau hired a new editor for the *Gazette,* respected journalist Pierre Audibert, a former political protégé of Premier Édouard Herriot. Under the supervision of his new boss, Audibert went to work on a special issue of the *Gazette* honoring the work of Frank Billings Kellogg, the American diplomat who won the Nobel Peace Prize in 1929, for negotiating a pact outlawing war as a national policy. Through his political connections, Audibert obtained signed photographs and letters from leading political and public figures of France and Europe, which he printed along with announcements of Hanau's various investment opportunities. Because of Audibert's political connections with Herriot, he was able to frank (mail free of charge) the Kellogg issue to European ambassadors as well as to every schoolteacher in France. Although the diplomats saw the picture spread in the Gazette as political advertising, the schoolteachers believed that the public figures pictured were endorsing Hanau's projects along with world peace, and began sending her their hard-earned money.

Hanau's rise was meteoric. By 1928, she was presiding over the Compagnie Générale Financière et Foncière, with impressive new offices on the Rue de Provence. Calling her business "a center of brokerage operations and administration of capital," she employed 450 local residents and 175 agents operating throughout France. Working 10-to-15 hours a day, Hanau advised 60,000 investors (mostly schoolteachers, clergy, widows, retirees, and small business owners), ran several syndicates, and published two daily customers' sheets. Using the *Gazette* to attack big business, Hanau came to be seen by her investors as a champion of the small entrepreneur who was being squeezed out by the devalued franc and postwar industrialization. "Her relations with her readers and investors became half avuncular, half demagogic," writes **Janet Flanner** in *Paris was Yesterday.* "Being a dominant personality, she was obeyed as if she were a man; being a woman, she was loved as if she were a friend." Her clients often sent gifts of baked goods and knitted wear along with their investment checks.

Hanau was generous with her profits, buying expensive gifts for her friends and giving away money to the needy. Although she dressed in oversized schoolgirl black dresses and lived in a modest suburban villa on the outskirts of Paris, she indulged in cars, expensive jewelry, and sable coats and purportedly kept a half-million francs in her checking account. While Hanau's coffers swelled, the French government became increasingly alarmed. Savings banks

were reporting large withdrawals; at one point, it was estimated that 600 billion francs had been given to Hanau for speculation. Furthermore, there were rumors of bribery between Bloch and some of the government officials who had appeared in the Kellogg edition of the *Gazette.*

On December 3, 1928, after a special Cabinet meeting was held to discuss her case, Hanau was arrested on charges of swindling, abuse of confidence, and infraction of corporate laws. She was taken to Saint-Lazare Prison, while her ex-husband Bloch and editor Audibert, booked as accomplices, were incarcerated at La Santé Prison. Hanau's offices were seized, her promotion schemes uncovered as dummies, and her investment syndicates declared bogus. Her complicated trial, beginning early in 1929 with a 16-month preliminary "instruction," went on for close to two years, during which time the public was as shocked about the government's complicity and corruption as they were by Hanau's crimes. During the trial's first two weeks, the Hanau suicides began—hangings, drownings, guns to the head, all involving distraught victims of Madame's business practices. Denied bail, Hanau went on a protest hunger strike. On the 25th day, when she was brought to the prison's hospital ward for forced feeding, she escaped through a window, sliding down a sheet that had been tied to a radiator by her devoted maid during a prison visit. Returning to prison on her own after only an evening of freedom, Hanau, close to death, was finally released on 800,000 francs, half of which was raised by some of her still devoted clients, who by now began to view her as a martyr.

Due to her weakened condition, Hanau's "real" trial was delayed until October 1930. It was five months in duration and, according to Flanner, was totally dominated by Hanau, who shouted herself hoarse in her defense, often leaving her lawyer standing idly by. On March 28, 1931, despite her pleas, Hanau was pronounced guilty and sentenced to two years in prison and fined 3,000 francs and costs of half a million. Her ex-husband, Bloch, got 18 months, and Audibert was acquitted. (Upon receiving the news, he suffered a heart attack and died.)

Six months later, Hanau successfully appealed her sentence, left prison, and promptly opened another brokerage house which remained in business until 1934, when her appeal was finally heard. Publishing a customers' sheet called *Le Secret des Dieux,* Hanau attracted 2,000 investors who paid 2,000 francs each for her predictions from the "gods." Surprisingly accurate in determining stock market swings, Hanau also profited by "going short," holding back money and buying stocks at a lower price than her customers thought she had paid for it.

By the time the Paris Court of Appeals got around to dealing with Hanau's case, she had aged considerably and could barely walk, due to a leg injury sustained in an automobile accident. Given an augmented sentence of a year in prison, she again appealed, but lost a second time. In February 1933, she was taken to the Prison de Fresnes, where she poisoned herself six months later. In a farewell note to her lawyers, Hanau, who had busied herself reading Montaigne, Marcus Aurelius, and Epictetus, denounced the pursuit of riches that had dominated and corrupted her life. "I'm sick of money—money has crushed me," she wrote. "The thought of earning money fills me with horror and perhaps impotence." Declaring herself finally at peace, she continued, "I desire that mercenary hands should burn my body and the ashes be cast to the four winds." Unfortunately, it was illegal in France at the time for anyone dying by violent means to be cremated, so Hanau was laid to rest in Montparnasse Cemetery. In attendance at the burial were her ex-husband, her loyal maid, and a half-dozen former investors.

SOURCES:
Flanner, Janet. *Paris was Yesterday.* NY: Viking, 1972.

Barbara Morgan,
Melrose, Massachusetts

Hanbury, Elizabeth (1793–1901)

British philanthropist. Born in 1793; died in 1901; daughter of Quakers; married Cornelius Hanbury, in 1826; children: Charlotte Hanbury (1830–1900).

The daughter of Quakers, Elizabeth Hanbury accompanied *Elizabeth Fry on her prison rounds in the early 1800s and advocated prison reform. She was also an active abolitionist. Her daughter **Charlotte Hanbury**, who worked side by side with her mother, would later establish a mission in Tangier for improving the lives of Moorish prisoners. Elizabeth Hanbury's autobiography was published in 1901, the year of her death.

Hancock, Florence (1893–1974)

British trade unionist. Name variations: Dame Florence Hancock. Born in Chippenham, Wilshire, England, in 1893; died in 1974; one of 14 children of a woolen weaver; attended Chippenham Elementary School until the age of 12; married John Donovan (a unionist), in 1964.

One of 14 children of an English weaver, unionist Florence Hancock was strongly influenced by her radically inclined father, who took her with him when she was ten to hear an address by David Lloyd George, the future prime minister. One of her lasting childhood memories was a phrase that Lloyd George uttered that day: "To deceive is always a contemptible thing, but to deceive the poor is the meanest trick of all." Building on that message, Hancock devoted her life to upholding the rights of England's laboring class.

At age 12, Hancock went to work as a kitchen maid in a cafe, then at 14 was employed at a condensed milk plant, where she worked for six years. She received an early lesson in gender and age discrimination when she was denied the highest wage for a woman (eight shillings, nine pence), because she had yet to reach the age of 21. In 1913, when the Workers' Union sent an organizer into the plant, she became one of the union's first recruits and was also instrumental in signing up 20 of her fellow workers. When the recruits were threatened with dismissal for their actions, Hancock helped organize a strike which lasted two weeks, but ultimately brought the workers a pay raise of three shillings a week. When work resumed, Hancock became dues collector, then branch secretary of the union. By 1917, she had risen to district officer for Wiltshire and Gloucester. The added responsibilities added hours to her day, as she had also been keeping house and caring for her brothers and sister since her mother's death in 1901.

As district officer, Hancock participated in a number of strikes, one of the bitterest against a laundry in 1918. The work stoppage lasted a month but resulted in a 100% raise for the employees. With the merging of the Workers' Union with the Transport and General Workers' Union in 1929, Hancock was sent to Bristol as a woman's officer, a post she held until 1942. In 1935, she was elected to the general council of the Trades Union Congress, which at the time controlled 7,500,000 organized workers. Elected president of the Congress in 1947, she became one of only two women to ever hold that British labor post. During World War II, she had also served as an advisor to the Ministry of Labor on women's war work.

In Hancock's ongoing campaigns for better standards for workers, she insisted on pay equity for women performing the same work as men, a principle that had the backing of the entire Trades Union Congress. She also worked to improve conditions and raise the status of domestic workers in the country (mostly women at the time). She once said that she would like to see the future domestic worker a college-trained girl, "not a left-over in a last-resort job." Hancock was equally concerned with children's issues, working to establish day nurseries for the children of married women.

During the 1950s, Hancock, who was described as an energetic, cheerful woman, full of good will, served on several government commissions. She was also governor of the BBC (1955–62) and director of Remploy (1958–66). In 1964, at age 71, she married a fellow unionist, John Donovan. She had been named a Dame of the British Empire (DBE) in 1951.

SOURCES:
Rothe, Anna, ed. *Current Biography 1948.* NY: H.W. Wilson, 1948.

Hancock, Joy (1898–1986)

U.S. naval officer who was a top-ranking woman line officer and the third and last director of the WAVES. Born Joy Bright in Wildwood, New Jersey, on May 4, 1898; died in Bethesda, Maryland, on August 20, 1986; daughter of William Henry Hancock (a banker and one-time lieutenant governor of New Jersey) and Priscilla (Buck) Hancock; graduated from Wildwood High School; graduated from the Pierce School of Business Administration, Philadelphia, Pennsylvania; attended Catholic University, Washington, D.C.; attended the Paris branch of the New York School of Fine and Applied Arts, 1926–27; married Charles Gray Little (a naval aviator), on October 9, 1920 (died 1921); married Lieutenant Commander Lewis Hancock, Jr. (a naval aviator), on June 3, 1924 (died 1925); no children.

Joy Hancock began her 35-year career with the U.S. Navy in 1918, when she enlisted in the Naval Reserve for the duration of World War I. In September 1919, after service at various naval stations in her home state of New Jersey, she left active duty to become a civilian employee at the Cape May (New Jersey) Naval Station. In 1920, she married Lieutenant Charles Gray Little, a naval aviator who was killed ten months later in the crash of the dirigible ZR-2 in England.

Hancock completed some courses at Catholic University, then took a position at the Navy Department's Bureau of Aeronautics in Washington. In 1924, she married Lieutenant Commander Lewis Hancock, Jr., also a navy pilot. In an ironic and tragic turn of events, Hancock's second husband was also killed in the crash of a dirigible (the U.S.S. *Shenandoah*), on September 3, 1925, in Caldwell, Ohio. Following his death, Hancock, who had been serving as a stenographer-clerk in the construction office of the Lakehurst Naval Air Station, decided to pursue her career more aggressively. She attended the Paris branch of the New York School of Fine and Applied Arts, then began pilot's training, receiving her civil license in 1928. After additional study at George Washington University and elsewhere, she rejoined the Bureau of Aeronautics, where for eight years she headed the Bureau's editorial and research section. Establishing herself as an expert on the evolution of naval aeronautics, she authored the book *Airplanes in Action* (1938) and contributed articles to such periodicals as *Flying, Aero Digest,* and *Popular Mechanics.*

In July 1942, Hancock became a lieutenant in the newly created Women's Naval Reserve, then called Women Accepted for Volunteer Emergency Services (WAVES). Rising quickly through the ranks, she was named assistant director of the WAVES in February 1946, and in July of that year, she became director, with the rank of captain. As the third and last director of the WAVES (succeeding Captain *Mildred McAfee Horton and Captain Jean T. Palmer), Hancock served during the period just before the Reserve passed out of existence in October 1948. Since the Navy planned to continue employing women personnel, Hancock had a leading role in the preparation and promotion of what finally emerged as the Women's Armed Services Integration Act (signed by President Harry Truman on June 12, 1948), under which the Navy was authorized to offer regular commissions to women. On October 15, 1948, she was one of the first eight women to receive a commission in the Navy, at which time she was accorded the permanent rank of lieutenant commander and appointed assistant to the Chief of Naval Personnel, with the temporary rank of captain. As adviser to the administration on women's affairs, Hancock was a key figure in activating a total force of 500 officers, 30 warrant officers, and 6,000 enlisted women in the Navy. Upon her retirement in 1953, she was succeeded by Captain Louise K. Wilde. Hancock published an autobiography, *Lady in the Navy,* in 1972.

SOURCES:
Current Biography 1949. NY: H.W. Wilson, 1949.
McHenry, Robert, ed. *Famous American Women.* NY: Dover, 1983.

Handel-Mazzetti, Enrica von (1871–1955)

Austrian novelist who wrote many novels reflecting the religious struggles that convulsed Central Europe in the 16th and 17th centuries. Name variations: Baroness Enrika von Handel-Mazzetti; (pseudonym) Marien Kind. Born Enrica Ludovica Maria Freiin von Handel-Mazzetti in Vienna, Austria, on January 10, 1871; died in Linz, Austria, on April 8, 1955; daughter of Heinrich von Handel-Mazzetti and Irene Cshergö de Nemes-Tacskánd von Handel-Mazzetti; never married.

In 1871, Enrica von Handel-Mazzetti was born into an aristocratic Viennese family that exemplified the multinational nature of the Habsburg imperial state of Austria-Hungary. Her maternal grandmother was a Dutch Protestant, whereas her maternal grandfather was a Hungarian state official and adherent of the liberal ideals of Emperor Joseph II. On her paternal side, her grandmother was the offspring of Italian civil servants, while her grandfather had a distinguished military career that culminated in his becoming a member of the Austrian army's general staff. Enrica's father, a captain in the Austrian army, died when she was an infant. Enrica attended the finishing school of the English Sisters in St. Pölten, Lower Austria, an institution which had a profound impact on her. This convent school kept alive a religious neobaroque tradition of celebrating festive events with theatrical performances. The power of this tradition can be seen in the fact that other alumnae of the English Sisters school, including **Paula von Preradovic**, **Paula Grogger**, and **Maria Veronika Rubatscher**, all became distinguished literary figures. The convention, first experienced by Handel-Mazzetti in St. Pölten, would be a major influence on her intellectual and literary development. After graduation, she returned to Vienna to live with her mother, moving to Steyr after her mother's death, and then finally to Linz, where she would spend the rest of her life.

By 1890, Enrica was publishing short stories in, among other journals, Vienna's semi-official newspaper, the *Wiener Zeitung*. During this early phase of her career, she also wrote plays. In 1897, she made her debut as an author of novels by allowing *Meinrad Helmpergers denwürdiges Jahr* (*Meinrad Helmperger's Memorable Year*) to appear in installments in a periodical (it was published in book format in 1900). Set in the 17th century and based on fact, this novel tells the story of a Protestant boy, the son of English refugee parents, who must first witness the torture and execution of his father (who had been accused of the crime of atheism) before he is received into the Roman Catholic faith at Kremsmünster abbey. Encouraged by the positive response of critics and readers alike, Handel-Mazzetti was emboldened to write more

large-scale works. She was encouraged by Professor Robert Zimmermann of the University of Vienna, who gave her valuable ideas on how to achieve verisimilitude in a literary work through the study of contemporary archival documents.

Jesse und Maria (1906), which many critics consider to be Handel-Mazzetti's best novel, was based on her research into the parish church of Krummnussbaum, a small hamlet in the Pöchlarn region of Austria. Set in the years 1658–59, the plot centers around the historical confrontation between the Protestant noble Jesse von Velderndorff and Maria Schinnagel, the Catholic wife of the forester to the local bishop. The story ends tragically, but not before the author has explored the complex psychological and historical processes of the Catholic Counter-Reformation of the 16th century as it affected individual lives. Carl Muth, editor of the respected Catholic periodical *Hochland*, praised *Jesse und Maria* as a harbinger of more sophisticated Catholic literature that could compete on equal terms with the great tradition of German letters. Muth announced to his *Hochland* readers that the young Austrian novelist's psychological insights matched those of another rising literary star, Thomas Mann. Mann himself praised her work, as did two past masters

Austrian postage stamp issued on January 11, 1971, in honor of Enrica von Handel-Mazzetti.

of Austrian letters, *Marie von Ebner-Eschenbach and Peter Rosegger.

Encouraged by positive reviews and strong sales of her first books, Handel-Mazzetti would write a large number of novels over the next half-century. All are based on the lives of saints, including the virgin martyrs of the early centuries of the Catholic Church. The substructure of all of her major books were the Stations of the Cross, and it is more than likely that her inspiration for this technique was the immensely popular 1854 British work by Cardinal Wiseman, *Fabiola, or the Church of the Catacombs. The basic action is then set into neobaroque Austrian settings in which invariably a self-sacrificing heroine is able to convert an errant man to the path of goodness by means of her virtuous steadfastness. As part of her literary formula, Handel-Mazzetti customarily included detailed scenes of the execution of her heroes. The inspiration for these gory episodes, she freely admitted, came not only from the Passion of Christ but also from personal memories of her religious instructors' vivid stories of stigmatization and the countless paintings and prints of the sufferings of Christian martyrs over the centuries.

In two novels published between 1909 and 1914, *Die arme Margaret* (*Poor Margaret*) and *Stephana Schwertner,* Handel-Mazzetti depicted the tragic nature of religious conflicts in 17th-century Austria, when human frailty and the desire to impose religious orthodoxy inevitably clashed. In both novels, young men attempt to rape women of the opposing religious faith, and pay for their transgressions with their lives. The strength of the author's prose rises above the melodramatic aspects of the stories, creating an epic canvas in which both human flaws and strengths are depicted in meticulous detail. Despite her own deep Catholic faith, Handel-Mazzetti was careful to avoid the trap of creating stereotypes on either side of the religious divide of the 17th century. While celebrating the revival of the Catholic spirit in Austria, she did not succumb to a mindless triumphalism.

Like virtually all Austrian intellectuals, Enrica Handel-Mazzetti rallied to the national cause when World War I began in the summer of 1914. Already famous, she became even more popular while serving as vice-president of the Austrian Red Cross. Wealthy from the sales of her books, she was generous in dispensing gifts to various charities. During part of the war, she worked as a nurse's aide in hospitals, experiences that inspired her to write the 1917 short story, "Ilko Smutniak, der Ulan" ("Ilko Smutniak, the Lancer"). The

military defeat and political collapse of the Austro-Hungarian monarchy was a severe blow to conservatives like Enrica Handel-Mazzetti. Not only a political and social regime, but a complex multinational, indeed supranational, Habsburg way of life was swept away, leaving behind little more than chaos and confusion. The loss is mirrored in Handel-Mazzetti's post-1918 writings, many of which are distinctly weaker than her earlier works. Her 1920 novel *Der deutsche Held* (*The German Hero*), set in the period of the Napoleonic Wars, is an unsuccessful attempt to create a modern version of Heinrich von Kleist's classic work *The Prince of Homburg*. Critical judgment of her final trilogy—*Das Rosenwunder* (*The Miracle of the Roses,* 1924–26), *Frau Maria* (1929–31), and *Graf Reichard* (*Count Reichard,* 1939–49)—is also essentially negative, the consensus being that these works are wordy, superficial and unconvincing.

Although Enrica von Handel-Mazzetti's literary skills appeared to have entered a period of decline after 1918, there is one exception. In her 1934 novel *Die Waxenbergerin* (*The Woman of Waxenberg*), the author appears to once again have found her true voice, strong, eloquent and vibrant in its celebration of religious faith and human strength. Set in the year 1683, when Austria and indeed all of Central Europe was threatened by the military might of the Ottoman Empire, the story centers around the exploits of the indomitable Aloysia Silbereissin, an apothecary's daughter. Aloysia saves lives by nursing wounded soldiers, organizing the rationing of scarce food supplies, and generally helping to keep her community from disintegration. At the same time, she makes preparations to begin the next phase of her life as an Ursuline nun. The novel received critical praise because of its clear focus on everyday details of life in the 17th century, as well as on its accurate and sympathetic use of the dialect spoken by ordinary folk in the district of Waxenberg and the Mühlviertel.

As a conservative Roman Catholic author and representative intellectual figure of the old Habsburg order, Enrica von Handel-Mazzetti was *persona non grata* in Nazi-occupied Austria. None of her works could appear in print after 1941, and when World War II ended in 1945 and Austria was liberated from seven years of dictatorial rule, she appeared to many of the younger generation to be a ghost from a vanished past. A new generation of readers now found her works to be old-fashioned and irrelevant. When she died in Linz on April 8, 1955, Enrica von Handel-Mazzetti was largely forgotten. In the 1980s, however, her novels began to be rediscovered by scholars and readers alike, and her strengths as an author were being savored once more by a growing number for whom a good story well told was sufficient reason to open a book. Enrica von Handel-Mazzetti was honored by Austria on January 11, 1971, when a commemorative postage stamp was issued on the occasion of the centenary of her birth.

SOURCES:

Bourgeois, Joseph Earl. "Ecclesiastical Characters in the Novels of Enrica von Handel-Mazzetti." Ph. D. dissertation, University of Cincinnati, 1956.

Doppler, Bernhard. *Katholische Literatur und Literaturpolitik: Enrica von Handel-Mazzetti, eine Fallstudie.* Königstein im Taunus: Verlag Hain, 1980.

"Enrica Freiin von Handel-Mazzetti," in *Der Österreicher.* Vol. 6, no. 1. January 24, 1931, p. 5.

Freylinger, Maria J. *Enrica von Handel-Mazzetti: Biographie und Werke.*

Grenzmann, Wilhelm. "Enrica von Handel-Mazzetti," in Frederick Ungar, ed., *Handbook of Austrian Literature.* NY: Frederick Ungar, 1973, pp. 108–110.

Handel-Mazzetti, Enrica von. *Jesse and Maria.* Translated by George N. Shuster. NY: Henry Holt, 1931.

Hemmen, Alcuin Ambrose. "The Concept of Religious Tolerance in the Novels of Enrica von Handel-Mazzetti." Ph. D. dissertation, University of Michigan, 1945.

Kern, Elga, ed. *Führende Frauen Europas: Neue Folge, in fünfundzwanzig Selbstschilderungen.* Munich: Ernst Reinhardt Verlag, 1930.

Schmidt, Josef. "Enrica von Handel-Mazzetti (1871–1955)," in Donald G. Daviau, ed., *Major Figures of Austrian Literature: The Interwar Years 1918–1938.* Riverside, CA: Ariadne Press, 1995, pp. 107–128.

John Haag,
Associate Professor, University of Georgia, Athens, Georgia

Handler, Ruth (c. 1918—)

American businesswoman who, with her husband Elliott, co-founded Mattel Toys and created the Barbie doll. Born Ruth Moskowicz (shortened to Mosko) around 1918 in Denver, Colorado; married (Issadore) Elliott Handler, around 1940; children: Barbara Handler; Ken Handler.

The daughter of immigrant Polish Jews, Ruth Handler describes herself in her autobiography *The Ruth Handler Story,* as "a fiercely independent woman, one who has always felt the need to prove myself, even when I was just a child." She was born in Denver, Colorado, around 1918 and moved to Los Angeles in 1936. Handler's scrappiness and entrepreneurial spirit was put to the test in 1945, when she and her husband Elliott, her hometown sweetheart, founded Mattel Toys, a company that made its mark under her innovative leadership. It was reportedly Handler's idea to begin marketing directly to children through tele-

vision ads in 1955, and four years later, in 1959, it was she who introduced the Barbie doll. Fashioned after a German adult toy named "Lilli," and named for her daughter **Barbara Handler**, the doll, according to Ruth, was "created to project every little girl's dream of the future," but Barbie's overproportioned adult figure and long blonde hair were controversial from the start. According to M.G. Lord, a journalist and an expert in Barbie lore, kids loved the new doll, but their mothers were less receptive. "Mothers felt she was their worst nightmare [their fearful fantasy] of their husband's secretary," she writes in her 1994 book *Forever Barbie.* "In order to get around this attitude, a marketing genius at Mattel positioned the doll as a grooming tool for little girls." Hence, the doll was marketed with outfits, including shoes, jewelry, and handbags, a "fashion system."

Barbie's success put Mattel on the map. The company went public in 1960, and sales rocketed from $25 million to $75 million over the following two years. Within eight years, more than $500 million in profits were realized from Barbie alone. Around that time, Mattel introduced Barbie's male counterpart, Ken, named after Handler's son. Siblings and friends of Barbie followed, although the original doll, in countless personas and special editions, dominated the market. Those early dolls became big business in the collector's market; a 38-year-old mint-condition Barbie could fetch more than $5,000 by the year 2000.

As a business executive in what was still a male-dominated workplace, Handler faced more than her share of prejudice. She describes the indignity of being escorted through kitchens and up service elevators so as not to offend male members of clubs that barred women, and of the particularly pointed hostilities she encountered while conducting business in Japan. Handler also grappled with her own ambivalent feelings about being a working mother during a period when women were expected to stay at home with their children. Her greatest challenges, however, came during the 1970s, when she was diagnosed with breast cancer and underwent a mastectomy, and was then found guilty—along with several other employees—of financial misdoings at Mattel. "After the mastectomy, I never was able to grab hold of things at Mattel and regain control," she wrote about her troubles at the company. Handler pleaded *nolo contendere* to crimes which included manipulating stock prices by not reporting significant losses and withholding $2.4 million from the employees pension fund. Though steadfastly claiming that charges against her were "totally untrue," Handler was, nonetheless, forced to retire. She subsequently

Ruth Handler

formed the Ruthton Corporation, manufacturing and marketing breast prostheses for women who had undergone mastectomies. In 1991, she sold the company to a division of Kimberly-Clark. In 1992, Handler was named the United Jewish Appeal's first "Woman of the Year."

During the 1980s, Mattel faced further woes unrelated to Handler. After some ill-advised purchases and a substantial loss in 1983, the company was all but broke at the end of 1987. A turnaround began that year with a new chair, John Amerman, who closed plants, cut jobs, and found new ways to exploit two of Mattel's biggest money-makers: Barbie and Hot Wheels race cars. New entries into the Barbie market included a motor home, a cruise ship and various ethnic friends of Barbie. By 1988, Mattel reported earnings of $36 million. In January 1997, Amerman was succeeded by **Jill Barad**.

SOURCES:

Business Section. *Time.* Vol. 149, no. 21. May 26, 1997, p. 62.

Jacobs, A.F., and Jessica Shaw. "Legend of the Doll," in *Entertainment Weekly.* February 24, 1995.

McCombie, Mel. "Barbie benders," in *Women's Review of Books.* June 1995.

"Q & A," in *The Day* [New London, CT]. Sunday, January 29, 1995.

Sheets, Ken. "How this bodacious babe got Mattel in her clutches," in *Kiplinger's Personal Finance Magazine.* Vol. 51, no. 8. August 1997.

SUGGESTED READING:

Handler, Ruth. *Dream Doll: The Ruth Handler Story.* Longmeadow Press, 1997.

Barbara Morgan,
Melrose, Massachusetts

Haney, Carol (1925–1964)

American dancer and choreographer. Born in New Bedford, Massachusetts, in 1925; died in New York City, on May 10, 1964; married actor Larry Blyden (divorced); children: two.

A talented dancer and choreographer, Carol Haney was at the peak of her career when she was stricken with bronchial pneumonia and died suddenly at age 39. Born in New Bedford, Massachusetts in 1925, Haney studied dance as a child and had her own studio by the time she turned 15. Her career was launched in Hollywood where she danced in nightclubs with Jack Cole and assisted Gene Kelly in choreographing the movie musicals *An American in Paris* (1951), *Singin' in the Rain* (1952), and *Brigadoon* (1954). She also danced with Bob Fosse in the movie *Kiss Me Kate* (1953). Haney's first major role on Broadway was in the musical hit *Pajama Game* (1954), in which she dazzled the audience in the dance number "Steam Heat." She went on to choreograph the stage musicals *Flower Drum Song* (1961), *Bravo Giovanni* (1962), *She Loves Me* (1963), *Jennie* (1963), and *Funny Girl* (1964). She also choreographed the annual Oldsmobile industrial show and the Garry Moore television show. Haney was married to actor Larry Blyden with whom she had two children. They were divorced at the time of her death.

Hanim, Latife (1898–1975)

Turkish feminist and wife of Kemal Atatürk. Name variations: Latife Muammer. Born Latife Hanim in 1898; died in 1975; daughter of a family in Izmir; married Mustafa Kemal Atatürk (1881-1938, Turkish officer, son of **Zübeyde Hanim** *and Ali Riza, who created the modern secular Turkish republic), in 1922; children: none.*

Latife Hanim, born in 1898, was the well-educated daughter of a wealthy family in Izmir. When she married Mustafa Kemal Atatürk, a Turkish officer, in 1922, the marriage was contracted in the modern manner, not in the tradition of Islam. From 1922 to 1938, her husband remade the Turkish state. The new government was a republic with Kemal as president, and with its capital at Ankara (formerly Angora). There followed over several years a massive program of secularization. The caliphate was abolished, and Islam ceased to be the official state religion. Men could no longer wear the fez, or women the Muslim veil. Women were also raised to legal equality with men; Turkey dropped the Arabic alphabet and replaced it with a Latin alphabet. The Grand National Assembly became the font of sovereignty, and both men and women could vote for, and be elected to, membership. Religious shrines were closed and even private religious organizations were outlawed. Hagia St. Sophia, the former Byzantine imperial cathedral in Istanbul which had become the Ottoman imperial mosque, now became a national museum which included exhibits containing pictorial representations of former Turkish leaders. Good Muslims had never allowed pictorial representations in places of worship because they believed it violated the injunctions against idolatry in the Koran and the Old Testament. All Turks were ordered to adopt surnames as in the Western world. Kemal chose Atatürk, which meant Father of the Turk.

The new secular Turkish republic faced two interrelated sources of opposition and turmoil. Devout Muslims led by conservative religious leaders fought secularization every step of the way. Non-Turkish ethnic minorities such as Kurds, Armenians, and Arabs often joined forces with the Muslim fundamentalist opposition. Kemal saw such alliances as the only serious threat which his new republic need fear, and he treated them accordingly. Martial law, drumhead court martials, and ruthless use of the Turkish army soon restored order. But these same methods and attitudes carried over into internal Turkish politics. Kemal always claimed he wanted to mold Turkey into a modern Western state. He also admitted that modern Western states were legislative democracies with a recognized and accepted opposition party. Despite Kemal's stated intentions, the Turkish republic became increasingly a one-party dictatorship led by a sometimes paranoiac and vengeful *führer*.

This ambiguity between the stated ideal and the real can also be seen in Kemal's private life. He often criticized the old oriental Turkish attitude towards women and deliberately pushed one of the most feminist legislative programs in the world. Yet his own lifestyle reflected the Turkish past. In the 1920s, he became involved with two women. The first served as a concubine during the years of national revolt and was then hustled out of the country when Kemal emerged as president of Turkey. The second, Latife Hanim, became his official wife. She was considered a modern woman, and they appeared publicly together as role models for the new Turkish family. However, when Latife tried to assert herself and control his drinking and his carousing, Kemal became resentful. He finally divorced her

by the old Islamic method of repeating four times the phrase, "I divorce thee," and had her removed from his house. This method became illegal in Turkey less than a year later when Kemal's new Western civil law code came into force. In the 1930s, he became more aggressive toward the wives and daughters which he met socially. He also started adopting numerous attractive teenage girls who came to live with him: Zehra, Rukiye, Sabiha, Afet, and Nebile.

SOURCES:
Churchill, Winston S. *The World Crisis: The Aftermath.* Scribner, 1929.
Kinross, Lord. *Ataturk.* Morrow, 1965.
Lewis, Bernard. *The Emergence of Modern Turkey.* 2nd ed. Oxford, 1968.
Nyrop, Richard F. *Turkey.* 3rd ed. Department of the Army, 1980.

Hanim, Leyla (1850–1936)

Turkish composer, pianist, poet, and writer who composed 200 instrumental and vocal compositions and wrote articles on Turkish women. Name variations: Leyla Saz. Born in Istanbul, Turkey, in 1850; died in Istanbul on December 6, 1936; daughter of the court doctor to the vizier and governor, Ishmal Pasha; married Shiri Pasha (governor of various provincial capitals and prime minister).

Leyla Hanim was born in 1850 and grew up in the Ottoman court where her father was the court physician. From the age of seven, she studied piano with an Italian pianist. Later, she mastered all details of traditional Turkish music under the tutelage of Medini Aziz Efendiu and Astik Aga. Hanim—who was nicknamed Leyla Saz after the saz, a Turkish stringed instrument which was her passion—played both Turkish and Western music with the palace orchestra. Extremely well-educated, she was fluent in Greek, French, and Arabic. Hanim and her husband lived in a series of provincial towns while he served as governor before moving to Istanbul when he became prime minister. In the capital, Hanim created an artistic circle of women in which Turkish and Western literature and music were cultivated. She composed hundreds of pieces and wrote lyrics for 50 of them. Hanim also contributed many articles about the lives of women to Turkish journals of the period.

John Haag,
Athens, Georgia

Hani Motoko (1873–1957)

Japan's first female newspaper reporter, who was editor and publisher of Fujin no tomo *(Woman's Friend),*

HANI MOTOKO

Japan's longest-surviving woman's publication, and co-founder of Jiyū Gakuen, a private, co-educational school. Name variations: Matsuoka Moto (birth name). Pronunciation: HA-nee Moe-toe-koe. Born Matsuoka Moto on September 8, 1873, in Hachinobe, Aomori Prefecture, Japan; died in 1957; granddaughter of Matsuoka Tadataka (a former samurai); her father, a lawyer, was adopted into her mother's family, taking the name Matsuoka; attended elementary school in Hachinobe, Aomori; Daiichi Kōtō Jogakkō (Tokyo First Higher Girls' School); Meiji Jogakkō (Meiji Girls' School); married in 1896 and divorced in less than a year; married Hani Yoshikazu (1880–1955); children: Setsuko (daughter, 1903–1987); Keiko (daughter, b. 1908).

Was a member of the premiere graduating class of the Tokyo First Higher Girls' School (1891); was first female newspaper reporter in Japan (1897); edited and published Fujin no tomo *(Woman's Friend), Japan's longest-surviving women's publication (1906–57); co-founded a private, co-educational school, Jiyū Gakuen (1921).*

Periodicals published by Hani Motoko and Hani Yoshikazu: Katei no tomo *(Household Friend, 1903, renamed* Katei jogaku kogi *[Homestudy for Women], 1906, renamed* Fujin no tomo *[Woman's Friend], 1908—);* Kodomo no tomo *(Children's Friend, 1914–29);* Shin shōjo *(New Girls, 1915–20);* Manabi no tomo *(Learning Companion, 1920).*

Hani Motoko was born on September 8, 1873, in Hachinobe, Aomori Prefecture, Japan, only five years after the establishment of a government which promised to transform the country into a modern nation state. In this rapidly changing society, Hani was in the first generation of women who sought to shape their own lives and the destiny of Japan. She had the character traits of a trailblazer: moral courage, self-reliance, competence, and unfettered ambition. As is the case with women who succeed in "being the first," Hani had mentors, both female and male, who shaped her dreams and gave her opportunities. Over the course of a long career, she developed lasting institutions which have molded Japanese women's values in the 20th century.

Hani Motoko often recalled the disadvantages of the old, traditional society in which she grew up. Specifically, she regretted that she had not received moral guidance from her family. "My family was not uncaring nor negligent," she wrote, "but in those days no one, even in the more educated families, knew better." Although she was the descendant of samurai and her family was comfortably well-off, neither her grandmother nor her mother was literate, and Hani considered them naive. Her father, a lawyer, had been adopted into her mother's family as heir. He was, however, a ne'er-do-well, who was divorced from her mother and disinherited, following an extramarital affair and suspicious business dealings that tarnished the family's reputation. Hani's estrangement from her father was a deeply felt loss.

In her telling, Hani "clung tenaciously" to her "own ideas and beliefs." She was a stubborn perfectionist and not a well-liked child. Looking back, she continued to rue incidents in which she failed to act on her moral convictions and remembered, with some pleasure, when she took the initiative, particularly when she showed up the boys. Though not competitive when it came to her class standing, she had a growing intellectual curiosity and, in 1884, won an award for academic excellence, presented by the Ministry of Education.

The year of Hani's birth, 1873, was the same year in which Japan's modern public-school system was established. While elementary school was compulsory, only 16% of Japanese girls were in school at the time Hani was a student. It was her maternal grandfather—the family member with whom she most identified—that enabled Hani to continue her education in Tokyo. Nationwide, there were only nine women's schools. In 1891, Hani enrolled in the first graduating class of the Daiichi Kōtō Jogakkō (Tokyo First Higher Girls' School).

Tokyo was intellectually heady for a young woman from rural Japan. "I was still a good student," she recalled, "but my earlier enthusiasm had waned, while my interest and curiosity were captured by the metropolis around me." The first session of the Imperial Diet (national legislature) was about to begin and street circulars announced a wide variety of public lectures. Said Hani: "I went to listen to the speeches, but less often after the school advised us not to attend political gatherings." At the time, women were prohibited by law from participating in political organizations. Hani was a regular reader of *Jogaku zasshi* (Magazine of Women's Learning), the first major women's magazine in Japan, which published articles with the intention of enlightening women about education, foreign affairs, and culture. During this time, she also attended Christian churches and was baptized.

Hani completed her secondary education with high objectives but limited opportunities.

At the time, no college in Japan admitted women. "My ambition . . . was to go on to higher normal school and eventually become a teacher," said Hani, "the only meaningful way of life that I knew." Most young women who were employed outside their parental homes worked as textile-mill operatives or domestic servants. Schoolteaching, however, had become a possible career after the establishment of compulsory education, though only 5.9% of teachers in Japan were women. It was not mere coincidence that most of the first generation of professional women in Japan, like Hani, began their careers as elementary school teachers, even though they later moved into other endeavors. Teaching was the most prestigious and lucrative career opportunity available. As Hani surveyed the landscape, she saw that only Christian women's schools were opening their doors to women for post-secondary education. She set her mind on attending one of them—Meiji Jogakkō (Meiji Women's School)—because its male president, Iwamoto Yoshiharu, was the editor of *Jogaku zasshi*, and the school embodied the progressive intellectual goals of the magazine. Hani's family, however, could not afford the tuition. Thus, she plucked up her courage, presented herself in Iwamoto's office for an interview, and persuaded him to admit her with a tuition waiver and a job as a copy editor for *Jogaku zasshi*. This enabled her to pay for her dormitory room and board. She had also found, in Iwamoto, her first mentor.

Meiji Women's School afforded Hani a stimulating intellectual and social environment. As a copy editor, she met prominent people in the fields of literature, religion, and education who wrote for the magazine. Hani's memoirs indicate that living in the dormitory with other women students, under the guidance of wise and gracious "mother figures," was perhaps, ultimately, more influential than the actual lectures she attended. This setting provided Hani with the moral guidance which she had missed in her own family. In Japan, these Christian women's schools were unprecedented, because they trained students in the discipline of daily living as well as in academic subjects. Unlike public elementary and secondary schools for women, which still espoused traditional feminine virtues like docility and submission to authority, Christian schools aspired to mold "modern" women and advance their social status by preparing them for leadership roles in society. Christian schools cultivated women's identity as individuals. While the values they espoused—dedication to socially useful work, self-reliance, and a sense

of mission—were not incompatible with traditional samurai values, the teaching of these values to women, was, indeed, revolutionary. The school's stated intent was "to educate women by providing them with a model of ideal womanhood in which both the Western concept of women's rights and Japan's own traditional female virtues are embodied." If Hani was typical of its graduates, however, it might more accurately be said that the school developed in its women students the character traits and values which had enabled men to be successful in both Western and Japanese societies.

For reasons which Hani does not make clear in her autobiography, she withdrew from Meiji Women's School in 1892 and returned to her hometown to teach elementary school. But she found no intellectual satisfaction teaching there, in a public school, nor spiritual satisfaction in teaching in a Catholic girls' school, where she worked in the company of Western nuns. For Hani, Christianity had become an inspiring set of moral values, rather than a source of spiritual fulfillment. "At Meiji Women's School we had been taught Christian thought, but not faith," she wrote. That Christian morality continued to be the standard by which she lived her life was perhaps most clear in her decision to marry the man she loved as a means of saving him from a lifestyle which she found vulgar. (Hers was not, as was most frequently the case, a marriage arranged by her family.) The marriage was unsuccessful, however, and within a year she sought a divorce. After the dissolution of her parents' marriage, her own divorce was the second emotional crisis of her life. Later, she wrote: "I have always feared that this painful episode of my life, of which I am ashamed even today, might jeopardize the effectiveness of my public service. Not for a moment, however, do I regret my decision to liberate myself from the enslaving hold of emotion, for my life had been rendered meaningless by the selfish and profane love of another." For Hani, as was the case with many of the educated women of her generation, divorce was the beginning of a self-directed life, finding satisfaction in public service.

Keeping her divorce a secret from family and friends, Hani returned to Tokyo to make her way in the world. Once more, she was fortunate to find a mentor. "Opportunity always reached out before suffering could claim me," she wrote. She obtained a position, first as a maid, later as a live-in student, in the household of Dr. *Yoshioka Yayoi, one of Japan's first female doctors, founder and president of Tokyo Women's Medical School, and publisher of the schools newspaper, *Joikai* (Women Doctors' World). In the Yoshioka household, which included Dr. Yoshioka, her husband, Yoshioka Arita, director of a German-language academy, as well as women medical students and a woman pharmacist, Hani's professional ambitions were nurtured, and she was introduced to a dual-career marriage in which professional work and personal lives were mutually supportive and beneficial.

In the challenging environment of the household, Hani developed the dream of becoming a writer. Armed with her experience as a copy editor for *Jogaku zasshi,* she sought a staff position on a newspaper. At first, the doors to employment were closed to her—the only position open to a woman in a newspaper office was as a receptionist. But again, with perseverance, she was allowed a trial run as a copy editor at the prestigious *Hōchi* newspaper. Since her work was deemed more accurate than that of the men with whom she worked, she was given the job with the proviso that, "as the first woman to work in the editing room, you will have to prove yourself." Hani appears to have been the victim of some verbal harassment, but she claimed to have been too pleased with her job to have taken notice of it.

But her dream was to write, not merely edit, and she eagerly looked for an opportunity. The *Hōchi* ran a popular column entitled, "Fujin no sugao" (Portraits of Leading Women). Although male writers were already assigned to the column, Hani seized the initiative, used her contacts from her former school, Tokyo First Women's Higher School, and wangled an interview with a prominent aristocrat. Her article was immediately accepted, and, within six months of having come to Tokyo, she realized her dream of becoming a newspaper reporter— the first woman reporter in Japan. Hani was convinced that women should not be limited to the society page. She wrote articles about women, education, and religions, and even police reports yielded subjects that required a woman's perspective. She was gratified when readers' responses backed her up. One of her favorite interviews was with a prominent Zen Buddhist monk, Nishiari. Hani described him not only as an open, cooperative subject, but also one who extended sympathy and understanding about the pain which still lingered after her divorce. Hani continued to have conversations with Nishiari and, for a time, contemplated becoming a Buddhist nun—particularly after learning from Nishiari that, historically, Bud-

dhist nuns had been moral counselors as well as political advisors to government officials. Of her journalistic style, it has been said that she endeavored to find wisdom in mundane settings. Thorough research was her hallmark, and her writing was clear and straightforward, a refreshing contrast to the overblown rhetoric that characterized the popular press of the day.

During her tenure as a reporter at the *Hōchi,* Hani Motoko met and married a fellow reporter, Hani Yoshikazu. It appears to have been a love match between equally independent writers who were devoted to their careers. Initially, their marriage was disruptive. While progressive with respect to hiring a woman, the *Hōchi* staff was not prepared to employ both a husband and wife in the same offices. Hani felt pressured to resign, and Yoshikazu was transferred. In the long run, however, their marriage was the basis of a professional partnership that mirrored the one which Hani had earlier witnessed in the Yoshioka household.

After leaving the *Hōchi,* Hani embarked on her career in magazine publishing, becoming, in 1903, the editor, clerk, and manager of a journal published by the Fujin Kyōikukai (Women's Education Association), the most influential women's organization of the day. That same year, she launched her own project, *Katei no tomo* (Friend of the Home), serving as sole editor and writer. The first issue, which she had totally written, was published the day after the birth of her first child. In 1906, due to mergers at the *Hōchi* newspaper, Yoshikazu joined Hani at *Katei no tomo*; in 1908, they parted with their publisher, renamed the magazine *Fujin no tomo* (Woman's Friend), and began publishing it themselves. It is the longest surviving women's magazine in Japan.

It might be said that the model for *Fujin no tomo* was the magazine for which Hani had worked as a copy editor, *Jogaku zasshi.* No longer in print when the couple began publishing *Fujin no tomo,* the earlier magazine had differed from other women's monthlies of the late-19th century because it denounced customary feminine roles. While *Fujin no tomo* urged women to develop their own identities, the magazine was politically neutral. In contrast to a number of short-lived, early 20th-century women's magazines, particularly those published by socialist groups, *Fujin no tomo* never advocated women's rights or the revision of the social and political order. True to Hani's own values, the magazine urged self-transformation. Appealing to an audience of lower- and middle-class housewives, the magazine put forth the idea that the home was the most important social unit and its improvement would result in significant social reform and progress. With the motto, "education in daily life," experts addressed issues of marriage, education of children, health concerns, and household finance. Hani used the magazine to initiate popular campaigns for reform, such as Western clothing for children, that she thought would bring reason and efficiency to matters of daily life. In an implied criticism of the more theoretical and political women's magazines, she said, "The world needs social critics and commentators, but the mission of our magazine, *Fujin no tomo*, lies somewhere beyond mere theorizing. It is our ultimate goal to give concrete form to our visions and to substantiate our theories in practice."

In 1921, Hani and her husband established Jiyū Gakuen (Freedom School), a private school as a means of developing the values they championed in their magazine. As was the case with Hani's early mentors, Hani Motoko and Hani Yoshikazu expressed their unique social vision by simultaneously publishing a magazine and administering a private school. The goal of the school (initially a girls' school, later it would become co-educational) was to foster a totally free individual—free as a result of her capacity to make her own way in the world. The representation of values designed to achieve this goal was drawn both from Confucian classics and the Bible. In practical terms for the education of young girls, the result of this combination of values was to develop the "good wife, wise mother" (a traditional Confucian formulation) who could efficiently manage a household without the assistance of servants. Over the years, the school became known for its success in combining the practical lessons of self-sufficiency (e.g. growing and preparing the food the students ate) with an academic curriculum. In the sense of combining a residential community, which developed lessons on daily living, with intellectual pursuits, the school was modeled on the Christian women's school which Hani had attended.

While there were many women of her generation who became professionals and rose to positions of leadership, Hani Motoko was in many ways unique among them. Unlike most, Hani had a profoundly spiritual, rather than a political, perspective. Consistent with this view, she believed in the capacity of a woman to transform herself, her family, and ultimately, society; individual transformation, rather than legal reform or the overthrow of the existing political

economy was, to her, the key to human liberation. For these reasons, Hani appeared to be more optimistic about improving the status of women than others. Perhaps it was this relatively optimistic message that best explains Hani's popularity and the success of her projects.

SOURCES:
Mulhern, Chieko Irie, ed. "Hani Motoko: The Journalist Educator," in *Heroic with Grace: Legendary Women of Japan*. Armonk, NY: M.E. Sharpe, 1991.

Linda L. Johnson, Professor of History, Concordia College, Moorhead, Minnesota

Hanisch, Cornelia (1952—)
West German fencer. Born on June 12, 1952.

In the 1984 Los Angeles Olympics, 32-year-old Cornelia Hanisch won the Foil team gold for West Germany (with teammates **Christiane Weber, Sabine Bischoff, Zita-Eva Funkenhauser,** and **Ute Wessel**). She also took the Foil silver individual, losing the gold to 25-year-old **Luan Jujie** of China. Hanisch had entered the final at 16-1.

Hankford, Anne (d. 1457).
See Montacute, Anne.

Hankford, Anne (1431–1485)
*Countess of Ormonde. Name variations: Anne Hankeford. Born in 1431; died on November 13, 1485; daughter of Sir Richard Hankford and *Anne Montacute (d. 1457); married Thomas Butler, 7th earl of Ormonde (r. 1477–1515), before July 11, 1445; children: Anne Butler (b. 1462, who married Sir James St. Leger and Ambrose Griseacre); Margaret Butler (1465–1539, who married Sir William Boleyn). Thomas Butler later married Lore Berkeley.*

Hanks, Nancy (1783–1818)
American mother of Abraham Lincoln. Born in 1783; died in 1818; became first wife of Thomas Lincoln (a carpenter), June 12, 1806; children: Sarah Lincoln (d. 1828); Abraham Lincoln (b. February 12, 1809); a third child, a son, died in infancy.

Nancy Hanks, the mother of the 16th U.S. president Abraham Lincoln, was a handsome young woman of humble circumstances; she was known for her intellect and exemplary character. In June 1806, she married the carpenter Thomas Lincoln, and the couple settled in Hardin County, Kentucky. They had three children: the oldest, daughter **Sarah Lincoln**; the second, Abraham; the third, a son who died in infancy.

The Lincolns lived plainly in a log cabin. Described as shiftless, Thomas Lincoln could not read or write and was always poor. Nancy Hanks could read but not write. A woman of piety and discernment, she left an indelible impression on her son. From her, Lincoln is said to have inherited his serious temperament which was brightened by a spirit of playfulness that was a prominent trait throughout his troubled career. Abraham Lincoln was closer to his mother than his father. When Nancy Hanks died in 1818, the nine-year-old boy deeply mourned the loss and turned to his older sister Sarah for guidance. (She would die ten years later.) In later years, Lincoln would say of his mother: "All that I am, and all that I hope to be, I owe to my angel mother." Following her death, Thomas Lincoln married a widow, **Sarah Bush Johnston**.

Hanna or Hannah.

Variant of Ann, Anna, or Anne.

Hannah (fl. 11th c. BCE)

Biblical woman. Name variations: Anna; Hannah is possibly an abbreviation of Hananiah. Flourished in the 11th century BCE; one of two wives of Elkanah of Ephraim, the Levite (Elkanah's other wife was Peninnah); children: Samuel the prophet, as well as three other sons and two daughters.

The better beloved of the two wives of Elkanah, an Ephraimite from Ramathaim-zophim, Hannah (meaning "Grace") was long childless. On an annual visit to Shiloh (an ancient administrative and religious center northeast of Jerusalem, later destroyed by the Philistines), Hannah vowed to God that she would dedicate a son to his service, if only she could conceive. This prayer apparently was answered, and Hannah gave birth to Samuel. Because of her vow, Samuel was raised at Shiloh by the site's chief priest, Eli. In time, Samuel became an influential prophet who anointed the first two Israelite kings, Saul and David. According to the Old Testament's *First Book of Samuel* 2.1-10, Hannah authored a prayer in which God is proclaimed the source of victory, justice, fertility and legitimacy, as well as the source of humility for the proud and exaltation for the meek. In addition to Samuel, she gave birth to three other sons and two daughters, none of whose names are known. In the *Talmud*, Hannah is considered one of seven important prophetesses, and her prayer is recited in the first day service of

Rosh Hashana as an example of a successful plea put before God.

William Greenwalt,
Associate Professor of Classical History,
Santa Clara University, Santa Clara, California

Hanover, electress of.

See Sophia (1630–1714).
See Sophia Dorothea of Brunswick-Celle (1666–1726).

Hanover, queen of.

See Frederica of Mecklenburg-Strelitz (1778–1841).
See Mary of Saxe-Altenburg (1818–1907).

Hansberry, Lorraine (1930–1965)

African-American dramatist, essayist and social activist whose play Raisin in the Sun *brought her great acclaim. Born on May 19, 1930, in Chicago, Illinois; died on January 12, 1965, in New York, of cancer; youngest of four children of Charles and Nannie Hansberry; attended University of Wisconsin through sophomore year; married Robert Nemiroff (a musician), in 1953 (divorced 1964); children: none.*

Began writing plays and short stories while working as a journalist in New York City for a progressive African-American newspaper; her first play, Raisin In The Sun, *opened on Broadway to great acclaim and earned her a New York Drama Critics' Circle Award, the first given to a black playwright (1959); saw her second play,* The Sign in Sidney Brustein's Window, *produced (1964); also wrote television drama, poetry and literary and social criticism while taking an active and vocal part in the civil rights and "Black Power" movements (1960s).*

One summer's day in 1954, Robert Nemiroff found a letter from his wife in his Greenwich Village mailbox. It was one of many Lorraine Hansberry wrote to him during a summer spent as a counselor at an interracial camp for children—certainly an unusual concept in the 1950s, although the same could be said of her own marriage, as an African-American writer to a Jewish musician. "The poets have been right in all these centuries, darling," she wrote to him from her verdant summer vantage point. "Even in its astounding imperfection, this earth of ours is magnificent. But, oh, this human race!" Her exasperation pinpointed the very source of her creative impulse, for it was the glories and weaknesses of her fellow humans that inspired Hansberry's remarkable artistic output during a tragically short career.

The lessons began during her childhood in Chicago, where she had been born on May 19, 1930, into the relatively affluent household of Charles and **Nannie Perry Hansberry.** Charles Hansberry had made a comfortable living in real estate, and was especially known for renovating homes abandoned by whites on Chicago's South Side as the influx of Southern blacks increased during the 1920s. Each of the small apartments he carved from these larger homes had a small cooking area for its residents, a trademark that built Charles Hansberry's reputation as "the kitchenette king." Like many of their tenants, the Hansberrys had come to Chicago from elsewhere—Charles from Mississippi and Nannie from Tennessee, where she had been a schoolteacher. By the time of Lorraine's birth, as the last of Charles and Nannie's four children, Hansberry Enterprises was a well-established and prosperous real-estate and construction firm.

The Hansberry household was a center of black Chicago's social and intellectual life. W.E.B Du Bois, the father of vigorous African-American progressivism, was a frequent visitor. A copy of his 1903 *The Souls of Black Folks* held a prominent place in the family library. Actor Paul Robeson and poet Langston Hughes, whose work would be such a powerful influence on Lorraine, were other familiar houseguests. All three men were, in different ways, articulate and outspoken defenders of black culture and pride. In addition to these luminaries, Hansberry could listen to the stories of a number of visitors from Africa brought to dinner by her uncle, Leo Hansberry, a prominent professor of African history at Howard University. Along with her family's vibrant social conscience, Lorraine would inherit the Hansberry's penchant for political activism. Charles, a frequent and generous donor to the NAACP and the Urban League, ran unsuccessfully for Congress in 1940 on the Republican ticket, while Nannie was a longtime ward committee member for the local GOP.

The difference between Hansberry's own upbringing and that of the majority of urban African-Americans was pointed out to her one day at the age of five, when she arrived at the Betsy Ross Elementary School wearing a luxurious white ermine coat given to her as a Christmas present by her doting parents. The beating spurred by the jealous anger of her schoolmates, many of whom had no coat at all, remained in her memory for years. "Ever since then," Hansberry wrote in a third person memoir, "she had been antagonistic to the symbols of affluence. In fact, after that day, she had chosen her friends

with intense fascination from among her assailants." Three years later, when the Hansberrys moved to a racially mixed neighborhood in a more prosperous section of Chicago, Lorraine narrowly missed injury from a brick thrown at her by a fleeing crowd of angry whites who appeared outside their home. Because of her father's prominence and his refusal to accept social boundaries dictated by whites, racial tensions were never far from the Hansberrys' door. "American racism helped kill him," Lorraine said of her father's sudden death in 1946, of a cerebral hemorrhage.

On her graduation from Englewood High School in 1947, Hansberry became the first in her family to attend a predominantly white college and the first African-American student in campus housing at the University of Wisconsin, where she was a liberal arts major. Within a year, she was coordinating campus campaign activities for 1948's Progressive Party presidential candidate Henry Wallace; by 1949, she was president of the Young Progressive League. Student theatricals were another area of special interest for her, especially a production of Sean O'Casey's *Juno and the Paycock.* "O'Casey never fools you about . . . the genuine heroism which must naturally emerge when you tell the truth about people," she later wrote. "This, to me, is the height of artistic perception." She was particularly impressed by O'Casey's talent for using his Irish themes and settings to illuminate the human condition as a whole, a lesson she would remember well when she began writing about her own race. Her infatuation with the theater, which she said embraced "everything I like all at one time," did not extend to academics. She later admitted that "the point of things . . . like classes and note-taking and lecture and lab" eluded her. In 1950, after completing her sophomore year, Hansberry quit school and moved to New York.

She arrived in a city which was giving new and energetic expression to a long tradition of political and social liberalism, especially to the growing civil-rights movement. Hansberry's first job in New York was with *Freedom,* a progressive black newspaper founded by Robeson and edited by Louis E. Burnham, who became Lorraine's mentor. "The things he taught me," she later wrote, "were the great things: that all racism is rotten, white or black; that *everything* is political; that people tend to be indescribably beautiful and uproariously funny." As the paper's youngest staff reporter, she covered civil-rights and women's issues, New York politics, and her beloved theater, all of which would find a place in her own writing for the stage. Her assignments began to impress upon her the inferior status of schools and housing in predominantly African-American sections of the city, which Hansberry traced to a pervasive lack of self-esteem. She urged in print that schools with a high percentage of black students include such topics as African history and the study of prominent African-Americans as part of their curricula. In 1951, she was promoted to associate editor, traveling as far afield as Paraguay to attend an international peace conference in 1952, at which she spoke out against the Korean War. All the while, Lorraine worked steadily at a growing body of unpublished short stories, poems, and plays.

By 1953, she had left *Freedom* to devote more of her time to writing and to social causes, especially discrimination against blacks in jobs, housing, and education. That winter, Lorraine joined a protest rally at New York University, which had been accused of deliberately excluding blacks from its basketball team. Among her fellow protestors was a musician named Robert Nemiroff, the son of Jewish immigrants, who was as passionate as Hansberry about social justice. The two were married on June 20, 1953, in the Hansberrys' Chicago home, by which time the inevitable tensions of an interracial marriage (then still illegal in 13 states) had eased somewhat. "We hadn't done anything interracial really with someone in our immediate family," said Lorraine's sister Mamie, while recalling how she and her mother chose to walk ahead of Lorraine and her white boyfriend on their way to a neighborhood restaurant the night of their first meeting.

The why of why we are here is an intrigue for adolescents; the how is what must command the living.

—Lorraine Hansberry

The young couple moved into an apartment over a laundry on Greenwich Village's Bleecker Street, working at a number of different jobs to support their respective artistic habits while plunging enthusiastically into the Village's social and cultural life. Nemiroff worked as a waiter, copywriter, and typist, while Hansberry found a position with the folk-music magazine, *Sing Out!*, which was the first to publish those stalwarts of the '60s protest movement, "This Land Is Your Land" and "We Shall Overcome."

In 1956, the Nemiroffs' finances were decidedly improved when one of Robert's folk ballads became a number one hit. Now able to devote all her time to writing, Lorraine began to concentrate on a play she had begun some time

earlier. It tells the story of an African-American family living in a Chicago apartment (not unlike the ones Charles Hansberry had provided for his tenants) who receives a $10,000 insurance check upon the death of a grandfather. Hansberry uses the conflicts that erupt among three generations of a family over the way to spend the money to explore the hopes, fears, and dreams of her race, weaving traditional African myth and dance into her story to underscore her belief that pride in one's heritage brings the strength to fight for equality. "It is a play that tells the truth about people," Lorraine wrote to her mother back in Chicago, "and I think it will help a lot of people to understand how we are just as complicated as they are." She called the play *Raisin in the Sun*, taking her title from Langston Hughes' poem *Harlem*:

> What happens to a dream deferred?
> Does it dry up
> Like a raisin in the sun?
> Maybe it just sags
> Like a heavy load
> Or does it explode?

One night, Lorraine read a first draft of the play to a dinner guest, Phillip Rose, a music publisher for whom her husband worked. Even though he had never been involved with a theatrical production in his life, Rose was so taken with her writing that he offered to option the rights. He and a partner managed to raise enough money from investors to introduce the drama outside of New York, successfully mounting it in Chicago, Philadelphia, and New Haven, by which time *Variety* was predicting that the play "would ripen into substantial Broadway tenancy." Within 18 months, *Raisin in the Sun* opened at Broadway's Ethel Barrymore Theater on March 11, 1959, directed by Lloyd Richards, starring Sidney Poitier, *Diana Sands, Claudia McNeil, and *Ruby Dee.

"Never before in the entire history of the American theater has so much of the truth of black people's lives been seen on the stage," James Baldwin noted. Walter Kerr told his *New York Herald Tribune* readers that Hansberry had found "the precise temperature of a race at that time in its history when it cannot retreat and cannot quite find the way to move forward. Three generations stand poised, and crowded, on a detonation cap." Lorraine found herself a celebrity overnight. *Raisin* was awarded the New York Drama Critics' Circle Award as Best Play of 1959, making Hansberry not only the youngest playwright to receive the award, but also the first black and only the fifth woman.

Variety named her the most promising playwright of that year. *Raisin in the Sun* ran for 530 performances, was successfully adapted for the screen, and was named the best film in competition at the 1961 Cannes Film Festival.

Just a week before *Raisin in the Sun* opened, Hansberry was asked to deliver the keynote address at a writer's conference sponsored by the American Society of African Culture. Her subject, "The Roots of the Negro Writer," pointed to the sources of her own inspiration in the emerging black social consciousness of her time. It was in this speech that she coined the phrase "young, gifted, and black." But recalling her college-age admiration for Sean O'Casey, Lorraine urged her audience to use their art to emphasize the common struggles of humanity in general. "All art is social," she said; it was writer's duty to get involved in "the intellectual affairs" of everyone, "everywhere." She attempted just that in her opening segment of a planned NBC series on the Civil War, written for producer Dore Schary in 1960. The episode examined the effects of slavery, and Hansberry took care to include in her script, called "The Drinking Gourd," slavery's

Lorraine Hansberry

impact on poor whites as well as blacks. But the network considered her treatment of the subject too controversial and eventually canceled the entire project over Schary's objections.

As the "Black Power" movement of the 1960s gained strength, Hansberry proved that her call to action was entirely serious by becoming a leading figure in fundraising and organizational efforts. She helped found the Student Nonviolent Coordinating Committee (SNCC), to unify the bewildering array of protest groups forming throughout the country, and, like her father before her, gave generously of her time to the NAACP, the Urban League, and the Congress of Racial Equality (CORE). She called publicly for the abolition of the House Un-American Activities Committee, which was then turning its McCarthy-inspired eye on the civil-rights movement, and criticized the Kennedy Administration's handling of the Cuban missile crisis as a threat to world peace. During her hectic schedule, Hansberry found time to buy and renovate a country house in Croton-on-Hudson, less than an hour from the city, along with Nemiroff. But their marriage had been suffering for some time from the constant publicity surrounding Lorraine. The couple began spending less and less time together and had separated by 1960. A discreet Mexican divorce would end their marriage in 1964.

All the while, Lorraine kept up an active writing schedule. By 1963, she was working on a musical adaptation of Oliver LaFarge's *Laughing Boy,* a dramatic adaptation of Charles Chesnutt's *The Marrow of Tradition,* and an original drama, *Les Blancs,* set during a revolution in a fictional African country. These works-in-progress were in addition to a constant stream of published literary criticism. Notable among them was an essay on *Simone de Beauvoir's *The Second Sex,* a book Hansberry said changed her life, although strong women characters had always been present in her work. The main action in *Raisin in the Sun,* for example, is driven forward by Walter Lee's mother and grandmother, while it is his sister, Beneatha, who provides the cultural traditions that save him from despair. In "The Drinking Gourd," it is the house slave Rissa who defies her white masters and arms her son for escape to the North, setting the main conflict of the play in motion; while in *Les Blancs,* a beautiful African dancer propels the male lead to join the struggle for his people's freedom.

In April of 1963, as the first draft of her next complete play was nearly ready, 33-year-old Hansberry began to suffer from fainting spells and attacks of nausea. Tests indicated what was at first suspected to be a duodenal ulcer, but which was later discovered to be colon cancer that had spread to her pancreas. As her health rapidly deteriorated, Lorraine worked feverishly to prepare *The Sign in Sidney Brustein's Window* for rehearsal.

Her inspiration was an incident from her Greenwich Village days in which a politically reticent friend had been prevailed upon to place a campaign sign for a local candidate in his window, only to have a brick thrown through it for his trouble. Hansberry's new play used the incident to call on intellectuals to abandon their ivory towers and take part in the social struggle around them; but the quasi-absurdist form she chose to relay her message left critics puzzled. In addition to the contrast from its sublimely dramatic predecessor, this new play of ideas attempted to take on issues as disparate as abstract art, prostitution, and marriage, and dealt only peripherally with black cultural issues. Indeed, there was only one African-American role in the play.

The new work was in trouble almost as soon as it opened in October of 1964. "A limbo play, full of insights, in which the playwright has not broken through with that touch of finality," wrote critic Max Lerner; while *The New York Times* critic Howard Taubman gently suggested that "the truth must be faced that Miss Hansberry's play lacks concision and cohesion."

The Sign in Sidney Brustein's Window nearly closed in the face of such negative reviews but was kept open through the dedicated efforts of some of Hansberry's theatrical peers who embraced its universalist message. While Lorraine's illness worsened, Ossie Davis, Ruby Dee, James Baldwin, and Sammy Davis, Jr., were just a few of the names appearing at the bottom of a full-page ad in *The New York Times* urging theatergoers to judge her play for themselves. Other actors contributed to a fund to prevent a closing. Their efforts were successful, even as Lorraine entered the final stages of her suffering. Five days after the play opened, she lapsed into a coma at New York's University Hospital. She seemed to rally two days later but remained hospitalized for the next three months as cancer slowly robbed her of life. She passed away on January 12, 1965, at 35 years of age. That night, *The Sign in Sidney Brustein's Window* closed.

At her death, Hansberry left behind an impressive body of unpublished work—unproduced plays, sections of an autobiography, a film script, and a collection of essays. Much of this output reached its audience through the efforts of Robert Nemiroff, whom Lorraine had named her literary executor. He published her unfinished autobiography under the title *To Be Young, Gifted and Black,* and shortly afterward adapted it for the off-Broadway stage; he produced *Les Blancs* on Broadway in 1970, starring James Earl Jones, *Lili Darvas, and Cameron Mitchell; and he brought a Tony-winning musical version of *Raisin in the Sun* to the stage in 1974, which has since been revived several times and was adapted for television in 1989.

"I want to reach a little closer to the world, which is to say, to people," Lorraine Hansberry once said; "and see if we can share some illuminations together about each other." Because of Hansberry's ability to successfully blend her art and her social conscience, those illuminations remain sharp and clear.

SOURCES:

Cheney, Anne. *Lorraine Hansberry.* Boston, MA: Twayne, 1984.

Hansberry, Lorraine (adapted by Robert Nemiroff). *To Be Young, Gifted and Black.* Englewood Cliffs, NJ: Prentice Hall, 1969.

Hine, Darlene, ed. *Black Women in America: An Historical Encyclopedia.* Brooklyn, NY: Carlson Publishing, 1993.

Norman Powers,
writer-producer, Chelsea Lane Productions, New York

Hanschman, Nancy (1927–1997).

See Dickerson, Nancy.

Hanscom, Adelaide (1876–1932)

American photographer of portraits and narrative tableaux. Born in Empire City, Oregon, in 1876; died in California in 1932; studied at the Mark Hopkins Institute of Art, San Francisco, California; married Gerald Leeson (a mining engineer and former Canadian Mountie), in 1907 (died 1915); children: two.

Photographer Adelaide Hanscom, a native of Oregon, studied at the Mark Hopkins Institute of Art in San Francisco, California, and began her career in that city. In 1902, after taking two second prizes in the Channing Club Exhibit held in Berkeley, Hanscom took over photographer **Laura Adams'** portrait studio, where she photographed many of the area's most prominent families In 1904, she partnered with **Blanche Cumming** to establish Hanscom and Cumming, a firm also located in San Francisco. Between 1904 and 1907, Hanscom exhibited widely throughout California and contributed her photographs to magazines. During the San Francisco earthquake of 1906, her studio caught fire, destroying most

of her prints and negatives, among them the negatives she had produced for a special edition of *The Rubáiyát of Omar Khayyám,* which was issued between 1905 and 1912.

Hanscom then moved to Seattle, where she established a studio and, in 1908, married Gerald Leesom, a mining engineer and former Canadian Mountie. Within the course of the next six years, she had two children and moved three times: to Alaska, back to California, and then to Idaho. Following the death of her husband, who was killed in 1915 during the first battle of World War I, Hanscom's mental health began to deteriorate. She continued to work, producing the illustrations for *Elizabeth Barrett Browning's* *Sonnets from the Portuguese* in 1916, and moving yet again to Danville, California. Hanscom lived in a mental-health facility from 1922 to 1924, after which she used her inheritance to move to England to be close to her husband's relatives. She had returned to California to be near her daughter when she was killed in a hit-and-run accident in 1932.

Hansen, Julia Butler (1907–1988)

U.S. Democratic Congresswoman from Washington (November 8, 1960–December 31, 1974). Born Julia Caroline Butler on June 14, 1907, in Portland, Oregon; died on May 3, 1988, in Cathlamet, Washington; daughter of Don C. Butler and Maude (Kimball) Butler; attended public schools in Washington; attended Oregon State College, 1924–26; University of Washington, A.B., 1930; married Henry A. Hansen, on July 15, 1939; children: David Kimball Hansen.

During her 43-year political career, which included elective offices on the local, state, and federal levels, Julia Butler Hansen served seven consecutive terms as a U.S. congresswoman.

Born in Portland, Oregon, in 1907, Butler attended Oregon State College for two years and then worked her way through the University of Washington, receiving a degree in home economics in 1930. She settled in Cathlamet, Washington, where she entered politics in 1938, winning election to the city council and serving until 1946. She was a member of the state house of representatives from 1939 until her election to Congress in 1960, serving as speaker pro tempore for five years (1955–60) and becoming an expert on transportation issues.

Following the death of Third District Representative Russell V. Mack in March 1960, Hansen was elected to fill the vacancy in the

86th Congress and simultaneously elected to the 87th Congress. She was reelected for six more consecutive terms, during which time she served on numerous committees and chaired the Subcommittee on Interior and Related Agencies of the Committee on Appropriations. Hansen initiated joint resolutions calling for a national traffic safety agency and an independent Federal Maritime administration. She introduced legislation for a joint Congressional committee to investigate crime, for construction of a Veterans' hospital in Vancouver, Washington, and for the regulation of dairy imports. During the war in Vietnam, she urged President Lyndon B. Johnson to seek mediation through the United Nations and also supported UN peace-keeping forces.

During her final congressional term, Hansen chaired the Democratic Committee on Organization, Study and Review, which recommended the first changes in committee structure since passage of the 1946 Legislative Reorganization Act. Hansen's plan, approved in amended form in October 1974, stipulated the expansion of the per-

manent committee staff and prohibited voting by proxy in committee, among other changes.

After leaving Congress in December 1974, Hansen served a six-year term on the Washington State Toll Bridge Authority and State Highway Commission (1975–81) and chaired the Washington State Transportation Commission from 1979 to 1980. She spent her final years in Cathlamet, where she died on May 3, 1988.

SOURCES:

Office of the Historian. *Women in Congress 1917–1990.* Commission on the Bicentenary of the U.S. House of Representatives, 1991.

Hansford Johnson, Pamela (1912–1981).

See Johnson, Pamela Hansford.

Hanshaw, Annette (1910–1985)

American pop and jazz vocalist of the 1920s and 1930s. Name variations: recorded under Gay Ellis, Dot Dare, and Patsy Young. Born in New York City, on October 18, 1910; died in 1985; married Herman Rose.

Selected discography—albums: It Was So Beautiful *(Halcyon);* Benny Goodman Accompanies "The Girls" *(Sunbeam);* Sweetheart of the Twenties *(Halcyon);* The Rare BG 1927–29 *(Sunbeam).*

Singles: Black Bottom *(Pe 12286);* Song of the Wanderer/ If You See Sally *(Pe 12329);* It Was Only a Sunshower/ Who's That Knocking at My Door? *(Pe 12372);* I Just Roll Along/ There Must Be a Silver Lining *(Pe 12419);* Get Out and Get Under the Moon/ We Love It *(Pe 12444);* Lover, Come Back to Me/ You Wouldn't Fool Me, Would You? *(Do 1769-D);* That's You, Baby/ Big City Blues *(Co 1812-D);* Moanin' Low/ Lovable and Sweet *(OK 41292);* The Right Kind of Man/ If I Can't Have You *(OK 41327);* When I'm Housekeeping for You/ I Have to Have You *(OK 41351);* Cooking Breakfast for the One I Love/ When a Woman Loves a Man *(OK 41370);* Would You Like to Take a Walk?/ You're Just Too Sweet for Words *(Ve 2315);* Ho Hum!/Moonlight Saving Time *(Ve 2393);* We Just Couldn't Say Good-bye/ Love Me Tonight *(Me 12471);* Say It Isn't So/ You'll Always Be the Same Sweetheart *(Me 12846);* Moon Song/Twenty Million People *(Pe 12882);* Sweetheart Darlin'/ I Cover the Waterfront *(Pe 12921);* Give Me Liberty or Give Me Love/ Sing a Little Lowdown Tune *(Pe 12959);* This Little Piggie/ Let's Fall in Love *(Ve 2635).*

In her brief, eight-year singing career, vocalist Annette Hanshaw left an enduring impression. Born in New York City and discovered at age 15, she belonged to a cadre of radio stars

Julia Butler Hansen

who were popular during the 1920s and 1930s, and only made recordings as an afterthought. Hanshaw made guest appearances on the popular Maxwell House "Show Boat" program and with Glen Gray's band on "Camel Caravan." She also had her own singing series in the early 1930s. She recorded with such legendary jazz artists as Benny Goodman, Eddie Lang, Red Nichols, Tommy Dorsey, and Jack Teagarden, and, on many of her early recordings, she added a "That's all" tag at the end.

Dubbed "The Personality Girl," Hanshaw was cited for her rhythmic bounce and her instinctive reading of lyrics, but was best known for her ability to switch from uptempo tunes to emotional torch songs almost effortlessly. Her incredible versatility encompassed romantic ballads, jazz standards, comedy novelty songs, and her superb Betty Boop impression. Although she was popular on the radio and even made a few short movies for Paramount, Hanshaw grew to dislike show business and called it quits in 1934, at age 23. Except for a few radio shows, she settled into married life with Herman Rose. Following his death, she volunteered to work at a local hospital in New York. Hanshaw's recordings are her lasting legacy, among which the collection album *It Was So Beautiful* (Halcyon) provides the best example of her talent. "Give Me Liberty or Give Me Love" and "I'm Sure of Everything but You" are considered particular standouts. Annette Hanshaw died in 1985.

Hanska, Éveline, Countess
(1801–1882)
Polish-born patron and, eventually, wife of Balzac.
Name variations: Eveline Hanska; Madame Hanska;
Madame Balzac. Born Éveline Rzewuska in 1801 in
Poland; died in 1882; married Count Hanska (died
1842); married Honoré Balzac (the writer), in 1850
(died 1850).

In 1832, a wealthy Polish countess named Éveline Hanska sent a letter of admiration to the great French novelist Honoré Balzac, signing it *L'Étrangère* (The Stranger or The Foreigner). After an 18-year correspondence that led to a liaison, Hanska married Balzac shortly before he died in 1850. The letters are contained in *Lettres à l'Étrangère* (1899–1906, 2 vols.).

Hanson, Jean (1919–1973)
British biophysicist and zoologist. Born Emmeline
Jean Hanson in 1919 in England; died in 1973; edu-

Éveline
Hanska

cated at Burton-upon-Trent High School for Girls and Bedford College, London, first class, zoology, 1941; Ph.D., King's College, London.

Born in 1919, Jean Hanson worked at Strangeways Laboratory during World War II. In 1948, she joined the Biophysics Research Unit at King's College, London, where she received her Ph.D. in 1951. From 1953 to 1954, she studied electron microscopy, working on muscular contraction and other problems at the Massachusetts Institute of Technology (MIT). Hanson then returned to England to rejoin the Biophysics Unit and continued her study of molecular aspects of contraction mechanism of muscle. She was a professor of biology at London University in 1966 and director of the Muscle Biophysics Unit, King's College, London, from 1970 to 1973.

Hanson-Dyer, Louise (1884–1962)
Australian-born arts patron and music publisher of
the mid-20th century. Name variations: Louise Berta
Mosson; Louise Dyer. Born Louise Berta Mosson in
Melbourne, Australia, in 1884; died in 1962; studied
at the Royal College of Music, London; married James
Dyer; married a second time to a man named Hanson,
in 1939.

Founded the British Music Society of Melbourne
(1921); moved to Paris and founded a music-publishing house (early 1930s).

Louise Mosson was born in Melbourne, Australia, in 1884 and exhibited a talent for the piano at an early age. As a young woman, she traveled to Edinburgh, Scotland, for further musical study, which she pursued in London at the Royal College of Music. She returned to Australia, married James Dyer, and was active among Melbourne's music-loving set for a number of years. In 1921, she was responsible for establishing Melbourne's British Music Society. She and her husband moved to London in 1927, and later to Paris where she founded Éditions du Oiseau-Lyre, a music publishing house. Under her guidance, the house released complete editions of works of obscure composers, and issued some of the first "long-playing" recordings of the music of Italian composer Claudio Monteverdi (considered the founder of opera) and Baroque composer George Handel, among others. Remarried in 1939 to a man named Hanson, she began using a hyphenated name. Hanson-Dyer was an innovator who helped generate interest in early music. During World War II, she remained in France but moved to Monaco following the war. When she died in 1962, her fortune was willed to Melbourne University for the purpose of music scholarship.

Carol Brennan,
Grosse Pointe, Michigan

Hansteen, Aasta (1824–1908)

Norwegian artist, author, lecturer, polemicist, and pioneer of women's rights. Born on December 10, 1824, in Kristiania, Norway; died on April 13, 1908; daughter of Professor Christopher Hansteen and Johanne (Borch) Hansteen.

Aasta Hansteen was born on December 10, 1824, in Kristiania, the daughter of Professor Christopher Hansteen and a Danish mother, Johanne Borch Hansteen. Her parents' home was a meeting place for the liberal intelligentsia of the time, typified by the poet Johan Welhaven, whom Aasta detested, reserving her admiration for his rival, Henrik Wergeland.

Hansteen trained as an artist in Kristiania, Copenhagen, and Düsseldorf, and was successful as a portrait painter. Her work was bought by the National Gallery of Norway, and exhibited at the Paris Exhibition of 1855, to which she was able to travel, she noted proudly, using money she had earned herself.

Norwegian nationalism and the New Norwegian language movement (*Landsmål*) engaged her interest, and her first book was published on the subject in 1862, followed by poems written in New Norwegian. She was even more strongly influenced by John Stuart Mill's *On the Subjection of Women,* which appeared in Danish translation in the early 1870s. This led her to give lectures in the Scandinavian capitals and many Norwegian cities, culminating in her book, *Kvinden skapt i Guds billede* (Woman Created in God's Image). As the book's title implies, she felt the state church to be in the forefront of "the tyranny of the male" and resigned her membership. Because of her temperament and outspokenness, as much as her uncompromising views, she encountered much criticism and caricature; this drove her to leave Norway and to spend the 1880s in the United States, where she participated in the women's struggle in Boston and Chicago, and took up her portrait painting again. When, after nine years, she returned to Norway, she was welcomed and hailed for her pioneering work for women, which she continued until her death on April 13, 1908.

Aasta Hansteen was immortalized by Henrik Ibsen in the character of Lona Hassel in his play *Samfundets Støtter* (*Pillars of Society*) and by another Norwegian dramatist, Gunnar Heiberg, in *Tante Ulrikke* (Aunt Ulrikke). Her portrait, painted by **Oda Krogh**, hangs in the National Gallery in Oslo, a bust by the sculptor Gustav Vigeland was placed on her grave, and a statue by **Nina Sundbye** was erected at Aker Brygge, Oslo, in 1986.

SOURCES:

Aschehoug & Gyldendal. *Store Norske Leksikon.* Oslo: Kunnskapsforlaget, 1992.

Garton, Janet, *Norwegian Women's Writing 1850–1990* (Women in context series). London & Atlantic Highlands: Athlone Press, 1993.

Norsk Biografisk Leksikon (Dictionary of Norwegian Biography). Vol. V. Oslo: Aschehoug, 1931.

Elizabeth Rokkan,
translator, formerly Associate Professor,
Department of English, University of Bergen, Norway

Hansteen, Kirsten (1903–1974)

First woman member of the Norwegian ministry, who was active in resistance during World War II and whose husband was executed by the Germans. Born Kirsten Moe in Lyngen, Troms county, in the far north of Norway, in 1903; died in 1974; married Viggo Hansteen (1900–1941), in 1930.

Born Kirsten Moe in Lyngen, Troms county, in the far north of Norway, in 1903, Kirsten Hansteen became a Norwegian politician and member of the Communist Party. In 1930, she married the Oslo barrister Viggo Hansteen, one of the first two anti-fascist members of the Norwegian Resistance movement to be executed during the German Occupation of Norway, 1940–45. During the war, Kirsten Hansteen edited *Kvinnefronten* (The Women's Front), an organ of women's Resistance. After the Liberation of Norway in 1945, this publication changed its name to *Kvinnen og Tiden* (Women and Current Affairs). Hansteen was given the post of consultative Cabinet minister in Prime Minister Einar Gerhardsen's coalition government of June–November 1945, and she represented Akershus county in the Norwegian Storting (Parliament) from 1945 to 1949.

SOURCES:

Aschehoug and Gyldendal. *Store Norske Leksikon* (The Greater Norwegian Encyclopedia). Oslo: Kunnskapsforlaget, 1992.

Elizabeth Rokkan,
translator, formerly Associate Professor, Department of English,
University of Bergen, Norway

Han Suyin (1917—)

Chinese author and physician who wrote the much-acclaimed novel A Many-Splendored Thing. *Name variations: Elizabeth Chou; Chou Kuang Hu; Zhou Guanghu; Elizabeth Comber. Born Chou Kuang Hu or Zhou Guanghu on September 12, 1917, in Peking (Beijing), China; daughter of Y.T. Chou and Marguerite (Denis) Chou; attended Yenching University in Peking; graduated from University of Brussels, B.Sc.; graduated from London University, M.B., B.S., 1948; married General Pao H. Tang (Bao Dang), in 1938 (died 1947); married Leonard F. Comber, on February 1, 1952 (divorced around 1962); married Vincent Ruthnaswamy, in 1964; children: one daughter, Yung Mei (adopted 1941).*

Selected works: (autobiographical fiction) Destination Chungking *(Little, Brown, 1942);* A Many-Splendored Thing *(Little, Brown, 1952);* From One China to the Other *(Universe, 1956); . . . And the Rain My Drink *(Little, Brown, 1956);* The Mountain is Young *(Putnam, 1958); (novellas)* Two Loves *(Putnam, 1962, published in England as* Cast But One Shadow *and* Winter Love, *J. Cape, 1962);* The Four Faces *(Putnam, 1963);* The Crippled Tree *(Putnam, 1965);* A Mortal Flower *(Putnam, 1966);* China in the Year 2001 *(Basic Books, 1967);* Birdless Summer *(Putnam, 1968);* Asia Today: Two Outlooks *(McGill-Queens University Press, 1969);* The Morning Deluge: Mao Tse Tung and the Chinese Revolution, 1893–1954 *(Little, Brown, 1972);* My House Has Two Doors *(Putnam, 1980);* The Enchantress *(c. 1985).*

Han Suyin was born in a Chinese railroad station in 1917, while her mother was journeying to Peking. As the biracial offspring of a Chinese

father, Y.T. Chou, and a Belgian mother, **Marguerite Denis Chou**, the young girl felt that she did not belong either to the Chinese culture in which she lived or the European heritage of her mother. She was convinced that Marguerite preferred her other daughter, who was white, to "the yellowish object" she felt herself to be, and she could not find solace within her own family. Even the variety of her names reflect her dual identity. Feeling that her given name, Chou Kuang Hu (Zhou Guanghu), was unpronounceable to her non-Asian friends, she became known as Elizabeth Chou. She later took the pseudonym Han Suyin while writing her first book, *Destination Chungking* (1942). Though some translate the name to mean "a gamble," Han insisted that her name translates as "a common little voice."

Han Suyin started her college education at Yenching University in Peking, but soon left to study at the University of Brussels in 1936. She met her first husband, Colonel Pao Tang (Bao Dang), on a boat returning to China, and they

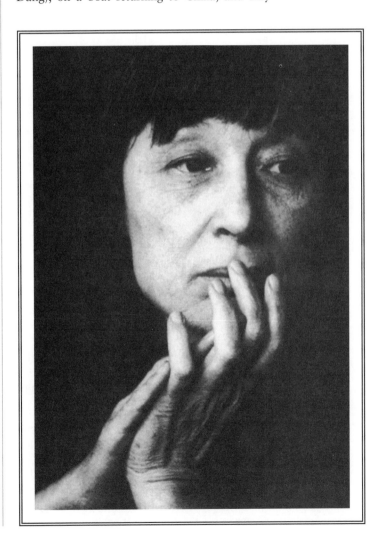

Han Suyin

married there in 1938. The marriage proved to be extremely unhappy. A brutal man, Tang beat his wife to discourage her from pursuing an education. Han was spared a life of misery when Tang was killed in the fighting with Communist Chinese in 1947. Meanwhile, she had adopted **Yung Mei,** a one-year-old girl in 1941 and, after her husband's death, moved to London with her young daughter to complete her medical studies. To supplement her small scholarship, Han worked as a stenographer, museum curator, and typist.

In 1949, Han Suyin took a position as resident physician at a hospital in Hong Kong, practicing medicine during the day and writing at night. There, she met and fell in love with British journalist, Ian Morrison. Their alliance encountered many obstacles, including the hostility of a society that disapproved of interracial relationships, and the fact that Morrison was married. The relationship ended in tragedy when, while covering the war in Korea, he was killed when a jeep he was riding in hit a land mine.

Han drew on her deep sorrow to write a largely autobiographical novel, *A Many-Splendored Thing* (1952), which closely mirrored their affair. The book was a huge success, earning a fortune for Han and establishing her international literary reputation. The novel managed to interweave an intimate personal narrative about a love story involving a Eurasian and a Westerner with an objective report on modern Asia. It was later made into a successful movie, *Love is a Many-Splendored Thing,* starring *Jennifer Jones.

In February of 1949, Dr. Han accepted an assistantship in the Obstetrics and Gynecology Department of Queen Mary Hospital in Hong Kong and married for the second time on February 1, 1952. Her husband, Leonard Comber, was a former British police officer. The marriage lasted for about ten years, ending in an amicable divorce around 1962. She traveled widely and frequently discussed political events with those in her social circle, including Mao Zedong and *Jiang Qing, Zhou Enlai, Lin Biao, Prime Minister Jawaharlal Nehru of India, Prince Norodom Sihanouk of Cambodia, and president Gamel Abdel Nassar of Egypt.

Han lived in numerous countries but spent most of her early to middle years in China. Her autobiography, *My House Has Two Doors* (1980), is a detailed account of the three decades between 1949 and 1980 when she experienced events that eventually formed Red China, including the Civil War, the Freedom of Expres-sion movement, the Great Leap Forward, and the Cultural Revolution. During the 1950s, the Chinese Communist government suspected her of being an American spy despite her earnest medical work for her compatriots—an ironic twist given the fact that she was simultaneously blacklisted as a Communist in the United States.

Han Suyin's publications were instrumental in providing insight into the governments of China, Cambodia and India, although many critics took offense at her virulent criticism of Western values. Always outspoken, she never apologized for her opinions and continued to lend her support to the government of Mao Zedong. Among her works are *Destination Chungking* (1942), written in collaboration with **Marian Manly;** *A Many-Splendored Thing* (1952); . . . *And the Rain My Drink* (1956); *From One China to the Other* (1956); *The Mountain is Young* (1957); *Four Faces,* about Cambodia (1960); *The Crippled Tree* (1965); *A Mortal Flower* (1966); *Lhasa, the Open City; Birdless Summer* (1967); *Asia Today: Two Outlooks* (1969); *The Morning Deluge: Mao Tse Tung and the Chinese Revolution, 1893–1954* (1972); *My House Has Two Doors* (1980); *The Enchantress* (c. 1985); and two novellas, *Cast But One Shadow* (1962) and *Winter Love* (1963).

Han met her third husband, Vincent Ruthnaswamy, an Indian military engineer, in Katmandu at the coronation of King Mahendra and Queen **Ratna Devi** of Nepal. Eight years after that first meeting, they married in 1964. As of 1985, they were living in Lusanne, Switzerland.

SOURCES:
Candee, Marjorie Dent, ed. *Current Biography 1957.* NY: H.W. Wilson, 1957.
Han Suyin. *My House Has Two Doors.* NY: Putnam, 1980.
Kinsman, Clare, ed. *Contemporary Authors* Vols. 17–20. Detroit, MI: Gale Research, 1976.
The New York Times Biographical Service. December 3, 1977, January 25, 1985.

RELATED MEDIA:
Love is a Many-Splendored Thing (102 min. film), starring Jennifer Jones and William Holden, screenplay by John Patrick, directed by Henry King, produced by 20th Century-Fox, 1955.

Judith C. Reveal, freelance writer, Greensboro, Maryland

Hao, Lady (fl. 1040 BCE).
See Fu Hao.

Hapgood, Mrs. Hutchins (1872–1951)
See Glaspell, Susan for sidebar on Neith Boyce.

Hapgood, Isabel (1850–1928)

American author and translator who offered the English-speaking world the first direct translations of Russian classics. Born Isabel Florence Hapgood on November 21, 1850, in Boston, Massachusetts; died on June 26, 1928, in New York City; daughter of Asa and Lydia (Crossley) Hapgood; attended the Oread Collegiate Institute, 1863–65, and Miss Porter's School in Farmington, Connecticut, 1865–68.

Isabel Florence Hapgood was born in Boston in 1850 into an old American family; her father traced his descent from Shadrach Hapgood, a New England settler of 1656. Isabel was one of a set of twins born to Asa and **Lydia Crossley Hapgood**; a younger brother rounded out the family. The Hapgoods moved several times during Isabel's childhood, living in Boston and Jersey City, New Jersey, before finally settling in Worcester, Massachusetts. Isabel, who soon distinguished herself with a gift for learning languages, attended the Oread Collegiate Institute from 1863 to 1865 and Miss Porter's School in Farmington, Connecticut, from 1865 to 1868. Her early studies included Latin and French, but she eventually mastered virtually all of the Germanic and Romance languages as well as several Slavic languages, including Russian, Polish and Old Church Slavonic.

Isabel Hapgood began her career in 1886 when she published her translations of Leo Tolstoy's *Childhood, Boyhood, Youth*, Nikolai Gogol's *Taras Bulba* and *Dead Souls*, and a collection of *The Epic Songs of Russia*. She traveled through Russia from 1887 to 1889, meeting members of the literary world, including Tolstoy who invited her to his home at Yasnaya Polyana. Hapgood followed her initial Russian translations with Tolstoy's *What to Do?* (1887), *Sevastopol* (1888) and *Life* (1888). She also published *Sophia Kovalevskaya's *Recollections of Childhood* (1895), Petr Sergeenko's *How Count L.N. Tolstoy Lives and Works* (1899) and, in 1901, produced two translations of Maxim Gorky, *Foma Gordyeeff* and *Orloff and His Wife*. Hapgood's translations of Russian works were the first direct translations of Russian classics available to the English-speaking world; prior to this, English-speaking readers read Russian literature translated from the French.

Hapgood also wrote her own books on the people and culture of Russia, starting with *Russian Rambles* in 1895. In 1902, she published *A Survey of Russian Literature* for the Chau-

Isabel Hapgood

tauqua Literary and Scientific Circle, but her major work was produced in 1903–04, a 16-volume edition of *The Novels and Stories of Ivan Turgenev*. In 1906, she published *Service Book of the Holy Orthodox Catholic Apostolic (Greco-Russian) Church* which was used by Orthodox churches in America. Hapgood was also a correspondent, reviewer, and editorial writer for the New York *Evening Post* and the *Nation* for 22 years.

In 1917, Hapgood visited Russia for a second time, and only escaped being caught up in the Russian Revolution through the intervention of acquaintances. Her last translations appeared from 1916 to 1924 with Nikolai Leskov's *The Steel Flea* (1916) and *The Cathedral Folk* (1924), and Ivan Bunin's *The Village* (1923).

Isabel Hapgood's exceptional language skills were not limited to Russian. She produced English versions of the French classics *Les Misérables* by Victor Hugo (1887), *Recollections and Letters* by Ernest Renan (1892), *The Revolution of France under the Third Republic* by Baron Pierre de Coubertin (1897), and *Méditations* by Abbé Joseph Roux (1903). Her Spanish translations included *Faith* by Armando Palacio Valdés (1892) and, from the Italian, *Coure* by Edmondo de Amicis (1887).

In 1887, Hapgood moved from Boston to New York where she remained for the rest of her life. She died of cancer on June 26, 1928, in New York City and was buried in Worcester, Massachusetts.

SOURCES:

James, Edward T., ed. *Notable American Women 1607–1950.* Cambridge, MA: The Belknap Press of Harvard University Press, 1971.

McHenry, Robert, ed. *Famous American Women.* NY: Dover, 1983.

Judith C. Reveal,
freelance writer, Greensboro, Maryland

Hapgood, Neith Boyce (1872–1951).

See Glaspell, Susan for sidebar on Neith Boyce.

Habsburg, Elisabeth von (1837–1898).

See Elizabeth of Bavaria.

Hara, Kazuko (1935—)

Japanese composer, librettist, singer, and professor. Born in Tokyo, Japan, on February 10, 1935; married Hiroshi Hara, the composer.

Awarded the second prize of the NHK and Mainichi Music Contest (1955); received the Takei Prize (1967) and the Ataka Prize; wrote orchestral pieces and operas, including The Case Book of Sherlock Holmes *and* The Merry Night.

Kazuko Hara, born in Tokyo in 1935, was thoroughly grounded in the composition of European music. She studied composition under Professor Romijiro Ikenouchi at the Tokyo Teijutsu Daigaku Faculty of Music, graduating in 1957. She then went to Paris in 1962 where she studied at the École Normale with Henri Dutilleux before attending the L'Academie International d'Été in Nice the following year to study with Alexander Tcherepnin. She also studied in Venice and then returned to Japan to explore Gregorian chant under Father R.F.J. Mereau. In 1968, Hara, whose work was in the Western style, became a professor at the Faculty of Music. She composed numerous works including three operas.

John Haag,
Athens, Georgia

Harand, Irene (1900–1975)

Austrian leader in Vienna who attacked the evils of Nazism, anti-Semitism, and religious intolerance and was honored by Israel for her efforts. Born Irene Wedl on September 6, 1900, in Vienna, Austria; died on February 3, 1975, in New York City; daughter of a modestly well-to-do Roman Catholic father and a Lutheran mother; attended the School of the Desmoiselles Diwisch for two years; married Frank Harand, in 1919; children: none.

Helped found Sterreichische Volkspartei (Austrian Peoples Party) with Moritz Zalman (1930); published first pamphlet, So? oder So?; *began newspaper* Gerechtigkeit (Justice) *and founded the Movement Against Anti-Semitism, Racial Hatred and Glorification of War, known as the Harand Movement (1933); published* Sein Kampf *to refute Adolf Hitler's* Mein Kampf *(1935); gave speeches warning against the Nazi menace in Austria, Poland, Latvia, Estonia, Finland, France, Switzerland, and U.S. (1936);* Sein Kampf *published in American and French editions (1937); French-language edition of* Gerechtigkeit *began publication in Brussels (1937); immigrated to U.S. (1938); gave countless anti-Nazi speeches in the U.S. and Canada and founded Austrian-American League to assist Austrian refugees fleeing Nazi rule (1938–45); became director of the women's division of the Anti-Nazi League of New York and began work at the Austrian Institute of New York (1943); honored by Israel as one of the "Righteous Among the Nations" for defense of Jews against Nazism (1969); praised by the Viennese press on the occasion of her 70th birthday (1970); honored by the lord mayor of Vienna in city hall ceremony (1971); ashes given place of honor in Vienna's Central Cemetery (1975); municipal housing project in Vienna named in honor of Irene Harand (1990).*

In the late 1920s, Irene Harand was a prosperous and happily married young woman when her innate sense of justice first drew her in the direction that was to change her life. The alteration began with a series of minor incidents seeming at first to have little to do with the often brutal world of Austrian politics. She had simply become concerned about the plight of an aged noble she was acquainted with, who had lost his fortune and then been refused assistance by his son who held the family castle and lands. Seeking justice on behalf of the old gentleman, Harand consulted a number of lawyers and paid a substantial amount in fees without seeing anything accomplished. Then she consulted Dr. Moritz Zalman, a well-known Jewish attorney who showed enthusiasm for the case. When the question of fees was raised, Zalman told Harand that if she could give of her energies to help the old man, he could volunteer his legal skills.

Years later, Harand explained this gesture as a turning point in her thinking. Although she had never acted as an anti-Semite, she realized that she had unconsciously held the notion, almost universal within Viennese Gentile society, that Jewish lawyers were avaricious and unscrupulous, and she had consulted only non-Jewish attorneys until she approached Zalman. "I blushed when I thought that a Jew . . . was ready to serve a non-Jew as no Christian I had met had been willing to serve," she said. "I determined then and there to give my life to wipe out this shame antisemitism was bringing upon Christians and Christianity."

In a country where religion was always politically significant, she had an early acquaintance with religiously mixed backgrounds. She was born Irene Wedl in 1900, into a moderately prosperous Viennese home to a Catholic father from the region of Moravia and a Lutheran mother from Siebenbergen. Irene grew up in comfortable circumstances during what is now considered Europe's golden age of security.

Although human relationships, not ideology, were paramount in Irene's personal world, anti-Semitism was rampant in the Austro-Hungarian empire into which she was born. During her childhood, she spent summer vacations with the family of her mother's older brother, who was unusually venerated in the family circle, and his wife, who was Jewish. A half-century later, Irene recalled this aunt and uncle and her two half-Jewish cousins, as "closer to me than any other of my relatives." During one such holiday, Irene was with her older sister Grete and several other children when they found themselves surrounded by local peasant children, taunting them with cries of "Jud! Jud! Jud!" With Grete in the lead, the youngsters ran back to the security of their summer cottage, but the memory of having been on the receiving end of anti-Semitic fury was to return again and again. Almost 60 years later, Irene Harand noted that "one never forgets the first time one feels oneself frightened to death, and sees the world as being full of nothing but enemies."

Harand's formal education ended after two years at the French School of the Mesdemoiselles Diwisch. She never attended university. In 1919, World War I had been over for less than a year when she married Frank Harand, a former captain in the Austrian army, five years her senior. Like Irene, Frank was a devout Christian. He was not interested in direct political involvement, but he was deeply conservative, believing in the "old Austrian" virtues of honor, integrity and the rule of justice. At a time when the Austro-Hungarian empire was in dissolution, his sympathies were close to monarchism. Irene and Frank Harand concentrated on rebuilding the comfortable life their families had known before the war. Frank became a successful business executive, and the couple remained childless, allowing them time and money to enjoy middle-class life in Vienna, a city whose pleasures remained undeni-

ably seductive in the troubled 1920s. During these relatively calm years, however, anti-Semitism did not disappear. Frank's business interests required frequent travel throughout the provinces, where most tourists from Vienna were assumed to be Jews. On an inspection tour to a small town, Frank was once greeted by the storekeeper who commented, "It must be summer if the Jews from Vienna are here."

> *I* fight anti-Semitism because
> it defames . . . Christianity.
> —**Irene Harand**

Meanwhile in postwar Vienna, the Roman Catholic Church was perceived as leading a "spiritual" struggle against Jewry, while the Christian Social Party had officially espoused anti-Semitic policies on the political front since the days of Vienna's colorful mayor, Karl Lueger. Depending on support from artisans, small shopkeepers, and entrepreneurs, Christian Social leaders never tired of condemning the destructive impact of Jewry, and even men of refinement, like Austria's Chancellor Ignaz Seipel, regarded the Jews "as natural materialists, deeply involved in the Communist movement." The political environment was made more confusing by the fact that rich Jewish industrialists occasionally supported Christian Socialist political activities as an alternative to the threat of communism.

Christians like the Harands were profoundly disturbed by examples of sanctioned intolerance, and even incitements to violence, that contravened the most basic teachings of the Catholic Church. The anti-Semitic diatribes of one Viennese priest were not banned by his superiors until the 1930s. In this atmosphere, Harand had already begun to question a fundamental assumption, that those holding the highest positions of church and state were always morally correct, when she first encountered Moritz Zalman and entered into the collaboration and friendship that was the genesis of her political involvement.

By 1930, Nazism was on the march in Austria. The rapidly expanding racist sect, on its way to becoming a mass movement, already dominated universities, technical colleges and gymnasiums throughout the country. In September of that year, Harand and her circle of Christians and Jews were alarmed by the electoral victory of the Nazi party in neighboring Germany. Two months later, when she witnessed a parade of Nazi youths, she was struck by the appearance of one 12-year-old boy, who seemed transformed before her eyes "from a human child into a bloodthirsty beast." Nazism, she was convinced, was "stealing our children from us and making criminals of them," and although the movement was still weaker in her country than its German counterpart, she saw it as a threat to the stability of the state.

In 1933, a few weeks after Hitler's accession to power in Germany, while parliamentary government was being extinguished in Austria, Irene Harand wrote her first major political statement. Her 24-page pamphlet entitled *So? oder So?* was a deeply personal document, declaring her refusal to accept the ascendancy of the growing totalitarian movement. Written for a mass audience, it attempted to identify and defuse the prejudices about Jews that the average Austrian absorbed almost from birth. The pamphlet first attacked the widely held notions of Jewish financial control of the world economy and Jewish domination of nefarious Freemasonry. As for the notion that Bolshevism was largely Jewish dominated, the author pointed out that neither Lenin nor Stalin were Jews and that the Jewish proletariat was largely Menshevik rather than Bolshevik in its loyalties. She characterized Jewish socialists in the West as "parlor revolutionaries" despite their radical rhetoric, and she refuted the generally held belief among unsophisticated Austrians that there was a vast Jewish conspiracy directed against the simple Christian people of town and village. Disputing claims of cowardice, she pointed out that Jews had not shirked their military duty in the World War I years of 1914–18, and had an ancient history of heroic acts on the battlefield, back to the Old Testament Maccabees, who had "fought like lions." In conclusion, *So? oder So?* listed the names of numerous physicians and medical researchers of Jewish descent, many of whom had worked in Vienna, whose gifts to humanity were discoveries that helped liberate mankind from pain, suffering, and disease.

If Harand's pamphlet voiced any quarrel with Jews, it was that they were too modest about their achievements. Her own experience working with Jewish intellectuals and professionals led her to observe that some did not hold strong feelings of Jewish racial pride, and she believed a sense of national pride, at least, might be a defense against anti-Semitism, while a pattern of behavior superior to that of Austria's non-Jews would help to discredit anti-Semitic arguments. Admitting that this approach represented a form of discrimination, Harand tried to confront the realities of a society in crisis, in which each individual would most likely be judged as representative of the entire group. In the national atmosphere of deep-seated prejudices, only "extraordinary achievements" (*Extraleistungen*) would prove the Jews' worthiness as law-abiding Austrian citizens, and therefore every one must be "crystal pure" in business and personal life; by the same token, as she put it, "one individual's dirt will soil the entire *Volksgemeinschaft*." If these arguments, putting Austria's Jews in a special category, and on probation until found acceptable, create a position that no longer seems morally defensible, it was politically realistic. *So? oder So?* was not novel in how it dealt with the "Jewish Question," but it differed from past works in being an intense statement by a non-Jew.

Thirty thousand copies of *So? oder So?* were printed and distributed, and a second edition of 30,000 was released a few months later. Interest increased when the venerable organ of Viennese Liberalism, *Neue Freie Presse*, publicized both the pamphlet and the philo-Semitic activities of Irene Harand and her followers in a short article entitled "A Woman's Courageous Words Against Anti-Semitism."

But it soon became clear that Hitler's dictatorship in Germany was to be of long duration, and that anti-Semitism was on the increase in both Germany and Austria. In fact, Austria's survival as an independent political entity was becoming increasingly questionable. Harand threw her full energies into the anti-Nazi struggle. In the summer of 1933, she secured financial support for a weekly newspaper entitled *Gerechtigkeit* (Justice) which she launched that September. Written in a popular style for the mass audience, the paper destroyed anti-Semitic myths, attacked Nazi barbarities in both Germany and Austria, and defended the policies of the conservative regimes that began to govern Austria in March 1933. It was to be the central focus of Harand's life for the next five years.

The simple ideas of *Gerechtigkeit* were repeated in each issue: anti-Semitism was a moral outrage, not only against the Jews, but against Christian ideals; Nazism was a pagan movement, and if not halted it would destroy European civilization; and the Christian spirit of love and charity could be made part of the social fabric of the West if enough men and women of good will joined together in a common undertaking. Soon after the inaugural issue, the organization for its publication began to call itself the World League Against Racial Hatred and Human Need (Weltverband gegen Rassenhass und Menschennot), more popularly known as

Irene Harand

the Harand Movement. Restricted at first to Vienna, its activities were confined to meetings and occasional rallies, then expanded to include a social welfare service in charge of several shelters for destitute citizens of Vienna in the bitter cold winter months.

Jewish support for the Harand Movement was not unanimous. Backing came almost immediately from Dr. David Feuchtwang, the chief rabbi of Vienna, who attended the inaugural rally of the Harand Movement and had kind words to say about Harand's courageous defense of Austrian Jewry. *Gerechtigkeit* and other activities of the organization were also made

possible by Jewish funding. One particularly generous supporter was Dr. Wilhelm Berliner, general director of the Phoenix Life Insurance Company, whose subsidies to many individuals and political groups during the early 1930s led to a major political scandal in 1936. While the Harand Movement was generally ignored by Austrian Zionists, who favored the formation of a Jewish state, it received public praise, and probably funding, from the assimilationist group, Union sterreichischer Juden, which commended Harand as late as 1937 as a noble woman who carried out her mission without fear of the consequences. There is also strong evidence that the Austrian monarchists supported her work, both politically and financially.

The years 1935–36 were the apogee of the Harand Movement. From 1934 to 1935, Irene Harand was at work on a major statement of her beliefs, and in late June 1935 a Polish-Jewish newspaper announced that publication of a book by Irene Harand was imminent. It appeared in Vienna in early August, under the title *Sein Kampf* (His Struggle), paralleling the title of Adolf Hitler's *Mein Kampf* (My Struggle). The fact that it was self-published (*Selbstverlag*), strongly suggests that leading publishing houses were afraid to offend either Nazi Germany or pro-Nazi elements within their own country.

The main arguments of *Sein Kampf,* directly challenging Nazi racial and political theories, had already been expressed in *So? oder So?* and *Gerechtigkeit.* Extreme nationalism was condemned as a "poison" which turned the youth of the world into irrational and hateful beings; there was a chapter on Jewish service to humanity in the arts and sciences; and Harand argued that the Jews, as authors of the Bible, deserved the highest possible respect from all Christians. The book was a passionate plea for racial tolerance.

Sein Kampf was reviewed in numerous European newspapers and journals, and editions in French and English eventually appeared. Despite a positive critical reception, sales were disappointing, and, after three months of intensive publicity, some copies of the initial printing of just 5,000 books remained unsold. The provocative title attracted the attention of Nazi Germany's supreme censorship board, the *Reichsschrifttumskammer,* which promptly placed the volume on its list of banned books, and Irene Harand was now regarded as an active and dangerous enemy of Nazi Germany. Her name was to remain on Heinrich Himmler's lists of those opposing the regime until the fall of the Third Reich, but the book did not seriously threaten the fascist German government, or even appreciably weaken Nazism in Austria.

Irene Harand and Moritz Zalman undertook a number of trips abroad to bring their work to the attention of Christian and Jewish communities in countries not yet directly threatened by Nazi Germany, but increasingly aware of the threat posed by Hitlerism. In the last months of 1935, Harand spoke in Denmark, Norway, and Sweden, and visited the cities of Warsaw, Riga, Talinn, Helsinki, Paris, Geneva, and Zurich. Zalman was equally active, bringing the message of the Harand Movement to Belgium, the Netherlands, and France, and was particularly optimistic about prospects in the Netherlands, whose Jewish community was increasingly alarmed by both domestic and German Nazism.

In late 1936, Irene Harand spent two months conveying her message in the United States, where she was received by many women and men of good will but could not stir them into action. As one dejected reviewer wrote about *Sein Kampf,* "If appeals to reason are still valid in a world like ours, Frau Harand's book will be helpful."

In 1937–38, Europe was imbued with a growing spirit of defeatism as the political situation continued to deteriorate. A world congress of the Harand Movement scheduled for May 1937 had to be canceled for lack of funds, but in the fall of that same year the group sponsored a meeting of national representatives from Poland, Belgium, Czechoslovakia, Hungary, Switzerland, and the Austrian provinces to discuss the future. That year, the Polish-language edition of *Gerechftgkeift* was abandoned for financial reasons, but the French-language edition, *Justice,* began publication in September. Czech and Hungarian editions appeared in print around the same time, and plans were made to revive the English and Polish version.

The Harand Movement found other innovative ways of supporting pro-Semitic activities, including a well-trained chorus, taken over from Austria's suppressed Social Democratic Party, composed of militant anti-Nazi young women and men, many of them Jewish. These folksong concerts became the talk of Vienna. A phonograph record, with a brief message by Irene Harand on one side and a song, "Gute Menschen," on the other, was issued. Yet another propaganda medium much favored by Harand and her collaborators were gummed stamps which spread the movements message. These were not postage stamps. Intended for use on envelopes, letters, or documents and printed in several languages, the stamps depicted great Jewish thinkers, artists, and scientists. Members of the Harand Movement used these stamps to challenge Goebbels' anti-Semitic extravaganza, "Der ewige Jude," by plastering them on the walls and display frames of the Nazi exhibit. In 1938, just a few days before the *Anschluss* that would see Austria become part of Germany's Third Reich, the Harand Movement announced production of a new set of stamps honoring a group that included Benjamin Disraeli, the Marquis of Reading, Heinrich Hertz, and Walter Rathenau.

By good fortune, the Harands were in England when the *Anschluss* took place. By September 1938, they were in the United States. While the Nazis killed millions of Jews, including her good friend Moritz Zalman, she continued to speak in the U.S. and Canada, warning the world against the dangers of Nazism. The Nazis in turn referred to her activities as "treasonable." In America, Harand founded the Austrian-American League to assist Austrian refugees fleeing Nazi rule (1938–45), became director of the women's division of the Anti-Nazi League of New York, and began work at the Austrian Institute of New York (1943).

In December 1969, Harand was awarded Israel's Yad Vashem medallion for her activities on behalf of persecuted Jews, in a ceremony that included her as one of the "Righteous Among Nations." One of the members of the commission that recommended her for the award noted the courage necessary for her activities in the 1930s:

> [T]o deliver public speeches at a time when Austria was swept by a wave of political assassinations meant exposing oneself to great risk. This woman waged a desperate and unceasing war which placed her in great peril. She sent her boys to hand out the newspaper at street corners. The children were beaten and she was beaten too. She stood her ground against vilification and threats. If this is not a struggle in which one risks one's life, then I don't know what risk means. She fought to save Austrian Jewry.

The following year, on the occasion of Harand's 70th birthday, Viennese newspapers carried accounts of her anti-Nazi efforts, and in July 1971 she was honored by the lord mayor in a ceremony at Vienna's city hall.

On February 3, 1975, Irene Harand died in New York City, and *The New York Times* carried a short obituary about the woman who had been decorated by the governments of Austria and Israel for her opposition to National Socialism. Her ashes have been given a place of honor in the Central Cemetery of the city of Vienna, and on April 20, 1990, her name was given to a municipal housing project in the city's First District, in recognition of the fact that her call for an end to racial intolerance continues to be essential. April 20th had been celebrated in the Third Reich with elaborate ceremonies, for it was the birthday of Adolf Hitler. After many decades, at least symbolic justice had triumphed in a small corner of Hitler's homeland.

SOURCES:

Bassett, Richard. *Waldheim and Austria,* Penguin Books, 1990.

"Champion of Justice: Irene Harand," in *Wiener Library Bulletin.* Vol. 9, nos. 3/4. May–August, 1955, p. 24.

Haag, John. "A Woman's Struggle Against Nazism: Irene Harand and Gerechtigkeit," in *Wiener Library Bulletin.* Vol. 34, new series 53/54, 1981, pp. 64–72.

Harand, Irene. *His Struggle (An Answer to Hitler).* Chicago, IL: Artcraft Press, 1937.

Paldiel, Mordecai. "To the Righteous among the Nations Who Risked Their Lives to Rescue Jews," in *Yad Vashem Studies.* Vol. 19, 1988, pp. 403–425.

Pauley, Bruce F. *From Prejudice to Persecution: A History of Austrian Anti-Semitism.* NC: University of North Carolina Press, 1992.

Weinzierl, Erika "Christliche Solidaritt mit Juden am Beispiel Irene Harands (1900-1975)," in Marcel Marcus et al., eds., *Israel und Kirche Heute: Beitrge zum christlich-jdischen Dialog/Fr Ernst Ludwig Ehrlich,* Herder, 1991, pp. 356–367.

SUGGESTED READING:

Geehr, Richard S. *Karl Lueger: Mayor of Fin de Siecle Vienna.* Detroit, MI: Wayne State University Press, 1990.

Parkinson, F. ed. *Conquering the Past: Austrian Nazism Yesterday and Today.* Detroit, MI: Wayne State University Press, 1989.

Pauley, Bruce F. *Hitler and the Forgotten Nazis: A History of Austrian National Socialism.* NC: University of North Carolina Press, 1981.

Whiteside, Andrew G. *The Socialism of Fools: Georg Ritter von Schnerer and Austrian Pan-Germanism.* CA: University of California Press, 1975.

John Haag,
Associate Professor of History,
University of Georgia, Athens, Georgia

Harari, Manya (1905–1969)

Russian-born co-founder of the influential Harvill Press, who was co-translator of Pasternak's Dr. Zhivago *and played a crucial role in bringing dissident works of Russian literature to the attention of the Western reading public. Born Manya Benenson in Baku, Russia (now Azerbaijan), on April 8, 1905; died in London, England, on September 24, 1969; daughter of Grigori Benenson and Sophie (Goldberg) Benenson; had three sisters; married Ralph Andrew Harari (1892–1969), in 1925; children: son, Michael.*

Throughout her life, Manya Harari appeared to be, in the words of Michael Glenny, "a frail wisp of a woman who might, one felt, be blown away if one coughed too hard." This was a complete misreading of a woman who pursued her varied interests "with passionate resolution." Born in 1905, a dozen years before the end of Tsarism, into an extremely wealthy Russian-Jewish family (her father Grigori was a successful financier), Manya Benenson grew up in her family's opulent St. Petersburg apartment, spending summers in a splendid country estate in nearby Redkino. At the start of 1914, the Benensons migrated from Germany, where they had been visiting, to London. Manya received an excellent education, first at Malvern Girls College and then at Bedford College, London, graduating in 1924 with second class honors in history. During these years, Manya's father was busy creating another financial empire, and the family enjoyed the fruits of his success, living not in a house but in a succession of luxury hotel suites.

In 1925, Manya visited the struggling Jewish community in Palestine, and while there she met and fell in love with Ralph Harari, a wealthy and cosmopolitan member of the Egyptian-Jewish community who divided his time between merchant banking and the collection and study of both Islamic and modern art. Manya married Ralph that same year and settled into the opulent lifestyle of Cairo's elite. Soon, however, she became bored with high society and began to search for greater fulfillment. She gave birth to a son Michael, worked briefly in a Zionist kibbutz, and was active in welfare work among Cairo's poor, all before the Hararis returned to London. After much thought, she became a Roman Catholic in 1932, but always emphasized that her decision in no way diminished her continuing identification with the Jews as a nation and people. Through her new religion, Harari began to move in Roman Catholic intellectual circles, including Cardinal Hinsley's Sword of the Spirit movement. She became actively associated with the *Dublin Review* and for several years in the early 1940s was editor of her own periodical, *Changing World*. When her journal ceased publication in 1942, Harari took a position as translator with the British government's Political Warfare Department.

In 1946, with **Marjorie Villiers** as her partner, Manya Harari founded a publishing house. Named the Harvill Press (after Harari and Villiers), the small but imaginative firm concentrated on translations of foreign works of fiction, as well as books on art, psychology, religion and philosophy (including an edition of Pascal's classic *Pensées*). From the start, Harvill Press showed an interest in publishing animal books with an African slant, an orientation that proved to be lucrative when Harari decided to publish a book that had been rejected by numerous publishers. *Joy Adamson's *Born Free* was a runaway international bestseller. In 1954, the Harvill Press was sold to the Collins publishing firm, but both Harari and Villiers were retained as directors of what was now an important subsidiary.

Harari's Russian origins, linguistic abilities, and discerning eye gave her a significant advan-

tage over other publishers. Throughout the 1950s and early 1960s, she discovered and published under the Harvill Press imprint, major works of contemporary Russian literature that for political reasons could not be published in the Soviet Union. By far the most famous of these works was Boris Pasternak's great novel, *Dr. Zhivago,* which appeared in 1958 in a joint translation by Harari and Max Hayward. She was also co-translator with Hayward of Alexander Solzhenitsyn's *The First Circle,* and published important works by other dissident Soviet authors, including Ilya Ehrenburg, Konstantin Paustovsky, Andrei Sinyavsky, and Yevgeni Yevtushenko. In effect, because of her intellectual advocacy and understanding of commercial publishing, she provided expression for a Russian literature shackled by censorship. Although she specialized in contemporary Soviet literature, Harari sometimes championed earlier Soviet works, like Mikhail Bulgakov's *The Master and Margarita,* and on occasion discovered a non-Slavic masterpiece, like Giuseppe de Lampedusa's *Il Gattopardo* (*The Leopard*).

A chain-smoker, Manya Harari paid little attention to her health, but all who met or worked with her commented on her gentle manner and soft voice. Her pallid, exquisitely drawn features were so intense that the rest of her body, slender in the extreme, hardly seemed to exist. Working in an attic room in her London home in Catherine Place, she could be seen poised between telephone and typewriter, as authors, authors' agents and advocates jostled for her attention. Oblivious of her material surroundings, Harari enjoyed long, demanding hours, rarely regarding her editorial and translating responsibilities as a chore. Because she bored easily and enjoyed travel, she went to Palestine in 1948 to report the birth pangs of the State of Israel. In 1955, with the onset of a cautious intellectual thaw in the Soviet Union as a result of the death of Stalin and a growing weariness over the perils and costs of the Cold War in both East and West, Harari made her first trip back to Russia since her childhood. Moved when she visited sites in Moscow, Leningrad, and Redkino, she returned to the Soviet Union in the spring of 1956, and for a third and final time in the winter of 1961.

In 1968, Manya Harari discovered that she was terminally ill and had only months to live. At the same time, her husband became seriously ill. She kept the knowledge of her incurable condition to herself, thus sparing him additional burden. Ralph Harari died in London on May 26, 1969. Manya dealt with her grief by continuing to write her autobiography (published in 1972), and by finding solace and serenity in her ever-deepening Roman Catholic faith. On September 24, 1969, she died in London, mourned by her son Michael and countless friends in the worlds of publishing, literature and art. In Glenny's assessment of her achievements, Manya Harari earned a place in world history as "the dauntless custodian of so much of the greatest Russian writing of our time—an exiled literature, driven out of its homeland, the country of her birth."

SOURCES:

Glenny, Michael. "Frail Patron of Russian Literature," in *The Times* [London]. November 23, 1972, p. 16.

Harari, Manya. *Memoirs 1906–1969.* London: Harvill Press, 1972.

Levin, Bernard. "Beyond Books Stands Life," in *The Times [London].* June 21, 1994.

Oxbury, Harold. *Great Britons: Twentieth-Century Lives.* Oxford: Oxford University Press, 1985.

Rolo, P.J.V., "Harari, Manya," in E.T. Williams and C.S. Nicholls, eds., *The Dictionary of National Biography: 1961–1970.* Oxford: Oxford University Press, 1981, pp. 487–488.

John Haag,
Associate Professor of History,
University of Georgia, Athens, Georgia

Haraszty, Eszter (c. 1910–1994)

Hungarian-American colorist, stylist, and designer of textiles. Born in Hungary around 1910; died of non-Hodgkin's lymphoma in Malibu, California, in November 1994.

Known for her Iceland poppy motif replicated on textiles, ceramics, and stained glass, Eszter Haraszty had her own design studio in New York City. Before coming to the United States in 1946, she was a costume designer in her native Hungary; she then shifted her focus to home design. Haraszty won five gold medals from the Association of Interior Designers for her textile designs. Her work is in the permanent collections of the New York Museum of Modern Art, the Victoria and Albert Museum in London, and Le Chateau Dufresne in Montreal.

Harb, Helen Hicks (1911–1974).

See Berg, Patty for sidebar on Helen Hicks.

Harbou, Thea von (1888–1954).

See von Harbou, Thea.

Harcourt, Johanna (d. 1488)

Duchess of Lorraine. Died in November 1488; daughter of William Harcourt; became first wife of Rene II, *duke of Lorraine (r. 1480–1508), on September 9, 1471 (divorced 1485).*

Hard, Darlene (1936—)

American who won the U.S. doubles titles for five consecutive years (1958–62) and was ranked #1 among U.S. women's tennis players (1960–63). Born in Los Angeles, California, on January 6, 1936; graduated from Pomona College, Claremont, California; never married; no children.

Among the top tennis players in the world from 1955 to 1964, Darlene Hard was born in 1936 and grew up in a modest neighborhood of Los Angeles, where she mowed lawns to help the family finances and left high school for a time to waitress. As a youngster, she played tennis at Griffith Park, learning the game from her mother, who was at one time a leading metropolitan player. When she began to show promise, the Los Angeles Tennis Club stepped in to help, as did Perry Jones, then the leading sponsor of Southern California tennis. Hard later credited much of her success to tennis great *Alice Marble, who suggested that she change from a Continental to an Eastern grip, thereby giving her more control on her flat and top-spin shots.

Hard began playing on the Eastern circuit in 1954 and was a semifinalist at Wimbledon the following year. It was not until 1957, however, that she achieved international recognition. That year, she reached the finals of the Wimbledon singles and won both the women's doubles and mixed doubles, with America's *Althea Gibson and Australia's Mervyn Rose, as respective partners. Hard was also a first-time member of the Wightman Cup team, which defeated England's top women players in July.

Hard played little competitive tennis in 1958, concentrating instead on her studies at Pomona College. She did become the first winner of the U.S. Intercollegiate title, and also made a respectable showing at Forest Hills, where she was runner-up in the singles and won the doubles with **Jeanne Arth.** In 1959, she again reached the finals at Wimbledon, losing the singles to *Maria Bueno but winning the mixed doubles while teamed with Rod Laver.

Hard's best year was probably 1960. She took the French singles with a 6-3, 6-4 win over **Yola Ramirez** of Mexico. In Paris, she aced the doubles with the help of Maria Bueno then, in June, captured the Northern England Tennis title at Manchester. Later that month, she helped

Darlene
Hard

WOMEN IN WORLD HISTORY

Sports Illustrated (September 18, 1961), Huston Horn wrote that "with almost embarrassing ease, Darlene the tigress gulped up the comparatively gentle lambs who opposed her." In November 1961, *World Tennis* magazine ranked Hard fifth among women then playing tennis, and in December, she placed third behind track star *Wilma Rudolph and golfer *Mickey Wright in the Associated Press poll for female athlete of the year. She was also once again ranked first among American women tennis players.

After an extended tennis tour of Australia in early 1962, Hard complained that the Lawn Tennis Association of Australia had treated her like a "puppet" rather than a player and called the $4.20-a-day living allowance "ludicrous." It was not the first time that she had openly spoken her mind, a habit that did not always sit well with tennis officials. Despite her occasional outbursts and fierce competitive spirit, Hard's ready smile and warm personality made her a favorite with both spectators and fellow players.

Later in 1962, Hard won the Italian doubles with Bueno, but lost in the quarterfinals at Wimbledon to **Vera Sukova** of Czechoslovakia. At Forest Hills, Hard also lost her singles title to Australian *Margaret Smith Court. The one bright note was her win of the national doubles in late August, partnered again with Bueno. Hard told Gene Roswell of the *New York Post* (September 6, 1962): "I like doubles. I like to have someone to talk to out there, someone to clown with or to encourage. . . . I play better if someone depends on me."

In 1963, her last full year on the circuit, Hard lost the singles title at Wimbledon and Forest Hill, and she and Maria Bueno also succumbed to Margaret Smith and **Robyn Ebbern** in the doubles championship. Hard and *Billie Jean King did, however, pace the American team to a triumph over the Australians in the Federation Cup tournament, and Hard also played magnificently against Margaret Smith in the finals of the Pennsylvania grass-court championships. In December 1963, she was ranked for the fourth consecutive year, as top American tennis player. In May 1964, Hard turned professional, taking a teaching position at a tennis ranch in Carmel Valley, California. She returned briefly to competition in 1969, winning the U.S. doubles with *Françoise Durr. Reflecting on her tennis career, Hard once said, "It's more fun to be on the way up than to be there."

America triumph over England again in the Wightman Cup matches by winning her two singles and the doubles. Only the Wimbledon championship continued to elude her. She lost a quarterfinal match to **Sandra Reynolds** of South Africa, although she shared the doubles title with Bueno. The two women also won the national women's doubles title at the Longwood Cricket Club in Chestnut Hill, Massachusetts. Playing perhaps the best tennis of her career, Hard battled it out with Bueno in early September at the U.S. Open championships at Forest Hills. It was her sixth bid for the national singles title, and Hard finally triumphed over the Brazilian in a 6-3, 10-12, 6-4 win. As the year wound down, Hard was ranked first among American women players by the U.S. Lawn Tennis Association.

Unfortunately for Hard, 1961 got off to a shaky start. After losing the final round of the Thunderbird tournament in Scottsdale, Arizona, she embarked on a tennis tour in the Caribbean and Europe. In Paris for the French championships, both she and her partner Maria Bueno were stricken with hepatitis. Although less seriously ill than Bueno, Hard was forced to take to her bed for six weeks. After her own recuperation, Hard nursed Bueno back to health. The hiatus resulted in exclusion from the 1960 Wightman Cup team. A turn-around began that August with a win at the Essex invitation tournament. Then, at Forest Hills, Hard captured the American doubles title with partner *Lesley Turner** and retained her national title, beating Britain's **Ann Haydon**, 6-3, 6-4. In

Harden, Cecil Murray (1894–1984)

American congresswoman, Republican of Indiana, who served from January 2, 1949 to January 3, 1959. Born in Covington, Indiana, on November 21, 1894; died in Lafayette, Indiana, on December 5, 1984; attended public schools; attended the University of Indiana at Bloomington; married Frost R. Harden (an automobile dealer), in December 1914.

Five-term congresswoman Cecil Harden was born and raised in Covington, Indiana, attended the University of Indiana at Bloomington, and taught school before her marriage to Frost R. Harden in 1914. She did not become active in politics until 1932, her interest piqued by meetings of the local Republican Party which were held in a room above her husband's car dealership. After chairing the Fountain County Republican Party from 1938 to 1950, she served as Republican national committeewoman from Indiana and was an at-large delegate to the Republican national convention of 1948, 1952, 1956, and 1968.

Harden ran for the Sixth District seat in July 1948, after Representative Noble J. Johnson left to assume a court judgeship. She was narrowly elected, beating her Democratic rival by only 483 votes, but she was ultimately reelected to four additional terms. During her tenure, she served on the Committee on Veterans' Affairs, the Committee on Expenditures in Executive Departments, the Committee on Government Operations, and the Committee on Post Office and Civil Service. She promoted flood control for the Wabash Valley and helped secure funds for a dam and a park facility. In 1956, she fought against Defense Department plans to close a water plant in her district, claiming that it would only add to the mounting unemployment problem.

Harden was one of five Indiana Republicans who lost seats in a national Democratic sweep of 1958, which ultimately cost the GOP 48 House seats. Two months after leaving Congress, she was appointed special assistant for women's affairs to Postmaster General Arthur E. Summerfield, a post she held until March 1961. In 1970, she served on the National Advisory Committee for the White House Conference on Aging. Cecil Harden died on December 5, 1984.

Hardenbrook, Margaret (d. 1690).

See Philipse, Margaret Hardenbrook.

Hardin, Lil (1898–1971).

See Armstrong, Lil Hardin.

Cecil Murray Harden

Harding, Ann (1902–1981)

American actress of stage and screen. Born Dorothy Walton Gatley on August 7, 1902, in Fort Sam Houston, Texas; died on September 1, 1981, in Westport, Connecticut (some sources cite place of death as Sherman Oaks, California); youngest of two daughters of Captain George G. (a career army officer) and Elizabeth (Crabbe) Gatley; attended school on Columbia Army Base in Cuba; attended public school in Montclair, New Jersey; graduated from the Baldwin School, Bryn Mawr, Pennsylvania; attended Bryn Mawr College for one year; married Harry Bannister (an actor), on October 22, 1926 (divorced 1932); married Werner Janssen (a symphony conductor), on January 13, 1937 (divorced 1962); children: (first marriage) daughter Jane Bannister.

Selected theater: New York debut as Madeline Morton in Inheritors *(Provincetown Players, Greenwich Village, March 21, 1921); Broadway debut as Phyllis Weston in* Like a King *(39th Street Theatre, New York City, October 3, 1921); Letitia Tevis in* Tarnish *(Belmont Theatre, New York City, 1923); Marie Millais in* Stolen Fruit *(Eltinge Theatre, New York City, 1925); Anna Schweiger in* Schweiger *(Mansfield Theatre, New York City, 1926); Marie-Ange in* A Woman Disputed *(Forrest Theatre, New York City, 1926); Mary Dugan in* The Trial of Mary Dugan *(National Theatre, New York City, 1927); toured as Nina Leeds in* Strange Interlude *(1929); London debut in title role in* Candida *(Globe Theatre, 1937); toured as Ann Murray in* Yes, My Darling Daughter *(1949); succeeded Ruth Hussey as Agatha Reed in* Goodbye My Fancy *(Martin Beck Theatre, New York City, 1949); succeeded Hortense Alden in the double-bill* Garden District, *appearing as Grace Lancaster in* Something Unspoken *and as Mrs. Venable in* Suddenly Last Summer *(York Playhouse, New York City, 1958); toured as the Mother in* September Tide *(1958); Rena Seeger in* General Seeger *(Lyceum Theatre, New York City, 1962); toured as Miss Moffatt in* The Corn Is Green *(West Coast, 1963); Amanda in* The Glass Menagerie *(West Coast, 1963); Myra Holliday in* Abraham Cochrane *(Belasco Theatre, New York City, 1964).*

Films: Paris Bound *(1929);* Her Private Affair *(1929);* Condemned *(1929);* Holiday *(1930);* The Girl of the Golden West *(1930);* East Lynne *(1931);* Devotion *(1931);* Prestige *(1932);* Westward Passage *(1932);* The Conquerors *(1932);* The Animal Kingdom *(1932);* When Ladies Meet *(1933);* Double Harness *(1933);* The Right to Romance *(1933);* Gallant Lady *(1934);* The Life of Vergie Winters *(1934);* The Fountain *(1934);* Biography of a Bachelor Girl *(1935);* Enchanted April *(1935);* The Flame Within *(1935);* Peter Ibbetson *(1935);* The Lady Consents *(1936);* The Witness Chair *(1936);* Love From a Stranger *(1937);* Eyes in the Night *(1942);* Mission to Moscow *(1943);* The North Star (Armored Attack, *1943);* Janie *(1944);* Nine Girls *(1944);* Those Endearing Young Charms *(1945);* Janie Gets Married *(1946);* It Happened on Fifth Avenue *(1947);* Christmas Eve *(1947);* Two Weeks With Love *(1950);* The Magnificent Yankee *(1951);* The Unknown Man *(1951);* The Man in the Gray Flannel Suit *(1956);* I've Lived Before *(1956);* Strange Intruder *(1956).*

Known for her blonde elegance and aristocratic manner, Ann Harding was a first-rate actress who made a substantial reputation on stage before beginning her film career. The daughter of a career army officer, she spent her childhood moving from one military base to another. While at the Baldwin School in Bryn Mawr, Pennsylvania, she made her first stage appearance as Macduff in a school production of *Macbeth*, directed by **Maud Durbin Skinner**, wife of actor Otis

Skinner, whose daughter *****Cornelia Otis Skinner** was playing Lady Macbeth. After appearing in another school play, Harding set her sights on an acting career, a goal that did not sit well with her father. After high school, she attended Bryn Mawr College for one year, but left to move with her family to New York, where she worked as an insurance clerk and free-lanced as a script reader for the Famous-Players-Lasky Company.

Through friends, Harding made her way to the Provincetown Players (then located in Greenwich Village), where she auditioned and landed the role of Madeline Morton in *****Susan Glaspell**'s play *The Inheritors* (1921). That year, she chose the stage name Ann Harding, an appellation she claims was picked out of the air, though the recent election of Warren G. Harding may have been influential. The play received such good reviews that it was extended beyond the usual two-week run. Harding made her Broadway debut later that year in an ill-fated play *Like a King*, after which her father, certain that his daughter was on the inevitable road to ruin, disowned her. Steadfast in her career choice, Harding refined her craft with several stock companies and on Broadway in Gilbert Emery's *Tarnish* (1923) and an unpleasant little drama called *Schweiger* (1926).

In 1926, she married actor Harry Bannister, an established leading man whom she met while with a stock company in Detroit. After a brief honeymoon, she opened in *The Trial of Mary Dugan*, which enjoyed a legendary run of 310 performances. In 1928, during a five-month summer vacation from the play, Harding gave birth to a daughter, Jane, then resumed her role. In 1929, the family moved to California where Bannister was appearing in *Strange Interlude*. That year, Harding signed her first movie contract with Pathé, which later merged with RKO. After her first three films, she was headed for stardom. For her leading role in *Holiday* (1930), playing a rich girl in love with a poor man, she received an Academy Award nomination as Best Actress. Her screen image—seemingly aloof, intelligent, and well-bred—mesmerized audiences and made her one of the top ten money-making stars of the early 1930s.

In 1932, Harding's popularity dipped somewhat when she divorced her husband and the studio canceled one of her projects. However, she was soon on track again, playing a vulnerable divorcée in *Westward Passage* (1932) opposite Laurence Olivier, who later commented, "It was unbelievable for a star of her reputation to be so nice." Co-starring with Richard Dix in *The Con-*

querors (1932), an epic picture about a late 18th-century family, Harding won accolades from the critics. *Picturegoer* wrote: "Although she does not share the glare of the big lights to the same extent as Garbo, Dietrich and Tallulah, she is certainly their equal in acting talent." Harding's next two films were former stage hits: Philip Barry's *The Animal Kingdom,* which was one of the best movies of 1932, and the first film version of *Rachel Crothers' play *When Ladies Meet* (1933). Although Harding was now at the peak of her film career, there were constant disagreements with RKO over the quality of her roles and the constraints regarding stage work. She had to pass up a starring role in the Theatre Guild's production of Eugene O'Neill's *Mourning Becomes Electra,* which she considered the major tragedy in her career. Amid rumors that she might retire, Harding signed a new contract which took her through a series of soapy films, including *The Right to Romance* (1933), *Gallant Lady* (1934), *The Life of Vergie Winters* (1934), and *The Fountain* (1934). She was then miscast in MGM's *Biography of a Bachelor Girl* (1935) but fared better with Paramount in *Peter Ibbetson* (1935), which many believe contains her best screen performance, though it was a box-office dud. After the failure of *The Witness Chair* (1936), RKO did not renew Harding's contract.

Surviving a nasty court battle with her former husband over custody of their daughter (during which Bannister won additional visitation rights), Harding went to Britain and made *Love From a Stranger* (1937), in which she was deemed wonderful as the victim of sinister husband, Basil Rathbone. That year, she also made her London stage debut in the first West End production of *Candida.* George Bernard Shaw, who attended one of the rehearsals, called her the best Candida he had ever seen. She also surprised everyone with a second marriage to orchestra conductor Werner Janssen. (They went through a bitter divorce in 1962, after which Janssen returned to Germany.)

Harding returned to Hollywood intending to play Mrs. Miniver for Louis B. Mayer, but the role ultimately went to *Greer Garson. She made some B movies before embarking on a series of "mother" roles in *Janie* (1944), *Those Endearing Young Charms* (1945), and *Janie Gets Married* (1946). Although she was as charming and capable as ever, her film career never revived, and she returned to the theater, touring in *Yes, My Darling Daughter* (1949) and replacing *Ruth Hussey as Agatha Reed in *Goodbye, My Fancy,* on Broadway. In 1950, she

played **Fanny Bowditch Holmes** in MGM's *The Magnificent Yankee,* the story of Oliver Wendell Holmes, Jr., which won her co-star Louis Calhern an Oscar nomination, but was seriously flawed in its historical representation of the Supreme Court justice. Harding made her last three films in 1956, after which she began acting on television with regularity. In 1958, she appeared off-Broadway in a Tennessee Williams' double bill entitled *Garden District* (playing Grace Lancaster in *Something Unspoken* and Mrs. Venable in *Suddenly Last Summer*). She made her final Broadway appearances in *General Seeger* (1962) and *Abraham Cochrane* (1964), both of which closed after a few performances. Harding then retired to Westport, Connecticut, where she enjoyed her family, a small circle of friends, and her garden. The actress died at home in 1981.

SOURCES:

Katz, Ephraim. *The Film Encyclopedia.* NY: Harper-Collins, 1994.

McGill, Raymond D., ed. *Notable Names in the American Theatre.* Clifton, NJ: James T. White, 1976.

Ann Harding

Ringgold, Gene. "Ann Harding," in *Films in Review.* March 1972, pp. 129–153.

Shipman, David. *The Great Movie Stars: The Golden Years.* Boston, MA: Little Brown, 1995.

Barbara Morgan,
Melrose, Massachusetts

Harding, Florence K. (1860–1924)

American first lady (1921–1923), wife of the 29th U.S. president Warren G. Harding, whose effort to give the White House back to the people was diminished by her husband's scandal-plagued administration. Born Florence Kling on August 15, 1860, in Marion, Ohio; died on November 21, 1924, in Marion; third child and first daughter of Amos Kling (a banker) and Louisa (Bouton) Kling; married Henry A. "Pete" De Wolfe, in March 1880 (divorced 1886); married Warren Gamaliel Harding (U.S. president), on July 8, 1891, in Marion, Ohio; children: (first marriage) Marshall Eugene De Wolfe (1880–1914).

*Florence
K.
Harding*

Florence Harding was born Florence Kling on August 15, 1860, in Marion, Ohio, the third child and first daughter of **Louisa Bouton Kling** and banker Amos Kling, the "wealthiest man in Marion." Had Florence been the boy her father wanted, she might have grown up to be president of the United States. She also might have done a better job than her husband, who distinguished himself as one of the worst presidents in the country's history.

Florence was educated locally and spent a short time studying piano at the Cincinnati Conservatory of Music. Little is known about her mother who by some accounts died when Florence was at the conservatory, forcing her daughter to abandon her studies and come home to keep house for her father. A willful, determined man, Amos ruled his children with an iron hand. Florence began to rebel at an early age by staying out late and roller skating with boys from across the tracks. It was not unusual for her to return home after the 11 PM curfew to find herself locked out of the house.

Described as tall and gawky, and as headstrong as her father, Florence was not very popular. When she was 20, she eloped with the boy next door, Henry "Pete" De Wolfe, an alcoholic and probably the only fellow in Marion who was not intimidated by her father. The couple moved to Galion, Ohio, where a son, Marshall Eugene, was born six months after the marriage. De Wolfe deserted Florence in 1884, and they were divorced two years later. Back home in Marion, Amos, who had never accepted the marriage, refused to help Florence unless she came home and resumed using her maiden name. Florence chose to live independently, supporting herself by giving piano lessons. After Amos adopted her son, Florence had little contact with the boy as he grew up.

Amos Kling was also enraged when Florence took up with Warren Harding, the struggling editor of the *Marion Star* and a renowned ladies' man. Amos denounced Warren as an "irresponsible scalawag" and claimed there was "Negro blood" in his family, a rumor that would never die. Despite her father, Florence set aside any of her own doubts about the motives of her new paramour and pursued him relentlessly for two years. When the couple finally married, not only did Kling shun the ceremony, he also disowned his daughter. It was another seven years before he spoke to her again.

"Duchess," as Warren called his wife, was the driving force behind her husband from the beginning. Filling in at the *Star* one day when Warren was ill, she stayed on for 14 years. With a

keen business sense picked up from her father, she handled the bookkeeping and advertising and organized home delivery to boost circulation. Meanwhile, Warren was the perfect front. Using his considerable charm and gift of gab, he easily won trust and gained enormous popularity. A transition into Ohio politics seemed natural. He became a state senator, then lieutenant governor, and won election to the U.S. Senate in 1915. Florence was closely involved in all of Warren's campaigns, and her pride in, and ambition for, her husband grew with each success. So, evidently, did her mistrust of others. Characterized by some as "jealous, suspicious, and vindictive," she kept a list of her enemies in a little red book.

When Warren was mentioned as a possible candidate in the 1920 presidential campaign, Florence energetically backed his nomination and election bid, but she also had serious misgivings. One of her greatest fears was exposure of her husband's extramarital affairs; one with her friend, Marion housewife **Carrie Phillips,** and another with ❧▸ **Nan Britton**, a younger woman who developed a crush on Warren while she was still in high school. (After Warren's death, Britton published *The President's Daughter,* detailing their affair and maintaining that her child was his.) Florence had once written in her diary: "To me, love seems to have been a thing of tragedy."

She also agonized over her age—now 60—and her own poor health. In 1905, she had one kidney removed, and her remaining kidney did not function well. She was prone to infections, which caused her frequent bouts of pain and fatigue. Finally, there is evidence that Florence, who often consulted with astrologers, had received a dire prediction from her favorite medium, "Madam Marcia," who warned that if Warren became president he would die in office, and Florence would die soon after.

The war-weary country responded to Warren's "back to normalcy" campaign and elected him in a landslide victory. The White House and grounds, closed during Woodrow Wilson's administration, were opened to the public again, and Florence exhausted herself with a lively social calendar. Garden parties for veterans and group tours were popular events. The "plain folks" image of the campaign, however, was double-edged. With Prohibition the law of the land, the Hardings held dry receptions downstairs in the mansion, while upstairs liquor flowed freely and poker was the game of choice. Florence even tended bar for her husband and his Ohio cronies, who were ever present.

❧▸ **Britton, Nan** (b. 1896)

American paramour of Warren Harding who wrote the infamous tell-all The President's Daughter. *Born on November 9, 1896, in Claridon, Ohio; children:* **Elizabeth Ann Britton.**

The long-time mistress of President Warren G. Harding, Nan Britton was only 14 when she saw his photograph in a newspaper and became hopelessly infatuated. At the time, the handsome 45-year-old was running for governor of Ohio, an office he was destined not to win. Britton's obsession continued throughout her high school years, when her English teacher ironically turned out to be Warren's sister **Daisy Harding.** As a teenager, Britton also visited Harding when he was editor-publisher of the *Marion* [Ohio] *Star.*

By 1915, Harding had been elected to the U.S. Senate, and Britton, upon completion of a secretarial course in New York City, was looking for work. She wrote to him in 1917, asking if he could assist her in finding a job, and Warren responded with a speedy trip to New York to see her, taking a room at the Manhattan Hotel. There, the couple quickly moved from matters of employment to matters of the heart. From that time until Harding's sudden death in 1923, the two carried on a clandestine love affair, supposedly with the full knowledge of Warren's wife Florence who kept quiet for political reasons. (***Florence Harding** had already dealt with her husband's philandering, when he had an affair with **Carrie Phillips**, whose husband owned a department store in Marion, Ohio.) In 1919, Britton gave birth to a girl named Elizabeth Ann, whom Harding took responsibility for and supported for a time, although he encouraged Britton to have the child adopted by her married sister in Chicago.

During Harding's presidential campaign in 1920, and throughout his years in the White House, the trysts and correspondence continued, aided by the Secret Service who sent notes and smuggled Britton in and out of the White House. Reputedly, many of the couple's meetings took place in an oversize coat closet next to the Oval Office.

Following Harding's sudden and mysterious death in August 1923, Britton, who was no longer receiving child support, was desperate for money. Failing in an attempt to secure $50,000 from the Harding estate following the death of Florence in 1924, Britton wrote *The President's Daughter*, a tell-all published in 1927, despite attempts from the Society for the Suppression of Vice to prevent its release. When the outspoken journalist H.L. Mencken reviewed the book in the *Baltimore Sun*, it flew off the shelves, making Britton a great deal of money and substantiating her claims in the eyes of the public.

She also was her husband's key advisor, frequently visited injured veterans at Walter Reed Hospital, was involved in many charities, and agitated for women's rights. But politically, Warren did not seem to grasp the serious demands of his position. Lacking intelligence, he relied heavily on the advice of friends and subordinates, who were at best unethical and at worst downright crooked. Scandals involving various appointees seemed to emerge daily. Although Florence put out what fires she could, the image of his administration began to tarnish. Warren, however, remained oblivious to the depth of his problems.

On the return leg of a transcontinental trip—a "Voyage of Understanding"—in the summer of 1923, Warren Harding fell ill and died in San Francisco. Mystery surrounded the tragedy, with hints by some that Florence may have been involved. Although the death was attributed to food poisoning, Florence refused to have an autopsy performed. (In another bizarre turn, Warren's personal physician died six months later.) Florence accompanied Warren's body cross country by train, and the public, still unaware of the far-reaching consequences of the administration's scandals, greeted the funeral procession in droves. While her husband's body lay in state in the Capitol, Florence made one final effort to protect his name by destroying every private paper she could find. She then returned to Marion, Ohio, where she died on November 21, 1924, 15 months after the president. She was buried in Marion Cemetery, at the Harding Memorial.

SOURCES:

Caroli, Betty Boyd. *First Ladies*. NY: Oxford University Press, 1987.

McConnell, Jane and Burt. *Our First Ladies: From Martha Washington to Lady Bird Johnson*. NY: Thomas Y. Crowell, 1964.

Means, Marianne. *The Women in the White House*. NY: Signet, 1963.

Melick, Arden David. *Wives of the Presidents*. Maplewood, NJ: Hammond, 1977.

Paletta, LuAnn. *The World Almanac of First Ladies*. NY: World Almanac, 1990.

SUGGESTED READING:

Anthony, Carl Sferrazza. *Florence Harding*. NY: William Morrow, 1998.

Harding, Rebecca Blaine (1831–1910).

See Olsen, Tillie for sidebar on Rebecca Harding Davis.

Hardinge, Belle Boyd (1844–1900).

See Boyd, Belle.

Hardwick, Elizabeth (1916—)

American novelist and essayist. Born in 1916 in Lexington, Kentucky; graduated from the University of Kentucky, M.A., 1939; married to Robert Lowell (a poet), in 1949 (divorced 1972); children: Harriet.

A professor at the Columbia School of the Arts, Elizabeth Hardwick was also a literary critic for the *Partisan Review* and, in 1963, cofounder the *New York Review of Books*. Her novels include *The Ghostly Lover* (1945), *The Simple Truth* (1955), and *Sleepless Nights* (1979). She also wrote *A View of My Own: Essays in Literature and Society* (1962), *Seduction and Betrayal: Women and Literature* (1974), which was nominated for the National Book Award, and *Bartleby in Manhattan and Other Essays* (1983), and was the editor for 18 volumes of *Rediscovered Fiction by American Women* (1977). Her recurring theme, writes **Joan Didion**, is of "the ways in which women compensate for their relative physiological inferiority."

Hardy, Catherine (b. 1932).

See Faggs, Mae for sidebar.

Harel, Marie (fl. 1790)

French inventor of Camembert cheese. Flourished in 1790 in the town of Camembert, Normandy, France.

Farmer Marie Harel is credited with inventing Camembert cheese during the French Revolution, when a resistant priest, Abbé Bonvoust, took refuge at her Beaumoncel Manner in Camembert in 1790. A year later, Bonvoust gave Marie a secret recipe to improve her cheese, and she readily heeded his advice. Following her death, her widowed husband reaped a fortune from her creation. "Mme. Harel's monument, a stone shaft," writes ***Janet Flanner** in *Paris Was Yesterday,* "unfortunately resembles a slice of Gruyère. There is no justice." Camembert became even more renowned in the 1890s with the invention of the circular wooden box which enabled it to be more easily transported. Marie Harel was posthumously awarded the French government's *palmes académiques* in 1927.

Harewood, countess of.

See Mary, Princess (1897–1965).
See Lascelles, Patricia (b. 1926).
See Stein, Marion (b. 1926).

Hargreaves, Alison (1962–1995)

English-born mountain climber. Born in England in 1962; died on Pakistan's K2 on August 13, 1995; grew up in Derbyshire, England; middle of three children of John and Joyce Hargreaves (both mathematicians); lived in Spean Bridge, Scotland; married James

Ballard (a climber), in 1988; children: To (b. 1989); Kate (b. 1991).

On August 13, 1995, Alison Hargreaves disappeared with five other climbers while scaling Pakistan's K2, situated in the Karakoram range bordering Pakistan and China. At 28,251 feet, K2 is the world's second highest summit and one of the most dangerous, because it is subject to sudden harsh storms and high winds. Only 134 climbers have conquered the mountain, while 50 have died trying. But Hargreaves, who maintained that she was just as vulnerable driving to London, felt "there was no gain without risk."

Four months earlier, she had entered the record books as the first woman, and second climber, to reach the 29,028-foot summit of Mount Everest, the world's highest peak, alone and without supplementary oxygen. She stood at the summit for 40 minutes and later told interviewers, "It was the best moment in my life."

Hargreaves became fascinated with mountaineering at an early age, when her parents took her climbing on Ben Nevis, Britain's highest peak. "I teamed up with another girl of my own ability," she told Bill Birkett. "We used to go to youth hostels and take a rope. Two girls in a youth hostel with a rope was highly novel, for all the other women were just walkers." At age 15, while climbing Black Slab at Stanage, Hargreaves was pulled to the ground, suffering a compound fracture of her left leg and a broken right heel, when a climber fell and grabbed her rope. Soon, her climbing companion lost interest, because, even with her injuries, Hargreaves was climbing higher and harder. "I started climbing with blokes. Just following them up routes, and for a long time I became a second."

But, despite her size at 5'2", she preferred to lead. Quitting school at 18, she moved in with another climber Jim Ballard; they were married in 1988. That year, while six months pregnant, she climbed the north face of Switzerland's Eiger. Unable to find a sponsor for Alison's climbing, the couple packed up the family—they now had two children—and camped in Switzerland, living out of an aged Land Rover. While Jim cared for the children, she climbed, becoming the first person in one season to conquer the six major Alpine north faces, including the Eiger and the Matterhorn. In 1986, she was the first from Britain to ascend the Kangtega in the Khumbu Nepal region of the Himalayas.

After two weeks at home in Scotland following her success on Mount Everest, Hargreaves left for Pakistan to prepare for her assault on K2, arriving on June 25. Reaching the second-stage camp at 22,500 feet in mid-July, she made a solo attempt to conquer the summit but was pushed back by a blizzard. For the next month, longing to be home with her husband and children, she sat out storm after storm on the mountainside. Finally, on August 13, despite signs of continued bad weather, she decided to make one last attempt. She set out with five others. By evening, they radioed that they had reached the summit. Soon after, another howling storm tore into the mountain and continued throughout the night. Experts theorize that the climbing party was literally blown off the side of the mountain. All told, seven were killed that night, and Hargreaves' body was seen out of reach near Camp 2. Because of the difficulties in retrieving the bodies, they will remain on the mountain.

Hargreaves' husband had been preparing for that fatal moment throughout their years together. "I suppose what's most comforting to me is that she was on her way down—she had conquered K2," he said. "I can hear her repeating her favorite saying," he continued. "'One day as a tiger is better than a thousand as a sheep.'"

SOURCES:

Birkett, Bill, and Bill Peascod. *Women Climbing: 200 Years of Achievement.* Seattle, WA: The Mountaineers, 1989.

People Weekly. September 4, 1995, pp. 69–70.

Harington, Lucy (c. 1581–1627).

See Russell, Lucy.

Harkness, Anna M. Richardson

(1837–1926)

American philanthropist who established the Commonwealth Fund (1918). Born Anna M. Richardson in Dalton, Ohio, on October 25, 1837; died in New York City, on March 27, 1926; daughter of James and Anna (Ranck) Richardson; married Stephen Vanderburg Harkness (a businessman), on February 13, 1854 (died 1888); children: Jennie A. Harkness (who died as a young child); Charles William Harkness (b. 1860); Florence Harkness (b. 1864); and Edward Stephen Harkness (b. 1874).

Most of what is known of American philanthropist Anna Harkness, who was born and raised in Dalton, Ohio, dates from her marriage at the age of 16 to Stephen Vanderburg Harkness, 19 years her senior and a widower with a young son. A successful businessman, Stephen moved his

Anna M. Richardson Harkness

education, medical research, and cultural institutions. In 1917, in memory of her son, she gave $3 million to Yale University to build the Harkness Triangle, a series of dormitory buildings. Additional gifts to Yale included $3 million in 1920 for faculty salaries, given with the stipulation that the university raise $2 million of its own. Harkness also contributed to other educational institutions, among them Hampton and Tuskegee institutes, two African-American schools.

Harkness, whose gifts were usually made anonymously, was also generous to the institutions of her adopted city, including the New York Public Library, The Museum of Natural History, and the Metropolitan Museum of Art. Her largest gift to the city was a 22-acre site in upper Manhattan (valued at $4 million) given to Columbia University for a new medical center for the College of Physicians and Surgeons and the Presbyterian Hospital.

By 1916, Harkness was finding it increasingly difficult to personally evaluate all the requests she received for aid. Two years later, after consulting with her son Edward, she established the Commonwealth Fund, a non-profit foundation with an endowment of $20 million and governed by a board of directors given full discretion to distribute the funds "for the welfare of mankind." The Fund, one of the few philanthropic foundations established by a woman at that time, helped support medical institutions, health organizations, and a program of fellowship which provided for British students to study in America.

Harkness continued to make personal charitable contributions until she died in 1926, at age 88. By that time, she had skillfully managed to increase the $50 million share of her inheritance to $85 million. Her will left $35 million to various charitable organizations and a large bequest to her only surviving child, Edward. Anna Harkness was buried in Cleveland's Lakeview Cemetery, next to her husband.

SOURCES:

James, Edward T., ed. *Notable American Women 1907–1950.* Cambridge, MA: The Belknap Press of Harvard University Press, 1971.

McHenry, Robert, ed. *Famous American Women.* NY: Dover, 1983.

Barbara Morgan,
Melrose, Massachusetts

family to Cleveland in 1866, where he invested a major portion of his considerable wealth in John D. Rockefeller's Standard Oil Company. While her husband amassed a fortune, Harkness managed an estate on Cleveland's millionaires' row and tended to her four young children (the eldest of which, a girl, died as a young child). When Stephen died suddenly in 1888, Harkness and her children divided an inheritance of over $150 million. Following her husband's death, Harkness moved to New York City, where her eldest son, Charles, established an office to administer the estate. Believing that her fortune was a public trust, Harkness embarked on a philanthropic career that would dominate the rest of her life. Her early charity centered on religious and welfare agencies, including the Fifth Avenue Presbyterian Church, the missions of the Presbyterian Church, the New York Association for Improving the Condition of the Poor, and the State Charities Aid Association.

After her son's death in 1916, Harkness broadened her philanthropic interests to include

Harkness, Georgia (1891–1974)

American scholar and one of the most prominent female Protestant theologians during the 20th century. Born Georgia Elma Harkness on April 21, 1891, in

Harkness, New York; died at Pomona Valley Community Hospital on August 21, 1974; daughter of Joseph Warren Harkness (a farmer) and Lillie (Merrill) Harkness; attended Keeseville, New York, high school; awarded A.B., Cornell University, 1912; M.A., Boston University, 1920; M.R.E., Boston University, 1920; Ph.D., Boston University, 1923; lived with Verna Miller; never married; no children.

Taught Latin and French at a high school in Schuylerville, New York (1912–14), and Scotia, New York (1915–18); was an instructor at English Bible, Boston University School of Religious Education (1919–20); was a member of faculty, Elmira College, advancing to rank of professor of philosophy (1922–37); was an associate professor of religion, Mount Holyoke College (1937–39); was a professor of applied theology, Garrett Biblical Institute (1939–50); was a professor of applied theology, Pacific School of Theology at Berkeley (1950–61).

Publications: The Church and the Immigrant *(George H. Doran, 1921);* Conflicts in Religious Thought *(Harper, 1929);* John Calvin: The Man and His Ethics *(Holt, 1931);* Holy Flame *(B. Humphries, 1935);* The Resources of Religion *(Holt, 1936);* Religious Living *(Association, 1937);* The Recovery of Ideals *(Scribner, 1937);* The Faith by Which the Church Lives *(Abington, 1940);* The Glory of God *(Abington, 1943);* The Dark Night of the Soul *(Abington-Cokesbury, 1945);* Prayer and the Common Life *(Abington-Cokesbury, 1948);* The Gospel and Our World *(Abington-Cokesbury, 1949);* Through Christ Our Lord: A Devotional Manual Based on the Recorded Words of Jesus *(Abington-Cokesbury, 1950);* The Modern Rival of the Christian Faith *(Abington-Cokesbury, 1952);* Be Still and Know *(Abington-Cokesbury, 1953);* Toward Understanding the Bible *(Scribner, 1954);* The Sources of Western Morality *(Scribner, 1954);* Foundations of Christian Knowledge *(Abington, 1955);* The Providence of God *(Abington, 1960);* Beliefs That Count *(Abington, 1961);* The Church and the Faith *(Abington, 1962);* The Methodist Church in Social Thought and Action *(Abington, 1964);* What Christians Believe *(Abington, 1965);* The Fellowship of the Holy Spirit *(Abington, 1966);* Christian Ethics *(Abington, 1967);* Disciples of the Christian Life *(John Knox, 1968);* Stability Amid Change *(Abington, 1969);* Grace Abounding *(Abington, 1969);* Women in Church and Society: A Historical and Theological Inquiry *(Abington, 1971);* The Ministry of Reconciliation *(Abington, 1971);* Mysticism: Its Meaning *(Abington, 1973);* Understanding the Kingdom of God *(Abington, 1974); (with Charles F. Kraft)* Biblical Foundations of the Middle East Conflict *(Abington, 1976).*

Until 1939, life had gone surprisingly well for Georgia Harkness. Two years earlier, *Time* magazine had referred to the middle-aged scholar as the "famed woman theologian," a unique compliment in a sphere dominated by men. Harkness was a theologian of the more liberal persuasion, a circumstance that undoubtedly helped her face the world with some confidence. She wrote in 1939:

> I believe in the essential greatness of man, in a Christian social gospel which calls us to action as co-workers with God in the redemptive process, in a Kingdom which will come in this world by growth as Christians accept responsibility in the spirit of the cross. My Christian faith has its central focus, not in Paul's theology or Luther's or Calvin's, but in the incarnation of God in the Jesus of the Gospels.

"A union of divine with human resources," she had written two years earlier, "is a possibility worth the effort." Indeed, it could create "an active saintliness of character."

Exhibiting the rare combination of being a highly productive academician and an articulate platform speaker, Harkness had always worked with frantic energy. In the process, she piled up an enviable number of "firsts" to her credit: the first woman participant of the Fellowship of Younger Christian Thinkers; the first woman member of the American Theological Society; the first full-time woman professor of theological studies at an American seminary; and the first major woman theologian to be part of the worldwide Protestant ecumenical circle.

Then, just as she was beginning her new faculty position at one of Methodism's leading seminaries, she found herself suddenly in deep melancholia. Although not yet 50, she started to experience a series of severe illnesses which included sacroiliac arthritis, a condition that precipitated several years of nagging pain. Her entire nervous system was disrupted. The result: one of the most energetic professors in the United States suddenly fell into severe lethargy. She later wrote, "This combination of low energy, a 'thorn in the flesh' and frustration at 'suffering many things at the hands of many physicians,' plunged me into insomnia and acute depression."

Worst of all, she felt that God was abandoning her. Always before, she found her Lord an abundant source of strength and support. Now, as she said in her letter to the seminary's president asking for a brief leave, she felt a "spiritual defeat in not being able to trust God and live triumphantly." She claimed to have no easy answers for the person who experiences "this the deepest hell," which she defined as a condition wherein one's reason "tells him there are things to live for, but to his emotions life is meaningless and the future bleak."

At this very point, however, when she felt absolutely cut off from her Creator, she experienced the realization that God was always bestowing his divine grace, irrespective of her subjective attitudes or efforts. No longer did it matter to be "well thought of as a servant of God" or to sense "satisfaction in being able to do the work of God." She wrote:

> It is the Christian's rightful faith that, however dark the night, God's love surrounds us. . . . When we are assured that God ceases not to love us, we can watch with patience through the night and wait for the dawn. . . . If with all our hearts we truly seek him, we can know that *God finds us* and gives rest to our souls.

While experiencing her new conversion, Harkness steeped herself in the works of the great Christian mystics of history, among them Thomas a Kempis, Brother Lawrence, George Fox, and John Bunyan. Although she never wrote directly about her experiences, the title of her more general study was more revealing: *The Dark Night of the Soul* (1945). It was borrowed from a Spanish mystic she much admired, St. John of the Cross. By the end of 1945, she had emerged from her ordeal a transformed woman.

*G*od lives, Christ lives, the church which is the carrier of Christ's gospel still lives, goodness lives. All of these will endure to the end of time, and beyond it to eternity.

—**Georgia Harkness**, *Grace Abounding*

Georgia Elma Harkness was born on April 21, 1891, the youngest of four children, in a rural Adirondack town named for her paternal grandfather. Indeed, she was raised in a large white farmhouse that had belonged to her father's family since 1801. Her father, whom she always called the greatest influence on her life, was not only a prosperous farmer, he was also a pious Methodist lay-leader who, from ages 16 to 84, taught his own Sunday School class. Furthermore, J. Warren Harkness organized the local grange, introduced free rural mail delivery, established a cooperative fire insurance company, and was the moving spirit behind the establishment of Plattsburgh Normal School. Her mother, the frail **Lillie Merrill Harkness**, was far more

retiring. Georgia remembers with gratitude Lillie's nursing efforts during the flu epidemic of 1918, for Lillie might well have sacrificed years of her own life to save that of her daughter.

As a child, Georgia was educated in a one-room schoolhouse that also served on Sunday as the community Methodist church. An extremely bright adolescent, she entered Keeseville High School at age 12, accumulated enough credits to graduate at age 14, and completed the equivalent of an eight-year program over the next two and a half years. When the school introduced a Greek class, she was its only student. Midway through high school, she experienced a religious conversion at an evangelistic meeting. "I felt no great upheaval of soul," she later wrote, "but I did feel that from then on I must be a Christian."

Always an outstanding student and highly competitive, Harkness won a state scholarship to Cornell University. "I was shy, green, and countrified," she recalled. "My clothes were queer; I had no social graces; and I did not come within gunshot of being asked to join a sorority." She found a congenial peer group, however, and a sense of direction in the Student Christian Association and the Student Volunteer Movement and, until prevented by the illness of her parents, planned to become a missionary. Moreover, through the teaching of Professor James E. Creighton, she also discovered philosophy, a field that—in Creighton's eyes—must center on the wisdom needed for "a common basis of life in society."

Upon graduating Phi Beta Kappa in 1912, Harkness taught Latin, German, and French in high schools in Schuylerville and Scotia, villages near Schenectady. Finding little stimulation in this experience, she enrolled in 1918 in Boston University's School of Religious Education and Social Science, a Methodist lay-training institution. She wrote a master's thesis that was later published under the title *The Church and the Immigrant* (1921), a most appropriate topic for a school that stressed the Social Gospel and urban ministry.

In 1920, Harkness began doctoral work under the direction of Edgar Sheffield Brightman, a scholar only seven years her senior. Brightman proved to be a warm personal friend, a hard taskmaster, and an astute theological mentor, who expounded a theology known as personalism. For the rest of her life, Harkness was influenced by this thought system, which centered on the individual person as the ultimate reality and personality as the explanatory principle of all life, human and divine. Her dissertation on an English exponent of philosophical idealism was entitled "The Relations Between the Philosophy and Ethics in the Thought of Thomas Hill Green." The final draft weighed six pounds and was 399 pages long.

Harkness first taught at Elmira College in Elmira, New York, where from 1923 to 1937 she was a member of the philosophy department. Despite the heavy teaching load characteristic of small colleges, Harkness—who often taught five courses per semester—was a prolific writer. Her *Conflicts in Religious Thought* (1929) dealt with universal problems of faith. Religion, she said, must be a way of life rather than a set of intellectual functions, offering the "strength to meet the storms and battles." In a study of John Calvin published in 1931, Harkness claimed to hold no brief for either the man or his theology. She nonetheless called Calvinism "an enduring structure, and one not wholly lacking in a stern sort of beauty." Somewhat like sociologist Max Weber, she saw in Calvinism many of the seeds of capitalism.

In *The Resources of Religion* (1935), she offered a more distinctly Christian focus than in *Conflicts*. The work epitomized the theological liberalism of her generation. The man Jesus embodied "the self-giving, suffering love of God for men"; the cross was "the eternal symbol of a loving, suffering God"; the resurrection conveyed the "triumphant living" that Christianity calls salvation; and the incarnation was "the high mark of ethical idealism." She went so far as to claim that a person could gain a "Christlike personality" through moral striving and wrote of creating an entire society patterned on the Kingdom of God.

Two other works—*The Recovery of Ideals* (1937) and *Religious Living* (1937)—contained a perfectionist thrust. In both, Harkness asserted that the truly dedicated believer was capable of fulfilling Christianity's highest ideals. As she said in *Recovery*, "Living in Christ, one could look the world in the face, do a mighty work, and know that nothing could daunt the soul." As noted by her biographer, **Rosemary Skinner Keller**, Harkness believed that a person could develop a genuinely Christlike personality "through high moral striving, not through a genuine grappling with a deeper experience of spiritual death and resurrection."

Harkness was busy on other fronts, almost compulsively so. She frequently contributed articles and poems to a host of religious journals, including the prestigious *Christian Century*. She

was a frequent speaker on campuses and at various Methodist conferences. Even though she spent much time caring for her aged parents, she took sabbaticals to study at Harvard University, Yale Divinity School (where she had been awarded the coveted Sterling Fellowship), and New York's Union Theological Seminary.

All during this time, the professor of philosophy was becoming increasingly attracted to theology. Harkness saw her intellectual quest centering increasingly less on philosophical objectivity, increasingly more on overt Christian commitment. In 1937, she leapt at the opportunity to join the faculty at Mount Holyoke College. She was hired by president *Mary Emma Woolley, an internationally known educator, to teach the history and literature of religion. She arrived amid faculty strife over a new president, and in 1939 she welcomed a bid to teach applied theology at Garrett Biblical Institute, a major Methodist seminary in the Chicago suburb of Evanston.

Georgia Harkness

Here began her ordeal, the illness that led her to believe that God had abandoned her. The years of speaking engagements and professional seminars, some of them overseas, had taken their toll. It took her several years to regain her footing. In 1944, the prominent Evanston minister Ernest Fremont Tittle introduced Harkness to **Verna Miller**, thinking that Miller—an administrative secretary and musician—might be an ideal companion for the overwrought professor. The two women became close friends, sharing a home for the rest of their lives.

Once she had recovered from her personal crisis, Harkness produced what was essentially a trilogy on the life of faith. Now a "chastened" liberal, she increasingly emphasized the power of evil and the role of sin. Yet in *Understanding the Christian Faith* (1947), she revealed that her theological liberalism was only tempered, not abandoned. Christians, she insisted, must remain continually open to new truth, at times even suspending judgment until relative certainty emerged. Her *Prayer and the Common Life* (1948) centered on her very definition of prayer: living one's whole life as a response to God and utilizing this relationship to foster the welfare of the world itself. *The Gospel and the World* (1949) showed her praising Protestant neo-orthodoxy for focusing on human pride and rebellion, but found it inadequate in recognizing divine grace and individual acts of love.

In 1950, Harkness again changed posts, becoming professor of applied theology at the Pacific School of Religion in Berkeley, California. She took a break in 1956–57, when she spent a sabbatical year teaching at Tokyo's International Christian University and Manila's Union Theological Seminary. Only in 1961, at the age of 70, did she retire; at which point, she moved to Claremont, California.

Again, Harkness' productivity could only shame many younger colleagues. *Towards Understanding the Bible* (1952) explained higher criticism to the laity and challenged the Fundamentalist belief in inerrancy. Offering her own criteria for the genuine "Voice of God," she said that one must hold up any passage to "the life, the words, and mind of Christ." In *Formulations of Christian Knowledge* (1955), she combined a rationalistic defense of Christianity with a call to the devotional life. "The Word of God" within the Bible, she said, "must be a living language, or it is not a word at all." Other works centered on providence (1961), the laity (1962), women in Western religious culture (1972), and mysticism (1973). Her final book, published two years after her death, centered on Middle East tensions and included an impassioned plea for dispossessed Palestinians.

In examining Harkness' career, certain themes predominate. Foremost is the status of women. Always steeped in Methodist life, Harkness was ordained locally as deacon in 1926 and elder in 1938. Under such local ordination, she was permitted to exercise most ministerial roles but denied membership in Annual Conference. To Methodist clergy, such membership was crucial, for it meant that district superintendents were obliged to find a parish for any willing applicant. She continually advocated full equality, calling the church in 1937 "the most impregnable stronghold of male dominance."

In 1948, at the World Council of Churches Assembly at Amsterdam, Swiss theologian Karl Barth—perhaps in jest—first cited Genesis to the effect that woman was made from Adam's rib, then quoted the passage in the Letter to the Ephesians on man as head of the woman. Harkness responded with Galatians 3:28: "There is neither male nor female; for you are all one in Christ Jesus." When Barth was reminded of the encounter a year later, he just remarked, "Remind me not of that woman."

When in May 1956 at the denominational assembly in Minneapolis, Methodist women were admitted to full pastoral status, Harkness attended but took no part in the debate. She later said, "The Bible says that there is a time to speak and a time to be silent. This was the time for me to be silent." Yet, when the entire gathering gave her a standing ovation later that evening, it was in recognition that she had been the leading spirit behind the move.

A second theme revolved around Harkness' pacifism. "War," she said in the late 1930s, "destroys every value for which Christianity stands, and to oppose war by more war is only to deepen the morass into which humanity has fallen." Denying that she was naive, she conceded that no motives were wholly pure and that life always involved choices between alternative evils. However, some evils were worse than others, war being primary. Indeed, it was precisely because humans were sinful and life full of conflict that no good could emerge from war. She realized, she said in 1938, that pacifists were unable to stop war from breaking out, but once it did, they were obligated to withhold support, even if it meant death.

Harkness became a pacifist in 1924, when she participated in a group tour of Europe directed by the prominent Christian reformer Sherwood Eddy. Made aware of Germany's grievances under the Versailles Treaty, she returned to America denying that Germany bore sole guilt for World War I; in fact, she accused the Allied blockade of starving over 700,000 people. She joined the international pacifist body, the Fellowship of Reconciliation (FOR), and she remained an anti-interventionist during World War II. During the conflict, she sought to earmark her taxes for strictly civilian use, but was told by the Treasury Department that such action was unlawful.

Late in 1950, Harkness was appointed to the Commission of Christian Scholars on the Moral Obligations of Obliteration Bombing and the Use of the Hydrogen Bomb for Mass Destruction. A task force sponsored by the Federal Council of Churches, it was chaired by Angus Dun, Episcopal bishop of Washington, D.C., and had in its ranks such eminent theologians as Paul Tillich, John C. Bennett, and Reinhold Niebuhr. The majority issued a statement approving American use of atomic weapons in retaliation for an atomic strike against the United States or its allies. Harkness, together with Robert Calhoun of Yale Divinity School, issued a strong dissent. Noting that the task force called for "all possible restraint" in Western use of nuclear weapons, she asked:

> Is this realistic? Can we have a major war that is not "all-out" war? Is not such restraint, if practiced, the very antithesis of military success? And is this not the very reason why some influential members of the commission refused during the last war to condemn food blockades and obliteration bombing of civilians?

During the Korean War, she supported the initial United Nations' action, though she opposed crossing the 38th parallel. While still calling herself a pacifist, she resigned from the FOR in 1951 over its tactics of tax and draft resistance. Once the Vietnam War broke out, however, Harkness strongly opposed it, calling it "so unjust and immoral that its continuance cannot be justified."

A third posture of Harkness involves her socialism. In the 1930s, seeing capitalism riddled with inequity and greed, she found it intrinsically contrary to Christian ethics. A more just distribution of goods was needed. On the international level, she believed, capitalism resulted in economic imperialism, which she saw as the root of both world wars. By 1967, she had mellowed, writing in *Christian Ethics* that the best economic order involved "a blend of free enterprise and state control in accordance with certain positive Christian principles."

Fourth, Harkness vehemently opposed all forms of racism. She fought segregation within the Methodist Church, even opposing the 1968 merger between Methodists and the Evangelical United Brethren Church on the race issue. The Methodist Church long had a segregated black administrative structure called the Central Jurisdiction. Harkness called the arrangement "a clear contradiction of Christian morality." She said, "This injustice I cannot stomach, and I hope my church cannot."

Fifth, Harkness had a strong sense of the church universal. She was always a leading figure in ecumenical circles, and there was seldom, if ever, a national or international assembly at which she was not present. Her participation reads like a history of the World Council of Churches and its immediate predecessors: the Oxford Conference on Life and Work (1937); the International Missionary Council at Madras, India (1938); the World Council organizational conference at Geneva (1939); the Amsterdam (1948) and Evanston (1954) assemblies of the World Council of Churches; the Commission of the Churches on International Affairs at Cambridge (1946); the conference on Faith and Order at Lund, Sweden (1952). Indeed, the Hymn Society of America selected her hymn, "Hope of the World," to honor the 1954 Evanston Assembly.

Harkness was extremely effective, even in the most sensitive of ecclesiastical matters, in part because of the cogency of her arguments, in part because she possessed a conciliatory personality. Whether dealing with colleagues on the Elmira faculty or delegates to a Methodist convention, she was tactful and fair-minded, trying to reconcile opposing views while pressing for what she saw as genuine reform.

One of the most widely read theologians of the mid-20th century, Harkness wrote over 30 books. No innovator, she sought to present the most profound of mysteries in clear, everyday language and to do so without violating the integrity of the Christian message. Among the first theologians to interpret ministry as the calling of all God's people, not simply the ordained clergy, she challenged pastors to show just how Christian teaching related to everyday life. She wrote in 1947:

> Laymen make the greater part of the political, economic, and social decisions on which human destinies depend. There are enough

Christian laymen in the world to establish "peace on earth, good will among men," if laymen understand the Christian gospel and act upon it.

At the same time, Harkness' strength—her self-designated role as theologian to the laity—was also her weakness. There is no point where her thinking forced the theological enterprise to take a new turn. Positive responses to her work invariably stress her lucidity of presentation, freshness of expression, and above all deep spirituality, whereas negative comments emphasize her oversimplification of argument, distilling the work of others, writing simply for the novice and the parish clergy—in short—popularization. In the 1990s, Harkness is seldom quoted, in part because contemporary parishes often ignore the entire theological quest, in part because many of her social concerns are obviously dated in the form in which they appeared. Perhaps the best place to begin appreciating Harkness is to start with her poetry which still conveys intensity and power.

God gave Isaiah then the vision high;
His unclean lips were purged with sacred fire.
Out of the smoke a Voice in challenge came;
Unhesitant, he answered, Here am I.
Again the days are dark, the outlook dire;
Lord, touch Thy prophets now with holy flame.

On August 21, 1974, Georgia Harkness suffered a heart attack at home. She died in Claremont.

SOURCES:

Frakes, Margaret. "Theology Is Her Province," in *Christian Century*. Vol. 69. September 24, 1952, pp. 1088–1089.

Keller, Rosemary Skinner. *Georgia Harkness: For Such a Time as This*. Nashville, TN: Abington Press, 1992.

COLLECTIONS:

The Georgia Harkness papers are located in the archives of Garrett-Evangelical Theological Seminary, Evanston, Illinois.

Justus D. Doenecke,
Professor of History, New College of the
University of South Florida, Sarasota, Florida

Harkness, Mary Stillman

(1874–1950)

American philanthropist. Born Mary Emma Stillman on July 4, 1874, in Brooklyn, New York; died on June 6, 1950, in New York City; third of four daughters of Thomas Edgar (a lawyer) and Charlotte Elizabeth (Greenman) Stillman; married Edward Stephen Harkness (1874–1940, a capitalist, benefactor of Harvard University, and trustee of the Metropolitan Museum of Art), on November 15, 1904 (died 1940); daughter-in-law of Anna M. Richardson Harkness (1837–1926); no children.

Born into considerable wealth, Mary Emma Stillman married into the Harkness family in 1904, and from that time on devoted herself to philanthropic concerns. Her husband Edward Harkness derived his own fortune from his father Stephen V. Harkness, whose early investment in John D. Rockefeller's Standard Oil Company yielded sizable dividends through the years. Before his marriage, Edward had made a number of substantial charitable contributions, and it was a habit he continued with the support of his wife. The fact that the couple had no children made them even more committed to their philanthropic ventures.

Edward's own philanthropic interests centered on medicine and education. In 1922, he and his mother, *Anna M. Richardson Harness, gave the first of several gifts to help build the Columbia-Presbyterian Medical Center in New York City, and after Anna's death in 1926, Edward made a series of grants to Harvard and Yale universities as well as to a number of independent preparatory schools, including St. Paul's and Phillips Exeter Academy. Mary Harkness, in addition to counseling her husband, made her own independent contributions. She also came up with the name "Pilgrim Trust" for the large British endowment Edward set up in 1930. In 1935, she gave $1 million for a convalescent facility in Port Chester, New York, to be operated in conjunction with Columbia-Presbyterian Medical Center. Other gifts included several buildings for Connecticut College for Women in New London, and a contribution to the restoration program of the Marine Historical Association at Mystic, Connecticut.

Following her husband's death in 1940, Harkness continued to support their combined interests until her own death in 1950. She made monetary gifts of over $3 million to the Columbia-Presbyterian Medical Center, Bennett Junior College, and Oberlin College, and also supported local charities, including the New York United Hospital Fund, the Red Cross, Y.W.C.A., and the Boy Scouts. The Metropolitan and Cleveland museums also benefited from her largess, receiving gifts of books and art objects, while she contributed her copy of the Gutenberg Bible to Yale Library. Mary Stillman Harkness' summer mansion on Long Island Sound, known as Eolia, with grounds landscaped by *Beatrix Jones Farrand, now comprises Harkness Memorial State Park in Waterford, Connecticut.

SOURCES:

James, Edward T., ed. *Notable American Women 1607–1950*. Cambridge, MA: The Belknap Press of Harvard University Press, 1971.

Barbara Morgan,
Melrose, Massachusetts

Harkness, Rebekah (1915–1982)

American composer, sculptor, dance patron, and philanthropist who founded the Harkness Ballet. Name variations: Betty Harkness. Born Rebekah Semple West on April 17, 1915, in St. Louis, Missouri; died on June 17, 1982, in New York City, second daughter and one of three children of Allen Tarwater (a stockbroker) and Rebekah Cook (Semple) West; attended Rossman and John Burroughs schools in St. Louis; graduated from Fermata, a finishing school in Aiken, South Carolina, 1932; married Charles Dickson Pierce, on June 10, 1939 (divorced 1946); married William Hale Harkness (an attorney and businessman), on October 1, 1947 (died, August 1954); married Benjamin H. Kean (a physician), in 1961 (divorced 1965); married Niels Lauersen (a physician), in 1974 (divorced 1977); children: (first marriage) Allen Pierce (b. 1940); Anne Terry Pierce (b. 1944); (second marriage) Edith Harkness.

Once one of the wealthiest women in America, Standard Oil heiress Rebekah Harkness was well known during the 1960s as a generous philanthropist and patron of the arts. She created a dance empire that included the 40-member Harkness Ballet, a ballet school and home for the company called Harkness House, and a refurbished 1,250-seat theater which presented the Harkness Ballet as well as other dance companies to New York audiences. Through the William Hale Harkness Foundation, named for her second husband, she also sponsored construction of a medical research building at New York Hospital and supported a number of medical research projects. Harkness was also a complex individual with a decidedly self-destructive edge. In *Blue Blood* (1988), author Craig Unger claims that the public image of Rebekah Harkness merely scratched the surface. Calling her story "a Rashomon-like affair," in which each of the central people in her life had a different take on her, Unger also maintains that much of what was written about Harkness was false. At the time of her death, he points out, her dance empire had been destroyed, she had been humiliated by the press, and most of her fortune had been lost through her capricious behavior. Saddest of all, he believes, were her problems as a mother. All three of the Harkness children led tortured lives. **Edith Harkness**, her only child with Bill Harkness, was in and out of mental institutions and eventually committed suicide; her other daughter, **Terry Pierce**, had a severely brain-damaged baby who died in childhood. Harkness' only son, obsessed with upholding the family honor, shot and killed a man in a brawl.

Born into a socially prominent St. Louis family, Rebekah Harkness was an irrepressible and mischievous youngster, an alter ego of her brother Allen, and quite the opposite of her sister **Anne West**, who was described as demure and sweet, with none of the "wildness" of her siblings. Raised primarily by a series of nannies, Harkness had every advantage money could provide but seemingly lacked warmth and affection. Her father was a tyrant who alternately terrorized and ignored her, and her mother was preoccupied with her own social life. By the time she was 16, Harkness (known to her friends as Betty) had grown from a pudgy, round-faced child into a striking, self-assured woman. She had taken up dancing and ice skating to lose weight and was compulsive and highly disciplined in both endeavors. After graduating from an exclusive Southern finishing school, where she was known for her pranks, she and a group of girlfriends formed the Bitch Pack, a kind of sub-culture of local debutantes who enjoyed subverting society events—lacing punchbowls with mineral oil or performing stripteases on banquet tables. Harkness continued both dance and piano lesson, studying ballet with **Victoria Cassau** (a student of *Anna Pavlova's), and performing in recitals and various Junior League events. She also had a small role in the chorus of *Aïda*, the first production in St. Louis' magnificent new Municipal Auditorium. Later, she spent several months at the Ned Wayburn Institute of Dance in Chicago. In 1937, she rounded out her youthful activities with an around-the-world cruise, accompanied by her brother Allen. Her outrageous shipboard antics resulted in an invitation to leave the ship.

In 1939, at 24, Harkness married the first of her four husbands, Charles Dickson Walsh Pierce, a Yale graduate who worked for an advertising firm and was described by friends as a Walter Mitty-like character with his head in the clouds. "As soon as I walked down the aisle," Harkness said later, "I knew that I had made a terrible, terrible mistake." The couple had a son Allen (1940) and a daughter Terry (1944), before divorcing in 1945. Pierce returned to St. Louis, while Harkness, who obtained custody of the children, stayed in Manhattan, where she worked briefly in advertising and studied music composition. In October 1947, she married William Hale Harkness, the handsome heir to the Standard Oil fortune, whom she met at Watch Hill, her parents' summer place in Rhode

Island. (Bill's great-uncle, Stephen V. Harkness, had staked John D. Rockefeller in the founding of the company.) The couple wed in a small private ceremony attended by Harkness' parents, her two children, and Bill's daughter from his first marriage to **Elizabeth "Buffy" Grant (Montgomery)**, who later married actor Robert Montgomery and was the mother of actress *Elizabeth Montgomery.

Despite Bill's restrained and aloof personality, and the fact that he was 15 years older than Harkness (he was 46, she 31), the marriage seemed to work. The couple commuted between a 40-room mansion Bill purchased at Watch Hill and a rambling duplex on Park Avenue in New York City. Harkness became the picture of the young society matron. "Bill looked on Betty as a naughty child and set about to reform her," said one friend of the couple. "She was scared of him," said yet another acquaintance. "But she loved him being the dominant figure. She'd never had that before, except possibly with her father, and she always thought he was a clown."

In October 1948, Harkness gave birth to her first child with her second husband, a daughter Edith. Bill adored the child, as he did his stepchildren, whom he treated as if they were his own. Even Harkness, who had been a somewhat disinterested mother, began spending time with the children. "She had been a real rip-roarer, and suddenly she was so prim and proper," said a friend. "She was simply not the same person." In 1953, a year after the death of Harkness' father, Bill suffered a serious heart attack. He had a second one a year later, from which he did not recover. When he died in August 1954, Harkness inherited his vast fortune. Friends worried, however, that without her father or Bill to guide and protect her, she might be headed for trouble.

Immediately following Bill's death, Harkness indulged in luxuries her husband would have frowned upon: a penthouse in Madison Avenue's elegant Westbury Hotel, a chalet in the Swiss ski resort of Gstaad, and a yogi named B.K.S. Iyengar. She launched herself into a world of cultural pursuits, turning the estate at Watch Hill into an artist's colony and purchasing the local firehouse for an Art Center. She became the patron of French sculptor **Guitou Knoop** and took up sculpting herself, although most of her time was devoted to her music. Having studied composition with *Nadia Boulanger and Frederick Werle among others, and written a hundred or so compositions, she was already gaining recognition as a composer. In 1955, her 20-minute tone poem "Safari Suite" (inspired by a

trip to Africa with Bill) was performed at Carnegie Hall to a polite reception. Another composition, "Il Palio," was performed in Washington, D.C., in 1957, and an album of her semiclassical pieces, *Music With a Heartbeat,* was also released that year. There soon followed a recording of a pop song "My Heart." According to Unger, much of Harkness' composing was accomplished with her regular piano teacher in New York, and some was done with the help of a Russian composer-arranger, Nicholas Stein. Unger further claims that she did none of her own copying or orchestrations and that most of her rave reviews came from society columnists, while real music critics, if they discussed her work at all, tended to dismiss it. "The only reason her works were ever played in public was because she subsidized the performances," he writes. "And in truth, she was not under contract to all those record companies at all: Her records were vanity pressings, paid for by her."

In 1957, Harkness was commissioned by her friend Marquis de Cuevas to compose a ballet score for his Grand Ballet, to be performed at the Brussels World's Fair in 1958. The resulting composition, *Journey to Love,* was extraordinarily well received, turning Harkness' ongoing interest in the dance into a full-blown obsession. Establishing the Rebekah Harkness Foundation in 1959 (later renamed The Harkness Ballet Foundation), she became a dance patron, helping to revive Jerome Robbins' Ballet U.S.A. in 1961, and backing *Pearl Primus for a four-month tour of Africa. Harkness began to combine her music studies with personal ballet instruction, hiring Leon Fokine (nephew of the great Russian dancer and choreographer Mikhail Fokine) as her teacher and later recruiting dancer Bobby Scevers as her exclusive dance partner. Their stormy love affair endured for 17 years.

Late in 1961, now married to her third husband, Dr. Benjamin Harrison Kean, whom she had met when he treated her for a parasitic infection, Harkness took the struggling Robert Joffrey ballet company under her wing. Sponsoring a 12-week summer workshop at Watch Hill, the goal of which was to prepare the ballet for an international tour, Harkness hosted the entire roster of dancers along with six choreographers commissioned to create new works for the company. Also included in the undertaking were dance teachers, administrators, lawyers, and, of course, her ever-present extended family of artists and musicians. Harkness went far beyond providing room and board and studio space for the entourage. "If a dancer required a nose job or orthodontics, she paid the bill," writes Unger. "Traveling accommodations for the troupe were always first-class. She showered them with gifts of perfume or scarfs or expensive leather purses." The unprecedented project prompted Walter Terry of the *New York Herald Tribune* (May 13, 1962) to remark: "The step made by Mrs. Kean, no matter what the result . . . is to be cherished by the choreographers and cheered by the dance world itself."

For two years, the Harkness Foundation continued to sponsor the Joffrey Ballet, underwriting

its tour of the Middle East, Europe, and Russia. At home, the foundation also sponsored dance company tours of the public schools, a season of modern dance at Hunter College, and an open-air dance festival in conjunction with the Shakespeare Festival in Central Park. Harkness' relationship with Joffrey endured numerous artistic squabbles, but ended abruptly when she proposed changing the name of the company to the Harkness Ballet. In April 1964, she took her plan further, forming her own company and endowing it with $2 million from both of her foundations. Although Harkness denied raiding Joffrey's com-

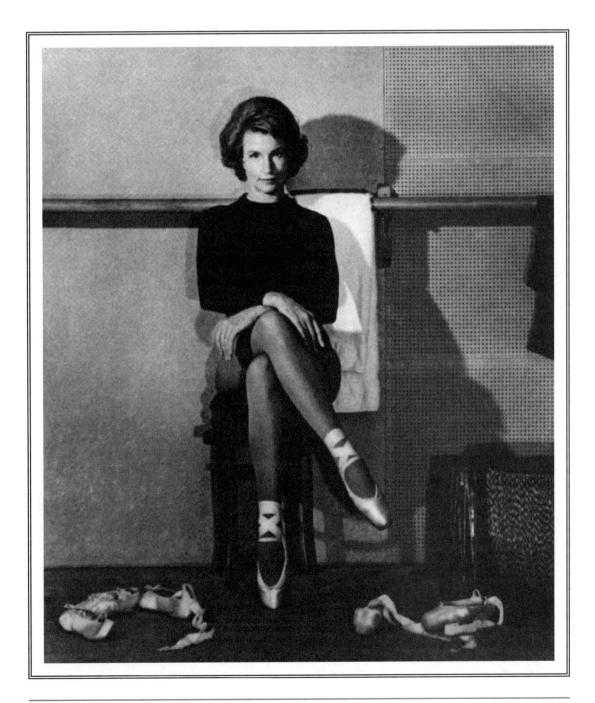

Rebekah Harkness

pany or taking over his repertory (which her foundation now owned), she contracted 14 of his dancers for her new company of 26. She admittedly asked Joffrey to stay on as artistic director of the new company, but he was outraged by her actions and refused her offer. The dance world rallied behind him, as did the press. Allen Hughes, in *The New York Times*, castigated Harkness for building her company "on the ruin of an old one." "The Rebekah Harkness Foundation has paralyzed the Joffrey Ballet for the present and imperiled the company's future," he said. "A moral issue is involved here."

Determined to create something uniquely her own and not merely a carbon copy of the Joffrey Ballet, Harkness launched her company during the summer of 1964, hiring George Skibine, former director of the Paris Opera Ballet, as artistic director. She also recruited some impressive talent—**Vera Volkova**, *Alexandra Danilova, Alvin Ailey, Richard Wagner, and Donald Saddler—among others—to create new works for her company. To provide her dancers with a home in New York City, she purchased the former Thomas J. Watson town house, a five-story, 35-room mansion that she transformed into the Harkness House for Ballet Arts. Completed in November 1965, it was as opulent as any of the European royal dance schools. As her ballet company prepared for its first performance, the press, who had crucified her a few months earlier, eagerly awaited the debut. "The first major cultural event of the new year is the launching of an American ballet company on a scale unprecedented in dance history," reported the *New York Morning Telegraph*.

Because of the lingering ill will over the Joffrey debacle, the Harkness Ballet did not debut in the United States. Instead it made its first appearance in Cannes, France, on February 19, 1965, followed by a European tour. Clive Barnes, who accompanied the ballet on the tour, called the first performance "shaky," but was generally optimistic about the future of the new company. In September 1965, the Ballet performed at the White House, after which it began a six-week tour of 30 American cities. After the company's first New York season in 1967, reviews were generally positive with regard to the dancers, but still questioned the repertory and the choreography. In the *National Observer* (November 20, 1967), Douglas M. Davis wrote that the principals "tower above their choreography . . . which is bland and uninspired for the most part." **Doris Harding**, in *Dance Magazine* (January 1968), objected to the dark themes of

the company's repertory, commenting that the dances "seemed to hark back to the anti-Victorian, new-Freudian churning of the thirties and early forties."

The "churning" on stage was nothing compared to the rumblings within the company, a result of Harkness' own artistic confusion and administrative naiveté. "It was disorganized and bizarre," recalled **Jane Remer**, who was made assistant director of the company, but had no clear-cut job description. "I sat at a desk worth more than my apartment! On any given morning when she and I had something to talk about, Rebekah would come down in her pink and blue leotards and literally stand on her head, and we would have the conversation with her standing on her head. It would be all very Proustian and never made too much sense." From 1965, when Harkness replaced original director Skibine with Bertrand Castelli (who later produced the musical *Hair*), the company began a series of shifts in leadership, although Harkness always retained the upper hand and exercised an iron will. Castelli was eventually replaced by Brian Mac-Donald, a Canadian choreographer who, in 1968, was replaced by company soloist Lawrence Rhodes. Although it was unusual for a principal dancer to become an artistic director of a company, Rhodes was embraced by both the dancers and the critics. A year later, finding himself unable to dance major roles as well as direct, Rhodes brought in Benjamin Harkarvy, a founder-director of the Netherlands Dance Theater, to codirect. By the end of that year, Clive Barnes wrote that the Harkness Ballet had survived a difficult rite of passage and was on the road to greatness. "We were a family," said one of the dancers. "Morale was high. We were a real unit. For the first time, we were proud of the repertory."

At the height of the company's success, Harkness apparently lost interest and devoted her time instead to the formation of a second company, the Harkness Youth Dancers. By 1970, she was so involved with the new company that she missed the main company's New York season premiere. In March 1970, quite unexpectedly, she called the company home from midpoint in a European tour, citing financial pressures that would no longer enable her to support two companies. In one devastating blow, Rhodes was fired and the rest of the tour was canceled. "It changed the lives of everybody in the company," said one dancer. "Nobody had any warning." Although 16 of the dancers were offered a place in the new company, all but one refused. A representative of the American Guild of Musical Artists called the situation tragic. "The company was built to a success and then dashed on the rocks. Every other company that's failed has failed for lack of money."

In May 1970, the Youth Dancers, who trained almost exclusively at the Harkness school, became the new Harkness Ballet, under Harkness' artistic direction, with Ben Stevenson as choreographer. "Many members were not even real professionals; they were trainees," writes Unger, "some of them just sixteen and seventeen years old. Within a few months, Clive Barnes wrote in *The Times* that the Harkness Ballet has 'descended beyond the necessity of serious consideration.' Rebekah's dream was over. Everybody knew it but her."

Unaware of her limitations, however, Harkness undertook her most ambitious project to date, the Harkness Theater. Purchasing the former RKO Colonial movie theater at Broadway and 62nd Street, she put $5 million into a renovation project, most of which was directed by her new love interest Niels Lauersen, a Danish gynecologist whom she would later marry. (Lauersen maintained that the marriage was annulled soon after the wedding. "It was an agreement, really not a marriage," he told Unger, "simply an agreement. The reason was to give her human support.") Inspired by the Kirov Theater in Leningrad, the finished theater facility boasted a 3,500-square-foot stage with absorption units beneath the floor to give it special resiliency. Marble and crystal from Spain lined the foyer and 16 crystal chandeliers hung from the ceiling. Harkness had 1,277 hand-carved Louis XIV chairs made in Spain and upholstered in velvet in her own shade of Harkness blue. She also commissioned Spanish artist Enrique Senis-Oliver to paint a 120-square-yard mural *Homage to Terpsichore* on the stage's proscenium arch. (*Newsweek* later called it "the ugliest mural ever painted.") The theater opened with a performance of the Harkness Ballet on April 9, 1974, a gala event that was attended by the most important figures in the dance world, as well as a roster of society swells and assorted royalty. The reviewers, although kind to the dancers, panned the choreography and the theater itself, for which they saved their most savage remarks. *New York* magazine called it a "garish bordello of a dance theater" and compared it to a "Staten Island beauty parlor." *Dance* magazine said it looked like "a lavish ladies' powder room."

After a two-week run in the theater, the ballet company embarked on a tour in Europe and the Middle East. Harkness, in the meantime, attempted, without much success, to rent out the theater to other dance companies. By 1974, as a result of the millions spent on the theater, a raging inflation, and the sluggish stock market, Harkness was in serious financial difficulty. Unable to pump enough money into the dance company, she began soliciting funds to save the company. The public, however, was not sympathetic. Clive Barnes echoed popular opinion when he wrote: "The Harkness Ballet is not at present artistically viable. Does any independent, experienced voice in the dance world say it is? So far as the dancers are concerned, Mrs. Harkness has already willfully disbanded a company of dancers far stronger than her present troupe." Within the year, the company had folded. Harkness was fed up. "I really want to go on to something else," she said.

The Harkness School of Ballet at Harkness House was all that remained of Harkness' ballet empire, although Harkness lost interest in it, too. The school had flourished under the direction of David Howard, a highly respected dance teacher, who attracted dancers like *Gelsey Kirkland, *Natalia Makarova, and Peter Martins to his classes. After he left, the school rapidly lost its edge, and even the building fell into disrepair. To put things right, Harkness recruited Bobby Scevers and named his friend and mentor Nikita Talin, a former dancer turned teacher, director of the operation. Talin's dictatorial leadership and gruff manner made him very unpopular, and the school soon began to lose teachers and students alike. "Harkness House had no bearing on what was happening in the dance world anymore," said a former employee. "The dance world was not enriched by anything that was happening there."

The decade of the 1970s took a personal toll on Harkness as well. Of major concern was her health and a growing dependency on drugs that had begun, according to Unger, in the 1960s, when she had started taking "vitamin injections" from Dr. John Bishop, whose practice at the time boasted such luminaries as Truman Capote, Cecil B. De Mille, Otto Preminger, and Alan Jay Lerner, among others. (Some of Bishop's patients reported that they suffered severe withdrawal symptoms when they were unable to get their injections, leading to speculation that the shots may have included something stronger than vitamins.) During the 1960s, Harkness, who was fascinated by medicine, also began injections of the male hormone testosterone, to strengthen herself as a dancer. She experimented with a variety of other drugs to keep her youthful, including some that were not yet approved for use in the United States. In the early 1970s, when she began to suffer with arthritis and hip problems, she started injections of Talwin, a powerful painkiller that caused physical and psychological dependence in some patients. Perhaps because of her drug problem, Harkness began to exhibit bizarre shifts in behavior, alternately drawing people close then shutting them out, leaving anger and confusion in her wake.

Few suffered more from Harkness' erratic shifts in attention than her three children, who ultimately kept their distance. By the spring of 1980, Harkness had lost most of her old entourage and had moved into a large apartment in a building adjacent to the Carlyle Hotel. Bobby Scevers and Nikita Talin, along with their friends, formed her new circle of admirers. Her health continued to worsen; now, stomach ailments accompanied her painful hip condition. After suffering a severe gastric attack on the way home from the theater one night, Harkness was hospitalized with what was believed to be an intestinal blockage. Surgery, however, revealed widespread stomach cancer from which she never recovered. In the final days of her illness, Harkness took responsibility for the pain she had caused her children. Edith, whose own mental health was fragile, spent a great deal of time with her mother in the days before she died, and Harkness was openly affectionate for the first time in her life. "She was grateful to see Edith every day," said a friend. "At the end she regretted all she had done and was warm and kind, and she was genuine about it." Harkness' daughter Terry also came but did not spend much time at her mother's bedside. Harkness also placed a phone call to her son, Allen, who was serving time in Raiford State Prison in Florida after being convicted of murder. "I want to apologize for making you the black sheep in the family," Harkness told Allen. He replied by telling her it was just as well. "I never had to put up with all the things you did," he said. (Allen's murder sentence was eventually reduced to manslaughter, and he was released from prison after serving eight years.)

Rebekah Harkness succumbed to her illness on June 17, 1982. Three days after her death, a memorial service was held at Harkness House, after which her body was cremated and her ashes placed in the Harkness family mausoleum in Woodlawn Cemetery. There was controversy over her will, which had undergone some 15 changes through the years and which Allen and

Terry later unsuccessfully contested. A tragic footnote to Harkness' death was Edith's suicide just two months later.

In assessing Harkness' legacy, most agree that her contribution to dance was extraordinary, both financially and artistically. Some likened her patronage to that seen only in aristocratic Europe. (Unger conjures up the name of *Catherine de Medici when discussing Harkness' powerful will and extravagance.) A former member of the Harkness Ballet maintained "that for everything that went wrong, Mrs. Harkness gave more to dance than anyone since Diaghilev." Her support of the dance continued for years after her death through the Harkness Ballet Foundation and the William Hale Harkness Foundation. On the philanthropic front, Rebekah Harkness quietly donated $2 million to New York Hospital for the construction of the William Hale Harkness Medical Research Building, and also supported medical research on Parkinson's disease and the work of the New York University Medical Center's Institute of Rehabilitation Medicine.

SOURCES:

Moritz, Charles, ed. *Current Biography 1974.* NY: H.W. Wilson, 1974.

———. *Current Biography 1982.* NY: H.W. Wilson, 1982.

Unger, Craig. *Blue Blood.* NY: William Morrow, 1988.

Barbara Morgan,
Melrose, Massachusetts

Harland, Marion (1830–1922).

See Terhune, Mary Virginia.

Harlem Brundtland, Gro.

See Bruntland, Gro Harlem.

Harley, Brilliana (c. 1600–1643)

British royal who sided with the Puritans. Name variations: Lady Brilliana Harley. Born between 1598 and 1600, most sources cite 1600; died while besieged at Brampton Bryan Castle in 1643; daughter of Edward (later 1st Viscount Conway, a member of Parliament, secretary of state, and governor of the Isle of Wight); became third wife of Sir Robert Harley, in 1623.

During the English Civil Wars of the mid-17th century, the Puritan Lady Brilliana Harley was accused of aiding the enemies of King Charles I. By mid-1643, she found herself besieged at Brampton Bryan Castle in Shropshire by a Royalist army of 700. Debilitated by a long illness, possibly pregnant, and deserted by many of her servants, she held out for six weeks. Parliamentary forces came to her aid, forcing the besiegers to withdraw; a few weeks later, however, the Cavaliers returned. Lady Brilliana then died, and early in 1644 Brampton Bryan surrendered to the king's army. Brilliana's children were well-treated, but the castle was ruined. Her letters, written from 1625 to 1643, were published in 1854.

Harlow, Jean (1911–1937)

American film actress who rose above her "blonde bombshell" image to become a fine screen comedian. Born Harlean Carpenter on March 3, 1911, in Kansas City, Missouri; died on June 7, 1937, age 26, from complications of kidney disease at Good Samaritan Hospital in Los Angeles, California; daughter of Jean (Harlow) Carpenter and Mont Clair Carpenter; married Charles McGrew, in 1927 (divorced 1929); married Paul Bern, in 1932 (committed suicide, 1932); married Harold Rosson, in 1933 (divorced 1934); no children.

At 16, eloped with a wealthy young businessman (1927); eventually moved to Los Angeles and found part-time work as a walk-on in features and comedy shorts; given first important role in Hell's Angels *(1930) but confined to vulgar, blatant roles until signing with MGM (1932), when her acting ability in both dramatic and comedic roles became apparent; developed into one of Hollywood's superstars (early 1930s), playing opposite such actors as Clark Gable and Spencer Tracy; fell seriously ill while shooting* Saratoga *(1937).*

Filmography—features: The Saturday Night Kid *(1929);* Hell's Angels *(1930);* The Secret Six *(1931);* The Iron Man *(1931);* The Public Enemy *(1931);* Goldie *(1931);* Platinum Blonde *(1931);* Three Wise Girls *(1932);* Beast of the City *(1932);* Red-Headed Woman *(1932);* Red Dust *(1932);* Hold Your Man *(1933);* Bombshell *(1933);* Dinner at Eight *(1934);* The Girl from Missouri *(1934);* Reckless *(1935);* China Seas *(1935);* Riffraff *(1936);* Wife vs. Secretary *(1936);* Suzy *(1936);* Libeled Lady *(1936);* Personal Property *(1937);* Saratoga *(1937).*

On an afternoon in early 1930, a car pulled up in front of a bungalow on Metro's lot in Hollywood to deposit a slim, blonde, statuesque young woman who walked timidly up to the cottage's screen door. She was not invited to enter; rather, she answered through the door the few questions posed to her by an invisible interrogator inside, then returned to the car, where an older woman was anxiously waiting. "He hired me, Mommie," the young lady murmured. *He*

was maverick film producer Howard Hughes; the older woman was **Jean Carpenter**, known to everyone as Mother Jean; and the young lady was her daughter, Harlean, known to everyone as "the Baby." Hughes had just hired Harlean for a picture that would launch a film career that Jean Carpenter had been denied but had always felt she deserved. Her daughter had even chosen her mother's maiden name, Jean Harlow, for her screen identity.

Mother and daughter shared another attribute; both were strikingly beautiful, though most used the word "angelic" to describe the daughter born to Jean and Mont Clair Carpenter in Kansas City, Missouri, on March 3, 1911. Young Harlean turned heads all over town with her pale blonde hair, green eyes, and flawless white skin. Few admirers, however, knew of her troubled home life. Mother Jean, the daughter of prominent real-estate developer Skip Harlow and one of Kansas City's most eligible and attractive women, had nearly created a scandal over her affair with a railroad conductor. Her father had hastily put an end to the relationship by marrying her off to Mont Clair Carpenter, a successful dentist with a chain of offices and a promising future. Although both father and grandfather doted on her child Harlean, Jean Carpenter took pains to keep her away from both men as much as possible and from other children who could carry tales of a loveless marriage to Kansas City's finer homes. The mother-daughter relationship was virtually exclusive during those early years. In a birthday note, an eight-year-old Harlean wrote to her mother, "I love you better than anything that ever its name was heard of. Please know I love you better than ten lives." Meanwhile, her mother confided to a friend that she wished every morning her husband had died in his sleep.

The Carpenters grew increasingly estranged until, in 1922, Mont Clair did not contest the divorce proceedings begun by his wife, granting her sole custody of their daughter and $200 a month in support. Neither he nor Skip Harlow could convince Jean Carpenter to abandon her stated plan to move to Los Angeles to become a movie star, for enough people had told her she was beautiful, and movie magazines, with their rags to riches yarns, had long been her favorite reading. Thus it was that Harlean entered the 1923 class of the Hollywood School for Girls while her mother made the rounds of studio casting calls. While Jean Carpenter, at 34, soon discovered she was considered too old for films, her daughter, at 11, was attracting the attention of both teachers and fellow students. She was the only student, jealous classmates noted, on which the school's required middy blouse and long, pleated skirt looked attractive—so much so that Harlean had to be admonished by school authorities for an excessive and alluring sway to her hips. **Cecilia De Mille**, who entered the school in the same year, complained to her father, director Cecil B. De Mille, that Harlean seemed unusually knowledgeable about sex and had so many boyfriends that there were no dates to be had. Harlean's notoriety grew even more when it became common knowledge that her mother, whom another classmate described as "a nightmare," had become the mistress of a wealthy European, disappearing for weeks at a time and leaving her daughter in the care of friends. When news of his daughter's scandalous behavior reached Skip Harlow, he threatened to cut off all support unless she returned to Kansas City. After barely two years in California, Jean and her daughter moved back to Missouri in 1925.

While Jean Carpenter promptly began an affair with a naturalized Italian named Mario Bello, Harlean was enrolled at her grandfather's insistence at Ferry Hall, a proper girl's boarding school in Illinois, where she had just as much impact as in Hollywood. "When we walked down the street, she would literally stop traffic," her "big sister" at the school later remembered. "Men would climb out of their cars and follow her." Also as in Hollywood, Carpenter was as much a subject of conversation as her daughter. "Harlean was passive, and Mother Jean was *strong*," another classmate at Ferry Hall noted. "She had complete control over that girl. Harlean had no willpower; she didn't stand up for *anything*." Nevertheless, nine months after Carpenter married Mario Bello, 16-year-old Harlean defied her by taking a husband herself. He was Charles McGrew, whom she met through a Ferry Hall classmate and married without her mother's consent on September 21, 1927. McGrew was the sole heir of a wealthy Chicago family, and rumors spread about how Mother Jean had threatened legal action unless McGrew promised to support her and her new husband as well as Harlean. Perhaps to remove Harlean as far as possible from her mother's influence, McGrew took his young bride to California, moving into a house in Beverly Hills in January of 1928.

Harlean's first exposure to a movie studio came shortly afterward, when she drove a friend to an audition at Fox. She later admitted to being fascinated by the environment, but said she had felt no compulsion to become an actress, even when her friend returned to the car with three Fox executives who took one look at her and produced a letter of introduction to Fox's head of casting. Weeks later, to win a bet that she would never use the letter, Harlean appeared at Fox's Central Casting department and signed in as "Jean Harlow." Central Casting was Fox's clearing house for extras, more than a hundred of which could be found on any one day milling hopefully and waiting for the next roundup to fill out crowd scenes. Jean Harlow was offered work almost immediately but turned down her first few offers until her mother, who had just moved back to Hollywood with husband Mario, ordered her to do otherwise. Jean Harlow accepted her next offer.

It was a brief appearance in *Honor Bound,* a prison drama starring matinee idol and former prizefighter George O'Brien. She was paid seven dollars for the day, was given a box lunch, and had sufficiently illuminated the few scenes in which she appeared for Fox to send her around to Paramount and to Hal Roach's studio. Roach decided Harlow was worth more than extra work and offered her her first contract to appear in a number of his two-reeler comedies. "She was different," he recalled many years later. "Her hair was an odd type, and she had a beautiful face and body. There was nobody like her." Roach offered her a five-year contract at $100 a week and saw his hunch pay off when Harlow strode through her first scene as a contract actress in a Laurel and Hardy comedy called *Double Whoopee*. In the scene, Stan Laurel, playing a hotel doorman, accidentally closes a taxi door on Harlow's dress, which gracefully rips away as she heads for the lobby, oblivious that she is wearing nothing but a thin slip below her waistline. The scene had to be shot twice, as it turned out, since Harlow had neglected to don the requisite, skin-colored tights for such "nude" scenes and revealed to one and all in the first take that she wore no underwear. It was a personal habit for which she would become famous in later years, and a possible indication of her complete innocence about displaying her considerable physical attributes.

After her third two-reeler for Roach, Harlow asked to be released from her contract, claiming that her husband objected to her film work. Roach, who agreed, suspected the real reason was that Mother Jean and Bello had visions of a bigger studio and more money. "Her mother made the decisions," he said. "Not that she was any good at business, but she and Bello

Jean
Harlow

were always around." The truth was that Harlow was pregnant. Carpenter and Bello, without Charles McGrew's knowledge, convinced "the Baby" that a child was not in her best interests and arranged for an abortion. "I wanted that child that was taken from me," Harlow later confessed to a friend. "My whole life would have been different if I'd been given that baby." Furious, McGrew struggled with Carpenter for control of her daughter and lost. On June 11, 1929, after only 20 months of marriage, Harlow and McGrew separated.

It ain't art, but it's box office.

—*Variety*'s critique of Jean Harlow (1935)

McGrew refused to pay any support money to Harlow, knowing full well it would land in her mother's pockets. Meanwhile, back home in Kansas City, Grandfather Harlow had seen *Double Whoopee* and had disinherited his granddaughter until she gave up films. For the first time in her life, Harlow—not to mention her mother and stepfather—was broke. "I turned to motion pictures because I had to work or starve," Harlow frankly admitted, although without Hal Roach's support the only work she could get was as an extra. She vented her hatred for the abuses and abasements of an extra's life in an unpublished short story, in which a young actress is told she will finally get a closeup only to discover it is of her legs, not her face.

But it was precisely her stunning good looks that got her noticed in 1929's *The Saturday Night Kid,* a Paramount vehicle for *Clara Bow in which Harlow was given a small part. Harlow was hired over the star's objections, for Bow, famous as the provocative "It" girl, rightly complained that she would be ignored in any scene with such a beauty. But Jean Harlow's naiveté and complete lack of guile eventually won over even Bow, who lent her some old costumes and insisted the two of them pose for publicity shots together. "See if you can help her out," Bow told Paramount's publicity director. "She's gonna go places." Bow's prediction proved accurate when, on the strength of her brief appearance in the film, Harlow was offered a management contract, a $500 advance, and an interview with Howard Hughes.

Two years previous, in 1927, Hughes had begun shooting a World War I aerial drama called *Hell's Angels* as a silent film. The son of a wealthy Texas oil baron, Hughes had arrived in Hollywood in the early '20s with deep pockets, an am-

bition to write, direct, and produce his own films, and a reputation as an eccentric playboy with a taste for beautiful women. *Hell's Angels* was his most ambitious film to date and would eventually cost some $4 million—an enormous sum at a time when most films were made for well under $1 million. Hughes had been caught off-guard by the rapidly rising demand for talking pictures and had decided to add sound effects to his aerial sequences and reshoot his dramatic scenes with sound, the only problem being that his tough-talking, brazen female love interest in the silent version was a Norwegian actress with a thick accent. No established actress would work with a producer of such shady reputation, and Hughes decided that Jean Harlow had the looks and sufficiently clear diction to play his Helen.

Harlow was the first to admit that her acting abilities at the time were minimal, calling herself at one point "the worst actress that was ever in pictures. But I can learn," she added, "and I will." Unfortunately, she got no help from *Hell's Angels'* director James Whale or from Hughes, who directed some of her scenes himself. No one was more surprised than Harlow when Hughes offered her a five-year contract at $100 a week. Hughes sensed that the public would be so impressed with Harlow's physical appearance that it would overlook the deficiencies in her acting. With the aid of a lavish promotional campaign and the kind of opening night ceremonies at Graumann's Chinese Theater that are the stuff of Hollywood legend, Hughes proved that he had guessed right. "It doesn't matter what degree of talent she possesses, for this girl is the most sensuous figure to get in front of a camera in some time," *Variety* told its readers the next morning, observing that "she'll probably always have to play these kinds of roles, but nobody ever starved possessing what she's got." *The New York Times*, in a more restrained mood, admitted she was "the center of attention" in an otherwise mediocre film; while *The New Yorker* bluntly called her "plain awful." But newspapers throughout the country carried a photo of Harlow taken on opening night. She looked celestially beautiful in a solid white, full-length gown, her arm through Hughes' on one side and through Mother Jean's on the other. Radio listeners had heard her effusively thank Hughes for having such confidence in her. Harlow was terrified of the crowds and the attention, as she would be throughout her career. "How I got through that night and talked in the microphone I'll never know," she later confided. "I don't remember seeing the picture at all, and what's more I never intend to."

Her work as the amoral predator in Hughes' film set the pattern for Harlow's career, leading her to confess her horror at the way audiences she met on nationwide tours equated her with the bra-less, cleavage-sporting harridans she played—"a bitch in heat," as she earthily put it. Hughes refused to cancel her contract or give her more dramatic roles in his other films, choosing instead to lend her out to other studios and make a healthy profit out of the sex queen he had created. Harlow dutifully portrayed the gun moll in MGM's underworld melodrama *The Secret Six,* the first of five films in which she played opposite Clark Gable; was panned in her first sympathetic role as a prizefighter's loyal wife in Universal's *The Iron Man* ("Harlow can by no means be classed as an actress," a more sober *Variety* said of her performance); and barely managed to attract attention in her most prestigious film up to that time, 1931's *Public Enemy* for Warner Bros., playing opposite James Cagney and **Mae Clark**. "She was an original," Clark said years later. "She had personality and presence, and that came through whether she could act or not." By May of 1931, Harlow had been loaned out to so many studios that she had three films open at once, *Secret Six, Iron Man,* and *Public Enemy,* the last of which was an overnight sensation. Harlow's style, movements, and mannerisms were mimicked by women throughout the nation, from the bell-bottomed pajamas she wore on screen to the white blonde shade of her hair.

If nothing else, Harlow had by now endeared herself to Hollywood, for her earnest desire to learn and for her comaraderie with the cast and crew of any set she graced. Numerous insiders told her she was being mismanaged by Hughes, and these same advisors wanted to take "the Baby" under their wing. Several studios tried to convince Hughes to sell them her contract, but Hughes turned them all down and insisted on sending her out on "personal appearance" tours before live audiences, as if offering the public the chance to gawk at his merchandise. Hughes took care to always include in Harlow's appearances a dropped handkerchief, a discarded flower, a lost earring—any excuse for her to bend forward and prove that the publicity about her aversion to bras was true. Typically, Hughes was paid $3,500 for each appearance, of which Harlow received $200.

Harlow's famous sobriquet "Platinum Blonde" was the idea of Harry Cohn, head of Columbia Pictures, to whom Harlow was loaned out to play in the studio's film *Gallagher,* a fast-paced comedy about a poor newspaper reporter who marries a society girl of loose morals (which was, of course, the role assigned to Jean). Hughes liked Cohn's appellation so much that he insisted it become the name of the film and devised a national promotion which offered $10,000 to any beautician who could reproduce Jean Harlow's hair color. The result was a 35% increase in peroxide sales (although the prize money was never won) and a box-office hit. Harlow publicly claimed she had never dyed or bleached her hair, concealing the fact that her natural color was ash blonde and that she spent every Sunday with a studio hairdresser, who used peroxide, ammonia, bleach, and soap flakes to produce the desired effect.

More important, *Platinum Blonde*'s director, Frank Capra, gave Harlow a much-needed education in acting for films. "She wanted to learn all the time," he recalled. "I remember telling her to go home when her scenes were finished, but she'd always stick around the set and watch the others." Capra's efforts and Harlow's willingness to learn paid off; she received her first positive reviews for her work in a sympathetic role in MGM's *Beast of the City,* an anti-gangster film in which she played opposite Walter Huston. "The Platinum Baby really acts this one!" *The Daily News* reported, while the *Times* devoted most of its review to her performance and called her "a shining refinement of Clara Bow." Harlow had won the part of Daisy Stevens in *Beast* through the efforts of Paul Bern, a production assistant to MGM's brilliant head of production, Irving Thalberg. Bern, who oversaw all of *Greta Garbo's pictures, had befriended Harlow two years earlier at a party Hughes had thrown to promote *Hell's Angels.* He had been quietly working to get her away from Hughes and into the fold at MGM, at the time Hollywood's most respected studio, famous for its careful handling and development of talent. Bern quickly followed up on the *Platinum Blonde*'s positive reception by negotiating a deal for MGM to pay Hughes $30,000 for Harlow's contract; and it was Bern who developed a problem property at MGM into the film that would make Jean Harlow a respected actress.

MGM had been struggling to develop a script based on a French novel which featured an adulteress who kills one lover, is acquitted of the crime, and lives happily ever after with another, wealthier paramour. After four years, all Louis B. Mayer had was a deadly serious script by F. Scott Fitzgerald and a letter from Will Hays, the government's movie censor, threatening to block the release of any story in which adultery goes unpunished. Paul Bern convinced Thalberg and Mayer that the story could be a star vehicle for Jean Harlow and sold the two men on hiring *Anita Loos to write a new script. Loos, who would later give the world Lorelei Lee in *Gentlemen Prefer Blondes*, turned the story on its head and made it a satirical sex comedy which she called *Red-Headed Woman*. "We made it over completely for [Jean]," said Loos. "It was, to all intents and purposes, a Jean Harlow story." Though nervous, Harlow was intrigued by the character of Lil Andrews, the stenographer who sails full steam ahead in her quest to win her boss' heart. Loos crafted an opening sequence displaying Lil's careful preparations for the coming battle:

> Lil, trying on a tight, revealing dress: "Can you see through it?"
>
> Salesgirl: "Yes, ma'am, I'm afraid you can."
>
> Lil: "I'll wear it."

Harlow's portrayal of the golddigger with a heart instantly won her audience's heart. "It was the first chance I ever had to do something in pictures other than swivel my hips," Harlow said later of the film that elevated her from a sex goddess to a comedic actress.

Harlow's gratitude to Paul Bern culminated in her marriage to him on July 2, 1932, the year of *Red-Headed Woman*'s release. "All I want is to sit at Paul's feet and have him educate me," she said. Friends quietly wondered about the future of the union, for while Bern was respected in the business, he was known as an emotionally cold man whom no one remembered having ever been romantically involved with a woman. It was rumored that he was inordinately interested in morbid psychology and always carried a handgun in his coat pocket.

After only a month or two of marriage, Bern was criticizing Harlow in public about her lack of education and making jokes about her character, but Harlow seemed to take it all in stride and went to work on her second picture for MGM and her second with Gable, *Red Dust*, a steamy jungle melodrama set in Indochina. Meanwhile, the studio's publicity department embarked on a campaign to soften her image by showing her cooking for Bern at home, sewing and crocheting on the set (long a favorite pastime of Harlow's), or having tea with Mother Jean, who by now had divorced Mario Bello but was maintaining a business relationship with him by appointing him Harlow's personal manager.

The *Red Dust* shoot was a long and difficult one, it being a challenge to recreate a humid

Southeast Asian jungle on a soundstage in Hollywood, and Harlow often spent the night at her mother's house, nearer to the studio, as she did the night of September 4, 1932. The next morning, a maid who arrived for work at the Bern household found Paul Bern dead of an apparently self-inflicted gunshot wound to the head, his naked body lying in a pool of blood in the bathroom and a now-famous note addressed to Harlow lying on a nearby table, in which he told her that "last night was a comedy." MGM made sure to comb the Bern household for evidence damaging to any of its stars or personnel before the police were called, a delay that further obscured what was a clear instance of suicide and led to speculation, which persists to this day, that Bern was murdered. Harlow was never directly implicated, and it appears that Bern's note had been written the day after an unexpected visit, while Harlow was at home, from a former common-law wife named **Dorothy Millette**, distressed at his marriage to Jean. (Millette herself committed suicide several days later.) There is also a good chance that Bern's desperate act was at least partly due to his impotence, which had long been rumored. Harlow, distraught at Bern's death and at the kind of relentless publicity she dreaded, quickly finished work on *Red Dust* and went into a seclusion jealously guarded by Mother Jean, who was unable to stop her daughter's increasing consumption of alcohol. Six weeks after Bern's death, *Red Dust* opened to great acclaim, grossing more than $1 million on the studio's $400,000 budget.

Friends later said privately that Harlow never fully recovered from the trauma of Bern's suicide, although her professional fortunes had never been better. She more than held her own in 1933's comedy of manners, *Dinner at Eight*, in such distinguished company as John and Lionel Barrymore, *Billie Burke and the venerable *Marie Dressler, and emerged victorious from another studio makeover of her screen persona after several boycotts of her films by the Catholic League of Decency and more threats from the Hays office. MGM dyed her hair light brown and cast her opposite Spencer Tracy in 1935's *Riffraff*. Harlow played a good-hearted cannery worker in San Francisco carrying the torch for Tracy's scruffy mariner. "Maybe it's the brownette hair that works the charm," *Louella Parsons speculated, "or maybe it's a more experienced little Harlow, but something has inspired her, because she gives her most sincere and convincing performance."

By now, Harlow had married and divorced her third husband, Hal Rosson, who had been

Opposite page

𝒥ean

ℋarlow

the cinematographer on several of her earlier films. The marriage had survived barely a year. Rosson, like Chuck McGrew before him, blamed Mother Jean for breaking it up. The divorce papers merely accused him of torturing Harlow by reading "in their bedchamber to a late hour." By the time of her divorce from Rosson in 1934, Harlow had already begun an affair with William Powell, her co-star in *The Girl From Missouri*, a liaison of which Mother Jean fully approved and which she thought might end in marriage.

Everyone hoped that Harlow's increasingly troublesome health was a temporary condition related to her incipient alcoholism. She had survived a bout of appendicitis in 1933 but complained of colds, aches, and vague abdominal pains throughout 1934 and 1935, when she collapsed on the set of *Wife vs. Secretary*, holding up production to recuperate from what was said to be fatigue. She reacted badly to anaesthesia during an operation to remove her wisdom teeth in 1936 and nearly died on the operating table; while later that same year, she was absent for several weeks from the set of *Suzy*, one of two musicals in which she starred, for what was said to be a bad cold. The truth in this case was that Carpenter and Bello had arranged for another abortion after Harlow became pregnant with what was probably Powell's child. By the time Harlow reported for work on 1937's *Saratoga*, everyone was shocked by her appearance. Her skin color, once so radiantly white, was now an ashen gray; and the figure that had once been the envy of millions of women appeared bloated and bruised. Considerable time was spent in makeup and wardrobe concealing the deterioration and shooting began on schedule in April of 1937.

Near the end of the shoot, in late May, it seemed as if Harlow could not possibly continue working, but she insisted on finishing her scenes to keep the picture on schedule. She shot her last scene on Thursday, May 27, with co-star Walter Pidgeon, whom she asked to hold her especially lightly during an on-camera embrace because her stomach hurt so badly. As soon as the cameras stopped rolling, she doubled over in pain and was driven home to bed, where a doctor diagnosed a gall bladder inflammation. News of her illness was first reported in the press on June 3; her mother was quoted as saying her daughter merely had a bad cold and was recovering. Carpenter denied that she had refused to take Harlow to a hospital because of her Christian Scientist beliefs and pointed out that several doctors and three nurses were in attendance around the

clock. She refused requests for visits, even from concerned family members who had traveled out from Missouri.

But two days later, even Carpenter had to admit that her "Baby" was gravely ill. She called in Harlow's favorite doctor who recognized that Harlow's condition had been misdiagnosed and that her kidneys had been failing for some time. Fluid retention was so severe by then that even Harlow's skull was swollen, and it was from cerebral edema and from uremic poisoning that Jean Harlow died on the morning of June 7, 1937, at Good Samaritan Hospital. She was 26 years old.

Despite her early death, Harlow had appeared in more than 40 films by the time of her passing and had transformed herself on screen from a mere sex object to a sensitive, funny, and warmly passionate woman. True to her word, she had learned her craft well. It has often been said that had she lived, Jean Harlow would have become one of the most accomplished actresses of American cinema. Harlow probably would have been as surprised as anybody. "I never quite believe," she once said, "that I am me!"

SOURCES:

Katz, Ephraim, ed. *The Film Encyclopedia.* 2nd ed. NY: Harper Perennial, 1994.

Stenn, David. *Bombshell: The Life and Death of Jean Harlow.* NY: Doubleday, 1993.

Thompson, David. *A Biographical Dictionary of the Cinema.* London: Secker and Warburg, 1975.

Norman Powers,
writer-producer, Chelsea Lane Productions, New York

Harlowe, Sarah (1765–1852)

English actress. Born in 1765; died in 1852; married Francis Godolphin Waldron (1744–1818, an actor-writer).

Following a triumph at Sadler's Wells, 25-year-old Sarah Harlowe appeared at Covent Garden in 1790. She also performed at the Haymarket, Drury Lane, and the English Opera House before her retirement in 1826. Career highlights included Lucy in *The Rivals,* Widow Warren in *Road to Ruin,* Miss MacTab in *Poor Gentleman,* and old Lady Lambert in *Hypocrite.*

Harmon, Ellen Gould (1827–1915).

See White, Ellen Gould.

Harnack, Mildred (1902–1943)

American-born anti-Nazi activist and member of the "Red Orchestra" spy network which supplied the So-

viets with important data, including the schedule for Hitler's attack on the USSR. Born Mildred Fish in Milwaukee, Wisconsin, on September 16, 1902; executed in Berlin, Germany, on February 16, 1943; grew up in Wisconsin; attended University of Giessen; married Arvid Harnack (1901–1942).

Born in Milwaukee, Wisconsin, on September 16, 1902, Mildred Fish was studying modern American literature at the University of Wisconsin, Madison, when she met Arvid Harnack, a serious, intelligent German graduate student from a highly distinguished academic family. They fell in love and married, moving to Germany in 1928 to complete their doctoral degrees. This they did at the University of Giessen, moving in 1930 to a Berlin already exploding with radical ideas and almost daily street clashes between unemployed Marxist workers and squads of equally desperate and ruthless Nazi brownshirts. Mildred Harnack observed these events with great interest while she worked as a translator and began her German academic career as a lecturer at the University of Berlin. By 1933, when the Hitler dictatorship was established, the Harnacks had become convinced that Nazism meant war and suffering and that the only reasonable alternative was a planned, Socialist society such as was apparently being created in the Soviet Union.

Despite the dangers inherent in such activities, both the Harnacks were involved in illegal anti-Nazi work virtually from the first day of the dictatorship. By the late 1930s, using his high position at the Reich Ministry of Economics, Arvid was able to secure important economic data and pass it on to the Marxist underground for study and dissemination; it could then be used in both secret seminars and the propaganda work of the anti-Nazi underground. By 1936, the couple was involved in the Communist underground organization led by John Sieg, one of the most dynamic resistance leaders in Nazi Germany at the time. By 1939, they had become acquainted with other anti-Nazi activist couples in Berlin, including Adam and *Greta Kuckhoff and Harro and *Libertas Schulze-Boysen. With the start of World War II in September 1939, this group was determined to assist the Soviet Union, which, despite the apparent stabilization brought about by the Hitler-Stalin pact of August 1939, remained in danger of Fascist aggression. The result of these concerns was the "Red Orchestra" spy organization, which for over a year was able to transmit extremely important military and political intelligence to Moscow.

In time, Nazi counter-intelligence broke into the "Red Orchestra" network, with tragic consequences for virtually all of its members. Both Mildred and Arvid Harnack were arrested on September 7, 1942. As a key leader of the spy organization, Arvid was sentenced to death and executed on December 22 of that year in Plötzensee prison. Mildred received a sentence of six years' imprisonment from the Reich War Tribunal, but when Adolf Hitler was apprised of the punishment he furiously demanded that the judgment be annulled and a new tribunal rule again in her case. This session took place on January 16, 1943, during the battle of Stalingrad, and the spirit of a vengeful Hitler hovered over the judges, who now ruled that a death verdict was appropriate punishment for Mildred Harnack. In her death cell in Plötzensee prison, the student of literature spent her final days translating verses by the German poet Goethe into English. Her mother had died in the United States at the beginning of the war, and Harnack decided not to write any farewell letters. Overheard by the prison chaplain, her last recorded words before her execution were, "And I have loved Germany so much." She was executed at Berlin's Plötzensee prison on February 16, 1943. Found among her effects was a poem by Goethe that she had translated while in her cell:

> Noble be man
> Helpful and good,
> For that alone
> Distinguishes
> Him from all beings
> On earth known.

SOURCES:

Biernat, Karl Heinz, and Luise Kraushaar. *Die Schulze-Boysen-Harnack-Organisation im antifaschistischen Kampf.* Berlin: Dietz Verlag, 1970.

Brysac, Shareen Blair. "She Spied, but Hitler was the Traitor," in *The New York Times.* February 20, 1993, section A, p. 19.

Kraushaar, Luise. *Deutsche Widerstandskämpfer 1933–1945: Biographien und Briefe.* 2 vols. Berlin: Dietz Verlag, 1970.

Rürup, Reinhard. *Topographie des Terrors: Gestapo, SS und Reichssicherheitshauptamt auf dem "Prinz-Albrecht-Gelände": Eine Dokumentation.* 7th ed. Berlin: Verlag Willmuth Arenhövel, 1989.

John Haag,
Associate Professor, University of Georgia, Athens, Georgia

Harper, Frances E.W. (1825–1911)

American educator, writer, lecturer, abolitionist, and human-rights activist. Name variations: Frances Watkins Harper. Born Frances Ellen Watkins on September 24, 1825, in Baltimore, Maryland; died on February 11, 1911, and buried in Eden Cemetery, Philadelphia, Pennsylvania; married Fenton Harper, on November 22, 1860 (died, May 1864); children: Mary Harper and three stepchildren.

After her mother died (1828), was raised and educated by uncle, Reverend William Watkins; was first woman instructor at Union Seminary (later Wilberforce) in Ohio (1851); taught in York, Pennsylvania (1852); was hired as lecturer for Maine Anti-Slavery Society (1854); was lecturer and agent for the Pennsylvania Anti-Slavery Society, one of the signers of the constitution of the Ohio State Anti-Slavery Society (1858); married Fenton Harper, a widower with three children in Cincinnati, Ohio (1860); spoke at the 11th Annual Woman's Rights convention in New York (1866).

Selected works: Poems on Miscellaneous Subjects (1854); Moses: A Story of the Nile; Sketches of Southern Life (1872); Iola Le Roy, or the Shadows Uplifted (1892).

From the Pennsylvania Anti-Slavery Society to the Pennsylvania Peace Society, Frances Ellen Watkins Harper aligned herself with those who shared her concerns about slavery, education, temperance, women's rights, and morality, issues often reflected in her literary work. Until Paul Laurence Dunbar, Frances Ellen Watkins Harper was the most popular 19th-century African-American poet. She enjoyed international fame as a lecturer with brilliant oratory skills.

In September 1992, an inter-denominational coalition of Philadelphia churches held a celebration of cultural and religious events to mark her life and achievements. "Philadelphians rediscover Frances Ellen Watkins Harper" reads the headline of *The Weekly Press*, a neighborhood paper. During the four-day commemoration, three Unitarian Universalist churches and Mother Bethel A.M.E. Church held the first-ever Continental Congress of African-American Unitarian-Universalists, and the Harper event was the centerpiece. This resurgence of interest in the works of Frances Ellen Watkins Harper has resulted in a reconsideration of both her literary career and her role as an activist.

Born Frances Ellen Watkins to a free African-American mother, Harper was orphaned in 1828 when her mother died. An aunt cared for her until she was old enough for school. Her uncle, the Reverend William Watkins, took her into his household, giving her an immediate family of siblings and the benefit of an educational institution, The William Watkins' Academy for Negro Youth, that he founded and administered. Entering both the Watkins' household and William Watkins Academy at age six, Harper was introduced to the key principles of self-discipline and personal responsibility. Free blacks lived an uneasy existence at best; if they were to survive and help African-Americans who had managed to escape slavery, it was necessary that they be imbued with extraordinary courage and focus. Reverend William Watkins possessed such courage, and, because of the kinship they shared, Harper would have an opportunity to observe a "Race Man"—one who cares deeply for his people and their welfare—in action.

Her path for a while was marked with struggle and trial, but . . . she met them bravely, and her life became not a thing of ease and indulgence, but of conquest, victory, and accomplishments.

—Frances E.W. Harper, "The Two Offers" (1859)

William Watkins, born free, was a self-made man. By avocation, he was a preacher and community leader, using his role as a preacher and self-taught medical expert to administer to the community. As headmaster of Watkins Academy, he influenced the education of African-Americans, enslaved and free. Interested in uplifting his people, he sought to discipline himself and those who occupied his sphere of influence. Watkins was a shoemaker by vocation who employed the skill he acquired as an apprentice to support himself and his family even as he ran Watkins Academy and founded a literary society in his church. In preparation for his role as headmaster of his own school, Watkins taught himself the basics of a classical education. Watkins Academy's curricula reflected his pragmatism and was grounded in Biblical studies overlaid with the classics. The school gained such an outstanding reputation that slave owners enrolled their "favorite slaves" there. In this environment, Harper had a chance to observe slavery, and resistance to it, through the presence of her uncle whose opposition to slavery or colonization was as strong as his loyalty to *The Liberator,* an anti-slavery publication.

During the years she attended her uncle's school, Harper studied oratory, grammar, composition, natural philosophy, music, mathematics, and—consistent with the founder's pragmatic philosophy—she also studied sewing and embroidery. Because free blacks in slave states were required to learn a trade, Harper was apprenticed out at 13 as a domestic to the Armstrong family where she was supposed to hone her "domestic science" skills. Because she had taught sewing at Watkins Academy, Harper required less training in the domestic sciences. This left her more time to pursue her studies in other areas. In *The Underground Rail Road,* William Still notes that the Armstrongs allowed the inquisitive teenager "occasional half-hours of leisure to satisfy her greed for books."

Before reaching the age of 21, Harper had written a volume of poetry and prose published under the title, *Forest Leaves.* At 26, having served her 10-year apprenticeship, Harper decided she wanted to live in a free state and moved to Ohio. She took a position at Union Seminary, a school for free blacks that would later become known as Wilberforce. In obtaining this position, Harper marked another milestone in her life as she was the first woman to obtain such a position. However, there was no need for her literary skills; she was hired to teach "domestic science." Remaining in Ohio for just one year, Harper traveled to York, Pennsylvania, where she began to grapple with the career dilemma she faced. She pondered how best to reconcile her literary aspirations with her desire to uplift her people. She doubted her ability to do this as a teacher, and her experience in York convinced her that she could only do a half-hearted job in the classroom.

Harper was attracted to the anti-slavery societies and their activism for the African American cause. Two important things happened to her while she was still in residence as a teacher at York. She met William Still who conducted the Underground Railroad in Philadelphia. Chair of the Acting Vigilance Committee, Still developed a network of safe hiding places for fugitives in the city's black community, raised funds for the refugees, and monitored the activities of the slave catchers. *The Underground Rail Road* is an important historical source because of the careful notes Still kept about the "passengers on the underground rail road." As their friendship developed, Still was convinced that Harper's desire to reach young children indirectly through adults could best be done in the forum she most desired. Buoyed by the possibility of a new career, Harper began shaping an essay in which she explored the ideas concerning education as a tool for elevating her race. Once she had decided to leave York, William Still and his wife **Letitia George** invited her to share their quarters over the anti-slavery office at 31 North Fifth Street. She arrived with a small volume of *Poems on Miscellaneous Subjects* (1854) that she hoped to publish.

Harper was also interested in becoming an agent for the Underground Railroad. Aware of the possibility of using literature to address social issues, she visited the anti-slavery office, read documents, and heard the stories of suffering from the escapees who traveled through the Underground Railroad. During this period, she began the fusion of her personal and political beliefs that informs her work and places her in the tradition of African-American women who maintain this fusion is necessary. Her growing interest in the anti-slavery cause was evident in the small volume she hoped to publish. Some of the poems she submitted separately to various anti-slavery publications such as *Frederick Douglass' Paper* and the *Liberator*. Harper's interest in the anti-slavery movement and her recognition of the usefulness of anti-slavery material is most evident in the poems influenced by *Harriet Beecher Stowe's *Uncle Tom's Cabin*. In a poem "To Mrs. Harriet Beecher Stowe," Harper reveals her recognition of the "power of the pen" as she thanks Stowe for her "grac'd . . . pen of fire."

Thus, Harper began to develop into a "Race Woman." Her concern for her people would eclipse her uncle's, as she eventually came to see a relationship between her literary aspirations and her attitude toward injustice, shaped by the racism she experienced firsthand. "Now let me tell you about Pennsylvania," she recalled: "I have been in every New England state, New York, Canada, and Ohio, but of all these places, this is the meanest of all as far as the treatment of colored people is concerned."

When Harper's convictions wavered, instance after instance of racism propelled her toward a reconciliation of politics and art. While she was still agonizing over where she would be most effective, Maryland passed a law forbidding free blacks who lived in the North to enter the state. Those who did so would be sold South into slavery. The account of one unfortunate free black who did not heed this law and was sold into slavery and sent to Georgia had a galvanizing effect upon Harper. As the ship carried him south toward enslavement, the man sought to hide in the wheel-house of the boat and was discovered. Having been exposed to the elements, and in weakened physical condition, this man died in slavery. "Upon that grave," Harper wrote to Still, "I pledge myself to the AntiSlavery cause."

Recognizing that slavery had effectively robbed many African-Americans of their humanity, Harper sought a way of uplifting her people while educating them, a way of speaking out against slavery in a large forum. Though she did not receive the job as agent for the Underground Railroad, she had gathered significant

Frances E.W. Harper

data and stiffened her resolve as to what role she should play in the anti-slavery movement. She traveled from Philadelphia to Boston to New Bedford; in New Bedford, Massachusetts, that "hot-bed of the fugitives," Harper found an audience eager to receive the ideas she had been mulling over since leaving York, Pennsylvania. Lecturing on "The Elevation and Education of our People," Harper was so compelling that she was hired by the Maine Anti-Slavery Society as a lecturer. For nearly two years, she traveled in New England states and Canada.

When she arrived in Philadelphia to take over her new role as a lecturer for the Pennsylvania Anti-Slavery Society in October 1857, Harper was convinced of her calling, and her oratory powers were acclaimed by her listeners. She was rated among the top two female orators during a period when oratory was an important communication skill. By the time her assignment with the Pennsylvania Anti-Slavery Society ended on May 1858, she had gained enough public recognition to begin speaking on her own. She was such a powerful public figure that she was enlisted to help frame the constitution for the new Ohio State Anti-Slavery Society even though African-American males, such as Frederick Douglass, William Nell, were not receptive to her and other African-American women.

As she gained a reputation and grew more successful, Harper continued to support William Still and the anti-slavery movement in any way she could. Writing to Still after a rescue attempt by the Anti-Slavery Society had failed, Harper reveals the depth of her commitment to the anti-slavery cause: "If there is anything that I can do for them in money or words, call upon me." Her commitment to the cause was total: "This is a common cause; and if there is any burden to be borne in the Anti-Slavery cause—anything to be done to weaken our hateful chains . . . I have a right to do my share of the work." Keeping her word, she lent her very public support to militant abolitionist John Brown and his family. When John Brown was captured at Harper's Ferry in October 1859 and sentenced to death, Harper wrote to Brown, "Although the hands of Slavery throw a barrier between you and me. . . . Virginia has no bolts or bars through which I dread send you my sympathy." She followed up this public show of support with financial contributions and her physical presence. During the two weeks before John Brown's execution, Harper remained with his wife **Mary Anne Brown**.

On November 22, 1860, Frances Ellen Watkins married Fenton Harper, a free black, in Cincinnati, Ohio. Using her savings, she purchased the family home, a farm in Grove City, Ohio. Harper devoted herself to being a housewife and later, when her daughter **Mary Harper** was born, a mother. Lecturing infrequently, she made and sold butter to help supplement the family's income. Her husband died in May 1864. The farm Harper had purchased with her own money, and all of her possessions were seized to pay off Fenton Harper's outstanding debts. To support herself and her child, Harper returned to giving lectures. This traumatic event would induce her to find common cause with women's rights groups despite racial tensions within some women's organizations.

Harper's role in the world took on another dimension with her commitment to the women's rights movement. In assuming this role she is numbered among *Sojourner Truth, *Mary Shadd Cary, *Harriet Tubman, *Ida B. Wells-Barnett, *Josephine Ruffin, and *Mary Church Terrell. She was among the speakers at the 11th annual Woman's Rights Convention, held in New York in May 1866. Then 41 years old, she told her audience that before her husband's death, the concerns of race had superseded the concerns of gender:

Born of a race whose inheritance has been outrage and wrong, most of my life has been spent battling these wrongs. But I did not feel as keenly as others that I had these rights in common with other women, which are now demanded. Had I died instead of my husband, how different might have been the result. By this time he would have another wife, it is likely; no administrator would have gone into his house, broken up his home, sold his bed, and taken away his means of support . . . justice is not fulfilled so long as woman is unequal before the law. We are all bound together in one great bundle of humanity.

Harper was not naive about her condition and the tenuousness of her alliance. She refused to engage in utopian notions: "I do not believe that giving the woman the ballot is immediately going to cure all the ills of life." Even when she was attempting to form new alliances, Harper was direct and to the point:

I do not believe that white women are dewdrops just exhaled from the skies. I think that like men they may be divided into three classes, the good, the bad, and the indifferent. The good would vote according to their convictions and principles; the bad, as dictated by prejudice or malice; and the indifferent will vote on the strongest side of the question, with the winning party.

The day after the Woman's Rights Convention, the American Equal Rights Association was formed to fight for equal rights for both black men and women. Harper found common ground with this organization alongside of other African-American abolitionists, including Frederick Douglass, Charles Remond, and Sojourner Truth. She joined with Douglass in arguing that African-American men in the South needed political power. Like *Harriet Jacobs, *Maria W. Stewart, and others, Harper devoted herself to the work of Reconstruction in the South. She felt that this could be achieved through enfranchisement, education, and morality. During this same period, she argued for both self-advancement and self-help and worked with the Women's Christian Temperance Union, even after serving as superintendent of the Philadelphia and the Pennsylvania "colored" chapters for nearly seven years. Though she gave freely of herself to reformist organizations, Harper supported herself by writing and lecturing. In 1892, she published *Iola Le Roy, or the Shadows Uplifted*. Until her death in Philadelphia in 1911, she remained actively involved in her community. Frances Harper is buried in Eden Cemetery in Philadelphia, Pennsylvania.

SOURCES:
Ammons, Elizabeth. "Frances Ellen Watkins Harper," in *Legacy 2*, 1985, pp. 61–66.

Bacon, Margaret Hope. "One Great Bundle of Humanity: Frances Ellen Watkins Harper (1825–1911)," in *The Pennsylvania Magazine of History and Biography*. Vol. CXIII, no. 1.

Foster, Frances Smith, ed. *A Brighter Coming Day: A Frances Ellen Watkins Harper Reader*. NY: The Feminist Press, 1990.

Graham, Maryemma, ed. *The Compete Poems of Frances E. W. Harper*. NY: Oxford University Press, 1988.

Van Dongen, Susan. "Philadelphians Rediscover Frances Ellen Watkins Harper," in *The Weekly Press*. Vol. 6, no. 8. March 5, 1993, pp. 1, 18.

SUGGESTED READING:

Harper, Frances Ellen Watkins. *Iola Leroy: Or, Shadows Uplifted*. Philadelphia: Garrigues Bros., 1892.

Harper, Ida Husted (1851–1931)

American journalist and women's rights advocate. Born Ida Husted on February 18, 1851, in Fairfield, Indiana; died of a cerebral hemorrhage, age 80, in Washington, D.C., on March 14, 1931; finished high school at 17 and entered Indiana University as a sophomore; left after one year to become principal of a high school in Peru, Indiana; married Thomas Winans Harper (a lawyer and friend of labor leader Eugene V. Debs), in 1871 (divorced 1890); children: one daughter, Winnifred Harper, who also became a writer.

Soon after her marriage in 1871, Ida Harper began a 12-year stint, writing for the Terre Haute *Saturday Evening Mail* under a male pseudonym. In 1883, much to the disgruntlement of her husband, she launched a weekly column, "A Woman's Opinions," under her own name. She joined the Indiana suffrage society in 1887 and divorced three years later.

Moving with her daughter **Winnifred Harper** to Indianapolis, Ida worked for the *Indianapolis News*. A few years later, she moved to California where she continued writing for the *News* while doing publicity for *Susan B. Anthony*'s campaign for California state suffrage (1896). Anthony was so impressed with Harper that she invited her to return to Rochester (N.Y.) as her official biographer. In 1898, having worked from papers tucked away in Anthony's attic, Harper published her two-volume *Life and Work of Susan B. Anthony* (a third volume was added in 1908, following Anthony's death). Ida Harper also assisted Anthony in the fourth volume of *History of Woman Suffrage*; in 1922, Harper would add volumes five and six. From 1909 on, Ida Husted Harper was a popular columnist for *Harper's Bazaar*.

$\mathcal{A}$CKNOWLEDGMENTS

Photographs and illustrations appearing in *Women in World History, Volume 6,* were received from the following sources:

Photo by Berenice Abbott, 1926, **p. 469**; Photo by Angleo Riverone Agrigento, **p. 251**; Alexander Korda Films, Inc., 1941, **p. 740**; Photo by Godfrey Argent, **p. 415**; Courtesy of Barnard College Archives, **p. 223**; Photo by Jerry Bauer, **p. 393**; Photo by Cecil Beaton, **p. 613**; Photo by Roloff Beny, **p. 598**; Courtesy of Benyas Kaufman Photographers, **p. 537**; Photo by Judy Blankenship, **p. 109**; From a portrait by Chardin, **p. 161**; Courtesy of Congressional Black Caucus, **p. 698**; Courtesy of Connecticut Historical Society (Hartford), **p. 459**; Fragment of painting by Paul Delaroche, **p. 531**; Courtesy of Dis (Paris), **p. 52**; © Her Majesty Queen Elizabeth II, **p. 155**; Courtesy of Enoch Pratt Free Library, **p. 314**; Courtesy of Felisa Rincon de Gautier Foundation (Santurce, Puerto Rico), **p. 115**; Courtesy of Fox Film Corp., 1935, **p. 121**; Painting by Fragonard, **p. 167**; Painting by Roger Fry, 1917, **p. 747**; Courtesy of Ghetto Fighter's Museum, M.P. (Western Galilee, Israel), **p. 139**; Courtesy of Gladney Center (Fort Worth, Texas), **p. 272**; Courtesy of HarperCollins (Australia), **p. 191**; Courtesy of HarperCollins (San Francisco), **p. 243**; Photo by Francois Hers, Viva (Paris), **p. 771**; Reprinted by permission of Houghton Mifflin Company, **p. 261**; Courtesy of Moorland-Spingarn Research Center, Howard University (Washington, D.C.), **p. 547**; Courtesy of the IMG Center (Cleveland, Ohio), photo by Heinz Kluetmeier, **p. 391**; Courtesy of the Embassy of India, Information Section, **p. 37**; Courtesy of the International Museum of Photography at the George Eastman House, **p. 607**; Courtesy of International Swimming Hall of Fame **p. 422**; Courtesy of the Jacob Rader Marcus Center of American Jewish Archives (Cincinnati, Ohio), **p. 463**; Photo by Bob Langrish, **p. 486**; Photo by Judy Lawne, **p. 281**; From the painting by Sir Peter Lely, **p. 659**: Courtesy of the Library of Congress, **pp. 231, 337, 357, 691, 711, 723**; Courtesy of Metro-Goldwyn-Mayer, **p. 43** (photo by Clarence Sinclair Bull), **p. 65** (photo by Eric Carpenter), **pp. 87, 88, 97**; Photo by Rollie McKenna, **p. 241**; Photo by Jack Mitchell, **p. 673**; Photos by Nadar, **pp. 116, 561**; Courtesy of National Handicapped Sports, photo by Hubert Schriebl, **p. 334**; Courtesy of the New York Public Library at Lincoln Center, **p. 275**; Courtesy of the Orangutan Foundation International, **p. 19**; Courtesy of Paramount (photo by A.L. "Whitey" Schafer), **p. 318**; Reprinted by permission of the Princeton University Library, **p. 399**; Courtesy of the Russian Information Agency-Novosti, **p. 387**; Engraving by Samuel Sartain, **p. 74**; Reproduced by permission of the Schlesinger Library, Radcliffe College, **pp. 15, 56**; Painting by J. Schmidt, 1800, **p. 737**; Courtesy of SIPA Press, **p. 591**; Courtesy of the Supreme Court Historical Society, Smithsonian Institution, photo by Richard Strauss, **p. 247**; Permission to reproduce courtesy of the Spastic Centre of NSW and NSW Society for Children and Young Adults with Physical Disabilities c/o Curtis Brown (Australia) Pty. Ltd. (Sydney), **p. 193**; Courtesy of the State Historical Society of Wisconsin, WHI (X3) 52341, Lot 310, **p. 23**; Courtesy of the Stewart Gardner Museum (Boston), painting by John Singer Sargent, **p. 70**; From the movie *South Pacific,* courtesy of Twentieth Century-Fox, 1958, **p. 125**; Courtesy of the Galleria degli Uffizi (Florence), **p. 157**; Courtesy of United Artists Corp., **p. 433**; Courtesy of the U.S. House of Representatives. **pp. 454, 483, 511, 768, 783**; Courtesy of the United States Tennis Association/Russ Adams, **pp. 199, 381, 429**; Courtesy of the University of Chicago, **p. 474**; Photo by Hugo van Lawick, **p. 369**; Courtesy of the Vancouver Public Library, photograph no. 13333, **p. 641**; Courtesy of Walt Disney Productions, **p. 665**; Courtesy of the Washington Post Company, **p. 437**; Based on a painting by G.F. Watts, 1854, **p. 593**; Courtesy of Wide World, **p. 133**; Photo by Geoff Wilding, **p. 694**; © Willard and Barbara Morgan Archives, Morgan and Morgan, Inc. (Dobbs Ferry, New York), photo by Barbara Morgan, **p. 443**; Photo by Crispian Woodgate, **p. 321**; Courtesy of Yale University Art Gallery, painting by Albert Heater, **p. 790**.